The Ultimate Wyoming

Atlas and Travel Encyclopedia

Compiled, edited, and written by
Michael Dougherty
and Heidi Pfeil Dougherty
and the Staff of Ultimate Press

UltimatePress
Bozeman, Montana

an *Ultimate*® book

ISBN: 1-888550-12-0

Ultimate Press
an imprint of Champions Publishing

1627 W. Main Street #148
Bozeman, Montana 59715
406-585-0237
800-585-0713
www.ultimatepress.com

Printed in Canada

Contents

Acknowledgment

We offer a sincere thank you to all of the sponsors who, without their financial support, this book would not have been possible. Throughout the book, you'll see their names in bold. Stop in and see them when you're in their area. They would like to hear from you.

We especially wish to thank our staff for their excellent help in bringing this first edition to press. A special thanks to Patricia DeWitt for her tireless efforts in obtaining our sponsors, without which, we would not exist.

Disclaimer

This guide focuses on recreational activities including traveling to some sites that are off the more frequently traveled roads. As all such activities contain elements of risk, the publisher, author, affiliated individuals and companies included in this guide disclaim any responsibility for any injury, harm, or illness that may occur to anyone through, or by use of, the information in this book. Although the author and publisher have made every effort to ensure that the information was correct at the time of going to press, the author and publisher do not assume and hereby disclaim any liability to any party for any loss or damage to person or property caused by errors, omissions, or any potential travel disruption due to labor or financial difficulty, whether such errors or omissions result from negligence, accident, or any other cause.

Throughout this book, public domain documents of government agencies (National Park Service, USDA Forest Service, Bureau of Land Management, and Wyoming State Parks and Historic Sites) were reprinted. Also, brochures published by local area chambers of commerce and from the various attractions were reprinted in part or in their entirety. Permissions were obtained where required.

Wyoming

The Cowboy State

Madison River north of West Yellowstone

The Cowboy State

When people think of Wyoming, they tend to think of cowboys, as the nickname shows. The cowboy is really a symbol of Wyoming's rugged, hard-working character. Covering nearly 98,000 square miles, the fourth largest state in the union is a land of wild, wide-open spaces and magnificent vistas.

Every corner of the state has natural wonders of world renown: from Yellowstone and the Grand Tetons in the northwest corner, to Devil's Tower and the Black Hills in the northeast, to the Vedauwoo Rocks and the Medicine Bow National Forest in the southeast, and Fossil Butte and the Flaming Gorge in the southwest. In between these marvels, numerous opportunities to explore Wyoming's varied, often awe-inspiring landscapes abound.

In the high heart of the Rocky Mountains, Wyoming is laced with a number of smaller ranges, including the Laramie Mountains, the Snowy Range, the Sierra Madres, the Salt Range, the Gros Ventres, the Absarokas, the Big Horns, the Tetons, and some of the regions highest peaks, the Wind Rivers, reaching nearly 14,000 feet elevation. Wyoming mountains are a spectacle of stark granite slopes, rolling foothills, and evergreen forests.

Between the various mountain ranges, you will find a variety of wilderness areas, pastoral valleys, grasslands, deserts, and amazing rock formations. You can find nearly every geological phenomenon imaginable, from deep canyons to majestic buttes and pinnacles to convoluted caverns. Geothermal curiosities occur all around the state, from geysers to hot springs.

Water is a precious commodity in the state, but it is crisscrossed with several streams, including the Green, the Snake, Bighorn, the Platte, the Powder, the Laramie and the Wind Rivers. Headwaters for the Missouri, Columbia, and Colorado Rivers also fall within Wyoming's borders. The continental divide, which cuts through the mountains, creates a place where water runs in three different directions. The landscape is dotted with a handful of lakes and reservoirs that provide not only recreational opportunities, but also much needed water conservation and dam-generated energy for the state.

Natural History

Taking its name from a Delaware word meaning "land of mountains and valleys", Wyoming has been a land of wonders for millions, even billions of years. The very minerals from which the earth is formed here harbor countless treasures, from silver and gold, to copper and iron ore, to semi-precious and even precious stones. The largest piece of solid jade ever unearthed came from Wyoming, and one of the largest diamonds ever found came from here as well.

Situated in an ancient volcanic caldera, the Yellowstone region boasts the most extensive area of geyser activity in the world, as well as boiling mud pots, hot springs, prismatic pools, and other hydrothermal phenomena. Waterfalls abound, and the deep and serene Yellowstone Lake is surrounded by multicolored cliffs, layered and carved from years of glacial activity.

Another vast ancient lake, really an inland sea, once covered much of Wyoming and left deposits of soda ash and other important minerals useful in a variety of industries today. Prehistoric life thrived around the tropical lake, leaving rich stores of fossil fuels and a host of archeologically significant remains, from several dinosaur graveyards to petrified trees. Some of the earliest ancestors of the modern horse have been unearthed within Wyoming's boundaries, as well as many other more ancient life forms.

Wildlife

Today, there are more animals than people in Wyoming, which is the least populated of any state in the union. Wyoming is home to numerous native species of ungulates, such as the bison (buffalo), pronghorn antelope, bighorn sheep, mule deer and white-tailed deer, moose, and elk, to name just a few. In the last couple of centuries, the state has also become host to a large population of domesticated cattle, sheep, horses, and even a few llamas and ostriches. Wild mustangs also roam the plains.

The animal population includes numerous prairie and mountain birds, from the Bald Eagle to the Meadowlark to the Sage Grouse. Several fish species inhabit the waterways, including many varieties of trout, bass, and even catfish. Beavers and otters can also be seen in streams and ponds. Marmots, rabbits, picas, chipmunks, and other small critters frequent the highlands and lowlands alike. Wolves, cougars, coyotes, foxes, badgers, and even a few bears also dwell in this largely untamed country.

Wyoming At a Glance

Population (2000): 493,782

Entered union: July 10, 1890

Capital: Cheyenne

Nickname: The Cowboy State or The Equality State

Motto: Equal Rights

Bird: Meadowlark

Flower: Indian Paintbrush

Song: "Wyoming"

Stones: Jade

Tree: Cottonwood

Animal: Bison

Fish: Cutthroat Trout

Fossil: Knightia (Fossilized fish)

Land area: 97,819 square miles

Water area: 714 square miles

Size ranking: 9th

Geographic center: Fremont, 58 miles ENE of Lander

Length: 360 miles

Width: 280 miles

Highest point: 13,804 feet (Gannett Peak)

Lowest point: 3,099 feet (Belle Fourche River)

Mean Elevation: 6,700 ft

Highest temperature: 114° on July 12, 1900, at Basin

Lowest temperature: -66° on Feb. 9, 1933, at Riverside

The History of Wyoming's People

Native Americans

Drawn by the mineral treasures and the wildlife, humans have been living here for millennia as well. Some of the oldest Native American campsites in North America have been discovered in Wyoming, dating back to over 11, 000 years ago.

Ever since that time, many groups of Native Americans have valued Wyoming as prime hunting ground. Early tribes utilized "buffalo jumps," cliffs where the bison were driven over the ledge to their deaths. Later on, hunting was done with weapons made from the flint and metals found in the region. The hunters left behind bones, pottery, petroglyphs, fire rings, and sacred stone circles known as Medicine Wheels, the use of which is still something of a mystery.

In more recent times, numerous plains tribes inhabited the Wyoming wilderness, and continued to vie for hunting rights in the region for centuries. Among these were the Cheyenne, Sioux, Arapaho, Shoshone, Lakota, Crow, Comanche, Ute, Paiute, Bannock, Blackfeet, Ogalala, Arikara, Gros Ventre, Nez Perce, and Miniconjou. These tribes had rivalries and alliances that sometimes changed and often lasted for generations.

Many Native Americans of great prominence called Wyoming home. The likes of Chief Washakie, Chief Joseph, Sitting Bull, Red Cloud, Crazy Horse, Dull Knife, White Bull, and Black Horse inhabited these parts during at least part of their lives. Even Sacajawea, the famous guide for Lewis and Clark, spent some of her life within the state's borders, and is thought by some to have been laid to rest near the Wind River Reservation.

Today, relatively few Native Americans remain in the state, many of who live on the sole protected remnant of their ancestral lands, the Wind River Reservation. They are increasingly reclaiming their heritage, and are making the most of opportunities to share their tribal traditions at a number of events and venues throughout the state.

Devils Tower. One of Wyoming's most recognizable icons.

Explorers And Mountain Men

John Colter, a member of the Lewis and Clark expedition, was probably the first white man to set foot in Wyoming, investigating the marvels of Yellowstone country in 1808. Over the next decade or so, Jacques LaRamee, a French-Canadian trapper traveled extensively in the eastern part of the state. Thereafter, Wyoming became the place many early European adventurers called home. Mountain men, in particular, were largely responsible for much of the investigation of the state. Lured here by the promise of riches from beaver pelts and other wild game, many men came to Wyoming with the John Jacob Astor expedition in the 1820s, and never left. William Ashley and Andrew Henry led the original party.

They befriended some Native Americans and were often rewarded with wives. In time and through often harrowing experience, they became familiar with the wonders and dangers of this magnificent state. They congregated at events called Rendezvous, exchanging goods, information, stories, a few punches, and a lot of liquor. These are still celebrated today in their honor, but fighting is now frowned upon. Names such as Jim Bridger, Kit Carson, and Jedediah Smith marked the paths that would be trod by Easterners for the next two centuries and beyond.

Tumbleweeds congregate along a fence line near Rocky Point.

Pioneers And Homesteaders

Not far behind the mountain men came pioneers, heading West to make new lives for themselves in Oregon country and Utah's Great Salt Lake Valley. Crossed by both the Oregon and Mormon Trails, innumerable wagons and hand carts traversed Wyoming, leaving ruts in the bedrock still clearly visible over 150 years later.

Immigrants left their marks in other ways, with names etched on cliffs and scattered graves. Winter in the high plains and mountains was harsh and often sudden, sometimes taking travelers by surprise. Martin's Cove was the site of the most extensive casualties. Disease and the occasional Indian raid took their toll as well. Making it across the state alive was no mean feat.

As the Utah Territory welcomed more and more Mormon immigrants, Prophet Brigham Young sent settlers north into Wyoming to tame the wild country there. The Mormon pioneers cultivated significant quantities of wilderness, from Fort Bridger to the Star Valley area to the Bighorn Basin, where they built an extensive canal system. They left behind a legacy of hard work and industry, and built many historic landmarks that still stand today.

Other settlers came from the East to homestead in relative peace, including German Lutherans from Iowa, who farmed land in the Bighorn Basin and near the Nebraska border. Their contributions have also stood the test of time, and made Wyoming part of what it is today.

The Overland Stage And The Pony Express

As traffic increased across Wyoming, a stage

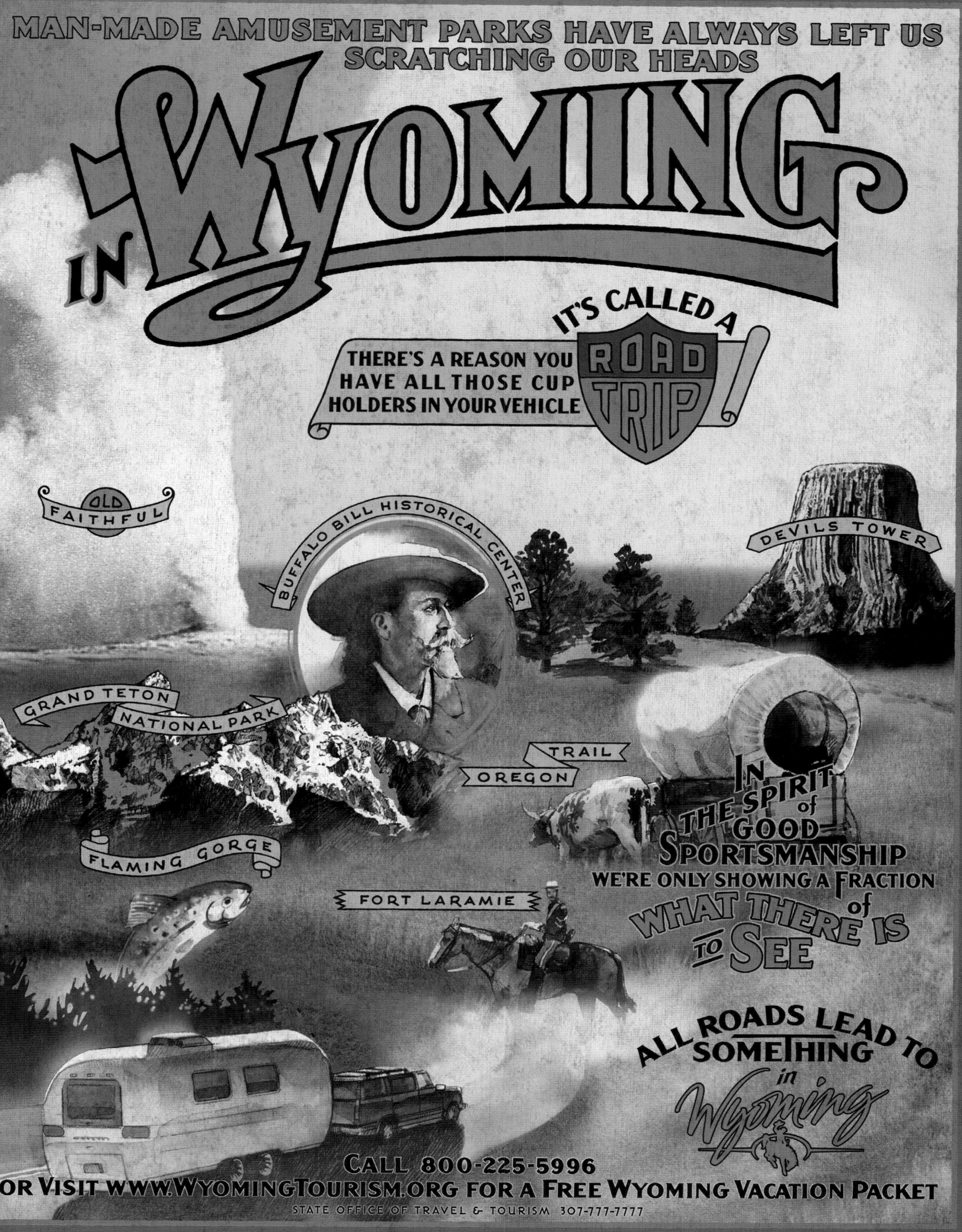

MAN-MADE AMUSEMENT PARKS HAVE ALWAYS LEFT US SCRATCHING OUR HEADS
IN WYOMING
IT'S CALLED A ROAD TRIP
THERE'S A REASON YOU HAVE ALL THOSE CUP HOLDERS IN YOUR VEHICLE
OLD FAITHFUL
BUFFALO BILL HISTORICAL CENTER
DEVILS TOWER
GRAND TETON NATIONAL PARK
OREGON TRAIL
FLAMING GORGE
FORT LARAMIE
IN THE SPIRIT of GOOD SPORTSMANSHIP
WE'RE ONLY SHOWING A FRACTION of WHAT THERE IS TO SEE
ALL ROADS LEAD TO SOMETHING in Wyoming
CALL 800-225-5996
OR VISIT WWW.WYOMINGTOURISM.ORG FOR A FREE WYOMING VACATION PACKET
STATE OFFICE OF TRAVEL & TOURISM 307-777-7777

North of Rawlins.

route was developed, with regular stops for weary travelers. With the Western population growing, many who rode the trail came to do business, not to settle. The Overland Stage Trail provided easier mobility for both eastern and western journeys. Stagecoaches ran freight and provided protection as well.

Many stage stations also served as stopovers for Pony Express riders, providing fresh horses for both. Sometimes, even the stage didn't travel fast enough for important information to be transmitted from coast to coast. A letter sent by Pony Express could travel from New York to California in about seven or eight days. Riding for the Pony Express was a dangerous occupation, mostly because riders were on their own, confronting uncertain conditions among the Indians, and unpredictable weather. Nevertheless, during the eighteen months it was in operation, only two riders died.

Treasure Seekers And Miners

The discovery of gold in California sparked a new wave of immigration in the 1850s and 60s. The pioneer influx was still ongoing, but now the byways were also filled with wanderers hoping to "strike it rich", if not in California then in Colorado, Montana, or South Dakota.

Wyoming, too, had its share of mineral wealth, and mining towns began to take root. The communities would thrive until the mine ran out of whatever it had provided, then the miners would move on. This was the start of the boom and bust cycle that would continue throughout Wyoming's development.

The hunt for gold inspired John Bozeman to pioneer a route north through Wyoming to the Montana gold fields. By 1864, the Bozeman Trail was yet another heavy traffic area across the state.

The Forts And The Indian Wars

As more and more white people began to come into Wyoming, the Native Americans became increasingly distressed about the impact the strangers were having on tribal lands. Some tribes, like the Shoshone under Chief Washakie, tried to maintain peaceful relations. Others chafed under the imposed sanctions, and misunderstandings and conflict became more frequent.

With the increase in Indian confrontations, the US government began to establish a presence in the area. Various forts, such as Fort Bridger and Fort Laramie, which had once been merely supply and trading posts, became barricaded citadels. Some of the most well known Indian battles were fought in Wyoming, including the brutal Fetterman Massacre at Fort Phil Kearney.

Both sides sustained many casualties in the Battle of the Red Buttes at Platte Bridge Station, later called Fort Caspar. The Battle of the Rosebud, which happened in the midst of the Powder River Expedition, had Native Americans fighting on both sides. Although the Battle of the Little Bighorn, or Custer's Last Stand, took place across the Montana border, it was the culminating campaign that began with a pioneer's missing cow near Fort Laramie, and the Grattan Massacre that followed. William F. "Buffalo Bill" Cody made a name for himself the summer after the Little Bighorn disaster by beating Cheyenne Chief Yellow Hand in one-to-one combat.

The Railroad And The Telegraph Line

Technology caught up with the call to head west, and steam engines became the preferred method of travel, telegraph messages the preferred form of communication. Plans were laid for a transcontinental railroad, and the race was on between the Eastern and Western builders as they hurried to meet somewhere in the middle.

The Union Pacific Railroad, and several smaller railroads such as the Burlington, Northern, and Santa Fe Lines, laid tracks all over the state, creating new "hell on wheels" communities, and bringing a variety of colorful people of different nationalities to the area. The logging industry and the coal industry rose up to meet the needs of the growing railways. The completion of the railroad in 1869 brought ever-greater numbers of Easterners to the west.

Before the railroad was finished, the state was filled with telegraph lines and offices, mostly where the stage and Pony Express stops had been. Mail delivered by Pony Express had taken about a week to arrive. With the telegraph, messages could be sent almost instantaneously. East and West were connected like never before.

Cattle And Cowboys

As the Eastern states filled with people, rangeland became harder and harder to find. Texas cattlemen, in particular, were on the lookout for new territory where their herds could graze cheaply,

Buffalo Bill Scenic Highway west of Cody.

unmolested. Pioneering ranchers like Nelson Story blazed the Texas Trail north, through Oklahoma and Colorado into the open range country of Wyoming, Montana, and the Dakotas. With the stabilizing presence of the army and the freight options brought by the railroad, Wyoming became ideal cattle country. Huge ranching companies sprung up, like the Swan Land and Cattle Company, and the Pitchfork and Sun Ranches.

With the cattle came the cowboys, tough and hard living, who made an art of the business of tending the herds. From their broad-brimmed hats, high-heeled boots, chaps and spurs, to their horsemanship, skills with ropes, and understanding of animals and nature, the cowboy became a breed apart. They lead a harsh and lonely existence, spending endless days on the windswept, open range, living off trail food and sleeping by solitary campfires. The cowboy became Wyoming's icon because Wyoming made him who he was.

Cattle ranching was so profitable during the late 1800s that it made many men rich. Other men, who were already rich, such as noblemen and aristocrats from Europe, found it useful to invest in the cattle industry. For either or perhaps both reasons, the most successful ranchers became known as "cattle barons."

The cattle barons had a great deal of influence in territorial politics and were able to strong-arm many agricultural settlers into giving up their land. Accusations of cattle rustling were rampant. Hired guns, known as "range detectives", intimidated homesteaders, and occasionally hung or shot someone. Tom Horn, Cattle Kate, and Calamity Jane became notorious for their roles in the range wars.

West of Dayton.

Sheep And Sheepherders

The cattlemen met their match with the advent of the sheep industry. Sheep were considered by some to be a more profitable investment because they provided two commodities: wool and lambs, and the wool was a renewable resource. Experienced European sheepherders, including many Basques from the Pyrenees, came to Wyoming to work for sheep ranchers.

Sheep ranching began to rival cattle ranching for power and money, but the real rivalry was over the rangeland and grazing rights. Eventually, tensions between the two industries and homesteaders escalated from hired guns making specific "hits" to an all out war in Johnson County. Federal troops had to be sent in to settle the raging dispute.

The Equality State

Wyoming made leaps in pioneering women's rights while it was still a territory. With such a scattered population, every able-bodied person had value. Wyoming became the first government entity in the world to grant women the vote and the right to hold office, as well as allowing them to own property in their own name.

The first female voter, perhaps in the entire world, was "Grandma" Louisa A. Swain of Laramie. The first female jurors in the world, Eliza Stewart, Amelia Hatcher, C.H. Hilton, Mary Mackel, Agnes Baker, and Sarah Pease, attended a trial in Laramie also. Wyoming had the first female Justice of the Peace in the world, Esther Morris, in South Pass City, and the first female governor in the US, Nellie Tayloe Ross, ran the state after her husband died in office. Jackson became to first town in the country to elect a group of city officials who were all women in 1920. Wyoming continues to be a place where women have great value.

Somewhere near Split Rock.

Outlaws

This rough country attracted many rough characters through the years, including:

Butch Cassidy (Robert Leroy Parker)
The Sundance Kid (Harry Longabaugh)
Kid Curry (Harry Logan)
"Flat Nose" George Currie
William C. "Teton" Jackson (Harvey Gleason)
James Butler "Wild Bill" Hickok
Tom Horn
John Henry "Doc" Holliday
Cattle Kate (Ellen Watson)
Calamity Jane (Martha Jane Canary)
Jesse James
Frank James (Jesse's brother)
"Big Nose George" Parrott (George Manuse)
"Dutch Charley" Burris

Bill Carlisle, Wyoming's (and perhaps the West's) last great "gentleman" train robber, who politely held up passengers several times between 1916 and 1919. He later was caught and served time in jail as a model prisoner.

Wide Open Spaces

While traveling on the backroads, you will sometimes get a sense that nobody lives here. You can travel for miles without seeing any sign of civi-

Ayres Natural Bridge.

lization beyond the occasional small herds of cattle. In many parts of the state, oil wells outnumber people. Occupied houses are rare and outnumbered by abandoned homesteaders shacks and log cabins. Fences often disappear entirely and are replaced by the infrequent "Open Range" signs that warn you cattle may be having their mid-day siesta in the middle of the road.

None-the-less, most of this land is privately owned unless posted otherwise. Before abandoning your car and heading out across these open spaces, it's a good idea and common courtesy to find the property owner and get permission. If you see fenceposts or gates with bright orange blazes, then getting permission isn't an option. They mean "no trespassing" in no uncertain terms.

However, I've never been shot at for stopping the car, getting out and smelling the sage, listening to the sound of silence, or to the voice of the wind, or the gurgle of a stream, the howl of a coyote, or the unidentified song of a prairie bird. I've never been asked to move along when I've stopped to admire a sunset, or simply marvel at the splendor of the endless sky.

Most of those that have bought and paid for a piece of this marvelous state don't mind sharing it with those who come to visit. They simply ask that you respect it and leave no trace you were there.

The Roads

Gravel roads are the rule rather than the exception in this part of the country. Almost all of Wyoming's paved roads are well maintained. There are posted speed limits and they are vigorously enforced.

Be prepared at any time to slow down for riders on horseback. Most horses are accustomed to cars, but can spook if you drive too near. Much of wyoming is open range. Cattle may be grazing on the road. A head-on with a steer can be just as deadly as a head-on with another automobile.

And speaking of cattle, don't be surprised if you come upon a cattle drive. If you do, follow the instructions of the drovers. They will make every effort to clear a path to allow you through. Usually the cattle just part ways and make a path, but don't go on unless you're given instructions to.

Beware of black ice! This is a virtually invisible layer of ice that forms on road surfaces after a fog. Be particularly careful of stretches of road that parallel rivers and creeks. The early morning fog rising from them can settle on the road freezing instantly. If you feel yourself sliding, tap your brakes gently. If you slam on the brakes, it's all but over. Gently steer into the direction of your skid (if your back end is going right—steer right).

Gumbo

We gave this subject its own headline. It is very important that you read it—and heed it.

While Wyoming isn't the only state that has gumbo, it has its fair share. If you become a resident, it is one of the first things you develop a respect (a healthy respect) for. Grizzlys and rattlesnakes might be the hazards you're warned of, but gumbo is the one that will get you.

You'll find it mostly in the eastern half of the state. It lies in wait on what in dry weather appears to be an ordinary rock hard dirt road. Your first clue is the occasional sign that reads *Road Impassable When Wet*. This is a clear understatement. When these roads become even mildly wet, they turn into a monster that swallows all sizes of vehicles—and yes, even 4-wheel drive SUVs. Think you'll get a tow? Forget it. No tow truck operator with a higher IQ than dirt will venture onto it until it dries. If you walk on it, you will grow six inches taller and gain 25 pounds all on the bottom of your shoes. It can coat your tires until they won't turn anymore. Of course, this is if it doesn't swallow you whole first like an unsuspecting native in a Tarzan movie who steps into quicksand.

Bottomline, heed the signs. If it looks like rain, head for the nearest paved road. When it comes to swallowing things whole, the Bermuda Triangle is an amateur compared to Wyoming Gumbo.

Wyoming Climate

Topographic Features

Wyoming's outstanding features are its majestic mountains and high plains. Its mean elevation is about 6,700 feet above sea level and even when the mountains are excluded, the average elevation over the southern part of the State is well over 6,000 feet, while much of the northern portion is some 2,500 feet lower. The lowest point, 3,125 feet, is near the northeast corner where the Belle Fourche River crosses the State line into South Dakota. The highest point is Gannett Peak at 13,785 feet, which is part of the Wind River Range in the west-central portion. Since the mountain ranges lie in a general north-south direction, they are perpendicular to the prevailing westerlies, therefore, the mountain ranges provide effective barriers which force the air currents moving in from the Pacific Ocean to rise and drop much of their moisture along the western slopes. The State is considered semiarid east of the mountains. There are several mountain ranges, but the mountains themselves cover less area than the high plains. The topography and variations in elevation make it difficult to divide the State into homogeneous, climatological areas.

The Continental Divide splits the State from near the northwest corner to the center of the southern border. This leaves most of the drainage areas to the east. The run-off drains into three great river systems: the Columbia, the Colorado, and the Missouri. The Snake with its tributaries in the northwest flows into the Columbia; the Green River drains most of the Southwest portion

Fall colors near Laramie. Photo courtesy of Laramie Area Chamber of Commerce.

and joins the Colorado: the Yellowstone, Wind River, Big Horn, Tongue, and Powder drainage areas cover most of the north portion and flow northward into the Missouri; the Belle Fourche, Cheyenne, and Niobrara covering the east-central portion, flow eastward: while the Platte drains the southeast and flows eastward into Nebraska. There is a relatively small area along the southwest border that is drained by the Bear which flows into the Great Salt Lake. In the south-central portion west of Rawlins, there is an area called the Great Divide Basin. Part of this area is often referred to as the Red Desert. There is no drainage from this Basin and precipitation, which averages only 7 to 10 inches annually, follows creekbeds to ponds or small lakes where it either evaporates or percolates into the ground.

Snow accumulates to considerable depths in the high mountains and many of the streams fed by the melting snow furnish ample quantities of water for irrigation of thousands of acres of land. The snowmelt also furnishes the water to generate electric power, and for domestic use.

Rapid run-off from heavy rain during thunderstorms causes flash flooding on the headwater streams, and when the time of these storms coincides with the melting of the snow pack, the flooding is intensified. When overflow occurs in the vicinity of urban communities situated near the streams considerable damage results.

Temperature

Because of its elevation, Wyoming has a relatively cool climate. Above the 6,000 feet level the temperature rarely exceeds 100° F. The warmest parts of the State are the lower portions of portions of the Big Horn Basin, the lower elevations of the central and northeast portions, and along the east border. The highest recorded temperature was 114° F on July 12, 1900, at Basin in the Big Horn Basin. The average maximum temperature at Basin in July is 92° F. For most of the State, mean maximum temperatures in July range between 85 and 95° F. With increasing elevation, average values drop rapidly. A few places in the mountains at about the 9,000 foot level have average maximums in July close to 70° F. Summer nights are almost invariably cool, even though daytime readings may be quite high at times. For most places away from the mountains, the mean minimum temperature in July ranges from 50 to 60 ° F. Of course, the mountains and high valleys are much cooler with average lows in the middle of the summer in the 30s and 40s with occasional drops below freezing.

In the wintertime it is characteristic to have rapid and frequent changes between mild and cold spells. Usually there are less than 10 cold waves during a winter, and frequently less than half that number for most of the State. The majority of cold waves move southward on the east side of the Divide. Sometimes only the northeast part of the State is affected by the cold air as it slides eastward over the plains. Many of the cold waves are not accompanied by enough snow to cause severe conditions. In January, the coldest month generally, man minimum temperatures range mostly from 5 to 10° F. In the western valleys mean values go down to about 5° below zero. The record low for the State is -66° F observed February 9, 1933, at Yellowstone Park. During warm spells in the winter, nighttime temperatures frequently remain above freezing. Chinooks, warm downslope winds, are common along the eastern slopes.

Numerous valleys provide ideal pockets for the collection of cold air drainage at night. Protecting mountain ranges prevent the wind from stirring the air, and the colder heavier air settles into the valleys often sending readings well below zero. It is common to have temperatures in the valleys considerably lower than on the nearby mountain side. Big Piney in the Green River Valley is such a location. Mean January temperatures in the Big Horn Basin show the variation between readings in the lower part of the valley and those higher up. At Worland and Basin in the lower portion of the Big Horn Basin, not far from the 4,000 foot level, the mean minimum temperature for January is zero, while Cody, close to 5,000 feet on the west side of the valley has a mean January minimum of 11° F. January, the coldest month, has occasional mild periods when maximum readings will reach the 50s; however, winters are usually long and cold.

Growing Season

Miner's Delight, the childhood home of Calamity Jane, is now a quiet ghost town.

Early freezes in the fall and late in the spring are characteristic. This results in long winters and short growing seasons. However, it is a county of rapid changes through the fall, winter, and spring seasons, with frequent variations from cold to mild periods. The average growing season (freeze-free period) for the principal agricultural areas is approximately 125 days. For hardier plants which can stand a temperature of 28° F, or slightly lower, the growing season is the agricultural areas east of the Divide is approximately 145 days. In the mountains and high valleys freezing temperatures may occur any time during the summer. For tender plants there is practically no growing season in such areas as the upper Green River Valley, the Star Valley and Jackson Hole. At Farson near Sandy Creek, a tributary of the Green River, the average is 42 days between the last temperature of 32° F in early summer and the first freeze in late summer. For the places like the Star Valley and Jackson Hole, the growing season is even shorter.

Sunshine

For most of the State, sunshine ranges from 60 percent of the possible amount during the winter to about 75 percent during the summer. Mountain areas receive less, and in the wintertime the estimated amount over the northwestern mountains is about 45 percent. In the summertime when sunshine is greatest – not only in time but also intensity – it is characteristic for the mornings to be mostly clear. Cumulus clouds develop nearly every day and frequently blot out the sun for a portion of the afternoons. Because the altitude provides less atmosphere for the sun's rays to penetrate and because of the very small amount of fog, haze, and smoke, the intensity of sunshine in unusually high.

Precipitation

Like other states in the west, precipitation varies a great deal from one location to another. The period of maximum precipitation occurs in the spring and early summer for most of the State. Precipitation is greater over the mountain ranges and usually at the higher elevations, although elevation alone is not the predominant influence. For example, over most of the southwest portion, where the elevation ranges from 6,500 to 8,500 feet, annual precipitation varies from 7 to 10 inches. At lower elevations over the northeast portion and along the eastern border, where elevations are mostly in the range from 4,000 to 5,500 feet, annual averages are from 12 to 16 inches. The relatively dry southwest portion is a high plateau nearly surrounded by mountain ranges.

The Big Horn Basin provides a striking example of the effect of mountain ranges in blocking the flow of moisture laden air from the east as well as from the west. The lower portion of the Basin has an annual precipitation of 5 to 8 inches, and it is the driest part of the State. The station showing the least amount is Seaver at 4,105 feet with an annual mean of about 5.50 inches. In the southern part of the Basin, Worland at 4,061 feet has an annual mean of 7 to 8 inches as compared with Termopolis at 4,313 feet and 11 to 12 inches. There is another good example in the southeastern part of the State where Laramie at 7,236 feet has an annual mean of 10 inches, while 30 miles to the west, Centennial at 8,074 feet receives about 16 inches. Only a few locations receive as much as 40 inches a year, based on gage records.

During the summer, showers are quite frequent but often amount to only a few hundredths of an inch. Occasionally there will be some very heavy rain associated with thunderstorms covering a few square miles. There are usually several local storms each year with from 1 to 2 inches of rain in a 24-hour period. On rare occasions, 24-hour amounts range from 3 to 5 inches. The greatest 24-hour total recorded for any place in Wyoming is 5.50 inches at Dull Center, near Newcastle, on May 31, 1927.

Humidity and Evaporation

The average relative humidity is quite low and provides delightful summer weather. During

Among the more famous of Wyoming's natives are:

Dick Cheney, Vice President under President George H.W. Bush

Lynne Cheney, author

Dean Conger, photo chief for National Geographic Magazine

Roulon Gardner, first man from Wyoming to win an Olympic gold metal in wrestling (Sydney, Australia, 2000 games)

Tom Browning, baseball player

Jim Bridger, frontiersman

Elas Spear Byron, photographer of Custer Battlefield survivors

Buffalo Bill Cody, entertainer and former Pony Express Rider

John Colter, first white man to enter Wyoming

Crazy Horse, Indian leader (Ogalala Sioux)

Peggy Simpson Curry, poet and author

Mike Devereaux, baseball player

Lavina Dobler, author

Thomas Fitzpatrick, mountain man

Harrison Ford, actor

Curt Gowdy, sportscaster

James Herdt, Master Chief Petty Officer of the Navy

Tom Horn, purportedly the fastest gun in the west

Isabel Jewell, actress

Mike Lansing, baseball player

Chris Ledoux, country music artist and rodeo cowboy

Thomas Moran, artist from England

Ester Morris, first woman judge

Edgar Wilson, known as Bill Nye, humorist and author

Ted Olson, writer

James Cash Penny, founder of JC Penney Stores

Frances Warren Pershing, wife of General Pershing

Jackson Pollock, abstract artist Conrad Schwiering, western artist

Jedediah Smith, mountain man

Gerry Spence, lawyer

Nellie Tayloe Ross, first woman elected Governor of a state

Willis VandeVanter, Supreme Court Justice

Francis E. Warren, first state governor

Chief Washakie, Chief of the Eastern Shoshone

James G. Watt, former Secretary of the Interior

Ella Watson (aka Cattle Kate), frontier legend

Darrel Winfield "Marlboro Man", advertising cowboy

Pete Williams, NBC correspondent

Lucille Wright, pilot

Owen Wister, author, The Virginian.

the warmer part of the summer days, the humidity drops to about 25 to 30 percent, and on a few occasions it will be as low as 5 to 10 percent. Late at night when the temperature is lowest, the humidity will generally rise to 65 or 75 percent. This results in an average diurnal variation of about 40 to 45 percent during the summer, but in the winter the variation is much less. Low relative humidity, high percentage of sunshine, and rather high average winds all contribute to a high rate of evaporation. Because of frequent spells of freezing weather before May 1 and after September 30, it is difficult to obtain consistent records of evaporation for more than the 5-month period from May through September. For this period, the average amount of evaporation is approximately 41 inches, as determined from evaporation pans at a few selected locations. The overall range is from 30 to about 50 inches.

Severe Storms

Hailstorms are the most destructive type of local storm for this State, and every year damage to crops and property from hail amount to many thousands ofdollars. Occasionally a hailstorm will pass over a city and cause severe damage. Most of the hailstorms pass over the open rangeland and damage is slight, although in small areas of crop producing land, some farmers occasionally lose an entire crop by hail.

Tornadoes occur, but records show they are much less frequent and destructive than those that occur in the Midwest. The relatively small amount of destruction is partly due to the fact that most of Wyoming is open range country and sparsely populated. However, records show that tornadoes which occur here are somewhat smaller and have a shorter duration. Many of them touch the ground for only a few minutes before receding into the clouds. The season extends from April through September. June has the greatest number on the average with May next and most occur in the eastern part of the State.

Wyoming is quite windy, and during the winter there are frequent periods when the wind reaches 30 to 40 miles per hour with gusts to 50 or 60. Prevailing directions in the different localities vary form west-south-west through west to northwest. In many localities winds are so strong and constant from those directions that trees show a definite lean towards the east or southeast.

Snow and Blizzards

Snow falls frequently from November through May and at lower elevations is light to moderate. About five times a year on the average, stations at the lower elevations will have snowfall exceeding 5 inches. Falls of 10 to 15 inches or more for a single storm occur but are infrequent outside of the mountains. Wind will frequently accompany of follow a snowstorm and pile the snow into drifts several feet deep. The snow sometimes drifts so much that it is difficult to obtain an accurate measurement of snowfall. An unusually heavy snow occurred at Sheridan on the 3rd and 4th of April 1955. During this period the snowfall amounted to 39.0 inches, had a water equivalent of 4.30 inches and blizzard conditions lasted more than 43 hours. High winds and low temperatures with snow cause blizzard or near blizzard conditions. These conditions sometimes last a day or two, but it is uncommon for a severe blizzard to last over three days.

Total annual snowfall varies considerably. At the lower elevations in the east, the range is from 60 to 70 inches. Over the drier southwest portion, amounts vary from 45 to 55 inches. Snow is very light in the Big Horn Basin with annual averages from 15 to 20 inches over the lower portion and 30 to 40 inches on the sides of the Basin where elevations range from 5,000 to 6,000 feet. The mountains receive a great deal more and in the higher ranges annual amounts are well over 200 inches. At Beckler River Ranger Station in the southwest corner of Yellowstone Park, the snowfall averages 262 inches for a 20-year period.

The weather pattern most favorable for precipitation is one with a low-pressure center a little to the south of the State. This will normally provide a condition where relatively cool air at the surface is overrun by warmer moist air. Studies of wind flow patterns indicate that Wyoming is covered most of the time by air from the Pacific. A smaller percentage of time the State is covered by cold air masses that move down from Canada.

Agriculture

Most of the State has been subjected to erosion for tens of thousands of years and less than 10 percent is covered with a mantle of recent (geologically speaking) water-transported soil. The lack of such soil and adequate moisture limits the natural vegetation to hardy plants, such as sagebrush, greasewood, and short grass. Low relative humidity and the high rate of evaporation add to the problem. A number of abandoned homesteads of onetime enthusiastic settlers bear silent testimony to the lack of moisture. Even so, dryland farming is carried on successfully in some areas. Approximately 42 percent of the State's total area is privately-owned land, the majority of which is used for grazing, although some is timberland. The fact that most of the State is still Government-owned attests to the semiarid climate which has make the land less attractive to homesteaders. Nearly 4 percent of the State is cultivated cropland, including both irrigated and nonirrigated. Another 13 percent is covered with forests, while parks and recreational areas take up about 4 percent.

The majority of the State is used for grazing and has a general appearance of dryness most of the time. The more abundant spring moisture brings a greener landscape often with myriad, varicolored wild flowers. As the season merges into summer, grasses and flowers turn brown, but continue to serve as food for livestock. Native grasses are nutritious, although scant. There are some very fine grazing areas with luxuriant grasses, especially in or near the mountains. Grass is generally so scarce that large ranches are required for profitable operation. The average for most cattle grazing is about 35 to 40 acres per cow. The mountain areas provide timber and a storage place for the winter snows which in the spring and summer feed lakes and reservoirs used in the irrigations districts. Most of the irrigated land is located in the valleys of the following river systems and their tributaries: North Platte, Wind River, Big Horn, Tongue, and Green. Principal crops in the irrigation districts are sugar beets, beans, potatoes, and hay. On the nonirrigated land the principal crops are hay and small grains, such as wheat, barley, and oats.

Tourism is increasingly important to Wyoming's economy and millions of persons, including many sportsmen, visit the State annually to enjoy Yellowstone and Grand Teton National Parks.

Weather article provided by National Climatic Data Center

The National Trails System

"I should compare the (South) pass to the ascent of the capitol hill from the avenue at Washington."
- John Fremont, 1843, describing the ease of using South Pass to cross the Rocky Mountains

In 1800, America's western border reached only as far as the Mississippi River. Following the Louisiana Purchase in 1803 the country nearly doubled in size, pushing the nation's western edge past the Rocky Mountains.

Yet the wilderness known as Oregon Country (which included present-day Oregon, Washington and part of Idaho) still belonged to the British, a fact that made many Americans eager to settle the region and claim it for the United States.

American Indians had traversed this country for many years, but for whites it was unknown territory. Lewis and Clark's secretly funded expedition in 1803 was part of a U.S. Government plan to open Oregon Country to settlement. However, the hazardous route blazed by this party was not feasible for families traveling by wagon. An easier trail was needed.

Robert Stewart of the Astorians (a group of fur traders who established Fort Astoria in western Oregon's Columbia River) became the first white to use what later became known as the Oregon Trail. Stewart's 2,000-mile journey from Fort Astoria to St. Louis in 1910 took 10 months to complete; still, it was a much less rugged trail than Lewis and Clark's route.

It wasn't until 1836 that the first wagons were used on the trek from Missouri to Oregon. A missionary party headed by Marcus Whitman and his wife Narcissa bravely set out to reach the Willamette Valley. Though the Whitmans were forced to abandon their wagons 200 miles short of Oregon, they proved that families could go west by wheeled travel.

In the spring of 1843, a wagon train of nearly 1,000 people organized at Independence, Missouri with plans to reach Oregon Country. Amidst an overwhelming chorus of naysayers who doubted their success, the so-called "Great Migration" made it safely to Oregon. Crucial to their success was the use of South Pass, a 12-mile wide valley that was virtually the sole place between the plains and Oregon where wagons could cross the formidable Rocky Mountains.

By 1846, thousands of emigrants who were drawn west by cheap land, patriotism or the promise of a better life found their way to Oregon Country. With so many Americans settling the region, it became obvious to the British that Oregon was no longer theirs. They ceded Oregon Country to the United States that year.

"When you start over these wide plains, let no one leave dependent on his best friend for anything; for if you do, you will certainly have a blow-out before you get far." - John Shivley, 1846

Before railroads or automobiles, people in America had to travel by foot, horse, boat or wagon. Some of these routes from our nation's early days still remain today as reminders of our historic past. A National Historic Trail (NHT) such as the Oregon NHT is an extended trail that follows original routes of travel of national historical significance.

In 1995, the National Park Service established the National Trails System Office in Salt Lake City, Utah. The Salt Lake City Trails Office administers the Oregon, the California, the Mormon Pioneer and the Pony Express NHTs.

The National Trails System does not manage trail resources on a day-to-day basis. The responsibility for managing trail resources remains in the hands of the current trail managers at the federal, state, local and private levels.

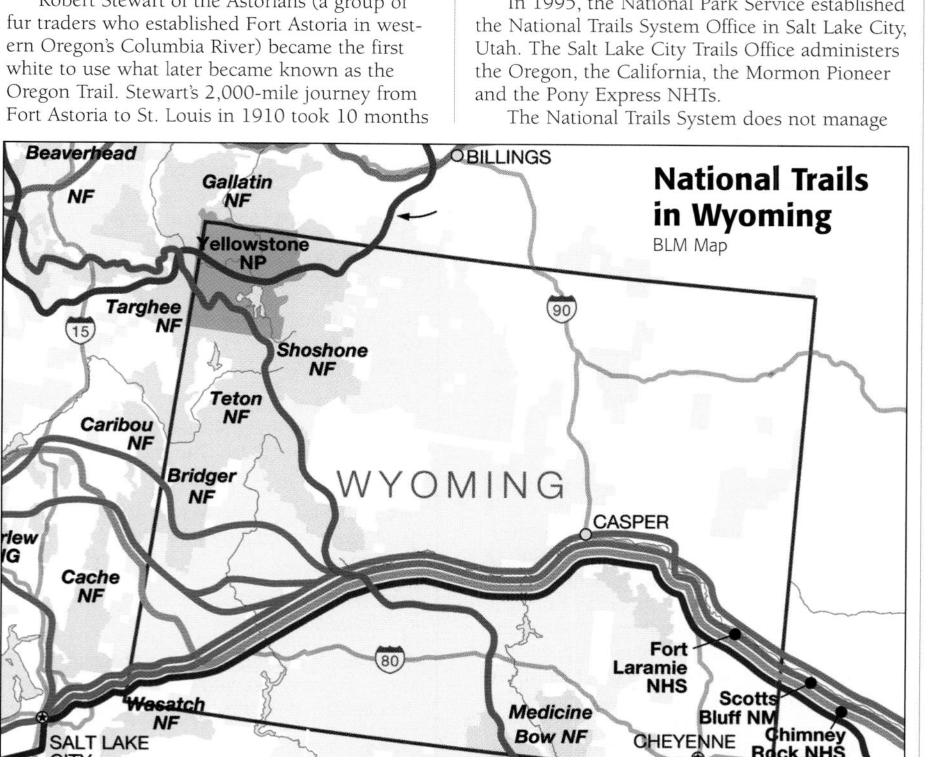

Jackelopes can be found everywhere in Wyoming, but Douglas is the home of the rabbit king.

The Office was established to improve interstate and interregional coordination. Specific responsibilities of this trails office include coordinating and supporting the protection of trail resources, marking and interpreting the trails, designating and marking an auto-tour route and identifying and certifying high-potential sites.

In 1968, Congress enacted the National Trails System Act and in 1978, National Historic Trail designations were added. The National Historic Trails System commemorates these historic routes and promotes their preservation, interpretation and appreciation.

National Historic Trails recognize diverse facets of history such as prominent past routes of exploration, migration, trade, communication and military action. The historic trails generally consist of remnant sites and trail segments, and thus are not necessarily contiguous. Although National Historic Trails are administered by federal agencies, land ownership may be in public or private hands. Of the 11 National Historic Trails, nine are administered by the National Park Service, one by the USDA Forest Service and one by the Bureau of Land Management.

If Americans today were to undertake a four-month, 2,000-mile journey on foot without the aid of modern conveniences, many would be in for a harsh jolt. Despite the lingering romance with which many view the emigrant tide on the Oregon Trail, the journey was tough.

Emigrants traveled under the dual yoke of fear and withering physical requirements. Rumors of hostile Indians coupled with unforgiving country, disease and dangerous work made life difficult.

Yet thousands did make it to Oregon. What was their journey like on a day-to-day basis?

First of all, timing was important to the emigrants' success in reaching Oregon. The most favorable time to depart from Missouri was in April or May. This would put them on schedule to make the high mountain passes when winter

The oil well is ubiquitous throughout the state.

snows would not be a threat.

Mistakes were often made before the journey even began. In preparing for the trip, many emigrants overloaded their wagons with supplies. As a result, not long after leaving Missouri, dumping excess items was a common sight along the trail. Tools, guns and food were considered vital—heirlooms were not.

The relatively gentle first leg of the route along the Platte River was a time for the emigrants to settle into travel mode. This meant getting used to hitching and unhitching the oxen, cattle and mules whenever a stop was made - hard and dangerous work. It also meant constant wagon maintenance, foraging for firewood and clean water, cooking over open fires and learning how to break and set camp every day.

When emigrants reached Chimney Rock and Scotts Bluff, their journey was one-third over. But more challenging terrain lay ahead as water, firewood and supply depots became more scarce. Buffalo herds that initially were a dependable food source for the emigrants also thinned out due to excessive killing.

The challenge of crossing many rivers and the Continental Divide created other severe tests for the emigrants. Summer temperatures, miles of shadeless trail and choking dust compounded to make life decidedly unenjoyable. Though confrontations with Indians were rare, the fear of attack was a constant worry.

The last leg of the trail was the most difficult. But thoughts of approaching winter snows kept emigrants motivated to move as quickly as possible. The Blue Mountains in eastern Oregon and the Cascade range in the west presented barriers that slowed progress.

Upon reaching Oregon City, the emigrants were faced with either taking their chances on the dangerous Columbia River, or, starting in 1846, taking the safer but longer Barlow Road. Sam Barlow's toll road became the preferred route for the emigrants. Finally, if money, animals, wagons, supplies and morale held out, the emigrants reached the Willamette Valley.

The Morman Trail

To the sounds of snapping harness and creaking wagon wheels the pioneers in the vanguard of westward expansion moved out across the North American continent. Between 1840 and 1870, more than 500,000 emigrants went west along the Great Platte River Road from departure points along the Missouri River. This corridor had been used for thou- sands of years by American Indians and in the mid-19th century became the transportation route for successive waves of European trappers, missionaries, soldiers, teamsters, stage coach drivers, Pony Express riders, and overland emigrants bound for opportunity in the Oregon Territory, the Great Basin, and the California gold fields.

The trunk of the corridor generally followed the Platte and North Platte rivers for more than 600 miles, then paralleled the Sweetwater River before crossing the Continental Divide at South Pass. Beyond South Pass the route divided several times, each branch pioneered by emigrants seeking a better way to various destinations. The route's importance declined with the completion of the transcontinental railroad in 1869 but continued to receive limited use into the early 1900s.

The Mormon Pioneer Trail

Few years in the Far West were more notable than 1846. That year saw a war start with Mexico, the Donner-Reed party embark on their infamous journey into a frozen world of indescribable horror, and the beginning of the best organized mass migration in American history. The participants of this migration, the Mormons, would establish thriving communities in what was considered by many to be a worthless desert.

From 1846 to 1869, more than 70,000 Mormons traveled along an integral part of the road west, the Mormon Pioneer Trail. The trail started in Nauvoo, Illinois, traveled across Iowa, connected with the Great Platte River Road at the Missouri River, and ended near the Great Salt Lake in Utah. Generally following pre-existing routes the trail carried tens of thousands of Mormon emigrants to a new home and refuge in the Great Basin. From their labors arose the State of Deseret, later becoming the Utah Territory, and finally the State of Utah.

The Trail Experience

The Mormon pioneers shared similar experiences with others traveling west: the drudgery of walking hundreds of miles, suffocating dust, violent thunderstorms, mud, temperature extremes, bad water, poor forage, sickness, and death. They recorded their experiences in journals, diaries, and letters that have become a part of our national heritage.

The Mormons, however, were a unique part of this migration. Their move to the Valley of the Great Salt Lake was not entirely voluntary; but to maintain a religious and cultural identity it was necessary to find an isolated area where they could permanently settle and practice their reli-

Wyoming First Ladies

Nellie Ross took the oath of office as Governor of Wyoming in January, 1925, the first woman governor in the United States. Mrs. Ross was later the first woman director of the U. S. Mint in Washington, D.C.

Irene Kinnear Mead was the first Shoshone woman elected to a Tribal Council.

Ella Mae "Cattle Kate" Watson, accused of cattle rustling, was the only woman ever lynched in Wyoming.

Narcissa Prentiss Whitman and Eliza Hart Spalding, missionaries, were the first white women in Wyoming.

Mrs. Esther Morris of SOUTH PASS CITY was the first female Justice of the Peace in the U.S., commissioned in 1870.

The first woman to cast her general election ballot in the nation was Eliza Swain of LARAMIE.

Women of Wyoming were granted suffrage in 1869, 21 years before the U.S. granted women the right to vote and hold office.

The first women jurors were in Wyoming, beginning in 1870.

The first woman in the country to be elected to a state office was Estelle Reel, elected Superintendent of Public Instruction in 1894.

Mary Bellamy, a Democrat from LARAMIE, was the first woman elected to a state legislature in the country. The election was in 1911.

Susan Wissler, elected mayor of DAYTON in 1911, was the country's first female in that position.

Rose Marshall was the first white baby born in Yellowstone National Park.

The nation's first female prison chaplain, Mrs. May Slosson, served at the Laramie Penetentiary in 1899.

Lorraine Lindaley, stationed at the Medicine Bow Peak Lookout in 1921, west of LARAMIE, was the world's first female fire lookout.

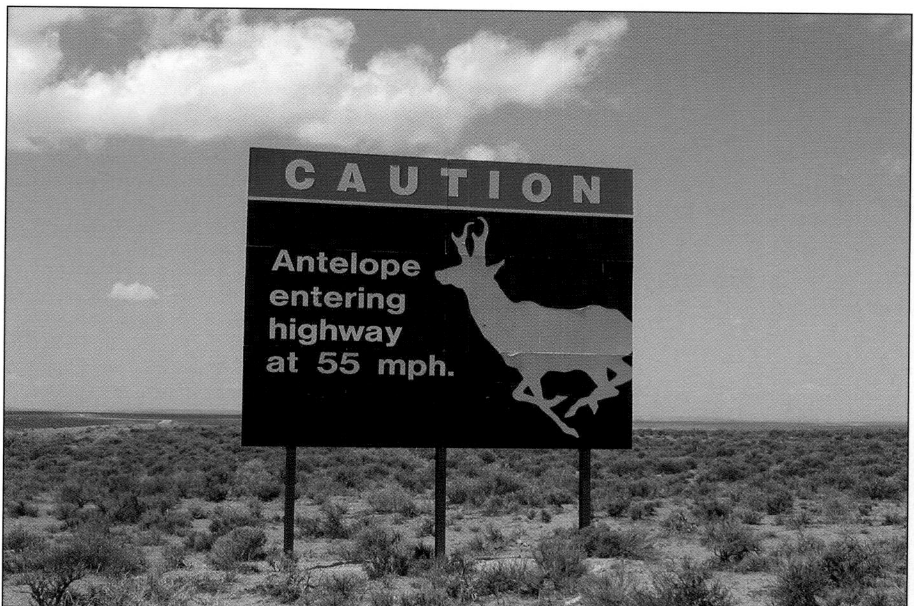

Traffic can often be heavy on Wyoming roads. Watch for merging traffic on all open highway.

Follow the Trail

To follow The Oregon National Historic Trail west through Wyoming, from Nebraska to Idaho:

1. Take U.S. Route 26 west to Interstate 25.
2. Turn north onto Interstate 25.
3. Take Interstate 25 west to State Route 220.
4. Turn west onto State Route 220.
5. Take State Route 220 to U.S. Route 287.
6. Turn west onto U.S. Route 287.
7. Take U.S. Route 287 west to State Route 28.
8. Turn West onto State Route 28.
9. Take State Route 28 west to State Route 372.
10. Turn southeast onto State Route 372.
11. Take State Route 372 east to Interstate 80.
12. Turn west onto Interstate 80.
13. Take Interstate 80 west to State Route 412.
14. Turn north onto State Route 412.
15. Take State Route 412 to U.S. Route 189.
16. Turn north onto U.S. Route 189.
17. Take U.S. Route 189 north to U.S. Route 30.
18. Turn west onto U.S. Route 30.

Total original route miles in Wyoming: 491

Source: National Park Service

gion in peace. This movement of an entire people, an entire religion, and culture was driven by persecution, religious fervor, and determination.

The Mormon pioneers learned quickly to be well-organized. They traveled in semi-military fashion, grouped into companies of 100s, 50s, and 10s. Discipline, hard work, mutual assistance, and devotional practices were part of their daily routine on the trail. Knowing that others would follow, they improved the trail and built support facilities. Businesses, such as ferries, were established to help finance the movement. They did not hire professional guides. Instead, they followed existing trails, used maps and accounts of early explorers, and gathered information from travelers and frontiersmen they met along the way. An early odometer was designed and built to record their mileage while traveling on the trail. In the end, strong group unity and organization made the Mormon movement more orderly and efficient than other emigrants traveling to Oregon and California.

The Mormon Church

The Mormon pioneer experience is closely tied to the formation, growth, and development of the Church of Jesus Christ of Latter Day Saints, which was founded by Joseph Smith, April 6, 1830, in Fayette, New York. According to the accounts of Mormon history, Joseph Smith translated a document from golden plates given to him by an angel. This document, The Book of Mormon, a record of Christ visiting America, became the cornerstone of the new religion. The name Mormon was applied to those who subscribed to these beliefs.

Driven from New York by detractors, the church headquarters subsequently moved to Ohio, Missouri, and, in the spring of 1839, to Nauvoo, Illinois. It remained there until 1846, when increasing hostility caused the church to move beyond the Rocky Mountains into then unsettled Mexican territory in the Great Basin. There, Mormon leaders hoped to be insulated from further harassment, antagonism, and persecution.

Membership grew rapidly from 1830 to 1845, and the church prospered. Hostility, fear, and controversy, however, surrounded the church. The rapid growth of church membership, the financial success of the members and the church, religious beliefs that were outside mainstream Christian tradition, the practice of plural marriage (polygamy), a large well-armed militia, the blurring of lines between church and state, and the perception by some non-Mormons that the church was a threat all fueled intolerance. Hostilities escalated, and on June 27, 1844, Joseph Smith and his brother Hyrum were killed by an angry mob while jailed in Carthage, Illinois.

By 1845, the Mormon population in and around Nauvoo had grown to more than 11,000, making it one of the largest cities in the state. In September of that year, foes burned more than 200 Mormon homes and farm buildings outside Nauvoo in an attempt to force the Mormons to leave.

A move to the Far West had been discussed by church leaders as early as 1842, with Oregon, California, and Texas considered as potential destinations. In 1844, Joseph Smith obtained John C. Fremont's map and report, which described the Great Salt Lake and its surrounding fertile valleys. Subsequently, the Rocky Mountains and the Great Basin became the prime candidates for settlement.

Establishing the Trail: The Treks of 1846 and 1847

The initial movement of the Mormons from Nauvoo, Illinois, to the Valley of the Great Salt Lake occurred in two segments: one in 1846 and one in 1847. The first segment, across Iowa to the Missouri River, covered around 265 miles. The second segment, from the Missouri River to the Valley of the Great Salt Lake, covered about 1,032 miles.

The Trek of 1846

The departure from Nauvoo began on February 4, 1846, under the leadership of Brigham Young, who succeeded Joseph Smith as leader of the Mormon Church. After crossing the Mississippi River, the journey across Iowa followed primitive territorial roads and Indian trails. The initial party reached the Missouri River on June 14 of that year, having taken more than four months to complete the trip. Some of the emigrants established a settlement called Kanesville on the Iowa side of the river. Others moved across the river into the area of present-day (north) Omaha, Nebraska, building a camp called Winter Quarters.

The Mormons left Nauvoo earlier than planned because of the revocation of their city charter, growing rumors of U.S. government intervention, and fears that federal troops would march on the city. This early departure exposed them to the elements in the worst of winter. Heavy rains later turned the rolling plains of southern Iowa into a quagmire of axle-deep mud. Furthermore, few people carried adequate provisions for the trip. The weather, general unpreparedness, and lack of experience in moving such a large group of people, all contributed to the difficulties they endured.

Along this first part of the trail, the Mormons developed skills for moving en masse. They established several semi-permanent camps, including Garden Grove and Mount Pisgah,

Most trails west passed through the South Pass shown above.

where they planted crops and built facilities to assist those who followed. It was during this leg of the journey that Brigham Young first organized them into companies of 1OOs, 50s, and 1Os. The lessons learned crossing Iowa were used by future companies of Mormons.

The Trek of 1847

The longest leg of the journey began at Winter Quarters on April 5, 1847, and ended on July 24, 1847, when Brigham Young entered the Valley of the Great Salt Lake. The trip went smoother than the previous year's journey because the Mormons were better organized, had better provisions, and began the trek when trail conditions were optimal. The lead pioneer party left with 148 people (143 men, 3 women, and 2 young boys), 72 wagons, 93 horses, 66 oxen, 52 mules, 19 cows, 17 dogs, and some chickens. This hand-picked group was organized into two large divisions and further split into companies of 50 and 10. This organizational structure was based on Brigham Young's plan for migrating west. The plan also included details on camp behavior and devotional practices to be followed during the journey.

The trail across the Great Plains traversed hundreds of miles along the north side of the Platte and North Platte rivers. At Fort Laramie the Mormons crossed to the south side of the river, where they joined the Oregon Trail. About 100 miles later, they left the North Platte River at present day Casper, Wyoming. They then followed the Sweetwater River for almost 100 miles and crossed the Continental Divide at South Pass. At Fort Bridger, they left the Oregon Trail and struck out on their own following a route first recommended by California promoter Lansford Hastings and pioneered in 1846 by four companies of emigrants bound for California. These four companies blazed two different routes into the Salt Lake Valley. The Mormons followed the faint, year-old track of the ill-fated Donner-Reed party through the Wasatch Mountains.

The final 116 miles, from Fort Bridger to the Valley of the Great Salt Lake, were the most difficult. The people were weary, their wagons worn, and livestock weakened by almost 1,000 miles of walking. Travel through the narrow, willow-choked canyons and over tree-covered slopes and rocky ridges of the Wasatch Range was so slow that it took the pioneer party 14 days to complete this part of their journey. On July 22, 1847, when Thomas Bullock caught his first full view of the valley he shouted "hurra, hurra, hurra, there's my home at last."

The pioneer party began planting late crops as soon as they reached the valley. During the next few weeks, they laid out streets, built temporary shelters, and prepared for winter. Mormon emigrants continued to arrive during the remaining weeks of summer and fall, and approximately 1,650 people spent their first winter in the valley. Shortly after their arrival, Brigham Young and

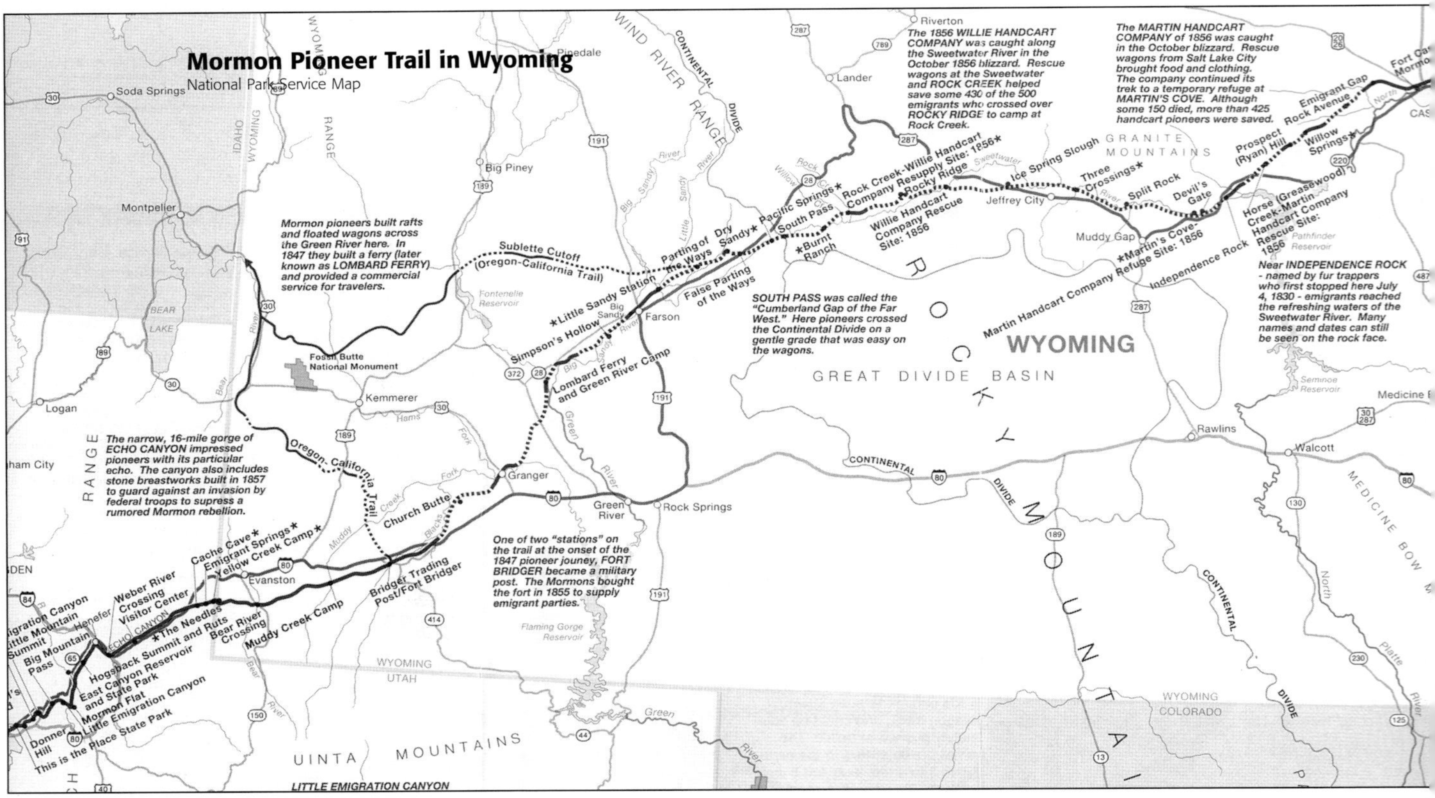

Mormon Pioneer Trail in Wyoming
National Park Service Map

Mormon pioneers built rafts and floated wagons across the Green River here. In 1847 they built a ferry (later known as LOMBARD FERRY) and provided a commercial service for travelers.

The 1856 WILLIE HANDCART COMPANY was caught along the Sweetwater River in the October 1856 blizzard. Rescue wagons at the Sweetwater and ROCK CREEK helped save some 430 of the 500 emigrants who crossed over ROCKY RIDGE to camp at Rock Creek.

The MARTIN HANDCART COMPANY of 1856 was caught in the October blizzard. Rescue wagons from Salt Lake City brought food and clothing. The company continued its trek to a temporary refuge at MARTIN'S COVE. Although some 150 died, more than 425 handcart pioneers were saved.

SOUTH PASS was called the "Cumberland Gap of the Far West." Here pioneers crossed the Continental Divide on a gentle grade that was easy on the wagons.

Near INDEPENDENCE ROCK - named by fur trappers who first stopped here July 4, 1830 - emigrants reached the refreshing waters of the Sweetwater River. Many names and dates can still be seen on the rock face.

The narrow, 16-mile gorge of ECHO CANYON impressed pioneers with its particular echo. The canyon also includes stone breastworks built in 1857 to guard against an invasion by federal troops to supress a rumored Mormon rebellion.

One of two "stations" on the trail at the onset of the 1847 pioneer jouney, FORT BRIDGER became a military post. The Mormons bought the fort in 1855 to supply emigrant parties.

Sublette Cutoff (Oregon-California Trail)
Parting of the Ways
Dry Sandy
False Parting of the Ways
Little Sandy Station
Simpson's Hollow
Lombard Ferry and Green River Camp
Pacific Springs
South Pass
Burnt Ranch
Rock Creek-Willie Handcart Company Resupply Site: 1856
Rocky Ridge
Willie Handcart Company Rescue Site: 1856
Ice Spring Slough
Three Crossings
Split Rock
Devil's Gate
Martin's Cove-Martin Handcart Company Refuge Site: 1856
Independence Rock
Horse (Greasewood) Creek-Martin Handcart Company Rescue Site: 1856
Prospect (Ryan) Hill
Willow Springs
Rock Avenue
Emigrant Gap
Oregon-California Trail
Church Butte
Bridger Trading Post/Fort Bridger
Muddy Creek Camp
Bear River Crossing
Cache Cave
Emigrant Springs
Yellow Creek Camp
The Needles
Hogsback Summit and Ruts
East Canyon Reservoir and State Park
Mormon Flat
Little Emigration Canyon
Weber River Crossing Visitor Center
Big Mountain Pass
Donner Hill
This is the Place State Park
WIND RIVER RANGE
GRANITE MOUNTAINS
GREAT DIVIDE BASIN
ROCKY MOUNTAINS
UINTA MOUNTAINS
WYOMING
LITTLE EMIGRATION CANYON

All Wyoming Area Codes are 307

Movies Made in Wyoming

Wyoming, with its diverse landscape and unspoiled vistas, has been the setting for a number of films. *Close Encounters of the Third Kind* (1977) used the Devil's Tower area. *Butch Cassidy and the Sundance Kid* (1969) was filmed near Hole-In-The-Wall. An area just north of Casper was the background for *Starship Troopers*, filmed in 1997, and for The *Hellfighters* (1968).

The Jackson Hole area was used in *Rocky IV* (1985), *The Cowboy and the Lady* (1922), *The Big Trail* (1930), *Shane* (1951), *Jubal, The Big Sky, Spencer's Mountain* (1963).

Clint Eastwood fans saw Wyoming scenery in *Any Which Way You Can* (1980).

Other movies made in Wyoming include: *Bad Bascomb* (1946), *Bright Angel* (1991), *The Cowpuncher* (1915), *End of the Trail* (1932), *The Far Horizons* (1955), *Ghosts Can't Do it* (1990), *Hike* (1998), *The Indian Wars* (1914), *The Last Resort* (1997), *The Vanishing* (1993), *The Wrong Guys* (1988).

many members of the pioneer party made the return trip to Winter Quarters to be with their families and to help organize the next spring's migration to the valley.

The next 20 years would see about 70,000 Mormons traveling by wagons and handcarts to the Valley of the Great Salt Lake. Overland wagon travel declined after the completion of the transcontinental railroad in 1869, when emigrants could travel across the plains by rail.

The Handcarts: 1856 to 1860

A unique feature of the Mormon migration was their use of handcarts. Handcarts, two-wheeled carts that were pulled by emigrants, instead of draft animals, were sometimes used as an alternate means of transportation from 1856 to 1860. They were seen as a faster, easier, and cheaper way to bring European converts to Salt Lake City. Almost 3,000 Mormons, with 653 carts and 50 supply wagons, traveling in 10 different companies, made the trip over the trail to Salt Lake City. While not the first to use handcarts, they were the only group to use them extensively.

The handcarts were modeled after carts used by street sweepers and were made almost entirely of wood. They were generally 6 to 7 feet long, wide enough to span a narrow wagon track, and could be alternately pushed or pulled. The small boxes affixed to the carts were 3 to 4 feet long and 8 inches high. They could carry about 500 pounds, most of this weight consisting of trail provisions and a few personal possessions.

All but two of the handcart companies completed the journey with few problems. The fourth and fifth companies, known as the Martin and Willie companies, left Winter Quarters in August 1856. This was very late to begin the trip across the plains. They encountered severe winter weather west of present-day Casper, Wyoming, and hundreds died from exposure and famine before rescue parties could reach them. While these incidents were a rarity, they illustrate that the departure date from the trailhead was crucial to a successful journey.

The Trail Today

Congress established the Mormon Pioneer National Historic Trail as part of the National Trails System on November 10, 1978. This historic trail commemorates the 1846-47 journey of the Mormon people from Nauvoo, Illinois, to the Valley of the Great Salt Lake. The designated corridor is almost 1,300 miles long and is managed as a cooperative effort among private landowners, trail associations, state and local agencies, the National Park Service, the Bureau of Land Management, and the U.S. Forest Service. Land ownership along the trail is comprised of 822 miles (64 percent) on private land, 264 miles (20 percent) under federal management, and 214 miles (16 percent) in state and local ownership. Much of the trail is no longer visible, though some trail segments and sites can be visited. Long stretches of the trail can still be seen in Wyoming.

Reprinted from National Park Service brochure

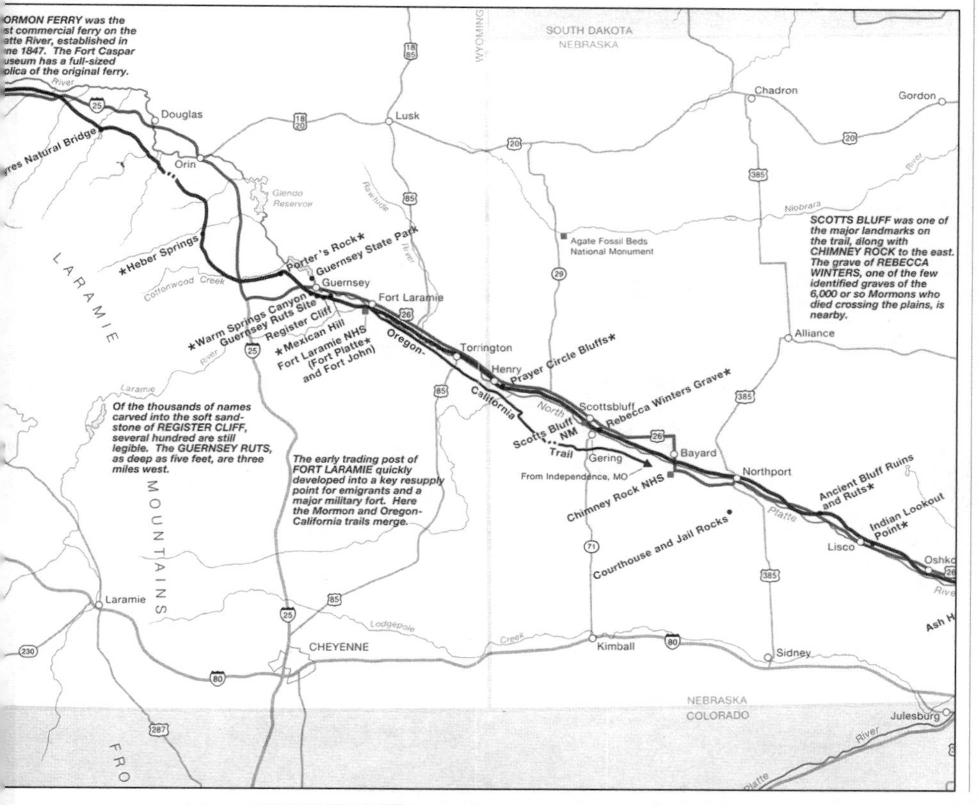

The Oregon Trail

"When you start over these wide plains, let no one leave dependent on his best friend for any thing; for if you do, you will certainly have a blow-out before you get far." —John Shively, 1846

Onto Oregon! It all began with a crude network of rutted traces across the land from the Missouri River to the Willamette River that was used by nearly 400,000 people. Today the 2,170-mile Oregon Trail still evokes an instant image, a ready recollection of the settlement of this continent, of the differences between American Indians and white settlers, and of new horizons. In 1840 only three states existed west of the Mississippi River. Maine's boundary with Canada was undefined. The western boundaries of the Nation lay roughly along the Continental Divide. Within 10 years the United States and Great Britain had drawn a boundary that stretched from the Atlantic to the Pacific. The western boundary moved from the Rocky Mountains to the Pacific Ocean. In another 40 years successive waves of emigrants completely eliminated any sense of frontier, changed the way of life of the American Indians, and ravaged many wild animal species, especially the herds of buffalo. Plows and barbed wire subdued the prairies. Transcontinental railroads knitted the great distances together.

The first Europeans to see the trans-Mississippi West were the mountain men, trappers, and the maritime explorers along the west coast. In Canada, the Hudson's Bay Company fur frontier was approaching the Columbia River basin. In 1812 John Jacob Astor established Astoria at the mouth of the Columbia in a countermove and sent Robert Stuart overland to carry dispatches east. Stuart found South Pass by following a Crow Indian trail. Only 7,000 feet above sea level, with easy gradients, South Pass has an attractive geographic proximity to the upper reaches of the Platte River. Both were determining factors in the routing of the Oregon Trail. The early frontiersmen found the passes, crossed the great rivers, and defined the vast reaches of the western interior. From the beginning these explorers contributed to a growing campaign to make the Oregon Country a part of either the United States or Great Britain, according to their own sometimes confused loyalties.

Economic depressions in 1837 and 1841 frustrated farmers and businessmen alike. The collapse of the international fur trade in 1839 intensified the hard times, and concerns of British domination of the Northwest grew. At the same time, eastern churches saw the American Indians of the Oregon Country as ready candidates for European ideas of civilization. Churches formed ardent missionary societies to create an active appetite for Christianity. In 1836 Marcus Whitman and his new wife, Narcissa, along with Henry and Eliza Spalding, headed for Oregon as missionaries. The letters they sent home publicized the opportunities and advantages of Oregon. Many people for many reasons had become interested in Oregon, but it was not until

Many travelers left their mark along the way at several locations. This man left his at Register Cliffs near Guernsey

1841 that the first group with serious intent to emigrate left the banks of the Missouri River and headed west. In 1843, nearly 1,000 completed the trip-an omen of the multitudes to follow.

The Oregon Trail was never a clearly defined track. In places the wagons passed in columns that might be hundreds of yards apart; those traces shifted with the effects of weather and use. In the course of time nature obliterated many of the fainter traces. Road builders followed the deeper, more permanent traces because they marked the best route. The Oregon Trail was quickly being forgotten. In 1906, 76-yearold Ezra Meeker, Oregon settler in 1852 and a tireless champion of the trail, set out in a covered wagon to retrace the route from west to east. Among his goals: to create a general interest in marking the route, to raise public awareness of the trail's history and heritage, and to point out the loss and damage resulting from careless disregard. Meeker met with Presidents Theodore Roosevelt and Calvin Coolidge, testified before Congress, and made several other publicity trips over the trail before his death in 1928. Today the National Park Service, in concert with the Bureau of Land Management, the Forest Service, and the states of Missouri, Kansas, Nebraska, Wyoming, Idaho, Oregon, and Washington strive to protect this legacy.

Across the Plains

Guidebooks

In book or pamphlet form, guidebooks were soon available for emigrants. Some provided good, solid, reliable information. Others contributed to the Oregon Fever that swept the country in the 1840s describing the land in almost Biblical terms.

Each part of the journey had its difficulties. For the first third of the way, the emigrants got used to the routine and work of travel. They learned to hitch and unhitch their livestock, to keep the wagons in good running order, and to make sure that their animals got the water and food they needed to survive. They learned to get along with their fellow emigrants, to agree on rules they would all follow on the journey, and to set up and break camp every night and morning. They learned to spread out in several columns so that they raised less dust and fewer of them had to breathe the choking air. They rotated positions in the line in a spirit of fairness. They learned to travel six out of seven days as experienced voices told them that some of the most difficult sections to travel would come at the end, when they would have to cross mountains before the winter snows. Fortunately the landscape was relatively gentle as they traveled through the Platte River Valley heading for the High Plains. Starting in the spring, too, provided them with abundant grass for the livestock. Water was also plentiful, and if they were early enough in the year campsites and waterholes would not be overgrazed or fouled. Cholera, whose cause was then unknown (but we now know can be traced to contaminated water), killed more travelers than anything else. How many emigrants died along the trail can never be known. The number of deaths varied from year to year. Most likely the death rate was little different from that for those who resisted the lure of the trail with all its potential disasters.

Loading the Wagon

Wagons usually measured 4 feet wide by 12 feet long. Into these 48 square feet were put supplies for traveling the trail and the wherewithal for beginning a new life. The emphasis was on tools and food, but a few family treasures and heirlooms were also carried. A typical load is shown at left. Using the wagon as shelter was almost an afterthought.

Over the Continental Divide

Excitement abounded when the emigrants passed the landmarks of Chimney Rock and Scotts Bluff, about onethird of the way on the

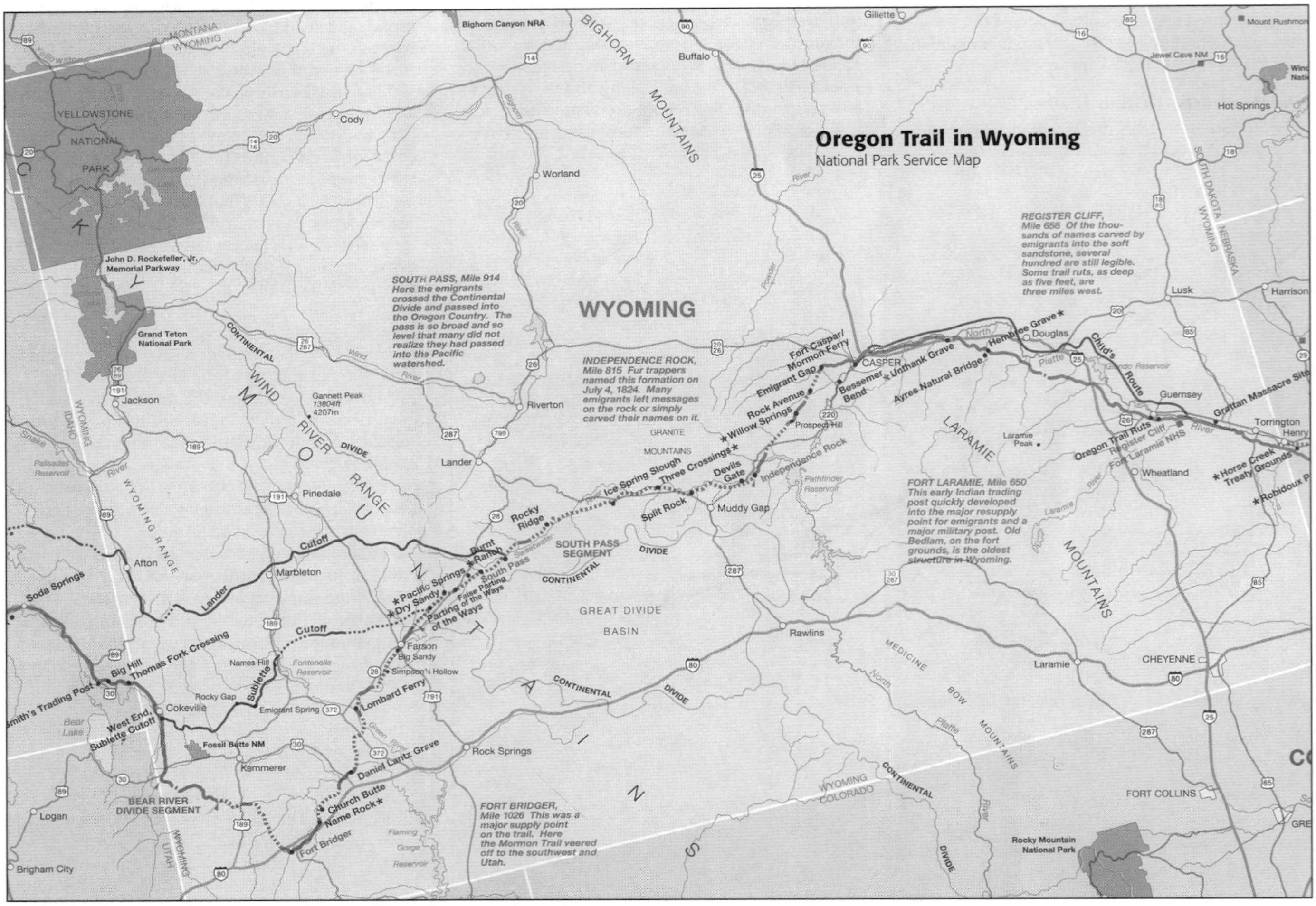

Oregon Trail in Wyoming
National Park Service Map

SOUTH PASS, Mile 914 Here the emigrants crossed the Continental Divide and passed into the Oregon Country. The pass is so broad and so level that many did not realize they had passed into the Pacific watershed.

INDEPENDENCE ROCK, Mile 815 Fur trappers named this formation on July 4, 1824. Many emigrants left messages on the rock or simply carved their names on it.

REGISTER CLIFF, Mile 658 Of the thousands of names carved by emigrants into the soft sandstone, several hundred are still legible. Some trail ruts, as deep as five feet, are three miles west.

FORT LARAMIE, Mile 650 This early Indian trading post quickly developed into the major resupply point for emigrants and a major military post. Old Bedlam, on the fort grounds, is the oldest structure in Wyoming.

FORT BRIDGER, Mile 1026 This was a major supply point on the trail. Here the Mormon Trail veered off to the southwest and Utah.

occurred often enough after 186010 keep both sides nervous when emigrant wagons crossed Indian lands. Wise members of both groups made an effort to avoid trouble, and they usually succeeded. Rather than fight, Indians often assisted emigrant parties on the way west. Countless instances of assistance in the form of extra wagon teams, food, and medical help were provided by Indians, who served as trail guides and pilots at dangerous crossings. Indian life was affected radically by the emigrants, who brought disease and killed the wild game. And despite popular fiction, emigrants circled their wagons to corral their livestock rather than to ward oft Indian attack.

Trail's End

Footsore, weary, and exhausted, traveler and beast alike faced the final third and the most difficult part of the trail. Yet speed was of the essence, for winter snows could close mountain passes or trap unprepared and tired groups of emigrants as they crossed both the Blue Mountains in eastern Oregon and the Cascades to the west. The photograph below shows a family entering Baker City, just east of the Blue Mountains, about 1864. In the early years, before the Barlow Road across the Cascades was opened as a toll road in 1846, emigrants had no choice but to go down the Columbia from The Dallas on a raft or abandon their wagons and build boats. The Columbia was full of rapids and dangerous currents; many emigrants lost their lives, almost within sight of their goal. Once the settlers arrived in the Willamette Valley they spread out to establish farms and small towns. Initially, few emigrants settled north of the Columbia, but once the United States and Great Britain agreed on an international boundary and the Hudson's Bay Company moved its post at Fort Vancouver to Vancouver Island, Americans settled in present-day Washington as well. The 1850 census showed that 12,093 people lived in Oregon. Ten years later, when Oregon had been a state for one year, 52,495 were counted. Small towns were on the verge of becoming cities. Frame houses replaced log cabins. Orchards grew to maturity. The land was acquiring the look of civilization that the emigrants had left behind.

Hundreds of thousands of travelers literally carved the trail into stone near Guernsey.

trail. It meant they were making progress. By this time, too, they would have an idea if their money would hold out. Tolls at ferries and bridges had to be paid. Supplies and food were bought at trading posts along the way or from other emigrants. A week's journey beyond Scotts Bluff brought them to Fort Laramie, the great supply depot and resting place. Here they could replenish dwindling stocks of food andother staples — br a price. Wheels could be repaired and wagon boxes tightened before they set out on the steepening ascent to the Continental Divide. Water-and grass for livestock-became more scarce. The drier air caused wooden wheels to shrink and the iron tires that held the wheels together loosened or rolled off. Buffalo herds on which the emigrants had depended for fresh meat to supplement their staples became increasingly hard to find the farther west they went. Cooking fuel, whether wood or buffalo chips, was also harder to find. To lighten their wagons, the emigrants left treasured pieces of furniture and other personal belongings by the wayside. Surviving the trip had become of paramount importance; food and tools were vital, heirlooms were not. From Fort Laramie to Fort Bridger, on the western edge of present-day Wyoming, the Mormon Trail flowed with the Oregon and California trails. At Fort Bridger the emigrants parted ways as those bound for Oregon turned northwest toward the Snake River Valley. Alternate routes included Sublette's Cutoff and the Lander Cutoff. Beginning just west of South Pass, Sublette's Cutoff crossed a barren, arid stretch of country where for 50 miles there was no water and little grass. Those who chose the grueling route and survived had saved 85 miles and a week of travel.

Wyoming Tidbits

The Oregon Trail extended from Independence, Missouri to the Columbia River. More than 300,000 people traveled the route between 1840 and 1869.

Emigrant and Indian

Early emigrants generally found the Indians they encountered to be cordial and helpful. Some never even saw any Indians As emigrant numbers multiplied, however, the friendly relationships became strained. Hostilities and casualties

The California Trail

Manifest Destiny-Paradise

"Ho for California!" Free land. Gold. Adventure. Between 1841 and 1869, more than a quarter million people answered this call and crossed the plains and mountains to the "El Dorado" of the West. By 1849 the lure of instant wealth and tales of gold beckoned at the end of the 2,000-mile California Trail. The story of the men, women, and children who traveled overland to the West coast has become an American epic.

Since the late 1700s, the West had held out the promise of boundless opportunity. After Lewis and Clark found a way to the Pacific in 1805, fur traders followed Indian trails up western river valleys and across mountain passes, filling in the blank spaces on early maps that represented unknown country. By the late 1830s, mountain men had explored most of the routes that became overland trails. In 1837 an economic panic swept the United States and gave people already itching to move an additional reason to go west.

Throughout the 1840s promoters and trail guides worked hard to create an idyllic picture of the prospects for greater fortune and better health open to Americans who made the journey to California. One young emigrant reported that a

Wyoming Tidbits

In 1865 a bill was introduced into Congress asking for a temporary government for the Territory of Wyoming. Had the tabled bill passed, Wyoming would have been included in what is now Nebraska and South Dakota.

pamphlet describing a lush California with its ideal climate and flowers that bloomed all winter "made me just crazy to move out there, for I thought such a country must be a paradise."

Why Go West?

Watching "one continual stream" of "honest looking open hearted people" going west in 1846, mountain man James Clyman asked why "so many of all kinds and classes of People should sell out comfortable homes in Missouri and Elsewhere pack up and start across such an immense Barren waste to settle in some new Place of which they have at most so uncertain information." Clyman's answer?—"this is the character of my countrymen."

What was the character of Americans in the 1840s? Many embraced Manifest Destiny, a phrase penned by journalist John O'Sullivan in July 1845 to explain the U.S. government's thirst for expansion. It was a new term but not a new idea. Since the beginning of the republic, leaders had aggressively claimed land for the United States. Manifest Destiny crystallized the idea that it was God's will and the rightful destiny of Americans to take over the continent. It became a rallying cry for overlanders to head west.

Personal motives of the emigrants varied. Some planned to build permanent homes or farms, but many hoped to make their fortunes and return east. One 1846 traveler noted that his companions all "agreed in the one general object, that of bettering their condition," but individual hopes and dreams "were as various as can well be imagined." Dreams spurred a diversity of emigrants too: Americans, African Americans, Indians, Canadians, Europeans-people of all ages and backgrounds crossed the plains.

Beginnings

The Bidwell-Bartleson party, the first emigrants to go to California, left Missouri in May 1841 with 69 people. At Soda Springs, Idaho, some continued on to Oregon. The others, knowing only "that California lay to the west," struggled across the north end of the Great Salt Lake Desert. They abandoned their wagons before reaching the Humboldt River, packed their livestock with necessities, and, in November, 39 travelers reached California.

In 1844 the Stephens- Townsend-Murphy party, traveling the Truckee route, reached the Sierra Nevada in November. Stalled by snow, they left some wagons at Donner Lake and packed onward. In the spring they retrieved their wagons, becoming the first emigrants to take wagons all the way to Sutter's Fort, California. In 1845 John C. Fremont explored a new route across the Great Basin. The next summer promoter Lansford W. Hastings convinced about 80 wagons of late-starting emigrants to try this new cutoff across the Great Salt Lake Desert. The last of them was the ill-fated Donner-Reed party.

In 1846 a party from the Willamette Valley opened a southern route to Oregon, now known as the Applegate Trail. Peter Lassen branched south from this route in 1848 to reach his ranch in northern California. Not all early traffic on the California Trail headed west. After marching across the Southwest during the war with Mexico, Mormon Battalion veterans left Sutter's Fort in 1848 for the Valley of the Great Salt Lake. They opened a wagon road over Carson Pass, south of Lake Tahoe, that became the preferred route for wagon travel during the gold rush.

Gold Rush

James W. Marshall discovered gold on January 24, 1848, at John Sutter's sawmill on the South Fork of the American River, about 40 miles east of Sutter's Fort. Fortune hunters from California, Oregon, and Sonora, Mexico, flooded the goldfields by June, but the news spread more slowly across the continent. In December 1848 President James Polk confirmed the discovery in a report to Congress, thus setting the stage for the largest voluntary migration in American history.

By the spring of 1849 gold fever was an epidemic. Single men headed west to find wealth and adventure. Married men left families and jobs, hoping to return home in a year or so with enough money to last a lifetime. Thousands of travelers clogged the trail to California. The size of the rush created a host of problems. Almost every blade of grass vanished before the enormous trail herds. Overcrowded campsites and unsanitary conditions contributed to the spread of cholera. Desperation created tension as Indians saw the plants and animals they depended on for food disappear.

The gold rush added new trails to California. Mountain man Jim Beckwourth and surveyor William Nobles opened routes across the Sierra Nevada, while thousands traveled to the goldfields across Mexico and the Southwest. Cherokee Indians from Arkansas and present-day Oklahoma opened a route through the Rockies, the first that did not use South Pass.

Cutoffs and Variants

Wyoming Tidbits

California, Arizona, New Mexico, Nevada, Utah, western Colorado, and southwestern Wyoming comprised the territory taken from Mexico following the Mexican War in 1846.

The California Trail eventually offered many ways to get to the West Coast. The network of cutoffs and variants became what is often described as a rope with frayed ends. Most emigrants set out from towns on the, Missouri River and followed the Oregon Trail along the Platte and North Platte rivers. The trails became a single cord (more-or-less) between Fort Kearny and South Pass in present-day Wyoming. At Parting of the Ways the strands unwound again. The western end of the rope fanned out at the Humbolt Sink into routes leading to California and the goldfields.

South Pass marked the halfway point on the

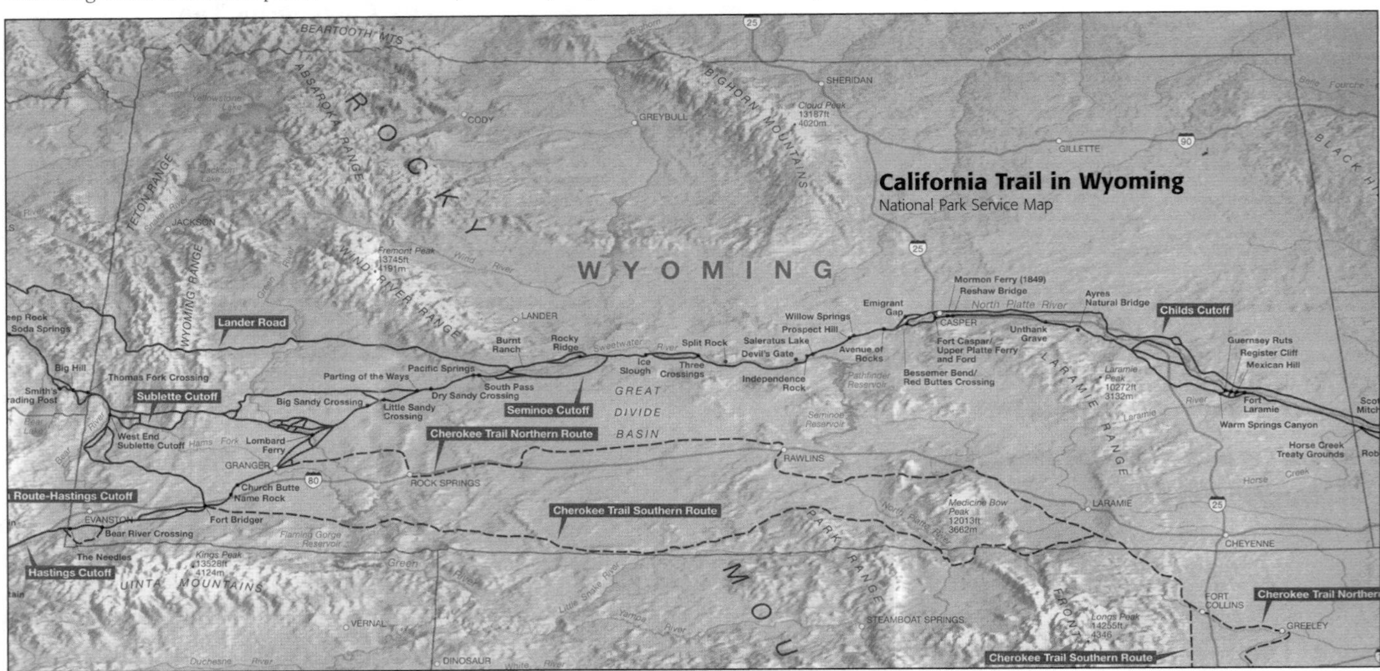

California Trail in Wyoming
National Park Service Map

trail and the end of the long ascent up the Continental Divide. West of South Pass travelers could go several ways: to Idaho and the Raft River area, where the main branch of the California Trail separated from the Oregon Trail; or to Utah and the settlements of the Latter-day Saints, Mormons, which were popular way stations. After visiting Salt Lake City, most emigrants followed the Salt Lake Cutoff back to the main trail at City of Rocks in present-day Idaho. For wagons the Humboldt River Valley provided the best practical wagon road through the basin-and-range country, but overlanders continually sought easier ways to cross the formidable Sierra Nevada.

By 1860 freight and mail companies, military expeditions, new settlements and trading stations, and thousands of travelers going in both directions transformed the California Trail into a road.

Seeing the Elephant

> ## *Wyoming Tidbits*
>
> Talk about home on the range - there are 2.8 cattle for every one person in Wyoming!

Every great human migration seems to have its own catchphrase, and the forty-niners were no exception. "Seeing the elephant" characterized emigrant encounters with vast plains and barren deserts and the difficulty of surviving the harrowing trek across the western landscape. The expression predated the gold rush and was based on the thrill of seeing these exotic beasts in circuses. For overlanders the elephant symbolized a challenging trip, the adventure of a lifetime.

If you had "seen the elephant" you had seen about all there was to see! People had never encountered anything like these prairies, canyons, deserts, and rugged mountains. The deserts of the Great Basin and the barrier of the Sierra Nevada made the California Trail the most difficult of all overland trails. Almost every emigrant recalled seeing the elephant somewhere along this arduous stretch. For many the encounter came on the Humboldt River-the Humbug, as some called it in disgust—a stream that got more sluggish and alkaline as it bent west and south until it finally disappeared into a shallow lake.

Others met the beast on the Fortymile Desert east of today's Reno, Nevada. The travelers lucky enough to escape the deserts of the Great Basin with animals and outfit intact were almost certain to see the elephant among the steep passes of the Sierra Nevada. Those who turned back often claimed to have seen the elephant's tail. One emigrant, who turned back after only 700 miles said "he had seen the Elephant and eaten its ears."

Wagons and Waybills

Going west was an expensive proposition. Emigrants needed supplies (food, utensils, stoves, bedding, lanterns, and more), hardware (axes, wagon parts, shovels, rope, other tools), livestock, and money to last for many months. Most travelers used light farm wagons that came to be called prairie schooners because their canvas tops reminded emigrants of sails on a ship. Schooners could carry about a ton of food and supplies, and often travelers packed their belongings into every bit of space. Treasures such as china, heirlooms, and furniture were jettisoned when it became obvious that the load was too heavy.

Overlanders preferred oxen to pull their wagons. They were slower than horses but cheaper, more reliable and powerful, and harder to steal. Oxen also fared better on prairie grass than did horses and mules, an important consideration because emigrants' lives could depend on the health of their livestock.

Getting started was one thing—getting safely to California was another. Guidebooks, or "waybills," became available almost as soon as the trail opened. Most waybills offered practical advice about routes, landmarks, distances, and what equipment and supplies to take. Some, such as <I>The Emigrants' Guide, to Oregon and California,<I> 1845, by promoter and guide Lansford W. Hastings, described California in almost heavenly terms and helped fuel what became "California fever."

Women and Families

Although single men made up the majority of early emigrants and forty-niners, women and families played an important role on the trail.

The first major wagon train, the Bidwell-Bartleson party, set out in 1841 with five women and about 10 children. At age 19 Nancy Kelsey (carrying her baby over the Sierra Nevada after the party abandoned its wagons) became the first covered-wagon woman to reach California. Iowans Catherine Haun and her husband caught gold fever in 1849. The Hauns, and about 25 of their neighbors in the wagon party, longed to go west, pick up gold off the ground, and return home to pay off their debts.

Catherine wrote in her journal that women and children on the trail "exerted a good influence, as the men did not take such risks, were more alert about the teams and seldom had accidents, [and] more attention was paid to cleanliness and sanitation." Even "the meals were more regular and better cooked thus preventing much sickness." Births on the trail were as common as deaths. As one girl recalled, "Three days after my little sister died... we stopped for a few hours, and my sister Olivia was born."

By 1852 about a third of all those crossing the plains were women. Five years later, it was common to find wagon parties made up largely of women and children. These women, as did all emigrants, left familiar homes and endured hardships to find a better life.

Indians and Emigrants

The quiet land along the California Trail may have seemed empty but Indian nations had lived there for more than 10,000 years. Unlike Hollywood stereotypes, Indians were more of a help than a danger to emigrants. In the 1840s fatal confrontations were rare. Travelers entrusted their wagons and families to Indians who guided them across swift rivers and through unfamiliar country.

In 1844 Paiute Chief Truckee guided emigrants along the route and the river that they named after him. Stories of Indian massacres far outnumbered actual hostile encounters. "We are continually hearing of the depredations of the indians," wrote Caroline Richardson in 1852, "but we have not seen one yet." Conflict increased in the 1850s and 1860s as thousands of emigrants and their livestock destroyed Indian food sources. Some Indians tried to collect payment for passage across tribal lands. A few emigrants paid, but most felt little sympathy for Indian claims to the land. Relations deteriorated: Indians killed travelers, and emigrants killed Indians.

The violence attracted attention, but it was not the reason most emigrants perished. Thousands died from drownings, accidents, and disease, especially cholera. Many incidents were the work of criminals called "white Indians," who were notorious for their brutality. One 1850 traveler concluded that "the savage Indians" were "afraid to come near the road" and "near all the stealing and killing is done by the Whites following the Trains."

An Enduring Legacy

Travel to California in days, not months! In 1869 the Union Pacific from the east and the Central Pacific from the west connected their rail tracks at Utah's Promontory Summit. A golden spike tapped symbolically to celebrate the union hailed a new, exciting way to travel the continent, and it signaled the demise of the wagon trails to the West.

Although dust from the wagons settled nearly 150 years ago, the California Trail's heritage lives on with the people who love its history and in the railroads, interstate highways, and powerlines that follow the routes of the old emigrant trails. Today, public lands preserve much of the original landscape. Surviving ruts offer silent testimony of the California Trail, but no one tells this epic better than the people who traveled it.

Westward travelers shared similar experiences: the drudgery of walking more than 2,000 miles, the struggle to cross forbidding landscapes, extremes of temperature and weather, shortages of food and water, fear of Indians, accidents, sickness, and death. These emigrants, who saw the elephant and more, remembered the trip west as their life's greatest adventure. Their experiences-often recorded eloquently in journals, drawings, and letters-inspired American popular culture and influenced art, literature, and the movies. Their stories are part of the legacy of the American West.

Reprint of National Park Service brochure.

> ## *Wyoming Tidbits*
>
> The Pony Express, though in operation only 18 months, was a vital form of communication. In those pre-telegraph days of 1860, riders carried mail on 10-day, 2,000 mile routes from St. Joseph, Missouri, to Sacramento, California, and back, crossing the mountains and plains of Wyoming.

THE PONY EXPRESS

"Men Wanted" The undersigned wishes to hire ten or a dozen men, familiar with the management of horses, as hostlers, or riders on the Overland Express Route via Salt Lake City. Wages $50 per month and found."
- Ad in Sacramento Union, March 19, 1860.

More than 1,800 miles in 10 days! From St. Joseph, Missouri, to Sacramento, California the Pony Express could deliver a letter more quickly than ever before.

In operation for only 18 months between April 1860 and October 1861, the Pony Express nevertheless has become synonymous with the Old West. In the era before electronic communication, the Pony Express was the thread that tied East to West.

As a result of the 1849 Gold Rush, the 1847 Mormon exodus to Utah and the thousands who moved west on the Oregon Trail starting in the 1840s, the need for a fast mail service beyond the

Rocky Mountains became obvious. This need was partially filled by outfits such as the Butterfield Overland Mail Service starting in 1857 and private carriers in following years.

But when postmaster general Joseph Holt scaled back overland mail service to California and the central region of the country in 1858, an even greater need for mail arose. The creation of the Leavenworth & Pike's Peak Express Company by William H. Russell, Alexander Majors and William B. Waddell became the answer. It was later known as the Pony Express.

Most of the original trail has been obliterated either by time or human activities. Along many segments, the trail's actual route and exact length are matters of conjecture. In the western states, the majority of the trail has been converted, over the years, to double track dirt roads. Short pristine segments, believed to be traces of the original trail, can be seen only in Utah and California. However, approximately 120 historic sites may eventually be available to the public, including 50 existing Pony Express stations or station ruins.

Wyoming Tidbits

In 1861, transcontinental telegraph lines were completed along the old emigrant trail. Builder Edward Creighton's project was subsidized by the federal government at $40,000 a year for ten years.

The First Ride

"...citizens paraded the streets with bands of music, fireworks were set off....the best feeling was manifested by everybody."

- New York times, April 14, 1860 on the success of the first Pony Express delivery

With only two months to make the Pony Express a reality, the team of William H. Russell, Alexander Majors and William B. Waddell had their hands full in January 1860. Over 100 stations, 400-500 horses and enough riders were needed - at an estimated cost of $70,000.

But on April 3, 1860, the first official delivery began at the eastern terminus of the Pony Express in St. Joseph, Missouri. Amid great fanfare and with many dignitaries present, a mail pouch containing 49 letters, five telegrams and miscellaneous papers was handed to a rider. At 7:15 p.m., a cannon was fired and the rider bolted off to a waiting ferry boat.

The Pony Express was set up to provide a fresh horse every 10-15 miles and a fresh rider every 75-100 miles. 75 horses were needed total to make a one-way trip. Average speed was 10 miles per hour.

On April 9 at 6:45 p.m., the first rider from the east reached Salt Lake City, Utah. Then, on April 12, the mail pouch reached Carson City, Nevada at 2:30 p.m.

The riders raced over the Sierra Nevadas, through Placerville, California and on to Sacramento. Around midnight on April 14, 1860, the first mail pouch was delivered via the Pony Express to San Francisco.

Despite the success and approval of the public, the Pony Express was by no means a trouble-free operation after the first delivery. Costs and difficulties of maintaining the extensive network of stations, people and horses were numerous. Yet the Pony Express, with the exception of delays caused by the Pyramid Lake War, stayed in operation until the telegraph's arrival in 1861.

The Pyramid Lake War

Of the many potential problems facing the Pony Express - weather, supply difficulties, rider fatigue, etc. - the biggest one was unforeseen.

The Pyramid Lake War crippled the operation of the Pony Express starting in May 1860, and continued to do so for many months following. A case of white mineral-seekers encroaching on traditional Indian lands led to the war.

Following the discovery of silver in the Washoe Hills of Nevada in July 1859, white settlers poured into the region from both east and west. The abrupt arrival of so many whites naturally brought them into conflict with the Paiute Indians who lived in the area. Prospectors claimed water, feed and land for themselves without regard for the Paiutes' rights.

The Pony Express was also guilty of taking Indian resources. In the desert of western Nevada, for example, relay stations were built at critical water sources that the Indians depended on. Conflicts between whites and Indians became inevitable.

On May 7, 1860, an incident at the Williams Station in Carson Valley, Nevada set off the Pyramid Lake War. An old Paiute man and a younger Pauite woman went to a house owned by J.O. Williams, a white. Four white men in the house tied up the man and attacked the woman. The Pauites were later set free but the Pauite man returned later with friends who forced the four white men into the house. The house was burned with the men in it.

The Pyramid Lake War had begun. The Paiutes claimed a big victory when they defeated U.S. Major William Ormsby's force in Nevada, but the Indians eventually were defeated.

Following the outbreak of the war, Indian raids became more common at the remote Pony Express stations in western Nevada. On May 21, 1860, a station keeper was killed and the station burned at Simpson Park Station. Major disruptions of the Pony Express ensued.

In June of 1860 the Pony Express cancelled operations between Carson City and Salt Lake City because of the depredations. Service continued between St. Joseph and Salt Lake City, but little revenue came in from this stretch.

By July 1860, with the help of federal troops and stepped-up security measures, the Pony Express again began delivering mail to California. Delays had cost the company around $75,000. But the delays were not yet over. In August, trouble erupted again at remote stations in Nevada.

More delays ensued, further crippling the already struggling Pony Express. By the following year, delays in deliveries and lack of federal assistance would help shut down the Pony Express. *National Park Service article.*

Wild Horses in Wyoming

In 1971, Congress passed legislation to protect, manage, and control wild horses and burros on the public lands. The Wild Free-Roaming Horse and Burro Act declared these animals to be "living symbols of the historic and pioneer spirit of the West."

Congress further declared that "wild free-roaming horses and burros shall be protected from capture, branding, harassment, or death..." and that they are "...an integral part of the natural system of the public lands." Furthermore, Bureau regulation requires that wild horses and burros be considered comparable with other resource values within the area.

The Bureau of Land Management maintains and manages wild horses or burros in herd management areas (HMAs). In the ten states where BLM manages horses, there are 270 HMAs. In Wyoming, about 3,000 horses are managed within 16 different HMAs scattered across the state. Wyoming has no wild burros.

The Bureau establishes an appropriate management level (AML) for each HMA. The AML is the population objective for the HMA that will ensure a thriving ecological balance among all the users and resources of the HMA, for example, wildlife, livestock, wild horses, vegetation, water, and soil.

McCullough Peaks HMA

The McCullough Peaks HMA is located 12 to 27 miles east of Cody, Wyoming (approximately 50 miles east of Yellowstone Park). The HMA encompasses 109,814 acres of land. The climate is typical of a cold desert. The average annual precipitation ranges from five to nine inches. Topography is highly variable, ranging from mostly flat to slightly rolling foothills carved by drainages, to colorful badlands and to desert mountains featuring steep slopes, cliffs and canyons. The current wild horse population in the McCullough Peaks HMA is estimated to be 150 animals. The appropriate management level is 70 to 140 animals.

A diversity of coat colors (bay, brown, black, sorrel, chestnut, white, buckskin, gray, palomino, blue, red and strawberry roans) and patterns (such as piebald and skewbald) can be found in the McCullough Peaks wild horses. The animals tend to be moderate- to large-sized and habitat conditions are such that the horses are in very good condition. The combination of size, conformation, coat colors and patterns, and excellent physical condition have become a draw for potential adopters and a matter of reputation for "McCullough Peaks" horses.

Horses in the McCullough Peaks HMA usually have adequate water from winter snows and spring runoff, which fill reservoirs and intermittent streams. No predation of wild horses has been documented in the HMA and it is considered to have little or no effect on the wild horse population. The McCullough Peaks HMA encompasses the McCullough Peaks Wilderness Study Area (WSA) and horses roam inside and outside the WSA.

Antelope Hills HMA

The Antelope Hills HMA encompasses 57,000 acres, of which 54,600 are BLM-administered public lands. The AML for this HMA is 60-82 adult horses. The area is located approximately 15 miles south/southeast of Atlantic, City,

Rockhounding in Wyoming

Where Is Collection Permissible?
Rockhounding is recognized as a legitimate recreational pursuit on nearly all of the 17.8 million acres of public land in Wyoming. These public lands administered by the BLM are open to everyone, to take limited amounts of rock material for noncommercial purposes without charge. Maps showing the location of public lands in Wyoming can be obtained from this office or the field offices (for addresses see information handout "WYNF-0007, BLM Offices in Wyoming"). You should check with the BLM field offices to become familiar with local procedures, policies and areas with authorized restrictions.

No Historic Artifacts, Please
The Archaeological Resources Protection Act of 1979 and the Antiquities Act of 1906 are designed to protect our Nation's cultural resources. These laws prohibit the unauthorized excavation, removal, damage, or alteration of any archaeological and historical site or object. Petroglyphs, human graves, old dwellings, pottery, stone tools, arrowheads, and other remains of Indians and early inhabitants are protected by law because they may provide important links to our past.

How About Fossils?
Fossil collecting has its own set of rules. Vertebrate fossils (which includes all bones and teeth) are off limits to rockhounders, but invertebrate and plant fossils that are not of special scientific interest may be collected in reasonable amounts for personal use. No fossils collected from public land can be sold, traded, or bartered. Please see the pamphlet titled Fossils on America's Public Lands available at BLM offices.

May Petrified Wood Be Collected?
Hobby collection has special rules. Please see Fossils on America's Public Lands pamphlet. A material site contract must be obtained from a BLM office for collection of more than 250 pounds a year, or for commercial use.

Collected But Not Destroyed . . .
Explosives or power equipment must not be used in excavating or removing petrified wood, and may apply to other collecting. Off-road vehicle use may also be restricted. Also, fossil and/or mineral collecting may be restricted or prohibited in some areas to allow dedication of the land for another purpose. Such restrictions follow official notice in the Federal Register and the areas are posted.

Permits?
The BLM grants permits to qualified individuals and institutions to conduct scientific research at archaeological, historical, and paleontological sites. These permits are issued and administered by the BLM Wyoming State Office in Cheyenne. Permits are given only to individuals holding advanced university degrees in archaeology, paleontology or a related field and are associated with an accredited institution.

Reporting Archaeological Or Fossil Sites
All archaeological or paleontological sites such as prehistoric campsites, buffalo jumps, and fossils of many kinds may be of scientific interest. The sites should be reported to the nearest BLM field office for evaluation by archaeologists or paleontologists.

How About Gemstones?
The private collector is welcome to take specimens of gemstones as well as common variety minerals from public lands. However, a permit must be obtained from the BLM field office if common variety minerals are to be taken in large quantities or for resale.

"Locating" Gemstones
Claims may be "located" for gemstones under the general mining laws if location requirements can be met. Collecting gemstone specimens on public land remains an accepted recreational use of the public land, however...

Don't Be A "Claim Jumper"
Care must be taken not to violate the rights of a mining claimant. Patented claims are private land and permission to collect specimens on them must be obtained from the property owner. Unpatented claims, however, are still public lands and rockhounders may pursue their hobby on such lands as long as they do not interfere with mining activities or collect locatable minerals or gemstones for which the claim is "located". In other words, if an unpatented claim is located for jade rockhounders can look for and collect any mineral except jade (claimants frequently locate claims for all locatable minerals). The claimant is entitled to the rights to the jade which is, for all practical purposes, his private property. A claim owner may not legally charge fees for recreational use of unpatented claims.

Article courtesy of Bureau of Land Management

Wyoming. Elevations in the HMA range from 7,100 to 7,250 feet along Cyclone Rim. The HMA is bisected by the Continental Divide National Scenic Trail. The area receives 5-7 inches of precipitation annually. The predominate vegetation type is sagebrush/grass. Riparian zones are infrequent but very important to wild horses, wildlife, and livestock. The topography ranges from rolling flatlands south of Cyclone Rim, uplifted ridges along Cyclone Rim, and abrupt rocky zones interspersed with rolling lands north of the rim to the Sweetwater River.

Crooks Mountain HMA

The Crooks Mountain HMA is located directly southeast of Sweetwater Station, Wyoming, and encompasses about 51,000 acres. The AML for this HMA is 65-100 adult horses. Elevations in the HMA range from 6,900 to 8,100 feet. The lower elevations receive approximately 10-14 inches of precipitation annually, and the upper elevations receive 15-20 inches annually. The major vegetation types are sagebrush/grass, woodland, and riparian. Topography within the HMA is generally rolling hills and slopes to the north and south of Crooks Mountain. The Crooks Mountain portion of the herd area is quite steep and broken with mountainous terrain. The area supports significant wildlife populations of elk, deer, and antelope. Livestock graze the area from May to December.

Muskrat Basin, Conant Creek, Rock Creek, and Dishpan Butte HMAs

These four HMAs are located in southeast Fremont County. They encompass about 375,000 acres of land, of which about 90% are BLM-administerd public lands. While the four HMAs are managed with recognized individual populations, there is no geographic separation of the HMAs and the gates between them remain open a significant part of the year. As a result, the horses move regularly among the HMAs, helping to ensure the overall genetic health of the horses. Topography of the area includes high ridges and steep terrain with grand vistas. Beaver Rim, located on the western edge of the HMAs, is a beautiful, high escarpment with amazing views of the Wind River Mountains, Copper Mountains, and Owl Creek Mountains. Elevations in the HMAs range from 5,300 to 7,200 feet. The area receives 5 to 12 inches of precipitation a year, depending on the elevation, most of it in the form of snow.

The AML for these HMAs is 320 horses. A full range of colors is present. Most horses are solid in color. The horses range from 11 to 15 hands and 750-1000 pounds mature weight. Health is good with few apparent problems. Domestic cattle and sheep utilize the area during spring, summer, and fall. Vegetation is dominated by various sage and grass species. Elk, deer, and antelope also inhabit this area.

Green Mountain HMA

The Green Mountain HMA encompasses 88,000 acres, of which 74,000 acres are BLM-administered public lands. Topography within the herd area is generally gently rolling hills and slopes north and south of Green Mountain. Green Mountain itself is quite steep with mountainous terrain and conifer/aspen forests. Elevations range from 6,200 to 9,200 feet with grand vistas of the Red Desert, Sweetwater Rocks, and Oregon Trail from the higher elevations. Precipitation ranges

from 10-14 inches at the lower elevations to 15-20 inches at the upper elevations. Most of the precipitation is in the form of snow.

The AML for this HMA is 300 horses. A full range of colors is present. Most horses are solid in color, but a noticeable number of tobiano paints are present. The horses range from 11 to 15 hands and 750-1000 pounds mature weight. Health is good with few apparent problems. Domestic cattle and sheep utilize the area in all seasons with summer cattle use predominating. Vegetation around the mountain is dominated by various sage, grass, woodland, and riparian species. The area supports significant wildlife populations of elk, deer, antelope, and moose.

Stewart Creek HMA

The Stewart Creek HMA encompasses

231,124 acres, of which 215,369 are BLM-administered public lands. The Continental Divide (eastern boundary of the Great Divide Basin) traverses the HMA in a north-south direction in its eastern portion along Lost Soldier and Bull Springs rims. Adjacent to these rims on either side are strongly rolling uplands. These areas transition to the gently rolling uplands which comprise the majority of the HMA. Elevation ranges from 6500 to 7900 feet. The most abundant plant community is sagebrush/grass. The climate in the Great Divide Basin is fairly harsh, with long, severe winters. Annual precipitation ranges from less than seven inches at the lower elevations to more than ten inches at some of the higher elevations. Most of the precipitation occurs as snow.

The AML for this HMA is 150 horses. The horses exhibit a full range of colors but most are solid in color. A noticeable number of tobiano paints are present, usually as entire bands. The present population has been influenced by the routine escape of domestic saddle stock from the surrounding populated areas. The horses range from 14 to 15 hands and 800-1000 pounds mature weight.

Lost Creek HMA

The Lost Creek HMA encompasses 250,000 acres, of which 235,000 acres are BLM-administered public lands. The HMA lies within the Great Divide Basin, a closed basin out of which no water flows. Some desert playa and vegetated dune areas are interspersed throughout the HMA. Several sensitive desert wetland riparian areas occur throughout the area, including both intermittent and perennial lakes and streams. Elevation ranges from 6500 to 6800 feet. Winters are long and severe. Annual precipitation averages a little less than six inches. The Lost Creek HMA is joined on the east by the Stewart Creek HMA, on the north by the Antelope Hills HMA, and on the west by the Divide Basin HMA.

The AML for this HMA is 70 horses. A full range of colors is present. The present population has been influenced by the routine escape of domestic saddle stock from the surrounding populated areas. The horses range from 14 to 15 hands and 800-1000 pounds mature weight. Genetic testing on horses in the Lost Creek HMA shows them to be closely identified with the Spanish Mustang breed.

Genetic testing on the Lost Creek wild horse herd has shown the horses to carry a very high percentage of genetic markers identified with the Spanish Mustang breed. This means the horses are genetically more like the Spanish Mustang and other New World Iberian breeds than they are like other breeds such as American Quarter Horse or Morgan. The characteristic makes the Lost Creek herd unique among the wild horse herds of Wyoming tested so far.

According to Chuck Reed, Rawlins Field Office, whose work is concentrated in the wild horse program, "The horses in the Lost Creek herd look a little different than other wild, free-roaming horses in Wyoming. They are just a tiny bit smaller, and their coloring is different than that of neighboring herds. Paints are less common in Lost Creek with solid colors predominant. Dorsal stripes and other so-called 'primitive markings' are more common."

The BLM has been working with noted equine geneticist Dr. Gus Cothran of the University of Kentucky to better understand the genetics of the wild horses it manages. This information will help the BLM develop a management plan for the horse herd that will ensure its longterm viability as a rare and unique genetic resource. The plan will identify ways the management of the Lost Creek herd and its habitat might need to be modified in order to protect the rare and unique genetic resource.

The Spanish Mustang breed was introduced to the Americas by the Spanish explorers and conquistadors in the 1500s. Genetic testing on the Pryor Mountain wild horse herd in southern Montana has shown it to also be closely related to the Spanish Mustang breed.

Adobe Town HMA

The Adobe Town HMA is located in southcentral Wyoming between Interstate 80 and the Colorado/Wyoming border. It encompasses 472,812 acres of which 444,744 are BLM-administered public lands. The topography of the area is varied with everything from colorful eroded desert badlands to wooded buttes and escarpments. In between are extensive rolling to rough uplands interspersed with some desert playa and vegetated dune areas. Limited, sensitive desert riparian areas are important features of the landscape. Winters are long and severe. Annual precipitation ranges from less than seven inches in the desert basins to more than twelve inches at some of the higher elevations. Elevation ranges from 6600 ft to 7800 ft along Kinney Rim, which forms the western boundary of the HMA. Some of the HMA is in the Adobe Town Wilderness Study Area. Other features in the area include the Cherokee Trail, the Haystacks, and Powder Rim.

The AML for this HMA is 700 horses. The horses exhibit a full range of colors, with roans and greys predominating. The present population has been influenced by the routine escape of domestic saddle stock from the surrounding populated areas. The horses range from 14 to 15 hands and 900-1100 pounds mature weight. Health is good with few apparent problems. One of the most famous wild horses of all times, named Desert Dust, came from this area.

Great Divide Basin HMA

The Great Divide Basin HMA encompasses 778,915 acres, of which 562,702 acres are BLM - administered public lands. The management area is located 40 miles east of Rock Springs, to the Rawlins/Rock Springs field office boundary, west to the Continental Divide, and north of I-80 to just south of South Pass City. The northern portion of the HMA consists primarily of consolidated public lands with state school sections and small parcels of private land making up the remaining lands. The southern portion is in the checkerboard land ownership area created by the Union Pacific Railroad grant. Topography within the herd area is generally gently rolling hills and slopes with some tall buttes and streams. Elevations range roughly from 6,200 to 8,700 feet. Precipitation ranges 6-10 inches, predominately in the form of snow.

The AML for this HMA is 500 horses. Most horses are bay, sorrel, black, brown, paint, buckskin, or gray, but many colors and combinations are present. The Wyoming horses have a diverse background of many domestic horse breeds. They are most closely related to North American gaited breeds such as Rocky Mountain Horse, American Saddlebred, Standardbred, and Morgan. The horses range from 14 to 15.5 hands and weighs up to 1,100 pounds mature weight. The health of the horses is good with no apparent problems.

Domestic cattle and sheep utilize the area lightly in summer and moderately in winter. Vegetation in the HMA is dominated by sagebrush and grass intermixed with greasewood and saltbrush. The area also supports significant wildlife populations including elk, deer, and antelope.

Salt Wells HMA

The Salt Wells HMA encompasses 1,193,283 acres, of which 724,704 acres are BLM- administered public lands. The majority of the HMA consists primarily of checkerboard land ownership area created by the Union Pacific Railroad grant in the Northern portion. Consolidated public lands with state school sections and small parcels of private land making up the majority of lands in the southern section of the HMA. Topography within the herd area is generally gently rolling hills. There are several small streams passing through the area, and some high ridges. Elevations range roughly from 6,300 to 7,900 feet. Precipitation ranges 7-10 inches in lower elevations and 15-17 inches at higher elevations, predominately in the form of snow. The area is unfenced other than portions of boundary fence and right-of-way boundaries along I-80.

The AML for this HMA is 365 horses. A full range of colors is present. This herd has a high number of palominos and sorrels with flaxen manes and tails. Other horses colors are bay, brown, black, paint, buckskin, or gray. The Wyoming horses have a diverse background of many domestic horse breeds. They most closely related to North American gaited breeds such as Rocky Mountain Horse, American Saddlebred, Standardbred, and Morgan. The horses range from 14 to 15.5 hands and weigh between 750 and 1,100 pounds mature weight. The health of the horses is good, with no apparent problems.

Domestic cattle and sheep utilize the area lightly in the summer and moderately in the winter, cattle use predominating. Vegetation in the HMA is dominated by sagebrush and grass, with juniper, aspen, and conifers interspersed. Horses typically use a high amount of grass species, the most favorable being needlegrass, Indian ricegrass, wheatgrass, and sedges. The area supports significant wildlife populations including elk, deer, and antelope.

White Mountain HMA

The White Mountain HMA encompasses 392,649 acres, of which 240,416 acres are BLM-administered public lands. The majority of the HMA consists primarily of checkerboard land ownership area created by the Union Pacific Railroad grant. Consolidated public lands with state school sections and small parcels of private land make up the remaining lands in the northeast section of the HMA. The HMA is a high plateau that overlooks Rock Springs. Elevations range roughly from 6,300 to 7,900 feet. Precipitation ranges 6-10 inches, predominately in the form of snow. The area is unfenced except for portions of boundary fence and right-of-way boundaries along I-80, and 191 north.

The AML for this HMA is 250 horses. A full range of colors is present. This herd has a lot of color in it, many of which are paints. Other colors are bay, sorrel, red roan, black, or gray. The Wyoming horses have a diverse background of many domestic horse breeds. They are most closely related to North American gaited breeds such as Rocky Mountain Horse, American Saddlebred, Standardbred, and Morgan. The horses range from 14 to 15.5 hands and weigh between 750 and 1,100 pounds mature weight. The health of the horses is good.

Wyoming Tidbits

Wyoming holds 30 percent of the nation's uranium ore reserves, ranks fourth in coal reserves, fifth in crude oil reserve and seventh in gas reserves.

Domestic cattle and sheep utilize the area lightly in the summer and moderately in the winter. Vegetation in the HMA is dominated by sagebrush and grass, with saltbrush, winterfat, and greasewood intermixed. Horses typically use a high amount of grass species, the most favorable being needlegrass, Indian ricegrass, wheatgrass, and Sedges. The area supports significant wildlife populations including elk, deer, and antelope.

Little Colorado HMA

The Little Colorado HMA encompasses 519,541 acres of BLM - administered public lands. The majority of the HMA consists primarily of consolidated public lands with state school sections, and a large portion to the south belonging to the Bureau of Reclamation. The Big Sandy River runs to the south and the Green River makes up the western boundary. The northern boundary is the Pinedale/Rock Springs Field Office boundary. Highway 191 makes up the eastern boundary. The area is mostly rolling hills with significant canyons breaking up the area. Elevations range from approximately 6,300 to 7,900 feet, and precipitation ranges from 6-10 inches, predominately in the form of snow. The area is unfenced except for portions of boundary fence between the Rock Springs Field Office and the Pinedale Field Office, and along Highway 191 north. The HMA is divided among Sublette, Lincoln, and Sweetwater counties.

The AML for this HMA is 100 horses. Most horses in this area are dark - bay, sorrel, brown, black or gray. The Wyoming horses have a diverse background of many domestic horse breeds. They are most closely related to North American gaited breeds such as Rocky Mountain Horse, American Saddlebred, Standardbred, and Morgan. The horses range from 14 to 15.5 hands and weigh between 750 and 1,100 pounds mature weight. The horse health is good with no apparent problems.

Domestic cattle and sheep utilize the area lightly in the summer and moderately in the winter. Vegetation in the HMA is dominated by sagebrush/grass, with saltbrush, winterfat, greasewood, and meadow species. Horses typically use a high amount of grass species, the most favorable being needlegrass, Indian ricegrass, wheatgrass, and sedges. The area supports significant wildlife populations including deer, antelope, and sage grouse.

Little Colorado HMA

The Little Colorado HMA encompasses 519,541 acres of BLM - administered public lands. The majority of the HMA consists primarily of consolidated public lands with state school sections, and a large portion to the south belonging to the Bureau of Reclamation. The Big Sandy River runs to the south and the Green River makes up the western boundary. The northern boundary is the Pinedale/Rock Springs Field Office boundary. Highway 191 makes up the eastern boundary. The area is mostly rolling hills with significant canyons breaking up the area. Elevations range from approximately 6,300 to 7,900 feet, and precipitation ranges from 6-10 inches, predominately in the form of snow. The area is unfenced except for portions of boundary fence between the Rock Springs Field Office and the Pinedale Field Office, and along Highway 191 north. The HMA is divided among Sublette, Lincoln, and Sweetwater counties.

The AML for this HMA is 100 horses. Most horses in this area are dark - bay, sorrel, brown, black or gray. The Wyoming horses have a diverse background of many domestic horse breeds. They are most closely related to North American gaited breeds such as Rocky Mountain Horse, American Saddlebred, Standardbred, and Morgan. The horses range from 14 to 15.5 hands and weigh between 750 and 1,100 pounds mature weight. The horse health is good with no apparent problems.

Domestic cattle and sheep utilize the area lightly in the summer and moderately in the winter. Vegetation in the HMA is dominated by sagebrush/grass, with saltbrush, winterfat, greasewood, and meadow species. Horses typically use a high amount of grass species, the most favorable being needlegrass, Indian ricegrass, wheatgrass, and sedges. The area supports significant wildlife populations including deer, antelope, and sage grouse.

Coal trains are a frequent reminder of Wyoming's vast natural resources. Photo by David Scott Smith. Photo courtesy of Gillette Convention and Visitor's Bureau.

Fifteenmile HMA

The first recorded wild horse roundup on federal rangeland took place in October 1938 on lands now adminstered by BLM's Worland Field Office. The Fifteenmile Wild Horse HMA was established in 1985 under the direction of the Wild Free-Roaming Horses and Burros Act of 1971.

The HMA is located in the upper Fifteenmile Creek watershed approximately 30 miles northwest of Worland, Wyoming. It encompasses over 83,000 acres of mostly public land with some intermingled state and private lands.

The HMA ranges from rolling hills to rugged canyons and badlands. The country is semi-arid with hot summers and cold winters. Precipitation averages eight inches. Sudden cloudbursts erode the area's badlands, turning the streams muddy reddish-brown. Part of the HMA lies in the Bobcat Draw Wilderness Study Area, with its colorful and intricately-carved formations known as hoodoos, goblins, mushrooms, and castles.

Bays and sorrels, along with some grays, roans and pintos, roam the range. BLM administers a wild horse population of 70 to 160 adults in the HMA. Counting foals and yearlings, there may be as many as 270 horses to view and enjoy. Periodically, excess horses are gathered and placed in the Adopt-a-Horse program.

The Legacy of Desert Dust

Few individual wild horses have made history, but one Wyoming horse made quite a name for himself more than half a century ago. From the fall of 1945 to June 1946, the Rawlins (Wyoming) Republican-Bulletin ran several stories about a particular wild horse from southern Wyoming.

It seems that in those days, ranchers, and probably others, helped themselves to the unbranded horses roaming federal lands both in and outside of the grazing districts. A Glenrock, Wyoming, rancher rounded up horses as a business, using an airplane to spot and then haze the horses into a trap. Traps from this era often used three sides of a draw or canyon with the fourth side made of fencing. Once rounded up, the horses were shipped to eastern markets for slaughter.

This particular spring, the rancher was rounding up about 40 miles south of Wamsutter, Wyoming, and invited Verne Wood, a Rawlins photographer, to accompany him for a day. One band of horses rounded up that day belonged to a beautiful palomino stallion. The rancher decided to keep the stallion for breeding and show purposes. Mr. Wood took several photos of the horses that day and obtained what all photographers hope for, a one-in-a-million photograph.

"With long, white mane and tail again against the rugged background of the corral, Mr. Wood's picture showed the stallion as it turned his head.

Wyoming Tidbits

A one percent severance tax from minerals and fuels helps Wyoming residents fund education and water development in the state.

All of the beauty, wildness and alertness was caught,." reported the newspaper. A few weeks later, Wood's picture was featured in the rotogravure section of the Denver Post. Wood had already enlarged, tinted, and sold several photos of the stallion, but after the photo appeared in the Post, the inquiries began to roll in. National Geographic, Western Natural Life, and Eastman Kodak all secured prints of the stallion.

In April of 1946, Wood announced that a 40x50 oil color print of the stallion, which by that time had acquired the name "Desert Dust," would be hung in the Wyoming Capitol in Cheyenne. A second enlargement was given to Sen. Joseph C. O'Mahoney for presentation to the national capitol. According to the Rawlins paper, "Prints of the original photo have gone throughout the world and it has become one of the most famous wildlife pictures ever snapped. The May [although it was actually June] issue of Wyoming Wildlife will feature the picture on its cover and carry a story of the wild horse chase which trapped Desert Dust. The feature article will be illustrated with other pictures of wild horses taken by Wood." It was estimated at that time that about 20 oil paintings of the horse by different artists had already been completed.

Desert Dust's fame resulted in the Glenrock rancher being invited to New York to appear on a radio program describing airplane roundups of wild horses. On his way to New York, the rancher stopped in Cheyenne and told reporters that only about 2,000 horses remained in the Red Desert area—about one summer's worth of roundups. The rancher estimated that six to seven thousand horses once roamed that part of Wyoming. Wood began receiving numerous letters favoring a program of protection for the animals. One stated that the "horses should be preserved as a symbol of the west and one of the last remnants of traditional western wild life." Proponents of protection urged immediate action since an airplane roundup scheduled for that summer was expected to almost eliminate the herd.

In 1959, passage of the Wild Horse Protection Act prohibited the roundup of wild horses by aircraft and motor vehicles. The 1971 Wild and Free Roaming Horse and Burro Act provided for protection and management of these animals on federal lands. In 1969, the BLM's first wild horse range was established in the Pryor Mountains along the Montana-Wyoming border. The BLM inaugurated its nationwide Adopt-A-Horse program in 1976 in an effort to resolve overcrowding of the public range by wild horses and burros. Since the program' inception, over 100,000 horses have been adopted across the nation (over 3,000 in Wyoming). Desert Dust may have started it all.

Article courtesy Bureau of Land Management.

Wyoming's Natural Resources

You know that when you drive your car you are using gasoline, and when you heat your home you are using natural gas. But did you know that when you turn on a light, chances are you're using coal? And when you drink that ice cold milk in a tall glass, you are using trona? And cosmetics and food additives on the market today use bentonite? Minerals contribute significantly to our way of life: to the products we use, the items we need, the comforts we are accustomed to. And Wyoming minerals managed by the Bureau of Land Management play a major role in how we live today.

Wyoming has huge reserves of low sulfur coal. The Eagle Butte Mine is one of several large open pit mines in the state.

Oil and Gas Production:

Oil

• Wyoming is the number one producer of federal onshore oil producing 46% of the nation's total.

• Wyoming produced a total of 104 million barrels of oil in 1990.

• Federal land in Wyoming produced 67 million barrels of oil, or about 60% of the states total in 1990.

• Oil production is expected to continue to decline as known reserves are depleted, to an estimated 88 million barrels total production in 1995.

Gas

• Wyoming is the number two producer of federal onshore natural gas producing 33% of the nation's total.

Wyoming Tidbits

The first telephones in Wyoming used barbed wire running from fences to houses. When a call was made, the phone in every house on the line rang. Listening in to other people's calls would earn you the reputation as a "rubbernecker."

• Wyoming produced 681 billion cubic feet of natural gas in 1990.

• Federal land in Wyoming produced 396 billion cubic feet of natural gas in 1990, or about 60% of the state's total.

• Natural gas production is expected to increase to over 900 billion cubic feet in 1995.

Trends

• New techniques such as horizontal drilling and carbon dioxide injection are being developed to increase the recovery rate of oil reserves.

• Coal bed methane is a natural gas which has received increased attention recently. When water is removed from underground coal seams, methane can be produced. It has been estimated that Wyoming coal beds may contain up to 77 trillion cubic feet of coal bed methane. So far, costs of development have been high, discouraging production.

Economics:

• The federal government received about $19 million from lease rental and bonuses in 1991, half going to the State of Wyoming.

• The federal government received about $232 million from royalties on oil and gas in Wyoming during 1991, half of which goes to the State of Wyoming.

• The oil and gas industry employs about 18,000 people in Wyoming.

Uses:

• Oil is refined into a variety of products, the most common being fuel and lubricants for vehicles.

• Natural gas is used in heating homes and other structures.

• Petroleum is used in a wide variety of products ranging from plastics, nylon and other synthetic fibers.

• Petroleum is also used in a wide variety of cosmetics and toiletries such as petroleum jelly.

Coal Production:

• Wyoming is the nation's largest coal producing state. The passage of the Clean Air Act will increase demand for Wyoming's low sulfur coal.

• 194 million tons of coal was mined in

Wyoming in 1991, 85-90% of which is produced from federal land.

• Total coal from federal leases in the United States was about 253 million tons in 1991.

• Wyoming produces about 70% of the total federal coal in the United States.

• Wyoming coal production is estimated to increase to 235 million tons of coal mined in 1995.

• Most of Wyoming mines are surface, strip mines.

• On site drying techniques are being developed to increase the heat content of Wyoming's coal which should make it even more marketable in the future.

Economics:
• Approximately $110 million was collected in federal royalties in 1991, half of which goes to the State of Wyoming.

• Coal mining employ s over 4,600 people in W yoming

Uses:
• Wyoming coal is primarily used in electric power generation.

Location:
• The largest mines are located in southeast Campbell County (the southern Powder River Basin).

• Coal is also mined in central Sweetwater County east of Rock Springs, Carbon County north of Hanna, Converse County north of Glenrock, and Lincoln County near Kemmerer.

• One underground coal mine is in Carbon County, and one is in Sweetwater County.

Bentonite

Production:
• Bentonite is a clay material which is formed through the weathering of volcanic ash or tuff.

• Wyoming bentonite mines are open pit mines.

• Wyoming is the leading producer in the United States, producing about 2.4 million tons per year.

• Wyoming produces about 68% of the bentonite mined in the United States.

• Only about 23% of Wyoming's production is from federal lands. However, most of the bentonite operations were started on mining claims on federal land which were subsequently turned over to operator ownership.

Economics:
• The bentonite industry in Wyoming employs about 550 people.

Uses:

• Bentonite is used in the oil and gas industry as a drilling mud for exploratory drilling.

• Bentonite is also used as a filler in cosmetics, food products and animal feeds.

• Bentonite is used as a sealant in water reservoirs and sanitary landfills.

Location:
• Bentonite mining takes place in northern Wyoming, primarily in Big Horn, Crook, Johnson, and Weston Counties.

> **Wyoming Tidbits**
>
> Wyoming's bucking horse on the car license is just one of the state's symbols. The state fish is the cutthroat trout, the only trout native to Wyoming.The state flower is the Indian paintbrush. The state fossil is the knightia. The state dinosaur is Triceratops. The state reptile is the horned toad, which is actually a lizard. When attacked, the horned toad hisses, bites, and ejects blood from the corner of its eyes. The state bird is the meadowlark; the state tree, the cottonwood. The largest cottonwood tree in the U.S., measuring 29 feet in circumference and almost 77 feet high, stood north of Thermopolis. The tree burned in 1955 when a grass fire grew out of control.

> **Wyoming Tidbits**
>
> These friendly folks in Wyoming are known as Wyomingites, not Wyomingans.

Uranium

Only about 10 years ago, Wyoming was a major uranium producing state. However, the price of uranium has fallen drastically and mining in the state has ceased. Several of the mines which were operating in Shirley Basin and Gas Hills are presently being reclaimed. There has been interest by industry in alternate mining methods, however the price of uranium would have to increase before more operations would open.

Trona

Production:
Wyoming is the number one producer of trona in the country. About 16 million tons of trona are mined annually in Wyoming. 90% of the nation's trona production comes from Wyoming. Wyoming supplies 30% of the world's trona. There are only 6 producers of trona in the United States, and five of them are in the Green River Basin in Wyoming. Nearly 50% of the trona in Wyoming is federally owned.

Economics:
Federal royalties from trona totaled over $10 million, half of which goes to the State of Wyoming. Trona mining employs approximately 3,100 people in Wyoming.

Uses:
Trona is refined into a white powder called soda ash. Soda ash is used to make glass, detergent, paper, water softeners, drugs, cleaning compounds, and baking soda.

Location:
The worlds largest deposit of trona, over 100 billion tons, are located west of Green River in Sweetwater County.

Other Mineral Commodities

Other mineral commodities mined on federal land in Wyoming include sand and gravel, limestone, gypsum, granite, clinker, and jade. Sand and gravel are used in varied construction activities, the largest being our road system. Approximately 6 million cubic yards of sand and gravel are mined annually in Wyoming. Limestone is used as building and decorative stone as well as being crushed and used as road aggregate. Gypsum's primary use is in the manufacture of wallboard for construction. Wyoming's jade industry is small, although well known, and jewelry from Wyoming jade is widespread. Collectively these minor mineral commodity industries employ about 400 people in Wyoming.

The minerals industry in Wyoming has had a major impact on the state's economy and the state's history. Without ready access to the mineral reserves found in abundance in the state of Wyoming, mostly on federal lands, the state and the nation would be without valuable products that are used in every day living. Since these reserves are a finite commodity, proper management of these reserves becomes more important every day. The Bureau of Land Management strives to ensure that mineral reserves are being produced in the most environmentally sound manner. New and emerging technologies are being developed to enhance the recovery of these minerals, and the Bureau of Land Management is working cooperatively with industry to ensure that the growing demands of the nation and the world are being met.
Article courtesy of Bureau of Land Management.

> **Wyoming Tidbits**
>
> The bucking bronco on the Wyoming license plate has a name, "Old Steamboat".

How to Use this Book

We have divided the state into six sections with separate chapters for Yellowstone and Grand Teton National Parks and Fort Laramie National Historic Site. Each section has a common personality and at least one major city or town (by Wyoming standards). The material in each section is loosely ordered along the highway routes through the section and organized by locator numbers.

Locator Numbers

These are the numbers on the map in white on a black circle (❶). All information relating to the area on the map marked by that number is presented together in the section. The sections of the book are ordered from northwest to northeast, then southwest to southeast. The numbers allow you to follow the routes mile by mile and quickly find information along your path relating to your location on the path. In a nutshell, find the number on the map, then find that number heading in the section and listed under that number is everything there is to see or do at that location on the map. If you know where you are on the map, you will know about everything there is around you.

Category Classification

Each item listed is classified under one of nine categories. The classification key is the shaded letter immediately preceding the item listed. This makes it very simple to find the type of information you're looking for immediately. If you're hungry, look for any items preceded by an **F**. Looking for something to do? Look for a **T** or **V**. Want to buy something to take home with you? Look for an **S**. Here is a key for the categories:

T Attraction
This category includes just about anything worth stopping for. It might be a museum, a ghost town, a park, or just some quirky thing on the side of the road that makes traveling through this state so interesting. Whatever it is, we've tried to provide enough information to let you decide whether you want to plan a stop or not.

H Historic or Interpretive Sign
We have taken the text from over hundreds of historical and interpretive signs throughout the state and reprinted them here. They're fun reading, and in total provide an excellent background on the history, growth, and features of Wyoming. They wouldn't have placed them there if they weren't of some significance. It would take you weeks, if not months, to travel the state and view them all personally, so we have provided the legends from each for you. We have entered them where they are located. Sometimes this is a different location than the actual item they are referring to. Even though, we've presented the text of these markers here, take the time to stop at everyone you can. They are only a label for the actual site or event they speak of, and the experience is only complete if you are able to view the area surrounding them.

V Adventure
This would be just about anything you would get out of your car and do. A whitewater raft trip, horseback ride, hike, etc.

A Auto
These are anything automobile related.

F Food
We didn't discriminate. If there is prepared food available, we list it. We've listed everything ranging from the finest restaurants in the state (and there are a lot of them), to fast food and hot dog stands. Bottom line, if they'll fix it for you, they're listed here. While we don't rate any of the establishments, we highly encourage you to try the mom and pop eateries and the locally owned fine dining spots. Dayton Duncan, in his excellent book *Out West: American Journey Along the Lewis and Clark Trail* (1987, Penguin Books) gave the best advice we've heard;

> *"Franchises are not for the traveler bent on discovery. Forsaking franchises, like forsaking interstates, means that you're willing to chance the ups and downs, the starts and the stops of gastronomy as well as motoring. It means sometimes finishing a supper so good that you order the piece of pie you hadn't realized you wanted and you're sure you don't need—and spending the night in town just so you can have breakfast in the same place."*

In Wyoming, you're pretty safe. Just consider the logic. Most of these towns are so small that any place not putting up good grub isn't going to last long anyway. Accountability. While much of America has forgotten that concept, it is still a harsh and unforgiving rule in Wyoming.

As for fine dining, we'd put scores of Wyoming's best against the best anywhere outside of Wyoming. Some of the most talented culinary artists in the world have settled here for the lifestyle and share their talents with residents and visitors alike.

L Lodging
If they'll put a roof over your head and a mattress under your back, they're listed here. Again, we don't discriminate. Truth is, it's hard to find a bad motel in this state. Surviving here is tough, and if you don't put up a good product, you don't last long.

C Camping
These are private campgrounds that wished to be included in the main portion of each section. Otherwise, all private campgrounds are listed in the camping reference chart later in this section.

S Shopping
Do we need to explain this one? Obviously, we don't list every place in the state you can buy something. Only those who wanted to be in here. And yes, they paid for the opportunity. It would be impractical to list every place in the state you can buy something. And you probably wouldn't want to wade through all of them to get to the ones that count. So we left it up to the merchants to decide whether or not they might have something of interest to you, and to choose whether or not to include themselves in this book.

M Misc. Services
This would be just about anything that doesn't fall into one of the other categories above.

Maps

We've included a map for just about anything you would need a map for. At the beginning of each section is a detailed map of the section. We've also included a map of any town too big to see everything on Main Street standing in one spot—sixty in all. We've also included a number of maps of special locations. On each of the section maps we've marked where campgrounds, fishing sites, and Lewis & Clark points of interest are.

Public Campgrounds

Campgrounds are marked on the map with a number. At the end of each section is a chart listing each campground along with pertinent information about that site. The listings are numbered and the numbers match those on the map. We listed every maintained campground, public and private, we could find. If you find any we missed, please let us know. There are countless primitive campgrounds in the state that are not maintained and have no facilities. You'll find almost all of Wyoming's campgrounds to be uncrowded most of the year. It's not unusual, even at the peak of tourist season, to be the only campers at a site. Most of the public campgrounds charge a small fee to cover the cost of maintaining them.

Fishing Sites

We've listed over hundreds fishing sites in the state and marked and numbered them on the maps. At the end of this section is a chart listing each site in the state along with species and facilities information. There are thousands of places to wet a line in Wyoming. We have listed the major drainages and and only those fisheries that are relatively easy to access.

Scenic Drives

We have tried to offer some scenic or interesting side trips wherever possible. Some take you on backroads, others just take you a different way. Some are day trips, some are longer. We feel the book itself offers one long scenic trip, but if you want to get off the path, these offer some choices. Heed the warnings about gumbo and other backroad hazards mentioned earlier in this book.

Hikes

We have offered you a number of hikes at the end of most sections. There are a few sections of the state that don't offer too many hiking options. We didn't provide a lot of detail about the hikes. We simply pointed them out and tell you how to get there.

Information Please

Here we give you phone number for just about anything we missed earlier in the section that might be of interest to you.

Dining and Lodging Quick Reference Guides

These charts allow you to take a quick scan of all of the dining and lodging facilities in a manner that allows you to find information quickly and make quick comparisons. The map locator numbers are listed with each entry to help you find their location and possibly additional information about them in the front of the section.

Notes

We've allowed you ample room at the back of each section to make notes about your trip or to record additional information about your trip. This is a good place to store reservation confirmation numbers, or schedule information.

We've made every effort to make this book a tool for you to get the most from your visit to the state. If you already live here, we hope it awakens you to the endless things there to do and see in the magnificent chunk of America.

And Finally...

This is a book that was not as much written as it was compiled and edited. We used articles and information provided by other sources whenever possible. To research and know about every resource and feature of the state intimately would take us years. If it was already researched and written, and written well, we used it when we could do so. We have credited every source as accurately as possible. It was our goal to provide you, the reader, the maximum amount of information possible to make your explorations of the state enjoyable, while providing all the resources you need in one book. Hopefully we accomplished that goal. We would certainly like to hear from you if there is anything we've overlooked.

Happy Trails!

Cowboy Wave

Wyoming is largely rural, and like largely rural states, it is pretty friendly to most who care to be friendly back. When you're traveling the back roads, particularly the gravel roads, you'll encounter a variety of waves from passing pickups and motorists.

The most common is the one finger wave, accomplished by simply raising the first finger (not the middle finger as is common in urban areas) from the steering wheel. If the driver is otherwise occupied with his hands or if it is a fairly rough road, you may get a light head nod. Occasionally, you may get a two finger wave which often appears as a modified peace sign if the passerby is having a particularly good day. On rare occasions, you may get an all out wave.

The most important things is that whatever wave you get, be sure and wave back.

Wyoming Glossary

Alkali - white powdery substance appearing on soil surface often around places that have been wet

Badlands - bleak, desolate, hostile-looking area

Basin - a bowl-shaped valley

Black ice - icy stretch of road or highway

Blizzard - a very heavy snowstorm with strong winds

Boothill - the cemetery usually located on the top of a hill in frontier towns. The term derived from the practice of nailing the boots of the deceased to a wooden cross planted on the grave.

Bull pine - common name for Ponderosa Pine

Borrow pit - a depression beside the road left after the dirt was removed to build the elevated roadway, out-of-staters call them "ditches"

Cattle Baron - a rancher with an unusually large herd of cattle and land. Editors note: never ask a rancher about the size of their herd. It's considered rude, kinda like asking you how much money you have in the bank. It's non'a yore business

Chains - actual chains attached to tires so you get better traction on snow and ice -required on many mountain passes

Chaps - ("shaps") leather leg protection for cowboys

Chinook - a warm winter wind in winter that melts snow and ice

Cooley - miniature valley

Creek - medium-sized flow of water, 10-20 feet wide, pronounced "crick"

Critter - usually refers to some form of livestock

Dog hair pine - very thick pine—trees, need to be thinned

Dogs - sometimes refers to coyotes

Doggie - a motherless calf

Down the road a piece - Not far - may be a quarter mile or twenty miles (distances seem different in Wyoming!)

Draw - same as a cooley, maybe bigger

Dryland Farm - Non-irrigated farm; watered only by rain/snow

Emigrants - those who move from one part of the country to another as opposed to immigrants who move in from another country

Sanded road - icy highwa

False front - a facade on the front of early frontier buildings which extended above the roof giving the building the appearance of containing a second story.

Foothills - gentle hills at base of mountains

Gelding - a male horse that has been castrated

Good handle - a good understanding or ability

Gulley - like a cooley, maybe smaller. but sharper, more vertical banks

Gulley washer - heavy rain storm

Happy Jack - a lamp or lanter made from a tin syrup can

Heave - where water gets into crack in a road, freezes and expands. When it melts in spring, many depressions and wide cracks are left in the roadways

Heifer - a female bovine that hasn't yet had a calf

Hog ranch - a whore house that serves up gambling and booze. Most of them in Wyoming were found near the forts and provided entertainment and diversion to the otherwise dreary, boring lives of the frontier soldier. The name either derived from the appearance of the women or the tiny stall-like rooms in which they practiced their trade.

Hogback - a long, narrow and somewhat steep hill. A ridge with a sharp summit and steeply sloping sides.

Jack fence - x-crossed posts that sit on top the ground, used where it's too rocky to dig post holes

Jackalope - a jackrabbit bearing antlers. Used to be found mostly around Douglas, but now proliferating throughout the West

A little gun shy - a little jumpy/has had some bad experiences

Mare - a female horse

Nester - a farmer or homesteader who settles on cattle grazing land. Nesters and catllemen often met in bloody confrontations

Outfit - usually refers to a vehicle, sometimes with horse trailer

Pair - means a cow and her calf

Plow - usually refers to snowplow - clears roads of snow - usually a pickup or truck

Plug-in - outlet at motel where you plug in engine heater of your vehicle so it won't freeze up overnight

Potbelly - semi-truck that hauls cattle

Pulling a big circle - taking a long trip

Range land - native grazing area

Rattler - a rattlesnake (beware - poisonous)

Ridge - abrupt change in elevation

Riding with a loose rein - relaxed, not heavily supervised

Rise - like a hill but maybe lower, can't see over it

River - a wide creek, maybe 30-40 feet across or more

Rode hard an' put away wet - really tired - could be animal or person who has worked hard

Row crop - type of farming, usually high-intensity crops planted in rows like potatoes, corn, sugar beets

Ruminate - think about something

Rustler - a cattle or horse thief

Sage Chicken - a sage grouse. Also known as sage hen or prairie hen

Salt grass - grass that grows in highly alkaline soil

Sanded road - icy highways and roads are sanded to cut down skidding and sliding

Scoria - also called "clinker" is formed when underground coal seams catch fire and burn nearby sandstone and shale creating a red slag. Used on gravel roads throughout Wyoming and mostly in Powder River Country.

Sheep fence - small mesh wire fence for securing sheep/goats

Short grass - doesn't require much moisture and is less than a foot tall

Snow fences - built to control drifting snow, usually seen along roadways to help keep roads clear

Snowblind - a winter condition where the snow is so bright from the sun it becomes difficult to see

Spring - area where water comes up from deep inside earth

Stallion - a male horse that has not been castrated

Steer - a male bovine that has been castrated

Stock - short for 'livestock'

Stream - a small creek, a few feet wide

Strip farm - method of farming which rotates crops and controls wind erosion

Studs - tires with metal studs imbedded give better traction in snow and ice

Swather - machine that cuts hay

Top a the mornin' to ya - good morning/have a nice day

Valley - lowland surrounded by hills or mountains

Varmint - any animal you don't take a liking to

Wapiti - the Indian word for elk. Pronounced WOP-i-tee

White Out - snowstorm so heavy that everything looks white, zero visibility, extremely dangerous to drive in

Wilderness Area - a Congressionally mandated area within Forest Service land that disallows roads, mining, logging and motorized vehicles

WYOMING ZIP CODES

*This community has more than one five digit zip code.

Acme	82839
Afton	83110
Aladdin	82710
Albin	82050
Alcova	82620
Alpine	83128
Alta	83422
Alva	82711
Arapahoe	82510
Arlington	82083
Arminto	82630
Arvada	82831
Atlantic City	82520
Auburn	83111
Baggs	82321
Bairoil	82322
Banner	82832
Basin	82410
Bedford	83112
Beulah	82712
Big Horn	82833
Big Piney	83113
Bill	82631
Bitter Creek	82901
Bondurant	82922
Bordeaux	82201
Bosler	82051
Boulder	82923
Buffalo	82834
Buford	82052
Burlington	82411
Burns	82053
Byron	82412
Carlile	82713
Carpenter	82054
CASPER*	
Centennial	82055
CHEYENNE*	
Chugwater	82210
Clearmont	82835
Cody	82414
Cokeville	83114
Cora	82925
Cowley	82420
Creston	82301
Crowheart	82512
Daniel	83115
Dayton	82836
Deaver	82421
Devils Tower	82714
Diamond	82210
Diamondville	83116
Dixon	82323
Douglas	82633
Dubois	82513
Eden	82932
Edgerton	82635
Egbert	82053
Elk Mountain	82324
Elmo	82327
Emblem	82422
Encampment	82325
Ethete	82520
Etna	83118
EVANSTON *	
Evansville	82636
Fairview	83119
Farson	82932
FE Warren AFB	82005
Fontenelle	83101
Fort Bridger	82933
Fort Laramie	82212
Fort Steele	82301
Fort Washakie	82514
Four Corners	82715
Frannie	82423
Freedom	83120
Frontier	83121
Garland	82435
Garrett	82058
Gas Hills	82501
GILLETTE	
Glendo	82213
Glenrock	82637
Granger	82934
Granite Canon	82059
Green River	82935
Greybull	82426
Grover	83122
Guernsey	82214
Hamilton Dome	82427
Hamsfork	83101
Hanna	82327
Harriman	82059
Hartville	82215
Hawk Springs	82217
Hiland	82638
Hillsdale	82060
Hoback Junction	83001
Horse Creek	82061
Hudson	82515
Hulett	82720
Huntley	82218
Hyattville	82428
Iron Mountain, (see Cheyenne)	
JACKSON *	
Jay Em	82219
Jeffrey City	82310
Jelm	82063
Jenny Lake	83012
Kaycee	82639
Keeline	82227
Kelly	83011
Kemmerer	83101
Kinnear	82516
Kirby	82430
Kirtley	82225
Kortes Dam	82327
La Barge	83123
Lagrange	82221
Lance Creek	82222
Lander	82520
LARAMIE *	
Leiter	82837
Leo	82327
Linch	82640
Lingle	82223
Little America	82929
Lost Cabin	82642
Lost Springs	82224
Lovell	82431
Lucky Maccamp	82501
Lusk	82225
Lyman	82937
Park	82190
Manderson	82432
Mantua	82435
Manville	82227
Marbleton	83113
Mayoworth	82639
McFadden	82083
McKinnon	82938
Medicine Bow	82329
Meeteetse	82433
Meriden	82081
Midval	82501
Midwest	82643
Mills	82644
Moneta, (see Casper)	
Moorcroft	82721
Moose	83012
Moran	83013
Morton	82501
Mountain Home, (see Laramie)	
Mountain View	82939
Muddy Gap	82301
Natrona	82646
Newcastle	82701
New Haven	82720
Node	82225
Opal	83124
Orin	82633
Osage	82723
Oshoto	82721
Otto	82434
Parkerton	82637
Parkman	82838
Pavillion	82523
Piedmont	82933
Pine Bluffs	82082
Pinedale	82941
Pine Haven	82721
Point of Rocks	82942
Powder River	82648
Powell	82435
Prairie Center	82240
Quealy	82901
Ralston	82440
Ranchester	82839
Rawlins	82301
Raymond	83114
Recluse	82725
Red Desert	82336
Reliance	82943
Riner	82301
Riverside	82325
Riverton	82501
Robertson	82944
Rockeagle	82223
Rock River	82083
ROCK SPRINGS*	
Rolling Hills	82637
Rozet	82727
Ryan Park	82331
Saddlestring	82840
Saint Stephens	82524
Sand Draw	82501
Saratoga	82331
Savery	82332
Shawnee	82229
Shell	82441
Sheridan	82801
Shirley Basin	82615
Shoshoni	82649
Sinclair	82334
Slater,	82201
Smoot	83126
South Pass City	82520
Story	82842
Sundance	82729
Sunrise	82215
Superior	82945
Sussex	82639
Sweetwater Station	82520
Ten Sleep	82442
Teton Village	83025
Thayne	83127
Thermopolis	82443
Tie Siding	82084
Tipton	82336
Torrington	82240
Turnerville	83110
Upton	82730
Veteran	82243
Walcott	82335
Wamsutter	82336
Wapiti	82450
Weston	82731
Weston, (see Gillette)	
Wheatland	82201
Willwood	82435
Wilson	83014
Wolf	82844
Woriand	82401
Wright	82732
Wyarno	82845
Yellowstone National Park (all locations)	82190
Yoder	82244

Wyoming Counties

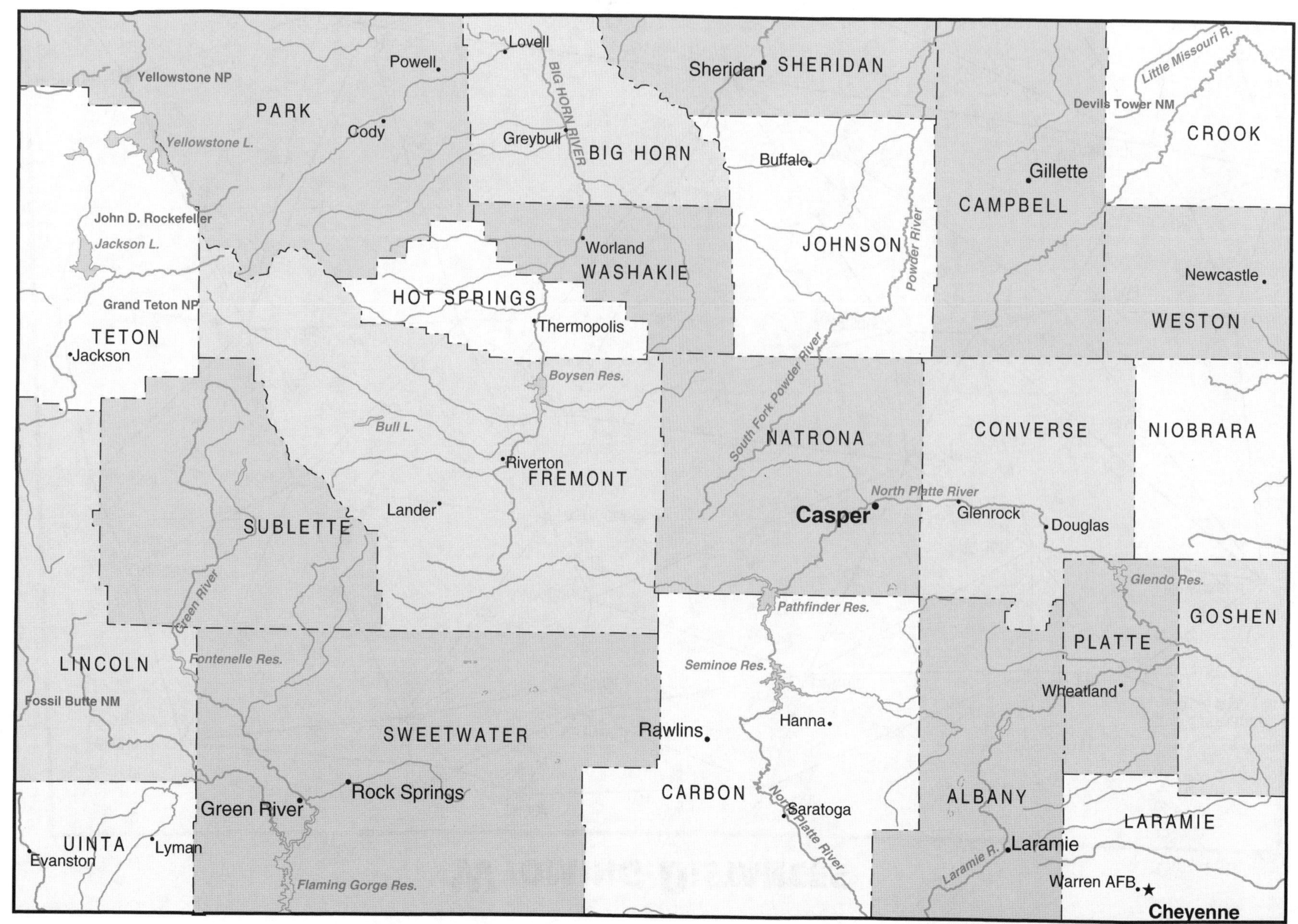

Wyoming Distances

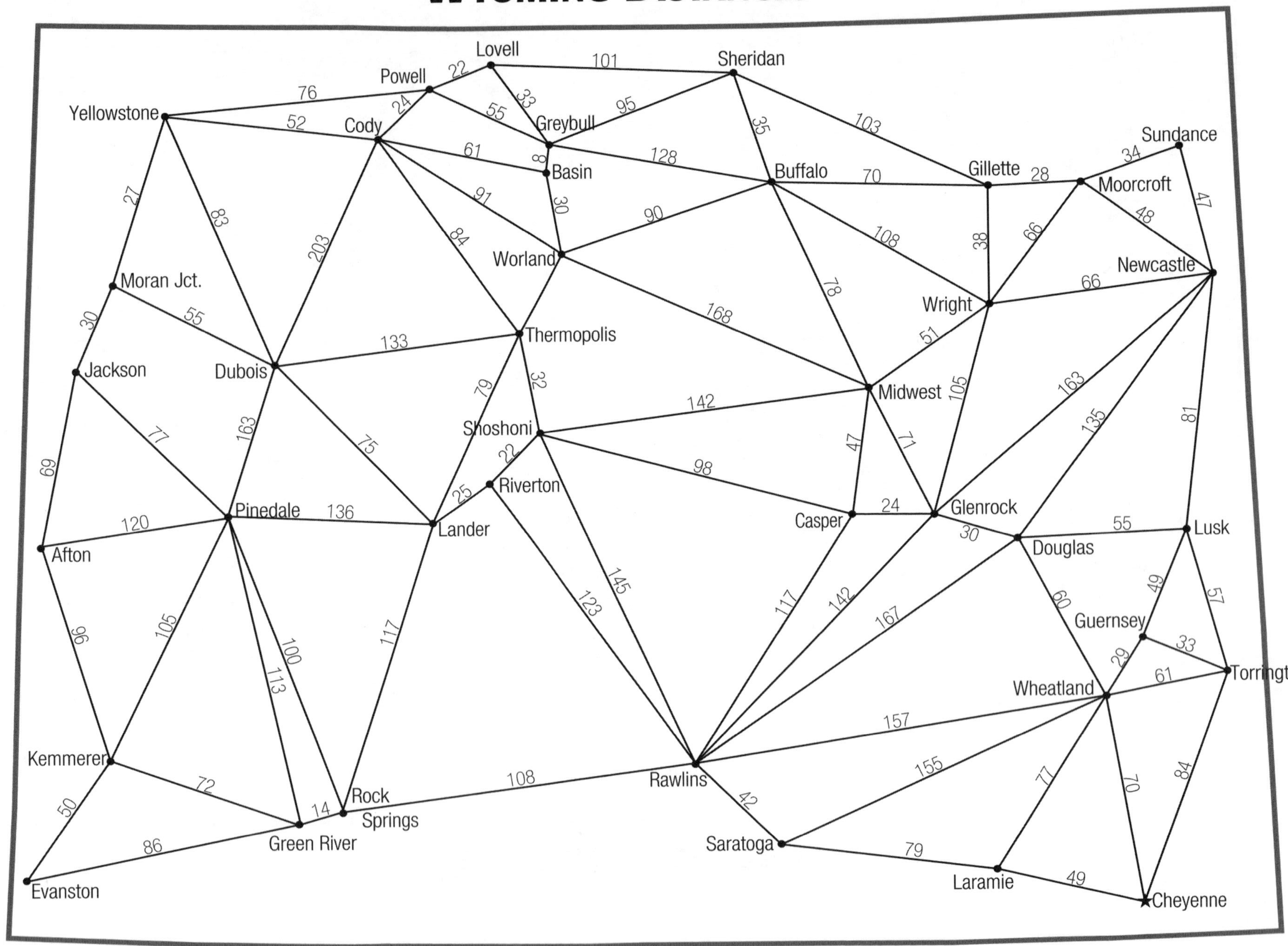

DRIVING DISTANCE

Afton to
Basin 308
Buffalo 411
Casper 353
Cheyenne ..436
Cody 247
Douglas 403
Dubois 155
Evanston ...120
Gillette 481
Glenrock ...378
Green River .165
Greybull 300
Guernsey ..464
Jackson 69
Kemmerer ...96
Lander 230
Laramie 387
Lovell 294
Lusk 457
Midwest 398
Moorcroft ..509
Moran Jct. ..100
Newcastle ..522
Pinedale ...120
Powell 271
Rawlins 288
Riverton 233
Rock Springs 179
Saratoga ...330
Sheridan ...394
Shoshoni ...255
Sundance ..543
Thermopolis 288
Torrington ..497
Wheatland ..445
Worland 321
Wright 478
Yellowstone .127

Basin to
Afton 308
Buffalo 120
Casper 194
Cheyenne ..372
Cody 61
Douglas 244
Dubois 196
Evanston ...343
Gillette 190
Glenrock ...218
Green River .272
Greybull 8
Guernsey ..305
Jackson 238
Kemmerer ..293
Lander 143
Laramie 339
Lovell 40
Lusk 298
Midwest ...198
Moorcroft ..219
Moran Jct. ..208
Newcastle ..267
Pinedale ...278
Powell 62
Rawlins 241
Riverton 118
Rock Springs 259
Saratoga ...282
Sheridan ...103
Shoshoni 96
Sundance ..252
Thermopolis .63
Torrington ..338
Wheatland ..303
Worland 30
Wright 228
Yellowstone .113

Buffalo to
Afton 411
Basin 120
Casper 112
Cheyenne ..290
Cody 182
Douglas 162
Dubois 256
Evanston ...403
Gillette 70
Glenrock ...136
Green River .332
Greybull 128
Guernsey ...223
Jackson 341
Kemmerer ..353
Lander 202
Laramie 260
Lovell 135
Lusk 216
Midwest 78
Moorcroft 98
Moran Jct. ..311
Newcastle ..146
Pinedale ...338
Powell 157
Rawlins 229
Riverton 178
Rock Springs 319
Saratoga ...259
Sheridan 35
Shoshoni ...156
Sundance ..132
Thermopolis 123
Torrington ..256
Wheatland ..221
Worland 90
Wright 108
Yellowstone .234

Casper to
Afton 353
Basin 194
Buffalo 112
Cheyenne ..178
Cody 214
Douglas 50
Dubois 198
Evanston ...326
Gillette 136
Glenrock 24
Green River .240
Greybull 201
Guernsey ...111
Jackson 284
Kemmerer ..288
Lander 145
Laramie 148
Lovell 233
Lusk 104
Midwest 47
Moorcroft ..164
Moran Jct. ..254
Newcastle ..170
Pinedale ...273
Powell 239
Rawlins 117
Riverton 120
Rock Springs 225
Saratoga ...148
Sheridan ...147
Shoshoni 98
Sundance ..197
Thermopolis 130
Torrington ..144
Wheatland ..109
Worland 164
Wright 98
Yellowstone .267

Cheyenne to
Afton 436
Basin 372
Buffalo 290
Casper 178
Cody 393
Douglas 129
Dubois 346
Evanston ...357
Gillette 242
Glenrock ...158
Green River .271
Greybull 380
Guernsey 98
Jackson 432
Kemmerer ..343
Lander 272
Laramie 49
Lovell 412
Lusk 140
Midwest 225
Moorcroft ..269
Moran Jct. ..402
Newcastle ..220
Pinedale ...355
Powell 417
Rawlins 149
Riverton 270
Rock Springs 256
Saratoga ...127
Sheridan ...325
Shoshoni ...276
Sundance ..265
Thermopolis 309
Torrington ...84
Wheatland ...70
Worland 342
Wright 204
Yellowstone .429

Cody to
Afton 247
Basin 61
Buffalo 182
Casper 214
Cheyenne ..393
Douglas 264
Dubois 203
Evanston ...364
Gillette 250
Glenrock ...239
Green River .293
Greybull 53
Guernsey ...325
Jackson 177
Kemmerer ..314
Lander 163
Laramie 359
Lovell 46
Lusk 318
Midwest 259
Moorcroft ..276
Moran Jct. ..147
Newcastle ..326
Pinedale ...254
Powell 24
Rawlins 262
Riverton 139
Rock Springs 280
Saratoga ...302
Sheridan ...147
Shoshoni ...116
Sundance ..311
Thermopolis .84
Torrington ..358
Wheatland ..323
Worland 91
Wright 288
Yellowstone ..52

Douglas to
Afton 403
Basin 244
Buffalo 162
Casper 50
Cheyenne ..129
Cody 264
Dubois 248
Evanston ...375
Gillette 113
Glenrock 30
Green River .290
Greybull 251
Guernsey 62
Jackson 334
Kemmerer ..337
Lander 195
Laramie 136
Lovell 283
Lusk 55
Midwest 97
Moorcroft ..140
Moran Jct. ..304
Newcastle ..135
Pinedale ...323
Powell 288
Rawlins 167
Riverton 170
Rock Springs 275
Saratoga ...198
Sheridan ...196
Shoshoni ...148
Sundance ..174
Thermopolis 180
Torrington ...94
Wheatland ...60
Worland 213
Wright 75
Yellowstone .316

Dubois to
Afton 155
Basin 196
Buffalo 256
Casper 198
Cheyenne ..346
Cody 203
Douglas 248
Evanston ...276
Gillette 325
Glenrock ...223
Green River .205
Greybull 204
Guernsey ..309
Jackson 86
Kemmerer ..225
Lander 75
Laramie 297
Lovell 236
Lusk 302
Midwest ...242
Moorcroft ..354
Moran Jct. ...55
Newcastle ..366
Pinedale ...163
Powell 227
Rawlins 200
Riverton 78
Rock Springs 192
Saratoga ...240
Sheridan ...290
Shoshoni ...100
Sundance ..387
Thermopolis 133
Torrington ..342
Wheatland ..307
Worland 166
Wright 296
Yellowstone ..83

Evanston to
Afton 120
Basin 343
Buffalo 403
Casper 326
Cheyenne ..357
Cody 364
Douglas 375
Dubois 276
Gillette 461
Glenrock ...350
Green River ..86
Greybull 351
Guernsey ..393
Jackson 190
Kemmerer ...50
Lander 201
Laramie 308
Lovell 384
Lusk 430
Midwest 372
Moorcroft ..488
Moran Jct. ..220
Newcastle ..495
Pinedale ...155
Powell 388
Rawlins 208
Riverton 226
Rock Springs 100
Saratoga ...250
Sheridan ...438
Shoshoni ...248
Sundance ..522
Thermopolis 280
Torrington ..425
Wheatland ..365
Worland 313
Wright 424
Yellowstone .247

Gillette to
Afton 481
Basin 190
Buffalo 70
Casper 136
Cheyenne ..242
Cody 250
Douglas 113
Dubois 325
Evanston ...461
Glenrock ...143
Green River .376
Greybull 198
Guernsey ...175
Jackson 411
Kemmerer ..423
Lander 272
Laramie 249
Lovell 203
Lusk 157
Midwest 89
Moorcroft 28
Moran Jct. ..381
Newcastle ...76
Pinedale ...408
Powell 226
Rawlins 253
Riverton 247
Rock Springs 361
Saratoga ...283
Sheridan ...103
Shoshoni ...225
Sundance 61
Thermopolis 193
Torrington ..208
Wheatland ..173
Worland 160
Wright 38
Yellowstone .301

Glenrock to
Afton 378
Basin 218
Buffalo 136
Casper 24
Cheyenne ..158
Cody 239
Douglas 30
Dubois 223
Evanston ...350
Gillette 143
Green River .265
Greybull 226
Guernsey 91
Jackson 308
Kemmerer ..312
Lander 169
Laramie 165
Lovell 258
Lusk 84
Midwest 71
Moorcroft ...170
Moran Jct. ..278
Newcastle ..163
Pinedale ...297
Powell 263
Rawlins 142
Riverton 145
Rock Springs 250
Saratoga ...173
Sheridan ...171
Shoshoni ...122
Sundance ..203
Thermopolis 155
Torrington ..124
Wheatland ...89
Worland 188
Wright 105
Yellowstone .291

Green River to
Afton 165
Basin 272
Buffalo 332
Casper 240
Cheyenne ..271
Cody 293
Douglas 290
Dubois 205
Evanston 86
Gillette 376
Glenrock ...265
Greybull 280
Guernsey ...307
Jackson 190
Kemmerer ...72
Lander 130
Laramie 222
Lovell 313
Lusk 344
Midwest 287
Moorcroft ..404
Moran Jct. ..220
Newcastle ..410
Pinedale ...113
Powell 317
Rawlins 123
Riverton 155
Rock Springs .14
Saratoga ...165
Sheridan ...367
Shoshoni ...177
Sundance ..437
Thermopolis 209
Torrington ..340
Wheatland ..279
Worland 242
Wright 338
Yellowstone .247

Greybull to
Afton 300
Basin 8
Buffalo 128
Casper 201
Cheyenne ..380
Cody 53
Douglas 251
Dubois 204
Evanston ...351
Gillette 198
Glenrock ...226
Green River .280
Guernsey ...312
Jackson 231
Kemmerer ..301
Lander 150
Laramie 347
Lovell 33
Lusk 307
Midwest ...306
Moorcroft ..226
Moran Jct. ..200
Newcastle ..274
Pinedale ...286
Powell 55
Rawlins 248
Riverton 126
Rock Springs 267
Saratoga ...289
Sheridan 95
Shoshoni ...103
Sundance ..260
Thermopolis .71
Torrington ..347
Wheatland ..312
Worland 38
Wright 160
Yellowstone .105

Guernsey to
Afton 464
Basin 305
Buffalo 223
Casper 111
Cheyenne ...98
Cody 325
Douglas 62
Dubois 309
Evanston ...393
Gillette 175
Glenrock 91
Green River .307
Greybull 312
Jackson 395
Kemmerer ..378
Lander 256
Laramie 104
Lovell 345
Lusk 49
Midwest 158
Moorcroft ...178
Moran Jct. ..365
Newcastle ..130
Pinedale ...384
Powell 350
Rawlins 184
Riverton 231
Rock Springs 292
Saratoga ...182
Sheridan ...257
Shoshoni ...209
Sundance ..174
Thermopolis 242
Torrington ...33
Wheatland ...29
Worland 275
Wright 137
Yellowstone .378

Jackson to
Afton 69
Basin 238
Buffalo 341
Casper 284
Cheyenne ..432
Cody 177
Douglas 334
Dubois 86
Evanston ...190
Gillette 411
Glenrock ...308
Green River .190
Greybull 231
Guernsey ..395
Kemmerer ..155
Lander 160
Laramie 383
Lovell 223
Lusk 388
Midwest ...328
Moorcroft ..440
Moran Jct. ...30
Newcastle ..451
Pinedale 77
Powell 202
Rawlins 284
Riverton 164
Rock Springs 177
Saratoga ...326
Sheridan ...324
Shoshoni ...186
Sundance ..473
Thermopolis 218
Torrington ..428
Wheatland ..393
Worland 251
Wright 392
Yellowstone ..57

Kemmerer to
Afton 96
Basin 293
Buffalo 353
Casper 288
Cheyenne ..343
Cody 314
Douglas 337
Dubois 225
Evanston 50
Gillette 423
Glenrock ...312
Green River ..72
Greybull 301
Guernsey ..378
Jackson 155
Lander 150
Laramie 294
Lovell 360
Lusk 392
Midwest ...334
Moorcroft ..450
Moran Jct. ..190
Newcastle ..457
Pinedale ...105
Powell 338
Rawlins 194
Riverton 175
Rock Springs .86
Saratoga ...236
Sheridan ...384
Shoshoni ...197
Sundance ..484
Thermopolis 230
Torrington ..411
Wheatland ..351
Worland 263
Wright 386
Yellowstone .217

Lander to
Afton 230
Basin 143
Buffalo 202
Casper 145
Cheyenne ..272
Cody 163
Douglas 195
Dubois 75
Evanston ...201
Gillette 272
Glenrock ...169
Green River .130
Greybull 150
Guernsey ..256
Jackson 160
Kemmerer ..150
Laramie 222
Lovell 183
Lusk 249
Midwest ...189
Moorcroft ..301
Moran Jct. ..130
Newcastle ..312
Pinedale ...136
Powell 187
Rawlins 125
Riverton 25
Rock Springs 117
Saratoga ...165
Sheridan ...237
Shoshoni 47
Sundance ..334
Thermopolis .79
Torrington ..289
Wheatlan ..254
Worland 112
Wright 243
Yellowstone .157

Laramie to
Afton 387
Basin 339
Buffalo 260
Casper 148
Cheyenne ...49
Cody 359
Douglas 136
Dubois 297
Evanston ...308
Gillette 249
Glenrock ...165
Green River .222
Greybull 347
Guernsey ...104
Jackson 383
Kemmerer ..294
Lander 222
Lovell 379
Lusk 166
Midwest ...195
Moorcroft ..276
Moran Jct. ..353
Newcastle ..246
Pinedale ...307
Powell 384
Rawlins 100
Riverton 221
Rock Springs 207
Saratoga 79
Sheridan ...294
Shoshoni ...243
Sundance ..290
Thermopolis 276
Torrington ..132
Wheatland ...77
Worland 309
Wright 212
Yellowstone .380

Lovell to
Afton 294
Basin 40
Buffalo 135
Casper 233
Cheyenne ..412
Cody 46
Douglas 283
Dubois 236
Evanston ...384
Gillette 203
Glenrock ...258
Green River .313
Greybull 33
Guernsey ..345
Jackson 223
Kemmerer ..360
Lander 183
Laramie 379
Lusk 338
Midwest ...213
Moorcroft ..232
Moran Jct. ..193
Newcastle ..280
Pinedale ...300
Powell 22
Rawlins 281
Riverton 158
Rock Springs 300
Saratoga ...322
Sheridan ...101
Shoshoni ...136
Sundance ..266
Thermopolis 104
Torrington ..378
Wheatland ..343
Worland 71
Wright 242
Yellowstone ..98

Lusk to
Afton 457
Basin 298
Buffalo 216
Casper 104
Cheyenne ..140
Cody 318
Douglas 55
Dubois 302
Evanston ...430
Gillette 157
Glenrock 84
Green River .344
Greybull 307

Guernsey ...49
Jackson ...388
Kemmerer ..392
Lander ...249
Laramie ...166
Lovell ...338
Midwest ...151
Moorcroft ..129
Moran Jct. ..358
Newcastle ..81
Pinedale ..377
Powell ...343
Rawlins ...221
Riverton ...224
Rock Springs 329
Saratoga ..244
Sheridan ..250
Shoshoni ..202
Sundance ..125
Thermopolis 235
Torrington ..57
Wheatland ..78
Worland ...268
Wright ...130
Yellowstone .370

Midwest to
Afton ...398
Basin ...198
Buffalo ...78
Casper ...47
Cheyenne ..225
Cody ...259
Douglas ...97
Dubois ...242
Evanston ..372
Gillette ...89
Glenrock ...71
Green River .287
Greybull ...206
Guernsey ..158
Jackson ...328
Kemmerer ..334
Lander ...189
Laramie ...195
Lovell ...213
Lusk ...151
Moorcroft ..117
Moran Jct. ..298
Newcastle ..123
Pinedale ..320
Powell ...235
Rawlins ...158
Riverton ...164
Rock Springs 272
Saratoga ..195
Sheridan ..113
Shoshoni ..142
Sundance ..150
Thermopolis 175
Torrington ..191
Wheatland ..156
Worland ...168
Wright ...51
Yellowstone .312

Moorcroft to
Afton ...509
Basin ...219
Buffalo ...98
Casper ...164
Cheyenne ..269
Cody ...276
Douglas ...140
Dubois ...354
Evanston ..488
Gillette ...28
Glenrock ..170
Green River .404
Greybull ...226
Guernsey ..178
Jackson ...440
Kemmerer ..450
Lander ...301
Laramie ...276
Lovell ...232
Lusk ...129
Midwest ...117
Moran Jct. ..409
Newcastle ..48
Pinedale ..436
Powell ...254
Rawlins ...280
Riverton ...275
Rock Springs 388
Saratoga ..311
Sheridan ..131
Shoshoni ..254
Sundance ..34
Thermopolis 221
Torrington ..185
Wheatland ..200
Worland ...188
Wright ...66
Yellowstone .330

Moran Jct. to
Afton ...100
Basin ...208
Buffalo ...311
Casper ...254
Cheyenne ..402
Cody ...147
Douglas ...304
Dubois ...55
Evanston ..220
Gillette ...381
Glenrock ..278
Green River .220
Greybull ...200
Guernsey ..365
Jackson ...30
Kemmerer ..190
Lander ...130
Laramie ...353
Lovell ...193
Lusk ...358
Midwest ..298
Moorcroft ..409
Newcastle ..421
Pinedale ..107
Powell ...171
Rawlins ...255
Riverton ...134
Rock Springs 207
Saratoga ..296
Sheridan ..2941
Shoshoni ..156
Sundance ..443
Thermopolis 188
Torrington ..398
Wheatland ..363
Worland ...221
Wright ...351
Yellowstone ..27

Newcastle to
Afton ...522
Basin ...267
Buffalo ...146
Casper ...170
Cheyenne ..220
Cody ...326
Douglas ...135
Dubois ...366
Evanston ..495
Gillette ...76
Glenrock ..163
Green River .410
Greybull ...274
Guernsey ..130
Jackson ...451
Kemmerer ..457
Lander ...312
Laramie ...246
Lovell ...280
Lusk ...81
Midwest ...123
Moorcroft ...48
Moran Jct. ..421
Pinedale ..442
Powell ...302
Rawlins ...287
Riverton ...288
Rock Springs 395
Saratoga ..317
Sheridan ..180
Shoshoni ..265
Sundance ..47
Thermopolis 270
Torrington ..137
Wheatland ..158
Worland ...237
Wright ...72
Yellowstone .379

Pinedale to
Afton ...120
Basin ...278
Buffalo ...338
Casper ...273
Cheyenne ..355
Cody ...254
Douglas ...323
Dubois ...163
Evanston ..155
Gillette ...408
Glenrock ..297
Green River .113
Greybull ...286
Guernsey ..384
Jackson ...77
Kemmerer ..105
Lander ...136
Laramie ...307
Lovell ...300
Lusk ...377
Midwest ..320
Moorcroft ..436
Moran Jct. ..107
Newcastle ..442
Powell ...279
Rawlins ...207
Riverton ...160
Rock Springs 100
Saratoga ..249
Sheridan ..373
Shoshoni ..183
Sundance ..469
Thermopolis 215
Torrington ..417
Wheatland ..364
Worland ...248
Wright ...371
Yellowstone .134

Powell to
Afton ...271
Basin ...62
Buffalo ...157
Casper ...239
Cheyenne ..417
Cody ...24
Douglas ...288
Dubois ...227
Evanston ..388
Gillette ...226
Glenrock ..263
Green River .317
Greybull ...55
Guernsey ..350
Jackson ...202
Kemmerer ..338
Lander ...187
Laramie ...384
Lovell ...22
Lusk ...343
Midwest ..235
Moorcroft ..254
Moran Jct. ..171
Newcastle ..302
Pinedale ..279
Rawlins ...286
Riverton ...163
Rock Springs 304
Saratoga ..326
Sheridan ..123
Shoshoni ..130
Sundance ..288
Thermopolis 108
Torrington ..382
Wheatland ..348
Worland ...93
Wright ...265
Yellowstone ..76

Rawlins to
Afton ...288
Basin ...241
Buffalo ...229
Casper ...117
Cheyenne ..149
Cody ...262
Douglas ...167
Dubois ...200
Evanston ..208
Gillette ...253
Glenrock ..142
Green River .123
Greybull ...248
Guernsey ..184
Jackson ...284
Kemmerer ..194
Lander ...125
Laramie ...100
Lovell ...281
Lusk ...221
Midwest ...158
Moorcroft ..280
Moran Jct. ..255
Newcastle ..287
Pinedale ..207
Powell ...286
Riverton ...123
Rock Springs 108
Saratoga ...42
Sheridan ..263
Shoshoni ..145
Sundance ..314
Thermopolis 178
Torrington ..217
Wheatland ..157
Worland ...211
Wright ...215
Yellowstone .282

Riverton to
Afton ...233
Basin ...118
Buffalo ...178
Casper ...120
Cheyenne ..270
Cody ...139
Douglas ...170
Dubois ...78
Evanston ..226
Gillette ...247
Glenrock ..145
Green River .155
Greybull ...126
Guernsey ..231
Jackson ...164
Kemmerer ..175
Lander ...25
Laramie ...221
Lovell ...158
Lusk ...224
Midwest ..164
Moorcroft ..275
Moran Jct. ..134
Newcastle ..288
Pinedale ..160
Powell ...163
Rawlins ...123
Rock Springs 142
Saratoga ..164
Sheridan ..212
Shoshoni ..22
Sundance ..309
Thermopolis .55
Torrington ..264
Wheatland ..229
Worland ...88
Wright ...218
Yellowstone .161

Rock Springs to
Afton ...179
Basin ...259
Buffalo ...319
Casper ...225
Cheyenne ..256
Cody ...280
Douglas ...275
Dubois ...192
Evanston ..100
Gillette ...361
Glenrock ..250
Green River ..14
Greybull ...267
Guernsey ..292
Jackson ...177
Kemmerer ..86
Lander ...117
Laramie ...207
Lovell ...300
Lusk ...329
Midwest ...272
Moorcroft ..388
Moran Jct. ..207
Newcastle ..395
Pinedale ..100
Powell ...304
Rawlins ...108
Riverton ...142
Saratoga ..150
Sheridan ..354
Shoshoni ..164
Sundance ..422
Thermopolis 196
Torrington ..325
Wheatland ..265
Worland ...229
Wright ...323
Yellowstone .234

Saratoga to
Afton ...330
Basin ...282
Buffalo ...259
Casper ...148
Cheyenne ..127
Cody ...302
Douglas ...198
Dubois ...240
Evanston ..250
Gillette ...283
Glenrock ..173
Green River .165
Greybull ...289
Guernsey ..182
Jackson ...326
Kemmerer ..236
Lander ...165
Laramie ...79
Lovell ...322
Lusk ...244
Midwest ..195
Moorcroft ..311
Moran Jct. ..296
Newcastle ..317
Pinedale ..249
Powell ...326
Rawlins ...42
Riverton ...164
Rock Springs 150
Sheridan ..294
Shoshoni ..186
Sundance ..344
Thermopolis 218
Torrington ..209
Wheatland ..155
Worland ...251
Wright ...246
Yellowstone .324

Sheridan to
Afton ...394
Basin ...103
Buffalo ...35
Casper ...147
Cheyenne ..325
Cody ...147
Douglas ...196
Dubois ...290
Evanston ..438
Gillette ...103
Glenrock ..171
Green River .367
Greybull ...95
Guernsey ..257
Jackson ...324
Kemmerer ..388
Lander ...237
Laramie ...294
Lovell ...101
Lusk ...250
Midwest ...113
Moorcroft ..131
Moran Jct. ..294
Newcastle ..180
Pinedale ..373
Powell ...123
Rawlins ...263
Riverton ...212
Rock Springs 354
Saratoga ..294
Shoshoni ..190
Sundance ..165
Thermopolis 158
Torrington ..290
Wheatland ..255
Worland ...125
Wright ...141
Yellowstone .199

Shoshoni to
Afton ...255
Basin ...96
Buffalo ...156
Casper ...98
Cheyenne ..276
Cody ...116
Douglas ...148
Dubois ...100
Evanston ..248
Gillette ...225
Glenrock ..122
Green River .177
Greybull ...103
Guernsey ..209
Jackson ...186
Kemmerer ..197
Lander ...47
Laramie ...243
Lovell ...136
Lusk ...202
Midwest ..142
Moorcroft ..254
Moran Jct. ..156
Newcastle ..265
Pinedale ..183
Powell ...130
Rawlins ...145
Riverton ...22
Rock Springs 164
Saratoga ..186
Sheridan ..190
Sundance ..287
Thermopolis .32
Torrington ..242
Wheatland ..207
Worland ...65
Wright ...196
Yellowstone .169

Sundance to
Afton ...543
Basin ...252
Buffalo ...132
Casper ...197
Cheyenne ..265
Cody ...311
Douglas ...174
Dubois ...387
Evanston ..522
Gillette ...61
Glenrock ..203
Green River .437
Greybull ...260
Guernsey ..174
Jackson ...473
Kemmerer ..484
Lander ...334
Laramie ...290
Lovell ...266
Lusk ...125
Midwest ...150
Moorcroft ...34
Moran Jct. ..443
Newcastle ..47
Pinedale ..469
Powell ...288
Rawlins ...314
Riverton ...309
Rock Springs 422
Saratoga ..344
Sheridan ..165
Shoshoni ..287
Thermopolis 255
Torrington ..181
Wheatland ..202
Worland ...222
Wright ...100
Yellowstone .364

Thermopolis to
Afton ...288
Basin ...63
Buffalo ...123
Casper ...130
Cheyenne ..309
Cody ...84
Douglas ...180
Dubois ...133
Evanston ..280
Gillette ...193
Glenrock ..155
Green River .209
Greybull ...71
Guernsey ..242
Jackson ...218
Kemmerer ..230
Lander ...79
Laramie ...276
Lovell ...104
Lusk ...235
Midwest ...175
Moorcroft ..221
Moran Jct. ..188
Newcastle ..270
Pinedale ..215
Powell ...108
Rawlins ...178
Riverton ...55
Rock Springs 196
Saratoga ..218
Sheridan ..158
Shoshoni ..32
Sundance ..255
Torrington ..274
Wheatland ..240
Worland ...33
Wright ...228
Yellowstone .136

Torrington to
Afton ...497
Basin ...338
Buffalo ...256
Casper ...144
Cheyenne ..84
Cody ...358
Douglas ...94
Dubois ...342
Evanston ..425
Gillette ...208
Glenrock ..124
Green River .340
Greybull ...347
Guernsey ..33
Jackson ...428
Kemmerer ..411
Lander ...289
Laramie ...132
Lovell ...378
Lusk ...57
Midwest ...191
Moorcroft ..185
Moran Jct. ..398
Newcastle ..137
Pinedale ..417
Powell ...382
Rawlins ...217
Riverton ...264
Rock Springs 325
Saratoga ..209
Sheridan ..290
Shoshoni ..242
Sundance ..181
Thermopolis 274
Wheatland ..61
Worland ...307
Wright ...169
Yellowstone .410

Wheatland to
Afton ...445
Basin ...303
Buffalo ...221
Casper ...109
Cheyenne ..70
Cody ...323
Douglas ...60
Dubois ...307
Evanston ..365
Gillette ...173
Glenrock ...89
Green River .279
Greybull ...312
Guernsey ...29
Jackson ...393
Kemmerer ..351
Lander ...254
Laramie ...77
Lovell ...343
Lusk ...78
Midwest ...156
Moorcroft ..200
Moran Jct. ..363
Newcastle ..158
Pinedale ..364
Powell ...348
Rawlins ...157
Riverton ...229
Rock Springs 265
Saratoga ..155
Sheridan ..255
Shoshoni ..207
Sundance ..202
Thermopolis 240
Torrington ..61
Worland ...273
Wright ...135
Yellowstone .376

Worland to
Afton ...321
Basin ...30
Buffalo ...90
Casper ...164
Cheyenne ..342
Cody ...91
Douglas ...213
Dubois ...166
Evanston ..313
Gillette ...160
Glenrock ..188
Green River .242
Greybull ...38
Guernsey ..275
Jackson ...251
Kemmerer ..263
Lander ...112
Laramie ...309
Lovell ...71
Lusk ...268
Midwest ...168
Moorcroft ..188
Moran Jct. ..221
Newcastle ..237
Pinedale ..248
Powell ...93
Rawlins ...211
Riverton ...88
Rock Springs 229
Saratoga ..251
Sheridan ..125
Shoshoni ..65
Sundance ..222
Thermopolis .33
Torrington ..307
Wheatland ..273
Wright ...198
Yellowstone .143

Wright to
Afton ...478
Basin ...228
Buffalo ...108
Casper ...98
Cheyenne ..204
Cody ...288
Douglas ...75
Dubois ...296
Evanston ..424
Gillette ...38
Glenrock ..105
Green River .338
Greybull ...160
Guernsey ..137
Jackson ...392
Kemmerer ..386
Lander ...243
Laramie ...212
Lovell ...242
Lusk ...130
Midwest ...51
Moorcroft ...66
Moran Jct. ..351
Newcastle ..72
Pinedale ..371
Powell ...365
Rawlins ...215
Riverton ...218
Rock Springs 323
Saratoga ..246
Sheridan ..141
Shoshoni ..196
Sundance ..100
Thermopolis 228
Torrington ..169
Wheatland ..135
Worland ...198
Yellowstone .340

Yellowstone to
Afton ...127
Basin ...113
Buffalo ...234
Casper ...267
Cheyenne ..429
Cody ...52
Douglas ...316
Dubois ...83
Evanston ..247
Gillette ...301
Glenrock ..291
Green River .247
Greybull ...105
Guernsey ..378
Jackson ...57
Kemmerer ..217
Lander ...157
Laramie ...380
Lovell ...98
Lusk ...370
Midwest ...312
Moorcroft ..330
Moran Jct. ...27
Newcastle ..379
Pinedale ..134
Powell ...76
Rawlins ...282
Riverton ...161
Rock Springs 234
Saratoga ..324
Sheridan ..199
Shoshoni ..169
Sundance ..364
Thermopolis 136
Torrington ..410
Wheatland ..376
Worland ...143
Wright ...340

Campgrounds

Map #	Description	Season	RV sites	tent sites	hook-ups	pull-thrus	dump station	restrooms	hot showers	pool	laundry	tables/grills	rec-room	drinking water
Section 1														
Afton														
1	Cabin Creek, 16 mi E of Alpine on US 89, USFS	5/27-10/31	10	•				•				•		•
2	Swift Creek, 2 mi E of Afton on Cty & FS Rds, USFS	5/27-10/31	13	•				•				•		•
Alpine														
3	Elbow, 14 mi E of Alpine on US 89, USFS	6/10-9/10	•	•				•				•		•
4	Forest Park, 37 mi SE of Alpine on US 89, USFS	5/27-10/31	13	•				•				•		•
5	Lynx Creek, 13 mi SE of Alpine on US 89, USFS	5/27-10/31	14	•				•				•		
6	Moose Flat, 19 mi SE of Alpine on US 89, USFS	5/27-10/31	10	•				•				•		•
7	Murphy Creek, 12 mi SE of Alpine on US 89, FS# 10138 Greys River Rd., USFS	5/27-10/31	10	•				•				•		•
8	Station Creek, 11 mi E of Alpine on US 89, USFS	6/10-9/10	15	•		•		•				•		•
Big Piney														
9	Middle Piney Lake, 25 mi W of Big Piney on WY & FS Rd, USFS	7/1-9/30	6	•				•				•		•
10	Sacajawea, 22 mi W of Big Piney on WY 35 & FS Rd, USFS	6/15-9/30	26	•				•				•		•
Bondurant														
11	Granite Creek, 10 mi NW of Bondurant on US 191-189, 9 mi NE of FS Rd, USFS	6/25-9/10	52	•		•		•		•		•		•
12	Hoback, 14 mi NW of Bondurant on US 191-189, USFS	6/5-9/10	8	•				•				•		•
13	Kozy, 7 mi W of Bondurant on US 191-189, USFS	6/1-9/5	8	•				•				•		
Boulder														
14	Boulder Lake, 11 mi NE of Boulder on WY 353, 6 mi N on Cty Rd, 3 mi E on FS Rd, USFS	6/20-10/15	•	•				•				•		
Dubois														
15	Brooks Lake, 23 mi W of Dubois on US 26/287, 5 mi N on FS Rd. 515, USFS	6/20-9/30	14	•				•				•		•
16	Circle-Up Camper Court, 225 Welty St. Box 1520, PH: 307-455-2238, E-mail jnowlin@wyoming.com	All	80	100	•	•	•	•	•	•	•	•	•	•
17	Double Cabin, 28 mi N of Dubois on FS Rd. 508 & 285, USFS	6/1-9/30	15	•				•				•		•
18	Falls, 25 mi W of Dubois on US 287, USFS	6/1-10/30	46	•				•				•		•
19	Horse Creek, 12 mi N of Dubois on FS Ad, USFS	6/1-10/30	9	•				•				•		•
20	Pinnacles, 23 mi NW on US 26/287, 5 mi on FS Rd 515, USFS	6/20-9/3	21	•				•				•		•
21	Pinnacle Buttes Lodge & Campground, 3577 Hwy 26, PH: 307-455-2506 or 800-934-3569, FAX: 307-455-3874	All	12	10	•	•	•	•	•	•		•		•
22	Riverside Inn & Campground 5810 Hwy 26, Box 642, PH: 307-455-2337 or 877-489-2337, www.dteworld.com/riversideinn	Seasonal	10	10	•	•		•	•			•		•
Freedom														
23	Haderlie's Tincup Mountain Guest Ranch, Hwy 34 #5336, Box 275, PH: 208-873-2368, Web: www.silverstar.com/html	6/1-8/31	2	4	•		•	•	•			•		•
Jackson														
24	Atherton Creek, 7 mi E of Kelly on FS Rd, USFS	6/5-10/30	20	20				•				•		•
25	Crystal Creek, 13 mi E of Kelly on FS rd, USFS	6/5-10/30	6	•				•				•		•
26	Curtis Canyon, 6 mi E of Jackson from Elk Refuge Entrance to Curtis Canyon, 3 mi E, USFS	6/5-9/10	12	•				•				•		•
27	Elk Country Inn & RV Park, 480 W Pearl St, Box 1255, PH: 307-733-2364, 800-483-8667, Web: www.townsquareinns.com	All	12		•			•	•		•	•		•
28	Hatchet, 8 mi E of Moran Jct on US 26-287, USFS	6/25-9/10	9	•				•				•		•
29	Lazy J Corral RV Park, 10755 S. Hwy 89, PH: 307-733-1554	4/1-11/1	23		•	•		•	•		•	•	•	•
30	Lone Eagle, 10755 S Hwy 89, Star Rt Box 45-C PH: 307-733-1090 or 800-321-3800, FAX: 307-733-5042	5/15-10/1	23	50	•	•			•		•	•		•
31	Signal Mountain, 5 mi NW of Moran via US 89-287, 2 mi SW on Teton Park Road, NPS	5/15-9/30	80	•			•	•				•		•
32	Snake River Park KOA, 1 mi N Hoback Jct, 9705 S. Hwy 89, 4/7-10/10 PH: 307-733-7078, 800-562-1878, FAX: 733-0412, Web: www.srpkoa.com	41	25	•		•	•	•		•	•		•	
33	Virginian Lodge RV Park, 750W Broadway, PH: 307-733-7189	5/1-10/5	105		•	•	•	•	•	•	•	•	•	•
34	Wagon Wheel Campground, 5 blks N of town square, 525 N Cache, Box 1463, PH: 307-733-4588	5/1-10/31	35	8	•	•	•	•	•		•	•		•
Marbleton														
35	Harper's Park & RV, 16 E 3rd St., Box 4478, PH/ Fax: 307-276-3611 or 276-3611	All	14	5	•	•	•	•	•		•	•	•	•
Pinedale														
36	Boulder Lake, 3 mi E of Boulder on 353, then 10 mi N on Boulder Lake Rd, USFS	6/1-10/15	20	•				•				•		
37	Fremont Lake, 3 mi NE of Pinedale on Cty Rd, 4 mi NE on FS Rd, USFS	5/25-9/10	53	•				•				•		•
38	Green River Lake, 25 mi N of Pinedale on WY 352, 31 mi N on FS Rd, USFS	6/15-9/10	36	•				•				•		•
39	Lakeside Lodge Resort & Marina, 4 mi N of town on S shore of Lake, PH: 307-367-2221	5/15-11/1	20	6	•		•	•	•			•		•
40	Narrows, 21 mi N of Pinedale on WY 352, 5 mi E on Cty Rd, 3 mi E on FS Rd, USFS	6/1-9/10	19	•				•				•		•
41	New Fork Lake, 21 mi N of Pinedale on WY 352, 5 mi E on Cty Rd, 3 mi SE on FS Rd, USFS	6/1-9/10	15					•				•		•
42	Pinedale Campgrounds, 204 S Jackson, PH: 307-367-4555, FAX: 307-367-2397	5/25-10/15	24	36	•		•	•	•		•	•		•
43	Scab Creek, 20 mi SE of Pinedale on Hwy 353, then N 10 mi, BLM	6/1-10/31	10	•				•				•		•

Map #	Description	Season	RV sites	tent sites	hook-ups	pull-thrus	dump station	restrooms	hot showers	pool	laundry	tables/grills	rec-room	drinking water
44	Trails End, 3 mi NE of Pinedale on Cty Rd, 11 mi NE on FS Rd, USFS	6/25-9/10	8	•				•				•		•
45	Warren Bridge, 24 mi N of Pinedale on Hwy 187-189, BLM	6/1-10/31	•	•				•				•		
46	Whiskey Grove, 36 mi N of Pinedale on WY 352, and FS Rd, USFS	6/15-9/10	9	•				•				•		•
Teton Village														
47	Teton Village KOA, 5 mi W of Jackson on Hwy 22/390, 5/1-10/12 PH: 307-733-5354 or 800-562-9043, FAX: 307-739-1298	150	•	•	•	•	•	•		•	•	•	•	
Thayne														
48	Flat Creek RV Park & Cabins, 74 Hokanson St, PH: 307-883-2231	All	23	6	•			•	•		•		•	•
Section 2														
Basin														
49	Rose Garden RV Park, Box 849, 704 South 4th St., PH: 307-568-2943, Email: rosegrrv@tctwestnet	4/15-11/1	12		•	•		•	•			•		
Cody (see also WAPITI)														
50	7K RV Park, 232 W Yellowstone Ave, PHI Fax: 307-587-5890	All	39	•	•	•	•	•	•		•	•		•
51	Absaroka Bay RV Park, 2001 Hwy 14-16-20, in town, Box 953 PH: 307-527-7440 or 800-557-7440, Web:www.cody-wy.com	5/1-9/30	98	10	•	•	•	•	•		•	•		•
52	Beartooth Lake, E WY 12 off WY 96, USFS	7/1-9/7	21	•										
53	Buffalo Bill State Park, 9 mi W of Cody on US 14-16-20, SP, PH: 307-587-9227	5/1-10/1	•	•		•	•	•				•		•
54	Big Game, 28 mi W of Cody on US 16, USFS	5/15-9/30	16	•				•				•		•
55	Camp Cody RV Park, 415 Yellowstone, PH: 307-587-9730	All	63		•		•	•	•	•	•	•		•
56	Clearwater, 31 mi E of Cody on US 16, USFS	5/15-9/30	32	•				•				•		•
57	Cody KOA, 5561 Greybull, PH/ Fax: 307-587-2369 or 800-562-8507, Web: www.koakampgrounds.com	5/1-10/1	200	100	•	•	•	•	•	•	•	•	•	•
58	Crazy Creek, 5 mi W WY 1 2 oft WY 96, USFS	6/1-10/20	19	•										
59	Dead Indian, WY 96 off WY 120, USFS	All	12	•										
60	Deer Creek, 47 mi SW of Cody on WY 291, USFS	All	7	•								•		
61	Eagle Creek, 44 mi W of Cody on US 16, USFS	5/15-10/30	20	•				•				•		•
62	Elk Fork, 29 mi W of Cody on US 16, USFS	5/15-10/30	13	•				•				•		•
63	Elk Valley Inn & Campground, 3256 Yellowstone Hwy, 5/1-9/30 PH: 307-587-4149, 877-587-4149, Web:www.tctwest.net/~elkvalley	60	30	•	•	•	•	•		•	•		•	
64	Fox Creek, WY 296 off WY 120, USFS	6/1-9/30	27	•										
65	Gateway Campground, 203 Yellowstone, PH: 307-587-2561	4/1-10/1	74	•	•			•	•			•		•
66	Hunter Peak, WY 296 off WY 120, USFS	All	9	•										
67	Island Lake, 16 mi E on WY 212 off WY 296, USFS	7/1-9/7	20	•										
68	Lake Creek, WY 296 off WY 120, USFS	6/1-9/30	6	•										
69	Lily Lake, WY 212 turn onto Forest Rd. 130 to Lily Lake, USFS	5/25-10/30	8	•										
70	Little Sunlight, Off WY 296 turn onto Forest Rd. 101 for 13 mi., USFS	5/1-11/30	4	•										
71	Newton Creek, 37 mi W of Cody on US 16, USFS	5/15-9/30	31	•				•				•		•
72	Parkway RV Campground, 132 Yellowstone Ave., PH: 307-527-5927	All	25	20	•	•	•	•	•		•	•		•
73	Ponderosa Campground, 1815 8th Yellowstone Hwy, PH: 307-587-9203	5/1-10/15	135	50	•	•	•	•	•		•	•	•	•
74	Rex Hale, 36 mi W of Cody on US 16, USFS	5/15-9/30	8	•				•				•		•
75	River's View RV Park, 109 W Yellowstone, PH: 307-587-6074 or 800-377-7253, FAX: 307-587-8644, Web: www.codyvacationproperties.com	5/15-10/15	5	4	•	•	•					•		•
76	Sleeping Giant, 47 mi W of cody on US 16, USFS	5/15-10/30	6	•				•				•		•
77	Three Mile, 48 mi W of Cody on US 16, USFS	5/15-10/30	•	•				•				•		•
78	Top of the World Store, 2823 Beartooth Hwy, US 212, 5/25-10/15 PH: 307-899-2482 or 754-1051, E-mail: topoftheworld@starband.net	10		•			•				•		•	
79	Wapiti, 29 mi W of Cody on US 16, USFS	5/15-10/30	•					•				•		•
80	Yellowstone Valley RV Park, 3324 Yellowstone Park Hwy, PH: 307-587-3961	5/1-9/30	25	30	•		•	•	•		•	•		•
Greybull														
81	Green Oasis Campground, Hwy 14-16-20 at 12th Ave N, PH: 3O7-7652856, 888-765-2856, www.greenoasiscampground.com	4/15-10/15	9	15	•	•	•	•	•		•	•		•
82	Greybull KOA, 333 N 2nd, Box 387, PH! Fax: 307-765-2555, 800-562-7508	4/15-10/6	32	22	•	•	•	•	•	•	•	•	•	•
Hyattville														
83	Medicine Lodge State Archaeological Site, 6 mi NE of Hyattville, SP, PH: 307-469-2234	5/1-11/6	•	•		•		•				•		•
Lovell														
84	Bald Mountain, 33 mi E of Lovell on US 14A, USFS	7/1-9/15	15	•				•				•		•
85	Camp Big Horn RV Park, Main St, E end of Lovell, PH: 307-548-2725, FAX: 307-548-7479	All	18	9	•		•	•	•		•	•		•
86	Horseshoe Bend, 2 mi E of Town on US l4A to Jct 37, l4 mi N, Box 487, NPS	All	128	•			•	•				•		•
87	Lovell Camper Park, 40 Quebec Ave, PH: 307-548-6551, FAX: 307-548-7614	5/1-9/30		13			•	•	•					•
88	Porcupine, 33 mi E of Lovell on US 14A, 1.6 mi N on FS Rd 13, USFS	7/1-9/15	16	•				•				•		•
Meeteetse														
89	Brown Mountain Campground, 25 mi SW of Meeteetse on Wood River Road	5/31-11/15	6	•				•				•		•

Map #	Description	Season	RV sites	tent sites	hook-ups	pull-thrus	dump station	restrooms	hot showers	pool	laundry	tables/grills	rec-room	drinking water
90	Jack Creek Campground, 30 mi W of Meeteetse Pitchfork Road	All	7	•				•						•
91	Oasis Motel & RV Park, 1702 Stale St., Box 128, PH: 307-868-2551 or 888-868-5270, Web: www.oaaismotelwyoming.com	All	10	30	•	•	•	•	•		•	•		•
92	Vision Quest Motel, 2207 State St., Box 4, PH: 307-868-2512, Fax: 868-2550 Web: www.vqmotel.com	6/1-12/1	5		•	•	•	•	•					•
93	Wood River Campground, 22 mi SW of Meeteetse on Wood River Road	5/31-11/15	5	•				•				•		
Powell														
94	Homesteader Park, Hwy 14A, E city limits, 307-754-9417, Fax: 754-5385, Web: www.cityofpowell.com	4/5-10/31	25	15			•	•				•		•
95	Park County Fairgrounds, 655 E 5th St. PH: 307-754-5421, FAX: 307-754-5947. Email: pcf@wir.net	5/1-9/1	130	•	•	•	•	•	•			•		•
Shell														
96	Cabin Creek Trailer Park, 15 mi NE of Shell on US 14, USFS	5/24-9/12	26	•				•				•		•
97	Medicine Lodge Lake, 15 mi NE of Shell on US 14. 25 mi SE on FS Rd. USFS	7/1-9/8	8	•				•				•		•
98	Paintrock Lakes, 15 mi NE of Shell on US 14, 25 mi SE on FS Rd 17, USFS	7/1-9/8	8	•				•				•		•
99	Ranger Creek, 15 mi NE of Shell on US 14, 2 mi on FS Rd. USFS	5/23-9/15	10	•				•				•		•
100	Shell Campground, 102 First St. & Hwy 14, PH: 307-765-9924, Web: www.shellcampground.com	4/1-11/01	12	100	•	•	•	•	•		•	•		•
101	Shell Creek, 15 mi NE of Shell on US 14, 1 mi S on FS Rd. USFS	5/30-10/31	11	•				•				•		•
Ten Sleep														
102	Big Horn Mountain Resorts, Box 86, PH: 307-366-2600 or 888-244-4070, Web: www.bighorn.com	6/1-11/1	18	20	•			•	•			•		•
103	Boulder Park, 13 mi NE of Ten Sleep on US 16. USFS	6/1-9/22	34	•				•				•		•
104	Bull Creek, 25 mi NE of Ten Sleep on US 16, USFS	6/1-9/22	43	•				•				•		
105	Castle Gardens, 1 mi W of Ten Sleep on Hwy 16-20 to Castle Gardens	6/1-10/31	•	•				•				•		
106	Circle S Campground, 300 Second Hwy 16, PH: 307-366-2320	5/1-11/1	•	•	•		•	•	•		•	•		•
107	Deer Park, 26 mi NE of Ten Sleep on US 16, USFS	6/15-9/22	7	•				•				•		•
108	Island Park, 23 mi NE of Ten Sleep on US 16, USFS	6/15-9/22	10	•				•				•		•
109	Lakeview, 15 mi NE of Ten Sleep on US 16, USFS	6/15-9/22	11	•				•				•		•
110	Leigh Creek, 9 mi NE of Ten Sleep on US 16, USFS	5/20-9/22	11	•				•				•		•
111	Sitting Bull Creek, 23 mi NE of Ten Sleep on US 16. USFS	6/15-9/22	43	•				•				•		•
112	Ten Broek RV Park & Cabins, 98 Second St., Box 10, PH: 307-366-2250, E-mail: tenbroekrv@t&twest.net	4/1-11/1	55	30	•		•	•	•		•	•		•
113	West Ten Sleep Lake, 27 mi NE of Ten Sleep on US 16. USFS	6/15-9/30	10	•				•				•		•
Thermopolis														
114	Country Campin' RV & Tent Park, 710 E. Sunny Side Ln, 4/15-10/30 PH: 307-864-2416, 800-609-2244. FAX: 864-2416. Web' www.camp@tnb.com	42	10	•	•	•	•	•		•	•		•	
115	Eagle RV Park, 204 Hwy 20 5., PH/FAX: 307-864-5262 or 888-865-5707, Web: www.interbasin.com/eagle/	All	46	12	•	•	•	•	•	•	•	•	•	•
116	Fountain of Youth RV Park, 250 N Hwy 20, PO Box 711, PH: 307-864-3265, FAX: 307-864-3388, Web: www.foyrvpk@trib.com	3/15-10/15	40	10	•	•	•	•	•	•	•	•		•
117	Grandview RV Park, 122 Hwy 20 S, PH: 307-864-3463	4/15-10/15	21	8	•	•	•	•	•		•	•		•
118	New RV Park, 113 N 2nd St. PH: 307-864-3926. Fax: 307-864-2291	4/1-11/1	15		•							•		•
119	The Wyoming Waltz RV Park, 720 Shoshoni, PH: 307-864-2778, Email: breed@trib.com	All	13	3	•	•		•	•		•	•		•
Worland														
171	Worland Cowboy Campground, 2311 Big Horn Ave., PH: 307-347-2329, Web www.worlandcowboycamnqround.com	4/1-10/31	38	8	•	•	•	•	•		•	•	•	•

Section 3

Map #	Description	Season	RV sites	tent sites	hook-ups	pull-thrus	dump station	restrooms	hot showers	pool	laundry	tables/grills	rec-room	drinking water
Alva														
120	Bearlodge. 7 mi SE of Alva on WY 24, USFS	All	8	•				•				•		
Big Horn Mountains														
121	East Fork, 17 mi SW of Big Horn, USFS	6/1-10/31	12	•				•				•		•
122	Ranger Creek, 19 mi SW of Big Horn, USFS	6/1-10/31	11	•				•				•		•
123	Twin Lakes, 22 mi SW of Big Horn, USFS	6/1-10/31	10	•				•				•		
Buffalo														
124	Big Horn Mountain Campground, 8935 Hwy 16 W, PH: 307-684-2307	All	48	25	•	•	•	•	•	•	•	•	•	•
125	Buffalo KOA Kampground, 87 Hwy 16 East. PH: 307-684-5423 or 800-562-5403	4/15-10/10	63	24	•	•	•	•	•	•	•	•	•	•
126	Circle Park, 17 mi W of Buffalo on US Hwy 6, USFS	5/15-10/31	10	•				•				•		•
127	Crazy Woman, 26 mi W of Buffalo on US Hwy 16, USFS	5/15-10/31	6	•				•				•		•
128	Deer Park Campground, 146 US Hwy 16 E, Box 568 PH: 307-684-5722 or 800-222-9960, Web: www.deerparkrv.com	5/1-9/30	85	40	•	•	•	•	•	•	•	•	•	•
129	Doyle, 31 mi W of Buffalo on US Hwy 16, USFS	5/15-10/31	19	•				•				•		
130	Hunter Corrals, 16 mi W of Buffalo on US Hwy 16, USFS	5/15-10/31	19	•				•				•		•

Map #	Description	Season	RV sites	tent sites	hook-ups	pull-thrus	dump station	restrooms	hot showers	pool	laundry	tables/grills	rec-room	drinking water
131	Indian Campground, 660 E Hart St., PH: 307-684-9601, Web: www.indiancampground.com	4/10-10/31	85	40	•	•	•	•	•	•	•	•		•
132	Lost Cabin, 27 mi SW of Buffalo on US Hwy 16, USFS	5/15-10/31	19	•				•				•		•
133	Middle Fork, 14 mi SW of Buffalo on US Hwy 16, USFS	5/15-10/31	9	•				•				•		•
134	Mountain View Motel & Campground, 585 Fort St., PH: 307-684-2881	All	15	3	•	•	•	•	•		•	•		•
135	South Fork, 15 mi W of Buffalo on US Hwy 16, USFS	5/15-10/31	15	•				•				•		•
136	Tie Hack, 15 mi W of Buffalo on US Hwy 16, USFS	5/15-10/31	9	•				•				•		•
Dayton														
137	Arrowhead Campground, 22 mi from Dayton		•		•			•	•			•		•
138	Bear Lodge Resort, P0 Box 159, 25 mi past Burgess Jct. on Hwy 14A PH: 307-752-2444, Fax 752-6444 www.bearlodgeresort.com	All	•	•	•			•	•	•	•	•	•	•
139	Dead Swede, 34 mi SW of Dayton on US 14, 4 mi SE on FS Rd 26, USFS	6/15-9/15	22	•				•				•		•
140	Foothills Motel & Campground, 101 Main, Box 174, PH: 307-655-2547, Web: www.tiberpipe.net/-foothill/Home.htm	5/1-11/1	22	30	•	•	•	•	•		•	•		•
141	North Tongue, 29 mi SW of Dayton on US 14, 1 mi N on FS Ad, USFS	6/15-10/31	12	•				•				•		•
142	Owen Creek, 34 mi SW of Dayton on US 14, USFS	6/1-10/31	7	•				•				•		•
143	Prune Creek, 26 mi SW of Dayton on US 14, USFS	6/15-9/15	21	•				•				•		•
144	Sibley Lake, 25 mi SW of Dayton on US 14, USFS	6/15-9/15	25	•	•			•				•		•
145	Tie Flume. 34 mi SW of Dayton on US 14. 2 mi E on FS Rd 26, USFS	6/15-9/8	25	•				•				•		•
Devils Tower														
146	Devils Tower KOA, entrance gate at Devils Tower Nall Monument, PH: 307-467-5395 or 800-562-5785	45 5/1-9/25	100	•	•	•	•	•		•	•	•	•	
147	Devils Tower National Monument. Hwy 110. Box 10. PH: 307-467-5283. Fax: 307-467-5350 Web: www.nps.gov/deto	4/15-10/15	30	•	•	•		•				•		•
Gillette														
148	CAM-PLEX (Rallies Only) 1635 Reata Dr., PH: 307-682-0552, 800-358-1897, FAX: 307-682-8418, Web: www.cam-plex.com	May-Sep	1821	100	•	•	•	•	•					
149	Greentree / Crazy Woman Campground, 1001 W 2nd St., PH: 307-682-3665	All	102	25	•	•	•	•	•	•	•	•	•	•
150	High Plains Campground, 1600 Garner Lake Rd., PH/Fax: 307-687-7339	All	65	50	•	•	•	•	•		•	•		•
Kaycee														
151	Hole in the Wall Campground, 17 mi W of Kaycee on Barnum Rd, PH: 307-738-2340	5/1-11/1	11		•									•
152	Kaycee Town Park, Adjacent to town, Box 265 (City Park)	All		•				•				•		•
153	KC RV Park. 42 Mayoworth Rd,PH: 307-738-2233. Email: kcrv@kaycee.smalltown.net	All	18	5	•	•	•	•	•		•	•		•
Moorcroft														
154	Keyhole Marina, Motel & Campgrounds, 215 McKean Rd., PH: 307-756-9529	4/1-9/30	10	10	•		•	•	•			•		•
155	Keyhole State Park, 12 mi E of Moorcroft on 1-90, use exit 165, 6 mi N on paved Rd, SP, PH: 307-756-3596	5/1-10/1	•	•		•	•	•				•		•
156	Wyoming Motel & Camping Park, 112 E. Converse, Jct. Hwys 14-16 & 1-90, PH: 307-756-3452 or 756-9836	5/15-11/15	10		•	•								•
Newcastle														
157	Cambria Inn RV & Campground, 23726 Hwy. 85, 5/1-10/31 PH: 307-746-2096, FAX 746-9569, Web: www.trib.com/-flyingv	15	7	•		•	•	•		•	•		•	
158	Corral Rest RV, 2206 W Main, PH: 307-746-2007	4/1-10/31	45	10	•		•	•	•	•	•	•		•
159	Crystal Park Campground, 2 Fountain Plz., PH: 307-746-4426 OR 800-882-8858, FAX: 746-3206	6/1-10/1	37	63	•	•	•	•	•	•	•	•		•
160	Four Corners RV Campground, 24695 US Hwy 85, PH: Fax: 307-746-4776 Web: www.trib.com/~hjohnsn	All	6		•							•		•
161	Rim Rock RV & Camp, 2206W. Main, 1911 W. Main PH: 307-746-2007 or 746-9775	All	42	10	•	•	•	•	•		•	•		•
Ranchester														
162	Connor Battlefield State Historic Site, I-90 to Ranchester, PH: 307-684-7629	5/1-10/1	•	•		•		•				•		•
163	Lazy R Campground RV Park, 652 Hwy 14, PH: 307-655-9284 or 888-655-9284, Email: davejudy@wavecom.net	All	25	6	•	•	•	•	•					•
Sheridan														
164	Big Horn Mountain KOA Campground, 63 Decker Ad. Box 35A. PH: 307-674-8766. Fax: 674-7190	5/1-10/5	90	32	•	•	•	•	•	•	•	•	•	•
165	Sheridan RV Park, 807 Avoca Aye, PH: 307-674-0722	4/1-11/1	26	12	•	•	•	•	•		•			•
Story														
166	Wagon Box Campground. 103 N Piney, PH: 307-683-2445	All	24	12	•		•	•	•		•	•		•
Sundance														
167	Cook Lake Camping, 1 mi E of Sundance on US 14, USFS	All	34	•				•					•	•
168	Mountain View Campground, N Govt. Valley Rd., Box 903 4/1-10/31 PH: 307-283-2270 or 800-792-8439. Fax: 307-283-2884	75	45	•	•	•	•	•	•	•	•	•	•	
169	Reuter, 2 mi W of Sundance on US 14, USFS	All	24	•				•				•		•
Upton														
170	Country Market Conoco, 909 2nd St. PH: 307-468-2551	All	6		•							•		

Map #	Description	Season	RV sites	tent sites	hook-ups	pull-thrus	dump station	restrooms	hot showers	pool	laundry	tables/grills	rec-room	drinking water
Wright														
172	Sagebluff RV Park, 387 at Sagebluff Dr., PH: 307-464-1305 or 464-1306	All	76	50	•	•		•	•		•			•
Section 4														
Cokeville														
173	Hams Fork. 12 mi N of Cokeville on WY 232. 4 mi NE on Cty Rd. 13 mi E on FS Rd. USFS	6/15-9/10	10	•				•				•		•
Evanston														
174	Phillips RV Park, 225 Bear River Dr, PH/ Fax: 307-789-3805 or 800-349-3805	4/1-11/1	56	3	•	•		•	•		•	•		•
Farson														
175	Big Sandy State Rec Area. N of Rock Springs on US 191, 5 mi N on paved road, 2 mi W on dirt road. SR PH: 332-3684	5/28-10/15	•	•		•		•				•		
Fort Bridger														
176	Ft. Bridger RV Camp, 64 Groshon Ad., Box 244, 82933, PH: 307-782-3150 or 800-578-6535	4/1-10/15	39	2	•	•	•	•	•		•	•		•
Green River														
177	Buckboard Crossing. 23 mi SW of Green River on WY 530. 5/17-9/12 2 mi E on FS Rd to Marina, PH: 800-280-CAMP, USFS	68	•			•	•	•					•	
178	Tex'sTravel Camp, Inc., 36OWashinoton St., State Rt. 2, Box 101, PH: 307-875-2630	5/1-10/1	80	10	•	•	•	•	•		•	•		•
Kemmerer														
179	Foothills Residential Community & RV Park, 310 US Hwy 189 N, PH: 307-877-6634, Fax: 307-877-6634	4/15-11/1	41	0	•		•					•		•
180	Lake Viva Naughton, 16 mi N of Kemmerer on WY Hwy 233, PH: 307-877-9669	All	35	100	•		•	•	•			•		•
181	Riverside RV Park, 216 Spinel St, PH: 307-877-3416	5/1-10/15	30		•	•	•					•		•
Lyman														
182	Lyman KOA. 1532 Hwy 413. Exit 41. 1 mi S. 5/15-9/30 PH: 307-786-2188 or 800-KOA-2762, E-mail: LymanKOA@bvea.net	34	15	•	•	•	•	•	•	•	•		•	
Rock Springs														
183	Albert's Trailer Court, 1560 Elk St. S (off I-80) Hwy 191	All	•	•	•		•		•			•		•
184	Firehole Canyon, 13 mi S on WY 191, W on FS 106 8 mi, PH: 800-280-CAMP	5/17-9/12	40	•		•		•	•					•
185	Rock Springs KOA, 86 Foothill Blvd. PH: 307-362-3063. 800-KOA-8699	4/1-10/15	106	20	•	•	•	•	•	•	•	•	•	•
Section 5														
Albany														
186	Bobbie Thompson, 7 mi W of Albany, USFS, FAX: 307-745-2398	6/15-9/30	18	•				•				•		•
187	Holmes, 10 mi W of Albany, USFS, FAX: 307-745-2398	6/15-9/30	11					•				•		•
188	Lake Owen, 3 mi S of Albany, USFS, FAX: 307-745-2398	6/1-11/1	35	•				•				•		•
189	Rob Roy, 7 mi NW of Albany, USFS, FAX: 307-745-2398	6/15-10/1	65	•				•				•		•
Casper (see also EVANSVILLE, MILLS)														
190	Alcova Lake Campground, 28 mi W of Town on Cty Rd 407, PH: 307-235-9311	4/30-10/1	100	•	•		•	•				•		•
191	Casper KOA East, 2800 E Yellowstone, PH: 307-237-5155 or 800-562-3259, E-mail: moman@aol.com	All	75	10	•	•	•	•	•	•	•	•	•	•
192	Casper KOA North, 1 101 Prairie Lane, PH: 307-577-1664 or 800-992-1460	4/1-11/1	65	5	•	•	•	•	•	•	•	•		•
193	Fairside Trailer Park, on Wyoming Blvd Hwy 258, between WY 220 & US 20-26, 3635 Fairside St	All	14		•				•			•		•
194	Fort Caspar Campground, 4205 Fort Caspar Rd. PH: 307-234-3260 or 888-243-7709, Email mbotdng@sprynet.com	All	86	24	•	•		•	•		•	•		•
195	Gray Reef Reservoir, 26 mi W of Town on WY 220, PH: 307-235-9325, FAX: 307-235-9611	4/1-10/15	11	•				•				•		
196	Lodgepole, 9 mi S of Casper on Casper Mtn Rd, 6 mi to Muddy Mtn, BLM	6/15-10/31	15	•				•				•		•
197	Pathfinder Reservoir, 32 mi SW of town on WY 220, PH: 307-235-9311	4/1-10/15	•	•			•	•				•		
198	Rim Campground, 9 mi S of Casper on Casper Mtn rd, 6 mi to Muddy Mtd, BLM	6/15-10/31	8	•				•				•		•
Centennial														
199	Brooklyn Lake, 10 mi NW of Centennial, USFS, 307-745-2398	7/15-9/15	19	•				•				•		•
200	Nash Fork, B mi NW of Centennial, USFS, FAX: 307-745-2398	7/1-10/5	27	•				•				•		•
201	North Fork, 5 mi NW of Centennial, USFS, 307-745-2398	7/1-11/1	60	•				•				•		•
202	Silver Lake, 12 mi W of Centennial, USFS, 307-326-5250	7/1-10/15	19	•				•				•		•
203	Sugar Loaf, 8 mi NW of Centennial, USFS, 307-745-2398	7/15-9/27	16	•				•				•		•
204	TMP Libby Creek. 2 mi NW of Centennial. USFS	5/28-10/13	38	•				•				•		•
Elk Mountain														
205	Bow River. 15 1/2 miSof Elk Mtn. USFS	5/24-10/31	13	•				•				•		

Map #	Description	Season	RV sites	tent sites	hook-ups	pull-thrus	dump station	restrooms	hot showers	pool	laundry	tables/grills	rec-room	drinking water
Encampment														
206	Bottle Creek, 7 mi SW of Encampment on WY 70, USFS, FAX: 307-326-5250	5/28-11/1	16	•				•				•		•
207	Haskins Creek, 15 mi SW of Encampment on WY 70, USFS	6/15-10/31	10	•				•				•		•
208	Lakeview Campground, 28 mi SE of Encampment, USFS, FAX: 307-326-5250	6/15-10/31	50	•				•				•		•
209	Lost Creek. 17 mi SW of Encampment on WY 401. USFS. FAX: 307-326-5250	5/24-10/31	13	•				•				•		•
Foxpark														
210	Boswell Creek, 8 mi SE of Foxpark, USFS	6/1-9/15	•	•				•				•		
211	Pelton Creek, 10 mi SW of Foxpark, USFS	6/15-10/15	15	•				•				•		•
Hanna														
212	The Miracle Mile Ranch & RV Park, 48 mi. N. of Hanna on Cty. Rd. 291, PH: 307-325-6710	All	21		•	•		•	•					•
Jeffrey City														
213	Cottonwood, 6 mi E of Jeffrey City on US 287, 8 mi S on Cty & BLM Rds, BLM. PH: 307-322-8420	5/22-12/1		18					•			•		•
Lander														
214	Atlantic City, 25 mi S. of Lander on WY 28, Atlantic City Rd, BLM	5/8-11/15	•	•				•				•		•
215	Big Atlantic Gulch, 25 mi S. of Lander on WY 28, Miner's Delight, Rd, BLM	6/1-10/31	•	•				•				•		•
216	Dickinson Creek, 34 mi NW of Lander, USFS	6/20-9/15	6	15				•				•		
217	Fiddlers Lake, 25 mi SW of Lander, USFS	7/1-9/30	13	•				•				•		•
218	Hart Ranch Hideout RV Park & Campground, 8 mi SE of Lander at Jct 28 & 789-287, PH: 307-332-3836 or 800-914-9226	All	55	28	•	•		•	•		•	•		•
219	Holiday Lodge Campground, 210 McFarlane Dr., PH: 307-332-2511 or 800-624-1974, Fax: 307-332-2256	5/1-9/30	2	8	•			•	•		•	•		•
220	Lander City Park, 240 Lincoln, PH: 307-332-4647	5/1-9/30	7	•				•				•		•
221	Louis Lake, 30 mi SW of Lander, USFS	7/1-9/30	9	9				•				•		•
222	Maverick Mobile Home & RV Park, 1104 N. 2nd St, PH/ Fax: 307-332-3142	4/1-9/30	50	10	•	•	•	•	•		•	•		•
223	Popo Agie, 28 mi SW of Lander, USFS	7/1-9/30	1	3				•				•		
224	Ray Lake Campground & Cafe, 39 Ray Lake Rd, PH: 307-332-9333, Fax: 307-332-1345	5/1-9/30	10	25	•	•	•	•	•			•		•
225	Rocky Acres Campground, 5700 US Hwy 287, PH: 307-332-6953, FAX: 307-322-8505	5/1-9/30	13	28	•		•	•	•		•	•		•
226	Sinks Canyon, 11 mi S of Lander, USFS	5/1-10/31	9	•				•				•		•
227	Sinks Canyon State Park, 6 mi SW of Lander on WY 131, SP, PH: 307-332-6333	5/1-11/1	•	•		•		•				•		•
228	Sleeping Bear RV Park & Campground, 715 E. Main, PH: 307-332-5159 or 888-757-2327, Web: www.sleeping-rv-park.com	All	44	6	•	•	•	•	•		•	•	•	•
229	Worthen Meadows, 18 mi SW of Lander, USFS	7/1-9/30	20	•				•				•		•
Mcfadden														
230	Arlington Outpost, at Arlington on I-80, 38 mi W of Laramie at exit 272, PH: 307-378-2350	5-1/10-31	50	20	•	•	•	•	•	•		•	•	•
231	White's Recreation Reservoirs, 5 mi NE of I-80 (Arlington Exit) on WY 13	5/1-10/1	25	25				•						•
Powder River														
232	Hell's Half Acre, US Hwy 20/26, 45 mi W. of Casper, PH: 307-473-7773 or 473-7772	3/1-11/15	10	10	•			•	•			•		•
Rawlis														
233	American Presidents Campground, 2346 W Spruce St, 6/15-10/30 PH: 307-324-3218 or 800-294-3218, FAX: 307-324-3509	72	•	•		•	•	•					•	
234	KOA Kampground, 205 E. Hwy. 71. PH: 307-328-2021 or 800-KOA-7559, E-mail: gattfarr@vcn.com	4/1-10/31	51	6	•	•	•	•	•	•	•	•		•
235	RV World Campground, 3101 Wagon Circle Rd, 3/1-10/1 PH: 307-328-1091 or 800-478-9753, Fax: 307-324-5031	100	5	•	•	•	•	•	•	•	•	•	•	
236	Western Hills Campground, 2500 Wagon Circle Rd. Box 760, PH: 307-324-2592. 888-568-3040. Web' wwwwesternhillscampground.com	All	171	50	•	•	•	•	•			•		•
Riverside														
237	Lazy Acres Campground & Motel, on Hwy 230, PH: 307-327-5968 Web: wwwwyomingcarboncountycom/lazy.htm	5/1-11/1	28	5	•	•	•	•	•		•	•		•
Riverton														
238	Owl Creek Kampground, 11124 US Hwy 26-789, PH: 307-856-2869 E-mail: campowlcreek@tcinc.net	5/15-9/15	19	21	•	•	•	•	•		•	•	•	•
239	Rudy's Camper Court, 622 E Lincoln, PH: 307-856-9764	All	21	3	•		•	•	•			•		•
240	Wind River RV Park, 1618 E Park Ave, PH: 307-857-3000. 800-528-3913, Fax: 307-856-9559	All	60	2	•	•	•	•	•		•	•	•	•
Saratoga														
241	Deer Haven RV Park, 706 N 1st St., 307-326-8746	5/15-10/15	45		•	•	•					•		•
242	French Creek, 39 mi E of Saratoga, USFS, 307-326-5258, FAX: 307-326-5250	5/25-10/31	11	6				•				•		•
243	Jack Creek, 19 mi W of Saratoga. USFS. FAX: 307-326-5250	5/24-10/31	16	•				•				•		•
244	Ryan Park, 23 mi. SE of Saratoga, Hwy 130, USFS, FAX: 307-326-5250	5/28-11/15	48					•				•		•
245	Saratoga Lake, 1 mi N of Saratoga. 307-326-8335 or 326-5811	4/15-11/1	25	20	•		•	•				•		•
246	South Brush Creek, 20 mi SE of Saratoga, USFS, FAX: 307-326-5250	5/28-11/15	20	•				•						•

Map #	Description	Season	RV sites	tent sites	hook-ups	pull-thrus	dump station	restrooms	hot showers	pool	laundry	tables/grills	rec-room	drinking water
Shoshoni														
247	Boysen State Park, Hwy 20 & Hwy 26, south end of Wind River Canyon, SP, PH: 307-876-2796	5/1-10/1	•	•		•	•	•				•		•
Sinclair														
248	Seminoe State Park, 34 mi N of Sinclair on Cty Rd 351, SP, PH: 307-320-3013	5/1-10/15	•	•		•	•	•				•		•
Section 6														
Buford														
249	Buford Trading Post, I-80 exit 335, PH: 307-632-3999 or 800-318-0009, FAX: 307-632-4244	5/1-9/1	50	20		•		•						
Cheyenne														
250	AB Camping, 1503W College Dr, 82007, PH/ Fax: 307-634-7035	3/1-10/31	130	40	•	•	•	•	•		•	•	•	•
251	Cheyenne KOA, 8800 Archer Frontage Road, PH: 307-638-8840 or 800-KOA-1507, Web. www.cheyennekoa.com	All	42	11	•	•	•	•	•	•	•	•		•
252	Curt Gowdy State Park, 24 mi W of Cheyenne on WY 210, SP, PH: 307-632-7946	5/1-10/1	•	•		•	•	•				•		•
253	Greenway Trailer Park, 3829 Greenway St., PH: 307-634-6696, Fax: 635-8555	All	41	3	•	•	•	•	•		•	•		•
254	Hide-A-Way, 218 S Greeley Hwy, 82007, PH: 307-637-7114	All	20		•			•	•		•	•		•
255	Hyland Park, I-25 at Missile Or, Exit 1 OD	5/1-10/1	30		•									•
256	Jolley Rogers RV, 3102 Hwy 30, 82001, PH: 307-634-8457 or 800-458-7779	5/1-10/1	128	•	•	•	•	•	•		•	•		•
257	Restway Travel Park, 4212 Whitney Rd, PH:307-634-381 1 or 800-443-2751, FAX: 307-637-4117	All	110	35	•	•	•	•	•	•	•	•	•	•
258	T-Joe's RV Park, 12700 E -80 Service Rd, PH: 307-635-8750, FAX: 307-632-5210	All	28	10	•	•	•	•	•		•	•	•	•
259	Terry Bison Ranch, 511-25 Service Rd E, PH:307-634-4171 or 800-319-4171, FAX: 307-634-9746	All	93	50	•	•	•	•	•		•	•		•
260	WYO Campground P0 Box 5201, Exit 377 on I-80 E, 5/1-10/1 PH: 307-547-2244, Web: www.wvocamooround@worldnet.att.net	50	93	•	•	•	•	•	•	•	•		•	
Chugwater														
261	Diamond Guest Ranch, 12 mi W on Diamond Rd, Box 236, PH: 307-422-3564, 800-932-4222, Web: www.diamondgr.com	5/15-10/15	106	30	•	•	•	•	•	•	•	•	•	•
262	Pitzel RV Park, 3rd & Clay St, PH: 307-422-3421		8	•	•						•			•
Douglas														
263	Ayres Natural Bridge Park, 208 Natural Bridge Park, PH: 307-358-3532	4/1-11/1	7	25				•				•		
264	Campbell Creek, 1 mi W of Douglas on US 26, 20 mi SW on WY 501, 6/1-10/31 13 mi SW on Cty Ad, USFS. FAX: 307-358-3072	8	•				•				•		•	
265	Curtis Gulch, 1 mi W of Douglas on US 26, 20 mi SW on WY 501, 5/1-10/31 14.5 mi S on Cty Ad, 4 mi NE on PS Ad, USFS	6	•				•				•		•	
266	Douglas Jackalope KOA, 168 Cold Springs Ad, PH: 307-358-2164 or 800-562-2469	All	80	20	•	•	•	•	•	•	•	•	•	•
267	Esterbrook, 1 mi W of Douglas on US 26, 30 mi S on WY 94, 3 mi E on FS Rd, USFS	5/1-10/31	12	•				•				•		
268	Esterbrook Lodge, 32 Pine-Esterbrook	All	5	5	•	•		•	•			•		•
269	Friend Park, 35 mi S of Douglas, USFS. FAX: 307-358-3072	6/1-10/31	11	•				•				•		•
270	River Side Park, 420 W Grant	All	20	20			•	•	•			•		•
Fort Laramie														
271	Bennett Court, 3 1/2 blocks N on Laramie Ave & Otis, PH: 307-837-2270	All	7	3	•		•	•	•		•	•		•
272	Carnahan Ranch, HC 72 Box 440, Hwy 160, PH/FAX: 307-8372917 or 800-837-6730, Emai': bcarnahan@scottsbluff.net	5/1-10/1	25	•	•	•		•	•			•	•	•
273	Chuck Wagon RV Park, 306 Pioneer Ct, Box 142, PH: 307-837-2828, E-mail lizbubba@prairieweb.com	4/15-10/1	13	5	•	•	•	•	•		•	•		•
274	Pony Soldier RV Park, Hwy 26, 5 mi W of Lingle, 5 mi E of Ft. Laramie. PH: 307-837-3078	4/15-10/15	53	12	•		•	•	•		•	•	•	•
Glendo														
275	Glendo State Park, 1.5 mi E of Glendo, SP, PH: 307-735-4433	All	•	•		•	•	•				•		•
276	Hall's Marina, 383 Glendo Park Rd in Glendo St. Park, Box 187, PH: 307-735-4216, FAX: 307-735-4203, hallmarina@ucn.com	5/1-10/1	7		•	•								
277	Lakeview Motel & Campground, 422 N 6th St., Box 231, PH: 307-735-4461	All	20	10	•			•	•		•			
Glenrock														
278	Deer Creek RV Campground, 302 Millar Ln, PH: 307-436-8121, FAX: 307-4365779	4/1-11/15	40	25	•	•	•	•	•		•			•
Guernsey														
279	Guernsey State Park, 3 mi N of Guernsey, SP, PH: 307-836-2334	5/1-10/1	•	•		•	•	•				•		•
280	Larson Park Campground, 100 5. Guernsey Rd. Box 827, PH: 307-836-2255, Web:www.golfandcamp.com	4/15-10/15	16	20	•			•	•			•		•
Hawk Springs														
281	Hawk Springs State Recreation Area, at Hawk Springs on Hwy 85, E 3 mi on dirt road, SP, PH: 307-836-2334	5/28-10/1	•	•		•		•				•		•
La Grange														
282	Bear Mountain Station. 32 miS of Torrington US 85, W Rt, PH: 307-834-2294	5/27-9/2	12		•		•	•	•			•		•

Map #	Description	Season	RV sites	tent sites	hook-ups	pull-thrus	dump station	restrooms	hot showers	pool	laundry	tables/grills	rec-room	drinking water
Laramie														
283	Laramie KOA, 1271 W. Baker St., PH: 307-742-6553, Fax: 721-3841, E-mail KOAlaramie@vcn.com	All	116	50	•	•	•	•	•		•	•	•	•
284	Tie City, 12 mi SE of Laramie, USFS, FAX: 307-745-2398	5/24-10/31	18	•				•				•		•
285	Vedauwoo, 21 mi SE of Laramie, USFS	5/5-11/1	28	•		•		•				•		•
286	Woods Landing, 9 State Hwy 10, Jelm, WY 82063, PH: 307-745-9638 or 307-745-5770, Web: www.woodslanding.com	All	10		•		•	•	•			•		•
287	Yellow Pine, 15 Mi SE of Laramie, USFS, FAX: 307-745-2398	6/15-9/30	19	•		•		•				•		•
Lusk														
288	BJ's Campground, 902 S. Maple, PH: 307-334-2314, (limited services 10/16-4/30)	5/1-10/15	26		•	•		•	•		•	•		•
289	B Q Corral, 702 5 Main, PH: 307-334-0128	4/1-10/15	6	6	•		•	•	•			•		
290	Prairie View Campground, 3925 Hwy 20, Box 1168, PH: 307-334-3174 or 334-2827, Fax: 307-334-2827	4/15-10/15	35	15	•	•	•	•	•		•	•	•	•
Pine Bluffs														
291	Pine Bluffs RV Park, 10 Paint Brush, PH: 307-245-3665, Fax: 307-778-4899, Email: snowardt@aol.com	All	100	30	•		•	•	•		•	•		•
Torrington														
292	Goshen County Fairgrounds, Hwy 85-26 W, PH: 307-532-2525	All	20	•	•		•	•	•			•		•
293	Pioneer Municipal Park, W 15th & Ave "E" St	5/1-9/30	10	•	•		•	•	•			•		•
294	Travelers Trailer Court & Campground, S on US 85, 750 Main, Box 6	All	30	25	•			•	•			•		•
Wheatland														
295	4-W Ranch Campground, I-25 at Fish Creek Rd, 15 mi N of Wheatland, PH: 307-332-4764	All	28	16	•		•	•	•	•		•		•
296	Arrowhead RV Camp, 2005 N 16th St, PH. 307-322-3467	All	12	8	•	•	•	•			•	•		•
297	Kemp Dakota Ranch Campground, 13 mi N of Wheatland to exit 94,13 mi W, PH: 307-322-2772	5/20-10/15	60	30	•		•	•	•			•		•
298	Wheatland City Park (Lewis Park), 600 9th St, PH 307-322-2822	All	28	5	•		•	•	•			•		•
Grand Teton National Park (see also KELLY, MORAN)														
	Colter Bay Campground, 25 mi N of Moose, NPS,	seasonal	350				•	•	•		•		•	
	Colter Bay RV Park, Box 250, PH: 307-543-2811, 800-628-9988, FAX: 543-3143, Web:www.gtlc.com	5/24-9/29 112	•	•	•	•	•	•	•	•	•			
	Colter BayTent Village, Box 250, PH: 307-543-2811, 800-628-9988, FAX: 543-3143, Web:www.gtlc.com	5/24-9/29	66											
	Gros Ventre Campground, 11.5 mi S and E of Moose, NPS	seasonal	360				•	•				•	•	
	Jenny Lake Campground, 8 mi N of Moose, NPS	seasonal	49			•			•	•				
	Lizard Creek Campground, 32 mi N of Moose, NPS	seasonal	60					•				•		•
	Signal Mountain Campground. 16 mi N of Jenny Lake, NPS, PH: 307-543-2516, Web: www.NPS.GOV/GRTEL	seasonal	86	•			•	•				•		•
Kelly (see also Grand Teton National Park, Moran)														
	Gros Ventre. 2 mi SW of Kelly on Gros Ventre Rd. NPS	5/1-10/10	•	•			•	•		•	•			
Moran (see also GRAND TETON NATIONAL PARK, KELLY)														
	Flagg Ranch Village, 2 mi S of Yellowstone on US 89-287, Box 187, PH: 307-543-2861	5/15-10/15	170	•	•	•	•	•	•		•	•		•
	Grand Teton Park RV Resort & Cabins, 1 mi E of Grand Teton Nat'l Park, Box 92, PH: 307-543-2483 or 800-563-6469	All	120	60	•	•	•	•	•	•	•	•	•	•
Yellowstone National Park, PO Box 165, 82190, PH: 307-344-7311 or 344-2114 (Recordings), Web: www.travelyellowstone.com														
Canyon Country														
	Canyon Village, at Canyon Jct., Box 165, PH: 307-344-7311, Fax: 307-344-7456	5/31-9/8	272	•			•	•	•		•	•	•	
Geyser Country														
	Lewis Lake, 10 mi N of S entrance, N PS	6/22-11/4	75	•				•				•	•	
	Madison Junction, 1/4 mi W of Madison Jct., Box 165, PH: 307-344-7311. Fax: 307-344-7456	5/3-10/20	280	•		•	•	•				•	•	
Lake Country														
	Bridge Bay, 3 mi SW of Lake Village, Box 165. PH: 307-344-7311, Fax: 307-344-7456	5/24-9/15	430	•			•	•				•	•	
	Fishing Bridge RV Park, NE of Lake area on East entrance Rd, Box 165, 5/17-9/22 PH: 307-344-7311, Fax: 307-344-7456	344		•		•	•	•		•	•	•		
	Grant Village, 2 mi S of West Thumb Jct. on the West Thumb of Lake Yellowstone, Box 165, PH: 307-344-7311	6/21-9/29	425	•			•	•	•		•	•	•	
Mammoth Country														
	Indian Creek, 7 mi S of Mammoth. NPS	6/8-9/17	75	•				•				•	•	
	Mammoth, 1/2 mi N of Mammoth Jct., NPS	All	85	•				•				•	•	
	Norris, 1 mi N of Norris Jct, NPS	5/18-9/24	116	•				•				•	•	
Roosevelt Country														
	Pebble Creek, 9 mi S of NE entrance, NPS	6/1-9/24	36	•				•				•	•	
	Slough Creek, 6 mi NE of Tower Jct., NIPS	5/25-10/31	29	•				•				•	•	
	Tower Falls, 2 mi S of Tower Jct., NPS	5/18-9/24	32	•				•				•	•	

Fisheries
By Drainage

Yellowstone Park

Map Number/Fishery		Brook Trout	Brown Trout	Cutthroat Trout	Grayling	Lake Trout	Mountain Whitefish	Rainbow Trout
Rivers & Streams								
1	Bechler River	•	•					•
2	Firehole River	•	•					•
3	Gallatin River		•	•			•	•
4	Gardner River	•	•	•			•	•
5	Gibbon River	•	•		•		•	•
6	Lamar River			•				•
7	Madison River		•		•		•	•
8	Slough Creek			•				•
9	Snake River		•	•			•	
10	Yellowstone River	•	•	•				
Lakes								
11	Heart Lake			•		•		
12	Lewis Lake	•	•			•		
13	Shoshone Lake	•	•			•		
14	Yellowstone Lake			•		•		

Snake River Drainage

Map Number/Fishery		Brook Trout	Grayling	Lake Trout	Mountain Whitefish	Snake Rvr Cutthroat
Rivers & Streams						
15	Flat Creek (Above Refuge)	•				•
16	Flat Creek (on Refuge)	•			•	•
17	Granite Creek				•	•
18	Greys River				•	•
19	Gros Ventre River				•	•
20	Hoback River				•	•
21	Pacific Creek				•	•
22	Salt River	•			•	•
23	Snake River				•	•
Lakes						
24	Grassy Lake			•		•
25	Jackson Lake	•		•	•	•
26	Jenny Lake			•	•	•
27	Lake of the Woods		•			•
28	Leidy Lake					•
29	Phelps Lake			•	•	•
30	Slide Lake, Lower			•	•	•
31	Topping Lake		•			

Introduction

Big Horn River Drainage

Map Number/Fishery

Rivers & Streams

#	Fishery	Bear River Cutthroat	Black Crappie	Brook Trout	Brown Trout	Burbot	Channel Catfish	Golden Trout	Grayling	Lake Trout	Largemouth Bass	Mountain Whitefish	Rainbow Trout	Sauger	Snake River Cutthroat	Splake	Stonecat	Walleye	Yellow Perch	Yellowstone Cutthroat
32	Bear Creek														•					•
33	Big Horn River, Lower					•	•							•				•		
34	Big Horn River, Upper				•	•						•	•							
35	Brooks Lake Creek			•									•							
36	Bull Lake			•				•		•			•		•					•
37	Clarks Fork River, Lower			•	•								•							•
38	Clarks Fork River, Upper			•									•							•
39	Greybull River				•															•
40	Horse Creek			•	•							•	•							
41	Jakeys Fork Creek			•	•							•	•							
42	Medicine Lodge Creek			•	•							•	•							
43	Medicine Lodge Unit			•	•							•	•							
44	Paintrock Creek			•	•							•	•							•
45	Popo Agie River, North Fork				•							•	•							
46	Popo Agie River, Middle Fork			•	•								•							
47	Popo Agie River, Little				•								•							
48	Popo Agie River, Little			•									•							
49	Shell Creek			•	•							•	•							
50	Shoshone River	•			•							•	•		•					•
51	Shoshone River, N Fork				•					•		•	•							•
52	Shoshone River, S Fork			•	•					•		•			•					•
53	Sunlight Unit			•									•							•
54	Tensleep Creek			•	•							•	•		•					
55	Torrey Creek			•	•	•							•							
56	Wind River (section I)				•	•						•	•		•			•	•	
57	Wind River (Dubois Area)			•	•							•	•							
58	Wind River (section II)				•	•						•	•		•			•		
59	Wind River, East Fork														•					•
60	Wind River, Little				•	•						•	•							
61	Yellowstone River																			•

Map Number/Fishery

Big Horn River Drainage

Lakes

#	Fishery	Bear River Cutthroat	Black Crappie	Brook Trout	Brown Trout	Burbot	Channel Catfish	Golden Trout	Grayling	Lake Trout	Largemouth Bass	Mountain Whitefish	Rainbow Trout	Sauger	Snake River Cutthroat	Splake	Stonecat	Walleye	Yellow Perch	Yellowstone Cutthroat
62	Alp Lakes, Wind River Mtns			•	•	•		•	•	•		•	•		•	•				•
63	Atlantic Gulch, Big			•											•					
64	Beartooth Lake			•					•	•			•							•
65	Beck Lake				•		•				•		•						•	•
66	Big Horn Lake		•		•	•	•				•	•		•			•	•	•	
67	Bighorn Mtns, Alpine Lakes			•	•	•		•	•	•		•	•		•	•				•
68	Boysen Reservoir		•		•	•	•			•	•		•	•	•			•	•	
69	Bridger Lake																			•
70	Brooks Lake, Upper			•									•			•				
71	Brooks Lake			•						•			•			•				
72	Buffalo Bill Reservoir				•					•		•	•		•					•
73	Bull Lake				•	•				•		•	•		•					•
74	Cameahwait Lake										•		•						•	
75	Christina Lake			•						•										
76	Deaver Reservoir												•					•		•
77	Depression Res, Middle				•								•							
78	Fiddlers Lake			•									•							

Map Number/Fishery

Big Horn River Drainage

Continued

Lakes

No.	Fishery	Bear River Cutthroat	Black Crappie	Brook Trout	Brown Trout	Burbot	Channel Catfish	Golden Trout	Grayling	Lake Trout	Largemouth Bass	Mountain Whitefish	Rainbow Trout	Sauger	Snake River Cutthroat	Splake	Stonecat	Walleye	Yellow Perch	Yellowstone Cutthroat
79	Fish Lake														•					
80	Frye Lake			•									•							
81	Hogan Reservoir				•										•					
82	Jade Lakes Upper & Lower									•					•					
83	Louis Lake									•			•		•					
84	Luce Reservoir												•							
85	Meadowlark Lake			•	•								•							•
86	Newton Lake, East			•	•											•				
87	Newton Lake, West																			•
88	Ocean Lake		•			•												•	•	
89	Pelham Lake																			•
90	Pilot Butte Reservoir				•	•							•						•	
91	Ray Lake				•	•						•	•		•			•		
92	Renner										•									
93	Ring Lake				•	•							•			•				
94	Shoshone Lake			•																
95	Sunshine Res, Lower					•						•			•	•				•
96	Sunshine Res, Upper											•			•	•				•
97	Swamp Lake			•																
98	Torrey Lake				•	•				•			•			•				
99	Trail Lake				•	•				•			•			•				
100	Worthen Meadows Res			•									•							

Powder/Belle Fourche Drainage

Map Number/Fishery

Rivers & Streams

No.	Fishery	Crappie	Black Bullhead	Bluegill	Brook Trout	Brown Trout	Channel Catfish	Cutthroat Trout	Grayling	Green Sunfish	Lake Trout	Largemouth Bass	Mountain Whitefish	Northern Pike	Rainbow Trout	Rock Bass	Smallmouth Bass	Splake	Stonecat	Tiger Musky	Walleye	Yellow Perch
101	Beaver Creek				•	•				•												
102	Belle Fourche River		•				•			•									•			
103	Belle Fourche River		•				•			•							•					
104	Bighorn Rvr, Little (Lower)					•							•		•							
105	Bighorn Rvr, Little (Upper)				•			•							•							
106	Blue Creek				•	•																
107	Bull Creek							•														
108	Clear Creek				•	•		•							•							
109	Crazy Woman Crk, N Fork				•										•							
110	Fool Creek							•	•						•							
111	Goose Creek, East Fork				•	•									•							
112	Goose Creek, West Fork				•										•							
113	Powder River, North Fork					•									•							
114	Powder River, Mid Fork				•	•									•							
115	Sand Creek					•									•							
116	Tongue River					•							•		•							
117	Tongue River, North				•	•		•							•							
118	Tongue River, South				•	•									•							
119	Willow Creek, Big				•			•							•							

Powder/Belle Fourche Drainage

Map Number/Fishery — Lakes	Crappie	Black Bullhead	Bluegill	Brook Trout	Brown Trout	Channel Catfish	Cutthroat Trout	Grayling	Green Sunfish	Lake Trout	Largemouth Bass	Mountain Whitefish	Northern Pike	Rainbow Trout	Rock Bass	Smallmouth Bass	Splake	Stonecat	Tiger Musky	Walleye	Yellow Perch
120 Bighorn Mts Alpine Lakes				•	•		•	•		•				•							
121 Blackhills Pl Reservoir											•			•							
122 Buffalo Wetlands Pond				•	•						•			•		•					•
123 Calvin Lake							•														
124 Cloud Peak Reservoir				•			•							•							
125 Cook Lake		•		•	•		•		•					•							
126 De Smet, Lake					•		•							•	•						•
127 Dull Knife Reservoir				•	•									•							
128 Duncan Lake														•							
129 East Iron Creek Reservoir			•				•				•			•							
130 Gillette Fishing Lake				•		•					•			•							
131 Healy Reservoir							•							•	•						
132 Kearny Lake				•			•			•				•							
133 Keyhole Reservoir	•		•			•							•			•				•	
134 Kleenburn Ponds	•	•				•					•					•					
135 LAK Reservoir					•				•		•			•					•	•	
136 Little Thunder Reservoir		•	•								•			•							
137 Mavrakis Pond		•							•					•							
138 Muddy Guard Reservoirs					•									•			•				
139 MW Reservoir				•					•					•							
140 Panther Pond						•			•		•			•							
141 Park Reservoir					•		•							•							
142 Ranchester City Pond					•				•					•							
143 Sawmill Lakes				•			•														
144 Sawmill Reservoir				•													•				
145 Sibley Lake					•		•							•							
146 Tie Hack Reservoir				•	•		•							•							
147 Turner Creek Reservoir											•										
148 Twin Lake Reservoir				•			•			•											
149 Willow Park Reservoir				•										•							

Green River Drainage

Map Number/Fishery — Rivers & Streams	Bear River Cutthroat	Brook Trout	Brown Trout	Channel Catfish	Colorado Rvr Cutthroat	Cutthroat Trout	Golden Trout	Grayling	Kokanee Salmon	Lake Trout	Largemouth Bass	Mountain Whitefish	Rainbow Trout	Smallmouth Bass	Snake River Cutthroat	Splake	Tiger Musky	Yellowstone Cutthroat
150 Blacks Fork River		•	•			•							•					
151 Battle Creek		•			•							•	•					
152 Boulder Creek		•				•							•					
153 Cottonwood Creek, North		•			•							•						
154 Cottonwood Creek, South		•			•							•						
155 Duck Creek		•	•															
156 East Fork River (BLM Access)		•	•									•	•					
157 East Fork River (By Hatchery)		•	•									•	•					
158 Green River (Natl.Forest)		•	•									•	•					
159 Green River (above Warren Brdg)		•	•									•	•					
160 Green River (above N. Fork Rd.)		•	•									•	•					
161 Green River (below N. Fork Rd.)			•			•						•	•					
162 Green River (Daniel)		•	•									•	•					
163 Green River (Fear)			•			•						•	•					
164 Green River (lower)			•	•						•		•	•	•	•			
165 Hams Fork		•	•			•						•	•					

Green River Drainage

Continued

Map Number/Fishery

Rivers & Streams

#	Map Number/Fishery	Bear River Cutthroat	Brook Trout	Brown Trout	Channel Catfish	Colorado Rvr Cutthroat	Cutthroat Trout	Golden Trout	Grayling	Kokanee Salmon	Lake Trout	Largemouth Bass	Mountain Whitefish	Rainbow Trout	Smallmouth Bass	Snake River Cutthroat	Splake	Tiger Musky	Yellowstone Cutthroat
166	Labarge Creek		•	•		•							•	•					
167	New Fork River (below E. Fork)		•	•									•	•					
168	New Fork River		•	•									•	•					
169	Pine Creek		•	•										•					
170	Salt Creek	•																	
171	Sandstone Creek, Big		•				•						•						
172	Sandy River, Big	•		•			•							•		•			
173	Savery Creek		•	•		•							•	•					
174	Smiths Fork (USFS)	•		•									•						
175	Smiths Fork, East Fork		•			•	•							•					
176	Smiths Fork, West Fork		•														•		
177	Tepee Creek		•			•	•												
178	Thomas Fork	•																	
179	Tosi Creek		•			•	•												
180	Vermillion Creek, North Fork		•																
181	Woodruff Narrows/Sear River	•		•			•												

Green River Drainage

Map Number/Fishery

Lakes

#	Map Number/Fishery	Bear River Cutthroat	Brook Trout	Brown Trout	Channel Catfish	Colorado Rvr Cutthroat	Cutthroat Trout	Golden Trout	Grayling	Kokanee Salmon	Lake Trout	Largemouth Bass	Mountain Whitefish	Rainbow Trout	Smallmouth Bass	Snake River Cutthroat	Splake	Tiger Musky	Yellowstone Cutthroat
182	Alice, Lake	•																	
183	Big Sandy Reservoir			•	•		•							•					
184	Boulder Lake									•	•			•					
185	Bridger Wilderness		•	•		•	•	•	•		•			•		•			•
186	Burnt Lake		•								•			•					
187	CCC Ponds		•											•					
188	Dollar Lake												•	•					
189	Flaming Gorge Reservoir			•	•					•	•			•	•				
190	Fontenelle Reservoir			•						•				•					
191	Fremont Lake			•						•	•			•					
192	Green River Lake, Lower		•								•			•					
193	Halfmoon Lake			•							•			•					
194	Halfmoon Lake, Little			•							•			•					
195	Jim Bridger Pond													•	•	•	•		
196	Kemmerer City Reservoir			•									•	•					
197	Meadow Lake								•										
198	Meeks Cabin Reservoir					•													
199	New Fork Lake		•							•	•			•					
200	Piney Lake, Middle									•	•			•		•			
201	Piney Lake, North		•			•													
202	Soda Lake		•	•															
203	Sulphur Creek Reservoir	•		•										•					
204	Sylvan Pond													•					
205	Viva Naughton												•	•					
206	Willow Lake										•			•					

Introduction

Platte River Drainage

Map Number/Fishery **Rivers & Streams**	Bear River Cutthroat	Black Bullhead	Bluegill	Brook Trout	Brown Trout	Channel Catfish	Crappie	Cutthroat Trout	Golden Trout	Kokanee Salmon	Lake Trout	Largemouth Bass	Rainbow Trout	Smallmouth Bass	Snake River Cutthroat	Tiger Musky	Walleye	Yellow Perch
207 Big Creek					•													
208 Douglas Creek				•	•								•					
209 Encampment River				•	•								•					
210 Laramie Peak Streams				•										•				
211 Laramie River (Jelm)					•													
212 Laramie River (Monolith)					•								•					
213 Laramie River (Spring Creek)					•								•					
214 Laramie River, Little					•													
215 Platte River, N. (Six Mile Gap)					•								•					
216 Platte River, N. (Bennet Pk)					•								•					
217 Platte River, N. (Treasure Is)					•								•					
218 Platte River, N. (Foote)					•								•					
219 Platte River, N. (Pick Bridge)					•								•					
220 Platte River, N. (Frazier)					•								•					
221 Platte River, N. (Ft.Steele)					•								•				•	
222 Platte River, N. (Steel Bridge)					•								•				•	
223 Platte River, N. (Dug Way)					•								•				•	
224 Platte River, N. (Miracle Mile)					•			•					•				•	
225 Platte River, N. (Cardwell)					•								•					
226 Platte River, N. (Grey Reef)					•								•					
227 Platte River, N. (PP&L)					•	•							•				•	
228 Platte River, N. (Bixby)					•	•							•				•	
229 Platte River, N. (S. Douglas)					•	•							•				•	
230 Platte River, N. (Glendo)					•	•							•		•		•	
231 Rock Creek				•	•								•					
232 Sweetwater River				•	•			•					•					

Notes:

Platte River Drainage

Map Number	Fishery — Lakes	Bear River Cutthroat	Black Bullhead	Bluegill	Brook Trout	Brown Trout	Channel Catfish	Crappie	Cutthroat Trout	Golden Trout	Kokanee Salmon	Lake Trout	Largemouth Bass	Rainbow Trout	Smallmouth Bass	Snake River Cutthroat	Tiger Musky	Walleye	Yellow Perch
233	33 Mile Ponds				•			•	•										
234	Alcova Reservoir					•								•				•	
235	Allen Lake, East	•												•					
236	Alsop Lake													•					
237	Country Club Lake								•					•					
238	Crow Reservoir, North													•					
239	Crystal Lake													•					
240	Diamond Lake	•			•									•					
241	Dome Rock Reservoir								•					•		•			
242	Festo Lake												•				•		
243	Gelatt Lake													•					
244	Glendo Reservoir					•	•	•					•					•	•
245	Goldeneye Reservoir								•					•				•	
246	Granite Lake										•			•					
247	Grayrocks Reservoir						•	•							•			•	•
248	Hattie, Lake					•					•	•		•					
249	Hawk Springs Reservoir						•	•					•					•	•
250	Hog Park Reservoir				•									•					
251	Johnson Creek Reservoir													•					
252	Lake Owen				•									•					
253	Meeboer Lake													•					
254	Packers Lake						•						•	•				•	
255	Pathfinder Reservoir					•								•		•		•	
256	Pole Mountain				•														
257	Rim Lake													•					
258	Rob Roy Reservoir				•									•					
259	Rock Creek Reservoir													•					
260	Rock Lake		•				•	•					•	•				•	•
261	Saratoga Lake					•								•					
262	Seminoe Reservoir					•								•		•		•	
263	Sloans Lake						•						•	•					
264	Snowy Range Lakes	•			•									•					
265	Sodergreen Lake													•					
266	Teton Reservoir					•								•					
267	Toltec Reservoir				•									•					
268	Turpin Reservoir				•														
269	Twin Buttes Reservoir					•								•					
270	Walker Jenkins Lake													•					
271	Wheatland Reservoir #1						•											•	•
272	Wheatland Reservoir #3					•			•					•				•	

Notes:

Master Map and Section Guide

Detailed enlargements of each section can be found at the beginning of each section. Enlarged sections also include camping and fishing sites.

All Wyoming Area Codes are 307

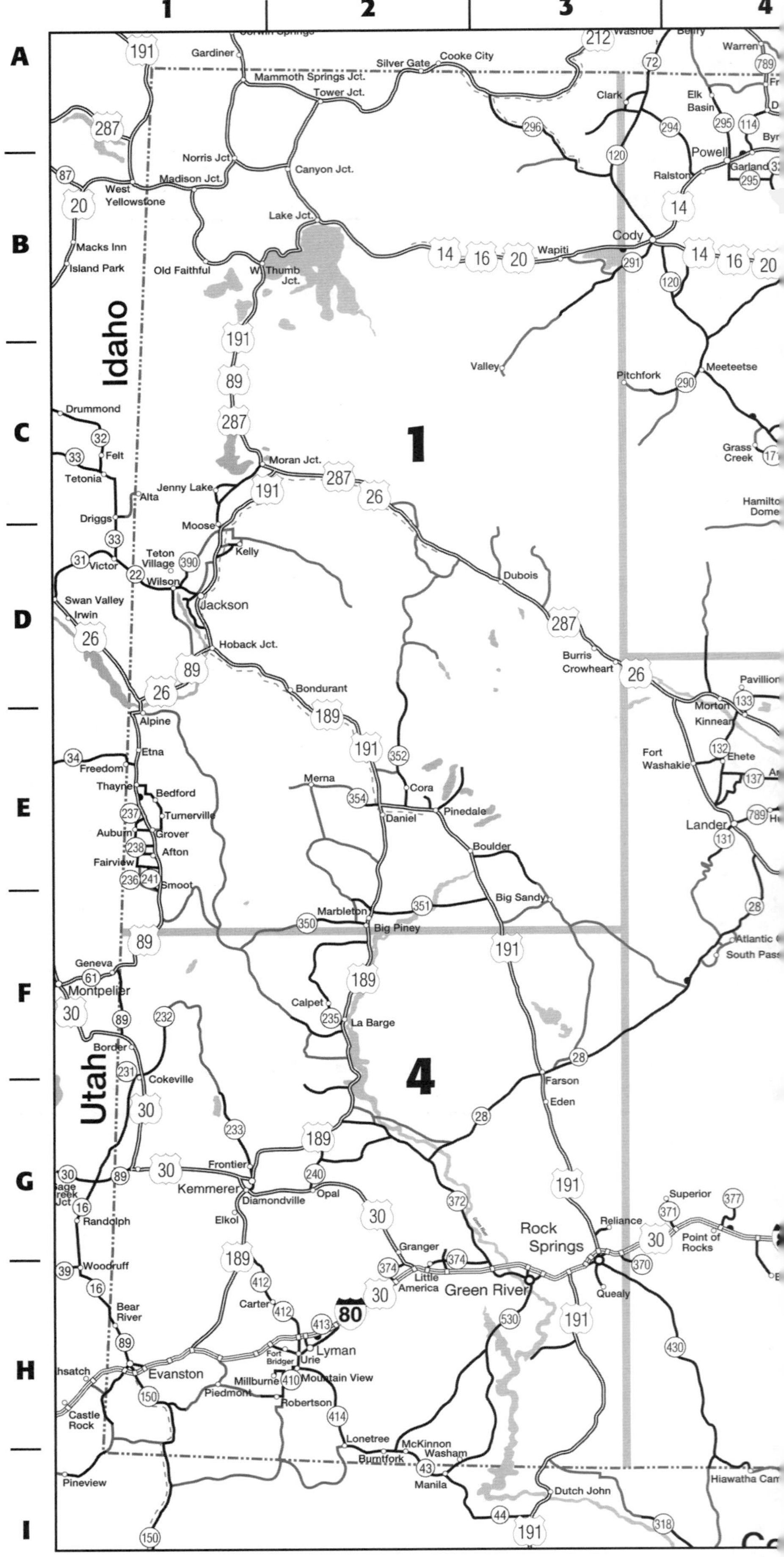

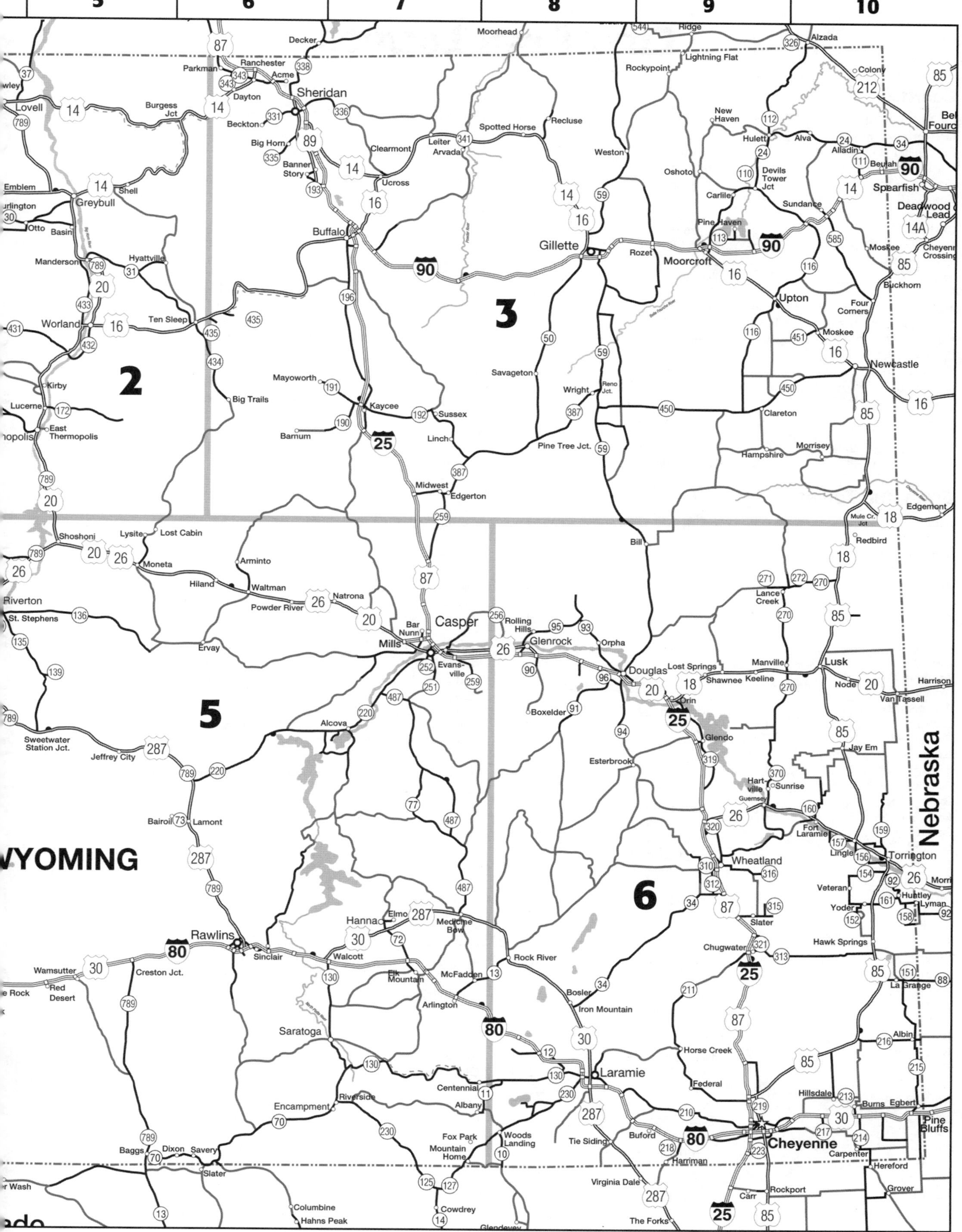
5
6
7
8
9
10
2
3
5
6
WYOMING
Nebraska
Decker
Moorhead
Ridge
Alzada
Lightning Flat
Rockypoint
Colony
Parkman
Ranchester
Acme
Dayton
Sheridan
Lovell
Burgess Jct
Beckton
Big Horn
Banner
Story
Clearmont
Leiter
Arvada
Spotted Horse
Recluse
New Haven
Hulett
Alva
Alladin
Beulah
Spearfish
Deadwood
Lead
Weston
Oshoto
Devils Tower Jct
Carlile
Sundance
Emblem
Shell
Greybull
Burlington
Otto
Basin
Ucross
Buffalo
Gillette
Rozet
Moorcroft
Pine Haven
Moskee
Cheyenne Crossing
Buckhorn
Manderson
Hyattville
Upton
Four Corners
Worland
Ten Sleep
Moskee
Newcastle
Savageton
Wright
Reno Jct.
Kirby
Mayoworth
Big Trails
Kaycee
Sussex
Clareton
Lucerne
East Thermopolis
Barnum
Linch
Pine Tree Jct.
Hampshire
Morrisey
Midwest
Edgerton
Mule Cr. Jct
Edgemont
Shoshoni
Lysite
Lost Cabin
Bill
Redbird
Moneta
Arminto
Hiland
Waltman
Riverton
St. Stephens
Powder River
Natrona
Lance Creek
Bar Nunn
Casper
Rolling Hills
Glenrock
Orpha
Mills
Ervay
Evansville
Douglas
Lost Springs
Shawnee
Manville
Keeline
Lusk
Node
Van Tassell
Harrison
Orin
Boxelder
Alcova
Glendo
Sweetwater Station Jct.
Jeffrey City
Esterbrook
Jay Em
Hartville
Sunrise
Guernsey
Fort Laramie
Lingle
Torrington
Bairoil
Lamont
Wheatland
Veteran
Huntley
Morrill
Lyman
Yoder
Slater
Hanna
Elmo
Medicine Bow
Rawlins
Sinclair
Walcott
Rock River
Chugwater
Hawk Springs
Wamsutter
Creston Jct.
Red Desert
Elk Mountain
McFadden
Bosler
Iron Mountain
La Grange
Arlington
Saratoga
Horse Creek
Albin
Laramie
Centennial
Federal
Hillsdale
Burns
Egbert
Pine Bluffs
Encampment
Riverside
Albany
Fox Park
Mountain Home
Woods Landing
Tie Siding
Buford
Harriman
Cheyenne
Carpenter
Hereford
Baggs
Dixon
Savery
Slater
Virginia Dale
Carr
Rockport
Grover
Columbine
Hahns Peak
Cowdrey
The Forks
Glendevey

City/Town Locator

Counties

Albany (5), 32014 . . . . .G-8
Big Horn (9), 11461 . . . . .B-5
Campbell (17), 33698 . . . . . . .C-8
Carbon (6),15639 . . . . .G-6
Converse (13), 12052 . . . . . . .E-8
Crook (18), 5887 . . . . .B-9
Fremont (10), 35804 . . . . .E-4
Goshen (7),12538 . . . . .F-10
Hot Springs (15), 4882 . . . . . .C-4
Johnson (16), 7075 . . . . .C-7
Laramie (2), 81607 . . . . .H-9
Lincoln (12), 14573 . . . . .F-1
Natrona (1), 66533 . . . . .E-6
Niobrara (14), 2407 . . . . .E-10
Park (11), 25786 . . . . .B-3
Platte (8), 8807 . . . . .G-9
Sheridan (3), 26560 . . . . .B-6
Sublette (23), 5920 . . . . .F-2
Sweetwater (4), 37613 . . . . . .G-4
Teton (22), 18251 . . . . .C-2
Uinta (19), 19742 . . . . .H-1
Washakie (20), 8289 . . . . .C-5
Weston (21), 6644 . . . . .C-9

Cities and Towns

Acme .A-6
Afton,1818 . . . . .E-1
Aladdin B-10
Albany H-7
Albin, 120 . . . . .H-10
Alcova F-7
Alpine, 550 . . . . .E-1
Alva B-10
Arapahoe E-4
Arlington H-7
Arminto E-6
Arvada B-7
Atlantic City F-4
Auburn E-1
Baggs, 348 . . . . .I-5
Bairoil, 97 . . . . .F-5
Banner B-6
Bar Nunn, 936 . . . . .E-7
Basin, 1238 . . . . .B-5
Bear River, 441 . . . . .H-1
Beckton B-6
Bedford E-1
Beulah B-10
Big Horn B-6
Big Piney, 408 . . . . .F-2
Big Sandy F-3
Big Trails C-6
Bill D-9
Bitter Creek H-4
Bondurant D-2
Border F-1
Bosler G-8
Boulder E-3
Boxelder F-8
Buckhorn C-10
Buffalo, 3900 . . . . .B-7
Buford H-9
Burgess Jct. A-5
Burlington, 250 . . . . .B-4
Burns, 285 . . . . .H-10
Burntfork I-2
Burns D-3
Byron, 557 . . . . .A-4
Calpet F-2
Canyon Jct. B-2
Carlile B-9
Carpenter I-10
Carter H-1
Casper, 49644 . . . . .E-7
Centennial H-7
Cheyenne, 53011 . . . . .H-9
Chugwater, 244 . . . . .G-9
Clareton D-9
Clark A-3
Clearmont, 115 . . . . .B-7
Cody, 8835 . . . . .B-3
Cokeville, 506 . . . . .G-1
Colony A-10
Cora .E-2
Cowley, 560 . . . . .A-4
Creston Jct. G-5
Crowheart D-3
Daniel E-2
Dayton, 678 . . . . .A-6
Deaver, 177 . . . . .A-4
Devils Tower Jct. B-9
Diamondville, 716 . . . . .G-1
Dixon, 79 . . . . .I-6
Douglas, 5288 . . . . .E-9
Dubois, 962 . . . . .D-3
E. Thermopolis, 274 . . . . .D-5
Eden G-3
Edgerton, 169 . . . . .D-7
Egbert H-10
Elk Basin A-4
Elk Mountain, 192 . . . . .G-7
Elkol .G-1
Elmo G-7
Emblem B-4
Encampment, 443 . . . . .H-7
Ervay E-6
Esterbrook F-9
Ethete E-4
Etna .E-1
Evanston, 11507 . . . . .H-1
Evansville, 2255 . . . . .E-7
Fairview E-1
Farson G-3
Federal H-9
Fort Bridger H-1
Fort Laramie, 243 . . . . .F-10
Fort Washakie E-4
Four Corners C-10
Fox Park H-7
Frannie, 209 . . . . .A-4
Freedom E-1
Frontier G-1
Garland B-4
Gillette, 19646 . . . . .B-8
Glendo, 229 . . . . .F-9
Glenrock, 2231 . . . . .E-8
Granger, 146 . . . . .G-2
Grass Creek C-4
Green River, 11808 H-3
Greybull, 1815 . . . . .B-5
Grover E-1
Guernsey, 1147 . . . . .F-9
Hamilton Dome C-4
Hampshire D-9
Hanna, 873 . . . . .G-7
Hartville, 76 . . . . .F-9
Hawk Springs G-10
Hiland E-6
Hillsdale H-10
Hoback Jct. D-1
Horse Creek H-9
Hudson, 407 . . . . .E-4
Hulett, 408 . . . . .B-9
Huntley G-10
Hyattville C-5
Iron Mountain H-9
Jackson, 8647 . . . . .D-1
Jay Em F-10
Jeffrey City F-5
Jenny Lake C-1
Kaycee, 249 . . . . .C-7
Keeline E-9
Kelly D-1
Kemmerer, 2651 . . . . .G-1
Kinnear E-4
Kirby, 57 . . . . .C-5
La Barge, 431 . . . . .F-2
LaGrange, 332 . . . . .G-10
Lake Jct. B-2
Lamont F-6
Lance Creek E-9
Lander, 6867 . . . . .E-4
Laramie, 27204 . . . . .H-8
Leiter B-7
Lightning Flat A-9
Linch D-7
Lingle, 510 . . . . .F-10
Little America H-2
Lonetree H-2
Lost Cabin D-5
Lost Springs, 1 . . . . .E-9
Lovell, 2281 . . . . .A-4
Lucerne D-5
Lusk, 1447 . . . . .E-1 0
Lyman, 1938 . . . . .H-2
Lysite D-5
Madison Jct. B-1
Mammoth Springs Jct. A-1
Manderson, 104 . . . . .C-5
Manville, 101 . . . . .E-10
Marbleton, 720 . . . . .F-2
Mayoworth C-6
McFadden G-7
McKinnon 1-2
Medicine Bow, 274 G-7
Meeteetse, 351 . . . . .C-4
Merna E-2
Midwest, 408 . . . . .D-7
Millburne H-1
Mills, 2591 . . . . .E-7
Moneta E-5
Moorcroft, 807 . . . . .B-9
Moose D-1
Moran Jct. C-2
Morrisey D-10
Morton D-4
Moskee B-10
Mountain Home 1-7
Mountain View, 1153 . . . . . .H-2
Mule Cr. Jct. D-10
Natrona E-7
Newcastle, 3065 . . . . .C-10
New Haven B-9
Node E-10
Norris Jct. B-1
Old Faithful B-1
Opal, 102 . . . . .G-2
Orin F-9
Orpha E-8
Osage C-10
Oshoto B-9
Otto B-5
Parkman A-6
Pavillion, 165 . . . . .D-4
Piedmont H-1
Pine Bluffs, 1153 . . . . .H-10
Pine Haven, 222 . . . . .B-9
Pine Tree Jct. D-8
Pinedale, 1412 . . . . .E-2
Pitchfork C-3
Point of Rocks G-4
Powder River E-6
Powell, 5373 . . . . .B-4
Quealy H-3
Ralston B-4
Ranchester, 701 . . . . .A-6
Rawlins, 8538 . . . . .G-6
Recluse B-8
Red Desert G-5
Redbird D-10
Reliance G-3
Reno Jct. C-8
Riverside, 59 . . . . .H-7
Riverton, 9310 . . . . .E-4
Robertson H-2
Rock River, 235 . . . . .G-8
Rock Springs, 18708 . . . . . . .G-3
Rockypoint A-9
Rolling Hills, 449 . . . . .E-8
Rozet B-9
Sage G-1
St. Stephens E-4
Saratoga, 1726 . . . . .H-6
Savageton C-8
Savery I-6
Shawnee E-9
Shell B-5
Sheridan, 15804 . . . . .A-6
Shoshoni, 635 . . . . .D-5
Sinclair, 423 . . . . .G-6
Slater G-9
Smoot E-1
South Pass City F-4
Spotted Horse B-8
Story B-6
Sundance, 1161 . . . . .B-10
Sunrise F-9
Superior, 244 . . . . .G-4
Sussex D-7
Sweetwater Station Jct. F-5
Table Rock G-4
Ten Sleep, 304 . . . . .C-6
Teton Village D-1
Thayne, 341 . . . . .E-1
Thermopolis, 3172 . . . . .D-5
Tie Siding H-8
Torrington, 5776 . . . . .G-10
Tower Jct. A-2
Turnerville E-1
Ucross B-7
Upton, 872 . . . . .C-9
Urie H-2
Valley C-3
Van Tassell, 18 . . . . .E-10
Veteran G-10
Walcott G-7
Waltman E-6
Wamsutter, 261 . . . . .G-5
Wapiti B-3
Washam H-2
W. Thumb Jct. B-1
Weston B-8
Wheatland, 3548 . . . . .G-9
Wilson D-1
Woods Landing H-8
Worland, 5250 . . . . .C-5
Wright, 1347 . . . . .C-8
Yoder, 169 . . . . .G-10

All Wyoming Area Codes are 307

SECTION 1

NORTHWESTERN AREA

INCLUDING JACKSON, DUBOIS, PINEDALE AND STAR VALLEY

The Teton Mountain Range is visible from many parts of this area.

1 *Lodging*

Smoot

Pop. 100, Elev. 6,619.

Once named Cottonwood, this settlement was renamed for Mormon Apostle Reed Smoot, who was also a Utah State Senator.

H Lander Cut-Off of the Oregon Trail

Three miles south of Smoot on U.S. Highway 89

Beginning in 1843, emigrants traveled across the continent along what became known as the Oregon Trail. Increased traffic during the 1850s resulted in the first government road construction project in the west. The 345-mile Central Division of the Pacific Wagon Road went from South Pass, Wyoming, to City of Rocks, Idaho, a geologic formation, which marked the Division's western boundary. Superintendent Frederick W. Lander of Salem, Massachusetts, supervised construction for the U.S. Department of the Interior. The 256-mile section of the road leading from South Pass to Fort Hall, Idaho, is known as the Lander Cut-Off. The cut-off traversed this Salt River Valley for 21 miles and parallels Highway 89 through this area. The new route afforded water, wood, and forage for emigrants and their stock. Between 1858 and 1912, it provided travelers with a new, shorter route to Oregon and California, saving wagon trains seven days. Lander, with a crew of 15 engineers, surveyed the route in the summer of 1857. The following summer, 115 men, many recruited from Salt Lake City's Mormon emigrants, constructed the road in less than 90 days at a cost of $67,873. The invention of the automobile led to its abandonment.

Stock Trail

Travel along the Oregon Trail was not restricted to one direction. Between 1875 and 1890, drovers herded vast numbers of cattle, horses and sheep eastward from Oregon to Wyoming. The animals were moved along the Lander Cut-off and into the Green River and Big Horn Basins and the Wind River drainage. There, they were used as initial range stock for the large ranches of cattle and sheep barons.

H Lander Cut-off

About 18 miles south of Afton on U.S. Highway 89

The Lander Cut-off left the Oregon Trail at Burnt Ranch on the Sweetwater River near South Pass City, Wy. Frederick Lander surveyed the trail in 1857. Tens of thousands of people passed over the trail during its use. With the Transcontinental Railroad being completed in 1869, emigrant travel over the trail rapidly declined. The last wagons over the trail were observed at Fort Piney Wy. between 1910 and 1912. The Lander Cut-off rejoined the Oregon Trail in Idaho northeast of Pocatello at Ross Fork Creek.

2 *Gas, Food, Lodging*

Afton

Pop. 1,818, Elev. 6,134

Named ironically for the line in a Robert Burns poem, ("Flow gently, sweet Afton") this town below the Salt Range is situated by the turbulent Swift Creek. A genuine small town, it is the central business hub of Star Valley, which was settled by pioneers from the LDS (Mormon) church in 1879. The winter of 1879-1880 was brutal, but they endured the near starvation and frigid temperatures. In the center of town, the Afton Tabernacle still stands as a monument to their fortitude. The signature Elkhorn Arch nearby, which spans Main Street, is made of over 3,000 antlers. Afton celebrated its first 100 years in 2002. Though still a dominantly agricultural community, locals have embraced tourism, which has resulted from the overflow of visitors to the Jackson and the Wind River areas. Dairy farming made the valley famous for its cheese, especially hard-to-make Swiss. Afton is probably most recently associated with being the hometown of Rulon Gardner, Greco-Roman wrestling Gold Medallist in the 2000 Summer Olympics. He was not the first Afton Gardner to gain national attention as an athlete. In 1947, Vern Gardner was named an All American basketball player, and became the MVP at college basketball's National Invitational Tournament. Afton is near one of only three intermittent springs in the world, Periodic Spring, about 5 miles east of town. The spring is situated in a lush and craggy canyon, which the Shoshone considered a sacred healing place. It runs constantly during the spring runoff, but pulses about every 18 minutes in the late summer and fall.

Fairview

The beautiful view of the Crow Creek Valley gave this town its name. Settled by Mormons in 1885, this was once a stopping place for caravans of cheese freighters.

T Call Air Museum

Look for a large hangar at the south end of Afton.

Over the centuries, man has dreamed of taking to the skies. In 1937 this dream took flight for Reuel Call over the mountains of Western Wyoming. Reuel, with the assistance of his Uncle Ivan, brothers Spencer and Barlow, and Carl Peterson, designed and built the original CallAir aircraft. With no aviation background, this visionary group of civil engineers and businessmen tinkered until their plane was airborne. Come relive

Jackson

	Jan	Feb	March	April	May	June	July	Aug	Sep	Oct	Nov	Dec	Annual
Average Max. Temperature (F)	27.3	32.5	40.8	52.2	62.8	72.3	81.7	80.4	71.1	58.5	39.6	28.0	53.9
Average Min. Temperature (F)	5.1	8.0	15.6	24.5	30.6	36.7	40.5	38.5	31.4	23.3	15.9	6.1	23.0
Average Total Precipitation (in.)	1.48	1.00	1.16	1.12	1.88	1.68	1.06	1.15	1.29	1.14	1.44	1.54	15.94
Average Total SnowFall (in.)	20.2	12.5	9.1	3.9	0.8	0.1	0.0	0.0	0.1	0.9	9.4	17.7	74.7
Average Snow Depth (in.)	12	14	10	1	0	0	0	0	0	0	2	7	4

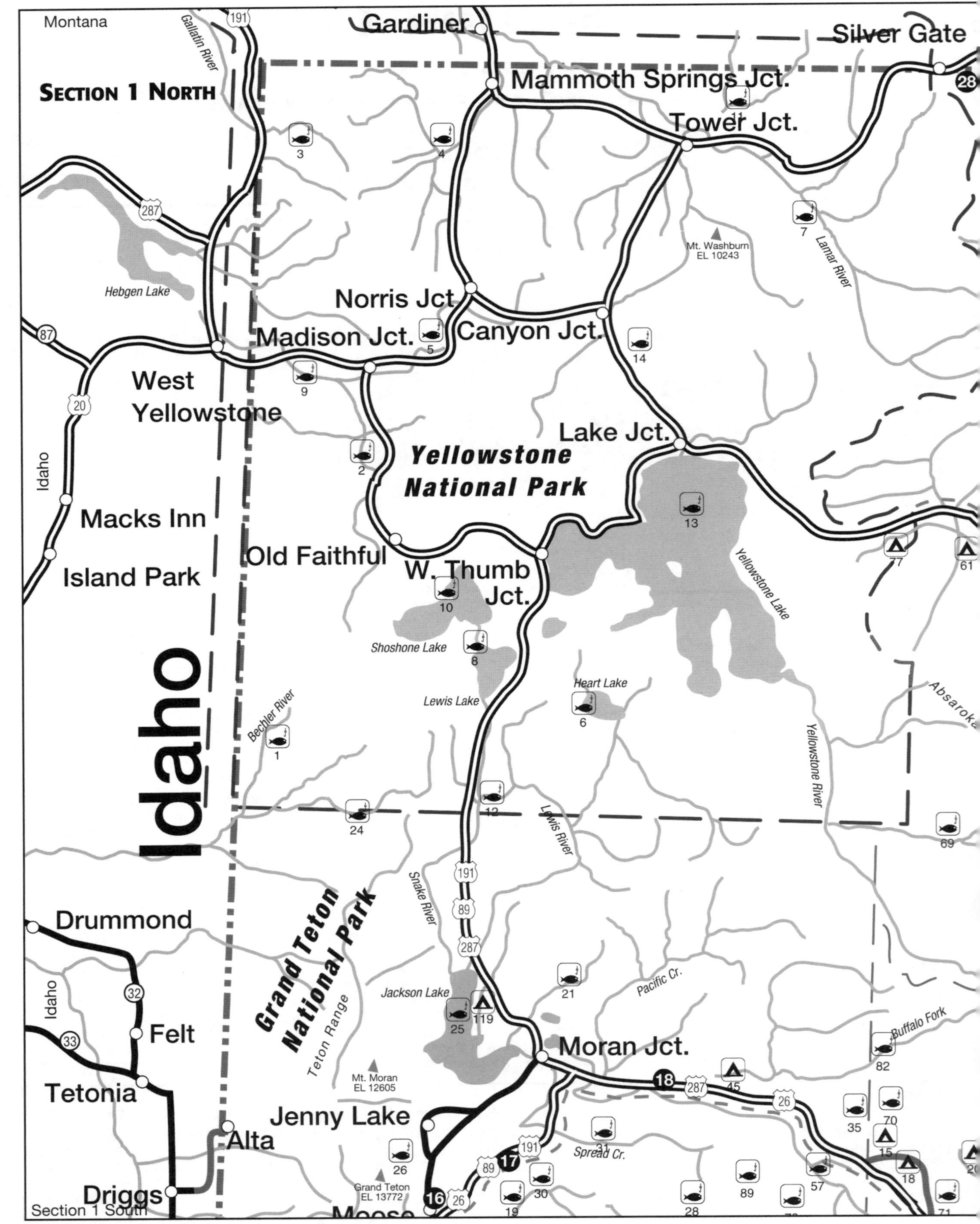
Montana
Gallatin River
Gardiner
Silver Gate
Section 1 North
Mammoth Springs Jct.
Tower Jct.
Mt. Washburn
EL 10243
Lamar River
Hebgen Lake
Norris Jct.
Madison Jct.
Canyon Jct.
West
Yellowstone
Lake Jct.
Yellowstone
National Park
Idaho
Macks Inn
Island Park
Old Faithful
W. Thumb
Jct.
Yellowstone Lake
Shoshone Lake
Lewis Lake
Heart Lake
Bechler River
Absaroka
Yellowstone River
Idaho
Lewis River
Snake River
Grand Teton
National Park
Drummond
Felt
Tetonia
Teton Range
Jackson Lake
Pacific Cr.
Buffalo Fork
Moran Jct.
Mt. Moran
EL 12605
Jenny Lake
Alta
Spread Cr.
Driggs
Grand Teton
EL 13772
Section 1 South

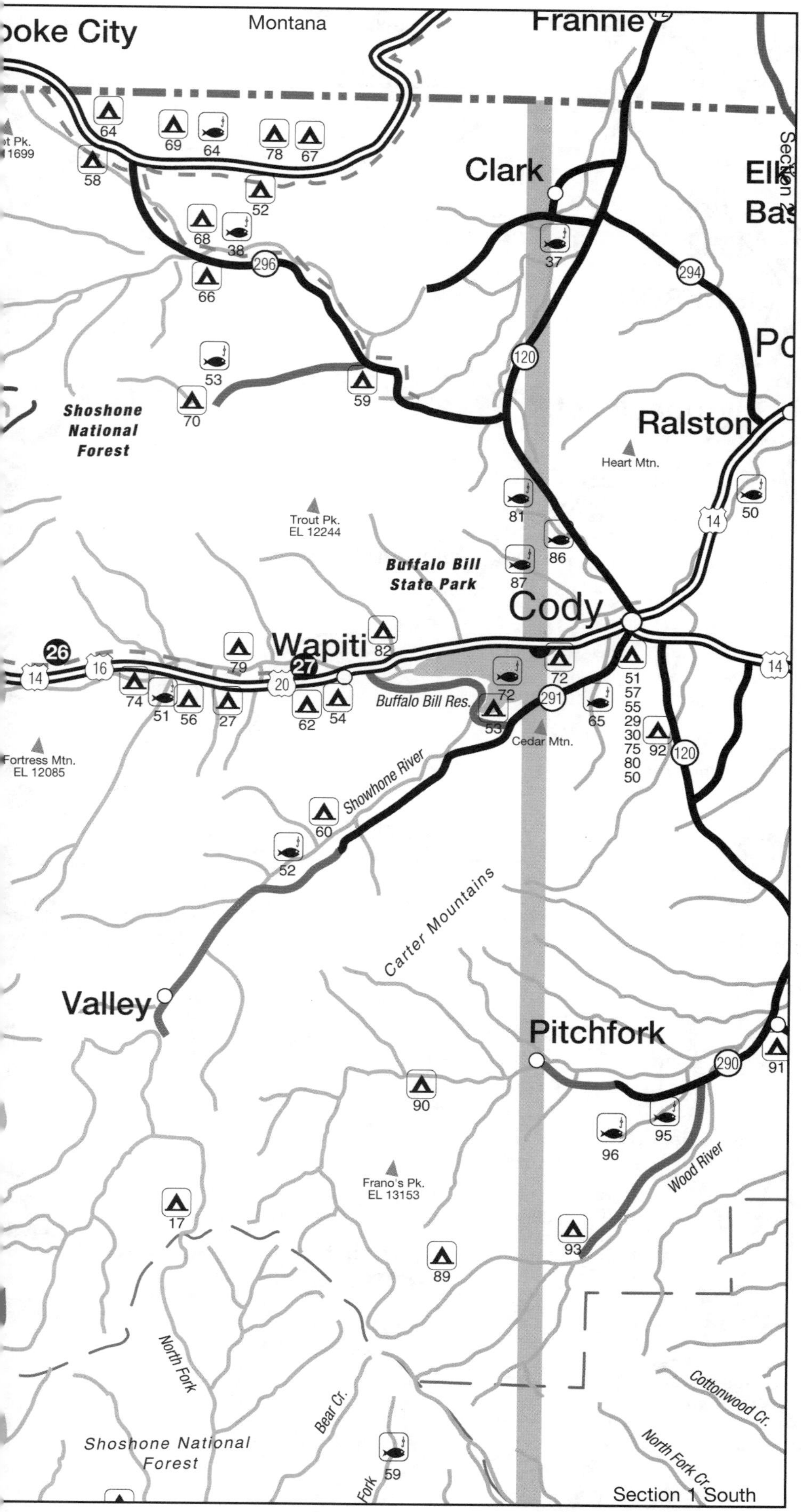

oke City
Montana
Frannie
Clark
Elk Bas
Section 2
Po
Ralston
Heart Mtn.
Shoshone National Forest
Trout Pk. EL 12244
Buffalo Bill State Park
Cody
Wapiti
Buffalo Bill Res.
Cedar Mtn.
Fortress Mtn. EL 12085
Showhone River
Carter Mountains
Valley
Pitchfork
Wood River
Frano's Pk. EL 13153
North Fork
Bear Cr.
Fork
Shoshone National Forest
Cottonwood Cr.
North Fork Cr.
Section 1 South

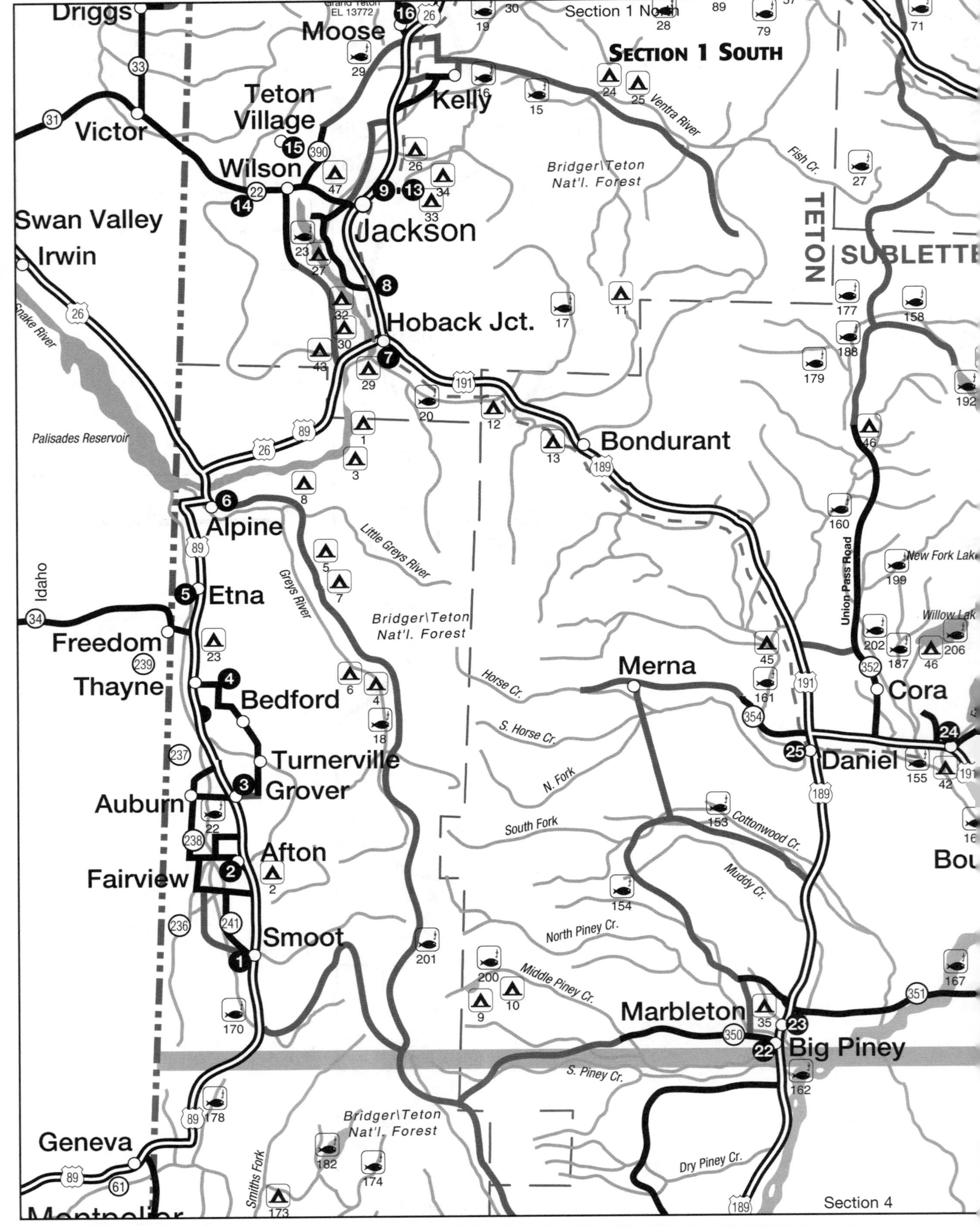
Section 1 South
Section 1 North
Driggs
Moose
Teton Village
Kelly
Victor
Wilson
Swan Valley
Irwin
Jackson
Hoback Jct.
Bondurant
Alpine
Etna
Freedom
Thayne
Bedford
Turnerville
Grover
Auburn
Afton
Fairview
Smoot
Merna
Cora
Daniel
Marbleton
Big Piney
Geneva
Idaho
TETON
SUBLETTE
Bridger\Teton Nat'l. Forest
Ventra River
Fish Cr.
Snake River
Palisades Reservoir
Little Greys River
Greys River
Horse Cr.
S. Horse Cr.
N. Fork
South Fork
Cottonwood Cr.
Muddy Cr.
North Piney Cr.
Middle Piney Cr.
S. Piney Cr.
Dry Piney Cr.
Smiths Fork
Union Pass Road
New Fork Lake
Willow Lake
Section 4

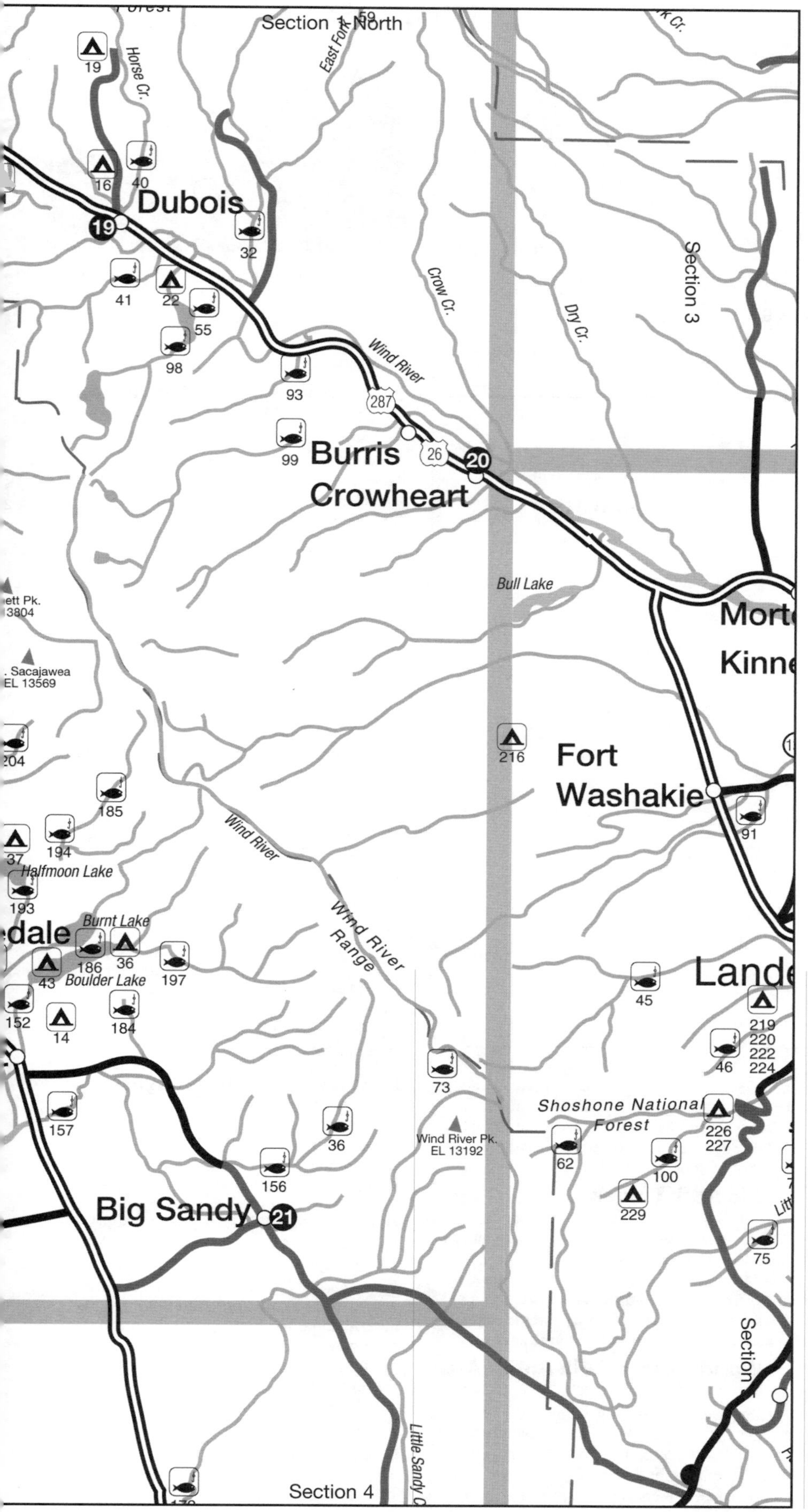

Section 1 North
East Fork
Horse Cr.
19
16
40
Dubois
19
32
41
22
55
98
93
Wind River
287
Crow Cr.
Dry Cr.
Section 3
99
Burris
26
20
Crowheart
Bull Lake
Mort
Kinne
ett Pk.
3804
. Sacajawea
EL 13569
204
216
Fort
Washakie
185
91
37
194
Wind River
Halfmoon Lake
193
Burnt Lake
dale
186
36
Wind River
Range
197
43
Boulder Lake
Lande
45
152
14
184
219
220
222
224
46
73
Shoshone National
Forest
226
227
157
36
Wind River Pk.
EL 13192
62
100
156
229
Big Sandy
21
75
Section
Little Sandy C
Section 4

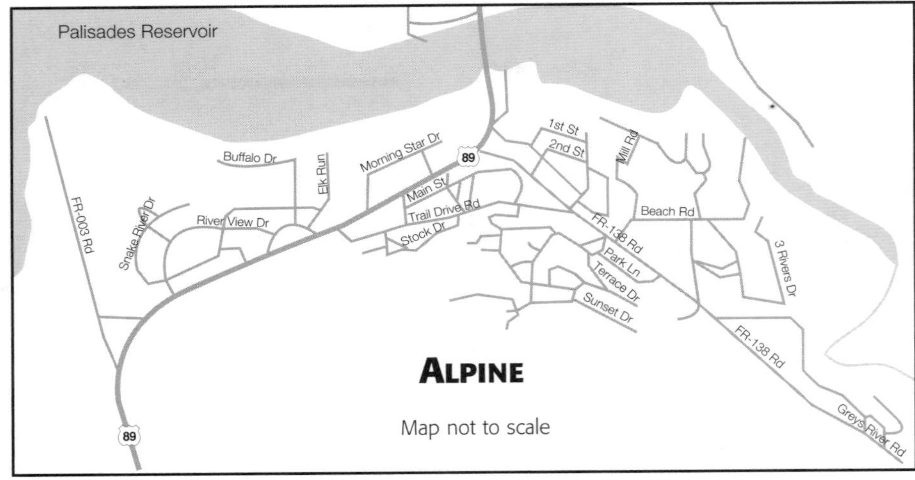

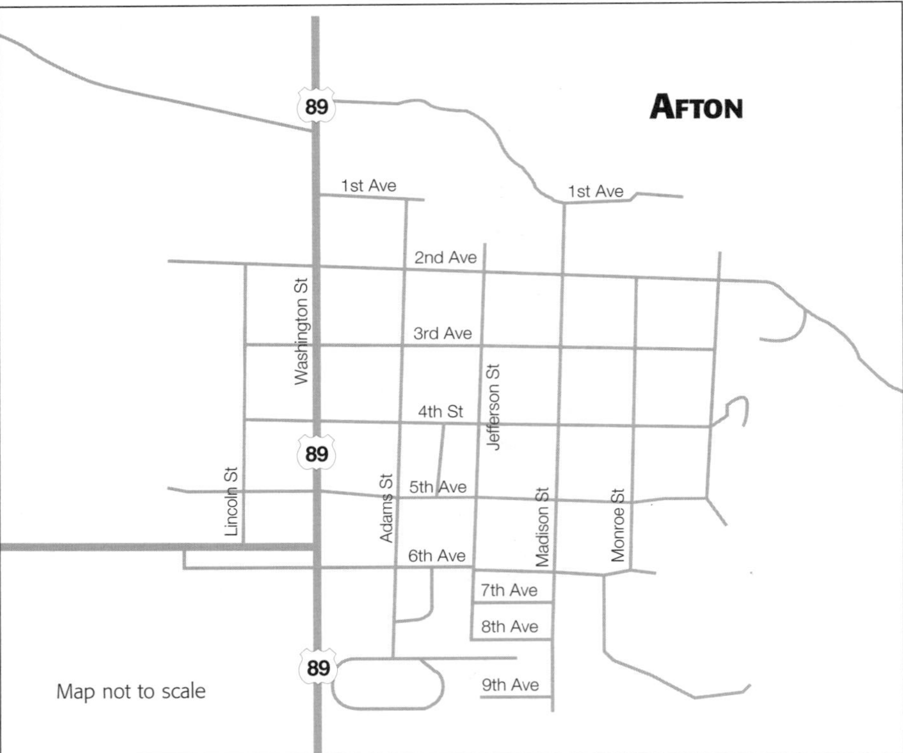

Plains Indian Powwow

Each June, the Plains Indian Powwow, sponsored by the buffalo Bill Historical Center, attracts visitors from around the world. Held at the Robbie Powwow Garden on the south end of the histroical center grounds, the event is an ideal way for non-Indians to experience and appreciate the value and history of the Indian world. Fancy dancers and traditional dancers entertain crowds to the beautifully hypnotic drum beat and song of the Indian world.

the magic of their dream while learning the dynamics of flight. Peer into the cockpits of original CallAir aircraft and imagine yourself flying among the snow-capped peaks of Wyoming. See the CallAir snow cars (forerunners of the snowmobile) and visit with our personnel as they restore vintage aircraft. The CallAir Museum offers free admission and sponsors the annual CallAir Fly In/ Star Valley Aviation Days, the last Saturday of June.

T Old Rock Church

Butch Cassidy and his gang wintered in the Auburn area. Heavy snowfalls made Star Valley a safe place to "hole up". Using aliases, Butch Cassidy and his partners were occasionally seen at church socials and dances held in the Old Rock Church in Auburn. Today the rock church is used as a melodrama theater in the summer.

T World's Largest Elk Antler Arch

Downtown Afton

Arching over Main Street in Afton is the "World's Largest Elk Antler Arch" consisting of over 3,000 antlers. This 18-foot high arch was built in 1958 and continues to be a favorite photo stop. In Asia powdered elk antlers are considered to be a prized aphrodisiac, making the antler arch worth over $300,000.

Downtown Afton is home to the world's largest elk antler arch.

H Periodic Spring–"The Spring that Breathes"

North edge of Afton on U.S. Highway 89

What Is It? The Periodic Spring is North America's only cold water geyser and is the largest of the three known fluctuation springs in the world. Its name is descriptive of the periodic flow, which during the fall and winter, turns on and shuts off every 12-20 minutes. These periodic flows are less noticeable during high water months in spring and summer.

The water at Periodic Spring has given life to the land, the wildlife, and the people of Star Valley. Historically, Native Americans traveled great distances to cure their ills by bathing in "the spring that breathes." Since 1958, the spring's water has been piped to the City of Afton for its municipal water supply, and is used for drinking, irrigation, and generating electricity.

No one knows for certain what makes the Periodic Spring start and stop. One theory is that underground streams carry melting snow and rain water to a lake deep in the Salt River Mountains. When the lake level gets high enough, a natural siphon draws the water from the lake to the surface like a faucet being turned on and off. The water then gushes out of a sheer ledge and cascades down a wild, moss-covered ravine to join Swift Creek. The flow continues until the water level in the lake drops below the siphon's intake level, allowing air to enter the siphon from the lake cavern. The flow stops until the lake rises again and the cycle repeats.

H Sawyer Expedition fight

About two miles east of Dayton on U.S. Highway 14.

Where the Bozeman Trail crosses tongue River Valley at this point, Colonel J.A. Sawyer's wagon train and road building expedition of 82 wagons fought the Arapahoe Indians for 13 days, August 31 through September 12, 1865. Captain Cole of the military escort was killed on the ridge across the valley, E. G. Merrill and James Dilleland, drovers, were killed in the wagon circle located between here and the river. All three are buried in an unknown common grave. From 1879 to 1894 the Patrick Brothers Stage Line used this road from Fort Custer to Rock Creek Station. Brigham Post Office and Stage Station was located here at Tongue River Crossing.

H Periodic Spring

About 18 miles south of Afton on U.S. Highway 89

Located 4 miles east of Afton in the Salt River Range, is the largest of three natural springs in the world that naturally turn off and on. Water flow is interrupted from anywhere between 3 to 30 minutes, generally between the months of August-May. It is thought that a cave behind the spring creates a siphon which causes interruption of the water flow. Its ability to turn off and on during low discharge stages has fascinated visitors since prehistoric times. Access to the spring is via the Swift Creek road and requires a 3/4 mile hike by trail.

H Star Valley
347 Jefferson Street in Afton

In the spring of 1879 a group of pioneers from Bear Lake settled here. Moses Thatcher explored the area, dedicated it as a home for the Latter-day Saints calling it Star Valley. Freedom and Auburn settled in 1879 and Afton in 1885. The first public building was located on this square. A log house with dirt roof served the settlers as a church, school, and public meeting place from 1886 to 1892 when it was replaced by a large frame building. The bell on this monument calling the people together could be heard throughout the valley.

L Mountain Inn Motel
83542 U.S. Highway 89 in Afton. 885-3156

L Lazy B Motel
219 Washington in Afton. 885-187

L The Old Mill Log Cabins
3497 Dry Creek Road in Afton. 886-0520

The Old Mill Log Cabins are nestled in the mountains of beautiful Star Valley. Exquisitely appointed and spacious cabins offer surroundings of peace and quiet. Your hosts, the Erickson's, have devoted many hours to making your stay a memorable one—from harvesting, shaping, and hand fitting the logs to tastefully decorating the interiors of each cabin. Let the sound of a crystal clear stream lull you to sleep as you snuggle under the handmade comforters on your queen size bed following a soak in the hot tub. The wide and varied outdoor activities await you in "their back yard" of Wonderful Wyoming. They can also board your horse or rent you theirs.

3 *No services*

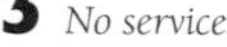

Grover
Settled by the Mormons in 1891, this little town was named for Jacob Grover, one of the early pioneers.

Turnerville
This little town was named for a Mormon family named Turner who settled here.

Auburn
First settled by Mormons in 1879, Auburn was abandoned for a time. When the growing Star Valley population revived it a few years later, one woman said the empty buildings reminded her of Goldsmith's "Deserted Village," and the poetic name Auburn stuck. The old rock church, built in 1889, was the only stone building in the valley until 1900. Butch Cassidy and his friends would sometimes attend socials and dances here when they were hiding out at the nearby Davis Ranch.

4 *Gas, Food, Lodging*

Thayne
Pop. 341, Elev. 5,950

When the post office opened here in 1889, the town was named for postmaster and storeowner Henry Thayne. Thayne became a significant community in the valley with the opening of the cheese factory, which processed milk from the many dairy farms in the area. Thayne is also known for being the place where cutter racing first evolved in the 1920s.

H Star Valley
Star Valley Rest Area just south of Thayne

Often termed the star of all valleys, the Shoshone Indians referred to the valley as a "heap fine hunting ground." Unusually high precipitation and topographic features make the Salt River Valley one of the most productive and diverse of all wildlife areas found in Wyoming. Sandhill cranes, Canada geese, ruffed grouse and bald eagles are among the birds nesting in the area. The valleys of the Greater Yellowstone Ecosystem, including Star Valley, are important waterfowl production areas for western North America. In 1987, trumpeter swans were transplanted to the valley from Montana and since have wintered here.Protection and improvement of the streambanks and wetlands along the river for both fish and wildlife resources are important to the area and its people. The big game animals summering and wintering in the mountains and foothills surrounding the valley provide some of the best hunting in Wyoming. Trophy elk, mule deer and moose abound in the rugged mountains of the Caribou, Salt, Wyoming and Palisades ranges. Thousands of visitors are attracted to this scenic area to hunt and fish or observe and enjoy wildlife in its wild surroundings—a testimonial that Wyoming's wildlife is a precious commodity for the state and its citizenry.

Bedford
Mormon pioneer and bishop, William B. Preston named this town for his childhood home, Bedford, England. Settled in the 1880s, this part of Star Valley specialized in sheep ranching, and large herds can still be seen in the fall when they come down from summer grazing in the mountains.

H First Post Office
U.S. Highway 89 just north of the Riggs Avenue and Wright Street intersection in Thayne.

Thayne, formerly called Glencoe, was founded in 1888, at which time mail was brought into Star Valley by team and wagon and distributed to the people from a log cabin owned by Joseph Thayne. The building was one room 12x15 feet with a dirt roof. Three years later it was moved to the center of town and Henry Thayne and his wife occupied it. This log cabin, located one and one-half rods west of this site, became the first post office May 8, 1891 with Laura Thayne post mistress.

FLC Star Valley Ranch Resorts & RV Camping
3522 Muddy String Road in Thayne. 883-2670.

Set between the majestic mountains of Bridger and Caribou National Forests on the Wyoming/Idaho border, the peaceful valley (called by many "Little Switzerland") is one of the most beautiful spots in the Western U.S. This is where you will find Star Valley Ranch Resorts, just 50 miles south of Jackson Hole. This is a golfer's paradise with 3 golf courses within a one-mile radius. There are 451 RV sites, plus 88 pull-throughs for members and guests, Coast to Coast, and RPI. This is a Five-Star Coast to Coast Resort with all hook ups and 10-room motel, along with swimming, tennis, Jacuzzi/hot tub, and clubhouse. RV sites are for sale including golf membership. Call for reservations or a site tour.

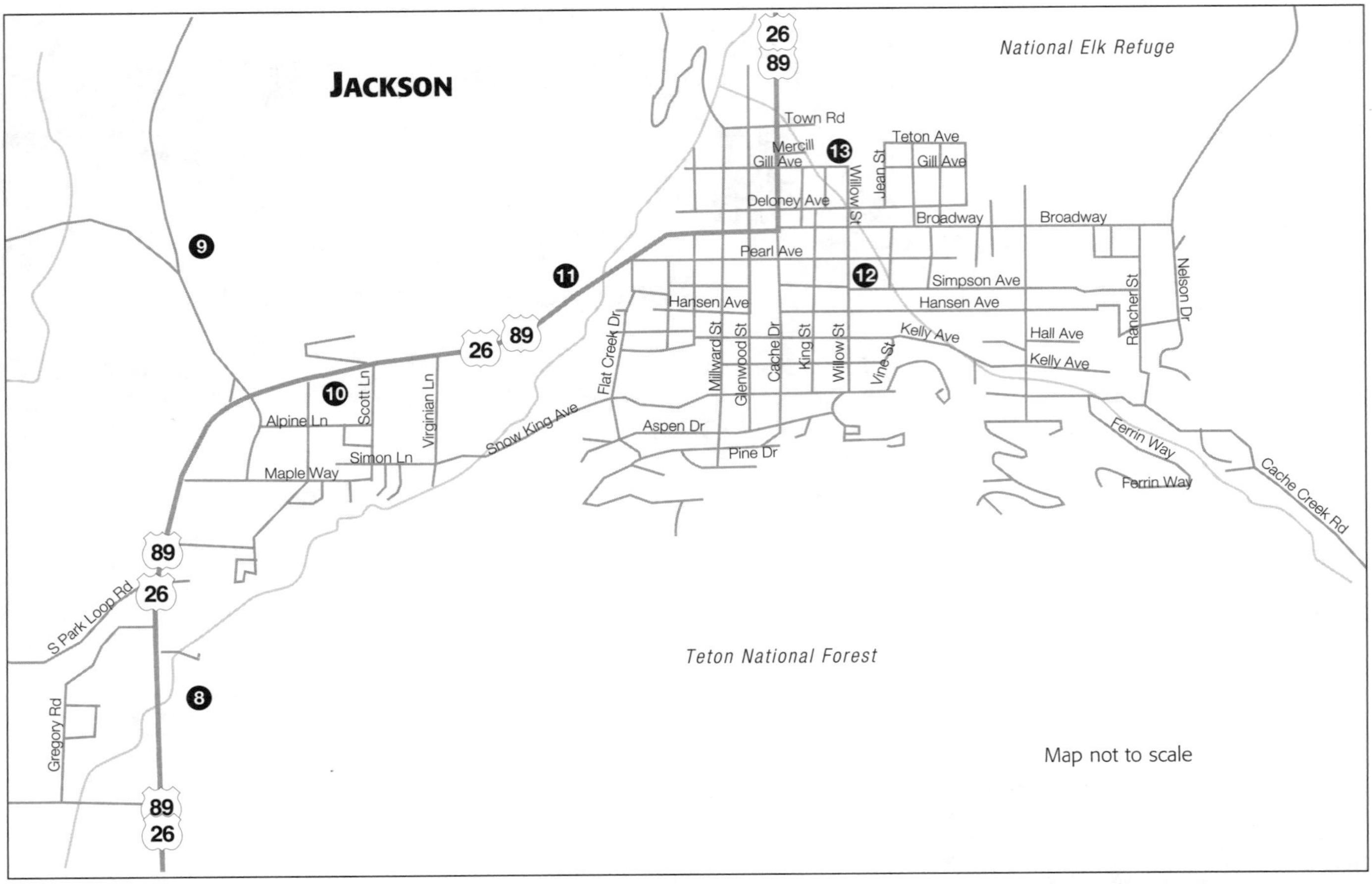

M Ellis Big Game Realty
235 S. Main in Thayne. 883-2424. www.ellis-biggame.com or email: kits@silverstar.com

5 *Gas, Food, Lodging*

Etna
Pop. 200, Elev. 5,815

Mormon pioneers, trying to name their community, picked this out of an insurance book because it was short, and easy to spell. The town is centered around a spacious LDS church and has a charming view of the surrounding pastureland.

Freedom
Pop. 100

This border town got its name from the freedom it gave early Mormon polygamists from having to outrun Idaho law. All they had to do was walk across the street and be in another jurisdiction. Established in 1879, this is the oldest settlement in Star Valley.

H Baker Cabin
On U.S. Highway 89 in Etna

Oldest surviving house in Star Valley is this two room dwelling built in 1889 by Anna Eliza Baker and her 12 year old daughter May. The logs are hand-hewn on four sides and dovetailed at the corners. It was the first home in this area to have a shingled roof and wood floors. The Baker family; Alonzo, Anna Eliza and their 12 children, were the first permanent residents on the east side of Salt River in the lower valley.

V Fool's Gold Day Hiking Excursions with Burros & Llamas
Freedom. 883-3783.
www.foolsgoldwyoming.com

S Blue Fox Studio/Gallery
107452 U.S. Highway 89 in Etna. 883-3310.
www.bluefoxgallery.com

Out of the ordinary! Blue Fox Studio/Gallery is fast becoming a favorite spot for returning tourists. It is a welcome experience to visit the working studios of artists Tony Ivie and Wayne Noffsinger. Both have a passion for working with clay. Tony is an experienced potter and clay mask sculptor. He was commissioned by the State of Wyoming to do the 1985 Governor Awards. Wayne started in jewelry but has become a highly collected mask artist himself. It is often possible to see numerous art pieces in various stages of completion. The gallery showcases stoneware, wood-fired and raku pottery along with jewelry and original masks representing both Wayne and Tony's unique styles.

M Stage Coach Realty
286 Main Street in Thayne. 883-8830.
www.starwalleywyoming.com.

6 *Gas, Food, Lodging*

Alpine
Pop. 550, Elev. 5,700

This border town is half in Wyoming, half in Idaho. Named for it's lovely mountain scenery, some of the buildings also reflect the old-world alpine influence of early settlers. Robert Stuart camped here in 1812 while trying to lose a party of Indians hot on his tail.

T Palisades Reservoir

Palisades Reservoir is formed by Palisades Dam, which is a major feature on the Palisades Project. Recreation on this 25 square mile (16,100-acre) reservoir with 70 miles of limited access shoreline is administered by the Caribou-Targhee National Forest. Located in scenic southeast Idaho and west-central Wyoming, east of Idaho Falls. Palisades' fish species include cutthroat and brown trout, kokanee and mackinaw. The fishing season is year-round, but fluctuations in the reservoir level during the summer months result in inconsistent fishing. Spring, fall and winter ice fishing are most productive. Reservoir acre feet and total reservoir capacity and cubic feet/second release rates for rivers below Upper Snake River Basin reservoirs and select river locations are updated daily and graphically provided. Site offers restrooms, boat ramps, and campgrounds. Information available at Idaho Falls Interagency Visitor's Center at 208-523-3278.

T Wyoming State Bird Farm

The Wyoming Game and Fish Department, along

with sportsmen and women, rallied to build a game bird farm outside of Sheridan, Woming. George R. Wells was chosen to build and manage the farm. Pheasant eggs from Oregon and Montana were the first to be hatched and released in 1937. Currently, the Sheridan Farm produces nearly 13,000 birds each year. Touring the farm is encouraged. For private tours, the bird farm may be contacted directly.

Wyoming Tidbits

The Federal Weather Bureau chose Big Piney for an official weather station in 1930 because it had the coldest year-round average temperature of any spot in the United States.

H A Changing View of Wildlife

Just south of Alpine on U.S. Highway 89 at Wildlife Watching Area pullout.

Many early beaver trappers left their moccasin tracks where you now stand. In the early part of the 19th century, from this location, the view of wildlife and wildlands was very different from what we see today. Nature's sights and sounds are still here, but not without the evidence of humans. Humans and wildlife occupy the same earth. Native Americans remind modern man that all life on earth is interconnected. Air, water, space and natural resources important to humans are also important to wildlife. We have an enormaous responsibility to protect and conserve our air, water, soil and natural resources and thereby "save a place for wildlife." An earth with diverse and abundant wildlife is also an earth healthy for the well-being of human life. The view of wildlife and wildlands has changed dramatically since the trapping era, and so has our un derstanding of the relationship of all life to planet earth..., 200th century wildlife if it is to endure, will need an understanding hand and wise use of earth's resources.

F Kringle's Birdhouse Cafe

161 U.S. Highway 89 in Alpine. 654-7536 or toll free at 888-900-5072. www.kringlescafe.com.

The chef owned Kringle's Birdhouse Cafe not only serves outstanding cuisine, you'll also enjoy one of the largest birdhouse collections you will ever see. The owner is a master chef who has cooked for Hollywood notables such as Frank Sinatra, Liberace, Frank Capra, and many others. At the cafe in Alpine, you will find such items as Danish style meat loaf, country fried steak, chicken and dumplings, Danish pastries, and unique salad choices. They are renowned for their 3-layer carrot cake and superb wedding cakes. The friendly staff and clean, fresh atmosphere will complete your dining experience.

L Three Rivers Motel

60 Main Street in Alpine. 654-7551.

FL The Nordic Inn & Brenthoven's Restaurant

East of Junction of U.S. Highway 89 & 26 in Alpine. 654-7556. www.starvalleywy.com/nordic/index.htm

The Nordic Inn Resort is located at the mouth of the Snake River Canyon. Enjoy the stunning surroundings, comfort, charm, and personalized service provided by the lodge. Before jumping into bed at night, you'll want to explore the amenities this popular country lodge has available. Start with dinner at Brent's. Enjoy a drink or two in the lounge, and shop at Anne's delightful gift shop. The Nordic Inn offers fine dining and a full service bar where you can enjoy breathtaking view from the outdoor patio or the quaint interior of one of Wyoming's oldest bars and finest restaurants. During the summer months, on Sundays, the Brenthoven Quartet plays familiar melodies and show tunes on the lawns.

Wyoming Tidbits

Which is both the oldest and the largest national park in the country? Yellowstone National Park, with more than two million acres, was declared by President U.S. Grant on March 1, 1872, to be our country's first park.

L Alpine Inn

1180 U.S. Highway 26 (1 mile west of Alpine Junction) in Alpine. 654-7644. www.starvalleywy.com/alpineinn.htm.

Are you heading for Yellowstone Park? Hunting or snowmobiling in the Star Valley area? The Alpine Inn is an affordable and easily accessible stopping point along the way. The charming cabins and rooms were recently remodeled. Some offer kitchenettes. The spacious grounds offer a quiet environment and breathtaking views. There are picnic areas and even teepees the kids can stay in. Pets and horses can also be accommodated at the Alpine Inn. This is an ideal and affordable location for family reunions and great headquarters for winter or summer outdoor activities. They are located close to town for dining, shopping, and all services.

7 *Gas, Food, Lodging*

Hoback Junction

John Hoback was a trapper and guide familiar with the Teton region. He led Wilson Price Hunt's party, a segment of the Astorian expedition, through the area in 1811. Hoback Junction is where the Hoback River meets the Snake River, and U.S. Highway 189/191 meets U.S. Highway 26/89. For the most part, the somewhat newly sprung community is an outgrowth of Jackson's popularity.

Bondurant
Pop.100 Elev. 6,588 Gas

Benjamin Franklin ("B.F.") Bondurant, the first settler, gave his name to the post office, which was run from his ranch. He was naturally the postmaster. His spread became one of Wyoming's first dude ranches in the early 1900s, and he and his wife, Sarah Ellen, were known for their wild pets, including elk, antelope, and bear cubs. The valley in which Bondurant is situated is rich in country beauty. The first Protestant sermon in the Rockies, delivered here by the Rev. Samuel Parker in 1835, was attended by the likes of Jim Bridger, Jedediah Smith, and Kit Carson. It was interrupted when a herd of bison passed through, and the listeners couldn't resist chasing them.

T River Runners Museum
At the Mad River Boat Trips "Wedge", about two miles south of Jackson Town Square on U.S. Highway 89.

Historic boats and rafts hang from the walls of the new River Runners Museum. Follow William H. Ashley's bull boat expedition on the Green River and John Fremont's 1842 voyage in the first inflatable raft. Artifacts and replicas thoughout the musem backpaddle visitors into another era, when river runnig was a courageous and risky means of travel.

T Granite Creek Hot Springs
East of Hoback Junction.

A large cement pool—a product of the Civilian Conservation Corps in the 1930s. Bathing suits are required. Open summer and winter. The roads are groomed in the winter for snowmobiles and cross country, but not plowed.

T Granite Falls

Enjoy great views of the Gros Ventre Mountains and the 50 foot drop of Granite Falls. A parking area and trails nearby offer a closer view via a short hike where you can enjoy Granite Creek cascading over a falls near Granite Hot Springs. It is a fairly easy drive and a nice day trip destination for the family. There is also a National Forest campground nearby. You'll enjoy the Granite Hot Springs, a secluded hot pool with wonderful mountain views.

H On the Ashes of Their Campfires
About 16 miles south of Hoback Junction on U.S. Highway 189/191.

This nearby canyon was a way through the mountains. Its game and Indian trails were followed by the white men. On September 26, 1811, the Astor party, with Wilson Price Hunt, 61 people and 118 horses entered the canyon here, making their way westward to the Pacific Ocean.The three legendary trappers, Hoback, Reznor, and Robinson, guided the party. These were the first white men to pass this way. From this time on, the stream and canyon became known as the Hoback.On October 10, 1812, Robert Stuart of the Astor Firm and his 6 companions camped here on their way to St. Louis from Fort Astoria with the message of the failure of Fort Astoria.On Sunday, August 23, 1835, Jim Bridger's and Kit Carson's brigade of trappers and Indians, and the Reverend Samuel Parker bound northward from the rendezvous on the Green River camped in this area. This basin was known then as Jackson's Little Hole. The Reverend Parker was delivering a sermon to the motley group when buffalo appeared. The congregation left for the hunt without staying for the benediction, This was the first protestant service held in the Rocky Mountains.

H John Hoback, Guide of Astorians
Approximately one mile southeast of Hoback Junction on U.S. Highway 191/189.

John Hoback, Jacob Reznor and Edward Robinson, trappers from Kentucky, in 1811 guided the Astorian land expedition under Wilson Price Hunt across the northern part of present Wyoming to the Snake River. From this junction of the Snake and Hoback Rivers the Hunt group passed through Jackson Hole, over Teton Pass and on to Henry's Fort in Idaho. In this area, Hoback and his companions were detached from the expedition to trap beaver. The following summer the eastbound Astorians led by Robert Stuart, met them in the wilderness, starving and destitute, having been robbed by the Indians. They were given clothing and equipment and continued hunting and trapping until the winter of 1813 when they were killed by the Indians. The River here was named by Wilson Price Hunt for his guide.

8 *Gas, Food, Lodging*

Jackson
Pop. 8,647

Perhaps the most famous town of the "Old West", Jackson has had its share of both attention and visitors. Featured in many movies, from John Wayne's *Big Trail* to Clint Eastwood's *Any Which Way You Can*, Jackson and its environs have appeared on the silver screen numerous times. Many Hollywood celebrities frequent the area in their down time, as well as presidents, politicians, diplomats, and royalty from around the world. First class amenities of all kinds exist here to accommodate such a crowd. Since so much glamour is associated with this rather small town, it's amazing that it still retains so much of its old time charm. But residents call their home "The Last and Best of the Old West." It's hard to believe that less than 200 years ago, the only people here were Indians like the Blackfeet, Gros Ventres, Nez Perce, Shoshone, Crows, Bannocks, and Flatheads, and they only came in the summer.

The town was named for "Jackson's Hole" (now Jackson Hole), which is inclusive of that portion of the Snake River Valley. The upper part of the valley is the Big Hole, and the lower valley is the Little Hole. "Hole" was trapper slang for a valley basin surrounded by mountains. John Colter is believed to have been the first white man here, exploring much of northern Wyoming on his own after he parted with Lewis and Clark in 1807. Astorian trappers were not far behind, who followed the Native Americans here in the warm months for the abundant game. Trapper/entrepreneurs Jedediah Smith and William Sublette named the area for their partner, David E. Jackson, a mountain man of hardy repute who was largely responsible for further exploration of the Snake River and Teton region.

Few others came to this rugged area until a band of outlaws discovered that it made an excellent hideout in the 1870s. William C. "Teton" Jackson, who was born Harvey Gleason in Rhode Island, adopted the names of the area where he dodged the long arm of the law. Jackson came west as part of the campaign against the Sioux in 1876, then discovered that being a horse thief

The elk antler arch at the entrance to Jackson Park in the heart of downtown Jackson.

was more profitable than being a pack train scout. He and his gang accumulated stolen horses from all over the western states, re-branded them, and sold them in South Dakota. They even had a plan to kidnap President Chester Arthur when he came to visit the newly designated Yellowstone National Park in 1883, but the president came with a sizeable military contingent to prevent any trouble.

That same year, permanent settlers arrived. Johnny Carnes and John Holland came to the valley to build homesteads for their families. In 1889, the Wilson family, led by Mormon Bishop Sylvester Wilson, crossed over Teton Pass from Idaho, in essence creating the first road there. Carnes and Holland, who hosted the new settlers until they could build their own homesteads, greeted them. Carnes and Holland continued to be the official welcome committee for other new families coming to settle in the valley throughout their lives. Bishop Wilson's brother, Elijah "Uncle Nick" Wilson, was once a Pony Express Rider, the youngest of the lot. He was said to have run of with the Shoshones for an adventure when he was young.

In 1873, another famous "Jackson", William H. Jackson, came to the area with the Hayden Geological Survey Expedition, and was the first to photograph both the Tetons and Yellowstone. His pictures helped to persuade Congress to set aside the Yellowstone area as a National Park.

When Jackson became an official town with a post office in 1897, it was named Marysvale, for postmistress Mary White. The name changed when the town became incorporated in 1901. By 1909, the town boasted three sawmills, a newspaper, two general stores, a hotel and restaurant, a blacksmith shop, a school, two churches, and a saloon.

Around this same time period, photographer and conservationist Stephen Leek was drawing national attention to the plight of the elk in the area. Over-hunted for their "tusks" (ivory teeth), and starving due to unusually harsh winters in the early part of the century, the government was called upon to aid the majestic animals. Both state and national agencies came together to create the National Elk Refuge in 1912. The four elk antler arches which surround the Town Square in downtown Jackson remind visitors of the remarkable creatures, known to Native Americans as "wapiti."

In 1920, Jackson again received national attention when it was the first town in the nation to elect an all-female city council and mayor. Shortly after their election, they appointed several other women to positions such as marshal, town clerk, and town health officer. In addition to other significant town reforms, this group of city officials was responsible for building the wooden sidewalks, which are still a trademark of Jackson's streets.

It has only been over the past thirty years or so that Jackson has become a hot spot for tourists. But the community has a long history of hospitality, from the trapper days to the homestead days, and current residents hold this tradition sacred. Although it is surrounded by many scenic wonders, Jackson is most popular for the friendliness of the people who live here.

L Super 8 - Jackson
750 S. Hwy. 89 in Jackson. 733-6833 or 800-800-8000

Enjoy the comfort and value at the Jackson Super 8. This 97-room motel will pamper you in a western ambiance and is conveniently located 1 mile from the Town Square. Guest rooms are accessed with interior corridors and electronic locks. Other amenities include in-room safes, micro fridges, expanded cable TV, on-site guest laundry, and 24-hour desk. Enjoy the complimentary fresh coffee bar all day long and fresh hot popcorn every evening in the lobby. A traveler workstation with high-speed access is available for you to keep in touch. Ski packages are available and a shuttle bus service is nearby. Children stay free. Ask about senior and group discounts.

L **Days Inn of Jackson Hole**
350 S. U.S. Highway 89 in Jackson. 733-0033 or 800-DAYS-INN ((733-0044). www.daysinn-jacksonhole.com

The Days Inn of Jackson Hole provides lodging and amenities as one would expect to find in a world class vacation destination. Choose from 78 rooms and 12 suites, some with hot tubs and fireplaces. All rooms come with in-room coffee, in-room ski racks, ski boot and glove dryers, and cable TV. They also provide a 24 hour giant hot tub and dry sauna. Guests are served a complimentary continental breakfast and children 17 and under stay free. Yellowstone National Park is just 50 miles away and they are just minutes from Grand Teton and the Jackson Town Square, an endless selection of fine dining and shopping establishments, as well as three local ski resorts.

9 *No services*

T **Antelope Flats**
13 miles east of Jackson.

Near the majestic backdrop of the Teton Mountains, Antelope Flats was settled in 1893 by Kansas pioneers who abandoned the area in 1912 after discovering the climate was too cold to grow crops.

T **Astoria Mineral Hot Springs**
On U.S. Highway 26/89, 17 miles south of Jackson.

An outdoor swimming pool and separate kiddie pool celebrate the natural mineral water flows. Bathing suits required. Open mid-May to Labor Day.

T **Huckleberry Hot Springs**
North of Jackson

Primitive hot springs on the north bank of Polecat Creek, Grand Teton National Park. Open all year. rock-and-mud soaking pools throughout have an average water temp of 100 degrees. Clothing is optional.

10 *Gas, Food, Lodging*

FL **The Virginian Lodge & Restaurant**
750 W. Broadway in Jackson Hole. 733-4330 or 800-262-4999, fax 733-4063. Email: info@virginianlodgejackson.com. www.virginianlodge.com

11 *Gas, Food, Lodging*

L **Town Square Inns - Cowboy Village Resort**
120 Flat Creek Drive in Jackson. 733-3121

Wyoming Tidbits

Rodeo may be the sport for which Wyoming is famous, but in the 1880s the most popular sport in the state was rollerskating.

12 *Gas, Food, Lodging*

T **Jackson Hole Museum**
Corner of N. Glenwood & Deloney in Jackson

The Jackson Hole Museum can be found under the covered wagon at North Glenwood and Deloney, just one block west of the Square. It is open daily from late May through early October. The museum captures the essence of history in the Jackson Hole and surrounding area. Ten thousand years of prehistory, Native American stone tools, weaponry, and clothing are displayed. You will also see artifacts and exhibits that show the lives of the Mountain Man and the Fur Trade Era, along with that of early settlers. Enjoy seeing exhibits of clothing, tools, guns, and old-time photographs. A collection of Boone & Crockett record game heads from the Jackson Hole area are also on display. Books, old-time wooden toys, Old West memorabilia, and Native American jewelry are available in the Museum Shop for you to purchase. Visit their web site to learn more.

F **Anthony's Italian Restaurant**
62 S. Glenwood in Jackson. 733-3717.

It's easy to see why Anthony's is a local favorite. It has been an institution in downtown Jackson since 1977. Three course family-style meals all include soup, salad, and garlic bread. They bake their own breads daily. Enjoy the eclectic Art Deco surroundings, reasonable prices, a children's menu, and a comfortably priced wine list and full bar. Entrees are served in large portions and you can choose from choices of fettucine, veal. chicken, duck, shrimp, scallops, clams, calamari, pizza, and vegetarian dishes. Make sure you arrive with a healthy appetite. The New England seafood chowder made with lobster stock is unsurpassed. They are open 7 days a week year round.

L **Ranch Inn**
45 E. Pearl, 1/2 mile south of Town Square in Jackson. 733-6363 or 800-348-5599. www.ranchinn.com or Email: info@ranchinn.com

L **Town Square Inns - 49er Inn & Suites**
W. Pearl & Jackson in Jackson. 733-7550 or 800-4-TETONS (800-483-8667). www.townsquareinns.com

The 49'er Inn and Suites, part of the Town Square Inns, features 150 rooms and suites in a great location with many amenities. There are 30 beautiful new fireplace suites, including 2-room luxury suites, with fireplace, Jacuzzi, kitchen, and steam shower. Guests will enjoy the complimentary extended continental breakfast, 35-person indoor hot tub, 12-person outdoor hot tub, fitness room, sauna, and complimentary ski shuttle. Handicap facilities and winter car plug-ins are also available. The 49'er Inn and Suites can accommodate all of your lodging needs and has earned AAA's 3 Diamond rating. Visit them on the web to learn more.

S **Wild Hands Art for Living**
70 S. Glenwood in Jackson. 733-4619

If you are looking for unique furniture, functional pottery, handmade jewelry, or just a humorous postcard, be sure and visit Wild Hands Art for Living. They can help you choose the perfect picture frame or a clever table by Sticks, for your dining room, that will keep your guests talking. Whimsical animal clocks built by Bryan McNutt adorn, alongside colorful mirrors adorn the walls in this fun store. Don't be surprised if you feel the urge to read all of Brian Adreas' Story People or Anne Taintor's sometimes shocking refrigerator magnets. Wild Hands sells functional American handcrafts in a delightful setting.

13 *Gas, Food, Lodging*

T **Jackson Hole Historical Society**
Log cabin on the corner of North Glenwood & Mercill in Jackson. 733-9605. www.jacksonholehistory.org

All Wyoming Area Codes are 307

Jackson Hole Historical Society

The Jackson Hole Historical Society is a research facility dedicated to the collections and study of local and regional history. Its mission is history education. Open year-round. The public will find historical exhibits, archival and biographical files, maps, oral histories, videos, a library, and a 7,000-item photograph collection available for reprinting. The Society offers history excursions, school programs, genealogies, oral histories, and various exhibits throughout the year. All areas are available for public viewing and research. Call for more information or visit the web site for current schedules and exhibits.

T National Museum of Wildlife Art

2 Miles North of Jackson on U.S. Highway 26/89, across from the National Elk Refuge. 733-5771. www.wildlifeart.org.

Just inside the doors of this museum's main gallery, a bronze mountain lion crouches, as if ready to pounce. This is just the first of many artworks. For the kids, the museum hosts a hands-on children's gallery. Adult visitors will enjoy the artwork displayed throughout twelve galleries, as well as a theater, 200 seat auditorium, gift shop, and Rising Sun Cafe.

The collection features the works of Carl Rungious, George Catlin, Albert Bierstadt, Karl Bodmer, Alfred Jacob Miller, N.C. Wyeth, Conrad Schwiering, John Clymer, Charles Russell, Robert Bateman, and numerous others. Especially interesting are the reconstructed studio of John Clymer and the Carl Rungius Gallery, where the most complete collection of his paintings in the nation resides.

Another notable exhibit is a feature on the American bison, documenting the once-abundant animals and the slaughter that took place. Six of the galleries host changing displays of photography, painting, and artwork. For those who want to see live animals, spotting scopes are located in the lobby and the members' lounge (open to public) to watch the inhabitants of the nearby National Elk Refuge.

A 45-minute museum tour is given daily at 11 a.m., or by request for groups. The museum is open from 8 a.m. to 5 p.m. during the summer. During the winter, hours are 9 a.m. to 5 p.m. Monday through Saturday, and 1 to 5 p.m. on Sundays.

T National Elk Refuge

Northeast of Jackson at 532 North Cache Street. 733-9212

In late October and early November thousands of elk begin their traditional migration from high summer range in Grand Teton National Park, southern Yellowstone National Park, and the neighboring national forests to lower elevation winter range in Jackson Hole. Heavy snows force the animals to lower elevations in search of food, and usually more than 7,500 elk make their way to the National Elk Refuge to spend the winter.

Establishment of the National Elk Refuge

Hundreds of years before the settlement of this country, elk ranged from the eastern states through central and western North America. They grazed the open prairies, mountain valleys, and foothills. As settlers pushed slowly westward, the distribution of the elk was rapidly reduced to the western mountains. By 1900, elk had disappeared from more than 90 percent of their original range.

When settlers arrived in Jackson Hole in the late 1800s, there may have been as many as 25,000 elk in the entire valley. The town of Jackson was built in a large portion of elk winter range.

Establishment of farms and ranches further forced elk from their traditional wintering areas. Livestock competed for winter food, and hungry elk raided haystacks. These severe conflicts between humans and elk diminished the Jackson elk population.

In the early 1900s, severe winters with deep, crusted snow also took a serious toll on the wintering elk. The refuge was created in 1912 as a result of public interest in the survival of the Jackson elk herd. Today the refuge continues to preserve much of the remaining elk winter range in the valley, approximately one-quarter of the original Jackson Hole winter range. Elk stay on the refuge for approximately six months each winter. An eight-foot high fence along the main highway and along the northern border of town prevents elk from moving through Jackson and onto private lands.

The nearly 25,000-acre National Elk Refuge is administered by the U.S. Fish & Wildlife Service and is one of more than 500 refuges in the National Wildlife Refuge System. This system was established to preserve a national network of lands and waters for the conservation and management of the fish, wildlife, and plants of the United States for the benefit of present and future generations.

History

The Jackson Elk Herd, estimated at approximately 14,000 animals, probably owes its prosperity to local citizens who were here about 1906-1912.

Following the removal of most of the beaver by trappers prior to 1840, the Jackson Hole country was virtually uninhabited by settlers until 1884. Only hunting/gathering native Americans (mostly Shoshone, Bannock, and Arapahoe) summered here until about the end of the Civil War (1865). Sixty-four people lived in Jackson Hole when the Wyoming Territory became a state in 1890. Nearby Yellowstone had become the world's first national park 1972. By the late 1890s and early 1900s, conversion of historic elk winter range to domestic livestock use began to pose a hardship situation for the elk.

However, even before the Jackson hole environment was changed somewhat by the arrival of settlers, significant numbers of elk died from starvation in winter. Early hunters and settlers noted that winters of unusually heavy snow resulted in death by starvation for thousands of elk. Survival of large numbers of elk was complicated further by the severe winters of 1909, 1910, and 1911 that put the herd in serious trouble. In order to survive, the elk raided ranchers' haystacks, but many still starved to death. Although the ranchers did not want to see the elk die, they could not afford to lose their hay and remain in the ranching business.

The first official suggestion for a permanent elk refuge in Jackson Hole was made in 1906 by the Wyoming State Game Warden, D.C. Nowlin, who, following his retirement from that post, became the first manager of the National Elk Refuge. Area residents gained statewide sympathy for the continuing elk losses, and appeals for assistance spread through many other states. As a result, in 1911 the Wyoming Legislature asked Congress to cooperate with the State in appropriations for "feeding, protecting, and otherwise preserving the big game which winters in great numbers within the confines of the State of Wyoming." Less than a month later, Congress appropriated $20,000 for feeding, protecting, and transplanting elk and ordered an investigation of the elk situation in Wyoming.

After this assessment by the Federal Government, $45,000 was appropriated by an act of Congress on August 10, 1912, for the purchase of lands and maintenance of a refuge for wintering elk.

By 1916, from a combination of public domain lands and private lands, 2,760 acres had been acquired for the National Elk Refuge.For more than ten years no additions were made to the refuge itself. In 1918 the U.S. Forest Service lands adjacent to the east side of the refuge were classified as big game winter range, and although they were not made part of the refuge, livestock grazing was restricted.

In 1927 Congress accepted title to 1,760 acres of private ranch lands that had been acquired and donated by the Izaak Walton League of America, expanding the refuge to 4,520 acres.

Congress, in a 1935 act that became known as the "Six Million Dollar Fund," designated money for purchase of wildlife lands throughout the United States. From this, about 16,400 additional acres of private lands were acquired for the National Elk Refuge. Also, 3,783 acres of public domain lands were added by Presidential Executive orders in 1935 and 1936.

Today the refuge consists of nearly 25,000 acres devoted to elk winter range. This represents the last remaining elk winter range in Jackson Hole.

That portion of the Jackson Elk Herd that winters on the National Elk Refuge averages approximately 7,500 animals yearly. Elk are on the refuge for about six months each year from November to May, freeranging for about 3.5 months and using supplemental feed for about 2.5 months, usually from late January until April.

Supplemental feeding began in 1910 when the Wyoming Legislature appropriated $5,000 to purchase all available hay in the valley to feed the elk. The supply of hay was inadequate and hundreds of elk died that winter. This was followed in 1911 with feed for elk from the $20,000 appropriated by Congress. Supplemental feed has been provided for the elk in all but nine winters since then. In 1975 a change was made from baled hay to pelletized alfalfa hay.

A Presidential "Commission on the Conservation of the Elk of Jackson Hole, Wyoming," was established and active from 1927 through 1935. Its membership, which included the Governor of Wyoming, developed the following tenet: The Jackson Elk Herd in the State of Wyoming is a national resource combining economic, aesthetic, and recreation values in which the State of Wyoming, the Federal Government, private citizens, and civic and sportsmen's organizations are actively and intensely interested.

In 1958 currently active Jackson Hole Cooperative Elk Studies Group was formed, composed of the Wyoming Game & Fish Dept., the U.S. Fish & wildlife Service, the U.S. Forest Service, and the National Park Service. The principal purpose of this group is to coordinate plans, programs, and findings of studies, and to provide an exchange of ideas, information, and personnel to study the elk herd and its habitat. All four agencies have legal responsibilities for management of the elk herd and its habitat. A better understanding and appreciation of individual agency objectives and responsibilities and closer cooperation have been attained since the establishment of the study group.

The refuge is dedicated primarily to the perpetuation of the nation's majestic elk, for us and future generations to enjoy.

Refuge Management

Refuge grasslands are managed to produce as much natural forage for elk as possible through extensive irrigation, seeding, prescribed burning, and other practices. These management practices enhance elk winter habitat and reduce the need for supplemental feeding. However, when deep or crusted snow prevents the elk from grazing, or the natural forage is depleted, refuge personnel feed the herds pelletized alfalfa. These 2- to 3-inch pellets have higher nutritional value than average baled hay and are easier for refuge staff to store and distribute to the elk. Elk are usually fed about 7 to 8 pounds per animal per day, which equals about 30 tons per day for a herd of 7,500 elk.The elk receive supplemental alfalfa for approximately 2.5 months during an average winter.

The number of elk wintering on the refuge must be limited to avoid overuse of the range and to reduce the potential spread of diseases common when herd animals are crowded. Refuge staff, in consultation with the Wyoming Game & Fish Department, have determined that a maximum of 7,500 (more than half the total Jackson elk herd) elk is optimum for the refuge. Herd numbers are maintained through a late fall controlled hunt on the refuge and adjacent public lands.

Elk Facts

Elk are the second largest antlered animals in the world; only moose are larger. Bull elk are 4.5 to 5 feet tall at the shoulder and weigh 550 to 800 pounds. Cow elk weigh from 450 to 600 pounds. The refuge elk herd consists of approximately 20% bulls, 65% cows, and 15% calves.

The majority of adult elk on the refuge are between 3 and 10 years old. The oldest animals in the herd are 15-30 years old, but these individuals represent a very small part of the refuge population. The age on an elk can be determined by examining milk tooth replacement, wear on permanent teeth, and annual dental rings.

While most members of the deer family are primarily browsers (feeding on twigs and leaves of shrubs and trees), elk are both browsers and grazers, feeding extensively on grasses and forbs, as well as shrubs.

Grizzly bears, black bears, mountain lions, wolves, and coyotes prey on elk. By weeding out the weak, predators help maintain healthy, vigorous elk herds.

More Elk Facts

Adult bull elk have large, branched antlers. Contrary to popular belief, there is no exact relationship between age and number of antler points, but the number of points may be used to estimate an animal's age. Bulls between 1 and 2 years old have short, unbranched antlers called spikes. By age 3, bulls usually have antlers with three to four points on each side. Older bulls carry antlers with five, six, or sometimes seven points on each side. Mature bulls with six points per side are called royal bulls, and those with seven points are called imperial bulls. On rare occasions you might see a bull displaying antlers with eight points on each side; these bulls are known as monarchs.

Large bulls shed their antlers during March and April every year, while the smaller bulls lose their antlers during April or early May. Mice, squirrels, and other animals chew on the shed antlers to get needed minerals. Antlers dropped on the refuge are collected by local Boy Scouts, who sell them at an annual public auction (the 3rd Saturday in May) to help raise money for both the scouts and for winter elk feed management. The public may not collect or remove antlers from the refuge.

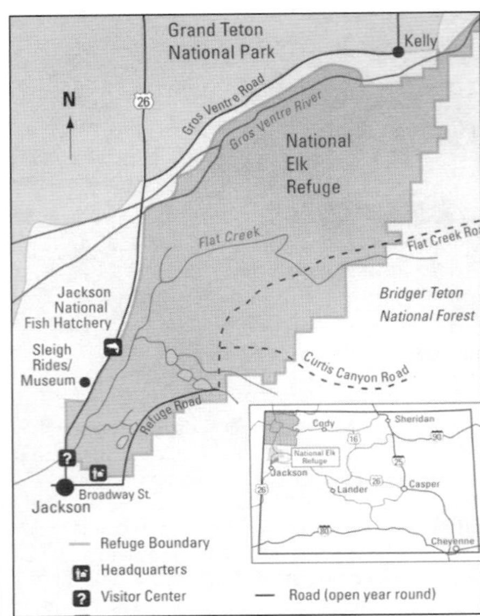

New antlers begin to grow as soon as the old ones are shed. They develop through the summer and reach maturity by mid-August. By this time, the antler's "velvet," or outer blood-rich skin has dried, and the bull rubs the dead velvet off on small trees and shrubs. A bull's antlers are hard and shiny by the fall breeding season (the "rut").

Elk leave the lower elevations in April and May, following the receding snowline back into the cool, high country, where they spend the summer. These animals travel distances varying from a few miles up to 100 miles during migration from the refuge to Grand Teton National Park, southern Yellowstone National Park, and national forest lands to the north and northeast of Jackson Hole. A few elk remain near the wooded areas of the refuge during the summer months.

From late May to mid-June, cows bear their young in secluded thickets on higher terrain. A cow typically has one calf that weighs 30 to 40 pounds. The calves are reddish colored and spotted at birth. Very few calves are born on the refuge, since the majority of elk migrate back to the high country before calving occurs.

The breeding season (or "rut") occurs in September and early October, while the elk are in the high country. At this time, the high-pitched "bugling" of the mature bulls can be heard as they gather harems of cows and challenge rival bulls. During the rut, bulls vigorously defend their harems of half a dozen to 15 or more cows.

In late fall, snow begins to fall in the high country, and the elk herds migrate back to their lower elevation winter range.

Wildlife and Their Habitat

Refuge habitat includes grassy meadows and marshes spread across the valley floor, timbered areas bordering the Gros Ventre (GroVONT) River, and sagebrush and rock outcroppings along the foothills. This habitat diversity provides a variety of food, water, and shelter that support the rich mixture of wildlife species found at the refuge.

While elk are the primary reason the refuge

was established, 47 species of mammals are found here year-around or during seasonal migration to and from surrounding areas. Moose, bighorn sheep, bison, and mule deer are common winter residents on the refuge. Wolves, coyotes, badgers, and Uinta ground squirrels are also seen. Other common wildlife species include muskrat, beaver, porcupine, long-tailed weasel, and voles or meadow mice.

Visitor Opportunities

The National Elk Refuge lies northeast of the town of Jackson, Wyoming, and directly south of Grand Teton National Park. The winter season, between November and April, is the best time to view elk and other wildlife on the refuge. To protect refuge wildlife and their habitats, public use activities are primarily confined to the main, unpaved roads on the refuge. Paved turnouts on the west side of the refuge along U.S. Highway 26 (leading to Grand Teton and Yellowstone national parks) are provided for viewing and photographing refuge wildlife.

From mid-December through late March, daily horse-drawn sleigh rides (or wagons, if weather conditions require them) offer visitors a close-up look at the elk herd. Sleigh rides begin at the National Museum of Wildlife Art, two-and-a-half miles north of Jackson on U.S. Highway 26, 89, 191. Visitors to the museum can also learn about elk and management of the refuge through a slide show, videos, exhibits, and by talking with refuge personnel. Sleigh riders are encouraged to bundle up, since they are likely to be exposed to very cold temperatures and chilling winds.

Limited hiking opportunities exist on the refuge, and there is no overnight parking or camping. Camping is available in nearby national parks and national forests.

Source: U.S. Fish & Wildlife Service

V Jackson Hole Whitewater/Teton Expeditions & Scenic Floats

650 W. Broadway in Jackson. 733-1007 or 800-700-RAFT(7236). www.jhww.com

Jackson Hole Whitewater Teton Expeditions, established in 1963, is committed to quality and customer satisfaction when they take visitors on scenic float trips and expeditions on the Snake River. They offer several trips for all levels of experience and distances. All trips come with the magnificent Teton range for a backdrop. The professional guides will treat you to an experience of a lifetime, great food, outstanding wildlife viewing, and photo opportunities. They can answer all your questions about the river, the flora and fauna, rock formations or any questions about the area. Give them a call to reserve your trip or visit them on the web.

F Off Broadway Grill

30 S. King Street in Jackson. 733-9777.

F Jedediah's Original House of Sourdough

135 E. Broadway in Jackson. 733-5671

F Harvest Bakery. Cafe & Organic Foods

130 W. Broadway in Jackson. 733-5418.

Harvest is a store that satisfies the needs of the organic consumer, providing the products to sustain one in a healthy way. The store offers an eclectic array of foods, supplements, and gifts. They carry items that provide the local, as well as the traveling shopper an oasis of products. The organic artisan bakery is famous for whole wheat cinnamon rolls and oatmeal raisin cookies, all featuring fine organic ingredients. The cafe offers everything: an organic salad bar, huevos rancheros, and their famous curried burrito, as well as living foods items. Find gifts that stir the imagination and warm the heart. Harvest's guiding principle of selfless service is reflected in all aspects of the business.

L Painted Buffalo Inn

400 W. Broadway in Jackson. 733-4340. www.paintedbuffalo.com

The Painted Buffalo Inn is just three short blocks from the Town Square, offering convenient, comfortable accommodations in the heart of downtown Jackson. Your comfort will be assured with queen beds, cable TV, air conditioning, and indoor swimming pool. Children under 18 stay free. Guests receive a membership to the Jackson Hole Athletic Club during your stay. On site is the Betty Roack Coffee House serving baked goods, sandwiches, salads, and pizza. The Body Essence Day Spa and Hair Art is a full beauty salon on site. Indulge yourself. Their friendly reservationists are happy to answer any questions you may have about things to do while in Jackson Hole.

L Anvil Motel & El Rancho Motel

215 N. Cache in Jackson. 733-3668 or 800-234-4507. www.anvilmotel.com

The Anvil Motel is just one boardwalk block from Jackson's Town Square and is convenient to shopping, dining, and Jackson's famous watering holes. Start Bus pickup is available at the office providing easy access around town and to ski and recreational areas. All rooms are air-conditioned with microwaves and refrigerators, irons, ironing boards, hair dryers, and clock radios. There is also a hot tub for pure relaxation. Also, at the

Anvil Motel & El Rancho Motel

same great location is the El Rancho Motel offering some rooms with the same amenities as the Anvil Motel. You're a stranger here but once. A cowboys' favorite for affordable, quality lodging since 1947. Visit them on the web.

L Bunkhouse Hostel

215 N. Cache in Jackson. 733-3668 or 800-234-4507.

LM Black Diamond Vacation Rentals & Real Estate

290 E. Broadway in Jackson. 733-6170 or 800-325-8605.Email: stay@bdjh.com. www.bdjh.com.

Since 1989, Black Diamond Vacation Rentals and Real Estate has evolved to provide a multifaceted approach to second home/rental investment ownership in Jackson Hole by providing all aspects of real estate sales, property management, and construction. All are coordinated in-house through one entity—Black Diamond. They offer a convenient and simple concept. They can find the right home for you or the right piece of land, rent it or take care of it in your absence. They can also build your home, provide property management services such as housekeeping and maintenance, or even remodel if necessary. Visit them at the web site.

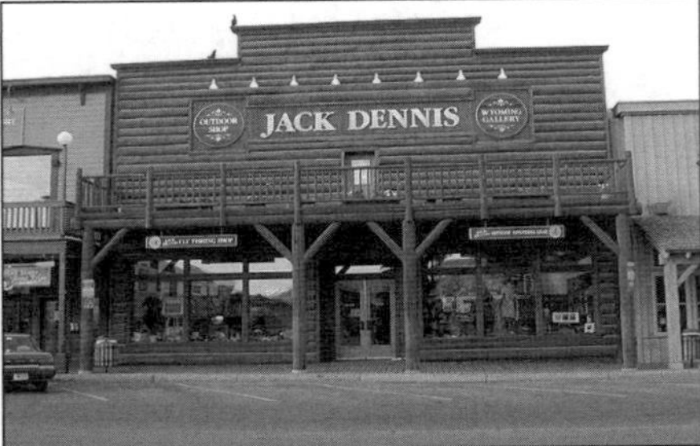

S Jack Dennis Outdoor Shop

50 E. Broadway on the town square in Jackson. 733-3270. www.jackdennis.com

Jack Dennis Sports Outdoor Shop is famous for fishing trips on the Snake River. Their guides are expert casters and happy to teach their methods of presenting and working a fly. All of their trips are limited to artificials only. While they do take spin fisherman on trips, they emphasize learning to fly fish. The Outdoor Shop offers complete pro fly fishing gear and an extensive selection of flies. They also carry outdoor gear, footwear, sporting arms, skis, and snowboards for enjoying the outdoor recreation in the area. Be sure and visit the Wyoming Gallery, which features fine art, gifts and distinctive furnishings. Visit them on the web.

S Boyer's Indian Arts and Crafts

30 W. Broadway in Jackson. 733-3773. Email: boyers@boyersindianart.com. www.boyersindianart.com

Boyer's Indian Arts and Crafts was established in 1962 and is devoted to the finest quality Indian art. A large selection of Navajo, Zuni, and Hopi silverwork is on display. The store features a wide variety of Navajo rugs from various areas of the Navajo nation. You'll find heshi from Santo Domingo as well as baskets, pottery, kachina dolls, drums and beadwork represented by several different tribes of Indian artisans. Boyer's also offers an excellent selection of local Native American beadwork. For an unusual and distinctive gift, visit their store in the heart of Jackson or visit them on the web.

S The Grand Basket

145 W. Gill in Jackson. 739-1139 or 800-967-2339. www.grand-basket.com

The Grand Basket provides unique gifts of gourmet foods and wonderful accessories with the Western flavor of Wyoming and the Rocky Mountains. When you want to send something really special to friends and family across the country they have the solution. For holidays, birthdays, thank yous, or just to let someone know you are thinking of them. Their tantalizing selections include Wyoming gifts, gourmet chocolates, a variety of buffalo meats, soup and sauce mixes, jams, candies, and Western snacks. Most items are made right in Jackson Hole. Choose from themes for New Babies to Get Well to New Home to Welcome. A Grand Basket is always welcome. Delivery and shipping are available.

S Davies Reid Rugs, Objects & Decor

15 E. Ave. in Jackson. 739-1009. www.davies-reid.com

Davies Reid specializes in authentic oriental carpets and tribal rugs. Their own line of vegetable dyed, handmade, Turkman rugs are produced through their Refuge Weaving Project. Also, on display is an extensive collection of Asian antique home furnishings, accessories, architectural elements, and exotic jewelry. Other unique items include antique textiles, earthenware, and antique carpets. All items are hand selected on the owners' twice-yearly trips to Central Asia and beyond. Their consistent, reliable service and fine quality products are available every week, all year long. Visit Davies Reid at their web site.

S The Country Woman
155 W. Gill Ave. in Jackson. 739-1865

When in Jackson you won't want to miss this very popular consignment shop. The Country Woman offers a fantastic selection of new and consigned clothing, jewelry, accessories, home decor, all wrapped up in a fun shopping experience. The upscale shop offers exciting collections, and can suit every budget. A large selection that includes everything from fabulous furs to great looks on the slopes to the ultimate hike. The Country Woman is a unique and satisfying shopping experience with fresh items added almost every day. You never know who you might see shopping for treasures here—celebrities, locals, or your next door neighbor.

S West Lives On Gallery
75 N. Glenwood in Jackson. 734-2888 or 800-883-6080. www.westliveson.com

Located in the heart of Jackson Hole, "Art Center of the Rockies", The West Lives On Gallery reflects the rich heritage of the American West. They feature Western wildlife and landscape art in original oils, acrylics, watercolors and bronzes. They represent over 50 local, regional, and national artists including Alfredo Rodriquez, the premier painter of mountain men and Plains Indians. Among the many artists represented you'll find the works of Roger Ore, Gary Robert Swanson, and Ray McCarty. Find them conveniently located across from the street, west from the Wort Hotel or visit them on the web.

S Beaver Creek Hat & Leather Co.
36 E. Broadway in Jackson. 733-1990 or 800-533-4522. www.beavercreekhats.com

S Home Resource Center
485 W. Broadway in Jackson. 732-1020.

The Home Resource Center is an outstanding source for the most current and unique items to finish your home with personal and unique custom features. Their showroom opens to a world of the most recent innovations and products for your home. They feature custom and architectural doors, Kolbe & Kolbe windows, custom cabinetry, and kitchen design. Select from products such as marble and granite, reclaimed wood flooring and timbers, antique and new siding, millwork, custom iron work and hand-carved fireplaces, and fixtures. The designers on staff can assist you in creating that perfect finishing touch in your own home.

S Jackson Moore Lighting
980 W. Broadway in Jackson. 734-8986. www.jacksonmoore.com

Jackson Moore Lighting can assist you in making important decisions about lighting, an integral part of the total design for your home interior and exterior. Their lighting designers can recommend what elements best provide for your home lighting functions. They specialize in professional lighting design, decorative, architectural, and outdoor lighting for mountain homes. Lighting fixtures are available from around the world, along with custom fixtures. Jackson Moore is a full service lighting source, including service, repair, and large selection of shades. Additionally, the store carries outdoor furniture. Excellent service is always a priority at Jackson Moore Lighting. Visit them on the web.

Grand Teton Music Festival

The beginning of July each summer brings the Grand Teton Music Festival to Jackson Hole. A weekend of impressive orchestra music draws thousands in for the world-class classical music the festival has to offer. The concerts are held at the state-of-the-art Walk Festival Hall which is home to a 200-member resident orchestra and internationally acclaimed music director. In addition, the Jackson Hole Wine Auction is held around the same time featuring private wine dinners in homes throughout the valley and wrapping up with a feast and gala auction including more than 200 lots of rare wines. Walk Festival Hall in Jackson, 733-1128.

Wyoming Tidbits

During World War II, the U.S. carefully patrolled the Wind Rivers area outside Dubois with bombers, fearing the Germans might poison the waters. This area, confluence of the Mississippi, Columbia and Colorado Rivers, is home to two thirds of the headwaters for our country. One of the patrol bombers crashed.

S Elkhorn Industries
36 E. Broadway in Jackson. 733-0067 or 800-848-4676. www.flatcreekcrossing.com

Discover Flat Creek Crossing at Elkhorn Industries located on the Town Square, south side. Find beautiful, enduring gifts from nature that are combined with fine craftsmanship to create classic antler accents for home and office. John Bickner, Jr., senior artist and owner, creates unique art exhibited worldwide and accenting everything from rustic hunting cabins to the most elegant homesteads. John is a fifth generation craftsman, and shows his appreciation of nature through his creations of fine art. The gallery features an exquisite selection of lighting fixtures, chandeliers, lamps, candleholders, furniture, cutlery, and jewelry. The artwork is superior in quality and impeccably designed to accentuate the natural beauty of the material. Visit them on the web.

M Coldwell Banker, The Real Estate Company
Montana, Idaho, & Wyoming. 733-7970 or 800-967-1482. www.theranchbrokers.com

Coldwell Banker, The Real Estate Company, serves buyers and sellers in Wyoming, Idaho, and Montana. Cyril K. Richard, "The Ranch Broker", specializes in resort properties, ranch and fishing properties, and commercial acquisitions. Cy has over 25 years experience in real estate. He has served as Vice President of the Wyoming Association of Realtors, past President of the Teton Country Board of Realtors, past president of the Rotary Club of Jackson, and has been a past Realtor of the Year. To better serve their customers, Coldwell Banker, The Real Estate Company has locations in Big Timber, MT, Jackson, WY, and Driggs, ID. Be sure and visit them on the web.

14

Wilson

Named for a family of Mormon pioneers who came to settle in the Jackson area, this little town is now primarily a preparation point for trekkers headed into the Tetons.

Teton Village

Teton Village is a ski and summer resort community open year round. The town consists of chalets, assorted lodging accommodations, restaurants, and shops.

L The Painted Porch Bed & Breakfast
3755 Moose-Wilson Road four miles southwest of Jackson Hole Ski Area and about 3 miles northeast of junction of State Highways 22/390, in Jackson Hole. 733-1981. www.jacksonholebedandbreakfast.com

Country elegance abounds at The Painted Porch Bed and Breakfast. This beautifully restored turn-of-the century farmhouse, is nestled in three acres of aspen and pine trees at the foot of the Teton Range. They are located just off the Teton Village Road (Moose-Wilson Road), eight miles from the town of Jackson. Four thoughtfully decorated unique rooms are available. Each is furnished with cable television and private bathrooms. A full, delicious breakfast is served in their cheery, light-drenched dining room or on the porches. Play board games or read from their large selection of local and regional books. The living room offers Teton views and a large rock fireplace. The Painted Porch is an inn for all seasons.

L Rendezvous Mountain Rentals
3600 N. Moose Wilson Rd in Wilson. 739-9050 or toll free at 888-739-2565. www.rmrentals.com or Email: lodging@rmentals.com.

Rendezvous Mountain Rentals and Property Management offers an exceptional selection of properties at an outstanding value for your Jackson Hole vacation. Fully furnished condominiums and unique vacation homes located in the Jackson Hole Racquet Club at the Aspens, the Teton Pines Resort, Teton Village and throughout Jackson Hole are all available to you. Nightly and monthly rentals are offered in properties ranging in size from cozy one bedroom condominiums to spacious four and five bedroom homes. Whether you are planning to ski one of Jackson Hole's three nearby ski areas or explore Yellowstone and Grand Teton National Parks, they are centrally located for all of your adventures. Their 30 years of lodging expertise comes with great service.

L A Teton Treehouse Bed & Breakfast
6175 Heck of a Hill Road between Jackson Hole and Wilson. 733-3233. www.crusing-america.com/tetontreehouse.

H Elijah Nicholas "Uncle Nick" Wilson April 8, 1843-Dec. 27, 1915
Wilson next to Post Office.

In 1889, Uncle Nick led the first Mormon settlers over Teton Pass into Jackson Hole. It took 14 days to travel from Victor, idaho, to Wilson, Wyoming, the town that bears his name. As a child, Uncle Nick lived with Chief Washakie's band of Shoshone Indians. He later was a Pony Express rider, a scout for General Albert S. Johnston, and an Overland Stage driver. In Wilson, Uncle Nick was the first Presiding Elder for the Mormon Church and had the first hotel, general store, and post office. This monument is dedicated summer, 1989, on the 100th anniversary of the pioneer crossing of Teton Pass.

15 *Gas, Food, Lodging*

L Jackson Hole Resort Lodging
3200 W. McCollister Drive in Teton Village. 733-3990 or 800-443-8613. www.jhresortlodging.com

Jackson Hole Resort Lodging offers rental accommodations in and around Teton Village at the base of the Jackson Hole Mountain Resort, Jackson Hole Racquet Club, and Teton Pines. Enjoy their recuperative accommodations that range from one-bedroom condominiums to five-bedroom luxury homes. All properties have a fully equipped kitchen, living area, dining area, fireplace or woodstove and access to washers and dryers. Most properties include a complimentary membership to Sundance Swim Club or Teton Sports Club depending on location. Concierge services are available. They are conveniently located three miles from Grand Teton National Park and 53 miles from Yellowstone National Park. Group rates and packages area available. Visit them on the web.

16

Kelly

This town was initially named Grovont, an Anglicized spelling for the nearby Gros Ventre River. Another post office had already used the name, however, so they had to change it in 1909. The new name honored Bill Kelly, local sawmill owner and rancher.

A landslide shook the little ranching community in 1925, when the end of Sheep Mountain crumbled in just three minutes and dammed the Gros Ventre River, creating Slide Lake. Some 50 million tons of rock, soil, and other debris, including some ancient trees, made up the dam. Some thought it would hold indefinitely, but in 1927, the dam gave way. Kelly residents had only a few minutes to get to higher ground and watch the fifteen foot wall of water sweep their town away, leaving only the church and the schoolhouse behind. Six people lost their lives in the flood

C.E. Dibble, a forest ranger, became a hero that day, when he recognized a hayrack that had been floating on the lake coming downstream. He raced in his Model T ahead of the river, cutting fences to free livestock and warning the town of the coming disaster.

Moose

Named for the animals that frequent the area, the world's largest ungulates, Moose is the headquarters for Grand Teton National Park.

T Grand Teton National Park Colter Bay Indian Arts Museum

At Colter Bay National Park Office.

This museum houses the David T. Vernon collection of Indian pieces, the most impressive in the park, and one of the finest anywhere in Wyoming. Included in the exhibition are beautifully beaded buckskin dresses, moccasins, masks, kachina dolls, ceremonial pipes, shields, bows, warbonnets, a blanket that belonged to Chief Sitting Bull, and numerous other decorated items.

Craft demonstrations are given daily through the summer months.

From mid-May to Memorial day, and Labor Day through mid-October, the museum is open from 8 a.m. to 5 p.m. daily. Early June to Labor Day, hours are 8 a.m. to 8 p.m. daily. The museum is closed for the rest of the year. Admission is free.

T Murie Museum/Teton Science School

Just south of Moran Junction in Kelly. 733-4765. www.teton-science.org.

Part of the Teton Science School, the Murie Natural History Museum displays thousands of specimens, including birds, mammals, and plants. Of particular interest are the casts of animal tracks used by Olaus Murie, famed wildlife biologist, in production of his Peterson's Guide to Animal Tracks. While this museum is open to the public, it is recommended that you call ahead to arrange an appointment.

T Grand Teton National Park Colter Bay Indian Arts Museum

In Moose at the Forest Service visitors center. 739-3594.

This museum houses the David T. Vernon collection of Indian pieces, the most impressive in the park, and one of the finest anywhere in Wyoming. Included in the exhibition are beautifully beaded buckskin dresses, moccasins, masks, kachina dolls, ceremonial pipes, shields, bows, warbonnets, a blanket that belonged to Chief Sitting Bull, and numerous other decorated items. Craft demonstrations are given daily through the summer months.From mid-May to Memorial day, and Labor Day through mid-October, the museum is open from 8 a.m. to 5 p.m. daily. Early June to Labor Day, hours are 8 a.m. to 8 p.m. daily. The museum is closed for the rest of the year. Admission is free.

T Jenny Lake

Situated by the lake of the same name, Jenny was the Shoshone wife of Dick Leigh, a trapper and guide for the Hayden Geological Survey Expedition of 1871. The town has become an amenity village for travelers. The Jenny Lake Ranger Station is a required stopover for climbers, who must register before entering either Teton or Yellowstone Parks.

T Kelly Warm Springs

Drive north on U.S. 189/191 from Jackson, turn on Gros Ventre Road, through the town of Kelly.

Located within the Grand Tetons National Park, this serene pond is open all year. Clothing is optional. This is the only place in the world where the tiny fish, Kendall dace are found. To protect these fish that only grow to two inches in length, no wading is allowed in the waters of Kendall Warm Springs.

T The Gros Ventre Slide

7 miles north of Jackson on U.S. Highway 89; turn right and travel 11 miles on the Gros Ventre Road.

On June 23, 1925, one of the largest fast-moving landslides in generations occurred near the village of Kelly, Wyoming. In just three minutes, huge amounts of rock and debris cascaded down the north slope of Sheep Mountain, changing the area forever.

Hurling down the slope at 50 m.p.h., the mile-wide slide carried 50,000,000 cubic yards of

Moose

	Jan	Feb	March	April	May	June	July	Aug	Sep	Oct	Nov	Dec	Annual
Average Max. Temperature (F)	25.8	31.0	39.1	49.1	61.0	70.6	80.0	79.0	69.0	55.8	38.1	26.1	52.1
Average Min. Temperature (F)	0.9	3.3	11.9	22.1	30.8	37.2	41.2	39.5	32.1	23.0	13.6	1.3	21.4
Average Total Precipitation (in.)	2.58	1.99	1.58	1.47	1.95	1.77	1.19	1.32	1.46	1.26	2.13	2.48	21.19
Average Total SnowFall (in.)	43.4	29.9	20.4	9.2	2.8	0.1	0.0	0.0	0.5	4.4	25.4	39.7	175.7
Average Snow Depth (in.)	27	34	32	13	0	0	0	0	0	0	4	16	11

debris. The mass rode 300 feet up the opposite slope, blocked the Gros Ventre River, and formed a five-mile long body of water known today as Lower Slide Lake. The piles of debris seen today contain large chunks of Tensleep Sandstone, along with remnants of the original forest.

Throughout the years, many people have wondered what caused this tremendous slide. Three primary factors are thought to have contributed to the unusual event:

(1) heavy rains and rapidly melting snow saturated the Tensleep Sandstone, causing the Amsden Shale rock layer on Sheep Mountain to become exceptionally slippery;

(2) the river, cutting through the sandstone, produced a "free side" with no extra support holding it in course;

(3) swampy pools with no outlets, on top of the mountain, indicating water-saturated soil.

Earthquake tremors (which were occurring) added to these already unstable factors and could have precipitated a landslide.

William Bierer, a long-time native to the area, predicted a slide in the near future. Convinced of the validity of his theory, Bill sold his ranch on Sheep Mountain to Guil Huff, an unsuspecting cattle rancher, in 1920. Bierer died in 1923 before his prophecy became reality.

Two years later, on the afternoon of June 23, 1925, Guil rode horseback down the river to the north side of Sheep Mountain where he had heard loud rumblings. He arrived at 4 p.m., in time to witness 50 million cubic yards of land mass descending rapidly toward him. He and his horse escaped the impact by a mere 20 feet. Along with Guil, two other men witnessed the phenomenon of nature — Forney Cole and Boyd Charter.

In a matter of minutes, debris covered 17 choice acres of the Huff ranch. Guil, along with his wife and daughter, escaped. Ranger Dibble took Mrs. Huff and the child to safety at the Horsetail Ranger Station. By 4 a.m. the next morning, the Huff house was standing in 18 inches of water. By June 29, after heavy rains caused the dam to fill and overflow, the Huff house was floating in the lake, to be joined by the ranger station on July 3.

Ranger Dibble moved his family to Kelly, Wyoming, where he kept a wary eye on the slide dam. A man-made dam has a built-in spillway so that the waters cannot top the dam, erode, and breech it. The slide dam, made by nature, was not equipped with a spillway.

Engineers, geologists, and scientists came to the area to study the slide; they determined that the dam formed as a result of the slide was permanent and safe. Most of the local people accepted that decision and ceased worrying about a possible disaster, especially when the spring runoff in 1926 passed with no major problems.

The winter of 1927, however, was one of the most severe ever recorded in the state to that time. When spring arrived, the unusually deep snowpack melted quickly, aided by days of rain. On May 17, water began spilling over the low places of the dam. The Gros Ventre River was rising.

Ranger Dibble and Jack Ellis, along with some other men, were poling driftwood and floating debris away from lodging against the Kelly bridge and endangering the structure. Suddenly Ranger Dibble saw a hayrack—one that had been in the lake above the dam since 1925—floating down the river.

He and Ellis jumped into Dibble's Model T and drove toward the dam to assess the situation.

The International Pedigree Stage Stop Dog Sled Race

This is the largest dog sled race in the lower 48 states. A $100,000 purse attracts world class mushers to this 8 day event is usually held around the end of January. The race begins and ends in Jackson. The race travels from Jackson, through Dubois, Lander, Evanston, Bridger Valley, Kemmer, Alpine, Pinedale and back to Teton Village. www.wyomingstagestop.org

On the way, they were met by the main thrust of water and debris. The top 60 feet of the dam had given way under the pressure of the excess water.

Dibble and Ellis turned around and headed for Kelly to warn the residents of the impending danger. By the time they arrived, the people had only 15 minutes in which to flee to safety.

Despite the warning, Henry ("Milt") Kneedy refused to believe the water was coming, and would not permit his wife and foster son, Joe, to leave. Ranger Dibble tried to rescue little Joe, but he got away and ran back to his mother. Later, Joe was reportedly seen clinging to the top of a barn floating down the river. The Kneedy family died in the flood.

Through field glasses, a rancher watched May Lovejoy and her sister, Maude Smith, load their wagon with valuables and drive off, but the horse became frightened and raced out of control toward the oncoming water. A wall of water rolled the wagon over and over. May's body was never found. Maude's body was retrieved after the water subsided.

Max Edick and Clint Stevens were trying to save their livestock when the water came. Quickly, they climbed to the top of a small chicken coop. Though Clint managed to jump onto a passing hayrack, he did not survive. Max was swept into the swift water. He somehow managed to catch hold of a tree branch, and was later found alive.

By 4p.m. the water receded. Six lives had been lost in the tragedy. Along with the human lives lost, hundreds of domestic animals perished. Property damage was estimated at $500,000. The little town of Kelly was almost completely obliterated.

As a result of the flood, Kelly was not awarded the special recognition of becoming the county seat. That distinction was given, instead, to Jackson.

Lower Slide Lake

This lake was formed when the landslide dammed up the Gros Ventre River. Many of the trees that once grew along the river were submerged, and today the tops of several of these trees can be seen at the far side of the lake.

Lake trout, Snake River cutthroat, mountain white fish, Utah suckers, and Utah chubs inhabit the lake.

Upper Slide Lake, formed long before man roamed this area, has no connection with the Gros Ventre Slide disaster.

Trees On The Slide

Several of the trees at the base of the slide are growing at abnormal angles. These trees were swept downhill with their roots still intact in the soil. They came to rest in the position in which you see them today.

It is interesting that trees over 40 years of age succumbed to the shock of that traumatic transplanting, while the younger trees were able to adapt and continue growing.

In the crystal clear water of the lake, some trees can still be seen standing erect where they were transported by the slide more than half a century ago.

Trees found in the Gros Ventre area are lodgepole pine, Englemann spruce, subalpine fir, Douglas fir, Rocky Mountain juniper, and aspen.

Life On The Rocks

Pikas, the smallest members of the rabbit family, also known as coneys, range from approximately 6 to 8 inches in length. They are grayish brown in color. These small herbivores do not hibernate; instead, they store little piles of dried plants under the snow for use in winter. Pikas make their homes under the rocks that were transplanted in the slide. They can be heard "bleating" as they travel along their trails under the rocks.

Lichens are plants composed of two different organisms: microscopic green or blue-green algae and colorless fungal threads. Lichens grow on the surface of rocks. Their colors vary from black to gray, rust, green, and brown. These small plants are important because they break rocks down into small pockets of soil on which other plants will grow.

Article courtesy of National Forest Service

H The Gros Ventre Slide

About five miles east of Kelly on paved road that parallels river.

Before you lie the remnants of one of the largest earth movements in the world. On June 23, 1925, earth, rock and debris moved rapidly from an altitude of 9000 feet, across the valley bottom and up the slope of the red bluffs behind you. The action lasted only minutes but a river was dammed and the landscape changed.

H Jackson Lake Dam

Grand Teton National Park at Jackson Lake Dam.

Main sign:

Jackson Lake Dam, a vital link in the development of the water and land resources of the Upper Snake River Basin, was built and is operated by the Bureau of Reclamation, U. S. Dept. of the Interior. It was originally authorized for irrigation–some 1,100,000 acres of the fertile Snake River Valley–and for flood control along the Snake and lower Columbia Rivers. Outdoor recreation and fish and wildlife conservation have become important project benefits.

History sign:

The Reclamation Service first surveyed Jackson Lake in 1902-03, leading to construction in 1905-07 of a temporary pole-crib dam to store 200,000 acre-feet of water. It rotted and failed in July of 1910, and in 1911 a new concrete structure was begun to restore the vital water supply for the farmers on the Minidoka Project. An unending string of freight wagons hauled cement from the railhead at Ashton, Idaho, over 90 miles away, often through deep snow and at temperatures down to 50 below zero. The 70-foot high structure, completed in 1916, raised the maximum lake elevation 17 feet, and increased the storage capacity to 847,000 acre-feet.

17 *No services*

H Cunningham Cabin

Just south of Moran Junction on U.S. Highway 26/89/191

With a sod roof and a covered walkway called a dogtrot connecting these two log cabins, this historic residence dates back to 1890. It was originally built by Pierce Cunningham when he and his wife Margaret came into the valley to raise cattle.

18 *Gas, Food, Lodging*

T Tie Hack Memorial

18 miles northwest of Dubois on U.S. Highway 26/287.

Dubois has long been connected with the timber industry. Beginning in 1914, the Wyoming Tie and Timber Company ran tie-cutting operations near Dubois, supplying ties to support the CB&Q railroad. With the combined efforts of the Wyoming Recreation Commission, the Wyoming Highway Department and the US Forest Service, a memorial dedicated to the hardy tie hacks was built.

Source: Dubois Chamber of Commerce brochure

H Tie Hack Monument

18 miles northwest of Dubois on U.S. Highway 26/287.

Erected to perpetuation of the memory of the hardy woods and river men who made and delivered the cross ties for building and maintenance of the Chicago and North Western Railway in this western country.

H The Hack Boss

On U.S. Highway 287/89 between Moran Junction and Dubois

Tie cutting on the Wind River started in 1914. Martin Olson became foreman of all woods operations in 1916. Ricker Van Metre, of Chicago, formed the Wyoming Tie and Timber Company in 1926 and hired Martin Olson as Woods Boss.

Martin, a Norwegian, was a veteran tie hack of Wyoming's pine forest. He started with a crew of 20 men who turned out 100,000 ties his first year as foreman. The crew grew each year, reinforced by young, woodswise immigrants from Norway, Sweden and other European countries, until 100 hacks were in the woods.

Martin Olson was held in respect. He had a way of getting the best from any man. He was boss, also a leader. He worked with, cajoled, humored, mothered or drove any hack that got out of line. Martin's ability as Woods Boss was measured by the number of ties out and delivered to the railhead at Riverton, Wyoming.

After supervising tie hacks and the drives for 31 years, Olson retired in 1947, when the Wyoming Tie and Timber Company was sold to the J. N. (Bud) Fisher Tie and Timber Company. The change of ownership brought new ideas and methods to the timber industry, marking the end of the tie hack era.

Lydia Olson, widow of Martin Olson, furnished the photographs and many of the historical facts presented here at the Tie Hack Memorial.

H The Cross-Tie

On U.S. Highway 287/26 between Moran Junction and Dubois

The tall, slightly tapered lodgepole pine is ideal for a cross-tie. The tie hack chose his tree and felled it with a double-bitted ax. Using the same tool, he walked the log from end to end cutting a series of parallel slashes on each side of the log. The slightest miscalculation could mean the loss of a toe or foot. Retracing his steps, he hewed the two side faces smooth with the broad ax. The faces were exactly 7 inches apart and so smooth that not even a splinter could be found with the bare hand.

The tie hack then traded his ax for a peeler and removed the bark from the two rounded sides. The final operation was to cut the peeled and hacked log into the 8 foot sections required by the railroad.

Each tie hack owned and cared for his own equipment which cost him his first 10 days of work.

Cross-ties were in demand by the Chicago and Northwestern Railroad as it spanned Wyoming. The Wyoming Tie and Timber Company was formed in 1916 in Riverton to supply the ties—it took 2,500 ties for a mile of track.

The main center of tie production was the lodgepole pine forest that surrounds you. Three to five ties, eight feet in length, were hewn from the clear, limb-free trunks.

Wyoming was undeveloped country with few roads. Water was the most economical method of moving the ties from forest to the railhead at Riverton.

H Togwotee Pass

U.S. Highway 287/26 between Moran Junction and Dubois

Captain William Jones, Army Corps of Engineers, named Togwotee Pass in 1873 in honor of his Shoshone Indian guide. Togwotee (pronounced toe-go-tee) was a Sheepeater Indian who aligned himself with Chief Washakie. Jones' mission was to find passage to Yellowstone National Park from the Wind River-Bighorn watersheds.

H Breccia Cliffs

U.S. Highway 287/26 between Moran Junction and Dubois

Breccia Cliffs—a remnant of volcanic activity 50 million years ago. Composed of angular fragments of lava cemented together after being torn from a volcanic crater during a massive explosion.

Scoured by glacial ice eons ago, its present physical form is being sculptured by wind and water.

H Union Pass

On U.S. Highway 267/26 between Moran Junction and Dubois

Jim Bridger knew this pass as the "Triple Divide" – a point forming headwaters of three different continental drainage basins. One stream eventually feeds into the Green River, which in turn drains into the Colorado, and finally the Pacific Ocean in Southern California. Another feeds the Snake River, adding to the Columbia which heads for the Northwestern Pacific. The third stream drains into the Wind River, which feeds the Missouri, then the Mississippi, and ends up in the Gulf of Mexico.

Captain William F. Reynolds, of the Army Corps of Engineers, named the pass for the Union Army. He thought it was the center of the continent. Reynolds was on an 1860 mission for the War Department to find an immigration route from Fort Laramie to the source of the Yellowstone River.

H Washaki Wilderness

On U.S. Highway. 287/26 between Moran Junction and Dubois

These high mountains are snowclad most of the year and only a brief cool summer. Few areas in the USA are more spectacular. Geologically, the formations are new. The large areas of exposed rock are interspersed with mountain meadows and mantles of unbroken forests.

H Tie Hack Interpretive Display

About 17 miles northwest of Dubois on U.S. Highway 26/287

Lower Level

Plaque #1:

Rough, tough, sinewy men, mostly of Scandinavian origin, whose physical strength was nearly a religion. The millions of cross ties they hacked out of the pine forests kept the railroad running through the West.

The tie hack was a professional, hewing ties to the exact 7 inches on a side demanded by the tie inspector. For years he was paid 10 cents a tie up to $3.00 for his dawn to dusk day. Board and room cost about 1.50 a day.

Mostly bachelors, they lived in scattered cabins or tie camps and ate hearty meals at a common boarding house. Entertainment was simple and spontaneous. A few notes on a "squeeze box' ' might start an evening of dancing, with hob nailed boots scarring the rough wooden floors. The spring tie drive down the Wind River usually ended with one big party in town with enough boozing and brawling to last them another year back in the woods.

These hard-working, hard-drinking, hard-fighting men created an image that remains today only in tie hack legend. By the end of World War II, modern tools and methods brought an end to an era that produced the proud breed of mighty men—the tie hack.

Plaque #2
The Cross-Tie

Here are the tools of his trade:

Double-Bit Ax—with two sharp edges

Broad Ax—an 8 pounder with a broad 12-inch long blade, looks like an executioner's ax!

Peeler—a slightly curved dull blade to slip easily under the bark

Crosscut Saw—designed to cut across the grain of the wood

Peavey—a stout spiked lever used to roll logs

Cant Hook—a toothed lever used to drag or turn logs

Pickaroon—a pike pole with a sharp steel point on one side and a curved hook on the other—used to guide floating logs.

They also carried a sharpening file and a jug of kerosene to clean pitch off their equipment.

Plaque #3

Cross-ties were in demand by the Chicago and Northwestern Railroad as it spanned Wyoming. The Wyoming Tie and Timber Company was formed in 1916 in Riverton to supply the ties—it took 2,500 ties for a mile of track.

The main center of tie production was the lodgepole pine forest that surrounds you. Three to five ties, eight feet in length, were hewn from the clear, limb-free trunks.

Wyoming was undeveloped country with few roads. Water was the most economical method of moving the ties from forest to the railhead at Riverton.

Middle Level

Section #1
Flumes

A cut, shaped and peeled tie weighs 120 pounds. Each tie hack was responsible for shouldering his own ties and carrying them to a decking area located by one of the narrow roads through the forest.

The hacks marked one end of the tie with his own symbol—a letter or number, and was paid by the number of ties marked with his symbol.

When winter snows arrived, horse drawn bobsleds moved the ties to a banking area next to a dammed up pond. A bobsled loaded with 120 ties weighed 7 tons and was pulled by two horses.

When the spring thaws came, tie hacks dumped their ties into the ponds on smaller creeks and fed them into flumes for the journey to the Wind River.

Flumes are great V-shaped wooden troughs built to float ties down to the main river—bypassing the rock-choked mountain streams.

Dams were built on the streams to impound enough water to carry the ties down the flumes. When the spring floods came in May or June, tie hacks fed the ties into the flumes for their downward journey.

A section of the Canyon Creek flume was constructed with a 41 degree grade, and one year they tried to slide the ties down it without water. This dry fluming attempt failed when the friction of the ties shooting down the trough set fire to the flume.

This portion of the Warm Springs Flume was trestled and guyed with steel cables to sheer rock walls. Ties traveling this flume emptied into the Warm Springs Dam. Notice the catwalk used by drivers to prod the ties on their way down the flume.

Part of the famous Warm Springs flume follows the creek underground through a water curved arch. The flume is suspended inside the arch by steel cables anchored in the roof. The last tie to float this flume was in 1942.

The smaller flume on the left brought the ties from the forest, the flume on the right transported ties to the Wind River.

Section #2
Booms

Barricades across the stream held the ties together in what is called a log boom. When the danger of spring floods had passed, the trap was sprung and the tie drive was on.

Section #3
The Tie Drive

It took an experienced Woods Boss to choose exactly the right time to start the drive. Too early, and the spring floods scattered the ties on the banks. Too late, and there wasn't enough water.

Martin Olson usually picked mid-July to put his half a hundred men on the river with peaveys and pike poles to steer a half million ties 100 miles down stream to Riverton.

A tie-drive looked like a river full of giant shoestring potatoes tumbling and rolling along with ant-like men running over the sea of ties, loosening a tie here or unjamming a pile-up there.

The drivers, half in and half out of the water, punched holes in their hobnailed boots to let the water out as fast as it ran in.

A drive lasted about 30 days, with the largest one having 700,000 ties. In the 31 year history of the Wind River drives, over 10 million ties floated to Riverton. The final drive in 1946 contained only machine sawn ties. The colorful tie hack and his river drives were history

Massive jams occasionally filled the river from bank to bank with tangled piles of ties. A good tie driver could find the 'key" tie to "spring" the jam.

Section #4
The Tie Hack Boss

The peak year was 1927 when 700,000 ties were driven down the Wind River to Riverton. The Wyoming T and T Company harvested 10 million railroad cross-ties under Olson's supervision and in cooperation with the Forest Service's timber management plan.

After supervising tie hacks and tie drives for 31 years, Martin Olson retired in 1947, when the Wyoming Tie and Timber Company was sold to the J. N. (Bud) Fisher Tie and Timber Company. The change of ownership brought new ideas and methods to the timber industry, marking the end of the tie-hack era.

Wyoming Tidbits

According to one source, two words from the Delaware Indians combine to make "Wyoming": Mecheweami-ing, "a land of mountains and valleys". Another source claims the Algonquin word for "large prairie place" is 'wyoming'.

H Union Pass Interpretive Plaques

About 8 miles west of Dubois, Wyoming, on U.S. Highway 287/26 and 15 miles south on Union Pass Road.

Union Pass

At this pass-midst a maze of mountain ranges and water courses which had sometimes baffled and repulsed them-aboriginal hunters, mountain men, fur traders and far-ranging explorers have, each in his time, found the key to a geographic conundrum. For them that conundrum had been a far more perplexing problem than such an ordinary task as negotiating the crossing, however torturous, of an unexplored pass occurring along the uncomplicated divide of an unconnected mountain chain.

Hereabouts the Continental Divide is a tricky, triple phenomenon wherein the unguided seeker of a crossing might find the right approach and still arrive at the wrong ending. In North America there are seven river systems that can be cited as truly continental in scope but only in this vicinity and at one other place do as many as three of them head against a common divide. Indians called this region the Land of Many Rivers and mountain men named the pass Union, thereby both—once again-proving themselves gifted practitioners of nomenclature.

Union Pass is surrounded by an extensive, rolling, mountain-top terrain wherein elevations vary between nine and ten thousand feet and interspersed water courses deceptively twist and turn as if undetermined betwixt an Atlantic or a Pacific destination. This mountain expanse might be visualized as a rounded hub in the center of which, like an axle's spindle, fits the pass. Out from this hub radiate three spokes, each one climbing and broadening into mighty mountain ranges-southeasterly the Wind Rivers, southwesterly the Gros Ventres and northerly, extending far into Montana, the Absarokas.

The Rendezvous

Twelve thousand foot mountain plateaus dominating this view of Green River and Snake River headwaters seemingly provide a southwesterly buttress for loftier peaks forming the core of the Wind River Range. Beyond them it is 43 miles from Union Pass to where confluence of the Green and its Horse Creek tributary marks the most famed of several "rendezvous" grounds relating to that epoch in American history known as the Rocky Mountain Fur Trade.

"Rendezvous", defined as a trade fair in wilderness surroundings, was held in diverse locations throughout the Central Rocky Mountain region. It required spacious, grassy environs for grazing thousands of horses, raising hundreds of trapper and Indian lodges and for horse races and other spectacles exuberantly staged by mountain men and Indians then relaxed from vigilance against dangers which otherwise permitted no unguarded carrousels. A favorite area for "rendezvous" was along the Green, recognized for producing the primest beaver peltry, and for conveniently straddling the South Pass logistic route utilized for transport of trade goods and furs between St. Louis and the mountains. On the Green the finest "rendezvous" grounds—rendered especially famous through Alfred Jacob Miller's paintings of the 1837 scene—were those at Horse Creek.

Depending on arrival of St. Louis supply caravans, 'rendezvous" usually extended through early July. At the close of revels—leaving many mountain men deeply in debt—there remained up to two months before prime furs signaled the start of fall hunting. The intervening time was pleasantly occupied in traveling and exploring high mountain terrain; then trails around Union Pass were furrowed by Indian travois only to be leveled again by the beating hoofs of the trapper's pack trains.

Cultural Heritage

High in mountains where the natural environment changes swiftly, eroding or burying its past, for how long a time can vestiges of man's frailer achievements withstand obliteration? No matter!, for here man has brought or developed cultures which are already heritages— treasured in memory if lost in substance.

Presented is a natural scene, a park surrounded by forest and parted by a virgin stream. But it is crossed by a road and also by a zigzag fence of rotting logs. Reconnaissance might reveal a campsite of prehistoric aborigines or discover a beaver trap once the property of a mountain man. Thus, is a cultural environment incorporated with the natural one.

Indians hunted these environs far into historic time. From exits of Union Pass, tribal trails branch in all directions. The road mentioned above, elsewhere explained, might cover ruts made by travois, Camps of mountain tribes, their chipping grounds, drivelines and animal traps exist throughout the area. Earliest among far western fur traders came this way—possibly Colter in 1807, certainly Astorians under Hunt in 1811. Mountain men camped here, Jim Bridger surely during the 1820s and, much later, guiding Captain Raynolds in 1860. Others, whose camping grounds may some day he ascertained, include: Bonneville, soldier, explorer, fur trader, enigma-recording carefully in 1833; Gannett, of the 1870's Geologic Survey with Yount his hunter-packer; Togwotee, a Shoshone Sheep Eater; Wister, famous author; Bliss, horse thief; Anderson, precursory forester; and, not far distant, Sheridan, a general and Arthur, a President of the United States.

The zigzag fence of rotting logs is a vestige of a continuing culture. Pastoral in nature it relates to the 1920 decade when cattlemen, under U.S. Forest Service permit, fenced rich grasslands to hold beef herds, fattening for the market.

Wyoming Tidbits

An oddity in Wyoming weather is the "chinook", a warm, moist wind that melts snow and allows game to reach grass.

Fauna of Union Pass

Before primitive man discovered this pass between rich hunting grounds native ungulates grazed here during summers, migrating to the river valleys and plains for winters. These high plateaus and mountain meadows then harboured thousands of bison.

Though bison are gone, hundreds of elk (wapiti), mule deer and pronghorn antelope summer on Union Pass and in the near vicinity. Bighorn sheep live the year-round on high peaks and plateaus, venturing occasionally to timbered slopes and mountain meadows, Black hear are much in evidence and Lord Grizzly-"Old Ephraim" to mountain men and, in Indian lore, sometimes "Our Brother"-still occasionally roams the nearby forests and crags. Only the Shiras moose had not yet arrived in the days of mountain men, having only migrated this far south since about 1870.

Around 1900 the canine teeth of bull elk were worth their weight in gold. Northwestern Wyoming, isolated midst an abundance of game, was a favorite base of operations for notorious tusk hunters until early day game wardens, forest rangers and private citizens combined to drive the outlaws out.

Except for loss of bison and gain of moose, native fauna is much the same as it was in the days of fur trade. Beaver and trout still inhabit streams. Occasionally an otter may be seen cavorting along stream banks and mink are common to such environs. Pine Martin their peltry prized next to Siberian Sable and much sought by a later generation of mountain men, porcupines and red squirrels inhabit coniferous forests. Marmots and ground squirrels are found in rocky ledges and grassy meadows along with many lesser four-footed denizens. At Union Pass the prehistoric hunter or the most recent recreationist might have seen:

"A golden eagle in the sky and 'Ole Coyote' on the sly."

and thought:

"All snowshoe hares and the little blue grouse had better peel an eye."

Resources—Ownership—Exploitation—Administration

Aesthetic and economic resources surround Union Pass, extending far to the west, north and southwest. These include grass, browse and forest plus animals living thereby and therein. Ownership of lands and vegetation repose in the nation's people; Wyoming's citizens own the wild animals; livestock, seasonally pastured, are privately owned.

Separate laws enacted in 1869 by Wyoming's first Territorial Assembly pertained to branding livestock and protecting wildlife. An incipient but immediately popularized livestock industry received credit for the first. But sponsors of the second, even following its augmentation in 1870 by a rudimentary wildlife agency, went, in that era of materialism, unnoticed. Few territorial fields of endeavor possessed sufficient background for practitioners to appreciate benefits stemming from conservation. Only the fur trade—flourishing in 1826, impoverished by 1840—had produced a second generation cognizant of dangers inherent in ruthless exploitation. Throughout such environs as Union Pass its diminished members trapped and hunted, sometimes outfitting (guide service, pack trains, supplies) clients attracted to the Territory by both its mountain wildernesses and continuing bonanza in open range livestock operations. From such relationships emerged types of outfitting and mountain valley ranching operations predisposed to conservation practices.

Spearheading a long overdue national conservation movement, Theodore Roosevelt found among such ranchers and outfitters men who played leading roles in organizing the first national forests out of the unwieldy Yellowstone Timberland Reserve and in developing an administrative structure adopted by the subsequent U.S. Forest Service.

Searching for complementary talents the Forest Service and the Wyoming Game and Fish Commission have both recruited personnel experienced in ranching and outfitting as well as the graduates of professional schools. Subject—as are all human efforts—to occasional errors, the administrators of Union Pass surroundings have successfully protected and enhanced its natural environment.

Flora At Union Pass

Union Pass the cultural site must first have been Union Pass the natural site. As a natural site it commenced to produce vegetation and was afterwards inhabited by animals before it ever became attractive to man—for any purpose other than the thrill of exploration.

Development of present flora at Union Pass is an evolvement of recent time. The connection between conspicuous boulders and glaciers lately covering the area is mentioned elsewhere, but lichens still thriving grew on those boulders before all local ice had melted. Other flora, needing more favorable conditions, probably didn't attain a flourishing status until following the altithermal period causing cessation of glaciers—about 7,000 years ago.

The forest's development into a climax, a spruce-fir culmination, has been slowed by wildfires. But forest cover is now expanding through man's protective measures plus continuing evolution of soils as in the filling of ponds and marshes from sedimentation and organic matter.

Fortunately, Union Pass is in a park, not in the forest. From its view the foreground is covered on the drier, higher area by sagebrush, bunchgrasses and forbs favoring semi-arid conditions; low grounds support grassland communities, patches of willows and sedge meadows bordering ponds. Common plants are big sage brush, shrubby cinquefoil, Idaho fescue, slender wheat grass, Indian paintbrush and lupine along the streams grow willows, sedges, rushes, little red elephant, march marigold and globe mallow.

Southeast—toward the Wind River Range—Engleman Spruce-subalpine fir growth is in wetter areas and whitebark pine along hilltops and ridges. To the west—forward—is a younger growth of Engleman Spruce and lodgepole pine fringing expanding forests while within older lodgepole stands are in various stages of transition to the spruce-fir climax. Understory plants are grouse whortle berry, lupine, sedges and grasses.

The Ramshorn

Jutting like the topsail of a ship from beyond the apparent horizon, a tip of the Ramshorn is seen. It serves to remind the viewer of the Absarokas, a cragged mountain range broader and longer than the Wind Rivers but slightly less elevated. These mountains take their name from Indians identified as Crows or Ravens in the Journals of Lewis and Clark. Fur traders adopting that appellation passed it along to subsequent generations excepting only Absarokas themselves who, echoing forefathers, Anglicize their name to Bird People.

Tip rather than peak is used advisedly; there are peaks in the Absarokas but they are not a dominant feature of that range. Originating in a typical anticlinal fold, the Absarokas have been capped by lava strata measuring to thousands of feet, a geological evolvement known as a volcanic pile. Accordingly, their summits tend to be flat although simultaneous erosion throughout periods of flowing lava prohibited the forming of an all-encompassing tableland. Continued erosion has resulted in a range marked by deep canyons, precipitous ridges, notched passes and escarpment delimited plateaus. Summits rising above a plateau's general elevation are composed of harder materials and sometimes indicate proximity of a former lava fissure. The Ramshorn is one such plateau but its name derives from its escarpment-3,000 feet of cliffs and talus slopes, curving for miles around its southwestern flank like the horn of a mountain ram.

It is appropriate that this mountain be named Ramshorn. The Absarokas offer habitat to a variety and an abundance of wildlife but escarpments and plateaus, producing grass and browse swept free of snow by winter gales, make ideal mountain sheep ranges. Trails established by sheep-eating Shoshones, now followed by other wilderness enthusiasts, attest to mankind's fascination with the wild sheep of the Absarokas.

Road Through A Pass

A road, component of a cultural environment, is the most noticeable feature of this otherwise natural landscape. In present form it is not old, not a pioneer route hacked by frontiersmen. Based and graded to support rapid haulage of ponderous loads of logs, this road was built by specialists operating specialized machines. It is a product of 20th century technological culture.

A road of a sort is an ancient and, originally, a natural feature at Union Pass. Wild animals, some camels, indigenous horses, mammoths now extinct, found this passageway and, following easiest grades during seasonal migrations, trod out—wide in places as a road—a trail, Perhaps 10,000 years ago progenitors of Nimrod trailed these animals around the edges of a receding glacier and on through Union Pass—leaving along that route its first traces of human culture. Around 1700 A.D. Shoshones, descendants or replacements of the earliest hunters, acquired the horse and, among other impacts made by them on the natural environment, the dragging ends of their travois poles widened and deepened this road.

Chronological stages in the Union Pass cultural environment have been: aboriginal, for trade, explorations and geological surveys, outfitting (recreational industry) and ranching, and management of natural resources—including forestry. Forestry, defined as "cultivating, maintaining, and developing forests", implying harvesting, came last owing to local patterns of development. Although Wyoming was a bellwether in Theodore Roosevelt's early conservation movement, pressing local concern regarding new national forests centered on livestock grazing and wildlife and watershed protection—forestry waited. Substantial timber harvesting, a tie hack era, only began after 1900; upgrading a Union Pass wagon road to high speed hauling standards was a mid-century project.

Wind River Range

Postulating the traverse of the Continental Divide the eye climbs to Union Peak, some four airline miles but nearer six by that tortuous route. At 11,491 feet Union Peak is a nondescript rise that draws attention only because it is the final timberline topping elevation on the northwestern end of the Wind River Range. Appearing slightly behind and more to the right, but actually seven miles further along the traverse of the divide, is Three Waters Mountain. That is as far into the Wind Rivers as can be seen from Union Pass. However, if vision could continue to follow the southeasterly bearing of the divide, the viewer might estimate 20 and 30 miles to where nearer 13,804 foot Gannett Peak and farther 13,745 foot Fremont Peak mark the scope of the heart of that range.

The Wind River Range is the highest mountain mass in Wyoming. Basically it is a broad uplift which originated about 60 million years ago during a period of "mountain building" called the Laramide Orogeny. The core of the range reveals Precambrian crystalline rocks, and Paleozoic and Mesozoic sedimentary rocks are upturned on the flanks. The Wind River Range, although south of continental ice caps, was extensively glaciated during the Pleistocene epoch and such sizable lakes as Newfork, Boulder, Fremont, Bull, Green River and Dinwoody, filling canyons and valleys along its widespread flanks, are dammed behind moraines. Existent glaciers in the highest parts of the Wind Rivers are small by comparison, yet they are often cited as the largest ice fields within the contiguous states of the Union.

Boulders strewing Union Pass environs are surface evidence that this northern margin of the range was subdued, by spreading glaciers which have left a blanket of till and moraine material.

Three Waters Mountain

Southeast rises a mountain given a lyrical name, one such as Indians or mountain men discovering a geographical phenomenon might have chosen. Midway of its four-mile long crest is the key point, one of only two in North America, where as many as three of the continents seven major watersheds interlock.

Here a raindrop splits into thirds, the three tiny driblets destined to wend their separate ways along continuously diverging channels to the oceans of the world. One driblet arrives in the Gulf of Mexico, 3,000 miles distant by way of Jakeys Fork, Wind River, Bighorn, Yellowstone, Missouri, and Mississippi; another joins currents running 1,400 miles to the Pacific through Fish Creek, the Gros Ventre, Snake and Columbia; the final one descends more than 1,300 miles to the Gulf of California; via Roaring Fork, Green River and the Colorado.

Seemingly neither Indians nor fur trappers named this mountain. Locally it has been called Triple Divide Peak, but only a bench mark (11,642 ft.) and lines denoting a junction of divides point to it on the Geological Survey's map of 1906. The Survey's 1968 map (correcting the B.M. to 11,675 ft.) officially names this long crest projecting in a northwesterly descent from the 13,800 foot glacier swathed peaks at the heart of the Wind River Range—Three Waters Mountain. That latter day cartographer, possessing the imagination and finding the inspiration to contrive this name, thus proved himself a worthy disciple of Ferdinand Vandeveer Hayden and his competent assistants who were precursors and, in 1879, helpers in the founding of the United States Geological Survey.

H Union Pass

About 8 miles west of Dubois on U.S. Highway 26/287

Westbound Astorians led by Wilson Price Hunt in September, 1811, passed through Dubois region, over Union Pass, and on to the mouth of the Columbia River to explore a line of communication and to locate sites for fur trading posts across the continent for John Jacob Astor. In the party were Mackenzie, Crooks, Miller, McClellan, Reed, 11 hunters, interpreters and guides; 45 Canadian engages, an Indian woman and her 2 children.

H Togwotee Pass/Continental Divide

U.S. Highway 26/287 at Togwotee Pass between Moran Junction and Dubois.

Named in 1873 by Captain W. A. Jones honoring his Shoshone Indian guide, Togwotee. Elevation 9,658 feet, Shoshone and Teton National Forests

Interpretive Signs

Togwotee Pass

Blackfoot, Crow and Shoshone Indian hunting parties, following the trail of elk, deer and buffalo, made the first human trail through this pass. Next came such courageous mountainmen as John Colter, Jim Bridger, Joe Meeker and Kit Carson who courted death in the search for prime beaver pelts.

Capt. Jones, Corps of Engineers, U.S. Army was on reconnaissance for a wagon road across these mountains when he was guided by Togwotee. In 1898, the army built the first wagon road over Togwotee to assist troop movements protecting the westward flow of pioneers. The first auto road was constructed in 1922. TOGWOTEE (pronounced toe-go-tee) means Lance Thrower in Shoshone.

Parting of the Waters

Here, on the Continental Divide, the course of mighty rivers is decided. Moisture from melting snow and summer showers filters into the soil, later emerging as small streams which form the rivers. The Wind and Missouri Rivers to the East, the Snake and Columbia to the West.

Two Ocean Creek, not far from here, was so named because its waters cascade both east and west from the top of the Divide watershed to finally reach both Atlantic and Pacific Oceans.

Moving Mountains

Natural forces sculptured the scene before you over 15,000 years ago. Glaciers gouged out the huge valleys from massive layers of lava. The Breccia (bretch-yuh) cliffs are composed of angular pieces of rock cemented together with finer materials. The ground you stand on constantly changes as nature continues to shape it. Wind tears at the thin soil. Rains attacks and erodes the bare ground. In such ways "mountains are moved." Where possible man seeks to slow this process slowing the force of water with dams, and maintaining a protective cover of vetetation in the form of grass or timber.

H The Old Blackrock Station

U.S. Highway 26/287 east of Moran Junction at Teton National Forest Ranger Station.

In days gone-by, this log cabin served as the Ranger's Office for the Buffalo District of the Teton National Forest, located 35 miles north of the town of Jackson. The building brings back some of the historic flavor of the Jackson Hole Country. The furnishings are typical of a District Forest Ranger's Office in the early days. This small rustic cabin was sufficient to meet the needs of the hardy Forest Rangers of that era. Their primary duties of forest protection and law enforcement kept them in the woods most of the time. Simple as it was the cabin was a welcome sight to the Ranger, especially during the long cold winter months. Please look inside for a brief glimpse into the past.

C Grand Teton Park RV Resort

17800 E. U.S. Highway 287, six miles east of Moran. 733-1980 or 800-563-6469. www.yellowstonerv.com

The Grand Teton Park RV Resort is a year-round recreation resort conveniently located near Yellowstone Park and Grand Teton National Park. This spacious Resort offers nearly every amenity possible for camping enjoyment. There are pull-through RV sites including hookups for all sizes of vehicles. Camping cabins, Teepee village, and tent sites complete the selection. There is a heated pool and hot tub for you to enjoy, playground, recreation room with pool table and video arcade, Chuckwagon dinners, and trail rides. Conveniences also include a fully stocked grocery store, gas station, firewood, immaculate showers and restrooms, laundries, RV supplies, and fishing tackle and hunting or fishing licenses. You can also rent a snowmobile or arrange a trip on the Snake River. All this and great views.

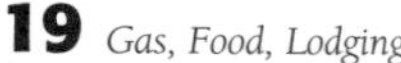

19 *Gas, Food, Lodging*

Dubois

Pop. 1,000, Elev. 6,917

At the head of the Absaroka and Wind River Mountains, and surrounded by the varigated Badlands, is the town of Dubois. A peaceful yet bustling hamlet surrounded by many natural wonders, Dubois was not always the calm, pastoral place it has become. Situated in the upper valley of the Wind River, a gathering place for wildlife, the area of Dubois was once a battleground for Crow, Shoshone, and Blackfeet Indians, disputing hunting rights. In 1811, the Astorians passed through, and not far behind were trappers Jim Bridger, Kit Carson, and others looking for beaver and game.

The most famous Indian battle was the Crowheart Butte Battle of 1866. That same year, the first homesteaders arrived and settled just up the river. As more people arrived, a saloon opened up, and the town grew around it. Finally, in 1886, the community applied for a post office, but postal officials considered the name they wanted (Never Sweat, for the ease of life there) too improper. Instead, they proposed naming the town after Idaho Senator Dubois, who was a proponent of homesteader rights. The townsfolk found this agreeable, and the name stuck.

In many ways, Dubois hasn't changed much since then. You can still spot ranch folk tying their horses to a rail on the main street, Rams Horn, which has a wooden sidewalk. Cattle drives and wildlife can also be seen in the middle of town. Locals can't feel too far removed from nature with bears and moose wandering into their backyards.

Downtown Dubois

T National Bighorn Sheep Interpretive Center

907 W. Ramshorn in Dubois. 455-3429 or 888-209-2795. www.bighorn.org.

The Center is devoted to educating the public about a variety of sheep living in the nearby Habitat area; including desert bighorn, Rocky Mountain Bighorn, stone sheep, and Dall sheep. The central exhibit, "Sheep Mountain" is as the name suggests; a 16 foot tall mountain with mounted sheep. Surrounding scenes and hands-on exhibits show and teach how the sheep live in their rugged environment.During the winter the Center hosts wildlife tours of the nearby Whisky Basin Habitat Area.Open year round. Summer hours (Memorial Day weekend through Labor Day weekend) are daily 9 a.m. to 8 p.m. Call for winter hours.

TV Fitzpatrick Wilderness Area

On U.S. Highway 26/287 between Moran Junction and Dubois

Designated in October of 1976 and named for Tom Fitzpatrick, a mountain man and partner of Jim Bridger, the Fitzpatrick Wilderness Area contains approximately 200,000 acres. Most of the area was previously classified as the Glacier Primitive Area and is known for its numerous glaciers and mountain peaks. The Fitzpatrick covers the northern half of the Wind River Mountains on the east side of the Continental Divide and is bordered on the west by the Bridger Wilderness. The Wind River Indian Reservation lies to the east. The Fitzpatrick is an area of immeasurable beauty and grandeur. The topography is extremely rugged, carved out of granite and limestone by the action of glaciers and glacial streams. There are 44 active glaciers covering approximately 7,760 acres.

Two of the largest glaciers in the Continental United States, the Dinwoody Glacier at the foot of Gannett Peak and Bull Lake Glacier at the base of Fremont Peak, are also found here which cover more than 15 square miles. Gannett Peak, 13,800 feet is the highest point in Wyoming and is in the Fitzpatrick, along with several other peaks over 13,000 feet. Accessible only by foot or horseback on established National Forest Trails.

Source: Dubois Chamber of Commerce brochure.

T Wind River Historical Center

909 W. Ramshorn in Dubois. 455-2284. www.windriverhistory.org/

The museum presents the history of Native Americans and settlers of the area. It houses a range of exhibits, from those depicting the Sheepeater Indians to various cultural artifacts to displays on ranch life, natural history, and the Tie Hacks. Tie hacks were men who cut trees around Dubois for 10 million railroad ties in the years

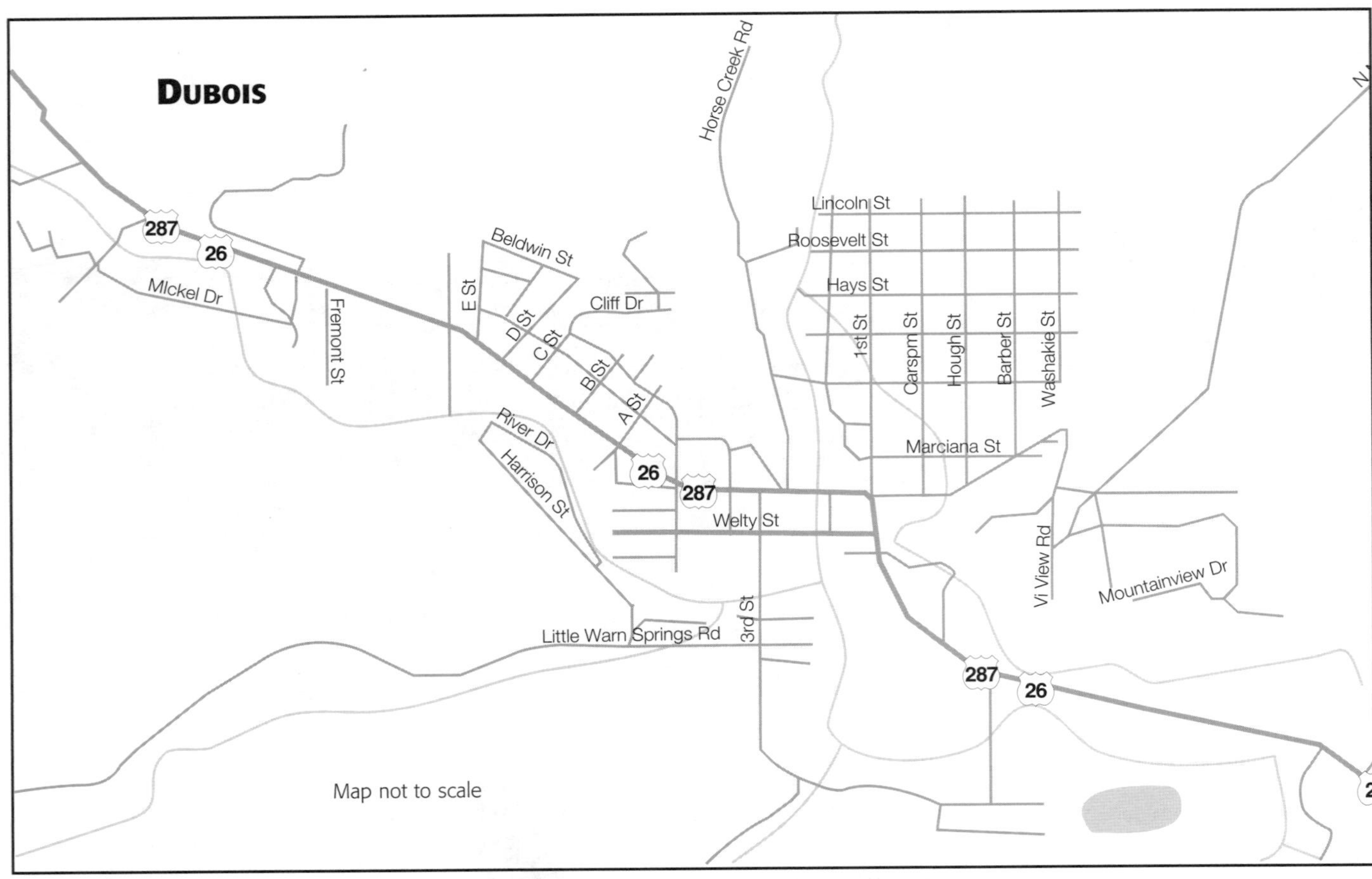

between 1914 and 1946. Artifacts from this logging era and mementos from the lumberjack's gambling houses are also shown.

Outside the museum are five historic log cabins, and the upstairs hosts the Headwaters Community Arts and Conference Center, showing the artwork of local artists.The museum is open year round. Call for hours.

T Headwaters Community Arts and Conference Center

Downtown Dubois. 455-2687

Built in 1995, the 17,000 sq. foot facility is for the use of the Dubois community and to encourage conventions, seminars and symposiums to come to Dubois. With one large conference room (48' x 100') built to divide into three meeting rooms which will hold 30-100 people each or accommodate 350-600 when left open. The building is also home of the Wind River Valley Artists' Build Art Gallery with a permanent art collection of over 60 original works of art. Source: Dubois Chamber of Commerce brochure.

T Dubois Fish Hatchery

South of U.S. Highways 26/287, five miles east of Dubois.

Situated at the base of the Whiskey Mountain bighorn sheep winter range on the east slope of the Wind River Mountains, the state of Wyoming maintains a fish hatchery. A fish rearing station was in use at this location in the 1930s, this was abandoned in 1937, and the present hatchery replaced it in 1940. In 1944 it was further expanded with 44 cement "raceways" providing outdoor homes for developing fish. Two natural springs, together, supply more than a million gallons of water a day to the hatchery. The springs are located 1 1/4 miles from the hatchery on Jakey's Fork Creek, and numerous land grants, easements and long-term leases were procured by the Wyoming Game and Fish commission in order to pipe the water to the hatchery facility farther down the canyon. Due to its location, the Dubois hatchery serves an extremely important function by caring for eggs taken from the cutthroat (native) spawning operation each spring at Lake of the Woods in the Union Pass area, 30 miles southwest of Dubois. This spawning operation furnishes a major portion of the cutthroat eggs for the entire state of Wyoming. The Dubois hatchery also cares for rainbow, golden, brook and brown trout. Visitors are welcome.
Source: Dubois Chamber of Commerce brochure.

T Tie Flumes and Old Campsites

18 miles northwest of Dubois on U.S. Highway 26/287 in vicinity of Tie Hack Memorial

Many old logging camps stand as mute testimony to the tie-hacking days. Little remains of the logging camps due to weathering of the old buildings. However, may artifacts of the tie cutting days are still to be found at the old sites. The oldest camps were established in 1914. Up until 1913, colorless glass was manufactured with an impurity that resulted in its turning purple after years of exposure to sunlights. The earliest tie camps can be dated by fragments of glass that have turned purple from 90 years of exposure to the sun on the trash heaps near the camps. Other artifacts to be found in the tie camps are cross-cut saws as they are still occasionally used. But, the broad axe has long since passed from use and become an antique. Source: Dubois Chamber of Commerce brochure.

T Union Pass Historical Site

15 miles south on Union Pass Road, about eight miles south of Dubois on U.S. Highway 26/287.

The road on Union Pass is very scenic. The Union Pass monument includes a history and monument of Three Waters Mountain (Triple Divide Peak); Ramshorn Peak, Union Peak, Roaring Fork Watershed Vista, Cattleman's Drift Fence, Bacon Ridge and logging roads. There is also a story of Aboriginal use, the explorers and the mountain men.

T Wind River Lake-Brooks Lake

Just west of Togwotee Pass north of U.S. Highway 26/287 of Brooks Lake Rd.

It is not necessary to journey into the wilderness area to find spectacular mountain scenery. Many panoramas may be viewed from your car as you travel the roads leading from Dubois. A very popular side trip is the road to Brooks Lake Lodge. The lodge was originally constructed in 1922 to serve bus travelers on their way to Yellowstone National Park. It has undergone a series of owners and restoration efforts since then. In 1989 the lodge restoration was completed and rededicated. Listed in the National Register of Historic Places, the lodge represents a unique time in the history of the Wind River Country.
Source: Dubois Chamber of Commerce brochure

T Ramshorn Basin Area

Directly north of downtown Dubois

The rugged Ramshorn Peak (11,635 feet) hovers north of downtown Dubois. The basin of the Ramshorn is surrounded on three sides by rugged peaks and the alpine basin is abundant with wildflowers in the summer.*Source: Dubois Chamber of Commerce brochure*

T Petrified Forest

37 miles north of Dubois.

The Washakie Wilderness north of Dubois has within its boundaries an area of particular interest to the scientist and amateur geologist. 30 to 40 million years ago this area was covered by massive volcanic ash deposits. The wood cells were replaced by minerals and water before they could rot creating petrified wood. The varying colors and textures of the petrified wood are the result of varying colors and textures of certain minerals in the stone. As the petrified forest is within boundaries of the Wilderness, all travel is restricted to foot and horseback. Petrified wood can not be taken from the area. For the rock hounds, the regions around the lower end of the creeks flowing into the Wind River are excellent places to hunt for pieces of the petrified wood which have been washed down from the slopes of the Wilderness area. *Source: Dubois Chamber of Commerce brochure*

T Wind River Indian Reservation

South of Dubois

This reservation is home to the Shoshone and Arapahoe tribes. Tourists who arrive in the Wind River area while either of the tribes's sun dances are in progress may stop to watch. The sun dance is a form of sacrifice, as the dancers neither eat nor drink during the three day ceremony. These dances are held during the summer months. The Arapahoes also have a Pow-Wow each summer during which numerous tribes compete in costume performing their traditional dances. Cameras and tape recorders are not allowed.*Source: Dubois Chamber of Commerce brochure*

T Red Rocks and Badlands

12 miles east of Dubois

On the north side of the highway through Dubois, the badlands offer the visitor spectacular scenery. The road winds through red rock country providing views of the red cliffs. The badlands stretch for many miles to the east in the Wind River Indian Reservation. The color of this barren wasteland is uniquely beautiful.

H Dubois Museum Interpretive Signs

At Dubois Museum

School House

The first Dubois high school, established in 1925, originally had approximately 12 students who attended for only two years. Those who wished to continue their education beyond what was offered locally had to make arrangements to board with friends or relatives in nearby Lander or Riverton, about 88 miles away. The first Dubois curriculum consisted of Latin, American History, English, Algebra and Geometry.

Like most rural schoolhouse, the Dubois high school contained only the bare essentials. It was the teacher's job to start the wood burning stove on cold mornings, fill the water bucket and care for the kerosene lamps. Toilet facilities consisted of an outhouse, located "outback" which required a quick dash in cold weather.

Swans Service Station

Swan's Service Station, which opened in 1930, was built by Swedish immigrant Swan Swanson (or Swenson). Swanson first came to Dubois in 1914. After a six year stay, he returned to Sweden and became engaged to his wife Sigrid. The couple immigrated officially in 1921 and settled in Dubois where Swan's father was a contractor for the Wyoming Tie and Timber Company.

Swan worked as "tie-hack" and Sigrid was employed as a cook at the Dunoir tie camp for their first nine years. Many other Scandinavian immigrants were also employed in the tie camps. In 1930, the Swansons moved to town to operate the service station and run a trucking buisness between Riverton, Lander and Dubois.

The filling station originally consisted of two small rooms with an office in front and sleeping room in the back. To the left of the station was a pit with wooden tracks on each side to hold vehicles while the oil was being changed.

Bunkhouse

Cowboys and other hired hands seldom found much in the way of luxury or home comforts in the ranch "bunkhouse" that served as their living quarters; a bed, wash basin and a place to store personal gear was about all their employers offered. Picture magazines, mail order catalogs, copies of Shakespeare (which could be bought with coupons that came with the Bull Durham brand of chewing tobacco) and card games were among the few sources of entertainment.

Tim McCoy, who worked for the Double Diamond Ranch east of Dubois, describes the winter montony of bunkhouse life in his autobiography, Tim McCoy Remembers the West:

"The thing that put a bee in my britches and got me moving from the Double Diamond was that I had spent the long, cold and boring Wyoming winter of 1909-1910 in the confines of the ranch's bunkhouse, with only occasional, dreary forays outside. I remember vividly at some point during the seemingly endless frost reading a poem in a magazine which extolled the virtues of lush Wyoming. Somehow it didn't jibe with what I saw outside the window and between furtive glances at the bunkhouse thermometer which frequently registered a teeth-shattering forty-degrees below zero, I wrote an answering piece."

Saddle Shop

Maxwell's saddle shop, a small buisness located behind what is now the Ramshorn Inn, provided horse tack and supplies for dude and working ranches in the Dubois area.

The equipment displayed here represents a cross-section of the types of horse gear used in this part of the west. The large stock saddle in the front (right) is typical of the heavy duty roping saddles used in Wyoming around the late 1930s and 1940s. Both saddle and saddle bags show the traditonal "California rose" pattern, typical of the decorative tooling of this era. The saddle to the left is a somewhat earlier model with larger square-cornered skirts, similar to those that came up from Texas with the start of the first cattle drives in the 1870s.

On the back wall are two pairs of "chaps," protective leggings worn by cowboys to shield them from the cold or thick brush. The pair on the left made from Angora goat, are straight or "shot gun" style chaps which would have been used in colder weather. Those on the right, with wide, flared edges are known as "batwings." Made of heavy cowhide, this pair was designed to protect the rider from the heavy willows and underbrush in the wrangle pasture at the T Cross Ranch at the head of Horse Creek.

Hanging by the horse collars on the left-hand wall are reins made out of braided horse hair. This kind of work and the braided leather reins and quirt to the left of the window on the right of the shop are typical of the kind of craft work that used to be done by ranch hands during the long Wyoming winters.

The center two bridles on the back wall have "spade" bits with extremely high ports. Their use required considerable training and sensitivity on the part of the horse and a high level of skill on the part of the rider. The bridle on the left is decorated with the brass brad or stud work typical of the late teens, twenties and thirties.

The mule pack saddle on the right of back wall is typical of the "saw" or "cross-buck" pack saddle used by outfitters and dude ranchers in this area. Pack saddles were used by working cowhands to transport salt to summer feeding grounds and bedrolls and other gear to mountain cowcamps.

Side-saddles, like that on the back wall (right), were used by a few women in the early west when riding astride was considered unlady like. The flat hornless English Saddles (center-right) wereused by the more "modern eastern women, "dudines" who brought the liberating fashion for riding "cross saddle" west with them when they began coming out as tourists, shortly after the turn of the cenntury. (The Ladies Astride, a kind of hybrid version of the English saddle and the stock saddle flurished briefly in the west's more urban areas around the turn of the century but was soon discarded in favor of lighter versions of the more practical stock or roping saddle.)

In the center of the shop is a McClellan saddle originally used by the miltary's calvary units. Some McClellans had horns attached and could be used for ranch work. With a large number of surplus McClellans on hand after World War I, these saddles were also issued to the Forest Service, which continued to use horses well into middle of the century, and other government agencies.

Forest Service Cabin

This cabin may have originally served as a bunkhouse at the Sheridan Creek ranger station west of Dubois.

What is now called the "Wind River District" of the Shoshone National Forest was initially part of the Yellowstone Forest Reserve. It was later designatied the Bonneville National Forest, and most recently, the Washakie National Forest, in honor of the Shoshone leader, Chief Washskie.

Beginning in 1891, when President Harrison established the first federal forest lands, the United States Forest Service has monitored timber sales and grazing allotments as well as recreational use. The history at Dubois is closed, linked to its National Forest resources. Public forest lands provided timber for a number of early sawmills and for the large railroad cross-tie industry which produced ties for the Chicago-Northwestern Railroad and timber products such as fence posts and mine props, along with dude and cattle ranching, were the area's most important economic industries during the 1920s through the 1940s.

Homestead Cabin

Originally located about eight miles east of

> ### *Wyoming Tidbits*
>
> Butch Cassidy was sent to jail by William "Bill" Simpson, who was Senator Alan Simpson's grandfather.

Wyoming Tidbits

Wyoming was the first state to have a county public library.

Dubois, this cabin is in many ways typical of homestead buildings around the turn of the century. Exceptions are the large windows and relatively high ceiling which would have made the cabin harder to heat. These more spacious features may indicate the influence of a woman's interest in the planning: most earlier cabins tended to be squat and low with narrow, horizontal windows.

Many of the articles in the cabin kitchen belonged to Nettie Stringer who came to Dubois in 1901. Nettie and her family, her mother and 6 brothers, settled west of Dubois where she filed her own claim in 1985.

Keeping house for her brothers, mending and ironing, cooking and tending outdoor chores kept Nettie busy year around On a typical day, in May of 1908, her diary reads as follows: "I washed early—baked bread and four pies, dress two chickens. Carl and Albert and two other men were here for dinner. I ironed the boys collars and basted up a bonnet, then did several turns (chores) and took a bath…"

We have left the cardboard and newspaper insulation on the kitchens back wall in place to show visitors how homesteaders "made do" with materials on hand. When the cabin was first moved to the museum grounds, this early insulation was covered with the same cardboard panelling and of the original outside chinking has been left visible on the west side of the cabin, above the boardwalk, to show how the outside looked before restoration work.

Meat House
Originally located in a pine grove on the Dennison Ranch along the west fork of Wind River, on Bear Creek, this building served to keep meat cool and safe from bears and flies. The pyramid shape and screen sidings provided natural cooling and ventilation.

The Dennison Ranch was a 5,500 acre ranch belonging to millionaire Richard Dennison. A true eccentric, Dennison also ran an exclusive dude operation which catered to the likes of Clark Gable and Carole Lombard. The ranch was also famous for the many safari trophies which decorated its extravagant interior. Dennison owned and bred a string of Kentucky racehorses and ran a herd of registered Jersey cattle which he kept in a three-story barn with hardwood floors. The barn has since been moved to the Thunderhead Ranch.

Two-Seater Outhouse
This large "privy" was originally located at the first Dubois Airport, on Table Mountain. Airport facilities were constructed as part of a WPA project in 1936.

Buffalo Bill and the Long Ride
Legend says that Pony Express rider William "Buffalo Bill" Cody exchanged horses here on a record ride from Red Buttes Station to Rocky Ridge Station and back. Due to another rider's untimely death, Cody was forced to add an extra leg to his relay and eventually covered a total of 322 miles in 21 hours and 40 minutes, using 21 horses. On another occasion, he rode one horse at top speed for 24 miles when chased by Indians from Horse Creek Station east of Independence Rock to Plant's Station just east of here.

V Emerald Creek Outfitters
103 S. 1st in Dubois. 455-3371. www.emeraldcreekoutfitters.com

Emerald Creek Outfitters provides an experience of a lifetime, taking you on horseback through the beautiful Absaroka Range. Whatever you are interested in—hunting, one of their artist or photo trips, or a custom family or corporate getaway, ECO will make it a great one. ECO prides themselves on quality food, a knowledgeable staff, and environmentally friendly pack trips. At ECO you will be provided with a true wilderness adventure. Emerald Creek Outfitters is a licensed outfitter with BGO #19, and permitted by the Shoshone National Forest. For more information give them a call or visit their website at www.emeraldcreekoutfitters.com.

F Cafe Wyoming
106 E. Ramshorn in Dubois. 455-3828

At the Cafe Wyoming, Chef Ken Wolfe will provide you a truly memorable dining experience. Everything is made from scratch daily, including breads, soups, and salad dressings that accompany delicious entrees. The famous catfish sandwich and hearty B.L.T. bring diners back again and again. House-smoked entrees are among their popular specialties with the dinner menu changing weekly. The Cafe Wyoming's signature barbecue sauce and rubs are made in house and sold nationally. Finish your meal with a cup of fresh organic coffee. The cafe is open for lunch and dinner. Dinner reservations are suggested. Seasonal outdoor dining is available on the deck overlooking the river.

F Rustic Pine Tavern & Steakhouse
119 E. Ramshorn in Dubois. 455-2430

The Rustic Pine Tavern and Steakhouse is famous for steaks, seafood, and other fine value oriented cuisine, served up nightly. The draw to this

Rustic Pine Tavern & Steakhouse

unique bar goes beyond the famous food. The 1930s building is a reminder of how colorful the Old West was. It is chock full of rustic furniture, game mounts, and relics from the Old West. The warm, friendly atmosphere makes this a big favorite for locals and visitors alike. Live entertainment and dancing is featured on summer weekends. Visit the Rustic Pine, step back in time, enjoy a great steak or the chef's nightly special, and relax in a friendly Western atmosphere.

F Bernie's Cafe
1408 Warm Springs Drive in Dubois. 455-2115

L Twin Pines Lodge & Cabins
218 W. Ramshorn in Dubois. 455-2600 or 800-550-6332. www.twinpineslodge.com or email: twinpines@wyoming.com

The Twin Pines Lodge and Cabins were built in 1934 and is listed on the Wyoming National Historic Register. The Lodge and Cabins have recently been remodeled with modern fixtures, while preserving the rustic atmosphere. Kick back and enjoy the western style and hospitality at the Twin Pines. They pamper you with large plush towels, refrigerators, coffee, tea, and hot chocolate in every guest room. Each room also has a VCR and they supply hundreds of movies for your enjoyment, free of charge. Guests are treated to a complimentary deluxe breakfast bar. Located in walking distance to restaurants, taverns, and shopping. Visit them on the web.

Wyoming Tidbits

Wyoming is called the Equality State because in 1890 the Wyoming Territorial Legislature sent a telegram to the 51st Congress, regarding its impending statehood. It read: "We will remain out of the union a hundred years rather than go in without women's suffrage."

L Branding Iron Inn
401 W. Ramshorn in Dubois. 455-2893 or toll free at 888-651-9378.
www.brandingironinn.com

The Branding Iron Inn is located 85 miles south of Yellowstone National Park, along one of America's most beautiful drives. Their Swedish Cope log cabins were hand built in the 1940's, and have all the modern conveniences you'll need while maintaining an authentic Old West atmosphere. The cabins feature king and queen sized beds, cable TV, some with kitchens, one full apartment, and some adjoining rooms. On-site horse corrals are available along with plenty of parking for snowmobiles and boat trailers, and including winter plug ins. They are within walking distance of the great historical attractions. Shopping, and dining that is available in downtown Dubois. Visit them on the web!

L Stagecoach Motor Inn
103 Ramshorn Street in Dubois. 455-2303 and reservations at 800-455-5090.
Email: stagecoach@wyoming.com.
www.wyomingcom/~dte/stagecoach/

The Stagecoach Motor Inn once had cabins along Horse Creek heated with wood stoves and a shared community bath house. Today, visitors to Dubois will enjoy 50 fine units that have replaced those cabins and offer electric heat, private bathrooms with tubs and showers, direct dial phones, cable television, hot tub, and seasonal outdoor pool. Some units are available with kitchens. Quite a change from the old days. The Stagecoach is a well established property and a cost affordable place to make your headquarters. Under the same ownership for the past 27 years. They pride themselves for the service and value that travelers expect.

L Trail's End Motel
511 W. Ramshorn in Dubois. 455-2540 or toll free 888-455-6660. www.trailsendmotel.com

The Trail's End Motel is the only motel with units on the Wind River in Dubois. The 21 native log units are newly remodeled. They come with amenities including king and queen sized beds, suites, cable TV, and direct dial phones. Some units have refrigerators, microwaves, and coffee makers. Decks with tables, chairs, and grills are available for the use of all guests. Catch and release fishing is featured on the property. The paved parking lot can accommodate large vehicles. Free local transportation is also provided for guests. The folks at the Trail's End can also help you with booking hunting, fishing, and pack trips.

VL MacKenzie Highland Ranch
3945 U.S. Highway 26 in Dubois. 455-3415

The MacKenzie Highland Ranch is located within the Shohone National Forest and specializes in independent living. Their primary summer business is renting cabins and houses. During the hunting season they are outfitters offering 3 levels of hunting services. The Independent package is for those hunters familiar with the area. The Intermediate package is for those who are independent, but desire a little backup. The Fully Guided package includes a guide with you at all times. Prices include cabins, stock and necessary equipment. Horses and four-wheelers can be rented as part of Independent package. They are fully licensed with the Wyoming State Board of Outfitters and professional Guides and permitted on the Shoshone National Forest and BLM. The winter months provide opportunities for snow sports.

VL Absaroka Ranch
U.S. Highway 26/287, 10 miles west of Dubois.
455-2275

Here in the West, very few places remain that offer both solitude and beauty on a grand scale. The Absaroka Ranch, located at the headwaters of Wyoming's Wind River and at the base of the spectacular Absaroka mountain range, is such a place. Your hosts, Budd and Emi Betts, invite you to come and enjoy all that this fabulous hideaway has to offer. Enjoy horseback riding, fishing, hiking, cookouts, photography, and wilderness pack trips. It is everything the complete guest ranch vacation can be. Secluded within the beauty of the wilderness, and among the most friendly and personal surroundings.

Dubois

	Jan	Feb	March	April	May	June	July	Aug	Sep	Oct	Nov	Dec	Annual
Average Max. Temperature (F)	33.5	36.6	41.4	49.8	60.5	69.9	78.8	78.1	67.2	56.2	42.1	34.8	54.1
Average Min. Temperature (F)	10.8	11.9	16.4	23.8	31.6	38.5	42.4	41.0	33.6	26.1	17.9	12.3	25.5
Average Total Precipitation (in.)	0.30	0.26	0.48	1.08	1.35	1.35	0.97	0.75	1.12	0.59	0.43	0.28	8.96
Average Total SnowFall (in.)	4.1	3.8	5.2	6.5	2.1	0.4	0.0	0.0	1.7	2.0	4.5	4.5	34.9
Average Snow Depth (in.)	1	0	0	0	0	0	0	0	0	0	0	1	0

LC Riverside Inn & Campground

5810 U.S. Highway 26 in Dubois. 455-2337 or toll free at 877-489-2337.
www.dteworld.com/riversideinn

The Riverside Inn & Campground is located on a fifty-acre ranch conveniently located 3 miles east of Dubois near the Wind River, surrounded by towering cottonwood trees. Wonderful family accommodations are available for lodging and full hookups for camping. Bring your pets and horses too. The 14 motel units are clean and comfortable, some with kitchenettes. Camping sites accommodate everything from large RV's to tent sites. Large clean showers and restrooms are included. At Riverside you will find ample parking, spacious grounds, a picnic area, and a playground area. The Suda's also offer outfitting services with trail rides available right from the motel and campground.

S Absaroka Western Designs Interior Furnishings & Custom Tannery

1416 Warm Springs Drive in Dubois. 455-2440.
www.absarokawesterndesign.com

The Absaroka Western Designs showroom is a wonderful source for beautiful home furnishings that bring out the best in western decor for your cabin and lodge. They design and construct lodge pole and aspen furnishings, rawhide and leather shades, and metal art. A selection of soft supple skins may be purchased direct from their custom tannery. They also carry a wonderful selection of western rugs. If you need that special Western gift this is a perfect place to find it. Be sure and explore the many choices of fantastic Western design at their web site.

Absaroka Western Designs & Home Decor

S Mountain Legacy Traditional Outdoor Clothing & Equipment

103 S. 1st in Dubois. 455-3265.

Mountain Legacy is a varied shopping experience under one roof. Carrying a full line of outdoor clothing and equipment, Mountain Legacy can outfit you with everything from sleeping bags and pads to biodegradable soap and toothpaste. From big names like C.C. Filson and Barbour to more obscure brands you may not find anywhere else. They have a large selection of high quality clothing with an emphasis on natural fibers like wool and oilskin. Mountain Legacy also sells Royal Enfield Motorcycles, which are new reproductions of the 1955 classic model. Test rides are available. A section of the store is dedicated to motorcycle clothing and accessories, especially hard to find items that harken back to the 1950s.

AFS Exxon Country Store

404 W. Ramshorn in Dubois. 455-2677

The Exxon Country Store is a full service travel stop, complete with a gift shop, soda fountain, candy shop, and bakery. The soda fountain is a fun place to enjoy your choice from over 50 flavors of shakes or nearly 20 different flavors of ice cream. The candy shop is stocked with over 30 flavors of Jelly Belly gourmet jelly beans, gourmet chocolates, and fudge. Homemade baklava is a special treat offered in the bakery. Great with Starbuck's coffee and espresso drinks. There is a game room with video games and pool table. You can have your picture taken riding the giant jackalope and discover how the jackalope came to be.

20 *Gas*

Burris

The first postmistress, a Mrs. Morrison, named this place for her first husband, not for "Dutch Charley" Burris, who was hung by vigilantes on his way to Rawlins to be tried for attempted train robbery and the murder of two deputies.

Crowheart

Like nearby Crowheart Butte, this town's name honors the great battle on the butte between Shoshone Chief Washakie and Crow Chief Big Robber. They fought one-on-one in 1866 to prevent all-out war between their people. The victor was supposed to eat his enemy's heart. When asked later if he did just that, Chief Washakie replied, "Youth does foolish things." The butte itself is considered sacred ground, and visitors are not permitted there, restricted both by law and by courtesy. Legends tell of trespassers disappearing. Better to view it from afar.

The town itself consists of a classic country store and gas station.

H Crowheart Butte

Four and one half miles southeast of Crowheart on Highway 26/287

In March, 1866, a battle was fought in this vicinity between Shoshone and Bannock Indians on one side and Crow Indians on the other. The contest was waged for the supremacy of hunting grounds in the Wind River basin. Crowheart Butte was so named because the victorious Washakie, Chief of the Shoshones, displayed a Crow Indian's heart on his lance at the war dance after the battle. The major portion of the battle was fought near Black Mountain several miles to the north.Washakie, in his youth and middle age, was a very mighty warrior. He was a wise chief and friendly to the white people. No white man's scalp hung in this chief's tepee.

Crowheart Butte

21 *Gas, Food, Lodging*

Big Sandy

Another town dubbed for a creek of the same name, Big Sandy was once a Pony Express station. Indians burned the station to the ground in 1862. At the foot of Wind River Peak (elev. 13,192 ft.), and practically within throwing distance of the Bridger-Teton National Forest, Big Sandy has an abundance of alpine scenery.

Boulder

Pop. 75, Elev. 7,016

The nearby creek of the same name was so called for the large boulder in its midst, fallen from a cliff overhead. The Boulder Store is about a century old. Other amenities such as a dancehall, a blacksmith shop, a post office, and a hotel once made Boulder a frontier hot spot. Now it is a quiet community with the main attraction being the ospreys which nest just to the west.

H Grass or Sand Springs–An Oregon Trail Campsite

North of 191/351 Junction

Here crosses the Lander cutoff–the northern fork of the Oregon Trail following a route of the fur traders. It was suggested as an emmigrant road by mountain man, John Hockaday in order to avoid the alkali plains of the desert, shorten the trip to the Pacific by five days, and provide more water, grass and wood. In 1857, it was improved as a wagon road by the government under the supervision of F. W. Lander and termed the Fort Kearny, South Pass, Honey Lake Rd. As many as three hundred wagons and thousands of cattle, horses and mules passed here each day. An expanding nation moved with hope and high courage. The trail-cut deep into the dirt of the plains and the mountains-remains as a reminder of a great epoch. Sublette County Historical Society, United States Department of the Interior Bureau of Land Management. This trail has been marked at all accessible points with brass caps.

H Buckskin Crossing–a Landmark

About eight miles south of Big Sandy on County Road 1804 where road crosses Big Sandy River.

This part of the Big Sandy River has been known as the Buckskin Crossing since the 1860s. Legend is that a trapper and hunter named Buckskin Joe lived here with his wife and daughter. The daughter died here. This marker is near his cabin site. This crossing was used by the fur companies and trappers, Captain Bonneville, Captain Wm. D. Stewart, and later by John C. Fremont. Captain Stewart's artist–the noted Alfred Jacob Miller–made the first painting of this area in 1837. This ford of the Lander Cutoff of the Oregon Trail, campsite and burial ground was heavily used by the emigrants, their hundreds of wagons and thousands of mules, cattle and horses. This was the mail route from the east to the west side of the Wind River Mountains in the early 1900s. Big Sandy Creek was named by William Ashley on his trapping expedition in 1825. Of the thousands of people who passed this way only the wagon tracks and graves remain.

H Fremont's Week in Sublette County

About Seven miles east of Boulder on State Highway 353.

On June 10, 1842, Lt. J.C. Fremont left St. Louis to explore the Wind River Mountains, with Kit Carson as guide, Charles Preuss, as topographer, L. Maxwell, hunter, and 20 Canadian voyageurs, including Basil LeJeunesse. Eight two-wheeled mule-drawn carts were used as far as the Platte River. The party crossed South Pass August 8 and camped here at "Two Buttes" August 9. Leaving 10 men at Boulder Lake, the lieutenant ascended Fremont Peak August 15, stayed here again August 17, and on the 19th re-crossed South Pass. So ended Fremont's Exploration of the Wind River Mountains and his stay in Sublette County.

22 *Gas, Food, Lodging*

Big Piney

Pop. 408, Elev. 6,798

Pines once lined the Big Piney Creek, for which the town was named, but none of the native trees grow in town anymore. Dan Budd, Sr., whose ranch housed the post office for a time, named both. Prior to that, the post office had been at the Mule Shoe Ranch of A.W. Smith. Big Piney is often the coldest spot in the nation.

T Green River Valley Museum

In Big Piney

The Historic Green River Valley Museum was formed to pertpetuate and preserve the history and culture of the Green River Valley. Featured exhibits include prehistoric Indian artifacts, early ranching and branding equipment, and historic oil field tools. The area oil and gas history is actively displayed, along with exhibits about family-operated coal mine histories. There is a restored homesteader cabin along with the history of homesteading and townsite development. Other unique displays include Campfire Girls and old Big Piney Examiner Presses. The museum is open mid-June to Mid-October.

23 *Gas, Food, Lodging*

Marbleton

Pop. 720, Elev. 6,798

Named for Cheyenne cattle man A. H. Marble, this small town was built up by ranchers. Author Ethel Mills Black, who wrote *They Made Wyoming Their Own*, spent her childhood in Marbleton in the late 1800s.

H Historic Sublette County Of Cattle and Men

About three miles north of Big Piney on U.S. Highway 189.

Thousands of people, cattle and horses passed this way to the Northwest when the Sublette Cut-off of the Oregon Trail was opened in 1857. None settled in this county. At the close of the Indian Wars in 1877, cattle herds from Oregon came this way to meet the railroad and to stock Wyoming ranges. The first Sublette County herds were started with other western cattle. In 1878-79 Ed Swan's PL, Otto Leifer's O Circle, Bud's 6 Quarter Circle, Hugh McKay's 67 and A.W. Smith's Muleshoe outfits settled on nearby Piney Creek. Their cattle were not Longhorns. The county's first barbed wire was unrolled in 1881 on the Circle outfit.

24 *Gas, Food, Lodging*

Pinedale

Pop. 1412, Elev. 7,175

Established near Pine Creek, this town was named by first postmaster Charles Peterson in 1899. At that time, it was farthest away from all the railroads of any town in Wyoming. Before that, this was Rendezvous country, where the biggest get-togethers of trappers, traders, and Native Americans took place from 1832 to1840. The tie-hack industry also contributed to the town's growth. Pinedale is still a ranching center, but is increasingly benefiting from the overflow of tourism from the Jackson area. With its proximity to the Wind River Mountains, however, it still retains its wild, rustic charm.

Cora

Pop. 3, Elev. 7,340

Named for Cora House, an old maid cowgirl who worked on the nearby Elmer Ranch, this post office was established in about 1890. A decade later, in 1900, the post office moved to the ranch of Mrs. Minerva Westphall, best known for her bootlegged whiskey and her big gray stallion, on which she carried the mail from Big Piney. In

1902 it moved again to the ranch of James Noble. When it finally developed into a town, it served the nearby railroad tie camp with its saloon and dance hall, blacksmith shop, and local newspaper. It had to move one last time to be near a paved road, but the post office was finally restored to its original building. Today, Cora is the place to catch up on news for the area ranchers.

V Pinedale Entertainment Center

153 S. Entertainment Lane in Pinedale. 367-5056 or Movie Line at 367-6688.

Your favorite big-city entertainment is available in Pinedale. The Pinedale Entertainment Center is a new concept multi activity center offering recreation for all ages. The center offers everything from bowling to two state of the art movie theaters. The 24,000 square foot building offers a fresh clean environment with an 8 lane bowling alley, game arcade, billiards, in addition to the movie theaters. An extensive snack bar serves up fresh pizza, sandwiches, and all of your favorite snacks, you can enjoy while watching the movies. There is also a large community/ballroom.

T Museum of the Mountain Man

700 E. Hennick off Fremont Lake Road in Pinedale. 367-4101 or toll free 877-686-6266. www.museumofthemountainman.com

The Museum of the Mountain Man is located at the base of the Wind River Mountains. The men of the Fur Trade, or Mountain Men, were among the greatest overland explorers that the world has ever known. The purpose of the museum is to interpret this important era of history to all who pass this way. The exhibition area includes special displays and interpretative text on equipment, tools, techniques, interaction with the American Indian, the Rendezvous and the role of the mountain man as an explorer and guide for the westward expansion. The museum also offers a research library, special programs and history demonstrations, children's hands on activities, and a gift shop. The museum is open May through October, admission is charged, and there is plenty of large vehicle parking. During the second weekend of July history comes alive with the Green River Rendezvous commemoration when local residents reenact the events of the fur trade era.

The Wind River

H Osprey

Just south of Pinedale on Highway 191.

The power pole near the highway has supported an osprey nest for many years. Ospreys normally build their nests (eyries) on top of large columns of rock or in trees with broken tops. Utah Power and Light Company built this nest site by adding an extension and platform to an existing pole. This provides the birds a safer place to nest and prevents powerline damage due to falling nesting material. Other such devices have been constructed within several miles of this location.

Osprey nests are generally constructed of large sticks, driftwood, grasses and bark. Ospreys lay 2 to 4 cream-colored eggs with brown to lavender blotches. Eggs are generally laid in May and hatch in approximately 28 days. About eight weeks after hatch, the young take their first extended flights.

Throughout the summer the adults can be observed bringing fish to the young at the nest. Fish are the primary food of the osprey, and are the reason they are commonly referred to as "fish hawks". Ospreys dive from 20 to 100 feet in the air and almost completely submerge in their attempt to catch fish, then take it back to a tree perch or the nest for their meal.

While ospreys are generally more tolerant of disturbance than other raptors, they will defend their nest from any intruders. It is important to maintain a reasonable distance from the nest to avoid too much disturbance that could cause the birds to abandon their eggs or young.

Wyoming Tidbits

Gannett Peak, at 13,804 feet in elevation, is Wyoming's highest peak. Located on the crest of the Continental Divide in the central Rockies, the peak was discovered by American explorer Henry Gannett.

H Green River Rendezvous

Just West of Pinedale

A marker place of fur trade, from the Mississippi to the Pacific, from Canada to Mexico, where trappers, traders and Indians came to barter for the first great resource of the west. Six rendezvous were held here, gathering not only furs but information of geographic importance to weld the final link in exploration of the new world. It is a tribute to the brave men, both red and white, who blazed the trails for culture and progress, and the lowly beaver who gave it impetus. Commemorated each year, the second Sunday in July. Sublette County Historical Society, Inc.

H Welcome to the Riparian Community of Duck Creek

Just west of Pinedale on U.S. Highway 191

Duck Creek riparian community is a diverse and complex society of living organisms. Wild brown trout feed on caddisfly nymphs, that live in self-made stick and stone shelters, clinging to the rocks. Yellow warblers and flycatchers nest in willow bushes. Beaver harvest willows to bild dams and lodges. A mallard hen raises its brood on the beaver pond. In the wet meadows beyond the creek, sandhill cranes and long-billed curlews raise their chicks. On a good morning you can see more than 30 kinds of wildlife from this spot.

People are also important members of this

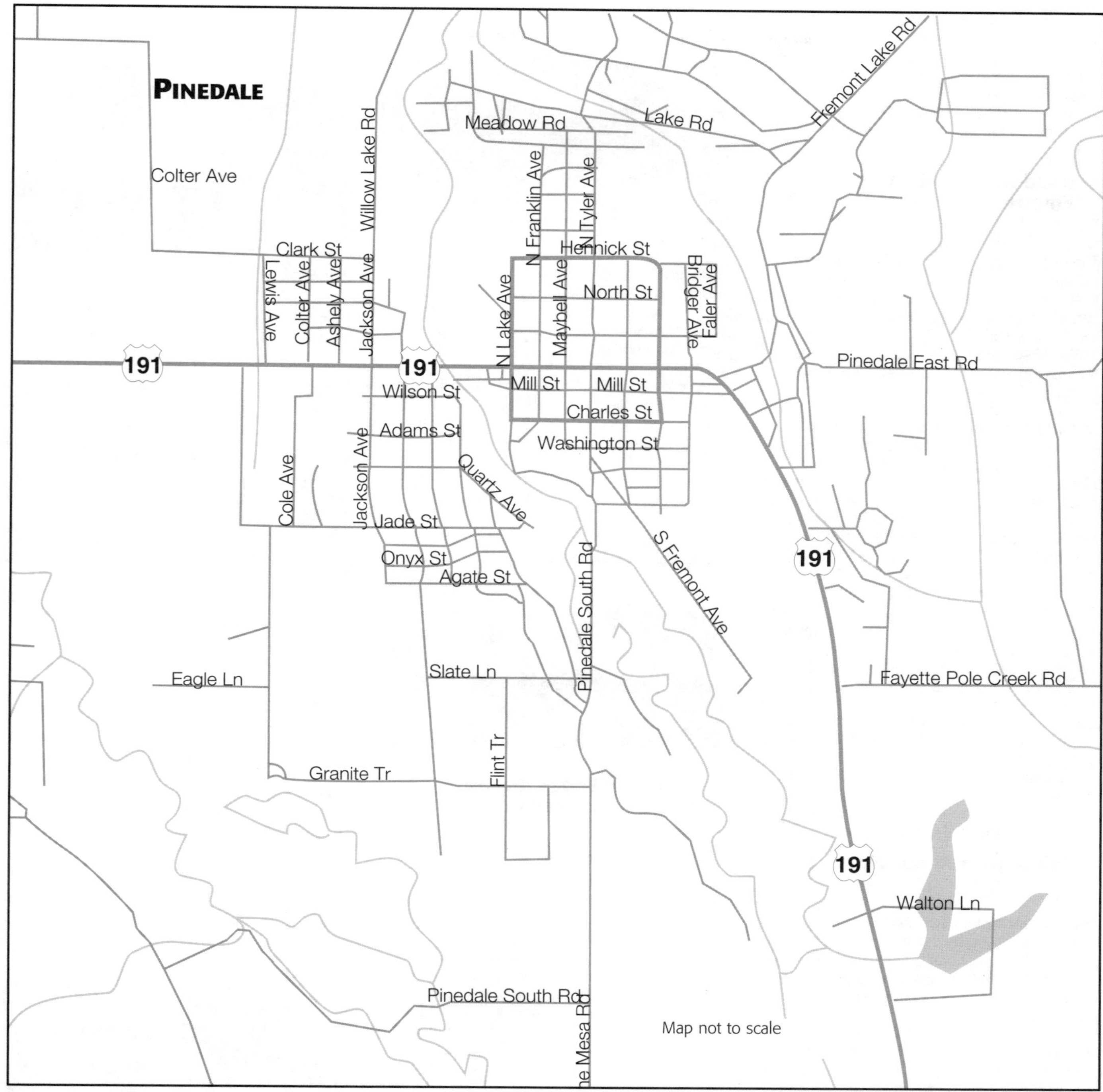

community. Ranchers harvest meadow grasses for winter livestock hay. Anglers test their skills on the wily brown trout, while you enjoy the sights and sounds of the wildlife.

The foundation of the Duck Creek community is water and soil. Willow bushes and sedges growing along the creek banks, have long roots that hold the soils in place against the force of flood water. Duck Creek is a role model for clean water, diverse wildlife and lush plant growth.

This community is made possible because of the good stewardship of ranchers, land managers, wildlife managers, anglers and groups like Trout Unlimited. While visiting Wyoming tread lightly and view wildlife from a distance—be a good steward and responsible member of our wild land communities.

H The Naming of the Lake

About three miles north of Pinedale at Fremont Lake.

On the edge of this magnificent sheet of water, Capt. William Drummond Stewart of Scotland camped many times with Jim Bridger, other Mountain men, and Indians from 1833 to 1844. In 1837, his artist, Alfred Jacob Miller, painted the first pictures of this area. On Stewart's last trip in August 1844, eight men in a rubbber boat, first boat on the lake, honored their leader by christening these waters as Stewart's Lake, in a joyous ceremony near the Narrows, with six jugs of whiskey. Years later, this glacier-formed lake with its shoreline of twenty-two miles and over six hundred foot depth was named after Gen. John C. Fremont—the map makers knew not that it had been named long before.

H Historical Sublette County: A Pause on a Journey

U.S. Highway 191 in Pinedale.

On October 16, 1812, the Astorians: Robert Stuart, Ramsey Crooks, Robert Mcclellan, Joseph Miller, Benjamin Jones, Francis LeClair and Andy Vallee, traveling from Astoria to St. Louis, all their horses having been stolen by Indians, passed this way on foot and forded Pine Creek near here, the first white men known to have seen it.

From Stuart's Journal: "We forded another stream whose banks were adorned with many pines—near which we found an Indian encampment–deserted about a month ago, with immense numbers of buffalo bones strewed everywhere–in center of camp a great lodge of pines and willows–at west end–three persons lay interred with feet to east–at head of each a large buffalo skull painted black–from lodge were suspended numerous ornaments and moccasins."

H Rendezvous–Birth of an Empire

About six miles west of Pinedale on U.S. Highway 191.

The river below is the Green. The mountains to the west are the Wyomings (Bear Rivers). Those to the east, the Windrivers. Along the river banks below are the Rendezvous sites of 1833, 1835 (New Fork), 1836, 1837 (Cottonwood), 1839, 1840, and Fort Bonneville. Trappers, traders and Indians from throughout the west here met the trade wagons from the east to barter, trade for furs, gamble, drink, frolic, pray and scheme. The Indians, Delaware and Iroquois brought in by the Hudson Bay Company, Snakes, Bannocks, Gros Ventre, Flatheads, Nez Perce, Crows, and Chinooks here made their first contact with the white man. The warring Blackfeet did not participate. The Rocky Mountain Fur Company, Hudson Bay Company, Captain Bonneville, Wyeth and free trappers controlled the trade. The people of God, Marcus and Marcissa Whitman, Mr. and Mrs. Spalding, Samuel Parker, Father DeSmet, Jason Lee, and W. H. Gray tempered the hilarity. Jim Bridger, Milton and Bill Sublette, Tom Fitzpatrick, Joe Walker, Joe Meeks, Kit Carson, Baptiste Gervais, Bob Jackson, Moses (Black) Harris, Lucien Fontenelle, Etienne Provost, Henry Fraeb, Andry Dripps, Robert Campbell, Henry Vandenbury, Sir W. D. Stewart and the artist A. J. Miller were all part of this and left their names imbedded in the annals of the West. Scattering for the value of a beaver plew and to see what was beyond the horizon, their trails became the highways of an empire at the cost of many a violent death.

H Wind River Mountains

About six miles west of Pinedale on U.S. Highway 191.

You are looking into the Wind River Mountain Range. So named by Indians and translated into English. These mountains are still in the ice age. The seven largest glaciers in the Rocky Mountains are here. Numerous smaller glaciers also remain.

This side of the mountains comprises the Birdger Wilderness. These 383,000 acres can be traversed only by foot or by horseback. The renewable resources of these national forest lands are managed in the combination that best meets the needs of the American people. The Wind River Mountian country provides some of the best fishing in the United States. There is also good hunting for elk, deer, moose, bighorn sheep, and bear.

Six major lakes just outside of the wilderness are being developed by the Forest Service to provide picnic and camp sites. Tourist accomodations are available in the Pinedale area. Additional information on this area may be obtained from the Chamber of Commerce or the Forest Ranger in Pinedale.

F McGregors Pub, Fine Dining, & Catering

21 N. Franklin in Pinedale. 367-4443.

The Old Pinedale Hotel was constructed in 1905

McGregors Pub

and has continuously housed a line of colorful businesses before McGregors Pub and Fine Dining opened there in the early 1980's. People drive for miles to enjoy menu offerings that range form Chateaubriand, lobster pasta, pork, veal, to the hand cut steaks and the Pub's prime dip and rib eye steak sandwiches. Before your meal with choice from a large variety of appetizers. McGregors is a local favorite, perhaps attributed to their unique recipes with "return appeal." Be sure and try their famous pepper steak skillet served with sizzling garlic mushrooms. They offer an extensive wine list and full line of premium liquors.

FL Lakeside Lodge Resort & Marina on Fremont Lake

Fremont Lake, four miles north of Pinedale. 367-2221 or 877-755-LAKE(5253). www.lakesidelodge.com

Lakeside Lodge Resort and Marina is located on the shore of beautiful Fremont Lake four miles north of Pinedale in the Bridger Teton National Forest. Fremont Lake is the largest and deepest glacially formed lake in the Green River Basin offering over eight sq. miles of recreation and enjoyment on one of the cleanest lakes in the United States. Lakeside Lodge offers Western hospitality, privacy, and informal comfort on fifteen acres surrounded by pristine wilderness. The resort includes a main lodge and restaurant, deluxe log cabins, rustic cabins, RV campground and a marina. Area activities include boating, horseback riding, biking, golf, hiking, lake fishing and fly-fishing on the nearby Green and New Fork Rivers.

FL Half Moon Lake Resort

On Half Moon Lake at Pinedale. 367-6373. www.halfmoonlake.com

Half Moon Lake is a short nine miles from Pinedale, at the base of the majestic Wind River Mountain Range. Hidden among the pines and aspen on the lake's shore is the historic guest ranch, Half Moon Lake Resort, rich in history and the spirit of the West. The perfect location for a relaxing fun filled getaway or fine dining with lakeside views. Enjoy the majesty and serenity of the Rocky Mountains, while boating, fishing, on trail rides or pack trips, or just relax in one of the

Half Moon Lake Resort

8 cozy cabins. Enjoy the outstanding western dining and fine cuisine in a cozy restaurant with huge windows overlooking the lake.

L The Sundance Motel

148 Pine Street in Pinedale. 367-4336 or reservations at 800-833-9178.

The Sandance Motel is a family owned and operated business located in the heart of Pinedale. Camping, world class fishing, backpacking and other great outdoor adventures abound in the surrounding area. Beautiful Fremont Lake is only 4 miles away and Jackson Hole is only 76 miles north. They take great pride in clean rooms and friendly service. All rooms are equipped with refrigerators and microwaves, and some rooms are available with kitchenettes. Sample their homemade fudge when you check in. You'll want to buy some to take with you and they'll even ship worldwide. During the winter they offer weekly and monthly rates.

L The Lodge at Pinedale

1054 W. Pine Street at Pinedale. 367-8800. www.pinedalelodge.com

The Lodge at Pinedale offers some of Pinedale's newest lodging with many of your favorite amenities. They are conveniently located adjacent to restaurants, service stations, and the Pinedale Entertainment Center. The Lodge is only minutes from fishing, golf, skiing, hiking, and the Continental Divide snow machine trail. Outside you'll find plenty of parking for large vehicles, including winter plug-ins. For the added comfort of guests the front desk is open 24 hours, data-port access is provided in all rooms, there is a guest laundry, two-room suites, and elevator. Relax in the indoor pool or Jacuzzi and wake up to a complimentary continental. breakfast.

L Chambers House Bed & Breakfast
111 W. Magnolia Street in Pinedale. 367-2168 or 800-567-2168. www.chambershouse.com

The Chambers House is a Pinedale landmark, built in 1933 with logs from the local forest. The current owner of the house is Ann Chambers Noble. The elegant, large old log house has been renovated and is decorated with a mixture of antiques and new furnishings. There are five bedrooms, two with fireplaces, three bathrooms, and a formal dining room. The central sitting room is reserved for conversation or reading around the fireplace. The Master Bedroom is handicapped accessible and has a private entrance. The Inn is located in charming downtown Pinedale and walking distance to shopping and dining. They are open year-round and welcome your children and dogs.

L Log Cabin Motel: A National Historic Place Built in 1929
49 E. Magnolia in Pinedale. 367-4579

M Hatch Real Estate
110 West Pine in Pinedale. 367-SOLD(7653). www.hatchrealestate.com

The staff at Hatch Real Estate is sold on offering their clients high quality real estate services in Sublette County and the surrounding area. Through their extensive marketing experience, the friendly professional service they offer will open doors for you. Whether you are buying or selling commercial, residential, agricultural or unimproved land, feel confident that they will be tracking down great deals for you. Visit their web site and view some of the many properties they offer. Hatch Real Estate can help you find your dream property in Wyoming.

M High Mountain Real Estate
107 E. Pine Street in Pinedale. 367-4600 or toll free at 877-367-4600. www.highmtn.com or Email: highmountain@wyoming.com

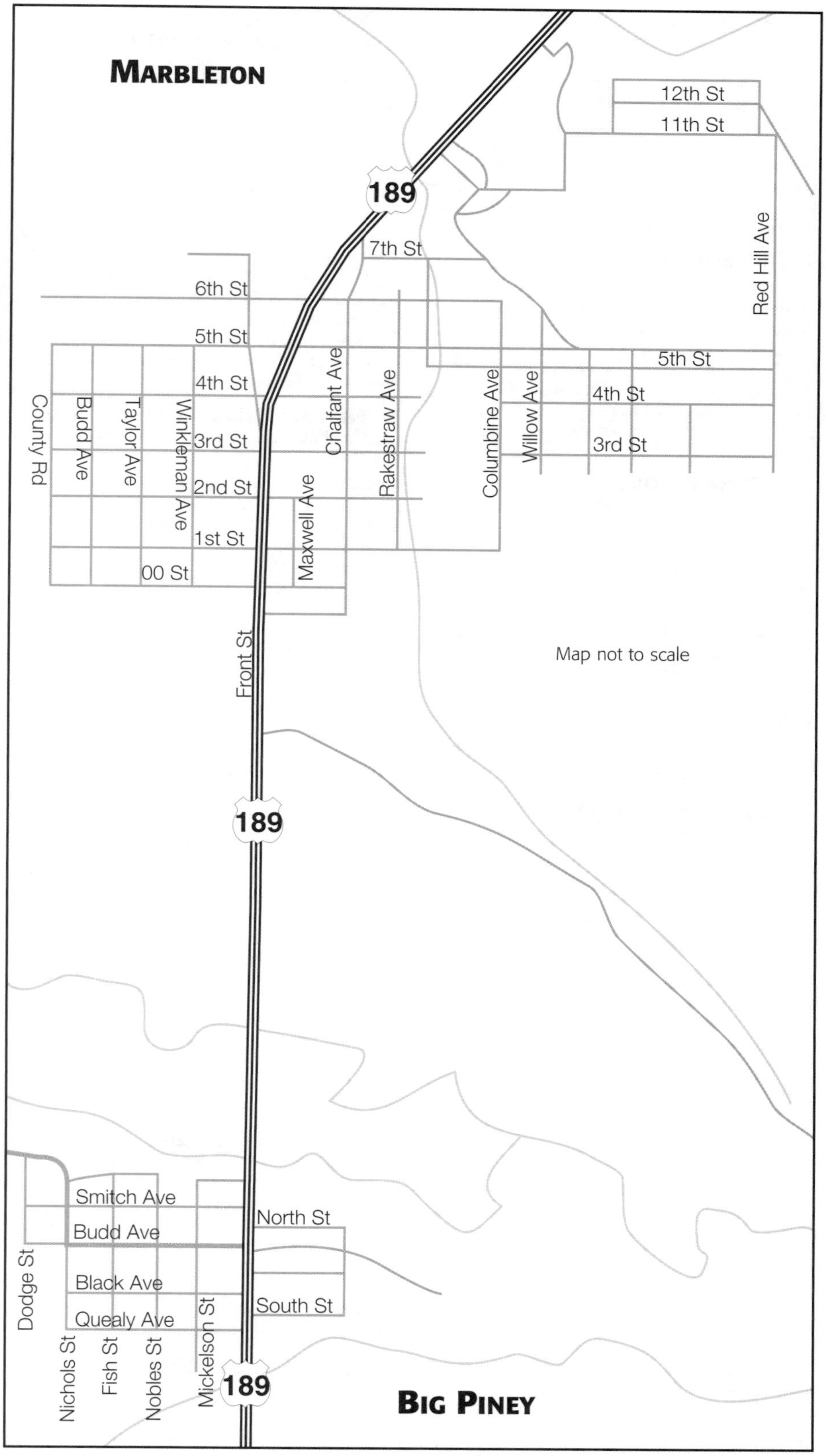

MARBLETON

Map not to scale

BIG PINEY

25 *No services*

Merna
Postmistress Grace Snyder named this post office for her hometown of Merna, Nebraska.

Daniel
Pop. 110, Elev. 7,192

When the post office moved here from the previous site of "Burns" (a problem name, since there was another Burns in Laramie County), it was named for Thomas P. Daniel, the owner of the general store in 1900. About two miles to the west is old Ft. Bonneville, named for founder Capt. Benjamin L.E. Bonneville. Built in 1832, it became the site of the original Green River Rendezvous, which was held yearly over the next eight years for the exchange of goods between trappers, traders, and Indians. The event is now celebrated in Pinedale. One mile to the east of Daniel is the site of the first Catholic Mass in Wyoming, held by Father Pierre DeSmet in 1840. A monument was built here in 1925.

T Fort Bonneville

Three miles northwest of Daniel

Established in 1832 by Captain Benjamin Bonneville as a fur trading post, the camp consisted of blockhouses bordered by towering log posts. The fort soon became known as "Bonneville's Folly" or "Fort Nonsense". Deep snow and frigid winds made the fort unusable in the winter, and it was abandoned after a little more than a year.

H Astorian Incident

North of 191/189 Junction on U.S. Highway 191/189

On this site, October 18, 1811, sixty one Astorians of the American fur comany, the squaw of Pierre Dorian and her two children, with one hundred and eighteen horses camped for 5 days. They were on their way to the pacific Ocean from Montreal via St. Louis. Here they met, traded and powwowed with the Snake Indians, killed buffalo and cured meat. Continuing their journey, they crossed the divide one mile north of here on to the waters of the Columbia River. These were the first white men in what is now Sublette County.

H Gros Ventre Lodge

About 23 miles north of Cora on State Highway 352

This Lodge, one of the earliest dude ranches in Wyoming, was built on the hill beyond in 1897 by William (Billy) Wells and operated until 1906. It was named for the little Gros Ventre (now tosi Creek) and was locally known as "Dog Ranch" because of the foxhounds Wells kept for hunting. Wile Wells guided guests on summer trips through the Green River Valley and Bridger National Forest, the Gros Ventre was the most notable as a hunting lodge that served prominent American and British big game sportsmen. The ranch included a central lodge, guest cabins and one of the first wooden bathtubs in western Wyoming.

By 1906, the Gros Ventre was no longer profitable, in part due to the stricter game loaws and a shorter hunting season. It was dismantled that year and the main lodge moved across the Green River and converted into a ranch house.

H Fort Bonneville Sisk-ke-dee Agie (Green river) Oregon 1832

About 3 miles west of Daniel on State Highway 354.

Here, in July, 1832, Captian Benjamin Bonneville erected a fort, two block houses and a stockade, for protection from the Blackfoot Indians. He was on leave from the U. S. Army, with his trapping and exploring group of 110 men and 20 wagons. These were the first wagons to cross Southpass. The party scattered and trapped for several years, doing valuable exploring as far as California and the Columbia River. In the party was the famed Joe Walker, Joe Meeks and many Delaware Indians. The fort, a strategic site, was not used in winter. Bonneville and most of his party returned to Missouri August 22, 1835.

H First Tie Drive on Green River

About 20 miles north of Cora on State Highway 352.

Because timber was scarce in neighboring states along the first transcontinental railroad line, the tie business flourished here and in other Wyoming mountain locations. Ties were cut in winter, stored on the river bank until spring, and floated downstream during high water.

Charles DeLoney was a youthful Michigan Civil War veteran who came to Wyoming after the war. An experienced timberman, he contracted with the Union Pacific Railroad in 1867 to supply ties. A crew of 30 men hauled equipment and supplies upriver and constructed a combined office-bunkhouse-cookshack-commissary building between this marker and the river. Cabins were built high in the timber, forcing the men to snowshoe for meals. DeLoney's was the first drive down the river, a trip of 130 miles. Ties were skidded down nearby mountains and held by a boom across the river until the drive. Another boom at Green River City caught the ties near the railhead. The operation continued successfully for two yars, and newspaper advertisements as late as fall, 1868, solicited tie hacks to work at the head of the Green River.

Charles DeLoney was a versatile person. He was a rancher, a pioneer merchant in jackson and helped found the town of Evanston. He was the state's first forest supervisor and served in Wyoming territorial and state legislatures.

H Prairie of the Mass

About two miles south of Daniel on U.S. Highway 189.

Rev. Pierre DeSmet (1802-73) was born in Belgium but came to America in 1821, joined the Jesuit society and began his work with the Indians. In his work he established sixteen treaties, crossed the ocean nineteen times and traveled 180 thousand miles on his errands of charity for the indians who knew him as the "Sincerest Friend."

On July 5, 1840, in the presence of two thousand Indians, trappers and traders, he offered the first Holy Mass in what is now Wyoming on an altar of native stone decorated with wild flowers. In Father DeSmet's own words, "It was a spectical truly moving to the heart of a missionary that this immense family, composed of so many different tribes should prostrate themselves in equal humility before the "Divine Host." The monument at the site was erected in 1925 and a commemorative mass is offered there annually in July. On July 4, 1940, the one hundredth anniversary of the first Mass, a Pontifical High mass was offered by the Most Rev. Bishop McGovern assisted by more than thirty priests and attended by about two thousand people.

26 *No Services*

Wapiti Valley

A quiet valley named after an Indian word for elk, this little piece of heaven on earth is located between Cody and Yellowstone Park, and is the most direct route to the park from Cody. Its beautiful mountain scenery, volcanic features and abundance of wildlife make travel in the Wapiti Valley a true Western experience.

H Absaroka Volcanic Field

Just west of Wapiti on U.S. Highway 14/16/20.

The valley of the North Fork of the Shoshone River passes through a series of volcanic rocks over 9,000 feet thick covering 3,000 square miles. The rocks include lava, volcanic ash, and other sorts of volcanic material. Agglomerate is a common type and consists of rounded masses of volcanic rock in a finer matrix. Numerous dikes which were feeders for lava flows, show in the canyon walls as thin, narrow bands resembling stone walls. The peculiar castle-like forms are the result of weathering and removal of softer material by water.

H Fire Fighters Memorial

U.S. Highway 14/16/20 about 18 miles west of Wapiti.

Shoshone National Forest Black Water Fire August 20-24, 1937. This marks the beginning of the Fire Fighters' Memorial Trail which follows Black Water Creek five miles to the place of origin of the Fire, and thence to other points of interest. This fire was controlled after burning over 1,254 acres of forest. Fifteen fire fighters lost their lives and thirty nine others were injured when the fire was whipped up by a sudden gale on August 21. Signs and monuments mark the important locations along this trail, including the fire camps, the first aid station, Clayton Gulch where eight men were killed, and the rocky knoll where Ranger Post gathered his crew to escape the fire.

Big Piney	Jan	Feb	March	April	May	June	July	Aug	Sep	Oct	Nov	Dec	Annual
Average Max. Temperature (F)	25.9	30.6	38.9	50.9	62.1	71.0	80.0	78.4	69.3	57.6	39.6	28.3	52.7
Average Min. Temperature (F)	-5.3	-1.5	8.4	19.6	29.0	36.4	39.7	36.1	27.3	17.7	7.1	-3.1	17.6
Average Total Precipitation (in.)	0.38	0.31	0.44	0.65	1.05	0.92	0.74	0.81	0.84	0.55	0.38	0.40	7.46
Average Total SnowFall (in.)	4.1	4.2	4.3	3.6	1.3	0.2	0.0	0.0	0.7	2.1	4.2	3.9	28.6
Average Snow Depth (in.)	4	5	3	0	0	0	0	0	0	0	1	3	1
Wind Speed (mph / kmh)	6 / 9	6 / 9	7 / 12	8 / 13	8 / 13	8 / 13	8 / 13	7 / 12	7 / 11	6 / 10	6 / 9	6 / 9	
Wind Direction	WSW	WSW	WSW	WSW	WSW	WSW	WSW	WSW	WSW	WSW	WSW	WSW	
Cloud Cover (out of 8)	5.0	5.0	5.1	5.2	5.2	4.2	3.6	3.6	3.6	4.2	4.9	4.6	

The Holy City in the Wapiti Valley.

27 *No services*

Valley

Traces of Valley remain as an old dude ranch named back around 1890 for its location in the valley of the south fork of the Shoshone River. Named by hunter and trapper, James McLaughlin.

Wapiti

Named for the Native American word for elk, Wapiti is a small community of fairly recent settlers, here to enjoy the scenery between Cody and Yellowstone.

T Buffalo Bill State Park

The history of Buffalo Bill Reservoir and "Cody Country" is rooted in the rich lore of the old West. Buffalo Bill State Park was named for Colonel William F. "Buffalo Bill" Cody, famous as a wild west showman, promoter and developer. He first came to the region in the 1870s as a guide for a survey expedition and spent the next 20 years guiding and sponsoring hunting parties in the area.

"Buffalo Bill" Cody was influential in bringing irrigation and agricultural development into the area and founded the town in 1896 that bears his name. Some of the land now occupied by Buffalo Bill State Park was originally owned by Colonel Cody and was acquired from him by the federal government to implement the reservoir project.

Work began on the dam in 1905. When completed in 1910, it was the highest dam in the world at 325 feet. Buffalo Bill State Park was established in 1957 and provided recreational areas and facilities along the original shoreline. In 1993 an eight year project was completed which raised the crest of the dam 25 feet and increased the reservoir storage capacity. The enlarged reservoir inundated the former recreation areas which required removal of the old park facilities. Buffalo Bill State Park has been redeveloped as part of the project.

Surrounding mountains dominate the scenery at Buffalo Bill State Park. Shoshone Canyon, the location of the dam, is framed by Rattlesnake Mountain to the north and Cedar Mountain (also known as Spirit Mountain) to the south. Further west, along the north shoreline, lies Logan Mountain. The north and south forks of the Shoshone River are divided by Sheep Mountain while prominent on the southern skyline is Carter Mountain. All are part of the Rocky Mountain Absaroka (Ab- Sor'-ka) Range. Elevations vary from approximately 5,400 feet in the state park to over 10,000 feet in the Absarokas.

Reprint of Wyoming State Parks and Historic Sites brochure.

H A Burning Need

Approximately five miles west of Wapiti on U.S. Highway 14.

The Shoshone National Forest provides habitat for more Rocky Mountain bighorn sheep than any other national forest. Grazing on nutritious bunchgrasses, bighorn sheep evolved in open, high visibility habitats near steep, rocky cover, making it easier for sheep to detect and avoid predators.

Due to fire suppression by humans over the past 60 plus years, limber pine, juniper, sagebrush, and other shrubs have increased on seasonal bighorn sheep habitats within the Shoshone National Forest and other portions of range.

In cooperation with the Wyoming game and Fish Department, the Foundation for North American Wild Sheep (FNAWS), and the Wyoming Chapter FNAWS, the US Forest Service has implemented a prescribed burning program, to maintain and improve habitat quality for bighorn sheep. On the slopes of Jim Mountain, bighorns are finding new foraging areas, thanks to this cooperative effort.

H Born of Fire and Ice, The Holy City

Approximately eight miles west of Wapiti on U.S. Highway 14.

Resembling a silhouette of the ancient city of Jerusalem, these formations reveal the earth's history in records before human timekeeping. Created millions of years ago by volcanoes, these unique formations reveal a geologic era of chaos and fury. Erosion of these rocks continues to shape the earth's landscape just as it has for the last 50 million years? Fifty million years ago Volcanoes were erupting one afer another with each eruption equalling the magnitude of Mt. St. Helens in 1990. A thick, soupy mixture of rock and ash blanketed the entire region. Known as "breccia", this mixture of rock and ash slowly cooled. Runoff from the streams and gullies began carving through the soft breccia, sculpting these unique rock formations. Wind blew tiny bits of sand and dust at the rock further eroding it. Small streams widened to gullies carving deeper into the breccia on its way down to the river.

H Protection Proves Profitable

Approximately five miles west of Wapiti.

This valley has sustained life for thousands of years. Early Native Americans were drawn here to hunt buffalo, elk, deer, moose sheep and bear. It has always been considered a unique place. The establishment of the nation's first park and timber reserve in the late 1800's spurred angry protests among local settlers. They were outraged that vast tracts of land were no longer available for personal gains. Soon residents realized the profits to made from tourism. A new road through the valley brought more people into the region. While in many other parts of the west resources were being spent for profit, these protected resources would prove profitable for local citizens. Lodges along the byway date back to this early era in our nation's history. The highway, Buffalo Bill Dam and the town of Cody were born from this visionary planning over a century ago. Relish this country, its legends and heros where a window of the "Wild West" remains for future generations.

H Wapiti Ranger Station, First in the Nation

Approximately nine miles west of Wapiti on U.S. Highway 14.

Before you stands the first forest supervisor's headquarters in the country, authorized and built in 1903 with government funds. When the supervisor's headquarters was moved to Cody, Wyoming in 1907, this building became a ranger station. Its unique role in the history of the conservation movement earned this station status on the National Register of Historic Places.

Originally a log structure, the Wapiti Ranger Station has expanded as the Forest Service mission evolved. It is still a hub of Forest Service activity today with men and women performing a variety of duties.

The life of the nation's first forest ranger wasn't easy. Early advertisements for these positions read: "A ranger must be able to take care of himself and his horses under very trying conditions, build trails and cabins, ride all day and night. Pack, shoot and fight fire without losing his head. All this requires a very vigorous constitution…the hardest kind of physical work from beginning to end."

C.G. Poole, North Fork District Ranger - 1908

H Castle Rock

About 18 miles southwest of Cody on South Fork Road.

John Colter, famed among the famous breed of "Mountain Men", passed this landmark late in the fall of 1807 while on business for the fur trader Manuel Lisa. Searching for Indians in order to conduct trade, he also hunted salt caves reputedly located near headwaters of this stream, then known as the "stinking water".

On his journey Colter not only discovered

Section 1

Bighorn sheep crossing on the Buffalo Bill Scenic Highway.

this later named Shoshone River but he also became the first recorded white man to visit the upper Wind River, Jackson's Hole and Yellowstone Park. His lonely trek, compunding the normal dangers of savage wilderness by mid-winter passage of a broad and lofty mountain range, lives in history and legend an epic of fortitudinous exploration.

28 *No services*

H Shoshone National Forest Blackwater Fire August 20-24, 1937

Just east of Yellowstone East Gate on U.S. Highway 14.

This marks the beginning of the fire fighters' memorial trail which follows Blackwater Creek five miles to the place of origin of the fire, and thence to other points of interest. This fire was controlled after burning over 1,254 acres of forest. Fifteen fire fighters lost their lives and thirty nine others were injured when the fire was whipped up by a sudden gale on August 21. Signs and monuments mark the important locations along this trail, including the fire camps. The first aid station, Clayton Gulch where eight men were killed and the rocky knoll where Ranger Post gathered his crew to escape the fire.

H A Day in the Life of an Early Forest Ranger

Approximately nine miles west of Wapiti on U.S. Highway 14.

Early rangers faced immense challenges. Due to lack of trained forest rangers, early national forests were the training grounds for "men who were to range far and wide over the nation's forests." A "jack of all trades", these rangers had to be innovative, resourceful and persuasive. Their duties on any given day could include a diversity of tasks, as a journal records: July l901 : "I was offered a job in July, 1901 as a forest ranger on the Shoshone Division of the Yellowstone Timberland Reserve. The rangers job was only for the summer months and paid $60 per month with nothing furnished. I had not only to furnish the necessary pack and saddle animals, camp equipment and supplies, but also the necessary tools with which to work. My duties consisted largely in patrolling to prevent trespass of all kinds and to suppress such forest fires as occured." Sept. 1902. I found a bunch of sheep about a mile up Elk Fork. The owners, on being questioned, stated he was looking for range for his sheep, but decided to move when the matter was explained to him". June 1905: "One of my many duties as ranger in those early years, as now, was the inforcement of State fish and game laws. This caused some confusion and controversy for a few years, but a more wholesome respect for and compliance with state game laws and Federal regulations were soon established."

Oct. 1905: "My district was bordered on the west by Yellowstone National Park and I spent considerable time in that part of the district in the fall during the hunting season and watching for fires."

June 1906: "The weekly mail brought into the basin news of the passage of this new Homestead Law. Immediately one of the settlers adjoining the ranger station came down to the station and ordered me to move, stating that he was taking the ranger station as a homestead. After some discussion he became convinced that I was not going to be forcibly evicted, so he went home rather disgruntled."

J.W. Nelson, Ranger on the Shoshone July, 1901 - March, 1907

H Dead Indian Summit Altitude 8,000 Feet

Chief Joseph Scenic Highway about 13 miles west of junction with State Highway 120.

This pass is the summit of Dead Indian Hill. Through this portal great herds of wild game seasonally migrated from the mountains to the plains. This high pass was the gate way for countless indian hunting and war parties, and through this portal Chief Joseph, in 1877, led his Nez Perce Indians in a strategic and defensive retreat, persued by U.S. Army soldiers. Over this one and only opening of the valleys to the west traveled a vast army of miners to seek wealth of cooke city, and down this steep hill the early settlers of Sunlight Basin braved its dangers. the first road improvement was made possible in 1909, by dwellers of Sunlight Valley whose names are here inscribed. Adophus J. Beam, William V. Campbell, Siras J. Davis, Oliver Whitney, Hervey g. Marvin, Samual Thompson, Mary E. Painter, Wm. T. Painter, Marguerita M. Painter, Wade M. McClung, Augustus A. Lafond, John R. Painter, Evelyn T. Painter, John K. Rollinson, Willard D. Ruscher.

Scenic Drives

Chief Joseph Scenic Byway

This scenic byway, on Wyoming 296, links the town of Cody with the Beartooth Highway and the Northeast Gate of Yellowstone National Park. The route crosses the Shoshone National Forest through the Absaroka Mountains to the Clarks Fork Valley. The 47 paved miles of the Scenic Byway run from the junction with US 120, 17 miles north of Cody, northwest to their connection with US 212, the Beartooth Highway. The Beartooth Mountains and the Clarks Fork of the Yellowstone River lie to the north of the road, and the Absaroka Mountains and North Absaroka Wilderness are to the south. Allow one hour minimum driving time over this stretch of Byway.

The most predictable times to travel this highway are during the summer and fall. During the winter months snow plows keep the roadway open to just east of the entrance to Yellowstone National Park. The road is at times steep and winding, and boasts the highest highway bridge in Wyoming - over Sunlight Creek. The road crests at 8060-foot Dead Indian Pass. The Pass is a good place to observe some 25 rugged peaks rising more than 12,000 feet above sea level.
Reprinted from Wyoming Department of Transportation Brochure

Beartooth Scenic Byway

On US 212, this is the most northern route across the Shoshone National Forest in the Beartooth Mountains. The 70 miles of the Scenic Byway run from Red Lodge, Montana to the eastern border of Yellowstone National Park. Beginning at Red Lodge, the Absaroka-Beartooth Wilderness and the Custer and Gallatin National Forests lie to the north as the road heads southwest into Wyoming. The North Absaroka Wilderness lies to the south as the road follows the Clarks Fork of the Yellowstone River toward Yellowstone Park. Allow at least three hours driving time from Red Lodge to Yellowstone Park on this Byway.

US 212 is the highest paved, primary road in Wyoming, cresting at 10, 947-foot Beartooth Pass. The scenery along this two-lane paved highway proves that the beauty of Yellowstone National Park does not diminish at its borders. The alpine country and high mountain lakes are accessible to highway travel only from late May to mid-October due to heavy snows.

Growing in the wet meadows, you may see Indian Paintbrush, monkey flower, senecio and buttercups. Lupines, arrow leaf, balsamroot, beardstongue, and forget-me-nots are found in drier areas. Snow banks often remain until August near Beartooth Pass, and some remnants of drifts may remain all summer. A pink color often appears on the snow later in the summer, caused by the decay of microscopic plants that grow on the surface of the snow.
Reprinted from Wyoming Department of Transportation Brochure

Buffalo Bill Cody Scenic Byway

This byway, along US 14/16/20, follows the North Fork of the Shoshone River through scenic Wapiti

Valley to the East Entrance of Yellowstone National Park. The 27 mile segment of paved road starts about 25 miles west of Cody at the Shoshone National Forest border. Normal driving time from the forest boundary to the Park is approximately 45 minutes.
Reprinted from Wyoming Department of Transportation Brochure

Centennial Scenic Byway

The 163 miles between Pinedale and Dubois, via Jackson, comprise the Centennial Scenic Byway. This horseshoe-shaped combination of highways includes US 26/287 and US 26/89/191. The route crosses diverse landscapes from badlands and ranch land to forests and mountain passes. It traverses Fremont, Teton, and Sublette counties in northwestern Wyoming.

The entire route is open year-round and could be driven straight through in about four hours, but few people do so because of the many attractions and outstanding scenery that make this region of Wyoming one of the top tourist destinations in America. Among other things, there are more moose, beaver, and greater sand hill cranes along this route than any other place in the Rocky Mountains. Coyotes, ravens, badgers, Swainson's hawks, and Northern harriers can be seen in the summer. During the winter, mule deer, magpies and cottontail rabbits can often be spotted.

The northern end of the Byway begins at Dubois, on Us 26/287, while the southern end of the tours begins at Pinedale on US 191. The route follows a modern, two-lane, paved highway that crosses the Continental Divide and crests at an elevation of 9658 feet at Togwotee (Toe-ga-tee) Pass. From Dubois, a 39-mile stretch meets US 26-89-191 at Moran Junction. From there the Byway takes a mostly southerly route through the town of Jackson, to Hoback Junction and Bondurant before reaching its conclusion at Pinedale. Many side roads to the area's diverse attractions can be accessed from this Byway.
Reprinted from Wyoming Department of Transportation Brochure

Buffalo Valley Road

A great drive to view moose in the winter and access Teton Wilderness trailheads. Also offers wonderful views of the Teton Range. Buffalo Valley Road is a 14 mile scenic by-way of US 26/287. It intersects the highway three miles east of Moran and is paved for ten miles to Turpin Meadows.The last four miles are gravel and is not plowed during the winter.

Fall Creek Road

A scenic alternative for those heading south from Jackson. Fall Creek Road connects Wilson with the Snake River Canyon.Varied habitats and bird watching opportunities make this 18 mile by-way an excellent choice. Twelve miles south of Wilson are paved, the remainder of the road is graveled or natural surface.The road is generally in good condition and clearance is not a problem. Fishing and hiking opportunities can also be found.

Greys River Road "Watch me Grow"

Following the river for 58 miles provides an excellent opportunity to watch a small stream become a river. Camping, fishing, hiking, horseback riding, hunting and wildlife viewing are all popular activities. The gravel and natural surface road climbs gradually from Alpine to Tri-Basin Divide. Although passable to low-clearance vehicles, the upper ten miles can be rough or slick when wet. Several other Forest Service roads connect to Greys River Road, accessing Afton, Big Piney and LaBarge.

Hams Fork Road

A 66 mile road between Kemmerer and Cokeville.The first 20 miles from Kemmerer are paved; the remainder of the road is gravel or natural surface.There are some rough places, but driven with care, clearance is not a problem. The road follows the Hams Fork River–named after mountain man Zacharias Ham. There are many scenic views along the road and moose are frequently seen.

Hatchet/Flagstaff Road

Offering splendid views of Buffalo Valley and the Teton Range, there is also the meadows, sagebrush and forested areas.

A 19 mile long scenic by-way of US 26/287.The west end of the road is at the Hatchet Campground, next to the Buffalo Forest Service office, and returns to the highway two miles east of the Cowboy Village Resort at Togwotee.The road is also popular with mountain bikers and snowmobilers in the winter.

LaBarge Road

Attractions include a spring with travertine deposits, the Lander Cut-Off Trail and wildflower meadows.

The 48-mile road follows the river named for mountain man Joseph M. LaBarge. The first 11 miles from LaBarge are paved, while the remaining 37 miles are gravel or natural surface.

McDougal Gap Road

Crossing the Wyoming Range and connecting the Green and Greys Rivers, the scenery along this by-way can't be beaten. From the agricultural lands to the subalpine forests, tremendous habitat diversity is passed through and many recreation opportunities await.

McDougal Gap Road meets US 189 south of Daniel and intersects the Greys River Road one mile north of Forest Park-a distance of 35 miles.The 12 mile Forest portion is gravel or natural surface and some sections can be rough.The road is usually snow covered until early July.

Middle Piney Road

A scenic drive passing two campgrounds ending at Middle Piney Lake is great for boating and fishing. Several Forest Service roads and trails can be accessed from the Middle Piney Road.

The road begins as WY 350 in Big Piney and is paved for 11 miles. It is another 9 miles to the Forest boundary, and then 6 miles to Middle Piney Lake, a total distance of 26 miles.The last mile of road is usually not open until early July.

Skyline Drive

A short, 16 mile paved road to the popular Trail's End Campground and Trailhead offering spectacular views of the Wind River Range. Skyline Drive climbs into the mountains from Pinedale. Between Pinedale and Trail's End are several scenic overlooks and roads to Fremont and Halfmoon Lake to explore.

Smith's Fork Road

Connecting Upper Star Valley to the Greys River Road, Smith's Fork offers a scenic diversion for those traveling US 89.The 22 mile road is natural surface which can be rough on passenger vehicles.

Smith's Fork Road joins US 89 6.5 miles south of Smoot and two miles north of Salt River Pass.The road connects with the Greys River Road at Tri-Basin Divide. From here you may also head southeast towards LaBarge.

Union Pass

Crossing the north end of the Wind River Range and two National Forests, the 60 mile Union Pass Road offers spectacular scenery and many recreation opportunities. Wyoming 352, off US 191 north of Pinedale, takes you to the Forest boundary where the pavement ends.The Union Pass Road branches off at the Kendall Bridge, 3 miles north of the Forest boundary. Signed intersections help navigate you over Union Pass to US 26 north of Dubois.The road is gravel or natural surface.There can be a few rough spots, a high clearance vehicle is recommended. There are many side roads off the Union Pass road that should be explored, especially Green River Lakes.

Hikes

Teton Area

Huckleberry Mountain
Distance: 10 miles (round trip)
Climb: 2000 feet
Rating: moderate/ difficult
Usage: moderate
Location: The trail begins at Sheffield Creek Trailhead, 1 mile southeast of Flagg Ranch between Grand Teton and Yellowstone National Parks.

Breathtaking views of the Tetons, Yellowstone National Park, and the surrounding wilderness reward those undertaking this climb. Huckleberry Lookout is listed on the National Register of Historic Places. Fire lookouts lived here in the summer, keeping a watchful eye for fires.

Jenny Lake Trails
Distance: about 2 to 7 miles
Climb: gentle/ moderate
Rating: easy/ moderate
Usage: heavy
Location: Travel north on Hwy. 191 about 12 miles from Jackson to Moose Junction. Turn left, and follow the Teton Park Rd. west and north to South Jenny Lake Junction. The trailhead is by the boat dock.

Several trails go around Jenny Lake, and diverge from it as well. The most popular hike is the one leading to Hidden Falls and Inspiration Point. The trail winds west and somewhat south around the lake, splitting at a junction that leads to Moose Ponds about 3/4 mile away. The trail forks again a little farther along, but both forks lead to the falls eventually. The trails crisscross and intersect around Cascade Creek, which can be followed upstream to Hidden Falls. Don't worry about getting confused about which trail to go on. There are usually lots of people around to point you in the right direction. Continue across the creek to proceed to Inspiration Point, where there is a lovely view of the Tetons and Jenny Lake. These portions of the hike are more strenuous, due to the uphill climb of about 500 feet elevation gain. You can continue to follow the creek upstream for another 4.5 miles to Cascade Canyon (making this an overnight hike), or head back to the lake and return back the way you came. You can also take the ferry back across the

The Astorians

The first white men to cross an established Indian trail in what is today's Sublette County. They were the Astorians, led by explorer Wilson Price Hunt, in 1811, employees of John Jacob Astor and the American Fur Company. The party was seeking to establish cross-continental routes for the fur trade. While camping near present day Pinedale, they met and traded with Snake Indians. Here they gathered buffalo meat for the journey ahead. A small but steady stream of fur trappers and traders followed on their heels in the years that followed. The fur trade expanded rapidly during the 1820s and brought to Wyoming William H. Ashley who came up with the idea to have an annual rendezvous instead of trying to maintain a series of permanent trading posts. The annual Rendezvous was held at a different location each year and brought mountain men and natives together for fun and trade. Other lively mountain men such as Jim Bridger, John Hoback, Jedediah Smith, Bill Sublette, David E. Jackson, and Robert Campbell were also known to work the area. Increasing competition with the Hudson's Bay and American Fur companies depleted the beaver catch and brought an end to the fur trade by the 1840s.

lake, or take the boat from the East Shore Boat Dock to this point, and hike back. Another option is to finish circling the lake, and take the trail north to the base of String Lake, then follow it down the east side of Jenny Lake for another 2.9 miles back to the boat dock.

Leigh and String Lakes Trails
Distance: about 3 to 4 miles
Climb: gentle
Rating: easy
Usage: moderate
Location: Travel north on Hwy. 191 about 12 miles from Jackson to Moose Junction. Turn left, and follow the Teton Park Rd. west and north to the String Lake Picnic Area.

These trails are less well known than the Jenny Lake Trails, so they are usually less crowded, but still offer lovely views. The trail heads north from the picnic area, following the edge of String Lake and continuing up and around Leigh Lake to Trapper and Bear Paw Lakes, about 3.7 miles, or a fork at the top of String Lake takes you west for about 0.8 miles to another junction. The trail continues northwest for 4.5 miles to Holly Lake, or heads south, back to String Lake, and eventually to the road leading to the picnic area, about a 1.6 mile trek. This route also intersects with the Jenny Lake Trail (or Valley Trail) at the southern tip of String Lake.

Bradley and Taggart Lakes Trails
Distance: about 3 to 7 miles
Climb: moderate
Rating: moderate
Usage: moderate
Location: These trails can be accessed from two points. The first is at Lupine Meadows Parking Area, just south of Jenny Lake Junction, and the other is about 3 miles farther south on Teton Park Road, at Taggart Lake Trailhead. Teton Park Road is just off of Hwy. 191, about 12 miles north of Jackson, west at Moose Junction.

This area was burned by forest fires in 1985, but much re-growth has taken place since then. Grasses, flowering plants, small trees, and an abundance of wildlife populate the area now. The Lupine Meadow segment of the trail traverses about 1.7 miles before it forks to the west and south. The west branch goes another 3.1 miles to the Amphitheater and Surprise Lakes. The south branch heads towards the lakes, crossing the top of Bradley Lake then forking again below the lake at 1.3 miles. The right fork follows the shoreline of Taggart Lake, while the left fork heads cross country, about one mile either way. The shoreline trail has two more junctions, the first being a choice between crossing the south tip of the lake or doubling back to the cross-country trail. The second offers a detour to Phelps Lake, another 6.1 miles of travel (definitely overnight), or returns east to again connect with the cross-country trail, which terminates at the Taggart Lake Trailhead.

Phelps Lake Trails
Distance: about 3 to 7 miles
Climb: gentle/ steep
Rating: moderate
Usage: light
Location: Travel north on Hwy. 191 about 12 miles from Jackson to Moose Junction. Go west at the junction, and turn left when the road forks, taking the Moose/Wilson Road. Take a right about 3 miles south to the Death Canyon Trailhead. This is a narrow, winding road, and is closed to RV's, trailers, and buses.

This trail (the Valley Trail) goes either northeast, towards Taggart Lake for about 4 miles, or you can head west , towards Phelps Lake and its surrounding area. The west trail goes gradually up for about a mile to the Phelps Lake Lookout, where you will find a panoramic view of wet meadows, aspen groves, and the lake. Several switchbacks take you down to the lake, making for a strenuous return climb. About midway, the Death Canyon Trail intersects with the Valley Trail, which leads to the Death Canyon Patrol Cabin, about 3.7 miles farther west. This is a good place to turn around for a day hike. You can continue on the Death Canyon Trail another 9.2 miles, climbing about 3000 feet over the highest point of public trails in the park, to arrive at Static Peak. This is a not a technical climb, but it is strenuous, and would require a permit and at least an overnight stay.

Continuing on the Valley Trail, about a mile farther south of the Death Canyon Junction, the trail forks again, the left fork following the shoreline, and the right fork taking a scenic loop towards the Open Canyon Trail. The Valley Trail, which originates at Jenny Lake, continues on south to the Granite Canyon Trailhead, another 3.5 miles below Phelps Lake.

Hermitage Point Trails
Distance: 3 or 4 miles
Climb: flat
Rating: easy
Usage: moderate/heavy
Location: Travel north of Jackson about 25 miles to the Colter Bay turn off. Park at the Colter Bay Visitor Center.

These trails meander around the eastern shore of Jackson Lake, encompassing Swan Lake, Heron Pond, and the Second and Third Creek areas. As the names indicate, this is prime bird-watching territory, as well as ideal for viewing elk, moose, beaver, otters, and other wildlife. The most popular trail is a loop which follows the shore of Jackson Lake for about a half mile, cuts between Heron Pond and Swan Lake for about one mile, then returns a little farther east. An alternative 4.5 mile trail from Jackson Lake Lodge ends at the horse corrals of Colter Bay. Other trails continue south, both along Jackson Lake and around the other nearby bodies of water. Some trails may be closed to allow for revegetation so please observe the signs. Further information on the trails can be obtained at the visitor center.

Jackson Area

Black Canyon Overlook Trail
Distance: 2 miles
Climb: gentle
Rating: easy
Usage: moderate
Location: From Jackson follow Hwy. 222 west to the summit of Teton Pass. Park at the south side turnout. The trailhead is well marked at the parking area.

This trail follows the ridge south of the pass, through sub-alpine meadows and forest, with views of Jackson Hole and the surrounding mountains. Wildflowers of all kinds can be seen throughout the summer along this trail. To make a loop on the trail, follow it on Black Canyon to the end of Trail Creek Road at the bottom of the pass. This option requires a shuttle from the bottom of Teton Pass back to the parking area.

Cache Creek Trail #3025
Distance: 6 miles
Climb: gentle
Rating: easy
Usage: heavy
Location: From the Town Square, travel east on Broadway to Redmond St. Follow Redmond to Cache Creek Drive, then go the parking lot at the end.

This hike is very close to town, and offers stunning views of the town and surrounding area. The trail follows an old road and has a consistent and gentle grade. The creek flows along the entire trail and is easily accessed at various points. During the summer months you may see moose, deer, elk, and other wildlife. This easy hike is great for the whole family, but plan for it to take the better part of a day. The Tiny Hagen and Putt Putt Trails both diverge from the Cache Creek Trail. Either trail can be followed downhill to the parking lot. Both trails are more strenuous than the Cache Creek Trail, adding as much as two hours to the total travel time.

Granite Creek Falls Trail
Distance: 2 miles
Climb: gentle
Rating: easy
Usage: moderate
Location: From Jackson follow Hwy. 89 south to Hoback Junction. Go east on Hwy 191 about 11 miles to Granite Creek Road, and turn left. Follow this road to a parking area at the junction of Swift Creek and Granite Creek. Parking is also available at Granite Hot Springs. From there, follow the trail downstream on the east side to the falls.

This trail follows the east side of Granite Creek upstream to the falls. Continuing up the trail you will reach Granite Hot Springs, open year round. A fee is required to take a dip in the springs. Beyond this point the trail goes on to the Gros Ventre Wilderness. No bicycles are permitted beyond the wilderness border.

Ski Lake Trail
Distance: 3 miles
Climb: moderate
Rating: moderate
Usage: moderate
Location: From Jackson travel west on Hwy. 22 up Teton Pass to an unmarked dirt road, about 4 miles west of Hungry Jack Store. There is no developed trailhead. Parking is on the dirt road or across the highway. Walk up the road about 1/2 mile to fork. Go left to sign board, where trail begins.

This trail follows a side slope to a rocky viewpoint with spectacular views of the Snake River Range and Jackson Hole. From there, the trail enters the forest and emerges in a meadow. A sign marks the trail junction. Go left to Ski Lake, climbing through forest and open slopes to the beautiful alpine lake. Then, go right to Phillips Pass, which follows another side slope through pine and aspen stands, and avalanche chutes, then drops in elevation to Phillips Canyon. The trail then climbs into sub-alpine meadows and up to Phillips Pass. This is a great place to see midsummer wildflowers.

East Table Trail
Distance: 2 miles
Climb: steep
Rating: moderate
Usage: light
Location: From Jackson, follow Hwy. 89 south about 20 miles along the Snake River to East Table Campground. The trailhead is located across the highway from the campground. Parking is available here.

This trail follows the steep, narrow canyon of East Table Creek, which quickly turns into a branched, intermittent drainage. The trail continues up a slope to the west and through meadows to a flat bench, from which there are spectacular views of the Snake River Canyon and the mountains to the south. Beyond this overlook, the trail continues through meadows and climbs steeply to the east side of a long ridge, which eventually meets the Red Pass Trail at Wolf Mountain. This section of the trail is not well marked or maintained, but the view makes the climb worthwhile. This option adds considerable time and distance to the hike.

Snow King Trail
Distance: 5 miles
Climb: steep
Rating: moderate/ difficult
Usage: heavy
Location: This trail is accessed at the bottom of the Snow King charilift. From the Town Square in Jackson, travel south on South Cache to the Snow King Ski Area. Parking is available at the bottom of the ski hill.

This trail is basically the service road for Snow King Mountain. It switches back up the ski slope to the top of the ridge, where there is a shelter and view area. Many tracks take off in other directions along the way. The view of the Jackson Hole area is spectacular. The chairlift operates in the summer, so hikers can either hike up and ride down, or vice versa. On top of Snow King there is also a well-marked nature trail.

Grizzly Lake Trail
Distance: 3.5 miles
Climb: steep
Rating: moderate
Usage: light
Location: From Jackson, travel north on Hwy. 89/191 for about 6 miles to Gros Ventre Road and turn right. Continue on this road through the town of Kelly, about one mile, then turn right again on Gros Ventre Road and go about 11 miles to the Red Hills Campground. Parking is available here.

This trail is well marked and easy to follow. Along the way it crosses several slopes and deep drainages, so the first two miles are strenuous. High points along the way offer terrific views of the Red Hills and the Gros Ventre River Valley. At the junction with the Blue Miner Lake Trail, the trail levels off and drops into the basin of Grizzly Lake.

Willow Creek Trail
Distance: 5 miles
Climb: steep
Rating: difficult
Usage: light/ moderate.
Location: From Jackson, travel south on Hwy. 89 to Hoback Junction, then go east on Hwy. 191 about 5 miles to FDR 30460, and turn right by the moose statue. Travel 1.5 miles down dirt road to the parking area at the right, with sign board and information.

This trail skirts a fence on a sagebrush-covered slope west of the trailhead, then climbs through open forest and meadows to a ridge overlooking Willow Creek. At the ridge, the trail forks. To stay on this trail, follow the sign, and at the base of the hill, turn left to follow Willow Creek. When it reaches Lick Creek, turn left again and follow the Wyoming Spur Trail to the ridge, then back on same trail to the trailhead. If you want to add another 1/3 mile to the trek, turn right at the top of the ridge, and head for the top of Ann's Mountain. You will return by the same route.

Shoal Falls Overlook
Distance: 5 miles
Climb: steep
Rating: difficult
Usage: light
Location: From Jackson, follow Hwy. 89 south to Hoback Junction. Go east on Hwy. 191 about 11 miles to Granite Creek Road, and turn left. Follow this road to a parking area at the junction of Swift Creek and Granite Creek. A sign indicates the trailhead.

This trail follows an old two-track road for the first half mile, then turns south and angles up a forested side slope, which reaches a dissected bench at the base of the Gros Ventre Mountains. The trail continues to Deer Ridge, where you'll find the overlook for Shoal Falls, then drops into Shoal Creek. To reach the falls, you need to follow the creek upstream, off the trail, about 1.5 miles.

Alpine Area

Bailey Lake
Distance: 4.5 miles from Waterdog Lake, 5.5 from McCain Guard Station.
Location: To reach the trailheads, follow the Greys River Road 71/2 miles east from Alpine, to the Little Greys River Road Junction. After approximately 12 miles on the Little Greys River Road, you will reach a turn-off for McCain Guard Station. The next intersection, reached in 2.5 miles, goes left to the guard station or right to Waterdog Lake.

This is a great!little lake for fishing or bird watching and solitude.

Pinedale Area

CCC Ponds
Distance: short
Location: The trailhead is located near Sandy Beach, off Skyline Drive, 2.5 miles north of Pinedale.

This is a short hike, to peaceful ponds close to the town of Pinedale. The ponds offer good fishing and excellent wildlife observation opportunities. The trail is paved, suitable for wheelchairs; benches along the way provide rest spots.

Cliff Creek Falls
Distance: 12.4 miles (round trip)
Location: The Cliff Creek Road leaves US 189/191 15 miles east of Hoback Junction or 5 miles west of Bondurant. Follow the gravel road 7.1 miles to the trailhead.

A beautiful two-tiered waterfall, Cliff Creek has a short upper falls followed by a fifty-foot plunge. The hike to the falls and return requires a full day. This is also a popular mountain bike ride.

Fontenelle Lakes
Distance: varies
Climb: varies
Rating: moderate
Usage: moderate/ heavy
Location: There are two trailheads on the LaBarge Road. The South LaBarge Trailhead is located a few miles from Scalar Guard Station. The Shaffer Creek Trailhead has a horse corral and larger parking lot.

A cluster of small lakes in the scenic Fontenelle Basin, the Fontanelle Lakes can be explored by horseback, mountain biking, or on foot. The South LaBarge Trail is an uphill climb. The Shaffer Creek Trail is less steep.

Monument Ridge
Distance: 10 miles (round trip)
Climb: 440 feet
Rating: moderate
Usage: light
Location: The trailhead is accessed from Clark's Draw Road (Forest Road 30530) two miles east of Bondurant. When the road forks at 1/2 mile, follow the right fork to the road's end. The road is natural surface and often in poor condition.

A panoramic view rewards those undertaking this gentle climb through aspen forests and wildflower meadows.

Information Please

Tourism Information

Big Piney/Marbleton Chamber of Commerce 276-3815
Dubois Chamber of Commerce 789-2757
Chamber of Commerce of Jackson 733-3316
Chamber of Commerce - Pinedale 367-2242

Government

BLM Pinedale Field Office 367-5300
Shoshone National Forest - Wind River Ranger District 455-2466
Bridger-Teton National Forest 739-5400
Bridger-Teton National Forest - Big Piney Ranger District 543-2386
Bridger-Teton National Forest - Greys River Ranger District 885-3166
Bridger-Teton National Forest - Jackson Ranger District 739-5400
Bridger-Teton National Forest - Pinedale Ranger District 367-4326

Car Rentals

Aspen Rent-A-Car • Jackson 733-9224
Alamo Rent A Car • Jackson Hole 733-0671
Budget • Jackson Hole 733-2206

Dollar Rent A Car • Jackson 733-9224
Eagle Rent A Car • Jackson 739-9999
Hertz • Jackson 733-2272
Leisure Sports Car Rental • Jackson 733-3040
Thrifty • Jackson 739-9300

Hospitals

Alpine Clinic • Alpine 654-7138
St John's Medical Center • Jackson 733-3636
Teton Village Clinic St John's Medical Center • Teton Village 739-7346

Airports

Big Piney 276-3386
Dubois 455-3339
Jackson Hole 733-5454
Pinedale 367-4151

Golf

Valli Vu Golf Club • Afton 886-3338
Antelope Hills Golf Course • Dubois 455-2888
Rendezvous Meadows Public Golf Course • Pinedale 746-2639
Teton Pines Country Club • Jackson 733-1733
Jackson Hole Golf & Tennis Club • Jackson 733-3111
Aspen Hills at Star Valley Ranch Country Club • Thayne 883-2230

Ski Areas

White Pine Ski Area & Resort 367-6606
Jackson Hole 733-3990
Grand Targhee Ski & Summer Resort 353-2300

Guest Ranches

MacKenzie Highland Ranch • Dubois 455-3415
Absaroka Ranch • Dubois 455-2275
Box R Ranch • 367-4868
Jensen's Guest Ranch • Afton 886-3401
Box Y Lodge & Guest Ranch • Alpine 654-7564
Sheep Mountain Outfitters • Alpine 654-7564
Preston Ranch • Bedford 883-2742
High Wild & Lonesome • Big Piney 276-3208
Wood Canyon Retreat • Big Piney 276-5441
Darby Mountain Outfitters, Inc • Big Piney 386-9220
Triple Peak • Big Piney 276-3408
Boulder Lake Lodge • Boulder 537-5400
Green River Guest Ranch • Cora 367-2314
Flying U Ranch • Cora 367-4479
David Ranch • Daniel 859-8228
CM Ranch • Dubois 455-2331
Ring Lake Ranch • Dubois 455-2663
T Cross Ranch • Dubois 455-2206
Lazy L & B Ranch • Dubois 455-2839
Moose Head Ranch • Dubois 733-3141
Triangle C Ranch • Dubois 455-2225
Bitterroot Ranch • Dubois 545-3363
Crooked Creek Guest Ranch • Dubois 545-3035
Elk Trails Riding Ranch • Dubois 545-3615
Double Bar J Ranch • Dubois 545-2681
Mill Iron 4 Mill Guest Ranch • Dubois 545-3478
Triple E Ranch • Dubois 555-2304
EA Ranch • Dubois 455-3335
Haderlie's Tincup Mountain Guest Ranch • Freedom 208-873-2368
Split Creek Ranch • Jackson 733-7522
Jackson's Hole Adventure • Jackson 654-7849
Mill Iron Ranch • Jackson 733-6390
A-OK Corral • Jackson 733-6556
Beard Mountain Ranch • Jackson 576-2694
Darwin Ranch • Jackson 733-5588
Flat Creek Ranch • Jackson 733-0603
Goosewing Ranch • Jackson 733-5251
Spotted Horse Ranch • Jackson 733-2097
Spring Creek Ranch • Jackson 733-8833
R Lazy S Ranch • Kelly 733-2655
Red Rock Ranch • Kelly 733-6288
Gros Ventre River Ranch • Moose 733-4138
Triangle X Ranch • Moose 733-2183
Cottonwoods Ranch • Moose 733-0945
Lost Creek Ranch • Moose 733-3435
Cowboy Village at Togwotee • Moran 733-8800
Togwotee Mountain Lodge • Moran 543-2847
Box K Ranch • Moran 543-2407
Flagg Ranch & Village • Moran 543-2861
Turpin Meadow Ranch • Moran 543-2000
Diamond D Ranch Outfitters • Moran 543-2479
Heart 6 Ranch • Moran/Jackson Hole 543-2477
Flying A Ranch • Pinedale 367-2385
Fort William Guest Ranch• Pinedale 367-4670
Green River Outfitters • Pinedale 367-2416
Pinedale Creek Ranch • Pinedale 367-2544
DC Bar Guest Ranch • Pinedale 367-2268
UXU Ranch • Tie Siding 587-2143
Crossed Sabres Ranch • Wapati 587-3750
Rocking D River Ranch • Wapati 587-8329
Sweetwater Lodge • Wapati 527-7817
Trail Creek Ranch • Wilson 733-2610

Lodges and Resorts

Twin Pines Lodge & Cabins • Dubois 455-2600
The Virginian Lodge & Restaurant • Jackson 733-2792
The Lodge at Pinedale • Pinedale 367-8800
Lakeside Lodge Resort & Marina on Fremont Lake • Pinedale 367-2221
Half Moon Lake Resort • Pinedale 367-6373
Jackson Hole Resort Lodging • Teton Village 733-3990
Star Valley Ranch Resorts & RV Camping • Thayne 883-2670
Silver Stream Lodge & Cabins • Afton 883-2440
Box Y Lodge & Guest Ranch • Alpine 654-7564
Royal Resort • Alpine 654-7545
Sheep Mountain Outfitters • Alpine 654-7564
Snake River Resort and RV Park • Alpine 674-7340
Teton Teepee Lodge • Alta 353-8176
Boulder Lake Lodge • Boulder 537-5400
Elk Ridge Lodge • Cora 367-2553
Rendezvous on the Green • Cora 367-2278
Chinook Winds Mountain Lodge • Dubois 455-2987
Brooks Lake Lodge • Dubois 455-2121
Lake's Lodge, Inc. • Dubois 455-2171
Camp Creek Inn & Fine Dining • Hoback Junction 733-3099
Rusty Parrot Lodge & Spa • Jackson 733-2000
Amangani Resorts • Jackson 734-7333
Elk Country Inn • Jackson 733-2364
Hoback River Resort • Jackson 733-5129
Jackson Hole Lodge & Motel • Jackson 733-2992
Lodge at Jackson Hole • Jackson 739-9703
Split Creek Ranch • Jackson 733-7522
Snow King Resort • Jackson 733-5200
Teton Pines Resort • Jackson 733-1005
Cowboy Village at Togwotee • Moran 733-8800
Hatchett Resort, Restaurant & Bar • Moran 543-2413
Jenny Lake Lodge • Moran 543-4647
Jackson Lake Lodge • Moran 543-2811
White Pine Ski Area & Resort • Pinedale 367-6606
The Alpenhof Lodge & Restaurant • Teton Village 733-3242
Snake River Lodge & Spa • Teton Village 732-6000
Jackson Hole Mountain Resort • Teton Village 733-2292
Four Seasons Lodge • Teton Village 734-7888
Grand Targhee Ski & Summer Resort • Alta 353-2300

Vacation Houses, Cabins & Condos

The Old Mill Log Cabins • Afton 886-0520
Twin Pines Lodge & Cabins • Dubois 455-2600
MacKenzie Highland Ranch • Dubois 455-3415
Riverside Inn & Campground • Dubois 455-2337
Rendezvous Mountain Rentals • Jackson 739-9050
Black Diamond Vacation Rentals & Real Estate• Jackson 733-6170
Jackson Hole Resort Lodging • Teton Village 733-3990
Aspen Chalet Cabins • Alpine 654-7962
Westviero Mountain Log Home & Log Cabin • Dubois 455-2552
Pinnacle Buttes Lodge • Dubois 455-2506
Cottages at Snow King • Jackson 733-3480
Dornan's Inn • Moose 733-2415
Luton's Teton Cabins • Moran 543-2489
Colter Bay Village Cabins • Moran 543-2811
Monte Vista Family Vacation Rentals • Thayne 886-9348
Baily House Guest Cabin • Wapati 587-3342
Four Bear Ranch • Wapati 527-6048
Kinkade Guest Kabin • Wapati 587-5905

Bed and Breakfasts

The Painted Porch Bed & Breakfast • Jackson Hole 733-1981
Chambers House Bed & Breakfast • Pinedale 367-2168
A Teton Treehouse Bed & Breakfast • Jackson Hole 733-3233
Davy Jackson Inn - Bed & Breakfast • Jackson 739-2294
Geyser Creek Bed & Breakfast • Dubois 455-2707
The Stone House Bed & Breakfast • Dubois 455-2555
Wildflower Inn Bed & Breakfast • Jackson 733-4710
Jakey's Fork Homestead • Dubois 455-2769
The Huff House • Jackson 733-4164
Teton View Bed & Breakfast • Wilson 733-7954
Cottonwood Cottage Bed & Breakfast • Smoot 866-9348
Rocking P Bed & Breakfast • Smoot 886-0455
Inn at Deer Run Bed & Breakfast • Thayne 883-3444
Inn on the Creek • Jackson 739-1565
Ramsview Bed & Breakfast • Dubois 455-3615
Wapiti Ridge Ranch Bed & Breakfast Inn • Dubois 455-2219
Salt River Bed & Breakfast • Etna 883-2453
Horseshoe Inn Motel • Etna 883-2281
Window on the Winds • Pinedale 367-2600
Branding Iron Bunkhouse Bed & Breakfast • Pinedale 367-2146
Stockman's • Pinedale 367-4562
Sassy Moose Inn Bed & Breakfast • Jackson 733-1277
Bentwood Bed & Breakfast • Jackson 739-1411
Pole Creek Ranch Bed & Breakfast • Pinedale 367-4433
Don't Fence Me Inn Bed & Breakfast • Jackson 733-7979
Mountain Top Bed & Breakfast • Dubois 455-2304
Horseman's Paradise Bed & Breakfast •

Wapati 587-2017
Alta Lodge Bed & Breakfast • Alta 353-2582
Teton County Bed & Breakfast • Alta 353-2208
Wilson Creekside Inn • Wilson 353-2409
Rocky Mountain Wilderness Adventure • Jackson 734-2636
Moose Meadows Bed & Breakfast • Wilson 733-4550

Outfitters and Guides

Fool's Gold Excursions G 883-3783
Half Moon Lake Resort FEG 367-6373
Emerald Creek Outfitters EG 455-3371
Jackson Hole Whitewater/Teton Expeditions & Scenic Floats R 733-1007
Absaroka Ranch FHE 455-2275
Riverside Inn & Campground FHEG 455-2337
Suda Outfitters FHE 455-2866
Outfitters of Wyoming Wilderness FHE 455-2725
CM Ranch E 455-2331
Press Stephens Outfitter FHE 455-2250
Deadman Creek Outfitters H 654-7528
Jackson's Hole Adventure G 654-7849
TJ's Sports, Inc G 654-7815
Fort William Guest Ranch FGE 367-4670
High Wild & Lonesome EG 276-3208
Darby Mountain Outfitters, Inc FHE 386-9220
Jensen's Guest Ranch H 886-3401
Green River Outfitters FHE 367-2416
Crossed Sabres Ranch FHRE 587-3750
Heart Six Ranch FHEG 543-2477
Triangle X Ranch FHER 733-2183
Camp Creek Inn H 733-3099
Turpin Meadow Ranch FHE 543-2000
Castagino Outfitters H 543-2403
Western Cross Outfitters H 543-2840
Ron Dube's Wilderness Adventures H 527-7815
Rocking D River Ranch FG 587-8329
Mill Iron Ranch FHE 733-6390
Wolf Mountain Outfitters H 886-9317
Wagons A+Cross Wyoming EG 859-8629
Grand Slam Outfitters H 486-2269
Highland Meadow Outfitters H 455-3478
Taylor Outfitters G 455-2161
Arrowhead Outfitters H 733-5223
Barker-Ewing River Trips R 733-1000
Charlie Sands Wild Water R 733-4410
Crystal Creek Outfitters FHEG 733-6318
Darwin Ranch FGE 733-5588
Fred Mau's Outdoor Adventure FHRE 637-6906
Jackson Hole Llamas G 739-9582
Jackson Hole Snowmobile Tours G 733-6850
John Henry Lee Outfitters HF 455-3200
Lewis & Clark River Expeditions R 733-4022
Mad River Boat Trips R 733-6203
Rocky Mt. Wilderness Adventure R 734-2636
Spotted Horse Ranch FHE 733-2097
Two Ocean Pass Outfitters FHE 886-4664
Wagons West & Yellowstone Outfitters HE 886-5629
O'Kelley Outfitting FGE 367-6476
Barlow Outfitting FHR 654-7669
Greys River Trophies HE 859-8896
Elk Antler Outfitters H 733-2649
Bald Mountain Outfitters FHER 367-6539
C 4 Outfitters H 734-4414
Coulter Creek Outfitters H 543-2111
Double Diamond Outfitters FHEG 885-4868
East Table Creek Hunting Camp H 886-9517
Elk Ridge Outfitters FHRE 367-2553
Gilroy Outfitting FHE 734-0440
Gros Ventre Wilderness Outfitters HF 733-4851
Hoback Outfitters FHRE 886-3601
Horse Creek Outfitters HFE 733-6556
Indian Summer Outfitters H 733-3974
Jackson Hole Outfitters G 886-3356
Jackson Peak Outfitters H 733-3805
Lazy TX Outfitting H 455-2688
Linn Brothers Oufitting H 733-5414
Mule Shoe Outfitters H 537-5655
Rendezvous Outfitters FHE 733-8241
Shoal Creek Outfitters FH 733-1310
Skinner Brothers Outfitters FHER 367-2270
Diamond D Ranch Outfitters FHE 543-2479
The Last Resort H 859-8294

NOTES:

Dining Quick Reference

Price Range refers to the average cost of a meal per person: ($) $1-$6, ($$) $7-$11, ($$$) $12-up. Cocktails: "Yes" indicates full bar; Beer (B)/Wine (W), Service: Breakfast (B), Brunch (BR), Lunch (L), Dinner (D). Businesses in bold print will have additional information under the appropriate map locator number in the body of this section.

MAP#	RESTAURANT	TYPE CUISINE	PRICE RANGE	CHILD MENU	COCKTAILS BEER WINE	MEALS SERVED	CREDIT CARDS ACCEPTED
2	Valleon Café	Family	$$	Yes		B/L	
2	Timberline Steak House	Steakhouse	$$$/$$	Yes	Yes	D/L/B	Major
2	Taco Time	Mexican	$	Yes		L/D	M/V
2	Rocky Mountain Pasta & Pizzaria	Italian/Pizza				L/D	
2	Red Baron Drive In	Fast Food	$	Yes		L/D	
2	Pizza Hut	Pizza	$$	Yes	B	L/D	Major
2	Noodle's Bar & Restaurant	Steakhouse	$$/$$$		Yes	B/L	Major
2	Subway	Sandwiches	$	Yes		L/D/B	M/V
2	Outlaw Saloon			Yes			
2	Golden Spur	American	$$			L/B	Major
2	Silver Stream Lodge Restaurant & Cabins	Steak & Seafood	$$$	Yes	Yes	D	Major
2	Rocky Mountain Seafood Market and Fish & Chips	Seafood					
2	Melina's Mexican Restaurant	Mexican	$$	Yes		L/D	
2	Homestead Restaurant	Coffee Shop	$$/$	Yes		L/D/B	M/V/Major/D
2	Burger King	Fast Food/	$	Yes		D/L/B	M/V
4	Star Valley Ranch Resorts & RV Camping	Family	$$			B/L	D/V/M
4	Field of Greens Putting Club & Pizza Pub	Pizza	$$/$$$		Yes	L/D	Major
4	Eidelweiss Restaurant	FineDining	$$$		B/W	D	M/V
4	**Star Valley Cheese Restaurant**	Family	$$			B/L	D/V/M
4	Melina's Mexican Food	Mexican	$$	Yes		L/D	M/V
4	Mavis' Restaurant	Family Dining	$$	Yes		L/B	M/V
4	Flat Creek RV Park	Family	$$			B/L	D/V/M
4	Edelweiss Restaurant	Family	$$	Yes		L/B/D	M/V
4	Tootsie's Take or Bake Pizza	Pizza	$$	Yes		L/D	M/V
4	Star Valley Pizza	Pizza	$$			B/L	D/V/M
4	Dad's Steakhouse	Steakhouse	$$$		Yes	D	Major
5	Home Cookin' Café	Family	$	Yes		L/D/B	
6	**The Nordic Inn & Brenthoven's Restaurant**	Fine Dining	$$		Yes	B/L/D	D/M/V
6	**Kringle's Birdhouse Café**	American Dining	$$	Yes	Yes/W/B	L/D/B	Major
6	Los Dos Amigos	American/Mexican	$$	Yes	Yes	L/D	Major
6	Bull Moose Saloon	Steakhouse	$$/$$$	Yes	Yes	L/D	Major
6	Frenchy's Bar-B-Que	Chicken & Ribs	$$	Yes		L/D	
6	Buffalo Station Café	Family	$$	Yes		L/D/B	M/V
6	Flying Saddle Lodge & Restaurant	Fine Dining	$$/$$$	Yes		B/D	Major
6	Gunnar's Pizza	Pizza	$$	Yes		L/D	
6	Red Baron Restaurant	American	$$	Yes		L/D/B	
6	Royal Ridge Restaurant	Fine Dining	$$$	Yes	Yes	D/L/B	D/M/V
6	Best Western Flying Saddle Lodge Restaurant	Eclectic	$$/$$$		Yes	B/D	Major
7	Horse Creek Station	Steakhouse	$$$/$$	Yes	Yes	L/D	Major
7	Camp Creek Inn & Fine Dining	Steakhouse	$$$/$$	Yes	Yes	L/D	Major
8	Huey's Restaurant	Pub	$$		Yes	L/D	Major
8	Gordo's Southpark Market & Deli	Deli	$$		W/B	B/L/D	M/V
8	Denny's	Family	$$	Yes		D/L/B	Major
8	Domino's Pizza	Pizza	$$			L/D	Major
8	Mill Iron Ranch	Family	$/$$		Yes	B/L/D	Major
9	Hanger Cantina	Mexican	$$	Yes	B/W	B/L/D	Major
10	**The Virginian Lodge & Restaurant**	Family	$$$	Yes	Yes	B/L/D	Major
10	Out of Bounds Pizzaria & Deli	Pizza & Deli	$			L/D	
10	Pizza Hut	Pizza		Yes	Yes	L/D	Major
10	McDonald's	Fast Food	$	Yes		L/D/B	Major
10	Beantown Cafe & Coffee House	Coffee House	$			L/B	M/V
12	Village Inn	American	$$	Yes		B/L/D	Major
12	Pearl Street Bagels	Deli	$			B/L/D	
12	Philly's Finest	Subs	$$	Yes	B	L/D	
12	Rendezvous Bistro	Fine Dining	$$$		Yes	D/L	Major
12	Merry Piglets Mexican Grill	Mexican	$$	Yes	Yes	L/D	Major
12	Million Dollar Cowboy Steakhouse	Steakhouse	$$$		Yes	L/D	Major
12	Lejay's Sportsmen's Cafe	Steaks/Game	$$$	Yes		B/L/D	Major
12	Subway	Sandwiches/	$	Yes		L/D	Major
12	Sweetwater Restaurant	Mediterranean	$$$		Yes	L/D	Major
12	Taqueria Sanchez	Mexican	$	Yes		L/D	M/V

Dining Quick Reference-Continued

Price Range refers to the average cost of a meal per person: ($) $1-$6, ($$) $7-$11, ($$$) $12-up. Cocktails: "Yes" indicates full bar; Beer (B)/Wine (W), Service: Breakfast (B), Brunch (BR), Lunch (L), Dinner (D). Businesses in bold print will have additional information under the appropriate map locator number in the body of this section.

MAP#	RESTAURANT	TYPE CUISINE	PRICE RANGE	CHILD MENU	COCKTAILS BEER WINE	MEALS SERVED	CREDIT CARDS ACCEPTED
12	Terroir Restaurant	Fine Dining	$$$		Yes	D	Major
12	Teton Steakhouse	Family	$$		W/B	B/L/D	Major
12	Teton Thai	Thai					
12	Thai Me Up	Thai	$$$	No	Yes	D	Major
12	Grill at Amangani	Italian	$$		Yes	L/D	Major
12	The Bunnery	American Bakery	$$$/$$	Yes		B/L/D	Major
12	Cadillac Grille	Fine Dining	$$$		Yes	D/L	Major
12	Betty Roack Cafe	Deli	$	Yes			M/V
12	Billy's Giant Hamburgers	American	$	Yes		L/D	V/M
12	Chili Pepper Grill	Mexican	$$	Yes	Yes	L/D	M/V
12	McDonald's	Fast Food	$	Yes		B/L/D	
12	Atrium Restaurant	Family	$$/$$$	Yes	Yes	B/L/D	Major
12	Cafe a Mano	Mexican	$$	No		L/D	M/V
12	Bar T-5 Cover Wagon Cookout & Wild West Show	American	$$$			D	Major
12	The Downtowner	American	$$		B	L/D	Major
12	The Granary	Fine Dining	$$$		Yes	D/L	Major
12	Bobby Rubino's Place for Ribs	Steakhouse	$$$	Yes	Yes	D	Major
12	Café 245	Eclectic	$$/$$$		Yes	D/L/B	Major
13	**Off Broadway Grill**	Eclectic	$$$	Yes	Yes	D	Major
13	**Jedediah's Original House of Sourdough**	Sandwiches	$$	Yes		B/L	Major
13	**Harvest Bakery. Café & Organic Foods**	Organic Foods	$$			B/L	V/M
13	Old Yellowstone Garage	Italian	$$$		W/B	L/D	Major
13	Pato Restaurant	Mexican	$$		W/B	D	Major
13	Wendy's	Fast Food				L/D	Major
13	Red Oak Grill	Fine Dining	$$$		Yes	D	Major
13	Rising Sage Cafe	Family	$$	Yes		L/D	Major
13	Route 89 Smokehouse Diner	Steak & Burgers	$$	Yes	Yes	B/L/D	Major
13	Shades Cafe	American	$$	Yes		B/L/D	M/V
13	Sidewinders Smokehouse & Tavern	American/Sports Bar	$$		Yes	L/D	Major
13	Silver Dollar Bar & Grill	Fine Dining	$$$		Yes	B/L/D	Major
13	Snake River Brewery & Restaurant	Pizza/Sandwiches	$$		Yes	L/D	Major
13	Snake River Grill	Fine Dining	$$$		Yes	D	Major
13	Hong Kong Buffet	Chinese	$$			L/D	Major
13	Mountain Dragon Chinese Restaurant	Mandarinn/Chinese	$$	Yes	Yes	L/D	Major
13	Nikai Sushi & Asian Fusion Cuisine	Asian/Fusion	$$$		Yes	D	Major
13	Taco Bell	Fast Food	$	Yes		L/D	
13	JH Soda Fountain	Ice Cream/Deli					
13	Gun Barrel Steak & Game House	Steak/Game	$$$	No	Yes	D	Major
13	The Blue Lion	Eclectic American	$$$		Yes	D	Major
13	El Abuelito	Mexican	$$$	Yes	B/W	L/D	Major
13	Bagel Jax	Bagels/Sandwiches	$			B/L/D	
13	Chinatown Restaurant	Chinese	$$$		Yes	L/D	M/V
13	Dairy Queen	Fast Food	$	Yes		L/D	
13	Mountain High Pizza	Pizza	$$		W/B	L/D	V/M/D
13	Acadian House	Cajun	$$$		Yes	D	Major
13	Burger King	Fast Food	$	Yes		D/L/B	M/V
13	Golden Palace Chinese Restaurant	Chinese	$$				
13	Jamba Juice	Juice Bar	$			L/D	Major
13	Koshu Wine Bar	Asian/Latin	$$$		Yes	L/D	Major
13	Bubba's Bar-B-Que	Barbeque	$$	Yes		L/D/B	
14	Bar J Chuckwagon Suppers & Western Show	Chuckwagon	$$$			D	Major
14	Stagecoach Café	Family	$$	Yes		D/L/B	Major
14	Nora's Fish Creek Inn	Steakhouse	$$	Yes		D/L/B	Major
15	**Anthony's Italian Restaurant**	Italian	$$/$$$	Yes	Yes/W/B	D	Major
15	Subway	Sandwiches/	$	Yes		L/D	Major
15	Mangy Moose Restaurant & Bar	Steak/Seafood	$$$		Yes	D/B/L	Major
15	Game Fish at Snake River Lodge	Fine Dining	$$$		Yes	L/D/B	Major
15	Vertical Restaurant	American Bistro	$$$		Yes	D	Major
15	Calico Italian Restaurant & Bar	Italian	$$$		Yes	D	Major
15	Stiegler's Restaurant & Bar	Austrian	$$$		Yes		Major
15	Alpenhof Bistro	American	$$$		Yes	L/D	Major

Dining Quick Reference

Price Range refers to the average cost of a meal per person: ($) $1-$6, ($$) $7-$11, ($$$) $12-up. Cocktails: "Yes" indicates full bar; Beer (B)/Wine (W), Service: Breakfast (B), Brunch (BR), Lunch (L), Dinner (D). Businesses in bold print will have additional information under the appropriate map locator number in the body of this section.

MAP#	RESTAURANT	TYPE CUISINE	PRICE RANGE	CHILD MENU	COCKTAILS BEER WINE	MEALS SERVED	CREDIT CARDS ACCEPTED
15	Alpenrose Dining Room	Fine Dining	$$$	No	Yes	D/B	Major
15	Solitude Cabins Dinner Sleigh Rides		$$$			D	Major
15	Teton Pines	Fine Dining	$$$		Yes	D	Major
15	Cascade Gull House & Spirits	New Western	$$$	Yes	Yes	B/L/D	Major
15	The Alpenhof Lodge & Restaurant	French European	$$$	Yes	Yes	D	Major
15	Jenny Lake Lodge Dining room	Family	$$$	Yes	Yes	B/L/D	Major
16	Vista Grande	Mexican	$$$		Yes		Major
16	Dornan's Inn	Italian	$$$/$$	Yes	W/B	L/D	Major
18	Strutting Grouse Restaurant	Fine Dining	$$$	Yes	Yes	L/D	Major
18	Grizzly Steakhouse	Steakhouse	$$$/$$	Yes	Yes	B/L/D	Major
18	Hatchett Resort, Restaurant & Bar	Family	$$		W/B	B/L/D	Major
18	Flagg Ranch & Village	Family	$$	Yes	Yes	L/D/B	Major
19	**Café Wyoming**	Hearty Homecooking	$$		Yes	L/D	M/V
19	**Bernie's Café**	Home-cooking	$$	No	B/W	L/D	D/M/V
19	**Rustic Pine Tavern & Steakhouse**	Steakhouse	$$$	No	Yes	D	V/M
19	Nani's Genuine Pasta House	Italian	$$/$$$	No	Yes	D/L	Major
19	Daylight Donuts & Village Café & Pizza	Family	$$	Yes	W/B	B/L/D	Major
19	Cowboy Café	Family	$$	Yes		B/L/D	
19	Dos Banditos	Mexican	$$	Yes	Yes	L/D	M/V
19	Pinnacle Buttes Wild Bunch Café	Home cooking			Yes		M/V
19	Ramshorn Bagel & Deli	Deli	$	No	Yes	B/L	
19	Sawmill Lodge	Fine Dining	$$$		Yes	L/D	Major
19	Taylor Creek	Deli	$			B/L	
19	Kathy's Koffee	Espresso/Deli	$	Yes		B/L	
19	Outlaw Saloon & Wild Bill's	American	$$	Yes	Yes	L/D	
19	Line Shack	Family	$$		Yes	L/D/B	Major
19	Edith's When It's Open	Family	$$$			D	
19	Wild Bunch Cafe	Family	$$	Yes	Yes	L/D	Major
21	Boulder Motor Inn & Restaurant	Family	$$	Yes	Yes	D/L	Major
21	Basecamp Restaurant	Steakhouse	$$$/$$	Yes	Yes	B/L/D	Major
22	Food Factory	Fast Food	$	Yes		L/D	
22	Happy Trails Café	Pizza	$	Yes		L/D	
23	Gordon's Corner Café	Family	$$	Yes		D/L/B	
23	Marbleton Inn Motel & Restaurant	Family	$$	Yes	Yes	L/D/B	Major
23	Three Pines	Family	$$	Yes	Yes	D/L	Major
23	Prairie Café	Family	$	Yes		B/L	
23	Rio Verde Grill	Mexican	$$/$$$	Yes	W/B	D	M/V
23	Gatzke's Grubhouse	Steakhouse	$$	Yes	Yes	D	Major
24	**McGregors Pub, Fine Dining, & Catering**	Fine Dining	$$$		Yes	D	Major
24	**Lakeside Lodge Resort & Marina**	Fine Dining	$$$	Yes	Yes	D/L/B	Major
24	**Half Moon Lake Resort**	Fine Dining	$$$		Yes	D	Major
24	Bottoms Up Brewery & Grill	Pizza & Grill	$$	No	Yes	D	Major
24	Café on Pine	Fine Dining	$$/$$$	Yes	Yes	L/D	Major
24	Calamity Janes/Corral Bar	Pizza/deli	$$	Yes	Yes	L/D	M/V
24	Fort William Guest Ranch & Restaurant	American	$$$		W/B	D	Major
24	Pitchfork Fondue	Western Cookout	$$	Yes		D	Major
24	Rumors Deli	Deli	$$/$	Yes		L/B	Major
24	Stockman's Steak Bar & Lounge	Steak/Seafood	$$	Yes	Yes	D/L/B	Major
24	Wrangler Café	Family	$$	Yes	W/B	D/L/B	Major
24	Wind River Rendezvous Pizza	Pizza	$$	No		D/L	Major
24	Freemont Peak Restaurant	German/American	$/$$/$$$			L/D/B	M/V
24	Pitchfork Fondue	Western	$$$			D	
24	Taqueria del Gallo Cantina	Mexican	$$	Yes	B	D/L	V/M
24	Moose Creek Trading Co.	American	$$/$$$	Yes	Yes	B/L/D	M/V
24	Patio Grill and Dining Room	Family	$$	Yes	Yes	L/D/B	
24	Trappers Tidbits	Fast Food	$			L/D	
24	Kat's Steakhouse	Steakhouse	$$/$$$	Yes	Yes	B/D/L	Major
24	Taqueria del Gallo Cantina	Mexican	$$	Yes	B	D/L	V/M
24	Corral Bar	American	$$		Yes	D	Major
24	Fat Daddy's Deli & Diner	Deli	$$			L/D	
24	Los Cabos Mexican Restaurant	Mexican	$$	Yes	W/B	L/D	M/V

Motel Quick Reference

Price Range: ($) Under $40 ; ($$) $40-$60; ($$$) $60-$80, ($$$$) Over $80. Pets [check with the motel for specific policies] (P), Dining (D), Lounge (L), Disabled Access (DA), Full Breakfast (FB), Cont. Breakfast (CB), Indoor Pool (IP), Outdoor Pool (OP), Hot Tub (HT), Sauna (S), Refrigerator (R), Microwave (M) (Microwave and Refrigerator indicated only if in majority of rooms), Kitchenette (K). All Wyoming area codes are 307.

MAP #	HOTEL	PHONE	NUMBER ROOMS	PRICE RANGE	BREAKFAST	POOL/ HOT TUB SAUNA	NON SMOKE ROOMS	OTHER AMENITIES	CREDIT CARDS
2	**Mountain Inn Motel**	885-3156	20	$$$	FB	OP/S	Yes	P	Major
2	**Lazy B Motel**	885-3187	25	$$$		OP	Yes	P/DA/R/M/K	Major
2	**The Old Mill Log Cabins**	886-0520	3	$$$$	Yes			R	V/M
2	Colters Lodge	885-9891	20	$$$			Yes	D/L	Major
2	Bar H Motel & Cabins	855-2274	40	$$$			Yes	D/L	Major
2	Corral Motel	885-5424	15	$$	CB		Yes	M/R	Major
2	Trailside Village Motel	885-8204	12	$$			Yes		Major
4	**Star Valley Ranch Resorts & RV Camping**	883-2670	14	$$$		HT/OP/S	Yes	R	M/V
4	Cabin Creek Inn	883-3262	19	$$$	CB		Yes	R/DA/M/K	Major
4	Swiss Mountain Motel	883-2227	9	$$			Yes	P/R/K	Major
4	Snider's Rustic Inn	883-0222	8	$$$			Yes	P/K/R/M	M/V
5	Horseshoe Inn Motel	883-2281	4	$$			Yes	P	
6	**The Nordic Inn & Brenthoven's Restaurant**	654-7556	10				Yes	L/D	D/M/V
6	**Three Rivers Motel**	654-7551	21					P	Major
6	**Alpine Inn**	654-7644	18	$$		HT	Yes	P/K	Major
6	Best Western Flying Saddle Lodge Restaurant	654-7562	26	$$$$/$$$		OP	Yes	L/D	Major
6	Lakeside Motel	654-7507	11	$$			Yes	D/K/P	M/V
6	Alpen Haus	654-7545	22	$$$			Yes		Major
8	**Days Inn of Jackson Hole**	733-0033	90		CB	S/HT	Yes	DA/R/M	Major
8	Motel 6	733-1620	155	$$		OP	Yes	P/D	Major
8	**Super 8 - Jackson**	733-6833	97	$$$/$$$$	CB		Yes	DA	Major
8	Teton Gables Motel	733-3723	36	$$$			Yes	P/D	Major
10	**The Virginian Lodge & Restaurant**	733-2792	170	$$$$		HT	Yes	D/L/DA/K	Major
10	Best Western Lodge at Jackson Hole	739-9703		$$$$	CB		Yes	D/L/DA	Major
11	**Town Square Inns - Cowboy Village Resort**	733-3121	82	$$$$/$$$		HT	Yes	R/M/K	Major
12	**Ranch Inn**	733-6363	57	$$$$/$$$	CB	HT	Yes	K	Major
12	**Town Square Inns - 49er Inn & Suites**	733-7550	150	$$$	CB	HT/S	Yes	K/P/D	Major
12	Town Square Inns - Antler Inn	733-2535	100	$$$			Yes	P	Major
12	Town Square Inns - Elk Country Inn	733-2364							
12	Buckrail Lodge	733-2079	12	$$		HT	Yes		M/V
12	Rawhide Motel	733-1216	23	$$/$$$				P	
12	Western Motel		38	$$$		IP	Yes	P/K	Major
13	**Black Diamond Vacation Rentals & Real Estate**	733-6170							
13	Painted Buffalo Inn	733-4340	136	$$$		IP/S	Yes	DA/D/P	Major
13	Anvil Motel & El Rancho Motel	733-3668	48	$$$		HT	Yes	R/M	M/V
13	Bunkhouse Hostel	733-3668	Dorm	$			Yes	K	M/V
13	Flat Creek Inn	733-5271	75	$$$	CB	S/HT	Yes	P/D/R/M/K	Major
13	Parkway Inn	733-3143	49	$$$$	CB	IP/S	Yes		Major
13	The Wort Hotel	733-2190	60	$$$$		HT	Yes	D/L/DA	Major
13	Alpine Motel	739-3200	18	$$$		IP	Yes	K/P	D
13	Anglers Inn	733-3682	28	$$				K/D	M/V
13	Cache Creek Motel	733-7781	37	$$			Yes	P/K	Major
13	Davy Jackson Inn - Bed & Breakfast	739-2294		$$$$		HT	Yes		
13	Four Winds Motel	733-2474	21	$$$/$$$$			Yes		Major
13	Golden Eagle Inn	733-2042	23	$$$		IP	Yes		Major
13	Jackson Hole Lodge & Motel	733-2992	26	$$$		IP			Major
13	Kudar Motel	733-2823	30	$$$			Yes	L/D	Major
13	Pioneer Motel	733-3673	21	$$			Yes		
13	Pony Express Motel	733-3835	24	$$$		OP		K/P	
13	Prospector Inn	733-4858	19	$$$	CB	HT	Yes	P/DA	Major
13	Sagebrush Motel	733-0336	24	$$$			Yes	K	Major
13	Stagecoach Motel	733-3451	21	$$$					
13	Sundance Inn	733-3444	27	$$$	CB		Yes	K	
13	Trapper Inn	733-2648	50	$$$		HT	Yes	R/M	Major
13	Wagon Wheel Village		97	$$$$		HT	Yes	D/L/K	Major
13	Inn on the Creek	739-1565	9	$$$$	CB		Yes		Major
13	Wyoming Inn of Jackson, Red Lion	734-0035	73	$$$$	CB		Yes	K/DA/P	Major
13	Best Western Inn at Jackson Hole	733-2311	83	$$$$		OP/S/HT	Yes	DA/K	Major
13	Elk Refuge Inn	733-3582	22	$$$			Yes	R/M/K	Major
13	Teton Inn	733-3883	14	$$$			Yes		Major

Motel Quick Reference-Continued

Price Range: ($) Under $40 ; ($$) $40-$60; ($$$) $60-$80, ($$$$) Over $80. Pets [check with the motel for specific policies] (P), Dining (D), Lounge (L), Disabled Access (DA), Full Breakfast (FB), Cont. Breakfast (CB), Indoor Pool (IP), Outdoor Pool (OP), Hot Tub (HT), Sauna (S), Refrigerator (R), Microwave (M) (Microwave and Refrigerator indicated only if in majority of rooms), Kitchenette (K). All Wyoming area codes are 307.

MAP #	HOTEL	PHONE	NUMBER ROOMS	PRICE RANGE	BREAKFAST	POOL/ HOT TUB SAUNA	NON SMOKE ROOMS	OTHER AMENITIES	CREDIT CARDS
14	**The Painted Porch Bed & Breakfast**	733-1981	3	$$$$	FB	HT	Yes	K	Major
14	**Rendezvous Mountain Rentals**	739-9050		$$$/$$$$					
14	**A Teton Treehouse Bed & Breakfast**	733-3233	6	$$$$	FB	HT	Yes		V/M/D
15	**Jackson Hole Resort Lodging**	733-3990		$$$/$$$$					
15	The Alpenhof Lodge & Restaurant	733-3242	42	$$$	CB	OP/HT/S	Yes	P/L/D	Major
15	Teton Mountain Lodge	732-6911	129	$$$$		IP/OP/HT	Yes	D/L/DA/R/K	Major
15	Village Center Inn	733-3990	16	$$$			Yes	D/K	Major
15	Jackson Hole Mountain Resort	733-2292							
15	The Hostel	733-3415	54	$				P	
16	Red Rock Ranch	733-6288		$$$/$$$$	FB		Yes		Major
18	Signal Mountain Lodge	543-2831	385	$$$$		OP	Yes	L/D/P/K	Major
19	Branding Iron Inn	455-2893	23	$$			Yes	P/K	Major
19	**Stagecoach Motor Inn**	455-2303	50	$$$/$$		HT/OP	Yes	DA/K/P	Major
19	**Twin Pines Lodge & Cabins**	455-2600	16	$$	CB		Yes	R/DA	Major
19	**Trail's End Motel**	455-2540	84	$		IP	yes	P/D/L/K	Major
19	**MacKenzie Highland Ranch**	455-3415	8	$$$$			Yes	K	
19	**Absaroka Ranch**	455-2275	4	$$$$	FB				Major
19	**Riverside Inn & Campground**	455-2337	14	$$			Yes	K/P	D/M/V
19	Line Shack Hotel & Lodge	455-2171	16	$$$			Yes	L/D/P	Major
19	Westviero Mountain Log Home & Log Cabin	455-2552		$$$			Yes		
19	Wind River Motel	455-2611	13	$$			Yes	P/D	M/V
19	Geyser Creek Bed & Breakfast	455-2707							
19	Wapiti Ridge Ranch Bed & Breakfast Inn	455-2219							
19	Bald Mountain Inn	455-2844	16	$$			Yes	P/K	Major
19	Black Bear County Inn	455-2344	16	$$			Yes	P/K	Major
19	Super 8 -Dubois	455-3694	34	$$		HT	Yes	P	Major
21	Boulder Motor Inn & Restaurant	537-5626	9	$$	CB		Yes	DA/L/D	Major
22	Big Piney Motel	276-3352	26	$$			Yes	R/M	M/V
22	Frontier Hotel	276-3329	10	$$			No		M/V
23	Marbleton Inn Motel & Restaurant	276-5231	35	$$			Yes	D/L	Major
23	Country Chalet Inn Motel	276-3391	14	$$			Yes	P	M/V
24	**Lakeside Lodge Resort & Marina**	367-2221	20	$$$$			Yes	P/D/L/DA/R/M	Major
24	**Half Moon Lake Resort**	367-6373	8	$$$$	CB		Yes	D/P/R	Major
24	**The Sundance Motel**	367-4336	19	$$$$/$$$			Yes	R/M/K/P	Major
24	**The Lodge at Pinedale**	367-8800	43	$$$	CB	HT/IP	Yes	P/R/M/DA	D
24	**Log Cabin Motel: A National Historic Place**	367-4579	10				Yes	R/K/P	M/V
24	**Chambers House Bed & Breakfast**	367-2168	5	$$$	FB		Yes	P/DA	Major
24	Fort William Guest Ranch & Restaurant	367-4670							
24	Best Western - Pinedale	367-6869	59	$$$$	CB	IP/HT	Yes	P/D/R/M	Major
24	Riviera Lodge	367-2424	8	$$$$			Yes	P/K	M/V
24	ZZZZ Inn	367-2121	10	$$$$/$$$			Yes	K/DA	M/V
24	Teton Court Motel	367-4317	17	$$$$/$$			Yes	K/P	Major
24	Wagon Wheel Motel	367-2871	15	$$$			Yes		Major
24	Camp O' the Pines Motel	367-4536	14	$		IP	Yes	P/K	Major
24	Super 8		43	$/$$	CB	IP	Yes		Major
24	DC Bar Guest Ranch	367-2268							
24	Pine Creek Inn	367-2191	16	$$$	CB		Yes	P/K	Major
24	Half Moon Lake Motel	367-2851	19	$$$			Yes	K/P	Major
27	Green Creek Inn & RV Park	587-5004	17	$$$				P	Major

NOTES:

SECTION 2

NORTHCENTRAL AREA

INCLUDING CODY, WORLAND, POWELL, LOVELL AND THERMOPOLIS

"Cody is Rodeo" is the slogan for the Rodeo Capital of the World.

1 *No services*

T Clark
Gas

This town was named for Len Clark, an early rancher, not for William Clark, the explorer, as might be supposed.

H Nez Perce Trail
28 miles north of Cody on Highway 120 at Clark's Fork River.

In 1877, the Nez Perce Indians of Idaho, led by Chief Joseph, fled the U.S. Army. They crossed the Clark's River near this point, while trying to outrun the soldiers to Canada.

2 *Gas, Food, Lodging*

Cody
Pop. 8,835 Elev. 5,016

Named for its famous promoter, William "Buffalo Bill" Cody, this little city was originally named Richland when George T. Beck established the post office in 1895. Prior to that, it was the homestead of Otto Franc, a wealthy Prussian rancher who may have helped finance the Johnson County War. Incorporated in 1901, the year that the Burlington railroad arrived, the trains brought curious visitors to "Cowboy Town," which was the eastern gateway to nearby Yellowstone.

Cody, Beck, and Horace C. Alger were responsible for developing the Shoshone Land and Irrigation Company, which brought water and agricultural prosperity to Cody and its environs. The region quickly became populated with both farmers and business people, hoping to capitalize off of Cody's name and Yellowstone's proximity. The famous National Park is not the only scenic marvel nearby. Cody is surrounded by the Beartooth and Absaroka Mountains, as well as Sunlight Basin and the Wapiti Valley.

In 1904, oil was discovered near Cody, and Park County went on to become the second biggest oil producer in the state. Marathon Oil Company is the town's largest employer, but tourism and agriculture continue to be significant moneymakers.

T Cody Country Visitor's Council
836 Sheridan Ave. in Cody. 587-2297 or 800-393-2639. www.pctc.org

T Park County Historical Society Archives Center
1002 Sheridan Ave. in Cody. 527-8530

A complete collection of records available to the public. Find photographs, biographies, obituaries, school information, oral histories, maps, military information, artifacts and many more areas of historical significance. Located in the Park County Courthouse they are open 9 a.m. to 4 p.m. Monday through Friday.

T Foundation for North American Wild Sheep/Wild Sheep Exhibit
720 Allen Ave. in Cody. 527-6261. www.fnaws.org

FNAWS is the leading voice in wild sheep conservation. Their message is built on protection of habitat, professional management based upon sound biological principles, educating the public, and protecting sportsmen's rights. Inside their headquarters are a number of exhibits of wild sheep. There is also a multi-media presentation to view.

T Buffalo Bill Historical Center
720 Sheridan Ave. in Cody. 587-4771. www.bbhc.org

The Buffalo Bill Historical Center is located in northwestern Wyoming, 52 miles from Yellowstone National Park's East Gate. The Center is comprised of five internationally acclaimed museums devoted to Western cultural and natural history: the Buffalo Bill Museum, the Cody Firearms Museum, the Plains Indian Museum, the Draper Museum of Natural History and the Whitney Gallery of Western Art, plus the Harold McCracken Research Library. Admission is good for two consecutive days to all five museums. Call for hours and rates or visit them on the web.

V North Fork Anglers
1107 Sheridan in Cody. 527-7274. www.northforkanglers.com

North Fork Anglers offers everything you need for the flyfishing trip of a lifetime: experienced guides, custom designed trip-planning, and a full-service pro shop with top-of-the-line equipment and supplies. All this and lots of blue ribbon trout water. Choose from walk-in or wading trips, float trips, horseback wilderness trips or float tube trips. They are an authorized Orvis dealer and the full-service pro ship is open all year. They offer special seminars and clinics throughout the year to help you hone your skills. You've proba-

Cody

	Jan	Feb	March	April	May	June	July	Aug	Sep	Oct	Nov	Dec	Annual
Average Max. Temperature (F)	35.7	40.2	47.2	56.7	66.3	75.7	84.7	82.7	72.1	60.9	45.8	38.0	58.8
Average Min. Temperature (F)	12.5	16.2	22.4	31.1	40.0	47.8	54.3	52.3	43.1	34.2	22.9	15.6	32.7
Average Total Precipitation (in.)	0.35	0.29	0.53	1.08	1.61	1.65	1.07	0.80	1.05	0.76	0.48	0.31	10.01
Average Total SnowFall (in.)	6.3	5.0	6.6	5.2	0.6	0.0	0.0	0.0	0.4	3.8	5.7	5.8	39.5
Average Snow Depth (in.)	1	1	0	0	0	0	0	0	0	0	0	0	0

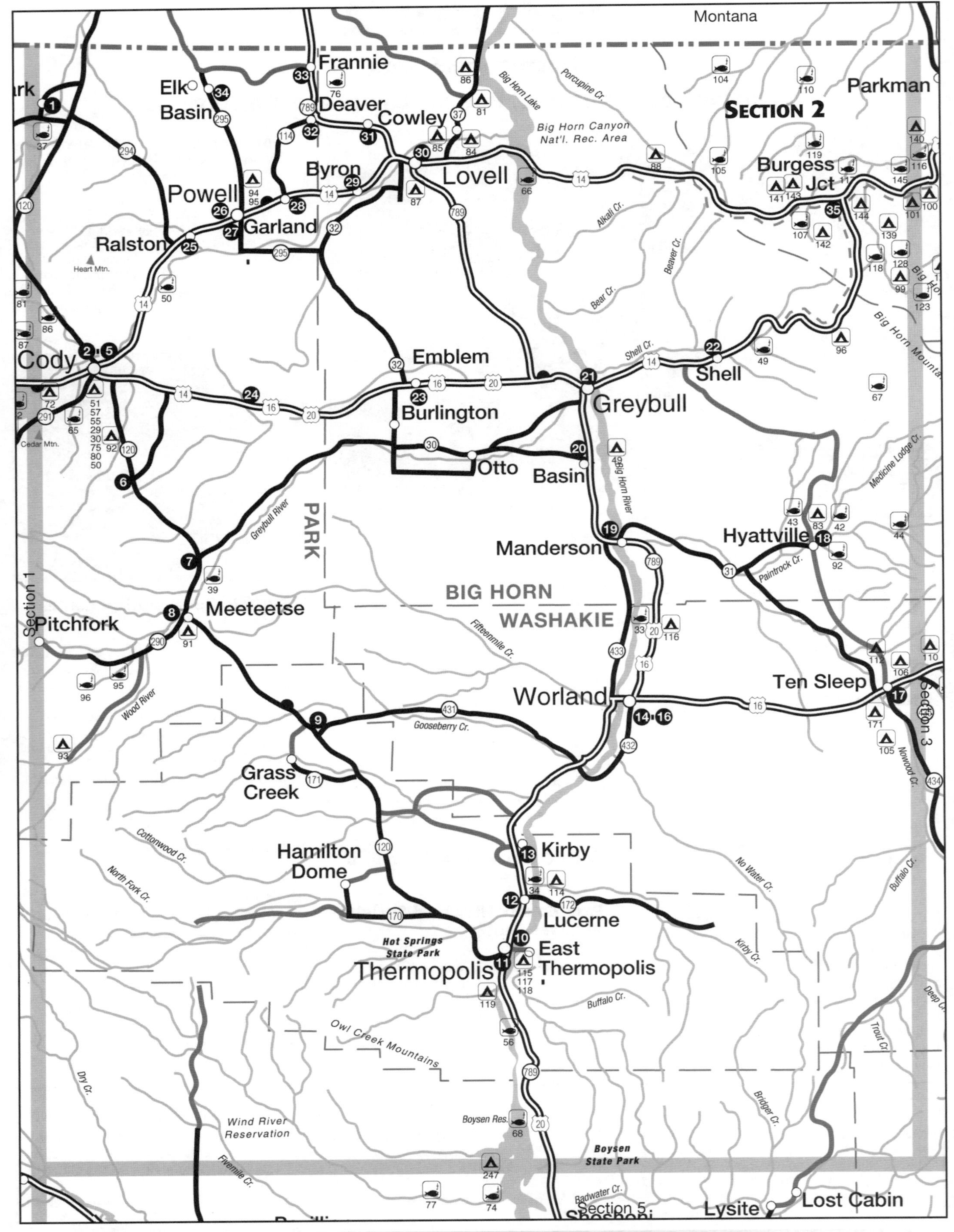
Montana
Section 2
Frannie
Elk
Basin
Deaver
Cowley
Parkman
Big Horn Lake
Porcupine Cr.
Big Horn Canyon Nat'l. Rec. Area
Byron
Lovell
Burgess Jct
Powell
Garland
Ralston
Heart Mtn.
Alkali Cr.
Beaver Cr.
Bear Cr.
Big Horn Mountains
Emblem
Shell Cr.
Shell
Cody
Greybull
Burlington
Cedar Mtn.
Otto
Basin
Medicine Lodge Cr.
Big Horn River
Greybull River
PARK
Hyattville
Manderson
Paintrock Cr.
BIG HORN
WASHAKIE
Section 1
Pitchfork
Meeteetse
Fifteenmile Cr.
Ten Sleep
Worland
Section 3
Wood River
Gooseberry Cr.
Nowood Cr.
Grass Creek
Cottonwood Cr.
Kirby
Hamilton Dome
No Water Cr.
Buffalo Cr.
North Fork Cr.
Lucerne
Hot Springs State Park
East Thermopolis
Kirby Cr.
Thermopolis
Deep Cr.
Buffalo Cr.
Owl Creek Mountains
Trout Cr.
Dry Cr.
Bridger Cr.
Wind River Reservation
Boysen Res.
Boysen State Park
Fivemile Cr.
Badwater Cr.
Section 5
Lysite
Lost Cabin

North Fork Anglers

bly seen them on one of 14 appearances made on ESPN. Their Worldwide clients find them on Cody's main street at the leaping neon trout sign or by visiting online. They're no small fish!

V Red Canyon River Trips & Wild Mustang Tours

1374 Sheridan Ave. in Cody. 587-6988 or toll free at 800-293-0148

Red Canyon River Trips takes pride in their more than thirty years experience as guides on the Shoshone and Clark's Fork rivers. Their professional guides are dedicated to offering a quality adventure full of fun and excitement, always with your safety as their priority. They guarantee a personalized trip for you and your family, accommodating all levels of experience. Red Canyon Wild Mustang Tours is an adventure and educational opportunity for the entire family. You will travel by van and observe these fabulous horses in their natural habitat. They enjoy an excellent reputation earned by their experienced and knowledgeable staff, committed to making your adventure safe and pleasant.

Map Legend

 Locator number (matches numeric listing in section)

 Campsite (number matches number in campsite chart)

 Fishing Site (number matches number in fishing chart)

 Rest stop

 Interstate

 U.S. Highway

 Paved State or County Road

Gravel/unpaved road

0 Miles 13 22

One inch = approximately 13 miles

FLS The Irma Hotel, Restaurant & Saloon

1192 Sheridan Ave. in Cody. 587-4221 or 800-745-4762. www.irmahotel.com

Step back into the old West at the Irma Hotel, a place that Buffalo Bill Cody called a "gem." He should know. He built the Irma in 1902 and often stayed in his personal suite, now open to the public. The 40 guest rooms and suites, with private bathrooms and air conditioning, have housed some famous personalities from around the world. The restaurant is famous for Prime Rib and serves breakfast, lunch and dinner daily, with breakfast, lunch, and dinner buffets served during the summer months. You'll love the Irma Hotel. It's a place fancy enough for royalty and plain enough for cowboys and cowgirls. While at the Irma, don't miss visiting Col. Cody's Wild West Emporium Gift Shop and watching the gunfights at 6 p.m. Monday thru Friday.

FL Best Western Sunset Motor Inn & Sunset House Restaurant

1601 8th Street in Cody. 587-4265 or toll free 800-624-2727 or fax 587-9029. www.bestwestern.com/sunsetmotorinn

The Best Western Sunset Motor Inn provides all the comforts you expect from a Best Western, along with convenient access to the many attractions in Cody Country. Accommodations are available to suit every guest requirement—king and queen size beds, suites, nonsmoking rooms, in-room coffee, seasonal outdoor pool, indoor pool, exercise room, and guest laundry. All rooms are ground floor with parking at your door. The Sunset House Restaurant serves breakfast, lunch and dinner, specializing in reasonably priced, fresh prepared food and great service in a warm western decor. Special menus are available for smaller appetites and the health conscious. Complete wine and cocktail lists are available.

Cody Gunfighters

Six nights a week throughout the summer, visitors to Cody can witness a gunfight between notorious Old West characters such as Wyatt Earp, Miss Lily Brown, Mad Dog, Longhair, Buffalo Bill and Teton Jack. All re-enactments of course, but the Cody Gunfighters keep the spirit of the Old West alive through their dramatic skits. Each 45 minute program features actors in full costume and is free of charge. Donations and poster sales benefit local charities including the Children's Resource Center and the Humane Society of Park County. Held on the street beside the Irma Hotel.

F The Noon Break

927 12th St. in Cody. 587-9720

F QT's Restaurant

1701 Sheridan Ave. Cody. 587-5555. www.blairhotels.com

L Robin's Nest Bed & Breakfast

1508 Alger Ave. in Cody. 527-7208 or toll free at 866-723-7797. www.robinsnestcody.com and Email: robinsnestcody@hotmail.com

L Burl Inn

1213 17th St. in Cody. 587-2084 or reservations only at 800-388-2084

Experience unique Western furnishings and hospitality at the Burl Inn. The unique handcrafted furnishings are designed and built after the historic works of Thomas Molesworth. Each piece is crafted from wood twisted by burls or other natural events. Rooms available are, singles, doubles, a Honeymoon suite, and two rooms specially equipped for disabled guests. They are located adjacent to Cody's downtown area with shopping, art galleries, dining, and historic attractions. Public transportation, including carriage rides, is available to the Historical Center and rodeo grounds throughout the visitor season and they are within walking distance of Cody's convention facilities. AAA and AARP discounts are honored.

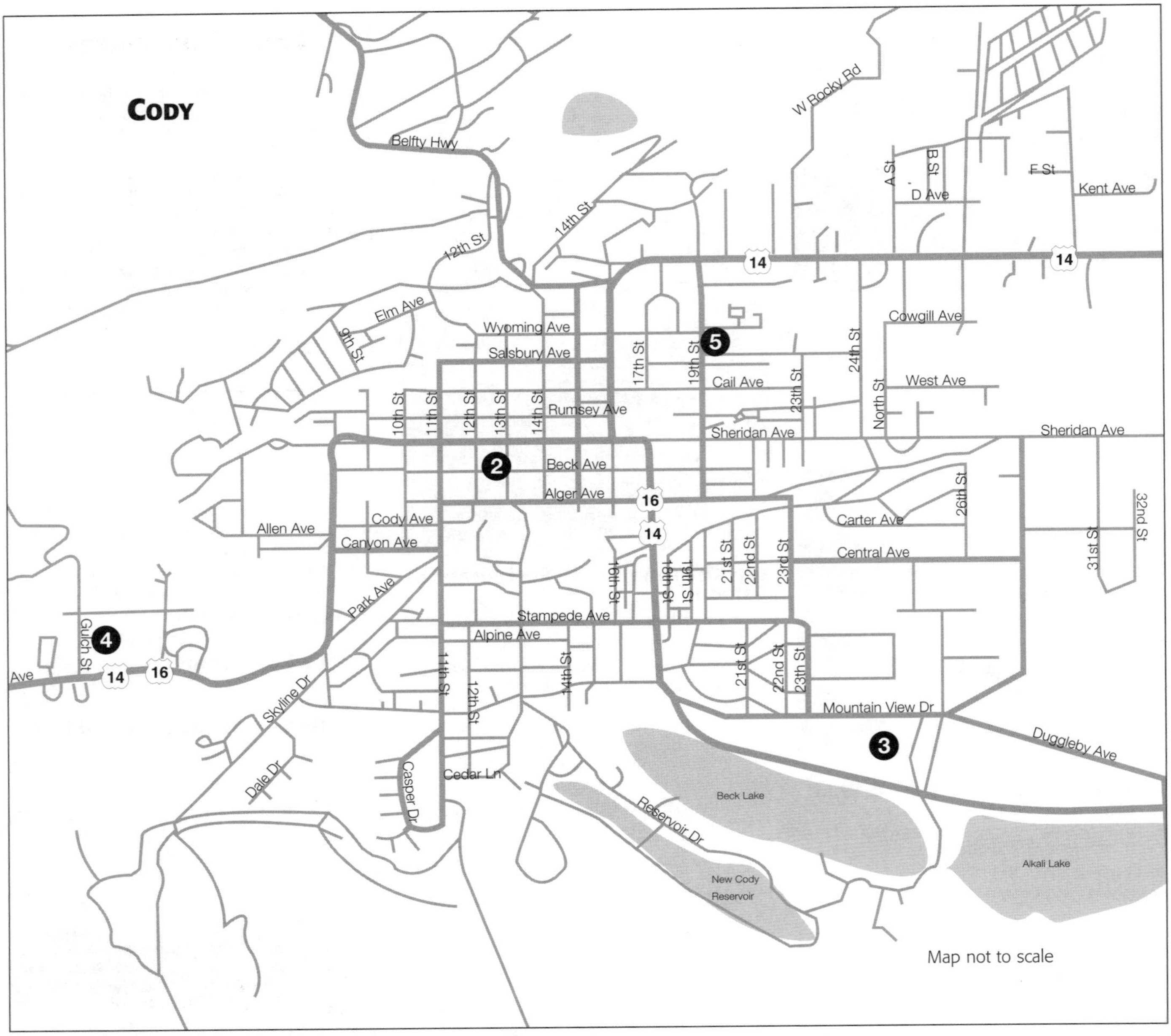

Cody

Map not to scale

Wyoming Tidbits

As many as 60 million buffalo once grazed on the great plains. "Buffalo Bill" Cody reportedly killed more than 4,000 in one year. By the end of 1883, herds were decimated by hunters and overgrazing.

L Cody Guest Houses & The Victorian House Bed & Breakfast

927 14th St. in Cody. 587-6000 or toll free at 800-587-6560, fax 587-8048. www.codyguesthouses.com

L Parson's Pillow B&B

1202 14th St. in Cody. 587-2382 or toll free at 800-377-2348

Guests of the Parson's Pillow Bed and Breakfast relax and enjoy a sense of coming home in a 1902 former church that has been caringly restored. Experience western homestyle hospitality and linger in individually designed rooms. Wake up to a delectable full breakfast. Each of five guest rooms is uniquely furnished for comfort and pleasure: the Rose is romantic and warm in aura, the Garden is bright and airy and filled with afternoon sun, the Western is Wyoming and cowboys, Memories will take you into the past, and the Sandstone is filled with wonderful Indian artifacts. The innkeepers are happy to assist you with reservations and excursion plans.

Parson's Pillow B&B

L Buffalo Bill Village Resort

1701 Sheridan Ave in Cody. 800-527-5544. www.blairhotels.com

Remember when it was fun to go on vacation? At the Buffalo Bill Village Resort, it still is! Experience the nostalgia of a Cowboy Cabin (but enjoy the conveniences you're entitled to. You'll enjoy in-room coffee makers, hairdryers, remote television, and full bath. Even private bedrooms!

Buffalo Bill Historical Center—Crown Jewel of the American West

One of the best-kept secrets in the West is the Buffalo Bill Historical Center, a complex of five internationally acclaimed museums and a research library.

The late author James Michener once called the Buffalo Bill Historical Center "The Smithsonian of the West," and with good reason.

The Buffalo Bill Historical Center stands as the largest history and art museum between Minneapolis and the West Coast, encompassing over 300,000 square feet of space on three levels. Because it is located in Cody, Wyoming, a town with a population of just 9,000, 52 miles from the east entrance of Yellowstone National Park, many visitors are stunned when they venture inside its doors. Nowhere else in the United States is such an important museum located in such a remote location.

The Buffalo Bill Historical Center has positioned itself as the single most important cultural attraction in the region surrounding Yellowstone National Park. Its collections include thousands upon thousands of priceless treasures related to the art, cultural and natural history, ethnology, and technology of the American West.

Originally begun in a small log cabin in 1927 and known as the Buffalo Bill Museum, the facility then housed memorabilia belonging to William Frederick "Buffalo Bill" Cody. Cody, for whom the town of Cody is named, was an authentic western hero whose career paralleled or became linked with most of the significant events in western American history. As a mere boy, he worked as a bullwhacker and mounted messenger for a freight-hauling company, and later joined the gold rush to Pike's Peak and rode for the Pony Express. During the Civil War, he served with a Union guerrilla group known as the Kansas Jayhawkers.

But it was not until after the War Between the States that he began to grow in fame. As a hunter supplying meat for workers building the transcontinental railroad, he earned the nickname Buffalo Bill. Later, his fame was cemented as a civilian scout for the Army, when he won the Medal of Honor. His career as the consummate showman followed, beginning with his appearance in stage plays in the East and later as the head of his own world-famous theater troupe.

Buffalo Bill's showmanship found its widest audience with Buffalo Bill's Wild West, an extraordinary outdoor touring show that he called "an educational exhibition on a grand and entertaining scale." Through this show, which ran for 30 years, Buffalo Bill brought the West to the world, showing people who didn't have the opportunity to travel to the West what America's frontier legacy was all about.

Today, the Buffalo Bill Historical Center does much the same thing — it brings the West to a world that would otherwise know about it only through television and motion pictures, sources that are not necessarily reliable. Nearly 250,000 people each year visit the Historical Center, making it the most heavily visited single attraction, outside of the park itself, in the entire Yellowstone National Park region.

And the institution has become far more than a monument to the life and times of Buffalo Bill. The Whitney Gallery of Western Art, dedicated in 1959, houses one of the most important collections of Western American art in the world. Masterworks are on display by George Catlin, Alfred Jacob Miller, Albert Bierstadt, Thomas Moran, Frederic Remington, Charles M. Russell, William R. Leigh, N.C. Wyeth and many others.

In 1968, the Buffalo Bill Museum was moved into a new building attached to the Whitney Gallery of Western Art, forming the core of today's Buffalo Bill Historical Center. The Plains Indian Museum, housing one of the richest collections of American Indian artifacts in the world, features the art and culture of the most important tribes of the Northern Plains. This museum was added in 1979 and reinterpreted in 2000. That 2000 $3.8 million reinterpretation truly moved the Plains Indian Museum into the 21st century and created "a living breathing place where more than just objects are on display," Advisory Board Member and Crow tribal historian Joe Medicine Crow said.

And in 1991, the Cody Firearms Museum, housing the world's largest collection of firearms of the American West, as well as European arms dating back to the 1500s, was added to the complex. The heart of the Cody Firearms Museum collection of over 6,000 firearms is the Winchester Collection, which was moved to Cody from New Haven, Connecticut in 1976.

The Draper Museum of Natural History opened in June 2002. Challenging the traditional approach of exhibiting objects in glass cases, the new museum leads visitors down an interactive trail through the sights and sounds of the Greater Yellowstone Ecosystem. This museum presents natural history in the context of the humanities and promotes increased understanding of and appreciation for, the relationships binding humans and nature in the

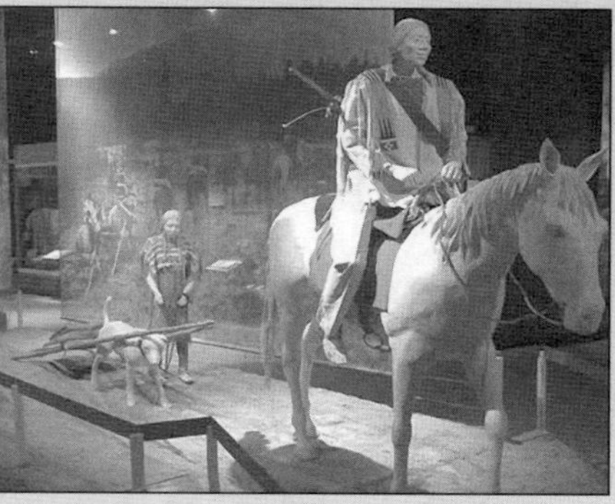

American West.

Rounding out the Historical Center complex is the McCracken Research Library, which is an important resource for scholars around the United States.

The Historical Center annually hosts important events and programs. Besides special exhibitions that often travel to important venues throughout the nation, annual events include Cowboy Songs and Range Ballads (April), a program that features some of the nation's best performers of authentic cowboy music and the Plains Indian Powwow (June), attracting the best dancers and drummers of the Northern Plains; and the Larom Summer Institute in Western American Studies (June), featuring education courses for college credit. In fact, the active education department creates a myriad of programming for children and adults covering a broad spectrum of topics about the West throughout the entire year.

One of the West's premier social events, the Buffalo Bill Historical Center Patrons Ball in September is combined with the Buffalo Bill Art Show and Sale and the Western Design Conference. The entire week of activities is known collectively as Rendezvous Royale, a celebration of the arts in Cody, and serves as a major fund-raiser for the institution.

The Buffalo Bill Historical Center is open year round and hours vary. Adult admission rates are $15; Senior rates are $13; students 18 and over (with current valid student identification) are admitted for $6. Youth aged 6-17 are admitted for $4 and children 5 and under are admitted free. This summer will also see the introduction of the $22 "Inside-Outside Tour," which will include museum admission plus a historic guided tour of Cody upon the charming Cody Trolley. While 2-3 hours will give visitors a fast, general overview of the Center, admission is good for two consecutive days to give visitors as much time as possible to enjoy the vast collections.

For a closer look at the Buffalo Bill Historical Center, please see the web site at www.bbhc.org.

Experience the original Buffalo Bill (Cabin) Village. Or, center yourself in western hospitality at Cody's largest hotel–the Holiday Inn–deluxe accommodations, deluxe dining, deluxe service. Treat yourself and your family to a complimentary welcome party each evening for guests, shopping, swimming–everything designed to compliment your visit to Cody and the Yellowstone Park area.

L Holiday Inn Buffalo Bill Village Resort

1701 Sheridan Ave in Cody. 800-527-5544.
www.blairhotels.com

The Holiday Inn has 189 rooms, six of which are ADA compliant, and one suite. In addition to the above, the Holiday Inn sports a fitness center and of course, *Kids Eat Free, Kids Stay Free* at every Holiday Inn. Guests receive a 10% discount in the General Store Shopping Emporium. The Comfort Inn has 75 rooms, two of which are ADA compliant and one suite. A complimentary Deluxe Continental Breakfast is served each morning, during the summers the breakfast is in the Sarsaparilla Saloon. The original Buffalo Bill (Cabin) Village is a bit of history not often found. The 83 individual cowboy style cabins are individual units, most with private parking. The cabins vary in size from those suitable for 1 or 2 persons (king/queen bed) to family units with two bedrooms, a total of three double beds. All Cabins have full bath, cable/remote television, and air conditioning.

L Comfort Inn Buffalo Bill Village Resort

1701 Sheridan Ave. in Cody. 800-527-5544.
www.blairhotels.com

S Beartooth Harley-Davidson/Buell of Cody

1137 Sheridan in Cody. 257-7776 or toll free 877-292-0526. www.beartoothharley.com

S TimberCreek Interiors

1371 Sheridan Ave. in Cody. 587-4246.
email: FIFIS@cowboystate.net

Let TimberCreek Interiors help you "experience the West" with fine furnishings for your home or office. The unique cowboy western and mountain lodge-style furnishing they offer range from gifts, accessories, area rugs, mirrors, lamps, and furniture. The interior design services available also include window and wall treatments for the perfect finish. They incorporate work from a variety of talented artisans who create custom furniture and accessories. Exceptional traditional home

Timber Creek Interiors

decor and accessories are also available to create the environment you are looking for. TimberCreek designers are allied members of ASID and will guide you through a pleasurable experience. Worldwide shipping is available.

S Rocky Mountain Atmosphere

1356 Sheridan Ave. in Cody. 587-6323.
www.rma.com or email: rma@rma.VNC.com

Rocky Mountain Atmosphere features a great selection of rustic gifts and accessories. Visitors to Cody will enjoy the variety of unusual souvenirs. The store is full of unique home furnishings with styles ranging from country and antique, to western and lodge. You can find something to dress your walls, tables and beds all under one roof. They showcase furniture, lighting, and upscale crafts by local craftsmen. Their selection of quilts, gourmet foods, hand-painted ceramics, and pottery is exquisite. With brands like Woolrich, True Grit, and Crabtree & Evelyn, gift ideas are easy to come by. Browse online at www.rma.com.

S Yellowstone Gift Shop

1237 Sheridan in Cody. 587-4611 or toll free at 800-788-9429

The Yellowstone Gift Shop has been pleasing visitors to Cody since 1967. This exciting store offers gifts and souvenirs for every interest and budget. The extensive Indian artifact department, also

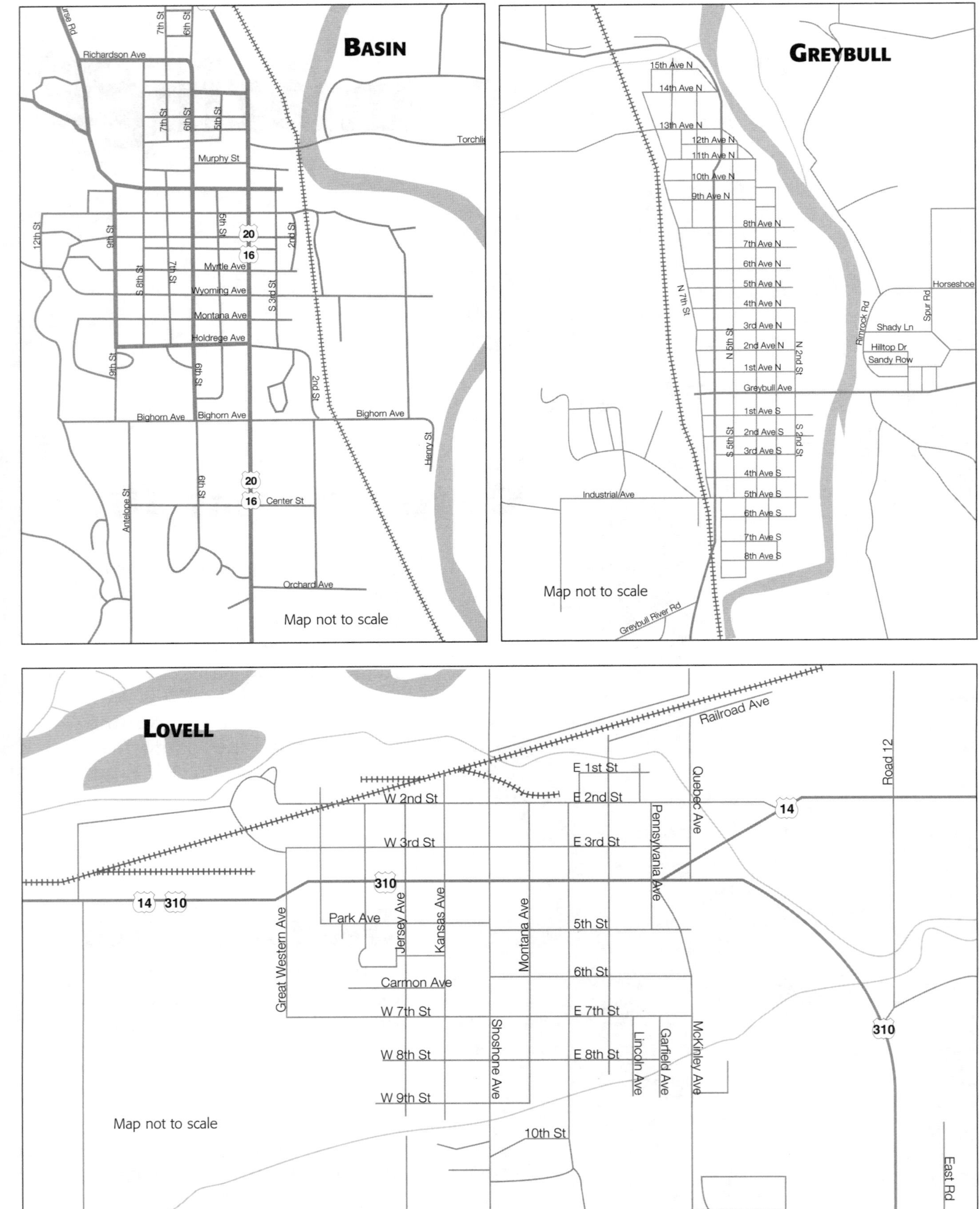
BASIN
Richardson Ave
Murphy St
Myrtle Ave
Wyoming Ave
Montana Ave
Holdrege Ave
Bighorn Ave
Center St
Orchard Ave
Map not to scale
GREYBULL
Greybull Ave
Industrial Ave
Greybull River Rd
Rimrock Rd
Shady Ln
Hilltop Dr
Sandy Row
Map not to scale
LOVELL
Railroad Ave
E 1st St
W 2nd St
E 2nd St
W 3rd St
E 3rd St
Park Ave
5th St
6th St
Carmon Ave
W 7th St
E 7th St
W 8th St
E 8th St
W 9th St
10th St
Lane 12
Great Western Ave
Jersey Ave
Kansas Ave
Montana Ave
Shoshone Ave
Pennsylvania Ave
Quebec Ave
Lincoln Ave
Garfield Ave
McKinley Ave
Road 12
East Rd
Map not to scale

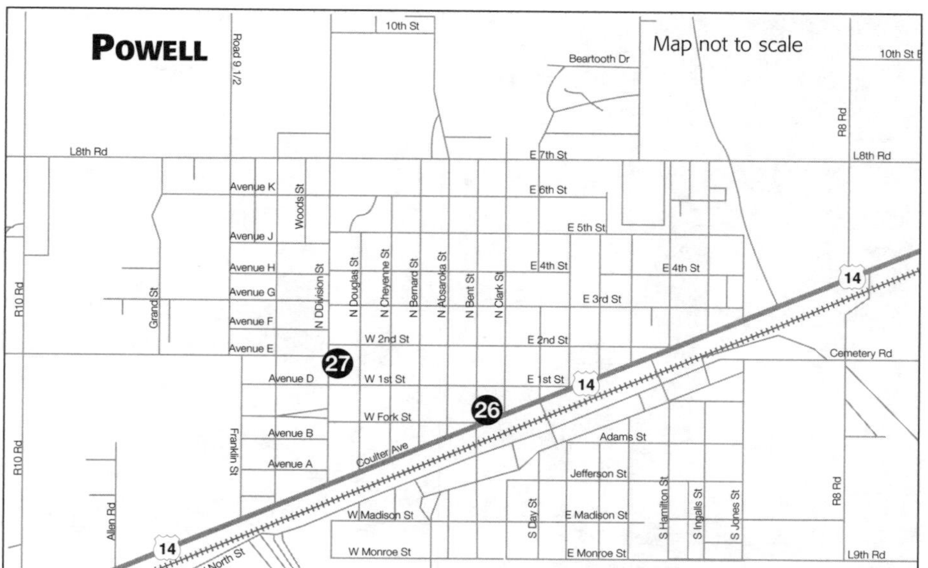

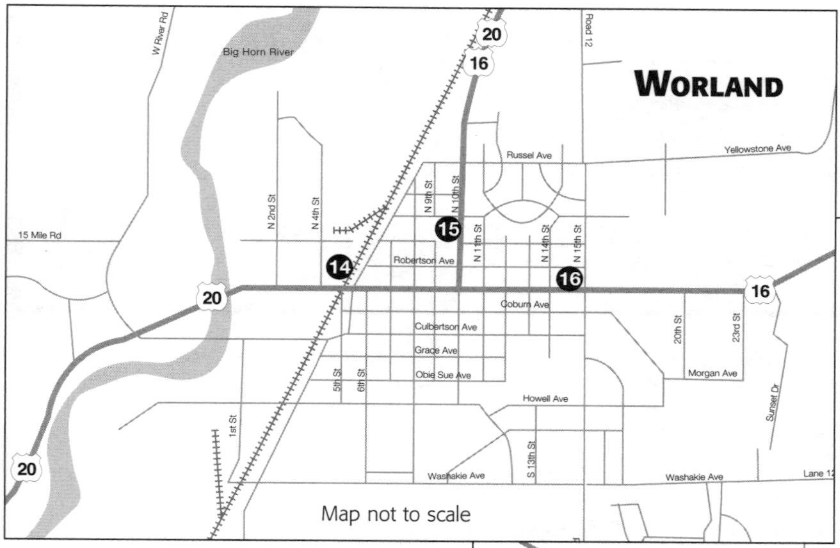

WORLAND

Map not to scale

Wyoming Tidbits

The Wapiti Ranger Station west of Cody is the first station established in the U.S.

THERMOPOLIS

Map not to scale

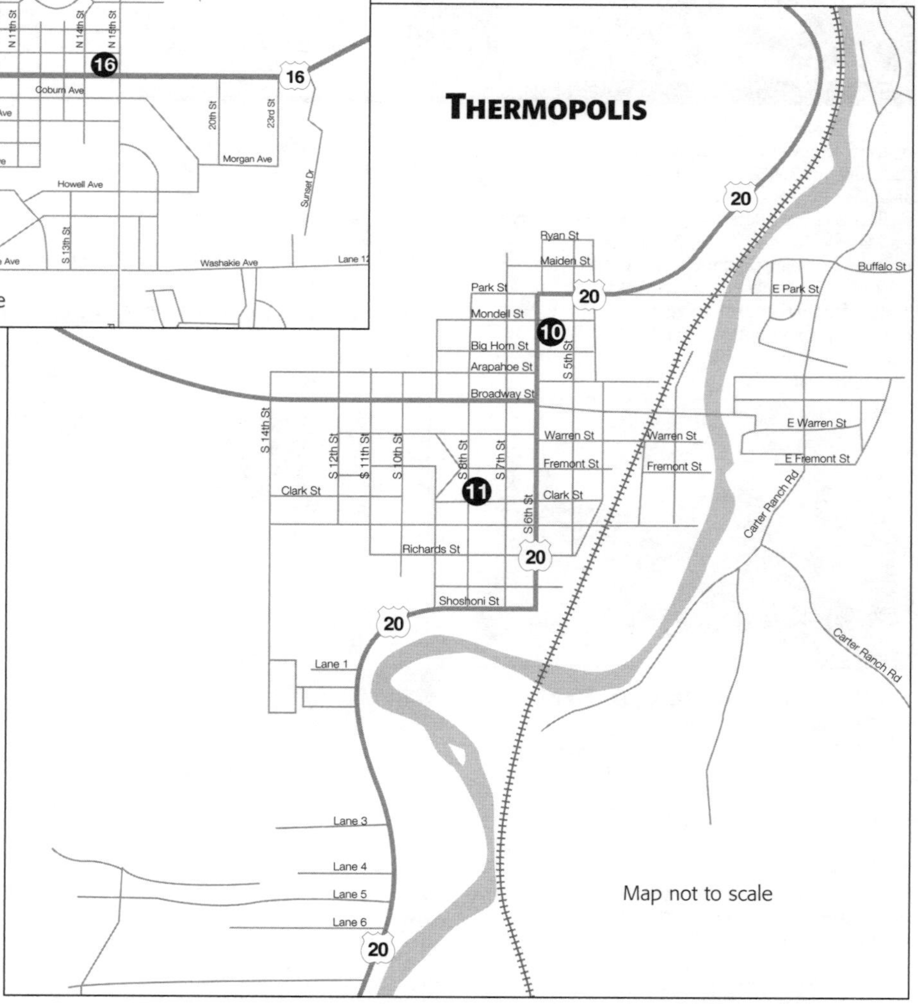

opens a window to the area's history. Throughout the store you will find exquisite jewelry, pottery, antiques, knives, music, toys, books, and cards. Collectibles are offered featuring Big Sky Carvers, Mill Creek Wildlife, Dept. 56, along with Christmas ornaments, including cowboy and western. This is also the place to find that perfect T-Shirt from an enormous selection. Don't forget to pick up some of their own fresh fudge. Shop and relax—shipping is available to get your treasures home safely.

S Sierra Trading Post Outlet Store
1402 8th Street in Cody. 578-5802 or 800-713-4534 (for free catalog). www.SierraTradingPost.com

Visit Sierra Trading Post and save 35-75% on name-brand outdoor clothing and equipment. You'll find The North Face, Marmot, New Balance, Carhartt, Columbia, Polaris, Vasque, Kelty, Lowe Alpine, and more. They are conveniently located just 1/2 block south of the Buffalo Bill Historical Center, across from Best Western Hotels. This is a great place to find savings on gear for hiking, biking, camping, fishing, hunting, or any Wyoming adventure, and beyond. Sierra Trading Post stores are open all year and located in Cody, Cheyenne, and Reno, Nevada. Visit their Bargain Barn where every item is always at least 60% off. Visit them on the web or call their toll free number for a free catalog.

M Eagle Real Estate LLC-GMAC
1234 Sheridan Ave. in Cody. 587-5266 or fax 587-5883. email: Eagle@trib.com. www.eaglerealestate.com

M ERA Beartooth Realty
1301 Sheridan Ave. in Cody. 587-7505 or fax 587-0222, call toll free at 877-578-9774. www.beartoothcodyrealty.com

Beartooth Realty is a full-service real estate company dedicated to personal service for you, the buyer. They offer 125 years of combined experience for services in residential, recreational, farm/ranch, commercial, building sites, investment and 1031 exchanges. Their goal is to provide superior quality service through teamwork. The close-knit staff provides a team that collaborates on all aspects to ensure the best transaction possible. Their objective is to give the best service with the highest professional and ethical standards. Small enough to be personal, but big enough to provide outstanding quality services for customers and clients. Visit them on the web.

M Homestead Realty, LC
1273 Sheridan in Cody. 587-4750 or fax 587-4780, or toll free 800-244-9510. www.homesteadrealty.us and Email:info@homesteadrealty.us

3 *Gas, Food, Lodging*

H Alkali Lake
Southeast of Cody at junction of U.S. Highways 14 and 120

Over 40 species of water-dependent birds are observed here throughout the year, including various ducks, geese and shorebirds. During the summer, a few ducks and Canada geese will nest and raise their young along the lake's limited shoreline habitat. Ducks like mallards, teal, widgeon, shoveler, gadwall and redheads are most often seen during spring and fall migration.Shorebirds are also common in the summertime and often walk this same shoreline in search of food. Explore the area, and you may see an avocet, black-necked stilt, killdeer, lesser yellowlegs or Wilson's phalarope. Viewing opportunities are usually best here during migration.

Alkali Lake gets its name from the extremely

The Old Trail Town Cemetery

The Old Trail Town Cemetery might be one of the smallest cemeteries you'll ever see, but its inhabitants all carved their niche in Wyoming History. Here are the stories behind them.

Belle Drewry

1867-1897

Belle Drewry was born in 1867, just two years after the Civil War. Her birth place and family are unknown. It is known that she left home at an early age and changed her name. Belle was a rather attractive young woman; about five foot six inches tall, medium to heavy boned with auburn hair. No one knows how or why Belle showed up in Wyoming Territory in the 1880's. However, it is suspected that she drifted west from mining towns in the Black Hills. She seemed to be drawn to the dark side of life and felt comfortable with the lawless element. A news item in the "Sundance Gazette" stated that in 1888, Belle Drewry was arraigned in court, for theft, with a piano player who was known to be an outlaw with an unsavory reputation. She was 21 years old.

By 1890 Belle had arrived (probably by stage coach) at the frontier town of Arland, Wyoming. Arland was located about twenty-five miles south of present Cody, Wyoming and was the first settlement in northwest Wyoming. It was a lawless town with a reputation for unrestrained violence and murder. Belle Drewry worked in the saloon and dance hall. Here she got to know W.A. Gallagher, Blind Bill Hoolihan, Robert Parker (Butch Cassidy), Jack Bliss and other suspected members of a gang known as the "Woodriver Horse Thieves".

Belle soon developed a close relationship with W.A. Gallagher a well known cowboy and horse thief. In 1891 Gallagher was lodged in the Fremont County Jail where he was held on charges of stealing a bay mare from the L U Ranch on Gooseberry Creek. Belle Drewry and Ed Lanigan put up $200.00 in bond money to get Gallagher out of jail.

Gallagher had the reputation of being a quarrelsome and vicious man. By the spring of 1894 Belle's relationship with Gallagher was deteriorating and she had developed a friendship with Bill Wheaton, another cowboy in the area. This resulted in a dispute in which Gallagher was shot and killed by Wheaton. Blind Bill, Gallagher's friend, attempted a show down with Wheaton to avenge Gallagher's death. However, Blind Bill was shot in the back and died in his cabin in Arland after writing a farewell letter to the undertaker. Belle Drewry and Bill Wheaton were charged with premeditated murder in the death of Gallagher, apprehended, and taken to the County Jail in Lander, Wyoming. However, the charges against Belle were dismissed at the preliminary hearing. Bill Wheaton's charge was later reduced to second degree manslaughter and was sentenced to eight years in the Wyoming Penitentiary at Laramie.

Belle continued her activities in the Arland-Meeteetse country and was well known. Early in 1897 Belle Drewry and three of her followers gave a party, one night. Everyone was drinking and the cowboys proceeded to shoot up the place. In the uproar that followed Belle pulled a six-shooter from a hiding place and shot the leader of the cowboy gang. A few days later, an unknown assassin came into the house and killed Belle Drewry, apparently in revenge, for their comrade's death.

Belle was given a respectable burial on the hill overlooking Arland. Thirty year old Belle Drewry was laid to rest in a red wood coffin, wearing a cobalt blue silk dress with a black sash. When Belle was disinterred for reburial at Old Trail Town, fired 45-70 and 45-60 cartridge cases were found in the ground around the coffin. It appears that a parting salute was fired, and the cartridge cases were dropped into the open grave.

One might imagine the boom of the rifles, the rolling echo across the hills and the black powder smoke drifting away with the wind like departing ghosts. Perhaps, a fitting farewell from a wild land.

Jack Stilwell

Frontiersman • 1850-1903

Simpson E. Stilwell, better known as "Comanche Jack", was born in Kansas in 1850 and served on the frontier during his youth as a scout and hunter. He is best known for his heroic deeds at the Battle of Beechers Island in September of 1868.

August 1868 were trying times in Kansas Territory as bands of marauding Sioux and Cheyenne were killing many settlers in what is now western Kansas and eastern Colorado.

It was well known that the regular troops had little effect against the hit-and-run tactics of the Indians.

On August 24, 1868 General Sheridan ordered Colonel G.A. Forsyth to enlist "50 first class hardy frontiersmen" and arm them with the new "Spencer Carbine", a repeating cartridge rifle that could fire nine shots without reloading. These guns were far superior to the single shot muzzle loading guns that had been in use for many years.

The ranks were soon filled, and among the volunteers was 18 year old Jack Stilwell, described as "a youth of six feet three or more, short of years but long on frontier lore."

Forsyth's contingent left Fort Hayes on August 29, 1868, and headed north-westward into the Indian country. On the morning of September 16, the scouts crossed the trail of a large band of Indians. That evening Forsyth's party camped along the north bank of the Arikaree Fork of the Republican River. Before dawn some young warriors tried to steal some of the scouts horses. Then, shortly after dawn, the entire horizon seemed filled with mounted and unmounted Indians. It is said that Jack Stilwell pointed to a small island in the river and the officers and scouts made a mad dash for it. Almost immediately, approximately six hundred Cheyenne and Sioux warriors began their charge down the slope toward the island. The scouts killed their horses for breastworks and dug into the sand behind them. Then, like a cyclone, the massive screaming force hit the island. When the first warriors were within twenty-five yards of the scouts, they opened fire with the new repeating guns. Horses and men fell in the first volley, many of which rolled over the defenders of the island. Colonel Forsyth's leg was shattered by a bullet, Lt. Beecher and Surgeon Moore were fatally wounded while others received lesser wounds.

The warriors, surprised by the rapid fire of the new guns, changed their tactics. They began riding in and swerving off as they fired, while others sniped at the defenders from hidden positions. After the first day of fighting Forsyth realized that without food and medical supplies their situation was hopeless. That night Jack Stilwell and Pierre Trudeau volunteered to try to sneak through the Indians and bring help from Fort Wallace, 125 miles away. Everyone feared that they would not make it. But after several close calls and a great deal of hardship, they did make it. On the 25th Jack Stilwell arrived with the 10th Cavalry and saved the survivors on the island.

After the Beecher Island battle, Stilwell remained a scout for the army for a length of time. Later in life he became a deputy United States Marshal in Oklahoma Territory, where he killed and captured several outlaws. Later he became the Police Judge at El Reno, Oklahoma and in the mid 1890s became a government cattle inspector for the Comanche Agency at Anadarko, Oklahoma. After that, Sttlwell became a United States Commissioner and the Master of the Masonic Lodge at Erwin Springs, Oklahoma.

Through the influence of his friend Buffalo Bill Cody, he came to Cody, Wyoming in 1897 where he took care of Cody's interests while he was away with the Wild West Show. Jack Stilwell had a small ranch on the South Fork of the Shoshone River, near Cody, Wyoming and died, from a sudden illness, in Cody in 1903.

John Jeremiah "Liver Eating" Johnston
1824-1900
Reburied at Old Trail Town June 8, 1974

John Johnston was born of Scotch-English descent in New Jersey in 1824. Johnston, described as a 6'6", 250 pound giant, came west in the early 1840's as a trapper. He began his career in the Medicine Bow mountains of Wyoming, gradually working his way northward through the Wind River, Owl Creek, and Absaroka Mountains, then into the Yellowstone Region and Montana.

About 1850 Johnston had acquired a Flathead Indian wife, of whom he was very fond, and had built a cabin on the Little Snake River in Wyoming. One day, on returning from trapping, he found his wife and unborn child dead and mutilated on the cabin floor. They had been killed by Crow Indians.

This started a personal revenge war against the Crows, which lasted nearly twelve years. According to legend, Johnston would on occasion remove the liver from a dead enemy and take a bite of it, or pretend to, in order to make a fierce impression on his savage foes. Consequently, he received the name "Liver Eating" Johnston.

Johnston went to Colorado in 1862 and enlisted in the Second Colorado Cavalry to fight in the Civil War. He was wounded in Missouri at the Battle of Newtonia, but remained in the service until his Honorable Discharge on September 23, 1865.

The winter after the war was spent in Fort Laramie, Wyoming, where he was hired to help supply buffalo and elk meat for the Army post. Johnston worked his way north to the Missouri River in Montana where he started a wood yard, supplying firewood for the steamboats that were traveling the river in those days.

In 1868, at the mouth of the Musselshell River, Johnston and some companions defeated a Sioux war party that intended to wipe out the group of trappers and wood cutters.

In 1877 Johnston became Chief of Scouts for General Nelson A. Miles. Johnston and ten scouts were credited with saving Miles command in a battle with the Cheyennes on Muddy Creek in 1877.

Johnston became the first Marshall at Coulson (Billings) Montana in 1882, and later in 1888, the first Sheriff of Red Lodge, Montana.

In old age he developed rheumatism, and in the late 1890's would treat his ailment at the DeMaris Hot Springs, near the river just below the site of Old Trail Town. His camping spot was just beneath the cliffs that can be seen from the grave site.

In the winter of 1899 Johnston's health failed him and he was sent to the old soldiers home in Santa Monica, California, where he died January 21, 1900.

"Liver Eating" Johnston, also known as Jeremiah Johnston from the Warner Bros. movie based on his life, was reburied near the mountains he loved on June 8, 1974.

The reburial was made possible through the efforts of Tri Robinson, and his seventh grade class of Lancaster, California.

The bronze statue of Johnston was sculpted by Peter Fillerup of Cody, Wyoming and donated by Larry Clark of Salt Lake City, Utah.

Jim White
Buffalo Hunter • 1828-1880
Reburied May 6, 1979

Jim White was born in Missouri in 1828. He found his way into the southwest as a young man, where he was a freighter with ox-drawn wagons.

When the Civil War broke out in 1861, Jim White served the Confederate Army as a grain buyer and wagon boss. At the end of the Civil War, Jim White married and returned to the southwest.

In 1868 he drifted down into Mexico, where a rich Spaniard won his wife away. White killed him and wounded several others in the fracas that followed.

There was a large reward offered for him, dead or alive. This was when he dropped his original name and adopted the name Jim White, for which he is known. His original name is unknown.

White walked 700 miles back into Texas where he got into the buffalo hunting profession. White kept several skinners busy as he preyed on the wandering herds.

One day a group of ciboleros rode over a hill and scared away a small herd of buffalo that White was firing on. In a fit of temper, he shot the horses out from under four of the party.

Jim White was hunting in the Texas Panhandle during the mid 1870s. He was in the region at the time of the Battle of Adobe Walls and other lesser battles with the Kiowas and Commanches.

White had the reputation in Texas for being a tough character. He operated best alone or with his own men.

By 1878 the buffalo on the Southern Plains were gone. Many hunters started looking toward the unspoiled Northern Plains of Wyoming and Montana.

Jim White was among the first hunters to reach the northern buffalo range. By late summer,1878, he had reached the Big Horn Mountains with two big span of mules. two wagons, 700 pounds of lead, five kegs of gun-powder, three 16 pound Sharp's rifles, varied equipment, and an old buffalo skinner named Watson.

White soon met Oliver Hanna, who had been a scout with General Crook in 1876. and they became hunting partners.

During the winter of 1878-79 the two men had a contract to furnish 5,000 pounds of game meat to the Army at Fort McKinney, near present Buffalo, Wyoming.

The following winter of 1879-80, White and Hanna had a buffalo hunting camp north of the Yellowstone River near Miles City. The two hunters kept six buffalo skinners busy. By spring, they had collected 4,600 buffalo hides which were freighted to the Yellowstone River by ox teams and then hauled down the river by steam boats.

In the following fall of 1880, White and Hanna came into the Big Horn Basin and set up a hunting camp on Shell Creek, near the foot of the Big Horn Mountains. They were hunting and trapping in the area. In late October, Hanna made a quick trip over the Big Horns. When he returned he found Jim White dead. He had been shot in the head by thieves who had stolen their horses, mules. wagons, guns, hides, furs, etc.

Hanna buried Jim White on the upper bank, on the north side of Shell Creek, presently on the ranch of Irvy Davis near Shell, Wyoming.

Hanna later stated that Jim White was the greatest buffalo hunter the world has ever known. Hanna stated that White had a ledger book that contained records of hide sales for over 16,000 buffalo.

Jim White, who had lived by the gun, now, also died by the gun.

Recent examination of his remains revealed that he was killed by a 50 caliber bullet; probably from a Sharp's buffalo rifle. Possibly from the same gun that killed his own victims.

The bronze statue of White was sculpted and donated by Tom Hillis of Stanton Michigan.

W. A. Gallagher and Blind Bill—Murdered
1894
Reburied December 17, 1978

William Gallagher and his friend, Blind Bill, were killed on Meeteetse Creek below the old town of Arland in mid-March of 1894. Both men, about thirty, were born during the Civil War period.

Gallagher, who was somewhat of an outlaw, was tall, lean and wore a drooping dark mustache. He wore a gun most of the time, had a severe temper, and was a hard case in general.

Blind Bill was short, muscular, and wore a patch over his left eye, which was blind. Blind Bill was a good friend of Gallagher's. Both men were working as cowboys in the Greybull River Country, and had probably found their way into the region on one of the early trail drives.

Gallagher was once described by A. A. Anderson, for whom he had once worked, as being one of the best horse-men and ropers he had ever known. However, his reputation was not as good as his figure. Gallagher told Anderson, one time after getting out of jail in Thermopolis, that; "I captured the town and was about to trade it off to the Indians when they threw me in jail." On another occasion, Gallagher was accused of horse stealing and tried at the district court in Lander, Wyoming in 1891. Later in that year he was tried for forgery. He escaped being jailed each time, due to technicalities.

In 1893, Gallagher had become involved with 27 year old Belle Drewery, one of the single women that hung out around the town of Arland. Early in 1894 Belle began seeing Bill Wheaton. When Gallagher became aware of the friendship, he went into a jealous rage. On March 15th Gallagher took Belle over to the ranch house where Wheaton was. An argument developed and Gallagher pulled his six-shooter and held Wheaton and Belle at gun-point for two hours, while he threatened them and kept cocking his six-shooter. Finally, Gallagher passed the incident off as kind of a joke and holstered his gun.

Belle informed Wheaton as to where a gun was hidden in the house. A little later she went out of the house and started walking toward Meeteetse.

When she didn't return, Gallagher went out to see where she went. Wheaton then got the gun that was in the house. Gallagher was walking across the yard when Wheaton rested the gun against the side of the door frame and shot him from behind. Wheaton then got on his horse and left.

When Blind Bill learned of Gallagher's death, he was very upset and swore he would kill Wheaton in revenge for the death of his friend.

Wheaton was soon informed that Blind Bill intended to kill him. Gallagher's loyal friend never fulfilled his vow, for he was found a few days later, shot in the back by an unknown assassin. Although it was believed that Wheaton killed Blind Bill, it was never proven.

Both Gallagher and his friend, Blind Bill, were buried on a sage brush hill near Meeteetse Creek.

Wheaton was tried in the death of W. A. Gallagher and sentenced to eight years in the Wyoming State Penitentiary. He was released in 1898 after serving four years. Belle Drewery had been killed the year before in a gun-fight at a saloon in Arland.

Phillip H. Vetter
1855-1892
Reburied June 10, 1978

Phillip Henry Vetter was born February 7, 1855 near Woodstock, Shenandoah County, Virginia. He was killed by a grizzly bear on the Greybull River in Wyoming in 1892.

A few years after the Civil War, Phillip's family came West by wagon train and settled in the Wind River Country near Lander, Wyoming Territory.

Through the 1880's, Phillip Vetter pursued the occupation of market hunter and trapper. About 1890 he moved over to the Greybull River above Meeteetse, Wyoming. Here he built a log cabin and continued his hunting and trapping.

On September 1, 1892, Vetter left a note at his cabin which said, "Jake, if you come to get your horses, I'm going down to the river after some bear."

A week or so later John Corbett, an old buffalo hunter, was riding over to John Gleavers on Wood River. When he was near Vetter's cabin, black clouds threatened a heavy rain. Corbett decided to wait out the storm in shelter with Vetter.

He rode up to the cabin. The door stood open. Inside, Corhett found Vetter's body on the floor. Dishes from Vetter's last meal stood unwashed on the dusty table. The storm was forgotten. Corbett jumped on his horse and raced to the Gleaver ranch.

The two men returned and sought to piece the story together. They found Vetter's neatly written note to Jake. In contrast, scribbled on the edge of a newspaper in Vetter's handwriting, in what they believed was his own blood, were several terse messages. The first said something about a battle with a grizzly hear. A later notation said, "Should go to Franc's but too weak." Vetter's handwriting grew shakier. "It's getting dark. I'm smothering." The final message read, "I'm dying."

One of Vetter's arms had been badly mangled and his chest was crushed. He had tried unsuccessfully to stop the flow of blood.

The men walked down to the river to look for more clues. Near the stream the men found a water bucket and Vetter's hat, and not far away was his rifle. A shell had jammed in the chamber. On the ground lay two empty casings.

The wounded bear had mauled him severely before leaving him for dead. Vetter was able to drag himself back to his cabin where he wrote his death message in his own blood. Thirty-seven year old Phillip Vetter died alone, far from help.

Corbett and Gleaver built a casket of rough boards with timbers hewn from logs for a lid. Vetter was buried on upper river bank, near his cabin. A slab of sandstone with the inscription "P. H. Vetter — 1892" was placed at the grave.

high concentration of soluble alkali metals, especially sodium. The lake's water falls as precipitation, seeps in as groundwater and flows in as surface runoff in the spring or after a rain. As the water level drops from evaporation, the alkalinity increases. Fish cannot survive in this water, however small invertebrates such as fairy shimp thrive here. During migration, waterbirds need places like Alkali Lake to rest and refuel before continuing on their journey. Fairy shimp, salt tolerant vegetaion and the agricultural land in and around Cody, provide the necessary food sources for these birds.

From the tiny solitary sandpiper to the rare and regal trumpeter swan, Alkali Lake is an important oasis and refuge.

Wyoming Tidbits

John Colter named the Stinking River due to the sulfur odor permeating the area. It was not until nearly a hundred years later the name was changed to Shoshone River.

L Super 8 Cody
730 Yellowstone Hwy. in Cody. 527-6214 or 800-800-8000.

4

T Cody Stampede
U.S. Highway 14/16, on the West Cody Strip. 587-2234. www.codystampederodeo.org

"Cody is Rodeo" is the slogan for the Rodeo Capital of the World. The Stampede Board works hard to put on the best rodeo for the cowboys and the spectators. 2003 marks the 84th anniversary of the Buffalo Bill Cody Stampede. The Stampede Board has won the "1998 & 1999 Large Outdoor Rodeo Committee of the Year" award and was nominated in 2000 and again in 2002. The local committee, the Stock Contractors and the community work very hard to please the contestants and see that the audience gets the best show they can for the money. Adding the announcer, clowns, pickup men and specialty acts, it is a good time had by all. Since 1937 the Cody Nite Rodeo has carried on the tradition of showing the world the Wild West every night from June 1st thru August 31st.

T Old Trail Town
On west edge of Cody next to Cody Stampede grounds

On this site in 1895, Western scout and showman William F. ("Buffalo Bill") Cody laid out the original townsite of Cody, Wyoming, which was named in his honor. Today Old Trail Town preserves the lifestyle and history of the Frontier West through a rare collection of authentic structures and furnishings. From remote locations in

Wyoming and Montana, these historic buildings were carefully disassembled, moved and reassembled here at Old Trail Town by Western historian Bob Edgar and friends.

Located here also are thousands of historic artifacts from the Old West, and gravesites of several notable Western figujres. Among them is the grave of mountain man John Johnson, who was portrayed by the actor Robert Redford in the 1972 motion picture "Jeremiah Johnson."

Here too are original cabins used by Old West outlaws Butch Cassidy and the Sundance Kid, and a Wyoming saloon frequented by Cassidy's "Hole-in-the-Wall Gang." Also on this site is the log cabin home of "Curley"—a Crow indian army scout who helped guide Lt. Col. George A. Custer and the U.S. 7th Cavalry to the battle of the Little Big Horn in 1876. Old Trail Town exists today as a memorial to the uniquely American experience known throughout the world as "the Old West."

Trail Town Information Signs

The Arland Cabin

Residential cabin built at the Arland and Corbett Trading Post on Cottonwood Creek, north of present Cody, WY, in 1883, WY Territory. The post was a trading center for hunters, trappers and Indians.

Blacksmith Shop (5004)

This building was built in lower Sunshine Basin, west of Meeteetse, WY, around 1900.

Buffalo Hunter's Cabin

Cabin built on Shell Creek at the hunting camp of Jim White and Oliver Hanna in 1880. Jim White was murdered at the camp in late October, 1880. The cabin was later used by Al Kershner when he homesteaded the property in 1889.

The Burlington Store

This building was built on the Greybull River, near Burlington, WY about 1897. It was moved to Burlington where it was used as a store for several years.

Bonanza Post Office

This building was built at Bonanza, Wyoming Territory, in 1885. This was one of the first settlements in the Big Horn Basin.

Carpenter Shop

One of the first buildings of Cowley, WY. It was built in 1901 and used by George Taggart. A Mormon pioneer that came to the Big Horn Basin by wagon train in 1900.

Carter Cabin

This cabin was built by William Carter's men on Carter MT about 1879, Wyoming Territory. Carter brought the first cattle into the region around Cody.

The Coffin School

This cabin was built at the W Ranch on Wood River, west of Meeteetse, in 1884. It was used as a school for several years. It derives its name from the tragic death of Alfred Nower, who died of gangrene in this cabin in 1885. He had chopped himself in the leg while hewing logs.

Commissary

This building was built on the W. B. Rice Ranch on Wood River about 1898. It was used as a bunkhouse and commissary.

Curly's Cabin

Log cabin home of Custer's Crow Indian scout, Curly. Curly escaped from the "Battle of the Little Bighorn" on June 25, 1876 and brought the news of Custer's defeat. The cabin was built near Crow Agency, Montana about 1885.

Hole in the Wall Cabin

Through this door walked Butch Cassidy, The Sundance Kid, and other outlaws of the famous "Hole in the Wall" Gang. The cabin was built on Buffalo Creek, in the Hole in the Wall Country, west of Kaycee, WY, Wyoming Territory, in 1883 by Alexander Ghent.

Homestead Cabin (5018)

This cabin was built on Wood River, west of Meeteetse, about 1899. It is a fine example of log craftmenship.

Homestead Cabin (5044)

Cabin built by homesteaders on Monument Hill, north of Cody, about 1900.

Homestead Cabin (5010)

Cabin built at the head of Dry Creek, between Cody and Meeteetse around 1900.

Livery Stable

This building was built near the Clarks Fork Canyon, north of Cody in the late 1890s.

Mayor's Cabin

Home of Frank Houx, the first mayor of Cody, WY. It was built about 1897.

Morrison Cabin

Cabin built at the foot of Copper Mountain, east of Shoshoni Wyoming, in 1884, by Luther Morrison. The Morrisons brought some of the first sheep into central Wyoming in 1882. Morrison had originally come west on the Oregon Trail in 1853.

The Rivers Saloon

This saloon was built in 1888 at the mouth of Wood River, west of Meeteetse, WY, by Henry Rivers. It was frequented by Butch Cassidy, W. A. Gallagher, Blind Bill Hoolihan and many other outlaws, cowboys, and colorful characters of the Old West. Bullet holes can be seen in the door.

The Shell Store

This was the first store in Shell, WY. It was built in 1892.

Trapper's Cabin

Cabin built on Cottonwood Creek, south of Meeteetse, about 1885.

T Wyoming Territory Old West Miniature Village and Museum

140 W. Yellowstone Ave. in Cody. 587-5362

This collection is the work of Jerry Fick, who has made a lifetime of assembling miniature figures and buildings into scenes depicting the Old West. His portrayals are historically accurate, though not always to scale, and feature such events as the Battle of the Little Big Horn, Buffalo Bill's Wild West Show, and the Green River Rendezvous. There are also Native American villages, wagon trains, forts, and railroad stations. A working train which travels through the other scenes operates with the push of a button. There are also a host of genuine Western artifacts on display here, including Geronimo's bow and arrows.

H Old Trail Town—Museum of the Old West

1831 Demaris in Cody. 587-5302

Old Trail Town is a collection of Frontier buildings and historical relics from northwest Wyoming. It is on the edge of the original townsite of Cody City.

In the cemetery, at the far end of the street is the grave of Liver Eating Johnston, better known as Jeremiah Johnson from the movie.

Old Trail Town is the largest collection of it's kind in Wyoming. Open Mid May through Mid September from 8 a.m. to 8 p.m.

The minimal admission fee is necessary for the maintenance and development of the Old Trail Town Project.

Section 2

to the park's geyser area—thereby causing a degree of historic confusion. The true Colter's Hell is here in view.

H Primitive Necropolis

North from Cody on State Highway 120 then west on County Road

The following pioneers were buried here, but not much of a record as to which grave was used and little information regarding the pioneers is available. We are indebted to Charles Hartung, a pioneer cowboy for what we do have. 1882—Tom Heffner, cowboy for Henry Lovel, gassed at springs. 1882—Johnnie Lincoln, murdered at the Trail Creek Ranch. Paul Bretache's baby was buried here. The wife and baby of Pete (Black Pete) Enzon, buried in separate graves. An unknown man walked over the cliff at the springs in the dark. 1900—Clarence Veonor Edick, died of internal injuries when crossing to the springs. An unknown invalid from the Red Lodge area died at the springs. 1903—Mrs. Wm. Brown of Bellfrey gassed in hot spring. Louis Wilde from the Greybull Valley died at the springs. His stock was branded with a cotton hook.

H Shoshone Canyon

Entrance to Shoshone Canyon west of Cody on U.S. Highway 14/16/20

Shoshone Canyon is a gorge cut across Rattlesnake Mountain by the wearing action of the Shoshone River over a long period of time. The mountain is an upfold in the earth's crust. Beds of sedimentary rock on the east flank slope eastward beneath the plains. The same units bend up and over the crest of the mountain and stand vertical along the west flank. Granite over two billion years old, is exposed around Buffalo Bill Dam. South of the dam is a vertical fracture, or fault, in the rocks along which the mountain was uplifted over 2,000 feet.

H The American Mountain Man

Historic Trail Town on west side of Cody

Dedicated to all Mountain Men known and unknown for their essential part in the opening of the American West. We gratefully acknowledge the way their uniue lifestyle has profoundly influenced our own. Erected by the Brotherhood of the American Mountain Men.

In Tribute to John Colter

First known white American explorer to enter this locale in the fall of 1807. Probably crossing the river 1/4 mile east of this point (right), before discovering "Colter's Hell" 1/2 mile to the west (left).

Born and raised in Virginia in 1770's. A valued member of the Lewis and Clark Expedition to the Pacific Ocean, 1803-1806. Among the first American "Free Trappers" in the Rocky Mountains, along with Joseph Dickson and Forrest Bancock, 1806-1807. First to explore Big Horn Basin, Yellowstone Park, and Grand Teton regions, 1807-1808. Immortalized by his legendary "run for life" escape, from the hostile Blackfeet Indians, 1808. Quit the mountains in 1810, married and settled on a farm near St. Louis, Missouri. Died of disease in 1813, unheralded, but not forgotten. His final resting place has since been lost. Erected by the John Colter Society, 1981. A legacy for all who adventure.

George Drouillard (c. 1775-1810)

Born to a French Canadian father and Shawnee mother, Drouillard joined the Lewis and Clark

William F. "Buffalo Bill" Cody

William F. Cody was born on February 26, 1846 near LeClair, Iowa. In 1854 his family moved to settle on lands in what would soon be Kansas Territory. Young William's father died in 1857, leaving the boy to help provide for his family.

William soon obtained a job as a messenger boy for Majors and Russell, who had a company store at Leavenworth, Kansas. In the next three years, William would try his hand at prospecting during the Pikes Peak gold rush, and at trapping. Neither ventures proved to be very successful.

In 1860, the partnership of Russell, Majors, and Waddell, in an effort to advertise and obtain a contract for a central route for mail to the Pacific, began the Pony Express. Cody, already acquainted with the principals in this partnership, was hired as a rider. The Pony Express operated from April 3, 1860 to November 18, 1861. The venture operated at a loss and failed to bring the desired contract to Cody's employers, whose partnership ended in bankruptcy.

Cody's mother died November 22, 1863. Shortly thereafter, in February, 1864, he enlisted in the 7th Kansas Cavalry, some say influenced by friends and alcohol. During the Civil War Cody saw action in Tennessee, Mississippi, and Missouri. He served 19 months, including one year of active duty.

After his discharge, Cody married Louisa Frederici on March 6, 1866. He worked briefly as a scout at Fort Ellsworth, where an old acquaintance, James Butler "Wild Bill" Hickok, was also employed. The following year Cody was hired by the Kansas Pacific Railroad to kill buffalo to feed track layers for eight months. This job apparently was the source of the nickname that would become known virtually worldwide: Buffalo Bill.

Later Cody distinguished himself as a scout for the U.S. Army. He was valued so highly that General Phil Sheridan endeavored to keep Cody on the Army's payroll even after the end of their campaign, something not done with scouts up to that time. This paved the way for the scout to become an established position in the Army during the years of the Indian wars. Cody was made chief scout of the 5th Cavalry by General Sheridan in October, 1868.

Cody first began to receive national attention in 1869, when a serial story about "Buffalo Bill" appeared in a New York paper. Then in 1872 he was assigned to guide the Grand Duke Alexis of Russia on a hunting trip. With the press following the Duke's every move, Cody received a great deal more exposure. This experience was followed by his first trip to the eastern states. He attended a play about himself and was talked into taking part in the performance. Thus began a period of years when Cody alternated between scouting duties and theatrical tours. Cody was awarded the Medal of Honor in 1872 for action against Indians at the South Fork of the Loup River in Nebraska. However, his name was stricken from the record of Medal of Honor recipients in 1916, since he was a civilian, and considered not eligible for the award. He later assisted General George Crook's campaign against the Sioux in 1876.

"Buffalo Bill's Wild West Show" had its beginnings in 1883. This was a propitious time for such an effort by Cody and his partners, during the height of popularity for outdoor shows such as circuses. The show in various forms would tour the United States and Europe for three decades.

Buffalo Bill was also commonly referred to as "Colonel Cody", rank was provided by Nebraska Governor John Thayer (former governor of Wyoming Territory) in 1887, when he was named aide-de-camp of the Governor's staff. He was never an officer in the U.S. Army.

Cody became interested in developing the Big Horn Basin in Wyoming in the 1890s. The Cody Canal was built in 1895, as part of the Shoshone Land and Irrigation Project. The company laid out a townsite, first calling it "Shoshone." With the Shoshoni Indian agency in the region this was rejected to avoid confusion. Therefore, in August, 1896 the Cody post office was established, with Buffalo Bill's nephew, Ed Goodman, as postmaster.

The water project led to the building of the Shoshone Dam, which was completed in 1910. The dam was renamed "Buffalo Bill Dam" in 1946. Buffalo Bill was also instrumental in bringing a rail line to the town of Cody in 1901.

William F. Cody died January 10, 1917 while staying in Denver, Colorado. He is buried on Lookout Mountain, west of Denver. Information in this article was drawn from, The Lives and Legends of Buffalo Bill by Don Russell, University of Oklahoma Press, 1960.

Courtesy of Wyoming State Archives

H Colter's Hell

U.S. Highway 14/16/20 on west edge of Cody.

John Colter, veteran of the Lewis and Clark Expedition, notably self-sufficient mountain man and indefatigable explorer, was the first white man known to have reconnoitered this locale. In 1807, possibly traveling alone but probably escorted by Crow guides, he crossed the Stinking Water (Shoshone River) via a major Indian trail ford located about a mile downstream from this observation point. here, extending along both sides of the river, he discovered an active geyser district. Steam mixed with sulfur fumes and shooting flames escaped through vents in the valley floor, subeterranean rumblings were ominously audible. Although mineralized hot springs continued to flow along the river's edge, the eruptions colter watched are now marked only by cones of parched stone.

This was primarily Shoshone and Crow country but other Indians came to the area. Particularly Bannocks and Nez Perce, journeying eastward over the mountains to hunt the plains buffalo, tarried to test the heralded medicinal values of these "stinking waters" baths. Ranged along bench-lands to the east and north are numerous tepee rings, evidence of former Indian encampments. Heart Mountain, famous landmark and geological oddity, is conspicuous on the northern horizon.

Honoring a respected predecessor, mountain men of the 1820s-1830s fur trade heyday named this place Colter's Hell. later, early-day officials of Yellowstone Park applied that name

Expedition in 1803 as chief interpreter and hunter. Lewis said of him, "I scarcely know how we should exist were it not for the exertions of this excellent hunter." While thus employed, he was possibly the first white man to trap on the upper Missouri River. In 1807, he joined Manuel Lisa's trading expeidtion. During two solitary winter treks on foot to notify various tribes of Lisa's fort on the Yellowstone, Drouillard journeyed up the Stinking Water (Shoshone River) near this spot. His explorations of this and other major rivers to the east totalled 500 miles, and he produced an important map upon which William Clark and later cartographers relied heavily. Trapping near the Three Forks with the Missouri Fur Company, he was killed by Blackfeet Indians in May 1810.

Jededian Strong Smith, January 6, 1799-May 27, 1831
Born in Jerico, New York, the 6th of 14 children, Jed was destined to influence the Westward expansion of the United States as few men have done. Influenced by Lewis and Clark's exploits he joined Ashley's trapping expedition in 1822, soon becoming a partner and then owner in 1827. A natural leader, devout Christian and tireless explorer, Jed's discovery popularized the South Pass crossing of the Rockies. He was the first man to travel overland to California and first to ravel the coast from California to the Columbia. He survived near death from thirst and starvation, maulings of a grizzly and attacks by Arikara, Mojava and Kelewatset Indians. Killed by Comanches near Fargo Spring, Kansas, his body was never found but his legacy live on as his trails of discovery became the highways for America's westward migration.

Born c. 1770, Died 1813, John Colter
A hunter for Lewis and Clark (1803-1806) Colter remained in the mountains to trap and explore. During his great journey of discovery he found "Colter's Hell" west of Cody, Wyoming. Captured by the Blackfeet in 1808, he was forced to run for his life. Outdistancing the entire tribe for seven miles he survived, naked and weaponless, to become a legend in his own lifetime. John Colter was the first true "Mountain Man."

A Tribute to James "Old Gabe" Bridger 1804-1881
Mountain man, hunter, trapper, fur trader, emigrant guide, and Army scout. Born in Richmond, Virginia in 1804 and moved to St. Louis, Missouri, in 1812. Served as a blacksmith's apprentice from 1818 to 1822. Came west with the 1822 Ashley-Henry Expedition. Discovered the Great Salt Lake in 1824 and visited what is now Yellowstone Park in 1830. In 1833 he became a full partner in the fur trading firm of Sublette, Fraeb, Gervais, Bridger, and Fitzpatrick. Anticipating the influx of immigrants he established Ft. Bridger to resupply and repair wagon trains. Jim served as a guide and scout for the Army until 1868. After his dischare Old Gabe retired to his farm in Missouri. However, by 1874, his health began to fall and he was blind. Jim's only regret was that he would never see his beloved Rocky Mountains before his death. On July 17, 181, the Lord laid Old Gabe's tired body to rest and set his spirit free to return at last to the mountains he loved.

In Tribute to Jim Bridger
Regarded most famous of the Rocky Mountain trappers and explorers who blazed the American West's early trails of continental destiny and who frequented these environs throughout the mid-1800's.

West 20 mile upriver towers Jim Mountain named for Jim Baker, a well known Bridger protege.

East 30 miles downriver the "Bridger Trail" crosses the "Stinking Water" (Shoshone River). This trail was established across the Big Horn Basin around 1864 by Jim Bridger (then working primarily as an emigrant and Army expedition guide). As a safer alternative route to the "Bozeman Trail" in traveling from the "Oregon-California Trail" to the Montana mines.

Jim Bridger epitomized the "mountain man" and his legacy endures, but only in context with many others. In all this breed never exceeded more than a few hundred. They came seeking adventure and fortune. Over half of them succumbed to the rigors of their profession: hostile elements, animals, Indeians, and starvation. Their names and remains are forever consigned-unrecorded-to the dust of the mountains and plains where they "went under", often in violent fashion. This marker also stands

Shoshone National Forest

The Shoshone National Forest was set aside in 1891 as part of the Yellowstone Timberland Reserve, making the Shoshone the first national forest in the United States. It consists of some 2.4 million acres of varied terrain ranging from sagebrush flats to rugged mountains. The higher mountains are snow-clad most of the year. Immense areas of exposed rock are interspersed with meadows and forests. With Yellowstone National Park on its western border, the Shoshone encompasses the area from the Montana state line south to Lander, Wyoming which includes portions of the Absaroka, Wind River and Beartooth Ranges.

Brief History...

The Shoshone National Forest was set aside by proclamation of President Benjamin Harrison as the Yellowstone Park Timberland Reserve on March 30, 1891. It was the first unit of its kind created after the passage of the Act of March 3, 1891, authorizing the establishment of forest reserves—as national forests were then called—to protect the remaining timber on the public domain from destruction and to insure a regular flow of water in the streams.

The Shoshone's historic and cultural links to the past are rich and diverse. An excavation of Mummy's Cave on the North Fork of the Shoshone River revealed artifacts of the "Sheepeater" Indians dating back 7,500 years. The Arapahoe, Blackfeet, Commanche, Crow, Nez Perce, Northern Cheyenne, Shoshone and Sioux tribes lived, hunted, traveled, traded and fought in the area. In 1877 the great Nez Perce leader Chief Joseph led his people through the thousand-foot-deep Clarks Fork Canyon, successfully evading the U.S. Army in his running battle to reach Canada. Such mountain men as John Colter and Jim Bridger were early visitors.

The ghost town of Kirwin, an early-day mining town, is a window to the past, recalling one of the colorful eras in Wyoming's history. The remains of tie hack flumes and cabins on the southern end of the forest are reminders of another era during which millions of railroad ties were produced.

The historic Wapiti Ranger Station in the North Fork Valley was the first ranger station built with government funds. Anderson Lodge, on the Greybull District, served as a home and workplace for A. A. Anderson, the first forest supervisor, and is listed as a National Historic Site.

Buffalo Bill was impressed with both the beauty and the hunting offered by the area. He built a hunting lodge on the forest called Pahaska Tepee and entertained numerous well known people including the Prince of Monaco. Teddy Roosevelt was equally impressed with the beauty of the area during several hunting forays.

Forest Facts...

The Shoshone consists of 2.4 million acres of varied terrain ranging from sagebrush flats to rugged mountain peaks and includes portions of the Absaroka, Wind River, and Beartooth Mountain Ranges. Elevations on the Shoshone range from 4,600 feet at the mouth of the spectacular Clarks Fork Canyon to 13,804 feet on Gannett Peak, Wyoming's highest point. Geologists delightedly call the Shoshone's varied topography an "open book." Formed under tremendous heat and pressure within the earth's interior were the granite monoliths of the Beartooth and Wind River Ranges. Born of the bubbling, spewing lava of prehistoric volcanoes was the Absaroka Range. Over aeons, wind and water have exposed strata and sculpted the rock into fascinating shapes to delight the visitor's eye. The Shoshone is unique in the Rocky Mountains for having so many glaciers and so many different kinds, four. There are 16 named glaciers and at least 140 unnamed ones. Fifty-three of them are over 11.4 square miles, which ranks Wyoming behind only Alaska and Washington in total glacier area.

The Shoshone National Forest is more than half (nearly 1.4 million acres) designated wilderness. There are five different wilderness areas. They include the Absaroka-Beartooth, the North Absaroka, the Washakie, the PoPo Agie and the Fitzpatrick.

Some 4,900 miles of streams flow through the Shoshone, and 11,700 acres of lakes and some 51,000 acres of additional wetlands dot the forest landscape. Hundreds of alpine lakes, many above timberline, lie in rugged cirques and high valleys of the Beartooth and Wind River mountain ranges.

Wildlife on the Shoshone includes deer, elk, moose, bighorn sheep, mountain goats, grizzly and black bears, as well as numerous smaller animals, birds and cold-water fish.

The Shoshone contains 940 miles of roads and 1,528 miles of trails. Roads include the Loop Road near Lander which offers spectacular scenery, fishing, camping and trailheads into pristine wilderness. The Beartooth Highway crosses the spectacular Beartooth Plateau at nearly 11,000 feet. The Buffalo Bill Cody Scenic Byway offers superb scenery and wildlife viewing. Hikers and horseback riders enjoy trails that follow willow-lined streams through long, winding valleys and cross high alpine meadows dotted with sparkling lakes.

in their memory. Erected 1982.

Plaque #7: Osborn Russell, 1814-1892

Born June 12, 1814 in Bowdoinham, Maine, Russell went to sea briefly at age 16 then for three years was a trapper in Wisconsin and Minnesota. He joined Nathanial Wyeth's 1834 expedition to deliver trade goods to the trappers' rendezvous in the Rocky Mountains. Wyeth met disappointment in his enterprise but moved on to build Fort Hall. Russell helped to build the fort and stayed to maintain it until spring when he joined Jim Bridger's trapping party. He soon declared his independence as a "free trapper" and pursued beaver until 1843.

Russell's travels took him from Montana to Utah Lake as he crossed and recrossed the Rockies many times. All this while he felt an obligation to record his observations in his journal.

In 1843 he moved to the California/Oregon country where he became a miner, a merchant and at one time a judge. He died August 28, 1892, in Pacerville, California. He is gratefully remembered by all who read his "Journal of a Trapper" with its daily account of the activities and adventures of a trapper.

Wyoming Tidbits

As many as 60 million buffalo once grazed on the great plains. "Buffalo Bill" Cody reportedly killed more than 4,000 in one year. By the end of 1883, herds were decimated by hunters and overgrazing.

Thomas Fitzpatrick, 1799-1854

Mountain man, business man, western guide, Indian agent; born and educated in Ireland, emigrated to America at age 16, he joined Ashley's trappers in 1823 and was appointed to leadership that year. He became a full partner in the Rocky Mountain Fur Co. in 1830. Tom battled with the Arickarees in 1823 and with the Gros Vents at Pierre's Hole in 1832. These same Gros Vents attacked him a few weeks earlier as he rode alone east of the Tetons. His horses and weapons lost in flight, barely alive when rescued many days later, his hair had turned white from the ordeal. Tom had two nicknames, "White Hair" and "Broken Hand", the latter from an encounter with a rifle ball during a Blackfoot attack. With the decline of the fur trade, Tom served as a guide to west-bound emigrants (1841-42), J. D. Fremont's explorations (1843-44) and Col. Kerney's expedition of 1845-46. Honorably served as a Federal Indian Agent from 1846 until his death February 7, 1854.

Hugh Glass, ?-1832(3)

Tough and independent, Glass had been a ship's captain and impressed pirate, captured and adopted by the Pawnees and finally made his way to St. Louis to join Ashley and his trappers. While ascending the Missouri he was wounded in a battle with the Arikarees (Rees). Several weeks later he was attacked by a grizzly and "tore nearly all to peases." Two men were paid to tend the old man until his death, but after several days they abandoned him knowing his death was certain and a Ree attack was imminent. Hugh recovered consciousness and crawled and hobbled 350 miles to Ft. Kiowa. When sufficiently recovered he headed back to the Rockies seeking those who had abandoned him.

Twice during the next ten months Glass was forced to flee for his life from Ree attack. He left Ashley's men to work the Santa Fe trade for a few years but later returned to the land of his old enemies.

Hugh was finally killed by Rees at a river crossing during the winter of 1832-33.

The Bighorn National Forest

Located in north-central Wyoming, the Bighorns are a sister range of the Rocky Mountains. Conveniently located half-way between Mt. Rushmore and Yellowstone National Park, the Big Horns are a great vacation destination in themselves. No region in Wyoming is provided with a more diverse landscape – from lush grasslands to alpine meadows, from crystal-clear lakes to glacial carved valleys, from rolling hills to sheer mountain walls.

Visit the Bighorn National Forest and enjoy the multiple reservoirs, 32 campgrounds, 3 scenic byways, 14 picnic areas, 7 lodges, miles and miles of streams, 189,000 acres of Wilderness, 1,500 miles of trails, and much more that provide a forest experience unique to the Big Horns.

Bits and Pieces About The Bighorn

- The Bighorn National Forest is 80 miles long and 30 miles wide.
- The Forest covers 1,115,073 acres.
- Elevations range from 5,500 feet to 13,175 feet
- Cloud Peak at 13,175 feet
- Black Tooth Mountain at 13,005 feet
- Most common tree is lodgepole pine.
- The Forest has 32 campgrounds, 14 picnic areas, 2 visitor centers, 2 ski areas 7 lodges, 2 recreation lakes, 3 Scenic Byways, and over 1,500 miles (2419 Km) of trails.
- The Bighorn River, flowing along the west side of the Forest, was first named by American Indians due to the great herds of bighorn sheep at its mouth. Lewis and Clark transferred the name to the mountain range in the early 1800's.

100 Years, One thousand uses:

For thousands of years, human cultures have inhabited the Big Horn region, using mountain resources to improve their quality-of-life.

During the 1800's the Big Horns provided teepee poles, lumber for nearby Fort Phil Kearny, beaver pelts, medicinal plants, abundant big game, summer grazing for cattle and sheep and clear, cool water. On February 22, 1897, Grover Cleveland signed legislation creating the Bighorn National Reserve, in recognition of the value these mountains hold for the American people and their livelihood.

Today, much remains the same. The Big Horns still provide products and uses like wood, water, livestock forage, and minerals. Of equal or even greater worth are the intangible resources that move our mind and soothe our souls – wildlife and wildflowers, magnificent scenic vistas, mountain trails, fresh air, and the freedom of wide open spaces.

F Cassie's Supper Club & Dance Hall

214 Yellowstone Ave. in Cody. 527-5500.
www.cassies.com

Cassie's is a historical landmark and has a long distinguished reputation for serving up great food and entertainment. It is one of the oldest clubs in the state of Wyoming, originally opened in the 192's. In the early days it was operated as a house of ill fame and served bootleg whiskey brewed in a cellar. Today it is known for serving the choicest cuts of meat, the freshest seafood, and an extensive list of beers and microbrews. In addition to excellent dining, your experience at Cassie's will include the dance hall, gift shop, and Old West art gallery. Voted one of the top 20 steakhouses of the West by Cowboys & Indians Magazine.

L Cody Vacation Properties AKA Grandma's House - Lockhart Bed & Breakfast Inn

109 W. Yellowstone Ave. in Cody. 587-6074 or toll free at 800-377-7255.
www.codyvacationproperties.com

Cody Vacation Properties offers Bed & Breakfasts, ranchettes, creek-side cabins, and vacation homes. One of the properties, Lockhart Bed & Breakfast Inn is Wyoming's first Bed & Breakfast and overlooks the Shoshone River. It was once the home of famous American authoress, Caroline Lockhart and has been featured on Home and Garden TV, in the LA Times, National Geographic Traveler, and other publications. The Lockhart houses seven rooms with private baths and oversized claw footed tubs, telephones, and televisions. Wake in the morning to an all-you-can-eat breakfast. Cabins by the Creek, is another property north of Cody in the beautiful Clark's Fork Valley. These secluded cabins are rustic, western, and modern, with abundant wildlife and outdoor activities. Learn more about their properties at their website.

L Skyline Motel
1919 17th Street in Cody. 587-4201 or reservations toll free at 800-843-8809

The Skyline Motel is located on the east side of Cody on the way to Yellowstone Park. This family owned and operated motel is convenient to Cody's great attractions, the airport, restaurants, and shopping. The motel has 46 lovely ultra-modern units with full baths, queen beds, baseboard heat, air conditioning, satellite TV, and phones. The staff can help you with tickets and information for local adventures. They also offer a heated swimming pool, playground, and breathtaking mountain scenery and beautiful sunsets to relax and rewind after a busy day of sightseeing. Special rates area available for weekly, monthly, off-season and large groups.

5 *Gas, Food, Lodging*

T Cody Murals Visitor Center
1719 Wyoming Ave. in Cody. 587-3290

The magnificent Cody Mural covers a domed ceiling 36 feet in diameter and 18 feet to the top of the dome. Perfectly blended into the mural are selected historical scenes from the first seventy years of the Church of Jesus Christ of Latter-day Saints. Edward T. Grigware, the artist, termed the mural his "masterpiece". He painted it after having worked and taught more than 40 years in the field of art. In an adjoining part of the building are displays and art telling the story of the colonization of the Big Horn Basn in Wyoming. This story is one of faith, sacrifice, and perseverance by Mormon pioneers who had moved from Utah and Idaho. Free guided tours daily.

T Harry Jackson Museum
602 Blackburn Ave. in Cody. 587-5508

Harry Jackson's works run the gamut from abstract expressionist paintings and cubist studies to his more recent sculptures of traditional western art: cowboys and indians. Several of his scultures are unusual in that they contain painted surfaces. Jackson's sculptures are for sale at the museum. Open M-F, 8-5.

H "Corbett's Shebang" at Stinking Water Crossing
Five miles northeast of Cody on U.S. Highway 14A

On September 10th 1880, Victor Arland and John F. Corbett set up the first mercantile establishment in the Big Horn Basin on the Indian Trace that follows Trail Creek. Looking to the cattlemen for business, they moved to Cottonwood Creek in1883, then to Meeteetse Creek in 1884 where Arland, their final trading post, was established.

Corbett, doing the freighting from Billings for company enterprises, set up a way station in the river bottom where the freight road crossed the Stinking Water River—later renamed the Shoshone. A bridge, the first of five to span the river at this point, was constructed in 1883 at a cost of $5,000 raised by subscription from cattlemen, the Northern Pacific Railroad and Billings merchants.

Accommodations provided were a small store, a saloon and overnight lodging. The post office was established in 1885 with Corbett the postmaster. It was a gathering place and social center long before Cody came into existence twelve years later.

Corbett died in bed at his Meeteetse home December 15, 1910. His partner, Arland, went to his reward in more traditional style—dying with his boots on. In December, 1889, a shot fired through a saloon window in Red Lodge, Montana, killed him while he is playing poker.

The name of Corbett lingers on but the need for "Corbett's Shebang" in the river bottom ended with the arrival of the railroad in November 1901.

H Corbett Dam
Seven miles northeast of Cody on U.S. Highway 14A

The Corbett Dam diverts water from the Shoshone River into the Corbett Tunnel, a three-and-a-half-mile-long concrete-lined structure. The tunnel transports the water into the Garland Canal, which is the irrigation artery for the Garland and Frannie divisions of the Project.

Corbett Dam

Water first flowed through the tunnel on April 27, 1908. Nearly 50,800 acres are irrigated by the waters carried through this system.

The dam is located 16 miles downstream from Buffalo Bill Dam and the storage reservoir, which supplies all the water for irrigation of the project.

Project History

On February 10, 1904, the Secretary of the Interior set aside $2,250,000 for the initial construction of the Shoshone Project, one of the first federal reclamation projects in the nation, and the largest federal project in Wyoming. The Project was settled in four divisions: the Garland in 1907, Frannie in 1917, the Willwood in 1927 and finally, Heart Mountain in 1846.

Today, the Project comprises 93,000 acres. Major crops are alfalfa hay, sugar beets, dry edible beans, malting barley and specialty crops.

6 *No services*

T Buffalo Bill Dam and Visitor's Center

Six miles west of Cody at the Buffalo Bill Dam, through the tunnels. 527-6076. www.bbdvc.org

One of the many legacies of Colonel William F. "Buffalo Bill" Cody is the Buffalo Bill Dam. Cody spent years promoting and attempting to raise money for his dream of irrigating thousands of arid acres east of Cody from the Shoshone River. Buffalo Bill Dam was the realization of his vision.

In 1897 and 1899 Cody and his associates acquired the rights from the State of Wyoming to irrigate about 169,000 acres of land in the Big Horn Basin. At the time their plans did not include a reservoir, only the diversion of water from the river through a canal. They were unable to raise the capital necessary to complete the plan. In 1903 they united with the Wyoming Board of Land Commissioners urging the federal government to become involved with irrigation development in the valley.

In 1903, the newly formed Reclamation Service (later to become the Bureau of Reclamation) began the Shoshone project. At that time, Service engineers recommended building a dam on the Shoshone River in the canyon just west of Cody. The dam was one of the first three major dams built by the Bureau of Reclamation.

Construction began on October 19, 1905 and was completed January 15, 1910. Building the dam at this location was a difficult project. Because of the remote area, it was difficult to recruit and keep workers. The steep granite canyon was a challenge. Excavation of the dam abutments required workers to hang from "spider lines" that were connected to cableway towers. To handle concrete, a riveted steel bridge was built across the canyon.

The Shoshone River itself was unpredictable with its flows. During one year, almost half of the annual runoff of the river occurred within a 30-day period, almost halting construction entirely.

A lack of natural sand and gravel deposits near the site forced the project to create it from the granite. Clean pieces of granite were hand-placed in the concrete. The boulders, weighing between 25 and 200 pounds each, make up approximately 25 percent of the masonry in the dam.

The total cost of the dam in 1910 dollars was $929, 658. It was the first high concrete arch dam built by the Bureau of Reclamation. At completion, the dam was the highest in the world at 325 feet. Its length at the base is 70 feet and 200 feet at its crest. It was 10 feet wide at the top and 108 feet wide at its base. Before raising the dam, it held about 400,000 acre feet of water.

Completed in 1993, an eight-year modification project raised the dam height by 25 feet to a total of 353 feet. This expansion increased the water storage capacity by about 250,000 acre feet. The project also added 25.5 megawatts of power generation capacity; the result of the addition of two new power plants about one mile below the dam. Refurbishments were also made to the old Shoshone power plant visible just below the dam.

The reservoir provides irrigation and drinking water for Cody and much of the Big Horn Basin. Because of its historical significance, the dam was added to the National Register of Historic Places in 1973.

The visitor center opened in May 1993 as a combination visitor center and Wyoming highway rest area. Inside the center are a number of exhibits and a gift shop.

H Buffalo Bill Reservoir

Buffalo Bill State Park at 47 Lakeside Rd. west of Cody. 587-9227

The development by the U.S. Reclamation Service of the great irrigation project in the lower Shoshone valley required sacrifice of their land by the settlers living in the upper part of the valley. Below the surface of this reservoir once stood the community of Marquette. Small ranches lined both the North and South forks of the river. The government bought all these properties for roughly $400,000 in 1905. The settlers were allowed to rmain until the reservoir began to fill in 1910.

More information on the development of the Shoshone Project can be found at Buffalo Bill Dam Visitors' Center 11.5 miles east of this site and at nine other Wayside Exhibits located on the Project.

Project History: On February 10, 1904, the Secretary of the Interior set aside $2,250,000 for the initial construction of the Shoshone Project, one of the first federal reclamation projects in the nation, and the largest federal project in Wyoming. The Project was settled in four divisions: the Garland in 1907, Frannie in 1917, The Willwood in 1927 and finally, Heart Mountain in 1946.

Today, the Project comprises 93,000 acres. Major crops are alfalfa hay, sugar beets, dry edible beans, malting barley and specialty crops.

H Upstream Cableway Winch

Buffalo Bill Dam west of Cody

This cableway winch, which was used to install and remove the ball plugs, trash racks, and the bulkhead gate for the left abutment outlet works, dates to the construction of the Shoshone Power Plant in 1922. It was originally housed in a hoist building on the north side of the Shoshone River Canyon about 75 feet upstream of the dam. The winch was manufactured by American Hoist & Derrick Company of

St. Paul, Minnesota, and powered by a Westinghouse electric 7.5 horsepower motor. This cableway winch was last used to aid divers using under water cameras in the inspection of the upstream dam face, trash racks and submerged debris prior to the Buffalo Bill Dam modification project. The winch was removed in 1985 and the hoist building was removed in 1986

H Balanced Plunger Hydraulic Valve

Buffalo Bill Dam just west of Cody

This 48-inch diameter valve is one of two which were originally installed at the base of Buffalo Bill Dam in 1922 to supply water to the Shoshone powerplant and low level river outlet works. The two valves were operational until they were replaced by new valves during the Buffalo Bill Dam modification project of 1985-1993. This specialized type of needle valve, known as a mechanically-operated, balanced plunger hydraulic valve, was manufactured in 1921 by the Wellman-Seaver-Morgan Company, Cleveland, Ohio.

H Ball Plug

Buffalo Bill Dam just west of Cody

This large wood and concrete ball plug was one of two used to halt the flow of water through the 42-inch-diameter power outlet works conduits, located in the base of the dam. The balls facilitated the repair and maintenance of downstream machinery and equipment. In order to access the submerged conduit openings on the upstream face of the dam, trash rack structures first had to be removed by divers and raised to the surface by a cableway winch. Then, assisted by divers, the ball plugs were lowered by the cableway winch into position, where water pressure forced the balls against the conduit openings, sealing off the flow of water. The construction of the ball plugs utilizing a combination of wood and concrete provided strength and also allowed easy maneuverability under water.

Two new ball plugs were obtained during the Buffalo Bill Dam modifications project (1985-1993), since the removal of the cableway winch in 1985, the installation of the new ball plugs must be accomplished using a barge mounted crane on the reservoir.

7 *No services*

H Arland

Seven miles north of Meeteetse on Highway 120

A few miles up Meeteetse Creek from here, stood one of the toughest settlements of Wyoming's frontier history. The town was founded in the spring of 1884 by Victor Arland, a French businessman, and John Corbett, a buffalo hunter. From 1880 to 1884, the men were partners in a trading post on Trail Creek and another on Cottonwood Creek, just north of Cody, Wyoming. They moved to Meeteetse Creek to be in the center of cattle country and the developing ranches.

"Arland" soon had a store, saloon, restaurant, U.S. Post Office, a two story hotel, blacksmith shop, red light district, coal mine, livery stables, residential cabins, and corrals. A mail and passenger stage ran weekly through Arland, helping the town to become a trade center for the area ranches and a mecca for the cowboys and other tough characters of the region. The nearest law was 150 miles away in Lander, Wyoming.

On February 22, 1888, Vic Arland shot and killed Broken Nose Jackson in self defense at a dance in Arland. Jackson's friend, Bill Landon, shot and killed Vic Arland in revenge, at Dunivan's Saloon in Red Lodge, Montana, on April 24, 1890. After Vic's death Arland degenerated into a hang-out for the outlaw element. There were names such as Black Jack Miller, John Bliss, Al Durant, Butch Cassidy, W.A. Gallagher, Blind Bill Hoolihan, Ed Nye, Rose Williams, Sage Brush Nancy, and Belle Drewry, known as the "Woman in Blue". Most of the above, and others, died entangled in a web of lawlessness, romance, intrigue, and murder.

By 1896, the nearby town of Meeteetse had sprung up and by 1897 Arland had died. Today, nothing remains of old Arland but the stories and ghosts of days gone by.

H Site of Halfway House Stage House

19 miles north of Meeteetse on Highway 120

At this spot in 1903 a rock dugout facing south, near a fresh-water spring in the hillside, was established as a stage "noon stop" where horses were changed and meals served. The primitive accommodation was halfway between Corbett Crossing on the Stinking Water River and the bustling frontier town of Meeteetse. In 1904 Halfway Stop had a newfangled telephone, complete with a large "Public Telephone" sign. The station was abandoned in 1908 after automobiles began to use the route, but the spring remained in use for many years, a favorite watering place in this arid country. This marker commemorates early station keepers and travelers who passed this way.

8 *Gas, Food, Lodging*

Meeteetse

Pop. 368, Elev. 5,797

Taken from a Shoshone word meaning "resting or gathering place", the town of Meeteetse took its name from the creek nearby. When the post office opened here in 1881, it was one of the first in the Bighorn Basin, and by 1890, Meeteetse was the biggest town in the area. Later, in 1893, the settlement was moved closer to the Greybull River. One-time mayor, John W. Deane, ran away from home in the East at age 15 to become a cowboy driving cattle up the Texas Trail in the 1870s. He lived with Indians for five months, and became a mail carrier for seven years before going into politics.

Pitchfork

This discontinued post office town, like the nearby creek, took its name from Otto Franc's Pitchfork Ranch, which had a pitchfork for a brand.

T Meeteetse Hall Museum, Bank Museum and Archives

1033 Park Ave. in Meeteetse. 868-2423

Meeteetse is one of the oldest settlements in the Big Horn Basin. The name is said to derive from an Indian word meaning "the meeting place". The area was well used by the Indians. There have been many Indian-killed buffalo skulls, arrowheads, and even the remains of Sheepeater teepee poles found in this area. The best preserved teepee is located on Sheep's Point.

The town was settled in the 1880s, and many of the original buildings are still in use. William McNally, who homesteaded the present site of Meeteetse, built the little house on the corner by the river in 1893. The Cafe next door was the first post office on that side of the river. Margaret Wilson started the first Post Office and the first school in the early 1880s. The Mercantile was established in 1899. The current Archives building was the Hogg, Cheeseman, and MacDonald's bank. It was built in 1901. The museum is in the process of restoring the bank to its former condition.

The Hall Museum was erected in 1900 by George Ed Heron, who became a judge in 1909. The Baptist parsonage next door was a school, and the stage at the hall was used for most school functions. The Masons, Woodsmen, and the IOOF all used the hall. It was also the center for political rallies. One of the most memorable was one at which one of the main speakers died in the middle of his speech. Many of the best community dances were also held at the Hall, with people from all over the country in attendance. At one dance, one of the cowboys decided that they needed a bonfire to liven things up, so he built one at the base of one of the support columns, which is why the columns no longer match. The fire put a damper on future dances, and the Hall gradually fell into disuse.

Meeteetse was never a "dry" town, not by a long shot. By 1906 they had seven saloons, one store, two banks, and two hotels. Since everything had to be freighted in by team and wagon, one wonders how much of every load had to have been the liquor required to keep the saloons in business. In addition to the bars in town, there were several scattered over the area. At the forks of the Greybull and Wood rivers used to stand one that was popularly called the "Bucket of

Wyoming Tidbits

The black-footed ferret, the rarest of all North American mammals, was thought to be extinct until a colony was discovered in Park County in 1981.

Blood". Since the only mode of transportation was afoot or on horseback, it was never too far between "watering holes". Meeteetse's reputation as a Wild and Woolly town lasted until fairly recently, and now it seems civilization has caught up with them because, for the first time, churches outnumber saloons.

In 1912 Josh Deane, who homesteaded on the Wood River, and had a Post Office there, started the Labor Day Celebration. Josh had been a freighter, mail carrier and rancher, but his biggest claim to fame was his "yarn spinning", hence the name "Josh". He moved to town, opened a restaurant, became a solid citizen, and was elected Mayor. He died in 1930. Meeteetse boasted of many "characters", with some very colorful and descriptive "monickers," Checkbook Smith, Poker Nell, Bronco Nell, Laughing Smith, Swede Pete. Of later vintage they had Airplane Jerry, Shorty the Crock, and Greasy Bill. The stories behind the names are interesting and funny. The purpose of the Museum and Archives is to gather and preserve the histories of these very unique people and their way of life. Settling the West was a hard and dangerous undertaking.

The people had to be tough, self-sufficient individuals. Meeteetse has produced some Senators, Governors, and not a few criminals. There were shootings over women, over cards, over land and livestock. They had their share of Rustlers, and the Pitchfork's Otto Franc is said to have helped bankroll the Cattleman's Association during the wars between the cattlemen and the homesteaders and sheepmen. Mr. Franc turned up dead of a gunshot wound and there were many people who thought it was a result of his affiliation with the Association. Dry-gulching, and a hanging here and there, settled a lot of squabbles and served as a warning to early entrepreneurs. The Ten Sleep Raid was an important event in Big Horn Basin History. A former Governor of Wyoming, Jack Gage, wrote several interesting books on events that shaped the history of the cattlemen and the sheepmen.

The Museum and Archives is open Monday through Saturday 10:00 a.m. to 5:00 p.m., Sunday 1:00 p.m. to 4:00 p.m. —May 15 through Labor Day. They also will open by appointment for special groups at any other time. Admission is free.

Reprinted from museum brochure.

T Charles J. Belden Museum

1947 State Street in Meeteetse. 868-2264

This museum features the work of Charles J. Belden, personal and family memorabilia, Western paintings, Indian artifacts, and sculptures. The photographic work of Charles J. Belden documents life on the Pitchfork Ranch earlier in this century. His photographs contributed much to establishing the current myth of the West. This building also houses the Meeteetse Museum collection, a wildlife display including a mount of one of the largest Grizzly bears ("Little Wab") ever taken in the lower 48 states. Also on display are artifacts from the Pitchfork Ranch, a Buffalo Bill Cody display and the Olive Fell collection.

Belden was born in San Francisco, California, on November 16, 1887. He was raised in California and graduated from the Massachusetts Institute of Technology in 1910. It was while at the Institute that he became friends with Eugene Phelps, who was to become his brother-in-law. After graduation Charles married Frances Phelps and came to the Pitchfork Ranch. During the 1920s, 30s, and 40s Charles Belden's photographs appeared in many newspapers across the country and in the National Geographic. His photographs appear today in western history books, calendars, and museums. Today there are over 4,200 negatives of his work. Part of the collection is in the archives collection at the Buffalo Bill Historical Center in Cody, Wyoming. The remainder is at the ranch and museum. Belden's abilities with the older type cameras were never surpassed. He captured scenes that have never been equaled, even with modern equipment. His artistry is evident in each of his photographs.

The museum is open daily from May 1 through September 30. Admission is free, but donations are encouraged.

Reprinted from museum brochure and web site.

T Double D Dude Ranch Site

Highway 290 east from Meeteetse, then south on Wood River Road. 4-wheel drive high clearance vehicle required for last two or three miles.

The beauty and natural resources of the area near Kirwin attracted the interest of several investors in the 1920s and early 1930s that formed the idea of establishing a dude ranch in the area. Carl Dunrud began the construction of the Double D Dude Ranch five miles below the townsite in 1931. Amelia Earhart visited the ranch in 1934 and was so attracted to the beauty of the area that she asked Dunrud to construct a home near the old townsite for her to use. She disappeared during her around-the-world flight before the construction was completed. The American Metals Climax Corporation eventually purchased the Kirwin townsite and the Double D Dude Ranch in the early 1960s. Today the site is abandoned. Amax donated the complex to the United States Forest Service in 1992.

T Kirwin Historic Mining Townsite

Highway 290 east of Meeteetse, then south on Wood River Road. Turnoff is just east of Lower Sunshine Reservoir. 4-wheel drive high clearance vehicle required for last nine or ten miles.

William Kirwin began prospecting in the area high in the Absaroka Mountains of the Shoshone National Forest in 1885. Gold, silver, copper, zinc and molybdenum were all found here during that time. Kirwin, Harry Adams, and sixteen others officially formed the Wood River Gold Mining District In 1891. In 1897, the first ore was shipped from Kirwin. By the turn of the century the Shoshone Mountain Mining Company, Wyoming Mining Company, and Galena Ridge Company had developed the site into one of the West's most promising mining camps. In late 1905 and early 1906 the population of Kirwin was around 200. The town had 38 buildings including a a general store, hotel, and a post office. The townfolk hoped for the construction of a smelter to process the ore and an extension of the Burlington Railroad to service the mines at Kirwin. These developments never materialized. The high altitude climate and the lack of significant quantities of ore combined with the factors above spelled the eventual end of the community.

In 1907 an avalanche nearly wiped out the town. Several buildings were buried and three people died. The town never fully recovered and eventually passed away.

Wolf Mine shaft in Kirwin. U.S. Forest Service Photo.

Located at 9,200 feet in the base of a bowl, the townsite is surrounded by peaks rising to 12,500 feet. In addition to many old buildings and remnants of the mining days, steep slopes, a high mountain meadow, and several waterfalls make this a unique and beautiful place.

H Amelia Earhart in Wyoming

Just north of Meeteetse on State Highway 120.

First woman to fly across the Atlantic June 17, 1928 and May 20, 1932. Was building a summer home near here when she left to fly around the earth and was lost in the South Pacific, July 2, 1937.

F Broken Spoke Cafe & Shirley's Pies

1947 State Street in Meeteetse. 868-2362

People in Wyoming will drive for miles to eat Shirley's Pies at the Broken Spoke Cafe, but that's not the only reason they love this place. Where else can you get a cup of coffee for a nickel? This popular restaurant serves breakfast, lunch, and dinner in a great western atmosphere in a building that is over 100 years old. The menu offers house specialties such as Shirley's own Centennial and Gunslinger breakfasts, and Bill's Special Chili. You can even build your own breakfast. Biscuits and gravy are served all day long. Open Sunday–Thursday, 8 a.m. to 2 p.m. and Friday–Saturday, 8 a.m. to 8 p.m.

9 *Lodging*

Grass Creek

This tiny town is named for the creek on which it is situated. Good grass land is a rare enough find in Wyoming to be noteworthy.

Hamilton Dome

The post office here was named for a Dr. Hamilton. His first name isn't certain. He was probably just known as Doc to the locals.

T Anchor Dam

Highways 120 and 170, 35 miles west of Thermopolis

Anchor Dam, a 200-feet high, thin-arch concrete dam, located approximately 35 miles west of Thermopolis Wyoming, was constructed by the

Bureau of Reclamation at a cost exceeding $5 million dollars during the dam building boom of the 1950s and 1960s. Sinkholes and earth fissures within the reservoir area continuously allowed drainage of the reservoir before, during and after construction. Additionally, attempts to plug solution-widened fractures in carbonate strata within the Pennsylvanian Tensleep Formation, which comprised the abutments, resulted in expensive change orders during construction. The reservoir and dam were doomed from the onset. Water continues to leak through the Madison limestone formations, preventing it from filling all the way. Efforts to improve its ability to hold water have reached the point it is able to be filled about halfway in some years.

H The Prairie Rattlesnake

About 16 miles south of Meeteetse at rest stop on Highway 120

Less conspicuous than the pronghorn antelope and the golden eagle is an even more ancient inhabitant of the high plains and valleys of Wyoming, the prairie rattlesnake. Feared by many and respected by most, these pit vipers so-called because of their heat sensing facial pits, used to detect warm bodied prey) are common in the eastern two-thirds of the state and all but alpine habitats. During winter these snakes hibernate in underground dens for up to eight months. In spring they migrate away from the dens in search of food (typically rodents and other small mammals) and mates. Studies show that they move from the den in virtually a straight line path covering perhaps several miles until they find a food source. They stay on their fixed angle course by using the sun as a navigational aid. When the temperature cools in fall, the snakes return to the same den.

The habitat around you no doubt contains many of these secretive and fascinating reptilian hunters, but there is really very little to fear. Though they are poisonous and seemingly hostile, evidence indicates the chances of being bitten are virtually nill, as long as the snake is not touched, provoked, or frightened. Since rattlesnakes are deaf and cannot actually hear rattling, this behavior is believed to be defensive. The rattling rattle snake is simply trying to warn or drive off another creature it perceives be a threat. if you encounter a prairie rattlesnake, give it plenty of room and you will be in no danger - it's probably more frightened than you are. Allow the snake to go on its way and hunt prey like it's ancestors have done in this area for thousands and thousands of years The prairie rattler may not earn your admiration, but it deserves respect as a fascinating and important element of Wyoming wild land.

10 *Gas, Food, Lodging*

Thermopolis

Pop. 3,172, Elev. 4,326

Founded in 1897, Thermopolis is a name derived from the Latin thermae (meaning hot spring) and the Greek polis (meaning city). With the world's largest natural hot spring, running at 2575 gallons per minute at a consistent 135 degrees Fahrenheit, the town grew quickly as people were drawn to the therapeutic waters. The Shoshone and other Native Americans had appreciated its healing properties for generations, and called it the "smoking waters". This was once sacred ground, and part of the Wind River Reservation when it was first established. Shoshone Chief Washakie and Arapaho chief Sharp Nose, as part of efforts to make peace with the white men, made a portion of the waters available for public use. Washakie Fountain commemorates this "Gift of the Waters".

Aerial view of Thermopolis. Photo by Richard Coffenberry, RAC Digital Photography in Thermopolis.

T TePee Spa

144 Tepee Street at Hot Springs State Park in Thermopolis. 864-9250

Exhilarating hot water fun is packed in to several attractions at the TePee Spa also known as the Hellie's Tepee pool. Pools are available inside and out, along with a sauna and steam room. Several outdoor hot tubs offer varying water temperatures. There are also wildly popular water slides, including a 162-foot indoor slide and 272-foot outdoor breath taker. Free water aerobics are offered Monday, Wednesday, and Friday evenings from 7-8 p.m. A shaded patio area is available with a large grassy area for sunbathing. There is also a massage therapist available, featuring watsu, water massage. A gift shop features swim suits, T-shirts, along with great gifts. If you don't have a suit, rentals are available.

> **Gift of the Waters Pageant**
>
> Held in Hot Springs State Park in early August, this annual pageant is performed by members of the Shoshone and other Indian tribes and local residents. Activities centered around the pagent include parades, merchant promotions, Indian dancing and other entertainment.

T Hot Springs County Museum & Cultural Center

700 Broadway in Thermopolis. 864-5183

The Hot Springs County Museum is larger than it looks. Visitors are astounded at the two full floors of exhibits, plus the five annex buildings that complete the amazing collections. The annex includes a Burlington Northern caboose, agriculture building, petroleum building, old school house, and poverty flats cottage. The two floors of the main building feature an exhibit of over 8,000 Native American artifacts, Gebo coal mine model, and original historic photographs. That's just for starters! Shoshone and Arapaho beadwork and elk hide paintings by Chief Washakie of the Shoshone are also on display. The original cherry-wood bar from the Hole-in-the-Wall Bar, once frequented by some of the West's most famous outlaws, like Butch Cassidy, is on the first floor. The museum has a long association with jackalopes. You can even get a jackalope hunting license at the museum. The entire family will enjoy this enormous display of Native American, pioneer and cowboy memorabilia, that will take you to the old west and before. The museum is open year round and admission is charged.

Photo by Richard Coffenberry, RAC Digital Photography in Thermopolis.

T Wind River Canyon

A panorama of over one billion years of geology is exposed in the Wind River Canyon between Thermopolis and Boysen Dam. Much of the geology is identified with informative signs along US Hwy. 20. The canyon is about ten miles long. See variegated rock units of the eocene Wind River formation, and severely-faulted Paleozoic rocks which reflect a faulted arch. At Boysen, the narrow canyon begins, with walls rising 2,500 feet above the river. Precambrian crystalline rocks and northward-ipping Cambrian shales highlight the area. A complete section of Paleozoic formations may be observed northward. The road emerges from the canyon at the north end, where extensive areas of Triassic red beds dazzle visitors.

Photo by Richard Coffenberry, RAC Digital Photography in Thermopolis.

T Legend Rock Petroglyphs

Hot Springs State Park. Inquire locally for directions

Big Spring at Hot Springs State Park is the source of the hot mineral water. Photo by Richard Coffenberry, RAC Digital Photography in Thermopolis.

Legend Rock is one of the most impressive petroglyph areas in the world. Hundreds of yards of sandstone cliffs contain rock art of thunderbirds and elk. An archaeological survey using test pits found there are at least 283 pictures on 92 rock panels. The oldest works date back from 500 to 1700 A.D. demonstrating the characteristics and beliefs of many prehistoric cultures. One area is representative of the early Plains Indians. Visitors must obtain a key from Hot springs State Park headquarters on Park Street in Thermopolis (Monday through Friday) in order to drive the final half mile to the site.

T Hot Spring State Park and State Bathhouse

Northeast edge of Thermopolis

Bison Viewing

The Hot Springs State Park Bison Herd is the central herd for Wyoming State Parks. Herd size is dependent upon the carrying capacity of the available range areas and the site specific requirements necessary to manage a healthy and safe bison herd.

The park maintains a free roaming herd of 24-27 adult and yearling bison on a year round basis. This number increases by 10-15 animals during the months of April, May and June as new calves become a welcome addition.

In addition to the "natural" feed that the bison receive from the pasture areas, the park's bison are provided with a daily "cake" supplement that provides necessary minerals and helps to ensure good health. This feeding occurs daily between 8 a.m. and 9 a.m. and offers park visitors a unique opportunity to view the "monarch of the Plains" up close.

Please remember that bison are wild animals and should be viewed ONLY while you remain in your vehicle.

The Swinging Bridge

The suspension foot bridge across the Bighorn River is commonly called "The Swinging Bridge."

The structure was removed in July 1991 and was replaced during 1992. The bridge offers a unique vantage point from which to view the Bighorn River and Mineral Terrace.

The State Bath House

In 1896 a treaty was signed with the Shoshone and the Arapaho which gave the public use of one of the largest mineral hot springs in the world. The hot mineral water is maintained at 104 degrees Fahrenheit to provide the safest soaking water possible. Attendants are available to assist you with your need. The Bath House hours are: Monday – Saturday, 8 a.m. To 5:30 p.m.; Sundays noon to 5:30 p.m. The Bath House is closed on holidays during the winter and open on holidays during the summer, noon to 5:30.

Boat Ramp Facility

On the Bighorn River, by the Terraces, is a boat ramp. The sister to this ramp is located at the mouth of the Wind River Canyon south of Thermopolis. These two ramps were built by the Wyoming Game & Fish Department with the needs of physically impaired persons in mind. These fit with the many other facilities in the state park that are also designed for physically impaired individuals.

While the Terrace ramp will be used primarily for removing boats from the water, there is still lots of water below the Terrace that can be floated and /or fished.

Wyoming Tidbits

Trapper Edward Rose was the first white settler in Wyoming. He came into the area in 1807 with a trapping party led by Ezekel Williams, and settled in the Big Horn Basin.

Flowers

Hot Springs State Park has long been known for its beautiful flower gardens. Make a point of bringing your camera with you and capture the exciting splash of color all summer long.

Legend Rock State Petroglyph Site

Legend Rock State Petroglyph Site has been developed for public viewing of the cliff face.

The facilities include an improved access road, a public restroom and picnic tables.

The site is approximately 30 miles northwest of Thermopolis and visitation must be arranged through Hot Springs State Park headquarters or the State Bath House. For information call park staff.

Reprinted from Wyoming State Parks and Historic Sites brochure.

H Hot Springs State Park

Hot Springs State Park In the foreground across the river are Rainbow terraces, formed of mineral deposits from the world's largest mineral hot spring. Algae forms the multicolor of the terraces. The spring flows 18,600,000 gallons every 24 hours, temperature 135 degrees Fahrenheit. The site was a former Indian shrine where Shoshones and Arapahos bathed and held ceremonials. Washakie, chief of the Shoshones, led the tribes in signing a treaty which gave the healing waters to the Great White in Washington. An Indian pageant annually depicts the gift of these waters. Now a state park, with buffalo herd, picnic areas, playgrounds, swimming pools, tourist accommodations. No entrance fee.

H The Swinging Bridge

The suspension foot bridge across the Bighorn River is commonly called "The Swinging Bridge." It is under reconstruction as rust has become a major concern and large portions of the bridge are currently being replaced.

The Wyoming and North Dakota National Guard are completing the removal and replacement work in cooperation with the Wyoming Transportation Department, Hot Springs State Park, Hot Springs County, the local Historical Society and many other interested individuals.

The structure was removed in July 1991 and replaced during 1992. The bridge offers a unique vantage point from which to view the Bighorn River and Mineral Terrace.

T World's Largest Mineral Hot Spring

Hot Springs State Park Loop Road

History: These springs were included in the Shoshone Indian Reservation created by the Treaty of 1868. Later the reservation was also used for the Arapahoes. As information that the springs have "magnitude, health giving properties" became more generally known, Congress was requested to set aside this area for a "National Park or Reservation." In 1896 upon authority from Congress, the Indian Commissioner sent John McLaughlin to negotiate a treaty for the purchase of these springs. He secured an agreement whereby a part of the reservation, approximately 10 miles square was ceded

to the United States Government for the sum of $60,000.00. Among the signers of this treaty were the Shoshone Chief Washakie and the Arapahoe Chief Sharp Nose. Chief Washakie said that when game was bountiful in this area, he used to camp near the spring. But by 1890 hunting was so poor in this vicinity that it was seldom visited by the Indian.

Geology: Most of the water in these springs is thought to come underground from the Owl Creek Mountains. Rain falling in the mountains enters porous rock layers, moves slowly downward, and is here forced through crevices in the rocks.

The heat and chemicals in the water are derived from the rock through which it passes and from gases that rise from deeply buried volcanic rocks.

The terraces are made chiefly of lime and gypsum which separate from the cooling water. The colors are due mainly to primitive plants (algae) which grow in the warm water.

Chemistry:

Minerals Chemical Composition Parts per million
Silica SI O2 24.0
Aluminum AL2O3 11.6
Iron FE2O3 14.8
Calcium CA0 624.0
Magnesium MGO 121.0
Sodium NA20 326.2
Potassium K20 89.6
Sulphur SO3 606.8
Chloride CL 217.6
Carbon Dioxide C02 382.9
Hydrogen sulphide H2S 4.5
Total solids 2,396.0
Flow 18,600,000 gallons every 24 hours.
Temperature 135 degrees Fahrenheit.
Reprinted from State Park brochure

H World's Largest Mineral Hot Springs

State Highway 120 about one mile from the junction of State Highway 120 and U.S. Highway 20/789.

See this natural phenomenon while you are in Thermopolisl Monument Hill, … visible from this site, overlooks the 'Big Spring"—begin your tour of State Park here.

See other springs and beautiful terraces created by the mineral deposits of these healing waters. Learn the history of the Indians' "Gift of the Waters" to the white man. See large buffalo herd. Avail yourself of many park facilities. No entrance fee.

H Thermopolis Hot Mineral Water

Hot Springs County Museum and Cultural Center in Thermopolis

50 million gallons daily 135 degrees Farenheit, in springs and wells. It contains 13 of 16 mineral salts which are essential to all life. and this water has an alkaline base. Counteracts acids, Removes leidosis the cause of some forty diseases. These soluble mineral solids are similar to those in vegetables and fruit and our system can assimilate them. The two main acid forming salts are left out.

Hydro Therapy (or Hot Bath)

It has been demonstrated in laboratory that Hot Bath kills many germs by producing artificial fever, increases resistance, hastens multiplication white cells of blood. This water contains 8 anticeptics or cleansers. No chance for infection.

Analysis vans pr. cal.
Silica (SiO2) 727
Oxides Iron (Fe2O3) 105
Oxides Aluminum 222
Carbonate lime 21,584
Sulphate lime 49,402
Carbonate magnesia 15,926
Potassium Sulphates 7,437
Sodium Sulphates 5,249
Sodium Chlorides 29,920
Carbon dioxide gas (dissolved) 83.6
Oxygen gas (dissolved) pts. pr. mil. 5.7

F Las Fuentes Restaurant

530 Arapahoe in Thermopolis. 864-2695

People from all over Wyoming drive to dine at Las Fuentes Restaurant. The North Mexico menu has received critical acclaim in publications throughout the state. This is truly fine Mexican dining in a casual and relaxed Wyoming atmosphere. All menu items are freshly made. While dining and sipping one of their famous Margaritas, enjoy the 500+ original Mexican and Western artifacts and artwork that are displayed throughout the restaurant. Enjoy your favorite cocktail. Dine upstairs, downstairs, or outdoors in quaint oversized booths or custom designed furniture. The ambiance is completed with Mexican music from classical to Meriachi. A children's menu is available.

LS The Rainbow Motel, Gifts & Tackle Shop

408 Park in Thermopolis. 864-2129 or 800-554-8815. www.thermop.com

The Rainbow Motel offers visitors high standards and low rates. This clean and quiet motel has one and two bedroom suites, with tub/shower combinations, queen beds, telephones, 45 cable channels, and some kitchenette units. They are close to the many area attractions and next to Hot Springs State Park and the rodeo grounds. Let them help you with Blue ribbon trout fishing trips on the Big Horn River or on beautiful Boysen Lake Reservoir. The gift shop includes a complete fishing and tackle store, plus great souvenirs, toys, picnic supplies, snacks and sundries. They have mostly nonsmoking and no-pet rooms.

L Plaza Inn - Best Western

116 E. Park in Thermopolis. 864-2939 or reservations at 888-919-9009. www.bestofwyoming.com

Quality Inn & Suites, Plaza Inn is located in Hot Springs State Park on the banks of the Big Horn River. This historic landmark was renovated and reopened to the public in 1999. Visitors are treated with the hospitality of years gone by while receiving the conveniences of modern times.

Plaza Inn & Suites

Suites are available with microwaves and refrigerators. Guests enjoy a luxurious soak in the healing mineral waters of the mineral spa from water piped directly from its source in the park. There is also an outdoor pool open during the summer. All guests are served a complimentary continental breakfast. Visit them on the web.

S Jeanne's On Broadway Gallery

518 Broadway in Thermopolis. 864-4244

Jeanne's on Broadway is an adventure in art, jewelry, antiques, and handmade gourmet chocolates. You will find a plethora of Indian jewelry including Zuni and Navajo, Santa Domingo, along with colorful and classy vintage jewelry. Tickle your taste buds with Huckleberry jams and syrups, and the always popular Jelly Bellies. Along with an ever changing collection of antiques large and small, you'll find vintage clothing, handmade soaps, hand appliqued denim clothing for the entire family, Wyoming Red Dirt Shirts, and pottery. They also carry local artwork. Over 4,500 square feet filled with treasures from the past and present.

M Properties West, Inc.

110 N. 5th Street in Thermopolis. 864-2192 or toll free at 800-353-4558. www.propertieswest.biz

Properties West is a full service real estate agency and has been serving the real estate needs of Thermopolis and the surrounding area since 1984. As ambassadors to this area they can help you find what you need in commercial, residential, recreational, farm and ranch properties. They can also help with rental management for property owners or those with rental needs. Phyllis Christianson and Carol Zancanata are managing partners and brokers and know the area well. Visit them on the web and preview some of the properties they offer. They welcome all questions about the area—even the best places to fish and swim.

M Wyo-West Real Estate

545 Broadway in Thermopolis. 864-5588, fax 864-5655. www.wyowestrealestate.com

Wyo-West Real Estate is a long established agency, located in downtown Thermopolis near the only stop light in town. They are a service provider whose main business is listing and selling real estate including residential, rural, commercial, recreational, lots and vacant lands, and farm and ranch properties. Property management is another service they provide. The staff provides professional service and assistance in a friendly relaxed atmosphere. When you are in town stop in. They'll have the coffee ready. Call or fax to receive a copy of the Hot Springs County Real Estate Guide or visit their web site.

11 *Gas, Food, Lodging*

T The Wyoming Dinosaur Center and Dig Sites

110 Carter Ranch Road in Thermopolis. 867-2997 or 800-455-DINO (3466). www.wyodino.org

Interpretive displays, dioramas and life-size dinosaur mounts greet you as you enter the museum. Over 12,000 square feet of exhibits covering all facets of early life on the planet. Fossils

The Wyoming Dinosaur Center. Photo by Richard Coffenberry, RAC Digital Photography in Thermopolis.

and life-forms from the earliest geologic time periods are displayed in a time perspective. There are over 200 displays throughout the museum. The central hall houses 20 full-size mounted skeletons, including 10 dinosaurs.

T Thermopolis Hot Springs Chamber of Commerce

119 S. 6th in Thermopolis. 864-3192 or toll free at 800-786-6772

Thermopolis is home to the World's Largest Mineral Hot Spring and Hot Springs State Park. The park offers swimming, soaking, and sliding in the hot mineral water. The park includes historical and geological sites and a ten-acre bison pasture. The Wyoing Dinosaur Center offers a world-class museum, working dig sites and complete modern preparation laboratory. The town hosts three other museums, whitewater rafting and other water sports, and horseback riding. Enjoy year around events including weekly rodeos and the historical Gift of the Waters Indian Pageant. For a free information packet call the Chamber at their toll free number listed above.

T Old West Wax Museum and Dancing Bear Folk Center Complex

Highway 20 in downtown Thermopolis. 864-9396

The wax figures in the Old West Wax Museum were developed more than 30 years ago by Kenneth Bunn, now nationally recognized for his bronze sculptures of Western wildlife. There are more than 80 of the original figures with their backdrops. A recently acquired collection of historic documents that can also be seen here includes historic photographs and maps dating from 1772. An extensive collection of historic newspapers and early printed etchings shows the West as it was portrayed by America's writers, journalists, and artists in the 1800s and early 1900s.

Also here, at the Dancing Bear Folk Center, are the Textile Studio and Teddy Bear Den. No scrap of fabric went unused on the frontier. Clothes were passed down from one child to the next. When past wearing, they were made into other useful items. Old coats and blankets became rugs and bed spreads. Cottons and silks became quilts that rival modern art in their complexity. Sacks that once held flour became undergarments, sheets, and tablecloths. New dresses could be made from chicken feed sacks. The studio includes spinning wheels, looms, early sewing machines, and examples of folk handiwork, such as rug-making, crochet, knitting, tatting, basket-making, weaving and other needle arts.

The Teddy Bear Den is an unusual collection of soft-sculpture "teddy bears" representing England, Scotland, Ireland, Germany, Holland, Canada, New Zealand, Australia, and the United States. They are arranged in settings representing historical events, geographical areas, and other unexpected scenes.

Call for hours, and to learn about visiting speakers, craftspeople, and demonstators.

Thermal pool at Thermopolis Hot Springs.

C Grandview RV Park

122 Hwy 20 S. in Thermopolis. 864-3463 or toll free at 800-475-7230

S The Wild Bunch Gallery

426 S. 6th Street in Thermopolis. 864-2208 or toll free at 800-637-5340. www.wildbunchart.com

12 *No services*

Lucerne

Pop. 527, Elev. 4,298

This name was taken from the French word for alfalfa, "luzerne", which is a major crop in the region, used to feed cattle.

H Bridger Trail-Bighorn River Crossing

On County Highway 433 at Lucerne.

The Bridger trail crossed the Bighorn river near this location in 1864. Passing over the Bridger Mountains to the Southeast, the trail came down Kirby Creek, crossed the river and proceeded north to the Yellowstone River, then west to the gold fields in southwestern Montana.

Within months following the 1863 gold discovery at Alder Gulch located in present-day Montana, a flood of miners and settlers were traveling to the mining communities of Bannack in Virginia City. Jim Bridger blazed a new trail in 1864. His trail through the big horn basin west of the Big Horn mountains avoided Sioux Indian hostility along the Bozeman Trail which lies to the east. It also eliminated the extra week's travel along the OregonTrail Fort Hall - Bannack road which lies to the West.

Use of the Bridger trail was short-lived. However, many variants evolved from the trail in 1880s and 1890s. The trail was the ancestor of a freighting network that connected remote ranches and early communities with Casper, Wyoming, and Billings, Montana.

Jim Bridger was the most renowned mountain man, explorer, and guide of the American West. This trail served as a safer route for emigration to Montana during a period of Native American resistance to Euro-American encroachment. Equally important, the trail acted as a foundation for the development of late nineteenth and early twentieth century transportation routes that made settlement possible in a region previously lacking any system of roads.

13 *Food*

Kirby

Pop. 57, Elev. 4,270

This little post office and railroad stop town was named for Kris Kirby, a cowboy from Texas who came north to become a rancher. He followed the Bridger Trail to settle here in 1878. The nearby creek, which also bears his name, was once a hide out for Butch Cassidy and the Wild Bunch.

T Crosby

County Highway 433 between Kirby and Lucerne

Tailing piles and a mine superstructure mark the spot of this ghosttown, named for Mormon pioneer Jesse W. Crosby. Coal from Crosby supplied Thermopolis and the surrounding area in the early 1890s and at one time, more than 100 children attended the Crosby school. The mines closed in 1932.

T Gebo

US Highwy 20 south from Worland for 22 miles to Kirby. West on Sand Draw Road

Remains at Gebo include a graveyard, rock-fortified dugouts used as homes for miners, and several stone houses. A larger blower that pumped air into the mine is still in evidence, as are many

Section 2

of the mine shafts with timbered entrances.

Named for Samuel Gebo, coal mine developer, the town once had more than 600 residents, mostly miners.

F Butch's Place Restaurant

101 E. Main in Kirby. 864-2669

14 *Gas, Food, Lodging*

Worland

Pop. 5,250, Elev. 4,061

Some of the earliest paleo-Indian artifacts were found near Worland, where ancient hunters killed mammoths over 11, 000 years ago. Eohippus (dawn horse), one of the modern horses oldest ancestors, was also discovered nearby. White men did not settle the area until 1903, when Charlie R. "Dad" Worland set up camp on the Bridger Trail by Fifteen Mile Creek. He soon set up a stage station and a saloon. When the Burlington Railroad came two years later, a store and a school had already been built. The community was built up by agriculture, both ranching and farming, and had the first sugar mill in Wyoming. The mill is still in operation, and continues to boost the economy, along with a Pepsi bottling plant and other agrarian concerns.

T Pioneer Square

The downtown entrance to Worland is a park dedicated to the hard working ancestors of the community. There are several interesting sculptures that pay tribute to the settlers.

H County of Washakie-Dedicated to Those Who Came First.

Pioneer Square in Worland

Sheltered by formidable mountains, the Big Horn Basin for ten thousand Great Suns nurtured hunting tribes of Crow and Sioux. Arapahoe and Shoshone following Pte Tanka, the Buffalo, their livelihood. Trappers and gold seekers ripped and ran, Bluecoats came and went. Ranchers and farmers brought courageous wives to put down roots, to weave a new civilization here in the wilderness. They built sand and sage and water into Worland and Washakie. We honor these first families who fulfilled Isaiah's prophecy....and the desert shall rejoice and blossom as the rose.

H City of Worland

U.S. Highway 16 on west of Worland, half mile past bridge over Big Horn River

Charles H. "Dad" Worland in 1900 dug his underground stage stop here on the old Bridger Trail. From Dad's dugout grew the City of Worland, drawing pioneer men and women possesing an indomitable spiritual force, dreaming that Big Horn River water would create a new way of life here in th desert. With muscles and guts, horses and hand tools, they dug miles of irrigation canals. With precious water, the parched land became an oasis. We cheer those who persevered and conquered the desert, making Worland the Jewel of the Big Horn Basin.

Pioneer Square in Worland.

H "Dad" Worland Monument

U.S. Highway 16 on west of Worland, half mile past bridge over Big Horn River

To all pioneers and in memory of C.H. "Dad" Worland for whom the town was named. He erected the stage station on the old Bridger trail about 100 yards north of here. That spot was the original town site established in 1904. The town moved across the river in 1906.

F The Ram's Horn Cafe

629 Big Horn Ave. in Worland. 347-4541

M McGarvin & Taylor Real Estate Specialists

114 N. 9th Street in Worland. 347-4271.
www.worlandwyo.com

The cornerstone of McGarvin and Taylor Real Estate Specialists is great customer service, achieved through work ethic, integrity, and character. They offer over 40 years combined experience in Washakie County and a wealth of professional education, which means they can offer abundant up-to-the-minute real estate guidance in selling, purchasing, or renting a home. Their services include educating their customers in the buying/selling process and will always go that extra step to assure confidence with the service they receive with residential, commercial, recreational properties, and financing options. Visit them on the web and learn more about why their customers keep coming back.

M Hake Realty/GMAC Real Estate

744 Big Horn in Worland. 347-3271.
wwww.hakerealty.com

15 *Gas, Food, Lodging*

H Jim Bridger Historic Trail

About two miles north of Worland on State Highway 433.

In 1864 an alternate route to the goldfields of western Montana was needed due to frequent hostile actions along the Bozeman Trail. Though the Civil War raged on, the nation continued its westward expansion through the efforts of men like Jim Bridger. A trapper, explorer, trader, hunter, scout and guide, Jim Bridger led miners north from the area we now call Fort Caspar. From there the trail led northwesterly through the southern Big Horn Mountains, across the Big Horn Basin, crossing the Shoshone River, into Montana through what was known as Pryor Gap, and finally rejoining the Bozeman Trail. The Bridger Trail reduced the threat of hostile actions against emigrants heading north and proved an important route in the settlement of the Northwest.

The Bridger Trail crossed the Big horn River approximately 12 miles southwest of here, near where the community of Neiber stands today. The original Bridger Trail passed very close to this location as it paralleled the Big Horn River on its way north.

This commemorative site was developed jointly by the Wyoming Highway Department, the Wyoming Centennial Wagon Train, Inc., and

Thermopolis	Jan	Feb	March	April	May	June	July	Aug	Sep	Oct	Nov	Dec	Annual
Average Max. Temperature (F)	36.3	43.2	51.1	62.3	72.2	82.5	90.6	90.2	79.1	65.5	47.6	38.6	63.3
Average Min. Temperature (F)	8.1	15.2	21.8	31.7	41.5	48.6	54.4	53.4	43.5	32.0	19.5	11.6	31.8
Average Total Precipitation (in.)	0.41	0.39	0.80	1.40	1.94	1.65	0.86	0.53	1.07	1.00	0.74	0.33	11.11
Average Total SnowFall (in.)	5.2	5.0	5.1	1.6	0.5	0.0	0.0	0.0	0.2	1.8	5.3	5.2	30.0
Average Snow Depth (in.)	2	1	1	0	0	0	0	0	0	0	1	1	1

Wind River Country

Breathtaking views of a range that boasts 53 peaks over 13,000 feet in elevation and an area containing nearly 600 lakes and over 2,000 miles of rivers and streams. This is truly a fishermans paradise. Tourists also have the opportunity to immerse themselves in Native American culture from powwows and petroglyphs. Or take in real cowboys and rodeos. Also on this adventure travelers will find the Oregon-Mormon-California-Pony Express trails, abundant wildlife and mountain man rendezvous re-enactments. Don't forget to visit the Continental Divide at South Pass which is the lowest spot on the divide. Here visitors have the opportunity to experience the land as the nineteenth century emigrants did 150 years ago as they traveled through. There is also a plethora of activities one can do throughout the area from horseback riding to camping and attending local unique events. A journey through this area will provide plenty of oohs and ahhs, as well as a sense of what life was like more than 100 years ago.

the Department of the Interior Bureau of Land Management, for your use and enjoyment.

L C's Bed & Breakfast

1000 Howell Ave. in Worland. 347-9388

16 *Gas, Food, Lodging*

T Washakie Museum

1115 Obie Sue in Worland. 347-4102.

The Washakie Museum provide visitors the opportunity to relate to the living environment of the early settlers from thousands of years ago. The museum is named for the Eastern Shoshoni statesman, Chief Washakie, whose philosophy of "Making the best of what you cannot change" led the Shoshoni tribe to offer peace to emigrants. Nine thousand pioneers signed a thank you document to Washakie and his people for safe passage through their territory. Washakie secured the Wind River Mountain Range for his tribe's homeland.

Many fine exhibits pay tribute to local history. The Colby site is a display of the earliest mammoth kill site in North America to settlers of the west one hundred years ago. Other exhibits include a covered wagon, sheep wagon, sod house, and beautiful display of western tack, including the first full term governor's saddle, along with an extensive collection of early settlement in the Big Horn Basin. There are also extensive displays on local anthropology and geology. The Family Discovery Center, introduces children to art and technology through hands on exhibits.

Call for information on changing displays and exhibits featured at the museum. The Museum offers several educational programs along with tours of museum exhibits. Programs at the museum are free and there is no admission fee. There is also a museum gift shop. Summer hours are Monday through Saturday, 9 a.m. to 5 p.m. and winter hours are Tuesday through Saturday 10 a.m. to 4 p.m.

H Colby Mammoth Kill Site

Highway 16, five miles east of Worland

Extinct species of mammoths, horses, camels, and bison roamed this area 11,000 years ago and were being killed by humans known as the Clovis hunters. South of this spot 400 meters is the location of one of the largest known Clovis mammoth kills in North America. A deep arroyo with steep walls was present when the mammoths were killed. Clovis hunters would stalk a family of mammoths and spear a young animal that was careless enough to wander away from the protection of the family. As the animal became weak from the effects of the wound, it became further removed from the herd and the hunters maneuvered it into the deep arroyo where it could not escape. The hunters needed only to wait for the wound to weaken the animal enough that it could easily be killed. This kind of event was repeated many times over the years.`

One pile of bones consisted of the left front quarter of a mature female mammoth with bones of other mammoths stacked around it and the skull of a young male mammoth placed on top. This is believed to have been a frozen meat cache that was never utilized and spoiled with the approach of warm weather. Another pile of mammoth bones was probably a similar cache that was utilized. A front quarter of a young mammoth would represent over 500 kilograms of meat. These caches suggest that at least some of the animals were killed during the cold weather months.

This site was excavated by the Department of Anthropology at the University of Wyoming under the direction of Dr. George Frison, during 1973, 1975, and 1978. Materials from the site can be seen at the Washakie County Museum and Cultural Center and at the University of Wyoming Anthropological Museum.

L The Wild Sage Inn

1895 Big Horn Ave. in Worland. 347-2222

The Wild Sage Inn is locally owned and operated, and new to Worland. This totally smoke-free motel is equipped with data ports, HBO, and coffee pots in every room. There is a handicap accessible room and a suite complete with a kitchen. The property is surrounded by a beautifully landscaped lawn for relaxing and soaking up the Wyoming sun. Local art is displayed throughout the motel for the enjoyment of guests. This is a great central location for the area's excellent hunting and fishing. They are located within walking distance to local dining and shopping.

Worland

	Jan	Feb	March	April	May	June	July	Aug	Sep	Oct	Nov	Dec	Annual
Average Max. Temperature (F)	28.8	37.2	48.4	59.9	70.4	80.6	89.7	87.5	75.5	62.1	44.1	32.0	59.7
Average Min. Temperature (F)	0.8	8.5	20.4	31.2	41.5	49.6	54.7	51.5	41.2	30.6	17.5	6.0	29.5
Average Total Precipitation (in.)	0.29	0.21	0.37	0.92	1.37	1.26	0.68	0.53	0.83	0.65	0.36	0.23	7.69
Average Total SnowFall (in.)	3.8	2.6	2.6	1.2	0.1	0.0	0.0	0.0	0.1	0.8	2.3	3.2	16.7
Average Snow Depth (in.)	1	1	0	0	0	0	0	0	0	0	0	1	0

17 *Gas, Food, Lodging*

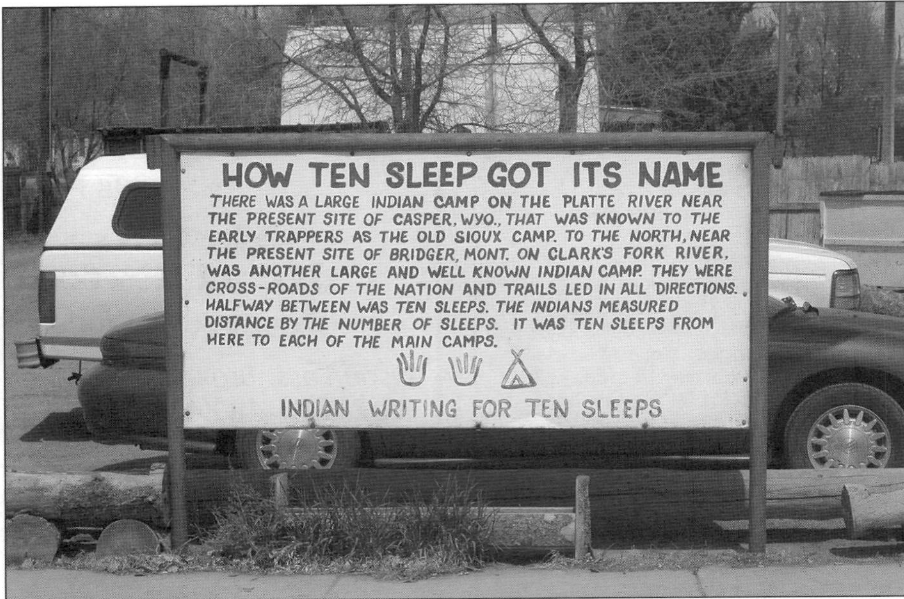

Ten Sleep
Pop. 304, Elev. 4,206

Native Americans measured the length of journeys in the number of "sleeps" (days) it took to arrive. The location of Ten Sleep was a ten-day (ten sleep) trip from both Fort Laramie and the Yellowstone region, the halfway marker for the journey from one to the other. An Army engineer who mapped the area, Col. Sackett, named the place Sackett Fork in 1867. The sheep industry brought growth in the 1890s and early 1900s, despite conflicts over grazing rights with cattlemen. This culminated in the Tensleep Raid of 1909, in which three sheepmen were killed. Today, Ten Sleep is a rustic, pastoral town and one of the few places in Wyoming where fruit trees can actually thrive.

Big Trails

Big Trails was first named Red Bank but changed for the four main Indian trails which converged here from all points of the compass. The name change seemed right because there was confusion with the mail and other towns that started with Red. The post office was closed in 1940.

T Ten Sleep Pioneer Museum
436 2nd St. in Ten Sleep. 366-2759

The Museum exhibits cover the everyday life of pioneer families and include tools and clothing. A special exhibits recreates the Spring Creek raid which was a major turning point for the relationships of the sheepmen and the cattlemen. The museum is open from 9:00 a.m. to 4:00 p.m. Admission is free and donations are welcomed.

H Tensleep Canyon
East of Ten Sleep on U.S. Highway 16

Ages ago, these mountains were deep within the Earth's crust, and the area that is known today as the Bighorn Mountains was a basin. Beginning about 75 million years ago the land began to slowly rise above the sea bed reaching an elevation of nearly 20,000 feet. Since that time, the eroding forces of wind, water, and ice have removed thousands of feet of rock resulting in what you see today.

The cliffs of Tensleep Canyon are composed predominantly of massive layers of limestone. This limestone layer underlies the towns of Tensleep and Worland and serves as their major source of water. The water is removed from the layer by deep wells.

Glaciers carved out the valley of Tensleep Canyon within the last 250,000 years. Evidence of these ancient glaciers can be seen in the U-shape of the valley bottom, and piles of boulders, or glacial moraine, left along West Tensleep Creek. The "West Moraine" stretches for 10 miles, making it the longest moraine in the Big Horn Mountains. 'Weathering forces and the flow of the creek continue to wear away the rock in Tensleep Canyon. In the winter, ice flows can be seen on the canyon walls.

Ten Sleep paddy wagon.

H Managing the Range
East of Ten Sleep on U.S. Highway 16

In the summer, domestic sheep and cattle graze the rangelands of the Bighorn National Forest. These rangelands are the vast, grassy hillsides and sagebrush-covered valleys that dominate the plateau of the Big Horn Mountains. Without the natural control of wild fire, sagebrush will spread, killing the grasses, and reducing the rangeland for livestock and wildlife. Today, the Forest Service is trying to restore the balance of sagebrush and grass by the use of controlled burns.

H Powder River Pass
East of Ten Sleep on U.S. Highway 16

This is Powder River Pass, 9,666 feet above sea level, is the highest point on Highway 16 in Bighorn National Forest.

At this elevation the harsh weather conditions and shallow soil discourages the growth of trees. Growing on the slopes of the pass are the fragile plants of the Alpine Tundra. These tiny plants survive by clinging to the thin rocky soil, which provides just enough water and nutrients.

The Big Horn Mountain Divide is the high-elevation backbone of the mountain range, which has its southern end in Wyoming and its northern end in Montana. The Big Horn Mountains serve as a major watershed, providing water to rancers, farmers, and communities in the valleys and basins to east and west.

Along the highway you will see long segments of tall wooden fences, standing at an angle to the roadway. These are snow fences, erected and maintained by the Wyoming State Highway Department. Their purpose is to divert blowing and drifting snow away from the road. In the winter, drifts as high as 10 feet line the side of highway.

Ten Sleep	Jan	Feb	March	April	May	June	July	Aug	Sep	Oct	Nov	Dec	Annual
Average Max. Temperature (F)	36.7	41.2	49.6	59.4	69.4	79.0	87.6	86.1	75.4	62.6	46.2	38.0	60.9
Average Min. Temperature (F)	13.3	18.1	25.9	34.0	42.4	50.5	56.9	55.5	45.4	35.1	23.9	15.4	34.7
Average Total Precipitation (in.)	0.54	0.39	0.85	1.42	2.19	2.07	0.94	0.72	1.33	1.14	0.81	0.62	13.02
Average Total SnowFall (in.)	9.6	6.9	8.4	5.5	1.9	0.0	0.0	0.0	0.8	3.0	7.8	9.7	53.7
Average Snow Depth (in.)	3	2	1	0	0	0	0	0	0	0	1	2	1

H First Washakie County Church

Highway 16 east of Ten Sleep at Circle J Ranch

March 14, 1901, Rev. L.C. Thompson, Rev. E.E. Tarbill, Mortimer Lewis, J.W. Carpenter, Kate Lynch and Mark Warner signed papers incorporating the Methodist Church of Ten Sleep and accepted land for a church building and cemetery from David Moses. The community raised $600, supplementing $200 given by Extension Society of Philadelphia. The building started in 1901 by volunteer labor with lumber donated by Milo Burke, was completed in 1904 and dedicated January 8, 1905. Each assisting family was given a lot in the cemetery, where many pioneers rest. The church was moved to its present location in 1925. The annex was added in 1952. Moved to Circle J in 1975.

H Bighorn National Forest

Ten Sleep Canyon. 674-2600

You are standing at the bottom of Ten Sleep Canyon near the western edge of the Big Horn Mountains. The steep rocky cliffs were the native territory of the Bighorn sheep. Disease and the activities of human and livestock have led to their eventual disappearance. They have been reintroduced to this forest through cooperative efforts of the U.S. Forest Service and the Wyoming Game and Fish Department.

Lewis and Clark's expedition was the first organized exploration into the area. The great numbers of Big Horn sheep noted in their journal in 1808 gave the river, basin, mountains, and National Forest its name.

H Leigh Creek Monument

U.S. Highway 16 nine miles east of Ten Sleep

Across the canyon, on the point, the Leigh Creek Monument topped with the cross was erected in 1889 in memory of an English nobleman who fell 200 feet to his death over the canyon wall, while in pursuit of mountain sheep. The monument was laid up of native stone in dry mortar and is approximately ten feet square at the base. It contains a marble slab facing west with the inscription. Gilbert E. Leigh died October 23rd, 1884. He was the guest of the Bar X Bar cattle company a remittance man, and had spent most of his adult life as a big game hunter.

H Spring Creek Raid

About 7 miles south of Ten Sleep on State Highway 434.

Cattlemen of the Big Horn Basin dominated the range for many years and set up boundaries or "deadlines" where sheep were forbidden. Fierce animosity grew between the opposing sheep and cattle ranchers as several sheep camps were raided during the late 1800s and early 1900s.

In late March, 1909, Joe Allemand, a Basque sheepman, and Joe Emge, a cattleman turned sheepman, left Worland headed for Spring Creek with 5000 head of sheep. They were accompanied by Allemand's nephew, Jules Lazier, and two sheepherders, Bounce Helmer and Pete Cafferall. Talk spread like wildfire across the western slope of the Big Horn Mountains as the deadline was crossed and plans were soon made to head off this intrusion.

On the moonlit night of April 2, 1909, seven masked riders approached the sheep camp's two wagons where the herders slept. Gunfire lit the night as rifles blazed. Emge and Lazier were killed in their wagon and both wagons were set afire. Allemand emerged from the flames, but was quickly shot down.

The monument on this side of the road is situated at the site of the south wagon. The monument on the north side of Spring Creek is near the location of the wagon where the sheepmen were killed. Five of the perpetrators were convicted and sent to prison. Public reaction against this brutal and tragic act left no doubt that violence on Wyoming's open range would no longer be tolerated.

F Dirty Sally's Gifts, Quilts & Soda Fountain

112 2nd Ave. in Ten Sleep. 366-2500.
www.tctwest.net/~kmoore/

M Hake Realty/GMAC Real Estate

104 2nd Street in Ten Sleep. 366-2208.
www.hakerealty.com

18 *Food*

Hyattville

Pop. 100, Elv. 4,457
No gas

Originally named Paintrock for the Indian pictographs found on a cliff nearby, Hyatt got its name from general store owner and postmaster Samuel Hyatt. When his store burned to the ground in 1900, he took up ranching.

Another pioneer settler in Hyattville was Asa Shinn Mercer. He was known for bringing shiploads of young women to the West Coast by way of Cape Horn to become frontier brides. This enterprise took place mostly in the 1860s, and he chose to retire here when it was finished.

T Medicine Lodge State Archaeological Site

Six miles northeast of Hyattville. 469-2234

Archaeology Makes Medicine Lodge Unique

The Medicine Lodge site has long been known for its Indian petroglyphs and pictographs, but not until 1969 did the full archaeological wealth of the site come to light. In that year, Dr. George Frison, then Wyoming State Archaeologist, began a series of digs that uncovered a human habitation site that has been continuously occupied for over 10,000 years. Medicine Lodge has thus become a key to the interpretation of the archaeology of the entire Big Horn Basin area.

The archaeological investigation involved digging through approximately 26 feet of soil and rocky sediments, discovering over 60 cultural levels spanning some 10,000 years of human occupation. This important aspect of the site enables the archaeologists to examine particular lifestyles and to study how these styles changed over time. Some of the material items found during the dig included fire pits, food storage pits, manos and metates (grinding stones) and projectile points.

The information gleaned from the archaeological investigation provides interesting educational and interpretive insight into the life of this area's inhabitants throughout the years. Interpretive signs located at the base of the petroglyph cliff and exhibits in the log cabin visitor center give an overview of the information accumulated by the archaeologists. They also explain some of what you see around you at Medicine Lodge State Archaeological Site.

From Ten Sleep to Hyattville

The excavations at Medicine Lodge Creek are part of long term archaeological research by Dr. George Frison. This includes investigations at several other rock shelters in nearby Paintrock and Medicine Lodge canyons and at several quarry sites where raw materials for prehistoric stone tools were obtained.

Frison has also conducted major excavations at the Colby site near Worland and the Hanson site near Shell. Results from this research have been published in Frison's 1978 book, "Prehistoric Hunters of the High Plains," and several other professional articles and books.

Data from all these sites are being used to reconstruct different aspects of prehistoric life and settlement systems ranging from those of the 11,000 year old Paleo-Indian to the historic Crow Indians who lived in the area.

Analyses of stone artifacts, flaking debris, seeds, bones, pollen, and charcoal from the site, as well as aspects of the local geology and site stratigraphy are all used to reconstruct the past. For example, bones found in the site can be used

Basin

	Jan	Feb	March	April	May	June	July	Aug	Sep	Oct	Nov	Dec	Annual
Average Max. Temperature (F)	29.5	38.7	50.4	62.1	72.4	82.4	90.9	89.2	77.2	63.6	45.0	32.9	61.2
Average Min. Temperature (F)	2.5	11.0	21.7	31.7	41.8	50.1	55.4	52.6	42.1	30.8	18.0	7.2	30.4
Average Total Precipitation (in.)	0.22	0.16	0.30	0.72	1.14	1.14	0.52	0.45	0.75	0.51	0.29	0.26	6.47
Average Total SnowFall (in.)	3.8	3.2	3.2	1.9	0.3	0.0	0.0	0.0	0.6	0.5	2.8	4.0	20.3
Average Snow Depth (in.)	2	1	0	0	0	0	0	0	0	0	0	1	0

Spring Creek Raid Exhibit

In the 1870s, in Wyoming, Texas and Colorado, sheep ranchers with their herders and "woolies" began to encroach on the open range in significant numbers. There was immediate dislike and antagonism on the part of the cattlemen and their cowboys towards the newcomers. The ensuing battles were, however, really being fought over the use of the rangeland grass and the wealth it could provide in the form of beef or mutton and wool.

The 1909 raid in Wyoming was a particularly brutal attack by cattlemen on a sheepherder's camp. It received protracted and widespread news media coverage at the time and marked the beginning of the end of such conflicts. The cattlemen involved were tried in the local court and, for essentially the first time, convicted of major crimes. All prior such cases that made it to court were either dismissed or won by the cattlemen because of expensive legal defenses and/or sympathetic jurors.

After this raid, the battle for use of public land for grazing would continue sporadically until about 1921. During their half-century duration, cattlemen-sheepmen battles numbered more than 120 over 8 states. They caused at least 54 human deaths along with the slaughter of more than 53,000 sheep. The cowboys found a number of ways to kill the hated sheep during their raids, including "rimrocking", i.e., driving a flock over a high cliff.

The Spring Creek Raid began in the Spring of 1909 when two sheepmen, Joe Allemand and Joe Emge, along with their three sheepherders, drove 2,500 head of sheep from Worland, Wyoming, east to Tensleep, some 25 miles distant. Allemand was well liked by both the cattlemen and the sheepmen of the area even though he ran sheep. Allemand was having some financial difficulty for some of his sheep had been lost in a couple of raids so he had sold a partnership to another Spring Creek rancher, Joe Emge. The latter, a squatty dark man, was not so well thought of. Emge had at one time been with the cattlemen but after taking over the sheep he had boasted that he'd graze his sheep any place he liked and that he'd run the cattlemen off the range.

On this April day in 1909, the two sheepmen were driving two bands of sheep across the badlands from Worland to the Spring Creek ranches. Allemand had telephoned his wife to say that he would be home that evening. Listeners over the party line hurried to inform some of Emge's enemies that Allemand would not be in the camp that night and Emge would be alone with the herder and the camp tender. But after camp had been made with one band of sheep and a sheepwagon on each side of the creek, two brothers who lived nearby stopped to visit and eat supper and by the time they left, Allemand thought it was too late to ride on home. So Allemand and his young nephew, Jules Lazier, a French subject, and Emge went to sleep in the upper wagon. A newly hired young herder, 16 year old Bounce Helmer and another Frenchman, Pete Cafferal, were in the lower wagon.

When it grew dark the raiders struck, two headed toward the wagon with the sheepmen and the other five after the sheep. Shots were fired at the herds and Helmer, fearing for his dog sprang, half-dressed out of the other wagon. He was immediately captured by the raiders as was Cafferal and both were tied up. Helmer who had lit a lantern was able to see and recognize some of the men but Cafferal could not.

When no one came out of the upper wagon, the two men who were near it started firing into it. One of them started a fire by throwing Kerosene from Helmer's lantern on the sage brush that had been piled under the sheepwagon to build the morning fire. As Allemand came out of the wagon he was shot and killed. The fire grew so rapidly that Emge and Lazier were trapped. When the raiders realized that they had killed the wrong man, they fled in a panic. In the meantime, Helmer and Cafferal freed themselves and ran to the neighbors for help.

It was almost noon the next day before Big Horn County sheriff, Felix Alston and Judge Percy Metz reached the scene of the raid. Joe Allemands body was lying near the smoldering embers of the sheep wagon and one of his sheep dog's puppies was curled up on his chest. The burned bodies of Emge and Lazier were found nearby.

Seven men were eventually arrested for the crime. Albert Keys and Charles Ferris turned states evidence and told the whole story. They were jailed in Sheridan and the other five in the Basin jail. A long trial was held in the fall of 1909. Herbert Brink was found guilty of first degree murder. George Henry Saban and Milton Alexander were found guilty of second degree murder. All three were sentenced to five years in the penitentiary. Tommy Dixon, and Ed Eaton were sentenced to two years on arson charges.

The Spring Creek Raid did indeed prove to be a major turning point in the relations between cattlemen and sheepmen. However, while such conflicts continued for the following decade, the day of the gunman in Wyoming was rapidly fading.

to infer dietary habits of the prehistoric occupants, as well as the particular time of year the site was occupied.

One interesting find was the recovery of rodent, deer and bird bones which appeared to be refuse from a cooking pit. Dated at about 9,500 years old, this discovery greatly increased our knowledge about some of the earliest Americans who were traditionally thought to have been only big game hunters.

Reprinted from Wyoming State Parks Brochure

H Medicine Lodge Creek Informative Plaques

Seven miles northeast of Hyattville about 2 miles off of Cold Spring Road.

Nature's Storehouse

For at least 10,000 years, this area where the Medicine Lodge Creek flows out of the Big Horn Mountains has provided a home for man. From the earliest hunter-gatherers to today's ranchers, Medicine Lodge is an ideal site for human habitation. Everything man needed is located at or near this site. Fruits, berries, greens and roots from the lush plant growth surrounding the creek bottom provided food, medicine, firewood and material for weapons and building. The abundance of animal life from wood rats to bison were an important part of the native diet. Within a few miles of the site there are excellent sources of high quality quartzite and chert—a rock resembling flint. These materials were used to make projectile points, arrowheads and other weapons and tools. The eastern exposure of the sandstone cliffs creates warm, sunny winter mornings and the slight overhang causes cool, shady summer afternoons at the base of the cliff. Add the constant availability of running water and you have an ideal camping spot that has been used throughout the ages.

Petroglyphs and Pictographs

Rock art at Medicine Lodge and throughout the Big Horn Basin falls into two categories—PETROGLYPHS which were pecked into the sandstone surfaces and PICTOGRAPHS that were painted onto the surfaces. Human-like figures and animals were common motifs. The meaning of rock art is difficult to decipher, but most archaeologists agree that the drawings are symbolic and represent the complex mythological and religious concepts of the artists. The figure illustrated here is located above you on the cliffs and has probably been chalked at some point in time and appears bluish in color. This type of figure petroglyphs appear throughout Wyoming and may symbolize the importance of hunting to the prehistoric economy. Rock art is extremely difficult to date, but art at this particular site is probably no more than 1000 years old.

Petroglyphs and pictographs are a priceless legacy from the Indian people who inhabited this area in years gone by. The elements are gradually dimming these fragile drawings and vandalism such as the carving of initials, painting over the figures and even chalking to make the art visible are leading to their destruction. Please let your foot-prints be the only sign of your visit!

Excavating and Recovery

Beginning in 1973, Medicine Lodge Creek was the scene of one of the most significant archaeological excavations in North America. For 2 years, anthropologists from the University of Wyoming carefully excavated the layers of silt

Greybull	Jan	Feb	March	April	May	June	July	Aug	Sep	Oct	Nov	Dec	Annual
Average Max. Temperature (F)	30.4	38.8	51.2	61.5	72.8	82.0	90.1	88.6	75.6	61.9	45.1	32.4	60.9
Average Min. Temperature (F)	4.1	10.4	22.2	34.8	42.2	50.5	56.0	52.8	44.7	30.5	18.5	7.3	31.2
Average Total Precipitation (in.)	0.36	0.27	0.31	0.68	1.22	1.23	0.54	0.47	0.74	0.49	0.36	0.30	6.98
Average Total SnowFall (in.)	4.1	3.2	2.6	1.7	0.3	0.0	0.0	0.0	0.7	0.6	2.9	4.3	20.4
Average Snow Depth (in.)	2	1	0	0	0	0	0	0	0	0	0	1	0

Days of '49

In 1949 a group of men attending a Junior Chamber of Commerce meeting in Greybull talked themselves into sponsoring the first Days of '49 Celebration. The first rodeo was memorable. The Jaycees saddled and gathered horses out of the hills. By the 1950s, the Days of '49 celebration annual drew several times the 2,500 population of Greybull. Colorful parades and two days of fun mark the Days of '49. Held the second weekend in June, this is an event not to be missed!

and clay to depths of well over 20 feet below where you are standing. Thousands of artifacts, bones, and seeds were recovered, and cooking and heating hearths, food storage pits, and evidence of these structures were unearthed. These discoveries revealed over 60 cultural levels, documenting the entire history of human occupation in the Big Horn Basin. The information gleaned by the anthropologist along with the geological, chemical, botanical, and related studies are being used to reconstruct the life ways of man and how he adapted to changing environmental conditions from the end of the Ice Age to modern times. Some physical evidence of the remains, such as the rectangular depressions at the base of the cliff which have been backfilled for preservation purposes.

Clues from the Past

Thousands of years ago, while the Indians camped here, the banks of Medicine Lodge Creek were only a few feet away from the base of the cliff. Throughout the years, the creek changed its course and meandered across the width of the valley. Massive rockfalls from the cliffs, such as the one before you, diverted the creek back out into the middle of the valley, thus preserving the silt and clays which held the remains of the campsite of the ancient hunter-gatherers. Only through this accident of geological action has any evidence of human habitation at Medicine Lodge Creek been preserved. From the stratigraphy exposed during the excavations, geologists and archaeologists can interpret the history of the valley. Each layer exposed produced clues that give us information on past environmental conditions and the cultural activities that took place. You can envision the original slope of the valley before it was leveled for corrals and before archaeological excavation began by looking at the undisturbed land adjacent to the rockfall and the line of red earth on the cliff approximately 10 feet above the existing ground level.

19 *Food, Lodging*

Manderson

Pop. 104, Elev. 3,890

Named for a Burlington Railroad official, this little town was originally called Alamo.

Scores of historic airpcraft are available for viewing at the Museum of Flight and Aerial Firefighting in Greybull.

20 *Gas, Food, Lodging*

Basin

Pop. 1,238, Elev. 3,870

Named for the Big Horn Basin, this is the county seat of Big Horn County. A bitter battle for this title ensued in 1897 between Basin City (as it was then called) and Otto. Basin won by 38 votes, thanks to the fact that Cody entered the race at the last minute and split the vote in the west. It is known as the Lilac City, and the major crop is beans, although the economy relies on ranching too. Along with Greybull, Basin was one of the first towns in the whole Northwest to make use of natural gas for utilities.

Otto

This little town was named for cattle mogul Otto Franc, owner of the Pitchfork Ranch. It was once a contender for county seat, but won out to Basin when Cody entered the race at the last minute, dividing the vote.

21 *Gas, Food, Lodging*

Greybull

Pop. 1,815, Elev. 3,788

It is said that an albino buffalo, held sacred by the Indians, once roamed in this area, giving both the river and the town its name. Pictographs of the animal can be seen on bluffs near the river. John Borner, an immigrant from Saxony, was probably the first white man to build a home here in 1886. A farming community developed, settled by German immigrants and Mormons. Natural gas was discovered here in 1908, and the following year the town was officially established. In 1915, several plentiful oil wells were drilled and two refineries were built. Energy production has dominated the economy ever since.

The area has been prone to flooding, experiencing two major floods in the early part of the 20th century. But the tendency of the river to overflow has left a treasure trove of fossil remains, including dinosaur bones, cycads, ammonite and bentonite deposits, and an early horse species called Eohippus (dawn horse). The landscape is also dotted with Indian fire rings, the small Bear Creek Medicine Wheel, and many other stone arrows, cairns, and circles left by the early occupants. Now the fertile, well-irrigated flatlands are mostly filled with ranging cattle and pronghorn antelope.

T Chamber of Commerce - Greybull

521 Greybull Ave. in Greybull. 765-2100

T Greybull Museum

325 Greybull Ave. in Greybull. 765-2444

This is a free museum in a friendly town where the entire family can relax and enjoy a new

Shell

	Jan	Feb	March	April	May	June	July	Aug	Sep	Oct	Nov	Dec	Annual
Average Max. Temperature (F)	32.5	40.4	50.9	60.8	70.0	80.4	88.8	87.3	75.6	62.5	44.8	34.6	60.7
Average Min. Temperature (F)	6.0	12.6	21.6	29.8	37.3	47.1	53.7	50.2	39.7	29.2	17.3	7.5	29.4
Average Total Precipitation (in.)	0.54	0.46	0.53	1.04	1.46	1.63	0.78	0.58	1.12	0.84	0.56	0.49	10.03
Average Total SnowFall (in.)	6.0	3.5	2.2	0.4	0.5	0.0	0.0	0.0	0.2	0.6	1.7	5.2	20.3
Average Snow Depth (in.)	3	2	1	0	0	0	0	0	0	0	0	1	1

approach to the world in which we live. The displays include Indian apparel and artifacts, guns and old weapons, and other bits of Western and pioneer heritage. For those interested in geology and the earth sciences, the museum offers perhaps the most outstanding agate collections and polished petrified tree sections around, dating back millions of years. Dinosaur bones and other prehistoric fossil remains can also be seen here. Call for hours.

T Museum of Flight and Aerial Firefighting

South Big Horn County Airport in Greybull. 765-4482

This area has long been a magnet for lovers of beauty and adventure. A significant part of that is reflected in the collection of the Museum of Flight and Aerial Firefighting. A nationally renowned historic assembly, you will find several of the last remaining examples of World War II's mighty bombers and transport aircraft. These magnificent planes are restored and retired here to whet the imaginations of many a true or would-have-been flying ace. Among other exhibits, you can see five of the last flying PB4Y-2 planes used against the Japanese in the South Pacific. So heavily fortified, the awesome firepower of the PB4Y-2 caused the Japanese to flee from several islands they occupied when they heard these planes were coming. The museum also features planes used in fighting fires over the decades since Orville and Wilbur Wright first flew. Planes have been used to help fight fires for most of the century, to transmit information before radio, to spot fires, and to drop fire retardant (once beer kegs full of water) on fires from above. In 1953, the first modern air tankers were developed and began testing in the Western US. We hope to add more planes to our collection to commemorate the history of flight, both in war and firefighting. Please make a donation.

T Greybull Elevator

In Greybull

As a way for farmers and ranchers from the Emblem Bench and Shell Creek Valley to market grain without the need to travel long distances in horse-drawn wagons, the Greybull Elevator was founded. This elevator is one of the oldest building in Greybull and is a point of interest in town today. When the present owner need to replace the siding, local artist Karyne Dunbar was hired to paint western scenes on the panels prior to installation. One tower features the legendary Greybull Buffalo who is unarmed and an Indian carrying a Buffalo spear on the other. The question on many minds is whether they face each other in greeting, or challenge. To uncover the legend, ask one of the folks at the Graybull elevator. They would be happy to share the story.

T Devil's Kitchen

Five miles east of Greybull

This exposure of rocks is part of the Cloverly formation, a million year old sequence of sediments containing dinosaur remains. The soft colorful sandstone and shales of the Cloverly Formation form a badlands landscape of isolated spires and weathered hills. In this rock formation is the fossilized remains of Deinonychus, a velociraptor. A map to the area may be obtained from the Greybull Chamber of Commerce.

T Stone Schoolhouse

Located between Greybull and Shell, on Highway 14 East.

Built in 1903 and used as a school until the early 1950s, the Stone School is an outstanding example of the vanishing one-room schoolhouse. It embodies the construction type employed by pioneer masons who used indigenous building materials. The school is one of the few remaining intact one-room schoolhouses in Wyoming and has received recognition on the National Register of Historic Places.

T Borner Cabin

In Greybull

In 1886, John Borner and his hired man, J. A. Benjamin, traveled from Lander, Wyoming and built a large cabin on the site of the present Greybull City Park. The cabin's chimney remains intact on the park site. Borner, who was born in Saxony, Germany, came to America as a child. He served in the Civil War, then headed west. he married Jennie Canary, a sister of "Calamity Jane" Canary, in Lander and remained there until his wife died. In 1887 he brought his children to the cabin and began the settlement which would become known a Greybull. Known as "Uncle Johnny" to many, he was remembered as a kind, generous man. He passed away in December of 1919.

H Wyoming's Prehistoric Wildlife

Greybull rest stop northwest of Greybull

The Big Horn Basin is famous for its dinosaur discoveries. During the 1930's, some of the world's significant dinosaur fossils were excavated by the American Museum of Natural History. The Basin received renewed interest in the early 1990's with the discovery of the world's most complete skeleton of an Allosaurus fragilis, a meat-eating dinosaur of the Jurassic Period (150 million years ago). The largest carnivorous dinosaur of its time, allosaurs stood 10 feet high and measured 35 feet in length. Dinosaur excavations continue today.

The Big Horn Basin also yields animal remains from recent times. Natural Trap Cave on the west slope of the Big Horn Mountains is an ancient sinkhole in the limestone where, for more than 20,000 years, animals fell 80 feet to their deaths. The bottom of the cave is littered with bones of extinct mammals such as mammoths, short-faced bears, saber-toothed cats. American lions and dire wolves.

Scientists study bones and fossils of the Big Horn Basin to help determine past climatic and enveronmental conditions. By researching the earth's past, scientists can better predict and evaluate future global changes and their effects on wildlife and humans.

H Sheep Mountain

10 miles north of Greybull on WY- 310

The prominent hill to the east is known as Sheep Mountain. It is the surface expression of an upward fold in the earth's crust that geologists refer to as an anticline. Sheep Mountain is a textbook example of an anticline fold. It is 15 miles long and the involved rock formations, which were originally horizontal, have been bent and uplifted over 1000 feet. The surface sedimentary rock formations that are exposed in the fold, range in age from 66-360 million years. Anticlines form when deep seated, compressive forces within the earth's crust, squeeze and shorten the crust. The geologic event, which resulted in the creation of Sheep Mountain Anticline, along with many other anticlines in the Big Horn Basin began approximately 66 million years ago. This is the same time period during which dinosaurs became extinct. The present Sheep Mountain has evolved over the past 3 million years. It resulted from down cutting of the land surface by rivers and streams and the removal of much of the original basin fill sediment.

H Lower Shell Schoolhouse

On U.S. Highway 14 about 6 miles east of Greybull

The Lower Shell Schoolhouse was one of the first non-log community buildings built in the Big Horn Basin. Using a classic one room schoolhouse design, it was constructed on this site in 1903 on land which had been donated to the Odessa School District. The school district was named for the nearby Odessa Post Office which had operated from 1891 to 1895. Local

Powell	Jan	Feb	March	April	May	June	July	Aug	Sep	Oct	Nov	Dec	Annual
Average Max. Temperature (F)	30.7	38.1	47.4	58.8	68.5	77.7	86.8	84.4	73.7	61.6	44.2	34.2	58.8
Average Min. Temperature (F)	7.8	13.8	20.9	31.3	41.5	49.6	55.9	53.5	43.5	33.2	21.0	12.1	32.0
Average Total Precipitation (in.)	0.19	0.14	0.20	0.51	1.08	1.25	0.66	0.58	0.78	0.41	0.23	0.16	6.19
Average Total SnowFall (in.)	3.1	2.2	2.6	2.4	0.3	0.1	0.0	0.0	0.4	0.8	2.6	2.7	17.2
Average Snow Depth (in.)	1	1	0	0	0	0	0	0	0	0	0	1	0

homesteaders quarried sandstone from the surrounding hills and assisted in the construction of the 24' by 46' building. During the 1905-1906 school year forty students were enrolled here demonstrating the early settlers' high regard for education.

Although the building was mainly used as a school, it also functioned as a church for traveling preachers and as a community dance hall. A wide variety of organizations, from cemetery boards to the farm bureau, held meetings here as well. Use as a school ended in the early 1950s, but the building continued to be used as a meeting hall until the early 1970s.

In 1980 the foundation received new footings and the roof was reshingled as an effort was made to stabilize the building after nearly a decade of neglect. The addition to the rear of the building was completed in 1988, using the same architectural design as the original construction. The historical appearance was thus retained, while at the same time the building could serve as an art gallery, bookstore and information center.

The simple form of the schoolhouse epitomizes the austere life of the region's early pioneers. Shell Valley's lush irrigated farm fields contrast with the arid topography of the basin demonstrating the current results of their earlier endeavors. As one of a few remaining one room schoolhouses in Wyoming the "old stone school", as it was often called, has received recognition by enrollment in the National Register of Historic Places.

The building houses the Stone School Gallery & Bookstore which has books, maps, and artwork of the region.

F Buffalo Rose Restaurant

601 N. 6th St. in Greybull. 765-4718

The entire family will enjoy dining at the Buffalo Rose Restaurant in a warm and friendly atmosphere. The newly remodeled dining room is complete with a cozy fireplace. Daily home-cooked specials are popular locally. On Friday and Saturday nights they serve up mouth watering prime rib. Accompany your meal with a cold beer or enjoy a glass of wine. They welcome children and will always have a special surprise for them. Delivery is available. Check at the desk of your motel for a Buffalo Rose menu. They are open 6 a.m. to 9 p.m. and until 10 p.m. during the summer months.

L Wheels Motel

1324 N. 6th in Greybull. 765-2105, Fax 765-2105 or Reservations at 800-676-2973

L Antler Motel

1116 N. 6th St. in Greybull. 765-4404 or toll free 877-849-7527

The Antler Motel is a true "mom & pop" business. The newly renovated rooms are extra clean and many of them are decorated with western themes. This cozy motel focuses on families and even provides guests with nine holes of Goofy Golf and a playland with swings, slide, trapeze, and a huge sandbox. Complimentary continental breakfast is served to guests daily. Occasional "meet-your-neighbor" nights complete with a steak barbecue and all the trimmings are offered. Some units are available with kitchenettes. Laundry facilities are also available. The Antler Motel caters to hunters too. A great place to stay on your way to Yellowstone National Park.

L Greybull Motel

300 N. 6th St. in Greybull. 767-2628 or fax 765-2933

This owner-operated motel has been completely remodeled and is an entirely smoke-free property. You'll enjoy central air conditioning, individually controlled electric heat and cable/HBO TV with remotes. They take pride in their crisp bed linens, fluffy pillows, large plush towels, and great water pressure. All rooms are computer friendly. They have two rooms for guests with pets. The motel is one-story, with a large paved parking lot, and an an abundance of flowers during the summer. A pleasant and comfortable stop whether you are heading for the Big Horn Mountains or Yellowstone Park.

22 *Gas, Food, Lodging*

Shell

Pop. 50, Elev. 4,210

This town, like the creek, was probably named for the fossilized invertibrate shells which line the creek bed and are found throughout the area. It also may have been named for Dick Shell, who founded the town.

Bureau of Land Management photo

T Red Gulch Dinosaur Tracksite

10 miles east of Greybull on U.S. Highway 14 to Red Gulch Scenic Byway turnoff, then five miles south

Red Gulch Dinosaur Tracksite

At BLM's Red Gulch Dinosaur Tracksite, you can imagine yourself walking along an ocean shoreline 167 million years ago with dozens of other dinosaurs, looking to pick up a bite of lunch from what washed up on the last high tide. The ground is soft and your feet sink down in the thick ooze, leaving a clear footprint with every step you take.

The discovery of rare fossil footprints on public lands near the Red Gulch/Alkali National Back Country Byway close to Shell, Wyoming, could alter current views about the Sundance Formation and the paleoenvironment of the Middle Jurassic Period.

Discovery/Background

The Red Gulch Dinosaur Tracksite is the largest tracksite in Wyoming and one of only a few worldwide from the Middle Jurassic Period (160 million to 180 million years old). Until the tracks were reported in 1997, most scientists thought the entire Bighorn Basin and most of Wyoming was covered by an ancient ocean called the Sundance Sea.

Scientists thought that only sea-dwelling creatures could have lived in this area. There shouldn't be any dinosaur footprints at all. Not only are there hundreds of tracks, but in this 40-acre area there could be thousands. The dinosaur tracks were clearly made just at the shoreline, not in deep ocean water, and there must have been large areas of dry land to support not only dinosaurs but other animals and plants.

The limey mud that the dinosaurs were walking in probably felt similar to cement just starting to harden. The tracks were perfectly preserved when the mud hardened and was covered by more layers of ooze, and then by fine sand, filling the tracks and preserving their shape. Over the

Lovell

	Jan	Feb	March	April	May	June	July	Aug	Sep	Oct	Nov	Dec	Annual
Average Max. Temperature (F)	29.6	37.8	47.6	58.7	68.9	78.7	87.8	86.2	73.8	61.1	44.1	33.2	58.9
Average Min. Temperature (F)	4.8	12.0	20.8	30.8	41.5	49.6	54.6	51.7	41.0	30.4	18.8	8.8	30.4
Average Total Precipitation (in.)	0.22	0.16	0.29	0.62	1.15	1.21	0.65	0.57	0.71	0.53	0.25	0.22	6.58
Average Total SnowFall (in.)	4.1	2.2	2.3	0.9	0.1	0.0	0.0	0.0	0.6	0.6	1.4	4.5	16.7
Average Snow Depth (in.)	2	0	0	0	0	0	0	0	0	0	0	0	0

years, layer upon layer of sediment filled in over the top. Much later, erosion went to work and removed those layers, exposing the tracks that had been made all those millions of years ago.

The tracks were reported in 1997 by Greybull native Erik Kvale while enjoying the scenery with Allen Archer, Rowena Manuel, Cliff Manuel and Fran Paton on BLM-administered lands.

Scientists Come to Study

In 1998, paleontologists and geologists from around the country descended on the Tracksite to study this intriguing site. The scientists from the University of Wyoming, Dartmouth College, Department of Geological Sciences - Indiana University, Kansas State University, BLM National Science & Technology Center, South Dakota School of Mines and Technology and the Smithsonian Institution formed the Red Gulch Dinosaur Tracksite Science Team. These scientists are working at the Tracksite under a BLM Paleontology permit.

They are mapping, measuring and comparing the rocks and fossils at this site with other previously studied tracksites. Working as a group, the team is breaking new ground in the study of the Middle Jurassic in central North America.

What We Now Know!

Scientists have been working for the past four years, trying to unlock the Red Gulch Dinosaur Tracksite (RGDT) puzzle. They had many questions and now have some of the answers.

What dinosaur made the tracks? All the tracks identified so far were formed by two-legged (bipedal) dinosaurs. Some, and perhaps all, of the tracks appear to have been made by meat-eating dinosaurs (theropods). They weighed between 15-400 pounds. Because Middle Jurassic dinosaurs are so rare, it is very difficult to match the tracks to any particular dinosaur.

Typically, a well-preserved theropod dinosaur track is three-toed and nearly symmetrical, exhibits tapering toes and preserves a slightly "S" shaped impression of the middle toe. Identifiable theropod trackways preserve prints that are slightly "pigeon-toed" having an inward rotation of the feet.

However, many other tracks and trackways do not exhibit such features. Although clearly made by two-legged dinosaurs, these less well-defined prints may have been made by a different type of dinosaur such as a plant-eating ornithopod. In many cases, it is impossible to identify the track-maker as to ornithopod or theropod.

How many tracks are there? 1,000 tracks have been located, 600 of them are in the Ballroom. Nearly 600 dinosaur tracks have been located by surveying instruments. A network of one-meter-square grids has been surveyed in the "Ballroom and Discovery" area. Scientists estimate there are at least 1,000 tracks in the "Ballroom" area of the Tracksite.

How big are the tracks? The tracks are 8 - 28 cm. long, have three distinct toes, and may also show the heel and claws.

Where were the dinosaurs going? Most of the hundreds of identifiable trackways go in the same south-southwesterly direction. The orientations of most of the tracks indicate that the dinosaurs were moving to the south-southwest.

This could indicate herding or migratory animal behavior. Or it could indicate the presence of a physically constrained pathway (such as a tidal flat or beach next to an open body of water).

A logical interpretation would be that the dinosaurs may have been moving parallel to the shoreline. However, the shapes of the ripples associated with the RGDT surface shows this was not the case. The presence and orientation of the ripples indicate that relatively deeper water conditions existed to the southwest. Since the dinosaurs were moving in a southwesterly direction, it appears the dinosaurs were moving perpendicular to the shoreline and not parallel. The ripples reveal the dinosaurs may have been moving toward the water.

Cross sectional view of a ripple showing an asymmetric shape. The steep side to the right of the ripple crest is the down-current side. Flow was therefore left to right. Figure modified from Reineck and Singh, 1980.

What do the ripples tell us? The Tracksite exhibits a well-developed rippled surface. Ripples can be used to determine the direction of current movements. The coated-grain limestone consists of tiny sand-sized spheres of calcium carbonate and fossil shell fragments cemented together. The ripple surface formed before the grains were cemented together. The ripples are very similar in shape to those formed by relatively gentle waves in very shallow water. The dinosaur trackways appear to have formed shortly after the formation of the ripples.

Some tracks have been cross-sectioned or "sliced" to find out what the rock looks like within the footprint. The geologists are studying how the soft, limy mud was deformed as the weight of the dinosaur pushed it down.

What was the geography and climate like? During the Red Gulch Dinosaur Tracksite time, large portions of the western interior of North

Wyoming Tidbits

Hyattville wa originally named 'Paintrock" for the petroglyphs on Medicine Lodge Creek. It was renamed for postmaster Sam Hyatt.

Deaver	Jan	Feb	March	April	May	June	July	Aug	Sep	Oct	Nov	Dec	Annual
Average Max. Temperature (F)	30.7	39.1	49.4	61.2	71.0	80.0	88.6	87.1	75.6	62.7	44.6	33.5	60.3
Average Min. Temperature (F)	4.5	11.0	19.2	28.7	39.4	47.6	53.4	50.8	40.7	29.8	17.4	7.8	29.2
Average Total Precipitation (in.)	0.14	0.12	0.19	0.43	0.98	1.19	0.63	0.55	0.54	0.29	0.15	0.13	5.35
Average Total SnowFall (in.)	3.1	1.1	1.5	1.4	0.1	0.0	0.0	0.0	0.4	0.2	1.1	1.5	10.4
Average Snow Depth (in.)	1	1	0	0	0	0	0	0	0	0	0	1	0

Wyoming Tidbits

In 1901, a farmer in Byron noticed gas escaping from a fence post hole on his land. He lit it, and the gas continued burning for several years.

America were inundated by a shallow sea. To the west, a volcanic arch extended north from Mexico to southwestern Canada. To the east, the sea was bounded by very shallow water, low-lying coastline conditions that extended from central Wyoming into the present day Dakotas.

The climate during this time was extremely arid, at least seasonally.

The geology team has traveled to Florida, Texas, New England and elsewhere to visit other ancient environments. The ichnology team has visited sites throughout Colorado and Utah. Track expert Beth Southwell, UW, has been to Dinosaur State Park in Connecticut and even to China!

How old is the Tracksite? The Red Gulch Dinosaur Tracksite surface dates to approximately 167 million years old. This puts it in the mid-Bathonian Stage. How do we know this? Scientists used several factors to determine the date:

1. The occurrence of the oyster Gryphea nebrascensis, just above the track bed;

2. The occurrence of a complete specimen of the ammonite Cadoceras muelleri just above the track layer;

3. Two microfossils of marine planktonic protozoans called "Dinoflagellates."

The ages of these fossils have been well established in many places around the world. By finding these fossils here in the RGDT area, scientists can deduce the age of the surrounding area including the Tracksite.

The Tracksite preserves an ancient tidal environment. Scientists have traveled around the world to get clues to the Tracksite puzzle. Even though the daily rise and fall of the tide is small, because the tidal flat slopes at a very low angle towards the sea, a very broad expanse (several kilometer wide) is exposed at low tide. This is similar to the type of tidal flat preserved in the Tracksite area.

Why were the footprints preserved? Team members are studying modern environments where footprints may be preserved and trying to find out why such delicate structures were not immediately washed away but instead preserved and turned to rock.

What is a trace fossil? A fossil is any physical evidence of ancient life. A body fossil would include bone material or shell. A trace fossil, however, is evidence of the activity of ancient animals or plants. The physical evidence in the rock record of burrowing, crawling, walking, etc., constitutes a trace fossil. Therefore, the footprints at the Tracksite are vertebrate trace fossils.

What other kinds of trace fossils were found at the Tracksite? The older trace fossils on the Tracksite are classified as belonging to a Skolithos burrow type. The primary example are round, vertical tubes approximately 0.5 cm in diameter, similar to those made by modern annelid worms. These were probably made at the same time the dinosaurs were making their tracks.

The second, younger generation of invertebrate faunal traces is also present. These were made after the dinosaur tracks had been buried by sediment. The younger traces consist of U-shaped burrows ranging from 5 cm to greater than 12 cm in width and 2 cm to 3 cm in diameter. These may have been made infaunal crustaceans, bivalves such as clams or lugworms.

What are ABs? Shallow, irregularly shaped depressions are also present on the Tracksite. They have been nicknamed "AB's" for "amorphous blob."

The Tracksite AB's appear to have formed through a combination of both biological and physical erosional processes. The depressions are very similar to features observed on modern intertidal flats.

What else has been found? Samples of pollens, collected by scientists during the summer of 1998 have been processed in the laboratory. So far, it appears that there are pollens of cycads and several different conifers, fern spores and a variety of one-celled organisms in the layers directly overlying the Tracksite. The pollen is the only remains we have of these plants and could have been blown or washed in from vegetated areas tens to hundred of miles away.

Paleontology in the Bighorn Basin

The 260-plus million acres administered by the BLM are rich in fossils. Most public lands are simply those rejected by homesteaders as too steep, too dry, and too barren to support a family. What is unsuitable for agriculture is perfect for fossil discoveries.

Paleontologists have been collecting fossils in the Bighorn Basin since before 1880. Rocks in the Basin and along the flanks of the Bighorns and Absaroka ranges from about 600 million years to about three million years old, and all but one geologic period is represented.

The Bighorn Basin, and Wyoming in general, has yielded many kinds of fossils. The region is arid, so little soil or vegetation forms to obscure the exposures of bare rock. Also, when rain falls, it often does so violently and quickly erodes the surface, exposing more and more fossils.

Collecting

Much of the surface is administered by the BLM, so while hobbyists may collect petrified wood, invertebrates, and plant fossils, vertebrates are kept in the public trust through BLM's collecting permit process.

May I Collect Fossils? You may collect a variety of fossils on public lands, with certain restrictions. Special management designations restrict access and types of activities on some public lands. It is always a good idea to stop by the nearest BLM office to check on local conditions such as land status, fire danger, or road closures. On private lands, fossils may be collected only with the permission of the landowner.

Invertebrates: No permit is required to collect reasonable amounts of invertebrate fossils such as:

- trilobites
- brachiopods
- ammonites

Wyoming Tidbits

The Shoshone National Forest was the first national forest established. President Teddy Roosevelt, an ardent conservationist, signed the bill in 1902, designating the forest the nation's first.

The invertebrate fossils you collect are for your personal use and enjoyment, and may not be bartered or sold. Please remember to leave some for the next collector, too.

Petrified Wood You may collect:

- up to 25 pounds of petrified wood, plus one piece, each day.
- no more than 250 pounds in any calendar year without a permit.

You may not combine your allowance with another collector's allowance to obtain larger pieces of petrified wood. And you can't sell it without a special permit.

Other Plant Fossils :No permit is required to collect reasonable amounts of plant fossils such as leaves. They are for your personal use and may not be bartered or sold.

Vertebrates Vertebrate fossils may only be collected with a permit because of their relative rarity and scientific importance. They include not only bones and teeth, but also footprints, burrows and other traces of activity.

Vertebrate fossils are fragile and complex and permit applicants must be able to show a sufficient level of training and experience in order to collect them. In addition, all vertebrate fossils collected under a permit must be held in an approved repository.

Article courtesy of Bureau of Land Management

T Chimney Rock

In Shell Canyon

As a focal point for numerous paintings and photographs over the years, Chimney Rock is quite the landmark. This Chugwater sandstone formation was originally coined White's Monument due to its significance as the grave of trapper, cowboy, buffalo hunter and prospector, Jim White. History has it that in 1881 White and Riley Kane set off on a journey to combine trapping and prospecting. On route to Shell Creek the duo picked up an unknown third partner. The trio stopped along the base of the mountains to pitch camp and settle for the winter. As spring approached they discovered a shortage in supplies, Kane then set off with a team of oxen for Lander 200 miles southwest for more supplies. Shortly after his departure, the third partner murdered White and took off with the remaining supplies, oxen, as well as their collection of furs, hides and gold. Later, a group of cowboys stumbled upon his body and buried him in a shallow grave protecting it from wild animals. Kane eventually returned and upon discovering his partners death, searched with no avail for the murderer. Whites body was later found by Mr. A. Kershner who moved the body to Trail Town in Cody.

T Shell Falls

Near Shell

Shell Falls has been described as the thundering heartbeat of the magnificent Big Horn Mountain Range!

About sixty million years ago the area that is now the Big Horn Mountains began to bow upward, and the basins on either side began to sag downward. Today the highest point is Cloud Peak, about twenty-six miles south of here, a respectable 13,175 feet high. Millions of years of erosion have removed almost all the sedimentary rocks from the top of the Big Horns, exposing the ancient "basement" rocks, the granite over which Shell Falls now roars. Colorful layers of sedimentary rock still clothe the flanks of the Big Horns, making the ride over Highway 14 one of the most spectacular in the west.

Shell Canyon has been formed by the headward erosion of Shell Creek over millions of years. The creek has incised a deep chasm through the three billion year old granite you see around you. The water of Shell Falls, falling at the rate of some 3,600 gallons per second, follows the course of fractures in the resistant granite. This grey and pink granite is among some of the oldest rock on earth, while the softer Flathead sandstone which rests on top of it, some 550 million years old, contains some of the earliest fossils of hard shelled creatures you can find. Such ancient shells gave Shell Canyon, and Shell Falls, their names.

There is a quality of the sublime in all waterfalls, but especially in Shell Falls. The thudding sensation of falling water can be felt through the soles of your feet, and the water's voice has a way of soothing the traveler. The memory of Shell Falls, cool and green, has stayed with generations of visitors as they traveled on through the harsher basins bordering the Big Horn Mountains.

The People of Shell Falls

It would be fascinating to know how the Falls were perceived by the native Americans: the prehistoric Indians, and the Shoshone, Sioux, Crow and Cheyenne that followed them. Indian people have occupied the Big Horn country for at least eleven thousand years.

The journals of many settlers in the Big Horn Basin mention Shell Falls. Whole families would often forsake the summer heat of their lowland ranches and farms and make a special trip to the Falls. This part of the Big Horn country was very remote to outside visitors until recently. The Burlington Northern Railroad reached the Greybull area in 1909, but few tourists ventured into the Shell area until the 1920's. The first road up Shell Canyon was completed in 1932.

The modern highway through the canyon is surprisingly young. Much of it was completed in the mid-1960s, with major improvements performed in the 1980s.

An interesting point of local history concerns the massive limestone promontory called Copman's Tomb. This conspicuous landmark forms the northwest skyline as seen from Shell Falls, and is visible from the town of Shell far below in the Big Horn Basin.

In 1879, pioneer cattleman Henry Lovell, trailed several large herds of Shorthorn cattle from Oregon into the country on the west side of the Big Horns. Working for Lovell was a young man named Jack Copman. Copman decided to establish himself as a trapper, and set up a camp on a tributary of Shell Creek that became known as Trapper Creek.

Long before the invention of the airplane, visitors to Copman's camp were amazed to see his "flying machine." This was an elaborate model glider which Copman would hurl into the air by hand. Copman dreamed of constructing a full-sized glider and knew just where he wanted to launch it, with himself as pilot. He eyed the impressive wedge-shaped prow of what we now call Copman's Tomb. Copman was intelligent, mechanically inclined, and shared his dream of flight with many local people.

Years later, a successful businessman and devoted husband and father, Copman knew that he would likely never fulfill his quest. He asked only that, when someone finally invented a flying machine, his ashes be scattered from such a device over the butte that figured so prominently in his young dreams. With his family in Europe at the time of his death in 1907, his wish could not be fulfilled. Copman is remembered as a visionary—his ideas well ahead of his era. Though he is buried in the Greybull cemetery, his real burial monument remains "Copman's Tomb."

The Animals of Shell Falls

There is an animal that loves the rumble and roar of falling water, that seeks it out as the place to feed and rear its young. Fast water does not deter it, and the bone-chilling cold of Shell Creek does not seem to touch it. The most surprising thing of all is that this is not a huge, fur-covered creature, but a diminutive, delicate-looking bird! The water ouzel, or dipper, is a tiny, slate grey bird, inconspicuous but for its unusual habit of repeatedly raising and lowering itself, dipping, on its tiny ouzel legs. The ouzel, which looks very much like a wren, can be seen entering the frigid waters of mountain streams without hesitation. While under the water its oily plumage protects it, and it uses its wings and feet to navigate through the stream, searching for aquatic insects, larvi and worms. It builds a large, moss-insulated nest, often close to waterfalls, and lays three to six eggs.

Another classic resident of the Shell Falls area is the rainbow trout, a lover of cold, well-oxygenated water. You can often see them lying quietly in the big plunge pools directly below the Falls. The "rainbow' comes by its name honestly. Its flanks are colored iridescent pink and electric blue. The rainbow is not native to the Big Horns, but was originally found only in localized areas of the California Sierras. Decades of transplanting this handsome fish now cause it to be found in mountain streams and lakes all over the west.

The trip to Shell Falls is often enlivened by the sight of moose. This largest of North American antlered mammals is frequently seen grazing the willow bottoms between Shell Falls and Burgess Junction. Moose are uniformly dark brown or black, with "scoop shovel" antlers and curved-down noses. There are no records of moose having inhabited the Big Horn Mountains prior to 1948, when eight were captured near Moran, Wyoming, and released on the east side of the Big Horns. Since then, aided by other "plants:" a large, healthy herd of moose now live in the Big Horn Mountains.

Many visitors to Shell Falls also see mule deer as they ascend either flank of the Big Horns. The name "mule deer" derives from their large, prominent ears. Mule deer prefer a diet of sagebrush, chokecherry, mountain mahogany, serviceberry, and other brushy species. The curlyleaf mountain mahogany you can see growing at the Shell Falls visitor center looks like it has been pruned. It has! Hungry mule deer love to feast on the tender leaves of this plant.

Reprinted from U.S. Forest Service brochure.

AFS Dirty Annie's

1669 U.S. Highway 14, east of Shell. 765-2304

Dirty Annie's, located at the foot of the Bighorn Mountains, has a big reputation for great breakfasts, burgers and old fashioned hard ice cream and malts. Not only will you get a great meal at Dirty Annie's, but you'll find all those last minute necessities like gas, ice, and film. Pick up some special souvenirs from an outstanding selection of western apparel, jewelry, art, books, and Rocky Mountain foods. That's not all! This is also a complete stop for fishing and hunting supplies, licenses, and information. Stop by on your road trip or bring a busload, Dirty Annie's offers plenty of friendly service, travel tips, and talks on local history.

FL Snowshoe Lodge

Snowshoe Lodge in the Big Horn Mountains near Shell. 899-8995 or 800-354-8637. www.thesnowshoelodge.com

The Snowshoe Lodge is an outstanding choice when you feel like combining the outdoors with intimacy and good taste! Stay in one of three log cabins in a secluded location at 8,600 feet in the Big Horn Mountains. The log cabins are furnished with private bathrooms and kitchenettes, accommodating two to six persons each. Relax in the main lodge, lounge and dining room, while enjoying the hospitality and home cooked food. The main lodge is equipped with telephone and TV/VCR for guests. Soak in the hot tub or unwind in the sauna. Hiking, backpacking, snowmobiling, cross country skiing, fishing, hunting, and wonderful views will energize you at this year-around paradise.

L Bear Creek Ranch

2098 Bear Creek Road near Shell. Phone or fax, 765-9319 or toll free at 888-770-8769 or cell, 899-9319. www.bilbrey.net

Bear Creek Ranch specializes in family ranch vacations in an area rich with Native American, pioneer, and dinosaur history. Geological formations are breathtaking. Hunting and fishing are fantastic. Deer, elk, and varmints abound for the serious hunters/wildlife viewers. This working ranch operates on 57,000+ acres and offers several camper sites and unlimited tent accommodations. They offer a "no frills" horseback/4WD experience and you'll go home with pleasant memories of living the "cowboy life," participating in actual ranch activities, sleeping under the stars, and too much good food! Book your visit for as long as you like.

23 *Food*

Emblem

Pop. 10, Elev. 4,438

Once called Germania for the German homesteaders who settled here, the name was changed during World War I to represent the flag.

Burlington

Pop. 250, Elev. 4,430

Probably named for the railroad, Mormon settlers hoped the trains would help their town grow. When that didn't happen, they had to rely on complex irrigation techniques to make agriculture viable on this high, arid bench. Between 1893 and 1907, they built a series of canals (the Sidon Canal System), channeling water from the Greybull River into ditches, which covered some 15,000 acres of land. As the crops began to flourish, more immigrants arrived, including many from Germany. The benchland came to be known as Germania Bench, until World War I, when they changed the name to Emblem Bench.

24 *No services*

T Wild Horses—An ancient Visitor Returns to the Bighorn Basin

Wild horses are often seem to the north around Bridger Butte. It's hard to imagine that their ancestors, called dawn horses, might have roamed here over 50 million years ago. Horses first developed in North America. However, they disappeared in the post-Pleistocene time about 11,000 years ago. They were reintroduced by the Spanish in the early 1500s and became a vital part of Western life.

What are wild horses?

A wild horse is an unbranded and unclaimed free-roaming horse found on public lands in the western United States or one that has been removed from the public lands and has not lost this status by giving title to an adopter. These animals are protected by a law passed in 1971. Wild horses are descendants of animals turned loose or escaped from early Spanish explorers, settlers, ranchers, prospectors, Indian tribes, and the U.S. Cavalry from the 1600s through the Great Depression of the 1930s to more recent times.

Where are Wyoming's wild horses?

Wild horses in Wyoming are found primarily in the southwestern part of the state near Rock Springs and Rawlins, but some can be seen near Lander, Worland, and Cody. Wild horses may often be seen from I-80 just north of the rest area between Red Desert and Point of Rocks, on the west side of Wyoming Highway 191 beginning about 10 miles north of Rock Springs to Eden, on the south side of Wyoming Highway 789 from Muddy Gap to the rest area, on either side of Wyoming Highway 135 from the junction with Highway 789 to where the road drops over the high rim, and on Wyoming Highway 16, 14, 20 from about 25 miles east of Cody to Emblem on the North side of the road. For the more adventurous, wild horses may be seen from many other back country roads. Directions may be obtained at the local BLM offices.

Where did wild horses come from?

The animals ranging through the West are considered mixtures of Spanish mustangs that escaped from early explorers and missions, along with Indian ponies and domestic horses that have strayed or were abandoned by their owners. Only one generation is needed to change a domestic breed to a wild one.

What is the "mustang"?

The name "mustang" from the Spanish mestano, means a horse that has strayed and become wild. Indians tamed some and used them to reign over the west until the coming of the railroads, ranchers and homesteaders.

What happened to the mustang?

Westward spread of civilization meant an end to the way of life of many Indians and their ponies, as domestic livestock and fences took over the open range. By the end of World War I, many domestic horses were simply abandoned on the range, but a strain of Spanish mustangs still remains in the bloodlines of many wild horses.

What is BLM's responsibility?

The Wild Horse and Burro Act passed by Congress in 1971 says that the Bureau of Land Management is responsible for protection, management, and control of wild horses.

Do wild horses need to be controlled?

The 1971 Wild Horse and Burro Act declared that these horses are living symbols of the historic and pioneer spirit of the West, and mandated BLM to manage the wild herds in perpetuity. The law directs that the horses are to be maintained in a thriving ecological balance with livestock, wildlife and the habitat. What is a thriving ecological balance and how many horses can be maintained to ensure the balance? The herd areas are continually monitored to accurately determine how many horses an area can accommodate. Information such as climate data, precipitation, vegetation, grazing utilization by horses, cattle, sheep and big game are all combined to come up with a manageable horse herd number. Wild horses are hardy animals, stronger than livestock or big game. If their numbers were left unchecked, they could easily dominate the winter range and other animals would suffer before the horses would. There are few natural predators or diseases to limit the horses, so, the number of horses has to be controlled.

How are wild horse populations controlled?

BLM rounds up excess wild horses using a helicopter and a crew of mounted wranglers. This is done on the average of once every 3 years in each herd area, and has proven to be a very effective and humane method of control. However, roundups are costly if they have to be done often and the law dictates that management be to the minimum level possible. Some fear that the roundups are harmful to the horses. For these reasons, BLM allows the horse populations to fluctuate so the number of roundups any one herd is subject to is minimized.

How many wild horses are there in Wyoming?

Currently, there are about 5,000 head in Wyoming

What happens to the horses that BLM rounds up?

Most of the horses that are captured are offered to the public under BLM's adopt-a-horse program. Anyone of legal age who can provide the proper facilities and care for a horse can adopt a wild horse for a minimum fee of $125. Horses that are unadoptable are returned to the range. More information about the adopt-a-horse program is available at any BLM office.

Can wild horses be trained?

Yes! In fact, most are easily trained to lead, ride, pull or anything any horse can be trained to do. In Wyoming, the BLM has an agreement with the Wyoming Honor Farm in Riverton, a state correctional facility, where wild horses are trained by the residents.

Today's wild horses are descendants of animals that either escaped or were turned loose by the various cultures who depended on them. The McCullough Peaks herd roams about 100,000 acres of public land, which includes Bridger Butte. In the distance and to the right of Bridger Butte are the Prior Mountains, home to another wild horse herd. These horses are unique because they still have many of the markings of the Spanish Mustang.

Wild horses are the responsibility of the Bureau of Land Management (BLM), which is an agency of the US Department of the interior. The BLM manages free roaming horses and burros as living symbols of the historic and pioneer spirit of the West, and as an important part of the natural system on public lands.

Because horses have few natural predators, and many more are born each year than die, the BLM has periodic round ups. Wild horses are available to the public through the Adopt-a-horse program. For more information, contact any BLM office.

Article courtesy of Bureau of Land Management

25 *Gas*

Ralston

Pop. 100, Elev. 4,700
Gas

This little railroad siding town took its name from the local saloon owner back in the days when it started as a railroad siding. The tiny town gained fame in Ripley's Believe It or Not when unusual bridges were recognized. The original highway bridge crossed Alkali creek at the same point the railroad bridge crossed. The railroad bridge passing over the highway bridge.

T Heart Mountain Historic Relocation Camp

10 miles northeast of Cody on U.S. Highway 14A, or six miles southwest of Ralston.

On a more sober note, 11 miles east of Cody, you will find the remains of the Heart Moutain Japanese Relocation Camp. This was where over 10,000 Japanese-Americans from the west coast were forced to settle after the attack on Pearl Harbor in 1941, when their patriotism was questioned unjustly. Conditions in the camp were primitive. Poorly insulated barracks contained small "apartments" with several occupants crowded into each. Internees came with few belongings,

Section 2

had little furniture, and shared bath facilities. The perimeter was surrounded by barbed wire, and guards with machine guns and searchlights watched from nine different towers, day and night.

But most residents remained true to the United States, and their mantra for survival was "shikata ga nai" (I guess it cannot be helped). Over 600 of the internees joined to Army and served in the war in Europe. Twenty-one of them gave their lives for their country. Those who remained behind found work in local agriculture, filling in for sons who had gone off to war. Mostly, their wages were less than what prisoners-of war were making on the other side of the state, near Douglas.

The Heart Mountain Wyoming Association is working at preserving this site as a reminder of social injustice, so that we may avoid such folly in the future.

H Heart Mountain Relocation Center

Six miles southwest of Ralston

During the World War II years, Heart Mountain Relocation Center was located on a 740-acre tract of land across the Burlington Railroad right-of-way westward from where you stand facing this monument and Heart Mountain itself, on the Heart mountain Division of the Shoshone Irrigation Project.

Eleven thousand people of Japanese ancestry from the three west coast states were loosely confined by the United States Government in the center for about three years. They lived in barracks as singles, or as families, according to their marital status.

The camp was equipped with modern waterworks and sewer system and a modern hospital and dental clinic, staffed with people from the ranks of the evacuees. First rate schooling was provided for the children of the evacuees through the high school grades.

H Heart Mountain Relocation Center

Six miles southwest of Ralston

History

After the bombing of Pearl Harbor on December 7, 1941, many parts of the West Coast were declared military defense zones. The government ordered the removal of all persons of Japanese ancestry and the War Relocation Authority was established in March 1942 to house them in inland camps. The Heart Mountain Relocation center was one of ten temporary camps constructed to confine over 110,000 men, Wahington and part of Arizona. It was the only camp located in Wyoming. Construction on the center began in June 1942 and the first internees arrived in August of that year. At the peak of its population, the Heart Mountain Center, which covered over 740 acres, contained nearly 11,000 people housed in 450 barracks. Although surrounded by barbed wire and armed quards, the internees kept the camp functioning as a small city with its own public works, grade schools, a high school, hospital and newpaper. At the time it was the third largest city in Wyoming.

The camp was closed in November 1945, the buildings removed and the land, made arable by irrigation ditches completed by the internees, was opened up for homesteading.

A portion of the Heart Mountain Center was listed on the National Register of Historic Places on December19. 1985. The area listed includes the immediate vicinity of this Honor Roll and structures located to the east.

H Honor Roll

Six miles southwest of Ralston

This monument was erected lby the internees at the Heart Mountain Relocation Center in August 1944 to honor those from the camp who served in the United States armed forces in World War II. The photographs to the right and below show the Honor roll as it was in 1944. Although the elements have erased the names ofthose listed, the structure still remains as it was originally.

In 1978 the Honor Roll was preserved as a memorial not only to those Japanese-Americans who served in the military, but also to recognize the sacrifices of those who were interned here throughout the war.

In 1985 a plaque was erected memorializing those people from Heart Mountain who gave their lives in World War II.

T Ralston Mystery Bridges

At the curve in U.S. Highway 14A east of Ralston

Listed in Ripley's Believe It or Not, this railroad bridge over a highway bridge over a creek is unique, not only to the area, but in the world. The most peculiar thing of all, however, is that the road on either side of the bridge goes nowhere.

H The Ralston Reservoir

Southwest of Ralston

The Ralston Reservoir was completed in 1907 and provides some operational control of the Garland Canal. It is also used as an emergency spill route during heavy rain storms which occasionally hit the area during the summer.

The reservoir has been set aside to provide wildlife viewing and waterfowl hunting. This designation came about through mitigation measures as part of a previous Rehabilitation and Betterment Program to modernize the irrigation delivery system on the Heart Mountain Division.

Today, Ralston Reservoir is "for the Birds" due to cooperation of the Shoshone-Heart Mountain Irrigation districts, Bureau of Reclamation and Wyoming Game and Fish Department.

Today, the primary importance of the reservoir is as a wild life habitat area.

H Willwood Dam

Five miles southwest of Ralston

The Willwood Dam diverts water from the Shoshone River to irrigate 11,400 acres of land on the Willwood Division of the Project, which was settled beginning in 1927.

Construction of the 70-foot-high dam began in 1922, and work was completed just a year later. Work on the canal, located across the river looking to the East, was completed in the spring of 1927, and the first unit homesteaders received water for their new farms on April 21, 1928.

The dam is located 22 miles downstream from Buffalo Bill Dam.

H Eagle's Nest Stage Station

Five miles southwest of Ralston

Established in the 1890's by Tom Lanchberry to accommodate passengers and horses on the Red Lodge to Fort Washakie run, Eagle's Nest Station, one-half mile north, operated until early in the century when railway expansion limited it's usefulness. Stout four and six-horse teams, under salty drivers, pulling tough, coach-type wagons, were changed every 15 to 20 miles. Stages traveled 60 to 80 miles a day, tying together cattle ranches and army posts. One dollar a night for supper, bed and breakfast was the usual charge to dust-covered passengers on the long rough route from Montana's Northern Pacific to the Union Pacific railroad in southern Wyoming.

26 *Gas, Food, Lodging*

Powell

Pop. 5,373, Elev. 4,365

Named for famed explorer John Wesley Powell, this community first grew up around the crews that came to build dams and irrigation systems for the Shoshone Project in the 1890s. Powell himself conceived of utilizing damming and canals to "reclaim" the land for agricultural purposes. Homesteaders swelled the population during the early part of the twentieth century, and the Burlington Railroad turned the town into a major shipping hub for the Bighorn Basin. With the discovery of oil in 1915, Powell found its fortunes rising still more as the Elk Basin Oil Field brought further growth. The oil industry is still a

Powell's elevator is its welcome sign.

factor in the town's economy, but it is first and foremost an agricultural town, churning out sugar beets, beans, and malting barley year after year.

Powell is also home to Northwest Community College, one of the state's two years schools, which brings educational and cultural opportunities to local residents. Founded in 1946, the college serves some 2000 students in the area, most of whom live on campus.

T Homesteader Museum
Corner of 1st and Clark off U.S. Highway 14A

The museum building has a lively history. Built by the American Legion in 1933, the log and hardwood space served as a dining area, banquet hall, community dance hall, roller rink and youth center. During WWII, it housed German prisons of war until Camp Deaver was ready. Artifacts include early day items, military memorabilia, geological displays, a caboose, photographs and maps. The museum is open Tuesday through Saturday. Call for hours. Tours and appointments can be arranged. Admission is free.

H An Island in the Sage
Homesteader Park Rest Area at the east edge of Powell

Powell is named for the famous one-armed explorer Major John Wesley Powell. In 1889, Powell reported on the agricultural potential of these western sagebrush grasslands. He declared the value of irrigation in "reclaiming" these area through a series of dams and canal systems funded by the government. So, the Shoshone Project started, including the nearby Buffalo Bill Dam and a series of canals to feed water to the fields along the Shoshone River. Because of the successful irrigation project and the arrival of the railroad, Powell became an agricultural shipping point.

The vast native prairie, which once provided for the needs of wildlife, was converted to fields of sugar beets, malt barley and beans for human needs. Although there is evidence of agricultural irrigation projects throughout the Big Horn Basin, there are vast areas of native prairie still remaining. Almost 50 percent of Wyoming's 96,000 square miles is covered by sagebrush grassland. Abundant sagebrush habitat is the reason Wyoming supports more than half the world's population of sage grouse and pronghorn antelope.

Wyoming's agricultural areas are like small islands in a vast expanse of sagebrush prairies. Many wildlife species, like the sage grouse, pronghorn antelope, coyotes and songbirds, have adapted to life in both the agricultural and sagebrush grassland habitats. Wildlands and vast open spaces are crucial parts of the formula required to ensure wildlife diversity, making Wyoming a unique place for wildlife and people!

27 *Gas, Food, Lodging*

T Northwest Galleries & Diorama
Northwest College campus in Powell. 754-6000

Visit the college's two galleries and permanent science exhibits on campus. Call for information on current exhibits.

M Northwest College
231 West 6th Street in Powell. 754-6000 or 800-560-4692

Northwest College is located in Powell about 70 miles from the east entrance to Yellowstone National Park, in the valley of the Shoshone River between the Big Horn and Absaroka Mountains. Northwest College opened in 1946 with nearly 100 full- and part-time students and three instructors who met in classrooms borrowed from the public school district. The name was changed to Northwest College in 1989. Over the years the campus developed with an enrollment of over 1,700 students. Northwest College is a community of people dedicated to providing an environment that fosters excellence in education. The college responds to the educational, career, cultural, and social needs of students and the larger community. At Northwest College, students may pursue transfer, occupational, developmental, life-long learning, and personal enrichment goals.

Wyoming Tidbits

No Wood Creek near Ten Sleep was so named because settlers were unable to find firewood along the creek banks.

28 *No services*

Garland
Pop. 50, Elev., 4,247

A respected forest ranger, John Garland, gave his name to this little intersection town. It sits alongside the Bridger Trail.

H The Shoshone Project Story–Project Overview
Three miles north of Garland

The Shoshone Project is located in a desert-like valley surrounded by mountains. Annual precipitation is between 5 and 6 inches, not enough to grow crops.

The success of farming in this area is directly related to the amount of snow which falls in the mountains. The water supply for the Project is obtained from this snowmelt above Buffalo Bill Dam and Reservoir. The reservoir stores water

Bighorn Canyon

At first glance, time seems to have stopped at Bighorn Canyon. The lake and the steep-sided canyons provide a peaceful setting for those seeking a break from the daily routine. The focus of the area is 71 -mile-long Bighorn Lake, created by Yellowtail Dam near Fort Smith. Dedicated in 1968, the dam provides electric power, water for irrigation, flood control, and recreation. Boating, water skiing, fishing, swimming, and sightseeing are main attractions.

While you enjoy the play of light and shadow on rock and water, take time to contemplate the changes that the land and the life upon it have undergone. Time and water are keys to the canyon, where the land has been shaped by moving water since upheavals of the Earth's crust built the Pryor and Bighorn mountains millions of years ago. For 15 miles upstream from the dam, the lake bisects a massive, arching anticline, exposing fossils that tell of successive times when this land was submerged under a shallow sea, when it was a tropical marsh, and when its conifer forests were inhabited by dinosaurs. Humans arrived here more than 10,000 years ago, living as hunters and gatherers. In modern times people have further altered the land.

Most of Bighorn's visitors come to enjoy the recreational opportunities the lake offers. Boaters, water skiers, anglers and scuba divers are all attracted here. But the park offers more than just the lake: from the wild flowers in spring and summer to more than 200 species of birds; from the stories of life forms adapting to a harsh environment to the modern search for energy. You can get more information on what the park offers at visitor centers near Lovell, WY, and Fort Smith, MT. Find your own place of solitude to relax and to enjoy the diversity and timelessness of this uncommon canyon water land.

A Challenging Land

In North America people have traveled and made their living along rivers and streams for more than 40,000 years. But the Bighorn River was too treacherous and too steep-walled. People here lived near the Bighorn but avoided navigating it—until the dam tamed the river.

The broken land here also challenged the ingenuity of early residents, forcing them to devise unusual strategies of survival. More than 10,000 years ago, Indian hunters drove herds of game into land traps. These Indians lived simply, gathering wild roots and seeds to balance and supplement their meat diet. They made clothes of skins, baskets and sandals of plant fibers, and tools of stone, bone, and wood. The many caves of the Bighorn area provided seasonal shelters and storage areas for the Indians, as well as for early traders and trappers.

Absaroke means "People of the largebeaked bird," in the Siouan language of the Crow. Their reservation surrounds most of Bighorn Canyon. Originally a farming people, the Crow split off from the Hidatsa tribe more than 200 years ago. They became a renowned hunting people, described by one of the Lewis and Clark Expedition as "the finest horsemen in the world."

After 1800, explorers, traders, and trappers found their way up the Bighorn River. Charles Larocque met the Crow at the mouth of the Bighorn in 1805; Captain William Clark traveled through a year later. Jim Bridger claimed he had floated through the canyon on a raft. Later fur traders packed their goods overland on the Bad Pass Trail, avoiding the river's dangers.

During the Civil War the Bozeman Trail led to mines in western Montana by crossing the Bighorn River. Open from 1864 to 1868, the trail was bitterly opposed by Sioux and Cheyenne; the Crow were neutral. The Federal Government closed the trail in 1868 after the Fort Laramie Treaty. Fort C.F. Smith, now on private land, guarded the trail as an outpost. A stone monument commemorates the Hayfield Fight, a desperate but successful defense against Sioux and Cheyenne warriors. In this skirmish a party of soldiers and civilian haycutters, working three miles north of Fort C.F. Smith, fought for eight hours until rescued by the fort's troops on August 1, 1867.

After the Civil War, cattle ranching became a way of life. Among the huge open-range cattle ranches was the Mason-Lovell (the ML); some of those buildings remain. Dude ranching, reflected in the remains of Hillsboro, was popular in the early 1900s.

The Crow made the transition from hunter-gatherers to ranchers in one generation. In 1904, after 12 years of labor, they completed an irrigation system and opened 35,000 acres of land to irrigated farming. Water was diverted into the Bighorn Canal by a 416-foot diversion dam, moving 720 cubic feet of water per second. Near Afterbay Campground is Bighorn Canal Headgate, remains of this human response to the challenge of the land.

Congress established Bighorn Canyon National Recreation Area in 1966 as part of the National Park System to provide enjoyment for visitors today and to protect the park for future generations.

Bighorn Canyon Visitor Center

The solar-heated visitor center near Lovell, WY., symbolizes the energy-conscious concerns of the National Park Service and of modern Americans. The heating is accomplished by storing heat from the sun in a rock bin, then blowing hot air through the building. The Yellowtail Dam Visitor Center, in the park, is two miles past the community of Fort Smith. It is approachable from the north by car.

Bighorn Wildlife

The wildlife of the Bighorn Canyon country is as varied as the land, which can be divided into four climate or vegetative zones. In the south is desert shrub land inhabited by wild horses, snakes, and small rodents. Midway is juniper woodland with coyotes, deer, bighorn sheep, beaver, wood rats, and porcupine. Along the flanks of the canyon is pine and fir woodland with mountain lions, bear, elk, and mule deer. In the north is shortgrass prairie, once home to herds of buffalo. Many of the smaller animals, such as cottontails, skunks, coyotes, and rattlesnakes, are seen frequently throughout the park. More than 200 species of birds, including many kinds of water fowl, have been seen here. Each plant and animal species is adapted to the particular conditions of temperature, moisture, and landform within one or more of the park's four primary zones.

Yellowtail Dam

The dam is named in honor of Robert Yellowtail, former Crow tribal chairman and reservation superintendent. The dam creates one of the largest reservoirs on the Missouri River tributary system. This arch type dam is 525 feet high.

Yellowtail Wildlife Habitat Management Area

Riparian, cottonwood forest, shrub land, and wetlands provide habitat for whitetail deer, bald eagles, pelicans, heron, water fowl, wild turkeys, and other species. The area is managed by the Wyoming Game and Fish Department through agreements with the National Park Service, Bureau of Land Management, and Bureau of Reclamation.

Ranch Sites

Mason-Lovell Ranch: A.L. Mason and H.C Lovell built cattle ranch headquarters here in 1883. Cattle roamed the Bighorn Basin in a classic open-range operation.

Hillsboro: A one mile round trip trail takes you to the site of Grosvenor William Barry's Cedarvale Guest Ranch and the 1915 to 1945 Hillsboro post office.

Lockhart: Caroline Lockhart, a reporter, editor, and author, began ranching at age 56. The well preserved buildings give a feel for ranch life; one mile roundup.

Ewing-Snell: This site was in use for nearly 100 years.

Bad Pass Trail

American Indians camped along this trail 10,000 years ago, and in prehistoric and historic times Shoshone used it to get to the buffalo plains. Early trappers and traders used it to avoid the dangers of the Bighorn River. You can see rock calms left along the route between Devil Canyon Overlook and Barry's Landing. Before the arrival of the horse, life changed little here for thousands of years. Small family groups wintered in caves near the canyon bottoms. In early spring they moved out of the canyon bottoms in search of plants and small animals, and in summer they moved to the highlands in search of game and summer maturing plants. Large groups gathered in fall for a communal bison hunt.

Devil Canyon Overlook

Here the canyon crosscuts the gray limestone of the Devil Canyon Anticline, a 1,000-foot high segment of the fault blocks that make up the Pryor Mountains.

What to See and Do

A film at Bighorn Canyon Visitor Center highlights park activities. Exhibits explain the canyon's history and natural features.

Boating enthusiasts will find a marina, snack bar, camp store (gas and oil), and boat ramp at Horseshoe Bend and OkABeh. Ramps are also at Afterbay Dam and Barry's Landing. All boaters should sign registration sheets at the ramps when entering and leaving the lake. If mechanical problems develop while you are on the lake, stay with your boat; hail other boaters and ask them to notify a ranger. Carry both day and night signaling devices. Do not try to climb the lake's steep canyon walls.

Swimmers are encouraged to use the lifeguarded areas at Horseshoe Bend and Ok-A-Beh.

Camping is restricted to designated sites in developed areas. It is also allowed in the back country and below the highwater mark along Bighorn Lake. Fire restrictions during periods of high fire danger may close certain areas to camping. Check with a ranger for the restrictions on fires or back country camping.

Hiking is available in the national recreation area and in nearby forests. Ask at the visitor centers for more information.

Hunting is allowed in designated areas in accordance with state laws. Trapping is prohibited.

Fishing in Montana or Wyoming requires the appropriate state fishing license. Fine game fish, such as brown and rainbow trout, sauger, ling, and perch, abound.

The most popular game fish, a gourmet's delight, is the walleye. Winter ice fishing around Horseshoe Bend is good. The Bighorn River provides excellent brown and rainbow trout fishing.

Regulations and Safety: Firearms are prohibited in developed areas and areas of concentrated public use, unless they are unloaded and cased. Pets must be on a leash in developed areas and in areas of concentrated public use. Trash and waste disposals into area waters are prohibited; all vessels must have a waste receptacle on board. Carry a first-aid kit as a precaution against poisonous snake bites.

All plants, animals, natural and cultural features, and archeological sites are protected by federal law. Collecting is prohibited.

Reprinted from National Park Service brochure.

from the approximately 1,500-square-mile Shoshone River drainage for use during the irrigation season, which runs from April 15 to October 15.

The elevation of the project ranges from about 4,200 feet above sea level in the Frannie Division to about 4,800 feet in the Heart Mountain Division.

The Garland, Willwood and Heart Mountain divisions of the Project can be seen from this vantage point. The Frannie Division is located about 10 miles northeast.

29 *Gas*

Byron

Pop. 557, Elev. 4,020

Mormon pioneer Byron Sessions, this town's namesake, was largely responsible for the Sidon Canal irrigation system in the area. A fence posthole unearthed a natural gas vent in a farmers field here, which —accidentally ignited — burned for years. Later, around 1906, the gas was intentionally tapped at 700 feet, and the Byron area became a prominent gas field.

H Sidon Canal

West of Byron

Following Mormon settlement of the Salt Lake Valley beginning in 1847, church leaders envisioned colonization of the entire inter-mountain region. In following decades, Mormons emigrated from Utah into Idaho, Arizona and Wyoming. Seeking to improve their economic status and following Mormon pioneering tradition, several hundred people in 1900 emigrated from Utah and Idaho to Wyoming's Big Horn Basin where they built a canal and a community.

Under the Carey Act of 1894 states were encouraged to sell arable public land cheaply following reclamation. But private reclamation projects required capital, and some were aborted as investors lost faith. Unlike other privately-financed projects, the Sidon Canal was built without a large amount of capital. Emigrants were organized into the Big Horn Colonization Company, an irrigation cooperative which offered company shares in return for labor. Upon arriving in the Basin workers plunged into canal construction, excavating with horse-drawn plows and slip scrapers. Near this point work was blocked by a sandstone boulder known as "Prayer Rock." According to legend, prayer and divine intervention caused the rock to split, allowing construction to continue and strengthening the emigrant faith in the canal project.

The 37-mile long canal was completed in less than two years. It still transports water from a headgate on the Shoshone River near the Big Horn-Park County line to a land segregation of approximately 20,000 acres. Its successful completion serves as an outstanding example of the cooperative effort and spirit of determination exhibited by Mormon pioneers in the American West.

30 *Gas, Food, Lodging*

Lovell

Pop. 2,361 Elev. 3,814

Lovell is known as the "City of Roses" for its renowned late citizen, Dr. William Horsely (d. 1971), who spent a lifetime cultivating the flower, becoming one of the nation's foremost authorities. The town honors his memory with a brilliant display of roses all over the place every summer, near homes and businesses. It's a quiet town, with the lowest crime rate in Wyoming. Still, Lovell has seen its share of booms and busts with the discovery of natural gas and oil in the area. The persistence of agricultural concerns has provided some stability, and a sugar beet factory and gypsum plant also contribute to the economy.

The Lovell area was originally part of the large ML Ranch, founded in 1880 by Anthony Mason and Henry Clay Lovell. By the turn of the century, several Mormon pioneers and German emigrants had come to the area to homestead, and were part of the irrigation project (the Sidon Canal) which made the Bighorn Basin flourish. In 1920, a glass factory was established, which later burned down. During the 1930s, Lovell was known for its brick and tile production.

While driving through town, note the solar powered street lights that line the main thoroughfare through town.

Veteran's War Memorial in Lovell.

T Bighorn Canyon Visitor's Center

U.S. Highway 14A east of Lovell. 548-2251

The center includes an interpretive area and large 3-D model of the Bighorn Canyon and Reservoir. There is also a small giftshop.

H Wildland Romance

U.S. Highway 14A one mile east of Lovell. Bighorn National Recreation Area Headquarters. 777-4600

Many native Americans and early 19th century beaver trappers left their moccasin tracks at this very site, while crossing between the Bighorn Mountains to the east and the Absaroka Moutains to the west. The view of wildlife and wildland landscapes has changed dramatically since that time, and so has our understanding of all life's connection to the land, water and air.

Wildland spaces and contrasting landscapes make Wyoming a special place for people and wildlife. Wide-open spaces provide a special need for free-ranging herds of elk, deer, bighorn sheep and pronghorn antelope. From this agrcultural island on the north edge of the Bighorn Basin you are surrounded by wildland expanses and a contrast of mountains, rivers and prairie. The Pryor Mountains to the north, the Owl Creek Mountains to the south, and Bighorns and Absarokas all contribute to the basin's wildlife diversity.

Pioneers began farming and raising livestock in this area in the late 1800s because of its temperate climate, wide open spaces and landscape diversity. Both wildlife and people have benefitted and share the wide open spaces and contrasting landscapes.

Abundant wildlife, natural wonders and western culture have always allured and enchanted the human spirit. We hope your spirit will be strengthened by your visit to this special piece of Wyoming's Wildlands.

H Lower Big Horn Basin

East of Lovell on Highway 14A.

John Colter visited this area in 1807. Many trappers and hunters followed later. The first wheeled vehicle was brought into this region in 1860. Permanent ranches were established near the mouth of the Shoshone River before 1888. Other ranchers soon settled along the Shoshone and Big Horn Rivers, and on Crooked, Gyp and Sage Greeks.

Later homeseekers settled in the lower Shoshone Valley, notably a large Mormon colony in 1900 which constructed irrigation systems and thriving towns. This log house, erected before 1894, and once occupied by one of Big Horn County's first officers, William F. Hunt, is typical of the homes built by the early settlers of this region.

H Bighorn Lake

U.S. Highway 14A 14 miles east of Lovell

Before you is Bighorn Lake. Yellowtail Dam at Fort Smith, Montana backs up the Bighorn River 71 miles to this point. Completed in 1968, the dam provides hydroelectric power to the region, water for irrigation and opportunities for recreation.

Fluctuation in river flow and differing demands in electric power will cause extreme change in the lake elevation. At this location a 30 foot change in water level could move the lake shore 5 miles.

At normal pool, the surface of the entire lake covers 12,685 acres. At this time the area before you is under water to the left of the causeway. This represents a 30 foot rise over the normal annual low water level, a difference amounting to 90 billion gallons of water capable of producing 111 million kilowatt hours of electricity at the dam.

For several months each year the water level is too low to cover this area of the reservoir. While the reservoir is drawn down, the ground exposed by the receding water provides breeding habitat for amphibians and aquatic insects, which provide food for fish in Bighorn Lake.

H Henry Gilbert, Jr. Memorial

Pennsylvania and Main Streets in Lovell

The Flying Tigers were American boys from 41 of our states, fighter pilots trained in our own Army and Navy, who became members of the new A.V.G. (American Volunteer Group) employed by the government of Generalissimo Chiang Kai-shek to protect the lifeline of China, the Burma Road. The Flying Tigers began under the leadership of Claire Lee Chennault with 100 Curtiss-Wright P-40B Tomahawks and the volunteer pilots to fly them.

They went on from there. They went on in smoke and flame and blood and death to compose their epic—one of the most spectacular in the annals of air warfare. They saved Rangoon and the Burma Road for 65 precious days. They became the demigods of fighting China.

Wingman Henry Gilbert, Jr. of Lovell, Wyoming was the youngest of the Flying Tigers at the age of 22.

On December 23, 1941, two waves of Japanese bombers accompanied by fighters were approaching Mingaladon. Fourteen P-40's and 16 Brewsters of the R.A.F. took off to meet the attack.

Gilbert dived on one of the bomber formations, shooting out bursts and striking two of them but without hitting vital spots in the attack. His P-40 was hit by a cannon shell and streamed out of the battle to crash into the jungle below.

There had been no parachute, and Henry Gilbert was the first Flying Tiger to die in combat.

H John Winterholler Gymnasium

Johnny Winterholler Gymnasium in Lovell

John Winterholler was born February 3, 1916 in Billings, Montana of Russian immigrants. He came to Lovell, Wyoming in 1932. John graduated from Lovell High School in 1935. While attending LHS he excelled in sports and was named All-State in basketball and football.

John started his meteoric rise to athletic fame at the University of Wyoming in the fall of 1935. "The Cowboy campus has produced no athlete who has attained the Lovell youth's heights," wrote Larry Birleffi of him in 1939. Birleffi noted "He is the athlete's idea of an athlete and a coach's answer... He earned a first berth in every all-conference selection among Big Seven's offerings for All-American honors... His achievements were in baseball, football and basketball."

During World War II he was captured at Corregidor and was a Japanese prisoner of war for 34 months, subsequently becoming paralyzed. John was a recipient of the Silver Star and promoted to a full colonel, all by the age of 30.

John captained a wheelchair basketball team after the war and was once again a leading figure in sporting news, termed "Spider", "Demon on Wheels" and "The Accurate Shooting Colonel Winterholler."

His Alma Mater, UW, called him home to Laramie for "Johnnie Winterholler Day" October 31, 1964. John's brief but poignant words of award acceptance were followed by thunderous applause, as John seemed to all to represent that flag of liberation, "The Stars and Stripes", "Old Glory."

M West Agency Real Estate

250 Nevada Ave. in Lovell. 548-7468 or 548-7404, fax 548-6988

Broker Dick Gifford offers over 20 years of real estate experience and is licensed in Wyoming and Montana. The professional service his staff at West Real Estate offers, covers Big Horn and Park Counties, as well as southern Montana. They can help you with a new home, farm and ranch properties, business investments, and recreational properties. Let them help you find that dream property in the shadow of the Big Horn Mountains or a piece of ranch country in southern Montana. Call Dick at West Real Estate and let him help you make your dreams come true.

31 *Gas, Food, Lodging*

Cowley

Pop. 560, Elev. 3,976
Gas

Established in 1901, this little town was named in honor of Mathias F. Cowley, a Mormon apostle. He was an instrumental figure in the building of the Sidon Canal, which irrigates the area's farmland. In addition to agriculture, Cowley came to depend on natural gas for its livelihood.

T Cowley Pioneer Museum

Main Street in Cowley. 548-7700

Cowley recently finished renovating a 1910 Frontier stone building for use as its town hall and historical center. Established by Mormon emigrants, cowley has a population of 500, and the bucolic setting welcomes visitors to the Museum where items of local historical interest are displayed. The community celebrates has been celebrating the pioneer history the third week in July annually since 1907.

H The Big Horn Academy

In Cowley

The Latter-Day Saints have always believed in the importance of education. Wherever they have settled they made building of schools a first priority. The Mormons had hardly finished putting up their own log cabins when they started planning for their schools. They built a large stone grade school dedicated in 1909, then began construction of a high school building. It was to be church-supported and called The Bighorn Acadamy. The first classes of this academy-to-be met in the grade school building while construction proceeded.

Though the Mormon Church supplied the actual money required to build and equip the facility, by far the major portion of the project was accomplished with donated labor, expertise, aqnd machines which were quite primitive by modern standards. The building was completed in 1916.

Its program was essentially that of a high school although in the context of that time, it was thought of, almost, as a college. Students came to the Academy from a wide area to live and board, somewhat as students leave home today for higher education.

The Academy was operated as a church school until 1924 when its facilities and responsibilities were transferred to the Cowley School District thereafter known as the Cowley High School.

During its life as the Big Horn Academy 178 students graduated from the school.

H The Log Community Building

In Cowley

During the Great Depression, President Franklin D. Roosevelt began the Works Progress Administration (WPA) to help stimulate economic activity. In 1933, the Cowley town leaders sought help from the WPA to build a community hall. It was built from lodge pole logs, cut and hauled from the Pryor Mountains north of Cowley. The WPA furnished a grant to pay laborers wages of thirty cents per hour. No records remain to tell exactly how much was spent or how many local citizens donated time, horses, wagons, tools, or equipment, but it is estimated that nearly a hundred people worked on the project without compensation. The actual money spent was perhaps around $10,000. A group of workers from five to a dozen stayed with the operation from beginning to end.

Adolf Anderson, a man of very little formal education, became both the designer and superintendent. He obviously knew what he was doing. Although the exterior is quite conventional, the interior has almost a cathedral effect with its soaring, open trusswork built of 14 inch logs.

Through the years the building has been used for public meetings, church conferences, annual celebrations, family gatherings, class reunions, dances, political rallies, musicals, dramas, school athletics, and even prize fights.

32 *No services*

Deaver

Pop. 177, Elev. 4,105

Once a tent town on the Burlington Railroad, Deaver was named for D. Clem Deaver, a Burlington agent who was very interested in developing the Big Horn region.

H Deaver Reservoir

State Highway 114 two miles west of Deaver. 527-2175

The Deaver Reservoir is an equalizing, or regulating, reservoir which serves water to about 1,800 acres on the Frannie Division of the Shoshone Project. For 75 years, the reservoir provided the domestic water supply for the town of Deaver. Water is now transported to Deaver by the nearly 60-mile-long Shoshone Municipal Pipeline, which was constructed in 1991.

In addition to serving as a strategic part of the irrigation system, the Deaver Reservoir today is used as a family recreational area. Fishing, picnicking and bird watching are popular pastimes at this reservoir, which has developed through a cooperative effort of the Deaver Irrigation District, The Wyoming Game and Fish Department and the U.S. Bureau of Reclamation.

33 *No services*

Frannie

Pop. 180, Elev. 4,219

This town was named for a six-year-old girl, Frannie Morris, whose father received permission to open a post office on the Wyoming-Montana border. Frannie grew up to be in Buffalo Bill's Wild West Show.

34 *No services*

Elk Basin

Elk Basin has been an active oil field since 1915 and continues to be highly productive. Today the oilfields are just about all that you'll fnd here. A recent discovery at Elk Basin, believed to be devoid of fossils, lead to a new and very productive Late Cretaceous site.

35

T Medicine Wheel

Between Sheridan and Lovell on Highway 14A

Located near the top of a mountain in Wyoming is the Medicine Wheel, a large wheel measuring approximately 80 feet in diameter. In this area of intense beauty, game is plentiful and the hills are filled with life. From the Wheel a magnificent view of distant, high peaks and the vastness of the Big horn Basin can be seen below. The Wheel is somewhat isolated and lacks large stands of shrubbery, water or shelter. The trees and plants that thrive here are bent and beaten annually by mighty snows and winds that are ccommon at altitudes of 9,642 feet6 above sea level. There is solitude here, where the Medicine Wheel sits above timberline on Medicine Mountain. It is a sacred site, an historic site, and an archaeological site.

The Medicine Wheel was designated a National Historic Landmark in 1970. It was probably constructed between 1,200 and 1,700 A.D. An exact date has not been determined. It is approximately 245 feet in circumference with a central cairn, a small donut-shaped structure. From this central cairn 28 spokes radiate to the outer rim of the circle. Placed at varying intervals around the rim are six smaller cairns. Five of the peripheral cairns touch the outer rim. One is located approximately ten feet outside the circle. Of these six cairn, four face the center of the circle, one faces north and one faces east. The central cairn is much larger than the rest and measures 12' x 7'. Some of the cairns may have been covered with skins supported by wooden posts.

There are many legends and traditions which may explain the Wheel's origin. But there are no specific artifacts which determine exactly when or who constructed this unusual landmark. It is clear that this place has been visited by many people over the last few hundred years because of the well-traveled trail that parallels the current access road.

There are some who suggest the spoke-like structure resembles the "Sun Dance Lodge," or "Medicine Lodge". The Sun Dance Ceremony is a celebration which is part of the fabric of Native American culture and religion. Some researchers have also suggested the Medicine Wheel is an aboriginal astronomical observatory.

A contemporary Cheyenne cultural leader stated, "the tribes traditionally went and still go to the sacred mountain. The people sought the high mountain for prayer. They sought spiritual harmony with the powerful spirits there. Many offerings have always been left on this mountain. The center cairn, once occupied by a large buffalo skull, was a place to make prayer offerings. Vision questors would have offered prayers of thanks for plant and animal life that had and would, sustain them in the future. Prayers of thanks were offered for all of creation. Prayers are made for families and for loved ones who are ill. Atonements are made for any offense to Mother Earth. When asking for guidance, prayers for wisdom and strength are always part of this ritual. All of this is done so that spiritual harmony will be our constant companion throughout the year."

A Crow Chief stated that Medicine Wheel was built "before the light came." Other Crow stories say the Sun God dropped it from the sky. And still others say it was built by the "Sheepeaters," a Shoshonean band whose name is derived from their expertise at hunting mountain sheep. Many Crow feel it is a guide for building tipis. Some explain the Wheel was built by "people without iron." At present there are no concrete answers as to who actually constructed this landmark.

One Crow speaks of a man named Scarface. He was handsome and was fond of strutting in his finery before young women. One day while entering his mother's tipi, he fell into the fire which severly burned his face and was thereafter embarrassed to be seen. Shamed at his appearance he left his people and went to live in the mountains. Scarface lived alone for many years. One day while a young woman and her grandmother were hunting berries, they became sparated from their people and couldn't find their way back. They traveled along a trail which took them into the mountains. They occasionally saw Scarface and one day made contact with him. Scarface later married the youngest woman. On their travels back to his people, Scarface supposedly built the Medicine Wheel as their shelter. On the second day he built another tipi near the Big Horn River in the valley below. The tipi rings are believed to still exist.

It is also said that Red Plume, a great Crow Chief during the time of Lewis and Clark, found great spiritual medicine at the Medicine Wheel. The legend states that following four days without food or water, Red Plume was visited by little people who inhabited the passage to the Wheel. They took him into the earth where they lived and told him that the red eagle was his powerful medicine guide and protector. He was told to always wear the small feather from the back of the eagle above its tail feathers. Thus Red Plume received his name. Upon his deathbed, he told his people his spirit would live at the Wheel and that they might communicate with him there.

You can do your part to protect the Medicine Wheel. Do not disturb or remove any cultural resources within or around the historic site. Respect the privacy of others at the Wheel. Do not remove the sacred prayer offerings left by Native Americans.

The Medicine Wheel and Medicine Mountain reflect 10,000 years of Native American culture. The site is sacred and revered by Indian people. It is important that the Medicine Wheel be treated with the utmost respect given any holy place. The site is protected by Federal Laws such as the Antiquities Act (1906), Historic Sites Act (1935), the National Historic Preservation Act (1966), The Archaeological Resources Protection Act (1978). Since 1993 the road which leads to the Wheel has been closed to vehicular traffic. A one and one-half mile foot trail now leads to the summit.

Reprinted from U.S. Forest Service brochure.

H Medicine Wheel

U.S. Highway 14A 22 miles west of Burgess Junction

The builders and purpose of the Medicine Wheel are unknown. It is currently thought that it was religious in nature, or it may have had astronomical implications, or both. It is constructed of stones laid side by side, forming an almost perfect circle 74 feet in diameter with 28 spokes. An associated radio-carbon date is about 1760. Crow Indian legend says that when they came, the wheel was there. They migrated to the Big Horn Basin around 1776.

Modern Indians use the Medicine Wheel for religious ceremonies. At times, flags, or offerings are left about the wheel, signifying that a ceremony has taken place. The Forest Service does not interfere with these ceremonies, so please do not destroy, or remove the objects. As part of their ceremonial activities the Indians may build an open fire and you may see evidence of this. However, open fires by the general public are prohibited.

The Medicine Wheel is designated a National Historic Landmark, which means it has national significance. It is not only the responsi-

Ten Sleep Canyon.

Sheep Mountain just north of Greybull.

bility of the Government to protect this national landmark but also every American.

Scenic Drives

Big Horn Scenic Byway

This is the middle route across the Bighorn National Forest in the Big Horn Mountains. The official 47-mile stretch of US 14 shares its western boundary with the forest. From the west, the route begins around four miles from the town of Shell. At Burgess Junction, the Big Horn Scenic Byway meets the Medicine Wheel Scenic Byway (US 14A). The eastern boundary of the Scenic Byway is 6.5 miles west of the town of Dayton.

The two lane highway can close for short periods of time due to heavy snows during winter or early spring, but summer an fall travel are normally not interrupted by inclement weather. Granite Pass, at 9033 feet, marks the apex of this scenic route that has switchbacks through a canyon on the western side and descends more gradually on the eastern slope of the mountains.
Reprinted from Wyoming Department of Transportation Brochure

Medicine Wheel Passage

This byway is the northern-most route across the Bighorn National Forest in the Big Horn Mountains. The 27 miles of this section of highway constitute nearly the entire length of US 14A, ending at the western edge of the Bighorn National Forest. Just to the west of the boundary are the Bighorn Canyon National Recreation Area and the nearby town of Lovell. On the east end is Burgess Junction, where the Scenic Byway merges with US 14 and becomes the Bighorn Scenic Byway. The Gown of Dayton provides access to the route from the east.

This two lane paved highway follows one of the highest routes in the state. The steep, winding road sports numerous truck turnoffs and a maximum 10-percent grade. Heavy snow keeps the road closed in winter and early spring, so summer and fall are the only practical seasons to make this trip.

A high point (literally) along th route is the 9430-foot view looking southwesterly into the Big Horn Basin, thousands of feet below. Mountain peaks tower above 13,000 feet in this high-altitude neighborhood. The rapid change in elevation along the Byway provides a variety of habitat types. During the summer, deer and an occasional elk can be viewed feeding at the edge of timber stands. Blue grouse, with their young, are found near the many springs on the forested area. Mourning doves are also common near water.
Reprinted from Wyoming Department of Transportation Brochure

Red Gulch/Alkali Scenic Backway

This 32-mile route through a mostly unraveled section of th Big Horn Basin traces two road of historic importance to Native American and frontier history: Alkali Road (CR 1111) and Red Gulch Road (BLM 1109). This country has been inhabited since Paleo-Indians first hunted mammoth here, 12, 000 years ago. In more recent times, the late 1800s and early 1900s, sheepherders built rock cairns here to provide landmarks and kill time while they watched the sheep.

Depending on weather conditions, driving this byway is not recommended from November through April. Even light precipitation can cause muddy, impassable conditions. In dry conditions, a high-clearance, two wheel drive vehicle, can manage without much difficulty. The road can be bumpy and rutted in places, so large vehicles, trailers, campers, and RV's may want to avoid this route. Road grades do not exceed seven percent.

Travelers should allow at least one hour to make this drive. Frequent stops to enjoy the scenery can extend the trip into a day's adventure or more. There are no towns, stores, gas stations, or telephones along the way. Some services are available in Shell and Tensleep, and more can be found in Greybull.
Reprinted from Wyoming Department of Transportation Brochure

Hikes

Crystal Creek Ridge

Distance: 1 mile
Climb: gentle
Rating: easy
Usage: light
Location: Take Alternate Hwy. 14 west from Burgess Junction, turning south on FDR 122, across from the Medicine Wheel Road. Follow this road for about 1.5 miles to where it intersects FDR 132. Turn right here, and take the road to its end.

This is an easy stroll of a hike with views of the badlands, the Bighorn Basin, and the Absaroka Mountains.

Porcupine Falls

Distance: 1 mile
Climb: 400 feet
Rating: difficult
Usage: light
Location: Take Alternate Hwy. 14 west from Burgess Junction to FDR 14 (Devil Canyon Rd.). Take this for 3 miles, continuing past the junction with FDR 11for another 5.7 miles. Here, the road meets up with FDR 146, which will take you to the trailhead.

This trail follows an old mining road, which climbs steeply up the canyon towards the 200 foot-high falls. A deserted mining camp is situated near the falls, across Porcupine Creek. Please respect it as a historic site and do not take souvenirs.

Bucking Mule Falls

Distance: 5.2 miles
Climb: about 300 feet
Rating: easy
Usage: light
Location: Take Alternate Hwy. 14 west from Burgess Junction to FDR 14 (Devil Canyon Rd.). Take this for 3 miles, bearing left at the junction with FDR 11. Follow this road 8 miles to the trailhead.

This is a vigorous day hike to the top of the 500 foot-high falls and back. Hikers interested in a longer hike can follow the rough trail another 8 miles along Porcupine Creek, to camp overnight at Porcupine Creek Bridge or Tillets Hole. The first portion of the trip, to the falls, descends to Big Teepee Creek, passes a junction then climbs to the overlook. Return to the junction for the overnight trek, following the less-worn path across a bridge and along the ridge of Railroad Springs Creek. Turn left at the junction with Mexican Hill Trails, heading south to Devil Canyon. Keep following the path through the valley until it turns west into Tillets Hole. Stay on the Bucking Mule Trail until it reaches a stock bridge across Porcupine Creek. Beyond this it connects with the Long Park Creek Trail, then continues to another bridge across the creek. The trail ends at FDR 137.

Lodge Grass Creek

Distance: 9.3 miles
Climb: 3350 (descent)
Rating: difficult
Usage: very light
Location: Take Alternate Hwy. 14 west from Burgess Junction to FDR 14 (Devil Canyon Rd.). Take this for 3 miles, turning right on FDR 11, and taking the steep road (no trailers or RVs) 6.7 miles to FDR 110. Turn left, staying on FDR 11, and continue to the trailhead.

A still-active stock trail, this route takes you along the creek across grassy terrain, surrounded by rocky cliffs lined with evergreens. An abrupt descent takes you past an old cabin, then follows the stream down to a meadow. You must pass through a gate at the top of the ridge, then cross a small stream before continuing along the creek to a boulder field. After going through another fence gate, the valley opens up to afford views of unusual glacial rock remnants, and the scars of a fire that swept the area in 1970. The trail continues on to a woodland area which is good for camping. For those who wish to travel a little farther, the trail terminates at the fenced Montana state line, where the Crow Reservation begins.

Cottonwood Canyon
Distance: 2.5 miles, one way
Climb: 1700 feet
Rating: difficult
Usage: light
Location: Take Alternate Hwy. 14 east from Lovell across Bighorn Lake, then turn left (north) on John Blue Road. Immediately make a right onto a little-used road which will take you about 6 miles to Cottonwood Canyon. Park near the gravel pits.

This trail follows a jeep road into the canyon, which broadens into an amphitheater and an overlook of Melody Falls. The road turns into a stock trail as the canyon narrows, and passes a number of smaller falls as it climbs steeply along the creek. The canyon turns north, and eventually fades into uncertain paths, indicating a return along the route you just traveled.

Rainbow Canyon
Distance: 4. 8 miles, one way
Climb: 60 feet
Rating: moderate
Usage: light
Location: Take Alternate Hwy. 14 east from Lovell across Bighorn Lake to the turnoff for Five Springs Campground. Take a right (south) onto the road across the highway, taking the right fork after about 100 yards and continuing to the parking area at the end of the road.

This hike travels through a colorful canyon towards the badlands west of the Bighorn Mountains. It begins along a jeep road that descends along a gulch, then takes you along Five Springs Creek and on into the canyon. Leave the road where it diverges into a deeply cut gully which follows the rim of the canyon for a while, then descends to the floor of the wash. Eventually, the canyon will diminish in height, and the stream bed will empty into Black Gulch, a barren valley which makes a good turn-around point. This hike can be very hot and dry, so bring lots of water.

Horse Creek Canyons
Distance: 11. 5 miles
Climb: 3900 feet
Rating: difficult
Usage: light
Location: Take Hwy. 14 south from Burgess Junction to FDR 10, north of Granite Pass. Go 12.6 miles to FDR 207 (Sunlight Mesa Rd.) and turn left (south), then bear left again at the first junction, heading towards Horse Creek Cow Camp Cabin. This is a rough road, and high clearance, 4WD vehicles are recommended. Continue past the cabin, bearing right, and then left onto FDR 208. Another mile will take you to Deer Spring and the trailhead.

This loop trail can be completed in a day by vigorous hikers. The trail emerges about 1.6 miles north of the starting point on FDR 207. It's best to take the loop in a clockwise direction, as finding the route can be difficult when approached in the opposite direction. Begin at the aspen grove that marks Deer Spring. Follow the faint trail to the dry fork of Horse Creek, a stay on the stock trail to the south of the meadow. The trail emerges onto an old road, which lads into a draw heading for the dry creek bed. As the trail fades, continue along the draw past a small spring, and on to Dry Fork. Here you can pick up a washed out path heading east as it meanders back and forth across the streambed. As the canyon walls rise and recede, continue following the north bank until a jeep track descends to the confluence with Horse Creek.

Follow another jeep track along the south bank of Horse Creek and up into the water filled canyon. Cross the stream and head northeast, climbing towards Horse Creek Mesa. Continue past the East and West Fork Confluence, keeping to the south along the East Fork. A climb out of the valley and across a burn area will take you past a natural arch and into Torry Gulch. Stay right until cattle trails take you across a meadow to FDR 207.

**(The Shell Canyon trails require an extra dose of caution because the area is known for its abundance of rattlesnakes. Please beware.)*

The Beef Trail*
Distance: 5.9 miles, one way
Climb: 1940 feet (descent)
Rating: moderate/ difficult
Usage: light
Location: From Greybull, take Hwy. 14 east, beyond Shell, to mile marker 27.6. Turn north here onto FDR 264, which is a rough road, and high clearance, 4WD vehicles are recommended. Take this about 2 miles to Brindle Creek, where the trail begins. The trail ends on Hwy. 14, at mile marker 20.6, where there is a pullout and a bridge.

Lovely views of Shell Canyon are the best part of this hike, as well as glimpses of Elephant Head Rock, Copmans Tomb, and Pyramid Mountain. Still an active stock trail, hikers may encounter cattle if they take this route in midsummer or early fall. Where the road forks, continue on the main trail towards the boulders. Follow this into the valley, where the trail climbs and then descends towards Cedar Creek, crossing Fender Creek along the way. A bridge across Cedar Creek offers a beautiful prospect of the chasm. Beyond the bridge, stay on the clearest stock trail until you cross Cottonwood Creek. Follow the trail towards Sunlight Mesa, where the trail skirts the edge of Shell Creek. A final descent to this creek's bottoms concludes the hike.

Cedar Creek*
Distance: 4 miles, one way
Climb: 1100 feet
Rating: difficult
Usage: light
Location: From Greybull, take Hwy. 14 east, beyond Shell, to mile marker 27.6. Turn north here onto FDR 264, which is a rough road, and high clearance, 4WD vehicles are recommended. Take this about 2 miles to Brindle Creek, where the trail begins.

This trail has many of the same views as the Beef Trail. Where the Beef Trail splits near Brindle Creek, take the right fork towards the northwest, where you will eventually pass a pond. Beyond this are vistas which include Sunlight Mesa, Elephant Head, and Copman's Tomb. Farther along the trail, you will climb through the trees and over some grasslands to Fender Creek. Continue on across the ridge of Copman's Tomb to a meadow where you can take in the grandeur of the mountains all around. After dropping below the meadow, the trail heads towards Cedar Creek, where it climbs down to the bottoms and terminates in the canyon.

The Bench Trail*
Distance: 10 miles
Climb: 3140 descent
Rating: moderate/ difficult
Usage: light
Location: From Greybull, take Hwy. 14 east, beyond Shell, to mile marker 31.3. Turn south onto FDR 17, taking this 2.8 miles to the Ranger Creek Campground. At the campground, take the first left to arrive at the trailhead. The end of the trail will be at mile marker 22.8 on Hwy. 14, by Post Creek.

Although this trail also passes through Shell Canyon, there are fewer opportunities to view the surrounding area through the trees. On the other hand, the trees provide much-appreciated shade along the way. This trail is especially popular for mountain bikers, so be alert. Follow the trail into the forest below the old road, past the junction and through the aspens. Look for the sign here about Rocky Mountain Irises. Follow the trail down into the valley, where it steeply drops towards Granite Creek. Along the way, you'll see some unusual destruction of the woodlands, wrought by a freak tornado in 1959. Another sign explains sheep ranching traditions of the late 1800s. After passing through more trees, the trail comes across an area burned by fire in 1984, a result of illegal fireworks. Re-growth is underway, and a variety of plants and wildlife still abound here. The burn area also provides the best views of the surrounding mountains and rock formation. Continue along the trail across some grassland until it drops down to the highway, near Post Creek.

Meyers Spring Draw
Distance: 2.5 miles
Climb: 400 feet
Rating: easy/ moderate
Usage: light
Location: From Greybull, take Hwy. 789 south about 20 miles, turning east (left) onto Hwy. 31, at Manderson. After about 22 miles, right before Hyatteville, turn north (left) onto Alkali/ Cold Springs Road, which turns to dirt quickly, then takes you about 8 miles to Alkali Flats and over a small ridge. Park just beyond the jeep road.

This badlands hike takes you through an unusual collection of scenic oddities. Starting at the jeep road, follow it along the edge of the ridge until it encounters a game trail leading down into the basin. Pass through the burnt brush, following the streambed past the first mesa. Around the mesa, you will see a gap in the cliffs to the southeast. Head towards the gap, which will take you to the draw. The draw itself passes through more burnt scrub surrounded by intriguing rock formations. You'll encounter another jeep road along the way, which will take you over a saddle to a jeep crossroads. Follow the jeep trail that heads west, going back to the esarpment a little less than a mile from where you began. Follow the ridge again back to the starting point.

Dry Medicine Lodge Creek Canyon
Distance: 5.6 miles, one way
Climb: 1730 feet
Rating: difficult
Usage: light
Location: From Greybull, take Hwy. 789 south about 20 miles, turning east (left) onto Hwy. 31, at Manderson. After about 22 miles, right before Hyatteville, turn south (right) onto Alkali/ Cold Springs Road. Take a right onto Cold Springs Road, following

the signs for the Medicine Lodge Archeological Site. After reaching the site, go north on the jeep road that heads into the canyon for 3 miles. Park where the road climbs out of the canyon.

This hike takes you past some truly remarkable rock formations, including a natural arch and some spires. The trail begins by following an old road that is sometimes blocked by rock fall and thorny brush, but its still rather easily negotiated. As the road leads you through some trees, the walls climb around you and shortly you'll arrive at the arch over the dry streambed. Here, the canyon merges with Sheep Creek Canyon, and several spires mark the confluence. Beyond this the trail becomes a little more challenging, and the creek is above ground, so a few minor crossings will come your way. The canyon eventually dissolves into the trees and a grassy meadow, then broadens as the trail ends at an old cabin below Spanish Point.

Medicine Lodge Canyon

Distance: 6.4 miles
Climb: 2850 feet (descent)
Rating: difficult
Usage: light
Location: From Greybull, take Hwy. 789 south about 20 miles, turning east (left) onto Hwy. 31, at Manderson. After about 22 miles, right before Hyatteville, turn north (left) onto Alkali/ Cold Springs Road, which turns to dirt quickly, then takes you about 9.6 miles to Alkali Flats and over a small ridge, and past a jeep road. Just before the road turns south, another jeep road marks the trail's beginning. The trail ends at Dry Medicine Lodge Road, off Cold Springs Road, by the Pictograph Site,

This area has been designated a Wilderness Study Area by the BLM, so it is likely you will see wildlife along the way. The jeep road will take you down to Captain Jack Creek, and turns into a stock trail that drops rather precipitously to the valley floor. The scenery makes the struggle through the scrub worthwhile. High colorful canyon walls soon surround you and the creek emerges from its underground course. Stick to the trails, as the creek area can be a tangle of vegetation. The canyon eventually diminishes and the trail becomes more grassy. As the canyon turns to the south, a rounded gap affords passage through the west side of the walls and into the Dry Medicine Lodge Creek Canyon. The canyon floor leads you to a jeep road which then takes you to the Pictograph Site.

The Paint Rock Badlands

Distance: 2.7 miles
Climb: 500 feet
Rating: easy/ moderate
Usage: light
Location: From Greybull, take Hwy. 789 south about 20 miles, turning east (left) onto Hwy. 31, at Manderson. After about 22 miles, right before Hyatteville, turn north (left) onto Alkali/ Cold Springs Road, which turns to dirt quickly. Follow the road about 15 miles, past the Paint Rock Canyon Trailhead, and park here.

Some of the area's most distinctive and colorful rock formations can be seen on this hike. The soil here is extremely delicate, however, so please walk only on exposed rock and established trails. From the trailhead, follow a game trail over a rim to the south. Follow the rim, past mushroom shaped pedestals, and into a gulch carved with hoodoos. As the cliffs rise around you, head northwest past more mushrooms and into a cleft of solid sandstone. After then turning northeast, the trail crosses some sandhills and heads into another gulch, climbing the ridge to a view of more mushrooms. Stay west as you reach another hoodoo which will take you to an ATV track at the base of a red butte. A nearby formation can be climbed easily to take in the colorful landscape. Continue along the ATV track over a saddle, to climb back to Cold Springs Road about a half mile from where you began.

Paint Rock Canyon

Distance: 12.8 miles, one way
Climb: 2570 feet
Rating: Difficult
Usage: light
Location: From Greybull, take Hwy. 789 south about 20 miles, turning east (left) onto Hwy. 31, at Manderson. After about 22 miles, right before Hyatteville, turn north (left) onto Alkali/ Cold Springs Road, which turns to dirt quickly. Follow the road about 15 miles, past the Paint Rock Canyon Trailhead, and park here.

A more extensive hike for overnight, this trip will take you to the Bighorn National Forest by way of a blue-ribbon trout stream. It passes over private land (the Hyatt Ranch) so be considerate, stay on the trails, and close all the gates behind you. The trail heads across an area of burnt scrub, heading southwest towards a draw and across it. Soon you will encounter the abundant vegetation surrounding Paint Rock Creek. Beyond this is the ranch's land, and a dirt road takes you past some pastures towards the canyon, and back onto public land. Follow the creek through a bend in the canyon, where a natural arch graces the north rim. The trail then climbs up to the Island, a large butte overlooking a basin, then passes through a gate to descend back to towards the creek. The creek then splits, and a bridge passes over the main fork. After passing over a swampy area and a meadow, the trail emerges from the canyon and passes below a tree covered mesa. Here it turns into an ATV trail and heads towards the Bighorn National Forest. The creek again splits, and another bridge provides a crossing. A final climb takes you to where the trail emerges onto FDR 349.

Information Please

Tourism Information

Basin Chamber of Commerce	568-3371
Cody Country Visitor's Council	587-2297
East Yellowstone Chamber of Commerce	527-9959
Chamber of Commerce - Greybull	765-2100
Bighorn Canyon Visitor's Center	548-2251
Powell Valley Chamber of Commerce	754-3494
Thermopolis Hot Springs Chamber of Commerce	864-3192
Chamber of Commerce - Worland	347-3226

Government

BLM Worland Field Office	347-5100
BLM Cody Field Office	578-5900
Shoshone National Forest	527-6241
Shoshone National Forest - Wapiti/Clarks Fork/Greybull Ranger Districts	527-6241

Car Rentals

Budget Rent A Car • Cody	587-6066
Hertz • Cody	587-2914
Rent A Wreck • Cody	527-5549
Thrifty • Cody	587-8855
Rent A Wreck • Thermopolis	864-5571

Hospitals

Hot Springs County Memorial Hospital • Thermopolis	864-3121
North Big Horn Hospital • Lovell	548-2771
Powell Hospital • Powell	754-2267
Washakie Medical Center • Worland	347-3221
West Park Hospital • Cody	527-7501

Airports

Thermopolis	864-2488
Greybull	765-7600
Cody	587-9740

Golf

Midway Golf Club • Basin	568-2255
Powell Country Club • Powell	754-7259
Foster Gulch Golf Club • Lovell	548-2445
Olive Glenn Golf & Country Club • Cody	587-5551
Green Hills Municipal Golf Course • Worland	347-8972

Ski Areas

Big Horn Mountain Ski Lodge	366-2600
Sleeping Giant Ski Area	587-4044

Guest Ranches

Bear Creek Ranch • Shell	765-9319
Bighorn Rodeo Ranch •	762-3535
Wayfaring Traveler Ranch • Burlington	762-3536
Rimrock Ranch • Cody	587-3970
DNR Ranch at Rand Creek • Cody	587-7176
Hunter Peak Ranch • Cody	587-3711
Beteche Creek Ranch • Cody	587-3844
Blackwater Lodge • Cody	587-5201
Bill Cody Ranch • Cody	587-6271
Red Pole Ranch & Motel • Cody	587-5929
Absaroka Mountain Lodge • Cody	587-3963
Schively Ranch • Cody	548-6688
Seven D Ranch • Cody	587-9885
Double Diamond X Ranch • Cody	527-6276
Mooncrest Ranch • Cody	587-3620
K Bar Z Guest Ranch And Outfitters • Cody	587-4410
Early Ranch Bed & Breakfast • Crowheart	455-4055
High Island Guest Ranch • Hamilton Dome	867-2374
Paintrock Ranch • Hyattville	626-2161
Wood River Lodg • Meeteetse	868-9211
Ranch at Meeteetse • Meeteetse	868-9266
Snowflake Ranch • Powell	754-5892
The Hideout at Flitner Ranch • Shell	765-2080
Ranger Creek Guest Ranch • Shell	751-7787
Bilbrey Guest Ranch • Shell	765-9319
Kedesh Guest Ranch • Shell	765-2791
Shell Creek Guest Ranch • Shell	765-2420
Ranger Creek Guest Ranch • Shell	751-7787
Deer Haven Lodge • Ten Sleep	366-2449
Meadowlark Lake Lodge • Ten Sleep	366-2449
Big Horn River Ranch • Thermopolis	864-4224
Sanford Ranches • Thermopolis	864-3575
Paintrock Outfitters • Greybull	765-2556

Lodges and Resorts

Buffalo Bill Village Resort • Cody	587-5556
Holiday Inn Buffalo Bill Village Resort • Cody	587-5555
Snowshoe Lodge • Shell	899-8995
Wagon Wheel Lodge •	765-2561
Elephant Head Lodge • Cody	587-3980
Pahaska Tepee • Cody	527-7701
Goff Creek Lodge • Cody	587-3753
Wyoming High Country Resort •	

Lovell 548-9659
Big Horn Mountain Resorts • Ten Sleep 366-2424
Big Horn Mountain Ski Lodge • Ten Sleep 366-2600
Deer Haven Lodge • Ten Sleep 366-2449
Meadowlark Lake Lodge • Ten Sleep 366-2449

Vacation Houses, Cabins & Condos

Cody Guest Houses & The Victorian House Bed & Breakfast • Cody 587-6000
Cody Vacation Properties AKA Grandma's House - Lockhart Bed & Breakfast Inn • Cody 587-6074
Cabins by the Creek • 587-6074
Cozy Cody Cottages • 587-9253
Rustler's Roost • Cody 587-8171
Trapper's Rest Bed & Breakfast and Guest Cabins • Shell 765-9239
Herzberg Hideaway • Worland 347-2217
Ten Broek Campground RV Park • Ten Sleep 366-2250

Bed and Breakfasts

Robin's Nest Bed & Breakfast • Cody 527-7208
Cody Guest Houses & The Victorian House Bed & Breakfast • Cody 587-6000
Cody Vacation Properties AKA Grandma's House - Lockhart Bed & Breakfast Inn • Cody 587-6074
C's Bed & Breakfast • Worland 347-9388
Angel's Keep • Cody 587-6205
The Mayor's Inn • Cody 587-0887
Shoshone Lodge • Cody 587-4044
Trapper's Rest Bed & Breakfast • Shell 765-9239
Lambright Place • Cody 527-5310
Heart to Heart Bed & Breakfast • Cody 587-2906
Casual Cove Bed & Breakfast • Cody 587-3622
Cody Victorian House • Cody 587-5000
Greybull Hotel • Greybull 765-2012
Horned Toad Bed & Breakfast • Ten Sleep 366-2747
Harmony Ranch Cottage • Manderson 568-2514
Early Ranch Bed & Breakfast • Crowheart 455-4055
4-Bears Outfitters • Powell 645-3375
Taylored Tours • Ten Sleep 366-2250

Outfitters and Guides

North Fork Anglers F 527-7274
Red Canyon River Trips & Wild Mustang Tours RG 587-6988
Double Diamond Outfitters H 868-9211
Wyoming River Trips R 587-6661
Wyoming Adventures F 864-2407
Wind River Canyon Whitewater R 864-9343
Bill Cody Ranch H 587-6271
Gary Fales Outfitting H 587-3970
Triple Creek Outfitters H 587-6178
Horseworks Wyoming E 867-2367
Hot Springs Outfitting H 864-2417
LZ Ranch Horseback Tours EG 867-2367
Outlaw Trail, Inc G 864-2287
Renegade Rides Inc. HE 366-2689
Deer Haven Lodge HFE 366-2449
Meadowlark Lake Lodge FGE 366-2449
Geoscience Adventures, Inc G 765-2259
Goff Creek Lodge FEG 587-3753
Cresent B Outfitters FHE 587-6937
Paintrock Adventures FH 469-2274
Grub Steak Expeditions 5276316
Mooncrest Ranch FHE 587-3620
River Runners, Inc. R 527-7238
Idgie Poo Outfitters FGE 486-2261
4-Bears Outfitters H 645-3375
Frontier Outfitting H 754-7156
Taylored Tours G 366-2250
Shoshone River Outfitters H 548-7069
Wyoming High Country EG 548-2301
Big Horn Mountain Adventures H 765-2420
Big Horn Outfitters 899-1858
Bliss Creek Outfitters FHRE 527-6103
Butte Creek Outfitters H 587-6016
Coy's Yellow Creek Outfitting H 587-6944
Diamond Tail Outfitters H 765-2905
Elk Mountain Outfitters FHE 587-8238
Fish Hawk Creek Outfitters H 754-749
Flying H Ranch & Outfitters HFE 587-2089
Grassy Lake Outfitters H 527-5494
Grizzly Ranch HF 587-3966
Ishawooa Outfitters HFE 587-9250
Johnson Outfitting HFE 587-4072
K Bar Z Guest Ranch Outfitters HFE 587-4410
Lee Livingston Outfitting HFE 527-7415
Lost Creek Outfitters FHE 527-6251
Majo Ranch H 587-2051
Morning Creek Outfitting H 587-5343
Pennoyer Outfitting H 867-2407
Sheep Mesa Outfitters FHE 587-4305
Two Diamond Outfitters H 587-3753

Notes:

Dining Quick Reference

Price Range refers to the average cost of a meal per person: ($) $1-$6, ($$) $7-$11, ($$$) $12-up. Cocktails: "Yes" indicates full bar; Beer (B)/Wine (W), Service: Breakfast (B), Brunch (BR), Lunch (L), Dinner (D). Businesses in bold print will have additional information under the appropriate map locator number in the body of this section.

MAP#	RESTAURANT	TYPE CUISINE	PRICE RANGE	CHILD MENU	COCKTAILS BEER WINE	MEALS SERVED	CREDIT CARDS ACCEPTED
2	**The Noon Break**	New Mexican	$	Yes		B/L	
2	**Sunset House Restaurant**	Family	$$	Yes	Yes	B/L/D	
2	**QT's Restaurant**	American	$$	Yes	Yes	B/L/D	Major
2	**The Irma Hotel, Restaurant & Saloon**	Family	$$$/$$	Yes	Yes	B/L/D	Major
2	Pizza on the Run	Pizza	$$			L/D	Major
2	Beta Coffeehouse	Coffee Shop	$	Yes		B/L	
2	Black Sheep Restaurant & Gibs Sports Pub	American	$$$	Yes	Yes	L/D	Major
2	Breadboard	Sandwiches	$	Yes		L/D	Major
2	Cody Coffee Company & Eatery	American	$$			L/B	
2	New Dragon Wall	Chinese	$$	No		L/D	Major
2	Gardens/Mack Brother's Brew. Co.	Mediterranean	$$	Yes	B	L/D	Major
2	Granny's Restaurant	Family	$/$$	Yes		D/L/B	
2	Maxwell's Fine Food & Spirits	Italian	$$/$$$	Yes	Yes	L/D	Major
2	Mustard's Last Stand	Fast Food	$	Yes		L/D	
2	Zapata's Mexican Restaurant	Mexican	$$		Yes	L/D	Major
2	Wendy's	Fast Food	$	Yes		L/D	Major
2	Stefan's Restaurant	Fine Dining	$$$/$$	No	Yes	L/D	Major
2	Peter's Café & Bakery	Sandwiches	$$			B/L/D	
2	The Proud Cut Saloon	Western		No	Yes	L/D	Major
2	Papa Murphy's Take & Bake Restaurant	Pizza	$$			L/D	Major
2	Tommy Jack's Cajun Grill	Steakhouse	$$$		Yes	D/L	Major
2	Dairy Queen	Fast Food	$	Yes		L/D	
2	Domino's Pizza	Pizza	$$	No		L/D	Major
2	Subway	Sandwiches	$	Yes		B/L/D	M/V
2	Taco John's	Fast Food	$	Yes		L/D	
2	Pahaska Tepee Restuarant	Fine Dining	$$$/$$	Yes	Yes	L/D	Major
2	Annie Oakley's Cowgirl Café	Family		Yes		D/L	Major
2	Trail Shop Inn & Café	Family	$$	Yes	Yes	L/D/B	Major
2	Yellowstone Valley Inn	Homestyle	$$	Yes	Yes	B/L/D	Major
2	Main Street Ice Cream	Ice Cream/	$	Yes		D/L	
2	Hong Kong Chinese Restaurant	Chinese		Yes		L/D	V/M
2	La Comida Mexican Restaurant	Mexican	$$	Yes	Yes	L/D	M/V
2	Daylight Donuts	Coffee Shop	$			L/B	
3	Bubba's Bar-B-Que	Barbeque	$$			L/D/B	Major
3	McDonald's	Fast Food		Yes		B/L/D	Major
3	Royal Palace Restaurant	Family	$$	Yes		B/L/D	Major
3	Pizza Hut	Pizza	$$	Yes	B	L/D	Major
3	Our Place	Homestyle	$$	Yes		B/L/D	
3	Bill Cody Ranch Restaurant	Family	$$$	Yes	Yes	B/D	Major
4	**Cassie's Supper Club & Dance Hall**	Steakhouse	$$/$$$	Yes	Yes	L/D	Major
4	Quizno's	Sandwiches	$	Yes		D/L	Major
4	Burger King	Fast Food	$	Yes		B/L/D	M/V
4	Subway	Sandwiches	$	Yes		B/L/D	M/V
4	Taco Bell/KFC	Fast Food	$	Yes		L/D	
4	Crosswinds Café	Family	$$			B/L/D	M/V
4	Taco Bell/KFC	Fast Food	$	Yes		L/D	
8	**Broken Spoke Café & Shirley's Pies**	Family	$$	No	Yes	B/L/D	Major
8	Elkhorn Bar & Grill	American	$$	No	Yes	L/D	M/V
8	Outlaw Parlor Café	American	$$	No	Yes	L/D	M/V
8	Lucille's Café	Family	$$	Yes		B/L/D	
10	**Las Fuentes Restaurant**	North Mexico	$$	Yes	Yes	D/L	Major
10	Granny's Bakery, Ice Cream & Grill	Sandwiches	$	Yes		B/L/D	
10	Sideboard Restaurant	Family	$	Yes		B/L/D	Major
10	Pumper Nick's	American	$$	Yes	Yes	B/L/D	Major
10	Safari Lounge & Restaurant	Family	$$	Yes	Yes	B/L/D	Major
10	Manhattan Café	Eclectic	$$/$$$	Yes	Yes	B/D/L	Major
10	Coyote Coffee Co.	Coffee Shop	$	Yes		L/B	M/V
10	Dairyland	Family	$$	Yes		L/D	
11	**Ballyhoo Restaurant**	Steak & Seafood	$$$/$$	Yes	Yes	D	Major
11	Subway	Sandwiches	$	Yes		B/L/D	M/V

Dining Quick Reference-Continued

Price Range refers to the average cost of a meal per person: ($) $1-$6, ($$) $7-$11, ($$$) $12-up. Cocktails: "Yes" indicates full bar; Beer (B)/Wine (W), Service: Breakfast (B), Brunch (BR), Lunch (L), Dinner (D). Businesses in bold print will have additional information under the appropriate map locator number in the body of this section.

MAP#	RESTAURANT	TYPE CUISINE	PRICE RANGE	CHILD MENU	COCKTAILS BEER WINE	MEALS SERVED	CREDIT CARDS ACCEPTED
11	A&W	Fast Food	$	Yes		L/D	
11	McDonald's	Fast Food	$	Yes		L/D/B	
11	Lil's Wrangler Restaurant	Family	$$	No		B/L/D	V/M
11	Pizza Hut	Pizza	$$	Yes	B	L/D	Major
13	**Butch's Place Restaurant**	Steak & Burgers	$$		Yes	D	M/V
14	**The Ram's Horn Café**	American	$$	Yes	Yes	B/L/D	Major
14	Ranchito Restaurant	Mexican	$$	Yes		D/L/B	D
14	China Garden	Chinese	$$	No		L/D	M/V
14	C&D Bowling Alley Snack Shop	Fast food	$		B	L/D	
15	A&W	Fast Food	$	Yes		L/D	
15	Subway	Sandwiches	$	Yes		L/D/B	M/V
15	Taco John's	Fast Food	$	Yes		L/D	
15	Brass Plum Restaurant	American	$$		Yes	L/D	Major
16	Cross-Bow Family Restaurant	Family	$$	Yes		B/L/D	M/V
16	Arby's	Fast Food	$	Yes		L/D	Major
16	McDonald's	Fast Food	$	Yes		L/D/B	
16	Maggie's Café	Family	$	Yes		B/L	
16	Pizza Hut	Pizza	$$	Yes	B	L/D	Major
16	Season's Supper Club	Steakhouse	$$$		Yes	L/D	Major
16	Office Lounge Cafe	American	$$/$$$		Yes	L/D	Major
16	Antone's Supper Club	Family	$$/$$$	Yes	Yes	L/D	Major
16	Coffees & Cakes	Coffee Shop	$			B/L	
16	Hot Stuff Pizzaria	Pizza	$$			L/D	Major
17	**Dirty Sally's Gifts, Quilts & Soda Fountain**	Soda Fountain	$	Yes		L/D	D
17	Flagstaff Café	Family	$$		W/B	B/L/D	
17	Deer Haven Lodge	Family	$$		Yes	L/D	Major
17	Meadowlark Lake Lodge	Steak House	$$	Yes	Yes	L/D/B	Major
17	Mountain Man Café	Family	$$			B/L/D	
17	Fireside Café & Lounge	Family	$$	Yes		L/D	Major
17	Other Side Bar & Grill	American	$$	No	Yes	L/D	Major
17	Tom & Jerry's	Steakhouse	$$$	Yes	Yes	D/L	Major
17	PerCup Expresso	Bakery/Deli	$		W/B	B/L	
18	Paintrock Inn Bar & Grll	Family	$$	Yes	Yes	B/L/D	
18	Hyattville Café	Family	$$/$	Yes		B/L/D	
19	Manderson Kwik Stop	Fast Food	$			B/L/D	Major
19	3 Sisters Truck Stop	Family	$$	Yes		B/L/D	Major
19	Blimpie's	Sandwiches	$	Yes		L/D	Major
19	Hi Way Bar & Café	American	$$		Yes	B/L/D	Major
20	Tom's Cafe	Family	$/$$			B/L/D	
21	**Buffalo Rose Restaurant**	American	$$	Yes	W/B	L/D	V/M
21	A&W	Fast Food	$	Yes		D/L	
21	Subway	Sandwiches	$	Yes		D/L	M/V
21	Wheels Inn Restaurant	American	$$	Yes		D/L/B	
21	Sugar Shack	Soda Fountain	$				
21	Uptown Café	American	$/$$	No	Yes	B/L/D	Major
21	Bejing Garden	Chinese	$$	No		D/L	M/V
21	Sidekick Pizza & Subway	Pizza/Sandwiches	$$/$$$/$	No		D/L	Major/M/V
21	Lisa's Fine Dining	Fine Dining	$$$	No	Yes	D/L	Major
22	**Dirty Annie's**	American	$/$$	Yes	W/B	D/L/B	Major
22	**Snowshoe Lodge**	Family	$$	Yes	Yes	D/L/B	Major
23	Burlington Café	Family	$			B/L	
26	Pizza Hut	Pizza	$$	Yes	B	L/D	Major
26	Burger King	Fast Food	$	Yes		L/D/B	M/V
26	Skyline Café	Coffee House	$$	Yes		L/B/D	
26	Domino's	Pizza	$$	No		L/D	Major
26	Taco Bell	Fast Food	$	Yes		L/D	
26	Taco Johns	Fast Food	$	No		L/D	
26	Pepe's	Mexican	$$	Yes		L/D/B	M/V
26	Chinatown Gourmet Chinese	Chinese	$$	No		L/D	M/V
26	Back Street Pub	Brew Pub	$$	Yes	Yes	L/D	Major
26	McDonald's	Fast Food	$	Yes		L/D/B	

Dining Quick Reference-Continued

Price Range refers to the average cost of a meal per person: ($) $1-$6, ($$) $7-$11, ($$$) $12-up. Cocktails: "Yes" indicates full bar; Beer (B)/Wine (W), Service: Breakfast (B), Brunch (BR), Lunch (L), Dinner (D). Businesses in bold print will have additional information under the appropriate map locator number in the body of this section.

MAP#	RESTAURANT	TYPE CUISINE	PRICE RANGE	CHILD MENU	COCKTAILS BEER WINE	MEALS SERVED	CREDIT CARDS ACCEPTED
26	Pizza on the Run	Pizza	$$	Yes	B	L/D	Major
26	Subway	Sandwiches	$	Yes		B/L/D	M/V
26	Hamilton House	Steakhouse	$$$/$$	Yes	Yes	B/L/D	Major
27	Bent Street Bakery	Bakery	$	Yes		L/B	
27	Lamplighter Inn	American	$$/$$$	No	Yes	L/D	Major
27	El Tapatio	Mexican	$$	No		L/D	
27	Peaks	Brew Pub	$$	No	Yes	L/D	M/V
27	Hansel & Gretel's	Family	$$	Yes	Yes	L/D	M/V
27	Linda's Sandwich & Ice Cream Shoppe	Sandwiches	$	No		L/D	
27	Powell Drug & Espresso	Coffee Shop	$	Yes		L/B	Major
27	Time Out Lounge	American	$$	No	Yes	L/D	Major
27	Parlor News Coffeehouse	Coffee House	$			B/L	
30	Lange's Kitchen	American	$$	Yes		B/L/D	V/M
30	Taco John/Blimpies	Fast Food	$	Yes		B/L/D	
30	Bighorn Restaurant	Family	$$	Yes	Yes	D/L/B	Major
31	Cowtown Café	Family	$$	Yes		B/D/L	Major
43	McDonald's	Fast Food	$	Yes		L/D/B	
43	Highwayman Café	Homestyle	$$/$	Yes		D/L/B	Major
43	Gannett Grill	Sanwiches	$	Yes		D/L	
50	Noble Roman's Pizza	Pizza	$/$$	Yes		L/D	Major

NOTES:

Section 2

Motel Quick Reference

Price Range: ($) Under $40 ; ($$) $40-$60; ($$$) $60-$80, ($$$$) Over $80. Pets [check with the motel for specific policies] (P), Dining (D), Lounge (L), Disabled Access (DA), Full Breakfast (FB), Cont. Breakfast (CB), Indoor Pool (IP), Outdoor Pool (OP), Hot Tub (HT), Sauna (S), Refrigerator (R), Microwave (M) (Microwave and Refrigerator indicated only if in majority of rooms), Kitchenette (K). All Wyoming area codes are 307.

MAP #	HOTEL	PHONE	NUMBER ROOMS	PRICE RANGE	BREAKFAST	POOL/ HOT TUB SAUNA	NON SMOKE ROOMS	OTHER AMENITIES	CREDIT CARDS
2	**Best Western Sunset Motor Inn**	587-4265	120	$$$$/$$$		HT/OP/IP	Yes	P/D	Major
2	**Robin's Nest Bed & Breakfast**	527-7208	3		FB		Yes	P	Major
2	**Burl Inn**	587-2084	40	$$$$			Yes	DA	Major
2	**Cody Guest HousesThe Victorian House B&B**	587-6000	20	$$$$			Yes	P/K	Major
2	**Parson's Pillow B&B**	587-2382							
2	**The Irma Hotel, Restaurant & Saloon**	587-4221	40	$$/$$$				DA/L/D	
2	**Buffalo Bill Village Resort**	587-5556							
2	**Holiday Inn Buffalo Bill Village Resort**	587-5555-1	189	$$$$		OP	Yes	L/D/DA	Major
2	**Comfort Inn Buffalo Bill Village Resort**		75	$$$$	CB	OP	Yes	DA	Major
2	Yellowstone Valley Inn	587-3961	36	$$$			Yes	D/K/L/P/DA	Major
2	Best Western Sunrise Motor Inn	587-5566	40	$$$$/$$$	CB	OP	Yes	P	
2	Best Value Inn	587-4258	24	$$$$/$$$	CB		Yes		Major
2	Cody Motor Lodge	527-6291	31	$$$$	CB		Yes	P/DA	Major
2	Econo Lodge - Moose Creek	587-2221	56	$$/$$$	CB	IP	Yes	DA	Major
2	Carriage House	587-2572	25	$$			Yes		
2	Red Pole Ranch & Motel	587-5929	8	$$$			Yes	K/P	Major
2	Summit Inn	587-4040	18	$$$			Yes	DA	Major
2	Uptown Motel	587-4245	10	$$				P	Major
2	Wise Choice Motel	587-5004	17	$$				P/D	M/V
2	Rainbow Park Motel	587-6251	39	$			Yes	D/K	Major
2	Rustler's Roost	587-8171							
2	Pawnee Hotel	587-2239	18	$$			Yes		Major
2	Bison Willy's Bunkhouse	587-0629	12	$			Yes	K	
3	**Super 8 - Cody**	527-6214	64	$$			Yes	DA/P	Major
3	Days Inn	527-6604	52	$$$	CB	HT/IP	Yes	DA	Major
3	AmericInn Lodge & Suites	587-7716	46	$$$$	CB	OP/S/HT	Yes	DA	Major
3	Frontier Motel	527-7119	28	$$$				K/L	
3	Big Bear Motel	69	42	$$		OP		L/P	Major
3	Elk Valley Inn & Campground	587-4149	9	$$		OP	Yes	P/L/D/K	V/M
3	Seven K's Motel & RV Park	587-5890	16	$$		OP		P/K	Major
3	Streamside Inn & Campground	587-8242	21	$$	CB	OP	Yes	K	Major
3	Western Six Gun Motel	587-4835	40	$$				P/K	Major
4	**Grandma's House/Lockhart B&B**	587-6074	7	$$$$	FB	HT	Yes		M/V
4	**Skyline Motel**	587-4201	46	$$$/$$/$		OP	Yes	P	Major
4	Parkway Inn	587-4208	39	$$$$/$$$	CB	OP	Yes	P	Major
4	Green Gables Inn		15	$$$	CB		Yes	DA/P	Major
4	Carter Mountain Motel	587-4295	28	$$$$			Yes	P/K/R	Major
4	Beartooth Inn of Cody	527-5505	50	$$$	CB	HT/S	Yes	R/M	Major
4	Grizzly Bear Lodge	587-5960	44	$$$					Major
4	River's View Motel & RV Park	587-6074							
4	Stage Stop	527-5065							
8	Vision Quest Motel	868-2512	14	$$			Yes	P/R/K/M	M/V
8	Oasis Motel & RV Park	868-2551	12	$$				P/R	M/V
10	**The Rainbow Motel**	864-2129	17	$$			Yes		M/V
10	**Plaza Inn - Quality Inn & Suites**	864-2939	36	$$$$	CB	HT/OP	Yes	P/DA/R/M	Major
10	Holiday Inn of the Waters	864-3131	80	$$$$		OP/HT/S	Yes	DA/L/D/P	Major
10	Budget Host Moonlighter Motel	864-2321	30	$$$		OP	Yes		Major
10	Hot Springs Motel	864-2303	11	$$				D/K	
10	Roundup Mountain Motel	864-3126	12	$/$$$/$$			Yes	K/P	D/M/V
11	Elk Antler Inn	864-2325	12	$$				K/P	
11	Cactus Inn	864-3155	11	$$/$			Yes	K/M/R/P	D/M/V
11	Super 8	864-5515	58	$/$$		IP		P	Major
11	El Rancho Motel	864-2341	13	$$				P	Major
11	Jurassic Inn	864-2325	16	$$$/$$			Yes	P	Major
11	Coachman Inn Motel	864-3141	19	$$		IP		P	
15	**C's Bed & Breakfast**	347-9388	1		FB		Yes	P	
15	Days Inn	347-4251	42	$$$	CB		Yes	P/DA	Major
15	Town & Country	347-3249	22	$$			Yes	P/K	Major
16	**The Wild Sage Inn**	347-2222	10	$$			Yes	DA/K	Major
16	Comfort Inn	347-6734	50	$$$	CB	IP/HT	Yes	P/DA	Major
16	Town House Motor Inn	347-2426	23	$$		OP	Yes	P	Major

Motel Quick Reference-Continued

Price Range: ($) Under $40 ; ($$) $40-$60; ($$$) $60-$80, ($$$$) Over $80. Pets [check with the motel for specific policies] (P), Dining (D), Lounge (L), Disabled Access (DA), Full Breakfast (FB), Cont. Breakfast (CB), Indoor Pool (IP), Outdoor Pool (OP), Hot Tub (HT), Sauna (S), Refrigerator (R), Microwave (M) (Microwave and Refrigerator indicated only if in majority of rooms), Kitchenette (K). All Wyoming area codes are 307.

MAP #	HOTEL	PHONE	NUMBER ROOMS	PRICE RANGE	BREAKFAST	POOL/ HOT TUB SAUNA	NON SMOKE ROOMS	OTHER AMENITIES	CREDIT CARDS
16	Super 8	347-9236	35	$$			Yes	P/DA	Major
16	Pawnee Motel	347-3206	8	$$					M/V
17	Log Cabin Motel & Campground	366-2320	8	$$				K/P	D/M/V
17	Valley Motel	366-2321	20	$$			Yes	P/K	D/M/V
17	Taylored Tours	366-2250							
20	Lilac Motel	568-3355	9				Yes	P	M/V
21	**Wheels Motel**	765-2105	22	$$$		S	Yes	R	Major
21	**Antler Motel**	765-4404	12	$$	CB		Yes	K/R/M	Major
21	**Greybull Motel**	765-2628	12	$$$		S	Yes	P/R/M	Major
21	Maverick Motel	765-4626	7	$$			Yes	DA	Major
21	Greybull Hotel	765-2012					Yes		
21	Yellowstone Motel	765-4456	34	$$		OP	Yes	DA/P/K	Major
21	Sage Motel	765-4443	17	$$		OP	Yes	DA/M/R	Major
21	K-Bar Motel	765-4426	12	$			Yes	P	Major
22	**Bear Creek Ranch**	765-9319							
22	**Snowshoe Lodge**	899-8995	3	$$$$	FB	HT	Yes	R/M/K	Major
22	Kedesh Guest Ranch	765-2791		$			Yes	P	
22	Wagon Wheel Lodge	765-2561							
26	Super 8 Motel	754-7231	35	$$			Yes	L/P/DA	Major
26	Best Western/King's Inn	754-5117	49	$$$/$$		OP	Yes	DA/D/P	Major
26	Park Motel	754-2233	18	$$		HT	Yes	DA/D/P/K	Major
27	Best Choice Motel	754-2243	20	$$			Yes	754-7231	Major
30	Super 8 Motel	548-2725	34	$$	CB		Yes	P/DA	Major
30	Cattleman Motel	548-2296	14	$$		HT	Yes	P/DA	Major
30	Western Motel	548-2781	23	$$		OP/HT	Yes	P/K	M/V
30	Horseshoe Bend Motel	548-2221	22	$$	CB	OP	Yes	P/M/K/R	Major

Notes:

NOTES:

SECTION 3

NORTHEAST AREA

INCLUDING SHERIDAN, BUFFALO, GILLETTE AND NEWCASTLE

Devils Tower near Sundance.

1 *Gas, Food, Lodging*

Ranchester

Pop. 701, Elev. 3,775

Named by English born senator, D.H. Hardin, Ranchester was the site of two significant battles during the Plains Indian Wars. In 1865, General Patrick E. Connor, an aggressive, anti-Indian commander at Fort Laramie, was responsible for the slaughter of 63 men, women, and children in an Arapaho village on the Tongue River. Only eight of his troopers died in the fight, and the victors took home 1100 ponies. Two days later, the Arapaho retaliated by attacking a road-building expedition headed by Col. James Sawyer. Three soldiers were killed, and Connor had to return to rescue the rest. Peace movements in the East prevented Connor from killing "all male Indians over the age of twelve," as he had planned. In 1894, Ranchester became a shipping stop on the Burlington railroad for the McShane Tie Company.

Acme

From the Greek for "high grade," Acme was named for its prime coal, known as "black diamonds." Once a coal mine camp, Acme was also a station on the Burlington railroad. It later gave its name to the Acme Petroleum Corporation, a large Wyoming oil company founded around 1900.

T Connor Battlefield State Historic Site

In Ranchester

Once the site of a bloody battle when General Patrick E. Connor's army attacked and destroyed Arapahoe Chief Black Bear's settlement of 250 lodges. The battlefield is now located in the peaceful and beautiful city park. The site marks the military engagement that was part of the Powder River Expedition of 1865. The battle caused the Arapaho to ally with the Sioux and Cheyenne at the Fetterman Fight the next year.

T Little Blue Schoolhouse

In Ranchester

One of the areas oldest schools, it was moved to Ranchester in 1988. This 1902 one-room school from the Parkman area has been completely restored.

T Ranchester Museum

145 Coffeen in Ranchester. 655-2284

H The Battle of Tongue River

Ranchester at Connor Battlefield Site.

On this site during the early morning hours of August 29, 1865, General Patrick Edward Connor led over 200 troops in an attack on Chief Black Bear's Arapaho village. Connor had departed from Fort Laramie on July 30th with 184 wagons, a contingent of Pawnee scouts, nearly 500 cavalrymen, and the aging Jim Bridger as guide. His column was one of three comprising the Powder River Indian Expedition sent to secure the Bozeman and other emigrant trails leading to the Montana mining fields.

During the Battle of Tongue River, Connor was able to inflict serious damage on the Arapahos, but an aggressive counter attack forced him to retreat back to the newly established Fort Connor (later renamed Reno) on the banks of the Powder River. There he received word that he had been reassigned to his old command in the District of Utah.

The Powder River Expedition, one of the most comprehensive campaigns against the Plains Indians, never completely succeeded. Connor had planned a complex operation only to be defeated by bad weather, inhospitable terrain, and hostile Indians. Long term effects of the Expedition proved detrimental to the interests of the Powder River tribes. The Army, with the establishment of Fort Connor (Reno) increased public awareness of this area which in turn caused more emigrants to use the Bozeman Trail. This led to public demand for government protection of travelers on their way to Montana gold fields.

L Ranchester Western Motel

350 E. Dayton Road in Ranchester. 655-2212 or toll free, 866-655-2213

2 *Food, Lodging*

Dayton

Pop. 678, Elev. 3,926

Dayton was named for banker, Joseph Dayton Thorn. It was established 1n 1882 and gained fame in 1911 when Susan Whissler, the first woman mayor in the nation was elected. Dayton is also home to Wyoming's first rodeo held in the 1890s.

Parkman

No Services

Named for Francis Parkman, author of *The Oregon Trail*, this railroad station town was established in 1894.

T Hans Kleiber Museum

520 Story in Dayton. 655-2217

The log cabin studio of watercolor artist Hans Kleiber has been preserved for use as a museum

Sheridan

	Jan	Feb	March	April	May	June	July	Aug	Sep	Oct	Nov	Dec	Annual
Average Max. Temperature (F)	33.3	38.5	45.6	56.5	66.6	76.4	86.2	85.5	73.7	61.3	45.5	36.3	58.8
Average Min. Temperature (F)	9.0	14.4	20.9	30.4	39.6	47.6	53.8	52.4	42.4	31.9	20.0	11.9	31.2
Average Total Precipitation (in.)	0.72	0.67	1.05	1.86	2.31	2.18	1.07	0.85	1.30	1.24	0.81	0.65	14.69
Average Total SnowFall (in.)	10.9	10.3	12.4	10.5	1.7	0.1	0.0	0.0	1.4	4.7	8.5	11.1	71.5
Average Snow Depth (in.)	3	3	1	0	0	0	0	0	0	0	1	2	1
Wind Speed (mph / kmh)	8 / 13	8 / 13	9 / 15	10 / 17	9 / 15	8 / 13	8 / 12	8 / 12	8 / 13	8 / 13	8 / 12	8 / 13	
Wind Direction	NW	NW	NW	NW	NW	NW	NW	NW	NW	NW	NW	NW	
Cloud Cover (out of 8)	5.7	5.7	5.6	5.4	5.3	4.5	3.6	3.7	4.0	4.7	5.4	5.4	

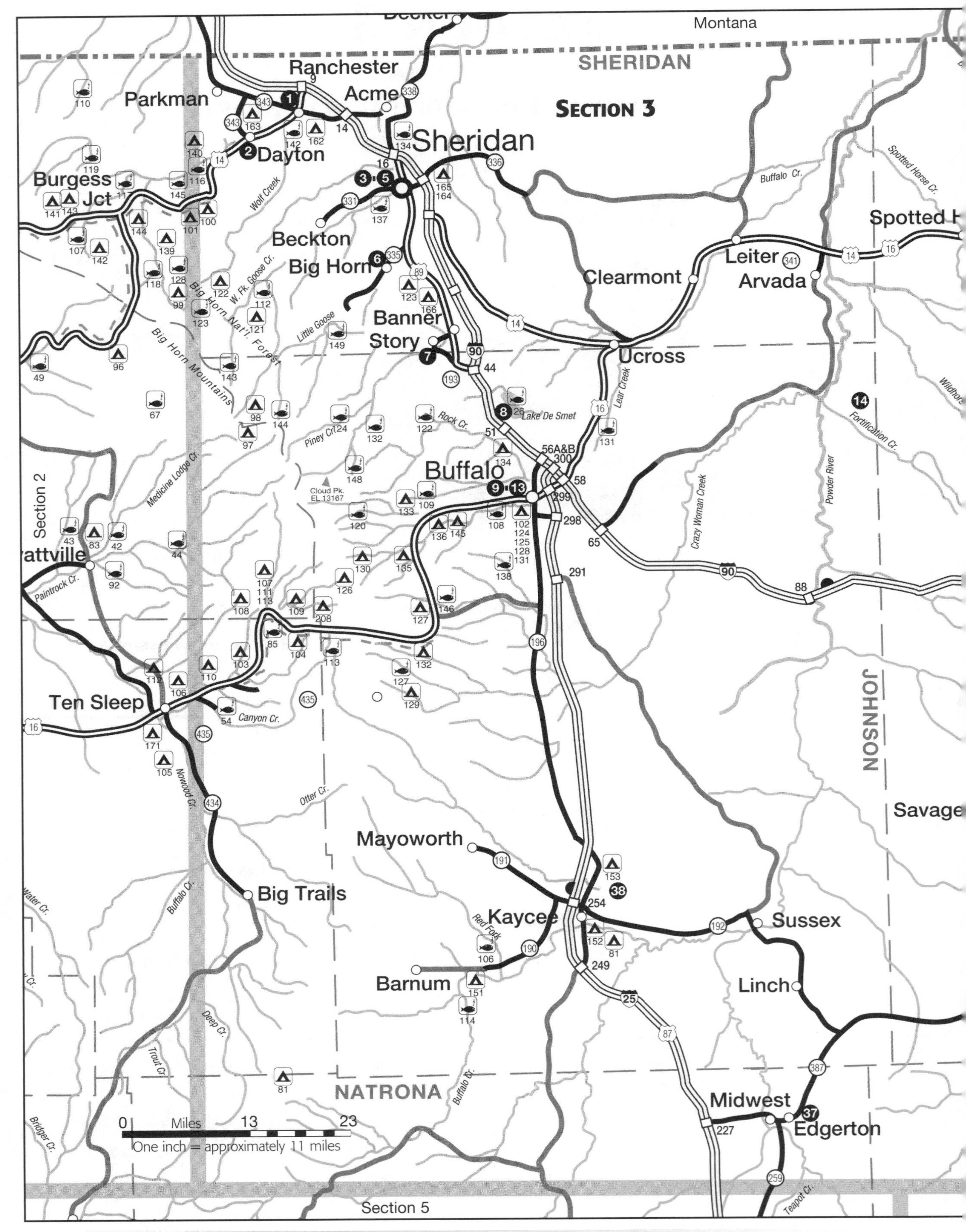
Montana
SHERIDAN
SECTION 3
Ranchester
Parkman
Acme
Sheridan
Dayton
Burgess Jct
Beckton
Big Horn
Banner
Story
Clearmont
Leiter
Arvada
Spotted H
Ucross
Buffalo
Lake De Smet
Cloud Pk. EL 13167
Big Horn Nat'l. Forest
Big Horn Mountains
Section 2
Ten Sleep
Mayoworth
Big Trails
Kaycee
Barnum
Sussex
Linch
Midwest
Edgerton
JOHNSON
Savage
NATRONA
Section 5
0 Miles 13 23
One inch = approximately 11 miles
Wolf Creek
W. Fk. Goose Cr.
Little Goose
Piney Cr.
Rock Cr.
Medicine Lodge Cr.
Paintrock Cr.
Canyon Cr.
Nowood Cr.
Otter Cr.
Buffalo Cr.
Red Fork
Deep Cr.
Trout Cr.
Bridger Cr.
Teapot Cr.
Lear Creek
Crazy Woman Creek
Powder River
Fortification Cr.
Spotted Horse Cr.

Section 3

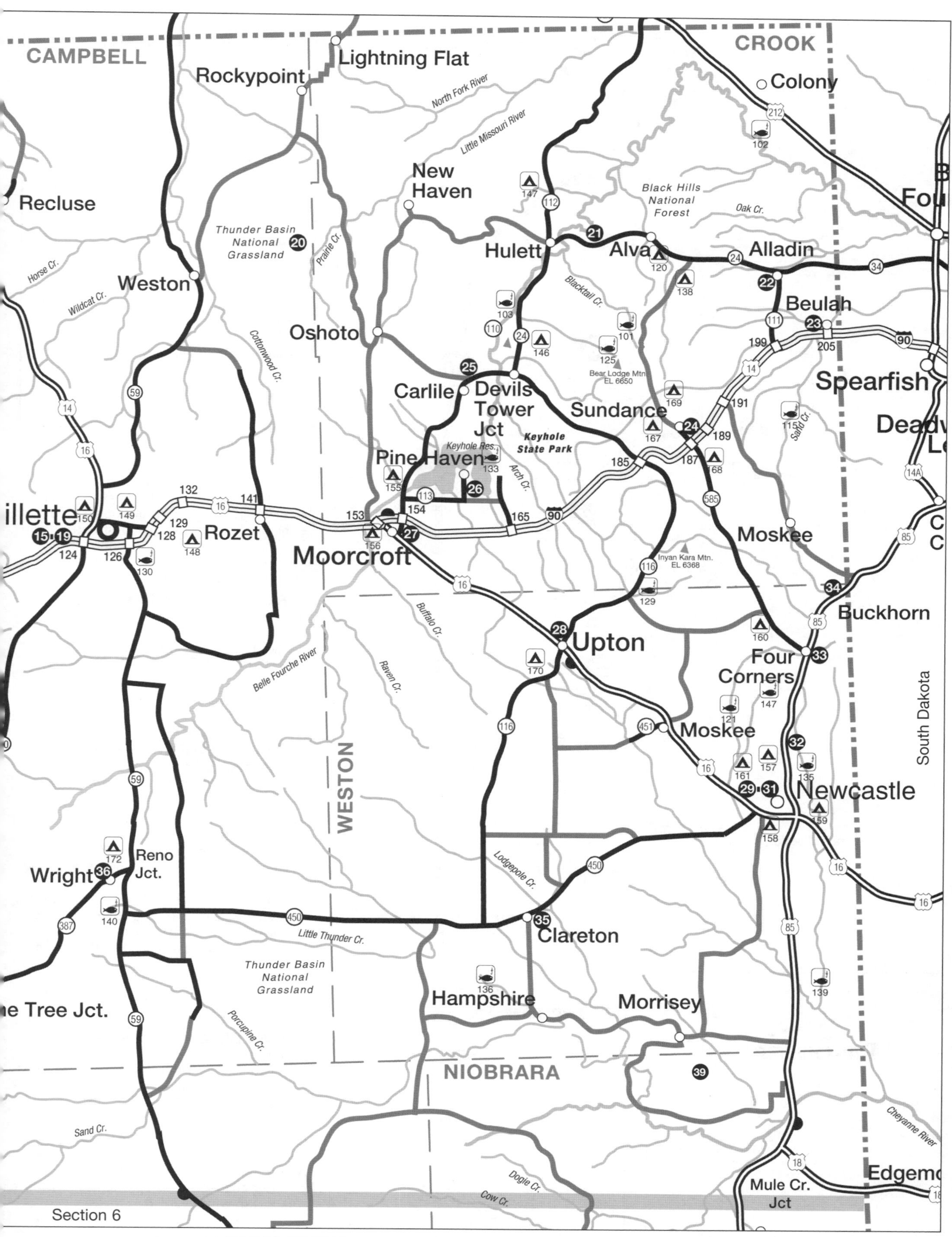
CAMPBELL
CROOK
WESTON
NIOBRARA
Lightning Flat
Rockypoint
Colony
Recluse
New Haven
Thunder Basin National Grassland
Black Hills National Forest
Hulett
Alva
Alladin
Weston
Oshoto
Beulah
Spearfish
Carlile
Devils Tower Jct
Sundance
Keyhole State Park
Keyhole Res.
Pine Haven
Bear Lodge Mtn EL 6650
Rozet
Moorcroft
Moskee
Inyan Kara Mtn. EL 6368
Buckhorn
Upton
Four Corners
Newcastle
South Dakota
Reno Jct.
Wright
Clareton
Hampshire
Morrisey
Mule Cr. Jct
Section 6
North Fork River
Little Missouri River
Prairie Cr.
Oak Cr.
Horse Cr.
Wildcat Cr.
Blacktail Cr.
Cottonwood Cr.
Arch Cr.
Sand Cr.
Buffalo Cr.
Raven Cr.
Belle Fourche River
Lodgepole Cr.
Little Thunder Cr.
Porcupine Cr.
Cheyanne River
Dogie Cr.
Cow Cr.

Section 3

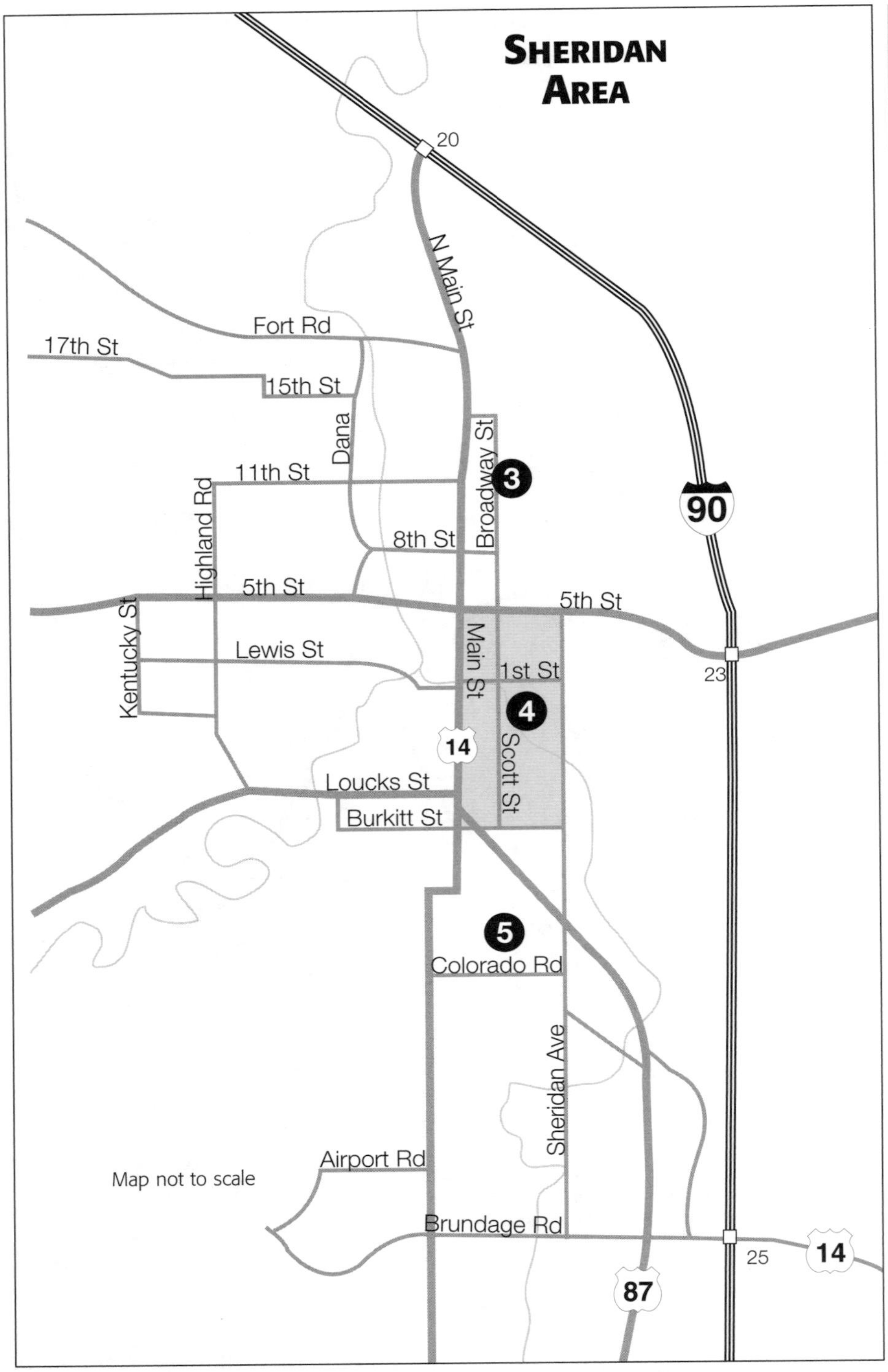

SHERIDAN AREA
20
N Main St
Fort Rd
17th St
15th St
Dana
Broadway St
11th St
Highland Rd
3
90
8th St
5th St
Kentucky St
Lewis St
Main St
1st St
23
4
14
Scott St
Loucks St
Burkitt St
5
Colorado Rd
Sheridan Ave
Airport Rd
Map not to scale
Brundage Rd
25
14
87

Legend for Section Map

- Locator number (matches numeric listing in section)
- Campsite (number matches number in campsite chart)
- Fishing Site (number matches number in fishing chart)
- Rest stop
- Interstate
- U.S. Highway
- Paved State or County Road
- Gravel/unpaved road

RANCHESTER
87
90
9
14
90
345
14
Railway St
Betty St
345
Coffeen St
Map not to scale
Hardin St
3rd Ave
2nd Ave
1st Ave
Wests St
Gillette St
Main St
Campbell St
Halbert St
14
Barker Rd

DAYTON
Dayton-Ohlman Rd
14
Map not to scale
1st Ave
2nd Ave
3rd Ave
4th Ave
Broadway Ave
Smith St
Tongue River Canyon Rd
14

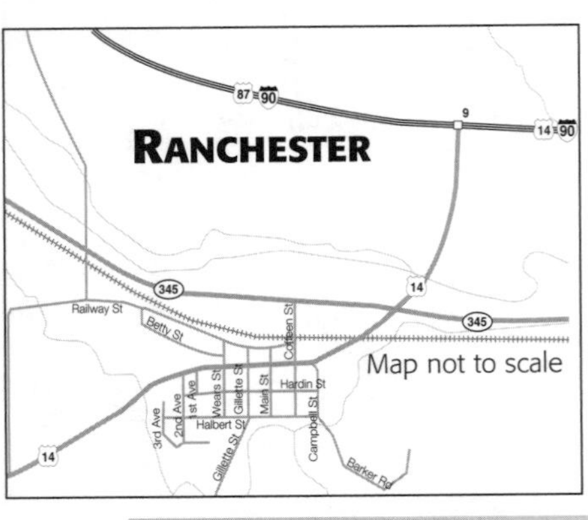

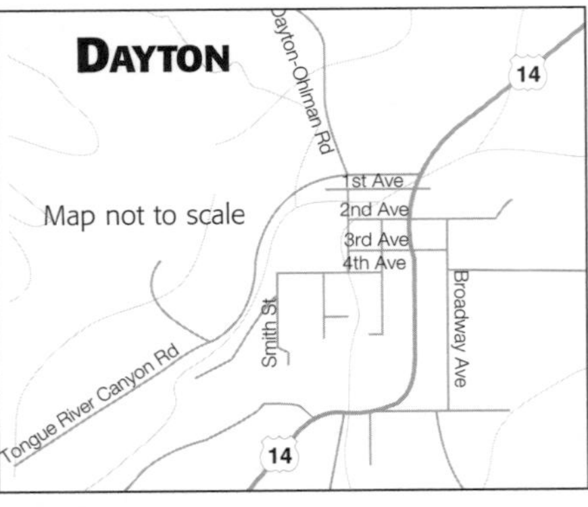

and visitors center. Known as the "Artist of the Big Horns", Kleiber's work is world renown. Born in Cologne, Italy in 1887, his family moved to Massachusetts in the early 1900s. He later moved West and after various jobs, moved to Dayton and established himself as an artist. The museum contains his press, art books and a number of etchings. The museum is open Monday through Saturday during the summer, closed in winter.

T Bald Mountain City

Fine-grained gold was discovered here in 1890, and for the next decade, prospectors flocked to the area. In 1892, the Fortunatas Mining and Mlling Company helped establish the town, one of the largest settlements in the Big Horn Mountains. The cost of panning, however, outweighed the value of the yields, and gold fever in the area ended by 1900.

H Connor Battlefield State Historic Site

Dayton and Gillette Streets in Dayton.

In 1865 General Patrick E. Connor led the Powder River Expedition into this area. This expedition was part of a broad military program to bring the Indians north of the Platte River under control and halt their depredations along the Western Trails.

At this site Connor's command located and attacked a large party of Araphao under Black Bear and Old David, destroying 250 lodges. Much of the fighting was hand-to-hand combat, and many women and children were killed and captured.

Later events proved the campaign of 1865 to be undecisive.

H First Woman Mayor in Wyoming

Bridge Street and West 3rd Avenue in Dayton.

Mrs. Susan Wissler, on May 9, 1911, was elected mayor of Dayton, Wyoming, then a community of about 175 people. She served two terms of two years each. Her administration was marked by civic improvement and community betterment as her campaign promise to curb gambling and regular the operation of saloons was, in a measure, fulfilled.

Mrs. Wissler was truly a pioneer. She taught

in the public schools of this area for several years and actively encouraged her students to go on for further study. As a practical nurse she is remembered for her ministrations in time of trouble. She also owned and operated a millinery and drygoods store for a number of years. Dayton became her home in 1890. She died in 1938.

H Susan Wissler 1853-1938

406 Main St. in Dayton.

Mrs. Susan Wissler owned and operated a millinery shop at this location while serving as mayor of Dayton from 1911 to 1913. Mrs. Wissler was the first woman mayor in Wyoming and the first woman to serve consecutive terms as mayor in the United States. Mrs. Wissler was an excellent teacher and a successful business woman. It is appropriate that she was elected in the first state to grant equal suffrage to women.

H Sibley Monument

About 20 miles west of Dayton on U.S. Highway 14.

Through this vicinity, a scouting party of the 2nd Cavalry, led by Lt. Frederick W. Sibley, was attacked by Sioux and Cheyenne Indians on July 7, 1876. In the fight Chief White Antelope was killed. The party abandoned its horses, took to the rugged terain, and scouts Frank Gruard and Baptiste Poirier guided the 26 soldiers and Chicago Times reporter John F. Finerty over the mountains without food, back to their main camp.

VFL Big Horn Mountain Lodge

U.S. Highway 14, Burgess Junction, Scenic Route to Yellowstone, near Dayton. 751-7599. www.bighornmountainlodge.com

The Big Horn Mountain Lodge is a place to live an adventure you'll always remember. Red stag, buffalo, various deer species, sheep, antelope, and other game have been stocked to provide the hunter with many options to meet their needs. From their accommodations and outstanding food, to the renowned wildlife, you will always find what you're looking for. Whether you are relaxing by the fire, dining in the restaurant, searching for that perfect trophy mount, or enjoying abundant wild flowers, you're sure to have a memorable experience. They also offer camping and RV sites, along with a convenience store and gift shop. Snowmobile rentals are available in the area.

Dayton Days

The last week in July, Dayton Days boasts a large parade, games, duck races, crafts and food vendors in the park, pet parade, fun walk, softball games, Rotary Club breakfast, entertainment, outdoor dances, barbecue and firemen's water fights.

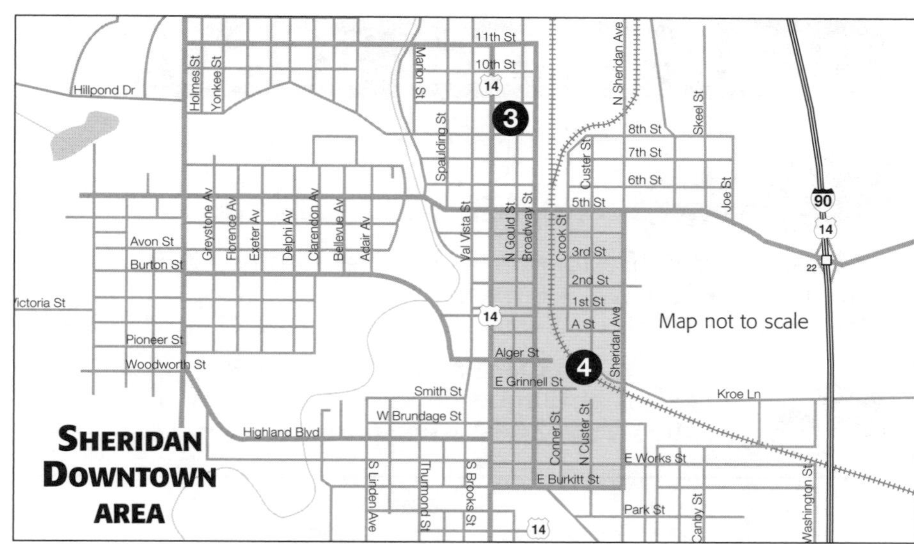

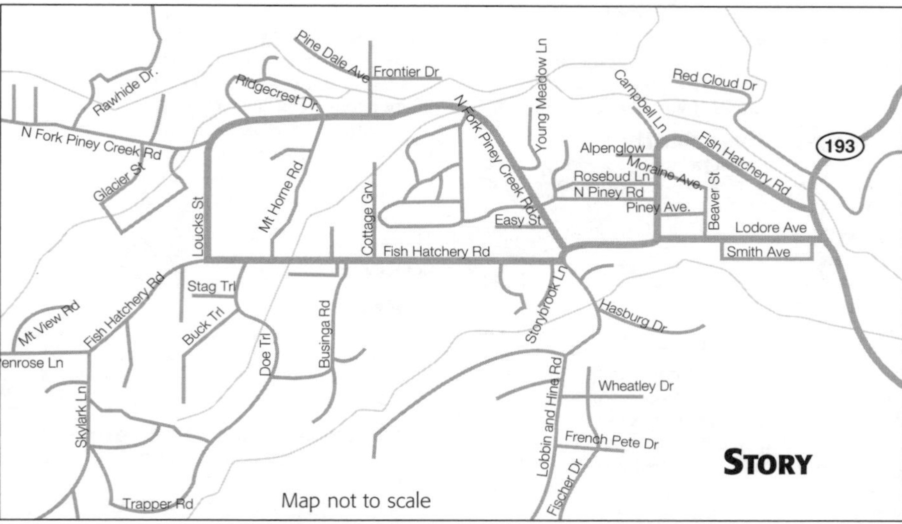

FL Bear Lodge Resort

U.S. Highway 14A, 1/4 mile past Burgess Junction near Dayton. 752-2444 or 752-5444. www.bearlodgeresort.com

The Bear Lodge Resort is located on top of the beautiful Big Horn Mountains in Bighorn National Forest. The full service, all-season alpine resort, open all year, provides a range of services and recreational opportunities for individuals, families, weddings, reunions, banquets, and company retreats. Choose from beautifully furnished motel rooms or rustic cabins. The full service restaurant, is open for breakfast, lunch, and dinner. An adjoining lounge offers a big screen TV, pool table, and games. Relax in the indoor pool or hot tub. The Snowmobile Shop offers sales, service, rentals and guided tours. The Gift Shop and Store is an oasis for Wyoming souvenirs, groceries, fishing supplies and licenses, maps, and gasoline.

F Aspen Creek Galleria & Restaurant by the Creek

841 Main in Dayton. 655-3974

L Four Pines Bed & Breakfast

114 Dayton East Rd., 1-1/4 miles from Dayton. 655-3764 or toll free, 866-366-2607. www.fourpines.com

The Four Pines Bed and breakfast is a quiet, comfortable, peaceful oasis located just outside of Dayton. Enjoy the lovely country setting surrounded by three acres of private gardens at the base of the Big Horn Mountains. The entire family is welcome to relax and explore at the Four Pines, including pets and horses. There is plenty of space for boarding and grazing livestock. Your day will start with a hearty, homemade breakfast. Snacks and beverages are also available. Visit nearby attractions, take a stroll on the property, or just sit back and relax on the spacious decks, or the expansive and comfortable common area.

M Tongue River Realty

311 Main Street in Dayton. 655-9556 or toll free, 888-625-9556. www.tongueriver.com or www.tongueriverrealty.com

Tongue River Realty specializes in all phases of real estate. Well established in the Dayton and surrounding areas, they are located at the base of the Big Horn Mountains surrounded by many ranch properties including the Padlock Ranch, one of the nation's largest ranches. Not only do they provide real estate services in the Sheridan County area, but they are licensed in Wyoming, Montana, and Colorado. They can list, show, and sell properties in all three states. Feel confident that when you call on Tongue River Realty, if they don't have the solution they will know someone who does. Call them for more information or visit them on the web.

3 *Gas, Food, Lodging*

Sheridan

Pop. 15,804, Elev. 3,745

The Sheridan area has been valuable territory since the days when only Native Americans roamed here, along with the buffalo and other wild game. Once a prized hunting ground, it was often disputed even before white men came. It was not until the establishment of the Bozeman Trail, however, that the Sioux, Cheyenne, Arapaho, and other tribes came together to fight off the increasing influx of settlers.

Some of the bloodiest battles of the Plains Indian War, which took place in the 1860s and 70s, occurred nearby. The Fetterman Fight, Wagon Box Fight, Connor and Sawyer Battles, the Battle of the Rosebud, the Dull Knife Battle, and the Battle of the Little Bighorn all took place within just miles of Sheridan. For that reason, this portion of the Bozeman Trail became known as the Bloody Bozeman. It was not until the surrender of leaders such as Red Cloud, Crazy Horse, and Sitting Bull that hostilities eased, and the area was open to settlement.

In 1878, mountain man Jim Mason built the first permanent building here. A store and post office opened in 1881. Storeowner Harry Mandel sold the place to Jim Loucks, who planned the town and named it for his Civil War commander, General Philip Sheridan. Homesteaders and cattle ranchers moved into the area, creating an agricultural crossroads where the Burlington Railroad set up a stop in 1892. The discovery of coal in the area added to the towns growing prosperity. The building of several flourmills and a sugar beet factory contributed to the economy as well. The twentieth century brought several booms and busts, but now the city has settled into a serene mix of agriculture, energy production, and tourism.

The lowest city in Wyoming, Sheridan's elevation is 3745 feet.

Beckton

Also known as Beckton Junction, pioneer George W. Beck built a flourmill here and established a post office in 1883. The post office was discontinued. There are only a few houses here today.

T Sheridan Travel and Tourism

I-90 & E. 5th Street in Sheridan. 673-7120 or 888-596-6787. www.sheridanwyoming.org

T Sheridan Rest Stop & Visitor's Center

I-90 exit 23 in Sheridan

T Wyoming Game and Fish Dept. Visitor Center

Across road from Sheridan Rest Stop

View taxidermist displays of native Wyoming creatures, and find out more about wildlife, hunting, and fishing in the West.

H Big Horns

The abundance of Rocky Mountain bighorn sheep led the Indians to name this mountain range after these majestic animals. The Big Horn Mountains are a wildlife viewing paradise. Several native Indian tribes competed with each other and later with settlers for access to the mountains and surrounding river basins. Eventually settlers took possession of the land. Due to excessive hunting and introduced diseases, the once abundant bighorn sheep were almost eliminated from this area by the turn of the century. Today, bighorn sheep are being reintroduced to the Big Horn Mountains.

At high elevations, mountain meadows are interspersed with timber stands which provide food and summer habitat for elk and mule deer. Willow stands provide forage for moose. The forests house black bears, snowshoe hares, marmots, chipmunks and blue grouse.

At lower elevations, white-tailed deer, mountain lions, sharp-tailed grouse, wild turkeys, black-billed magpies and over 300 other kinds of wildlife inhabit the foothills and riparian areas. Notice the diverse habitat types which make this area so productive for wildlife. The riparian zones bordered by stands of cottonwood trees and cropland provide excellent feeding areas. The steep foothills of the Big Horns furnish crucial winter range for big game.

Discover more about the current status of bighorn sheep and the diverse wildlife communities of Wyoming by touring the Wyoming Game and Fish Department Visitor Center across the highway.

F Pablo's Mexican Restaurant & Cantina

1274 N. Main in Sheridan. 672-0737. Email: pablos@fiberpipe.net

At Pablo's Mexican Restaurant & Cantina, owner Brent says, "Let us salsafy your life." Be careful! It gets hot in Pablo's! Step into a Mexican experience replete with traditional Mexican architecture, music, furnishings, and stunning hand painted murals. Their homemade salsas have made a major contribution to making salsa a huge favorite around the world. Enjoy their fresh salsa along with the taco buffet, soup and salad bar, and all your favorite dishes made from authentic recipes and the freshest ingredients. Get "salsafied" for lunch or dinner and top off your meal with with their famous Margaritas and tons of fun.

4 *Gas, Food, Lodging*

T Chamber of Commerce - Sheridan

707 Sheridan in Sheridan. 672-2485 or 800-453-3650. www.sheridanwy.com

T Sheridan Heritage Center Inc

856 Broadway in Sheridan. 674-2178

TS King's Saddlery Museum

184 N. Main in Sheridan. 672-2702

This collection features over 500 custom-made saddles, including (but not limited to) several made by famed saddlemaker Don King. One of the museum's most treasured item is a Japanese saddle from the 1600s. There is more craftsmanship on displays than just saddles. The museum also houses guns, chaps, spurs, wagons, Native American and frontier clothing, and an old horse drawn hearse. Admission is free. Call for hours.

T Historic Sheridan Inn Museum

Take the Fifth Street exit off of I-90 at Sheridan. 674-5440

The Old Sheridan Inn was once the place to be if you were part of the elite in nothern Wyoming. It was originally built to accomodate passengers on the Burlington and Missouri Railroad. Over the years, such famous people have been here as Calamity Jane, Ernest Hemingway, President Herbert Hoover, and even Bob Hope. Buffalo Bill Cody used to stay here when he came to town to audition acts for his show. It became the first place in Sheridan to have steam heat, telephones, and electricity around the turn of the century. The Inn was partially restored in 1965, and then refurbished again when the Sheridan Heritage Center took responsibility for it. The SHC accepts donations to help further restore the Inn and keep it running. Call for hours.

T Sheridan County Fulmer Public Library

335 West Alger in Sheridan. 674-8585

Permanent exhibits feature works of regional artists and Native American artifacts. There are also changing monthly exhibits. The Wyoming room features collections including local and regional history and U.S. genealogy. Open Monday through Thursday, 9 a.m. to 9 p.m., Friday and Saturday, 9 a.m. to 5 p.m. Sundays, September to May, from 1 p.m. to 5 p.m.

H Crook's Campaign, 1876

W. Dow and Alger in Sheridan.

On this site, the junction of Big and Little Goose Creeks, General George Crook, with 15 troops of cavalry, 5 companies of infantry, 1325 men and 1900 head of transport animals, headquartered. Joined by Indian allies, the Crows under chiefs Old Crow, Medicine Crow and Plenty Coups, and Shoshoni under Washakie, he battled 2500 Sioux 40 miles northeast, on the Rosebud, June 17. Defeated, Crook returned here, occupying these valleys, awaiting reinforcements which arrived in August. He then united with General Alfred Terry's army, which included remnants of Custer's 7th Cavalry, to campaign in Montana. Buffalo Bill, Calamity Jane, Frank Grouard, noted western characters, were with this expedition.

F Wyoming's Rib & Chop House

856 N. Broadway in Sheridan. 673-4700

The Wyoming's Rib and Chop House is located in the historic Sheridan Inn, built in 1893. The whole family will enjoy the menu they are famous for. Favorites include baby-back ribs, Certified Angus Beef steaks, and Louisiana-style seafood selections. They are open year round and patio dining is available in the summer. The Sheridan Inn was owned and housed Buffalo Bill for many years. It is believed to be haunted by long time housekeeper, Miss Kate. The bar and backboards were sent to Wyoming by Queen Victoria in 1896. For a truly pleasurable dining experience be sure and stop by for lunch or dinner. Catering for large groups is available.

L Cameo Rose Bed & Breakfast

306 W. Loucks Street in Sheridan. 673-0500

S Best Out West

109 N. Main in Sheridan. 674-5003

This truly unique store is housed in one of Sheridan's historic landmark buildings on Main Street. It's a true treasure trove offering 10,000 square feet of antiques and collectibles from over 100 dealers. Best Out West features an extraordinary selection of old and new items that capture the flavor of the Old West, including locally handcrafted items. There is something for every taste and budget including shabby chic, western and lodge decorative items as well as your favorite collectibles and antiques.

Wyoming Tidbits

The geographical center of Wyoming is Fremont, 58 miles northeast of Lander.

S Crazy Woman Trading Company

120 N. Main in Sheridan. 672-3939. www.CrazyWomanTradingCo.com

The Crazy Woman Trading Company specializes in one-of-a-kind items featuring a variety of art, antiques, fun gifts, fantastic jewelry, and logo clothing. Their T-shirts are worn around the world. A full line of Aspen Bay candles are also available. The shop is a truly unique and fun shopping experience. The courtyard is chock full of yard art. Stop in and meet Ms. Murphy McDougal, the CEO and resident Labrador. You'll also want to take a minute to meet the proprietors, Linda and Willis. Located in historic Downtown Sheridan. Be sure and visit them on the web.

S BigHorn Design Custom Embroidery & Screenprinting

201 N. Main in Sheridan. 674-8808 or toll free at 888-322-8607. wwwbighorndesign.com

BigHorn Design offers the convenience of catalog shopping with built-in hometown service. You can also visit their store in downtown Sheridan and experience the variety of colors, textures, and styles of garments and accessories they offer first hand. Visit their web site to review the thousands of garments they offer in their catalog. Whether you shop in person, by phone, or on line you can be assured that your order will receive close attention and care. All embroidery design, digitizing and production is done in-house. When choosing apparel for yourself, family, or company you can count on BigHorn Design's commitment to providing quality garments and outstanding customer service at a competitive price.

Wyoming Tidbits

A "nester" is a farmer or homesteader who settled in cattle-grazing country. Cattlemen and nesters were in constant conflict, and one of the most historic events in Wyoming's history involves such a conflict in the Johnson County War of 1892.

M ERA Carroll Realty Co.

306 N. Main in Sheridan. 672-8911 or 800-585-8911. www.eracrc.com

In 1913, George C. Carroll entered the real estate business and the first Carroll Realty office opened its doors with his son Granville Carroll, operating the company until 1955. The company continued to grow under the leadership of Don Carroll, grandson of George Carroll, affiliating with ERA, (Electronic Realty Associates) in 1978. The family-owned business developed the reputation for honesty and reliable service, which it upholds today. In 1990 the company was sold to long time employee, Dixie See, who aggressively expanded the business, always striving to provide new and enhanced services. The agency recently merged with Banner Realty which brought with it a strong ranch and rural real estate department. Tom Belus and Jane Clark joined Dixie as owners of this full service real estate organization.

5 *Gas, Food, Lodging*

T Sheridan College Martinson Gallery

3059 Coffeen Ave. in Sheridan.674-6446

T Wyoming National Guard Armory Museum

3219 Coffeen in Sheridan. 672-6442

T Trail End State Historic Site

400 Clarendon Avenue in Sheridan. 674-4589. www.trailend.org

From its authentically furnished rooms to its finely manicured lawns, the Trail End State Historic Site displays an elegantly different aspect of Wyoming's colorful ranching history. Built in the Flemish Revival style in 1913, Trail End was the home of John Benjamin Kendrick. A cattle rancher who started out a Texas cowboy, Kendrick ended up as Governor of Wyoming and a United States Senator. Trail End is the perfect place to take a moment and just imagine what life might have been like in Wyoming during the early years of the 20th century.

From laundry room to ballroom, Trail End offers an intriguing glimpse into life during the period 1913 to 1933. Exhibits and displays throughout the home's fully-furnished historic interior provide information on daily life, entertainment, interior design and technology. The house and grounds were placed on the National Register of Historic Places in 1970. A state-held property since 1982, Trail End is currently operated by the State Parks & Historic Sites Division of the Wyoming Department of Parks and Cultural Resources.

The house is closed to the public from December 15 through March 31. The site grounds are open year round until sunset. A fee is charged.

T Kendrick City Park

Near the Kendrick Mansion on Clarendon in Sheridan

This is the home where the buffalo roam! The park's small game preserve is home to bison and elk. An outdoor swimming pool, 90-foot long water slide, band shell, walking path, ice cream shop, and all-season playground add to the park's charm.

T Trail End

400 Clarendon Avenue in Sheridan. 674-4589. www.trailend.org.

Trail End viewed from its spacious park-like grounds.

The Building at Trail End

Located on 3.5 acres of groomed grounds, Trail End is an example of Flemish Revival architecture, one of the few found in the western United States.

There are three main floors plus a basement, an attic, four balconies and four porches.

Materials used on the outside include Kansas brick, Indiana limestone, Missouri roofing tile and Wyoming granite. Both the mansion and the Carriage House (located to the west of the mansion) were designed by architect Glenn Charles McAlister of Billings, Montana.

Trail End took five years to finish, but not all that time was spent actually building. Workers were idle for over a year due to the combined effects of labor unrest in the eastern furniture mills and low prices in the midwestern cattle markets. During the delay in construction, the Kendricks lived in the Carriage House, completed in 1910.

Instead of relying on the taste and judgement of strangers, John and Eula Kendrick acted as their own general contractors. They then employed designers and consultants from all over the United States to help them put together the home they envisioned. The wall paneling, cabinets, stairs and other carved pieces were custom made for the house, using the newest automated equipment. All of the woodwork was machine-tooled in Michigan and shipped to Sheridan via railroad.

Like most large homes of the period, Trail End contained many labor saving devices: intercom, built-in stationary vacuum, laundry chute, dumbwaiter and elevator. Although never used, there was also an emergency fire suppression system with fire hoses located on each floor.

Very few structural changes have been made at Trail End. You will see, however, several rooms that were redecorated over the years by the family. The alterations have not been removed because they are part of the history of the house.

The Kendricks and Trail End

Trail End was the home of John Benjamin Kendrick, former Wyoming Governor and United States Senator. Born in Texas in 1857, Kendrick was orphaned at an early age and raised by relatives until he went out on his own at age fifteen. In 1879, Kendrick came to Wyoming territory for the first time, as a trail rider on a cattle drive.

John Kendrick married 17 year old Eula Wulfjen in 1891. For the next 18 years, they lived on the OW Ranch in southeastern Montana. This property was the start of what later became the Kendrick Cattle Company, a 200,000 acre collection of cattle ranches in northern Wyoming and southern Montana.

While at the OW Ranch, the family's size doubled. Rosa Maye (1897-1979) and Manville (1900-1992) were both born in Sheridan, but lived their early lives at the ranch.

Construction began on Trail End in 1908. After it was finished in 1913, the family had only a short time to enjoy their new home. John Kendrick was elected Governor of Wyoming in 1914 and the family moved to Cheyenne. Two years later he was chosen to serve in the United States Senate, an office he held until his death in 1933. During that time, Trail End was used primarily as a summer home.

From 1933 to 1961, Eula Kendrick lived at Trail End with her son and his family. After her death, the others moved out and the house stood empty for seven years.

In 1968, when it was about to be torn down, Trail End was purchased by the Sheridan County Historical Society. They opened the home to the public as a community museum. Ownership was transferred to the State of Wyoming in 1982.

On a tour of the house you will find special features in every room.

Foyer: Hand-painted ceiling panels; dark mission oak woodwork; custom designed chandelier and wall sconces; elevator.

Drawing Room: French silk damask wall coverings; piano-finish mahogany beams and panels; Italian marble fireplace; 1922 portraits of John and Eula Kendrick; peonies painted by Paul de Longpres; hand- made Kurdistan rug.

Cloak Room: Intercom; coat closets.

Library: Quarter-sawn golden oak panels and bookcases; gothic style chandelier; stained glass windows; 1917 Declaration of War against Germany; Sharp reproduc- tion over fireplace.

Powder Room: Porcelain double pedestal sink with German silver fixtures.

Dining Room: Hand-painted ceiling and wall panels; piano-finish mahogany woodwork; Italian marble fireplace with carved mantle.

Vault: Walk-in combination safe.

Butler's Pantry: Glass-front cabinets; German silver sink; dumb waiter; laundry chute; icebox.

Kitchen: "Hospital White" porcelain tile walls, ceramic tile floor, marble trim; original wood/coal cookstove (later replaced by gas); porcelain sink; built-in spice cabinet and storage bins.

Back Hallway: Intercom; fusebox; fire hose; annunciator; stairs to basement; stairs to second and third floor (closed: please use main staircase).

The Carriage House

Second Floor Hallway: Replication of original wallpaper; stained glass windows; hand-painted canvas ceilings.

Manville's Bedroom: Navajo-motif wall stenciling; red fir trim.

Master Bedroom: Balcony overlooking rose garden; intercom.

Rosa Maye's Bedroom: Hand-tinted wall panels; custom designed light fixtures.

Maid's Closet: Hoses and nozzles for built-in stationary vacuum system; fusebox.

Guest Wing: Three bedrooms, each with private bath (closed to public; they're currently used as

Section 3

staff offices).

Ballroom: Tiffany-styled chandeliers with verdigris finish; maple dance floor; Georgia pine ceiling beams; horsehair cushions; rotating lead glass windows for ventilation; musician's loft.

Staff Quarters: Three bedrooms (each with sink and closets); pine wood trim; intercom; laundry chute; dumbwaiter; communal bathroom.

Attic: Musician's loft; storage area; pulley for dumbwaiter (closed to public).

Basement: Contains laundry room with three porcelain sinks, fireplace, stationary vacuum cleaner motor, vault; furnace room with boilers for steam heating system; coal bin; chauffeur's bedroom; storage facilities; public restrooms.

The Grounds

The Carriage House

Finished in 1910, it served as the Kendricks home during the construction of mansion. It was built to house carriages and horses, but never used for that purpose. By the time the family was ready to move out of their make-shift home, they were driving Cadillacs instead of buggies. It was converted to a theater and is currently the home of the Sheridan Civic Theater Guild. Phone 672-9886 for ticket information.

The Mandel Cabin was built in 1879 by George Mandel and purchased in 1882 by Sheridan founder John Loucks. It served as the area's first post office, store, school, law office, and bank. In 1976, the cabin was reconstructed from original logs and moved to Trail End State Historic Site. It is the property of the Colonial Dames of America.

Also found on the grounds are a sunken rose garden, an English sundial, an apple orchard, a circular back driveway with original clothesline/drying yard, a lawn tennis court, and a wide variety of trees and bushes, both native and exotic.

Reprinted from Wyoming State Parks and Historic Sites brochure.

Wyoming Tidbits

Wyoming's most famous outlaws were Robert LeRoy Parker ("Butch Cassidy") and Harry Longabaugh ("The Sundance Kid"). They were notorious for train robberies. Two other outlaws were "Persimmon Bill" and "Big Nose" George Parrott. Cattle rustling, horse stealing and murder were the most serious crimes in Wyoming in the late 1800s.

H Carneyville (Kleenburn) 1904-1924

I-90 Exit 25 at Sheridan Visitor's Center.

This mine was located 9 miles North of Sheridan. Traveling North along Interstate 90, as you approach the 2nd exit after leaving Sheridan, you will turn right. You will notice a great deal of subsidence in the hillside. This is where the Carneyville mining shafts were. This mine employed 450 miners and had two tipple loadouts. In the valley to the right of the shafts lay the mining community of Carneyville (Kleenburn). This community had 150 to 200 houses and approximately 2000 people residing there.

FL Holiday Inn Atrium Hotel & Conference Center

1809 Sugarland Drive in Sheridan. 672-8931 or fax 672-6388.
www.holiday-inn.com/sheridanwy

The Holiday Inn Sheridan offers 212 recently renovated luxuriously and thoughtfully appointed rooms designed for relaxation, style, and comfort. There are plenty of opportunities to rest, revive, and restore, including relaxing in the atrium at the waterfall where they proudly serve Starbucks coffee. Details make the difference from the superb staff to the fitness facilities to the banquet and conference facilities. The property is located just minutes from the Powder Horn Golf Club, affiliated with the Holiday Inn. Dine on the premises and enjoy their Chef's flair and creativity in a menu brimming with nutritious, delicious choices to suit any mood. More great food and great fun is found in Scooter's Bar and Grill.

L Days Inn - Sheridan

1104 E. Brundage Lane in Sheridan.
672-2888 or reservations at 800-329-7466

The Days Inn in Sheridan is close to I-90 at exit 25 and convenient to local attractions, shopping, and dining. This property offers plenty of amenities at reasonable rates. All rooms are provided with free local calls, cable TV, and HBO. All guests are provided with a complimentary continental breakfast. choose from smoking or non-smoking rooms, suites with in-room spas, and fully equipped handicapped facilities. Relax year around in the indoor pool.

S Tom Balding Bits & Spurs

655 Riverside off Coffeen in Sheridan.
672-8459 or 800-672-8459.
www.tombalding.com

Tom Balding moved to Wyoming in the early 1980's to find work as a ranch hand, bringing with him his considerable skills as a welder in the aerospace and sailboat industries. Soon after he began making bits and spurs, and is now one of the most respected and successful independent bit and spur makers in North America. His pieces are known for their precision and flawless finishing. The nation's leading trainers and competitors use and endorse Tom's products. While you're in Sheridan, stop by the Chrome Pony gift shop and showroom. Meet Tom, his wife Juanita, and the rest of the crew. Take a tour and see the art of real spur and bit making in progress.

M You WIN Realty

1263 Coffeen Ave. in Sheridan. 673-0641 or 800-665-UWIN (8946). www.youwinrealty.com

Mary Valdez and Associates You WIN Realty opened its doors in June 2002 with forward thinking and expansive vision. After a five-year history in selling real estate and becoming a top-producing agent in Sheridan County, in 2001 and 2002, Mary envisioned changes to benefit both buyers and sellers. Her commitment to change culminates by providing customers and clients with the utmost professionalism while providing powerful and progressive marketing and service at a fair price. Call their toll free number for up-to-date information on residential, commercial, and recreation properties in Wyoming. You can also visit them on the web.

M Farrington Realty

1760 S. Mountain View Drive in Sheridan. 672-3750. www.vickiefarrington.com

Vickie Farrington of Farrington Realty has the experience to help you find or sell property in the Sheridan and Big Horn Mountain area. She has lived in the Sheridan area since 1983 and after a successful teaching career began a real estate career in 1993. She has served as Past President of the Sheridan County Board of Realtors and is involved in many aspects of the community. She enjoys meeting new people and seeing new homes. She is a professional at helping buyers and sellers, facilitating relocating, and providing you with tools to make the right decisions and keep more of your own money. Visit Vickie on the web.

M Sheridan Realty Associates

371 Coffeen Avenue in Sheridan. 673-1000 or fax 673-7273 or cell at 752-379

M Sheridan College - Sheridan

3059 Coffeen Avenue in Sheridan. 674-6446 or 800-913-9139. www.sc.whecn.edu/

Sheridan College consists of the main campus in Sheridan Wyoming, a commuter campus in Gillette Wyoming as well as outreach centers in Buffalo, Kaycee and Wright. The Sheridan Campus consists of 64 acres featuring modern well-equipped facilities and attractive grounds. Twenty campus buildings house academic, student services and residential operations. Creating student success through educational leadership is the school's motto. A new facility is under construction. The completed project will find the Campus housed in a 66,000 sq. foot building located on 15.5 acres. The new campus will contain cutting edge instructional and networking technologies as well as science, presentational and video conferencing facilities. Completion of this facility is expected sometime in late 2003. Over 2,700 students are enrolled at Sheridan College. The Gillette Campus is currently in a transitional motto.

6 *Lodging*

Big Horn

Pop. 217, Elev. 4,059

At the foot of the mountains of the same name, Big Horn was once just a couple of cabins that sheltered outlaws. Officially founded as a town in 1878 by O.P. Hanna, this was a much-needed rest stop on the Bozeman Trail. By 1881, it was the first real town in Sheridan County. Later, in 1894, it became the home of the first college in the area, the Wyoming College and Normal School, begun by the Congregational Missionary Society. The school had to close in 1898 when the students couldn't pay the $100 tuition.

T The Bradford Brinton Memorial Museum

Just south of Big Horn on State Highway 335. Follow signs. 672-3173

This is ranch country; some of the finest in Wyoming and the Rocky Mountain West. It was settled late, in the 1870s and 1880s, but the well-watered, rich grasslands have produced excellent cattle and horse herds. The Quarter Circle A Ranch dates from this period and is typical of the more prosperous ranches of the Big Horn area. Here Bradford Brinton raised horses and cattle, entertained distinguished guests, enjoyed the scenic mountains and plains, and collected aspects of an older West. When he died in 1936, his sister, Helen Brinton, became the owner of the ranch. She kept it as a summer home until her death in 1960.

The house was built in 1892 by two Scotsmen, William and Malcolm Moncreiffe, and in 1923 was purchased by Bradford Brinton, who enlarged it to its present 20 rooms. Bradford, and later Helen, tastefully decorated and furnished the house with fine furniture, his collections of western art, Indian crafts, books, and historic documents.

Though a native of Illinois, Brinton loved the West and was particularly enamored of the work of western artists. He numbered many now famous artists among his friends, and they benefited from his encouragement and patronage. Helen Brinton, wishing to share her brother's fine collections with future generations, established the Bradford Brinton Memorial Ranch in her will to commemorate western art and culture. The Bradford Brinton Memorial Ranch opened in 1961. It is maintained and administered by The Northern Trust Company of Chicago, Illinois.

The Indian conflicts, nature's wonders, the harsh elements, and the often lonely but always exciting life of the cowboy inspired the artists of the West. The Brinton collection contains over 600 oils, watercolors, and sketches by American artists including: Charles M. Russell, Frederic Remington, Edward M. Borein, E. W. Gollings, Hans Kleiber, Will James, Frank W. Benson, John J. Audubon, Joe De Yong, Winold Reiss, and Frank Tenney Johnson.

Each year a different art exhibit is featured in the reception gallery, which is the only addition made to the ranch.

The memorial is open daily 9:30 a.m. until 5 p.m. May 15th through Labor Day.

Wyoming Tidbits

The first polo field in the United States was built north of SHERIDAN.

T Bozeman Trail Museum

Main Street in Big Horn.

Built in 1879 by the Rock Creek Stage Line, the Blacksmith Shop we now call the Bozeman Trail Museum originally satisfied the needs of travelers on the nearby Bozeman Trail, which connected southeastern Wyoming to Virginia City, Montana. O.P. Hanna was the first settler to make his permanent home here, also in 1879. John DeWitt, another early settler, was the original owner of the Blacksmith Shop. It changed hands several times before Mr and Mrs Goelet Gallatin bought it and restored it in 1936. Eventually, it became a storehouse for a variety of historic items, and was completely refurbished in 1976 by the Big Horn Bi-Centennial Committee. In 1990, with the official establishment of the Big Horn Historical Society, the site became an official museum.

T Bonanza

Big Horn Basin

Early travelers lubricated their wagon wheels in the natural oil seeps of this area. Settlers hoped to develop the town into an oil production center, but the industry never blossomed here. It is now a ghost town.

Story Day

Held the last Saturday in August, this is a day full of food, fun, parades, games, music, American indian art show, quilt show, garage sales and flea markets, craft fair, drawings and vendors. This is the annual fall-festival-type celebration.

H Bozeman Trail Blacksmith Shop

Big Horn

Near here emigrants traversed the Bozeman Trail, 1864-68, to Virginia City, Montana gold mines. Confronted with hostile Indians unwilling to share their hunting grounds, the trail became known as the "Bloody Bozeman" and was discontinued.

Crossing Little Goose Creek to the south and Jackson Creek to the west, the trail was later used from 1879-94 by the Patrick Brothers Stage Line from Rock Creek near Laramie, Wyoimng to Fort Custer on the Big Horn River in Montana.

This building was a blacksmith shop in the early 1880s to serve the stage line and ranchers of the valley.

7 *Food, Lodging*

Story

Pop. 650, Elev. 4,960

This cozy little community was probably named for Nelson Story, the first man to bring cattle up the Texas Trail, through Wyoming, and into Montana. Charles P. Story, an early newspaperman in Sheridan, may also have given his name to the town. Nestled in the pine-covered Bighorn Mountains, this was where timber was collected to build Fort Phil Kearny.

Banner

Pop. 40, Elev. 4,617

The first postmaster here, a rancher, had a flag as a cattle brand. The locals called it a banner, and when the post office opened out of his dining room, the name became the place.

T Story Fish Hatchery Visitor Center

311R Fish Hatchery Road, 2 miles west of Story. 683-224

The center is a popular for both locals and visitors, receiving more than 14,000 guests annually. The hatchery stocks nearly 250,000 fish each year and processes up to four million trout eggs that will eventually end up in the state's fish culture program or are shipped to other states in trade for species not raised in Wyoming's hatcheries.

Managed by the Wyoming Game and Fish Department, the hatchery is the oldest operating station in the state. The original hatchery was in Sheridan but was moved to the current location because of a better, colder water supply. Water is drawn from South Piney Creek 1.5 miles away. An underground waterway from the creek moderates the water's temperature.

The center is open from april 15 through September 15, and the grounds are open to visitors year-around.

T Fort Phil Kearny - History

Fort Phil Kearny

Named for a popular Union general killed in the Civil War, Fort Phil Kearny was established at the forks of Big and Little Piney Creeks by Col. Henry B. Carrington of the 18th U.S. Infantry in July, 1866.

The Mission of this fort and two other posts along the Bozeman Trail, Forts Reno and C. F. Smith, was three-fold: to protect travellers on the Trail; to prevent intertribal warfare between Native Americans in the area; and to draw attention of Indian forces opposed to Euro-American westward expansion away from the trans-continental railroad construction corridor to the south.

All three Bozeman Trail forts were stockade fortifications, with Port Phil Kearny being the largest. Enclosing seventeen acres, the fort wall was eight feet high, 1,496 feet in length, and tapered in width from 600 feet on the north to 240 feet on the south. More than four thousand logs were used to erect the stockade, while over 606,000 feet of lumber and 130,000 bricks were produced in 1867 alone for the extensive building construction.

During its two year existence, Fort Phil Kearny was the focal point of a violent war between the U.S. Army and the Sioux, Cheyenne, and Arapaho Indians opposed to intrusions into the last great hunting grounds on the Northern Plains. Besides the Fetterman and Wagon Box battles, many smaller fights took place in the area.

By 1868, the Union Pacific Railroad had reached a point to the west where travellers could bypass the Bozeman Trail route by going to Montana through Idaho, thus making the Bozeman Trail forts expensive liabilities. In the Treaty of 1868, the United States agreed to close the forts and the trail, Fort Phil Kearny was abandoned by the Army in early August, 1868, and burned soon afterwards by the Cheyenne.

In 1963, Fort Phil Kearny was designated a National Historic Landmark. Today, portions of the fort site and the Fetterman and Wagon Box battlefields are included within the Fort Phil Kearny State Historic Site boundaries .

Fetterman Fight.

On December 21, 1866, Sioux, Cheyenne, and Arapaho warriors engaged a military force commanded by Captain William J. Fetterman. Ordered to rescue a besieged wagon train, Fetterman's men pursued Crazy Horse and other warriors acting as decoys over Lodge Trail Ridge where over two thousand Indians waited in ambush The warriors attacked the soldiers, overwhelming the separated cavalry and infantry units. All eighty one men in Fetterman's command were killed within thirty minutes. Only the Battle of the Little Big Horn stands as a worse defeat for the United States Army and a greater victory for the Plains Indians.

"Portugee" Phillips Ride

Phillips is known for his heroic 236 mile ride to Fort Laramie following the Fetterman Fight. Riding in the deep of winter into the midst of a blizzard, he hid during the day and rode only at night as he passed through enemy territory. He pushed his horse beyond its limit and sacrificed it

Fort Phil Kearny State Historic Site

HANDICAPPED ACCESSIBLE
HISTORIC/INTERPRETIVE TRAIL
PARK HEADQUARTERS
RESTROOMS
PICNIC AREA
PAVED ROAD
GRAVEL ROAD

To Sheridan 20 miles
BOZEMAN TRAIL
Fetterman Fight
BIG HORN MOUNTAINS
STORY
North
South
Piney Creek
LODGE TRAIL RIDGE
Wagon Box Fight
Little Piney
SULLIVANT HILL
Portugee Phillips' Monument
Ft. Phil Kearny State Historic Site Visitor Center/Museum
Cemetery
PILOT KNOB
Exit 44
To Buffalo 17 miles

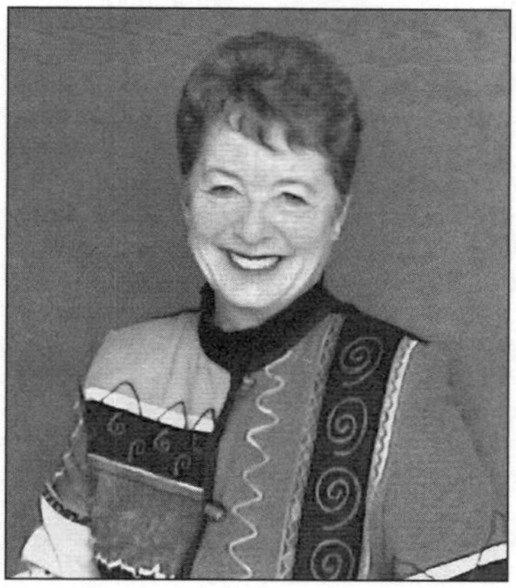

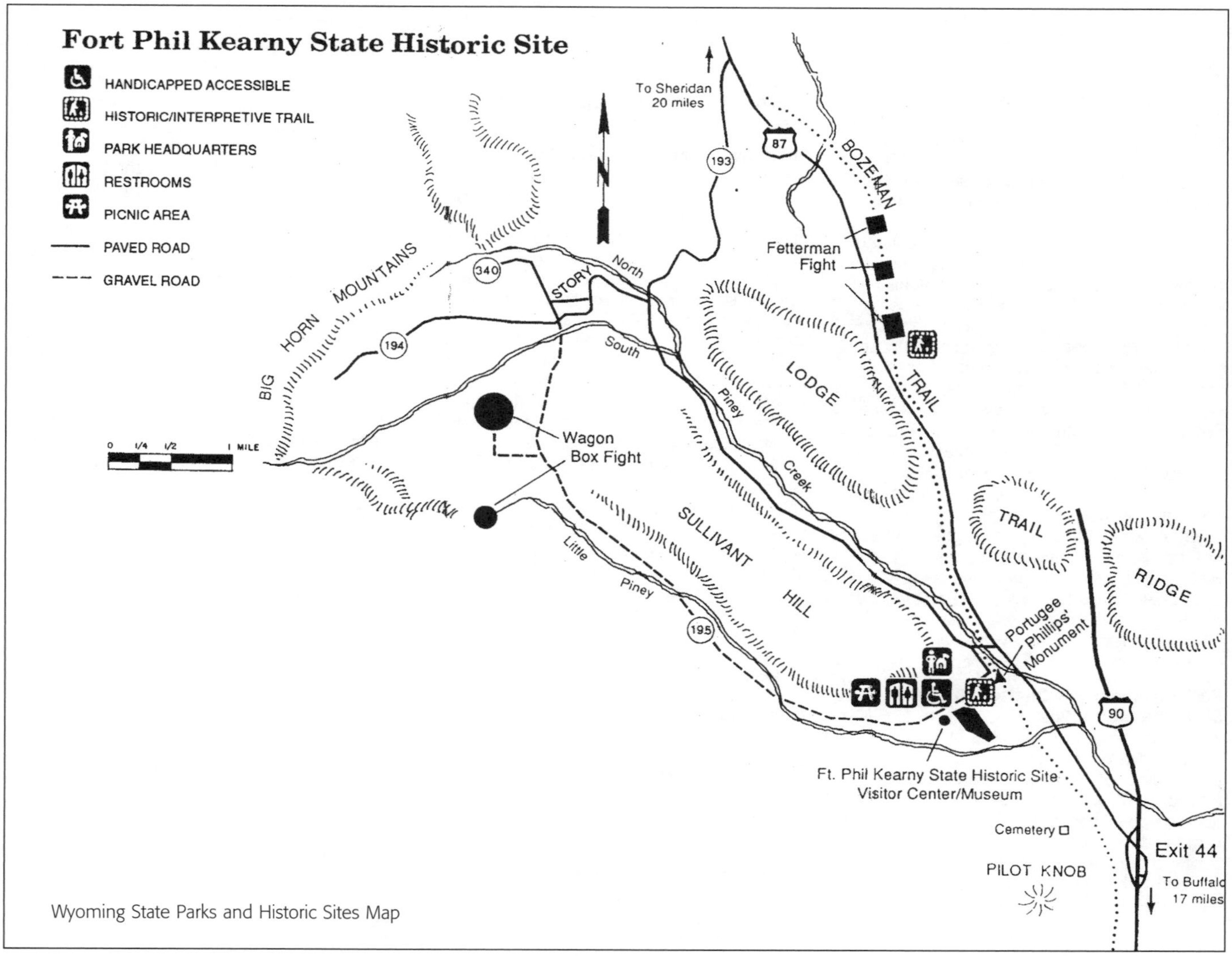

Wyoming State Parks and Historic Sites Map

in the process, completing the ride in just four days, and arriving at Fort Laramie during a ball on Christmas night.

Wagon Box Fight

Indian forces attempted to repeat the Fetterman victory in the summer of 1867. On August 2, about eight-hundred Sioux attacked wood-cutters and soldiers camped at a cutting area five miles from Fort Phil Kearny. During initial stages of the battle, twenty-six soldiers and six civilians took cover inside an oval of wagon boxes used as a stock corral.

After burning another camp, Sioux warriors launched a series of attacks against the corral. Armed with breechloading rifles, the soldiers and civilians commanded by Captain James Powell held off the massed warriors until a relief force arrived from the fort. Three men were killed and two wounded inside of the corral, while Indian casualties were estimated at from five to sixty or more killed, and five to one hundred twenty more wounded.

Reprinted from Wyoming Department of Commerce brochure.

H Fort Phil Kearny Interpretive Signs

Fort Phil Kearny

The Magazine: Storing Munitions and More

All military posts had a magazine for storing munitions. At Fort Phil Kearny the Magazine was 16 by 16 feet, with a 11 foot dirt covered ceiling and it was buried eight feet in the southwest quadrant of the parade ground. It is referred to in numerous historical records. Carrington shows its location on his as-built map, and he did a design for its construction. Samuel Gibson indicates its location on his map of the fort. Margaret Carrington describes the location as "being in the center of one of the squares".

There are many colorful accounts centered around the magazine. Colonel Carrington was constantly frustrated with his lack of munitions and the shortage of ammunition at the post. This became very apparent following the Fetterman Fight when men were sent to guard the stockade with only five rounds of ammunition each. When Carrington left the fort on December 22, 1866 to retrieve the bodies of Fetterman's command he left secret instructions which Francis Grummond recounted. "If, in my absence, Indians in overwhelming numbers attack, put the women and children in the magazine in a last desperate struggle, destroy all together, rather than have any captured alive". Results of the 1999 archaecological study provide no evidence of the magazine being in the southwest quadrant as historical records indicated. At present the magazine's exact location is unknown, still one of the many unanswered questions about Fort Phil Kearny.

Post Commander's Quarters: The Best Structure on the Post

1867 quartermaster inspections of Fort Phil Kearny indicated the poor condition of many of the buildings on post and that they needed rebuilding. These included the barracks, officer's quarters, post headquarters and more. The post commander's house was a 48 by 32 foot frame construction structure, built of fire dried trees, shingled with a 22 by 13 foot attached kitchen, and brick chimneys. This was probably the best structure on post.

The house was built by the regimental band for Colonel Carrington. It initially housed the Colonel, his wife Margaret, their sons Jimmy and Harry, and butler George. It was then occupied in turn by later Post Commanders Henry Wessells and Jonathan Smith.

Two archaeological pits have been left open for viewing. They show the remains of the interior ground structure of the commander's house.

The Guard House: Not Just a Jail

Even though Fort Phil Kearny, like most frontier posts, had plenty of use for a jail this was not the main function of the Guardhouse. The 50 by 43 foot, shingled building with a brick chimney, was used primarily for quard-mount. Guard-mount was the duty of protecting the post. Soldiers would be detached from their companies to this building on a repeated schedule for guard duty. From this building an individual soldier would be assigned to a guard-stand where he would quard the post on intervals of 2-hours-on 4-hours-off, for 24 hours. This was not an easy duty, During the harsh winter months the interval could drop to as little as 20 minutes to prevent injury or death to the guard. Francis Grummond recounts a story in My Army Life of Indians sneaking up and shooting guards off the stand. One had to be vigilant.

For soldiers convicted of serious crimes the building did serve as a jail. In August 1866 records indicate that 24 prisoners were being held under guard in tents awaiting the completion of this building. Their crime was desertion. Lessor crimes might be punished by extra duty, wearing a ball and chain, wearing a barrel with a sign stating your offense, or even flogging.

The Cavalryman's Quarters: Few and Far Between

It is a false perception that the frontier posts of the American West were garrisoned with large troops of cavalry. Actually a post's usual population was largely infantry with a rew cavalry for support, reconnaissance, escort, or mail delivery. Fort Phil Kearny was no exception. It was not until November 2, 1866 that any cavalry were stationed at the post. Though initially placed in a variety of quarters, they were finally housed in a large, new 100 by 25 foot log-panel constucted barracks with a shingle roof. Nearby was a 250 by 32 foot board and batten stable with corral, saddler's shop and a blacksmith.

Company C, of the 2nd U.S. Cavalry Regiment was assigned to Fort Phil Kearny. They arrived, armed with single-shot Starr Carbines on poorly conditioned mounts. Colonel Carrington replaced their weapons with the band's Spencer Carbines, but little could be done for the mounts. Few cavalry were ever at the Fort. They were constantly being requisitioned for mail, escort, or other duties by military inspectors traveling the trail. Unforunately, of those troops available on December 21, 1866, the majority wre killed in the Fetterman Fight, leaving their quarters sorrowfully near empty.

The Civilians: Living Outside the Post

Because the regulations would not allow non-military dependent civilians to reside inside Fort Phil Kearny, several civilian dwellings existed outside the post stockade on the valley plain below, and in the Quartermaster corral to the south. These homes varied in size and degree of construction. Some were built as notched cornered log cabins with shingled roofs, others were of pole construction with sod roofs, while others were mere dugouts in the northeast slope of the stockade line. Depressions from these dugouts are still visible today.

Civilians provided many services for the military and travelers of the Bozeman Trail. James Wheatley and Issac Fisher built a way-station and restaurant. Another eatery and the only known garden were managed by Mr. and Mrs. Charles Washington. Walter J. Harden and F.J. Fairbrast had a small "ranche" and billiard room. This building undoubtedly provided after-hours entertainment for the soldiers. One large group of about 40 gold-miners, under the leadership of Robert Bailey, arrived in the fall of 1866. They stayed through the winter working for both civilian contractors and the military. Occupations included wood cutters and forage gathers for civilian contractors and carpenters or blacksmiths for the military.

Unfortunately, the civlians often got caught up in the military activities. Wheatley and Fisher volunteered to go with Captain Fetterman's command on December 21, 1866 and lost their lives that day. Remarkably, Mrs. Wheatley continued to run the way-station until the fort's closure. John "Portugee" Phillips, part of the Bailey miners, rode for relief following the Fetterman fight and later settled in Wyoming.

Lessons Learned
Archaeology at Fort Phil Kearny

Documented archaeology began at Fort Phil Kearny in 1961 and reoccurred in 1970, 1991-92, 1999 and 2000. The initial work was done by Gene Gallaway who salvaged artifacts during the county road construction. In 1970-71 George Frison studied the site, determining stockade, gate, southeast blockhouse and flag-pole locations. Richard Fox searched for the southwest blockhouse, sutler store, and post commander''s residence in 1991 and 1992. In 1999-2000 Tom Larson and Lewis Somers studies, using subsurface mapping techniques, provided images of the under ground remains (see illustrations below) of the upper stockade and its diagonal blockhouses.

These studies have provided a great deal of insight into understanding the fort site. Many historic features have been confirmed, including locations of the upper stockade, main gate, blockhouse, gun bastion, sutler store, and commander's house. Various construction techniques have been identified, including frame and post/pole, and many personal artifacts have been recovered. We now know that the period historic maps are reasonably accurate, but questions remain. We do not know the exact location of the magazine, unidentified buildings have shown up on the ground radar research and historically recorded ones have not.

The archaeology has provided us a better understanding of Fort Phil Kearny. It has given us some understanding of the reliability of the historical record, and pointed out new directions for study. There is still much to be learned.

Quartermaster and Commissary Buildings: Supplying the Post

The quartermaster and commissary departments provided the two categories of supplies for maintaining military posts. Quartermaster supplies included items like weapons, clothing, saddles, blankets, beds, and more. Commissary supplies were mainly food stuffs. At this fort these items were stored in five or more warehouses varying in size from 24 by 84 feet to 32 by 160 feet. The buildings were of board and batten construction with shingle roofs and one building contained a cellar. Records indicate that some civilians bunked in the larger warehouse. Due to theft by soldiers and civilians, guards were placed at all warehouses.

Included in this complex of buildings was the Quartermaster's office. This building was 32 by 64 feet, board constructed with a shingle roof. It straddled the stockade wall and from here the Quartermaster acted as liaison between civilian workers and the military. Captain Frederick Brown was the first Quartermaster and upon his death Captain George Dandy took over the duties.

Fort Phil Kearny State Historic Site: A Guided Tour

Fort Phil Kearny State Historic Site is administered by the Wyoming State Parks and Historic Sites Department and supported by the Fort Phil Kearny/Bozeman Trail Association. All parties are committed to the preservation and interpretation of the many aspects of the site.

The Historic site has three components. Two of the components, the Getterman and Wagon Box fight sites, are approximately five miles from the fort. These sites offer interpretive trails with signing and help the viewer more fully understand the dramatic history of Fort Phil Kearny.

At the fort site the visitor has several options. The interpretive center offers many exhibits describing the fort's mission, archaeology, the Native Amercans, provides a video overview of the fort, distributes a site brochure, and offers a wide variety of books which further explain the area's history. The Civilian Conservation Corp cabin interprets the living conditions of an officer or enlisted man. Outside the fort-proper interpretive signs explain crucial landmarks surrounding the fort and oulying structures.

On the fort grounds visual and audio interpretive signs describe the structures, personalities, and short history of the post. To best view the fort grounds one should follow a clockwise route.

Protecting the Travelers or the Garrison?

The mission of the Fort Phil Kearny garrison was to quard travelers on the Bozeman Trail, but, it soon became apparent that the quards would also need protection. Therefore, on July 13, 1866, Captain Tenador Ten Eyck began building a fort which had been designed by Colonel Henry Carrington before they left Fort Stephen Kearny. The fort's 800 by 600 foot long walls were made of 11' by 12" logs buried three feet in the ground. There were firing notches cut along the banquet at every fifth log, and blockhouses or gun-bastions on two opposite corners to provide enfilading fire along the walls. The main gate was located on the east wall, and smaller, five foot wide officer's gates were originally located on each of the other walls. Each gate was provided with a locking mechanism. Five guard stands were located to provide 24 hour surveillance of the grounds both inside and outside the post.

Before you is a reproduction of the stockade, guard stand, officer's gate and artillery bastion as originally built at Fort Phil Kearny. From this position we knew Col. Carrington fired artillery at the Native Americans who opposed the fort.

At the time of construction few military forts in the West had stockades. Would it have been better to train the raw recruits to protect the travelers? Was the time used to build the 2,800 feet of stockade wasted?

Artist conceptual drawing prior to archaeological discoveries.

An Enlisted Man's Quarters Better than Nothing

Some of the first structures built at Fort Phil Kearny were the enlisted men's barracks. The first four were 24 by 84 foot, green log, panel constructed buildings with dirt roofs and floors. In 1867 one additional 26 by 100 foot barrack was built to house the cavalry; kitchens were installed as basements in some of the previous barracks. Each barrack was expected to house an infantry or cavalry company averaging 87 men. With the exception of noncommissioned officers, who lived in small rooms within the barracks, all men live in an open bay heated with cast-iron stoves. The buildings were said to be breezy in winter, cool in the summer and by 1867: "fit to be torn down."

The roofs leaked in the rain, and provided homes for snakes, mice, and all sorts of critters. The green log building material shrank as it dried, leaving gaps in the walls and the dirt floors turned to mud. All these factors made life in the barracks and for the enlisted men miserable.

Some men came right from the Civil War, armed and clothed with four-year-old equipment. Others avoiding famine, and persecution in Europe emigrated, joined the army and came here. Their base pay was thirteen dollars a month supplemented with soured food for long marches and back breaking work.The enlisted man was poorly paid, poorly fed, and poorly housed. But it was better than nothing, if only slightly.

The Military Stockade: Post Headquarters, Soldier Quarters and More

Fort Phil Kearny's design was based on standard military models of the time, with the post's buildings located around a 400 by 400 foot parade grounds. The parade grounds were divided into four 200 by 200 quadrants, with walkways surrounding the parade grounds and dividing the quadrants. Soldiers were forbidden to walk across the open areas of the parade grounds except when performing official duties such as drill, parades or answering the Call to Arms.

The military stockade was a constantly evolving complex of structures during the two years of Fort Phil Kearny's existence. Many of the original buildings were improved or replaced over the life of the post. Some examples of these changes were the addition of brick chimneys, and the building of basement kitchens under the existing barracks and those newly constructed during 1867-1868, which not only helped save space in the cramped confines of the fort, but also provided some additional warmth for the barracks' occupants.

A List of the Structures

1. Gun Bastion
2. Infantry Barracks
3. Officer Quarters
4. Permanent Hospital
5. Bakery
6. Band Quarters
7. Sutler Store
8. Post Headquaters
9. Guard House
10. Main Gate
11. Warehouses
12. Laundry Quarters
13. Saddle Shop
14. Temporary Hospital
15. Powder Magazine
16. Commander Quarters
17. Flag Pole Bandstand
18. Artillery Park
19. Guard Stand
20. Chapel
21. Civilian Dwelling (Wheatley)
22. Cavalry Barracks
23. Cavalry Stables
24. NCO Quarters
25. Guard Stands
26. Sinks
27. Quartermaster Office
28. Civilian Dwellings

Cloud Peak Wilderness Area

Cloud Peak Wilderness preserves many sharp summits and towering sheer rock faces standing above glacier-carved U-shaped valleys. Named for the tallest mountain in Bighorn National Forest–Cloud Peak at 13,167 feet–the Wilderness is blanketed in snow for a large part of the year. Most of the higher ground doesn't show bare ground until July. On the east side of Cloud Peak itself, a deeply inset cirque holds the last remaining glacier in this range. Several hundred beautiful lakes, many offering excellent trout fishing, cover the landscape and drain into miles of trout streams. The Cloud Peak Wilderness is part of the 106 million acre National Wilderness Preservation System. This System of lands provides clean air, water, and habitat critical for rare and endangered plants and animals. In wilderness, you can enjoy challenging recreational activities like hiking, backpacking, climbing, kayaking, canoeing, rafting, horse packing, bird watching, stargazing, and extraordinary opportunities for solitude. You plan an important role in helping to "secure for the American people of present and future generations the benefits of an enduring resource of wilderness" as called for by the Congress of the United States through the Wilderness Act of 1964. Use Leave No Trace techniques when visiting the Cloud Peak Wilderness to ensure protection of this unique area.

Unless otherwise specified, no motorized equipment or mechanical transport is allowed. This is true for all federal lands managed as designated wilderness.

Courtesy: U.S. Forest Service

The Post Headquarters: Administering Fort Phil Kearny and the Mountain District

From this building the commander of the Mountain District of the U.S Army isssued orders to Forts Phil Kearny, C.F. Smith, and the Reno. The Mountain District was made up of the 2nd Battalion 18th Infantry until 1867 when it was reorganized into the 27th Infaantry Regiment. During this building's existence, the 25 by 50 foot, one inch plank boxs and batten

Present Structures

A. Visitor Center
B. Exterior Restrooms
C. CCC Cabin (Employees only)
D. Interpretive Circle
E. Native American Memorial
In-situ archaeology displays on grounds

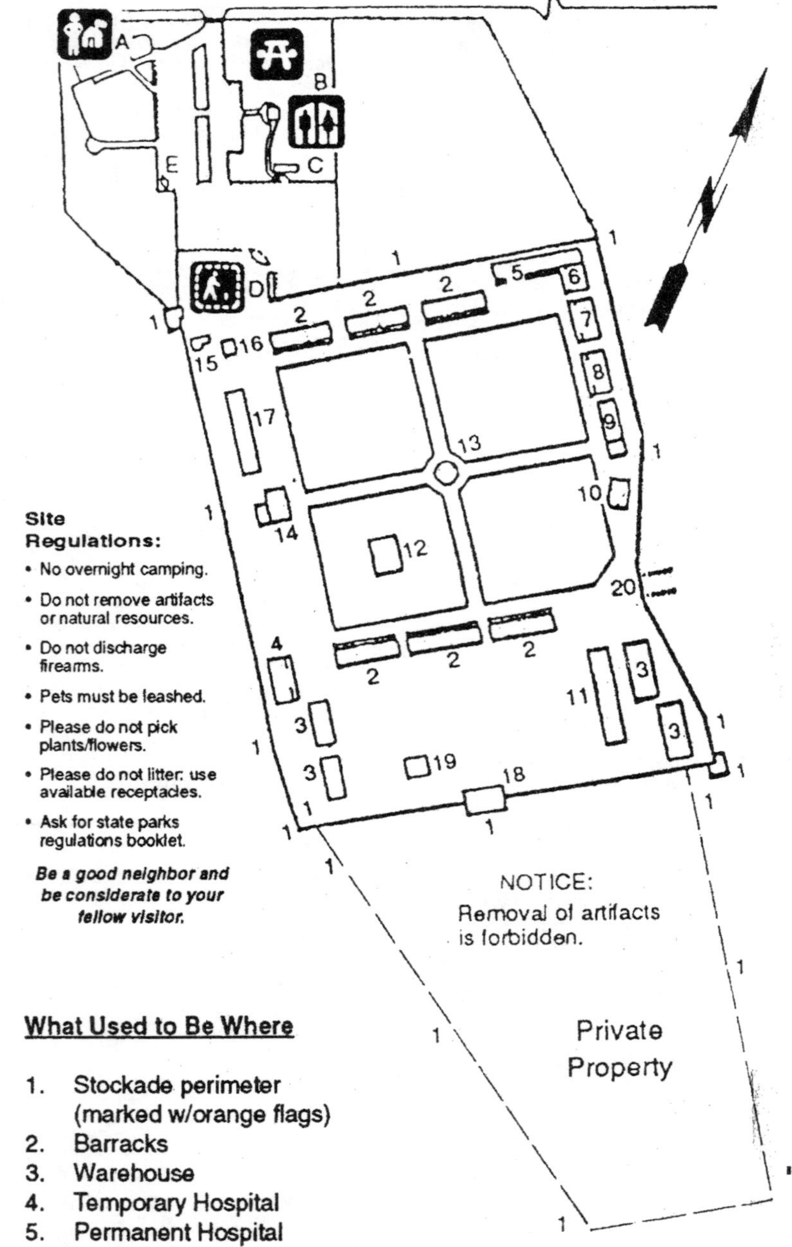

Site Regulations:

- No overnight camping.
- Do not remove artifacts or natural resources.
- Do not discharge firearms.
- Pets must be leashed.
- Please do not pick plants/flowers.
- Please do not litter: use available receptacles.
- Ask for state parks regulations booklet.

Be a good neighbor and be considerate to your fellow visitor.

What Used to Be Where

1. Stockade perimeter (marked w/orange flags)
2. Barracks
3. Warehouse
4. Temporary Hospital
5. Permanent Hospital
6. Bakery
7. Band Barracks
8. Sutler Store
9. Post Headquarters
10. Guard House
11. Laundry Quarters
12. Powder Magazine
13. Original Flagpole
14. Commander's Quarters
15. Post Chapel
16. Surgeon's Quarters
17. Officers' Quarters
18. Quartermaster's Office
19. Saddle Shop
20. A Main Gate (red flag with white flags on exterior of the two openings)

structure was an office for Colonels Henry B. Carrington, Henry Wessells, and John E. Smith. The building was also the commuynication center for Fort Phil Kearny. Flag signalmen located on a lookout stand attached to building received and sent messages to Pilot Knob and other points.

In 1887, Quartermaster Captain George Dandy described the building as "needing torn down".

Yet it continued to function in a number of ways until the closure of the fort. One use was as a school house, in which Chaplain White taught classes for the 10 children of 17 families on post.

The Quartermaster Corral: Civilian Quarters, Storage, and Shops

While not as well built and fortified as the military stockade to the north, the quartermaster's stockade provided protection for the Quartermaster Department's supplies, draft animals, work shops and civilian employees. Most of the supplies brought to the fort, either by wagons up the Bozeman Trail or by contractors working local resources, came into the quartermaster's corral.

By April 1867, the Quartermaster Department was employing 52 civilians, including mail carriers, guides, carpenters, wagon masters, coal miners, stock herders and others.

Maintaining Fort Phil Kearny was expensive; laborers were paid $35-$45 a month, three times the salary of an Army enlisted man, while guides made from $5 to $10 a day, almost as much as an Army colonel.

The Fort

On July 13, 1866, Colonel Henry B. Carrington, leading four companies of the 18th Infantry, arrived at this site. Carrington, a competent engineer, immediately put his men to work. Through diligent labor they built, by October of that year, the basic units of what became an outstanding example of the complete, stockaded, "Indian Wars" military establishment.

From here, as you face across this tablet, extends the ground where Fort Phil Kearny once stood. Replacement posts mark the original corners of the 800' x 600' stockade. Beyond, salient points of contiguous cavalry and quartermaster corrals are marked. At the southwest end an animal watering gap jutted into Little Piney Creek. The Bozeman Trail passed roughly parallel to the northeast side.

Fort Phil Kearny was usually garrisoned by four to six infantry companies, plus one or two companies of cavalry. However, so slosely did Sioux and Cheyenne warriors, under the tactician Red Cloud, invest the post that these troops were frequently unable to perform Bozeman Trail convoy duty. Incidents of hostility were the daily rule and several of the most famous engagements of "Indian Wars" relate to this fort.

The military abandoned the fort in August, 1868, and it was burned by a band of Cheyenne.

The Flagpole: A Relief to the Traveler

The sight of a 20 by 36 foot American flag flying atop a 124 foot flagpole came as a great relief to the traveler on the Bozeman Trail. It meant the viewer was in sight of safe haven, temporarily free from the rigors of the trail, and safe from Indian attak. The pole which supported the flag was constructed of two pieces in a design similar to a ship mast. Made of lodge-

Little remains of old Fort Kearny. The interpretive signs along the fort's grounds do much to give the visitor an idea of what the original fort was like.

pole pine hauled from the wood-cutting areas on nearby Piney Island, the round poles were carved into octagons, painted black and the two pieces pinned together under the direction of civilian builder William Daley.

The flagpole was raised on October 31, 1866, with much fanfare. The first United States garrison flag to fly over the land between the North Platte and Yellowstone Rivers was hoisted. The band played on an octagonal stand erected at the pole's base. Colonel Carrington addressed the post's residents, and soldiers, dressed in newly issued uniforms. He spoke of their haardships, losses, and tribulations, and he didicated the new fort after nearly four months of occupation, naming it for a fallen Civil War hero.

The Hospital: Any Attempt to Relieve the Suffering…

at Fort Phil Kearny was seldom successful at either of its two hospitals. The original hospital was a 24 by 84 foot structure similar to the barracks in construction. During this hospital's short service it sadly served as the morgue for Fetterman's command. During most of its existence the building functioned as an officer's quarters and was home to Captain Powell during his time at the post.

The second and primary hospital was built in 1867. It was an L—shaped structure incorporating panel construction and was 25 by 156 feet. The building either replaced or was attached to the bakery which was also located in this corner.The bakery attachment would have provided additional warmth and soothing aromas for the occupants. Little else is known abut this building.

Suffering at the post was considerable. There was constant skirmishing with the Indians ouside the post resulting in numerous battle injuries. In addition to combat wounds the occupants might be suffering from disease including dysentery, scurvy, or tuberculosis which, records indicate, were prevalent at the fort due to poor diet and sanitation.

The Band: For Conflict or Comfort

The 18th Infantry's 40-piece Regimental Band was housed at Fort Phil Kearny in a 24 by 64 green log, panel constructed, dirt roofed barrack. The band provided drummers and buglers for drill, ceremony, and combat commands during the day. In the evening they would gather at an octagonal bandstand surrounding the flagstaff to serenade the post with martial or popular music of the day. On special occasions they would orchestrate waltzes at post dances. Their duties were truly ones of extremes; besides sounding commands or music to march by, members might also be called on to act as messengers, medical orderlies, or combat soldiers. Band members at the fort also built Colonel Carrington's house in addition to serving as clerks or supply personnel.

There is more historical information on the band at Fort Phil Kearny than some of the other units. It is known that the band members carried Spencer Carbines even though the men seldom went into combat as a complete unit. Following the December 6, 1866 skirmish Colonel Carrington transferred these weapons to the cavalry, hoping to increase their fire power. All these weapons were lost in the Fetterman Fight two weeks later. Sadly, it is also known that the first death at Fort Phil Kearny was the Bandmaster, Master Serveant William Curry,who died of typhoid and pneumonia, leaving behind a wife and two boys.

"As we passed the Fort some distance we came to a halt for nearly an hour and a half…crossing the stream and ascending the bluffs beyond. As we lay there the brass band at the Fort commenced playing. Such sounds in such a scene! There was something in the wild, sweet strains that filled and floated through the deep reechoing valley that spoke of home; yet so far distant and in so wild a place that it partook of the nature of the scenes around it. It was like looking through the 'glass of time' into the dim Past…'

From the diary of Davis Willson, August 7, 1866, near Fort Phil Kearny

The Land

The land under view, where the Great Plains meet the Rocky Mountains, was once the Red man's land of milk and honey. Then, as now, teeming with wildlife, it was most productive—thus favorite—hunting ground. But it was also a natural route for north-south travel, used from time immemorial by nomadic men and migratory beasts. Lying hundreds of miles beyond the 1860 frontier it was treaty-confirmed Indian Country.

Here came a frontiersman, John Bozeman, pioneering a wagon road which followed buffalo, Indian and trapper trails. His time and energy saving short cut led to the booming mining fields of western Montana. This interloper was followed by others whose habitual frontier callousness easily stifled any scruple over trespass of an Indian passageway. Faint wheel marks soon became a beaten road known as the Bozeman Trail.

High plains and mountain Indians, notably Sioux and Cheyenne, watching this transgression, resented both the physical act and the implied contempt of solemn treaty. They made war. The white transgressors called upon their army for protection. In the end the Indians won a brief respite-partly because of developing railroad far to the south canceled the Bozeman Trail's short cut advantage.

Pilot Hill Picket Post

Pilot Hill—overlooking Piney and Little Piney Creek Valleys, the Bozeman Road, the Sullivant Ridge with its wood road was a constantly manned lookout. From this post the sentry signaled to the Fort news of events as they occured—how the wood detail progressed, what travelers fared the Bozeman Road, where and how a skirmish was developing, who was in desperate need of reinforcements.

A Monument Honoring John "Portugee" Phillips

One of history's great but little celebrated rides was made between midnight December 21st and Christmas night December 25th in the year 1866. From here at Fort Phil Kearny, where annihilation of Fetterman's force had left the garrison in desperate straits, this ride spanned 236 miles to strategic Fort Laramie, the nearest hope for any succor. John "Portugee" Phillips, shrouded in snow and driven by an arctic wind, made that ride. He rode the Commanding Officer's superb thoroughbred and he rode by night and hid by day, or used the bitter yet advantageous storm to hide his movements and blot his tracks. Thus he eluded pursuing Indians who, anticipating a necessary dash for aid, sought to intercept the speeding pair—resourceful messenger and courageous steed.

Site of a sawmill

As explained in No. 1 of this series, wood was the life blood of Fort Phil Kearny. The founding soldiers had carried into this wilderness a sawmill. It was set up without the walls of the stockade as here illustrated. And here, as supplied by logs carried in wagon trains returning from the Pinery, were sawed the boards from which the Fort's structures were built.

Sullivant Ridge

Fort Phil Kearny, built of wood and fueled by wood, required a never ending supply of wood. A supply obtained despite hostile activity by Sioux and Cheyenne. Source was the Pinery four miles west against the mountains. The

Fort Phil Kearny

route followed by the crest of Sullivant Ridge-permitting observation of hostiles and preventing opportunity for an ambush.

Lodge Trail Ridge
Lodge Trail Ridge divided the drainages of both Piney Creeks with the drainage of Peno (now Prairie Dog) Creek. Up this divide, north beyond Phil Kearny, climbed the Bozeman Trail on its route to Montana. There, December 21, 1866, in violation of explicit orders, Fetterman led his command of eighty-one men. There were no survivors to return.

Cemetery Site
Because of a healthy climate plus a short existence, Phil Kearny's cemetery might have remained an almost vacant place. But warfare prevented that idea. Here rested eighty-one victims of Fetterman's impetuosity; three heros of the masterful Wagon Box defense; and a few casualties of less celebrated incidents. On June 24, 1896 all bodies not previously exhumed were removed for re-interment in the Custer Battlefield National Cemetery.

The Bozeman Trail…its Approach from the South
…so ran, through treaty guaranteed Indian Land, a white man's route of commerce. Like any road it was an environment and ecology disturbing intrusion. Which, in this case, made it a challenge bound to produce a redman's reaction—a resort to arms. Thus the white man's government, supporting its citizens in violation of its own treaty, found justification to found a Fort Phil Kearny.

H Fetterman Massacre

Old U.S. Highway 87 just north of I-90 Exit 44.

Along this ridge on December 21, 1866, Capt. William J. Fetterman, 2 officers, 76 enlisted men and 2 civilians were decoyed into ambush and overwhelmed by a superior force of Sioux, Cheyenne, and Arapahoe Indians. Fort Phil Kearny, 2 miles south, was built in the summer of 1866 to protect travelers along the Bozeman Trail. The Indaians were bent on preventing such encroachment into their last hunting grounds which had been assigned them by the Fort Laramie Treaty of 1851. Sent out to relieve a wagon train that was under attack, Capt. Fetterman was ordered not to pursue the Indians beyond Lodge Trail Ridge. He disobeyed and led his command to this ridge, where they were engaged ina pitched battle. The final stand was made behind the large boulders at the monument. There were no survivors.

H The Fateful Decision

Old U.S. Highway 87 just north of I-90 Exit 44.

Fetterman relieved the wood train and chased its attackers to the limit prescribed in orders. His return was all that was necessary to complete a successful mission.

But he continued the chase. He did not return and his decision remains unexplained. The brash young Captain's decision to disobey orders and the resulting annihilation of his command has created a problem for generations of historians. Why did he continue pursuit? What "estimate of the situation" did he make? What thoughts influenced his decision? "None" appears to be a most charitable answer to the questions.

The mixed command of infantry and cavalry had no hope of catching the fleet Indian horseman. Fetterman knew he would be punished for disobeying orders unless he successfully engaged the warriors.

He gave little regard to the broken terrain, laced with pockets, ravines and ridges ideal fo concealment. He paid no heed to the fact that Indians did to fight according to the "rules of war" he learned in the Civil War. He descended the ridge and his comand stretched out—a tantalizing target for the attack. with little thought of the consequences, he charged blindly on, leading his command to its final engagement.

H Farthest Pursuit Trap Sprung Retreat-Defeat-Death

Old U.S. Highway 87 just north of I-90 Exit 44.

Pickets on Pilot Hill had signalled the fort when the wood train was attacked. They watched Fetterman's command advance to the relief and pursue the attacking Indians who retreated over the crest of Lodge Trail ridge. They saw Fetterman's men pause on the summit—the boundary that was supposed to be the limit of pursuit. But they only paused, then vanished over the ridge.

Indian accounts of the subsequent engagement were long in coming and proved fragmentary. The best reconstruction of events was made by relief and recovery parties who found the bodies of their comrades on the field of battle.

Fetterman, chasing decoys beond the ridge, met an overwhelming force of Indians. He turned about only to meet others who laid in ambush while he hotly pressed his pusuit.

Retreat along the Bozeman Road was impossible and within an hour, the fate of Fetterman's entire command was sealed.

H Recovery of the Dead

Old U.S. Highway 87 just north of I-90 Exit 44.

Two separate parties went forth from Fort Phil Kearny to recover the dead. The first party was sent while there was still hope that some of Fetterman's men might be alive. Captain Tenodor Ten Eyck and 76 men reached an observation point on Lodge Trail Ridge before the Indians left the battleground. Though seen and challenged by the exuberant victors, he refused to commit his command against such overwhelming odds. When the Indians withdrew, he ventured down the slope and recovered 49 bodies found in one group where the fight climaxed.

Next morning Colonel Carrington led a second party which found the remaining 32 bodies scattered along more than a mile of the Bozeman Road. Most of the bodies had been stripped, scalped and mutilated. The corpses of captains Fetterman and Brown had powder burns at their temples suggesting suicide. Three pools of blood—within ten feet of the body of Lieutenant George Grummond—evidence of Indian casualties—gave moot testimony to the frenzied fighting. James S. Wheatley and Isaac Fisher, two civilian volunteers, had wanted to test their new Henry repeating rifles. The hundred or more expended cartridges near their mutilated bodies showed how dearly they sold their lives.

The recovery parties found more than 60 separate pools of blood, suggesting removed Indian casualties. Indian spokesmen later acknowledged the loss of thirteen warriors.

H Fetterman Monument

At Fetterman Massacre Memorial near Banner

On July 3, 1908, Henry B. Carrington, Frances Grummond Carrigton and veterans of the Fort Phil Kearny garrison attended a memorial ceremony to dedicate this monument. Colonel Carrington and others recounted the events surrounding the battle of December 21, 1866, and their experiences at the fort.

To honor the battlefield dead, the monument had been constrcted during the previous two years by local stonemasons. There are however, several inaccurcies in the legend and some of language reflects the racial feeling of the times. Historical records show that only two civilians were killed, not the four mentioned in legend. Current scholars also question whether Red Cloud led or was even at the battle. Native Amercan histories do not mention his presence, but do mention numerous other Sioux and Cheyenne leaders. Finally, the plaque states"there were no survivors," but it obviously refers only to U.S. military casualties since approximately 1,500 Sioux and Cheyenne did

Fetterman Monument

in fact survive.

Today, this monument still honors the battlefield dead, but it should be remembered that members of two cultures died here, both fighting for their nations.

By 1866, twenty years of confrontation had occurred on the Northern Plains. European Americans pressured all the tribes in the quest of mineral wealth and settlement lands.

The Fort Laramie Treaty of 1851 attempted to curtail these confrontations. It established territorial boundaries for man of the Plains Indians and the United States Government was allowed to build roads and forts. All signators were allowed to cross on another's territory unmolested and unhindered. But the diminishing buffalo herds and discoveries of gold led to continuing and escalating confrontation.

The discovery of gold in southwest Montana led to the establishment of the Bozeman Trail in 1863. By the fall of 1865 numerous fights with the European Americans had allied the Sioux, Cheyenne and Arapaho. The Crow Indians supported the military against these tribes. The high cost of military campaigns and the need for new roads with safe travel impressed upon the United States Government the need for new negotiations with the Northern Plains Indians. These negotiations began at Fort Laramie in June, 1866.

While the intent of the Treaty of 1866 was to allow the construction of forts and roads in exchange for bi-annual annuities, government officials failed to recognize the complexity of tribal politics. Some Indian leaders did sign the treaty and government officials assumed they had a treaty with all members of the tribes. When Carrington's command arrived under orders to establish three forts on the Bozeman Trail, Red Cloud and other Indian leaders walked out of the talks declaring that war would occur if the trail was used and forts constructed. Carrington followed orders regarrisoning Fort Reno and established Forts Phil Kearny and C.F. Smith. The Indian leaders who refused to sign the treaty prepared for war.

With the arrival of reinforcements, supplies and two successive commanders, Fort Phil Keanry was reorganized and and the training of the soldiers increased. Skirmishes between the soldiers and the Indians continued through the spring and summer of 1867. Better arms and ammunition resulted in successful defenses at the Hay Field Fight and Wagon Box Fight on August 1 and 2.

News of the Fetterman Fight intensified the debate in the East between U.S. citizens with differing philosophies about the Indians. Some people avocated annihilation of the Indian nations while others advocated peaceful resolution of hostilities on the Western Plains.

The nation had survived four years of Civil War but the toll had been tremendous. Fighting Indians on the frontier was expensive and unpopular to those who wanted peace. Conflict in the West had created severe equipment and logstics problems for the post-war military.

In 1867, the military established Fort Fetterman, but the Treaty of 1868 closed the Bozeman Trail and Forts Phil Kearny, Reno and C.F. Smith. The treaty established reservations for the Sioux much like those set up for Cheyenne and Arapaho in 1866. The Interior Department became responsible for care and control of the tribes. It was hoped that the Indians would adopt Christian ways, become farmers and cease hostilities on the frontier

For six years, until gold was discovered in the Black Hills in 1874, an uneasy peace existed in the Powder River country. Soon thereafter, the Sioux, Cheyenne and Arapaho were at war on the Little Big Horn River.

H The Fetterman Fight... December 21, 1866

At Fetterman Massacre Memorial near Banner

During the fall of 1866, Red Cloud gathered Sioux, Cheyenne, and Arapaho warriors. As the Indians strength grew to the north on the Tongue River, they increased their raids on the Bozeman Trail forts. Colonel Henry B. Carrington received orders from the Department Commander to be more aggressive and carry out "punitive strikes against the raiding Indians." Carrington requested more troops, better arms and more ammunition. Captain William J. Fetterman, a recent arrival to the fort, said that he could ride through the Sioux nation with 80 men. The stage was set for the Fetterman Fight.

December 21, 1866 was a clear day, with snow drifted on the north slopes of the hills and ridges from earlier storms. That morning Captain Fetterman requested command of a force to relieve a wood train under attack by Indians. His command included Lieutenant George Grummond, Captain Frederick Brown, 49 infantry, 27 cavalry and civilians James Wheatley and Issac Fisher, totaling 81 men.

Earlier in the day 800 to1,200 Sioux, Cheyenne and Arapaho warriors had arrived in the Peno Creek Valley. Some were sent to attack the wood train, others to decoy the Army's relief party and the rest took up positions for the planned ambush. The decoys lured Fetterman's command over Lodge Trail Ridge. As the soldiers approached Peno Creek, the ambush was sprung. In the ensuing battle, as the troops retreated south toward Lodge Trail Ridge, they were surrounded and defeated.

In approximately one hour the battle was over. Captain Tenodor Ten Eyck's relief column arrived to find the bodies of Fetterman's command in three sparate groups along what is now known as Massacre Hill. Fort Phil Kearny had lost 81 men. Indian oral history indicates that their casualties were 20 or more.

H The Aftermath: Two Views of Victory

At Fetterman Massacre Memorial near Banner

By the end of the fight the Indians, through the heroics of fellow warriors, managed to remove all but one or two of their dead and wounded from the battlefield. These were taken to a spring near the present day Fish Hatchery for cleansing and treatment. Estimates very greatly as to the number of Indian caualties. Traditional Indian oral history places the number as low as six and as high as 100. Captain Powell estimated the dead at 60 and wounded at 120. As the Indians withdrew from the field, so did the soldiers. Following their rescue by Major Smith's column the surgeon treated the wouned and gave each survivor a drink of whiskey to settle their nerves. The military casualties consisted of three dead in the corral, four dead at the side camp, and two wounded in the corral.These caualties and the day long fight would cause the military to rethink their position at the pineries.

Although the military felt they had won the fight, which gave a great boost to the morale of soldiers on the western plains, they knew the existing corral had its weaknesses. Immediately following the fight Lieutenant Alexander Wishart created a new position south and west of the Wagon Box Fight corral. The new corral was placed further out in open, giving a better field of fire, and was constructed in a stronger defensive position. A trench was dug around the exterior, and the wagon boxes were placed upon the excavated dirt, creating a formidable barrier to any attack. A new camp site was located to south of this corral.

To the Indians the Wagon Box fight was also a victory. They had succeeded in destroying the side camp, burned several wagons, captured a large mule herd and killed or wounded several of the enemy. Their goal of harassing the forts had been fulfilled. One lesson learned was that the soldiers had new weapons and that if the Indians expected to win they would need modern guns. In November 1867, Lieutenant Shurley's command was attacked on Big Goose Creek and after a day long fight, the Indians were driven off. It is believed that the Indian objective was to capture a mountain howitzer and weapons. This ongoing fighting kept the Bozeman Trail closed to all but military traffic, and the maintenance of the forts became a great expense for the military. Through continuous skirmishing and the husbanding of his resources, Red Cloud was winning his war. The war continued into the summer of 1868 with raids at all three forts along the Bozeman Trail and at the new Fort Fetterman located on the North Platte River. In 1868 treaty negotiators were again ready to discuss the Bozeman Trail. The results of the negotiations would make "Red Cloud's War" one of the few, though temporary, victories by American Indians against the western expansion of the United States.

H The Interpretive Trail

At Fetterman Massacre Memorial near Banner

For an in-depth understanding of the Fetterman Fight, you are invited to walk the interpretive trail. Approximately one mile in length, it consists of two separate but overlapping trails traversing more than half of the actual battlefield.

The first trail provides specific information about the battle and its participants and is accessible for the physically impaired. The second trail requires you to use your imagination, to visualize the battlefield as it was in 1866 from the Indian and soldier perspectives, at positions occupied during the battle.

Archaeological studies have been conducted on the battlefield. Since artifact collecting began soon after the fighting, few artifacts remain, but you are reminded that their removal is UNLAWFUL. Please report any findings to the vistor center immediately.

H Attack-Relief-Decoy-Pursuit

Old U.S. Highway 87 just north of I-90 Exit 44.

By December, 1866, For Phil Kearny was in the final phases of construction. Logs for the stockaded post were hauled by wood train from the pinery six miles west of the fort.

On december 21, a heavily escorted wood train left for the pinery. It came under Indian attack about three miles to the west. When pickets on Pilot Hill signaled the train was being attacked, Colonel Henry B. Carrington ordered out a relief party and reluctantly put Captain William J. Fetterman in command. It included two other officers, 76 enlisted men and two civilians. the soldiers in the party were from four companies of the 18th Infantry and one company of the 2nd Cavalry.

The Indians had broken off the attack by the time the relief party was under way but Fetterman pursued them to the crest of Lodge Trail Ridge—so far keeping within range of his orders.

H Wagon Box Fight Interpretive Signs

At Wagon Box Memorial site about five miles northwest of Fort Phil Kearny

Wagon Box Monument

Before you stands a monument dedicated to the courage and bravery of the defenders in the Wagon Box fight of August 2, 1936. This monument was built in 1936 by the Civilian Conservation Corps. The legend was written by local historians and although it was accurate with the information available at the time,it is now known to contain several discrepancies. Also, it makes no mention of the Lakota warriors who died on this field in defense of their cullture.

It is not known if Red Cloud was the actual leader during this battle and the number of Lakota warriors who were involved in the Wagon Box Fight is now estimated to be 1,000 to 1500. Native American casualty estimates, based on oral histories, vary from six to sixty.

Two Lakota individuals mentioned in both white and Indian accounts of the battle should be noted: one is Red Cloud's nephew whose name is unknown; the other is a Miniconjou Sioux name Lipala. Both were killed during the battle, but they displayed unusual courage and leadership in their numerous attempts to defeat the corral defenders.

Wagon Box Fight, August 2, 1867

This monument is erected to perpetrate the memory of one of the famous battles of histor. It is dedicated to the courage and bravery of twenty-eight soldiers in Comany C.27th United States Infantry, and four civilians who held their improvised fort made of fourteen ordinary wagon-boxes, against 3000 Sioux warriors, under the leadership of Red cloud for a period of six or seven hours under continuous fire. the number of indians killed has been variously estimated from three hundred to eleven hundred. The following participated in this engagement: Capt. Jas. Powell, 1st Sgt. John M. Hoover, 1st Sgt. John H. Mcquiery, 1st Lt. John C. Jenness, corp. Max Littman, Corp. Francis Roberts, Privates: Wm. Baker, Ashton Barton, wm. Black Nolan, Chas. Brooks, Alexander Brown, Dennis Brown, John Buzzard, Frederick Clause, John Condon, Thomas Doyle, V. Deming, John Grady, John M. Garreett, Henry Gross, Samuel Gibson, Henry Haggerty, Mark Haller, Phillip C. Jones, Freeland Phillips, John L. Somers, Chas. A. Stevens, Julius Strache, 4 unknown civilians.

Battle, August 2, 1867

On August 2, 1867, 51 men of Company C, 27th Infantry under the command of Captain James Powell and Lieutenant John Jenness are assigned to the wood cutting detail. Fourteen of these men escort a wood train toward the fort. Another 13 are protecting wood cutters; nine at the upper pinery and four at the Little Piney Camp. While the soldiers at the corral prepared breakfast, the herders turned out the mules, and sentries took up position, the battle begins.

Crazy Horse and Hump led a small number of warriors across the hills to the west in a decoy attack on the Little Piney Camp. Here three soldiers are killed and the remaining wood cutters are chased into the mountains.

This attack is followed by attacks on the wood train at the upper pinery, and the mule herd.

Soldiers, drivers and wood cutters from the wood train and pinery escape into the mountains, but the mule herd is captured. Powell leads an attack to rescue the herders, as outlying sentries and hunters from the fort make for the safety of the corral. By nine o'clock 26 soldiers and six civilians are surrounded in the corral facing, by Powell's estimate, 800 to 1000 warriors.

Indian spectators, including leaders, women, and children watch from the surrounding hills, as mounted warriors make the first attack, charging the corral from the Southwest. The Indians expect a volley from the soldiers who will then pause to reload, and the warriors will then overrun the corral. But the pause never occurs as the soldiers quickly reload their new rifles. Discouraged by the continuous fire the Indians withdraw. During the lull, the soldiers pass ammunition about the corral, holding it in their caps and the Indians prepare to charge on foot from behind the ridge to the north.

The second attack is made from behind the ridge to the north by warriors on foot while mounted warriors demonstrate to the south and snipers located along the rim fire into the corral.

During this attack all the casualties in the corral occur. But again the soldier's firepower turns the Indians back. A third attack comes from the northeast. The soldiers hear loud chanting as Indians burst from cover singing their war song and surge to within a few yards of the corral before being turned back. The Indians again retreat to the protection of the rim, sniping at the corral as others attempt to retrieve the dead and wounded. The final attack comes on horse back from the southeast.

By now it is early afternoon and the fight has not gone unnoticed at the fort. Major Benjamin Smith leaves the fort with a relief column of 102 men and a mountain howitzer. As the column nears the corral, they fire on Indian spectators viewing from a high knob east of the corral. With the arrival of reinforcements for the soldiers, the Indians decide to withdraw and the Wagon Box Fight ends.

Wood Cutting: A Hazardous Harvest

Though construction of Fort Phil Kearny was complete by August of 1867, the need of wood for burning and alterations continued. Colonel John E. Smith, the post commander, located wood cutting camps on Big and Little Piney Creeks five miles west of the fort. A company of infantry armed with the 50-70 Allin Conversion Rifle (a converted Springfield musket, which was breach-loading and fired metal cased cartridges) were assigned to protect the cutters and wood train. Their duties were rotated with other companies on a monthly basis. The soldiers operated out of a camp located at a corral built by the wood contractors to hold the mules at night. The corral was made of 14 wagon boxes, removed from the running gears, and placed in an oval measuring 30' by 70'. It was located on a plateau between Big and Little Piney Creeks, at the junction of the wood roads, and visible from Pilot Knob, a lookout point near the fort. One box at the west end of the corral and another on the south side were covered to protect the supplies for the soldiers and civilains. An additional supply wagon was located ten feet to the west. The soldiers and civilains slept in tents ouside of the corral.

To Save The Powder River Country

In July, 1867, many Lakotas of the Ogalala, Miniconjou and Sans Arc tribes gathered with the Cheyennes along the Rosebud Valley to participate in the sacred Sun Dance ceremony. After fulfilling the religious duties, the headmen and fighting chiefs turned their attention once more to warfare against the Bozman Trail Forts.

One year of fighting had failed to drive the soldiers from the Powder River country. Small groups of warriors struck during the spring and summer, but there had been no victory to equal the winter battle known as "One Hundred in the Hands," which had annihilated Fetterman's soldiers near Fort Phil Kearny. Now, with almost one thousand fighting men concentrated on the Rosebud, the Indian leaders planned another great battle. Disagreement over which fort to attack led to a split in the Indian forces. Most of the Cheyennes would go to attack Fort C.F. Smith, while the Lakota and some Cheyenne chose Fort Phil Kearny.

Led by Crazy Horse, Hump, Thunderhawk, Ice and other war leaders, hundreds of Lakota and Cheyenne warriors rode to their destiny in battle. Traveling with them were Red Cloud, Flying By, other older headmen, and many woman and children. All hoped fo a great victory that would save and protect the land.

A Fight To Survive (See diagram)

Inside the corral the small body of soldiers expected defeat and the same fate as Fetterman's command. As they took up positions of their choosing, between, behind, or inside the wagon boxes, the men prepared for the worst. Some removed their shoe laces so that the string could be used to attach their toe to the rifle trigger when the end was near. Others stockpiled ammunition and weapons. While the Allin Conversion was the most prominent weapon of the fight, Spencer carbines and an assortment of pistols were also used. Some accounts indicate that only the marksmen fired

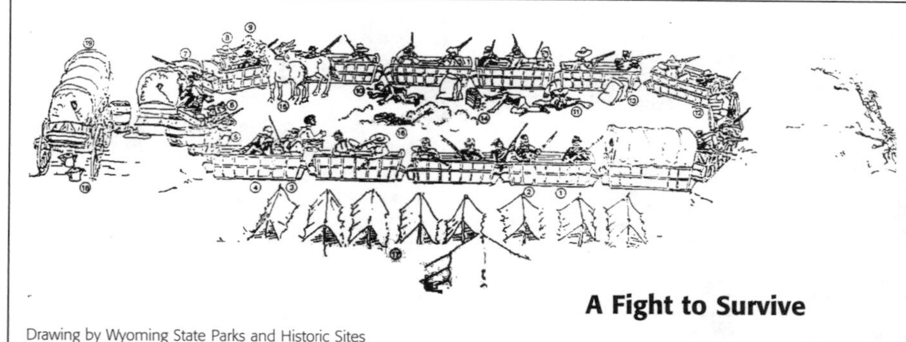

Drawing by Wyoming State Parks and Historic Sites

while others reloaded the rifles for them. During the fight Powell gave few orders other than an initial command of "shoot to kill." Jenness took up a position in the covered box with four civilians. It is reportedly here that after being told to keep down, Jenness replied "I know how to fight Indians" and promptly fell dead of a head wound.

Acts of valor were quite common in the corral. A private named Max Littman stepped from the safety of the corral to give covering fire for the retreating sentries at the beginning of the fight. On two occasions Privates Sam Gibson and John Grady ventured from the corral, once to knock down tents which were obscuring the field of fire, and a second time to retrieve water for the thirsting defenders. Indian fire arrows ignited the dry hay and manure, which, combined with the hot August sun and gun powder smoke, made conditions in the corral miserable. In the corral, in addition to death of Lieutenant Jenness, Privates Haggerty and Doyle were killed, and two others wounded.

1. Pvt. Gibson (drawing based on his descriptions)

2. Pvt. Gradey

3. Sgt. Hoover

4. Captain Powell

5. Max Littman (behind a barrel of beans, he provided cover fire as Gibson retreated to the corral)

6. Private Condon (behind a barrel of salt)

7. Lieut. Jenness killed

8. and 9 Bullwackers (6 civilians were in fight)

10. Private Doyle killed

11. Private Haggerty killed

12. Somers wounded in wagon box

13. Grain stored and used as protection in corral

14. Ammunition placed about corral, men would retreive it in their hats to their firing position.

15. A horse and mule were tied in the corral, they died of wounds suffered during the fight

16. Using fire arrows, Indians set fire to manure and straw within the corral, causing discomfort for the defenders

17. Civilian and soldier tents

18. Coffee pots containing the only water available during the fight

19. Supply Wagon

Valor in Attack

The Indian leaders had hoped the soldiers would pursue a small decoy party of warriors led by Hump into an ambush, but the soldiers refused to follow, and the last pickets retreated safely into the corral after wounding the Ogalala warrior Paints Yellow. The side camp was taken and some soldiers killed, but now the only option for quick success was to launch massed attacks at the corral, and hope to overrun the soldiers' improvised wagon box fortress.

Soon, mounted warriors circled around the corral. Using their horses as shields, they quickly rode in close to fire arrows or guns, and then zigzagged away from the soldiers' rifles. During the first attack from the south, Hairy Hand, a Miniconjou, rode straight at the corral to count coup. Hit by a soldier's bullet, he laid out in the open until a young warrior named White Bull ran in and dragged him to safety. The mounted charge failed, and the war leaders Crazy Horse of the Ogalalas and Hump of the Miniconjous organized the warriors for an assault on foot. As the foot charge moved toward the corral, the Ogalala Only Man rushed ahead, almost reaching the wagon boxes before the bullets killed him. The attack stalled, and some warriors concealed themselves in the brush and started firing into the corral with guns captured during the battle of One Hundred in the Hands. These snipers inflicted most of the casualties suffered by the soldiers.

During a lull before the next attack, one of the bravest acts of the day took place. Jipala, a tall, impressive Miniconjou, walked toward the corral, carrying a shield, lance and bow. Singing his death song, he ran forward, jumping in the air and firing arrows at the corral. Finally, the soldiers bullets found him, and he lay dead before the corral. Both warriors and soldiers talked of his bravery for many years to come.

Two more Miniconjous, Muskrat Stands of His Lodge and Packs His Leg, died in foot charges. During the final attack, the Lakota Young Duck was shot dead leading the assault, and three of his people wounded attempting to recover his body.

Once more, the warriors attempted a mounted charge, but the soldiers' guns kept up a fierce fire. The assault ended before reaching the corral, but not before Sun's Road of the Cheyennes was killed. His death was the last of the day.

The boom of Smith's howitzer signaled the end of fighting. As the Lakota and Cheyennes left the battlefield, they paused near local springs to care for their wounded and dead before moving north to their camps.

Red Cloud's Victory

By 1868 the Union Pacific Rail Road had been completed through southern Wyoming and northern Utah and a new and shorter road ran north to the southwestern Montana gold fields. The Bozeman Trail became obsolete. The U.S. Government once again sought negotiations with the Lakota and Cheyenne, hoping for a solution to the fighting along the trail. Red Cloud refused to talk until the forts and the trail were abandoned, but others did negotiate and a treaty was settled upon. The Fort Laramie Treaty of 1868 stipulated that in exchange for the military abandoning the forts along and the use of the Bozeman Trail, the Lakota would accept for their reservation the western half of South Dakota from the Missouri River to the Black Hills. The Powder River country was to remain unceded Indian land, open for hunting by all tribes. The United States Government signed this treaty as did several bands of Lakota, but it was not until the forts were actually abandoned that Red Cloud finally signed in October of 1868. For the Lakota and Cheyenne, even though greater conflicts lay in the years ahead, the Powder River Country had been saved.

Continuing Controversies

Over the years a controversy has arisen about the exact location of the Wagon Box Corral, Indian casualties, and the length of the battle.

Which Is the Best Way Over the Mountain?

There are three major highways traversing the Big Horns in an east-west direction. Each offers its own distinct and memorable scenery, with relatively equal travel distances and comparable surfaces. So the choice is up to you depending on your travel objectives.

Big Horn Scenic Byway (U.S. Hwy. 14) connects Sheridan and surrounding communities with Greybull, Wyoming and includes 45 miles of scenic mountain driving. Look out over spectacular valley views from one of several roadside turnouts. On a clear day, you can see for miles and miles. Interesting stops include Shell Falls, Burges Junction Visitor Center and Sand Turn. Open year-round.

Cloud Peak Skyway (U.S. Hwy. 16) traverses the southern Big Horn Mountains and offers breathtaking vistas of distant snow-capped peaks along its 45-mile length. This route connects Buffalo and Tensleep, Wyoming. Highlights include Hospital Hill, Powder River Pass, Meadowlark Lake and Tensleep Canyon. Open year-round.

Medicine Wheel Passage (U.S. Hwy. 14A) rises sharply from the Big Horn Basin near Lovell, Wyoming and winds 25 miles through steep canyon terrain and high alpine meadows to Burgess Junction. This route provides primary access to the medicine Wheel National Historic Landmark. This may not be the best choice for those pulling or driving an RV. Grades exceed 10%. Open from memorial Day to mid-November.

Source: U.S. Forest Service

The most disputed fact is the location of the corral. In the early 1900's area residents brought survivors of the fight, both Indian and white, to the area in hopes of pinpointing the exact location of the corral. Unfortunately, the survivors were not at the site at the same time and did not agree on the location. One site chosen is the location laid out near where you are standing. The other location is a brass marker several hundred yards to the southeast. There has been much study in an attempt to resolve this debate, including correspondence with early residents, aerial photography, and archaeological surverys. The strongest evidence come from archaeology done over several years, which indicates that the laid out corral may be close to correct. But if the actual participants could not agree on a location, then the best and most accurate description of the location of the corral is to say that it was placed somewhere atop the plateau, between Big and Little Piney Creeks. As to the other controversies, Indian casualties can probably be estimated at between six and sixty and the time of the fight from 8:00 A.M. to 1:00 P.M. As with all historical events research will continue and new facts will come to the surface.

F Tunnel Inn Dining Room and Bar

402 Hwy. 193 in Story. 683-2296.

Regular diners at the Tunnel Inn Dining Room and Bar call it the best little secret in the Big Horn Mountains. Superb dining is enjoyed in a rustic, comfortable, yet elegant setting among the pine forests. The menu features premium Black Angus beef, fresh seafood, and authentic pasta dishes. Various theme nights feature international dishes such as Indian, Cajun, Japanese with sushi, French, and others. Compliment your meal from a fine selection of wines, spirits, and micro brews. Live entertainment every other Wednesday nights includes nationally recognized musicians such as Jalan Crossland, national finger picking champion and Motor City Josh and the Big Three from Atlanta, and numerous local artists.

FS Piney Creek General Store & The Waldorf A' Story

19 N. Piney Road in Story. 683-2400

People travel from all over to shop and dine at the Piney Creek General Store and The Waldorf A' Story. The unique atmosphere inside and out of this intriguing store is always a great experience. The store is stocked with gourmet groceries, cookware, auto supplies, souvenirs, unique gifts, antiques, and a generous beer and wine selection. The Waldorf A'Story is a sophisticated little gem of a restaurant, popular among the local residents and visitors alike. Among their breakfast, lunch, and dinner menus you'll find biscuits and gravy, double-deck sandwiches and yummy bisques, and entrées with selections such as baby back ribs and fresh seafood. Many local events, including fairs and flea markets are held at the store throughout the year.

L Story Pines Inn, LLC

46 N. Piney Road in Story. 683-2120 or 800-596-6297. www.storypinesinn.com

The Story Pines Inn is a small country inn nestled in the pines at the base of the Big Horn Mountains, midway between The Black Hills, and Yellowstone National Park. Take the road less traveled and find paradise. Enjoy the intimacy and attention to detail that comes with a privately owned business. Six new clean and modern rooms are furnished with lodge pole pine furnishings. Amenities include: hot tub, cable TV, coin-op laundry, picnic area, complimentary coffee and tea. The Inn is conveniently located within walking distance to restaurants, country store, art gallery, library, post office, and churches.

L Mountain Cabin by the Stream

In Story. 672-8260 or 800-965-8059. www.mountaincabin.vcn.com

What Makes the Big Horns So Special?

No region in Wyoming is provided with a more diverse landscape; from lush grasslands to alpine meadows, and rugged mountain tops to canyonlands and desert.

Gorgeous canyon country is a hallmark of the forest. Shell, Tensleep and Crazy Woman Canyons are among those that can be enjoyed from your car window. Others, like Tongue and Devil's Canyon are better viewed on foot.

Geology is noteworthy in the Big Horns. Watch for highway signs that trace the geologic history of this regin as you travel the major highways.

One of our many treasures is an abundance of large mountain meadows. These natural openings, caused by soil type and moisture levels, favor grasses and wildflowers rather than trees. Wildflowers are truly extraordinary in the Big Horns during June and July.

Interspersed with mountain meadows are large patches of cool evergren forest extending from just above the foothills to timber line. Ponderosa pine and Douglas-fir populate the lower slopes with lodgepole pine, subalpine fir and Englemann spruce at the higher elevations.

Open landscapes make for great wildlife viewing as well. Watch for moose munching on a tasty bite of willow streamside or a family of mule deer bounding away, then stopping to look back with large ears raised and listening.

History buffs come to this region to explore the land that once felt the footsteps of legendary giants like Jim Bridger, Lewis and Clark, Red Cloud, Plenty coups and Buffalo Bill. Big Horn country was highly valued by tribes like the Crow, Sioux, Northern Cheyenne, Eastern Shoshone, and Arapahoe. Some of the most famous battles between American Indians and the U.S. military were waged at the foot of the Big Horn Mountains or in close proximity.

Source: U.S. Forest Service

8 *Gas, Food, Lodging*

T DeSmet Lake

At I-90 Exit 51

The lake was named for Father Pierre DeSmet, a Jesuit missionary back in the early 1800s. It is now known for its terrific fishing opportunities, boating and skiing, and swimming. There are many facilities at the lake including ramps, docks, campgrounds and picnic shelters. You might even see the legendary "Smetty", the lake monster.

T DeSmet Lake Monster

Lake Desmet not only attracts fishermen looking to catch the great rainbow trout or crappies it provides, but "Smetty" is another great attraction. Smetty is the legendary creature believed to inhabit Lake Desmet.

The lake is named for a Jesuit missionary priest to the Indians, Father Pierre DeSmet, back in the early 1800's. Rumor has it that the Indians were so frightened by this body of water, they refused to camp along the red shale shores. Some say that the Sioux Indians believed the waters had healing powers and the ability to prompt visions. The tribe legend was that a young brave turned against the love of his life because he was overpowered by the charms of a water maiden rising from its depths. His intended wife-to-be was so distraught by his rejection she subsequently drowned herself. Her father, the tribal chief seeking revenge, swiftly administered justice to the unfaithful young man. In the darkness of windy Wyoming nights, his spirit supposedly wanders around the shore bemoaning the loss of his Indian maiden.

Local ranchers often told stories about seeing a 30 to 40 foot long looking like a "long telephone pole with a lard bucket attached." Other recorded physical characteristics include a "bony ridge along the back, with a resemblance to a horse's head coming out of the water in a swimming motion."

There have been tales about the lake's dark side that range from a monster resembling an alligator rising from the waters to a Loch Ness-type creature that seized an Indian papoose and disappeared into the murky depths.

When imagination runs high, "Smetty" is said to dwell in the so-called bottomless lake's subterranean caverns sometimes speculated to be a faraway outlet from the Pacific Ocean.

Edward Gillette, author of "Locating the Iron Trail" wrote a book in 1925 chronicling the tales and observations surrounding "Smetty". Visit Lake Desmet and judge for yourself, but don't forget to take your fishing pole and bait so you don't miss out on some great fishing!

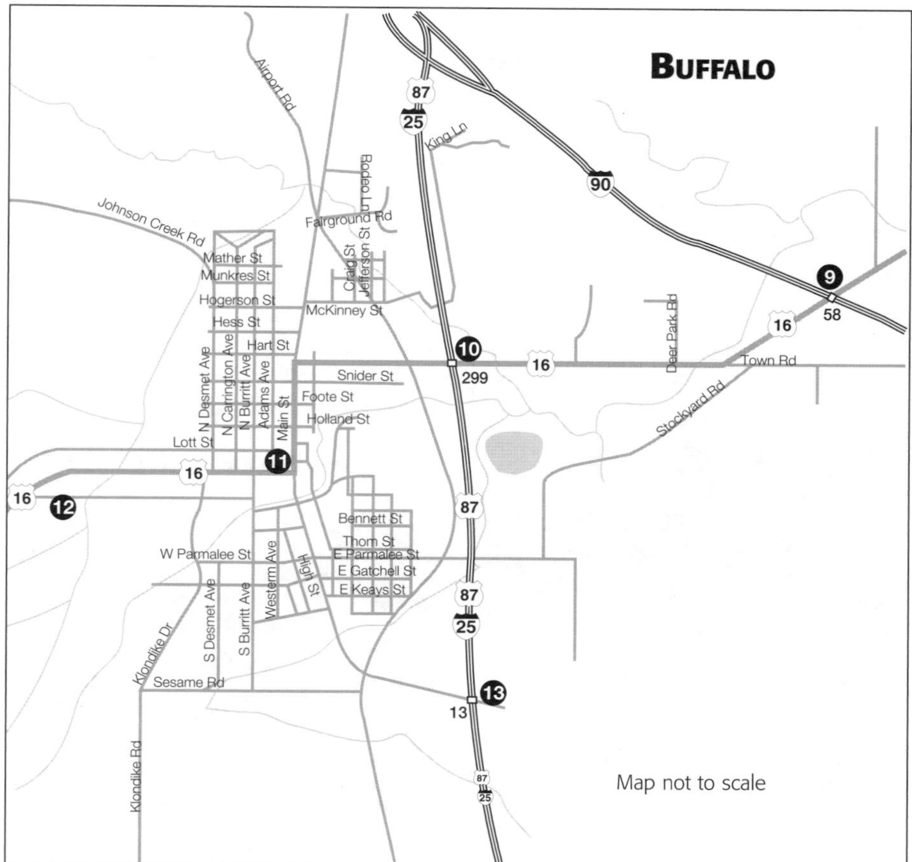

9 *Gas, Food, Lodging*

Buffalo

Pop. 3,900, Elev. 4,645

Founded in 1879 by homesteaders, cattle ranchers, and miners, Buffalo was not named for the animal, but for Buffalo, New York, hometown of one early settler, Alvin J. McCray. By 1883, there were a dozen saloons in town, but no churches. While an old buffalo trail did once run down Main Street, Buffalo's streets are most famous for being the only place in the US where you can make a legal U-turn on a highway bridge, right in the middle of town. As the Johnson County Seat, Buffalo also claims the distinction of having hosted the oldest county fair in the state in 1887.

T Dry Creek Petrified Tree Forest

I-90 east from Buffalo to the Red Hills exit, drive north off exit for seven miles to the Petrified Tree Area access road.

The Dry Creek Petrified Tree Environmental Education Area (EEA), set aside as such in 1978, is located about 9 miles east of Buffalo, Wyoming. A parking area, picnic table, and interpretive facilities can be found here.

As you travel around a loop nature trail about 0.8 mile long, you will go back 60 million years to the geologic era of the Early Eocene when this area was shaded woodlands and mossy glades. You will learn how the uplifting of the Big Horn Mountains helped to create the prairie ecosystem we see today. And you will also learn about early vegetation and the formation of coal, scoria, petrified trees and other indicators of the past.

This area was very different from what can be seen today. Giant trees grew in a jungle-like area somewhat like the Okefenokee Swamp in southern Georgia. A large system of rivers flowed north to a distant ocean. Huge swamps filled the wide, flat plain between the Big Horn Mountains and the Black Hills. There may have been turtles, crocodile-like creatures, large fished similar to modern gars, and primitive mammals and birds.

Scoria is a sort of natural brick formed from shale or sandstone that has been "fired" when coal seams caught fire and burned back into the ground. Scoria can be crushed and used as a rock aggregate for road pavement, hence some of the red color roads in the area, and as a road base for unimproved roads. The red color is produced by iron oxides in the rock. Scoria can be crushed and used as a rock aggregate for road pavement; hence, some of the red-colored roads in the area, and as a road base for unimproved roads.

Coal forms slowly over great periods of time. The coal beds in the area originally accumulated as peat deposits that formed from the leaves, branches, stems, and roots of trees and other plants that grew in the swamps. The peat beds probably were buried when a nearby river flooded, covering the area with sand and mud. After millions of years under thousands of feet of sediment, the peat gradually changed to coal. (One coal seam near Buffalo, the Healey, is about 200 feet thick in places.)

As erosion and uplifting began to change the earth's surface, many coal seams were exposed to air and caught fire. As the coal seams burned back into the hillsides, the intense heat changes the normally soft brown and gray rocks to a hard red material—scoria. At station 2 you will learn about plants that helped to form the coal.

The ecosystem of the swampy plain played a significant part in the development of coal, an important energy resource today.

Article courtesy of Bureau of Land Management.

S The Wolf Den

173 Hwy. 16 E. in Buffalo. 684-7943.

The Wolf Den represents old west excitement, adventure, and the drama of nature. They offer for sale some of the nation's most beautiful fur hats, ski bands, ear muffs, vests pouches and exquisite custom designed fur coats. Items are made from high quality local furs acquired and processed by the store's owners. They also offer a wide variety of native skulls as well as rare and unusual skulls. The store is also a source for quality materials for making decorative items using beads, bones, hemp, buckskin, and bear claws. Among the many other unique high-quality, hand crafted items available are knives, pipes, dreamcatchers, jewelry, and Indian replicas.

10 *Gas, Food, Lodging*

H Cloud Peak Ferris Wheel

Behind Bozeman Crossing Restaurant
I-25 Exit 299

A ride on this Ferris wheel will give the rider a beautiful view of the Big Horn Mountains and the Cloud Peak Wilderness area. This 195,000 acre wilderness area and Cloud Peak (elevation

13,165) are directly in front of the Ferris wheel.

The Ferris wheel gets its name from George Washington Ferris who designed a 250 foot wheel for the Columbian Exposition in Chicago in 1892. This Eli #16 wheel was built in 1936 by the Eli Bridge Co. of Jacksonville, Illinois. It is serial number 547 and originally ran at the Utah State Fair. It moved to Heritage Square, Golden Colorado in 1978 and ran there for twelve years. It has been totally reconditioned and now operates daily during the summer months.

H Six-Mule Army Wagon

At Bozeman Crossing restaurant, 1-25 Exit 299 near Buffalo

This replica of a six mule Army wagon was built on the running gear of an 1864 design for this military wagon. The first design of this wagon in 1857 and the Army brought out three models, the 1858 model, the 1864 model and the 1878 model.

Thousands of these wagons were built for use in the Civil War and design (with modifications) was in use by the United States military from 1858 until after World War 1.

The wagon had a payload of 2000 lbs. and was pulled by six mules. The teamster or mule skinner did not ride in the wagon, but rode the "nigh" or left wheeler mule. The two mules that were closest to the wagon were called the "wheelers", the next pair of mules were called the "swing team" and the front pair wre called the "leaders". The teamster controlled the wagon by use of a jerk line to the bit of the nigh leader. The nigh leader had a stick from his harness collar to the off or right leaders bit. This stick was called a jockey stick. The wagon was turned to the left by pulling the rein or jerks line in a steady pull causing the nigh leader to come left pulling the off leader with him. Sharp jerks on the jerk line caused pain on the nigh leaders mouth causing him to move away from the pain or to the right. The jockey stick then forced the off leader to the right and the swing team and wheelers went with them. A certain amount of strong language went with this maneuvering, but when you consider the mule skinner had no protection from the elements save what he wore, perhaps it was justified.

H Big Horn Mountains

At Bozeman Crossing restaurant I-25 Exit 299

The high country backdrop on top of the Big Horn Mountains encompasses much of the Cloud Peak Wilderness area. This 195,000 acre area was designated as wilderness by Congress in 1984.

The highest point in the wilderness area is Cloud Peak, which can be seen by looking through the peep hole on the right hand side of the sign. Cloud Peak is 13,005 feet high. The peak immediately to the South is Bomber Mountain, 12,436 feet high. It is named for a B-17 bomber that crashed there on June 28, 1943 with the loss of 10 lives.

There are 256 fishing lakes and 49 miles of fishing streams in the wilderness area. They feature Rainbow, Cutthroat, Brook, German Brown, California Golden, Mackinaw and Grayling fish species. Big game animals found in the wilderness area include elk, deer, moose, mountain sheep and black bear.

A closer look at Cloud Peak wilderness area and the beautiful Big Horns can be had by taking US Highway 16 to Worland or by taking Crazy Woman Canyon/Pole creek loop tour.

F Dash Inn Restaurant

620 E. Hart in Buffalo. 684-7930

F Colonel Bozeman Restaurant

665 E. Hart in Buffalo. 684-5555

FLS Historic Bozeman Crossing Super 8

655 E. Hart, I-25, Exit Hwy. 16 in Buffalo. 684-2531 www.bozemancrossing.com

The Historic Bozeman Crossing Super 8 is known for excellent lodging. However, unlike other Super 8s this one offers food, lodging, an amusement park, open air museum, and shopping. It is located on the famous Bozeman Trail at the foot of the Big Horn Mountains. Dine in Colonel Bozeman's Restaurant and Buffalo Room Tavern. See the only full-size bucking horse carousel in the world—the Cowboy carousel. Shop an incredible array of gifts and collectibles in the Cowboy Carousel Gift Shop. Stroll the grounds and take the history walk or play miniature golf. Enjoy snacks, fudge, espresso or caramel corn from the expanded Ice Cream Parlor. The Historic Bozeman Crossing Conference Center also offers banquet facilities for up to 200 people, equipped for all occasions.

L Motel 6 of Buffalo

100 Flat Iron Drive in Buffalo. 684-7000

The Motel 6 is conveniently located close to I-90 and I-25 on the Scenic byway to Yellowstone National Park only 4 hours away. The newly built motel is in a quiet location and offers more than the standard Motel 6 experience. The area offers great recreation, dining, and shopping. Play golf on a Four Star golf course, check out the area's great hunting and fishing, or shop till you drop in the Historic Downtown district. In the winter months there are great snowmobile and ski trails nearby. Enjoy your stay in Buffalo with comfortable surroundings and reasonable rates.

L Comfort Inn Buffalo

65 Hwy 16 E. in Buffalo. 684-9564. www.choicehotels.com

Plan to stop at the Comfort Inn in historic Buffalo on your trip between Yellowstone National Park and the Black Hills of South Dakota. They will assure your personal comfort with queen beds, and interior and exterior entries on ground level. All rooms are equipped with coffee makers and 27 inch color TV's. Enjoy a continental breakfast in the morning. They are conveniently located at I-25 Exit 299 and I-90 Exit 58. They are only a few blocks from historic downtown Buffalo, and great dining and shopping. The 24-hour desk is available for your added convenience and assistance.

11 *Food, Lodging*

T Johnson County Tourism Association

55 N. Main, Hwy 16 at I-90 & I-25, Buffalo Chamber of Commerce. 684-5544 or 800-227-5122. www.buffalowyo.com

T Chamber of Commerce - Buffalo

55 N. Main in Buffalo. 684-5544 or 800-227-5122

T Cattle Wars Sculptures

South edge of downtown on Main Street.

Plaques

Living on the Edge

Sculptor: D. Michael Thomas

An independent cowboy, or small rancher, brands a calf on the open range. Surprised at his work, he turns to see a rider from a large cattle outfit galloping threateningly toward him.

Small ranchers, like this cowboy, rode south from Buffalo on the morning of April 11, 1892, to confront "The Invaders" at the TA Ranch.

Wyoming Tidbits

Raising sheep was a hazardous occupation in the late 1800s in Wyoming. Sheepmen and cattle ranchers warred over the range, and cattlemen marked "dead lines" in the soil. Sheep and people could be killed for crossing the lines.

Sheriff Red Angus, citizens of Buffalo, and small ranchers laid siege to the gunmen. Three days later, troops from Fort McKinney, near Buffalo, arrived on the scene. The invaders surrendered and were escorted to the fort, then sent to Cheyenne. They were never brought to trial.

Ridin' for the Brand
Sculptor: D. Michael Thomas

In the late 1800s, independent Johnson County ranchers began branding calves before the spring and fall roundups. The practice angered larger ranchers of the day, who resented this infringement on the open range. So began the Johnson County Cattle War.

The conflict peaked on April 6, 1892, when a group of large ranchers and hired guns rode north from Casper toward Buffalo, "the invaders" carried with them a black list of alleged rustlers, two of whom they killed near present day Kaycee. On April 10th they fortified and spent the night at the TA Ranch 13 miles south of Buffalo. The stage was set for one of the most notable confrontations in frontier history.

This bronze portrays a rider for one of the big outfits challenging a homesteader branding a "maverick" calf.

Wyoming Tidbits

Built south of the Big Horn Mountains in 1890, the Sheridan Inn was featured in "Ripley's Believe it or Not" as "The House of 69 Gables".

FS The Sagewood Gift Store & Cafe

15 N. Main in Buffalo. 684-7670.
email: sagewood@vcn.com

Take a break from burgers and fries at the Sagewood Gift Store & Cafe. Enjoy food that is enticing, fresh, and delicious. The menu offers a selection of homemade soups made daily and served with cheese wedges and fresh bread and butter. Gourmet sandwiches, and vegetarian dishes are served with homemade breads. Be sure and save room for their homemade pies, cookies, and fabulous cheesecake. Call ahead and your order will be ready for take out. The gift shop features lodge accessories, including local pottery and food items. You'll find a delightful selection of gifts for the kitchen, kinfolk, and kids.

Wyoming Tidbits

A "nester" is a farmer or homesteader who settled in cattle-grazing country. Cattlemen and nesters were in constant conflict, and one of the most historic events in Wyoming's history involves such a conflict in the Johnson County War of 1892.

Buffalo

	Jan	Feb	March	April	May	June	July	Aug	Sep	Oct	Nov	Dec	Annual
Average Max. Temperature (F)	36.0	40.1	47.1	56.9	67.1	77.0	85.9	85.1	74.0	61.6	46.0	38.6	59.6
Average Min. Temperature (F)	9.6	14.3	21.2	30.4	39.5	48.3	54.3	52.4	42.2	31.7	20.0	12.4	31.4
Average Total Precipitation (in.)	0.52	0.43	0.72	1.56	2.23	2.27	1.37	0.82	1.31	0.97	0.58	0.44	13.23
Average Total SnowFall (in.)	5.8	5.3	5.0	2.6	0.6	0.0	0.0	0.0	0.1	1.9	5.1	6.7	33.1
Average Snow Depth (in.)	2	1	0	0	0	0	0	0	0	0	0	2	0
Wind Speed (mph / kmh)	8 / 13	8 / 13	9 / 15	10 / 17	9 / 15	8 / 13	8 / 12	8 / 12	8 / 13	8 / 13	8 / 12	8 / 13	
Wind Direction	NW	NW	NW	NW	NW	NW	NW	NW	NW	NW	NW	NW	
Cloud Cover (out of 8)	5.7	5.7	5.6	5.4	5.3	4.5	3.6	3.7	4	4.7	5.4	5.4	

M Coldwell Banker: The Smith Brokerage
75 North Main in Buffalo. 684-5563

M RE/MAX Mountain West Realtors®
490 N. Main Street in Buffalo. 684-8886 or toll free at 877-579-8874. www.buffalowyominghomes.com

The Realtors® at RE/MAX Mountain West Realtors® feel that their office reflects their love of Buffalo and Wyoming and their dedication to their community. While maintaining their heritage, they are also committed to staying at the forefront of modern technology and innovation in the real estate industry. Behind the walls of their turn-of-the-century offices, a computer network links their offices to the rest of the world. The global network capabilities and cutting edge philosophy of the RE/MAX franchise, along with old west values of honesty and integrity provide the best of both worlds to customers and clients in residential, commercial and land real estate needs.

12 *Food, Lodging*

T Jim Gatchell Memorial Museum
100 Fort Street in Buffalo.684-9331. www.jim-gatchell.com

In 1900, as the western frontier period was drawing to a close, Jim Gatchell opened a little drugstore in Buffalo, Wyoming. His customers included famous army scouts, cowboys, lawmen and cattle barons. He was also a trusted friend of the region's Native Americans, many of whom fought at the Battle of the Little Big Horn and who called Gatchell a "Great Medicine Man." For more than 50 years, Gatchell cherished these friendships. In turn, the old timers presented him with the priceless artifacts of a vanishing era. From this grassroots beginning in a crowded drugstore, the Jim Gatchell Museum today houses one of the most historically significant collections in the Rocky Mountain West.

Buffalo, Wyoming has been called the crucible of the American Frontier. More than a century ago, many of the pivotal events in the history of the west took place within 30 miles of here. Near the center of town, the Jim Gatchell Museum lends evidence to that time when this country was neither so tame nor so friendly. Scenes from the Wagon Box Fight, the Johnson County Cattle War and Buffalo's Main Street from the 1800s are depicted in detailed dioramas in the museum's main building.

The museum offers a large collection of American Indian artifacts, along with memorabilia from the Bozeman Trail and the Johnson County Cattle War of 1892. Mingled with the legends of Calamity Jane, Weasel Bear, Tom Horn, Red Cloud, Captain Fetterman and Portuguese Phillips is an extensive frontier guns collection, saddles of men who once rode the open range and items passed down through the families of pioneers who settled "in" and then "settled" the Powder River Region.

Museum visitors can view beadwork of Native Americans, relax outside near the restored western wagons, and meet the past face-to-face by viewing over 800 photographs of people who made history.

The Jim Gatchell Museum of the West is nestled near the tall pines at the corner of Main and Fort Streets overlooking historic downtown Buffalo. The museum is contained on four levels within two buildings: the main museum built in 1956 houses the original collection and the Carnegie Building built in 1909 is home to traveling displays, educational programs, children's hands on exhibits and the museum's gift store. It is open from mid-April through December 24. *Reprinted from museum brochure.*

T Mosier Gulch Recreation Area
5 miles west of Buffalo along U.S. Highway 16

This area lies at the foothills of the Big Horn Mountains (map). With almost 900 acres of ponderosa pine-forested lands, Mosier Gulch canyon is a popular hiking area.

A developed roadside picnic area complete with picnic tables, pedestal fire grates, and a vault toilet is available. In addition, the picnic area is a trailhead for the Clear Creek walking path which leads back to Buffalo.

At an elevation between 5,500 and 6,800 feet, this area is also home to mule deer, antelope, eagles, and ocassionally black bear and elk.

This area is open for hunting with a Wyoming Game and Fish Department. license. Trout fishing is available on adjacent city of Buffalo lands along Clear Creek.
Article courtesy of Bureau of Land Management.

T Bud Love Winter Range
West of Buffalo out Fort Street

Here you'll see some of the most scenic mountain views imaginable. As you pass through a wildlife preserve you will see mule deer, white tail deer, game birds including wild turkey, antelope, and in the winter, elk.

Burgess Junction	Jan	Feb	March	April	May	June	July	Aug	Sep	Oct	Nov	Dec	Annual
Average Max. Temperature (F)	27.3	29.6	33.8	40.4	50.9	60.6	69.8	68.5	58.0	46.9	34.7	28.3	45.7
Average Min. Temperature (F)	5.3	6.2	9.9	17.5	28.0	35.0	40.2	38.7	31.4	22.5	12.5	6.4	21.1
Average Total Precipitation (in.)	1.40	1.31	1.98	2.66	2.30	2.15	1.48	1.25	1.88	1.87	1.42	1.37	21.06
Average Total SnowFall (in.)	31.2	28.6	38.4	37.0	14.6	3.7	0.1	0.2	8.2	21.9	27.0	30.9	241.6
Average Snow Depth (in.)	28	33	34	28	10	0	0	0	0	2	9	18	14

H Fort McKinney

U.S. Highway 16 west of Buffalo just west of entrance to Soldier's and Sailor's Home.

Established at Powder River Crossing of the Bozeman Trail in 1876 as Cantonment Reno was moved to this site in 1878. The fort was built by two companies of the Ninth Infantry, in command of Captain Pollock, for the protection of the Powder River country from the hostile Sioux, Cheyenne, and Arapahoe Indians. The post was named for John McKinney, Lieut. of the Fourth Cavalry, killed in the Dull Knife fight on Red Fork of Powder River November 26, 1876.

It was abandoned in 1894 and the land was deeded to the State of Wyoming for a Soldier's and Sailor's Home.

L Z-Bar Motel

626 Fort Street in Buffalo. 684-5535 or toll free at 888-313-1227. www.zbarmotel.com

At the Z-Bar Motel guests enjoy clean, comfortable, modern air conditioned cabins nestled on quiet, shaded, park-like grounds with the Big Horn Mountains in the background. Choose from King or Queen beds and kitchenettes in rooms that have direct dial phones, cable TV and refrigerators. Parking is right at the door of your cabin. The Z-Bar is open year round with fishing, hunting, golf, tennis courts, hiking, boating, horseback riding, skiing and snowmobiling all nearby. They are located midway between Mt. Rushmore and Yellowstone Park. It is an ideal setting for quiet getaways, weddings, reunions, and seminars. The Z-Bar is AAA 2 Diamond rated.

Wyoming Tidbits

The country's first national monument, Devil's Tower, was dedicated by President Teddy Roosevelt on September 14, 1906. The 600 foot-high volcanic rock was later featured in the movie, "Close Encounters of the Third Kind."

13 *Gas, Food*

H Tisdale Divide

7 miles south of Exit 298 on Hwy 196

Wyoming in the 1880s was an open range controlled by cattle kings. Some of the powerful stockgrowers thought rustling was a problem, but others were just as concerned about the

influx of small operators who used government land grants which threatened the open range. John A. Tisdale, one of the small operators, was dry-gulched in a gully just north and east of this spot as he returned home from a shopping trip to Buffalo in late November, 1891. Locals were outraged by the killing of this respected family man.

Frank Canton, a former Johnson County sheriff was accused of the murder, but he was never brought to trial. Stock detectives, such as Canton, were hired by the Wyoming Stock Growers Association to protect their large herds and to intimidate would-be ranchers.

This incident, coupled with the murder of Orley E. Jones a few days earlier, set the stage for the infamous invasion of Johnson County in April, 1892.

14 *Gas, Food, Lodging*

T Ucross Foundation & Art Gallery

30 Bid Red Lane in Clearmont. 737-2291

Arvada

Originally named Suggs, the Burlington Railroad was responsible for renaming this town with a respectable biblical name.Natural gas, which flowed from an artesian well nearby, created a strange cocktail. Brave citizens would light it and drink the flaming water.

Clearmont

Pop. 115, Elev. 3,921

Situated on Clear Creek, Clearmont has an old hometown feel to it, with tree-lined streets and a friendly little park and an old jail.

Leiter

This post office was named for Joseph Leiter, who was a principle in the Lake DeSmet Irrigation Project.

Recluse

When this post office opened in 1918, it seemed very far away from the ranches it served. Only a recluse would want to be that far away, the ranchers thought.

Spotted Horse

This discontinued post office was named for a Cheyenne chief, Spotted Horse. The post office is gone, but the restaurant/ bar and gas station remain.

Ucross

Pop. 25, Elev. 4,085

Named for a cattle brand that had a U with a cross under it, this post office was once named Cedar Rapids, after the city in Iowa from which local settlers had emigrated.

H Powder River

On 1-90 halfway between Buffalo and Gillette

Too thin to plow, too thick to drink." That was the humor of early settlers describing the mud swept down stream each spring in the Powder. The river named the "Powder" because its banks have a black brittle gunpowder appearance. This river carries water from melting snows high in the Bighorn Mountains north to the Yellowstone River in Montana.

Powder River country is a land of heritage and tradition. Native Americans lived here for over 8000 years before the first explorers and immigrants. The famous "Hole-in-the-Wall" hide out of Butch Cassidy and the Sundance Kid was on the Middle Fork of Powder River, 60 miles southwest of where you now stand. Today these open expanses of prairie are home to hard working ranch families a cultural heritage

Moorcroft

	Jan	Feb	March	April	May	June	July	Aug	Sep	Oct	Nov	Dec	Annual
Average Max. Temperature (F)	31.4	36.3	43.9	55.0	65.8	76.7	86.1	85.4	73.7	60.2	44.4	34.4	57.8
Average Min. Temperature (F)	7.6	12.9	19.9	29.3	39.6	48.5	54.8	53.2	42.3	31.5	19.9	10.4	30.8
Average Total Precipitation (in.)	0.37	0.37	0.65	1.25	2.52	2.38	1.54	1.27	1.03	0.87	0.48	0.41	13.13
Average Total SnowFall (in.)	5.4	3.9	5.3	4.2	3.1	0.1	0.0	0.0	0.4	1.6	3.8	6.3	34.1
Average Snow Depth (in.)	2	2	1	0	1	0	0	0	0	0	0	1	1

passed on from the pioneer cattle barons of the late 1800's.

Once the habitat for great herds of bison, Powder River country now supports a blend of agriculture and native prairie wildlife. Cattle and sheep graze the lands along with herds of antelope, deer and elk. Riparian areas (the lush green areas bordering the river) are of special importance in fulfilling the habitat needs of people, livestock and wildlife.

This country has seen years of oil development, and is now a prime source of low sulfur coal for the U.S.- helping to reduce air pollution from power generation plants in many parts of the country. The Powder River basin now produces one-sixth of the world's energy.

As you pass through this area it appeaars endless and barren, but life abounds on the vast Powder River landscapes. Land ownership along the river is mixed between private, state and federal. Pioneers tended to homestead the low lands close to water, leaving the federal lands now administered by BLM. These lands are currently used for grazing. wildlife, minerals and other multiple uses. Prairie vegetation is produced on soil rich in nutrients and minerals and nourished by sunshine, snow and rain. Ranchers raise cattle and sheep, which convert prairie plants to meat, wool, leather and other products used to feed and clothe the nation. Through good stewardship and cooperative management of the prairies wildlife and livestock coexist.

You are in the Heart of Powder River country - a special place for wildlife and people. A land of cowboy culture and wildland romance.

H Stagecoach Roads in Sheridan County

Bingham Post Office and Stage Station

Bingham Post Office and stage station on the Rock Creek stage line was located from 1879 to 1885 at Benjamin F. Smith's ranch on the north side of the Tongue River, where the stage road crossed. The site is in a field west of the ranch buildings, about a half mile southeast of this sign. The ranch was one of twenty-three stage stations, eighteen to twenty miles apart, on the Rock Creek to Montana stage road. The stations consisted of stables and houses for the employees on the route, and nine of them, including Bingham, also served as post offices.

Bingham Post office was named for John T. Bingham, superintendent from 1879 to 1882 of the northern half of the stage line (from Powder River, Wyoming, to Junction, Montana). A bridge was built here in the early 1880's that washed out in 1884. B.F. Smith died about the same time, and Frank Mock took over the stage station and post office. In 1885 the post office was moved two and a half miles southeast to Frank McGrath's Keystone Ranch on Wolf Creek, retaining the name of Bingham until 1894. After the post office was moved, the Rock Creek line adopted a new route on the south side of the Tongue River to Dayton, where a bridge had been built.

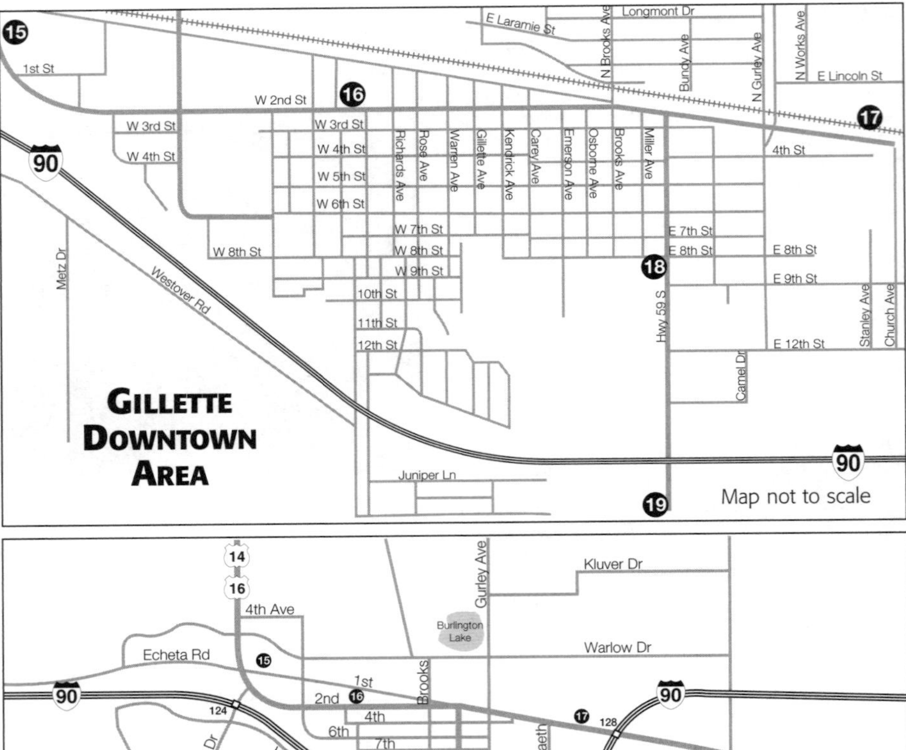

H Minnows and Mud

Rest area 30 miles east of Buffalo on I-90

Powder River, flowing north to Montana, has a far different character than the clear, trout-filled mountain streams that form it. Here the water is wide and shallow and in spring the run-off from the mountains transforms the river into a heavy current of muddy water.

Unique fish live in the Powder River and are adapted to life in murky conditions. The stonecat and three minnows (flathead chub, sturgeon chub and longnose dace) have flattened or streamlined bodies to help them stay near the bottom and fight the current. They have small eyes since good eyesight is of little use in muddy water. Near their mouth they have "Barbles" or "whiskers" which they use to smell and taste potential food. In June, the river is also host to the shovelnose sturgeon, channel catfish and goldeye, which swim by on their long trek to tributary streams to spawn.

The Powder River—one of the unique habitats, which supports unique species of Wyoming wildlife.

H 1811 Astorian Overland Expedition

At Spotted Horse

Gillette	Jan	Feb	March	April	May	June	July	Aug	Sep	Oct	Nov	Dec	Annual
Average Max. Temperature (F)	32.2	36.7	43.9	55.3	65.6	75.7	86.3	85.0	73.5	60.4	44.0	35.3	57.8
Average Min. Temperature (F)	11.1	15.2	21.2	30.5	40.0	48.3	55.6	54.0	44.0	33.8	22.1	14.5	32.5
Average Total Precipitation (in.)	0.57	0.54	0.99	1.87	2.62	2.75	1.49	1.14	1.29	1.11	0.70	0.60	15.67
Average Total SnowFall (in.)	8.2	7.4	10.4	8.6	1.7	0.1	0.0	0.0	0.7	3.5	7.5	8.4	56.7
Average Snow Depth (in.)	2	1	1	0	0	0	0	0	0	0	1	2	1
Wind Speed (mph / kmh)	8 / 13	8 / 13	9 / 15	10 / 17	9 / 15	8 / 13	8 / 12	8 / 12	8 / 13	8 / 13	8 / 12	8 / 13	
Wind Direction	NW	NW	NW	NW	NW	NW	NW	NW	NW	NW	NW	NW	
Cloud Cover (out of 8)	5.7	5.7	5.6	5.4	5.3	4.5	3.6	3.7	4.0	4.7	5.4	5.4	

The Astorians, first organized white expedition to enter this region, passed near this point on August 25, 1811. The party under the leadership of Wilson Price Hunt, was composed of 60 men, 1 Indian squaw and 2 children and was bound for the mouth of the Columbia River to help establish the Pacific Fur Company, headed by John Jacob Astor.

Leaving the Missouri River near the mouth of the Grand River in South Dakota, they traveled overland having one horse for each two men. After many hardships they reached their destination on February 15, 1812. Edward Rose acted as guide through this area.

L The Ranch at Ucross

2673 U.S. Highway 14 East between Ucross and Clearmont

Want to experience a vacation at a different pace? The serenity of the Ranch at Ucross is just the place! Nestled at the foothills of the Big Horn Mountains, Ucross is 27 miles southeast of Sheridan and 18 miles northwest of Buffalo, a convenient half-day drive from Yellowstone National Park or the Black Hills, South Dakota. The Ranch features deluxe accommodations, swimming, horseback riding, tennis, fishing. . . the list is as endless as your imagination. Get off the interstate.! Take a short ride on Wyoming Highway 14 or 16. You'll find a little piece of heaven—the Ranch at Ucross.

15 *Gas, Food, Lodging*

Gillette

Pop. 19,646, Elev. 4,544

The Founding of Gillette

The area now known as Gillette began when Frank Murrey, Robert, and George Durley, and Charles T. Weir filed homestead rights in Rockpile Draw. The new railroad crossed these homesteads, so the Lincoln Land and Livestock company bought them. In July, 1891, the livestock company planned the town of Gillette and sold lots. The town grew with the arrival of the railroad in August, 1891.

The Naming of Gillette

Edward Gillette was born December 14, 1854, in New Haven, Connecticut. He graduated from the Yale Scientific School in 1876. His first job was with the U.S. Geological Survey. Later, he became locating engineer and chief draftsman for the Rio Grande and Western Railway. He then worked as a surveyor and civil engineer for the Burlington and Missouri Railroad. While working for the Burlington and Missouri Railroad in Sheridan, he married the daughter of H.A. Coffeen, who at one time was Wyoming's congressman. After he quit working for the railroad, he was elected Wyoming State Treasurer on the Republican ticket. He served from 1907-1911. He also served as Wyoming Water Superintendent.

The city of Gillette was named after Edward Gillette because his survey saved the railroad money.

Gillette Grows

For several years after Gillette was formed, no doctors lived here. Until 1900, Dr. Baker would come from Sundance to see patients. At that time, he and his family moved to Gillette. Other doctors began coming to Gillette about 1902. Some of the early doctors also operated drug stores. One of the first hospitals in Gillette was established by Dr. A.G. Hoadley. Since there was no hospital, some of these early doctors kept patients in their homes.

The first bank, The Bank of Gillette, was started in Gillette in 1902. Before the first bank was started, John Larimore offered a check cashing service. He charged 10% to cash a check.

In 1904, Mr. Perry began printing the Gillette News. In 1913 a second newspaper was established. The Campbell County Record. The two newspapers were combined into one paper, The News-Record, in 1925 by Arthur Nisselius.

The First Baptist church was the first church built in Gillette. It was started in 1902 and was the only church until 1907. Most of the early churches did not have full-time ministers when they were started. Traveling ministers usually came about once a month.

The first telephone service in Gillette and Campbell County was started in 1905. At this time, several ranchers built telephone lines into town. Later, in 1910, the Northern Wyoming Telephone Company started an exchange in Gillette. Calls could be made in Gillette and to the towns of Moorcroft, Upton, Sundance, and Newcastle. The company offered telephone service from 7:00 a.m. to 10:30 p.m.

Electricity was first supplied to Gillette in 1915, and the first motion picture theater was opened in the same year. Admission was 10 and 15 cents. A regular feature at the first theater was a pianist and violinist to accompany the silent movies. Residents of Gillette also enjoyed roller skating and public dances as recreation.

The first school in Gillette was built in 1891. The first schools included students of all grades. The Gillette High School had its first graduating class in 1912 and there were two students in that first graduating class.

Agriculture in Campbell County

After the end of the Civil War, Texas cattlemen moved their herds of Longhorn cattle north looking for open range. The Longhorns were allowed to roam free all winter and fend for themselves until the spring roundup. Then the calves were branded and cattle selected for market.

The railroads were rapidly expanding west in the late 1880s, providing a way to market for Western beef and minerals. For a brief period Gillette was the rough and ready terminus of the Burlington and Missouri Railway, boasting twenty saloons, a large stock yard, and more than its fair share of rustlers, stock detectives, and shady characters. Then the railroad continued building to the west and Gillette matured into a typical small Western town serving as a division point on the railroad and a supply center for ranchers and farmers.

During the very dry years of the 1930s farmers learned that they must use the land more wisely. Today, farmers protect their land by using such methods as strip farming, shelter belts, crop rotation, and contour farming.

The G Bar M and 4J ranches raised as many as 40,000 sheep. Sheep were popular with ranchers because they provided two products, meat and wool.

Minerals in Campbell County

Early homesteaders found deposits of coal close to the surface. This provided an inexpensive

The Wild Bunch

Everyone knows the Hollywood version of "Butch Cassidy and the Sundance Kid," but the Wyoming mountains and trails hold many of their real stories and a lot of their secrets. The Wild Bunch, also known as the "Hole-in-the-Wall Gang" was an every changing group of outlaws that thrived during a period of five years from 1896 through 1901. The gang was a group of ten or so outlaws banded together by Robert Parker ("Butch Cassidy") and Harry Longabaugh ("Sundance Kid"). The membership included a Montana fugitive, Harvey Logan, known as "Kid Curry", George Currie, alias "Flat Nose", Bob Lee, and Lonny Logan, Bob Meeks and William Ellsworth, known as Elza Lay, Deaf Charley Hanks, William Carver, and Walter "Wat the Watcher" Punteney, among others.

Wild Bunch outlaws worked out of the Hole in the Wall, a well hidden hideout for the outlaws, located in the southern Big Horn Mountains of Wyoming west of Kaycee. A second home for the Wild Bunch Brown's Hole located in a desolate valley near the Wyoming, Colorado and Utah border In the winter Wild Bunch outlaws other 's worked out of Robber's Roost located in the desert of southeastern Utah a famous outlaw winter resort.

The Wild Bunch spent most of their time robbing banks, and collecting mine payrolls particularly from Union Pacific Railroad trains. The infamous train robbery portrayed in the movie, The Great Train Robbery, occurred on June 2, 1899 near Wilcox, Wyoming. The Wild Bunch outlaws flagged down the Union Pacific Railroad 's Overland Limited and detached the express car and dynamited the door wide and blew cash like rain as the outlaws scrambled to retrieve some of the loot. Other robberies took place, including one at Tipton, Wyoming, and another at Malta, Montana which netted them over $40,000. The Union Pacific finally got ahead of the outlaws and outfitted them with professional gunmen on horses packing high powered rifles.

With the last known holdup at Malta the Wild Bunch outlaws dispersed with Cassidy and Sundance leaving for South America in 1901, along with Sundance's beautiful lady friend, Etta Place. Some believed they were both killed in a shoot-out with Bolivian troops, following a series of robberies and living a quiet life there as peaceful ranchers for a few years. Some say that after Sundance was killed in the confrontation, that Cassidy shot himself.

Many of Wyoming's old timers believe that Cassidy returned to the United States and lived another 20 years of so, attempting to recover stolen loot hidden in the Wind River Mountains.

Section 3

Much of the nation's coal reserves are in the area surrounding Gillette. The Eagle Butte Mine shown here is one of the nation's largest open pit mines.

fuel for them to use in heating their homes. Starting in 1909, small mines were built around the county. The first major coal mine in Campbell County was Wyodak, east of Gillette. This was the first surface mine in the west, and the coal seam at Wyodak averages 80 feet thick. This mine continues to produce coal for the nearby power plant. Campbell County contains more coal than any other county in Wyoming. This coal has a very low sulfur content, and is clean burning. Increased concerns about air pollution in the United States encouraged the mining of Campbell County's low sulfur coal. During the 1970s coal companies planned and built large surface mines in Campbell County. Most of the coal produced in the County is shipped by train to coal-fired power plants in the Midwest. The increased coal production in Campbell County caused the railroad to build 116 miles of new track in the 1970s. In 1984, the Chicago Northwestern Railroad began serving southern Campbell County coal mines.

In 1999, Campbell County produced 316.9 million tons of coal. The state total for 1999 was 334 million.

The first oil explorations began in the 1940s. Although the first wells were dry, the constant visitations of geologists and their crews suggested that oil and gas would soon be found in Campbell County. The first commercial oil field discovery was made in 1948. Oil discoveries near the Crook County line in 1956 touched off the first oil boom. Other major oil and gas discoveries were made in the 1960s and 1970s at Belle Creek, Hilite, and Harzog. In 1983, 21,000,000 barrels of oil were pro- duced in Campbell County. Campbell County is the second largest producer of oil in the state. Some of Campbell County's oil is piped to refineries in Casper and Newcastle. There the oil is changed into gasoline and oil for your car and fuel oil for heating homes and buildings.

In 1969, a total of 758 oil wells were drilled. Four hundred thirteen were producing wells.

Gas is also produced in Campbell County. Most gas produced in Campbell County is piped south to Colorado and east to Nebraska. Most of the gas is used to heat homes and other buildings. Production of coal bed methane began in the late 1990s. Coal bed methane originates in coal beds and is recovered before the coal is taken from the ground. It is estimated that there will be over 100,000 methane gas wells in Northeast Wyoming by the year 2010. The importance of minerals in Campbell County has been increasing over the last 30 years. Campbell County now leads the state in assessed mineral valuation. The 1983 production of oil, gas, and coal was valued at $1,313,619,608.

The Future of Campbell County

Continuing mineral development will bring more growth to Gillette and Campbell County. Billions of tons of coal lie undeveloped in Campbell County. Future growth will come from existing coal mines and gas exploration and development. These continuing developments assure the citizens of Campbell County an exciting and promising future.

Reprinted from Gillette Convention & Visitors Bureau pamphlet.

16 *Gas, Food, Lodging*

T Rockpile Museum

900 W. 2nd Street in Gillette. 682-5723

The Campbell County Rockpile Museum is located in Gillette on the arid high plains of Northeastern Wyoming. Gillette had its start as a "tough as they come" railroad and ranching community. Many of the famous desperadoes and lawmen of the Old West, from the Tom Horn to Butch Cassidy and the Sundance Kid, plied their trades in the wild country of Wyoming. Cattle barons built ranches and homesteaders settled the country a quarter-section at a time. The Museum celebrates the rich history of the area exhibiting outstanding collections of stone Indian artifacts, saddles and other horse equipment, rifles, ranch and farming equipment. An original Homesteader's cabin from the early twentieth century helps demonstrate the sometimes bleak life early settlers endured.

Since the 1950's the Powder River Basin has been an important source of energy for the United States. Today a quarter of the Nation's coal is mined within 60 miles of the Museum and coal bed and methane is an increasingly important source of natural gas. Video presentations and static exhibits in the Rockpile Museum illustrate this vital history. Open daily, June 1 – September 1. Call for winter hours. Free admission.

F Coffee Friends

320 S. Gillette Ave., Villlage Square Mall in Gillette. 686-6119

Coffee Friends will let you pick your brew, have it ground, and served in fine bone china. The coffee bar offers 25 different whole beans, teas, and your choice of espresso drinks. Enjoy the great friendly atmosphere with friends or relax with a book on a comfy couch. This is a great place for a coffee break or lunch. They also serve delicious grilled and toasted sandwiches, with daily soup specials. Coffee Friends also sells lovely china coffee and tea sets. They are open Monday through Friday 7 a.m. to 5 p.m. Saturdays from 8 a.m. to 4 p.m. A meeting room is available for groups.

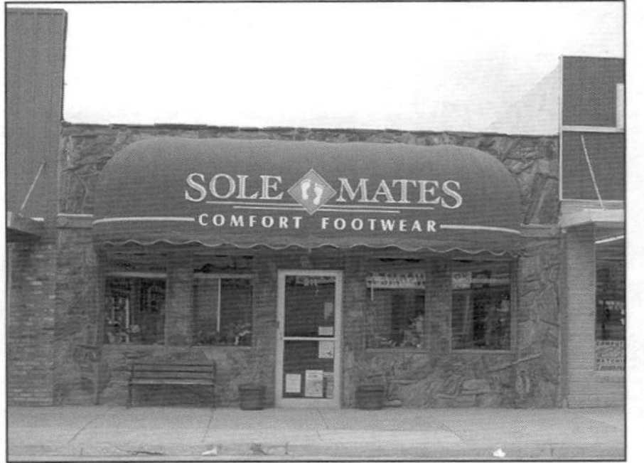

S Sole Mates

211 S. Gillette in Gillette. 685-2612

Kathy Bowman invites you to step into Sole Mates and step into comfort. Shoppers from near and far appreciate the large selection of comfort footwear for men and women, along with great customer service. The store offers a wide variety

Hulett

	Jan	Feb	March	April	May	June	July	Aug	Sep	Oct	Nov	Dec	Annual
Average Max. Temperature (F)	33.8	39.8	46.4	56.9	68.0	77.4	85.9	85.8	74.6	63.2	45.2	37.2	59.5
Average Min. Temperature (F)	7.5	12.7	19.1	28.3	39.0	48.0	53.3	51.2	41.0	30.9	20.0	11.7	30.2
Average Total Precipitation (in.)	0.65	0.60	0.95	1.85	2.52	3.05	1.88	1.33	1.28	1.41	0.83	0.59	16.94
Average Total SnowFall (in.)	11.6	9.1	11.2	9.4	1.0	0.2	0.0	0.0	0.7	2.9	8.9	9.9	64.8
Average Snow Depth (in.)	5	4	2	1	0	0	0	0	0	0	1	2	1

of brands including Birkenstock, Dansko, Born, Ecco, Naot, Clark's, and Josef Seibel, just to name a few. You'll be impressed with a variety of styles, colors, and sizes for every need from travel to every daily activity. Sole Mates is centrally located in Gillette's downtown area. Special orders are always available. Be sure and try out The Healthy Back by AmeriBag.

S Monogramming Plus Silkscreen
205 S. Gillette Ave. in Gillette. 682-5942

Monogramming Plus Silkscreen creates custom embroidery, silkscreen, and transfers, for hats, jackets, T-shirts and endless personalized items, in-house. There is no end to the possibilities of items that can be personalized to your specifications. Promotional items such as pens, key chains, cups, and just about anything you can think of are also available. They are licensed to use the Wyoming bucking horse logo to make any item a great souvenir. Check out the store for a large selection of camouflage children's clothing. They also offer a full line of Sabona bracelets and watches in copper and magnet styles.

S Deb's Bed & Bath Boutique
221 S. Gillette Ave. in Gillette. 686-4919

M Sheridan College - Gillette
720 W. 8th Street in Gillette. 686-0254. www.sc.whecn.edu/

Sheridan College consists of the main campus in Sheridan Wyoming, a commuter campus in Gillette Wyoming as well as outreach centers in Buffalo, Kaycee and Wright.

17 *Gas, Food, Lodging*

T Cam-Plex
1635 Reata Drive in Gillette. 682-0552

The CAM-PLEX Multi-Event Facilities just east of Gillette, provides 1,100 acres of activity for residents and vistors to Gillette and Campbell County. Located on the high rolling plains of Northeast Wyoming, this unique combination of facilities offers a performing arts theater, a convention/exhibit hall, two large multi-purpose pavilions, rodeo grounds, RV campgrounds, a horse race track and a 21-acre park and picnic area.

H Wyodak Coal Mine
On State Highway 51 about 8 miles east of Gillette.

This open pit coal mine is the source of fuel for generating electricity in northeastern Wyoming, southeastern Montana and the Black Hills region of South Dakota.

The coal was first mined in 1923 by removing the overburden with horse drawn scrapers and then hauling coal to the surface with horse drawn wagons.

The Marion shovel and the P & H crane seen here were used 40 years ago and were some of the first mechanized pieces of equipment purchased for the mine. Wyodak Resources Development Corp. was incorporated in 1958 at which time it purchased mining equipment and leased coal reserves from Homestake Mining Company.

Located in the upper portion of what is known geologically as the Fort Union Formation are three important and remarkable coal seams. The three seams are composed of the upper Wyodak with a thickness of 40 feet, the middle Wyodak with a thickness of 12 feet, and the lower Wyodak with a thickness of 40 feet.

The coal lies in a practically continuous bed varying in thickness from 70 feet to about 110 feet. It is classified as subbituminous coal with an average heat content of 8,000 BTU's per pound. The present coal reserves will provide home heating for the Gillette area and electrical generation until the year 2027.

Upon removal of the coal the area will be reclaimed providing rangeland for cattle grazing and additional habitat for deer and antelope.

L National 9 Inn
1020 E. U.S. Highway 14/16 in Gillette. 682-5111 or toll free 866-999-1449. www.national9gillette.com

18 *Gas, Food, Lodging*

F Polar Bear Frozen Yogurt & Espresso Cyber Cafe
900 Camel Plaza, behind McDonald's, in Gillette. 682-3155

S Marshall Jewelry
1103 E. Boxelder in Gillette. 686-6666

Marshall Jewelry is highly respected for original and custom designed jewelry. They carry an extensive variety of diamond rings, pendants, and earrings starting under one hundred dollars and going up to ten thousand dollars. The jewelry store is home to a Graduate Gemologist and 2 in-house goldsmiths, specializing in diamond and colored gemstone jewelry. A personal jewelry design can be created with your ideas and viewed on their Cad Cam computer program and viewed before the final piece "is set in stone." They also offer Montana sapphire jewelry. Landstroms says, "Marshall Jewelry sells more Landstrom's Black Hill Gold than any other retail store in Wyoming." Watch and jewelry repair services are available from the friendly staff at Marshall jewelry.

19 *Gas, Food, Lodging*

T Gillette Convention and Visitors Bureau
1810 S. Douglas Hwy in Gillette. 686-0040 or 800-544-6136. www.gillettewyoming.net

F Little Giant Cafe
500 O-R Drive, Southview Shopping Center in Gillette. 682-0001

The Little Giant Cafe has been a gathering place for the hometown Gillette crowd and visitors for over 25 years. It's not only the 55 cent coffee that people keep coming back for—The fresh made soups and baked goodies are consistently a big favorite. Old-fashioned lunch specials are served daily. Some of the regular offerings are home cooked meatloaf, lasagna, and other traditional favorites. Stop in for a great breakfast, lunch or

Section 3

Little Giant Cafe

coffee break, and enjoy the friendly atmosphere. They are conveniently located in the Southview Shopping Center and open from 6 a.m. to 3 p.m. Monday through Saturday.

FL Clarion Western Plaza Inn
2009 S. Douglas Highway in Gillette. 686-3000 or 800-686-3368. www.westernplaza.com

L The Jost House Inn Bed & Breakfast
2708 Ridgecrest Drive in Gillette. 687-1240 or toll free 877-685-2707

S Quilt Nook, Inc.
1001 S. Douglas Hwy #120 in Gillette. 682-9196 or toll free 888-268-3381

S Shell's Scrapbooking & Gifts
201 W. Lakeway, Suite 610 in Gillette. 685-1595

S Country Creations Gift Shop
2009 S. Douglas Highway, in Clarion Hotel Lobby, Gillette. 686-3000, ext. 136.

Country Creations has been owned by Vernetta Yantes for over 18 years. This extensive gift shop is conveniently located just inside the Clarion Hotel. Popular gift lines found in this delightful shop include Boyd's Bears, both in resin and plush, a complete selection of Burt's Bees Products, and lovely Bridgewater Candles. You will also find a great selection of luxurious creams and lotions to pamper yourself. The shop is a great place to find Wyoming souvenirs, quilts, jewelry, sweatshirts, and T-shirts. Country Creations is more than a gift shop. It is also a source for cross-stitch supplies, information, and classes.

20 *No services*

Lightning Flat
Right by the border of Montana, this one-time post office town was named for the violent lightning storms that often occur on the plain.

New Haven
Postmaster Harry Wilson named this post office for New Haven, Connecticut, where his favorite ball team played.

Oshoto
Sam Rathburn, a former Indian scout, suggested this Native American word for bad weather when clouds gathered over the meeting to decide the town name in 1911.

Rockypoint
Once only a post office, general store, and filling station named for their location.

Weston
Like the county of the same name, Weston was probably named for geologist/ surveyor John B. Weston, who was responsible for mapping much of the northeastern part of the state in the late 1880s.

T Weston Hills Recreational Area
25 miles north of Gillette on the west side of State Highway 59

At an elevation ranging between 3,800 feet to over 4,500 feet, the area is managed jointly between the Bureau of Land Management and Forest Service.

In this area, the lower elevations are grasslands with some juniper, while the upper elevations are ponderosa pine-covered hills and steep drainages interspersed with meadows and scoria outcrops. In the distance you can see the Big Horn Mountains and Devil's Tower.

With 7 miles of roads and trails, this area is popular for hunting, hiking, and ATV-riding. And you may even see mule deer, antelope, elk, turkey, and eagles. Of course, if you want to hunt in the area, you'll need to get a license from the Wyoming Game and Fish Department. Camping is permitted, and campfires are allowed (unless banned because of high fire danger) but must be kept under control. No water is available here.

The entire Weston Hills Recreation Area is a limited use vehicle travel area. This means that motorized vehicle travel is limited to roads and vehicle routes marked with "white arrows."

Tumbleweeds congregate along a fenceline in Rocky Point. They're pretty much the only residents of this town anymore.

The "ATV Loop Trail" is closed to motorized vehicles from September 15 to October 20 so as not to disturb wildlife before and during the big game hunting season.

Article courtesy of Bureau of Land Management.

21 *Gas, Food, Lodging*

Alva

Pop. 50, Elev. 3,995

Alva is another tiny town named for its first postmaster, Alva S. Bender, appointed in 1891. The first post office was merely a dugout. The Bear Lodge Mountains, the Belle Fourche River, and some grassy, cattle-filled hills surround Alva.

Downtown Hulett

Hulett

Pop. 408, Elev. 3,755

Lewis M. Hulett, first postmaster here, gave his name to the town when the post office opened in 1886. Located within sight of Devil's Tower, this little community depends mostly on logging and agriculture to thrive.

H Custer's Expedition

Midway between Alva and Aladdin

On July 20, 1874, General George A. Custer, leading the first official government exploring expedition in the Black Hills, crossed at this point en route to the Black Hills to investigate rumors of gold in paying quantities. The trail in the foreground was left by his party whch consisted of 110 wagons, 2,000 animals and 1,000 men, including engineers, scouts, geologists and practical miners. This expedition was in violation of the Treaty of 1868, which guaranteed the region to the Indians. In 1875, after government negotiations with the Indians to purchase the Black Hills broke down, miners and settlers poured into this area.

H Camp Devin

At Wyoming-Montana border on State Highway 112

The Ft. Laramie treaties of 1851 & 1868 set aside the Black Hills for the Sioux, for as long as the grass shall grow and the rivers shall flow. Nevertheless, in 1874 Lt. George Armstrong Custer was sent to investigate rumors of gold in the area giving rise to a flood of goldseekers and camp followers who poured into the hills violating the treaties. Sioux representatives were called to Washington to negotiate, but in November, 1875, before a new agreement could be reached, President Grant used attacks by Sioux on trespassing miners to order the Indians to give up their sacred hills and go to assigned agencies by January of 1876. That spring the military began a campaign to round up all remaining "hostiles" resulting in the Battle of the Little Big Horn, the Dull Knife Battle and the eventual forced surrender of all remaining Indian lands, Native Americans who had once roamed the high plains freely were confined to small reservations, often far from their sacred places.

Two years later the military was still at work protecting settlers and miners. June 1, 1878 Lt. Col. Luther P. Bradley and 520 men left Ft. Laramie following the Cheyenne-Deadwood Stage route to the Black Hills. Their mission was to construct a telegraph line between Deadwood and Ft. Keogh, thus tieing together Montana, Wyoming, and Dakota Territories. At the conclusion of a 30-day march they established a summer bivouac near here. Camp Devin, named for Col. Thomas Devin of the Third U.S. Cavalry, had a life of only two months. Although the existence of the camp was short, its occupants fulfilled their mission. The completed telegraph line resulted in improved communications between forts and white settlements, opening the way for domestication of northeast Wyoming.

L Diamond L Guest Ranch

850 Lame Jones Road south of Hulett. 467-5486 or 800-851-5909. www.diamondlranch.com

The Diamond L Guest Ranch located in the Wyoming Black Hills offers rides that are as diverse and interesting as the magnificent landscape. Their riding program offers unique opportunities for experiencing the outdoors on a well-trained, responsive horse. Their program accommodates all levels of riding experience from the beginner to the seasoned pro. Enjoy the hospitality that the west is known for. This family owned and operated guest ranch features a 4,000 square foot cedar log lodge, offering a warm and cozy atmosphere after a day in the saddle. Week stays include lodging, all meals, horseback riding, and all ranch activities. Their policy of limiting the number of guests each week to 12 allows personalization of each guest experience.

22 *Gas, Lodging*

Aladdin

Pop. 15, Elev. 3,740

Another stop on the Burlington Railroad to the Wyoming coalfields, this town was named for the character in Arabian Nights to inspire good luck and riches. The name was also given to the Aladdin Coal Mine Company which developed here. The "Liar's Bench" in front of the bright red Aladdin General Store is known for the tellers of tall tales who have sat there over the years. Aladdin is the lowest settlement in Wyoming, at 3740 feet elevation, and a basin just to the north is the lowest point in Wyoming, at 3125 feet. The Aladdin area is also rich in fossil remains, from petrified tree trunks to lizard footprints.

Colony

When homesteaders established a post office here, they hoped to start a colony for retired schoolteachers from the East. No colony formed, and the post office later closed.

23 *Gas, Food*

Beulah

Pop. 33, Elev. 3,510

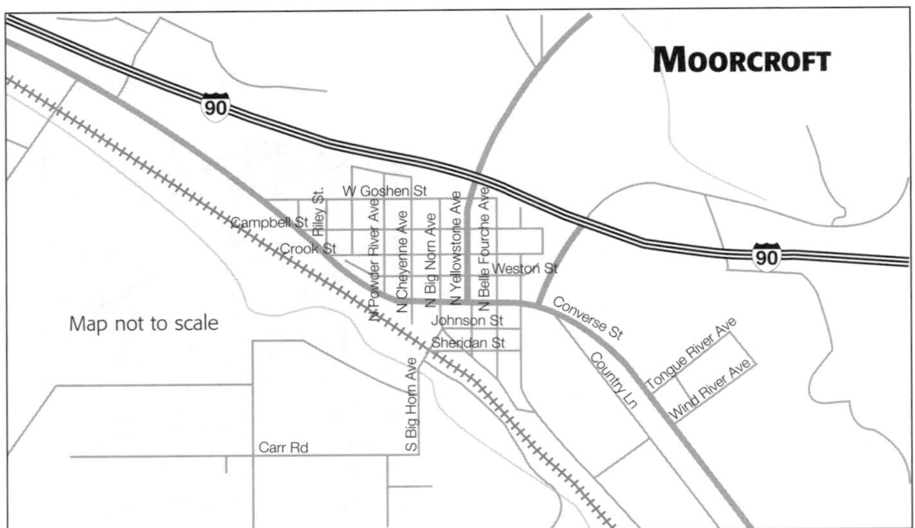

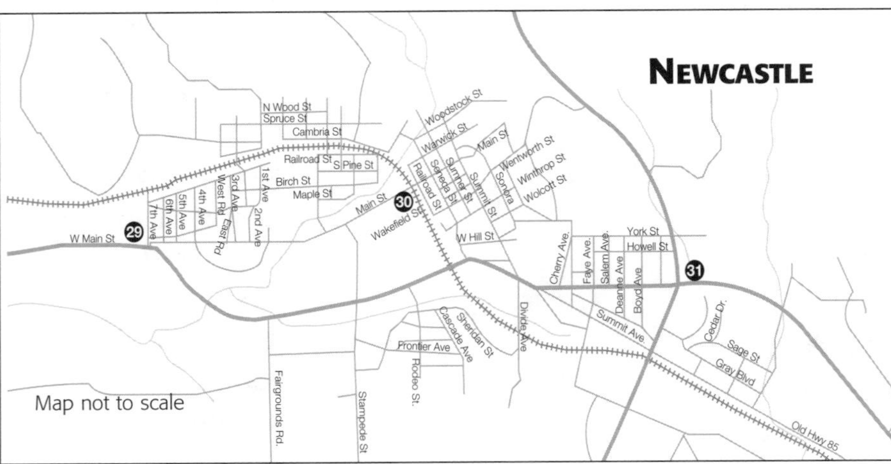

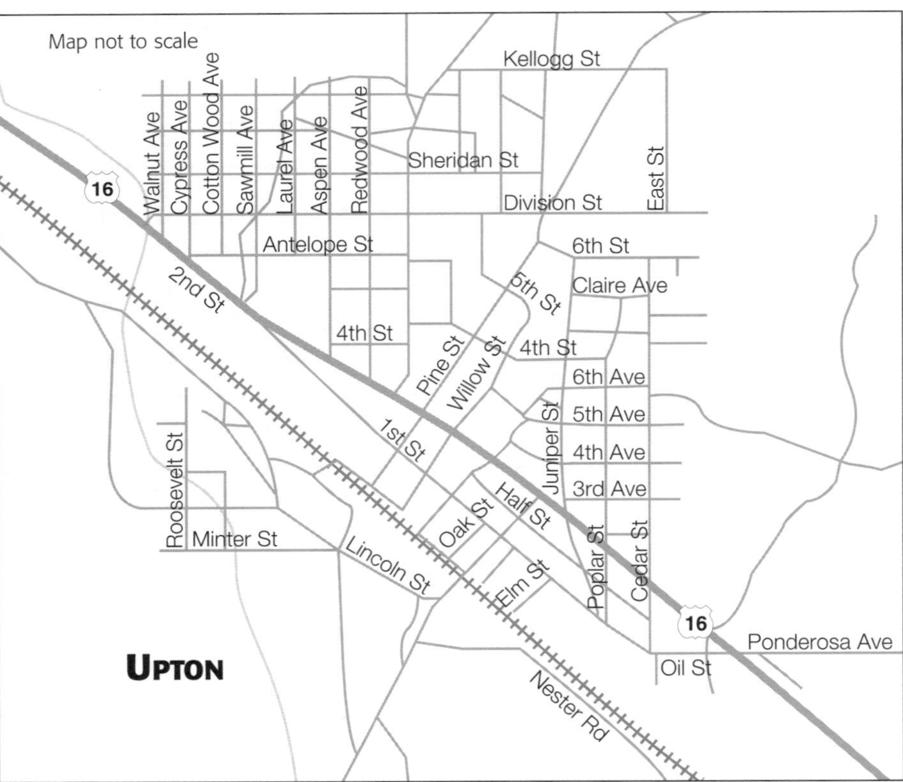

A well-loved schoolteacher, Mrs. Beulah Sylvester did not actually live here when some of her former pupils named this town for her. They were settlers from Exira, Iowa, and much to their delight, Beulah soon followed and taught in Crook County just a few miles west of South Dakota's Black Hills. The first post office was established in 1883 in the corner of one of the town's saloons.

T Tinton
On the Wyoming/South Dakota border

Initially a gold mining town, the deposits were thought to be mined out by the early 1900s. Recently, tantalum mining exploration has been conducted in the area.

T Vore Buffalo Jump
Five miles west of the Wyoming-South Dakota border on U.S. Highway 14, near I-90. 283-1192

The Vore Buffalo Jump is on U.S. Highway 14, near I-90 between Sundance and Beulah. This unique site is a natural sinkhole approximately 200 feet in diameter and 40 feet deep. The area was used by many Indian tribes for several hundred years to stampede buffalo into the hole. They were then salvaged for food, clothing, and supplies. The bones of thousands of buffalo remain at the site. The site is rich with artifacts in near perfect condition. A nonprofit corporation based in Sundance is beginning a major fund drive to pay for the first stage of an interpretive center site. Organizers promise that it will be a jewel for the region when it's finished, featuring a world-class museum and visitors center.

H Vore Bison Jump
U.S. Highway 14 between Sundance and Beulah. 283-1192

Between 1500 and 1800 A.D. the ancestors of at least five Plains Indian tribes killed and butchered as many as 20,000 bison at the Vore Buffalo Jump. Herds of bison were gathered from the surrounding valley and stampeded over the edge of this large round sinkhole providing tons of meat for winter storage thick layers of butchered bone extend almost 20 feet below the present bottom of the sink.

24 *Gas, Food, Lodging*

Sundance
Pop. 1,161, Elev. 4,750

The nearby mountain of the same name was a sacred spot for many Native American tribes. Numbers of people came here to participate in the sun dance, a grueling ceremony that involved, among other things, staring at the sun. The first white settler here, Albert Hoge, set up a supply station for ranchers in 1879. Cattle and lumber became the primary industries over the next century or so, with a few other influences on the economy coming and going, like an airfield and energy services.

Harry Longabaugh, the Sundance Kid, hailed from here. When Robert Redford played Longabaugh in Butch Cassidy and the Sundance Kid, it became his favorite character. He named the area where he built a home in central Utah Sundance. Later, he helped promote the Sundance Film Festival in Park City, which is known worldwide. So the name has come a long way from where it began.

T Crook County Museum
309 Cleveland Street in the lower level of the Crook County Courthouse in Sundance. 283-3666.

National Grasslands

Flowing east of the Rocky Mountains, from the badlands of North Dakota and Wyoimng to north-central Texas, spilling into the Great Plains, are 17 National Grasslands. West of the Rockies, in the Great Basin states of Oregon, California and Idaho, are three more National Grassland expanses. These wind swept seas of grass and wildflowers have witnessed the pageant of the frontier, the Dust Bowl and reclamation of 20 publicly owned National Grasslands totaling almost four million acres administered by the USDA Forest Service.

The grass seemed eternal, teeming with abundant buffalo herds, elk and other wildlife. It was also home to many tribes including: Sitting Bull's Hunkpapa Sioux, Apache, Arapaho, Arikara Assiniboine, Atsina, Bannock, Blackfeet, Cheyenne, Chippewa, Ojibwa, Bungi, Comanche, Cree, Crow, Hidsata, Kiowa, Klamath, Kootnei, Mandan, Metis, Modoc, Pawnee, Santee, Shasta, Shoshone, Teton, Wichita, Yankton and Yanktonia. The United States acquired most of the Great Plains and Great Basin from France with the Louisiana Purchase of 1803. Until the late 1860s, the Great Plains region was perhaps America's last frontier.

The Homestead Act of 1862 brought almost six million settlers by 1890 who tried to replace grass with crops more beneficial to economic aspirations. The settlers soon discovered, however, that while these vast grasslands were productive in wet years, they were also subject to serious drought and bitter winters. Land that should never have been plowed yielded its topsoil to incessant dry winds. Above parts of Oklahoma, Texas, Wyoming, Nebraska, Kansas, Colorado and the Dakotas, dust clouds rose to over 20,000 feet. Ten-foot drifts of fine soil particles piled up like snow in a blizzard, burying fences and closing roads.

During the same time, bison were largely eliminated by westward expansion. Ranchers filled the large open ranges of the plains and the Great Basin with cattle and sheep. Soldiers, prospectors, railroad builders and a host of others seeking the west helped push back the last frontier as they crossed and settled these lands.

By the early 1930s, the broad midsection of America was in trouble. Not only because of the Dust Bowls, but the Great Depression was reaching its economic depths. Emergency measures were taken to save the farmers and settlers. The National Industrial Recovery Act of 1933 and the Emergency Relief Appropriations Act of 1935 allowed the federal government to purchase and restore damaged lands and to resettle destitute families.

From these disastrous days, a hundred years after the Homestead Act, on June 23, 1960, the National Grasslands were born. Grass is the key to maintaining the productivity of these areas. Remove it, and the soil blows away. When rain falls, the barren ground can't absorb water and it runs off quickly carrying silt into streams and ponds. These grasslands must be used wisely for the benefit of the land and its inhabitants.

Our nation's 20 National Grasslands are an outstanding conservation success story. They are examples of progressive agriculture in arid grass country. Revegetated to provide for soil and water conservation, these intermingled public and private lands are managed to complement each other and to conserve the natural resources of grass, water and wildlife habitat.

Clean water flows off restored watersheds to be used miles downstream. Wildlife, including many declining, threatened or endangered species, thrives in reborn habitats. And, under a nurturing shield of vegetation, once wounded soil rebuilds its fertility. Water developments have provided additional wetland resources to benefit livestock operations, wildlife and recreation.

Private farmlands within the National Grassland boundaries add diversity to the prairie habitat. The presence of prairie dog colonies creates habitat favorable for such wildlife as burrowing owls, which use the abandoned burrows. The rare black-footed ferret preys on the prairie dogs and use their burrows, as well. Rattlesnakes are the only poisonous snakes found in the grassland; they are seldom seen during the heat of the day.

National Grasslands are rich in mineral, oil and gas resources. They also provide diverse recreational uses, such as mountain biking, hiking, hunting, fishing, photography, birding and sightseeing. Fossils, prehistoric and historic resources, as well as many cultural sites are being discovered. The National Grasslands are being managed to protect these important legacy resources.

The National Grasslands are important lands managed for sustainable multiple uses as part of the National Forest System. They have made important contributions to conserving grassland ecosystems while producing a variety of goods and services which, in turn, have helped to maintain rural economies and lifestyles.

Reprinted from U.S. Forest Service brochure.

Crook County was created in 1875, as part of the Wyoming Territory. The County is named for General George Crook, a famous Indian fighter. Crook County can boast of several other famous people who have touched its history. The Plains Indians who camped, hunted and held religious ceremonies here; General George Custer who in 1874, made several camps in the County on his Black Hills Expedition; The Sundance Kid, in 1887, spent 18 months in the county jail for horse stealing; and Teddy Roosevelt who visited and fished on Sand Creek in the early 1900s.

The Crook County Museum reflects the history of the count—the Indians, the cowboys and the pioneers who settled it. Step back in time and view a re-creation of a prehistoric buffalo jump, plus other early native American artifacts. Visit the turn of the century rooms for a glimpse of domestic life of these adventurous settlers. Take a look at authentic cowboy gear, including guns, saddles and branding irons. These are just a few of the exhibits on display. The museum is open year round and admission is free.

Excerpted from museum brochure.

H Crook County

Just east of Sundance at Sundance Rest Area on I-90 Exit 189

Serving as a western gateway to the Black Hills, Crook County, Wyoming is a place of beauty and diversity. The varied terrain includes the state's lowest elevation, 3,125 feet, situated north of the town of Aladdin, while rugged Warren Peak rises to a height of 6,800 feet. Among the county's many communities is nearby Sundance from which famous desperado Harry Longabaugh took the name 'Sundance Kid" after being imprisoned there for horse stealing.

Long a favorite hunting ground of Plains Indian tribes, a few white men had entered what is now Crook County before 1874. In that year an elaborate military expedition led by Lieutenant Colonel George A. Custer passed near this point prior to discovering gold in the Black Hills. Hoards of gold hungry prospectors quickly descended on the area, although the Fort Laramie Treaty of 1868 had reserved the Black Hills for the Sioux Nation. Bloody conflict ensued, but General George Crook, for whom the county is named, played an instrumental role in defeating the Indians and confining them to reservations. Crook County was thus opened to white settlement.

In 1876, gold seekers founded Beulah, Crook County's oldest town. Despite the initial lure of gold, ranching provided the county's enduring wealth. After the Civil War, great cattle drives brought Texas Longhorns to the Northwestern plains. Herds were driven through Moorcroft and western Crook County on the Texas Trail, leaving in their dusty wake the beginnings of a cattle kingdom in Wyoming. Stock raising, lumbering, oil and tourism all play an important role in the modern day Crook County economy. Tourists enjoy the abundant recreational opportunities offered by scenic Devil's Tower-the nation's first national monument-the Black Hills National Forest and Keyhole State Park. LOCATION: Sundance Rest Area and Information Center south of 1-90 just east of Sundance, Wyoming.

H The Custer Expedition

About 16 miles south of Sundance on State Highway 585.

Camped here July 22-23, 1874. General George Custer and officers climbed Inyan Kara Mountain. Two soldiers died while in camp and were buried on the mountain side to the east

H Inyan Kara Methodist Episcopal Church

About 11 miles south of Sundance on State Highway 585

One of the first country churches in Wyoming

Devils Tower

	Jan	Feb	March	April	May	June	July	Aug	Sep	Oct	Nov	Dec	Annual
Average Max. Temperature (F)	34.1	39.5	47.9	59.2	69.3	79.0	87.3	86.7	75.5	62.9	45.3	35.9	60.2
Average Min. Temperature (F)	4.7	10.2	18.5	27.8	37.6	47.0	52.6	50.1	39.7	28.3	16.9	7.4	28.4
Average Total Precipitation (in.)	0.61	0.59	0.89	1.82	2.61	3.16	1.89	1.45	1.39	1.31	0.73	0.69	17.15
Average Total SnowFall (in.)	9.3	7.9	9.1	6.6	0.7	0.0	0.0	0.0	0.5	2.2	6.5	10.5	53.3
Average Snow Depth (in.)	7	7	4	0	0	0	0	0	0	0	1	4	2

was built by Rev. O. B. Chassell, pastor of Sundance Circuit, and member of Inyan Kara Community in 1891. Site one mile west.

F Aro Restaurant

205 Cleveland in Sundance. 283-2000

The Aro Restaurant is a big favorite with the locals of Sundance. It's also a great reason to visit Sundance. Open for breakfast, lunch, and dinner, serving a menu loaded with burgers, steaks, and Mexican selections. Homemade breads, rolls, pancakes and soups will delight your palate. Wonderful luncheon wraps include vegetarian combinations with fillings including fresh broccoli, pearl onions, water chestnuts, and other fresh ingredients. Check out the daily specials. They are famous for juicy prime rib served on Fridays and Saturdays. Ask for your favorite beer, wine, or cocktail. The Aro is AAA approved and can accommodate banquets or parties up to 100 people.

S Sundance Mercantile Western Gifts & Antiques

109 N. 3rd in Sundance. 283-2274 or 800-299-2606

Nestled in downtown Sundance is the Mercantile where you can enjoy a bit of the West from long ago and the present day. Discover their collections of authentic western souvenirs from local and regional artisans. Items you will enjoy perusing include: pottery, jewelry, furniture, music, art, and hunting and fishing gear. Log furniture and accessories come from the mountains of Wyoming and the Black Hills. Authentic Arapahoe, Sioux, Northern Cheyenne, and Shoshone collectibles are also featured. Western collectibles and antiques will delight you as you find special treasures to take home. There is plenty of parking, even for RV's in the center lane.

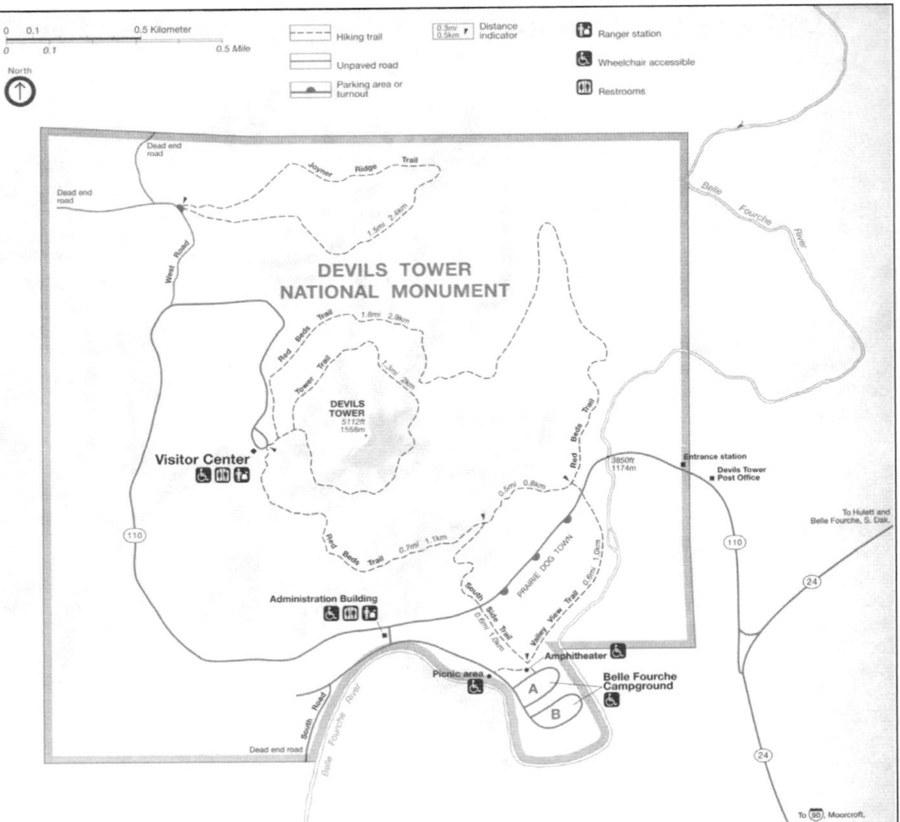

25 *Food, Lodging*

Carlile

Cecil S. Handcock, first postmaster, named this post office for an unknown relative in 1887. Also a railroad station, the post office later closed.

T Devils Tower National Monument Visitor Center

On Highway 110, at Devils Tower. 467-5283

Learn about the First National Monument Proclaimed September 24, 1906 by President Theodore Roosevelt. The Visitor Center is located at the end of the park road at the base of the Tower. See a variety of exhibits and a Natural History Association bookstore. There are outdoor wayside exhibits throughout the monument area. Open daily April through mid-October. Call for specific hours.

T Devils Tower

"A dark mist lay over the Black Hills, and the land was like iron," N. Scott Momaday wrote. "At the top of the ridge I caught sight of Devils Tower upthrust against the gray sky as if in the birth of time the core of the earth had broken through its crust and the motion of the world was begun. There are things in nature that engender an awful quiet in the heart of man; Devil's Tower is one of them." Several Indian nations of the Great Plains share similar legends on the origin of this prominent butte. The Kiowa people say:

"Eight children were there at play, seven sisters and their brother. Suddenly the boy was struck dumb; he trembled and began to run upon his hands and feet. His fingers became claws, and his body was covered with fur. Directly there was a bear where the boy had been. The sisters were terrified; they ran, and the bear after them. They came to the stump of a great tree, and the tree spoke to them. It bade them climb upon it, and as they did so it began to rise into the air. The bear came to kill them, but they were just beyond its reach. It reared against the tree and scored the bark all around with its claws. The seven sisters were borne into the sky, and they became the stars of the Big Dipper."

"Bear Lodge" is one American Indian name for the Tower. The name Devils Tower was affixed in 1875 by Col. Richard I. Dodge. Gen. George Armstrong Custer had confirmed gold reports in today's South Dakota portion of the Black Hills. Dodge's expedition was sent to survey the area. In the late 19th century, science had an explanation for every natural occurrenceor would shortly. Devils Tower was determined to be the core of an ancient volcano.

On July 4, 1893, with fanfare and more than 1,000 spectators, William Rogers and Willard Ripley made the first ascent, using a wooden ladder they had built that spring for the first 350 feet. The fact that they already had a flagpole waiting for raising Old Glory atop the Tower suggests the "first ascent" might have been one day before. The climbers' wives ran the refreshment stand and sold pieces of the flag as souvenirs. Such was life in the Old West. The Tower became a Fourth of July meeting place for families from area ranches, who might see each other but once a year. At the annual picnic in 1895, Mrs. Rogers used her husband's ladder to become the first woman to reach the summit.

Records of Tower climbs have been kept since 1937. Approximately 5,000 climbers come here every year from all over the world to climb on the massive columns. More than 220 routes have now been used in climbing the Tower.

But there is more to this area than the Tower. Life thrives around its base. Here in Wyoming's northeast corner, the Black Hills pine forests merge with rolling plains grasslands. At Devils Tower you can see every step in the process of establishing a forest-from bare rock to pines. And because mountains and plains converge here, you may find a great variety of birds. More than 150 species have been counted-including hawks, bald and golden eagles, prairie falcon, turkey vulture, and American kestrel. No one will miss the brightness of the male mountain bluebird, the industriousness of the nuthatches, or the feistiness of the black-billed magpie. Predominant mammals are the white-tailed deer and black-tailed prairie dog. You can spend hours watching busy, playful prairie dogs in their "town" on the grasslands below the Tower.

Wildlife has been protected here since 1906, when President Theodore Roosevelt proclaimed Devils Tower the first national monument under the new Antiquities Act. His action made Wyoming the home of our first national park-Yellowstone in 1872-and our first national monument. During the Great Depression, the Civilian Conservation Corps built road improvements, camping and picnicking facilities, and a museum. The roughhewn log museum still serves as a visitor center, book sales outlet, and the registration office for rock climbers.

1. About 60 million years ago molten magma forced its way into overlying sedimentary rocks and cooled underground. The cooling igneous rock contracted, fracturing into columns. An earlier flow formed today's Little Missouri Buttes. 2. and 3. Over millions of years the sedimentary rock eroded to expose Devils Tower and accentuate Little Missouri Buttes. The Tower rises 867 feet from its base, 1,267 above the river, and 5,112 feet above sea level. The area of its teardrop shaped top is 1.5 acres. Its base diameter is 1,000 feet.

Reprinted from National Parks Brochure

Devil's Tower–A Sacred Site to Indians

How is Devils Tower A Sacred Site to American Indians?

George L. San Miguel • August 1994
Courtesy of National Park Service

"A review of the ethnographic literature demonstrates that Devils Tower was a sacred area for several Plains Tribes, and that it has been encoded as an important landmark in tribal narratives."[1] According to the National Park Service, over twenty tribes have potential cultural affiliation with Devils Tower National Monument:[1]

Assiniboine & Lakota (MT), Blackfeet, Blood (Canada), Crow, Cheyenne River Lakota, Crow Creek Lakota, Devil's Lake Lakota, Eastern Shoshone, Flandreau Santee Dakota, Kootnai & Salish, Lower Brule Lakota, Northern Arapaho, Northern Cheyenne, Oglala Lakota, Pigeon (Canada), Rosebud Lakota, Sissteon-Wahpeton Dakota, Southern Arapaho, Southern Cheyenne, Standing Rock Lakota, Three Affiliated Tribes, Turtle Mountain Chippewa, and Yankton Dakota.

Tribes with historical and geographical ties to the Devils Tower area include: [1]

Arapaho, Crow, Lakota, Cheyenne, Kiowa, and

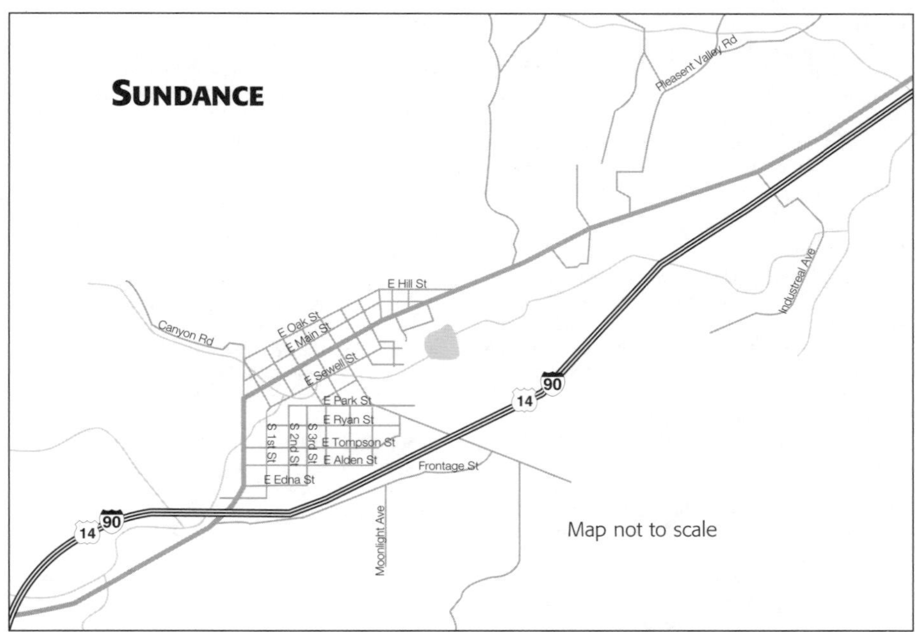

the Shoshone.

Traditional ceremonial activities which demonstrate the sacred nature of Devils Tower to American Indians include:[1]

Personal Rituals:

Prayer offerings (bundles and cloths), sweatlodge ceremonies, vision quests, funerals.

Group Rituals:

Sun Dance

Sacred Narratives:

Origin legends, legends of culture heros, and legends of the origins of ceremonies and sacred objects.

Among these rituals, all are still practiced at Devils Tower except for funerals. The Arapaho, Cheyenne, Crow, Kiowa, and Lakota all have a similar sacred origin legend for Devils Tower. See Gunderson 1988 for descriptions of these legends. [2]

Arapaho

The Arapaho call Devils Tower "Bear's Tipi."

The Arapaho people have a sacred narrative or legend on the origin of Bear's Tipi. 1

Sherman Sage, an Arapaho, said that his grandfather, Drying-Up-Hide, was buried near Devils Tower. [2]

Cheyenne

The Cheyenne call Devils Tower "Bear's Lodge," "Bear's House," "Bear's Tipi," and "Bear Peak."

The Cheyenne camped and hunted at Devils Tower in the winter.[1]

"This (Devils Tower) was a very holy place to us." [2]

The Cheyenne people have a sacred narrative or legend on the origin of Bear's Lodge.[1]

"A band of Cheyenne Indians went on one of its visits to 'Bear's Tipi' to worship the Great Spirit, as did many other tribes before the white man came. The Cheyenne braves took their families with them as they felt that would be safe, as Bear's Tipi was a holy place." [2]

Devils Tower is where Sweet Medicine died and it is his final earthly resting place. Sweet Medicine is the great culture hero of the Cheyenne who brought the Four Sacred Arrows to the tribe. The Four Sacred Arrows' sanctuary was located within a secret cave on the south side of Bear's Lodge.[1] Sweet Medicine also founded the Cheyenne Warrior Societies, tribal government, special laws, and ceremonies. As Sweet Medicine lay dying in a hut by Bear's Lodge, he foretold a dark prophecy of the coming of the horse; the disappearance of the old ways and the buffalo, to be replaced by slick animals with split hoofs the people must learn to eat (cattle). He told of the coming of white men, strangers called Earth Men who could fly above the earth, take thunder from light, and dig up the earth and drain it until it was dead.[2]

Crow

The Crow call Devils Tower "Bear's House" and "Bear's Lair."

The Crow have a sacred narrative or legend on the origin of Bear's House.[1]

The Crow people were known to fast and worship at Devils Tower and built small stone "dream houses" there as part of these vision quests.[2] The stone dream houses were about as long as a man is tall. A man would recline inside with his head to the east and feet to the west, "like the rising and setting sun."

The Crow believe Devils Tower was "put there by the Great Spirit for a special reason, because it was different from other rocks."[2] It is looked upon as a holy place.

Sundance

	Jan	Feb	March	April	May	June	July	Aug	Sep	Oct	Nov	Dec	Annual
Average Max. Temperature (F)	31.5	35.4	42.1	53.7	64.1	74.3	83.0	81.9	71.7	58.9	42.7	33.9	56.1
Average Min. Temperature (F)	9.2	12.5	18.7	28.9	38.9	47.7	54.5	52.8	42.9	32.5	20.9	12.7	31.0
Average Total Precipitation (in.)	0.74	0.70	1.06	1.89	2.75	3.30	1.99	1.45	1.42	1.32	0.87	0.74	18.25
Average Total SnowFall (in.)	11.2	10.7	12.1	11.1	2.4	0.3	0.0	0.0	0.7	4.7	9.3	12.0	74.5
Average Snow Depth (in.)	7	6	3	1	0	0	0	0	0	0	1	4	2

Kiowa

The Kiowa call Devils Tower "Aloft on a Rock" and "Tree Rock."

The Kiowa people have a sacred narrative or legend on the origin of Tree Rock.[1]

"...origin memories of American Indian people reveal none anywhere 'as bright- and remote-' as the Kiowas memories of their days in the Black Hills and at Devils Tower."[2]

Lakota (Sioux)

The Lakota call Devils Tower "Bear Lodge," "Bear Lodge Butte," "Grizzly Bear's Lodge," "Penis Mountain," "Mythic-owl Mountain," "Grey Horn Butte," and "Ghost Mountain." The Lakota people have a sacred narrative or legend on the origin of Bear Lodge.[1]

The Lakota often had winter camps at Devils Tower. 2 This is documented at least as far back as around 1816.[1]

The Lakota claim to have an ancient and sacred relationship with the Black Hills of South Dakota and with Devils Tower and Inyan Kara in the Black Hills of Wyoming. The Black Hills are the Lakota's place of creation.[1]

A Sioux legend tells of a Lakota band camped in the forest at the foot of Bear Lodge. They were attacked by a band of Crow. With the supernatural assistance of a huge bear, the Lakota were able to defeat the Crow.[2]

At Devils Tower, they fasted, prayed, left offerings, worshipped the "Great Mystery" (the essence of Lakota spiritual and religious life), and performed sweatlodge ceremonies. Lakota pray for health, welfare, and personal direction.[1]

The healing ceremony is known to have been performed at Bear Lodge, conducted by a healing shaman. The Great Bear Hu Nump imparted the sacred language and ceremonies of healing to Lakota shamans at Bear Lodge. In this way, Devils Tower is considered the birthplace of wisdom.[1]

"White Bull told of 'honor men' among the people who went up close to Devils Tower for four-day periods, fasting and praying. There they slept on beds of sagebrush, taking no food or water during this time. Once, five great Sioux leaders-Sitting Bull, Crazy Horse, Red Cloud, Gall, and Spotted Tail-went there together to worship. We did not worship the butte, but worshipped our God."[2]

Vision quests are a very intense form of prayer requiring much preparation, fasting, sweating (sweatlodge), and solitude[1]. It is a ritual integral to the construction of Lakota identity. In addition to learning lore and moral teachings, individuals who seek visions, "often regain clarity of purpose in their lives and a secure identity as a member of their tribe." Men and women may seek a vision for a variety of reasons: to give thanks, to ask for spiritual guidance, or simply to pray in solitude. 3 One of Devils Tower National Monument's archeological sites, assessed by archeologist Bruce Jones in 1991, is a post-1930's shelter made of stone and wood which could have been used for vision quests.

A Lakota legend tells of a warrior undergoing a vision quest at the base of Bear Lodge for two days. Suddenly, he found himself on the summit. He was frightened since he did not know how to get back down. After praying to the Great Spirit for assistance he fell asleep. Upon awakening, he found himself back down from the butte.[2]

The Lakota traditionally held their sacred Sun Dance at Devils Tower around the summer solstice. The Belle Fourche River was known to the Lakota as the Sun Dance River1. Bear Lodge is considered a sacred place of renewal. The Sun Dance is a group ceremony of fasting and sacrifice that leads to the renewal of the individual and the group as a whole. The Sun Dance takes away the pain of the universe or damage to Nature. The participant suffers so that Nature stops suffering. The Sun Dance is "...the supreme rite of intensification for the society as a whole..." and "...a declaration of individual bravery and fortitude..." "Young men went through the Sun Dance annually to demonstrate their bravery as though they themselves had been captured and tortured, finally struggling to obtain their freedom."[3] The tearing of the pierced flesh is symbolic of obtaining freedom and renewal. NPS records indicate that modern Sun Dance ceremonies have been held at Devils Tower since 1983.

The Lakota also received the White Buffalo Calf Pipe, the most sacred object of the Lakota people, at Bear Lodge by White Buffalo Calf Woman, a legendary spiritual being. The sacred pipe's sanctuary was located within a secret cave on the north side of Bear Lodge. 1 In 1875, General George A. Custer swore by the pipe that he would not fight Indians again. "He who swears by the pipe and breaks oaths, comes to destruction, and his whole family dies, or sickness comes upon them." 3 Pipes often are held as sacred objects used in vision quests, Sun Dances, sweatlodge rites, and in making peace.

Eastern Shoshone

The Eastern (Plains) Shoshone claim to have a sacred association with Devils Tower. Their religious world, however, is kept very secret and, as a result, cannot be documented at this time.[1]

1. Hanson, J. R. and S. Chirinos. 1991. "Ethnographic Overview and Assessment of Devils Tower National Monument." University of Texas, Arlington.

2. Gunderson, M. A. 1988. "Devils Tower - Stories in Stone." High Plains Press. Glendo, Wyoming.

3. Evans, M. J. et. al. "NAGPRA Consultation and the National Park Service." An Ethnographic Report on Pipe Springs National Monument, Devils Tower National Monument, Tuzigoot National Monument, Montezuma National Monument, and the Western Archeological and Conservation Center. March 4, 1993. Bureau of Applied Research in Anthropology, University of Arizona.

Devil's Tower Geology

The Tower's Geology

Devils Tower rises above the surrounding grassland and Ponderosa pine forests like a rocky sentinel. Northern Plains tribes worshipped at this remarkable geologic formation long before white men wandered into the West, and fur trappers, explorers, and settlers alike were awed by the Tower's majesty. In 1906, President Theodore Roosevelt established Devils Tower as our nation's first national monument. Many have gazed at the Tower and wondered, "How did this amazing formation get here? How did it form?"

The Stage is Set

Most of the landscape surrounding Devils Tower is composed of sedimentary rocks. These are rocks which are formed from broken or dissolved fragments of other rocks and are usually deposited by water or wind. The oldest rocks visible in Devils Tower National Monument were laid down in a shallow sea during the Triassic time, 225 to 195 million years ago. This dark red sandstone and maroon siltstone, interbedded with shale, can be seen along the Belle Fourche River. Oxidation of iron minerals causes the redness of the rocks. This rock layer is known as the

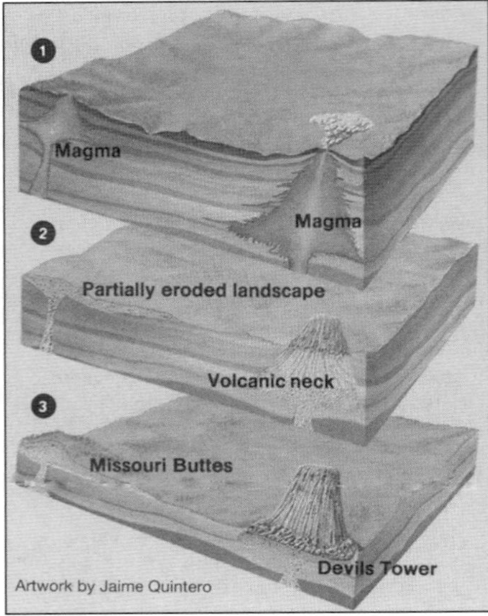

National Park Service Graphic

Spearfish formation. Above the Spearfish formation is a thin band of white gypsum, called the Gypsum Spring formation. This layer of gypsum was deposited during the Jurassic time, 195 to 136 million years ago. Seas retreated and returned. Climates changed and changed again. Gray-green shales (deposited in low-oxygen environments such as marshes) were interbedded with fine-grained sandstones, limestones, and sometimes thin beds of red mudstone. This composition, called the Stockade Beaver member, is part of the Sundance formation. The Hulett Sandstone member, also part of the Sundance formation, is composed of yellow fine-grained sandstone. Resistant to weathering, it forms the nearly vertical cliffs which encircle the Tower itself. Seas again retreated and advanced. Landforms were eroded; new sediments were deposited. About 65 million years ago, during the Tertiary time, pressures within the earth climaxed, uplifting the Rocky Mountains and the Black Hills. Molten magma welled up toward the surface of the earth, intruding into already-existing sedimentary rock layers.

The Tower is Formed—An Ongoing Debate

Geologists agree that Devils Tower was formed by the intrusion (the forcible entry of molten rock into or between other rock formations) of igneous material. What they cannot agree upon is how, exactly, that process took place!

Numerous theories have evolved since the official discovery of Devils Tower. Geologists Carpenter and Russell studied Devils Tower in the late 1800s and came to the conclusion that the Tower was indeed formed by an igneous intrusion. Later geologists searched for further explanations.

In 1907, scientists Darton and O'Hara decided that Devils Tower must be an eroded remnant of a laccolith. A laccolith is a large mass of igneous rock which is intruded through sedimentary rock beds but does not actually reach the surface, producing a rounded bulge in the sedimentary layers above. This theory was quite popular in the early 1900s since numerous studies had earlier been done on a number of laccoliths in the Southwest.

Other theories have suggested that Devils Tower is a volcanic plug or that it is the neck of

Indian Legends of Devils Tower

Arapaho Legend

An Arapaho lodge was camped at Bears Tipi. The father of this lodge was a head lodge and had seven children, five boys and two girls. The two girls had made an arrangement between themselves that the one who found the end bond (end rib) of a buffalo should receive the most favors from the brothers. The boys often made trips to other tribes. After a long search one of the girls found an end bone of a buffalo and on picking it up she turned into a bear and made some big scratches on her sister's back. The bear-girl told her sister, "if you tell the dogs will howl and this will be a signal so I will know that you have told." The sister did tell her brothers and when they heard the dogs howl and give the signal they were scared and started to run.

The bear-girl heard the signal and ran after them. The girl who had told was carrying a ball in her hand which she dropped and accidentally kicked. The ball bounded up on the big, high rock. The bear-girl reached over her sister's shoulder to grab the ball, slipped and made very big scratches on the big rock and fell on her sister and broke the sister's chest. The bear-girl climbed to the top of the big, high rock and told her family that there would be seven stars in the shape of a diamond appear in the east and the first star out would be off to one side and would be brighter than the other stars. This first star would be called Broken Chest Star. From this time on the Arapaho called this big, high rock "Bears Tipi".

This legend was told to Dick Stone by Sherman Sage, 81 years old. Otto Hungary, Interpreter.

Cheyenne Legend

A band of Cheyenne Indians went on one of their visits to Bears Tipi to worship the Great Spirit; as did many other tribes before the white man came. The Cheyenne braves took their families with them as they felt that would be safe as Bears Tipi was a holy place.

After having camped there for several days, one of the Cheyenne braves noticed that his wife was often gone from camp, staying away for a short time. As time went on he noticed that she was gone longer than before. This brave could not understand why his wife should be gone from their lodge so much as he had always been devoted to her and being a good hunter, as well as a brave warrior, she always had much buffalo, antelope, and deer meat. He furnished her fine skins to make nice clothes.

Becoming suspicious that some other brave in his band might be courting his wife, he watched to see what man was missing when his wife left camp. He found that no man was missing when his wife was gone. This man also saw that his wife had a skin over her shoulders now that she did not wear before coming to this camp.

One day when she had been gone longer than usual, he laid in wait for her, on her return he asked her where she had been and what drew her from camp so much of the time. She would not answer any of his questions. Then the man became mad and tore the skin from her shoulders and saw that she was covered with scratches.

He demanded that she tell him which man had abused her. Becoming frightened at the way her husband was acting she told him that she had been charmed by a very big bear that lived in the big rock. The bear had no mate and had become infatuated with her while she was out gathering fruit. Fearing for the safety of the camp, she had submitted to the bear's embraces, which accounted for the scratches on her shoulders.

Then the warrior told his wife to lead him to the bear so he could kill it. When they found the bear, the man had great fear because the bear was big, very big. The bear slapped the woman with his paw and changed her into a bear. The man ran to the camp to get the rest of the braves to help him kill the big bear.

They found the bear had crawled into a cave, leaving his hind feet in the door. The bear's feet were so big that nobody could get past them. They could not get close enough to the bear to kill him so they shot at his feet to make him come out. When the bear came out he was so big that all the warriors were scared and climbed up on a big rock.

There men were so scared that they prayed to the Great Spirit to save them. In answer to their prayers, the rock began to grow up out of the ground and when it stopped it was very high. The bear jumped at the men and on the fourth jump his claws were on the top. The Great Spirit had helped the men and now they had great courage and they shot the bear and killed him. When the bear fell, he fell backwards and pushed the big rock which made it lean.

After that, the bear-woman made this big rock her home, so the Cheyennes called it Bears Tipi.

This legend was told to Dick Stone by Young Bird. Samuel Weasel Bear, Interpreter.

Crow Legend

Once when some Crows were camped at Bears House, two little girls were playing around some big rocks there. There were lots of bears living around that big rock and one big bear seeing the girls alone was going to eat them. The big bear was just about to catch the girls when they saw him. The girls were scared and the only place they could get was on top of one of the rocks around which they had been playing.

The girls climbed the rock but still the bear could catch them. The Great Spirit, seeing the bear was about to catch the girls, caused the rock to grow up out of the ground. The bear kept trying to jump to the top of the rock, but he just scratched the rock and fell down on the ground. The claw marks are on the rock now. The rock kept growing until it was so high that the bear could not get the girls. The two girls are still on top of the rock.

This legend was told to Dick Stone by Rides the White Hip Horse. Goes to Magpie, Interpreter.

Kiowa Legend

Before the Kiowa came south they were camped on a stream in the far north where there were a great many bears, many of them. One day, seven little girls were playing at a distance from the village and were chased by some bears. The girls ran toward the village and the bears were just about to catch them when the girls jumped on a low rock, about three feet high. One of the girls prayed to the rock, "Rock take pity on us, rock save us!" The rock heard them and began to grow upwards, pushing the girls higher and higher. When the bears jumped to reach the girls, they scratched the rock, broke their claws, and fell on the ground.

The rock rose higher and higher, the bears still jumped at the girls until they were pushed up into the sky, where they now are, seven little stars in a group (The Pleiades). In the winter, in the middle of the night, the seven stars are right over this high rock. When the people came to look, they found the bears' claws, turned to stone, all around the base.

No Kiowa living has ever seen this rock, but the old men have told about it - it is very far north where the Kiowa used to live. It is a single rock with scratched sides, the marks of the bears' claws are there yet, rising straight up, very high. There is no other like it in the whole country, there are no trees on it, only grass on top. The Kiowa call this rock "Tso-aa", a tree rock, possibly because it grew tall like a tree.

Told by I-See-Many-Camp-Fire-Places, Kiowa soldier at Fort Sill, Oklahoma, 1897.

Sioux Legend

In the Sioux tribe long ago was a brave warrior who often went alone into the wilderness where he would fast and worship the Great Spirit in solitude. Being alone helped him to strengthen his courage so that in the future he could carry out his plans.

One day this warrior took his buffalo skull and went along into the wilderness to worship. Standing at the base of Mato Tipila after he had worshipped for two days he suddenly found himself on top of this high rock. He was very much frightened as he did not know how he would get down. After appealing to the Great Spirit he went to sleep. When he awoke he was very glad to find that he was again at the base of this high rock.

He saw that he was standing at the door of a big bear's lodge as there was foot prints of a very big bear there. He could tell that the cracks in the big rock were made by the big bear's claws. So he knew that all the time he had been on top of this big rock he had been standing on a big bear's lodge.

From this time on his nation called this big high rock Mato Tipila and they went there often to worship. The buffalo skull is still on top of this big high rock and can be seen on the highest point.

This legend told to Dick Stone by Short Bull, who lived a short distance west of Ogalala, South Dakota, on July 31, 1932. Mark Running Eagle, Interpreter.

Article courtesy of National Park Service.

BEFORE YOU CLIMB

Rock climbing at Devils Tower is a popular recreational sport. The tower is acclaimed as one of the premier crack climbing areas in North America and boasts a colorful 100-year climbing history. With this popularity, regulations are essential in order to protect climbers, the general public, and the Tower itself. We ask all climbers to act responsibly and observe park regulations.

The final climbing management plan for Devils Tower National Monument was released in March 1995 and currently guides climbing management. For the first time, Devils Tower National Monument will manage the Tower as a cultural resource as well as a natural and recreational resource. Management of recreational climbing will be approached from this broader perspective. The plan stipulates that there will be no new physical impacts to the rock. Out of respect to American Indian beliefs, a key element of the plan is a voluntary closure to climbing during the month of June. (See March 2000 Climbing Management Plan Press Release)

Regulations

- Register before your climb and check in immediately upon your return.
- Observe any route closures posted on bulletin boards and on the Tower Trail. Some routes are closed from mid-March to mid-summer to protect nesting Prairie Falcons. Contact the monument for specific closure areas.
- Camp only in the designated campground. Camping is not permitted on the Tower.
- Leave pets where they are comfortable and safe. Do not leave pets unattended. Pets are not allowed on trails or away from parking lots, the campground, or the picnic area. All pets must be leashed or confined in a vehicle.
- Pull your ropes when you are finished climbing for the day. Leaving unattended ropes on the Tower is not permitted. Please do not leave webbing on the Tower.
- Leave the rock as you found it. Chipping holds, gluing holds, gardening, and excessive route cleaning are prohibited.
- A permit is required to replace existing bolts or fixed pitons. Do not install new bolts or fixed pitons.
- Power drills are prohibited at Devils Tower National Monument. A permit is required to use manual drills.

Registration

All persons planning to climb or scramble above the boulder field are required to register at the Visitor Center April through October or at the Administration Building during winter months. Climbers are required to check in at the end of their climb. During off hours, a registration board with blank registration cards and check-in sheets is posted on the outside of the Visitor Center or Administration Building door. During peak visitation - May through September - climbers are asked to leave their vehicles in the lower parking lot, located immediately to the right as you enter the main visitor center parking lot.

Climbing Guides

Several climbing guide companies hold commercial use permits for Devils Tower. Check with Devils Tower for a current list of guides with permits. When using a commercial guide service make certain that the guide has a valid permit.

Establishing New Routes

Climbers completing new routes are asked to describe them on forms available at the Visitor Center. New route descriptions are made available to all interested climbers. Please remember that the installation of new bolts and fixed pitons is not permitted.

A Word of Caution

Rescue: The National Park Service does not maintain a rescue team at Devils Tower. Make plans for self-rescue or assistance from other climbers should an unexpected incident arise. Available park staff will provide assistance to the limit of their abilities. Response to an incident may take several hours.

Injury: The closest medical facility which can treat significant trauma is 60 miles from Devils Tower. Caution should dictate your actions while climbing!

Weather: Storms can develop quickly, creating danger from lightning, slippery rock surfaces, and hypothermia. Obtain forecast information before beginning your climb and observe changing weather conditions. Dehydration is common during hot, dry weather. Always carry plenty of water.

Rappelling: Accidents often occur when rappelling if proper care is not taken. The National Park Service does not maintain bolts. Inspect all anchors and back them up if you feel they are inadequate. Make sure that you know where your rappel route is before you begin. Always rappel over the nose of a column and take extreme care to prevent ropes from jamming in cracks when pulled. Avoid knocking off loose rock.

Other Hazards: Climbing helmets are strongly recommended due to frequent rock falls. Significant hazards should be reported to a ranger so that future climbers can be warned of the situation. Watch for snakes, spiny plants, poison ivy, falcon attacks, wasps, and falling rocks while climbing on the Tower.

Planning

Some routes are closed to protect nesting Prairie Falcons from mid-March to mid-summer. Please check for route closures when you register to climb.

A key element of climbing management at Devils Tower is a voluntary closure to climbing during the month of June. The National Park Service asks climbers to consider the voluntary closure in planning a climbing trip to Devils Tower.

an extinct volcano (an unlikely theory, for there is no evidence of volcanic activity - volcanic ash, lava flows, or volcanic debris - anywhere in the surrounding countryside)!

No one yet has a definite answer as to how exactly Devils Tower was formed - other than that it was an igneous intrusion into the sedimentary layers above and that the molten rock comprising the Tower did not surface.

In any case, geologists agree, the igneous material intruded and then cooled as phonolite porphyry, a light to dark-gray or greenish-gray igneous rock with conspicuous crystals of white feldspar. As the lava cooled, hexagonal (and sometimes 4-, 5-, and 7-sided) columns formed. As the columns continued to cool, vertical cracks developed as the columns shrank horizontally in volume.

The Tower is Uncovered

Until erosion began its relentless work, Devils Tower was not visible above the overlying sedimentary rocks. But the forces of erosion - particularly that of water - began to wear away the sandstones and shales. The much harder igneous rock survived the onslaught of erosional forces, and the gray columns of Devils Tower began to appear above the surrounding landscape.

As rain and snow continue to erode the sedimentary rocks surrounding the Tower's base, and the Belle Fourche River carries away the debris, more of Devils Tower will be exposed. But at the same time, the Tower itself is slowly being eroded. Rocks are continually breaking off and falling from the steep walls. Rarely do entire columns fall, but on remote occasions, they do. Piles of rubble - broken columns, boulders, small rocks, and stones - lie at the base of the Tower, indicating that it was, at some time in the past, larger than it is today.

Eventually, at some time far in the future, even Devils Tower itself will be eroded away!

Climbing Devil's Tower

How Do They Get Up There?

For over a hundred years, rock climbers have tested their skills on the vertical faces of Devils Tower. Using various techniques and innovative and specialized equipment, climbers have inched their way up - and down - the steep walls. As you gaze at the Tower, you will very likely see climbers clinging to the precipitous rock.

Brave Souls and Foolish

In 1875, an expedition under the leadership of Colonel Richard Dodge and geologists Walter Jenney and Henry Newton set out to look for gold in the Black Hills. Newton recorded the first detailed description of Devils Tower, "as inaccessible to anything without wings."

There are those, however, who are eager to take on any challenge, no matter how impossible it may at first seem. William Rogers and Willard Ripley, two local ranchers, were determined to climb Devils Tower!

The two ranchers made elaborate preparations for the climb. They built a 350-foot wooden ladder to the summit by driving pegs into a continuous vertical crack running between two columns on the southeast side of the Tower. The pegs were braced and secured to each other by a continuous wooden strip. Sometime before the "official" ascent scheduled for the 4th of July, the two men took a 12-foot flagpole to the top of the Tower and planted it solidly in the ground.

On July 4, 1893, a thousand spectators watched in awe as Rogers made the first ascent of the Tower. To the wild cheers of the crowd, William Rogers ascended the ladder and ran an

American flag up the flagpole. Devils Tower had officially been climbed!

Others quickly followed in Roger's footsteps, utilizing the ladder to ascend to the summit. (Portions of the ladder can still be seen from the south side of the Tower Trail.) On July 4, 1895, William's wife Linnie Rogers, wearing knee-high leather boots and navy-blue bloomers, became the first woman to climb the ladder to the top of the Tower.

Until the late 1930s, all who ascended the Tower utilized William Rogers' ladder. In 1937, Fritz Weissner led three mountain climbers from the American Alpine Club of New York City to the summit using rock-climbing techniques only. Their ascent took 4 hours and 46 minutes. The classic - and easiest - route to the top was pioneered the next year by Jack Durrance.

George Hopkins was the only person to climb down the Tower - without climbing up first! In 1941, as a publicity stunt, George parachuted onto the summit of Devils Tower. But his untried preparations for an easy descent did not work. Food and supplies were dropped by plane to the stranded man. For six days, George waited, eating well, while attempts were made to locate climbers with the expertise to rescue him. George was eventually - and successfully rescued - becoming the only person to reach the top of the Tower without first climbing up.

Today, modern rock climbers use a variety of techniques and equipment to scale the nearly vertical walls of Devils Tower.

Scaling the Heights

Most climbers free climb Devils Tower, utilizing naturally occuring ledges, cracks, and projections to inch their way up the Tower. Ropes and equipment are used only as safety precautions - to catch climbers if they should fall. Some climbers utilize aid climbing, using equipment for holds and upward movement. Climbers are NOT allowed to chip the rock or modify Devils Tower in any way.

Climbers usually wear climbing shoes which are very tight-fitting and have a special rubber sole to help the climber retain their foothold safely on the rock. Many climbers wear helmets to protect their heads from possible rock falls. On harder climbing routes, climbers may wear chalk-bags filled with gymnasts' chalk to keep fingers and hands dry while clinging to precarious holds. A harness enables a climber to be roped to their partner and to attach themselves to safety equipment on the rock.

The climbing rope is the most important piece of technical equipment. These ropes are made of nylon and are tested for flexibility and elasticity. Most ropes last for only two or three years before they are too worn to provide safety.

Pitons are steel wedges which are hammered into cracks. Climbers are no longer allowed to install fixed pitons into the rock at Devils Tower. Today, most climbers use chocks for protection rather than pitons. Chocks come in various sizes and shapes and are easily placed in and removed from rock cracks without damaging the rock. A carabiner is clipped to the chock, and the climbing rope is clipped through the carabiner, effectively attaching the climber to the rock face.

Climbers usually climb with partners. The leader ascends the rock first while their partner, who is anchored to the wall, belays them, feeding out or taking in the rope attaching them. When the leader reaches the end of the rope, they secure themselves well and belay their partner. The second climber then ascends, taking out whatever chocks have been placed in the cracks.

Most climbers rappel to descend from the Tower. With a rope well anchored, a climber can literally walk down the face of the rock, slowing the descent by braking on the rope as it slides through the harness. There are several standard rappel routes on Devils Tower. These have fixed anchors so that climbers do not have to leave any of their own equipment. The ropes pass through rappel rings and can be pulled down after the rappel.

Sacred Tower, Climbing Mecca

Climbing is considered an historical recreational use at Devils Tower. But long before climbers found their way to the area, American Indians regarded the Tower as a sacred site. Today, Northern Plains tribes still view Devils Tower as a sacred place. The Climbing Management Plan, implemented in 1995, allows for management of Devils Tower as a cultural resource as well as a natural and recreational resource. Out of respect for American Indian beliefs, climbers are asked to voluntarily refrain from climbing during the month of June.

Article courtesy of National Park Service

H Devils Tower

Midway between Devils Tower and Devils Tower Jct.

Devils Tower, an important landmark for Plains Indian tribes long before the white man reached Wyoming, was called Mateo Tepee, or Grizzly Bear Lodge, by the Sioux. A number of Indian legends describe the origin of Devils Tower. One legend tells about seven little girls being chased onto a low rock to escape attacking bears. Their prayers for help were heeded. The rock carried them upward to safety as the claws of the leaping bears left furrowed columns in the sides of the ascending tower. Ultimately, the rock grew so high that the girls reached the sky where they were transformed into the constellation known as the Pleiades.

Fur trappers may have visited Devils Tower, but they left no written evidence of having done so. The first documented visitors were several members of Captain W. F. Raynold's Yellowstone Expedition who arrived in 1859. Sixteen years later, Colonel Richard I. Dodge led a U.S. Geological Survey party to the massive rock formation and coined the name Devils Tower. Recognizing its unique characteristics, Congress designated the area a U.S. forest reserve in 1892 and in 1906 Devils Tower became the nation's first national monument.

Rising dramatically to a height of 1,280 feet above the Belle Fourche River, Devils Tower has become a rock climbing mecca. On July 4, 1893, local rancher William Rogers became the first person to complete the climb after constructing a ladder of wooden pegs driven into cracks in the rock face. Technical rock climbing techniques were first used to ascend the Tower in 1937 when Fritz Wiessner conquered the summit with a small party from the American Alpine Club. Today hundreds of climbers scale the sheer rock walls each summer. All climbers must register with a park ranger before and after attempting a climb.

H Devil's Tower

Midway between Devils Tower and Devils Tower Jct.

Although Devils Tower has long been a prominent landmark in northeastern Wyoming, the origin of the mammoth rock obelisk remains somewhat obscure. Geologists agree that Devils Tower consists of molten rock forced upwards from deep within the earth. Debate continues, however, as to whether Devils Tower is solidified lava from the neck of an ancient volcano, the wall of which eroded long ago, or whether it is a sheet of molten rock which was injected between rock layers. The characteristic furrowed columns are apparently the result of uniformly-arranged cracks which appeared during the cooling of the volcanic magma. Geologic estimates have placed the age of Devils Tower at greater than fifty million years, although it is likely that erosion uncovered the rock formation only one or two million years ago.

The unique geological attributes of Devils Tower stimulated several early preservation efforts. In 1892 Wyoming Senator Francis E. Warren persuaded the General Land Office to create a timber reserve which surrounded the tower. Senator Warren also launched an unsuccessful effort to declare the entire area a national park. In 1906 Congress passed the Antiquities Act, which empowered the President to bestow national monuments status upon federally owned land that contain historic landmarks, historic or prehistoric structures, and other significant historic or scientific objects. President Theodore Roosevelt quickly invoked the Antiquities Act, designating Devil's Tower the nation's first national monument in 1906. The National Park Service was created in 1916 and eventually assumed administrative control of all national monuments.

H Devil's Tower ... the first National Monument

Devil's Tower National Monument Visitor's Center

President Theodore Roosevelt proclaimed Devil's Tower a national monument on September 24, 1906.

President Roosevelt acted under the authority of the Antiquities Act of 1906 which declared, "that the President of the United States is hereby authorized, in his discretion, to declare by public proclamation historic landmarks, historic and prehistoric structures, and other objects of historic or scientific interest that

Upton

	Jan	Feb	March	April	May	June	July	Aug	Sep	Oct	Nov	Dec	Annual
Average Max. Temperature (F)	30.8	35.8	44.6	56.6	67.6	78.3	87.0	85.7	74.5	60.6	42.8	32.9	58.1
Average Min. Temperature (F)	6.0	11.1	19.4	28.9	39.7	48.9	55.3	53.4	42.4	30.8	18.4	8.7	30.2
Average Total Precipitation (in.)	0.44	0.48	0.63	1.53	2.37	2.61	1.84	1.45	1.03	1.05	0.58	0.54	14.55
Average Total SnowFall (in.)	7.0	6.5	7.4	4.9	0.4	0.2	0.0	0.0	0.3	1.9	6.3	8.4	43.3
Average Snow Depth (in.)	4	4	1	0	0	0	0	0	0	0	1	3	1

are situated upon the lands owned or controlled by the Government of the United States to be national monuments. . ."

FSM Devils Tower Trading Post

57 Hwy 110 at the Devils Tower. 467-5295.
www.devilstowertradingpost.com

Devils Tower Trading Post is located at the gateway to our nation's first national monument. It is also home to the world's largest Harley Davidson flag. It is flown only one week a year during the Sturgis Motorcycle Rally and dedicated to all the bikers that make it a huge success. Stop by for lunch and dinner and enjoy homemade BBQ Beef, pizza, chili. Enjoy a refreshing sarsaparilla

Devils Tower Trading Post

or a sweet treat from the ice cream parlor. You can find everything to fill your picnic basket or cooler. You will also find an enormous selection of souvenirs, apparel, gifts, books, calendars, magnets, glassware, and other unique items including buffalo hides and local crafts. They also carry official Sturgis Rally products and licensed Harley-Davidson products.

C Devils Tower KOA

60 State Highway 110 at Devils Tower. 467-5395 or reservations at 800-562-5785.

The Devils Tower KOA is located in the shadows of Devils Tower National Monument on the banks of the Belle Fourche River. Located on the filming site of the movie "Close Encounters of the Third Kind", the movie is shown nightly. There are 15 acres for tent campers, 56 shady and spacious RV sites, and 11 Kamping Kabins® and a full service cafe open for breakfast, lunch, and dinner, along with 2 gift shops. You can even enjoy hay rides, horseback rides, and hand dipped ice cream. Devils Tower KOA welcomes families, buses, groups, family reunions, and caravans. They are just 30 minutes off of I-90 from Sundance or Moorcroft.

26 *Food*

Pine Haven

Elev. 4,200 Pop. 222

On the banks of the Keyhole Reservoir, this community is named for the surrounding trees.

T Keyhole State Park

353 McKean Rd. 12 miles east of Moorcroft. 756-3596

History

The magnetism of names like "Sundance" and "Devils Tower" draw the traveler to this spacious park. The area was reserved by treaty for the Sioux tribes until the great Black Hills gold rush in 1874. Conflicts with Native Americans grew during this time, and the Sioux lost control of the lands.

Keyhole State Park was named for the "Keyhole" livestock brand that was used by two brothers by the name of McKean. They had established a ranch in the area.

Keyhole Dam, an earthfill structure, was completed by the Bureau of Reclamation in 1952.

Facts & Figures

The Keyhole area centers on the reservoir, approximately 14,720 acres of water recreation opportunity.

The elevation at Keyhole is about 4,100 feet. The four seasons are comparatively mild with glorious weather from spring through fall, and some of the finest ice fishing in the state during the winter months.

Attractions

Keyhole State Park is located on the western edge of the famed Black Hills, between Sundance and Moorcroft, and is easily accessed off 1-90 at exit 165, or take exit 153 or 154 in Moorcroft, then Hwy 14 north 6 miles, then take Hwy 113. Within sight of Devils Tower, Keyhole State Park is situated along the south east shore of Keyhole Reservoir and offers excellent fishing for walleye, catfish, small mouth bass, and northern pike.

Keyhole is a mecca for both resident and migrating birds of all species. Visitors have the opportunity to view many types of wildlife including white tailed deer and wild turkeys. A marina, motel and cafe are located on Headquarters Road, adjacent to the lakeshore.

Birds, Birds, Birds

Approximately 225 species of birds can be observed at Keyhole or within a mile of park boundaries. During the summer the most abundant species include the White Pelican, Osprey, Common Yellowthroat and Savannah Sparrow. Birds migrate from the area during the winter.

Winter birds that are commonly observed at the park include Bald Eagles, Red and White-Breasted Nuthatches and Red Crossbills.

Excerpted from Wyoming State Parks Brochure

27 *Gas, Food, Lodging*

Moorcroft

Pop. 807, Elev. 4,206

Alexander Moorcroft, the first white man to build a cabin in these parts, may have given his name to this town. The name might also have come from the English hometown of first postmaster, Stocks Miller. A "Dr. Moorcroft" also came here to hunt every year around the time the town was established, in 1889. Perhaps the town was

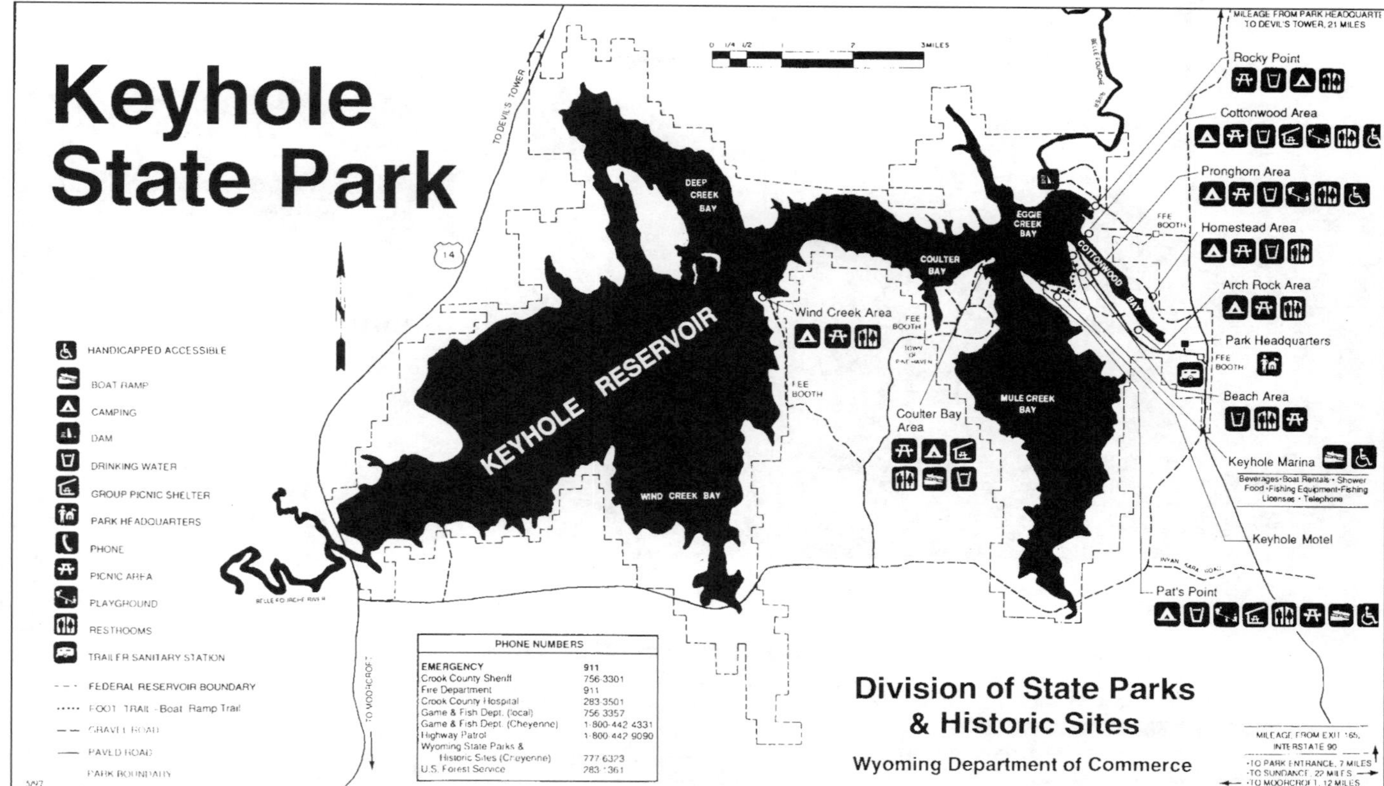

named for all three men.

Once a key point on the Texas Trail, Moorcroft was once the largest shipping point in the US during the 1890s. Cattle from all across the state, as well as Montana and South Dakota, rode the rails on the Burlington and Santa Fe trains from here to all points of the country. Although ranching continues to be at the heart of Moorcroft's economy, the oil and gas industries have impacted it in recent years, as has the attraction of the wild country that surrounds it.

Rozet

Elev. 4,286

This tiny town may have been named for the abundance of wild roses that grow in the area.

T Helen Robinson Zimmerscheid Western-Texas Trail Museum

in Moorcroft

Get a taste of the Western heritage that surrounds the Texas Trail. This small but charming collection of local historical artifacts is open M-F, Noon-4 summers only. There is no charge, but you'll gain a wealth of information from the museum's displays.

H Lifeline

At Moorcroft Exit Rest Stop

The arid basins and prairies of Wyoming lie in the rainshadows of our great mountain ranges. The shortgrass prairie of eastern Wyoming and Colorado are all that is left of this native grassland type. Buffalo grass and grama grasses typify the shortgrass prairie. The shortgrasses grow on the arid, wind blown prairies of the Rocky Mountain front.

Water on the shortgrass prairie is limited to a few potholes filled from early snow melt, holding water in early summer. Man has pumped water, using windmills, creating summer long water for livestock and wildlife. Some of the buttes in the area also provide spring and seep water.

The life line for wildlife on the prairies, however, are the rivers, like the Belle Fourche, providing water year-long. The winding Belle Fourche bisects a myriad of coulees and breaks and places water within daily travelling distance of large numbers of wildlife. Large cottonwoods and lush vegetation grow near the banks of the river, providing food and shelter for the pronghorn antelope, jackrabbits, sage grouse, mule deer and other wildlife that live on the shortgrass prairie.

Water, especially in arid areas, is an essential element in maintaining Wyoming's abundance and diversity of wildlife.

F Taco Time

600 E. Commerce in Moorcroft. 756-3899

F Subway

600 E. Commerce in Moorcroft. 756-3899

LC Wyoming Motel & Camping Park

112 E. Converse in Moorcroft. 756-3452

F Donna's Diner

203 W. Converse in Moorcroft. 756-3422

28 *Gas, Food, Lodging*

Upton

Pop. 872, Elev. 4,234

This railroad station town went through several name changes. Originally called Irontown, the water here had a rusty taste. It was later changed to Merino, reflecting a breed of sheep favored by sheepherders in the area. Finally, the town received its current name, Upton, from a Burlington Railroad surveyor, George S. Upton.

Osage

Pop. 350, Elev.4,300

Osage is an Indian name for "on top of the world". Named for the oil regions in Oklahoma, the first oil well was drilled here in 1890. Later when a gusher well was drilled in 1920 the tiny flag stop community along the railroad became a booming oil town with a refinery and a population of 1,500 in less than a year.

T Red Onion Museum

609 Pine St. in Upton. 468-2672

The Red Onion Museum is located in uptown Upton in the old time "Red Onion Saloon". The museum reflects the history of Weston and Upton counties. Various exhibits display tools and household items used during early settler's day. There is also an extensive collection of photographs, artwork, and items of interest including a 2-headed calf. The museum is open Monday through Friday from 10 a.m. to 5 p.m. and there is no admission charge

T Old Town (Old Upton)

West of Upton on Highway 16.

The "Old Town" project began in 1995 to relocate cabins and other structures essential to the late 1800s and early 1900s life in Wyoming. These cabins and structures have been moved to the original site of Upton, then known as Iron Town, and restored to preserve an important era of local heritage.

H Pine Paradise

Rest stop south of Upton

You are amidst a stand of ponderosa pines. These majestic trees, which can reach heights of 180 feet, provide a variety of habitats for wildlife.

Porcupines, pygmy nuthatches, red squirrels and mule deer inhabit ponderosa pine forests. Porcupines find abundant food here in the form

Section 3

Newcastle train depot.

of tree bark, buds and twigs. A slow-moving mammal, the porcupine climbs trees to escape danger. Porcupines are very fond of salt and because of this, they are often killed on roads where salt has been used to thaw ice.

Wyoming Tidbits

The unusual terrain outside Gillette results from layers of clinker (burned coal and clay) that is erosion resistant.

Ponderosa pine forests are sometimes the subject of attacks by insects and for this reason, the pygmy nuthatch is a very beneficial resident. A mere four inches long, this small bird eats insects which may attack the pines. Nuthatches are unique to the bird world because of their ability to travel head first down trees.

Red squirrels find abundant food in pine forests in the form of pine seeds. Look around and you may see a squirrel midden. A midden is a pile of cone scales which has been left after the squirrel has eaten the seeds inside the cone. Red squirrels may also find fungus, eggs and other seeds to eat.

29 *Gas, Food, Lodging*

Newcastle

Pop. 3,065, Elev. 4,334

Named for the English coal port town, Newcastle-on-Tyne, this Weston County seat is in the heart of one of Wyoming's best coal reserves at the Cambria Mines. In addition to sitting on plenty of "black diamonds," the economy has been built up by "black gold" (oil) as well, and signs hail it as the "Gateway to the Black Hills." Lumber and livestock also provide local employment.

Wyoming Tidbits

Frewen's Castle near Sussex was the home of Winston Churchill's Aunt Clara. The Castle was built by Clara and Moreton Frewen.

Wyoming Tidbits

Look out, Kentucky! In 1988, Wyoming became the top coal-producing state in the country, knocking out Kentucky with 163 million tons production.

The Newcastle area was first settled in 1875 by a group of army engineers, surveyors, and researchers led by Lt. Col. R. I. Dodge and Professor Walter P. Jenney. They built the Jenney Stockade, and set up a station for the Cheyenne-Deadwood Stage. In 1888, a community named Tubb Town sprung up, made up mostly of saloons. When the railroad swung further west, Newcastle took the place of Tubb Town, and the wilder elements drifted elsewhere.

M Black Gold Realty

2103 W. Main in Newcastle. 746-3655 or 800-385-5924. www.mls50.com/blgold.htm

30 *Gas, Food, Lodging*

H The Hanging of Diamond L. Slim Clifton

Downtown Newcastle across from train station

Beyond this sign, this side of the bridge on the main track, there was once a bridge on the spur that ran up the canyon to the Cambria Mining Camp. In imagination you might see the ghost of "Diamond L. Slim" Clifton hanging from this phantom bridge.

Slim was hung in 1903 for the murder of a young couple, Louella and John Church, Slim's neighbors and friends. People throughout north-eastern Wyoming, angered by the grisly deed, stormed the jail, took the prisoner from Sheriff Billy Miller at gun point and dragged Slim to the bridge. Masked men slipped the noose around Slim's neck and dropped him from the bridge neatly decapitating him. Such was vigilante justice.

M Arnold Realty, Inc.

505 W. Main in Newcastle. 746-2083 or 800-822-0002. www.eranches.net

Arnold Realty, Inc., is licensed to sell and market real estate in the beautiful Black Hills and surrounding areas of Wyoming, South Dakota, and Montana. Let them help you find that dream property whether you are looking for a ranch, farm, country home, cabin, acreage, recreational land, hunting property, mountain retreat, hobby ranch or lodge. The agents at Arnold Realty enjoy living in the Black Hills. They market some of the finest properties in the West. Helping people find their dream ranch or home is a top priority. Come discover the uniqueness of the Black Hills. Their office is located conveniently in the center of town across from the Old Mill Inn Restaurant.
Photo copywrite Julie Pederson

31 *Gas, Food, Lodging*

T Accidental Oil Company

5297 U.S. Highway 16, 4 miles east of Newcastle. 746-2042

Al Smith, a lifetime oilman, was convinced that oil could be found at shallow depths as well as at the usual depth of 4,000 feet or more. Seeking oil on land he had leased from the government in 1966 and unable to find a rig, he began to dig by hand, using only a pick and a shovel and a few sticks of dynamite. About four weeks later he astounded the experts by striking oil at a depth of 24 feet. At the peak of its production the well yielded a little more than five barrels of crude oil per day. At the Accidental Oil Company, a 120-foot ramp leads to a viewing room at the bottom of a 24-foot well. In the ultraviolet lighting the oil oozing from the cracks in the 100-million-year-old rock appears to be a bright fluorescent yellow, and the process of seepage is easy to see. Antique drilling equipment, including a 1912 steam-powered cable-tool drill rig, is displayed on the grounds. An 1880 derrick stands on a hill above the gift shop, which is located in an oil storage tank. Tours daily, June through August.

T Anna Miller Museum

401 Delaware in Newcastle. 746-4188

Built in the 1930s, the museum was originally a WPA project for Company !, 115th Cavalry of the Wyoming National Guard. The structure is built of hand-hewn sandstone blocks, quarried from nearby Salt Creek. Originally there were three main areas: the tack room, the stables and the sergeant's quarters, which all now house many of the exhibits.

Included with the museum complex is the Green Mountain School. This one-room building is typical of rural schoolhouses of the 1890-1930s. It contains a wood burning stove, school desks, maps, blackboards, globe, bell, water bucket and dipper along with lunch boxes and more.

Also on the complex is the Homesteader's House and the Jenny Stockade, true models of pioneer cabins and representative of how the westerners once lived. The Jenny Stockade Cabin is the oldest existing building of the Black Hills gold rush. It was also a stage station along the Cheyenne Deadwood Trail.

The museum houses many interesting artifacts from the Old Cambria Coal Camp. A crew of men, who worked for the Kilpatrick Brothers and Collins Co., discovered the coal in 1887, 7 miles northwest of Newcastle. Cambria was known as the "Model Coal Camp of the World." Saloons couldn't be built in the coal-mining town, because of a promise the Kilpatrick brothers made to their mother. A police force was never formed because the town of Cambria never incorporated. A lone sheriff, armed with brass knuckles and a gun, enforced the law.

The museums display of fossils thrills young and old alike. The collection includes the skull-cap of Pachysephalosaures, sections of Tyrannosaurs Rex and Triceratops.

Yesteryear comes alive in the museum's country store. It is filled with nostalgic items like P&G bar soap used by pioneer women to scrub clothes on washboards. The store brings back memories for some. For others it provides a glimpse of turn-of-the-century life.

The museum was named after Anna Cecelia McMoran Miller, the daughter of a pioneer family, and the widow of Sheriff Billy Miller, who was killed in what is known as the last Indian battle in the area. She was Newcastle's first librarian, a pioneer schoolteacher and school superintendent. It is open year round Monday through Friday from 9 a.m. to 5 p.m. Summertime it opens on Saturdays from 9 a.m. to 12 p.m.

H Camp Jenney

About 4 miles east of Newcastle on U.S. Highway 16

Campsite of the first authorized military expedition into the Black Hills. on September 12, 1857, Lt. G. K. Warren of the U. S. Topographical Engineers and his party, camped here and erected a log corral, 17 years before the famous Custer Expedition. On June 3, 1875 the expedition headed by Prof. Walter P. Jenney, under military escort commanded by Col. R. I. Dodge of Ft. Laramie, camped on the location of Lt. Warren's camp and corral. A stockade was erected and became known as Camp Jenney. The stockade was a stopover for gold seekers during the winter 75-76 and later became a stage station. The Stockade is now located by the Anna Miller Museum.

L Sage Motel

1227 South Summitt in Newcastle. 746-2724 or reservations at 877-746-2724

The Sage Motel offers 12 large newly remodeled large clean economy rooms all on ground level. You will find many features not usually offered with economy lodging. Each fully carpeted room also comes with in room coffee, refrigerators, microwaves, 25" color television with HBO, air conditioning, full baths, and radiant hot water heat. Along with direct dial phones, you will also find the provided convenience of data ports for your computer. Relax in the peaceful surroundings in the picnic area. There is plenty of parking for large vehicles too. The Sage Motel is AAA Diamond rated.

32 *Food, Lodging*

T Moskee

U.S. Highway 85 near the Hardy Ranger Station

In the early 1900s, the McLaughlin Tie & Timber Company started this sawmill town. In 1907, however, they ceased operations. In 1921, the Homestake Mining Company began lumbering and sawmilling for mine timbers. During the Second World War, the mill and town were closed and never reopened. Not much remains of this old site, which was almost all leveled by Homestake.

H Salt Creek Overlook

About 7 miles north of Newcastle on Hwy. 85

The Black Hills, named after the dark green carpets of pines that cover the hills, are a geological wonder. Covering some 125 miles north to south and 65 miles east to west, the Hills rise 3,000 to 4,000 feet above the red valley floor. Below you are Salt and Beaver creeks where the bur oak grows. Above the valley floor, ponderosa pine and aspen groves cling to the limestone cliffs, clay soil and red sandstone.

History, geology and wildlife are alive and well in the Salt Creek Valley. The Sioux believed the Great Spirit lived in these hills. Pioneers came here to mine for coal and oil. Small towns, like nearby Cambria, sprang up as fast as they were deserted. Tales of gunfights, stage robberies and gambling are kept alive by those who never left.

White-tailed deer roam through the pines and aspens. Wild turkeys scratch through leaves and needles along the creek bottoms, in search of acorns and seeds. Brought here from New Mexico in 1948, turkeys are now the most widespread game bird in northeastern

Wyoming. These shy, elusive birds don't let humans get too close. At night, they roost in treetops and return to the ground at daybreak to forage. Watch closely and you could see one of these magnificent birds!

H Flying V Cambria Inn
North of Newcastle on U.S. Highway 85

In 1923 Cambria Coal Company started construction of a resort retreat type facility for the town of Cambria and the surrounding areas. Completed in 1928 it was first known as Cambria Casino Park. Today the Flying V operates as a restaurant, B&B and Lounge.

H Cambria Salt Mine
Midway between Newcastle and Four Corners

In the early days of the development of the Black Hills, the nearest railroad was nearly 200 miles away. Wagon transportation costs to the mines were high, so a bulky, yet necessary, commodity like salt had high value. Springs with a heavy salt content were discovered in the canyon below on July 8, 1877. In November, 1878, James LeGraves came to the area to produce salt for the growing Black Hills mining market. He erected a furnace with two evaporating pans, the larger of the two being six feet wide and sixty feet long. For the next six years LeGraves produced salt by evaporating off spring water during the summer months and shipping his product to the mining districts. Some of the salt went to the general stores of Deadwood and Lead but its chief use was in chloridizing the gold and silver ores mined in the Black Hills.

N. H. Darton reported in 1904 that the spring along Salt Creek flowed at the rate of about 1 gps (gallon per second) and the water contained a little more than 5% sodium chloride (salt). According to Darton's calculations, about 35,000 pounds of salt were produced every 24 hours.

The Cambria Salt Company was organized in 1907 and prepared to manufacture and refine salt for the large western market. In an unsuccessful effort to locate the bed of rock salt from which the brine comes, several wells were drilled, one having a depth of 825 feet. The evaporating and purifying plant, arranged for coal fuel, was located over the divide to the west near the Cambria coal mine and the brine was pumped to it.

The Cambria Salt Company failed. The company's equipment was sold at a bankruptcy sale May 11, 1909 essentially ending salt production at the Salt Mine.

H Cambria Mining Camp
About six miles north of Newcastle on U.S. Highway 85.

About 5 miles west is the site of the once picturesque Cambria Mining Camp—now a vacantly ghostly place. In 1887 Frank Mondell, sent by the construction firm, Kilpatrick Brothers and Collins, discovered coal at Cambria. This was the first coal found along a proposed rail route suitable for use in the locomotives of the day.

It made possible the extension of the Burlington through previously isolated northeastern Wyoming, and the founding of Newcastle in 1889.

Cambria was a prideful community of three churches and nary a saloon. Fifteen hundred people of 23 nationalities lived harmoniously there; 13,000,000 tons of coal were mined before seams played out in 1928.

Reminiscing old-timers sigh, "there was never a place like it".

Wyoming Tidbits

Native Americans call the mountains of northaestern Wyoming and western South Dakota "Paha Sapa" (Black Hills) or Mess Sapa (Black Mountains). White people call them the Black Hills.

33 *Lodging*

Four Corners
At the intersection of Highways 85 and 585, this crossroads town has a post office and a small store.

H Canyon Springs Stage Station
U.S Highway 85 at Four Corners.

The scene of the only successful raid on a Deadwood treasure coach. On September 26, 1878, the treasure coach, carrying between 20,000 and 140,000-reports vary-was held up at this place. Hugh Cambell, a passenger, was killed and the driver, Gale Hill, was badly wounded. Scott Davis, the shotgun messenger, killed one of the outlaws and fatally wounded another, the others escaped.

Part of the treasure was recovered. Legend has it that some of the gold was buried near here. The little log station was torn down a few years ago.

Wyoming Tidbits

A billboard at the edge of GILLETTE touts the city as "America's Answer to OPEC". Geologists estimate nearly a trillion tons of coal lie beneath the region.

34 *Gas, Food, Lodging*

Buckhorn
A post office close to the South Dakota border, Buckhorn was named by the first postmaster, Isaac Sawyer, for the mountain sheep often seen in the area.

35 *No services*

Hampshire
Nestled within the Thunder Basin National Grassland, this tiny village has no services.

H Texas Trail—1866-1897
23 miles southwest of Newcastle on U.S. Highway 450

Following the Civil War, construction of the transcontinental Railroad opened the West, ensuring elimination of vast buffalo herds and forcing Native American Indians onto reservations where the military provided food.

Leggy Texas Longhorns were moved as far north as Canada to take advantage of open range grazing and lucrative government contracts. These routes became known collectively as the Texas Trail. One entered Wyoming near Cheyenne, headed north past Fort Laramie, Newcastle, Upton, into Moorcroft and then west to Powder River where it unraveled like a poor piece of rope. Cowhand Bob Fudge recalled a drive in northeast Wyoming. "We had been told that from the Cheyenne River to Powder River there was likely no water, which we surely found out....The weather was hot and at the end of the second day the cattle commenced to grind their teeth in their suffering...their groans were enough to raise the hair on a wooden Indian."

Drovers learned the best size herd to move a long distance was 2,500 head. The herd stretched out for a mile or more with cowboys placed along the edges depending on their skill. Experienced cowboys rode point to direct the herd. Others rode drag at the back, eating the dust of those ahead. The rest were spaced in between at flank and swing. Herds moved slowly to avoid stampede. Cattle could be moved 10-15 miles a day, 300-500 miles a month and could gain weight if skillfully managed. Cowboys were paid at the end of the ride and usually returned home with the wagon and horses. Some stayed behind and started ranches of their own. One cowboy, John B. Kendrick, came to Wyoming with a Texas herd, married the cattleman's daughter, and eventually became Governor. Such is the stuff of legend.

36 *Gas, Food, Lodging*

Savageton
This discontinued post office was not named for the Indians, as might be expected here in the heart of Powder River Country. Rather, it was named for storeowner and postmaster, Bailey Savage.

Black Hills National Forest

The Black Hills National Forest is located in southwestern South Dakota and northeastern Wyoming on 1.2 million ponderosa pine-studded acres ranging in elevation as high as 7,242 feet. Amid the splendid scenery are 11 reservoirs, 30 campgrounds, 32 picnic areas, 2 scenic byways, 1,300 miles of streams, 13,000 acres of wilderness, 353 miles of trails, and much more. As the forest is managed for multiple use, visitors will see mining, logging, cattle grazing, and summer homes on their travels.

Some of the more spectacular features nestled among the hills are seen from the Peter Norbeck National Scenic Byway with its one-lane tunnels that frame Mount Rushmore and curly pig-tail bridges along the Iron Mountain Road and Needles Highway. Breath-taking views of waterfalls, sheer cliff walls, springs, a roaring stream, and plenty of wildlife can be enjoyed along the Spearfish Canyon National Forest Scenic Byway.

Black Hills National Forest: A Brief History

For many people, from early Native Americans to today's visitors, the Black Hills has been a special place to come for physical and spiritual renewal. In August 1874, A.B. Donaldson, one of several newspaper correspondents with General George A. Custer's historic Black Hills Expedition, wrote the following:

The lover of nature could here find his soul's delight; the invalid regain his health; the old, be rejuvenated; the weary find sweet repose and invigoration; and all who could come and spend the heated season here would find it the pleasantest summer home in America.

Millions of visitors who come to the Black Hills each year still find it a pleasant place during any season.

The name "Black Hills" comes from the Lakota words Paha Sapa, which mean "hills that are black." Seen from a distance, these pine-covered hills, rising several thousand feet above the surrounding prairie, appear black. The Black Hills are in western South Dakota and northeastern Wyoming, covering an area 125 miles long and 65 miles wide. They encompass rugged rock formations, canyons and gulches, open grassland parks, tumbling streams, deep blue lakes, and unique caves.

The Black Hills area has a rich, diverse cultural heritage. Archaeological evidence suggests the earliest known use of the area occurred about 10,000 years ago. Later Native Americans, such as the Arapaho, Cheyenne, Kiowa, and Lakota, came to the Black Hills to seek visions and to purify themselves. The Black Hills was also a sanctuary where tribes at war could meet in peace.

Exploration of the Black Hills by fur traders and trappers occurred in the 1840s. In 1874, General George A. Custer led an Army exploration into the area and discovered gold. Settlement of the Black Hills rapidly followed the discovery of gold. The need for wood to build mines, railroads, towns and for use as a fuel increased demand for timber. As settlement continued, agriculture and livestock grazing added to the area's economic diversity.

A series of large forest fires in 1893 focused attention on the need to protect the timber resource. On February 22, 1897, President Grover Cleveland established the Black Hills Forest Reserve. This land was protected against fires, wasteful lumbering practices, and timber fraud. In 1898, the first commercial timber sale on Federal forested land in the United States was authorized in the area of Jim and Estes Creeks (near the town of Nemo). Cutting began around Christmas 1899. In 1905, the Black Hills Forest Reserve was transferred to the Forest Service, an agency of the U.S. Department of Agriculture. Two years later it was renamed the Black Hills National Forest.

The Black Hills National Forest Visitor Center at Pactola Reservoir includes exhibits on Black Hills natural history and a self-guiding nature trail. The Visitor Center is open daily from Memorial Day to Labor Day.

Congress established the Norbeck Wildlife Preserve in 1920 for the "protection of game animals and birds and to be recognized as a breeding place therefore." The preserve covers about 35,000 acres, 25,000 of which are managed by the Forest Service. Most of the rest of Norbeck is part of Custer State Park. Norbeck is home to a variety of wildlife, including elk, deer, bighorn sheep, and mountain goats. It also contains rugged granite formations, small lakes, scenic drives, and hiking trails.

Black Elk Wilderness is in the center of the Norbeck Wildlife Preserve. The 13,605-acre wilderness was named for Black Elk, an Oglala Lakota holy man. Congress established the wilderness on December 22, 1980; legislation in 2002 increased its size by 3,774 acres.

Harney Peak, at 7,242 feet above sea level, is the highest point in the United States east of the Rockies. From a historic lookout tower on the summit, one has a panoramic view of parts of South Dakota, Nebraska, Wyoming, and Montana, as well as the granite formations and cliffs of the Black Elk Wilderness.

Wright

Pop. 1,347, Elev. 4,980

Established in 1976, this is a coal-mining town that popped up almost overnight during the energy boom of the 70s. A very modern community, it was named for the first postmaster, R. A. Wright, in grand Wyoming tradition.

T The Wright Centennial Museum

In Wright

The mission of the Wright Museum is to interpret and preserve the history, culture and development of Southern Campbell County. Here you'll find historic mining equipment and supplies, artifacts from the homestead days, World War I memorabilia and various individual displays, and historic farm implements and tools. One of the items on display outside the museum is a 70-ton truck that was used at the Black Thunder Mine southeast of Wright until the mines began to use the much larger trucks in use today. ARCO donated this truck to the museum in 1990.

Wyoming Tidbits

The largest coal mine in the USA is Black Thunder located near Wright.

H # 100 First Truck

at Black Thunder Mine

Truck #100 - 170 Ton Unit Rig Mark 36 with

Dirt Box Commissioned October 13, 1976.
Retired June 1, 1989
Material Moved by Truck# 100
Overburden 12,325, 000 BCY-80BCY/Load
Coal 913,000 Tons-100 Tons/Load
Scoria 365,000 BCY-l00 BCY/Load
Topsoil 151,000 BCY-75 BCY/Load
Total number of Operating Hrs 36,741 hrs
Total Fuel Consumed 926,000 Gal.
Total Number of Tires Replaced 54
Total Number of Engines Replaced 6
Total Number of Miles 650,000
Truck #100 Specifications
Empty Vehicle Weight 194,825 Lbs.
Gross Vehicle Weight 534,825 Lbs.
Height 18' 3"
Width 22' 1"
Net Horsepower 1,600 HP
Fuel Tank Capacity 760 Gallons
Engine oil Capacity 48 Gallons
Hydraulic Oil Capacity 170 Gallons

37 *Gss, Food, Lodging*

Edgerton

Pop. 169, Elev. 5,000

This town was named for being right on the edge of the great Salt Creek oil field.

Linch

Named for the Linch family, who settled in the area, this little town became an oil-drilling site in the late 1940s.

Midwest

Pop. 408, Elev. 4,851

Named for the Midwest Oil Company, Midwest became the first town in the nation to have electric lighting for a football game in 1925.

T Salt Creek Museum

The Museum's exhibits cover the Salt Creek oilfields from 1889 to present. Exhibits include a furnished doctor's office that was in use from 1937 to 1993, a school room, kitchen, dining room, barber shop and various household artifacts. The Museum's research facilities include a full set of midwest Refining Company Books from 1920-1930, which detail the operations in Salt

Wyoming Tidbits

The country's first artificially lit football game was in Midwest in 1925.

Section 3

Teapot Dome Scandal

Long before the Watergate Scandal in Washington D.C. the Teapot Scandal shocked the nation. During the administration of Theodore Roosevelt the nation's first true interest in conservation began to emerge. While national parks and reserves were being developed, locations of vast mineral wealth were put under the control of the U.S. government. The National Oil Reserve Law passed in 1904. The purpose of this law was to provide necessary fuel for the Navy, which had converted from coal to oil around the turn of the century. President Taft designated an area of nearly 10,000 acres north of Casper as a Naval Reserve and closed it to private exploration. The area was called Teapot Dome, named for the huge rounded sandstone formation with a column and arch that appeared to have a handle, that has since eroded.

In 1920 Warren Harding was elected and the policies towards conservation were loosened and the oil field control was transferred to the Department of the Interior from the Department of the Navy. The Secretary of the Interior, Albert B. Fall, decided that the reserves were unnecessary. He leased the Teapot Dome Reserve to Harry F. Sinclair, an oil tycoon, of the Mammoth Oil Company. The lease had been arranged secretively and without competitive bids. Rumors began to fly with the largest gusher of oil that anyone had ever seen in Wyoming.

The "The Teapot began to steep" when Senator John Kendrick of Wyoming heard the rumors about the lack of competitive bidding. He forced the disclosure that Sinclair's oil company had received the sole lease. Hearings on the Teapot Dome oil lease began on October 15, 1923 before the Senate Committee on Public Lands and Surveys. Senator Thomas J. Walsh, a Democrat from Montana, led the committee's investigation.. Senate hearings in 1923 disclosed that Secretary Fall had received over $400,000 in no interest loans from Sinclair, along with other gifts. A civil suit filed against the Mammoth Oil Company in 1925 found the practices legal. However, the U.S. Supreme Court upheld a later government appeal and that decision was reversed. The lease was invalidated .

The government regained control of the reserves in 1928 and Sinclair was ordered to serve prison time and pay fines to the United States for the oil that had been pumped from Teapot Dome. Secretary Fall was convicted of fraud and bribery in 1929. He was fined and served prison time for his actions. The extent of President Harding's guilt in the scandal has never been fully determined.

Creek Oil Fields. The Museum is open by request. Admission by donations only.

T Pumpkin Buttes

30 miles east of Midwest on State Highway 387

These five flat-topped landmarks rise 1,000 feet above the surrounding plains of southern Campbell County. Col. James Sawyer rote in his diary, "Made 13 miles over good roads, to a gap in Pumpkin Buttes, from whence we looked down on an immense valley, if such an abyss of hill tops can be so called." The buttes boast hundreds of tipi rings. The area is rich with uranium deposits.

H 1863 Bozeman Trail

On State Highway 387 about 8 miles west of Pine Tree Junction

John Bozeman and John Jacobs laid out this route from Fort Laramie to the Virginia City, Montana gold fields. In 1865 the Powder River Military Expedition under Gen. P. E. Connor, established Ft. Connor on the Powder River. In 1866 Forts Reno, Phil Kearny, and C. F. Smith were built for its protection against the Indians who fought bitterly to hold their last hunting grounds. It became known as the Bloody Bozeman. Portugee Phillips rode over this trail to Ft. Laramie to report the Fetterman Massacre. In 1866 Nelson Story trailed the first herd of Texas longhorns to cross Wyoming along this road. Indian hostiles forced abandonment of the trail in 1868.

H Salt Creek Oil Field

Junction of State Highways 387 and 259 at Midwest.

Stockmen were aware of pools of oil in the creek bottoms during cattle trailing days. These oil seeps led to the discovery of Salt Creek, one of Wyoming's largest oil fields, nine miles long by five miles wide.

In 1883, the first claims were filed in the 22,000 acre Salt Creek Field. The first strike in the field occurred in 1908 at a depth of 1,050 feet. Many wells are still active.

Salt Creek was one of the first unitized oil fields in the United States. Under unitization one company operates properties for all owners and more efficient recovery methods can be used. Improved practices in Salt Creek have recovered many additional milions of barrels of oil.

38 *Gas, Food, Lodging*

T Hoofprints of the Past Museum

344 Nolan Ave. in Kaycee. 738-2381

What began as a Wyoming Centennial project in 1990 has grown into a great hands on collection of Powder River Country history. The Museum is headquartered in the oldest standing structure in Kaycee, but has since acquired a blacksmith shop, a country schoolhouse, a homestead cabin, and the original twn jail, relocated to be near all the rest. Collections include relevent artifacts from the Johnson County Cattle War, homesteaders and pioneers, Native American battles, and outlaws like the Wild Bunch and the Hole-in-the-Wall. The Museum is also the headquarters for area tours.

Mayoworth

This post office was named in 1890 for the postmistress's daughter, May Worthington.

Sussex

Mrs. Davis, the wife of the rancher who ran the first post office here, came from Sussex County, Delaware.

Kaycee

Pop. 249, Elev. 4,660

Kaycee has a wild history as home to infamous outlaws. Established as a cowman's town in 1900 and named for the brand, KC, owned by Peters and Alston. Kaycee is probably the smallest town to told a Professional Rodeo Cowboy's Association (PRCA) rodeo and the community pride shows. Kaycee was an important site of the Johnson County War, one of the most significant events in Old West history. The Bozeman Trail, which linked the Oregon Trail to the Montana gold mines, can still be viewed east of town. The infamous "Hole-in-the-Wall" country and outlaw cave where the legendary outlaws Butch cassidy and the Sundance Kid and the rest of the Hole-in-the-wall gang hid out is just west of town.

T Frewen Castle

Near Sussex

Two brothers, Moreton and Richard Frewen, left England bound for the wilds of Wyoming to hunt buffalo. Once they spotted the verdant Powder River country, however, they vowed to stay and invest in cattle. Moreton also invested in a wife, Clara Jerome of New York, aunt of Winston Churchill. Erecting an exquisite two-story log "castle", the Frewens filled the home with every known luxury. Locals dubbed the home Frewen Castle. English hunting parties and high teas filled their social calendar, and ladies who visited were treated to hothouse bouquets delivered on horseback. British nobility graced the castle with their presence, and it was a magical kingdom. Then, the disastrous winter of 1886-87 devastated the cattle herd. Moreton suffered financial losses from which he could not recover. He and his family returned to England, where he deposited Clara and their three children in an English countryside while he travelled extensively. Very little remains of the Frewen Castle today.

T Crazy Woman Battlefield

East of I-25 between Kaycee and Buffalo

The site of numerous skirmishes between native tribes and white travelers, the battlefield is bisected by a creek of the same name. There are two

Coal trains are as common as sagebrush in this part of the state.

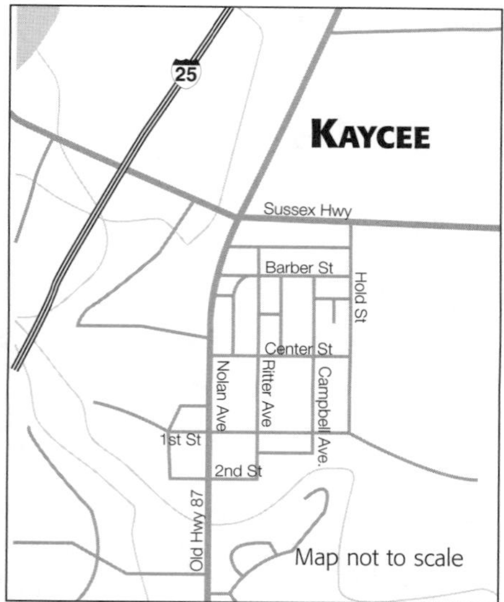

varying accounts of how the area received its name. One story is that an Indian woman living alone and slowly went mad. A second version is that a white traveler's wife went insane when she witnessed Indians scalp her husband.

T Outlaw Cave and Canyon

About 20 miles southwest of Kaycee

Outlaw Cave is a prehistoric rock shelter and Indian Pictographs can be found nearby. The Middle Fork of the Powder River is also viewed along this route as well as beautiful panoramas of the red mountain walls, the canyon at the Middle Fork of the Powder River and the Dull Knife Battlefield. The deep cave was also a popular hideout for outlaws including the Wild Bunch from the nearby Hole-in-the-Wall hideout.

H The Dull Knife Battle

Kaycee Rest Stop I-25 Exit 254

On November 25th the final battle of the Sioux campaign of 1876 was fought approximately 28 miles west of this point. Colonel Ranald Mackenzie with 750 cavalrymen and 400 Indian scouts and auxiliaries attacked a Northern Cheyenne encampment at dawn. Leaders Dull Knife and Little Wolf were among the Cheyenne.

This village consisted of about 175 lodges housing 1400 people, some of whom had participated in the defeat of Custer at the Battle of the Little Bighorn the previous summer. Cheyenne women and children fled to the surrounding mountains, but the men checked the army's advance during the day-long battle.

Wyoming Tidbits

The largest coal mine in the USA is Black Thunder located near Wright.

The army lost 1 officer, 6 soldiers and had more than 20 wounded. At least 25 Cheyenne died. Mackenzie ordered the village destroyed and 500 ponies were captured. This proved disastrous for the Cheyenne who were left destitute. They found sanctuary with the Sioux in Montana and South Dakota but by May 1877 surrendered. The U.S. government, thus, secured control of the Powder River country. In 1884 it established the present Northern Cheyenne reservation in southeast Montana.

H Mountain Lion

Kaycee Rest Stop I-25 Exit 254

Mountain lions, also known as pumas, cougars, panthers and catamounts, live in the rugged mountains and foothills of Wyoming. The foothills of the Bighorn Mountains provide some of the best mountain lion and mule deer habitat in America.

Mountain lions prefer rugged canyon country in mixed conifer or mountain mahogany cover. Mule deer and elk compose a majority of their diet. They also prey on small mammals like jackrabbits, snowshoe hares, porcupines, yellow-bellied marmots and other small rodents. In localized parts of the Bighorn Mountains, lion predation on domestic sheep is a chronic problem, thereby necessitating special management strategies and tightly regulated harvest to maintain a delicate balance between man and the cat.

Mountain lions once roamed from northern Canada to the southern tip of South America, but along with the colonizing of the Americas by European man, came the persecution and extensive habitat changes which greatly reduced the cat's range. In Wyoming, however, vast, unbroken expanses of habitat still remain.

The Bighorns are home to the big cat. While seeing one is rare, mere knowledge of their presence adds something special to that place called Wyoming. A place where quality of life is oftentimes defined in wildlife terms.

H Powder River Country

Kaycee Rest Stop I-25 Exit 254

Twelve thousand years ago, the rich grasslands and abundant wildlife attracted Native American hunters into the area. As the United States expanded, commerce and conflict occurred. The Portuguese Houses, east of Kaycee, were part of the fur trade industry during the early nineteenth century. The establishment of the Bozeman Trail in 1863 brought on warfare between some of the tribes and the United States Army ending with the expulsion of the Native Americans from the area in 1877. Historic sites like Fort Reno and Crazy Woman Battlefield reflect this struggle. During the last two decades of the nineteenth century, disputes between open range ranchers and homesteaders resulted in many confrontations, ending with the 1892 Johnson County War fights at KC and TA ranches.

Today, ranching exists alongside minerals and recreation industries. The land's wealth however, is not infinite. Only through careful stewardship can the land be cared for and maintained. Wildlife viewing, hunting and fishing, tours of museums and historic sites, traveling historic roads, and camping and hiking allow all to appreciate Powder River Country.

H Killing of Champion and Rae

U.S. Highway 87 just south of bridge over Middle Fork of the Powder River.

About 100 yards west of this point stood the buildings of the Kaycee Ranch, a log cabin and a barn. These buildings were surrounded before daylight on April 9, 1892, by invading cattlemen. Occupying the cabin were Nate Champion and Nick Rae, alleged rustler and two trappers who were captured by the cattlemen, but were unharmed. Rae appeared and was shot down. He was dragged inside the cabin by Champion, who fought off the attackers alone until late afternoon, when the cabin was set afire. He attempted to escape but was shot and killed. Rae died of his wounds during the forenoon.

F Invasion Bar & Restaurant

343 Nolan Ave. in Kaycee. 738-2211. Email: ctaylor@kaycee.smalltown.net

The Invasion Bar and Restaurant is the area's locals' office day or night. There motto is, "Everyone who comes in as a stranger leaves as a friend." Enjoy great family dining in a historical building restored in the 1960's. The menu offers great down home cooking with selections such as real mashed potatoes, homemade pies and soups, and daily lunch specials to make your mouth water. Be sure and try their specialties like pork fritters or Rueben sandwiches. Thursdays are Mexican Night and Fridays enjoy there own country style BBQ pork ribs. Check for nights when you can stop in and enjoy live music and dancing.

L Willow Creek Ranch at Hole-in-the-Wall

28 miles southwest of Kaycee off TTT Ranch Road on Willow Creek Road at Hole-in-the-Wall. 738-2294. www.willowcreekranch.com

The Willow Creek Ranch at the Hole-In-The-Wall is a 57,000 acre rustic cattle and horse ranch on the famous Red Wall at the southern end of the Big Horn Mountains. It is the former home to Butch Cassidy and the Sundance Kid and their famous hideout, "The Hole-In-The-Wall". There is a monument marking an outlaw shoot-out, Indian teepee rings, homestead cabins, the Sioux Indian trail and old stage coach routes. Their specialty is great food and tailoring a real ranch vacation to suit your individual desires, including cattle drives, branding, and lodging in a restored 1890 bunkhouse. There is great fishing and hunting in season! Photo provided by Gene Vieh

C KC RV Park

42 Mayoworth Road in Kaycee. 738-2233. Email: KCRV@Kaycee.smalltown.net

39 *No Services*

Morrissey

This discontinued post office was named for a rancher. It has been reported on various occasions that folks driving through this area see vivid tumbling lights or Ghost Lights.

H Robbers' Roost Station

Cheyenne and Black Hills Stage Route

About three miles north of Mule Creek Junction on U.S. Highway 85.

Along the Cheyenne-Deadwood Stage Route, stories still are told of outlaws and buried gold. But the swaying Concord stagecoaches stopped rolling in 1887, eleven years after beginning service to the gold regions of the Black Hills in 1876.

Located at the Cheyenne River crossing, Robbers' Roost was a station of the Cheyenne and Black Hills Stage and Express Company. Built in 1877 on a new shortcut, it derived its name from the many robberies in the area. The crossing was the spot most dreaded by stage driveres; steep river banks slowed the coaches to a crawl and provided concealment from which lurking road agents could watch the approach of their intended victims.

Station agent at Robber's Roost was D. Boone May, also a deputy U. S. marshall and a shotgun messenger for the gold-laden treasure coaches from the "Hills". In September, 1878, south of here, May and John Zimmerman surprised desperadoes in the act of robbin gthe southbound coach. the outlaws opened fire and one of them, Frank Towle, wa fatally wounded. Outnumbered, May and Zimmerman escorted the coach to safety and the outlaws made their escape. Towle was buried by his companions. May later found the grave, removed Towle's head and took it to Cheyenne in a sack to try to claim a reward.

The era of the gold rush to the Black Hills was a flamboyant one, bringing together a diverse gathering of frontier characters Indians, soldiers; miners, stage drivers; tradesmen, housewives; gamblers, prostitutes and outlaws.

According to legend Robbers' Roost Station was burned by Indians.

Scenic Drives

Beaver Creek Tour

The 50 mile Beaver Creek loop tour is designed to provide you an opportunity to explore a diverse and beautiful country. It is a trip through time and has 26 marked sites of historic, scenic or other interest.

Each site has an area where you may pull your vehicle off the road. The drive offers you the opportunity to see plenty of wildlife during your drive. Better opportunities exist in the early morning until about 10 a.m. and in the latter part of the afternoon from about 4 p.m. It seems most animals and birds have the sense to stay out of the noonday sun. The slant light accompanying these hours sculpts and contours the countryside in a most photogenic manner. This light is a pleasant contrast to the starkness of the harsh midday sun of the High Plains West.

You may begin or end the tour at the Anna Miller Museum—Site 1—on Delaware Avenue. Even if you don't take the tour a visit is time well spent and admittance is free. Don't miss this gem of a small museum and its displays. The mileage count for the tour begins at the intersection of U.S. 16 & U.S. 85.

To gain the most from this trip, let your imagination roam free—the history of this area is not just the history of man the past few hundred years, that is only part of the story, a small part—the real story began 2.5 billion years ago.

Two and one-half billion years; over one-half the Earth's history. The continent was coming together and geological forces were at work forming the base from which the Black Hills would finally thrust. Think about the passage of time, measured not in years, but in millions of years as the land evolves. Imagine a land covered by advancing and retreating marine and inland seas, eroding and laying down layers of black and gray sediment destined in time to become today's coal and oil. Imagine, as the seas recede for the last time, the land with its rivers and swamps, its dinosaurs and the red and green mud of its flood plains that will become their tomb. Finally, imagine, some 36 million years ago, the Black Hills' central core of hard metamorphic and igneous rock rising from the earth like a blister, pushing and tilting all above and around it.

What a difference time makes! Today, the Black Hills stand as a green oasis rising from a sea of grass, the last bastion of the mixed grass prairie before it gives way to the short grass prairies to the south and west. They are the same hills as that earlier blister—like a lot of us, they are just weathered and wrinkled by time—some 6,500 feet of sediment and softer formations having eroded away to leave today's diverse and varied landscape.

Like four ovals, one inside the other, the Black Hills cover some 120 miles north to south and 40 to 50 miles east to west. The hard core of weather resistant metamorphic and igneous rock that started the process is in the center. As you move outward from this center, the land opens to the Limestone Plateau. Densely covered with pine and aspen, this plateau is composed primarily of a variety of limestones and sandstones laid down during different geologic periods. The Limestone's cliffs tower above the Red Valley. This valley, the product of erosion, is named for its soft red sandstones, clays and shales and runs full circle of the Black Hills. Almost devoid of trees, except where streams follow its course, the Red Valley's grasslands have been valued by both man and beast for their forage.

The outer edge of the Black Hills is marked by the Hogback. Like a breastwork, the Hogback protects the Hills from intrusion by making entry difficult. An erosion resistant sandstone ridge covered by Ponderosa Pine, the Hogback rises from the surrounding shale plains on an incline, and then, abruptly and at times precipitously, drops to the Red Valley's floor. The only gaps in this almost continuous circle are those created by major streams as they leave the Black Hills for the surrounding prairie. Your trip will cover portions of the Red Valley and the Hogback.

Newcastle sits tucked into the outer edge of the Hogback on dark gray Belle Fourche shale dating from the upper part of the Cretaceous Period (65–140 million years ago). This was the time when South America and Africa separated, the dinosaurs and large reptiles reached their peak and then disappeared, and flowering plants and modern trees began their development. Newcastle owes its existence and economic well-being to the area's geology. The discovery of coal in a Hogback canyon brought the Burlington & Missouri River Railroad to the area and, in 1889, the town was built where the spur from the mine met the main track. Today, the area's geologic heritage still provides the basis for the area's economy: coal, oil, bentonite (a clay formed from volcanic ash and found in everything from face powder to kitty litter), timber, rich farming land and grass for grazing.

1. Anna Miller Museum—401 Delaware

The Anna Miller Museum is located in an old National Guard cavalry barn built by the WPA in the 1930s. Constructed of native sandstone quarried from the Hogback, the building was to be part of a larger complex for Newcastle's horse cavalry unit. The existing native stone armory downtown housed the adminstrative offices, arms room, an indoor range and dismounted drill area. This building was to provide living quarters for the full-time stable sergeant, a feed room and stalls for the horses, while immediately to the east and attached to it, there was to be a large indoor riding hall. Construction on the riding hall progressed to a point where the walls where up about halfway when Pearl Harbor occurred. With the outbreak of war, construction ceased, and the uncompleted riding hall was torn down after the war. The building has been enrolled in the registry of National Historic Places.

The Anna Miller Museum's varied and diverse collection makes description difficult, but its collection captures the history of the area and provides an excellent background for your trip. The museum contains Cambria mining camp displays, period rooms, a country store and early day doctor's office, Indian artifacts and a fossil collection which includes a Pachycephalosaurus skull cap and sections of both Tyrannosaurus Rex and Triceratops, to name but a few of its exhibits. On the museum's grounds, you will find also a homesteader's cabin, an early country school and the oldest standing building in the Black Hills—the Jenney Stockade—as well as a Burlington Northern train caboose.

Site 2-The Visitors Center-is located approximately 4 blocks east of the museum on U.S. 16/Washington Boulevard.

2. Visitor Center—U.S. Hwy 16

If you look to the east from the parking lot of the Visitors Center you can see a fountain spray-

Newcastle	Jan	Feb	March	April	May	June	July	Aug	Sep	Oct	Nov	Dec	Annual
Average Max. Temperature (F)	34.0	38.4	45.8	57.4	68.2	78.3	87.6	85.6	74.3	61.0	44.9	36.3	59.3
Average Min. Temperature (F)	11.3	14.9	22.0	32.1	42.4	51.6	59.0	57.0	46.6	35.3	22.7	14.4	34.1
Average Total Precipitation (in.)	0.45	0.47	0.72	1.50	2.45	2.64	2.02	1.66	1.15	0.99	0.59	0.48	15.11
Average Total SnowFall (in.)	6.3	5.6	6.8	3.9	0.5	0.0	0.0	0.0	0.2	1.9	5.0	6.2	36.2
Average Snow Depth (in.)	2	2	1	0	0	0	0	0	0	0	1	2	1

ing water into the air. (As you drive to Site 3 it will be on your left as you cross the junction of U.S. 16 & U.S. 85.) This fountain draws its water from a well drilled 2,700 feet into the Paha Sapa or Madison Limestone formation of the lower Carboniferous Period (280-345 million years ago). The water has been carbon dated as being about 2,500 years old. It has its source in the snow and rain that fell in the Big Horn Mountains some 150 miles to the west, or possibly even farther north in Canada. The fountain requires no pump and flows to the surface under 120 pounds of pressure. Newcastle has drilled four of these wells to supply its needs and others have been drilled either privately, or by water districts to provide service to outlying areas.

If you have not been born in the West, or lived here, you might not understand the preoccupation with water, or its importance to the residents here. The annual moisture in this area is 12 to 15 inches. A desert is defined as an area that receives 12 inches or less. The area is certainly arid and an adequate supply of water touches every aspect of the lives and livelihoods of the people who live here. As you drive this country you will notice almost every little draw with any drainage whatsoever is the proud possessor of an earthen dam to catch whatever bounty nature sends its way. You might also notice the number of pickup trucks with fiberglass tanks in their beds. They belong to individuals who have found that special place to live, but which is without water. They are willing to put up with the inconvenience of hauling water—water to drink, with which to cook and to wash—in order to live in this special place. It says something about their character. They are the true inheritors of the spirit shown by the early pioneers of Newcastle and the area.

When the town was founded there was no water on the site. Water was brought in barrels from a spring 3 miles up in Cambria Canyon or from Beaver Creek about 6 miles away. As an early resident wrote many years later, "A five gallon square tin kerosene can filled with water cost you fifty cents. But who cared about water, as very few drank water, and it was not then necessary to take a bath every morning. Water was all right to wash dishes in, and for the 'Milk Man' to mix with the cows' milk to make it go to more satisfied customers."

Now look south to the ridge with the orange water tank. (By the way, the colors, black and orange, are the school's colors and their teams are known as the Dogies.) There you see the light colored Pierre shale of the Upper Cretaceous. This is truly an important shale as it possesses the ability when wet to mire your vehicle like you would not believe—the plastic clays we know as "gumbo" weather from it. Gumbo can pack your fender wells so tightly your wheels won't move, or you might slip and slide so badly, even with a four-wheel drive vehicle, that you are positive you are driving on grease. This little byproduct of the Pierre is the reason we suggest that when you drive the country roads, you stick to the gravel.

From here to Site 5 watch for Mule (Black-tailed) deer in the open Ponderosa Pine habitat.

Johnson County War

The Johnson County War took place in northern Wyoming in April 1892, a short and bitter page in United States history. Hollywood has immortalized the event, but the real facts are found in the Big Horn Mountain country. Back in 1868 when Wyoming became a territory in 1868, and later, a state in 1890. It was settled with peace loving, honest and God-fearing people. This didn't stop a fierce battle to break in 1892 between the cattlemen and the homesteaders.

Cattlemen came in first, setting up ranches, and becoming quite wealthy in the process. The educated entrepreneurs from the East as well as those from England were drawn to the promises of the territory. Most of the land was free government land and cattle were not fenced in but allowed to graze freely. The cattlemen formed the Wyoming Stock Growers' Association. When Wyoming became a State in 1890, the Governor joined this association adding to its power.

Homesteaders began to move in along the Bozeman and Oregon Trails in the late 1880s claiming the land. The cattlemen accused the homesteaders of taking their watering holes and rustling their cattle which was a hanging offense. The homesteaders said they had not rustled the cattle and had the support and protection of Sheriff 'Red' Angus.

The 1880s eventually brought hardships for everyone. Cattlemen did not keep an accurate count of their herds and this would have disastrous results after the blizzards of 1886-87, which just wouldn't stop. The cattlemen who survived these years bitterly resented the farmers who had supposedly taken over their land. The losses and lack of records caused many of the ranchers to go bankrupt, thus leaving more land for the taking. Every time a farmer claimed land, especially near a water hole, and often fencing it off, the cattlemen's anger and resentment grew. The fences and the ownership of water holes led to two fiercely diverse factions.

It was actually the accusations of cattle rustling, more than the homesteaders' fences, that festered as a sore spot for cattlemen and their rift with the farmers. The ranchers' charge of rustling done by the farmers was probably unjust. Most of the farmers were hardworking folk who just wanted to make an honest living. Yep, it's possible though, that they might have needed a cow now and then.

The pot was boiling in 1889 when a rancher, A. J. Bothwell, wanted to take over some land that belonged to James Averill, a saloon owner. Averill lived on the land with a prostitute, Ella Watson, who was alleged to frequently receive payment in stolen cattle. James Averill accused Bothwell of being a land grabber. Bothwell accused Averill of rustling cattle. Averill and Watson were taken by force and hanged without trial. The men who lynched them were not brought to trial either.

The accusations exploded in 1892 when Wyoming cattlemen attempted to sort out the rustlers and were sponsored by some of the most powerful men in the state and the Union Pacific Railroad. The railroad people offered to transport a load of gunmen up from Texas. These regulators attacked the KC Ranch, killing two alleged rustlers, Nathan Champion and Nick Ray. They then headed for Buffalo, to the cattlemen friendly TA Ranch.

In the meantime, Sheriff Angus had been tipped off and the regulators found themselves under attack. The mission backfired and two of the Texans were killed. Governor, Amos W. Barber, supporter of the regulators, interceded and cabled President Harrison for help. Army troops rescued the Texas invaders and at the trial all were released under the pretense that the county was not able to pay for their keep. After receiving pay from the cattlemen they skipped back to Texas.

Governor Barber and Senators Carey and Warren, were later implicated as supporters of the raid. The invasion by the regulators had been a direct violation of the Wyoming State Constitution. Cattlemen remained, often living in fear of retribution, and the end of free range ranching. The Panic of 1893 followed and the Union Pacific Railroad folded. The fences continued to go up.

Your next site, Site 3, is Tubb Town-Field City. It is on the left of U.S. 16 going east, 3 miles from the Junction of U.S. 16 & U.S. 85.

3. Tubb Town—Field City

The state's site marker provides the broad outline of the short, but notorious history of "Satan's Toadstool of Prairie Dog Flats," as Tubb Town was sometimes called. It was a rowdy town located astride Salt Creek on the Custer-Belle Fourche Trail. As such, it saw its share of transients, to include Calamity Jane. Calamity came to town one day driving an ox team, stopped in a store, saw a bolt of bright pink, silk cloth. She bought 15 yards to have a wrapper made with Watteau Pleats on the back. Calamity Jane? It is an eyewitness account.

Salt Creek's water wasn't fit to drink in 1888. Still isn't. In fact, many argued that it was composed of equal parts water, alkali and Epsom salts. Mr. Tubb's public privy was very busy; as was one of his other businesses—hauling water from Beaver Creek and selling it for fifty cents a barrel. However, lousy water didn't stop the "crick" from being used for bathing.

With as many men as there were, the "girls" had followed. One young resident, whose family lived on the respectable west bank of the creek, recalled that there were at least 30 to 40 sporting ladies hanging around the saloons. These ladies used the crick to bathe, and more than one young man received part of his education doing a little spying. That probably didn't bother the "soiled doves" much; what bothered them was when

Kaycee

	Jan	Feb	March	April	May	June	July	Aug	Sep	Oct	Nov	Dec	Annual
Average Max. Temperature (F)	37.4	41.7	48.1	57.8	67.9	78.8	87.9	86.7	75.6	63.1	47.6	39.7	61.0
Average Min. Temperature (F)	6.6	12.6	19.7	28.3	38.2	46.4	52.3	50.1	39.9	29.3	17.5	9.5	29.2
Average Total Precipitation (in.)	0.41	0.37	0.70	1.47	2.26	2.09	1.14	0.82	1.05	1.00	0.52	0.38	12.21
Average Total SnowFall (in.)	6.7	6.3	7.3	6.7	1.3	0.1	0.0	0.0	0.4	2.4	5.6	6.6	43.3
Average Snow Depth (in.)	2	1	0	0	0	0	0	0	0	0	1	1	1

some young cowboy might happen on them, steal their clothes with great glee and leave them to find their way back to town dressed in a sagebrush chemise.

When the railroad changed its route and it was time to move, Tubb Town moved. And boy did it move! In no way was a little thing like moving allowed to interfere with business. One saloon owner just jacked up his bar, loaded it on a wagon, and sold drinks all the way to Newcastle. Didn't break a glass or spill a drop. On arrival, he set the bar on the ground, leveled it and built the new building around it. What one would call real customer oriented service.

The boisterous crowd from Tubb Town didn't seem to realize that they had been sitting on oil. Oil in sands that reached close to the surface. They must not have been paying attention. Ten years earlier in 1878 oil had been found in the area, "bubbling," or at least seeping, from a spring or outcropping. On this news, many miners from the hills flocked in and filed their claims. For a time claims cabins dotted the landscape to the south and west. The boom didn't last, though some continued to seek their riches in black gold.

These oil seeps were not infrequent. It was a common practice where one existed to dig a hole and let the oil and water accumulate. The sand filtered green oil rose to the top and when it was about three or four inches deep it was skimmed off and filtered through cheese cloth. Mixed with flour the oil made a very satisfactory axle grease. It was also used to treat animal cuts and wounds.

In 1966 a local resident decided to see if he could dig an oil well by hand. It took about three weeks of hard pick and shovel work with a bit of dynamite, but 21 feet down he found oil. Enough oil accumulates to pump to the surface with an old-fashion hand pump. If you look east across the creek (this was the disreputable side of Tubb Town), you will see the site of that hand dug oil well.

Site 4—Jenney Stockade—is located 1.0 miles to the east on the right side of the highway.

4. Jenney Stockade—LAK Ranch

Lt. Warren's expedition wasn't the first entry into the southern Black Hills by whites. The first recorded entry was by a party of twelve men under the command of famed mountain man Jedediah Smith who crossed the Cheyenne River near the mouth of Beaver Creek in 1823. [We need to clarify a point. The Beaver Creek you travel today is properly Stockade Beaver. It flows south and west into the Beaver Creek mentioned here.] The party entered the Hills through the Buffalo Gap and then crossed the southern part of the Hills on their way west. Given the terrain, it is logical to assume they passed nearby while moving west. While in the Hills, a member of the party, Bill Sublette, also to gain fame as a mountain man, found, or so it was reported, a "'putrified' forest with 'putrified' trees on which 'putrified' birds sang 'putrified' songs." Finding such "putrifaction" caused Sublette no harm, but Smith ended up losing an ear when a grizzly charged him and ripped it off. One story has Smith inventing the phrase, 'Well, don't just stand there, do something," after his companions killed the bear. According to the story, Smith then proceeded to take a hand in sewing his chewed up skin back on.

There were other scientific and military expeditions to the Black Hills that preceded or followed Warren's of 1857; however, none of these organized expeditions appear to have ventured far into this area until Custer's in 1874 which passed just north of this loop. The 1875 Jenney expedition was organized specifically to check Custer's report and determine as accurately as possible how much gold there was in the Black Hills. The party of geologists, topographers, astronomers, and "practical" miners, spent 5 months in the Hills protected by Lt. Col. Dodge's 400 infantrymen. They didn't find much gold—the miners accomplished that as they violated the treaty with the Indians and its off-limits rules and sneaked into the Hills in ever increasing numbers.

Colonel Dodge's own words describe best what the expedition felt and found when they reached the site of Warren's corral built some 18 years earlier; which according to another report had been occupied, at least for a time in the sixties, by a trading post run by one Nick Janis:

"As we go up the Beaver the country gets in every way worse. A dreary, monotonous, alkaline plain, no timber except an occasional scrubby cotton-wood. The water, acrid and bitter, irritating to the mouth, throat, and alimentary canal, stands in long, narrow, and deep pools, in which there seems no life, either animal or vegetable. Every man was more or less affected, and all were glad to turn our faces to what seems a gap in the apparently impenetrable mass of mountains to the north.

"A few hours brought us to this gorge, when we went into camp in a spot which, after our trying journey over the horrible alkaline desert, seemed a paradise. "A lovely stream, of apparently pure water, rushed swiftly from its mountain home, through a grassy mead, smooth as a lawn, green as emerald, and carpeted with flowers of every hue. Overhanging the stream, and dotted singly or in clumps about the lawn were hundreds of box-elder, the most graceful and picturesque of plains trees. Just at the entrance of a narrow canon, the mountains to the east and west tower to the height of from one thousand to fifteen hundred feet, their summits and the deep gorges scored in their sides clothed with dark forests of pine.

"The brook was named Spaulding's Creek. The spot, Camp Jenney. It is one of the most beautiful camps I ever saw."

The creek was named, no doubt, after Capt. Spaulding of Dodge's command. You can imagine it was his reward for having led the scouting party which brought them to this break in the hills and decent water.

The Jenney Party built a stockade on the east bank of Beaver Creek where Warren's corrals had been, just about where you see today's ranch buildings. The stockade was some 85 feet wide and 122 feet long. Two cabins were built within it to store provisions. One of these cabins is the same cabin you had the opportunity to see at the Anna Miller Museum. As the expedition moved on, the stockade and its remaining provisions were left in the care of one man and served as a stopping place for miners and others headed for the Black Hills.

In June of 1877, the stockade became a station for the Cheyenne and Black Hills Stage Company after it changed its route to Deadwood from the Red Canyon gap in the Hogback to the shorter one provided by the Beaver Creek gap. The stockade remained a stage stop until October 1878 when a new, much smoother and easier route well to the east was opened. Passengers were pleased with the change. The new route avoided the Hills entirely and they would not be "all shook up" as they had been before, particularly on that part of the trail north of Jenney Stockade.

J. C. Spencer and two other men bought the stockade and the land around it in the summer of 1877. That same winter, three Chicago investors put up money for Spencer to buy cattle in Texas and drive them north to the ranch. It was from their names—Lake, Allerton and King—the ranch received its name. The cabin served as the LAK's headquarters until 1924 when a new ranch house was built. A few years later the cabin, minus eight rooms that had been added over the years, was dismantled and moved to Newcastle.

Spencer continued to operate the ranch until 1914 when his health failed and he was forced to sell. Throughout the years he had been a pioneer—one of the first to bring ranching to the Black Hills and northeastern Wyoming, in stocking purebred Hereford cattle and in irrigating and raising alfalfa for hay. Those hay fields, the same fields as Colonel Dodge's grassy mead, are still in use as you can see, thriving on the rich alluvial soil washed from the canyon and on Beaver Creek's plentiful water. Today, the well-run ranch not only raises cattle, but also feeds them in its lots. The aroma can be "interesting," but it is a small price to pay for a good steak.

Site 5—Cheyenne-Deadwood Stage—is located 0.8 mile to the east on the left side of the road.

5. Cheyenne-Deadwood Stage

As the Cheyenne-Deadwood stage passed through this gap in the Hogback, it entered a new world, an entirely different world from the one characterizing the trip so far from Cheyenne. Up to this point on the average fifty to fifty-two hour trip to Deadwood, the passengers in the big red, yellow-wheeled Concord coaches with their six horse teams had been subjected in summer to sun and wind, the possibility of hail, and, if it rained, swollen creeks and that ever present gumbo. In winter, it was cold, with plenty of snow and wind. It could be bitterly cold, 20, 30, maybe 40 or more below zero, with blinding blizzards that would white-out the countryside and pile drifts high.

If it wasn't the weather, it was road agents between Jenney Stockade and the Hat Creek Station farther south. After 1876 the Indians were not the trouble they had been; but, road agents seemed to hit this section of the line with regularity, a great deal of impunity and a lot of gall. In fact, they once wrote a letter asking the stage company to send them a set of gold scales. In their letter they said, "dividing dust with a spoon is not always satisfactory." More than once the coaches had to be escorted by the cavalry. The passengers received all this for a fare which ranged from $30 for first class to $10 for third.

From this point on water was more plentiful, but the ride was rougher, the land rose and fell dramatically as the trail followed the Red Valley and crossed the Limestone Plateau. Stations were closer together as the horses needed to be changed more frequently. There wasn't as much wind and in summer it was cooler, but there were swift, sudden thunder storms and cloudbursts of rain or hail. In winter, while warmer than the open plains, the snow could be deep, requiring that the coaches be equipped with runners. In fact, it was entirely possible that there might be snow any month of the year.

What wasn't different was the food at those stops which served it and not all did. At some stops the food rated praise, but at most the fare consisted of fried salt pork, soda biscuits or hard tack and coffee "thick enough to float worn-out horses shoes." Just the meal to settle a queasy stomach on a coach which swayed enough on its leather slings to induce sea sickness. As you drive this road, look off to the sides and imagine what it would be like in a car, for all its power and modern suspension system, let alone in a stage coach.

Costing about $1,300 apiece, the great coaches were eight and a half feet long and eight feet tall. They required a high degree of skill on the part of their tough and resilient drivers in order to handle three sets of reins in one hand and a whip in the other.

Site 6—Frannie Peak-LAK Lake—is located 0.9 miles to the north on the gravel Beaver Creek Road.

6. Frannie Peak-LAK Lake

You should take a little time at this location. You are in the Red Valley, hemmed by the 360 million year old Devonian limestone cliffs of the Plateau to the east and the 160 or so million years old Jurassic sandstone walls of the Hogback to the west. Looking the way you came, you see the Beaver Creek gap, a gate standing open to the High Plains. In the other direction, drawing you on to the higher hills, lies a thin green line of well-watered rich alluvial soil bounded by arid slopes covered with Rabbit Bush, Rocky Mountain Juniper and Mountain Mahogany.

The Beaver Creek gap attracted more than miners and stage lines as a route into and out of the Hills. There is evidence that man has used this area for more than 12,000 years. Recent archaeological excavations just to the east of the gap have placed man in the Black Hills around 12,000 years ago. Rock art in the area has been dated at about 11,500 years old.

Imagine these early men as they lived and walked this area, seeking shelter in its canyons from the weather and the seasons as they bore and raised their children. There is evidence they quarried hard flints from outcroppings in the area to make tools for daily living and the weapons used to kill the big horned bison, elk and other large animals during their communal hunts. It is not difficult to imagine them fishing the creeks and drinking from the valley's springs as they gathered the abundant fruits, berries and other plants that could be easily found then as they can be now.

These early men must have climbed and used Frannie Peak as a lookout as did Dr. V.T. McGillicuddy, a topographer with the Jenney party. He went up to get a better look at the countryside and he probably had a better view than you would if you climbed it today. The Black Hills were not as forested then as they are now—wildfires kept them thinned and open. The lush, densely forested hills we see today came with the advent of modern forest and fire management practices. The pipe on the site marker will locate Frannie Peak for you.

There are no natural lakes in the Black Hills. Today's lakes are manmade and were built, with few exceptions, to provide water for the use of towns or crop irrigation. Any recreational use was considered secondary, the LAK Lake is no exception. Built and owned by the ranch, the present dam, constructed in the 1940s, replaced the original smaller dam. It serves to store and divert water to ditches which carry it to the fields below the ranch.

Each owner of the ranch has been most gracious and opened the lake for fishing and other recreation. In 1994 a unique private, public and civic cooperative development effort was undertaken when the ranch owners, the Wyoming Game and Fish Commission, the Weston County Commissioners and Newcastle's Cambria Lions Club joined to improve and expand the lake's recreational opportunities. If you wish to use the area, all that is asked is that you stop at the ranch, the Visitors Center or Crum's in Newcastle and ask for a permit. No charge.

Enjoy the lake and its opportunities, but please don't abuse the area. That's true for all the land along this trip. It is private land. Enjoy it, but don't leave your mark on it. A caution is well worth making at this point: The roads aren't wide, but they are wide enough if you keep to your side of the road. Be particularly careful on the curves and hills.

Around the lake, watch for waterfowl and water birds such as the Mallard Duck, Canada Goose, Phalaropes (shore birds), the Spotted Sandpiper and, occasionally, the Common Loon, as well as the Red-winged blackbird. Raptors to watch for include the Osprey and the Red-tailed Hawk in summer and the Bald Eagle in winter. During the next few stops, watch for Passerines (perching birds) and song birds like the Wood Thrush, Yellow Warbler, Common Yellowthroat in the shrubs and trees along the creek, to name but a few. Also, begin to watch for White-tailed deer along the brushy streamside and Mule (Black-tailed) deer in the higher open country.

Site 7—Sawmills—is located 2.3 miles to the north on the right.

7. Sweet Sawmill

While the buildings at this location are of recent vintage, there has been a ranch here since sometime before 1881 when the Stockade Ranch or Stockade Beaver Ranch was started along the old Cheyenne to Deadwood stage trail.

The Stockade Ranch was the location of one of the earliest saw mills in the area. With the abundance of timber and a growing demand for lumber, sawmills flourished wherever strong creeks flowed. Most of the lumber used in building Tubb Town came from this area and much of it came from the Hanson, Davis and Sweet sawmill which was in operation in 1888.

The mill was located on the creek and the creek powered its great wooden water wheel. The logs were cut high in the hills and reached the valley floor by way of dry flumes (chutes). The steepness of the grade caused the logs to gain such speed in their descent they would be on fire when they reached the bottom, where workers doused them with water to put the fire out. That is, according to one story. Others say they were just too hot to handle and needed the water to cool them down. You can see evidence of that flume if you look through the pipe attached to the site marker. The mill itself was located on the creek. The mill's location is also identified by a pipe on the site marker.

Along with dimension lumber, the mill undoubtedly produced wooden lath, those thin wood strips used to hold plaster to the walls in the days before metal lath or sheetrock. As you drove here, you probably didn't notice a large hole on the right hand side of the road. It is all that remains of a kiln where the area's limestone was burned to produce the lime used in mixing plaster.

This lime also had a mundane, but important, daily use: It was a common practice for every home or business to keep a small bucket of lime handy in their outhouse. Thoughtful users would throw a scoopfull down the seat hole to speed decomposition and control odors.

Between here and Site 11 drive slowly and watch for wildlife. Watch the meadows. Any turkeys you see are not some farmer's flock—they are wild. In the spring, you might just see them strutting and displaying. During the winter, Bald Eagles may be observed along the creek, as can other raptors in the summer. The Great Blue Heron is also around in the summer, drawn no doubt by the fish hatchery.

Site 8—Sweet School—is located one mile north on the right.

8. Sweet School

The memories stirred by this dying building are those of isolated rural communities and country schools. The building is actually two buildings. On the right is the original building on the site, the Sweet School. In the 1940s, the men of the Beaver Creek community moved the LAK School eight miles and built a kitchen between the two buildings so it could serve as a community center, as well as a school. For many who drive by today, the building sparks pleasant memories of parties, dances, meetings, romance—to say nothing of the "readin', writin' and 'rithmetic" of one room schools with as many as 32 students in eight grades.

The Sweet School remained open until 1959. After that, students were bussed to Newcastle. Community activities continued, but became fewer, until they finally died out in the 1970s—improved roads, the loss of activities associated with country schools, off-ranch jobs all took their toll and changed the fabric of rural community life.

While one of the earlier schools in the county, the Sweet School was not the oldest; that honor went to the Beaver Creek School located up the road. It opened in 1888 with six or eight books with the floor serving as its blackboard. In the early years, country school teachers usually found their room and board with a nearby family. Like the students, they sometimes had a ways to go by foot or horseback to the school. In winter, it was not at all unusual to find the inside walls of the school covered with frost when they arrived in the morning.

The Sweet School wasn't always located here. The moving of a school building was not at all uncommon. School board politics, large families moving in or out, a neighborhood feud, or a land dispute (whatever, sometimes it didn't take much) and the school would be on the road again. The building would be jacked up, put on log rollers or skids and hauled off to its new location by a team of 8 to 10 horses.

If you look 360 degrees you might conclude Colonel Dodge was describing the view from this spot when he wrote:

"The scenery is very grand and beautiful. The valley, owing to the number of streams, is a rich green. On each side rise ranges from one to two thousand feet, their tops covered with the dark, thick growth of pine which gives the name 'Black' to the 'Hills.' The face of these ranges shows near their tops a stratum of several hundred feet of red sandstone; below this, a belt of very uniform thickness of white limestone; below this, a greenish formation, which the geologists pronounce 'Jurassic;' near the bottom are beds of great thickness, of a stiff red clay; and against the base of these are immense dirty-white beds of gypsum; below all this is the green valley, graceful with trees and shrubbery. The combination and variety of colors, the towering precipices and broken crags, make a picture as delightful to the eye as may be found."

Site 9—Grist Mill—is located 0.6 of a mile north on the right.

Salt Creek Overlook

9. Harper Grist Mill

Up until the 1940s when it was torn down, a large two storied, rather plain Victorian building occupied the area next to the old shed which leans against the rock. The shed was the ranch's blacksmith shop and the larger building was used to house the hired hands working on the place. When the building was built is unknown, but the main ranch house across the road did have a parlor, dining room and three bedrooms added to what had been a kitchen in 1902.

This building was more than a little unique. It had a water wheel under the first floor—a wheel which reflected ingenuity, constructed as it was from the wheel of a horsedrawn hay mowing machine with cups attached. Water to move the wheel and drive the grinders of its attached grist mill came through a wooden flume from a spring located higher on the hill and some distance away. The spring is still there, but its water is diverted and now used for irrigation of fields down the creek.

The ranch was blessed with springs, as were many ranches along Beaver Creek. They provided good water for livestock and gardens, but they also created swamps and a bumper crop of brush that the rancher burnt out each year. It took (and still takes) a lot of hard work and a great deal of sweat to get ahead of Mother Nature to create and keep up the meadows you see along the creek today.

It would be an odd ranch that didn't have a large garden to provide for its own needs—enough to eat fresh in season and enough to can or store for the long winter months. The soil and water on Beaver Creek were productive and some early ranchers, in addition to their cattle, carried on market garden operations to supply the area's growing needs.

On your way to the next site, take note of the yellow Victorian house 0.6 of a mile up the road. The owner of this ranch purchased it in 1883, but didn't move on to it until 1900. He replaced the original log cabin with this house in 1904. Along its south side there was a long utility room through which ran a very small stream fed by a spring up the hill. This boxed-in stream served as the family's refrigerator, keeping milk and other perishables cool and unspoiled. Undoubtedly, the family also had an ice house where ice for warm weather use was kept. This ice was cut in winter from ponds and stored under sawdust for insulation. The ice lasted the summer. This system continued in use until the late 1940s when rural electrification was undertaken seriously.

Site 10—Fish Hatchery—is located 1.2 miles north on the left.

10. Fish Hatchery

The Cedar Ridge Hatchery takes advantage of spring water to raise Rainbow, Brook and German Brown trout. At any one time, about 20,000 to 150,000 are in residence. Of course, any beyond 25,000 are small fry. Some end up stocking streams, some end up on a dinner plate and some stick around to make sure that there are more next year.

The spring is a strong one, a million and a half gallons of pure mountain water per day. Its temperature is about 50 degrees Fahrenheit. The source of this water is the same as that of the fountain in Newcastle—the Paha Sapa (Madison) Formation. Here, however, the formation has been thrust far closer to the surface of the Limestone Plateau and, as you may have noticed as you drove the road, many springs exist. It is their flow which makes Beaver Creek the strong stream it is. Farther up the road, particularly at the point where the road crosses Beaver Creek there is no water. The natural flow of the creek disappears, going underground to reappear later. This is not an unusual occurrence in the Black Hills given its geology. The entrance to the hatchery is 0.2 of a mile from here. If the gate is open, you are welcome to drive in and see some very nice trout.

Site 11—Wooden Waterline—is 1.0 miles north on the right.

11. Wooden Waterline

For many years Newcastle received part of its water supply through a wooden waterline that had its start some twelve miles north of here on the EVA Ranch. Built in 1920, the line continued in use until the early 1950s when Newcastle drilled its wells into the Paha Sapa Formation. Constructed of oak planks and bound with spirals of heavy gauge wire, the line crossed hill and dale. You can still see from here where part of that line ran if you look through the pipe on the sign. You can only marvel at the skill of the surveyor who laid out the route for this gravity fed system unaided by modern maps or today's satellite surveying technology.

Relics of the line continue to exist. At one spot there is a manhole cover that even today when lifted reveals cold, clear water rushing through the pipe. Within hangs an old tin dipper, a clear invitation to drink. But, as good and plentiful as the water was, the line was not without its troubles. Simply, it was a maintenance nightmare and more than one Newcastle resident remembers water restrictions being enforced because the line was down. One of the jokes often repeated ran, "How do you fix a leak in a wooden water line?" Answer: "Just dump a couple of gunny sacks of sawdust into the line and pray some of it will catch in the holes, swell and stop the leak."

Even after drilling its wells, Newcastle did not relinquish its water rights to this source until sometime in the 1970s. It did so then only after some considerable thought and discussion. That it took some twenty years is not surprising when you consider how water is valued in this country.

As you leave this stop begin to watch for elk. A small herd resides in the area and you just might see them on the high meadows early in the morning or later in the afternoon or evening.

Site 12—Thomson Canyon—is 1.7 miles up the road on the left.

12. Thomson Canyon

The Thomson Ranch homesteaded by Ed Thomson was located on the left side of the road. The canyon is off to the right. His grandson, Keith, distinguished himself in World War II and was later elected to serve Wyoming in both the U.S. House of Representatives and the U.S. Senate.

Ed and his brother Dan came by rail to Deadwood in 1886 and then trailed their livestock here to homestead. They stayed the first winter in the old Beaver Creek stage station which was located up the road from here near the EVA ranch. Like most stations built to do no more than accommodate the changing of horses, it probably wasn't much more than a stable with a room for the stock tender.

The Winter of 1886-1887 was a tough one, a real tough one. One cattle company out on the open plains lost 93,000 head of cattle that winter. It was little better for the two Thomson families. They lived on turnips and wild game. By March they were in real trouble, so Ed hitched a team to a two-wheel cart made out of the rear wheels of a wagon and took off for supplies. For the newcomer, it was a long, hard winter trip through the hills to Buffalo Gap in South Dakota, but he made it there and back—120 plus miles of nothing but snow and cold.

With the coming of better weather that spring, they built log houses and barns, dug ditches and began irrigating their land. Later, they even farmed up on the Limestone, and for a while they ran a saw mill until it burned. They raised livestock, hay, grain, and vegetables. They milked cows and made cheese which they sold in Cambria along with beef and fresh vegetables.

Each of the Thomson families raised seven children and those children went to the first school on Beaver Creek. It was built on Thomson land. The Thomson brothers and their wives were typical of those who homesteaded this country and made it. Decent, tough, determined souls, they took the opportunities offered them by this new part of the nation and made something of those opportunities through hard work.

The next site, Site 13—Hank Mason—is 7.5 miles from here. As you drive to it, you are beginning the climb to the Canyon Springs Prairie. In those miles the land begins to change: You find fewer springs and Beaver Creek spends part of its time underground. The valley opens out and seems drier. The wildlife habitat ceases to be riparian, becoming more meadow-like with pines defining its edges. The elk herd may be here, and it's good Mule (Black-tailed) deer country. There is also the chance you just might see Mountain Bluebirds flitting across the road or American Kestrels, either sitting on a fence or hovering over the fields adjacent to the road.

13. Hank Mason

Jedediah Smith lost his ear to a bear, but gained fame as a mountain man. Hank Mason, who ran a saw mill on upper Beaver Creek, lost his life to a bear and thereby assured himself a place in local folk lore. Hank was an old-timer in the area and his buffalo camp had been the first habitation by whitemen in the area of Campbell County south of what is now Gillette, Wyoming. He had also been the first county road supervisor of Crook County, which originally encompassed what we now know as Weston, Crook and Campbell counties.

Hank had a saw mill, but the mill was not operating in the spring of 1893. A broken wheel caused a shut-down and the help had been temporarily laid off. Hank and his wife Rose were in the canyon alone when a couple of inches of snow fell on the night of May 18. When Hank got up on the morning of the 19th, he told Rose he was going up to the cabin on his mining claim and pick up some bacon as they were getting low. When he stepped outside there were large bear tracks near the doorstep. It is said that he picked up his rifle and told Rose, "I'm going up in the canyon and try to get my twenty-second bear."

Hank didn't come home that night. Worried, Rose kept a light burning all night. When morning came, alone and unarmed, she set out to find him. She followed his tracks in the snow for about three miles until they went into the brush. Another half mile on the trail she found him. Seeing he was dead, Rose removed her apron and covered his face. She also must have stretched him out on his back and folded his hands on his breast, as that is how the men later found him.

On foot, she worked her way 6 miles down the creek to the EVA Ranch. Arriving at the ranch about 11 o'clock, she told her story. Nobody believed her. She went on another half mile to where another rancher and his daughter were planting potatoes in a field. She told the daughter what had happened. The daughter went to her father and told him. He disbelieved the story also, but the daughter convinced him he should investigate. He agreed and sent his sons to gather some more men. With Rose, they then started out for the canyon in a wagon.

The wagon could only go so far in the rough canyon and the party walked the rest of the way in. What they found and surmised happened is best described by the rancher who gathered the party:

"There were bear tracks everywhere, going and coming, and we found where Mason had on the morning of the 19th trailed the bear to where he had a bed under the overhanging branches of a large spruce tree. When within fifty feet, the bear evidently jumped up and stood in his bed facing Mason. Or he may of charged. Mason had a 40-60 caliber Winchester repeating rifle and shells he had reloaded himself. He shot the bear in the shoulder, the bullet striking the shoulder blade and then following the blade a short distance, not doing any serious damage. Mason threw out the empty and threw another cartridge into the barrel. But it didn't go all the way in because it was too large. So he got out his jacket knife [sic-jack knife?] and tried to pry it out but the bear didn't give him time. He threw his gun down and started up a quaking asp tree tight by him but didn't quite make it. The bear got him by the heel and pulled him out. His fingers peeled the bark from the limb where he had a hand hold. An awful fight had taken place there. Man and bear blood was on the rocks, logs and snow. Now the bear evidently thinking that Mason was dead left him and went to a spring and got a drink. Mason could not walk so began to crawl down the canyon towards home. The bear came back and trailed Mason about one hundred yards or a little more, caught up with him and finished him there."

Hank put up a good fight, but he had 32 wounds and any one of five would have been fatal. It was a tough job for six men to get Hank's mangled body back over the rough terrain to where the rancher had left the wagon. On the 21st of May they buried Hank at the mill. He was quickly avenged when four heavily armed friends and two dogs went after the bear. Following the bear's trail, the dogs soon found the grizzly, but it took eight hits before he was finally brought down. He was an old bear with teeth worn down smooth. Six and half feet long, he was thin after the winter and dressed out at 600 pounds by one report. The old "silver-tips' was mounted by a Newcastle taxidermist in a standing position and more than one young man had his picture taken re-enacting the struggle.

There is also another story. Like married men everywhere, Hank had a mother-in-law. Mrs. Colclosure spent several years with Hank and Rose at the saw mill down in the canyon. She disliked the canyon passionately—she felt closed in. Quite ill her last winter, she made it very clear before she died that she didn't want to be buried in the canyon. It is reported she said, "Please bury me up on the ridge where I can see out." They honored her wish.

As you drive to the next stop, Site 14—Mallo Road—3.4 miles up the road, watch the fields for Mule deer and predators like the Coyote and the Red Fox and raptors like the Swainson's and the Red-tailed hawk.

14. Mallo Road

You entered the Canyon Springs Prairie when you broke out on top after leaving Beaver Creek canyon. This prairie is part of the Red Valley and better represents the general topographic nature of the Red Valley than does Beaver Creek. The "Prairie" has been Weston County's prime farming country since homesteaders started arriving with the opening of the Black Hills to mining.

You have two choices at this point. You can turn to the left and continue the tour or you can take a side trip to the location of the Canyon Springs stage robbery and Mallo Camp beyond. If you choose this option, you will then backtrack to this point and continue the tour to the west on Mallo Road. The station location—Site 15—is located 1.8 miles east on the right side of the road.

The area you just crossed does not seem to be much changed from Colonel Dodge's day and the Canyon Springs are probably the same springs he found as he escorted the Jenney party across the same area you have just traveled. Dodge found:

"The topographical features are here very remarkable, mountain and plain, forest and prairie, smooth level surfaces and rocky deep canons being all jumbled together. We stand on a high, level, treeless plain, apparently limitless to the west and northwest; behind us are the long slopes terminating in the valley from which we have recently emerged; in front, and on the same level with us is a heavy mass of pine forest; to the east, immediately to our right, is the canon of Spaulding's creek, five hundred feet deep, and impassable for anything but a bird; and close from its further brink, broken and precipitous mountains, covered with dense black forests of pine, rise yet a thousand feet above us.

"Our route led along the brink of the canon of Spaulding's Creek, from the almost precipitious sides of which gushed numerous springs of pure water. One of these, which could be got at by animals, was evidently a favorite resort of Indians, as many camps were found, of all ages. This we named 'Indian Spring."

15. Canyon Springs Robbery

Just through the trees in the open area sat a small building roughly constructed of logs. Primarily a stable, it had a room that served as living quarters for the station's stock tender. Think back on your trip and imagine the stage climbing up and out of the Beaver Creek canyon, the horses tired from pulling a heavily loaded road coach with as many as eighteen passengers up and over that rough country. The open and level terrain was a relief and the Canyon Springs station gave everyone a quick chance to stretch as the horses were changed.

Ten million dollars worth of gold had been taken out of the Deadwood area by the end of 1877. Road agents were always after it and they got more than a little, until the summer of 1877 when the stage company had the "salamander," a 16x30 inch iron safe lined with chilled steel, constructed. The manufacturer "warranted' that with the latest Yale lock, the safe could not be opened inside of six days, by any means except a knowledge of the combination." The stage company installed it in a regular coach for the weekly "treasure" run to Cheyenne.

With the use of the "salamander" widely known, the road agents' interest in gold waned and shifted to registered mail. As always, the passengers were fair game. However, it was obvious to the stage company this disinterest would not continue as times were changing: the day of the small mining operation was over, stamping mills were now operating and large capital intensive operations were becoming the norm. This development could only mean larger treasure shipments and renewed interest by the ever-present road agent. Consequently, the company decided to build a coach whose sole purpose was to carry valuable cargo. They lined a regular coach with five-sixteenth inch steel plate; that is, except the roof. Firing ports were added to the doors and the "salamander" was bolted to the floor. Only two were built—the first was called "The Monitor" and the second, "The Johnny Slaughter," after a stage driver who had been killed earlier by road agents just outside of Deadwood.

The Monitor was scheduled for the September 26, 1878 run to Cheyenne. Not long before it was due to arrive at the Canyon Springs station, five men rode in and took the station over. They locked the stock tender in the grain room and proceeded to knock the chinking from between the logs by the stable door where the stage pulled up. Having set the scene for the "most daring, biggest and bloodiest" holdup of the stage line, they waited and around 3 o'clock the Monitor rolled to a halt about ten feet from the stable door.

Five men were aboard the coach—the driver and an armed guard on the boot with him, two armed guards inside and an unarmed telegraph agent on his way to the Jenney Stockade. The guard climbed down to block the wheels after calling for the tender to help them with the seven minute change of horses. As he started for the stable he met a hail of bullets. Hit in the arm, he fired back and wounded a robber. Then, he was hit again, this time in the chest. Knocked down, he continued to fire and wounded another robber. Finally, he crawled behind the barn out of the line of fire.

A round through the top of the coach grazed and stunned one of the guards inside. The remaining guard, while firing through the ports, couldn't get a good view as close as the stage was to the door. He and the telegraph agent dismounted and ran for the trees. The telegraph agent was killed. After reaching the trees the guard wounded a robber trying to take control of the horses. Just then another holdup man got hold of the driver and used him as a shield in an attempt to get the guard to surrender. It didn't work. Believing the safe would hold for at least 24 hours, the guard took off on foot for the ranch nearest to the Beaver Creek station, a trip of seven miles. There he could get a horse and go for help from the station where three new armed guards were waiting to take over the stage.

With all opposition gone, the hold-up men loaded the driver and the remaining unwounded guard on the stage and drove off into the trees, leaving the wounded guard behind the barn and the stock tender locked in the feed room. The tender freed himself and headed north to the Cold Springs Ranch station for help. By the time any help arrived at the station the robbers were long gone. In the trees, they tied their "guests" to the coach wheels and with a sledge hammer and cold chisel had the "salamander" open in about two hours. Not much to be said for manufacturer's warrantees. It wouldn't happen again, at least not here; a month later the station closed when the stage line shifted its route to the east.

The loot? Twenty-seven thousand dollars mostly in bullion, but some currency, diamonds and jewelry. The hunt was extensive and justice sometimes swift. In less than six weeks some three-fifths of the loot was recovered. Eleven thousand two hundred dollars of gold were never recovered. That translates into some 650 ounces at $17.25 an ounce which appears to have been gold's value at the time. At today's prices—well over two million dollars. Local legend has it buried somewhere around here.

The stage company was not about to be outdone by road agents. They ordered another safe. This one was one ton in weight and guaranteed by its maker to hold up under 56 hours of uninterrupted work. What happened with this first one is not known, but a similar safe delivered five months later was opened by the line's superintendent after just one and a half hours of unassisted effort.

The Site 16—Mallo—is just 0.4 of a mile down the road.

16. Mallo

When you drive through the ranch style gates you arrive at Mallo, a recreational complex owned and operated by Weston County. In 1935, a pioneer Cambria resident purchased 160 acres from the Mallo family and then donated it to the county for use as a recreational center.

The upper camp to your right is known as the Mallo Resort. Some refer to it as the Russian Motel or the County Commissioner's Motel. It was built to house U.S. and Russian scientists when they come to monitor nuclear weapons tests from the seismic facility located up the road.

The lower camp, farther down the road at the bottom of the canyon, is known as Mallo Camp. Twenty-five men spent the winter of 1935-36 clearing trees downed by a strong storm. The development of the area was taken on as a WPA project and a large log lodge and eleven cabins were finished in 1938. The log lodge burned in 1977 and a new lodge was built in 1980 to replace it. It's a gorgeous place nestled in the spruce with Beaver Creek running through.

Together, the facilities provide exceptional recreational opportunities. Each February, Mallo hosts Weston County's Winter Festival with its horse drawn sleds, snowmobile races and a host of other winter activities aimed at both young and old. It sits next to a cross-county ski area developed through the cooperation of private landowners, Weston County and the US Forest Service, and it serves as a snowmobiler's base camp providing easy access to the over three hundred miles of groomed trails in the Black Hills. In warmer weather, it is home to school science camps, sports camps, church camps, conferences, family reunions—you name it.

You might want to give a second thought to going down to the lower camp during inclement weather. The road is steep with sharp curves and can be slippery coming back up. If you are driving one of the larger recreational vehicles, you probably shouldn't go down in any weather. Remember Colonel Dodge's 500 foot deep canon, impassable to anything but a bird? In a half mile the road will have you down in the bottom of that same canyon.

Site 17—Boyd Cemetery—is located 1.2 miles to the west of Site 14, Mallo Road, the intersection where you turned right. As you drive back along Mallo Road, compare the vegetation to that you saw when you were driving along Beaver Creek. Here spruce and quaking asp join the pine with spreading juniper in the gladelike open areas.

17. Boyd Cemetery

The Boyd Cemetery contains the graves of some of the Canyon Spring Prairies' earliest pioneers and it is still used by those families. It once had a church. Originally built as a community church, it became a Methodist Church in 1909. With infrequent use the building deteriorated and it was moved in 1957 at a cost of $700 to Four Corners to serve as a community hail and a place for 4-H and Farmer's Union meetings. This use did not last and for quite a few years the church sat quiet and boarded; like the settlers of the Prairie, it was resilient and refused to roll over, lie down and die. Today, it has a new life—it is again a church.

There was a Boyd Post Office from 1894 to 1917. You passed the site on your way here from Mallo. About 10 by 12 feet in size, it also served as a general store and living quarters for the postmaster. Nothing of note happened at the post office, but the Brown family, who lived nearby, had a friend named Stoian. Like most homesteaders, Stoian worked in the Cambria mines and proved up on his homestead at the same time. Stoian also made the best sauerkraut you ever tasted. The Brown's really enjoyed it and Stoian told them to come and get some whenever they ran out. One day they did. Stoian was happy to see them and led them to the kitchen where a big open sauerkraut crock sat with several hens roosted along its rim. It was the last time the Brown's ate Stoian's delicious sauerkraut.

Site 18—Inyan Kara Mountain-is located 0.6 of a mile down the road.

18. Inyan Kara

As you look northwest across the Canyon Springs Prairie, a series of mountains marking the Hogback rise on the horizon. The one on the extreme right is Inyan Kara Mountain. (There are so many different meanings given to those words we won't go into them and have someone tell us we are wrong.) What we do know is that Kara rises some 6,368 feet above sea level and covers an area of some 12 square miles. Geologically, Inyan Kara is not part of the Hogback; like the Devils Tower, it is an igneous intrusion that forced its way up through the formations lying over it. Early expeditions, such as Gore's in 1854 and Warren's in 1857, mentioned the mountain in their reports.

George Custer was sent on a reconnaissance of the Black Hills in 1874. Entering the Hills from the north, he traveled down the Red Valley roughly along what is now Wyoming Highway 585. He stopped 4 miles east of the mountain and remained in camp for a couple of days. On the 23rd of July, accompanied by his staff, the expedition's scientists, a reporter and some cavalry, Custer climbed the mountain. He hoped to get a good view of the Black Hills and the surrounding plains. However, he was frustrated as the area was obscured by smoke and haze from large prairie fires. Some surmise the fires were started by Indians, but the more likely case is that they were caused by lightning from summer thunder storms.

Custer left his mark. The expedition's journal records that "In the hard and flinty album of the summit, engraven with cold chisel and hammer, in large and distinct characters, Arabic and Roman is a date and an autograph thus, '74. CUSTER." It is still up there.

Custer also left a couple of his troopers in the area—Private Cunningham, who died on the 21st of diarrhea, and a Private Turner, who was killed by another trooper on the 22nd in a dispute over a horse. They were buried and a fire was built over their graves to conceal their location. [There is a historical marker for this site on WY 585.] Custer then departed to the east and crossed Cold Springs Creek in the area where the stage line later built its Cold Springs station. Present day Buckhorn, Wyoming on U.S. 85 is near that location.

19. Four Corners

There are more than a few places in Wyoming

known as "Four Corners," but there is only one Four Corners, Wyoming. Its story began when an early 1890's homesteader decided he needed to add something "more profitable than dry farming" to the family income So, sometime in the middle 1910s, he went up the road about a mile to where two country roads crossed and built the Four Corners Mercantile. The store was successful, very successful, as Prairie residents came from miles around to trade. There were no roads as we know them today to Newcastle, Sundance or Cambria and travel was difficult. In the winter, if you had a car, you put it away. Travel was by a horsedrawn sleigh. The store was located 1.3 miles north on WY 585 from the intersection of U.S. 85 and WY 585 at the junction with Pzinski Road. A large hole at the junction, the store's basement is all that remains.

The dry farmer turned merchant also saw the area needed a post office and in May of 1916 the Four Corners, Wyoming Post Office opened in his general store with himself as postmaster. The post office remained at this location until 1935 when it moved to the Prairie Store when the "Mercantile" finally closed its doors. Today, the post office is a rural branch of the Newcastle Post Office and is located in the Four Corners General Store and Diner.

The Prairie Store opened in 1932 and for fifty-eight years provided, the area's residents with gas, groceries, and mail, to say nothing of serving as a place to stop and learn what was going on in the area. Today, it is a bed and breakfast, but the role it played in the life of the area is not gone; it just moved next door to the Four Corners General Store & Diner located in the old school.

Stores like the Prairie Store were not uncommon. You didn't go to town more than once a week, if that. There were as many as five of these small stores open on U.S. 85 between Newcastle and the South Dakota line in the late 1930s. The 7-11s of their day, they offered travelers a chance to gas, the opportunity for a soda, a snack, and, the kids, car sick from rough, curvy, bumpy roads, a chance to stretch. Maybe even a bathroom, if they hadn't already had to go on the side of the road. The Prairie Store was a little different though; it had a refinery across the road, a few remnants of which are still visible. Oil was hauled from the Osage oil field and refined into gasoline and kerosene that the store then sold. Highly developed refining and distribution systems didn't exist in this sparsely populated part of the nation and if you desired the products at a reasonable price, it had to be done locally. For a time, almost every small town and by-way in this part of Wyoming had its own refinery, as did many small stores like this one.

As you can see, the old Boyd Church still stands. Again a church, nondenominational, its congregation numbers 40 to 50 on Sundays and they come from Newcastle, Osage, Upton and Sundance as well as the Prairie. Some remodelling work has been done (like the lean-to on the side) and the church has changed a little, but the old lines and feel are still there. One thing hasn't changed: the original and unique pot bellied stove still heats the church.

Site 20—The Roundhouse—is 3.1 miles south on U.S. 85 on the left.

As you drive to your next site at the Roundhouse notice how the Hogback rises to protect the Red Valley from intrusion. The mountain to your right, as you look south along the highway, is Sweetwater Mountain and the one to the left is Mt. Pisgah.

Water was piped from springs on Mt. Pisgah and Sweetwater Mountain to a tunnel at the bottom of Salt Creek canyon near the Flying V. From there it was piped through a tunnel in the Hogback as far as the mines at Cambria. While the line was built to supply the mines, some of it found its way to Newcastle. Early on, a water line had been built from Cambria down the canyon to Newcastle to supply the railroad. It was the day of the steam locomotive and a lot of water was required. The town tagged on to this supply.

The more than 6,000 feet high Sweetwater Mountain has an interesting climate and some species of sub-alpine shrubs and flowers are found on its heavily wooded slopes, along with the plants and other trees typical of a Ponderosa pine forest. It is a rare winter Sweetwater is not deeply buried in snow. When spring arrives, the mountain comes ablaze with high country flowers and blooming wild fruits like chokecherry, serviceberry, thorn apple and gooseberry, among others. In the fall of the year, the Sweetwater again puts on a spectacular show of color. The quaking aspens turn an almost fluorescent yellow and the sumac, chokecherry and wild currant add bright patches of red.

20. The Roundhouse

Doesn't look like much, it never did—BUT—What a Place! The Roundhouse had its grand opening on the 4th of July in 1932. From then until it closed it was dances, dances and dances. The 4th, Easter, birthdays, weddings, Christmas and just plain Saturday night dances. Everybody invited and everybody welcome. You made your way from wherever to the Red Butte Store for a dance at the Roundhouse. It didn't make any difference what the weather was, you came—ten below or not.

The Roundhouse had great hardwood floors to dance on, the walls were lined with benches and there was a small kitchen where the ladies fixed a bite to eat for the midnight "supper" break. That break was when all of the younger ones paired off and more than one romance got its start—all under the watchful eye of mom, dad, the grandparents, relatives and all the neighbors. The little and the littlest ones came with their folks, no one stayed home, and when they were tired of playing and devilling the dancers, or having mom or dad teach them how to dance, they just laid down on the benches and went to sleep as their folks danced the rest of the night away.

A dance at the Roundhouse was family, one great big family which extended itself throughout the better part of the county. One lady summed up what people thought of those dances and how they were one of the brighter spots of our history when she said, "I've never been to a dance at the Roundhouse. For the 28 years I've lived here, I have heard the stories and waited for them to have another one. Now they are and I'm going to be out of town. I don't want to wait another twenty-eight years." She didn't leave town. That dance took place on June 5, 1993 and the house was packed.

The small two story building to the south was the Red Butte Store, another of those 7-11s of their day.

Site 21-Red Butte-is 2.1 miles down the road.

21. Red Butte

Local folklore has it that the Indians and the whiteman used Red Butte as a lookout. That's probably arguable, but it is true that some bootleggers had their stills in the area during Prohibition and there are some stories that local law officers might have been in the habit of talking too much in public about when federal revenue authorities were to be around. Earlier, the Buck Hanby gang had their "hold-out" somewhere near Red Butte's base. This gang of murderers and holdup men were reported by an early resident of the area to have been "wanted by the 'law' all along the old Chisholm cattle trail from the Mexican border to Wyoming." In the Spring of 1889 sheriff's deputies killed Hanby nearby and broke up the gang. Hanby was "planted' where he fell in a slab board box of native pine from Tom Sweet's sawmill." This was the same sawmill you saw the location of on Beaver Creek.

Red Butte is also a good example of how a good roof of sandstone and greenish gray shale with fossiliferous limestone from the Jurassic's Morrison Formation can keep the weather at bay. The red soil is Spearfish shale from the Triassic. You have seen a lot of it as it is the dominate geologic feature in the Red Valley.

Site 22-Salt Springs-is located 2.4 miles ahead on the left.

22. Salt Springs

A group of prospectors found seventy or more salt springs in this area in 1877. The volume of water and the salt content was higher than it is today, yielding, according to reports, three-quarters of a pound of salt per gallon of water. One of the prospectors had past experience in salt production by evaporation and, realizing the find's value, he persuaded his partners to develop the springs and produce salt for sale. They did and the salt was well received in the area. Not only was it produced for table use, but a coarser variety was manufactured which cattlemen bought for their livestock and the mines in the central Black Hills at Galena purchased for use in the extraction of silver.

When and why production ceased is a mystery, but it did. In 1905 a new corporation was formed to exploit the springs. Stock was sold, some facilities were constructed and there was an attempt to drill well into the salt formation. More than one problem was encountered. One might be solved, but it seemed another quickly arose.

The crowning blow or excuse may have been

events associated with the following report from the Newcastle News Journal in July 1907: "The banks of Salt Creek from the milk ranch to a distance above the Salt Springs are lined with carcasses of dead cattle killed by drinking salt water. Most of the cattle killed in this manner are cattle that have been driven from the range around Sweetwater by sheep located there and as they are not accustomed to drinking the water it kills them." The news item indicates less concern with the salt water as the cause of the cattle's deaths than it does with sheep as the cause. A not unexpected view for the time as sheep really were not popular. The company went bankrupt and its assets were sold on the courthouse steps.

Site 23—Flying V—is 1.5 miles down the highway to the left. You will leave the highway at this point.

From here on back to Newcastle you may see large soaring birds. They are not eagles. They are just Turkey vultures, or buzzards as we would say. Graceful, they are a pleasure to watch as they look for something to eat—road kill or anything else that's dead.

23. Flying V

The Flying V-Cambria Inn was built by the mining company as a resort for and a memorial to the Cambria miners. It was completed in 1928, only months before the mine closed. Originally known as the Cambria Park and Casino, its construction of native sandstone from the Hogback was overseen by a master mason the company brought over from Germany. It had two swimming pools—one salt water and one fresh—with gravel bottoms. The bath house featured fresh and salt water showers. The stone entrance to the wooden bath house is now on the National Register of Historic Places. The lodge featured a dining room, six modern rooms with both tubs and showers, and upstairs a ballroom surrounded by a wide, open, covered porch. Across the hill behind the pools, there was a not unchallenging golf course.

The Flying V has had a varied history. In 1931, the mining company leased the park and casino, and the brothers who leased it renamed it after their livestock brand, the Flying V. At one time it was home to a bible college, but for the most part it has been a place to eat and play. Today, it is a restaurant and bed and breakfast. It is well worth a trip inside to see the building's stonework and the chapel which was originally built to be a museum focused on the mine and its miners.

It was in this area water brought from Sweetwater Mountain and Mt. Pisgah passed through the tunnel cut through the Hogback to the mines at Cambria.

Site 24—Salt Creek Overlook—is 2.8 miles up the hill.

24. Salt Creek Overlook

This is one spectacular view. You are on the side of the Hogback looking out over the Salt Creek and Beaver Creek valleys to the Limestone Plateau. From here you can see those same vertical cliffs that were to your east when you stopped at the LAK Lake.

A mile or so down in the valley is a ranch known as the 'Wantz Place." The original building was a road house and saloon located halfway between Tubb Town and the Cambria mining camp. The mining company did not allow the selling of liquor in Cambria, so the miners just walked over the hill to "Schuh's Saloon" for some socializing. (Later, the company did allow a beer wagon to come from Newcastle on Sunday and many miners imported grapes and made wine.) Old newspaper reports and passed down stories tell a tale of missing persons, rumored graves and other events that suggest it might have been wiser for the prudent traveler to choose another route. Mr. Wantz bought the saloon and homesteaded the place in 1899. Wantz family members recall that before Mr. Wantz enlarged and sided the house they could find bullet holes in the walls.

Site 25—Cambria—is 0.4 of a mile ahead on the right.

25. Cambria

The state's historical marker outlines Cambria's history, but it doesn't tell its story. One can only speculate what this country would have been like had the railroad not found its coal here. Where would the Burlington and Missouri River Railroad have laid its tracks as it reached to meet the Northern Pacific in Montana? If you look at a map of Wyoming, you will see that most of its towns, at least those that lasted, reached and maintained any size, are almost all located on a railroad.

While Newcastle has a town because coal was found here, it was Cambria itself which made them what they are today. No! Not the mine, but those adventurous, determined and independent souls from 23 countries who worked there as they sought a better life for themselves and their families. Twenty-three nationalities who lived in harmony, intermarried, and who, while working at the mine, homesteaded the surrounding area or gained their stake to build businesses. If the United States ever had an area that demonstrates all the good implied in the melting pot theory, it is here in this area.

Site 26—High Plains Overlook—is located 1.8 miles south on the right.

26. High Plains Overlook

You are standing on top of the Hogback. The view stretching before you is the last of the mixed grass and the beginning of the short grass prairie of the High Plains which extends west some 150 miles until they reach the Big Horn Mountains. To the south, they go all the way to Cheyenne and beyond. An idea of the distances you can see: On a clear day, an exceptionally clear day, you can see Laramie Peak 130 miles away; on most other days about 50 to 70 miles. The small butte, standing all alone, is Alkali Butte—out 20 miles; and the Rochelle Hills on the horizon are about 55 miles distant.

This is an ideal place to watch summer storms moving across the plains, to watch thunderheads form and drift east, and to watch a sunset. There is no such thing as a bad sunset in this country. This is a place to come at night, undisturbed by city lights, and watch the stars reach right down to the ground. It is a place to imagine cattle herds raising clouds of dust as they trail north across the arid plains. It is a perfect place to stand and imagine it covered with water in which the long necked Plesiosaurus and sharklike New Ichthyosaur swim and in which Ammonites, Belemnites, Baculites and Crinoids lived out their lives. Or, imagine the sights you might see after the seas recede, when the thickheaded Paschysephalosaurus, the duckbilled Antatosaurus, Tyrannosaurus Rex, and Triceratops walk the land—to name a few whose fossilized remains have been found.

Later, imagine early man emerging from the Hills to hunt on its grasslands the mammoth, the big horned bison, Pleistocene camels, elk and antelope. It's changed a lot since the dinosaur, but has it really changed that much from the time of early man? It is generally accepted that the prairie you see today, though changed by modern man, closely resembles and retains much of the character of its earlier state. What you see today is the same as what the Lakota found as they moved west in the middle 1700s and the early whiteman found in the 1800s. Today, deer, antelope and elk share the grasslands with cattle and sheep instead of sharing it the bison, the camel or the mammoth. This is the last site on the tour. The junction of U.S. 16 & 85 is 1.5 miles down the road. If you did not stop by the Anna Miller Museum, you really should do so. It is a gem. If you did visit, you are always welcome to come back again.

On the way back to the junction, you might notice to your left just a bit down the road a complex of buildings. They are the Wyoming Honor Camp, a part of the state penal system. The men there work for the state forestry department and have been superb in giving time to community projects. The camp is also home to a "boot" camp, designed to provide a disciplined program for youthful, first time offenders in an effort to give them a chance to straighten out without prison incarceration. The Honor Camp is a good and trusted neighbor.

If you go out on the prairie at night, the lights of the camp give the impression of a flying saucer soaring through the night sky over the seemingly never ending open space of this great part of the country.

This tour was developed by interested individuals with the cooperation of the Anna Miller Museum, the Weston County Museum District, the Weston County Preservation Commission, and the Weston County Historical Society. Special thanks to Pope & Talbot, Inc. for providing the site sign materials and the Honor Camp for making them. Reprinted with permission.

Cloud Peak Skyway

This is the southern-most route across the Bighorn National Forest in the Big Horn Mountains. The designated 47-mile stretch on US 16 shares its boundaries with the National Forest. The highway can be reached via Tenleep from the west of Buffalo from the east. Allow one hour minimum driving time.

The road is a paved tow-lane highway, with occasional pullouts as it ascends toward 9666-foot Powder River Pass. This route makes a more gradual ascent of the mountain range than routes to the north. Mountain weather can be extreme and snow can fall in any month at these elevations, but rarely does it affect travel in the summer and early fall.

Reprinted from Wyoming Department of Transportation Brochure

Bud Love Winter Range

On this drive, you'll see some of the most scenic mountain views imaginable, as well as deer, antelope, wild turkey, and in the winter, elk. It takes about one or two hours to drive it, depending on how much you stop and look at what surrounds you. Start in Buffalo at Fort Street and Main Street (US 16 west), then head west on Fort and turn right (north) on DeSmet. Follow this route out of town on CR 91.5 (French Creek Road). When the road forks at 5.4 miles, bear left and travel another 5 miles to the Bud Love Winter Range. The road forks again at 15 miles, where you should stay right and follow Rock Creek Road back to Buffalo.
Reprinted from Wyoming Department of Transportation Brochure

Crazy Woman Canyon

One of the favorite drives for Johnson County locals, and visitors as well, this tour takes you along a single lane dirt road past stunning canyon walls into the mountains. Begin at the intersection of Fort and Main in Buffalo, taking US 16 west towards the mountains. After about 25 miles, watch for a well-signed Crazy Woman Canyon Road, which branches left off of US 16. To return to Buffalo, follow the gravel road which brought you through the canyon and joins Wyoming 196. Turn left onto Wyoming 196 on which you'll drive ten miles back to Buffalo.
Reprinted from Wyoming Department of Transportation Brochure

Outlaw Cave/Dull Knife Battlefield

This tour takes you to the land of Butch Cassidy and the Sundance Kid. Johnson County locals and visitors favor the area's wildlife and scenery as much as the tales of these outlaws. This is also the area of the Middle Fork of the Powder River. High clearance vehicle are recommended for this route. Beginning at Kaycee, take the I-25 interchange and head west about a mile to the Barnum Road sign (Wyoinng 190). Follow Barnum Road 17.1 miles to a sign designating the Middle Fork Management Area of the Powder River. Turn left at the sign onto a gravel/dirt road. This will take you another 8.5 miles to the Outlaw Cave sign, where you should turn and drive another 2 miles to the hideout. Another .3 miles past the cave you can find a prehistoric rock shelter and Indian pictographs.
Reprinted from Wyoming Department of Transportation Brochure

Hikes

Black Hills Area

Carson Draw Trails

Distance: 6.8 miles total
Climb: 800 feet
Rating: easy to moderate
Usage: moderate
Location: Three miles north on FDR 838 off of US 14 from Sundance.

The Carson Draw Trails are Four-season, non-motorized trails that wind through Carson Draw. They are off the beaten path and offer solitude to those searching for a more primitive trail experience. Pine, aspen and oak stands surround the trails and provide habitat for the abundant wildlife that uses the area. From spring to fall, the trails are busy with multiple types of users, including hikers, mountain bikers, and horse riders. The trails are a pleasant diversion into the peaceful backwoods. Users may find that the trails are much like the Sundance system in their beauty and serenity, and offer a refreshing level of solitude.

Sundance Trails

Distance: 47.3 miles total
Climb: 1600 feet
Rating: easy to difficult
Usage: moderate
Location: Three and a half miles north on FDR 838 off of US 14 from Sundance.

This trail system weaves through the network of densely forested canyons and winding open ridges that form the Bearlodge Mountains. From some ridge tops you can see such sites as the Custer Expedition Route, Devil's Tower and the Twin Missouri Buttes. Elk, deer, and turkey are among the wildlife. This rugged but serene country is ideal for horseback riding. The secluded trails provide one of the most primitive recreational opportunities in the Black Hills. Water for horses is normally available along many of the trails. These trails are also popular for mountain biking because of the rough topography. Be sure to look for bypasses designed specifically for more challenging mountain biking, especially South Fork Tent, and Edge Trails.

Cliff Swallow and Cook Lake Trails

Distance: 3.5 miles and 1 mile
Climb: 600 feet/ 100 feet
Rating: difficult/ easy
Usage: moderate
Location: 20 miles north of Sundance on FDR 838, 843, and 842.

These trails are designed and maintained for hiking, mountain biking and nature study. Below Cook Lake and along Beaver Creek, you can see beaver in their natural habitat, plus many species of birds and other wildlife. Cliff swallows nest in the limestone bluffs above Beaver Creek. From the rim there is a stunning view of the surrounding Bearlodge Mountains as well as Beaver Creek Valley and Cook Lake. The trail takes you through ponderosa pines, aspen, birch and oak. You may see white-tailed deer, mule deer, and elk grazing in the meadows.

Bighorn National Forest (Tongue District, west of Dayton)

South Tongue Trail

Climb: gentle
Rating: easy
Usage: light
Location: Take FDR 193 off of Hwy. 14 about 10 miles south of Dayton, then go 150 yards south of Arrowhead Lodge.

This is a fairly easy day hike offering a variety of scenery. The trail goes through meadows, across several streams, through stands of timber, and past unique rock formations. There fishing opportunities in several pools and riffles along the way. The trail ends just off FDR 26, about 1/2 mile from the Tie Flume Campground.

Black Mountain Fire Lookout

Distance: 1 mile (plus)
Climb: steep
Rating: easy/ moderate
Usage: light
Location: Take FDR 16 off of Hwy. 14 about 9 miles south of Dayton, then turn onto FDR 222 on the east side.

> **Thunder Basin National Grassland**
>
> Thunder Basin National Grassland covers 572,211 acres of northeastern Wyoming's Powder River Basin between the Bighorn Mountains and the Black Hills. It offers wide expanses of rolling plateaus, steep rocky escarpments, and rolling plains. It is one of the largest intact grassland habitats left in the Northern Great Plains. This ecosystem is home to rare species that include the ferruginous hawk, swift fox, mountain plover, burrowing owl, and black-tailed prairie dog. The Bozeman and Texas trails cross a section of the grassland.
>
> Recreational activities abound. You can fish in mountain streams, stay in a campground or hike into the backcountry and find pristine solitude. Excellent opportunities await you, no matter what type of outdoor recreation you enjoy, from ATV trails and 4WD roads to mountain biking and hiking. From skiing champagne powder to visiting the largest coal mine in the Northern Hemisphere.
>
> For use information, permits, and othe questions, contact the Laramie Ranger District at at 2468 Jackson Street in Laramie or phone 745-2300. www.fs.fed.us

It's possible to drive to within a mile of the lookout if you have a high clearance vehicle. The trail up to the lookout is steep, but the bird's-eye view from the top, at 9489 feet, is worth it. At the summit you'll find a historic cabin and a 360-degree view of the Bighorn Mountains.

Blue Creek Loop Trail

Distance: 2.4 miles
Climb: moderate
Rating: easy/ moderate
Usage: light
Location: Take Hwy. 14 about 9 miles south of Dayton to the Sibley Recreation Area turnout.

This trail follows Prune Creek for a short distance then proceeds through a small meadow, to arrive in some lodgepole pine stands. The trail then loops and returns to the Sibley Lake Campground. There are also two other marked loop hiking trails accessible from the Blue Creek Trailhead. The Prune Creek Loop travels 2.7 miles and the Dead Horse Park Loop is 6 miles long.

Barrs Hill Trail

Distance: 6.5 miles
Climb: steep
Rating: difficult
Usage: light
Location: Take Hwy. 14 south of Dayton to FDR 196, about a mile north of Arrowhead Lodge. Follow this road past the stone cabin , then branch off to your right at the first fork. Continue following the main road until you come to the Barrs Hill sign. A high clearance vehicle is recommended.

This trail is on a steep slope, which drops into the Tongue River drainage area. The North and South Tongue Rivers meet along this riparian zone. The trail parallels the river on the south side, winding through aspen, pine, and cottonwood until it ends at the Cutler Creek and Box Canyon area. This is where the historic sawmill town of Rockwood once stood. There are several old cabins still standing and other interesting sawmill remnants. These are a part of our heritage, so please don't disturb them. You must travel the same trail back to the starting point, which is a considerable uphill climb.

Steamboat Point Trail
Distance: about 3 miles
Climb: steep
Rating: moderately difficult
Location: Take Hwy. 16 about 13 miles south and west. There is a parking area just across the highway from Steamboat Point.

Follow the tire ruts up to the Point. The trail then heads to the right side of the mountain and follows the base of the south wall. Reaching the back of the rock is challenging, but no ropes or equipment are necessary: just strength and caution. From the top, there is a sheer drop to the rocks below, and only a makeshift railing, so use extreme caution, especially if there is wind. Do not attempt this hike if a thunderstorm is threatening; lightning has struck here more than once. The view on all sides is breathtaking.

Tongue River Canyon Trail
Distance: 4 miles
Climb: moderate
Rating: easy/ moderate
Location: Turn right on County Rd. 92, between Dayton and Ranchester, and travel about 5 miles, staying to the left and heading into the canyon. This road is accessible to most vehicles. The trail is at the north end of the parking area.

This trail is a gradual climb through the canyon, with a few precarious overlooks down to the river along the way. There are also a few steep ravines leading down to the riverside.

Buffalo Area

French Creek Trail #42
Distance: 2 – 3.5 miles
Climb: gentle
Rating: easy
Usage: light
Location: Travel about 10 miles west of Buffalo on Hwy. 16, then turn right (north) on FDR 368 (French Creek Rd.). Cars and two wheel drive vehicles need to park about 1/4 mile down the rode. High clearance, 4WD vehicles can go another 1.5 miles in before parking.

The trail begins at the creek. You may follow it either west or east; the trail circles back to the same point. Either way, you'll see views of the Buffalo area and surrounding countryside.

Pole Creek Road
Distance: 11 miles
Climb: flat
Rating: easy
Usage: light
Location: Travel 19 miles west, then south of Buffalo on Hwy. 16, then turn right (west) on FH 31 (Pole Creek Rd.).

This is a gravel road, passable for most vehicles, which reconnects with Hwy. 16 about 11 miles south. There is seldom any traffic, and it is flat, so it's easy to walk or ride on. Along the way, you will find several old logging roads, which are gated and closed to motorized vehicles, but open to walkers, bikers, and horses.

Crazy Woman Canyon
Distance: varies
Climb: steep
Rating: difficult
Usage: light
Location: Travel 25 miles west, then south of Buffalo on Hwy. 16, then turn left (east) onto FDR 33 (Crazy Woman Canyon Rd.). The road drops quickly into some side drainages, which offer some challenging hiking.

There are no trails, so caution needs to be exercised on these hikes. Experience with mountaineering and orienteering is recommended. The main advantage is that very few people will be encountered in this canyon.

Poison Creek Road
Distance: varies
Climb: steep
Rating: difficult
Usage: light
Location: Travel about 29 miles west/southwest of Buffalo on Hwy. 16, then turn left (south) onto FDR 484 (Poison Creek Rd.). This road will take you to the base of the Hazelton Peaks area. The road is rough, but passable for most vehicles.

There are no marked trails on the mountains, but many routes along the drainages of the peaks will lead you to the top, where you will find a spectacular panorama of both the Powder River Basin and the Bighorn Basin.

Grouse Mountain Road
Distance: varies
Climb: gentle
Rating: moderate
Usage: light
Location: Travel about 10 miles west of Buffalo on Hwy. 16, then turn left (south) onto FDR 402/403 (Grouse Mountain Rd.). Park just off the road.

There are no trails maintained in this area, but the surrounding meadows and view of the valley make walking here enjoyable and easy.

(* These hikes are in the Cloud Peak Wilderness Area, so registration is required.)

Sherd Lake/ South Fork Trails*
Distance: varies
Climb: gentle/ moderate
Rating: easy/ moderate
Usage: heavy
Location: Travel about 16 miles west of Buffalo on Hwy. 16, then turn right (west) on FDR 20 (Circle Road). This will take you about 2.5 miles to the Circle Park Trailhead, where both trails begin.

The Sherd Lake Trail begins on TR 182, which turns into TR46, and goes about a mile to the lake. Beyond the lake, the elevation climbs, and the trail becomes the South Fork Trail. This trail turns into TR 095, then 1/4 mile farther along becomes TR 046 at Rainey Lake. Head south past Old Crow Trail. After crossing Duck Creek, go north on TR 095 to complete the loop back to Sherd Lake at the South Fork Ponds crossing.

Hunter/ Ant Hill Trail*
Distance: about 7 miles
Climb: steep
Rating: quite difficult
Usage: heavy
Location: Travel about 12 miles west of Buffalo on Hwy. 16, then turn right (west) on FDR 19 (Hunter Park Rd.). The Hunter Trailhead is about 3 miles west, where you can park.

This is a fairly strenuous hike, and should be planned for overnight, at least. Take FDR 496 northwest from the trailhead through the French Creek Swamp, to where it intersects with FDR 399. Follow this northwest to South Rock Creek, where it intersects with TR 7. Take TR 7 to TR 219 then follow it until you reach TR 38 at Elk Lake. This trail circles the lake, then heads south over the saddle of North Clear Creek, turning east into TR 24, then TR 44, which goes to the Seven Brothers Lakes. At Lake One, turn east onto TR 45 heading for Buffalo Park. Go east through the park, until you reach FDR 396, which will take you back to the Hunter Trailhead.

Solitude Loop Trail #38*
Distance: 50 miles
Climb: moderate
Rating: moderate/ difficult
Usage: light
Location: Travel about 12 miles west of Buffalo on Hwy. 16, then turn right (west) on FDR 19 (Hunter Park Rd.). The Hunter Trailhead is about 3 miles west, where you can park.

This hike takes about five days to complete, but it takes you past several of the prettiest lakes in the Bighorn Mountains. Go west from the trailhead on FDR 394 (Soldier Park Rd.) to TR 24. Continue west until you reach TR 38, which is the Solitude Loop Trail. It is well marked and will eventually lead you back to TR 24, and Soldier Park Rd. Other spurs diverge from this trail, including the West Tensleep Trail.

West Tensleep/ Misty Moon Trail #63*
Distance: about 7 – 57 miles
Climb: moderate
Rating: moderate/difficult
Usage: heavy
Location: Travel 44 miles west/ southwest of Buffalo or 17 miles east of Tensleep, then turn north on FDR 27, continuing 7 miles to the West Tensleep Trailhead.

This trail meets with the Solitude Loop Trail, which means hikers may chose to make it an overnight hike, or a several day trip. The trail follows West Tensleep Creek to Lake Helen, Lake Marion, and finally to Misty Moon Lake, which is the 7 mile portion of the journey. TR 63 intersects with TR 38 (the Solitude Loop Trail) north of Misty Moon Lake. Following this loop can add as much as 50 miles to your trip (see Solitude Loop Trail).

Lost Twin Lakes Trail #65*
Distance: about 6 miles
Climb: moderate
Rating: moderate/difficult
Usage: heavy
Location: Travel 44 miles west/southwest of Buffalo or 17 miles east of Tensleep, then turn north on FDR 27, continuing 7 miles to the West Tensleep Trailhead.

This trail climbs through lodgepole pine forest and meadows by the Middle Tensleep Creek to Mirror Lake, then on to Lost Twin Lakes. The forest changes from pine to often stunted spruce and fir along the way, until the treeline is crossed, and an open view of the area can be seen at the top of the trail.

Middle Tensleep Falls Trail
Distance: 2 miles
Climb: flat
Rating: easy
Usage: light
Location: Travel 44 miles west/ southwest of Buffalo or 17 miles east of Tensleep, then turn north on FDR 27, continuing 7 miles to the West Tensleep Trailhead.

This trail follows Middle Tensleep Creek south to the falls. Take the same route back.

Baby Wagon Creek Trail*
Distance: about 3 miles
Climb: gentle

Rating: easy
Usage: light
Location: Travel 38 miles west/ southwest of Buffalo or 27 miles east of Tensleep, then turn north on FDR 422, then north again onto FDR 419, which is a rough road, so high clearance, 4WD vehicles are recommended. The road ends at Baby Wagon Creek, which is where the trail begins.

This trail meanders along the riparian zone of the creek towards McLain and Maybelle Lakes. TR 69 runs east and west and connects with TR 98, which passes by the lakes, with a possible loop by way of TR 79, which leads to FDR 430 and returns east on TR 69.

Middle Rock Creek Trail*

Distance: about 8 miles
Climb: 4500 feet
Rating: very difficult
Usage: light
Location: In Buffalo, turn north off of Fort St. (Hwy. 16) onto N. DeSmet St. This street turns into French Creek Rd. Take this road 8 miles north to the entrance of the Bud Love Winter Game Refuge. Go through the gate and head west on the dirt road for 2 miles until you reach the Taylor Cabin site. The cabin is no longer there, but a barn is. Motor vehicles are not permitted beyond this point.

This is probably an overnight trek. From the cabin site, follow TR 51 to Firebox Park then take TR 41 to the junction of Middle and South Rock Creek. Take TR 41 south along Keno Creek, where it meets up with FDR 399/396. For a longer loop, head north along TR 40 until it intersects with TR 10, which will take you back down to FDR 399/ 396 also. This road connects with FDR 388, which will take you north to TR 41, then TR 51, which takes you back to Taylor Cabin.

Johnson Park/ Cougar Canyon Trail*

Distance: about 8 miles
Climb: steep
Rating: very difficult
Usage: light
Location: In Buffalo, turn north off of Fort St. (Hwy. 16) onto N. DeSmet St. This street turns into French Creek Road. Take this road 8 miles north to the entrance of the Bud Love Winter Game Refuge. Go through the gate and head west on the dirt road for 2 miles, until you reach the Taylor Cabin Site: The cabin is no longer there, but a barn is. Motor vehicles are not permitted beyond this point.

Take TR 51 west along the North Fork of Sayles Creek. At Firebox Park take TR 41 then go onto TR 549 about a half mile after that. Take this trail south onto TR 550, which intersects with FDR 396. Take this road south to TR 42, then head northeast to the National Forest boundary. As you drop in elevation, leaving the forest area, follow the tree line back to Taylor Cabin, about 2.5 miles.

Firebox Park Trail

Distance: varies
Climb: steep
Rating: moderate/difficult
Usage: light
Location: In Buffalo, turn north off of Fort St. (Hwy. 16) onto N. DeSmet St. This street turns into French Creek Road. Take this road 8 miles north to the entrance of the Bud Love Winter Game Refuge. Go through the gate and head west on the dirt road for 2 miles, until you reach the Taylor Cabin Site: The cabin is no longer there, but a barn is. Motor vehicles are not permitted beyond this point.

Take TR 51 up North Sayles Creek to Firebox Park. Turn onto TR 41 and go west along Middle Rock Creek to TR 43. Then follow TR 10 south to TR 41 on Keno Creek. Return on TR 41 north to TR 51 at Firebox Park and back to Taylor Cabin.

Battle Park/Paint Rock Creek Trail*

Distance: about 7 miles
Climb: moderate
Rating: moderate
Usage: moderate
Location: Travel 44 miles west/ southwest of Buffalo on Hwy. 16, or 17 miles east of Tensleep, then turn north on FDR 27. Continue 1 mile north, then turn left on FDR 24 (Battle Park Rd.). Drive 15 miles to reach to Battle Park Trailhead.

This trail passes through high mountain meadows, pine stands, and along several streams. From the trailhead, go north on TR 164 west of Grace Lake, then go west on TR 38. Continue on this trail to TR 62, on Paint Rock Creek, by the cow camp. Just south of the camp, turn southeast to TR 172, which returns to TR 164, then back to the trailhead.

Upper Paint Rock Lake Loop Trail*

Distance: 18 miles
Climb: steep
Rating: difficult
Usage: light
Location: Travel 44 miles west/ southwest of Buffalo on Hwy. 16, or 17 miles east of Tensleep, then turn north on FDR 27. Continue 1 mile north, then turn left on FDR 24 (Battle Park Rd.). Drive 15 miles to reach the Battle Park Trailhead.

Go north on TR 164 west of Grace Lake to TR 38, where you'll travel west, and then east, around Poacher Lake to TR 59 in the Teepee Pole Flats. Take this trail to Lower Paint Rock Lake, turning south onto TR 116 and then onto TR 94. This will take you to TR 62, then south to TR 173 and back to TR 164 and eventually the Battle Park Trailhead.

Lily Lake Trail

Distance: 3 miles
Climb: moderate
Rating: moderate
Usage: moderate
Location: Travel 44 miles west/ southwest of Buffalo on Hwy. 16, or 17 miles east of Tensleep, then turn north on FDR 27. Continue 1 mile north, then turn left on FDR 24 (Battle Park Rd.). Drive 15 miles to reach to Battle Park Trailhead.

This is a reasonable day hike - not too strenuous, not too easy. Go north on TR 164 until it intersects with TR 66. Follow this trail to the lake, and return by the same route.

Lake Angeline Trail*

Distance: 6 miles
Climb: steep
Rating: difficult
Usage: moderate
Location: Travel west of Buffalo on Hwy. 16 to FDR 391 (Schoolhouse Park Rd.). This road requires a high clearance, 4WD vehicle. The trail begins at Weber Park.

Follow TR 88 west up to Lake Angeline. The trail is rather difficult to follow through the Lost Fire area, with its many blown-down trees. Once above the timberline, it is marked with rock cairns. Lake Angeline and its environs offer excellent views and climbing opportunities. From the top of the surrounding peaks, climbers can get a magnificent view of the west slope of the Bighorn Mountains and the Bighorn Basin beyond.

Elgin Park Trails

Distance: varies
Climb: varies
Rating: moderate
Usage: light
Location: Travel 20 miles west/ southwest of Buffalo on Hwy. 16, then turn left (east) onto FDR 22 (Elgin Park Rd.). Go 1 mile east to FDR 460, then 1 ile north, to turn left on FDR 372. Follow this road 1.3 miles to the trailhead. This road accommodates large trailers and RVs.

There are numerous loop hikes or rides available from the Elgin Park Trailhead. The trails are marked with yellow diamonds, and a handout is available. The Elgin Park area offers exceptional views of the backbone of the Bighorn Mountains, camping, and stream fishing. Best of all, it receives little use. Designed for horse travel, but open to hikers, backpackers, and mountain bikers, there are exceptional views along the trails, and they are easy to follow. Motorized vehicles, such as ATV's and dirt bikes, are permitted here also, so use caution.

High Park Lookout Trail

Climb: moderate
Rating: easy
Usage: moderate
Location: Travel 41 miles west/ southwest of Buffalo, or 20 miles east of Tensleep, on Hwy. 16, then turn south on FDR 429. Follow the signs to the Lookout Parking Lot.

This trail goes up to the summit where an old fire lookout post stands. It is well marked, and easy to follow. From the top, there are spectacular views of the Bighorn Mountains and Bighorn Basin. The building itself cannot be entered because it is no longer safe.

Devil's Tower Hikes

Tower Trail - 1.3 miles (2 km)

The Tower Trail is the easiest and most popular trail in the monument. You will enjoy close up views of the Tower, while walking through strikingly different environments. Expect close views of the boulder field, ponderosa pine forest, and the fringe of meadow habitats.

Interpretive exhibits along the way point out such natural processes as the formation of the Tower, erosion of the landscape, local wildlife, and the flora of the base. The Tower Trail is paved with benches provided at various points. The steepest part of the trail is the very beginning but soon levels into a rolling trail. Plan to take 45 minutes to 1 hour to complete this loop trail.

Joyner Ridge Trail - 1.5 miles (2.4 km)

Joyner Ridge provides visitors with the full picture of different life zones of the area. Located away from the Tower in the northern section of the park, it takes hikers on a tour of the ridgetop forest, and provides fine views of the north and west faces of Devils Tower. The trail drops past sandstone cliffs into a secluded meadow, where you can often see deer and a variety of birds. Meander through a grove of deciduous trees and shrubs, into the prairie, and back to the trailhead. A few interpretive exhibits provide insight into the ecological checks and balances of the area. Joyner Ridge is a spectacular sunset hike with wonderful photographic opportunities. Allow 1 1/2 hours to complete this loop trail.

Red Beds Trail - 3 miles (4.5 km)

The Red Beds Trail is the longest trail in the monument. In a counterclockwise direction, the trail leaves the Visitor Center and takes you through pine groves and meadows with good views of the valley floor and distant hills, winding down toward the Belle Fourche River. You may choose to take a 30 minute loop down the South Side Trail through Prairie Dog Town to the campground or continue along the river via the Valley View Trail. The Red Beds Trail continues through the iron-stained bluffs known as the Red Beds and emerges into a broad prairie with good views of the Tower. From the prairie you climb back up through the forest to the Visitor Center. Allow yourself 2 hours to complete this loop trail.

Information Please

Tourism Information

Johnson County Tourism Association 684-5544
Chamber of Commerce - Buffalo 684-5544
Devils Tower Chamber of Commerce 467-5395
Gillette Convention and Visitors Bureau 686-0040
Hulett Chamber of Commerce 467-5430
Moorcroft Chamber of Commerce 756-3386
Newcastle Area Chamber of Commerce 746-2739
Chamber of Commerce - Sheridan 672-2485
Sheridan Travel and Tourism 673-7120
Sundance Chamber of Commerce 283-1000
Wright Chamber of Commerce 464-1312

Government

BLM Buffalo Field Office 684-1100
BLM Newcastle Field Office 476-6600
Gillette Project Office 686-6750
Bighorn National Forest - Tongue Ranger District 674-2600
Bighorn National Forest - Buffalo Ranger District 684-1100
Black Hills National Forest - Hell Canyon District 746-2782
Bighorn National Forest - Medicine Wheel/Paintrock Ranger District 548-6541
Black Hills National Forest - Bear Lodge Ranger District 283-1361

Car Rentals

Enterprise • Gillette 686-5655
Hertz • Gillette 686-0550
U-Save Auto Rental • Gillette 682-2815
Truck Corral Auto Rentals • Sheridan 672-7955
Enterprise • Sheridan 672-6910
Frank's Rentals • Gillette 682-5620

Hospitals

Campbell County Memorial Hospital • Gillette 682-8811
Memorial Hospital of Sheridan County • Sheridan 672-1000

Airports

Gillette 686-1042
Sheridan 674-4222

Golf

Horseshoe Mountain Golf Club • Dayton 655-9525
Powderhorn Golf Club • Sheridan 672-5323
Kendrick Golf Course • Sheridan 674-8148
Sundance Golf Club • Sundance 283-1191
Buffalo Golf Course • Buffalo 684-5266
Devils Tower Golf Club • Hulett 467-5773
Keyhole Country Club • Pine Haven 756-3775
Salt Creek Country Club • Midwest 437-6859
Newcastle Country Club • Newcastle 746-2639
Cedar Pines Golf Club • Upton 468-2847
Haycreek Golf Club • Wright 464-0747
Gillette Golf Club • Gillette 682-4774
Bell Nob Golf Course • Gillette 686-7069

Ski Areas

Antelope Butte Ski Area 655-9530

Guest Ranches

The Ranch at Ucross • Clearmont 737-2281
Diamond L Guest Ranch • Hulett 467-5236
Willow Creek Ranch at Hole-in-the-Wall • Kaycee 738-2294
Diamond Seven Bar Ranch • Alva 467-5786
Rocking Horse Ranch • Arvada 736-2488
Little Piney Ranch • Banner 683-2008
Canyon Ranch • Big Horn 674-6239
Klondike Guest Ranch • Buffalo 684-2390
Paradise Guest Ranch • Buffalo 684-7876
Dry Creek Ranch • Buffalo 684-7433
Gardner's Muddy Creek Angus • Buffalo 684-7797
Triple Three Ranch • Buffalo 684-2832
TA Ranch • Buffalo 684-5833
Sweetgrass Ranch • Buffalo 684-8851
Sky Bow Castle Ranch, Inc. • Gillette 682-3228
Heartspear Hideaway • Gillette 682-0812
7W Ranch • Hulett 878-4493
Lake Guest Ranch • Hulett 467-5908
Tumbling T Guest Ranch • Hulett 467-5625
Wyoming Edge Outfitters • Hulett 467-5588
Pine Ridge Ranch • Hulett 467-5843
Dampier Lodge • Newcastle 746-4797
Paleo Park • Newcastle 334-2270
Buffalo Creek Ranch • Recluse 682-8728
HF Bar Ranch • Saddlestring 684-2487
Spear-O-Wigwam Ranch • Sheridan 673-5543
Hawken Guest Ranch • Sundance 756-9319
Eaton's Ranch • Wolf 655-9285

Lodges and Resorts

Big Horn Mountain Lodge • Dayton 751-7599
The Ranch at Ucross • Clearmont 737-2281
Bear Lodge Resort • Dayton 752-2444
Bear Track Lodge & Outfitters • Buffalo 684-2528
South Fork Mountain Lodge • Buffalo 684-1225
Lake Stop Resort & Marina • Buffalo 684-9051
Pines Lodge • Buffalo 351-1010

Vacation Houses, Cabins & Condos

Mountain Cabin by the Stream • Story 672-8260
Wagon Box Inn, Restaurant & Cabins • Story 683-2444
Little Goose Coop Guest House • Sheridan 672-0886
Sundance Mountain Hideaway • Sundance 283-3766

Bed and Breakfasts

Four Pines B&B • Dayton 655-3764
Cameo Rose B&B • Sheridan 673-0500
The Jost House Inn B&B • Gillette 687-1240
The Bunkhouse • Aladdin 283-3542
White Horse B&B • Dayton 655-9441
EVA - Great Spirit Ranch B&B • Newcastle 746-2537
Graves B&B • Kaycee 738-2319
Historic Mansion House Inn • Buffalo 684-2218
Piney Creek Inn B&B • Story 683-2911
Bozeman Trail Inn • Big Horn 672-9288
Spahn's B&B • Big Horn 674-8150
Four Corners Country Inn • Four Corners 746-4776
Devils Tower Lodge B&B • Devils Tower 467-5267
Powder River Experience • Clearmont 758-4381
GranMa's B&B • Hulett 467-5410
Bozeman Trail B&B • Big Horn 672-2381
Double Eagles Nest B&B • Buffalo 684-8841
Empire Guest House • 756-9707
Bunkhouse Country Experience B&B • Adaddin 283-3542
Spear Ranch B&B • Big Horn 673-0079
Historic Old Stone House • Ranchester 655-9239
Greenhorn B&B • Kaycee 738-2548
Clear Creek B&B • Buffalo 684-2317
Stonehearth Inn • Buffalo 684-9446
Flying V Campbria Inn • Newcastle 746-2096
Foothills B&B • Parkman 655-9362
Kroger House B&B • Sheridan 674-6222
Meadows at the Powder Horn • Sheridan 674-9545
Ranch Willow B&B • Sheridan 674-1510
Auntie M's B&B • Sheridan 674-7035

Outfitters and Guides

Big Horn Mountain Lodge H 751-7599
Trail West Outfitters FHEG 684-5233
Just Gone Fishing F 684-2755
Bear Track Lodge & Outfitters H 684-2528
Nelson Outfitters H 672-6996
Triple Three Ranch FHE 684-2832
Simon's Hunting H 283-2664
Western Gateway Outfitters H 467-5824
P Cross Bar Ranch Trophy Hunts H 682-3994
Tumbling T Guest Ranch/Whitetail Creek Outfitters FEG 467-5625
Platt's Guides & Outfitters FHRE 327-5539
Edwards Outfitters HF 464-1518
Sagebrush Outfitters H 682-4394
Windows to the West G 682-3334
Wyoming Edge Outfitters H 467-5588
Double Rafter Cattle Drive EG 655-9463
Northern Wyoming Outfitters H 672-2515
Cloud Peak Llama Treks G 683-2548
Rimrock West Adventures H 683-2911
Baker Hunts H 750-2464
Eagle Creek Outfitters HFE 672-6520
Antelope Outfitters H 685-1132
Big Buck Outfitters H 751-0448
Bare Tracks Trophies H 896-3914
Big Horn Mountain Oufitters H 674-4691
Greer Outfitters H 687-7461
Little Bighorn Outfitters H 684-5179
North By Northwest H 684-9633
Rafter B Outfitters R 684-2793
Seven J Outfitters H 283-3443

Dining Quick Reference

Price Range refers to the average cost of a meal per person: ($) $1-$6, ($$) $7-$11, ($$$) $12-up. Cocktails: "Yes" indicates full bar; Beer (B)/Wine (W), Service: Breakfast (B), Brunch (BR), Lunch (L), Dinner (D). Businesses in bold print will have additional information under the appropriate map locator number in the body of this section.

MAP#	RESTAURANT	TYPE CUISINE	PRICE RANGE	CHILD MENU	COCKTAILS BEER WINE	MEALS SERVED	CREDIT CARDS ACCEPTED
1	Kelly's Kitchen	Family	$$	Yes		L/D	M/V
2	**Big Horn Mountain Lodge**	Family Style	$$$	Yes	Yes	B/L/D	M/V
2	**Bear Lodge Resort**	Family	$$	Yes	Yes	B/L/D	Major
2	**Aspen Creek Galleria & Restaurant by the Creek**	Sandwich/Desserts	$	No		L	V/M
2	Dayton Mercantile Restaurant	American/Pizza	$$			L/D	Major
2	Branding Iron Restaurant	Homestyle	$$	Yes		L/D/B	Major
2	Mountain Inn	Bar food	$	Yes	Yes	L/D	Major
3	**Pablo's Mexican Restaurant & Cantina**	Mexican/American	$$	Yes	Yes	L/D	Major
3	Trolleyline Restaurant	American	$$	Yes	Yes	B/L/D	Major
3	Domino's Pizza	Pizza	$$	No		L/D	Major
3	Kentucky Fried Chicken	Fast Food	$	Yes		L/D	
3	Pizza Hut	Pizza	$$	Yes	B	L/D	Major
3	Golden Steer	Steakhouse	$$$	No	Yes	D/L	Major
3	Grub Wagon Café	Family	$			B/L	
3	Silver Spur Café	Family	$/$$	Yes		B/L	
3	Kim Family Restaurant	Korean	$$			L/D	Major
3	Sutton's Tavern	Bar	$		Yes	D/L	
3	Trails End Restaurant	Family	$/$$	Yes		D/L/B	Major
3	Country Kitchen	Family	$$	Yes		L/D/B	Major
4	**Wyoming's Rib & Chop House**	Family	$$$/$$	Yes	Yes	L/D	Major
4	Sheridan Palace Restaurant	Homecooking	$	Yes		B/L	Major
4	Quizno's	Sandwiches	$	Yes		L/D	Major
4	Dairy Queen	Fast Food	$	Yes		L/D	
4	Dragon Wall	Chinese	$$	No		L/D	M/V
4	Oliver's Bar & Grill	New American	$$$	Yes	Yes	L/D	Major
4	Perkins	Family	$$	Yes		L/D/B	Major
4	Subway	Sanwiches	$	Yes		L/D	M/V
4	Subway	Sanwiches	$	Yes		L/D	M/V
4	Sanford's Grub & Pub	Brew Pub	$$/$$$	Yes	Yes	D/L	Major
4	Dutch Lunch	family	$$	Yes		L/D	
4	Main Street Diner	Family	$$	Yes		L/D/B	Major
4	Main Street Bagel	Sandwiches	$	Yes		L/B	
4	PO News Specialties & Tea Shoppe	Coffee Shop	$			L/B	
4	Paolo's Pizzeria Ristorante Vesuvio	Italian	$$/$$$	Yes	Yes	L/D	Major
4	Papa Guyos	Mexican	$$	Yes	Yes	L/D/B	
4	Bear Claw Donut Company	Coffee Shop	$	No	Yes	L/B	V/M
4	Quizno's	Sandwiches	$	Yes		L/D	V/M
4	Hardee's	Sandwiches	$	Yes		L/D/B	
4	Beaver Creek Saloon	American	$$	No	Yes	L/D	M/V
4	Java Moon Bakery & Deli	Coffee House	$$$/$	No		L/B	Major
4	Sheridan Center Restaurant	Family	$$	Yes	Yes	B/L/D	Major
4	Pony Grill	Family	$$	No	Yes	L/D	Major
4	The Mint Bar	Bar	$$		Yes	L/D	Major
5	**Holiday Inn Atrium Hotel & Conference Center**	American	$$$	Yes	Yes	B/L/D	Major
5	Arctic Circle	Burgers	$	Yes		L/D	Major
5	Blimpie/Nach-O-Fast/Ice Box	Fast Food	$	Yes		L/D	Major
5	Burger King	Fast Food	$	Yes		L/D	M/V
5	Golden China Restaurant	Chinese	$$	No		L/D	M/V
5	The Greenery Restaurant	Family	$$	No		L/D/B	Major
5	King Buffet	Buffet	$$	Yes		L/D/B	Major
5	McDonald's	Fast Food	$	Yes		L/D/B	
5	Taco Bell	Fast Food	$	Yes		L/D	
5	Taco John's/	Fast Food	$	Yes		L/D	
5	Wendy's	Fast Food	$	Yes		L/D	Major
5	Little Big Man	Family	$$		Yes	D	Major
5	Los Agaves	Mexican	$$		W/B	L/D	M/V
5	Las Margaritas	Mexican	$$	Yes	Yes	L/D	Major
5	JB's	Family	$$	Yes		L/D/B	Major
5	Scooters Bar & Grill	American	$$		Yes	L/D	M/V
5	Arby's	Fast Food	$	Yes		L/D	Major

Dining Quick Reference-Continued

Price Range refers to the average cost of a meal per person: ($) $1-$6, ($$) $7-$11, ($$$) $12-up. Cocktails: "Yes" indicates full bar; Beer (B)/Wine (W), Service: Breakfast (B), Brunch (BR), Lunch (L), Dinner (D). Businesses in bold print will have additional information under the appropriate map locator number in the body of this section.

MAP#	RESTAURANT	TYPE CUISINE	PRICE RANGE	CHILD MENU	COCKTAILS BEER WINE	MEALS SERVED	CREDIT CARDS ACCEPTED
5	Taco Bell	Mexican	$	Yes		L/D	
5	Perkins	Family	$$	Yes		L/D/B	Major
5	Subway	Sandwiches/	$	Yes		L/D	M/V
7	**Tunnel Inn Dining Room and Bar**	Fine Dining	$$/$$$	Yes	Yes	D	M/V
7	**The Waldorf A' Story**	Eclectic	$$$		W/B	L/D	M/V
7	Ladore Supper Club	Steakhouse	$$$/$$		Yes	D	Major
8	Lake Stop	American	$$	No	Yes	D/L/B	Major
9	The Virginian	Fine Dining	$$$	Yes	Yes	D	Major
10	**Historic Bozeman Crossing**	Family Dining & Steaks	$$$		Yes	L/D	Major
10	**Dash Inn Restaurant**	Fast Food	$	Yes		L/D	
10	**Colonel Bozeman Restaurant**	Eclectic	$$	Yes	Yes	L/D	M/V
10	The Breadboard Sub Shop	Sandwiches	$			L/D	M/V
10	Duffy's Bluff Café	Family	$$	Yes		D/L/B	Major
10	Hoot 'n Howl Pub	Family	$$	No	Yes	D/L	Major
10	Hardee's	Fast Food	$$/$	No		D/L/B	
10	La Crocevia	Family	$$	Yes	Yes	D/L/B	Major
10	McDonald's	Fast Food	$	No		D/L/B	
10	Pizza Hut	Pizza	$$	No	B	D/L	D
10	Subway	Sandwiches	$$/$	Yes		D/L	M/V
10	Taco Johns	Fast food	$	Yes		D/L	
10	Winchester Steak House	Fine Dining	$$$	Yes	Yes	D	Major
11	**The Sagewood Gift Store & Cafe**	Soup & Sandwich	$$			L	Major
11	The Virginian Restaurant	Fine Dining	$$$	Yes	Yes	D	Major
11	Creekside Café	Family	$$	Yes		D/L	Major
11	Deer Field Boutique & Espresso Bar Café	Coffee House	$			B/L	V/M
11	Tavern on the Creek	Homestyle cooking	$	Yes	Yes	L/D	M/V
11	Cowgirl Coffee Café	Coffee House	$	No		L/B	Major
11	Country Delight & Daylite Donuts	Family	$$	Yes		L/D	Major
11	China Garden	Chinese	$/$$	No		L/D	Major
11	Tom's Main Street Diner	Homecooked	$	No		L/B	
11	Pistol Pete's	Family	$	Yes		L/B	Major
12	Stagecoach Inn Restaurant	Western	$$	Yes	Yes	L/D/B	M/V
12	South Fork Mountain Lodge	Family	$$		Yes	B/L/D	Major
13	Domino's Pizza	Pizza	$$			L/D	Major
13	Dino's Pizza	Pizza	$$	Yes		L/D	Major
14	Red Arrow Café 7 & Bar	American	$		Yes	B/L/D	
15	Hong Kong Restaurant	Chinese	$$	No	Yes	L/D	Major
15	Long John Silver's	Fast Food	$	Yes		L/D	
15	Burger King	Fast Food	$	Yes		L/D/B	M/V
15	Sugar Shack	Family	$$	Yes		L/D	Major
15	The Great Wall	Chinese	$$	No		L/D	Major
16	**Coffee Friends**	Soup & Sandwich	$	Yes		B/L	M/V
16	Domino's Pizza	Pizza	$$	Yes	W/B	L/D	Major
16	Hardee's	Fast Food	$	No		L/D/B	
16	Pizza Hut	Pizza	$$	Yes	B	L/D	Major
16	Bailey's Sandwich Bar & Grill	American	$$	Yes	Yes	L/D	Major
16	Chophouse Restaurant	Steak/Seafood	$$$	Yes	Yes	L/D	Major
16	Subway	Sandwiches	$	Yes		L/D	M/V
16	Casa Del Rey	Mexican	$$	Yes	Yes	L/D	Major
16	Granny's Kitchen	Family	$$	Yes		L/D/B	Major
17	Lariat Café	American	$$	Yes	Yes	L/D	Major
17	Taco John's	Fast Food	$	Yes		L/D	
17	Village Inn	Family	$$	Yes		L/D/B	Major
17	Tully's-to-Go	Fast Food	$	No		B/L/D	Major
17	Boot Hill Nightclub	American	$$$	Yes	Yes	D	Major
17	Mona's Café	Mexican	$$	Yes	B	L/D	M/V
17	Perkin's	Family	$$	Yes		L/D/B	Major
18	**Polar Bear Frozen Yogurt/Espresso Cyber Café**	Soup & Sandwich	$			B/L	
18	Pizza Etc.	Pizza	$$	Yes		L/D	Major
18	Prime Rib Restaurant	Prime Rib	$$$	No	Yes	L/D	Major

Dining Quick Reference-Continued

Price Range refers to the average cost of a meal per person: ($) $1-$6, ($$) $7-$11, ($$$) $12-up. Cocktails: "Yes" indicates full bar; Beer (B)/Wine (W), Service: Breakfast (B), Brunch (BR), Lunch (L), Dinner (D). Businesses in bold print will have additional information under the appropriate map locator number in the body of this section.

MAP#	RESTAURANT	TYPE CUISINE	PRICE RANGE	CHILD MENU	COCKTAILS BEER WINE	MEALS SERVED	CREDIT CARDS ACCEPTED
18	Breanna's Bakery	Bakery/Sandwiches	$	Yes		L/B	
18	Main Bagel Co.	Deli	$	No		B/L	
19	**Little Giant Café**	Home Cooking	$	Yes		B/L	Major
19	**Clarion Western Plaza Inn**	Family	$$$/$$	Yes	Yes	B/D/L	Major
19	Godfather's Pizza	Pizza	$$	Yes	B	L/D	Major
19	Las Margaritas	Mexican	$$	Yes	Yes	L/D	Major
19	Papa Murphy's Pizza	Pizza	$$	No		L/D	
19	Perkin's	Family	$$	Yes		L/D/B	Major
19	Taco Bell	Fast Food	$	Yes		L/D	
19	Wendy's	Fast Food	$	Yes		L/D	Major
19	China Buffet	Chinese	$$	Yes		L/D	Major
19	Dairy Queen	Fast Food	$	Yes		L/D	
19	Applebee's	American	$$	Yes	Yes	L/D	Major
19	Arby's	Fast Food		Yes		L/D	Major
19	Blimpie's	Sandwiches	$	Yes		L/D	Major
19	Packard's Grill	Family	$$	No	Yes	B/D/L	Major
19	Subway	Sandwiches	$	Yes		L/D	M/V
19	Quizno's Subs	Sandwiches	$	Yes		L/D	Major
19	Burger King	Fast Food	$	Yes		L/D/B	M/V
19	Ole's Pizza	Pizza	$$	Yes	B	L/D	Major
19	Flying J Travel Plaza	Family	$$			B/L/D	Major
19	Countryside Café	Family	$	Yes		L/B	
19	Kentucky Fried Chicken	fast Food	$$	Yes		L/D	
19	Tully's-to-Go	Fast Food	$	No		B/L/D	Major
19	Golden Corral	Family	$$	Yes		L/D	Major
19	Lula Bell Coffee Shop	Family	$$	Yes		L/D/B	
19	Humphrey's Bar & Grill	Eclectic	$$/$$$	Yes	Yes	D/L	Major
21	Ponderosa Café	Steakhouse	$$	Yes	Yes	D/L/B	Major
22	Aladdin Cafe	Family	$$	Yes	B/W	B/L	M/V
23	Sand Creek Trading Post Steakhouse	Steakhouse	$$	Yes	Yes	D	Major
24	**Aro Restaurant**	Family	$$		Yes	B/L/D	Major
24	Flo's Place Restaurant	American	$$	Yes		B/L/D	M/V
24	Subway	Sandwiches	$	Yes		L/D	M/V
24	Higbee's Restaurant	Family	$	Yes	Yes	B/L/D	M/V
24	Log Cabin Café	Family	$$	Yes		B/L/D	Major
25	**Devils Tower Trading Post**	Family	$	Yes		L/D	Major
25	Crook Country Saloon & Dining Emporium	Steakhouse	$$	Yes	Yes	L/D	M/V
26	Anchor Bar	Bar	$	No	Yes	L/D	M/V
26	Haven Bar & Grill Restaurant	Family	$$	Yes	Yes	L/D/B	M/V
27	**Taco Time**	Mexican	$	Yes		L/D	D/M/V
27	**Subway**	Sandwiches/	$	Yes		L/D	M/V
27	**Donna's Diner**	Family	$$	Yes	Yes	D/L/B	Major
27	Bryan's Place	American	$$		Yes	D/L	
27	Rozet Bar & Grill	American	$$		Yes	L/D	V/M
27	Hub Café	Family	$			L/D	V/M
28	Cowgirl's Subs	Sandwiches	$	Yes		L/D	M/V
28	Penny's Diner	Family	$$			L/D	
28	Western Café	American	$$			L/D/B	
29	Hi-16 Drive In Restaurant	Family	$	Yes		L/D	
29	Old Mill Inn Restaurant	Family	$	Yes	Yes	L/D/B	
30	Howdy Drive In	Family	$	Yes		L/D	
30	The Hop Restaurant	Family	$$	Yes		L/D/B	Major
30	Taco John's	Fast Food	$	Yes			
30	Main Street Diner	American				L/D/B	
31	Subway	Sandwiches	$	Yes		L/D	M/V
31	Fountain Motor Inn & Crystal Campground	Family	$$		Yes	B/L/D	Major
31	Flying V Cambria Inn & RV Campground	Family	$$/$$$	Yes	Yes	D	Major
31	Pizza Hut	Pizza	$	Yes			
31	Pizza Barn	Pizza	$			D/L	M/V
32	Flying V Restaurant & Bar	Family	$$	Yes	Yes	D	
34	Buckhorn Bar & Grill	American	$$	No	Yes	D/L	Major

Dining Quick Reference-Continued

Price Range refers to the average cost of a meal per person: ($) $1-$6, ($$) $7-$11, ($$$) $12-up. Cocktails: "Yes" indicates full bar; Beer (B)/Wine (W), Service: Breakfast (B), Brunch (BR), Lunch (L), Dinner (D). Businesses in bold print will have additional information under the appropriate map locator number in the body of this section.

MAP#	RESTAURANT	TYPE CUISINE	PRICE RANGE	CHILD MENU	COCKTAILS BEER WINE	MEALS SERVED	CREDIT CARDS ACCEPTED
36	Little Thunder Café	American	$$	Yes		D/L/B	M/V
36	Subway	Sandwiches	$	Yes		L/D	M/V
36	Wright Slice	Pizza	$$			L/D	Major
36	Reno Junction Café	Family	$$	Yes		D/L	Major
37	Edgerton Café	Family	$$	Yes		B/L/D	V
37	Whiners	Family	$$	Yes		L/D	Major
38	**Invasion Bar & Restaurant**	Family	$$	Yes	Yes		M/V
38	Kaycee Sinclair Grab-n'-Dash	Fast Food	$	Yes		B/L/D	Major
38	On the Run	Fast Food	$	Yes		B/L/D	Major

Motel Quick Reference

Price Range: ($) Under $40 ; ($$) $40-$60; ($$$) $60-$80, ($$$$) Over $80. Pets [check with the motel for specific policies] (P), Dining (D), Lounge (L), Disabled Access (DA), Full Breakfast (FB), Cont. Breakfast (CB), Indoor Pool (IP), Outdoor Pool (OP), Hot Tub (HT), Sauna (S), Refrigerator (R), Microwave (M) (Microwave and Refrigerator indicated only if in majority of rooms), Kitchenette (K). All Wyoming area codes are 307.

MAP #	HOTEL	PHONE	NUMBER ROOMS	PRICE RANGE	BREAKFAST	POOL/ HOT TUB SAUNA	NON SMOKE ROOMS	OTHER AMENITIES	CREDIT CARDS
1	**Ranchester Western Motel**	655-2212	18	$$			Yes	P	
1	Eaton's Ranch	655-9285		$$$/$$$$	FB		Yes		V/M/D
1	Western Ranchester Motel	655-2212	18	$		OP	Yes		Major
2	**Big Horn Mountain Lodge**	751-7599	16	$$$/$$$$				P/D/L/DA/K	M/V
2	**Bear Lodge Resort**	752-2444	30	$$$		HT/IP	Yes	DA	Major
2	**Four Pines Bed & Breakfast**	655-3764	3	$$$	FB		Yes	P	Major
2	Wigwam Motel	587-3861	14	$				K	D/M/V
2	Foothills Motel & Campgrounds	655-2547	10	$			Yes	P/K	
3	BW Sheridan Center	674-7421	138	$$$		HT/IP/OP	Yes	P/D/L/R	Major
3	Alamo Motel	672-2455	19	$$			Yes	P	M/V
3	Aspen Inn	674-9064	24	$$			Yes	P/K	Major
3	Bramble Motel & RV Park	674-4902	15	$$			Yes	P/K	Major
3	Super Saver Inn	672-0471	37				Yes	P	V/M
3	Trails End Motel	672-2477	84	$/$$$		IP	Yes	P/K/D/L	Major
3	Evergreen Inn	672-9757	39	$$		HT	Yes	M/R/P	Major
3	Guest House Motel	674-7496	44	$$$			Yes	P	Major
3	Stage Stop Motel	672-3459	18	$			No	P/K	
3	Sundown Motel	672-2439	23	$$		OP		K/P	Major
3	Super 8 - Sheridan	672-9725	39	$$			Yes	P	Major
4	**Cameo Rose Bed & Breakfast**	673-0500	3		FB				M/V
5	**Holiday Inn Atrium Hotel & Conference Center**	672-8931	212	$$$		IP/HT/S	Yes	P/L/D/DA	Major
5	**Days Inn - Sheridan**	672-2888	47	$$/$$$/$$$$	CB	IP	Yes	DA	Major
5	Historic Mill Inn	672-6401	45	$$$	CB				Major
5	Apple Tree Inn	672-2428	24	$$$		S	Yes	P	Major
5	Comfort Inn	672-5098	61	$$$$	CB	HT	Yes	P	Major
5	Parkway Motel	674-7259	14	$$			Yes	K/P	Major
5	Rock Trim Motel	672-2464	18	$$/$				K/P	M/V
5	Triangle Motel	674-8031	7	$				P/K	
6	Spahn's Bed & Breakfast	674-8150							
6	Days Inn	234-9125	59	$$		OP	Yes	P/DA	Major
6	Hampton Inn	235-6668	122	$$$	CB	OP	Yes		Major
7	**Wagon Box Inn**	683-2120	6	$$$		HT	Yes	P	D/M/V
7	**Mountain Cabin by the Stream**	672-8260	1	$$$$			Yes	K	
10	**Historic Bozeman Crossing Super 8**	684-2531	48	$$	CB		Yes	P/D/L/DA	Major
10	**Motel 6 of Buffalo**	684-7000	44	$$			Yes	DA/P	Major
10	**Comfort Inn Buffalo**	684-9564	41	$$$	CB	HT	Yes	P	Major
10	EconoLodge	684-2219	44	$$			Yes	P/DA	M/V
10	Wyoming Motel	684-5505	27	$$		IP		K/P	Major
10	Best Western Crossroads Inn	684-2256	60	$$$		OP/HT	Yes	D/L/DA	Major

Motel Quick Reference-Continued

Price Range: ($) Under $40 ; ($$) $40-$60; ($$$) $60-$80, ($$$$) Over $80. Pets [check with the motel for specific policies] (P), Dining (D), Lounge (L), Disabled Access (DA), Full Breakfast (FB), Cont. Breakfast (CB), Indoor Pool (IP), Outdoor Pool (OP), Hot Tub (HT), Sauna (S), Refrigerator (R), Microwave (M) (Microwave and Refrigerator indicated only if in majority of rooms), Kitchenette (K). All Wyoming area codes are 307.

MAP #	HOTEL	PHONE	NUMBER ROOMS	PRICE RANGE	BREAKFAST	POOL/ HOT TUB SAUNA	NON SMOKE ROOMS	OTHER AMENITIES	CREDIT CARDS
11	The Occidental Hotel & The Virginian Restaurant	684-0451	14	$$$$	CB		Yes	P/D/L/K	Major
11	Blue Gables Motel	684-2574	17	$$		OP	Yes	P/L/D/K	Major
11	Big Horn Motel	684-7822	18	$$					Major
11	Historic Mansion House Inn	684-2218	18	$$$	CB		Yes		Major
12	**Z-Bar Motel**	684-5535							
12	Arrowhead Motel	684-9453	13	$$/$	CB		Yes	DA/K	M/V
12	Cowboy Town Motel	684-0603	19	$$				L/P/K	M/V
12	Mountain View Motel & Campground	684-2881	13	$$				P/K	
14	**The Ranch at Ucross**	737-2281							
14	Powder River Experience	758-4381							
15	Super 8 Motel	682-8078	60	$$	CB	IP	Yes	P/DA	Major
15	Best Western Tower West Lodge	686-2210	189	$$$		IP/HT	Yes	DA/P/R/M	Major
15	Motel 6	686-8600	74	$$		HT/S	Yes	DA/P	Major
15	Budget Inn Express	686-1989	50	$$	CB	HT/S/IP	Yes	DA/P	Major
16	Circle L Motel	682-9375	32	$			Yes	P	Major
16	Arrowhead Motel	686-0909	32	$			Yes	P/DA/K	Major
16	Hampton Inn	686-2000	60	$$	CB	IP/HT	Yes	DA	Major
16	Mustang Motel	682-4784	30	$$	CB		Yes	P	Major
17	**National 9 Inn**	682-5111	80	$$		OP	Yes	P/D/L	Major
17	Quality Inn	682-2616	62	$$	CB	IP/HT	Yes		Major
17	Econolodge Motel	682-4757	62	$$			Yes	P	Major
18	America's Best Value Inn	682-9341	76	$$	CB	HT/OP	Yes	DA/P	Major
19	**Clarion Western Plaza Inn**	686-3000	159	$$$		S/HT	Yes	P/D/L/DA/K	
19	**The Jost House Inn Bed & Breakfast**	687-1240	3	$$/$$$/$$$$	FB		Yes	P	Major
19	Holiday Inn Express	686-9576	83	$$/$$$	CB	IP/HT	Yes	DA/P	Major
19	Wingate Inn	685-2700	84	$$$$	CB	IP/HT	Yes	DA/P/R/M/K	Major
19	Days Inn	682-3999	130	$$$			Yes	P	Major
19	Holiday Inn	686-3000	158	$$$		IP	Yes	L/D/DA/P	Major
21	**Diamond L Guest Ranch**	467-5236							
21	Hulett Motel	467-5220	12	$$			Yes	L/P	Major
21	Pioneer Motel	467-5656	15	$$			Yes	L/P/K	Major
22	The Bunkhouse	283-3542		$$$	FB		Yes		Major
24	Arrowhead Motel, Budget Host	283-3307	12	$$			Yes		Major
24	Bear Lodge Motel	283-1611	37	$$			Yes	P	Major
24	Dean's Pineview Motel	283-2262	12	$			Yes	P/K	M/V
24	Sundance Mountain Inn	283-3737	42	$$		IP	No	P	Major
26	Empire Guest House	756-9707							
27	**Wyoming Motel & Camping Park**	756-3452	4	$			Yes	M/R/P	M/V
27	Cozy Motel	756-3486	23	$$				P	Major
27	Rangeland Court Motel & RV Park	756-3595	10	$					M/V
27	Keyhole Marina, Motel, & RV Park	756-9529	6	$				P	V/M
27	Moorcroft Motel	756-3411	30	$$/$$$				K/P	Major
28	Weston Inn	468-2401	24	$$			No	P	Major
28	Upton Motel	468-9282	13	$$				K/P	
29	Auto-Inn Motel & RV Park	746-2734							
29	Sundowner Inn	746-2796	35	$		IP	Yes	P/K	Major
29	Roadside Motel	746-9640	10	$			Yes	R/M/P	V/M
30	Stardust Motel	746-4719	16	$			Yes	P/K	M/V
31	**Sage Motel**	746-2724	12	$$/$			Yes	P/R/M	Major
31	Fountain Motor Inn	746-4426	86	$$		OP		P/D/L/K	Major
31	Hilltop Motel	746-4494	15	$$			Yes	P/R/M/K	Major
31	Mallo Camp & Motel	746-4094	16	$$/$			Yes	K/P	M/V
31	Morgan's Motel	746-2715	9	$$/$			Yes	P	M/V
31	Pines Motel	746-4334	12	$$			Yes	P/K	Major
36	National 9 Inn	464-1510	27	$$			Yes	P	Major
37	Teapot Motor Lodge	437-6541	20	$				P	Major
38	**Willow Creek Ranch at Hole-in-the-Wall**	738-2294							
38	Kaycee Bunkhouse	738-2213	4	$$			Yes	P	Major
38	Cassidy Inn Motel	738-2250	18	$			Yes	P	Major
38	Siesta Motel Country Inn	738-2291	13	$$			Yes	D/P	M/V
38	Riverside Inn	738-2659	19	$$				P	Major

NOTES:

Section 4

Southwest Area

Including Evanston, Kemmerer, Green River and Rock Springs

The Black's Fork River south of Green River

1 *No services*

I-80 Exit 111

2 *Gas, Food, Lodging*

Rock Springs

Pop. 18,708, Elev. 6,271

As you approach Rock Springs, you can almost imagine travelers bouncing along the Overland Stage route toward the stage station that was the beginning of this southwestern Wyoming town. Rock Springs derives its name from a large spring that flowed from the rocks. The springs disappeared when the coalmine operations interrupted the underground flow but a monument now commemorates the location.

In the mid 1850s, US Army Captain Howard Stansbury and his party stopped at Rock Springs and made detailed reports of the large coal outcroppings. Days later, at Salt Wells to the east of Rock Springs, the Captain's party learned from trappers that the Blair Brothers were working on the coal outcroppings in the site now known as Blairtown.

During August, 1868, the Union Pacific Railroad was completed to Rock Springs, and from that time on Rock Springs was the Central Terminal for the Stock herds being shipped to market on that side of the state. By 1875, the railroad was hauling supplies for the army, settlers had arrived, and the coalmines were working constantly.

Robert Parker ("Butch" Cassidy) spent some of his youth in Rock Springs, working in some butcher shops. It is believed that is how he got his nickname.

Rock Springs still has the largest coal reserves west of the Mississippi River. Rock Springs is also the center of the rapidly growing oil and gas production industry, power plant development, and the center of mineral resource development program that is marked by the continual expansion of the trona industry. Sweetwater County has been designated as the "Trona Capitol of the World".

As the most industrialized county in Wyoming, over half of the workforce in Rock Springs is employed by industry, principally mining, petroleum, power generation and related services. The coal mining industry continues to produce over ten million tons of coal annually, and the trona mines and plants are one of America's most important natural resources, producing approximately fifteen million tons of trona per year. The five plants in the area produce 95% of the world's natural soda ash. Sweetwater County's trona deposit is large enough to produce at the same rate for the next 6000 years.

The nearby Jim Bridger Power Plant is the largest electric generating plant in Wyoming. Located thirty-two miles east of Rock Springs, it has a generating capacity of 2000 megawatts. The plant is a coal-fired steam turbine. The county is also the largest producer of natural gas in the state. Some eleven billion cubic feet of gas can be produced annually.

Much of the history of Rock Springs is based on its multi-ethnic influence. Rock Springs was once known as the "Melting Pot" of the West, with over 57 nationalities having lived here. Most came to work in the coalmines, and later in the oil and gas fields. Although this was once an uneasy mixture (as with the Chinese Massacre of 1885), the town now embraces its cultural diversity.

Information courtesy of Rock Springs Chamber of Commerce

T Camp Pilot Butte

633 Brider in Rock Springs

Workers were encouraged by mining companies to migrate to Rock Springs. At one time, more than 56 different nationalities were represented, resulting in Rock Springs being named the "melting pot of Wyoming". The need for more workers brought Chinese contract laborers to work in the mines in 1875. This precipitated the Chinese Massacre of 1885 when white miners chased the Chinese out of town and burned Chinatown. Soldiers were sent to establish Camp Pilot Butte in the center of Rock Springs and were stationed there until 1898 when the Spanish American War broke out. The officers' quarters and buildings have been destroyed but the enlisted men's barracks now serve as a Catholic School.

T Weidner Wildlife Exhibit

Western Wyoming Community College.
382-1600

Situated on the Western Wyoming Community College Campus, this new museum showcases a collection of more than 100 wildlife mounts from around the world. Exhibits include an elephant, hipopotamus, zebra, lion, alligator, several bears, and the elusive jackalope. Open Monday and Wednesday, 10 a.m. to-1 p.m. and Thursdays 1 p.m. to 4 p.m. Admission is free.

Rock Springs

	Jan	Feb	March	April	May	June	July	Aug	Sep	Oct	Nov	Dec	Annual
Average Max. Temperature (F)	31.7	36.9	43.7	55.3	66.5	77.1	86.4	83.7	73.5	61.0	44.0	34.2	57.8
Average Min. Temperature (F)	10.6	15.2	20.7	28.8	37.5	45.3	51.8	49.5	40.0	30.6	20.7	13.4	30.3
Average Total Precipitation (in.)	0.44	0.42	0.59	0.96	1.29	1.07	0.56	0.66	0.76	0.74	0.53	0.48	8.51
Average Total SnowFall (in.)	8.0	6.6	7.1	6.2	1.9	0.1	0.0	0.0	0.6	3.8	6.7	8.2	49.2
Average Snow Depth (in.)	1	1	0	0	0	0	0	0	0	0	0	1	0

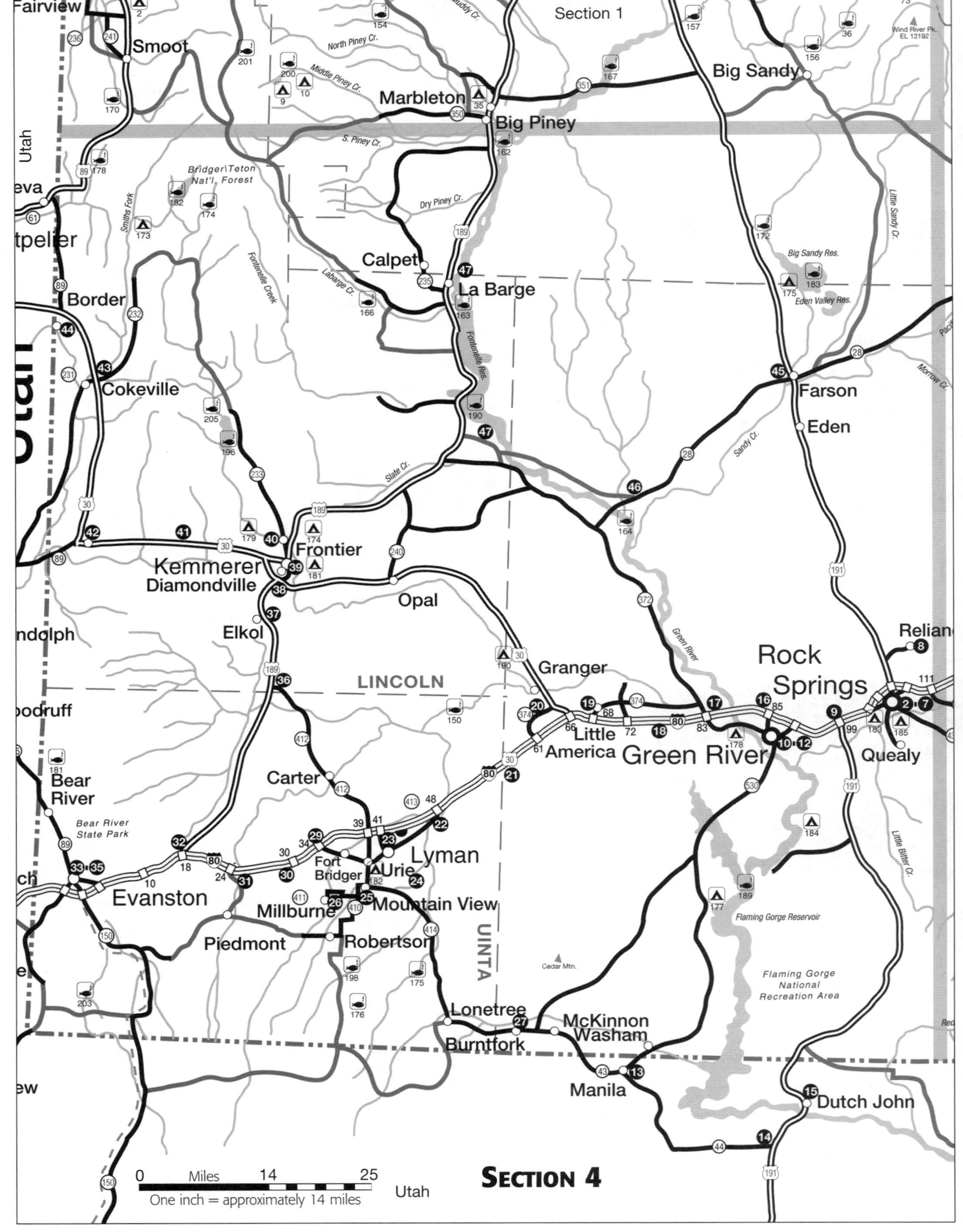
Section 1
Fairview
Smoot
Marbleton
Big Piney
Big Sandy
Calpet
La Barge
Border
Cokeville
Farson
Eden
Frontier
Kemmerer
Diamondville
Opal
Elkol
Granger
LINCOLN
Rock Springs
Little America
Green River
Quealy
Carter
Bear River
Bear River State Park
Lyman
Fort Bridger
Urie
Evanston
Millburne
Mountain View
Piedmont
Robertson
UINTA
Flaming Gorge Reservoir
Flaming Gorge National Recreation Area
Lonetree
McKinnon
Washam
Burntfork
Manila
Dutch John
Utah
Bridger\Teton Nat'l. Forest
Fontenelle Creek
Fontenelle Res.
Green River
Big Sandy Res.
Eden Valley Res.
Little Sandy Cr.
Little Bitter Cr.
Sandy Cr.
State Cr.
Dry Piney Cr.
North Piney Cr.
Middle Piney Cr.
S. Piney Cr.
Labarge Cr.
Smiths Fork
Muddy Cr.
Morrow Cr.
Wind River Pk. EL 13192
Cedar Mtn.
0 Miles 14 25
One inch = approximately 14 miles
SECTION 4

Legend

- Locator number (matches numeric listing in section)
- Campsite (number matches number in campsite chart)
- Fishing Site (number matches number in fishing chart)
- Rest stop
- Interstate
- U.S. Highway
- Paved State or County Road
- Gravel/unpaved road

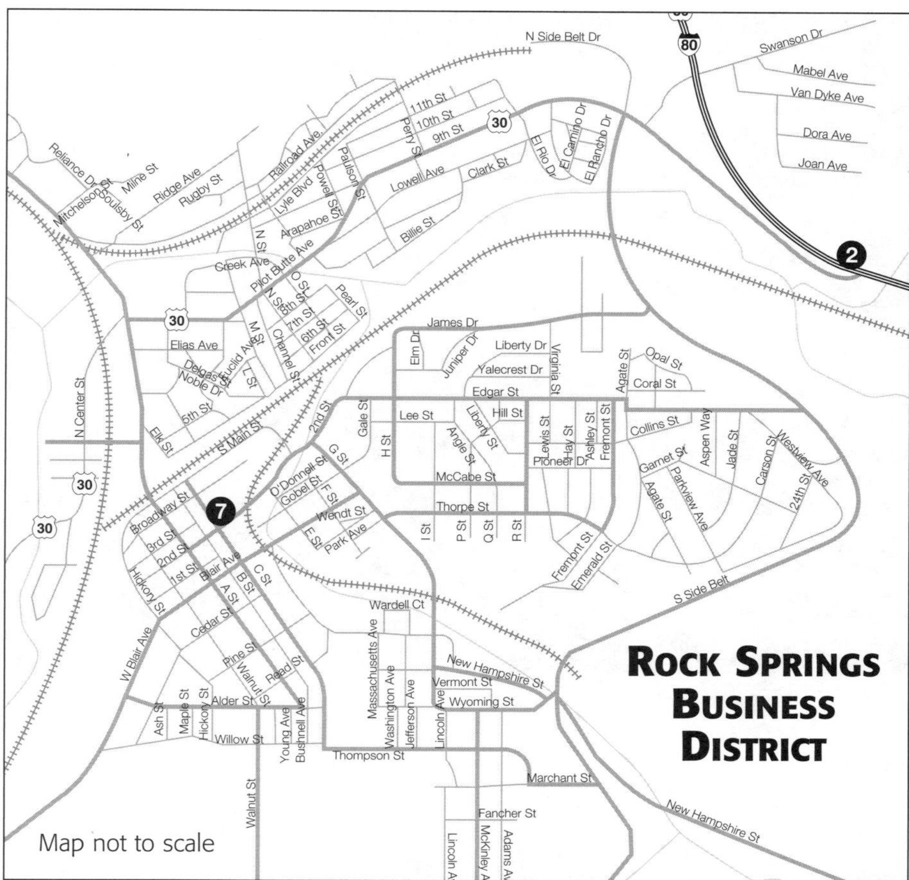

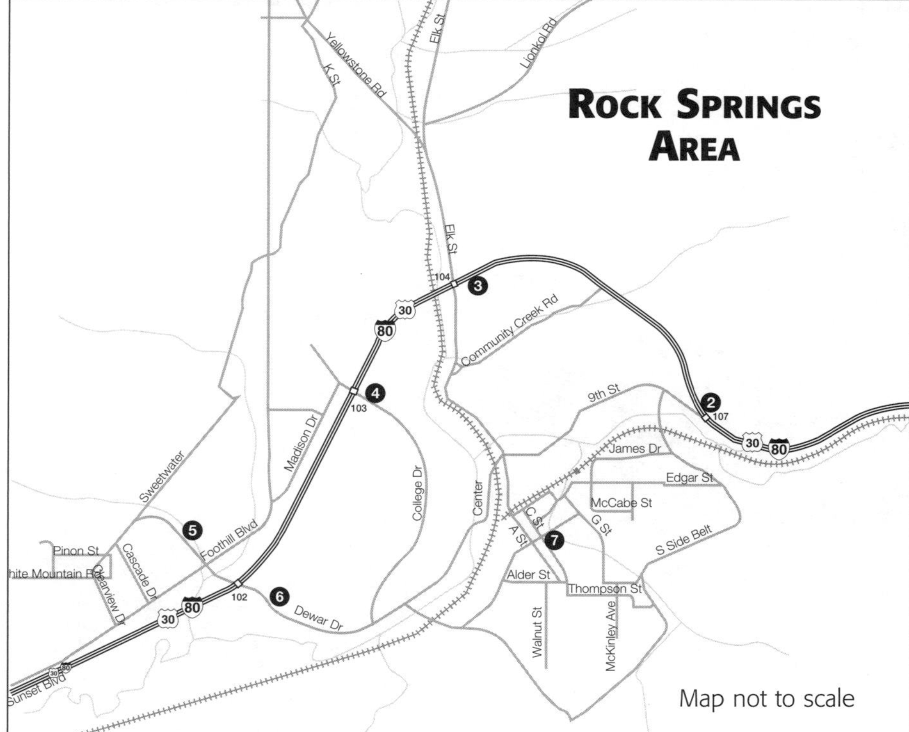

T Sweetwater Community Fine Arts Center
400 C Street in Rock Springs. 362-6212

This collection by local artists originated in 1939 and now numbers over 300 works of art, acclaimed the best owned by an American High School. The collection was featured in Time Magazine in 1952. The permanent collection includes original paintings by such notables as Norman Rockwell, Grandma Moses, Rafino Tamayo, and Rafael Soyer, to name a few. The facility has areas for traveling exhibits, sculptures and is used as a community events center. Open Monday through Thursday and on alternating Fridays and Saturdays.

3 *Gas, Food, Lodging*

I-80 Exit 103

4 *Gas*

T Western Wyoming Community College Art Gallery
2500 College Drive in Rock Springs. 382-1600

This gallery features regional and national artists representing a great variety of mediums. It features a semiannual art student exhibit and several ceramic exhibitions. Open Monday through Friday and admission is free.

T Western Wyoming Community College Natural History Museum and Archeological Services
At Western Wyoming Community College. 382-1666

The Museum of Natural History offers artifacts reflecting the archeology, geology, and natural history of the region. Several Wyoming dinosaur skeletons and fossils are displayed for public viewing throughout the campus facility.

T Rock Springs Family Recreation Center
3900 Sweetwater Drive in Rock Springs. 352-1440

Recreation facility for residents and visitors with swimming pool, ice arena, and fitness facilities. Open Monday through Saturday.

M Western Wyoming Community College
2500 College Drive in Rock Springs

Western Wyoming Community College, the fifth of seven community colleges in Wyoming, was established in the Fall of 1959 with forty students enrolled for college credit courses. Student numbers were over 5,000 in 2002. These figures include all students of varying ages and interests, enrolled in the credit, noncredit and extension programs. Western Wyoming Community College is located in Rock Springs and has an extended

Western Wyoming Community College.

campus center in Green River, Sweetwater County, Wyoming. The campus consists of 435 acres with modern facilities and equipment. Western Wyoming Community College envisions providing lifelong learning opportunities in an environment characterized by a commitment to quality and success.

L Ramada Limited

2717 Dewar Drive, Exit 102 in Rock Springs. 363-1770 or toll free at 800-272-6232 or Reservations at 888-307-7890

5 *Gas, Food Lodging*

I-80 Exit 102 North

6 *Gas, Food, Lodging*

F JB's Restaurant

1313 Dewar Drive in Rock Springs. 383-2727

JB's Restaurant is located in Rock Springs and Evanston. Visitors to the area love it as much as local residents do. The full service menu will please the entire family for breakfast, lunch or dinner. The breakfast buffet is a perennial favorite. A soup and salad bar is available for lunch and dinner to compliment any meal. The desserts are fabulous. Try a slice of pie from a great selection of custards, creams, and cheesecakes. The Volcano Lava cake is a big hit–chocolate cake filled with hot fudge, heated, and topped with ice cream. They are open 6 a.m. to 11 p.m. and until midnight Friday and Saturday.

7 *Food, Lodging*

T Union Pacific Freight Station

Downtown Rock Springs

The 1917 freight station serviced the Rock Springs coal field mines, which had a daily output of 2,000 tons of coal and operated for nearly forty years. It was the largest mine ever operating through one opening. Additions to the original freight station closed the street, and the railroad comany constructed a steel pedestrian viaduct above the tracks so residents could cross eight tracks dividing the town. Walk along the grass toward the train depot, and you'll see the dates and names inscribed near the tops of the buildings across the street.

T Rock Springs Historical Museum

201 B Street in downtown Rock Springs. 362-3138

Located in the 1894-95 City Hall, the most imposing exhibit of the museum, the building itself, houses a variety of long term and temporary exhibits. Restored in 1991, the building offers a sense of 1890s Rock Springs' pride at its growth and survival along the major East-West corridor. The history on display covers cowboys, outlaws, railroading, ethnic diversity, labor issues and, underneath it all, coal. Coal brought the Union Pacific Railroad, which, in turn, imported a great variety of workers. The museum is open year round, Monday through Saturday. Call for hours. Admission is free.

T Children's Discovery Foundation

501 S. Main Street (the Train Depot) in Rock Springs. 362-8306

The Children's Discovery Foundation promotes learning through hands-on or interactive activities in their exhibits at the Discovery Station. Open on Saturdays 10 a.m. to 4 p.m. and other times by appointment.

8 *Np servoces*

Reliance

Pop. 334, Elev. 6,510

The dependability of the coalmines established here in the 1870s gave rise to this name. Reliance was the original site of Western Wyoming Community College when it opened in 1958. It was later moved to Rock Springs.

H The Reliance Tipple

Five miles north of Rock Springs on Highway 191 at Reliance

This is one of only two such structures left in the state. The tipple was used to sort and grade coal and load it on to rail cars. The tipple is open during daylight hours. Interpretive signs are present for a self guided walking tour. The tipple is handicapped accessible.

It was in 1910 that coal mine operations began at Reliance. These mines were opened by the coal mining company of the Union Pacific Railroad. Here, where the tipple now stands, the first coal loading facility was constructed in 1912. The stone foundations for the earlier wooden tipple are still evident east of the metal tipple. The tipple you see today was completed in 1936 and still contains machinery from when it was in operation. Few tipples remain from the era when coal was king. Modern mining methods and a shift to gasoline and diesel powered locomotives made underground coal mining too expensive to compete in the energy market while using the technology of the early twentieth century. Tipples such as this one were torn down and the equipment sold as salvage. In Wyoming, only the Reliance tipple remains as an example of a large industrial coal handling facility. It is a silent marker of a by-gone age and serves as a tribute to the min-

Ashley National Forest

Forest Facts

- 1,384,132 National Forest System Acres (1,287,909 located in Utah, 96,223 in Wyoming)
- Of the total acres: 276,175 are High Uintas Wilderness (180,530 additional acres of High Uintas Wilderness are located on the Wasatch/Cache National Forest)
- Elevations range from 6,000 feet to over 13,500 feet.
- Remarkable features include Kings Peak (highest peak in Utah), Flaming Gorge National Recreation Area, Flaming Gorge-Uintas National Scenic Byway, The Green River Corridor (a world-class blue ribbon fisheries)

The Ashley National Forest, with headquarters in Vernal Vernal, Utah, comprises 1.3 million acres located in the northeastern portion of Utah and southwestern portion of Wyoming. National Forest System lands are located in three major areas: the northern and southern slopes of the Uinta Mountains, the Wyoming Basin, and the Tavaputs Plateau.

The Ashley National Forest is bordered by the Uintah and Ouray Ute Indian Reservation, the Uinta and Wasatch-Cache National Forests, private property, and lands administered by the Bureau of Land Management and State of Utah. Dinosaur National Monument is located approximately 10 miles east of the Forest.

The Ashley National Forest was established by President Theodore Roosevelt in 1908. Its forest and range lands are protected and managed to ensure timber, grazing, minerals, water, and outdoor recreation for the American people.

The vast Uinta Mountains watershed within the Forest boundary provides vital water supplies for power, industry, farm, and city use in Utah, Nevada, Wyoming, and California. Sheep, cattle, and horses graze under permit on over a half million acres of the Forest each season. Timber is managed in harmony with other resources to insure a continuing supply and a quality environment. Over 2.5 million visitors come to the Forest each year to participate in outstanding outdoor recreation activities, such as boating, fishing, camping, hiking, backpacking, horseback riding, cross-country skiing, and snowmobiling.

Forest landscape ranges from high desert country to high mountain areas. The elevation varies from a low of 6,000 feet to a high of 13,528 feet above sea level at the summit of Kings Peak.

Topographical diversity and intensive land management has served to protect the visual quality on the Forest. The existing vegetation patterns and the geological formations further add to the aesthetic value. The Forest boundaries include places such as the Sheep Creek Geological Area, the High Uinta Wilderness area, the Green River, and the Flaming Gorge National Recreation Area.

History of the Ashley National Forest

The history of the Ashley National Forest is a colorful parade of trappers, explorers, outlaws, and settlers. Their deeds and lives create a colorful and interesting picture in the development of this area.

Dominquez and Escalante, Spanish explorers, were probably the first white men to set foot in the Uintah Basin. They entered the Basin in 1776, traveling from Santa Fe, New Mexico, attempting to find a shorter route to Monterey, California. They did not cross the Uinta Mountains, but proceeded westerly across the south face of the Uinta Mountains, up the Strawberry River and into Utah Valley.

In 1822, Major Andrew Henry, a partner of General W. H. Ashley who organized a fur company, pushed his way through with a party of trappers from St. Louis, Missouri, up the Missouri River to the mouth of the Yellowstone River. Here he established a post and spent the winter of 1822-23. In the spring he came to the point where a stream, which now bears his name, enters the Green River. Here he was able to obtain a rich harvest of pelts. He then headed back to St. Louis.

The following year, General W.H. Ashley directed the expedition and arrived on the banks of the Green River in the spring of 1825. At this point, he dispatched his men in different directions. All were to attend his "general rendezvous" on the Green River on July 10.

Ashley, with six of his men, started down the river in boats constructed from buffalo hides and local timber on April 21, 1825. On Saturday May 2, Ashley wrote "we entered between the walls of this range of mountains, which approach at this point to the waters edge on either side of the river and rise almost perpendicular to an immense height." Thus, the explorers passed through the Flaming Gorge, the first recorded entry of white men into the area now included in the Ashley National Forest. Later as they were passing through Red Canyon, they found it necessary to portage their boats around some falls, "produced from large fragments of rock which had fallen from the wall and settled in the river." From this incident, "Ashley Falls" received its name.

General Ashley and his party pushed on down the river to the point near where Green River, Utah is now located apparently seeking an outlet for his fur business to the Gulf of Mexico. At this place he was finally convinced by the Indians that the Green River emptied into the western ocean. He secured horses from the Indians and worked back north to and across the Uinta Mountains, "through a maze of little streams and valleys over the top of the Uintas near what is now called "Mount Baldy" (Marsh Peak)".

It has been said that "the written history of the country west of the Rockies where Americans made their first stand for possession begins with a single name and a date painted high on a mountain precipice." The name is "Ashley" and the date is "1825". The precipice on which W. H. Ashley wrote his name overhung a river flowing through eastern Utah. The name and date are now covered by waters of the Flaming Gorge Reservoir.

Ashley National Forest, Ashley Creek, and Ashley Valley received their names from this early explorer. The imprint of Ashley's party is still evident in the name Bridger Valley named for Jim Bridger; David Jackson for which Jackson Hole is named; Etienne Provost, for which Provo River and the City of Provo is named; and William Sublette for which Sublette County, Wyoming was named.

In the year 1828, four white men, Toopeechee Reed, Jim Reed, Dennis Julien and Augustus Archambeaux, French traders from Kentucky, entered the Uintah Basin and set up a trading post near a spring of water just south and east of the present settlement of Whiterocks. They brought in the first butcher knives, coffee beans, and other articles traded to the Indians for fur.

Antoine Rubidoux entered the Basin in 1832. When he decided to build his fort, Reed and others sold out and eventually left the Basin. Fort Rubidoux, a center for fur traders, had a life of 12 years. In 1844, this fort was burned to the ground. Antoine Rubidoux and a guide were away from the fort at the time and escaped.

In 1861, all the valley of the Uinta River was set aside as an Indian Reservation. The reservation extended to the crest of the mountains.

The first settlement of the Uinta Basin took place in 1872 by Captain Pardon Dodds. Following Captain Dodds, Morris Evans trailed about 2,000 head of cattle into the valley. In 1874, A. Hatch and Company brought in about 2,500 cattle and a large band of horses. In a few years, all of the surrounding ranges were fully stocked.

Following the settlement, came another era of the west–the advent of the famous outlaws and rustlers. In the 1880s and 1890s Butch Cassidy and his gang, known as the "Wild Bunch", roamed the Intermountain Area. Butch shines in western legend as one of the brightest lights in his profession: leader of one of the largest organizations of cowboy outlaws the west has ever seen.

One of Butch's famous hideouts was found in the northeast corner of Daggett County known as Brown's Hole. It was here that he organized his famous band, composed of such notorious characters as Elza Lay, Matt Warner, George Cutty, Tom Horn, Tom O'Day, Harry Longabaugh, and others.

On July 15, 1905 President Theodore Roosevelt, by proclamation, added part of the area within the Indian reservation to the Uinta Forest Reserve. By executive order on July 1, 1908, he created the Ashley National Forest from that portion of the Uinta Forest Reserve east of the Rock Creek and Smith Fork drainages. These boundaries did not vary greatly until 1953 when a change in Forest boundaries between the Wasatch, Uinta, and Ashley National Forest was made. All of the north slope of the Uinta Mountains west of the Burnt Fork drainage was transferred from the Ashley National Forest to the Wasatch National Forest. The Ashley received the Rock Creek and Duchesne River drainages from the Wasatch Forest and Tabby Mountain and Avintaquin units from the Uinta National Forest. Today the boundaries are essentially the same, except the Phil Pico and Tabby mountain units were exchanged with the State of Utah in 1966-1968.

On October 1, 1968, President Lyndon B. Johnson approved legislation establishing the Flaming Gorge National Recreation Area as part of the Ashley National Forest. This legislation added approximately 120,000 acres to the Forest. From a small handful of dedicated men in 1908, the personnel force has expanded to more than 280 persons employed during the summer months on the Ashley National Forest.

Reprinted from U.S. Forest Service Brochure.

ers and their families who worked to establish homes in southwest Wyoming and to the men who lost their lives in the coal mines of Sweetwater County.

H Reliance Tipple: Placque #1

At Reliance Tipple in Reliance

The tipples constructed here were designed to serve all the Reliance coal mines. Union Pacific Coal Company opened their mines in phases. The coal mines were all located east of here with portals located along the sides of the valley. Coal from these mines was hauled to the surface by either electric locomotives or hoists. From the portal, the coal was shipped over a tramway to the tipple The distance from the No 7 mine portal to the tipple was about 1.2 miles. Once the coal cars were inside the tipple you see today, they were set on a rotary dump. The coal car was fastened down, rolled over, and emptied into the coal hopper. From the hopper, the coal moved over conveyors to the shaker screen. The screen sorted the coal by sizes. The coal then fell through the screens into a chute that carried it to the picking tables. At the picking tables, men, boys, and, later, women sorted through the coal looking for stones or checking the size of the coal. Good coal was loaded into waiting rail cars while stone and refuse were conveyed outside the tipple into the refuse bin. The tipple you see in front of you, contructed in 1936 at a cost of $232,700, was designed to be a model of efficiency.

H Reliance Tipple: Placque #2

At Reliance Tipple in Reliance

The wooden, coal-loading facility, which was completed in 1912, went through a number of changes during its life time. The original wooden tipple was a frame structure set on top of wooden piers. Windows were located on either side of the structure to let in light and let out coal dust. Coal came into the tipple from the south. The coal was sorted by men or boys and sized according to need. The Workers picked out stone or odd-sized pieces of coal and dropped these pieces into the appropriate conveyor or outside the tipple. The stone wall southwest of here is all that remains of the tipple today.

It was not uncommon for boys to work alongside men in the tipple. Some miners began their lives in the coal company's employ by first working in the tipple. The wooden tipple was contructed long before safety regulations were in force. Though working in the tipple was much safer than working underground, it was still dusty. Tipple workers often complained that you could not even see the person working beside you.

H Reliance Tipple: Placque #3

At Reliance Tipple in Reliance

From 1910 to 1955, the mines at Reliance produced coal for the Union Pacific Railroad. To staff these mines, people from a variety of countries were hired. During World War II there were not enough mine workers to extract the coal. People were brought in from Oklahoma and Arkansas and housed in railroad cars. Yet there were still not enough workers, and women entered the work force in the coal industry. Women had long been considered bad luck underground, and this superstition died slowly. One of the first places women found work was in the Reliance tipple. Working alongside men in the black dust, women sorted coal throughout the war years. Here, at the "picking tables" inside the Reliance tipple, dust-covered women sorted coal amidst the deafening noise of the now silent shaking screens.

TRONA

History

Ancient Egyptians first used soda ash over 5,000 years ago. They recovered the chemical from dry lake bed deposits or manufactured it by burning seaweed and other marine plants. This crude, impure product was used to make glass ornaments and vessels. The Romans also used it for baking bread, making glass and as a medicine.

When European cultures came to the New World, they continued to make soda ash, using the ancient process of burning plant materials. In the late 1700s a French scientist named LaBlanc invented a method for manufacturing soda ash using salt, limestone and coal. Belgian scientists Ernest and Alfred Solvay created a more efficient method in the 1860s using ammonia instead of salt. This is the method that is still used today in creating synthetic soda ash.

Trona was discovered in Sweetwater County in 1938 during oil and gas explorations. The first mine shaft was excavated in 1946 and commercial production of soda ash began in 1948. Up until that time all soda ash in the United States was produced synthetically using the LaBlanc and Solvay methods.

Since that initial discovery five mines and processing plants have been opened. These companies produce over 15 million tons of trona and over 8 million tons of soda ash each year as well as being the major employer in both Sweetwater and Uinta counties.

New uses are being found for soda ash, particularly in the areas of environmental protection. Soda ash is used to clean smoke stack emissions which, if left untreated, would cause acid rain.

Geology

Trona is a rare mineral found in only a few locations worldwide. There are deposits in Africa, China, Turkey, Mexico and the Green River Basin of Wyoming. Sweetwater County is the only site where trona is commercially mined.

Where did trona come from? About fifty million years ago the Green River Basin and surrounding areas were covered by a 20,000 square mile land-locked lake. As the climate changed over thousands of years the water evaporated, leaving behind several beds of a mineral mixture called trona wedged between layers of sandstone and shale. There are an estimated 100 billion tons of trona in the basin, enough to meet the world's needs for another 2000 years. These deposits cover about 1,000 square miles and vary in depth from 800 to 3500 feet below the surface. Actual mining occurs at a depth of 800 to 1600 feet in beds that are eight to ten feet thick.

What is Trona and Soda Ash?

Trona is a naturally occurring mineral that is chemically known as sodium sesquicarbonate. Trona is the raw material from which the chemical soda ash (sodium carbonate) is refined. Soda ash in turn is used to make glass, paper, laundry detergents and many other products. It is also used in the manufacture of other chemicals including sodium bicarbonate (baking soda) and sodium phosphates (detergents).

Over 90% of the soda ash produced in the United States and about 25% of the world's supply is natural soda ash from Sweetwater County.

Trona Capital of the World

In recognition of the importance of the trona/soda ash industry to the economy of the State of Wyoming, on November 3, 1989 Sweetwater County was proclaimed as Trona Capital of the World by Governor Mike Sullivan.

Reprinted from Sweetwater County Historical Museum brochure.

T Winton

Approx. 8 miles northwest of Rock Springs

Mining slag dumps, a roofless hotel, and the foundation and basement of the Union pacific store are all that remain of the former town of Winton. Six mines operated well into the 1940s. At one time, a boarding house, pool hall, doctor's office, tiple and bath house graced the area.

T Dines

North of Reliance, Wyoming

The town was named for Courtland Dines, one of the owners of the Colony Coal Company. The mining community once boasted its own baseball team. Dines whithered away in the early 1900s.

T Killpecker Dunes

North of Rock Springs approximately 11 miles to Tri-Territory Road past the Boars Tusk turnoff.

Don't let your first look at the seemingly barren Killpecker Dunes fool you. Upon closer inspection, as you walk over occasional patches of purple vetch and quiet, endless dunes you'll find much more. The constantly shifting sand, stretching out in a band for more than 55 miles, records, and then erases tracks of birds, coyotes, deer, even insects. Seasonal ponds, fed by melting snowdrifts and insulated by the creamy sand, pop up unexpectedly to greet visitors. Waterfowl frequent the waterholes in the springtime.

As with any desert clime, temperatures in the Dunes area are extreme. Bone-chilling winter nights may reach 40 below; summer's heat can bring temperatures well over 100.

H Greater Sand Dunes

At Killpecker Dunes parking area

The greater sand dunes area of critical environmental concern (ACECO), encompassing approximatelyu 38,650 acres, was established to protect unique resources in the Killpecker Sand Dunes. The Killpecker Dunes is one of the largest active dune fields in North America. The critical resources present include wildlife, cultural, wilderness, and scenic values, which offer outstanding recreation opportunities.

Part of the Killpecker Dune Field is a Wilderness Study Area. The spectacular nothern dunes show little sign of human activity. One of the unique features of the sand dunes is the Eolian Ice-Cells that feed pools at the base of many large dunes. These are formed as snow and ice accumulate on the leeward side of the

Killpecker Dunes

dunes and then are covered by blowing sand. The buried ice cells then slowly melt during the summer months to supply these ponds with fresh water.

Valuable haitat for big game is found throughout the area. The dunes help support the only herd of desert elk in Wyoming.

Cultural values vary from prehistoric Indian campsites to historic homesteads. Numerous scatters of ancient artifacts have been found at various points throughout the area.

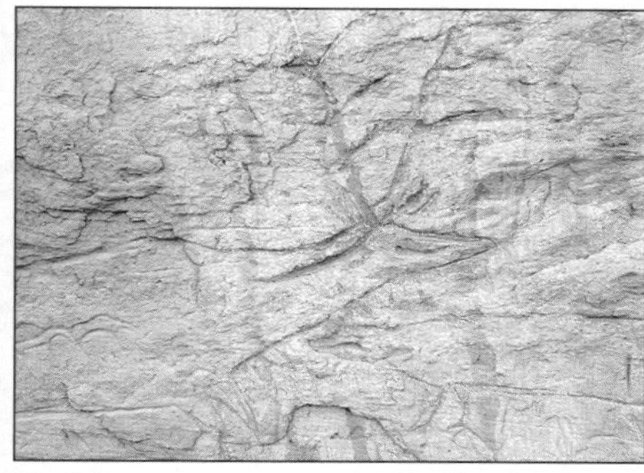

T White Mountain Petroglyphs

24 miles northeast of Rock Springs. Take Tri-Territory Road 12 miles east from U.S. 191, to turnoff, go 4 miles to sandstone cliff.

Before early settlers arrived in this area, the Shoshone people inhabited regions of the Red Desert. Carving their art into the soft sandstone cliffs, they recorded hunts of elk and bison. Over a dozen panels, including hundreds of figures, were etched more than 200 years ago into the sandstone bedrock of the Ecocene Bridger formation.Some of the petroglyphs may be as much as 1,000 years old. Because several of the drawings depict animals within animals, it is believed by some that the area was a birthing place for the Plains and Great Basin native American people. Handholds worn in the stone may have served for generations of women to grip the rock during labor. It is a sacred place for the Native American people, and visitors are encouraged to respect the reverence of the area.

T Boar's Tusk

East of U.S. Highway 191 between Eden and Reliance

Located in the heart of the Red Desert region is Boar's Tusk, a unique rock formation that juts up out of the desert. The remains of a volcanic plug, the Tusk looms 400 feet above the dunes, and is an open invitation to rock climbers and photographers alike.

9 *Gas, Food*

T Firehole Canyon

Highway 191, south from Interstate 80 near Rock Springs

See unique scenery and interesting geological features include two fingerlike projections known as North and South Chimney Rocks. Along with the interesting geology you will often see large flocks of sheep.

T Ute Mountain Fire Tower

Just west of Sheep Creek Geologic Loop, on Forest Road 221

This is an old wooden lookout with spectacular views, located at the southwestern end of the Flaming Gorge National Recreation Area. It was built in 1935 by the CCC. It is the first fire tower in the state and the last operating. The tower is open June through Labor Day.

H Chinese Massacre

I-80 Exit 99

In 1885, more than 700 Chinese miners lived in Rock Springs. Complaints about wages and competition for work, coupled with racial prejudice, sent mobs of white miners into the Chinese settlement, setting fire to their homes and beating all in their wake. More than one hundred Chinese men fled on foot, running to the hills for sanctuary. Governor Frances Warren sought help from President Grover Cleveland, who ordered federal troops into the melee. Soldiers from Utah arrived and escorted the Chinese back to Rock Springs. More than a dozen men were charged with crimes against the Chinese; all were released. The Union Pacific Coal Company reinstated the Chinese in their jobs, but as pressure built from the white community, the Asian men's positions were slowly phased out. Eventually, most of the Chinese left the area.

H Tri-State Corner of the States of Wyoming, Utah & Colorado

South of I-80 Exit 99 on U.S. Highway 191 for 31 miles. Turn east on dirt road. After 11 miles, directional signs lead you through last 10 miles to monument

This point was monumented by U.S. surveyor, Rollin J. Reeves, on July 19, 1879, while completing the survey of the western boundary of the State of Colorado and the east boundary of Utah Territory. The boundary line separating Wyoming Territory from Colorado and Utah Territories was surveyed by U.S. surveyor, A.V. Richards in 1873.

The original monument was found to be disturbed in 1931 and was remarked by U.S. Cadastral Engineer, E.V. Kimmel, with a brass tablet seated in a concrete monument.

This monument is one of the corners of the national Rectangular Cadastral Survey System, inaugurated in 1785, that has aided the development and orderly settlement of the public lands in the western states. From these monuments, state and local governments and private citizens are provided with easily identifiable boundaries. Such monuments serve as a base for the work of private surveyors in making accurate land subdivisions and descriptions.

M Rock Springs Realty

1413-A Dewar Drive at the Plaza Mall in Rock Springs. 382-2995.
Email: marsmith@sweetwater.net or www.realestatewyo.com

10 *Food, Lodging*

Green River

Pop. 11,808, Elev. 6,100

Established by the river of the same name, the Green River encampment area was known to the Crow Indians as "Seed-ska-dee," their name for the sage hens, or "prairie chickens," which gathered here. When trappers arrived, they called it the Spanish River, and then Rio Verde, Spanish for Green River. The river's bright color is a result of the soapstone cliffs dissolving their mineral content into the stream. The water source, abundance of game, and shelter of nearby rock formations made it a natural gathering place. Castle Rock, an impressive sandstone cliff, overlooks the area.

The site became an Overland Stage Station in 1861, a Pony Express Station, and finally, in 1868, a railroad camp and tie float station, where

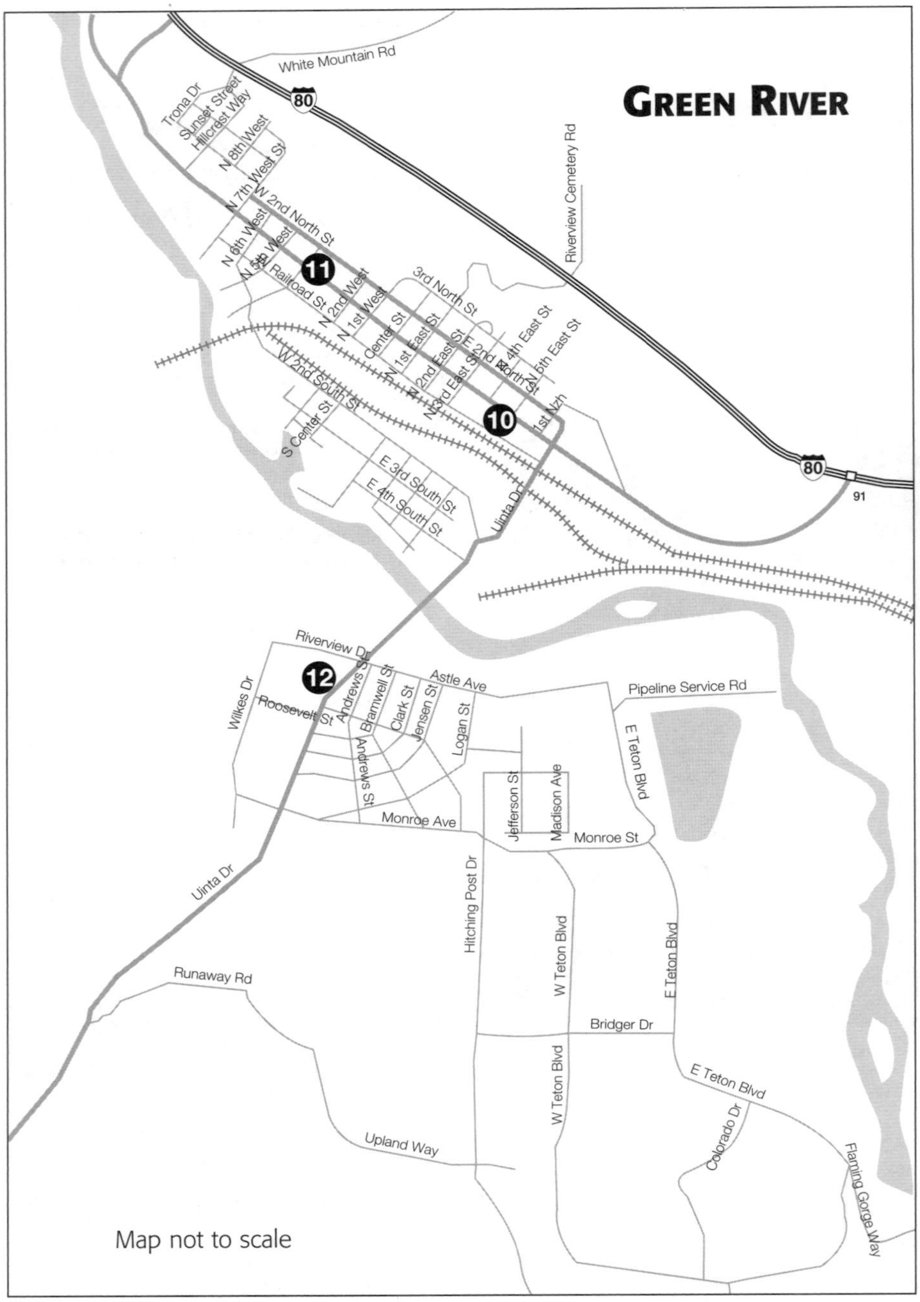

Green River

Map not to scale

over 300,000 ties were sent down the river while the railroad was under construction. In 1869, Maj. John Wesley Powell arrived on the train here to begin his expedition down the Green and Colorado Rivers, eventually exploring the Grand Canyon. He returned in 1871 with a large group of scientists who helped map the region, and later directed the US Geological Survey.

Green River is now largely supported by its extensive trona mining industry. Trona is an important mineral used in making glass, detergents, paper, metal refining, and baking soda. One third of the worldwide supply of trona is derived from the 1000 square mile bed deposited north of Green River by an ancient lake. Five different mining concerns delve into the area, but FMC Corporation has the world's largest mine, with tunnels more extensive than the streets of a large city. FMC alone extracts more than 900 tons of trona an hour. The massive size of the trona bed makes this rate of extraction sustainable for the next 600 years.

Green River is also noted for being the first town in the nation to ban door-to-door salesmen. They became a nuisance to the mine and railroad shift workers who often had to sleep during the day. The law became known as the Green River Ordinance, and was adopted by several other communities nationwide. The Fuller Brush Company fought it all the way to the US Supreme Court, and lost.

11 *Food, Lodging*

T Sweetwater County Historical Museum

3 E. Flaming Gorge Way in downtown Green River. 872-6435

Established in 1967 to preserve the history of Sweetwater County, the museum contains permanent and temporary exhibits, a large historical photograph collection, and local history research material.

Sweetwater County's history began long before written records. In prehistoric times the landscape was swampy and inhabited by great dinosaurs. Thousands of years later Native Americans, mostly Shoshone and Ute, claimed the land. The first white men moving through the area with any regularity were the mountain men. The first Rocky Mountain Rendezvous was held in 1825 in Sweetwater County, as was a later gathering in 1834 which is said to have been the largest rendezvous ever.

Several major emigrant trails passed through the county including the Oregon, California, Mormon, Overland and Cherokee Trails, as well as the 1861 transcontinental telegraph line and Ben Holladay's Central Overland Express stage

Wyoming Tidbits

Green River was the home to Wyoming's first brewery. The Sweetwater Brewing Company won medals at world fairs and at its peak, bottled nearly 20,000 bottle of beer a day. With the enactment of the Volstad Act (Prohibition), the company was forced to close.

Green River	Jan	Feb	March	April	May	June	July	Aug	Sep	Oct	Nov	Dec	Annual
Average Max. Temperature (F)	32.0	37.4	46.0	57.1	68.1	78.4	87.4	85.1	75.3	62.4	45.0	34.5	59.1
Average Min. Temperature (F)	4.3	9.4	18.9	27.8	36.3	43.5	49.9	47.5	37.6	27.5	16.4	7.3	27.2
Average Total Precipitation (in.)	0.38	0.42	0.58	0.94	1.14	0.82	0.62	0.72	0.78	0.83	0.47	0.37	8.08
Average Total SnowFall (in.)	4.7	4.8	4.6	4.0	1.1	0.0	0.0	0.0	0.2	2.0	3.9	4.2	29.5
Average Snow Depth (in.)	1	1	0	0	0	0	0	0	0	0	0	1	0

The old Green River Brewery

line. Vitally important to the history of the county was the coming of the transcontinental railroad in 1868. This was instrumental in the creation and development of Sweetwater County's two major population centers, Green River and Rock Springs. Green River was the major railroad town due to the nearness of a water supply, while Rock Springs became the coal mining center of the county.

The railroad and coal mining industries brought many people of different nationalities and races to Sweetwater County. European and Oriental immigrants as well as Americans from back east made the area their home. As a result the cultural diversity represented by the county's populace was unmatched in the state of Wyoming.

As coal mining decreased in the mid-1900s, trona mining became increasingly important to the county's economy. Trona is an ore which is refined into soda ash, a commonly used industrial chemical. In fact trona is in such great abundance in the county that Wyoming's Governor Mike Sullivan proclaimed the area "Trona Capital of the World" in 1989.

In an effort to preserve their rich mining heritage, the Sweetwater County Historical Museum acquired the Reliance Tipple in 1987. Visitors are encouraged to take the short drive to Reliance and examine the structure which was used to sort and grade coal and load it onto railroad cars. At the site you may take a self-guided walking tour along the paved path to view the tipple and the accompanying interpretive signs.

A highlight of the museum is a fine ethnic collection of items from Sweetwater County's diverse population. A Lakota Sioux pipe bag, Greek ceremonial sword and Chinese theater banner add color to the exhibits. The museum also contains an excellent mining collection of three-dimensional objects, photographs and documentary material which show the mineral exploitation industry and its impact on area history.

The museum is open from April through December, Monday–Saturday from 10 a.m. to 6 p.m. Winter hours are Monday–Friday from 9 a.m. to 5 p.m.

Wyoming Tidbits

Green River, Sweetwater County seat, was the home to so many railroaders working the night shift, that the town enacted the "Green River Ordinance" prohibiting door-to-door salesmen from soliciting during daytime hours. Adopted by other towns, the ordinance assured quiet so the shift workers could sleep during the day.

T Castle Rock, Tollgate Rock, and Mansface Rock

These distinctive rock formations above Green River have many stories behind them. Pick up a brochure at the visitor center to learn about these buttes and other fascinating rock formations in the area.

H Called to the River

At Expedition Island in Green River

You're standing on an historical landmark of the Green and Colorado Rivers exploration - Expedition Island. Named long after the Powell expeditions 1869 and 1871, the island commemorates early western river exploration.

As you walk around this path, you will read about the river runners who answered the "call to the river" and floated here in the Green River path before and after Powell's celebrated expeditions.

There were almost as many reasons for river travel on the Green as there were people floating. There were fur trappers, explorers, gold seekers, dam builders, developers, and finally the adventurers who came for the excitement and to see nature's wonders.

These signs were erected by the Green River Parks and Recreation Department in celebration of Green River's 100th birthday as an incorporated city and in honor of the men and women who answered the call and ran the river.

H Pavilion

At Expedition Island in Green River

This pavilion was built in the early 1930s with the bid for construction being awarded to the Green River Lumber Company for $17,790. Throughout the years it has been used for a dance hall, public gatherings, wedding receptions, a roller skating rink. National Guard Armory, Teen Town, and 4th-of-July and Flaming Gorge Days celebrations.

The building was renovated in 1979 through efforts of the Green River Bicentennial Commission and the Expedition Island Pavillion Restoration Committee at a cost of $256,412.

The island has been known by various names since it was originally claimed by S.I. Field when he platted Green River City in early 1868. It was known as the Island, Johnson Island, Island Park and Expedition Island. It had been in private ownership until Green River City purchased it in October 1909. The Island Park's name was changed to Expedition Island on May 24, 1969.

In 1949, a plaque was placed on the island by the Historical Landmark Commission of Wyoming "Marking the spot from which Major Weslely Powell and party departed May 24, 1869, to make first exploration of Green and Colorado Rivers, arriving mouth of Grand Canyon Aug. 29, 1869."

On April 16, 1969, Expedition Island was designated a Registered National Historic Landmark by the U.S. Department of the Interior National Park Service, indicated that "This site possesses exceptional value in commemorating or illustrating the history of the United States."

H William Ashley - 1825

At Expedition Island in Green River

Leaving Missouri in 1824, William Ashley led a large group of men west in search of riches-beaver. Ashley and his crew arrived on the banks of the Green River (or Seeds-ke-dee as it was called then) on April 9th, 1825 near the mouth of the Big Sandy River north of here. The men divided into four groups to explore the area for beaver.

Ashley supervised the building of "bull boats" - clumsy crafts of buffalo hides stretched over a willow frame and led 7 men down the Green River. His was the first recorded river trip on the Green.

The voyagers passed by Expedition Island on sunday, April 25th, 1825. They walked around many rapids including Ashley Falls, now under Flaming Gorge Reservoir.

They continued downriver through the Green's canyons until they arrived in the Uinta Basin (now Utah) on June 16th. From there, Ashley left the river and made his way back to this area for the first of the great annual rendezvous held on Henry's Fork in July 1825.

Though not widespread, word of Ashley's decent of the river gradually spread in the "States" letting others know that river travel down the Green was possible. Later mountain men used dugout canoes made from cottonwood logs to float the Green.

Expedition Island bridge.

H Norm Nevills & A.K. Reynolds - 1940's

At Expedition Island in Green River

Norman D. Nevills took his first major voyage in 1938, floating from Green River, Utah, through the Grand Canyon. This journey included the first woman ever to float Cataract and Grand Canyons.

In 1940, Nevills decided to float from Green

Section 4

River, Wyoming , to Lake Mead. The party included his wife Doris and one other woman. Their departure from Expedition Island on June 20th, 1940 was marked by ceremonies with Wyoming and Utah state officials who presented Nevills with special license plates for his boats. The trip was successful, but not without hardship.

During the 1940s, Nevills ran commercial river trips on several western rivers. On June 21st, 1947, Nevills returned to Wyoming for another commercial trip on the Green River to Jensen, Utah. By the time of his death in September, 1949, Nevills had run the Grand Canyon more times than any other person and was known as "the world's number one fastwater man."

When Nevills was at Expedition Island in 1947, he inspired a local man, A.K. Reynolds, to start his own river outfitting business. Reynolds, Mike Hallacy, and G.G. Larson all Green River residents, built cataract boats to Nevills' specifictions and started Reynolds-Hallacy River Expeditions. Reynolds ran trips on the upper Green until the early 1960s and the inundation of the river under Flaming Gorge Reservoir.

H The French Trio - 1938

In September 1938 on the eve of World War II, three young people from France came to southwest Wyoming for a trip down the Green River.

The Frenchmen spent a week in Green River making preparations and on September 14th, they launched - the first kayakers on the upper Green River. Though only 22 years old, Genevieve was the star of the trip. She ran her own boat, did her share of the work, and was the best boat "person" of the three. She kayaked much slower than the men, but never damaged her boat or flipped in rapids.

The trio continued downriver and resupplied in Jensen and Green River, Utah. They ended their journey November 9th at Lee's Ferry, Arizona. The river was icing up and they were unable to continue.

Returning to Europe in time for World War II, the three fought in the French Resistance, lived quiet lives in France and died in the 1970s.

H The Damsite Surveys 1914–1922

The search for "Practical" uses of the canyons of the upper Green River had been on since the turn of the century. In 1914, a U.S. Geologic Survey expedition led by Eugene LaRue floated to the Utah border and noted several damsites in the Flaming Gorge area.

In 1917, the Utah Power and Light Company floated their own men down the river to search for suitable sites for hydro-electric dams.

Head boatman for the trip was Bert Loper, a seasoned runner on the Colorado River. The other boatmen, who also served as rodmen for the servey, were E.B. Lunt and H.E. Blake. Additional men survey as cooks, helpers, and engineers completed the crew.

The party launched on July 22nd, 1922; again with tales of disaster from the townspeople. The group floated to Green River, Utah, located 14 potential damsites and thoroughly mapped the canyons of the upper Green River

Though still untamed, the "Great Unknown" of the Green River was reduced to lines on maps.

H Kolb Brothers-1911

At Expedition Island in Green River

Ellsworth and Emery Kolb were photographers with a studio on the south rim of the Grand Canyon. They wanted to make a complete photographic record of the canyons of the Green and Colorado Rivers themselves.

Arriving in Green River, Wyoming in early September 1911, the Kolbs brought a relatively new invention with them - a movie camera. They were to take the first moving pictures of the river and canyons.

Ellsworth Kolb later recorded the town's reception of their plan, "The whole of Green River City, it seemed, had learned of our project, and came to inspect, or advise or jeer at us. The kindest of them wished us well: the other sort told us "it would serve us right" but none of our callers had any encouragement. Many were the stories of disaster and death with which they entertained us."

The Kolbs' boats soon arrived on the Union Pacific railroad. With the arrival of James Fagin, a young man from San Francisco hired to help the brothers with their camp gear, the expedition launched on September 9,1911.

The brothers made it all the way to the Gulf of California without incident. They returned to their photo studio and lived at the Grand Canyon until they died in the 1970s.

H Julius Stone - 1909

At Expedition Island in Green River

An Ohio millionaire and no stranger to the river, Julius Stone wanted to duplicate Major Powell's run down the Green and Colorado Rivers. Stone even went to Washington to meet with the aging Powell. Major Powell, however, was jealous of his achievements and refused to help Stone.

Undaunted, Stone hired Than Galloway to travel to Ohio and build the boats. Stone had floated Glen Canyon on the Colorado River with Galloway in 1899 and the two had become friends.

On September 12th, 1909 the Stone-Galloway party launched from Green River, Wyoming. A local man, Mr. Morris, had let them use his barn to organize their gear and gave Stone a bottle of rye whiskey in case of an accident. Twenty five years later, Stone still had the bottle, unopened!

The party included Stone, Galloway, C.C. Sharp, Seymour Dubendorff, and Raymond Cogswell. Arriving in Needles, California on November 19th, 1909, the men made the entire journey in less than two months, the fastest descent of the rivers and canyons at the time.

Julius Stone's reason for floating the Green River was significant, he had no other motive than to seek the experience itself - which made him the first paying tourist on the river.

H Sunbeam - 1908

At Expedition Island in Green River

J.F. Moerke, Frank Briggs, M.C. Peterson and C.W. Johnson, the owners of the amusement park on Island Park, purchased the "Sunbeam" and a companion craft, the "Teddy R," in 1908. These were stern-wheeler, gasoline propelled motor launches which were to be used for pleasure excursions on Green River at the amusement park.

The boats were seven feet wide and twenty five feet in length and seated twenty adults. They were used at the amusement park for the enjoyment of those fond of a glide over the turbulent waters of the Green River.

These stern-wheeler launches were very popular at the amusement park, which made many pleasure excursions around the Island Park. Also, many pleasure trips were made up and down the river. The "Sunbeam" carried pleasure seekers as far down the river as Buckboard and up the river as far as Big Piney.

The "Sunbeam" was eventually converted from a stern -wheeler to a propeller-propulsion boat.

On its last river trip, the "Sunbeam" sheared its propeller at Big Piney. It was left there at Big Piney and eventually was hauled overland to Fremont Lake at Pinedale, where it was repaired and continued in service for long years afterward.

H George Flavell - 1896

At Expedition Island in Green River

Trapper, hunter, prospector, and tattoo artist - George Flavell and his passenger/partner Ramon Montez were the first men to float the "distance" of Green River, Wyoming to Needles, California primarily for the "adventure."

The two arrived in Green River in mid - August 1896, built their own boat - the Fanthon, and launched on August 27th, 1896. Far downstream in Yuma, Arizona, Flavell told a reporter the reasons for the journey, "First, for the adventure; second, to see what so few people have seen; third, to hunt and trap; fourth, to examine the perpendicular walls of rock for gold".

One of the major river controversies which remains today is whether it was actually George Flavell instead of Than Galloway who was the first to use the facing downstream method of running rivers and to build the newer style boats better suited for river travel.

In any event, Flavell's diary records running all the rapids except for six on the entire journey from Green River to the ocean.

H Nathaniel Galloway - 1890's

At Expedition Island in Green River

A sometime trapper and prospector from Vernal, Utah, Nathaniel "Than" Galloway revolutionized river travel on the Green and all other western rivers. Galloway was convinced that both beaver and gold could be found in the canyons of the green River.

He made several shore runs on the Green between 1891-94 and his first lengthy trip started from Green River, Wyoming in 1896.

Galloway's greatest historical contributions were the design of his boats and the way he ran the river, particularly rapids. Galloway designed and built his own boats - They were about 214 feet long and 4 feet wide with a "cockpit" for the oarsman, they had a slight rise both fore and aft, and they weighed only 400 pounds. His crafts were very maneuverable and could "turn on a dime."

Most significantly, though, Galloway's river running technique was brand new. Instead of rowing backwards for power and speed and looking over one's shoulder, Galloway simply turned around and faced downstream. This new approach allowed him to see rocks and obstacles in the river and steer around them.

The "Galloway" technique of river running is used to this day.

H Paddlewheeler Comet-1908

At Expedition Island in Green River

The paddlewheeler or steamship the Comet represented a new form of transportation on the upper Green River—the use of power other than oars. The flagship of the newly organized Green River Navigation Company, the Comet made its maiden voyage from Green River, Wyoming south to Linwood, Utah on July 4, 1908. The purpose of the steamship was to carry freight and passengers to ranches along the Green River to Linwood at the confluence with the Henry's Fork. The launching was the major event of the year combined with the Fourth of July celebration.

Built at a cost of $25,000, the Comet was not a success. The first trip to Linwood and back took 33 hours and was hampered by low water, swift current and rocks. After only a few trips, the Comet was abandoned in the river several hundred yards downriver from here.

Other boats which operated on the Green in that period included the power launch Teddy R which was made for pleasure excursions up and down the river, and a stern wheeler, the Sunbeam which was used until it broke down upriver from here at Big Piney, Wyoming. Afterwards, the Sunbeam was hauled to Fremont Lake and used as a pleasure boat for many years.

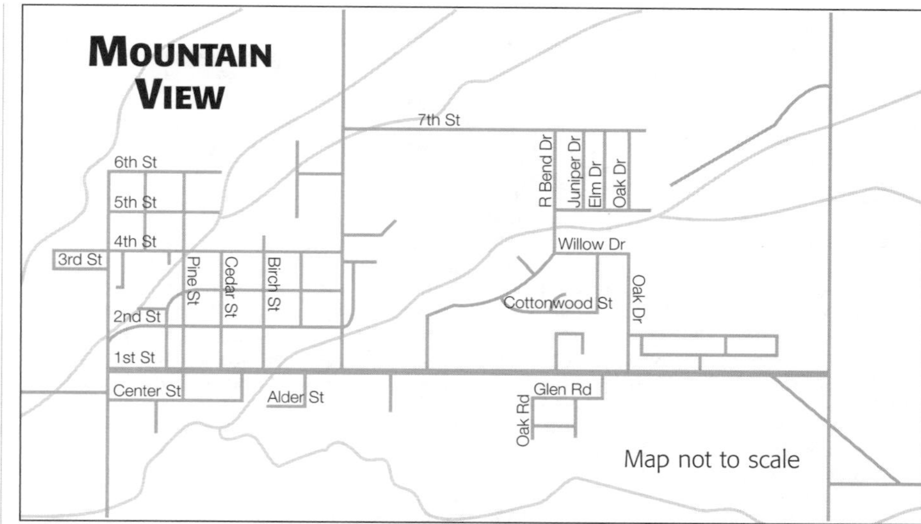

H Major Wesley Powell and party

Expedition Island in Green River

Marking the spot from which Major Wesley Powell and party departed May 24, 1869, to make the first exploration of Green and Colorado Rivers, arriving mouth of Grand Canyon August 29, 1869.

H Powell-Colorado River Expedition

Expedition Island in Green River

On May 24, 1869, the Powell-Colorado River Expedition, ten men and four boats strong, embarked from these environs on a voyage of adventure resulting in civilization's first definite knowledge of this continent's last unexplored major river drainage. Out of the still shaded but no longer unknown depths of that river's Grand Canyon came, 98 days later, six tattered river veterans to triumphantly beach two water-torn and rock-mauled hulks.

This adventure, no odyssey if measured by elapsed time alone, easily qualifies by the other standards of suspense, danger and action. Its successful completion captured and held the admiration of a nation.

John Wesley Powell himself—cast in the hero's role and endowed with rare executive and scientific talents—rode the crest of national acclaim into public service and the highest councils of the republic. Over the years his ever-sharpening executive ability resulted in the creation and productiveness of important federal agencies, while his scientific genius contributed to the advancement of such divergent disciplines as ethnology, geology and agronomy. Perhaps his greatest gift to the nation, conceived during Colorado River explorations, was the theory of arid-land culture. As developed, through his success in fathering the Bureau of Reclamation, this theory has changed the face of western landscapes and caused extensive geographic regions to blossom and thrive.

12 *Gas, Food, Lodging*

T Green River Greenbelt and Scott's Bottom Nature Area

At Expedition Park in Green River

This area contains assorted paved and dirt riverside trails beginning at Expedition Island. Water fowl and other types of birds nest in the tall grass and bushes which grow throughout the area. Further to the south of the southern edge of the river is Scott's Bottom Nature Area. Like the Green Belt, the Scott's Bottom Nature area has paths and interpretive signs which tell of the wildlife which live in this riparian habitat along the edge of the Green River.

H Linwood-Lucerne Valley Interpretive Sign

About 42 miles south of Green River on State Highway 530

Linwood Bay

Linwood—The Town that Drowned

From this point you can see Linwood Bay of the Flaming Gorge Reservoir. Beneath the surface of the reservoir at the far western end, lies the site of the town of Linwood. When Flaming Gorge Dam was built in the early 1960s, the rising waters of the reservoir covered the small town. It was laid out in 1900 by George Solomon who carefully planted many rows of cottonwood trees, giving the town its name "Linwood."

This area is a reminder of the colorful and exciting days of Indians, trappers, explorers, settlers, cowboys and outlaws. Although Linwood itself has vanished, the memory of one of the last towns of the "Old West" lingers on.

The Green River

In front of the vista point is the original bed of

Mountain View	Jan	Feb	March	April	May	June	July	Aug	Sep	Oct	Nov	Dec	Annual
Average Max. Temperature (F)	32.7	35.4	43.8	52.9	63.8	73.2	80.3	79.4	70.5	57.8	42.1	33.3	55.4
Average Min. Temperature (F)	11.8	12.7	19.9	26.0	34.1	41.6	47.4	45.9	37.9	28.9	18.5	11.3	28.0
Average Total Precipitation (in.)	0.44	0.37	0.52	0.93	1.20	1.02	0.97	0.86	1.01	0.94	0.57	0.44	9.28
Average Total SnowFall (in.)	5.6	5.0	5.1	6.1	2.9	0.3	0.0	0.0	0.5	3.9	5.6	5.3	40.3
Average Snow Depth (in.)	2	2	1	0	0	0	0	0	0	0	1	2	1

The Bear River Region

Beginning high in the Uinta Mountains south of Evanston, the Bear River meanders more than 500 miles through Idaho, Wyoming and Utah, ending in the Great Salt Lake, less than 100 miles from it's origin. This route makes the Bear River the Northern Hemisphere's longest river that does not flow into an ocean.

During the late 17th and 18th century, before the white man's arrival, this region was widely used by Shoshone, Arapaho, and Uintah Indians who camped here while hunting the abundant wildlife and gathering berries. They called the river "quee-yaw-pah" for a tobacco root growing along it's bank. Trappers called it the "Bear River" because of the many bears that frequented the area, Indians and trappers sometimes held rendezvous in this region. The Burnfork Rendezvous held in 1825, just 50 miles southeast of here, was the first rendezvous of traders and trappers to be held in the Rocky Moutains.

Between 1840 and 1870, more than 500,000 emigrants traveled through this area bound for opportunity in the Oregon Territory, the Great Basin, and the California gold fields. in 1843 famed mountain man, Jim Bridger, and his partner, Louis Vasquez, established a trading post that soon became Fort Bridger. Located just 35 miles east of here, it became a welcome spot to rest, resupply, trade animals, and get necessary blacksmith work done.

During the development of America's Transcontinental Railroad, tie hacks cut railroad ties in Uinta Mountains to the south. The Bear River's spring runoff was used to float them to the railway to construct and maintain the railroad you see on the west bank of the river. The Union Paific Railroad depended on this river as a source of water for their steam engines and for ice that was cut, stored in nearby ice houses and used to protect perishables before the advent of refrigerator cars.

Geologically, this region is part of the Overthrust Belt, a series of folds and faults that formed over a vast period as two enormous land masses compressed together. These land mass movements caused the crust of the earth to overlap by as much as 60 miles, burying petroleum source rocks deep beneath the surface where high tempertures stimulated the generation of oil and gas. Oil, gas and minerals play a major role in southwestern Wyoming as evidenced by the presence of many energy and mineral related companies. The world's laargest deposits of trona are located just east of here. Mines in this region produce two thirds of the world's supply of soda ash (a trona derivative).

Today the Bear River is used for recreation, agriculture and municipal water. Many species of wildlife use the river habitat. Visitors enjoy viewing antelope, deer, an occasional moose or elk, and many small animals. Bird watchers enjoy Eagles, Great Blue Herons, Sand Hill Cranes, several species of ducks, Canada Geese, and many song birds.

Bear River State Park, established lin 1991, provides visitors with the opportunity to hike the trails following in the footsteps of Jim Bridger, Cut Face Sublette, Hugh Glass, and Chief Washakie, or enjoy viewing the bison and elk herds. Visitors can fish for Bear River Cutthroat Trout or just relax under a large cottonwood tree and imagine what it might have been like to confront a 600 lb Grizzly along the river's edge. Winter provides unique viewing opportunities from numerous cross country ski trails.

Reprinted from State Park brochure

the mighty Green River, the major source of water for Flaming Gorge Reservoir.

The 41st Parallel

The Utah-Wyoming border, located on the 41st parallel, ran directly through the middle of Linwood making it an interesting community since it was in two different states.

Henry's Fork

Named for Maj. Andrew Henry, the fork was an early camping and gathering place for trappers, traders and explorers. Gen. William H. Ashley originated the "rendezvous" system for fur trade here. Early in July, 1825 , 120 trappers and mountain men arrive d at the first rendezvous site, approxijmately 15 miles up Henry's Fork, to trade furs and supplies.

Uncle Jack Robinson's Cabin

The first permanent settler in the area was John Robinson, known as 'Uncle Jack Robinson," who built a cabin on Lower Henry's Fork in 1834-35. The cabin was moved to a location near Flaming Gorge Recreation Area.

Other Points

Also located in the area was Jim Baker's Trading Post, established in 1839. Soon after, the famous explorer, Jim Bridger, built a fort at Bridger Bottom. The famous Colorado River expedition led by John Wesley Powell camped below this point in 1869.

Two Canals

The Lucerne Valley Land and Water Company Canal and the People's Canal were completed near the turn of the century. The canals brought irrigation to the settlers in the dry valleys.

Bob Swift's Bucket O'Blood Saloon

Located a few hundred yards from Uncle Jack's cabin, the "wild and wooly" saloon was frequented by such outlaws as Butch Cassidy and the Sundance Kid, the McCarty boys, and the Curry gang.

The Linwood S chool or "Stateline School"

The school, which was constructed in the fall of 1904, has the distinction of being the only school in the country to be run by two different state school boards–the north half of the school was in Wyoming and the south half was in utah. The school is now used as a grainary one mile north of its original location.

Octagonal Dancehall

The dance hall was a beautiful and magnificent structure and had the first real hardwood floor in the region.

Nearby Points of Interest

The Uinta Mountains

The only major mountain range in the Western Hemisphere to run east and west, the Uinta Mountains form the southern boundary of this area.

Flaming Gorge

Named by John Wesley Powell in 1869, Flaming Gorge is probably the most interesting and dramatic geological feature in the area. It is located in front of you to the left at the end of the range of mountains.

Different Geological Formations

It's interesting to note the different geological formations of the area. The rocks generally lie flat and are light colored and soft. In Utah, the rocks are more colorful and have been bent and forced upward by tremendous earth pressure.

13 *Gas, Food, Lodging*

McKinnon

Established by Mormon pioneer, Archibald McKinnon, this little town didn't get electricity until the 1960s. There is still a store and a post office.

Washam

When the post office opened here, it was named for postmistress Pauline Washam.

14 *No services*

T Flaming Gorge Dam and Reservoir

Near Dutch John south of Wyoming border in Utah. (435) 784-3445

History

Petroglyphs and artifacts suggest that prehistoric people of the Fremont culture hunted game near Flaming Gorge for many centuries. Later the Ute tribes, whose members spread throughout the mountains of present-day Colorado and Utah, visited Flaming Gorge country. During the early 1800s, fur trappers searched the mountains of the West for beaver. William H. Ashley, organizer of a large fur trading company, came to the Green River in 1825, loaded trade goods into buffalo hide boats, and set out on an epic first exploration of the Green River. Ashley returned the same summer for the first of the famous mountain men rendezvous, held on Henry's Fork, near Burnt Fork, Wyoming. The Ashley National Forest was named in honor of this early western explorer.

On a spring day in 1869, John Wesley Powell and nine men boarded small wooden boats at Green River, Wyoming to embark on a daring exploration of the Green and Colorado Rivers. Powell and his men slowly worked their way downstream, successfully completing their journey in late summer. On May 26, 1869, Major Powell named Flaming Gorge after he and his

Flaming Gorge National Recreation Area

men saw the sun reflecting off the red rocks.

In the 1870s, the first ranchers moved to the mountain valleys near Flaming Gorge. It was harsh, rough country for earning a livelihood. Backbreaking hours were spent grubbing sagebrush and laying irrigation ditches on the land. Many of the early pioneers gave up the struggle and moved on.

Many outlaws and fugitives would hide out in the isolated valleys along the Green River. Butch Cassidy and the Wild Bunch were the most notorious.

Flaming Gorge National Recreation Area

The Flaming Gorge National Recreation Area was established in 1968. The Forest Service administers recreation facilities in the area. With over 300 miles (483 kilometers) of shoreline, boat ramps and marinas, campgrounds, and full service lodges, Flaming Gorge Reservoir is an aquatic paradise. While motor boating, sailing, swimming, windsurfing, water skiing, and scuba diving are popular recreation activities, the reservoir is most famous for its fishing. Its cool, clear depths are ideal for growing enormous trout. These famous angling waters have produced fish of state and world record size, including lake trout ("Mackinaw") over 50 pounds (23 kilograms), German brown trout over 30 pounds (14 kilograms), and rainbow trout over 25 pounds (11 kilograms). Flaming Gorge also supports cutthroat trout, kokanee salmon, smallmouth bass, and channel catfish. Ice fishing is a popular pastime in the winter. Anglers should check with local offices or businesses for ice conditions as warm weather and fluctuating water levels may cause hazardous ice.

The Green River below the dam is famous for its trout fishing and rafting. White water rapids and gorgeous canyon scenery also lend to the popularity of river rafting below the dam and hiking Little Hole National Recreation Trail. Water that flows from the dam in the summer is cold, about 55 degrees Fahrenheit (13 degrees celsius) or lower. River levels may vary as power generation fluctuates. A permit is not needed when rafting to the Gates of Lodore — beyond that point, contact officials at Dinosaur National Monument for a permit. Special safety precautions are required when rafting. Rafters must wear life preservers at all times. Common sense and respect for the river will help make the trip safe and enjoyable.

Flaming Gorge Reservoir

Flaming Gorge Dam is a thin-arch concrete dam. From the streambed, the dam stands 502 feet (153 meters) high and contains 987,000 cubic yards (754,616 cubic meters) of concrete. Construction of the dam began in 1958 and was completed in 1964. The dam was dedicated in 1964 by former First Lady Mrs. Lyndon B. "Ladybird" Johnson. The Bureau of Reclamation operates and maintains the dam and powerplant. Water is released from the dam through large pipes called penstocks into the powerplant where the water turns turbines that generate electricity. Warmer water can be released through the penstocks, to benefit downstream fish, by adjusting the selective withdrawal structure located on the upstream face of the dam. Additional water can be released through the outlet works and the spillways.

Flaming Gorge Dam impounds waters of the Green River to form Flaming Gorge Reservoir which extends as far as 91 miles (146 kilometers) to the north. When the reservoir is full at elevation 6,040 feet (1,841 meters) above sea level it has a capacity of 3,788,900 acre-feet (4,674 million cubic meters) and a surface area of 42,020 acres (17,005 hectares).

There are two distinct types of land in the reservoir area: a mountainous area in Utah composed of benches, canyons, and forest; and a desert area in Wyoming composed of low hills, shale badlands, and desert shrubs. These diverse areas provide habitats for a variety of birds and animals, such as deer, elk, bighorn sheep, pronghorn antelope, prairie dogs, Steller's jays, Clark's nutcrackers and eagles.

Environmental Issues

The construction of Flaming Gorge Dam and Reservoir in 1964 resulted in permanent changes to the Green River and the immediate surroundings. Prior to 1964, the Green River was characterized by periods of high snowmelt runoff with low fall and winter flows. After 1964, the amount of water in the river was controlled by the dam, and much of the muddy snowmelt was captured in the reservoir and the regulated downstream releases were cold and clear. Consequently, the types and numbers of animal and plant species present in 1964 have changed and now represent those commonly found in cold water reservoirs and dam tailwaters throughout the United States. Both the reservoir and downstream fisheries at Flaming Gorge are among the best in the world for cold water species, including brown, rainbow and lake trout. However, there are native species of fish that inhabited the Green River prior to 1964 that now exist in very reduced numbers and are in danger of becoming extinct.

Since 1985, there have been numerous physical and biological resource studies and experimental flows from the dam, all directed at determining the needs of the surviving endangered fish. As a result, changes to dam operations have been made to benefit the endangered fish species. These changes have been in combination with other fish recovery activities being taken by many federal, state and local agencies and groups throughout the Upper Colorado River Basin. The goal is to recover the endangered fish so they are no longer in danger of extinction, while seeking to sustain the existing cold water fisheries and support future water development projects.

Excerpted from Bureau of Reclamation Brochure.

14 *No services*

H Red Canyon

Depth 1700 FT—Width About 4000 FT.
At Red Canyon Visitor's Area

General William H. Ashley, politician, fur trader, and explorer, descended the Green River through Red Canyon May 3, 1825 seeking a route to the Gulf of Mexico. He was followed by William Manley (on his gold venture to California) in 1849, Major John Wesley Powell in 1869, and again in 1871-72. Indians, explorers, mountain men, hunters, trappers, outlaws, stockmen and ranchers have given the canyons and valleys a colorful history. This area became part of the National Forest System by an executive order signed by President Theodore Roosevelt July 1, 1908.

H Explorers of the Green Had Lives of Rugged Adventure

At Red Canyon Visitor's Area

Legends of Indians hunting, explorers braving the unknown, mountain men trapping and trading, and outlaws and ranchers competing for living space give the Flaming Gorge area a colorful history.

Fur-trader William H. Ashley was the first to attempt to float the Green River to the Gulf of Mexico. He passed through Red Canyon on May 3, 1825, and was followed by William Manley, on a gold-seeking venture to California in 1849.

It was Major John Wesley Powell that gave us the names Flaming Gorge and Red Canyon in 1869, while exploring the rough water and unknown territory of the Green and Colorado Rivers.

After years of gunfights and land battles, the area became the Ashley National Forest, part of the National Forest System, signed into effect by Theodore Roosevelt.

The Green House

Across from the Cumberland Cemetery was once a thriving brothel known as the Green House, once the most impressive house for miles around. Built in 1896 by Madam Isabelle Burns with the money she recieved when her husband died in Salt Lake City, the establishment employed about 50 practitioners of the world's oldest profession. Local miners kept the place busy, even after Madam Isabell left town in 1926. That same year, scandall erupted when some murders involved certain occupants of the house. A confrontation with one of the fathers of a victim resulted in a fire which reduced the house to ashes. The Southern Hotel was built on the site, and the ladies carried on with business as usual. A new sheriff finally closed them down in 1967.

15 *Gas, Food, Lodging*

Dutch John

South of Wyoming border on U.S. Highway 191

Dutch John, Utah, located about two miles (three kilometers) northeast of the Flaming Gorge Dam, was founded by the Secretary of the Interior in 1958 as a community to house personnel, administrative offices, and equipment for construction and operation of Flaming Gorge Dam, Reservoir, and Powerplant. The community was named for a pioneer settler of the area. Since completion of construction, the community has been managed by the Bureau of Reclamation and has served primarily as a residential area for those involved in the operation, maintenance, and administration of the dam and surrounding area. In 1998, Congress passed legislation that provided for the disposal of most lands, structures, and community facilities in the Dutch John area and transfer of administration responsibility to local government. *Excerpted from Bureau of Reclamation Brochure.*

T Swett Ranch

West of U.S. Highway 191, northeast of Dutch John

Swett Ranch is located along the Flaming Gorge-Uintas National Scenic Byway and is administered by the Ashley National Forest. Homesteaded by Elizabeth Swett and her son Oscar in 1909, the buildings were built to secure the claim to the land. It is now offers a glimpse of local pioneer life, as well as a collection of tools used to work the land during the early 1900s This National Historic Site is open in the summers only for walking tours from 10 a.m. to 5 p.m. of the property. The setting and sunsets are spectacular and the wildlife abundant.

H Flaming Gorge Dam

South of Dutch John on U.S. Highway 191

This impressive view of the dam reveals its mass and height. The dam stands 455 feet (140 meters) above the river channel. It extends below the river bottom for another 47 feet (14 meters), where it is anchored in bedrock. One million cubic yards (765,000 cubic meters) of concrete were used to build the dam and powerplant. The project was started in 1958 and completed in 1963.

16 *No services*

I-80 Exit 85

17 *No services*

H Bryan

About 3 miles west of I-80 Exit 83. Access from westbound lanes only

One mile north of this spot stood the boom town of Bryan. Founded in 1868 as a division point of the Union Pacific Railroad, it grew rapidly and had, at one time, as many as five thousand inhabitants. A twelve-stall roundhouse and huge freight warehouses were constructed and from the latter canvas-topped wagons piled high with goods of all types, departed daily for the south Pass gold mines, eight miles northeast. The water supply soon proved inadequate and when the South Pass gold mining bubble had burst, the railroad moved its division headquarters to Green River and Bryan became a ghost town.

18 *No services*

I-80 Exit 72 to Trona Mines

19 *No services*

Granger

Pop. 146

Originally a stage stop and Pony Express station named for Gen. Gordon Granger, this town became a UP railroad camp in 1868. It was an important junction between the main line and the Oregon Short Line. Granger was also a railroad tie float station, where the timber could be received from Ham's Fork and loaded on the trains. Once a key point on early travel routes, from the days of covered wagons to the early highways, the current course of I-80 bypasses it to the south.

Oyster Ridge Music Festival

The third weekend of June, Kemmer hosts Wyoming's largest free music festival – the Oyster Ridge Music Festival (ORMF). The Oyster Ridge Music Festival started in 1993 as the brain child of Keith Chasteen a local Forest Service employee and a picker of some repute. He wanted to find a home for the newly created Wyoming State Flatpick Guitar championship. The holder of this title could represent Wyoming at the National Flatpick Guitar championships held each year in Winfield, Kansas. He approached the local Chamber of Commerce and the Music Festival was born. At the Kemmerer Triangle.

20 *No services*

T Church Butte

10 miles southwest of Granger on the Black's Fork Road, gravel road. Make local inquiry.

Like many trail landmarks, this butte in the valley of the Black's Fork of Green River, had more than one name. John Boardman, an 1843 pioneer called it "Soloman's Temple" and described it as, "...of the shape of a large temple and decorated with all kinds of images: gods and goddesses, everything that has been the subject of the sculptor: all kinds of animals and creeping things." The butte is said to have provided a spectacular backdrop for Mormon religious services conducted by Brigham Young early in July 1847. *Source: BLM brochure.*

H The Old South Bend Stage Station

Eastern edge of Granger

One of the river crossings on the Oregon Trail was at Ham's Fork. As with all river crossings, this afforded emigrants an opportunity to rest travel-weary livestock. Ham's Fork later became known as South Bend Station. In 1868, the Union Pacific Railroad came, and the town of Granger was established.

H Daniel Lantz

About 1.5 miles northeast of Granger on the Oregon Trail

On April 2, 1850, a California-bound company of gold seekers left their homes in the Wayne County, Indiana, towns of Richmond, Boston, and Centerville. Daniel Lantz, age 45, a wagon maker from Centerville, was a member of this party.

The company arrived here at Black's Fork on July 9. Daniel Lantz had been ill for several days, but on July 10 his condition was so much worse that the company agreed to stop "until there was change in him for better or worse." They camped all that day and the next. The dying man was tended by the company's doctor, Dr. David S. Evans of Boston, who did not believe that Lantz could live another morning.

James Seaton of Centerville recorded the death of Daniel Lantz in his diary entry for July 12, 1850: "Mr. Lantz is still alive but insensible. He lived until 9 1/2 o'clock A.M. When he was no more he was buried at sunset near the road in a very decent manner. His grave was marked by a neat stone. His disease was the bloody flux. There are 10 more get the same disease but none serious."

Daniel Lantz left a wife, Mary, and five children behind in Indiana to mourn their loss. The Centerville company reached Johnson's Ranch near Hangtown in the California goldfields on September 15.

21 *No services*

I-80 Exits 48, 53, 61

22 *Gas, Food*

H Wyoming Wildlands

At I-80 Exit 41 Lyman Rest Stop

Do yourself a favor! As you travel Wyoming slow down and enjoy a taste of wildness.

Wyoming is one of the lst places in North America with great expanses of wild lands.

Much of wyoming is similar to the way it was before the West was settled. Take a break-smell the sage, hear a meadowlark, and feel the freedom of these wildlands.

The migrations of many of our elk, mule deer and pronghorn antelope herds are extensive, as long as 200 miles, as they move through these vast habitats on seasonal treks as old as time itself.

The feelings of desolation you experience when traveling 1-80 across southern Wyoming are not shared by the mule deer or pronghorn antelope. Their survival depends upon being able to move freely between summering and wintering areas. Sagebrush and large expanses of native habitat in which to roam make Wyoming home to two-thirds of the world's population of pronghorns, numbering over one-half million animals.

So, while traveling throughout Wyoming, remember that much of what you see is still wide open, untrammeled wildland and part of the formula critical to conserving Wyoming's outstanding wildlife resources.

23 *Gas, Food, Lodging*

Lyman

Pop. 1,938, Elev. 6,695

Founded by Mormon apostles Francis M. W. Lyman and Owen Woodruff, the town was originally named Owen, and later changed to Lyman. Fort Supply was once nearby. Although the railroad did not come here, Lyman made its way by means of canal construction and agriculture. For a while, the University of Wyoming ran an agricultural experiment station from Lyman. Today, it houses many of the Bridger Valley's businesses, as well as several city and county offices.

T Trona Mining Museum of Bridger Valley

100 East Sage, Town Hall Complex in Lyman. 787-6916

Some people say trona is the most important mineral you've never heard of. It is a sodium carbonate/ bicarbonate compound used as a raw material in the soda ash manufacturing process. Soda ash is the ninth most widely used chemical in the US. Almost every day we come in contact with a product that uses soda ash as a raw material: glass, fiberglass, detergents, cleansers, sodium chemicals, petroleum precuts, paper, aluminum, baking soda, sugar refining, and pharmaceutical products. Come discover more about trona and how it is mined, processed, and used in your day to day world. Wyoming has the largest reserve of trona in the world and at the current rate of mining the supplies could last for about 1,300 more years. Open daily Monday through Friday year around. Call for hours.

S Valley Fabric & Quilts Shop

102 Meadow in Urie, between Fort Bridger & Lyman. 786-2653

24 *Gas, Food*

Urie

Elev. 6,787

This settlement was named for homesteader Nicholas Urie.

25 *Food*

Mountain View

Pop. 1,200, Elev. 6,760

With a view of the rugged Uinta Mountains to the south, this little community is the second largest in the Bridger Valley. The Town Park has over two miles of beautifully landscaped paths.

26 *No services*

Millburne

John Wade owned the first flourmill in the valley, built in a clearing here created by a fire.

Robertson

The first agricultural settlement in the Bridger Valley, Robertson was named for trapper and mountain man John "Uncle Jack" Robertson.

27 *No services*

Burntfork

The arid climate here often makes the land vulnerable to brush fires. Burntfork is named for the creek nearby which is lined with blackened timber. Although there's no longer a post office here, the site is still important for being the place where General William Ashley first met with trappers, traders, and Indians already in the area in 1825.

Lone Tree

Once a post office and stage stop, this town was known for its solitary pine tree, a landmark that travelers could see for miles.

H 1825 Rocky Mountain Rendezvous

State Highway 414 between Burntfork and McKinnon

"When all had come in, he (Ashley) opened his goods and there was a general jubilee…We constituted quite a little town, numbering at least eight hundred souls,…half were women and children. There were some…who had not seen any groceries, such as coffee, sugar, etc. for several months. The whiskey went off a freely as water, even at the exorbitant price he sold it for. All kinds of sports were indulged in with a heartiness that would astonish more civilized societies."

Taken from The Life and Adventures of James P. Beckwourth, as told to Thomas D. Bonner, this passage describes a raucus social event; the rendezvous. Here, mountain men swapped stories, tested their skills, and shared news of friends. The annual event was actually begun as a time saving measure whereby trappers could replenish supplies and trade furs without traveling to St. Louis each summer. North of this point on Henrys Fork of the Green River, between Birch and Burnt Fork Creeks, the first Rocky Mountain Rendezvous was held during June and July, 1825. Held under the direction of William Ashley the gathering was planned for the Green River, but was moved up Henrys Fork because that site provided better forage for animals. One-hundred twenty trappers gathered to barter their furs at Burnt Fork. Among those assembled were some of the industry's most colorful characters: General Ashley, Jedediah Smith, Bill Sublette, Davey Jackson, Tom Fitzpatrick, Etienne Provost, James Beckwourth and a still green Jim Bridger. On July 2, 1825, Ashley and his men headed for St. Louis with a load of furs worth $50,000.

Sublette Cut-Off

The Cut-off is the branch of the Oregon Trail 10 miles north of Kemmerer. The trail ruts are still noticeable along State Hwy. 233. The cut-off saved 52 miles for travelers as they made their way to join the Bridger Trail. The trail was not documented and to take this short cut, wagons followed the dead animals that were left behind by earlier wagon trains. It was not the most popular route as there was no water until Bear River. The trail was first used by the William Sublette around 1830. The time saved was at a cost with no water or supplies available along the way. It maintained its appeal as it did help the settlers cross the mountains before the first winter snowstorms.

Held annually throughout the region until 1840, when the demand for beaver pelts decreased, the rendezvous is remembered as one of the western frontiers most colorful traditions. Modern day mountain men still reenact these 19th century "for fairs".

28 *Gas, Food, Lodging*

Fort Bridger, the town

Pop. 150, Elev. 6,675

The town of Ft. Bridger provides practicalities for the nearby historic Fort. A few homes surround the curve in the highway, and the road by the post office will take you past the local cemetery, and on to other parts of the valley.

T Fort Bridger State Historic Site

I-80 Exit 34, 3 miles south on Highway 30. Fort Bridger

History of Fort Bridger

"I have established a small fort, with a blacksmith shop and a supply of iron in the road of the emigrants on Black Fork of Green River, which promises fairly…"

In the summer of 1842, mountain man Jim Bridger announced that he was building a trading post, in the road of the emigrants on Black's Fork of the Green River." From its beginnings as a log and mud trading post, Bridger's "fort" matured into a modern frontier military post before the days of the covered wagon emigration were over. The Mormons purchased the fort from Bridger's partner Louis Vasquez in 1855 and operated it, together with Fort Supply 12 miles to the south, until the fall of 1857. With the onset of the Mormon War and the approach of Johnston's Army, Mormon proprietor Lewis Robinson burned both forts to the ground before departing for Salt Lake. The U. S. Army assumed ownership and command of Fort Bridger the following year. A very successful ranching operation grew around the Fort under the direction of Post Sutler Judge William A. Carter. With the ranch came settlement and, eventually, the town of Fort Bridger, the only community in Wyoming with direct roots to the earliest days of the Oregon Trail. Today Fort Bridger is operated by the State of Wyoming as an historical attraction.

Thus spoke Jim Bridger in a letter he dictated to would-be suppliers in 1843. While that small fort only lasted a little more than a decade, Bridger's words did prove to be prophetic. Not only did the location "promise fairly," it proved to be one of the main hubs of westward expansion used by mountain men and Indians to emigrants

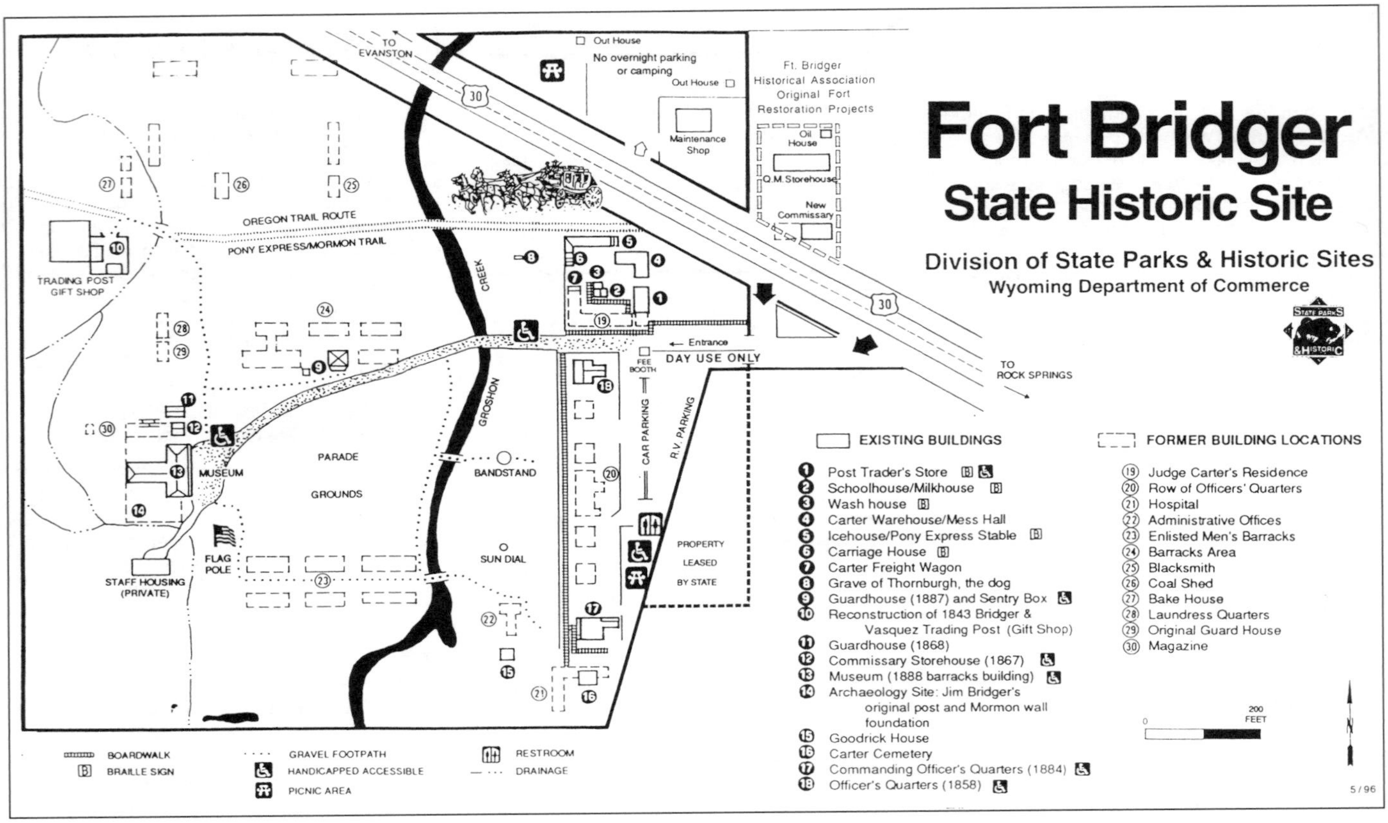

Fort Bridger
State Historic Site

Division of State Parks & Historic Sites
Wyoming Department of Commerce

EXISTING BUILDINGS

1. Post Trader's Store
2. Schoolhouse/Milkhouse
3. Wash house
4. Carter Warehouse/Mess Hall
5. Icehouse/Pony Express Stable
6. Carriage House
7. Carter Freight Wagon
8. Grave of Thornburgh, the dog
9. Guardhouse (1887) and Sentry Box
10. Reconstruction of 1843 Bridger & Vasquez Trading Post (Gift Shop)
11. Guardhouse (1868)
12. Commissary Storehouse (1867)
13. Museum (1888 barracks building)
14. Archaeology Site: Jim Bridger's original post and Mormon wall foundation
15. Goodrick House
16. Carter Cemetery
17. Commanding Officer's Quarters (1884)
18. Officer's Quarters (1858)

FORMER BUILDING LOCATIONS

19. Judge Carter's Residence
20. Row of Officers' Quarters
21. Hospital
22. Administrative Offices
23. Enlisted Men's Barracks
24. Barracks Area
25. Blacksmith
26. Coal Shed
27. Bake House
28. Laundress Quarters
29. Original Guard House
30. Magazine

BOARDWALK · BRAILLE SIGN · GRAVEL FOOTPATH · HANDICAPPED ACCESSIBLE · PICNIC AREA · RESTROOM · DRAINAGE

5/96

and Mormon pioneers, the U.S. Army, the Pony Express, the Overland Stage and the Union Pacific Railroad. If it happened in the opening of the American West, it affected, or was affected by, Fort Bridger.

Established by Jim Bridger and Louis Vasquez in 1843 as an emigrant supply stop along the Oregon Trail, it was obtained by the Mormons in the early 1850s, and then became a military outpost in 1858.

In spite of temporary times of abandonment during the Civil War and then again during the late 1870s, Fort Bridger remained U.S. Government property until 1890. After the post was abandoned, many of the buildings constructed by the army were sold at public auction and moved off of the fort grounds to become private homes, barns, bunkhouses and the like. For a time, the buildings that remained were allowed to fall into disrepair. But after a period of neglect, various groups and individuals took interest in preserving and restoring what remained of old Fort Bridger. In 1933 the property was dedicated as a Wyoming Historical Landmark and Museum.

Fort Bridger Annual Mountain Man Rendezous

This exciting annual event is always held on Labor Day Weekend. Over 200 lodges and tepees are set up for the four day event. Traders, buckskinners, mountain men and hunters demonstrate 1840-era crafts and occupations, trade and sell authentic goods, and compete in tomahawk throwing and muzzle loading contests.

Excerpted from Wyoming State Parks and Historic Sites Brochure

H Fort Bridger Interpretive Signs

Fort Bridger - Fort Bridger, Wyoming

Fort Bridger

Jim Bridger established Fort Bridger in 1843 as a fur trading post. It was composed of two double-log houses about 40 feet long that were joined by a pen for horses. The Mormon Pioneer Company reached the fort on July 7, 1847, and spent a day there but considered its prices too high.

Thomas Bullock commented, "several brethren go to make trades with the French & Indians, but few succeeded, as they could not obtain sufficient for their goods." Here the main Oregon-California Trail turned north toward Fort Hall, and the Mormon Trail/Hastings Cutoff continued west to the Valley of the Great Salt Lake. The fort served as a Pony Express, Overland Stage and transcontinental telegraph station in the 1860s and was garrisoned by the U.S. Army between 1857 and 1890.

The Post Trader

The buildings in this area are virtually all that remain of the once thriving commercial empire of Judge William Alexander Carter and his wife Mary, Fort Bridger's only two Post Traders. Carter arrived at Fort Bridger with Colonel Albert S. Johnston's Army in 1857 and soon received the appointment as Post Trader. Selling to soldiers, emigrants, railroad builders, cattlemen, settlers, and Indians, William Carter amassed a fortune and became one of Wyoming Territory's most influential citizens. His interest extended into lumbering, agriculture, livestock, mining, and politics. Carter's "Bug" brand was known on the cattle ranges of four states. Carter County, Dakota Territory (antedating Wyoming Territory) was named for him as was Carter Mountain in northern Wyoming. The Carters entertained such notables as President Chester A. Arthur, James Bridger, Chief Washakie, Mark Twain, Jay Gould, Sidney Dillon, Generals Sherman, Harney, Crook, Augur and Bisbee.

After William's death on November 7, 1881, Mary E. Carter assumed her husband's position and carried on the empire he began in 1857. With Fort Bridger's abandonment in 1890, Mary became the caretaker until the government auctioned off the buildings in 1895. The Carter family maintained the family business through the early Twentieth Century. Judge and Mrs. Carter's contrbutions to the Rocky Mountain west, though of different nature, compare with those of James Bridger.

The Post Trader's Store

Although Judge Carter dabbled in many areas, his main responsibility revolved around his activities as post trader at Fort Bridger. In this store he sold various items not supplied by the Army to the garrison, including limited amounts of liquor. A post council of administration set a ceiling on prices to make sure that the military received a fair deal. In addition to food, dry goods and other items regularly found in a general store of the period, Carter also provided a post office, as well as telegraph and even telephone service in the store's many years of operation. When Judge Carter died in 1881, his wife, Mary, continued in her husband's footsteps. She operated the store and its many facets, and when the government abandoned the fort in 1890, she became the custodian of the grounds until they were sold.

The building itself was an "L" shape with one wing of white washed wood running to the east and west for the store and a stone section which stood to the northeast for a tavern. The remains of this last section measures 25 feet 5 inches by 53 feet 4 inches. The walls rise 10 1/4 feet and the peak of the roof is 16 feet.

House, Warehouse and Mess Hall

At the northeast corner of Judge Carter's complex rose the log chinked ice house. Three doors at the southern side appeared one over the other, allowing this tall building of 18 feet 7 inches by 14 1/4 feet to be entered at all levels as the ice stock began to grow lower with the coming of warmer weather. Ice could be taken to the stone building next door, the two story warehouse and butcher shop-meat storage area. The lower story contained the beef and included a type of walk-in freezer while the upper portion of this large 24 feet by 60 feet facility could hold stock such as dry goods. An "L" off the southeast corner provided space for Carter's employees to take their meals. Two windows and a center door faced to the east to provide light and some additional warmth from the morning sun. This site measured 32 feet while the shorter ends were 18 feet.

School House, Milk House & Wash house

As an indication of his wealth and influence William Carter provided three buildings not commonly available to the average person on the American frontier. The first frame building served the family as a private school. It measured a mere 11 feet 3 inches by 14 feet 3 inches. Here the six children of Judge Carter received their rudiments of education. The adjacent stone structure was the milk house, an 11 feet by 16 1/2 feet processing and storage facility for luxury dairy products. The third building, the wash house, a 20 feet 2 inches by 11 feet 5 inches frame affair, made it possible for the Carters to bathe in relative comfort and also to have the servants do the wash. Inside this small edifice is a 'washing machine,' a new invention on the frontier. The walls of all these buildings rose less than 10 feet.

Post Trader's House

Judge Carter began building his home in 1858 and continually added onto it as his family grew and his status improved. The house was a frame structure with board and batten siding. Two bay windows flanked the front porch. The Carter's boasted one of the largest libraries in the region, and enjoyed several conveniences found in fine Eastern residences of the period. For this reason noted scientists, generals, railroad executives and other distinguished travelers welcomed an invitation to the house. A President of the United States and Mark Twain even visited the residence in its hayday. Unfortunately, a fire destroyed the historic structure in the early 1930s.

Carriage House, Stables and Chicken Coop

This set of buildings completed the holdings of the Post Trader. The first board and batten building with the large double doors served as the carriage house. Judge Carter owned several animal-drawn vehicles which lent an air of wealth to the isolated frontier outpost. He also constructed a stable next to the carriage house for his teams, as well as for use by the Pony Express for the little more than a year that this service kept a station at Fort Bridger. A tack room connected to the stables, as did a crude low wooden shelter for such stock as milk and beef cows. Adjacent to this shelter is the frame chicken coop. The Carriage House is the largest of these buildings at 21 feet by 16 feet 3 inches while the enclosed stable measures 12 feet 9 inches by nearly 16 feet. None of these structures stand more than 10 feet high.

Commanding Officer's Quarters—1884-1890

This structure was of frame construction and completed in 1884 during a period of extensive improvement at the Post. It supplanted the old log Commanding Officers Quarters which had been in use since 1858.

After the abandonment of Fort Bridger in 1890, the building was sold and moved to a new location a short distance to the northeast.

The structure subsequently served as a hotel for several years.

Post Commissary

The post commissary, erected in 1867, measured 28' x 100' and was built of cut stone quarried about two miles west of the fort. A portion of the old cobblerock Mormon Wall was utilized to form a section of the building's north wall.

The commissary provided a vital service to the men of Fort Bridger. It was from this building that the men received their rations. In addition, a wide variety of supplies, including lighting devices, stationery, pens and ink could be purchased here by the troops as well as by certain civilian employees.

During 1983 and 1984 the remaining part of the commissary was restored. The interior now consists of a room that served as an office and sleeping quarters for the clerk, and the sales or issue room where the men were given their rations. The rear of the building, now missing, was the storeroom for the supplies. Since such storerooms were frequently targets of theft, the clerk's sleeping quarters provide some extra security.

Due to the completion of a new commissary and increased concern regarding the building's deterioration, in 1884 the army converted this building into an indoor shooting gallery. By 1887 it was serving as a storage area for rough lumber, and when the army left in 1890, the commissary building's value had dropped to only $20

Bridger's Stockade

These log buildings and corrals are a reconstruction of the trading post operated by mountain men Jim Bridger and Louis Vasquez in 1846. The post was originally built in 1843 when the fur trade was rapidly dying due to a change in Eastern fashions and the depletion of beaver from Rocky Mountain streams. The establishment of this trading post, known as Fort Bridger, marked the end of the era of free roaming trappers and the beginning of the westward movement of civlization. Thousands of emigrants stopped here for supplies, smith work, or fresh animals on their way west to find land, gold, religious freedom, or a fresh start in a new land.

Jim Bridger's original fort consisted of two pole stockades. One measured 100' x 100' and contained two log cabins at right angles to one another. Each cabin was divided into two rooms. The proprietors and their families split one cabin and the other housed the blacksmith/carpenter shop and the traderoom. The other enclosure measured 100' x80' and was used to corral the livestock at night to guard them against theft.

Fort Bridger was brieflly occupied by the Mormons in the early 1850's and then established as a military post by the U.S. Army in 1858. This reconstruction was based on diary accounts and made possible by a donation by former local resident and his wife, George V. and Phila Caldwell. It was built during 1985-6 and according to archaeological evidence, sits about 60 yards northwest of the original.

The Carter Cemetery

The decendents re-interred here in 1933 represent a very significant cross section of those individuals whose names and contributions will

Section 4

All Wyoming Area Codes are 307

Jim Bridger

Mountain men were the essence of the frontier spirit, and Jim Bridger was the essence of the mountain man. His name graces many locations throughout the Rockies, but Wyoming was his primary stomping ground. Born in Virginia in 1804, he was orphaned at an early age, and was raised by relatives near St. Louis, Missouri. Since this was then the western edge of the American Frontier, he quickly learned the skills of survival, which included an apprenticeship as a blacksmith. When William Ashley's call for "100 enterprising young men" came out in the Missouri Gazette in 1822, young Bridger - then only 18 - was among the first to respond. He was on the leading keelboat which took the adventurers up the Missouri River to the wilds of the Rockies.

As the passage of time would demonstrate, Bridger was driven by a will to push boundaries. After his trek up the Missouri, he volunteered to explore the Bear River, which led him to be the first white man to see the Great Salt Lake in 1825, at the age of 21. He then volunteered to lead an expedition down the Big Horn River, during which he almost lost his life. By 1830, at just 26 years of age, he was well-respected as a serious explorer, and had accumulated the means to buy out Ashley's Rocky Mountain Fur Trading Company when the older man retired.

The 1830s were significant in Bridger's life as the Rendezvous years. He was always present, from the first get together at the Green River in 1832, to the last in 1840. While the other mountain men brawled and drank away their hard earned winter fur stores, Bridger would entertain them with his tall tales. He continued telling stories to travelers throughout his life. Most of them had a grain of truth in them, but many found the stories of the marvels of Yellowstone and the Black Hills hard to swallow, especially after he'd just told them a story about being chased by Indians in which he died or got scalped at the end.

Bridger did have one encounter with the Gros Ventre Indians in about 1833 which left him with an arrowhead in his shoulder that he carried with him for the next three years. When the Reverend Samuel Parker and Dr. Marcus Whitman brought religion and "modern medicine" to the West in 1836, the doctor performed a publicly viewed surgery to remove the arrowhead which established not only his expertise, but also Bridger's reputation as a tough customer. After this, the once far-ranging adventurer began to slow down a bit, especially when he saw the economic tide was turning away from the fur trade. He'd sold his share in the Fur Trading Company to William Sublette in 1835, and with the Rendezvous drawing to a close in 1840, he chose to throw in his lot with the fortunes of Ft. Laramie. There, the trappers could go year-round for supplies. Capitalizing on this new trend, he established his own "Fort" Bridger as a stopover for travelers coming down from South Pass in 1842.

Fort Bridger life had its perks, and kept his finances more or less stable with the constant influx of immigrants, but Bridger couldn't sit still for long. After the arrival of the Mormons in 1847, which Bridger directed to the Salt Lake Valley, he began to act as a scout for various parties. He led numerous survey teams around the region, enabling them to map much of the West. His knowledge was so extensive that he became known as "Old Gabe," because it was said he knew his way around as well as the angel Gabriel. Bridger also had an extensive knowledge of Indian sign language, as well as the customs of various tribes, which could prove very useful if people listened to it. They often didn't.

Bridger had three or four Indian wives (accounts vary) who tended to keep up young. Perhaps he was just hard to keep up with. His last wife, known as Mary, was the daughter of Chief Washakie. She must have been made of tougher stuff because she was with him into his old age. The only thing which could have kept Bridger from staying in the mountains forever was failing eyesight. As blindness overtook him, he was forced to return to Missouri, and lived his last days with Mary on a farm in Westport. When he died in 1881, at the age of 77, he left behind a legacy of adventure and discovery seldom rivaled in the annals of U.S. history.

ever be associated with Fort Bridger's early day history. Of particular interest are.......

"Uncle Jack" (John Robertson - an early mountain trapper who came to the vicinity in the 1830s and remained until his death. A colorful local character. It is said he was instrumental in convincing Jim Bridger of the wisdom of establishing a trading post on the Black's Fork.

Virginia Bridger Hahn - born at Fort Bridger on July 4, 1849, daughter of the intrepid Jim Bridger by his second wife, a Ute Indian.

"Judge" William Alexander Carter who came to Fort Bridger with the United States Army in 1857, stayed to become a merchant -cutler, and with his family and associates went on to establish one of the most extensive business enterprises in Wyoming Territory.

This Cemetery was established on the Fort grounds through the efforts of William A. Carter, Jr. and the Historical Landmark Commission of Wyoming.

The Road to Zion

From the late 1840s through the 1860s, an exodus of more than 70,000 Mormons passed by here on their way to their "New Zion" in Utah. Starting from Nauvoo, Illinois in February 1846, the first group of at least 13,000 Mormons crossed into Iowa to escape religious persecution, then spent the winter in the area of present-day Council Bluffs, Iowa and Omaha, Nebraska.

In 1847, Brigham Young led an advance party of 143 men, 2 women, and 3 children along the Platte River. At Fort Bridger, Wyoming they departed from the Oregon Trail to head southwest to the Great Salt Lake. Thousands of other Mormons soon followed. Today, a marked 1,624-mile auto tour route closely parallels their historic trek.

Many Mormon emigrants wrote diaries to describe their experiences. Appleton Harmon wrote his journal in 1847.

After arriving, the Mormon pioneers set up communities and ferry crossing along the trail to assist later wagon trains going to and from Utah.

From 1856-60, many European converts walked more than 1,200 miles to Salt Lake City pushing and pulling handcarts loaded with 500 pounds of supplies. After 1860, the Mormon church sponsored oxen-drawn wagons to bring emigrants to the "New Zion."

Old Fort Bridger-Pioneer Trading Post

The Fort was established about 1842 by Jim Bridger, discoverer of Great Sale Lake; notable pioneer, trapper, fur trader, scout and guide. Bridger was born at Richmond, Virginia, March 17, 1804, and died at Westport, Missouri, July 17, 1884. His unerring judgement regarding problems of trappers, traders, soldiers, emigrants, and gold seekers, bordered on the miraculous, and his advice was universally in demand in the early history of this state.

Bridger has been prominently recognized as America's greatest frontiersman and the west's most gifted scout.

Sutler's Store

The Post Trader's or Sutler's Store, shown as it appeared about 1871, was owned and operated by Judge W. A. Carter, a prominent citizen in Territorial Wyoming. The east-west wing on the left was removed sometime after the fort was abandoned by the Army in 1890. The Carter family is buried in the cemetery on Officer's Row.

Thornburgh was a dog...

Named after Major T. T. Thornburgh who was killed in a fight with the Ute Indians near the White River Agency, September 29, 1879. The dog was a survivor of a wagon train burned during the battle and grew up as a military camp follower. Eventually he ended up at Fort Bridger.

On several occasions Thornburgh distinguished himself by his heroic deeds including catching a commissary thief, warning a sentinel of marauding Indians, saving the life of a soldier in a knife fight and rescuing a small boy from drowning.

At fort Bridger, Thornburgh became the devoted companion of a freighter, "Buck" Buchanan, and the favorite of many who frequented the Post. Thornburgh died September 27, 1888 as the result of being kicked by one of Buchanan's mules.

It is said that Thornburgh's master lies in an unmarked grave in the city cemetery at Salt Lake City.

Fort Bridger in 1889

Above is a copy of a watercolor of Fort Bridger done by Merritt D. Houghton (1845-1918) known for his historic illustrations of Wyoming

Fort Bridger Rendezvous

Experience the mystique of the fur trade era at Wyoming's biggest mountain man celebration which takes place over Labor Day Weekend. Participate with this lively gathering of Mountain Men and Indians who gather as costumed revelers and traders of brightly colored goods. You'll see black powder shoots, Native American dancers, tepee village, primitive demos, knife and hawk throw, and cannon shoots. Traders Row features 1840s period trade goods with 140 different traders. See demonstrations of the skills needed to survive this era. At Fort Bridger State Historic Site.

Wyoming Tidbits

The mideast oil embargo of 1973 led to exploration in the Evanston area, known as the Overthrust Belt. The embargo resulted in sky-rocketing crude oil prices and increased the popularity of low-grade coal and natural gas as domestic fuel sources.

towns, ranches and mines. The view is toward the south and the Uinta Mountains.

In 1889, the date of this painting, the fort had but one year remaining in its existence as a United States military post. The following year, as a result of the vanishing frontier and the lack of a need for forts such as this one, the army abandoned Fort Bridger.

A number and name description is listed locating all of the sites at Fort Bridger.

Mormon Occupation

The involvement of the Mormons in the affairs of Fort Bridger constituted a short, but eventful period. A few remnants of their industry may still be found.

After the establishment of Fort Supply, twelve miles to the south, in 1853, Lewis Robison acquired Bridger's trading post in 1855, supported in his endeavor by Brigham Young. Under Robison's proprietorship, trade with the emigrants, trappers and Indians continued much as usual around the post for the next two years.

Early in 1857, Brigham Young instructed Robison to fortify his property for protection from the Indians. Brigham was probably also apprehensive about the clouds of discontent gathering between the Mormons in Utah and the United States government. Throughout the summer, as a punitive force of Federal troops marched westward across the plains toward Utah, Robison worked hard with cobblestone and mortar to construct a walled enclosure. The main Fort, was 100 feet square with walls 16 feet in height and 5 feet at the base. Attached was a horse corral, 80 feet by 100 feet, with walls 8 feet in height and 2 1/2 feet wide at the base.

Robison completed the walls in August of 1857, just before "Johnston's Army" reached Fort Bridger in November, the Mormons instituted a "scorched earth" policy and deserted and burned both Fort Bridger and Fort Supply. The fire-gutted stone walls then became a quartermaster storage facility. Subsequent military construction resulted in most of Robison's fort being leveled to the ground.

The Mormon Wall

On August 3, 1855 the Church of Jesus Christ of Latter-Day Saints concluded arrangements for the purchase of fort Bridger from Luis Vasquez, partner of James Bridger, for $8,000.00. final payment was made October 18, 1858. A cobblestone wall was erected in the fall of 1855, replacing Bridger's stockade. A few additional log houses were built within the Fort. The place was evacuated and burned on the approach of Johnston's Army September 27, 1857. A portion of the wall is here preserved. In 1855, Fort Supply was established by Brigham Young six miles south where crops were raised for the emigrants.

1st Commanding Officer's Quarters

From 1858 to 1890 the area in the foreground was occupied by the log and frame structure shown in the photograph. The building was the fourth log Officers' Quarters in a row of six constructed shortly after Fort Bridger was declared a military post in 1857. For sixteen years it served as the Commanding Officer's residence with frame extensions added in 1868 and 1873 to provide a kitchen, servants room, parlor and two bedrooms. A new frame Commanding Officer's Quarters was completed in 1884 after which this building was divided into an Officers' Quarters and into Court Martial and Military Board rooms.

The First School House in Wyoming

In 1860, Judge Wm. A. Carter erected this school house for the education of his four daughters, two sons and other children of the fort. Competent instructors from the East were employed and the students of this school were permitted to enter eastern colleges without further preparation. Thus, the way was paved for future education in Wyoming.

29 *No services*

T Encampment Museum

At Encampment. 327-5308

Two-Story Outhouse

Deep Snow Plumbing — Though most dwellings in the mining communities in the hills above Encampment in the early days were settled on solid earth (many of the nearby Chic-Sale structures were designed in higher fashion) to overcome the problem of deep, drifting snows. Some of these outhouses were erected high atop a base of cribbed up logs; others were slender, silo-like creations with doors opening high up on their fronts; a few were even impressive with newly shingled exteriors. Most were approached by wooden steps leading up five or six feet to railed platforms in front of the doors; others were reached by railed ramps from building to outhouse.

This two-story outhouse is part of the display at the Grand Encampment Museum complex.

History Of The Area

An abundance of fine pelts drew the first white men into this valley, long held sacred by the Indians. The trappers' day soon passed, and was succeeded by others, equally brief. Tie cutters, cattle barons, and hunting expeditions came and went. Thomas Edison accompanied one of these expeditions, taking time to do some fishing in Battle Lake. Homesteaders and ranchers, the first permanent residents, began to arrive in the 1870s.

The year of 1897 produced an electrifying change. A rich copper strike in the Sierra Madres precipitated the new city of Grand Encampment and several satellite settlements. The smelter was supplied by a 16-mile aerial tramway — longest in the world. Power was provided by water through a 4' wooden pipeline. The S & E Railroad was constructed, but its completion came a little late.

In 1908, the company which had produced two million dollars in copper ore, was indicted for over- capitalization and fraudulent stock sales. The mines closed, and Rudefeha, Dillon, Copperton, Rambler, Battle and Elwood became ghost towns. Encampment and Riverside survived but the "Grand" was quietly dropped.

Reprinted from museum brochure.

Wyoming Tidbits

The Wyoming Battalion of the National Guard raised the first United States flag in Manila during the Spanish-American War.

30 *Gas, Food*

I-80 Exit 30

31 *No services*

T Piedmont

I-80, Exit #24, 7.5 miles south

Almost a dozen wood cabins and structures, as well as a number of charcoal kilns, remain as testament to the productivity of Piedmont. The town was abandoned when the railroad tracks were moved father north in 1901. Legend has it that buried treasure from one of Butch Cassidy's bank robberies remains here. Calamity Jane's dad lies buried in an unmarked grave in Piedmont.

T Charcoal Kilns

About five miles south of I-80 Exit 24

Located at Piedmont, southeast of Evanston and Hilliard, south of Evanston. Wood was turned into coke and used by the Union Pacific Railroad for its steam engines. At Piedmont, treasure hunters still dig the area for the loot Butch Cassidy supposedly buried there.

H Muddy Creek Camp and Crossing

The Muddy Creek Camp, which was northwest of this marker and on the west side of the Muddy Creek, was used by Brigham Young's first group of Mormon Pioneers who arrived here on July 9, 1847. Thomas Bullock reported that the brethren sang hymns for President Brigham Young and they had a delightful evening. This camp had good water and plenty of grass, and the animals were well-fed by the tall bunch-grass growing along the creek. Erastus Snow described the campground as "very Pretty."

It was one of the most heavily used camps on the Overland-Mormon-California-Pony Express Trails. Approximately 70,000 Mormon pioneers crossed, passed through, or camped at Muddy Creek Campground. The U.S. Army camped here with 2,000 men in June of 1858. Both the Martin and Willie handcart companies crossed here in November of 1856 while traveling with rescue wagons. The Muddy Overland Stage Stop and Pony Express Station were locat-

Depot Square in Evanston.

ed at this site, and foundation stones my still be seen along the west bank of Muddy Creek. The road by this marker was the original Transcontinental Railroad bed of 1869. The Transcontinental Telegraph, automobile road and stageline either go through the campground or are very nearby, making Muddy Creek Camp an important part of this area's history.

32 *No services*

I-80 Exits 10, 18, 21, 23

33 *Gas, Food, Lodging*

Evanston

Pop. 11, 507, Elev. 6,748

The Uinta County Seat was named for James A. Evans, a railroad surveyor and engineer. The town was established in 1869. Sarah Bernhardt was once stranded here when a landslide delayed the train heading west. Downtown, the restored old Evanston Depot was once among the finest stopovers on the Transcontinental Railroad. As a result of the abundance of Chinese immigrants who came to work on the railroad, part of Evanston became a Chinatown. This was a gathering place for Chinese from all around Wyoming, until it was destroyed by fire in the 1920s.

Now that the railroad's glory days are past, Evanston has a more pedestrian quality. In addition to being the site of the State Mental Institution, Evanston claims agriculture, oil, mining, and logging as central to its economy. It is beginning to welcome tourism with a decent sampling of restaurants, shops, and activities. An excellent recreation center, golf course, cross-country ski trails, horseback riding, and other activities and adventures are available to entertain visitors.

Opal

Just outside the canyon of the Uinta Mountains near the Utah line of Wyoming lies Opal –a half dozen log houses, a saloon, and many corrals. For several years, 10,000 cattle and sheep were shipped annually to Chicago from this once bustling town. As with many towns of southern Wyoming, Opal sprang up as a result of the railroad boom. The rails of the Union Pacific spread west from Cheyenne in the 1860s, and along those tracks, Opal proved to be somewhat of an oasis for weary travelers.

Opal witnessed the discovery of petroleum, and soon after during the 1860s and 1870s, oil-well drilling was done in Uinta County.

T Bear River State Park

1-80 Exit 6 at east edge of Evanston. 789-6547

History

Bear River State Park is located in extreme southwestern Wyoming, within the city limits of Evanston and just south of exit #6 on 1-80, near the Bear River.

Native Americans named the river "Quee-ya-paw" for a tobacco root that grew along its banks. Trappers called it "Bear River," because of the many bears that frequented the area. Indians and trappers often held rendezvous in this area, including one in 1825 near Burnt Fork, just 50 miles southeast of the park.

The nearly 300 acres that make up Bear River State Park was opened to the public in 1991. The park is connected to the Bear Project, a greenbelt activity offered by the city. Although the Bear Project is not in the state park, it allows visitors to connect easily to downtown Evanston via an interconnecting trail system.

Summer and Winter Trails

Nearly 3 miles of foot trails are within park limits. This includes 1.2 miles of asphalt-surfaced trail and an arched footbridge that crosses the Bear River, allowing access to a natural area. Another 1.7 miles of packed gravel trails are located on the west side of the river.

The foot trails in the park also double as cross-country ski trails in the winter. Evanston's Parks and Recreation Department and Bear River State Park staff combine forces to provide high quality, cross-country ski trails as an excellent way to dump the "winter blues." When weather permits, the park road is closed to vehicles and open to skiing and hiking. Numerous other trails are maintained for those who ski and snowshoe. *Reprinted from park brochure.*

T Depot Square

Downtown Evanston

Depot Square was designed with the preservation of Evanston's history in mind. Newly refurbished Union Pacific Depot is the centerpiece of the square, and a UPRR dining car and caboose will be restored for use as a restaurant. The Beeman-Cashin building, a historic wooden structure built in 1883, hosts ballet, wedding receptions and other community activities. The Carnegie Library, built in 1906, now serves as the Chamber of Commerce and Uinta County museum. A gazebo in Martin Park, on the west end, is an area for concerts and picnics. The bandstand hosts weekly concerts. A replica Joss House, a Chinese sacred temple, serves as a Chinese museum and information center. Depot Square is designed to encourage people to stroll through the area and experience the history and nostalgia of the area.

H Evanston

Just east of fairgrounds on Bear River Drive in Evanston.

Evanston was established by the Union Pacific Railroad Company late in 1868. In the first county election, September 6, 1870, Evanston was chosen county seat. Union Pacific Railroad shops moved here in the fall of 1871. Timber and sawmill operations were the leading business. Cattle and sheep ranching became the

Evanston	Jan	Feb	March	April	May	June	July	Aug	Sep	Oct	Nov	Dec	Annual
Average Max. Temperature (F)	31.1	33.9	40.6	51.9	62.3	72.2	81.1	79.5	70.8	58.1	42.9	33.1	54.8
Average Min. Temperature (F)	7.4	9.8	16.3	25.2	32.3	38.6	44.6	43.2	35.1	26.6	16.7	9.0	25.4
Average Total Precipitation (in.)	0.83	0.90	1.06	1.20	1.36	1.02	0.84	0.97	0.99	1.14	0.87	0.76	11.95
Average Total SnowFall (in.)	10.1	9.8	9.3	5.1	2.0	0.2	0.0	0.0	0.7	3.1	6.8	8.3	55.5
Average Snow Depth (in.)	8	8	2	0	0	0	0	0	0	0	1	4	2

basic industry of Uinta county. In the 1870s and early 1880s, a Chinese Joss House, one of the three in the United States, attracted thousands of Chinese for Chinese New Year's Day ceremonies. About four hundred Chinese normally lived in "China Town" and worked in the Almy coal mines. The Joss House burned on January 26, 1922.

F Old Mill Restaurant

30 County Road, next to Super 8 in Evanston. 789-4040

The Old Mill Restaurant is located in a building built in 1892 as a flour mill and has been a landmark and part of Evanston's history for over 100 years. The restaurant is conveniently located to downtown shops and attractions. The Old Mill is popular in Evanston for breakfast, and open for lunch and dinner. Enjoy great sandwiches and burgers, along with a full steak and seafood dinner menu. Enjoy your favorite libations with your meal or just stop in and relax. There are four pool tables for your enjoyment. A private banquet room is available for up to fifty people.

L Super 8 Motel - Evanston

70 Bear River Drive in Evanston. 789-7510 or toll free at 866-298-4341. www.super8.com

34

T Uinta County Museum

36 10th St. in Evanston. 789-8248

The museum's exhibits focus on the general history of Uinta County and Wyoming. Permanent exhibit topics include Indians, pioneers, mining, the railroad, gambling, the Chinese, industries, equipment, costumes, ranches, schools, stores and parlors. It contains an extensive collection of Chinese artifacts, arrowheads, Indian artifacts, clothing, pioneer relics, furniture, and pictures. It also has a room furnished in 1880s furniture. M-F, 9-5; Summer: Sat/Sun., 10-4. Admission is free and donations accepted.

T Mormon Trail Crossing

Eight miles southeast of Evanston on State Highway 150.

The Mormon Trail crosses State Highway 150 about eight miles southeast of Evanston, near the Wyoming-Utah border. The Mormon Trail follows the Hastings Cutoff to California that was pioneered by the ill-fated Donner Party in 1846, a year before Brigham Young's initial trip west. A monument marks the site. *Source: BLM brochure.*

T Evanston Recreation Center

275 Saddle Ridge Road in Evanston. 789-1770

The Recreation Center has a wide variety of equipment and areas to suit all fitness needs. The facility has swimming pools, gyms, raquetball, range, classes, indoor track, nursery and more.

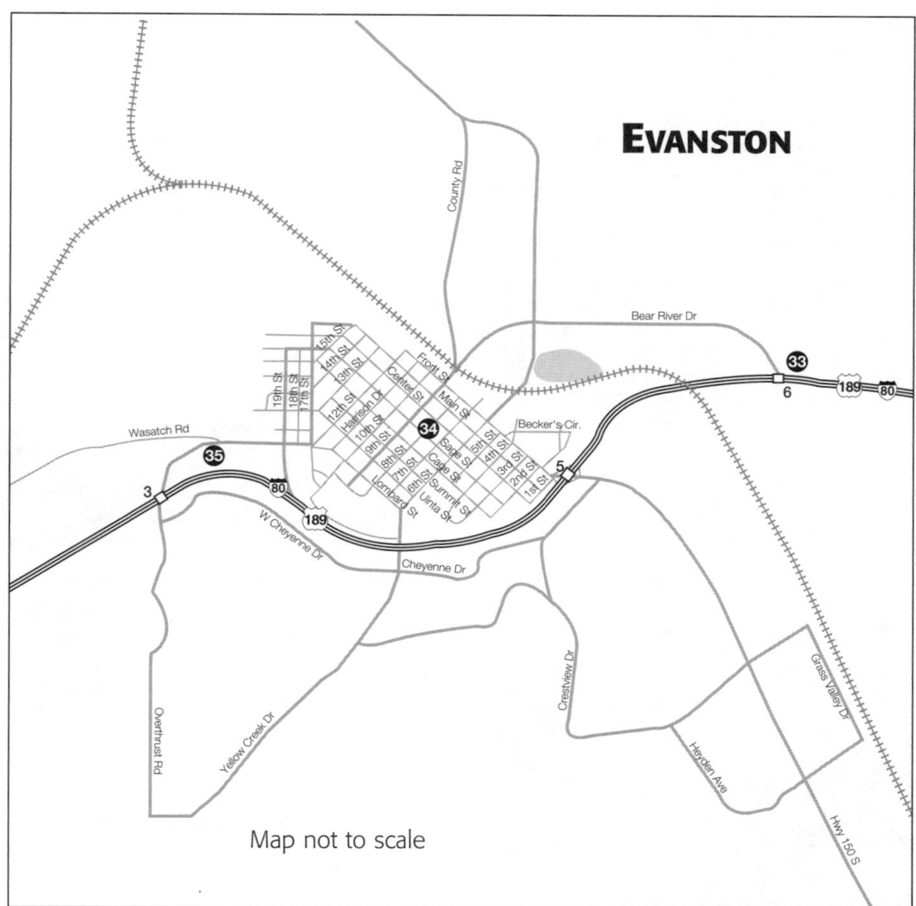

The Evanston Parks and Recreation District Offices are also located in this building.

T Chinese Joss House Museum

920 Front Street in Evanston. 783-6320

The museum is housed in a reproduction of the Joss House, a place of worship for the Chinese in the area from the 1894 through the early 1920s. Exhibits address the Chinese in Evanston from 1870–1939. Collections include artifacts from Chinatown Archaeological Digs, private Chinese collections (dates varying), historical photographs, pottery, books, paintings, and other Chinese items. Open Monday through Friday, 7 a.m. to 3 p.m. in winter, 8 a.m. to 7 p.m. in summer. Admission is free, donations are gratefully accepted.

H First Brick Church

Just south of Main and 7th Street in Evanston

In February, 1873, a branch of the Church of Jesus Christ of Latter-day Saints was organized in Evanston by President William Budge of Bear Lake Valley, Idaho. On May 23, 1873, William G. Burton was ordained Bishop. On June 24, 1890, this ward was incorporated under the laws of the State of Wyoming and named Evanston. The Board of Trustees were James Brown, Thomas Parkinson, John Whittle, Frank Mills and Arthur W. Sims. In 1890 this group, with James Brown as Bishop, built the first brick church in Wyoming.

T Bear River

There is little to see of what was once a bustling little lumber town. There was a mill and lumber was brought into town from the Uinta Mountains. Originally established in the late 1800s, along a railroad spur line, it was destroyed by a fire in 1900 and never rebuilt. Before that the Army briefly used the town as a fort.

H Bear River City

About 10 miles southeast of Evanston on State Highway 150.

Nothing remains today as a reminder that Bear River City was one of the notorious "end-of-track" towns along the original Union Pacific Transcontinental Railroad line. Initially called Gilmer, the town was first settled by lumberjacks, who arrived in 1867 and supplied ties to the approaching railroad. The population of the settlement swelled to nearly 2,000 as construction of the Echo Tunnel in Utah and the onset of winter held up track laying.

This railroad boom town, its name changed to Bear River city, developed a reputation for unparalleled rowdiness. The town consisted of a few stores and boarding houses standing alongside numerous saloons and gambling parlors.

Section 4

All Wyoming Area Codes are 307

These liquor and gaming establishments catered to a nefarious crowd, causing the Frontier Index to report Bear River City as "the liveliest city, if not the wickedest in America."

The Frontier Index, a traveling newspaper printed at various points along the Union Pacific route, outraged Bear River City's lawless element by endorsing vigilante activity as a means of eliminating undesirables. Whipped to a frenzy, on November 20, 1868 an unruly mob burned down the Index office. The town's law-abiding citizens retaliated against the mob and the ensuing battle lasted well into the night. Order had been restored by the time troops arrived from Fort Bridger the next morning.

The railroad, not riotous mobs, caused the town's demise when the Union Pacific refused to construct a siding connecting Bear River City to the main line. The populace hurriedly packed their belongings and moved on to Evanston, a town which offered better prospects. The hoopla, which marked the short history of Bear River City became only a memory.

F JB's Restaurant
1969 Harrison Drive in Evanston. 789-7537

JB's Restaurant is located in Evanston and Rock Springs. Visitors to the area love it as much as local residents do. The full service menu will please the entire family for breakfast, lunch or dinner. The breakfast buffet is a perennial favorite. A soup and salad bar is available for lunch and dinner to compliment any meal. The desserts are fabulous. Try a slice of pie from a great selection of custards, creams, and cheesecakes. The Volcano Lava cake is a big hit–chocolate cake filled with hot fudge, heated, and topped with ice cream. They are open 6 a.m. to 11 p.m. and until midnight Friday and Saturday. Sesasonal patio seating is available.

F Bear River Brewing LLC, Restaurant & Pub
1012 Main Street in Evanston. 789-6274.
www.bearriverbrew.com

Bear River Brewing LLC, Restaurant & Pub features the products of Bear River Brewing, including nonalcoholic sodas. Their signature beer has won the People's Choice Award at the Saratoga Beer Festival two years in a row–a record. Two national beer judges said, "They'd only fill their glasses at the BRB booth." Brewmaster, James Bond, oversees the enjoyable dining experience. This family-friendly, smoke-free restaurant serves pastas, vegetarian dishes sandwiches, and hearty main courses made fresh for each customer. Diners can watch the activity in the brew room. You can also order your favorite cocktail. A delicious, healthful menu is offered for lunch and dinner Wednesday through Saturday. Live entertainment is showcased on weekends.

S Quilt Trappings LLC
1029 Main Street in Evanston. 444-1675.
www.quilttrappings.com

M Real Estate HeadQuarters
645 Main Street in Evanston. 789-7821.
www.evanstonwyomingrealestate.com

Real Estate HeadQuarters offers personalized service for your individual needs, providing a superior level of informed, professional real estate services to buyers and sellers in the Evanston area. Broker/owner Barry Coster, has been a resident of Evanston for over 20 years, with over 17 years experience in real estate. Barry and his staff are committed to specific needs when representing clients either as a buyer agency or as a seller agency. The professionals at Real Estate HeadQuarters help you feel confident with commercial, industrial, residential, or business investments. They are conveniently located in downtown Evanston or visit them on the web. 34

M ERA Plowman Realty
625 Front Street in Evanston. 789-7700 or toll free at 866-789-7700. www.era.com

ERA Plowman Realty is licensed to service buyers and sellers in Wyoming and Utah and is a member of the Multiple Listing Service (MLS). They can help you with all your real estate needs from buying your first home to retirement homes. Their own mortgage company, available 7 days a week, makes it quick and easy for the buyer, even over the phone. They offer exclusive AON Home Warranties and the ERA Seller Security Plan—they will sell your home or ERA will buy it. Voted best agency by the people of Evanston in 2002. Deb Plowman was voted best real estate agent for 1999 and 2002. Ask them for a copy of the Answers Book or visit them on the web.

Father Pierre Jean DeSmet

A Belgian missionary born in 1801, Father Pierre Jean DeSmet was one of the first Catholic priests to stay among the native tribes. In 1840, Father DeSmet arrived at Green River and met with members of the Blackfoot nation near Yellowstone. DeSmet stayed in the region for years, working with the native tribes. In 1858, he helped negotiate peace treaties with various tribes. Black Robe, as the Native Americans called him, had a genuine concern for their welfare and they, in turn, trusted him.

M RE/MAX Results Realty, Inc.
848 Main Street in Evanston. 789-4411 or toll free at 888-739-4414.
Email: miakeeast@allwest.net.
www.homesinevanston.com

RE/MAX Results Realty and broker, Michael Eastman, will go the extra mile to help you achieve your goals in purchasing or selling your property. The agency specializes in residential properties, but also provide the same great service in commercial, recreational, and vacation properties. Michael Eastman has been in in the real estate market in Evanston for over twenty one years. He is one of 15% of Realtors in the USA with a CRS, certified residential specialist, certification. You will appreciate the friendly and professional service that will give you confidence and the results you are looking for. Visit them on the web or give them a call.

35 *Food, Lodging*

T Almy
3 miles northwest of Evanston on State Highway 89.

Named for James T. Almy, this rambling town encompassed nearly 5 miles along the Bear River. At one time, the town boasted nearly 4,000 residents. The coal mines at Almy were deemed some of the most dangerous in the state, with frequent methane gas explosions, and mining disasters took their toll on the population. In 1900 the mines were closed by the Union Pacific Railroad. With its primary industry gone, the town whithered and died. Today, millions of tons of coal remain unmined, and some still burns in the shafts.

H Almy

3 miles northwest of Evanston on State Highway 89

Ninteenth century railroads were dependent upon coal for fuel. The vast coal reserves of southern Wyoming helped determine the route of the transcontinental Union Pacific Railroad and were the basis for Wyoming's first energy boom. Communities sprang up along the line and several with coal deposits or rail facilities survived. Coal mines were opened in the surrounding Bear River Valley in 1868. Dreams of prosperity lured miners from England, Scandinavia, China, and from throughout the United States to settle in "Wyoming Camp", which later became Almy. Named for James T. Almy, a clerk for the Rocky Mountain Coal company and located three miles northwest of Evanston, Almy was strung out along the Bear river for five miles. This particular "string-town" owed its existence solely to coal mining. Her 4,000 residents suffered more than their share of mining tragedies. On March 4, 1881, the first mine explosion west of the Mississippi to claim lives, killed 38 men in just one of many serious disasters to strike Almy. In January of 1886, 13 more died and on March 20, 1895, the third worst mine explosion in Wyoming history, claimed the lives of 61 men. The State coal Mine Inspector determined the Almy mines "among the most dangerous in the state". Finally, in 1900 the mines were closed by the Union Pacific due to labor troubles and explosions. Almy lost its principal industry, the population dwindled, and the town suffered the fate of many railroad coal towns throughout Wyoming.

Overthrust Belt

A geologic term for the folding and thrusting of layers of the earth's crust. This narrow belt stretches from New Mexico to Wyoming. The belt is where the Kemmerer/Diamondville area gets much of its oil and gas resources.

F Rendezvous Smokehouse Restaurant and Sports Bar

339 Wasatch Road in Evanston. 789-2220

The Rendezvous Smokehouse serves up wildly popular dry-rubbed, smoked meats, featuring baby back and St. Louis-style ribs. But that's not all! They also serve up great pulled pork, smoked jumbo prawns, and prime rib. In addition to smoking their own meats, they also make fantastic soups, fresh baked cheese biscuits daily, and smoked apple pie. Open for breakfast, lunch and dinner and a children's menu is available. The Sports Bar is a great place to enjoy pool, darts, and shuffleboard. Watch your favorite event on one of nine TV's with the NFL Ticket, NBA Pass and ESPN's Gameplan. Located next to the Rendezvous Lodge.

L Comfort Inn - Evanston

1931 Harrison Drive in Evanston. 789-7799 or 800-228-5150. www.comfortinn.com

The Comfort Inn is an outstanding choice for business, relaxation, and relocations when in the Evanston area. 56 new, beautifully appointed guest rooms each include microwave, refrigerator, coffee maker, hair dryer, data port, iron and ironing board, clock radio, cable TV, and voice mail. Guests also receive a complimentary deluxe Continental breakfast. Other room options include a suite with hot tub, king business rooms, and large family room. Work out in the on-site fitness center and then relax in the indoor heated pool and hot tub. A large guest laundry is available for added convenience. A variety of restaurants are within walking distance. 35

FL Best Western Dunmar Inn & Legal Tender Restaurant
1601 Harrison Drive in Evanston. 789-3770 or 800-654-6509.
www.bestwestern.com/dunmarinn

The Best Western Dunmar Inn features 165 upscale guest rooms in a complex of buildings spread over 15 acres of beautifully landscaped grounds. All rooms come standard with microfridge, hairdryer, iron and ironing board, data ports, 2 telephones and one 2-line speaker phone, voice mail, pay-per-view and cable television, king or queen size beds, and 27" TV's, The Legal Tender Restaurant and Lounge, Gift Shop, an outdoor heated swimming pool, outdoor hot tub and an exercise room with sauna also compliment the Hotel. The restaurant is open daily for breakfast, lunch, and dinner and the lounge is open until 2 a.m. Visit them on the web.

L Rendezvous Lodge
339 Wasatch Road in Evanston. 789-2220

The Rendezvous Lodge is conveniently located to the interstate and downtown Evanston. This independently owned and operated takes pride in their courteous and service minded staff. 113 clean and spacious rooms and suites are affordable and have inside corridors. Suites with kitchenettes or Jacuzzi's are also available. Relax at the end of a busy day in the sauna or Jacuzzi available for all guests. The full service Rendezvous Smokehouse Restaurant and Sports Bar is located on site and open 6 a.m. to 10 p.m. daily. There is plenty of off street parking available for large vehicles. Pets are allowed.

36 *No services*

Carter

Judge William A. Carter, the first merchant and post sutler at Ft. Bridger, is the man for whom this railroad station town was named. Originally from Iowa, Carter became vice-president of the Wyoming Stock Growers Association in 1871.

T Cumberland Ghost Town
Near the junction of U.S. Highway 189 and State Highway 412 (approx. 36 miles north of Evanston)

Between 1920 and 1935, this flourishing coal-mining town boasted four underground mines in full production, named Cumberland 1, Cumberland 2, etc. Today only the Ziller ranch buildings and the cemetery remain. The abundance of children's graves may have been the result of a cholera epidemic in the early 1900s, which claimed many of the young in those days. The cemetery is located just past the junction on Highway 189.

37 *No services*

Elkol

Perhaps a merging of two of Wyoming's hallmarks, elk and coal, this mining town was established in 1908.

38 *Gas, Food, Lodging*

Diamondville

Pop. 900, Elev. 6,927

Prospector Harrison Church found a vein of coal just north of this town in 1868. It wasn't until 1894 that Church found enough investors to start the Diamond Coal and Coke Company, named for the pristine coal, "black diamonds." Riches of another kind came with the advent of Prohibition, which brought prosperity to Diamondville when its bootlegging operation became popular product in Chicago. The original coal mine played out in the 1930s, but the area continues to be coal-rich.

T Stolen Bell Museum
316 Diamondville Ave. in Diamondville. 877-6676

With exhibits covering the area's general history with wonderful mining exhibits, and even a moonshine still. The museum is open Monday thorugh Friday, 8 a.m. to 4:30 p.m., and will open upon request. Admision is free and donations are accepted.

39

T Fossil Country Museum
400 Pine Avenue in Kemmerer. 877-6551.
www.hamsfork.net/~museum

This museum chronicles the history of Kemmerer and Diamondville. Inside you'll see an early 1900s period dining room, a replica coal mine and assortment of coal mining equipment, bootlegging stills and wine presses, a Hadrosaurid footprint, a two-bodied lamb, mountain men memorabilia, the JC Penney Mother Store, Sawaya's Kemmerer Shoe Store, and Annie Richey, Cattle Rustler, memorabilia. The museum is open Monday through Saturday. Admission is free.

T Kemmerer
Pop. 2,651, Elev. 6,927

Situated on the Hamsfork River, Kemmerer is the Lincoln County Seat. Established in 1889, it became an incorporated city in 1902. Named for M. S. Kemmerer's Coal Company, who founded it, the town provided goods and services to the local miners and ranchers. Nearby Diamondville and Frontier, which were official company towns, served more as bedroom communities. Kemmerer today has the distinction of being the only community in the county with stoplights. There are two.

T J.C. Penney Home and Historical Foundation
722 J.C. Penney Drive in Kemmerer. 877-4501

The Penney's first home was restored in 1982 and moved to Penney Avenue on the Triangle, where it is now a museum operated by the J.C. Penney Foundation. The six room cottage is a National Historic Landmark. It is open during the spring and summer.

T Triangle Museum
800 Pine Ave. in Kemmerer.

J.C. Penney Mother Store and Home

The year was 1902 and a 27 year old man arrived by train in Kemmerer, Wyoming to start a new

Kemmerer	Jan	Feb	March	April	May	June	July	Aug	Sep	Oct	Nov	Dec	Annual
Average Max. Temperature (F)	29.0	32.0	39.4	51.2	62.8	72.3	80.9	79.3	69.1	56.8	40.4	30.4	53.6
Average Min. Temperature (F)	4.5	6.0	13.4	23.0	32.1	38.3	44.2	42.4	34.1	24.7	15.2	6.0	23.7
Average Total Precipitation (in.)	0.73	0.59	0.65	0.82	1.17	1.11	0.74	0.87	0.99	0.77	0.81	0.69	9.95
Average Total SnowFall (in.)	9.6	7.8	7.0	4.1	1.7	0.2	0.0	0.0	0.5	2.0	8.5	10.0	51.4
Average Snow Depth (in.)	9	8	3	0	0	0	0	0	0	0	1	5	2

business. He couldn't afford the train fare twice, so he made a committment in dollars before seeing the town. A scattered mining community, Kemmerer had about one thousand residents, a company store that operated on credit and 21 saloons where a good deal of spare cash was spent.

J. C. Penney mother store.

Two revolutionary ideas—cash only and do unto others as you would have them do unto you, were the basis for James Cash Penney's new business venture. (The middle name is a family name, not chosen to express his retail philosophy). He named the store the Golden Rule.

"When the sun rose over Kemmerer, Wyoming, April 14, 1902, it gilded a sign reading "GOLDEN RULE STORE, and I was in business as a full partner. The firm name was Johnson, Callahan and Penney, but it was used only for bookkeeping purposes. In setting up a business under the name and meaning of Golden Rule, I was publicly binding myself, in my business relations, to a principle which had been a real intimate part of my family upbringing. To me the sign on the store was much more than a trade name. We took our slogan "Golden Rule Store" with strict literalness. Our idea was to make money and build business through serving the community with fair dealing and honest value, and did business cash-and-carry."

"When we locked the store at midnight and went upstairs to our attic room after the first day's business to figure out how we stood, there wasn't a great deal of paper money or. for that matter, so many silver dollars; but there was an astonishing - to us - wealth in pennies, nickels, dimes, quarters, and half-dollars. Our first day's sales amounted actually to only $33.41 shy of the $500 savings we had put with the note for $1500 to pay for the partnership."

"Having made the point of a new store by opening up at sunrise on the first day, we then settled on an opening of 7 a.m. Closing time was when no more people in the streets seemed to be heading for the store. Saturday nights, that meant at least midnight. We couldn't make perpetual-motion machines of ourselves and on Sunday opened the store at 9 a.m."

During 1911 and 1912 twenty stores were added, bringing the total number of Golden Rule Stores to thirty-four. So it was Kemmerer, Wyoming, that gave Mr. James Cash Penney his start in business, and in 1913 the decision was made to change the Golden Rule Store to the J.C. Penney Company. The mother store is still a thriving business in Kemmerer.

The Penney's first home was restored in 1982 and moved to Penney Avenue on the Triangle, where it is now a museum operated by the J.C. Penney Foundation. The six room cottage is a National Historic Landmark. It is open during the spring and summer. Mr. Penney's home and the "mother store" are "must" photographs for thousands of tourists each year.

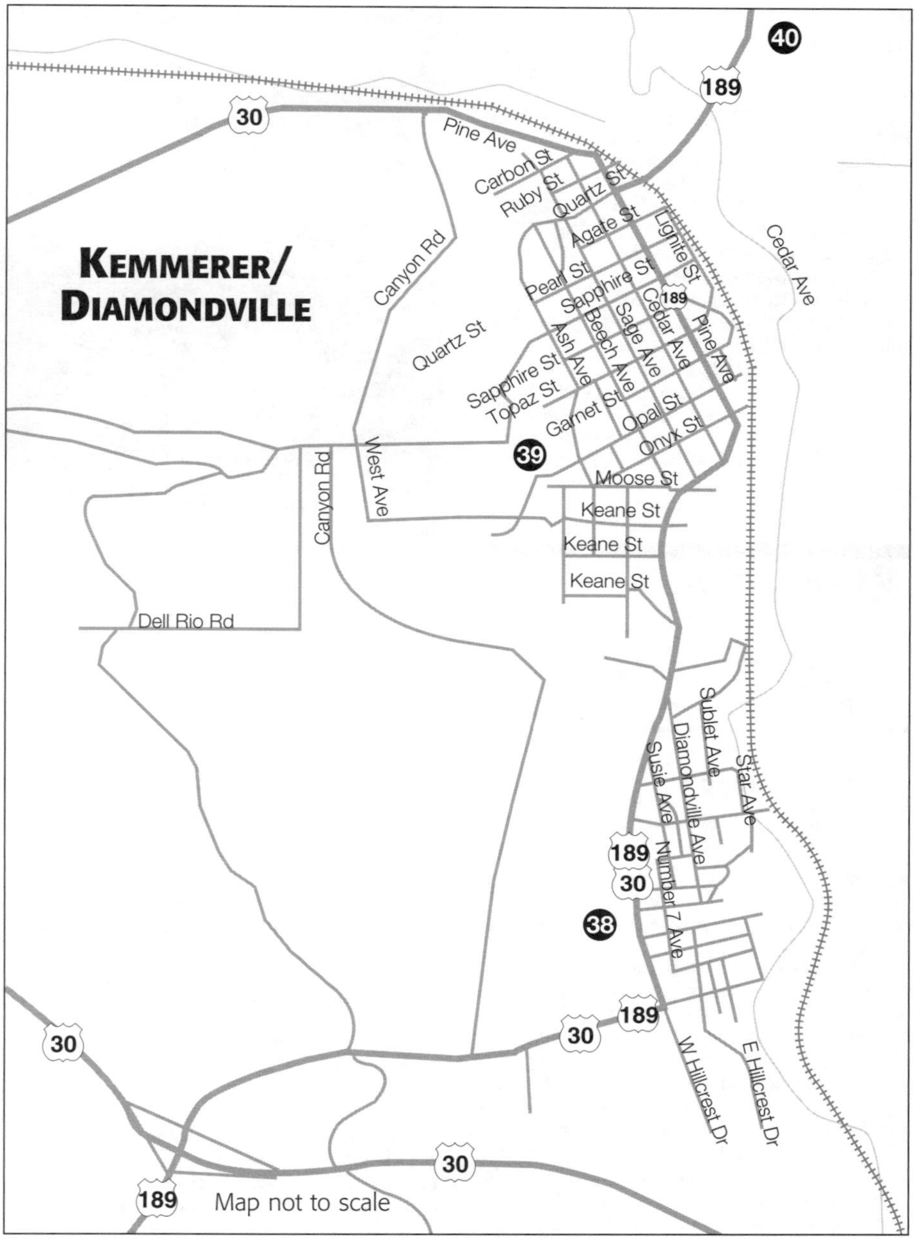

Article courtesy of Kemmerer Chamber of Commerce

KEMMERER/ DIAMONDVILLE

Map not to scale

T Fossil Murals
At the Post Office

These were painted by WPA artists in 1938.

T Ulrich's Fossil Quarry, Warfield Fossil Quarry, and Tynsky's Quarry

For a fee, you can dig for your own fossils at these sites. Children are not generally allowed, as digging conditions can be dangerous.

M Hams Fork Realty
717 Pine Ave. in Kemmerer. 877-2907.
www.hamsforkrealty.com

40 *Food, Lodging*

Frontier

Named for being on the edge of the Wyoming frontier, this is one of the oldest coal mining camp towns. In 1919, a mine explosion here killed 98 men.

Glencoe

Glenco's Scottish name came from Thomas Sneddon, a Scottish prospector who stumbled upon coal in this region. Here, Thomas built the mine he always dreamed of, as well as the town. Glenco attracted miners from all parts of the country, including foreigners. The work was dangerous and heavy; pay was calculated by the ton with $3.00 for a ten-hour day being as much as the strongest miner could earn.

Mine explosions were common, especially the one in 1927 where 100 men died in the Frontier mine. The wives of Glenco worried continuously about their husbands' dangerous occupation. The Frontier mine disaster and the depletion of coal served as the catalyst for the closing of the mines. By early 1940, Glenco was deserted.

H Alfred Corum Grave
About 18 miles northwest of Kemmerer on State Highway 233. Rough road, travel only in good weather.

Within this compound lie the graves of five or six pioneers who lost their lives while traveling to the gold fields of California and the fertile Willamette Valley of Oregon.

Alfred Corum and his brothers John, Herod, and Simeon left Cooper County, Missouri, on April 10, 1849, bound for the gold fields. Their wagon train reached the Hams Fork Plateau on July 3, 1849. and "laved over" as Alfred had been sick for a week or ten days. Some 200 wagons passed them on this day. On July 4 the wagon train pulled out, leaving six men behind to render aid to the dying Alfred. He died at 1:00 p.m. of unknown causes on the 4th of July, 1849.

Margaret Campbell is buried a few yards from Alfred Corum. She died on July 29, 1848 of unknown causes. Historians have been unable to determine the names and circumstances of death of the other emigrants buried here.

Fossil Butte National Monument Visitor's Center.

Wyoming Tidbits

J.C. Penney's first store was in Kemmerer. The first year, 1902, he sold $29,000 in merchandise. By 1929, he had 1,400 stores and a huge mail-order business.

H Nancy Jane Hill

About 18 miles northwest of Kemmerer on State Highway 233. Rough road, travel only in good weather

In April, 1852, four brothers, Wesley, Samuel, James and Steven Hill, together with their families, 62 persons in all, left Paris, Monroe County, Missouri, for California.

There were two deaths along the Platte River and here on the Hamsfork Plateau. Nancy Jane Hill, second eldest of the six children of Wesley and Elizabeth Hill, died of cholera, July 5, 1852, age twenty years.

Nancy's Uncle, James Hill, wrote: "She was in good health on Sunday evening taken unwell that knight worst in the morning and a corps at nine o'clock at knight."

On the Forty Mile desert in Nevada Nancy's father, Wesley Hill, died August 24, 1852, and was buried at Ragtown at the Carson River.

The Hill train settled in Soscol Valley, Napa County in California.

Legend has it that Nancy Jane's fiance returned three times over a period of 53 years to tend the grave.

41 *No services*

T Fossil Butte National Monument

15 miles west of Kemmerer on U.S. Highway 30

Fossil Butte National Monument was established on October 23, 1972, in order to preserve fossil bearing rock formations. These rocks contain traces of plants and animals from a lake that covered the area over 50 million years ago. Many species of fishes, insects, birds, and even crocodiles are wonderfully preserved, making the park's fossils of international scientific importance.

The 8,198 acre park is located just 15 miles west of the town of Kemmerer in southwestern Wyoming. At between 2000 and 2500 meters (6500' and 8000') in elevation, its climate is that of high desert. Summers bring hot, sunny days and pleasantly cool nights. Winters are cold with moderate snowfall.

The park has a visitor center featuring a display of museum-quality fossils, a bookstore, and an information desk. It is open year-round excluding federal holidays. There are also two groomed hiking trails.

Animals abound at Fossil Butte. Herds of elk, pronghorn antelope, mule deer, and even a few moose frequent the park. Smaller mammals such as jackrabbits, badgers, porcupines, coyotes and prairie dogs are resident year round. A variety of eagles, hawks, and falcons have become increasingly common.

Fees and Restrictions

There is no entrance fee at the Monument.

Licensed motor bikes, trucks, and automobiles are permitted in the Monument, but are restricted to designated roads and operators must be properly licensed. Bicycles must also remain on the roads and stay off of the trails for maintenance and safety reasons. There is no camping or overnight parking at the park.

Pets are allowed on trails, but must be under physical restraint at all times. Horse use is allowed in the Monument, but not on the trails. During the winter, hiking and cross-country skiing are encouraged, weather permitting. Snow machines are not permitted within the Monument boundaries.

The Fossils

Three ancient great lakes existed in the region of Wyoming, Utah, and Colorado 50 million years ago - Lake Gosiute, Lake Uinta, and Fossil Lake, the smallest. All are gone today, but they left behind a wealth of fossils in lake sediments that turned into the rock layers known as the Green River Formation, made up of laminate limestone, mudstone, and volcanic ash. The fossils are among the most nearly perfectly preserved remains of ancient life in the world. Some of the most extraordinary of these fossils came from Fossil Lake, represented today by a flat-topped remnant of rock that stands where the center of Fossil Lake once was. Fossil Butte National Monument preserves that butte and its invaluable, fascinating record of the past.

The fossils of Fossil Lake are remarkable for their abundance and the broad spectrum of species found here - more than 20 kinds of fish, 100 varieties of insects, and an as yet uncounted number of plants. Paleontologists, the scientists who study fossils, and private collectors have unearthed literally millions of specimens during the past 100 years. Many billions more still lie buried in the hills.

The fossils are remarkable for their detail. Many fish, for example, retain not only their entire skeletons, but their teeth, delicate scales, and skin as well. And perhaps most remarkable of all is the story the fossils tell of an ancient life and landscape.

The scene 50 million years ago, during the Eocene Epoch of the Cenozoic Era, was quite different from that today. Fossil Lake, 50 miles long and 20 miles wide at its maximum, nestled among mountains in a lush green forest of palms, figs, cypress and other subtropical trees and

Fossil Butte

	Jan	Feb	March	April	May	June	July	Aug	Sep	Oct	Nov	Dec	Annual
Average Max. Temperature (F)	29.1	31.9	41.1	52.9	64.0	73.5	82.7	82.2	72.0	57.4	39.6	29.0	54.6
Average Min. Temperature (F)	6.3	7.1	15.9	23.8	31.1	36.2	41.9	41.6	34.2	23.6	14.3	5.9	23.5
Average Total Precipitation (in.)	0.59	0.66	0.74	0.77	1.33	1.27	0.90	0.75	0.76	1.16	1.00	0.68	10.63
Average Total SnowFall (in.)	13.9	10.8	10.3	5.1	1.3	0.4	0.0	0.0	0.0	2.5	10.9	15.8	71.0
Average Snow Depth (in.)	12	12	7	0	0	0	0	0	0	0	1	7	3

Glossary of Geologic Terms

Alkaline
Having the qualities of a base. pH greater than 7.2. Such a chemistry has implications for the type of flora and fauna present. Ocean water has a pH of 8.1-8.3; saline water has a pH of 9.0 or higher.

Bioturbated
Sediment churned and stirred by organisms. The most bioturbated sediments of Fossil Lake indicate lake margins.

Butte
A small, isolated, flat-topped hill resulting from the erosion of near-horizontal strata. The sediments of Fossil Butte actually dip eastward a few degrees below the horizontal.

Calcium Carbonate (Calcite)
Fundamental component of limestone. Produced by a reaction of calcium and bicarbonate ions in water. In a lake these ions are provided primarily by the inflow of streams and rivers.

Chert (Flint)
A hard, dense, mostly quartz sedimentary rock formed by organic or inorganic precipitation or replacement. Chert nodules in Fossil Lake sediments indicate saline, alkaline conditions at the time of their formation.

Dolomicrite
Mud-size dolomite crystals in a carbonate rock. The presence of dolomicrites indicates a saline to hypersaline environment.

Dolomite
A carbonate (limestone) rock distinguished by a significant concentration of magnesium. Indicative of saline-alkaline conditions. Some ostracode fossils are found in these sediments.

Formation
Fundamental body of rock which is characterized by similarities such as rock type, chemical composition and structures, textures or fossils distinct from adjacent rock bodies. The sediments of Fossil Lake are found within the Green River Formation.

Fossil
Any evidence of past life. Bones, teeth, shells and plant material are the most obvious kinds of fossils, but burrows, trackways, footprints, molds and impressions are also considered fossils.

Kerogen
Mineralized organic material, similar to fossil fuels like coal and oil. Formed by the decay of the aquatic plants of Fossil Lake. This dark material gives the "oil shales" of Fossil Basin their distinctive color and odor.

Lamina
A layer of sediment or sedimentary rock less than 1 cm thick. Alternating couplets of lighter limestone and darker kerogen laminae are sometimes incorrectly called varves.

Limestone
A sedimentary rock consisting largely or entirely of calcium carbonate. The laminated limestones of Fossil Lake are characteristic of chemically-stratified lakes, and are the result of changes in temperature/pH or photosynthetic activity causing the calcium carbonate to precipitate out of the water.

Member
A specially developed part of a varied formation, distinguished by color, hardness, composition or fossil content. The Green River Formation has been subdivided into the Fossil Butte and Angelo Members in Fossil Basin. The middle unit of the Fossil Butte Member is the most fossiliferous in this area.

Micrite
Microcrystalline carbonate rock. Described in the Fossil Lake region as kerogen-rich laminated micrite (KRLM) or kerogen-poor laminated micrite (KPLM) it is primarily in this rock that the majority of Fossil Lake fossils are found.

Oil Shale
Dark gray or black shale containing kerogen. Some of the oil shales in this area are so rich in kerogen that early fossil hunters used to burn the rock in their campfires for fuel.

Ostracode
A small crustacean (other members of this superclass include crabs, lobsters, shrimp and barnacles) that is a good indicator of salinity and fluctuations in the positions of shorelines. The presence and concentration of ostracode fossils in the sediments of Fossil Lake distinguish near-shore from deeper water environments.

Paleontology
Paleo = "ancient" + onta = "existing things" + logy = "science". The study of fossil plants and animals. Careful examination of the diverse fossils in Fossil Basin helps establish this ancient environment.

Saline
Salty. Fossil Lake's salinity varied with the lake's size, depth, and amount of material washed in by streams.

Shale
Fine grained, easily-split (fissile) sedimentary rock composed primarily of clay minerals and quartz. Early discoverers described the fossils of Fossil Lake as being in shale instead of limestone because shale is often used as a generic term to describe any fine-grained fissile sedimentary rock rather than to distinguish its mineralogy.

Siliciclastics
Sediment which comprises particles composed of silicate minerals and rock fragments, such as the claystones, siltstones and sandstones of Fossil Basin.

Soft Sediment Deformation
Sedimentary beds, cross-beds, or laminae that were disrupted, convoluted or contorted prior to lithification. Much of the soft sediment deformation found in Fossil Basin may be soils or turbidites.

Tuff
Compacted (lithified) volcanic ash. There are a number of tuff layers in Fossil Lake sediments, indicating the region underwent a certain amount of volcanism during the life of the lake. These layers are important in dating the lake since it is from these sediments samples can be obtained for radiometric dating. Such volcanic material is considered to be "frozen in time" at the instant the minerals within them crystallized whereas sedimentary rocks are the products of the deterioration of preexisting material and are subject to weathering and erosion which corrupts the closed system required by absolute dating techniques. The K-spar tuff layers in Fossil Basin contain a high percentage of potassium (K) feldspar.

Turbidite
Sediment or rock deposited by a swiftly moving bottom-flowing current (turbidity current). The turbidites of Fossil Basin may reflect periods of rapid expansion of Fossil Lake.

Varve
A banded layer of silt and sand deposited annually in lakes especially near ice sheets. The sand layer represents summer deposition; silt represents winter deposits—hence a pair of these deposits signifies a one-year period in the life of the lake. Once used to determine the age of certain stages of Fossil Lake, the varve concept is no longer an appropriate model for Fossil Lake due to variations in laminae thickness and the mineralogical character of Fossil Lake sediments.

shrubs. Willows, beeches, oaks, maples, and ferns grew on the lower slopes, and on the cool mountain sides was a spruce and fir forest. In and around the warm waters of the lake animal life was diverse and abundant. A broad range of fish inhabited the tributaries, shallows, and deep water of Fossil Lake during its unusually long life of more than 2 million years. Gars, paddlefish, bowfins, and stingrays, though they may appear primitive to some, still survive today, as do herring, perch, and mooneyes. The lakeshore was alive with crocodiles and turtles; insects, dog-sized horses, and early primates inhabited the land; birds and bats mastered the air.

Ideal Conditions for Fossil-Making

What events led to the preservation of so much of Fossil Lake's life as fossils? No one knows for sure, but after careful study scientists have developed theories to explain the process. One essential ingredient for preservation, they believe, was rapid burial in calcium carbonate, which precipitated out of the water and fell like a constant gentle snow on the bottom of Fossil Lake. Whatever sank to the bottom - dead fish, fallen leaves - was covered by this protective blanket. Year after year for hundreds of thousands of years, this reoccurred. Some of the most perfectly preserved fossils come from the deep-water sediment layers of whitish to buff-colored calcite limestone alternating with brown oil shale commonly called the 18-inch layer. The fossils are generally adult fish. An equally important fossil-bearing layer comes from nearer the lake shallows and is composed of lighter colored limestone with faint lamination that splits easily due to the lack of organic material. Thus, its name: the split-fish layer, which averages 6.5 feet thick. Here one finds younger fish and species that would have survived better in near shore shallows - crayfish and stingrays, for example.

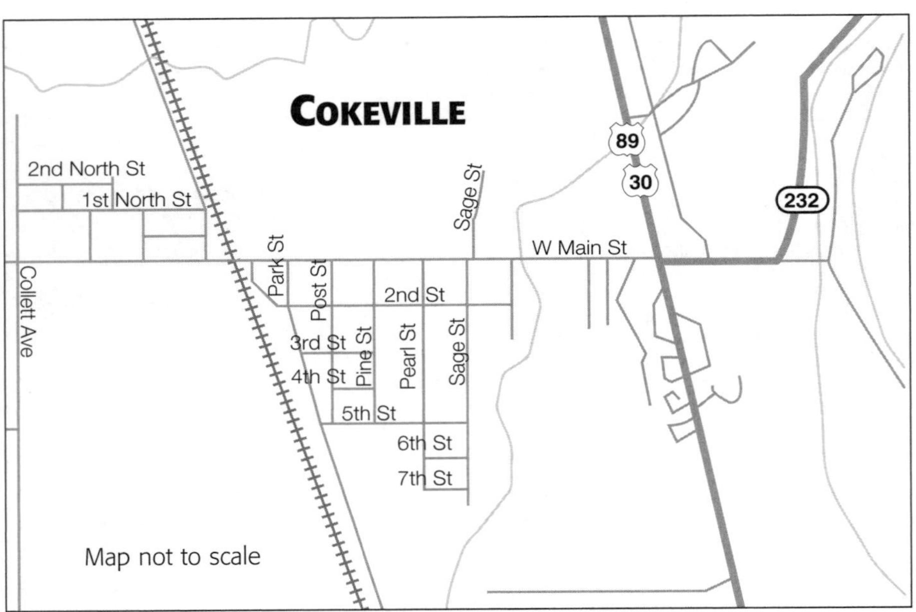

Unsolved Mysteries

While many of Fossil Lake's animals and plants probably died natural deaths, on several occasions huge numbers of fish were killed suddenly. These die-offs are recorded on great slabs of the Green River Formation called mass mortality layers. What killed these fish? A superbloom of blue-green algae that emitted poisons into the water? A sudden change in water temperature or salinity? All of these? Ongoing research may solve the mystery.

Fossil Collection Issues

Fossils: A Part of Our National Heritage

Fossils have been pondered and discussed since the time of the early Greeks. Throughout human history, fossils have been perceived as objects of awe and wonder, and scorned as tricks of the Devil. As we have come to understand earth history more fully, fossils have proven valuable tools for interpreting ancient climates and understanding the development of life forms throughout earth history.

When the science of paleontology was first established, fossils were often studied "out of context." Little attention was given to the study of ancient environments in which the fossil had once resided or the context in which the organism was deposited. With the increased sophistication of paleontology as a science, fossils are no longer considered isolated objects but as elements of a complex continuum of ancient ecosystems.

When fossils are collected by researcher, careful documentation is made of their location, their place in the geologic record, and the type of depositional environment. Also, any relationship with surrounding ancient organisms is noted. Paleontologists are now asking questions about how the earth's climate has changed through time and what forces were at work to cause the mass extinctions that occurred in the past.

Because fossils can provide such a wealth of information, they are considered an important national treasure to protect. On federal lands, the collecting of vertebrate fossils is allowed only for research purposes and the collectors must be associated with some type of public institution, usually a museum or university. The purpose of this regulation is to ensure that vertebrate fossils are collected with as much information as possible and that they remain in the public trust. Different regulations pertain to state lands, and private lands are unregulated.

Fossil Collecting in Fossil Basin

Fossil Basin contains some of the most complete and well-preserved fossils in the world. Fossil Basin also contains the remains of an ancient ecosystem. These detailed fossils and their ecological relationships have been studied extensively by researchers since the 1870s. Around the turn of the century, the first commercial quarriers "set up shop" in Fossil Basin. They collected and prepared fossil fish and sold them to private collectors and museums around the world. Today, the Bureau of Land Management (BLM) and Fossil Butte National Monument, a unit of the National Park Service (NPS), protect a portion of the land within Fossil Basin. Commercial quarrying activity in Fossil Basin occurs on private or state leased lands.

The State of Wyoming has developed a permit system through the State Land Commission that allows commercial quarriers to quarry for vertebrate fossils in the Green River Formation on State lands. However, they must report and relinquish any vertebrate fossils that are not one the seven most common genera (Knightia, Diplomystus, Priscacara, Mioplosus, Notogoneus,and Amphiplaga. The uncommon genera are sent to the University of Wyoming Museum of Geology where they are prepared and further studied.

Individuals who collect on private lands are not obligated to turn in rare or unique specimens. They can sell their fossils without restriction. However, many private collectors donate fossils to public institutions.

The Value of Protecting Fossils on Public Lands

- All fossils collected on public lands are documented and accounted for. Within the National Park Service, fossils are curated and available for loan to other institutions.
- Researchers with collecting permits are able to study paleontological deposits and purse pertinent questions on ancient environments, evolution, and paleoclimates.
- Fossils within the National Park Service are made available to the public through exhibits and interpretation. Specimens not on exhibit are accessible through study collections and loans.

Above article courtesy of National Park Service.

H Fossil Butte

About 11 miles west of Kemmerer on U.S. Highway 30 on access road to Fossil Butte National Monument

Fossil Butte is world famous for perfectly preserved fossil fish. The deposits were worked as early as 1877. There are specimens from this locality in museums all over the world.

The rocks in the Butte were laid down about 50 million years ago. Red rocks in the lower part are stream deposits named Knight Formation. Light colored beds in the upper part are of the Green River and are remnant of beds deposited in a lake once covering much of western Wyoming.

The fish-bearing layer and quarries are about half-way up the butte. The Green River Formation has yielded a great many varieties of fossil fish, including herring, perch, catfish and stingrays as well as fossil insects, birds and bat.

42 *No services*

Sage

This railroad station was named for the most prominent plant in the area: sagebrush.

H State Boundary Monument

(Utah, Idaho And Wyoming)

The state boundaries of Idaho, Utah, and Wyoming share one corner approximately 7.3 miles southwest from where you're standing.

Two corners were surveyed and marked in the 1870's. U.S. Astronomer and Surveyor Daniel G. Major and a party of 11 men surveyed the Idaho-Utah boundary during the summer of 1871. Using transits, chronometers, a sextant and steel measuring chains, Major projected a line northerly from Evanston to a point near the Bear River where a series of celestial observations were performed. A specified distance was measured westerly to the intersection of the 42nd Parallel of North Latitude with the 34th Degree of Longitude (west of Washington, D.C.), the place for the

"Initial Point". The point was marked by a "glazed white earthen bottle" deposited beneath a set pine post and witnessed by inscribed boulders.

Three years later in 1874 while surveying the western boundary of Wyoming, U.S. Astronomer and Surveyor A.V. Richards found the

"Major Monument" to be approximately 0.7 mile too far east, thereby creating a new point for the corner common to Idaho and Utah on the Wyoming boundary. Later surveys marked this point that became the accepted corner we recognize today.

A coordinated effort by local and government surveying organizations recently relocated the historic corner sites established more than a century ago. The original survey records were instumental in relocating these historic sites.

43 *Gas, Food, Lodging*

T Cokeville

Pop. 506, Elev. 6,191GAS

Originally dubbed Smith's Fork, for the nearby river, this town was officially settled in 1874. The year before, in 1873, mountain man Tilford Kutz and his Indian wife had dwelt alone here, run-

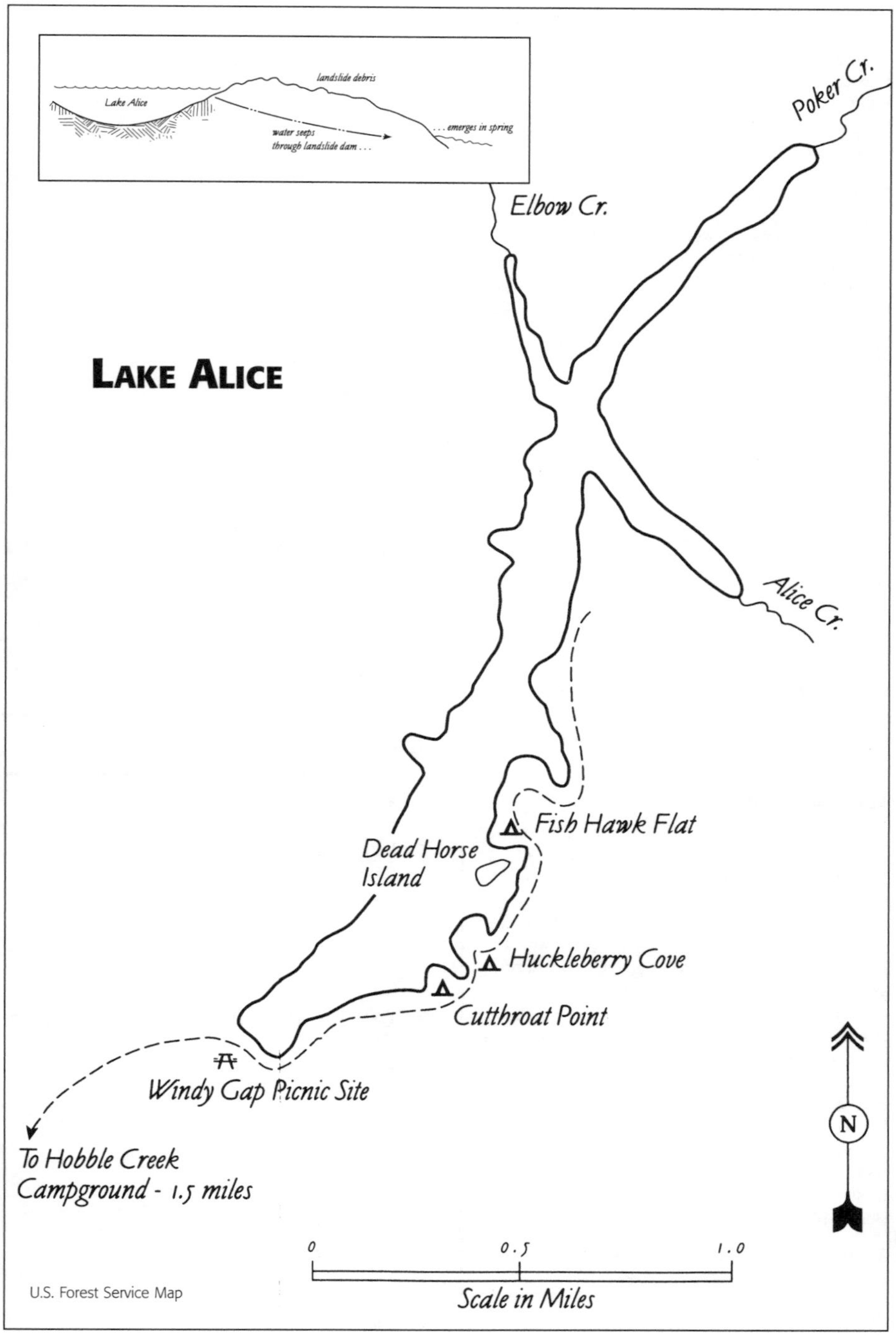

LAKE ALICE

Lake Alice
landslide debris
water seeps through landslide dam . . .
. . . emerges in spring

Poker Cr.
Elbow Cr.
Alice Cr.
Fish Hawk Flat
Dead Horse Island
Huckleberry Cove
Cutthroat Point
Windy Gap Picnic Site
To Hobble Creek Campground - 1.5 miles
N
0 0.5 1.0
Scale in Miles

U.S. Forest Service Map

ning a small ferry and trading post which catered to travelers on their way west. When pristine coal was found nearby, it was renamed Cokeville, for the highly refined form of carbon they could derive from it, called coke. Coke is made from carbonization of coal, and its byproducts include oven gas, ammonia, and tar. Coke fuel is extremely clean burning, and is used in both industry and modern home heating systems.

Cokeville is situated in a fertile valley, overlooked by majestic Rocky Point Mountain, which is ideal rangeland for livestock. By the turn of the twentieth century, it became known as the "sheep capital of the world," and ranching was it's dominant resource. It was said to have the highest number of millionaires per capita of any place in the world in 1900. In addition to the draw of big money, many outlaws found Cokeville a convenient location due to its easy access to Idaho and Utah, which made outrunning the short arm of the State law easier.

T Lake Alice

State Highway 232 northeast of Cokeville, right at the "Y" for about 13 miles, another 35 or so miles on gravel

Nestled in the depths of a canyon between peaks over 9,000 feet lies the largest natural lake in the southern ranges of the Bridger-Teton National Forest — Lake Alice. The Lake was created when a massive landslide peeled from the 9,325- foot Lake Mountain and dammed Poker Creek with a mile-long pile of debris. The resulting Lake Alice is three miles long and over 200 feet deep.

The Lake's outlet runs under the landslide material, which is porous enough to let the water slowly percolate through. Water from Lake Alice drains under the surface for over a mile, then emerges as a spring. This is the source of Spring Lake Creek, a short creek that flows .5 mile before reaching its confluence with Hobble Creek.

Lake Alice lies at 7,745 feet. High mountains rise on all sides, some cloaked with heavy forest, while others are more open with aspen stands and meadows. Mt. Isabel, at 10,162-foot elevation, stands above the north end of the Lake.

Several trails lead to Lake Alice from surrounding backcountry. The shortest route is a 1.5-mile trail from Hobble Creek Campground. There is a trailhead adjacent to the campground, with a bridge over Hobble Creek leading to the trail. The campground usually opens by July 1, depending on snow and weather conditions, and remains open through October.

At the Lake itself you will find a picnic site at the near end of the Lake. A trail continues along the south shore (right side as you are facing the lake) to three backcountry campsites equipped with tables, fire grates, a water system, and pit toilets. The trail ends about 1.5 miles up the lakeshore, after passing several points with excellent views and good fishing access.

Access to Lake Alice is by foot, horse, and mountain bike. No motor vehicles are allowed on the trails.

Because the lake's outlet flows below the surface through the natural dam, the fish population has been isolated. Only the Bear River (Bonneville) Cutthroat Trout, rarely exceeding 13 inches, lives in the lake. No other species have been introduced.

Fishing season in Lake Alice and its tributary streams runs from July 1 to March 31. The following rules apply: Trout 10 inches or less must be released; fishing must be with artificial flies or lures.

Humans aren't the only fishermen you may see at Lake Alice. Bald eagles, ospreys, and diving ducks may all be seen in the area. Many birds nest near the lake and in the surrounding forest.

The mountains above Lake Alice are home to moose, deer, and other wildlife. Black bear are not common but they may be seen, something to keep in mind if you are camping. Keep any food or other potential bear attractants well enclosed or hung in a tree.

L Hideout Motel

10763 U.S. Hwy 30 in Cokeville. 279-3281 or 800-770-5845

The Hideout Motel provides fun, quiet, and comfortable accommodations in Cokeville. All rooms come with true Western flavor with area themes; cowboy, Indian, mountain man, hunting, or fishing. There are also suites with kitchenettes that can comfortably sleep 6. For added convenience rooms come with data port hookups and digital

Eden Valley

This Is Eden Valley

The unincorporated communities of Farson and Eden form what is called the Eden Valley, named by early day promoters to suggest the agricultural potential of the soon-to-be-irrigated area. Although separated by four miles, the communities share a K-12 public school, post office, volunteer fire department and community hall.

Just Passing Through

The Eden Valley prior to settlement was a thoroughfare for various types of travelers. Evidence of Indian presence such as the Eden Point, one of the oldest types of arrowheads, was discovered by archaeologists along with ancient Indian camps in this area. Jedediah Smith, Thomas Fitzpatrick and William Sublette, mountain men looking for a practical overland route over the Rocky Mountains for the fur trade made the first east west crossing of South Pass in 1824. John C. Fremont surveyed South Pass in 184, mapping the route that would become the Oregon and Mormon Trails. Thousands of pioneers made their way to Oregon, California and Utah on the trail from the 1840s through the 1860s. Pioneer accounts talk of following the Big Sandy to the Green River which would have taken them through Eden Valley. Later the Pony Express arid telegraph lines followed the same route.

From Sagebrush Desert To Alfalfa Fields

Although there were a few attempts at settlement of the area in the 1880's, the majority of settlers came after a large scale irrigation project under the provision of the Carey Act was financed by John M. Farson, Sons & Company in 1907. Like the Homestead Act, the Carey Act allowed each settler 160 acres of Federal Land, but differed in requiring that they pay fifty cents per acre for the land and $30 per acre for the water right. Payment was due in ten years if they could irrigate at least 20 acres. The sources for irrigation are the Big and Little Sandy Rivers, which begin north in the snow fields of the Wind River Mountain Range.

To attract settlers to the area, the Farson company distributed pamphlets promoting the advantages of farming in the valley. Claims proved to be exaggerated, such as "fruit orchards will thrive and corn will grow higher than a man's head" and "the growing season in Eden Valley is as delightful as can be found in the country anywhere."

Lured by the promise of a prosperous new beginning, settlers started coming around 1907. Most traveled on the Union Pacific Railroad to Rock Springs, bringing furniture, farm equipment and even animals with them in emigrant cars. They continued by wagon to Eden Valley. Some of the earliest arrivals lived in tents during their first winter here. Early settler Ivan Dearth summed up the optimism of his neighbors when he said: "I like this place and with reasonable luck can do well here" The Farson irrigation company went bankrupt in 1923. After that, the project had several owners. Finally in 1940, the U.S. Bureau of Reclamation took over the irrigation project with a plan to use Civilian Conservation Corps labor to build a dam on the Big Sandy River. World War Two delayed construction until the 1950s when the Big Sandy reservoir and additional canals were completed. The Eden Valley Irrigation and Drainage district was then formed to oversee operation of the project. Flood irrigation was the predominate method used. Besides crop production, other types of agriculture supported area families. Between 1920 and 1960, independent dairymen provided milk to customers in Rock Springs.

Farmers also raised poultry, livestock, and potatoes for the Rock Springs market. To supplement their incomes early residents sometimes found it necessary to work in the coal mines of Rock Springs.

Eden Valley Today

During the 1980s farmers and ranchers were encouraged to change irrigation methods to increase efficiency and reduce salinity in the watershed. Today ranching operations grow hay and small grains to winter livestock or sell throughout the region. Some who are not employed in agriculture work for the school, various government offices and small businesses located here. In recent years increasing numbers of residents who live on small acreages or ranches commute to Rock Springs and Green River to work. Gas exploration nearby provides work for area residents and a boost for the local economy.

Settlers would be proud to know that Eden Valley, almost one hundred years later, is an oasis in the desert, just as they dreamed it would be.

Reprinted from brochure created by The Eden Valley History Project

TV service. The on-site game room is equipped with a pool table. Your pets are welcome to stay and a horse corral is available. For those with their own rigs there are three full RV hookups. A common patio area can be used for picnics or relaxing.

L Valley Hi Motel

10716 US Hwy 30 in Cokeville. 279-3251

44 *No services*

Farson

Pop. 325, Elev. 6,580

Just west of here, at the Little Sandy Opening, is the place where Jim Bridger met Brigham Young to give the Mormons directions to the Great Salt Lake valley. A betting man, Bridger is said to have offered Young $1000 for the first bushel of corn grown in the arid Utah soil. The town was later named for John Farson, a Chicago broker who funded an irrigation project to help the Farson and Eden area thrive. The arrival of homesteaders also brought the Pony Express, until the station burned in 1862.

The Farson Mercantile, an old time general store, sells some of the biggest ice cream cones around, in addition to being the best place to stop and stretch your legs before continuing your journey.

Border

Situated on the Wyoming-Idaho border, this place was once a railroad station and a post office. The post office was discontinued, but the trains still pass by, mostly carrying coke and soda ash from the nearby mines.

Wyoming Tidbits

Scientists have found fossils of a 13-foot alligator, fish, and plants imbedded in the slate at Fossil Butte.

45 *Gas, Food, Lodging*

Eden

Pop. 338, Elev. 6,590

Settled by Mennonites who hoped to create a little paradise, Eden is like a drink of cool water after the brown, arid drive through the Bad Land Hills and past the Killpecker Dunes. A little farming community, barely distinguished from Farson by a small gap in the highway, the two towns share a high school and other amenities.

T Big Sandy Crossing and Station Site

At the junction of State Highway 28 and U.S. Highway 191 in the town of Farson.

The Mormon Trail and the main Oregon Trail to Fort Bridger crossed the Big Sandy River at this point before following its north bank to the Green River. A stage and Pony Express station was located here in the 1860s. This was also the first meeting place between mountain man Jim Bridger and Brigham Young during the Mormon leader's initial trip to the Great Salt Lake Valley in 1847.

Excerpted from BLM brochure.

T Simpson's Hollow

On State Highway 28, about 10 miles southwest of Farson.

In 1857, President James Buchanan, for political reasons, decided to replace Brigham Young as acting governor of the Utah Territory. Anticipating the Mormon reaction, Buchanan ordered an Army force of 2,500 soldiers, under the command of

Farson	Jan	Feb	March	April	May	June	July	Aug	Sep	Oct	Nov	Dec	Annual
Average Max. Temperature (F)	25.8	31.2	40.5	53.4	64.9	74.6	83.5	80.8	71.7	59.8	41.9	29.6	54.8
Average Min. Temperature (F)	-6.4	-1.1	11.6	22.3	30.6	38.3	44.2	41.6	32.6	21.9	9.4	-1.9	20.3
Average Total Precipitation (in.)	0.39	0.38	0.46	0.71	1.05	0.94	0.67	0.66	0.72	0.66	0.38	0.33	7.35
Average Total SnowFall (in.)	4.6	4.5	4.9	3.5	0.8	0.0	0.0	0.0	0.1	1.7	3.9	4.4	28.4
Average Snow Depth (in.)	3	3	1	0	0	0	0	0	0	0	1	2	1

Brevet General Albert Sidney Johnston, to Utah to ensure that the his orders were carried out. Young responded by calling out the Utah Territorial Militia (also known as the Nauvoo Legion) and placed the territory on a war footing. At Simpson's Hollow, the militia captured and burned 22 army supply wagons under the leadership of Capt. Lewis Simpson (thus the name Simpson's Hollow) On October 5. The destruction of this and two other wagon trains carrying a total of 368,000 pounds of military supplies and the onset of winter snows which closed the passes to Utah, forced the Army to spend the winter at the recently burned Fort Bridger. By the spring of 1858, the federal government and the Mormons had settled most of their differences and Alfred Cumming was installed as territorial governor. *Excerpted fromBLM brochure.*

T Oregon Trail Baptist Church

In Eden

The Oregon Trail Baptist Church is built with sturdy brown log walls, quaint bell tower, and a long window with breathtaking views of the Wind River Mountains.

T Big Sandy Recreation Area

15 miles north of Farson

Situated in an open setting north of Farson at a 6,760-foot elevation, the recreation area and Big Sandy Dam are located on Big Sandy Creek. Recreation at the reservoir is directly managed by the Bureau of Reclamation. This is a popular recreation area for local residents.

T Haystack Butte

A few miles north of Farson

A small picturesque butte is immediately adjacent to the ruts of the Sublette Cutoff about a mile west of the crossing of the Big Sandy and a few miles north of Farson, Wyoming. It is unusual in that it stands alone on the flat prairie and is visible for many miles despite its relatively small size. Back in 1849 forty-niner J. Goldsborough Bruff estimated its height at eighty feet, but it is now greatly diminished in size.

H Pilot Butte & "Graves" of Unknown Emigrants

12 miles SW of Farson on Hwy. 28

Welcome to the Pilot Butte Emigrant Trails Interpretive Site. The purpose of the site is to help you gain a sense of what life was like for the 400,000 emigrants who left their homes to seek a new life in the West. They were seeking wealth, religious freedom, land of their own, a new life. Tlhey all found hardship and suffering along the trail.

At the bottom of the path you'll see the actual trail ruts of the Oregon, California, Mormon Pioneer, and Pony Express National Histroric Trails.

The signs along the path relate some of the history of the westward expansion. During your visit, look around. This area is largely unchanged from the days of the overland emigrants. Imagine what it would have been like to walk, ride a horse, or drive a wagon halfway across America and a long way from home.

Interpretive Plaques

Continuing the Journey West

Just a few miles from where your're standing, the emigrants would come to the first of several trail "splits" that would take them to a crossing on the Green River where they would camp for the evening.

Even with South Pass behind them, Oregon or California-bound travelers still faced more than half their journey and the roughest traveling portion of the trail. Emigrants headed to Utah were slightly better off as they were less than a month away from journey's end.

As you continue your own journey, think about the courage of the people who passed through this country and settled half our nation.

Emigrant/Indian Relations

Relations between emigrants using the trails and the Indians were inconsistent during the migration period. While hostile acts and violent confrontations did occur, they have been overemphasized in trail histrory. During the early migration period of the 1840s, there is documentation of the Indians helping emigrants with treacherous river crossings, giving directions, conducting peaceful trading, and providing food. It appeared that the native populations did not view the small numbers of emigrants as a threat, even though they were trespassing on tribal lands. Chief Washakie and his Shoshones were well-known for their kindness and assistance to the emigrants.

The California Gold Rush period, with its large increase in emigrant numbers, seems to mark the beginning of ill feelings and openly hostile acts, as large emigrant numbers disturbed the game herds upon which the Indians heavily depended. The emigrants' cut all the available wood and their livestock over grazed the trail corridor. Confrontations increased and the paying of tribute to cross tribal lands became a common practice.

Indians suffered heavier losses than did the emigrants. In the 20-year period from 1840 to 1860, only 362 emigrants were killed by Indians. Large groups of emigrants were seldom attacked, and most deaths resulted when individuals were out hunting or exploring. An emigrant was much more likely to die from disease, be run over by a wagon, trampled in a stampede, accidentally shot, or drowned while crossing a river.

First Transcontinental Telegraph

In 1859, the California legislature offered $6,000 a year for the first overland telegraph. This was followed by an act of the United States Congress on June 16, 1860, pledging $40,000 a year for ten years for carrying government messages. With these inducements, the first work was begun in 1860, but by the end of that year the line ran only to Fort Kearny, Nebraska, from the east and to Fort Churchill, Nevada, from the west.

There was some question of which route should be followed over the Rocky Mountains. The Western Union and Missouri Telegraph Company informed Colorado residents that if they would subscribe $20,000 worth of stock in the enterprise, the company would run the line through Denver, otherwise, the emigrant and mail route over South Pass would be followed. The support in Colorado did not come, and the telegraph was pushed across Wyoming in the summer and fall of 1861. The lack of trees along much of the western route posed a considerable construction problem, but in the fall of 1861, the transcontinental telegraph carried the first message from New York to San Francisco. The remains of the telegraph poles have long since disappeared, but it passed along the emigrant trail in front of this sign.

Wyoming Tidbits

Will "Buffalo Bill" Cody was only fifteen years old when he made what would become the longest Pony Express ride on record. Sarting from Red Butte on the Platte River, he rode 76 miles to Three Crossings. Upon his arrival there, he learned his replacement rider had been killed. He then rode 85 miles to Rocky Ridge, and returned to Red Butte after depositing his mail bags. He was still within the scheduled time when he completed his 322-mile run!

Pilot Butte

On the horizon about 25 miles to the south is Pilot Butte. An important landmark, Pilot Butte served as a guide post separating South Pass trails from the more southerly Overland Trail that crossed southern Wyoming. Oddly enough, Pilot Butte was more important to travelers headed east than it was for west-bound emigrants.

The name Pilot Butte appears on fur trade maps at least as early as 1837. Captain Howard Stansbury mentioned Pilot Butte on September 12, 1850, as his column of topographic engineers travelled east from Fort Bridger guided by Jim Bridger. Stansbury's journal reads, "...we came in sight of a high butte, situated on the eastern side of the Green River, some forty miles distant: a landmark well known to the traders, and called by them Pilot Butte."

The butte grew in importance as a land mark as traffic eastward increased in the 1850s and especially in 1862 when Ben Holladay moved his stagecoach and freighting operations from the Oregon Trail south to the Overland route.

Interestingly, the butte sits atop White Mountain and is just north of the original location of the Rock Springs airport. Thus, Pilot Butte was used as a landmark by early-day pilots - flying the first airmail routes across the nation.

Stand in the trail ruts immediately in front of this sign, look at Pilot Butte, and feel the passage of history.

Death on the Trail

Death was a constant companion for emigrants headed west. It is estimated thaat 10,000 to 30,000 people died and were buried along the trails between 1843 and 1869.

Cholera and other diseases were the most common cause of death. People didn't know that cholera was caused by drinking contaminated water. Poor sanitation and burial practices perpetuated the disease. People infected long before might die by a river crossing and would be buried near the river which would in turn infect more people. Cholera kills by dehydrating the body. Unfortunately, many of the recommended cholera remedies, such as wearing flannel shirts, increased body temperature and dehydration.

Remedies for other ills also decreased the likelihood of survival. Amputation was often the treatment for broken bones, and bleeding the sick was a common practice. Some treatments for dehydration and heat exhaustion cautioned against giving the patient water—when in fact it was lack of water that was killing the patient!

Accidental gunshots, drownings, murder, starvation, and exposure also took their toll. The very young and the very old were the most likely to perish. Whatever the cause of death might have been for each grave passed, it was a grim reminder to the emigrant of the hazards of overland travel.

"Graves" of the Unknown Emigrants

Graves were an all-too-frequent reminder of the dangers of overland travel. Most emigrant journals record death, burial, or passing graves during the day's travel. Most burials along the trail were hasty affairs.

The official Company Journal of the Edmund Ellsworth Company of Handcart Pioneers, dated September 17, 1856, stated,

"James Birch, age 28 died this morning of diarrhea. Buried on the top of sand ridge east side of Sandy. The Camp rolled at eight and traveled eleven miles. Rested . . .by the side of Green River"

In the two weeks prior to Birch's death, five other company members were buried along the trail. Birch's gravesite has not been found.

No one is buried in the graves in front of this sign. They are here as symbols of all the emigrants who died and were buried alongside the trail, lost forever.

As you look at these simple mounds of rock and dirt, imagine what it would be like to lose a spouse, child, or friend on the trail. You would dig a shallow grave, say your goodlbyes, and continue your journey West, saddened and bereft.

Burial on the Trail

Death on the trail did not allow for the fineries of the funerals back home. Emigrants made do with materials available. Black would adorn the clothes of mourners, and care would be taken to provide the best funeral possible. The most travelers could provide was often just a shallow trench beside the trail and no coffin for the deceased.

Many emigrants worried about the lack of propriety of a simple grave on the windswept prairie and vowed to return and provide a "proper" resting place.

Few of the thousands of emigrant graves have been located. The wind and snow soon obliterated any evidence of them. Markers disappeared, and in some cases, wild animals scavenged the graves. Stories of family members later returning to search for a loved one's final resting place are common, but the searches were usually fruitless.

H The Utah War-A Legacy of Distrust

Ten miles southwest of Farson on State Highway 28

In 1857, the Buchanan Adminstration faced a series of national challenges. Civil war loomed on the horizon, the New York stock market was in trouble, Federal troops were sent to quash unrest in Kansas and Washington D.C.

Mutual mistrust, suspicion, and poor communications between Washington and Salt Lake City had been festering for a decade. The perception in Washington was that church leader/Territorial Governor Brigham Young was challenging Federal authority in the territory.

President Buchanan decided to replace Young as Governor. Thinking his decision might meet with resistance, Buchanan dispatched 2,500 troops to Utah. They left Fort Leavenworth, Kansas in July marching 1,000 miles along the Oregon Trail. The commander, Brevet General Albert Sidney Johnston, did not reach the army until near Fort Bridger. In Utah, the territory was mobilized to resist "invasion." Plans were made for a "scorched earth" defense.

A brief brush with Utah miltiamen convinced acting commander Colonel E.B. Alexander to improve preparedness. The army and its supply trains were strung out along the trail for over 50 miles. Many supply trains had no military escort and were ordered to wait for soldiers before proceeding. For three such wagon trains, their escorts would arrive too late.

H Burning Wagons

Ten miles southwest of Farson on State Highway 28

Brigham Young sent the Utah Militia, also known as the Nauvoo Legion, to harass the Federal troops and delay their approach. In the early hours of October 4th, Major Lot Smith of the Utah Militia and 40 men captured and burned two supply trains, totalling 52 wagons, west of here near the Green River.

The next day, Smith and his men struck again near where you are now standing. Militiaman Newton Tuttle, wrote in his journal:

"Mond 5 We went on to the Sandy got breakfust then we went up to the road & found 24 waggons we burnt 22 of them & took 7 mules & 2 saddles we then went off from the road...".

Wagon train owners Russell, Majors, and Waddell valued the damage at more than $85,000. The only casualty of both wagon incidents was when one of Lot Smith's men who was wounded by Smith when his pistol discharged accidentally.

The loss of three months rations and livestock, as well as an early bitter winter stalled the army at Fort Bridger. The severe weather kept the militia and the army apart. During this lull in action, intermediary Thomas Kane negotiated a peaceful sttlement of the conflict. In the spring of 1858, the army peacefully entered Salt Lake City and Alfred Cumming was installed as Utah Territorial Governor.

H Little Sandy Crossing

U.S. Highway 191 in Farson

On Monday evening, June 28, 1847, Brigham Young and Mormon pioneers met James Bridger and party near this place. Both companies encamped here over night and conferred at length regarding the route and the possibility of establishing and sustaining a large population in the valley of the Great Salt Lake. Bridger tried to discourage the undertaking. In this conference he is reported to have said that he would give one thousand dollars for the first bushel of corn grown in the Salt Lake Valley.

H Tri-Territory Historic Site

State Highway 28 about 13 miles northeast of Farson; east on gravel road for 31 miles. Follow BLM markers. This trip should only be attempted in good weather

Bronze Plaque:

Marking the common boundary of the Louisiana Purchase (1803) the Northwest Territory (1846) and mexico (1848). The site is located where the Continental Divide crosses the 42 parallel North Latitude.

Permaloy Plaque:

This site, where the Continental Divide crosses the 42 degree parallel, North Latitude, was first claimed by Spain through the presumptive right of early discoveries and explorations. The area was also a part of Acadia, granted in 1603 by Henry IV of France, and part of New England as granted to the Plymouth Colony by James I, transferred to the Massachusetts Bay Colony in 1629. In 1682, LaSalle claimed for France the whole basin of the Mississippi River (thus including the northeastern portion of this site).

France ceded its claim to Spain in 1762 but regained them in 1800 and sold the region of "Louisiana" to the United States in 1803.

Great Britain claimed the western portion of the site in 1792 and the United States laid formal claims in 1818 until the 42 parallel was accepted as the boundary between United States and Spain in 1819. Mexico, after gaining independence from Spain in 1821, reconfirjmed the boundary lines. In 1824, Great Britain relinquished her claim to the area of the columbia River basin, reaffirming this action by the Treaty of 1846 establishing the right of the United States to the "Oregon Country." On July 4, 1848, the cession of territory by Mexico was proclaimed giving to the United States the undisputed right to all of Wyoming.

H Simpson's Hollow

Ten miles southwest of Farson on State Highway 28

Here on October 6, 1857, U.S. Army supply wagons led by a Capt. Simpson were burned by Major Lot Smith and 43 utah militiamen. They were under orders from Brigham Young, Utah Territorial governor, to delay the army's advance on Utah. This delay of the army helped effect a peaceful settlement of difficulties.

The day earlier a similar burning of 52 army supply wagons took place near here at Smith's bluff.

46

T Seedskadee National Wildlife Refuge

About 30 miles northwest of Green River

First Hunters

The first recorded humans in this area arrived as the great continental ice sheets were receding to the north. To survive, they constantly hunted and gathered whatever food was available. They stamped out trails along the rivers and streams as they followed the great herds of bison and pronghorn that migrated within this area. Using their ingenuity they constructed elaborate traps that funneled bison over cliffs and pronghorn into corrals where they could be slaughtered. Scattered campsites remain as testimony of these peoples' lives.

The Shoshone Indians spread into this area

Lombard Ferry Crossing on the Green River.

around 700 years ago. Before acquiring horses, they hunted bison and pronghorn much the same way as the first people upon this land. They were a nomadic tribe that traveled widely and, in the process, opened up trails over the mountains. From their arrival until the appearance of the white man, they were the lords of the Green River basin. In addition to bison, they hunted deer, elk, pronghorn, mountain sheep, and the abundant "prairie chicken:' or sage grouse. It was the Shoshone that gave the river its first name, "sisk-a-dee-agie' or "river of the prairie chicken:' Fur trappers later corrupted the Indian name to "seedskadee:'

Wheels Across the Rockies

Faced with having to resupply his trappers each summer, Ashley devised a plan to bring supplies to them at a pre-appointed place in the mountains, rather than bringing the party back to St. Louis. In 1825, Ashley and his men crossed the Green River near the Big Sandy, descended the Green to Henry's Fork, and held the first such "rendezvous:' This began a series of summer rendezvous renowned for their wild sprees of drinking, shooting, gambling, lying, and general celebration. Jedediah Smith, David Jackson, and William Sublette bought out Ashley's interests in 1826, and, in the summer of 1827, came rolling over South Pass pulling a two-wheeled cannon on their way to resupply the trappers. Five years later, independent fur trader Captain Bonneville pulled the first wagon train over South Pass and down to the Green River, forging a trail for wagons over the Rockies and across the Green River. When the beaver trade fell off sharply in the late 1830s, mountain man Jim Bridger soon realized that there might be a need for a trading post to serve trappers and the settlers he was sure would come over the trail from South Pass to the Green River. In 1839, a few miles south of the confluence of the Green and Big Sandy Rivers, Bridger and Henry Fraeb built a trading post. Unfortunately, Fraeb was killed by Indians in 1841, which led Bridger to abandon the post for a site on Black's Fork of the Green River.

Emigrant Tide

The circuit to Oregon was finally completed in 1841, when mountain man Tom "Broken Hand" Fitzpatrick led the Bidwell- Bartleson party over the Blue Mountains of Oregon. In 1843, enterprising mountain men constructed a commercial ferry at the primary Green River crossing on the Oregon Trail. Many emigrants followed, including Brigham Young and the great exodus of Mormons on their way to settle Salt Lake City in 1847. Settler traffic on the Oregon Trail increased to total about 12,000 people by 1848. When gold was discovered in California in 1849, the trickle of travelers suddenly turned to a tide. That year, tens of thousands of people used the trail and the crossings on the Green River. By 1850, the Oregon Trail had become part of the Mormon and California Trails as well. Alternate trail routes, or cutoffs, began to be developed, shortcutting the standard route. One such cutoff was known as the Kinney Cutoff and ran near the confluence of the Green and Big Sandy Rivers upstream along the east bank of the Green and crossed at a ford or ferry near Fontenelle, Wyoming. This cutoff, a variation of the Sublette Cutoff, saved considerable mileage for the traveler not wishing to go to Fort Bridger on Black's Fork. The old wagon ruts are still visible in places along the east bank of the Green. The fabled, but short-lived, Pony Express sprang up in 1860, and the route used by its riders followed much of the Oregon Trail. A Pony Express station was located on the west bank of Green River Crossing, just upstream from the Big Sandy-Green confluence. At this time, this little stretch of river was western Wyoming's largest community. A year later wire was strung for the transcontinental telegraph through this same spot, putting the Express out of business.

Settlers on the Green

Although this portion of the Green River was popular with Indians, fur trappers, and emigrants, the area originally offered very little attraction for settlers. The remote location, poor soil, and cold, arid climate made settlement unattractive. Indian uprisings along the Oregon Trail in the 1860s began to turn even more settlers away. However, gold was discovered on South Pass in 1867, and, once again, the Oregon Trail became a popular route. With the advent of gold and the last spike driven for the Union Pacific railroad, the route from the railhead at Bryan (near Green River) to South Pass City was improved and utilized as a stage road. The road improvement, gold strike, and railroad access, finally led settlers to homestead this area. A few remains of these homesteads can still be seen on the Refuge.

A Demand for Beef

With the end of the Civil War, many people returned anxious to pick up the pieces and start a new life. Due to a great demand for beef back East, cattle ranching sprang up in Wyoming and throughout the West. It soon became common practice to winter cattle from as far away as Utah and Nevada along the Green River. By the 1870s, the cattle industry was the biggest business in the Wyoming Territory. Sheep also moved into the area. Notorious range wars erupted between ranchers over precious forage. By 1886, the situation turned grim — the range was overstocked and in poor condition, a drought was on, beef prices were down, and, as a result, ranchers were leaving more stock on the range. A devastating blow struck that winter when savage blizzards ravaged the big herds, reducing them to half by spring. This disaster signaled the end of open range grazing and led to the fencing of the open range.

Elizabeth Markham, an early day Oregon Trail pioneer wrote this poem after her arrival in Oregon:

Road to Oregon

We left our friends in foreign lands-
Our native country dear;
In sorrow, took the parting hand
And shed the falling tear.

For Oregon, three cheers they gave,
From us to disengage-
Fearing that we might find our graves
Amidst the sand and sage;

Or met by cruel savage bands,
And slaughtered on the way-
Their spectered visions, hand in hand,
Would round our pathway play.

To the Pacific's temperate clime
Our journey soon begun-
Traversing through the desert sands
Towards the setting sun.

On Platte the rocks like battlements,
Were towering tall and high;
The frightened elk and antelope
Before our trains would fly.

And herds of buffalo appear-
On either side they stand;
Far as our telescope could reach
One thick and clustering band.

O'er sinking sands and barren plains,
Our frantic teams would bound-
While some were wounded, others slain,
Mid wild terrific sound.

And in those lone and silent dells
The winds were whispering low;
And moaning to the Pilgrims, tell
Their by-gone tales of woe.

Our toils are done, our perils o'er-
The weary pilgrims band
Have reached Columbia's fertile shore-
That far-framed happy land.

O'er mountains high and burning plains,
Three thousand miles or more-

We are here; but who can e'er explain
Or count the trials o'er?

Giver of Life

Just as the Green River was important to emigrants as a source of life-giving water and wildlife, it is important to us today a century and half later for the same reasons.

Siskadee Agie is a Crow Indian term meaning "River of the Praririe Hen." Along with sage grouse (also called Prairie Hens), Native Americans hunted deer, pronghorn, bison, waterfowl, eagles, and other wildlife. Explorers and mountain men trapped beaver in the Seedskadee area; and the hundreds of thousands of pioneers who crossed the Green River hunted game here.

Construction of the Fontenelle Dam about 20 miles upstream changed the natural flooding cycle of the Green River, affecting the fish and wildlife habitat along the river. The dam created prime trout habitat; yet it endangered the natural marshlands bordering the river that relied on spring flooding. These marshlands are critical nesting habitat for many species of waterfowl.

Seedskadee National Wildlife Refuge was established by Congress in 1965 to help offset the loss of marshlands habitat resulting from construction of both the Fontenelle Dam and The Flaming Gorge Dam which is about 100 miles downstream in Utah.

Since 1965, U.S. Fish and Wildlife Service refuge managers have used methods such as prescribed burning, flood irrigating, native grass planting, and fencing to enhance this valuable wildlife habitat and restore the lands to a condition similar to that in the days of the Oregon Trail.

Reprinted from Department of the Interior brochure.

H Overland to Zion
26 miles southwest of Farson on
State Highway 28

The migration of Mormon (Church of Jesus Christ of Latter-day Saints) converts to Utah is a fascinating chapter of the overall American westering experience of the 19th century. In search of religious freedom and an end to persecution, Mormon groups traveled to Utah. The Mormon wagon trains were highly orgainized compared to other west-bound emigrants.

Led by Brigham Young, the first group of Latter-day Saints (160 people, livestock, and 77 wagons) arrived on the east bank of the Green River on Wednesday, June 30, 1847.

William Clayton described the scene, "...At 11:30 we arrived on the banks of Green River, having traveled eight miles and formed our encampment in a line under the shade of the cottonwood timber. This river is about sixteen to eighteen rods wide (297 feet) and altogether too deep to be forded. Its banks are well lined with cottonwood but none large enough to make a canoe...."

Amidst bad weather and hordes of mosquitoes, the men worked three days chopping down trees, building two rafts, and floating the wagons across the Green. By Saturday, July 3rd the party was across the river. Three weeks later on July 24th, Brigham Young arrived in the Valley of the Great Salt Lake and the pioneers began a new life.

By 1869, when the completion of the Union Pacific Railroad ushered in a new era of transportaion, about 68,000 Mormons had traveled the overland route to Utah.

H One Day at a time
26 miles southwest of Farson on
State Highway 28

For the hundreds of thousands of people heading west, life was one day at a time. The travelers had settled into the monotonous routine of life on the trail - up before dawn, and early breakfast, hitch up the stock, and began the day's journey.

Upon safely crossing the Green River, emigrants could breathe a sigh of relief as another major challenge was now behind them. About 55 miles west on the trail was their next goal. Fort Bridger was less than a weeks journey from where you're standing now.

There were very few places for travelers to resupply with food staples or purchase fresh animals. The last resupply opportunity was Fort Laramie about 340 miles and one month east of here. At a pace of 12 to 16 miles per day, Utah was a few weeks away. California and Oregon were still months down the trail.

H Lombard Ferry
26 miles southwest of Farson on
State Highway 28

This site of the Lombard Ferry was one of the most used crossings on the Green River, lasting from about 1843 into the early 1900s. First established by mountain men, it was operated by Mormons in the 1850s during the peak years of the westward emigration.

Many famous emigrant parties are thought to have crossed here. These include: 1841 - Bartleson-Bidwell Party, the first wagon train of emigrants to California; 1843 - Applegate Party, the first large group of emigrants headed to Oregon; 1846 - Donner Party, the ill-fated group stranded by snow in the Sierras; 1847 - Brigham Young and the first Mormon emigrants who settled Utah; 1856 - the first Mormon Handcart Companies of emigrants who literally pulled their own belongings across the plains.

Mariett Foster Cummings, a young woman on her way to California, recorded the experience in her diary for June 28, 1852, "Started before sunrise in order to get to the ferry of Green River, which we did by eight o'clock. Green River is a deep, swift stream 200 feet wide. A rope ferry and the moderate charge of $3 per wagon, 25 cents per head of horses."

William Lombard, for whom this site is named, operated the ferry from about 1880 into the early 20th century when bridges across the Green River ended the need for ferries.

Look across the peaceful river flowing in front of you and imagine the line of wagons and the trail-weary people waiting to come across. Source: National Park Service

H Crossing the Green River
26 miles southwest of Farson on
State Highway 28

Crossing rivers was the most dangerous activity emigrants faced on their journey west. By the time weary pioneers enroute to Oregon, California, or Utah reached the east bank of the Green River, they had been on the trail for several months. Utah was close, but those going to Oregon or California were only about halfway there.

Though crossing the Green had its perils, most emigrants were happy to see the cool water and lush cottonwood groves with grass for their hungry animals, firewood instead of buffalo chips and the chance to camp under trees - a rare opportunity in western Wyoming.

Before spring runoff and in late summer when the water level of the Green was low, fords provided relatively safe crossings. However, most emigrants reached the Green River at the height of its annual flood when it flowed swift, wide, and deep.

Several enterprising pioneers settled along the river and established ferries to float emigrant wagons across the river. Ferry prices sometimes changed daily to correspond with the changes in the river level. It often took several days for large wagon trains to cross the river.

As the number of people headed west swelled into the tens of thousands each year, the number of ferries on the Green increased also. As many as 50 ferries are thought to have operated along the 50 mile corridor of the Green River Valley crossed by emigrant trails.

H Ferrying Across the Green
26 miles southwest of Farson on
State Highway 28

If you look down the river about 250 yards on the right side - there's a wooden ferry. The ferry you see was built by Forrest Cramer of Pinedale, Wyoming in 1997 for 150th anniversary celebrations of the Mormon Pioneer National Historic Trail. The ferry was used on July 6, 1997 to transport several wagons across the river. It sits on the exact location where an earlier one was used over 100 years ago. The new ferry was donated to Seedskadee National Wildlife Refuge.

Follow the path that starts here and go see the ferry. Built out of logs and planks, it's a very accurate reproduction. As you walk down the path, listen to the rhythms of the water and look at the grove of trees on the left side of the river. Whether people prepared to ferry or ford the Green, you can almost hear the shouts of the men positioning the wagons and oxen; and the calls of women as they watch out for their children. Imagine them all tired from 1,000 miles and months of trail behind them and more miles of rough travel yet to go.

H Fording the Green
26 miles southwest of Farson on
State Highway 28

Red Desert Round Up

This annual event, held in late July or early August, features a PRCA rodeo and Calcutta each night, a Saturday parade and a county fair in conjunction with the festivities.

'49ers on the Green River

Great events in the history of the American West are often viewed as one happening, the Gold Rush to California in 1849 for example. Gold was discovered at Sutter's Mill, the news spread like wildfire in the United States, and a lot folks headed west. Some by sea... some by land. Some folks got rich... some didn't.

However, the story of the Gold Rush is really a huge collection of individual stories. Every man, woman, and child who came west had an adventure to tell his or her descendants later in life. Each person's account is a part of the whole that makes the history of the west so fascinating. William Lewis Manly's experiences in southwestern Wyoming's Sweetwater Country and subsequent adventures are one of those obscure tales.

Manly was born in Vermont in 1820. He moved with his family to Ohio in 1827 and like so many Americans of the time, his family continued to drift around—to Michigan, Wisconsin, and then on to Maine—in search of better land and living conditions. In the course of his travels, Manly turned his hand at quite a few different jobs—trapper, farmer, railsplitter, bullwacker.

Like thousands of Americans in the winter of 1848-49, Manly heard the news and decided to take the Overland Route to California in search of gold. And like most of the folks on the Trail, he was in a hurry to get there and make his fortune, so, he joined a mixed group of soldiers and emigrants at St. Joseph, Missouri and headed west on the Trail.

Later in life, he wrote a book, Death Valley in '49, which tells what happened.

"When we came to the first water that flowed toward the Pacific coast at Pacific Springs, we drivers had quite a little ta1k about a new scheme. We put a great many "ifs" together and they amounted to about this: If this stream were large enough; if we had a boat; if we knew the way; if there were no falls or bad places; if we had plenty of provisions; if we were bold enough to set out on such a trip, etc., we might come out at some point or other on the Pacific Ocean. And now when we came to the first of the "ifs, "a stream large enough to float a small boat, we began to think more strongly about the other if." [Pacific Springs is northeast of Rock Springs, just west of the Continental Divide.]

When their party arrived at the banks of the Green River, fate intervened. Sitting on a sandbar, filled with sand, was a ferryboat. After putting the boat back into shape, the entire party ferried across the river and had a meeting. The time had come for decisions. The soldiers would split off to the northwest headed for Oregon, the emigrants would continue southwest towards Salt Lake City and eventually California. William Manly, with six other men, decided to try the river route.

"...So we parted company ...Each company wished the other good luck, and we then set to work in earnest to carry out our plans." Manly's next words have become something of a tradition among modern river running historians, "...All our worldly goods were piled up on the bank, and we were alone."

Standing on the west bank of the Green River on August 5, 1849, Manly and his six companions watched the soldiers and emigrant party disappear into the distance. Having split off from the main group in lieu of the "river" route to California, the men made preparations to begin their descent down the Green. In addition to Manly, the band of adventurers included John Rogers. Richard Field, brothers Charles and Joseph Hazelrig, M.S. McMahon, and Alfred Walton. Because of his travels and confident manner, Manly was elected captain of the group.

The ferryboat the men had found on the bank of the river was an ungainly craft approximately 12 feet long and 7 feet wide, but they thought it adequate for the task of floating to California. Drifting and poling through the Green River valley and the Firehole country proved a leisurely trip. The men shot game, fished, and were generally pleased with their decision to abandon the dusty, overland route. Manly described, "...I went on shore and sighted a couple of antelope, one of which I shot, which gave us good grub and good appetites we already had. As near as we could estimate we floated about thirty miles a day, which beat the pace of tired oxen considerably ... Thus far we had a very pleasant time, each taking his turn in working the boat while the others rested or slept."

The further they floated, though, the swifter the current became. In one spot above the upper Flaming Gorge, Manly was tossed out of the boat when the pole he was using jammed between two rocks. And as the current increased, so did the towering mountain walls until they were deep in the Flaming Gorge.

At Ashley Falls, the worst rapid in the Gorge, the men lost their boat when it was pinned on a large boulder. Working day and night, the men chopped down two pine trees, fashioned them into rough canoes, lashed them together and started out again. After going just a short ways downstream, they stopped

and made a third canoe, approximately 25 feet long. The party floated through Red Canyon, Brown's Park, and the Canyon of Lodore in what is now Utah and Colorado. The smaller canoes flipped in a rapid in Lodore and the men lost all their arms except one rifle and one shotgun. Alfred Walton was nearly drowned. By lining their canoes around the worst rapids, they eventually made it through Lodore, Whirlpool, and Split Mountain Canyons.

In Ashley Valley, the group met the famous Ute Chief Wakara (or Walker) who persuaded them that further travel down the Green River would be fatal. There the party split—McMahon and Field didn't trust Chief Walker and decided to continue down the river. The Ute Chiefs words proved true as McMahon and Field had to abandon the river in Desolation Canyon and wound up walking overland back to Wyoming. They eventually made it to Salt Lake City in December 1849, via Fort Bridger. Manly and the remaining four headed overland towards Salt Lake.

It's interesting to note that Manly and his six companions floated a major portion of the upper Green River system exactly 20 years before John Wesley Powell and his six companions. Yet Manly was still not the first. William Ashley and a group of trappers descended the Green in 1825, fur trapper Denis Julien left a legacy of carvings on the canyons of the Green in the late 1830s to the early 1840s, and an unknown party of travelers preceded Manly in 1848 or 49.

Stumbling into Utah Valley after a hard route from the Uinta Basin, Manly and his companions met up with a group of emigrants headed to California. By one of those unexplained coincidences, he met the Bennett wagon—people he had been trying to overtake since leaving Missouri. The Bennett's were even carrying some of his possessions—a gun, several shirts, and other provisions. Manly and Rogers joined the group and once again started off to complete their journey to California.

Alter their experiences floating the Green River, meeting Chief Walker, and walking overland across the high deserts of eastern Utah, joining a wagon train of emigrants was a relief. However, the adventures weren't over. The party they joined wound up trying a new route to California and became the group that gave Death Valley its name. But that's another story.

Bureau of Land Management article.

Although it was a surging torrent from spring until after mid-summer, Green River flowed moderately in late summer and autumn. Low water allowed wagon trains to ford the river, thus avoiding the expense and delays of ferry crossing. Emigrants who were members of the Church of Jesus Christ of Latter-day Saints (Mormons) and freighters bound for Utah typically arrived here in late summer and early autumn. A few late summer emigrants headed for California on the Salt Lake Road also arrived here during low water. Several good fording places dotted the banks of the Green River from here downstream for seven miles. Trail variants connected the main road to crossing points. Low banks and a gravelly bottom made certain places ideal for driving wagons and herding livestock across the river.

To prepare for fording, the emigrants sometimes raised their wagon beds and coated them with tar to keep the contents dry. Usually people rode in the wagons while the animals hauled them through the water, but some handcart emigrants pulled their two-wheeled vehicles across. After crossing, the emigrants and freighters rejoined the road which ran down the west side of the river.

In times of high water, fording could be dangerous. Some invited disaster by attempting to ford when the current was too strong. The river swept people, wagons, and animals downstream. Wagons sometimes capsized. Drownings were not uncommon. Horses or oxen occasionally lost their footing, toppling riders or wagons. The river was extremely cold in late autumn.

47 *Gas*

T Fontenelle Reservoir

Northwest of Green River on State Road 372.

The reservoir has a surface area of 8,000 acres. The lake is 20 miles long when full and has a shoreline of nearly 56 miles. Elevation of the reservoir is 6,500 feet. Water from the reservoir is used for irrigation and for electricity. Recreation use is low and seasonal, and fish species include rainbow, brown and cutthroat trout. Below the dam, float trips are relaxed and offer great scenery. Fontenelle Creek campground has developed campsites with restrooms and running water. Other campsites below the dam are more primitive. Stream fishing opportunities exist on the Green River above and below the reservoir.

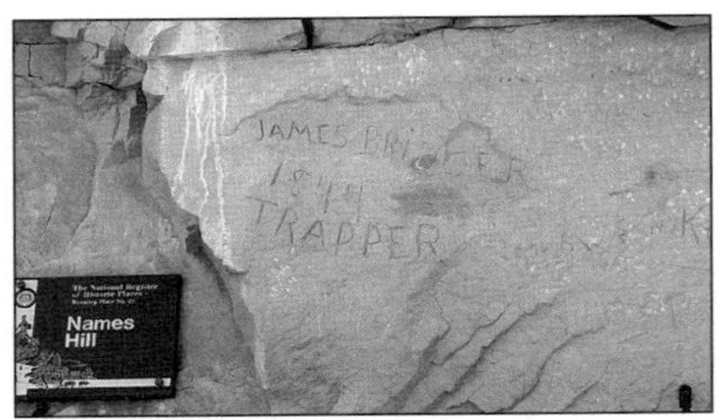

T Names Hill

On the west side of U.S. Highway 189 about six miles south of LaBarge

Some people equate the Names Hill site with the historic inscription, "James Bridger, Trapper, 1844" on the sandstone rock south of LaBarge. But few know they are standing in a region so important to the Oregon Trail system history. Everything from petroglyphs to 1880s surveyors' inscriptions can be found at Names Hill. The Mormons ran a ferry at Names Hill. In the 1850s, a village supporting emigrant use became established at Names Hill. The oldest name dates back to 1827.

48

LaBarge

Pop. 431, Elev. 6,600

LaBarge was named for the creek, which was thus dubbed by William Ashley. He named it for a member of his company, Joseph LaBarge, who came west at the age of 16 in the 1820s. Originally, when the town acquired a post office in 1926, it was named Tulsa, but in the 1930s they changed the name to avoid confusion with Tulsa, Oklahoma. Once a company town for the California Petroleum Company, like nearby Calpet, LaBarge is still in the heart of oil country, with oil pumps visible in most any direction.

Calpet

Named for the California Petroleum Oil Company, this was once a camp for oil workers. Established when oil was struck here in the early 1900s, it became home to some 300 men. A refinery and pipeline were built in 1927 and 1928. In 1956, the refinery closed, the post office closed, and Calpet became a ghost town.

H The Land

26 miles southwest of Farson on State Highway 28

The land under view, where the Great Plains meet the Rocky Mountains, was once the Red man's land of milk and honey. Then, as now, teeming with wildlife, it was a most productive—thus favorite—hunting ground. But it was also a natural route for north-south travel, used from time immemorial by nomadic men and migratory beasts. Lying hundreds of miles beyond the 1860 frontier it was treaty-confirmed Indian Country.

Here came a frontiersman, John Bozeman, pioneering a wagon road which followed buffalo, Indian and trapper trails. His time and energy-saving short cut led to the booming mining fields of western Montana. This interloper was followed by others whose habitual frontier callousness easily stifled any scruple over trespass of an Indian passageway. Faint wheel marks soon became a beaten road know as the Bozman Trail.

High plains and mountain Indians notably Sioux and Cheyenne, watching this transgression, resented both the physical act and the implied contempt of solemn treaty. They made war. The white transgressors called upon their army for protection. In the end the Indians won a brief respite—partly because a developing railroad far to the south canceled the Bozeman Trail's short cut advantage.

H James Bridger • Trapper 1844

About 6 miles south of La Barge on U.S. Highway 189

Little did he know that when he cut his name or had it cut in this stone, that it would be engraved in the annals of the history of the west deeper than that of any other man. As one of the world's outstanding explorers he guided emigrants, railroads, and army in the expansion of a nation. [At this site you can clearly see the name of Jim Bridger carved in the stone.]

H Seeds-Kee-Dee Agie, Spanish River, Rio Verde, Green River

South of La Barge on U.S. Highway 189

To the Shoshone Indian, this river was the Seeds-Kee-Dee Agie (Prairie Chicken River). On September 16, 1811 the Astorians near its headwaters termed it the Spanish River. To the Spaniards far to the south, it was the Rio Verde (Green River). Jedediah Smith and his ten mountain men, making the first westward crossing of the South Pass by white men, camped near here Mar. 19, 1824 on the Seeds-Kee-Dee. They trapped the river and its forks which were named for them; Labarge, Ham's, Black's, Smith's, Henry's etc. These waters were considered as the greatest beaver waters ever known. The upper reaches became the center of the fur trade and Rendezvous. In 1841 the fur trade had ceased but the trappers had blazed the trails for emigrants. For forty-nine years over the Oregon and California trails thousands of emigrants going west, crossed these waters near by. The many that drowned and died were buried along the river banks. The mountain men guided, manned the ferries, and traded with the emigrants. Graves, marked and unmarked, names cut in the rocks, and wagon trails worn deep, remain with the legend and lore of a great river of the west, The Green.

Scenic Drives

Mirror Lake Scenic Byway

This drive takes you from Evanston, Wyoming, to Kamas, Utah through the western portion of the Uinta Mountains. It is reached by taking Wyoming Highway 150 south of Evanston, off Interstate 80. After about 20 miles, Highway 150 reaches the Wyoming/ Utah border and continues as Utah Highway 150, taking travelers into Utah's Uinta Mountains and the Wasatch-Cache National Forest. Both Wyoming and Utah have designated this 78-mile stretch of highway as an official State Scenic Byway.

The entire length of the byway takes two to three hours to drive straight through, longer for visitors who wish to stop along the way. The Wyoming portion can take as little as 20 minutes. Services are available at both Evanston and Kamas, but not in between. There are 22 family oriented campgrounds along the route, operated by the Wasatch-Cache National Forest.

Along the Wyoming section, southbound travelers will get a splendid, panoramic view of the Uinta Mountains. The route peaks at an elevation of 10,620 feet on Bald Mountain Pass. The Uinta Mountain Range is the only range in the contiguous United States with an east to west axis.

Reprinted from Wyoming Department of Transportation Brochure

Big Spring Scenic Backway

This 68-mile route from Kemmerer to Cokeville criss-crosses historic immigrant trails, parallels willowy river valleys, and plunges deep into the uncrowded wilds of the Tunp Mountain Range and the Bridger National Forest. Traveler services are available in Kemmerer, Cokeville, and Diamondville, and limited services are available at the Viva Naughton Lake Marina.

The easternmost stretch of this byway begins with a two-lane, paved road that takes the traveler as far as the northern end of Lake Viva Naughton. It then becomes oiled gravel, and finally loose gravel at the forest boundary. Good tires are highly recommended, as well as high clearance vehicles beyond the Kelley Guard Station. Pavement resumes at Hwy 232, twelve miles east of Cokeville. Drive time for this byway is a minimum of two hours, not including time to stop and enjoy the scenery and recreational opportunities.

Reprinted from Wyoming Department of Transportation Brochure

Scenic By-Way 150

By Denise Wheeler of Evanston

Scenic By-Way 150 stretches between Evanston, Wyoming and Kamas, Utah, and includes some of Wyoming's most beautiful and historic areas. Ancestral tracks, footprints and wheels from Native Americans, wildlife, mountain men, pioneers, and countless forms of transportation have been imprinted on the land adjacent to the byway.

Travelers' interests will be piqued by the region's history, as it echoes with the excitement and adventure from the Shoshone and Arapahoe Indian tribal camps, the advent of the railroad, deserted ghost towns, and many historic sites.

The Mormon and California trails come into Uinta County from South Pass City. In 1847, more than 3,000 emigrants camped alongside this byway, leaving behind marked and unmarked graves.

Railroad construction swept westward into Wyoming in the latter part of 1867, bringing thousands of people. Along with railroad workers came hundreds of others looking for their fortunes in saloons, stores, and other "questionable" professions. The scenic by-way was the setting for this development and many sites along the way highlight the cycle of the construction that took place and transition into ghost towns. The infamous bear town— Hilliard City— and Piedmont Still, have structures and graveyards that will interest sight-seers. Not to be missed are the perfectly preserved Piedmont kilns that facilitated the making of charcoal for use by the railroad.

An Evanston scenic by-way committee consisting of volunteers, city employees, state highway officials, and forest service employees have worked for over eight years to obtain scenic byway status for highway 150 and are now completing magnificent information kiosks to be set

On the Trail to Tragedy...The Donner Party in Wyoming

Most people are familiar with the "end" of the Donner, or Donner/Reed Party in the winter of 1846/47. It was (and still is) the most famous incident of cannibalism in American history. The very horror of being snowbound in the Sierras helped spur the growth of various cutoffs on the Oregon Trail. In addition to death by cholera, childbirth, Indians, and a multitude of accidents, being eaten by your companions was added to the list of hazards of overland travel.

The "story" of the Donner Party in Wyoming is a story of chance meetings, poor communication, bad decisions, coincidence, uneasy feelings, bad luck, and perhaps simply fate.

To many historians, the outcome of the Donner Party was a culmination of small isolated mistakes. According to Dr. Gary Topping in a recent article in the Utah Historical Quarterly, "If ever a group was doomed at the beginning it was the Don-ners."

Other theories say that the Dormers were doomed when they purchased Lansford W. Hastings' *Emigrants Guide to Oregon and California*. In a brief aside in his guidebook, Hastings stated, 'The most direct route, for the California emigrants, would be to leave the Oregon route, about two hundred miles east from Fort Hall; thence bearing west southwest, to the Salt Lake; and thence continuing down to the bay of San Francisco, by the route just described." At the time of writing, Hastings had not actually traveled the route across the Utah desert.

The nucleus of the group, which later became known as the Donner Party, included two brothers, George and Jacob Donner, and James Reed. Each was wealthy, lived in Illinois, had a large family and they started out with three wagons each. One of Reed's wagons was literally a palace on wheels. It was a two-story affair heated with a stove. The wheelbase of the giant wagon was over 86 inches, as compared to an average width of 58 to 60 inches. The Reed wagon not only slowed the group's travel as it frequently fell behind the rest of the wagons, it also was a constant reminder of wealth to the poorer members of the group.

During the second week of May 1846, they joined a large group of emigrants and left Independence, Missouri on their way west. Although wealthy and influential, the Donners and Reeds were just part of another party under the leadership of Lillburn Boggs, ex-governor of Missouri. On May 30th, Reed's mother-in-law, Sarah Keys, died and was buried along the trail near present-day Manhattan, Kansas. Continuing across the plains without incident, the travelers crossed into Wyoming.

One of those chance meetings that makes people later ask "what if?" took place on the night of June 27th. While camped at Fort Bernard, a few miles from Fort Laramie on Laramie Creek, mountain man James Clyman walked up to the campfire. Clyman was a legend in the history of the fur trade. He came west with Ashley in the early 1820's and knew the country as well as any man. Besides, Reed and Clyman were old brothers-in-arms, having served in the same regiment in the Black Hawk War. Another comrade from that regiment, Abe Lincoln, also went on to make a name in history.

Clyman had just come across the route with Hastings heading east, and Clyman didn't think much of the new cutoff. He warned Reed and the Donner brothers to "stick to the main road" and not take the cutoff described in Hastings' Guide. Reed was unpersuaded. After all, he was holding the book in his hands. Many historians have written about the human nature involved at that fateful meeting. Do you believe a scruffy, dirty old mountain man who looked disreputable, or do you believe the well-written, recently published book you're holding in your hands?

One member of the party, journalist Edwin Bryant, decided he would take Hastings' route. Bryant didn't want to be encumbered with wagons (heeding part of Clyman's advice), so he sold and traded his outfit for a string of pack animals and pressed ahead.

Compounding the dilemma of Clyman's warning, a few weeks later on July 17th, Reed and the Donners were shown a letter from Hastings at South Pass offering to "personally" guide emigrants across his new route to California. So, their minds made up, the party continued west. On July 18th, they crossed South Pass and like so many emigrants before and since, camped at Pacific Springs.

Meanwhile, Hastings had met another group, the Harlan-Young party, and was at Fort Bridger preparing to guide them across the Utah Desert.

On July 19, the Reeds, Dormers, and their fellow travelers camped at the Little Sandy crossing. Here the original group decided to split. The next morning, most of the families headed over to the Sublette Cutoff on their way to Oregon or California and the remainder of the original group headed to Fort Bridger. Typical of politics along the Trail, an election was held to determine the leadership of the party and George Donner was chosen as captain of the company. From that point on the group was known as the Donner Party.

In his 60's, George Donner was more of a friendly patriarch than a dynamic leader. He was considered a kindly 'man who loved his family and many children. Some historians feel that the outcome of this election was one of those mistakes that added up to the final horror. Reed was also wealthy, but he was a younger, more robust man and perhaps better suited for leadership. The ratio of able-bodied men to women and children was also a factor in the group's eventual fate.

Another telling incident which occurred while the party was camped on the Little Sandy was the "adoption" of Luke Halloran. Halloran was "consumptive" and had been abandoned to die alone a few days before by the group with whom he was traveling. A charitable person, George Donner's wife Tamsen took Halloran in as one of her own and cared for him. Later, when Halloran died of his ailment in the Utah Desert, it turned out he wasn't a "penniless waif' as most of the party thought. Gold, totalling $1500, was found in his belongings and he had willed the money to the Donners. Because the Donners were already wealthy, this caused quite a bit of dissension in the poorer members of the party. Halloran's story has a bit of historical irony; imagine being left to die and being rescued by the Donners.

Somewhere between the Little Sandy and Fort Bridger, young Edward Breen, the son of Irish emigrants Patrick and Margaret Breen, fell from his horse and broke his leg. The recommended medical procedure for the broken leg was amputation, but the young lad refused it. His luck held and gangrene didn't set in. A month later he was able to walk without crutches.

On July 28th, the Donner Party arrived at Fort Bridger. It was here that one of the most fateful errors occurred. Hastings was several days ahead of the Donners leading the Harlan-Young group across his cutoff through the Wasatch Mountains. And the going was next to impossible. Edwin Bryant was also ahead of the Donners with his pack string and he was struggling with the route. Bryant sent a letter back to Fort Bridger to be delivered to his friends the Donners. The letter told the Donners NOT to take Hastings' route. Jim Bridger and his partner Louis Vasquez never delivered the letter. Not receiving the message has sparked controversy among historians which is still disputed to this day.

Bridger and Vasquez stood to gain financially from emigrants using the proposed route, all travelers on the Hastings Cutoff would pass by the fort which was a business establishment they owned.

Compounding the error of not getting the message from Edwin Bryant, the Donners didn't depart from Fort Bridger until July 31st. They had rested there four days, time which would haunt them a few months later.

Leaving Fort Bridger, the Donners headed toward Fort Hall on the Main Trail and after traveling a few miles north they turned west, following a recent set of tracks which led them out of Wyoming into the tangled canyons of the Wasatch, and eventually, into history.

Much of the Donner's path across Wyoming is on public lands managed by the Bureau of Land Management. Visiting the various sites along the Trail can be a rewarding experience. With a few exceptions, the land surrounding the Donner's route looks just like it did 144 years ago when they passed through Wyoming. Maps showing the route of the Oregon Trail are available at BLM offices.

Bureau of Land Management Article

up along the by-way. Dedication of the kiosks and the official opening of the scenic by-way are scheduled for June 2003. Both tapes and CD's will be available for purchase that give information by mile marker on the byway.

In addition to historic sites and view of the High Uinta Mountains, travelers may spot mule deer, elk, moose, hawks, eagles, coyotes and red fox along the road. The Bear River Watershed runs from Whitney Reservoir in the Uinta's to the Great Salt Lake in Utah. As it meanders along the by-way, one learns that it is the largest river in North America where the waters do not reach an Ocean. The river is 500 miles long and enters the states of Wyoming, Utah, and Idaho a total of five times and yet it is only 90 miles from its headwaters to the mouth of the lake.

The river runs by the historical Myers

Seedskadee History

1. Teal Island Cabin

The cabin among the cottonwoods is of 19th century vintage and is thought to have been constructed by a wintering mountain man. As with so many pioneer structures, subsequent use probably included ferry-boatmen, emigrants, and homesteaders.

2. Dodge Homestead

This site was first used by enterprising mountain men who constructed a commercial ferry in 1847. They operated the ferry until 1853, when Mormons chartered by Brigham Young took over. Mormon operation continued until their emigration was complete in 1858.

Harold H. Dodge homesteaded this area in 1916 and, by 1922, completed his masterpiece, a suspension bridge across the Green River. An A-frame still stands marking one of the bridge towers. The bridge was used to cross livestock and wagons for which Dodge charged a toll. He also sheared sheep for local ranchers in the spring. His wife, Mary, told of having to break the ice on the Green River in the winter so she could haul their household water. Everything went smoothly until 1936, when a local ranch hand was crossing the bridge with a wagon load of grain. Once he reached the middle of the bridge, a main support cable snapped and the entire outfit - horses, wagon, grain and driver - plunged into the river. The driver and horses made it to shore but the rest was lost.

3. Yancey Homestead

SW. Brazzil and F.H. Orcult originally homesteaded this land in the early 1900s. They later sold to Edlvin P. Yancey, a drifter who worked seasonally for several ranches in the region. The site still contains the remains of a 2-room stable with attached tool shed and corral and a side-hill root cellar.

4. Tailman Ranch

Carl H. Beckman filed the original homestead papers for this site in 1920, but it was the fourth owner, James A. Tailman who built most of the structures and improved the land. Like so many others, Tallman worked odd jobs around the area – herding sheep, irrigating, haying, punching cattle, and trapping.

Among the many ruins of the Tallman Ranch are two graves marked by an outline of stones. These are the final resting places for two of the Holden children who died of sickness while staying with the Tallmans. Other ruins include two cabins, a barn with a log corral, an old shed with a Model A Ford parked in it, and a self-cleaning outhouse on the river bank.

5. Concrete Houses

Ed Karel and his wife homesteaded here in 1916, and his half brother, Joe Startz, filed on the land across the river. It was rumored that Ed was a little mentally imbalanced and dangerous, which explains why Joe wanted to be on the opposite side of the river when he built a similar concrete house that he shared with an elderly gentleman named Mr. Shaw. When Mr. Shaw and Mrs. Karel were both away, an argument broke out between the brothers, both of whom had been drinking. Ed was known to have suspected an affair between his wife and Joe and may have wanted to settle the score. Both men palmed their guns and shots echoed across the prairie. A few days later, Mr. Shaw returned to find their bodies laying near each other, bloated and picked on by magpies.

6. Barnhardt Wild Horse Ranch

The two log buildings in the meadow are from a much earlier time. These are the original homestead buildings of J.E. Barnhardt, a drifting saddle tramp who homesteaded here in 1918. Barnhardt ran wild horses that he broke, gelded, and sold to ranchers in the region.

7. Lombard Ranch

Concealed by cottonwoods on the east bank of the river are the log buildings of the Lombard Wild Horse Ranch, homesteaded by William Lombard in 1889. A few years later, Gustave "Frenchy" Tronquet took over the property. Frenchy was a horse trader and rustler. He would sell wild horses to people in Missouri, Canada and places back east. During shipment, he would steal them back and sell them all over again. Ruins on the site include a large stockade-type corral with a cabin on each corner. During prohibition, many stills cranked out their illegal elixir here.

8-9. Oregon Trail Crossings (Lombard Ferry)

The Green River had many ferries operating on it during the emigration period, especially during the gold rush; however, these two sites were the ferry crossings for the primary route of the Oregon Trail. The ferries were built in 1843 by mountain men who ran them until 1850. Mormons chartered by Brigham Young took over the operation until 1858. William Lombard arrived to continue operation in 1889. Later, people referred to these as the Lombard Ferry. Ruts leading away from the river can still be seen on the private land of the northern crossing.

Writing in her diary, one pioneer woman had this to say about the ferry crossing on the Green River:

"This day at last we came in sight of the formidable Green River which we have so much dreaded. There is a good ferry boat kept by Mormons and worked by French and Indian half breeds. Mrs. S. and I visited their wigwams after we crossed. Disgusting looking beings... uncomfortable times ... ferry men dishonest"

During the peak emigration months of May, June, and July, the wait for a ferry could be several days. Rates were high too. It could cost as much as $16.00 per wagon to get across, which was a great deal of money. Impatient parties who risked fording the river at these crossings sometimes lost life and property if they misjudged the current or slipped off the narrow gravel bar that allowed safe progress.

10. Green River Crossing, Ferry, Stage Station, Pony Express Station and Transcontinental Telegraph Office

This is the site where a fur brigade led by Jedediah Smith crossed in 1824. His boss, William Ashley, crossed a year later on his way to organizing the first mountain man rendezvous. The ill-fated Donner Party crossed late in 1846, on a trip which subsequently led some of them to cannibalism and snowy graves in the mountains of California. By 1849, a ferry had been built near the old ford and was operated by Mormons until 1858. On April 3, 1860, the Pony Express established a station here that operated until its demise on October 24, 1861, by which time telegraph wires spanned the continent from this same spot. A stage station was built after gold was discovered on South Pass in 1867.

11. Robinson Ferry

On this site, a ferry was built by the Mormons in 1847, who ran it until 1856, when operation became the exclusive right of Isaac Bullock and Lewis Robinson, through a controversial court decision. A few years later, tragedy struck the Robinson family when their homestead was attacked by Indians. The entire family was killed, with the exception of their 10-year-old daughter. An old trapper who heard about the child's plight escorted her back east to relatives in New Jersey.

12. Rood/Branson Ranch
13. Rood/Branson/Johnson Ranch

The land that includes the ranch on the east bank of the river and another ranch 1/2 mile further down was homesteaded by Albert Rood in 1919, and taken over by P.C. Branson several years later. When one of Branson's daughters came of age, she married Albert Johnson who built the lower ranch. A unique sagebrush corral still exists at the Johnson ranch.

A word of caution: Federal law prohibits disturbing historic sites. Your cooperation will enable others to enjoy these historic places unmarred by human disturbance. • Bridger-Fraeb Trading Post, Palmer/Mormon Crossing

On this site, mountain men Jim Bridger and Henry Fraeb built a trading post in 1839. These men had seen the beaver trade flourish and decline in little over a decade. Bridger was probably the one man who knew that settlers would undoubtably come pouring through the area. In fact, he was the one who had inadvertently blazed the trails for them. Now, he and Fraeb had a plan to serve the fur traders still in the mountains, the Indians, and the settlers that would soon be coming. Unfortunately for Fraeb, a brigade of trappers he was leading stumbled upon a large party of Indians. The Indians attacked, and the trappers repelled them without a loss, except for poor Fraeb. This led Bridger to abandon this site in 1841, for a more favorable location along Black's Fork of the Green River.

Joel Palmer, who gained notoriety for writing a guidebook about the Oregon Trail, crossed here July 21, 1845. This is also the place where Brigham Young led the Mormons across the Green River in 1847, on their way to settle Salt Lake City, Utah.

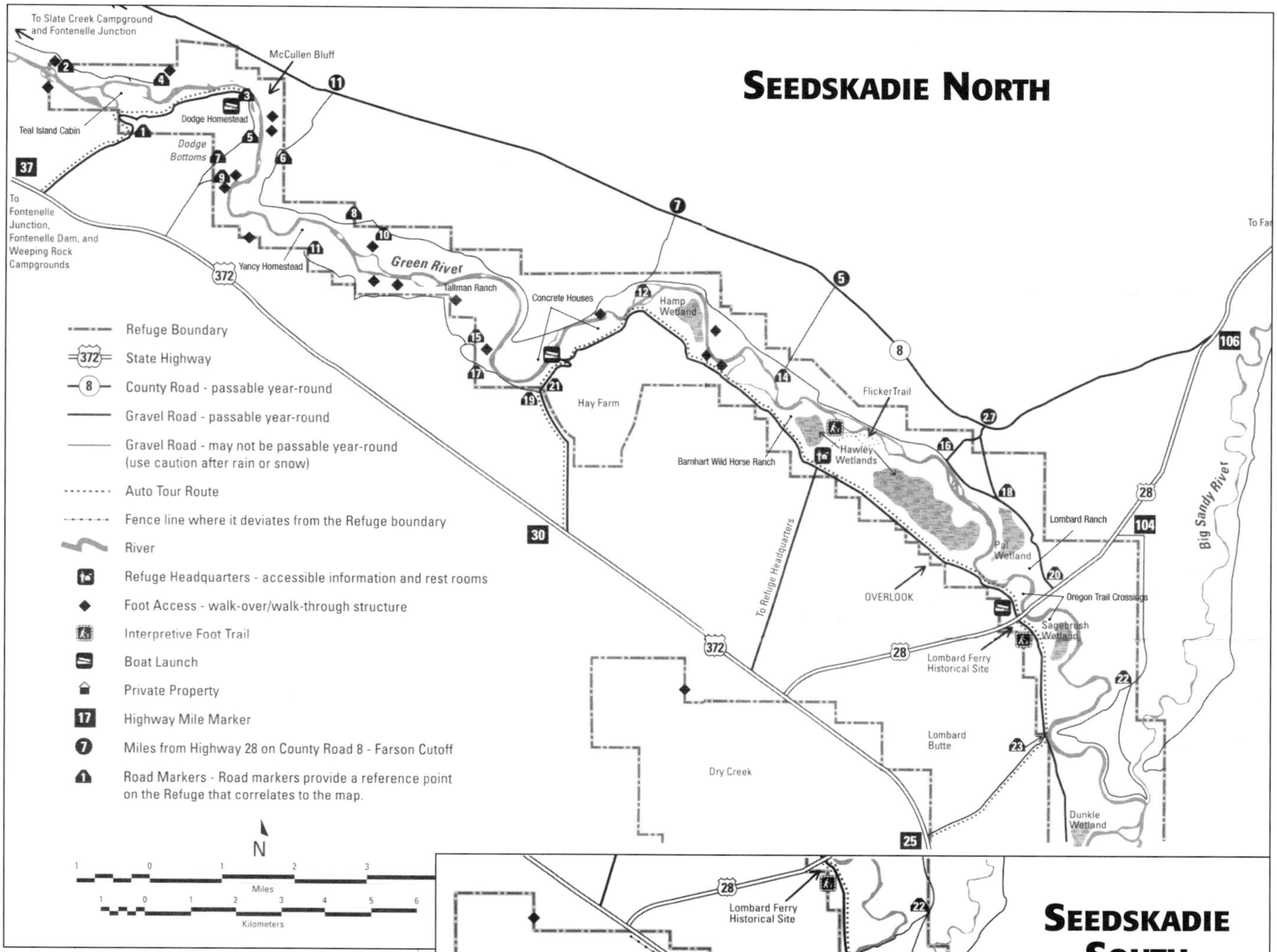

Seedskadie North

To Slate Creek Campground and Fontenelle Junction
McCullen Bluff
Teal Island Cabin
Dodge Homestead
Dodge Bottoms
To Fontenelle Junction, Fontenelle Dam, and Weeping Rock Campgrounds
Yancy Homestead
Green River
Tallman Ranch
Concrete Houses
Hamp Wetland
Hay Farm
Flicker Trail
Hawley Wetlands
Barnhart Wild Horse Ranch
To Refuge Headquarters
Lombard Ranch
Big Sandy River
Pal Wetland
OVERLOOK
Oregon Trail Crossings
Sagebrush Wetland
Lombard Ferry Historical Site
Lombard Butte
Dry Creek
Dunkle Wetland
To Far

Refuge Boundary
State Highway
County Road - passable year-round
Gravel Road - passable year-round
Gravel Road - may not be passable year-round (use caution after rain or snow)
Auto Tour Route
Fence line where it deviates from the Refuge boundary
River
Refuge Headquarters - accessible information and rest rooms
Foot Access - walk-over/walk-through structure
Interpretive Foot Trail
Boat Launch
Private Property
Highway Mile Marker
Miles from Highway 28 on County Road 8 - Farson Cutoff
Road Markers - Road markers provide a reference point on the Refuge that correlates to the map.

N
Miles
Kilometers

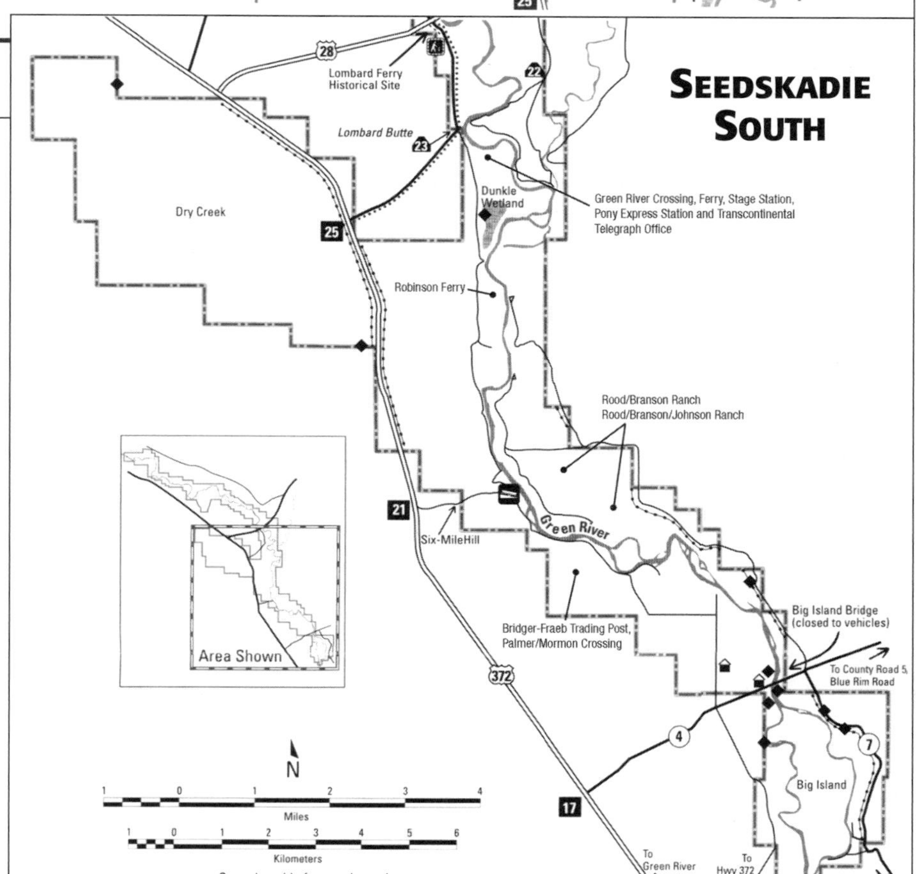

Crossing. It was here in 1858 that John Myers located his ranch. It was also called the Bear River Station on the Overland Stage Route and a changing station for the Pony Express in 1861.

Ranching dominates private property land use adjacent to the Mirror Lake scenic byway, and is an important industry in Uinta County. The area includes working ranches that span generations who have raised cattle, sheep, and hay. It would not be unusual for a traveler to see a cowboy herding sheep down the highway or a harvesting crew working in the fields. Livestock feeding, branding, roping and irrigating chores can be seen from spring to fall and visitors are especially excited during lambing and calving season.

Just off the highway, one can see the Sulphur Creek Reservoir that provides a wide variety of recreational opportunities. Summer activities include boating, water skiing, windsurfing, picnicking, hiking, and fishing. Winter activities include ice fishing, ice skating and kite surfing. Reservoir facilities include a boat ramp and dock, picnic shelter, vault toilets, and group camping.

Millions of years ago, an east/west fracture in the earth's crust led to an uplifting that resulted in the birth of the high Uinta Mountains. With an approximate span of 150 miles in length and 35 miles in width, this mountain range is one of only a few in North America running east to west. The High Uintas are a very old mountain range comprised primarily of quartzite rock. The forces of erosion and glaciers have shaped the rugged

Mule Deer Facts

• Over 55,000 mule deer roam BLM public lands in the Rock Springs District.

• Mule deer inhabit every major vegetation type in western North America and every climate zone except arctic and tropics. Mule deer in high elevation ranges may migrate up to 50 miles between summer and winter range. Snow depth and forage availability is considered to be the dominant factor in population control by many.

• Mule deer occupy a wide range of habitats. Food, cover, arid water requirements change with the seasons. Mule deer often must compete with livestock grazing practices and other human-caused disturbances. Proper land management can benefit deer.

• Mule deer gain weight during spring, summer, and fall. Deer must be in excellent condition in the fall of each year to survive the harsh winter weather.

• Deer eat a wide variety of foods. The major foods eaten by mule deer include sagebrush, serviceberry, snowberry, rabbitbrush, aspen, bitterbrush, juniper, willow, mountain mahogany, grasses, and forbs. In winter, more shrubs are eaten than dead forbs and grasses. Shrubs are alive and provide more protein and carbohydrates. Mule deer in North America have adapted to these long periods of nutritional stress caused by winter. Protection from human disturbance helps mule deer survive winter stress periods.

• Males gain and lose weight more rapidly than females.

• Both sexes essentially starve a little each day during severe winters because they can't eat enough forage to maintain their body weight.

• Good quality habitat may keep them from starving to death except in the very worst of winters.

• Antler growth in males begins in the spring. As fall and the rut approaches, the males' necks and shoulders swell, they become hyperactive and aggressive and begin to eat less food.

• Mule deer have their young in riparian areas and aspen stands when they are available.

• Under good conditions, most mule deer does have twins. Fawns average 7-8 pounds at birth.

• Mule deer nearly disappeared from the plains by the late 1930s, probably due to the combination of excessive hunting, several periods of severe drought, complicated by over-grazing by domestic livestock and several extremely severe winters. Mule deer populations have rebounded in most of their range.

Source: Bureau of Land Management Rock Springs District

peaks and formed the many beautiful lakes that provide great fishing. All along the by-way are campgrounds with water and toilets and hundreds of miles of hiking and biking trails. The Bear River Lodge on the Wyoming side of the mountains provides food, groceries, camping supplies and rental cabins. Off road vehicles may be rented in the summer and snowmobiles in the winter.

Early day timber cutting in the Headwater Drainages of the Bear River occurred between 1870 and 1900. Cut and burned-over areas indicate a large amount of timber was removed during this time frame. Large sawmills were established that used the logs that were floated down the river during the spring run-off. Railroad ties were an early product of timber cutting, and charcoal produced in the kilns at Hilliard and Piedmont were shipped to smelters in Utah and Colorado. An Historic tie-hack cabin is well-preserved at the Forest Service office at milepost 46.4. A guide to the Mirror Lake scenic byway with listings of all campgrounds and side trips may be purchased here.

The Wyoming side of the Mirror Lake scenic by-way 150 is open year round. Additional information may be secured by calling the Evanston Chamber of Commerce at 1-800-328-9708, the Bear River State Park at 1-307-789-6547 or the Bear River Ranger station at 1-435-642-6662.

Hikes

Flaming Gorge Area

Little Hole Trail
Distance: 7 miles
Climb: flat
Rating: easy
Usage: moderate/ heavy
Location: Take access road below Flaming Gorge Dam, off of Hwy. 191.

This trail follows the north side of the Green River below the dam and is the main angler access. For non-anglers, the trail offers a scenic walk along the Green River, with opportunities for viewing wildlife. Another section of the trail continues downstream from Little Hole, ascends to a scenic bench above the river, descends to the riverside, then fades out about two miles below Little Hole.

Bear Canyon/ Bootleg Trail
Distance: 3 miles
Climb: gentle
Rating: easy
Usage: moderate/ heavy
Location: Trailhead is found opposite Firefighter's Campground on Hwy. 191.

This trail marked with blue diamonds passes through open forest and meadows, ending at a scenic viewpoint overlooking the reservoir.

Canyon Rim Trail
Distance: 5 miles
Climb: gentle
Rating: easy/ moderate
Usage: moderate
Location: Trail begins at the Red Canyon Visitor Center, about 3 miles north of the junction of Utah 44 and Hwy. 191. It also has access points at Canyon Rim Campground (2 miles from junction) and Greens Lake Campground and Greendale Rest Area (1 mile from junction).

Marked with blue diamonds, this trail connects Red Canyon Visitor Center with Greendale Overlook. It follows the rim of the canyon for abut one mile to Canyon Rim Campground and offers spectacular views of 1400 foot deep Red Canyon. Past the campground, the trail makes a 2.75 miles loop giving hikers the opportunity to continue further along the rim or hike past scenic Greens Lake. It then drops down into Skull Creek for a short distance on its gentle ascent to Greendale Overlook. Quiet hikers may see moose, elk, deer, and other wildlife.

Dowd Mountain/ Hideout Canyon Trail
Distance: 5 miles
Climb: 1,600 feet (descent)
Rating: moderate
Usage: moderate
Location: Go four miles down Utah 44 at the end of Dowd Mountain road.

This trail descends from Dowd Mountain to Hideout Boat Camp. The first mile is relatively flat and offers scenic views of the Flaming Gorge.

Ute Mountain Trail
Distance: 2 miles
Climb: 600 feet (descent)
Rating: easy
Usage: heavy
Location: Take FDR 5, just south of FDR 221, to the Sheep Creek Geologic Loop.

This trail connects the Ute Lookout Tower with the Browne Lake Campground. The fire tower is open seasonally to the public.

Tamarack Lake Trail
Distance: 3 miles
Climb: gentle
Rating: easy
Usage: moderate/ heavy
Location: Trailhead begins at the west end of Spirit Lake Campground.

This trail begins between Spirit Lake Campground and Lodge. It ascends to Tamarack Lake. A side trail goes to scenic Jessen Lake. The high Uintas Wilderness is accessed by continuing west from Tamarack Lake.

Cokeville Area

Lake Alice
Distance: 1.5 miles
Climb: gentle
Rating: easy
Usage: moderate
Location: Take FDR 10069 off of Hwy. 232 just north of the Pine Creek Fish Hatchery. Follow it to FDR 1066, just past the Ranger Station, and bear right. At the junction with FDR 10193, bear left and follow the road to the campground. A trail from Hobble Creek Campground leads to the lake.

The largest natural lake in Bridger-Teton's south end, with magnificent scenery and recreation opportunities, Lake Alice is popular for hiking, horseback riding, and mountain biking. Several trails from other locations also lead to the lake.

Big Piney Area

Wyoming Peak
Distance: 2.5 to 5 miles
Climb: steep
Rating: moderate/ difficult
Usage: moderate
Location: The Shale Creek Road (10138) is located near the southern end of the Greys River Road (10126) and heads east. A parking area for trailers is located at 2.8 miles, vehicles without trailers can continue for another .8 miles. A small sign identifies the trail. From Middle Piney Lake, the trail begins at the Middle Piney Lake Campground at the end of Forest road 10024, 24 miles from the town of Big Piney.

A historic lookout cabin on the summit of

Wyoming Peak offers spectacular views of the surrounding mountain ranges. From Shale Creek, in the Greys River drainage, the trail climbs switchbacks 2.5 miles to the summit; Wyoming Peak can also be accessed from Middle Piney Lake, a 5-mile hike one way.
Historic Quarry Trail

Fossil Butte National Monument

Quarry Trail

This trail, just over two and one-half miles in length, leads to the site of a historic fossil quarry on the face of the butte. The interpretive signs along the trail will help you understand the natural and cultural history of this semi-arid environment. Comfortable walking shoes, water, and insect repellant will add to a safe and pleasant hike. Check at the Visitor Center for trail conditions.

The tops of the buttes are prone to lightning strikes. If you are hiking as a storm approaches, seek shelter in a low lying area such as a ditch or draw, avoid trees and metal objects. Crouch down and wait for the storm to pass.

The first documented discovery of fossil fish was in 1856. Originally the interest in the fossils and the Green River Formation was scientific, with references being made in various geographic surveys and associated reports. By the turn of the century, however, many fossil fishermen were collecting fossils. Little is known about these early collectors. Some were local workers who quarried for extra income. Many sold fossils to large museums back east and passengers on the trains passing through the old town of Fossil.

Take a few moments to enjoy the scenery and become familiar with the area around you.

This abandoned quarry site is 7,410 feet above sea level, about 600 feet higher than the beginning of the trail. In the time since the sediments were deposited in Fossil Lake some 50 million years ago, they have uplifted about 6,000 feet.

As you go up the trail following the arrows and numbered markers we remind you to watch out for people below. The trail is steep and cuts through a talus slope of loose rock. Do not throw or roll any objects from the trail or quarry.

Take time and be sure of your footing.

1. Ash Layers

Ash layers from ancient volcanoes periodically covered Fossil Lake. Although the volcanic activity had a definite effect on the lake environment, it did not "kill" the lake. Fossils are found after (above) these layers. The ash or "Tuff" layers are recognizable throughout Fossil Basin and are used as marker-beds by geologists. Minerals within these ash deposits can be radiometrically dated.

2. Salt Lake

The light tan rocks were formed in shallow water that was saline (salty). These beds typically do not have as many well preserved fossils or fine laminae (layers) as other layers on the butte.

3. Rock Layers

The Green River Formation has many distinctive horizontal layers. The natural tendency of this rock is to break along these flat-lying planes. This is due to the settling of fine particles through water that forms paper thin layers.

4. Oil Shale

Although often called oil shale, this finely laminated rock is a type of limestone that contains abundant layers of organic material. The original organic material was converted into kerogen by heat and pressure. Close examination of this unit will reveal very fine alternating light and dark bands. Each represents a change in the lake side environment. As many as 5,000 of these laminae can be counted in a one-foot thick section. Laminae counts vary in number based on where they occur in the lake. Geologists now question the classic "varve" model (seasonally deposited laminae), thought to have occurred at Fossil Lake.

5. Fossils!

As you look at this wall you will find a number of brown inclusions. These are fossils. The pores within the original skeletal material have been filled by mineral deposits. The coloring is derived from: iron (red, orange, brown); copper (blue); and carbon (brown).

Help to protect Fossil Butte!

All objects in the monument: rocks, fossils, artifacts, wildflowers and animals, must be left in place and undisturbed so that others may enjoy them. No personal collecting is allowed. This protection is not only the law, it is a matter of good citizenship and consideration for others.

Fossil Lake Trail Guide

This 1-1/2 mile trail provides a view of the flora and fauna on the monument. It winds through an aspen grove, high desert landscape and near a beaver pond. Outcroppings above the trail are limestone lake sediments. Here, and throughout the monument, you are likely to notice sites where these sediments have been scientifically sampled. Your assistance in not disturbing these fragile sites is important.

Fossil Lake Trail leads to the bottom layers of this now dry lake bed. Snow and rain filter down through the limestone, where lenses of clay trap the moisture. The water is slowly released, creating outflows, or springs, that support the aspen groves.

Markers have been placed at five locations along the trail. The numbered sections in this guide correspond with the markers.

Comfortable shoes, drinking water, and insect repellant will add to a safe and pleasant hike. Check with a ranger for trail conditions.

1. Beaver Pond

Beavers have been active in the aspen groves around you. Look carefully to see evidence of their presence. The beaver alters its environment more than any other animal except man. Beaver dams change the flow of springs and streams; create ponds that provide protection for the beavers, and habitat for various forms of life. These ponds also create an ideal ecosystem for plant growth. Beavers renew the environment of aspen groves by removing the older, larger trees and allowing the younger seedlings to regenerate.

2. High Desert

Although it may look sparse and unpopulated, the high desert ecosystem is abundant with plant and animal life. For plants and animals in this ecosystem, obtaining and retaining water is vital.

Sagebrush, the grayish-green plant that dominates the landscape, has several features that enable it to survive. Its leaves are narrow which reduce the surface area where evaporation can take place. The roots extend horizontally, like fingers, so that they can retain water on the surface and vertically (10-20 feet) to obtain ground water.

The tall green-leafed bush just in front of the marker is serviceberry. Its fruit provides food for mule deer, moose, and humans. Native Americans mixed serviceberries with fat and jerky to make "pemmican", which was stuffed into buffalo intestines and kept for the winter months. Today, people make preserves from serviceberry.

The large 6-8 inch holes, in the ground, are badger dens. Badgers feed on small mammals including the Uinta Ground Squirrel, mice, and other rodents. Once a badger abandons its den, a fox or jackrabbit may inhabit it.

3. Green River Formation

The tan to yellowish rock in front of you is part of the Green River Formation deposited as sediments in Fossil Lake 50 million years ago. At the time of its existence, Fossil Lake was at an elevation of about 1000 feet and approximately 50 miles long and 10 miles wide. Today, what remains of the lake bottom is approximately 7500 feet above sea level, the result of geologic uplift occurring 5-10 million years ago. Since then, wind and water have been at work carrying away the softer sediments leaving only remnants of Fossil Lake—like Fossil Butte and the ridge above you.

The rock layers are predominantly limestone, mudstone, volcanic ash, and dolomite, dispersed throughout the formation. Fossil fish are found in many layers of the Green River Formation. These include relatives of the herring family, paddlefish, gar, bowfin, and stingray.

Research and commercial quarrying has occurred in the Green River Formation since the late 1800s. The Historic Quarry Trail, located southeast of the Visitor Center, provides a closer look at an inactive quarry.

4. Aspen Grove

Aspen groves suggest the presence of water near the surface and support a variety of plants and animals. Mule deer, elk, and moose use the aspen groves for shelter and food. Beavers use the trees for building material and the bark and leaves for food. Height, not the number of trees, indicates the amount of moisture in an aspen grove. The taller the trees are, the more moisture there is in the ground.

5. Dead and Down Material

Some may see a dead tree as useless or unsightly. However, dead and dying wood is one of nature's most valuable resources. A large variety of organisms live in or on dead trees, including squirrels, woodpeckers, bats, lichen, fungi, and mosses. Tree cavities are important to a variety of animals because they provide a place to sleep, nest, rest, and breed. Dead and dying wood is more alive than a living tree, as it has more nutrients and can hold more water.

Help Us Protect Fossil Butte

All objects in the monument including rocks, fossils, artifacts, wildflowers and animals must be left in place and undisturbed so that others may enjoy them. No personal collecting is allowed. This is not only the law, but is also a matter of good citizenship and consideration for others.

Information Please

Tourism Information

Cokeville Chamber of Commerce 279-3200
Green River Chamber of Commerce 875-5711

Kemmerer Chamber of Commerce 877-9761
La Barge Chamber of Commerce 386-2221
Chamber of Commerce - Rock Springs 362-3771

Government

BLM Kemmerer Field Office 828-4500
BLM Rock Springs Field Office 352-0256
Bridger-Teton National Forest - Kemmerer Ranger District 877-4415
Ashley National Forest - Green River Office 875-2871
Wasatch-Cache National Forests - Evanston Ranger District 789-3194
Wasatch-Cache National Forests -Mountain View Ranger District 782-6555

Car Rentals

Rent A Wreck • Green River 875-4000
Affordable Used Car Rental • Evanston 789-3096
Hertz • Rock Springs 382-3262
Wayne's Car Rental • Rock Springs 362-6970

Hospitals

Evanston Regional Hospital • Evanston 789-3636
South Lincoln Medical Center • Kemmerer 877-4401
Memorial Hospital of Sweetwater County • Rock Springs 362-3711

Airports

Rock Springs 352-6880
Evanston 789-2256

Golf

Purple Sage Golf Course • Evanston 789-2383
Rolling Green Country Club • Green River 875-6200
White Mountain Golf Course • Rock Springs 352-1415
Kemmerer Field Club • Kemmerer 877-6954

Ski Areas

Pine Creek Ski Area 279-3201

Guest Ranches

Flying V Ranch • Kemmerer 386-2465

Lodges and Resorts

Little America • Little America 875-2400

Bed and Breakfasts

Clark Country B&B • Cokeville 279-3336
Pine Gables Inn B&B • Evanston 789-2069

Outfitters and Guides

Western Discovery Tours G 789-3655
Paintrock Outfitters FGE 765-2556
DT Outfitting EG 386-2499
Magic Mountains Outfitters FHER 279-3345

Notes:

Dining Quick Reference

Price Range refers to the average cost of a meal per person: ($) $1-$6, ($$) $7-$11, ($$$) $12-up. Cocktails: "Yes" indicates full bar; Beer (B)/Wine (W), Service: Breakfast (B), Brunch (BR), Lunch (L), Dinner (D). Businesses in bold print will have additional information under the appropriate map locator number in the body of this section.

MAP#	RESTAURANT	TYPE CUISINE	PRICE RANGE	CHILD MENU	COCKTAILS BEER WINE	MEALS SERVED	CREDIT CARDS ACCEPTED
2	Lew's Family Restaurant	Chinese American	$$	Yes	Yes	L/D	Major
2	City Limits			No			
2	Casa Chavez	Mexican	$$	No		L/D	M/V
3	Santa Fe Trail Restaurant	Family	$			B/L/D	Major
3	Burger King	Fast Food	$	Yes		D/L/B	M/V
3	Renegade Cafe	Family	$			B/L/D	
3	Thad's Restaurant	American	$	Yes		B/L/D/BR	Major
5	The Inn at Rock Springs	Steakhouse	$$	Yes	Yes	D	Major
5	Wyoming Cattle Company	Steakhouse	$$$	Yes	Yes	D	Major
5	Taco Time	Mexican	$	Yes		L/D	Major
5	Nacho Nana's	Fast Food	$	Yes		L/D	
5	China King Buffet	Chinese	$/$$			L/D	Major
6	**JB's Restaurant**	American	$$	Yes	W/B	L/D/B	Major
6	Pizza Hut	Pizza	$$	Yes	B	L/D	Major
6	Wonderful House	Chinese	$$	Yes	B/W	L/D	Major
6	McDonald's	Fast Food	$	Yes		L/D/B	
6	Taco Bell	Fast Food	$	Yes		L/D	
6	McDonald's	Fast Food	$			L/D/B	
6	Wendy's	Fast Food	$			L/D	
6	Village Inn	Family	$$	Yes		B/L/D	Major
6	Rocky Mountain Noodle	Italian	$/$$			L/D	M/V
6	Subway	Sandwiches/	$	Yes		L/D	M/V
6	Killpepper's	Family	$/$$	No		L/D	
6	KFC	Fast Food	$	Yes		L/D	
7	Los Cabos Mexican Restaurant	Mexican	$$	Yes	W/B	D/L	M/V
7	Fiesta Guadalajara	Mexican	$$	Yes		D/L	Major
7	Broadway Burger Station	Burgers	$/$$	No		L/D	
7	Boschetto's European Market & Caterers	Deli	$$			L/D	Major
10	Don Pedro Mexican Family	Mexican	$$	Yes	W/B	L/D	M/V
10	Sage Creek Bagels	Deli/Café	$$/$	Yes		L/B	M/V
10	Buckaroos Family Restaurant	Deli/Café	$$/$	Yes	Yes	L/B/D	M/V
10	Gerry's Snack Bar	sandwiches	$	Yes		L/D	
10	Arctic Circle	Burgers	$			L/D	Major
10	China Garden Restaurant	Chinese/American	$$	Yes	Yes	L/D	Major
10	Pizza Hut	Pizza	$$	Yes	B	L/D	Major
10	Penny's Diner	Family	$$	Yes		L/D/B	Major
10	Log Inn Supper Club	Steak/Seafood	$$$	Yes	Yes	D	Major
10	Krazy Moose Restaurant	Fine Family Dining	$$$/$$	Yes		D/B/L	Major
10	Sweet Inspirations	Bakery/Sandwiches	$	No		L/B	M/V
10	Red Feather Restaurant	Family	$/$$	Yes	Yes	B/L/D	Major
12	Denali Grill	Eclectic	$$/$$$	Yes	Yes	L/D	Major
12	Taco Time	Mexican	$	Yes		L/D	
12	Mi Casita Mexican Food	Mexican	$$	Yes	W/B	L/D	M/V
12	Java Connection	Coffee House/deli	$	Yes		D/L	Major
12	Other Place Restaurant	American	$$	Yes	Yes	D/L/B	Major
12	Taco Johns	Fast Food	$	Yes		L/D	
12	Subway	Sandwiches/	$	Yes		L/D	Major
19	Holding's Little America	Family	$/$$	Yes	Yes	B/L/D	Major
23	Taco Time	Mexican	$	Yes	Yes	L/D	
23	Cowboy Inn Restaurant	American	$$	Yes		B/L/D	Major
25	Mountain View Drive Inn	Fast Food	$	Yes		L/D	Major
25	Pizza Hut	Pizza	$$	Yes	B	L/D	Major
25	Pony Express Restaurant	American	$$	Yes		L/D	
28	Wagon Wheel Café	Family	$$	Yes		B/L/D	
28	Mrs. B's Restaurant	Family	$/$$	Yes		B/D/L	
33	**Old Mill Restaurant**	Steak & Seafood	$$		Yes	B/L/D	Major
33	Kelly's Roadhouse Grill	Family	$$	Yes	Yes	L/D	Major
33	Circle Star Grille	Family	$	Yes		L/D/B	Major
33	Country River Restaurant	Family	$			B/L/D	Major
34	**JB's Restaurant**	American	$$	Yes	W/B	L/D/B	Major

Dining Quick Reference-Continued

Price Range refers to the average cost of a meal per person: ($) $1-$6, ($$) $7-$11, ($$$) $12-up. Cocktails: "Yes" indicates full bar; Beer (B)/Wine (W), Service: Breakfast (B), Brunch (BR), Lunch (L), Dinner (D). Businesses in bold print will have additional information under the appropriate map locator number in the body of this section.

MAP#	RESTAURANT	TYPE CUISINE	PRICE RANGE	CHILD MENU	COCKTAILS BEER WINE	MEALS SERVED	CREDIT CARDS ACCEPTED
34	**Bear River Brewing LLC, Restaurant & Pub**	Creative Western	$$	Yes	W/B	L/D	Major
34	Domino's Pizza	Pizza	$$$/$$	No	Yes	D/L	Major
34	Don Pedro's	Mexican	$$	Yes	Yes	D/L	Major
34	Dragon Wall	Chinese	$$	Yes		D/L	Major
34	Main Street Artisan's Café & Gallery	Casual Gourmet	$$	No		L/B	Major
34	Papa Murphy's Pizza	Pizza	$$/$	No		D	V/M
34	Pizza Hut	Pizza	$$	Yes	B	D/L	Major
34	Taco John's	Fast Food	$	Yes		D/L	
34	Subway	Sandwiches	$	Yes		D/L	M/V
34	Wendy's	Fast Food	$	Yes		D/L	Major
34	Main Street Deli	Deli	$	No		B/L	V/M
34	El Rancho Grande	Mexican	$$	Yes	Yes	L/D	Major
34	Captain Ron's	Fish & Chips	$	Yes	Yes	L/D	
34	Aspen Restaurant	American	$$	Yes	W/B	D	Major
34	Hernandez Tacos & Restaurant	Mexican	$$	Yes	B	L/D	M/V
34	McDonald's	Fast Food	$	No		L/B/D	
34	Arby's	Fast Food	$$$/$	Yes		D/L	Major
34	Michael's Bar & Grill	Fine Dining	$$$	Yes	Yes	L/D	Major
34	Mother Mae's Kitchen	Family	$$	Yes	Yes	L/D	
34	Wally's Burgers	Fast Food	$	Yes		D/L	M/V
34	High Stakes Grill	Family	$$	Yes		B/L/D	Major
34	Hunan Garden	Chinese	$/$$	No			Major
35	**BW Dunmar Inn & Legal Tender Restaurant**	Steak & Seafood	$$$	Yes	Yes	B/L/D	Major
35	**Rendezvous Smokehouse Rest. & Sports Bar**	Barbeque	$$	Yes	Yes	B/L/D	Major
35	A&W	Fast Food	$	Yes			
35	Burger King	Fast Food	$	Yes		L/D/B	M/V
35	KC's Café & Latté	American	$$	Yes		L/D/B	M/V
35	KFC	Fast Food	$	Yes		L/D	
35	Flying J - The Cookery	Buffet	$$	Yes		L/D/B	Major
35	Lotty's Family Restaurant	Family	$$	Yes	Yes	L/D/B	Major
35	Blimpie's	Sandwiches/	$	Yes		L/D	Major
38	Bon Rico Restaurant	Fine Dining	$$$	Yes	Yes	D	M/V
38	Arctic Circle	Burgers	$	Yes		L/D	Major
38	Pizza Hut	Pizza	$$	Yes	B	L/D	Major
38	Luigi's Restaurant	Italian	$$	Yes		L/D	Major
39	Bootleggers Steakhouse & Grill	Family	$$	Yes	Yes	D	Major
39	Busy Bee Café	Family	$$	Yes		D/B/L	
39	King Cone Drive-In	Fast Food	$	No		D/L	
39	Westerner Café	Family	$$	Yes		B/L/D	Major
39	Taco Time	Mexican	$			L/D	
40	Hams Fork Buffet & Mesquite Grill	Buffet	$	No		D/L/B	Major
40	Polar King Drive-In	Fast Food	$	No		L/D/B	
40	Lake Viva Naughton Marina Hotel	Family	$$	Yes	Yes	B/L/D	Major
43	Country Market Restaurant	Family	$$	Yes		B/L/D	Major
43	A&W - Tri-Mart	Fast Food	$	Yes		L/D	
45	Mitch's Café	American	$$	Yes	Yes	B/L/D	M/V
48	Timberline Restaurant	American	$$	Yes		B/L/D	
48	Dry Creek Station Deli	Deli	$			L	Major
58	Dredge Station	American	$$	Yes	Yes	L/D	Major

NOTES:

Motel Quick Reference

Price Range: ($) Under $40 ; ($$) $40-$60; ($$$) $60-$80, ($$$$) Over $80. Pets [check with the motel for specific policies] (P), Dining (D), Lounge (L), Disabled Access (DA), Full Breakfast (FB), Cont. Breakfast (CB), Indoor Pool (IP), Outdoor Pool (OP), Hot Tub (HT), Sauna (S), Refrigerator (R), Microwave (M) (Microwave and Refrigerator indicated only if in majority of rooms), Kitchenette (K). All Wyoming area codes are 307.

MAP #	HOTEL	PHONE	NUMBER ROOMS	PRICE RANGE	BREAKFAST	POOL/ HOT TUB SAUNA	NON SMOKE ROOMS	OTHER AMENITIES	CREDIT CARDS
2	Econo Lodge	382-4217	95	$$$	CB	OP/HT	Yes	P/D/K	Major
2	Best Western Outlaw Inn	362-6623	101	$$$$/$$$		IP	Yes	D/L	Major
2	Economy Guest Village	362-3763	28	$				R/M	Major
2	Sands Inn	362-3739		$$			No		
3	Days Inn	362-5646	107	$$$	CB	OP	Yes	R/M/P	Major
3	Elk Street Motel	362-3705	18	$			No	P/R/M/K	M/V
5	**Ramada Limited**	362-1770	129	$$$	CB	OP	Yes	P/DA	Major
5	The Inn at Rock Springs	362-9600	150	$$	CB	HT/IP	Yes	DA/L/D/P/R/M	Major
5	Motel 6	362-1850	130	$		IP		P	Major
6	Motel 8	362-8200	91	$$			Yes	P	Major
6	Super 8 - Rock Spring	362-3800	49	$$	CB	IP	Yes	DA	Major
6	Budget Host Inn	362-6673	32		CB		Yes	P/R/M	Major
6	Comfort Inn	382-9490	103	$$$	CB	OP/HT	Yes	DA/K	Major
6	Holiday Inn	382-9200	114	$$		IP	Yes	K/P/D	Major
6	Sunset Suites	362-5155	41	$$		OP	Yes	P/K	Major
7	Walker's Motel	875-3567	6	$$/$			Yes	P	Major
7	Springs Motel	362-6683	23	$/$$				P	Major
7	Cody Motel	362-6675	37	$			No	P/M/R	Major
10	Coachman Inn Motel	875-3681	18	$$			Yes	P	Major
10	Mustang Motel	875-2468	19	$			Yes	P/R/M	Major
10	Flaming Gorge Motel	875-4190	17	$$			Yes	P/K	M/V
10	Oak Tree Inn	875-3500	190	$$	FB	HT	Yes	P/D/DA	Major
10	Western Inn	875-2840	31	$$	CB	HT	Yes	P/DA/M/R	Major
11	Super 8	875-9330	37	$/$$$/$$		HT	Yes	P/K	Major
11	Desmond Motel	875-3701	22	$$/$			Yes	P	Major
12	Sweet Dreams Inn	875-7554	30	$$/$$$		HT	Yes	D	Major
13	Steinaker Motel	784-3104	5				No	K	
15	Flaming Gorge Lodge	889-3773	5	$$$			Yes	D/R/M/K	Major
23	Valley West Motel	787-3700	42	$$			Yes	K/P	Major
28	Wagon Wheel Motel	782-6361	56	$$				P/D/K/L	Major
33	**Super 8 Motel - Evanston**	789-7510	87	$$				P/DA/R/M	Major
33	Prairie Inn Motel	789-2920	31	$$	CB		Yes	P	Major
33	Vagabond Motel	789-2902	30	$			Yes		
33	Alexander Motel	789-2346	12	$				P	M/V
33	Motel 6	789-0791	91	$$		OP	Yes		Major
34	Weston Plaza Hotel	789-0783	100	$$$		OP	Yes	D/L/P/K	Major
34	Weston Super Budget Inn	789-2810	115	$$		OP	Yes	D/L/P/K	Major
34	Hillcrest DX Motel	789-1111	40	$			Yes	P/L	M/V
35	**BW Dunmar Inn & Legal Tender Restaurant**	789-3770	165	$$$		HT/S/OP	Yes	R/M/DA	Major/V
35	**Comfort Inn - Evanston**	789-7799/	56	$$	CB	IP/HT	Yes	P/D/R/M/K	Major
35	**Rendezvous Lodge**	789-2220	113			HT/S	Yes	D/L/P/DA/K	Major
35	High Country Inn	789-2810	111	$$				L/D	Major
35	Economy Inn	789-2777	80	$$	CB		Yes	P/DA	Major
38	Energy Inn	877-6901	42	$$				K/P	M/V
38	Bon Rico	877-4503	24	$$				L/D/K/P	Major
39	Antler Motel	877-4461	58	$$/$			Yes	K	
39	Chateau Motel	877-4610	14	$				P/R/M/K	
39	Fairview Motel	877-3938	61	$$			Yes	P/M/R	Major
39	Fossil Butte Motel	877-3996	13	$$$			Yes	P/K/M/R	Major
39	Downtown Motel	877-3710	11	$			No		
40	Lake Viva Naughton Marina Hotel	877-9669-1	34	$/$$				K/L/D/P	M/V
43	**Valley Hi Motel**	279-3251	18				Yes	P/R	M/V
43	**Hideout Motel**	279-3281	11	$$			Yes	P/R/M	Major
45	Dwayne Mitchelson Motel	273-9200	10	$				P	
45	Sitzman's Motel	273-9246	10	$				D/P	
48	Red Cliffs Motel	386-9269	9	$$			Yes	K	
48	Wyoming Inn	386-2654	28	$$/$			Yes		
58	Dredge Station	339-7404	4	$$$				P/D/L/K/R	Major
58	Miner's Delight B&B	332-0248	8	$$$				L	M/V

NOTES:

Section 5

Southcentral Area

Including Casper, Riverton, Lander and Rawlins

North of Rawlins

1 *Gas, Food*

T Evansville

Pop. 2,255, Elev. 5,136

Named for W.T. Evans, early homesteader and blacksmith, Evansville was the original site of the Platte River Crossing for pioneers, used as early as 1834. From 1851 to 1853, the Reshaw Bridge stood here, an engineering marvel of its day. The Sioux burned the bridge when Fort Clay (an adjunct to Fort Casper) was abandoned after the Oregon Trail was rerouted south. With the discovery of oil, Evansville became a refinery town. Now it is a suburb of Casper.

Historic Evansville

One of the best-kept secrets in Wyoming is the vast amount of history held within the boundaries of the small Central Wyoming town of Evansville. Here can be found the Triangular Survey Point of Monument Hill, the highest point looking north across the Platte River, Richard's (Reshaw's) Bridge and Trading Post, a Memorial Cemetery and Mausoleum, Military Camps Davis and Payne and Fort Clay, Stroud's Crossing and Cabin, the convergence of the Oregon, California, Mormon Pioneer, Pony Express, Bridger, and Bozeman Trails, and where the Sioux, Arapaho and Cheyenne hunted the buffalo. In addition is the location of the "Mysterious Cross."

Richard's (Reshaw's) Bridge, Trading Past and Settlement

In operation from 1853-1965, constructed by John Baptiste Richard, a French Canadian, this was the first bridge across the North Platte River in this part of the country. It was also the first private business in Central Wyoming. The structure had 12 arches, was 835 feet long and 18 feet wide, and rested on 23 piers or cribs of hewn timbers filled with stone. Emigrants were charged as much as $5 per wagon during high water, thereby ensuring a more than adequate income to the partners in the endeavor.

Skylar Scott, in "Military Camps at Camp Payne" in a report on excavations at Camp Payne, edited by David Eckles of the Office of the Wyoming State Archaeologist, in The Wyoming Archaeologist, Volume 28. Number 3 and 4, 1985 states,

"Though not occupied over a long period of time by the United States Army, the military camp at Richard's Bridge played a significant role in the affairs of the region. The post protected a strategic crossing of the North Platte River on the Oregon Trail, and played a protective role with emigrants and a punitive one with hostile Indian tribes. The post provided a link between East and West in communications and supply transport. The Post at Platte Bridge, also known as Fort Clay, Camp Davis, and Camp Payne, was associated with two significant military campaigns, the Sioux Expedition of 1855-1856 and the Utah Expedition of 1858-1859. Furthermore, the military camp played an important role in Indian-Euro-American relations.

The post at Platte Bridge protected the most important river crossing in Wyoming, in the most hostile area of Wyoming, aiding in travel and communication on the Oregon Trail. Undoubtedly, the camp also played a significant role in relations between Plains Indian tribes and the U S. Army as the post acted out it's role as peacekeeper, protector, and aggressor."

Memorial Cemetery and Mausoleum

This site is located lust north of the Evansville Elementary School near the corner of 5th and Albany Streets on a tract of land known as the "Oregon Trail Memorial Park." This is the burial tomb of six skeletons recovered from an unmarked cemetery believed to be circa 1850s. Research indicated that the initial remains consisted of four males and two females. Later three skeletons, believed to be Native Americans, were included in the interment. Five of the skeletons, including one of the females, were clothed in military uniform, parts of which were recovered with military buttons and insignia attached. Army reports suggest that two of the dead may have been Sergeant John McCall, Co. E, 4th Artillery, who died in the area September 6, 1858 and the second a Private John Morgan. Co. A, 7th Infantry, who died August 25, 1858. The nine skeletons were interred in the mausoleum April 12, 1963.

At the time of discovery the evidence indicated that a small, little-known community existed at the location between 1847–1867, and was later destroyed by Indians. Symbols, words, and letters written or stenciled on the boards used in the manufacture of the coffins indicated that the remains had been in the ground for at least 100 years.

Military Camps Bevis and Payne and Fort Clay

These camps were in existence at various times from 1855 to 1859. Lieutenant Deshler and members of the 6th Infantry, 10th Infantry and 4th Artillery staffed Fort Clay in November 1855. The fort was renamed Camp Davis in March 1856 but was abandoned in November 1856. Captain Joseph Roberts of the 4th Artillery later established "Post at Platte Bridge," which became known as Camp Payne and was later abandoned in May 1859.

Continued on page 4

Casper

	Jan	Feb	March	April	May	June	July	Aug	Sep	Oct	Nov	Dec	Annual
Average Max. Temperature (F)	33.5	37.8	45.3	56.0	66.7	78.6	87.4	85.8	74.3	60.5	44.2	35.2	58.8
Average Min. Temperature (F)	12.7	16.4	21.5	29.4	38.6	47.2	54.2	52.7	42.7	32.5	22.1	15.1	32.1
Average Total Precipitation (in.)	0.52	0.57	0.90	1.43	2.10	1.39	1.14	0.62	0.94	1.01	0.73	0.55	11.91
Average Total SnowFall (in.)	10.2	10.0	12.9	12.4	4.0	0.2	0.0	0.0	1.4	6.2	10.4	10.3	78.1
Average Snow Depth (in.)	1	1	1	0	0	0	0	0	0	0	1	1	0
Wind Speed (mph / kmh)	17 / 27	16 / 25	15 / 23	13 / 22	12 / 20	11 / 18	11 / 17	11 / 17	12 / 19	13 / 21	15 / 24	17 / 27	
Wind Direction	SW	SW	SW	SW	SW	WSW	WSW	SW	SW	SW	SW	SW	

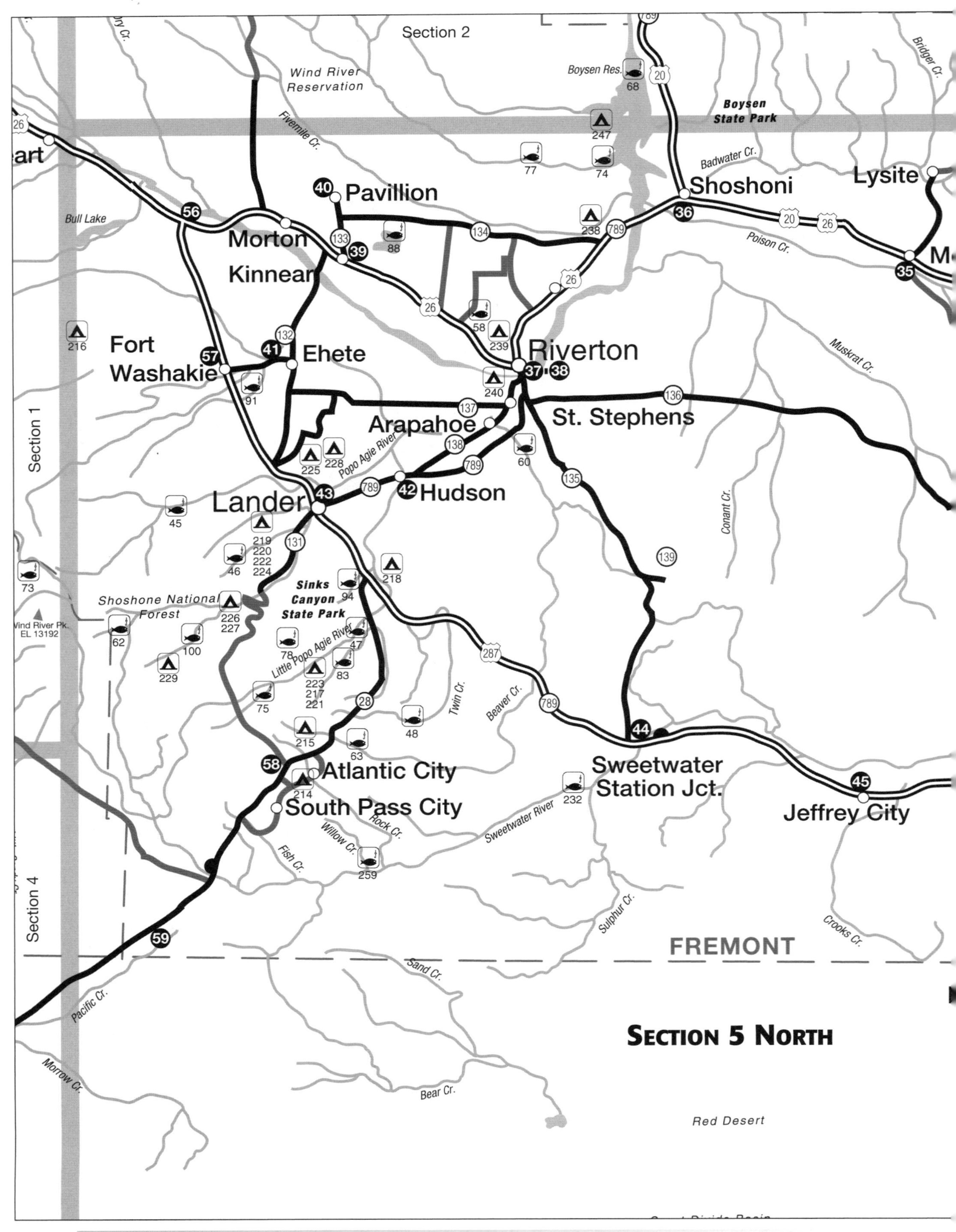
Section 2
Wind River Reservation
Boysen Res.
Boysen State Park
Fivemile Cr.
Badwater Cr.
Pavillion
Shoshoni
Lysite
Bull Lake
Morton
Kinnear
Poison Cr.
Fort Washakie
Ehete
Riverton
Muskrat Cr.
St. Stephens
Arapahoe
Popo Agie River
Section 1
Lander
Hudson
Conant Cr.
Sinks Canyon State Park
Shoshone National Forest
Wind River Pk. EL 13192
Little Popo Agie River
Twin Cr.
Beaver Cr.
Atlantic City
Sweetwater Station Jct.
South Pass City
Jeffrey City
Willow Cr.
Rock Cr.
Fish Cr.
Sweetwater River
Sulphur Cr.
Crooks Cr.
Section 4
FREMONT
Sand Cr.
Pacific Cr.
Section 5 North
Morrow Cr.
Bear Cr.
Red Desert

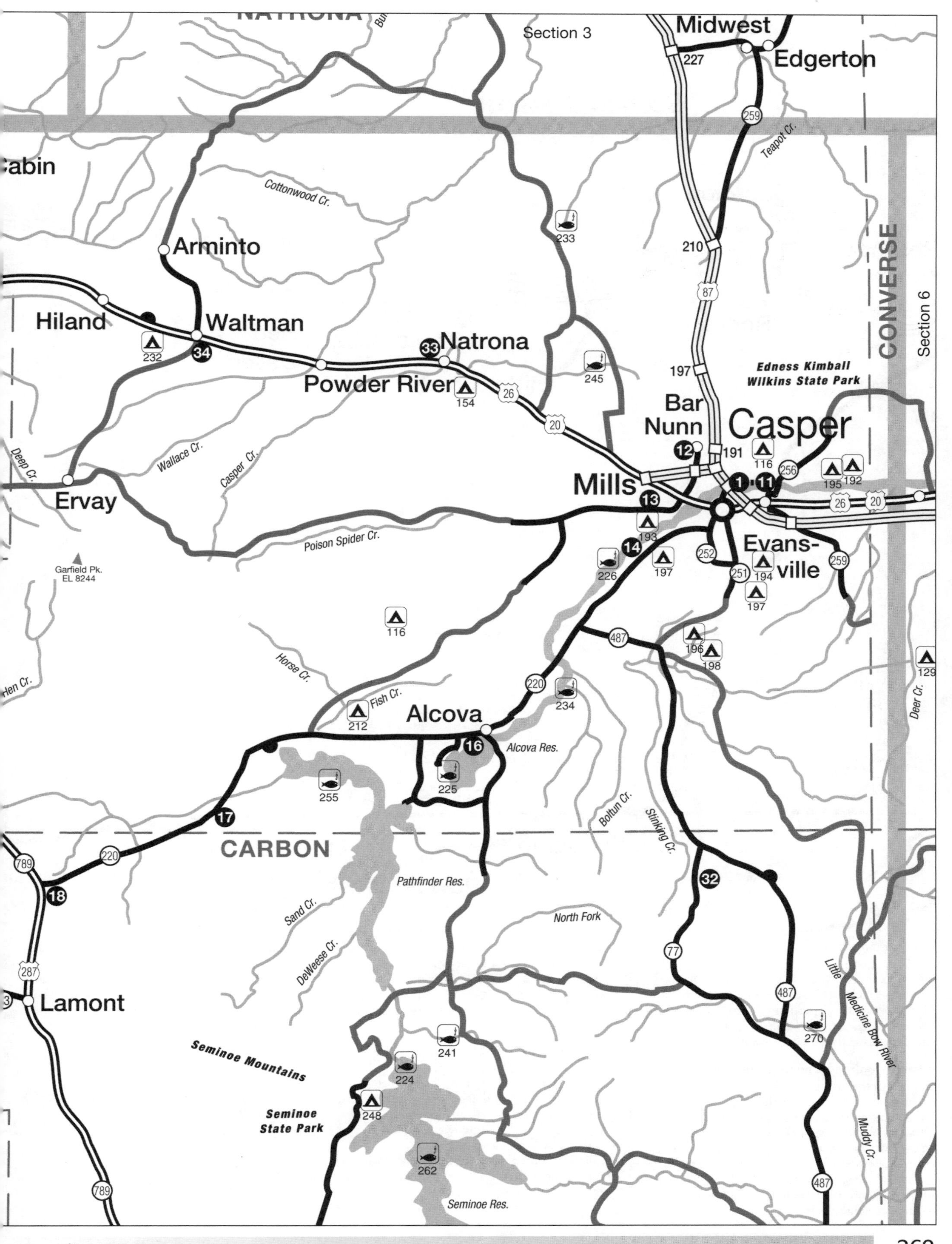

Section 3
Midwest
Edgerton
Cabin
Cottonwood Cr.
Teapot Cr.
Arminto
Hiland
Waltman
Natrona
Powder River
CONVERSE
Section 6
Edness Kimball Wilkins State Park
Bar Nunn
Casper
Mills
Evansville
Ervay
Deep Cr.
Wallace Cr.
Casper Cr.
Poison Spider Cr.
Garfield Pk. EL 8244
Horse Cr.
Fish Cr.
Alcova
Alcova Res.
Boltun Cr.
Stinking Cr.
Deer Cr.
CARBON
Pathfinder Res.
Sand Cr.
DeWeese Cr.
North Fork
Little Medicine Bow River
Lamont
Seminoe Mountains
Seminoe State Park
Seminoe Res.
Muddy Cr.

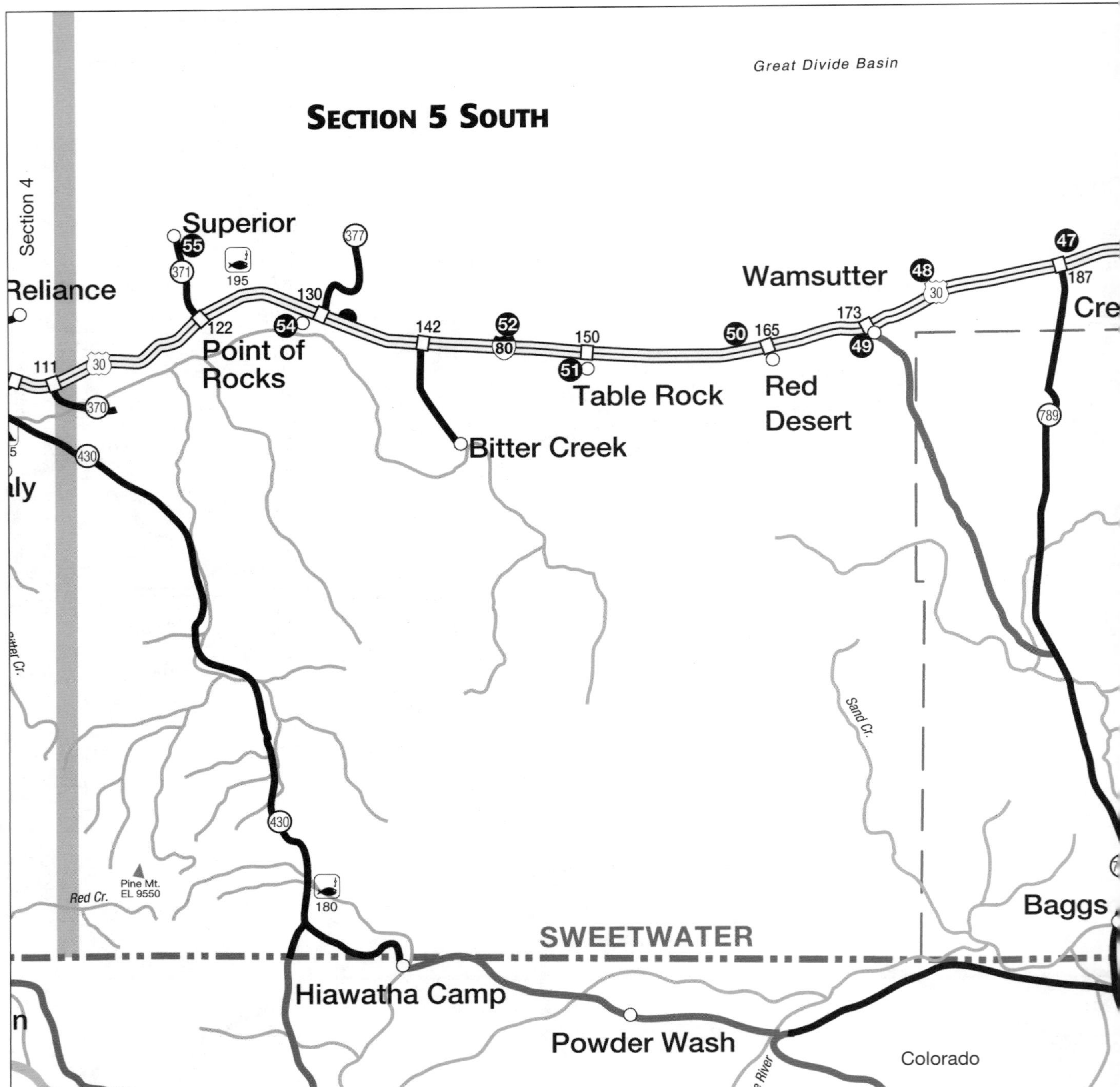

Continued from page 1

There is a small exhibit of artifacts from excavations of Richard's Trading Post and Camps Davis and Payne. A portion of Camp Payne is still preserved nearby, where approximately 40 stone fireplaces used by soldiers have been identified.

Stroud's Railroad Crossing and Cabin

Located in the area of the W. T. Evans original ranch land which includes the town of Evansville. Land areas were divided into sections in the early 1800s by the government. An old area map shows Strouds where Lathrop Feed is now located. Stroud's was the original name of the town started in 1888. Later the town of Evansville was developed and incorporated in 1923 where the town is currently located. The Chicago and Northwestern Railroad came out of Nebraska to Lusk and Douglas in 1886, Glenrock in 1887, and Casper in 1988. The Cheyenne and Burlington Railroad incorporated in 1867. Passenger services were discontinued in 1969.

Mysterious Concrete Cross

The crumbling cross is approximately 14 feet by 16 feet by 16 inches. It is thought that it may be a memorial to Maud Toomey, a woman killed in an airplane accident at this location in 1920. She was the first Wyoming woman to die in an aviation-related accident.

Maud Toomey was a sister of Howard Toomey of Newcastle, who owned the Toomey Flour Mill there. She was a Casper school teacher and a passenger in the plane flown by Burt Cole when the accident occurred. Cole survived the accident, although he was injured.

The airport at Evansville was the first airport to serve Casper, predating the Wardwell Airport and the present Natrona County Airport. Cole's plane was the first one in Casper. No evidence of the runways remain.

Reprinted from brochure compiled by the Evansville Historic Preservation Commission.

T Edness K. Wilkins State Park

Six miles east of Casper off I-25, exit 182

From Rock Quarry to Beautiful State Park

Edness K. Wilkins State Park is a serene day-use park where families, nature lovers and those looking for solitude can enjoy the huge old cottonwoods as they cast reflections on the historic

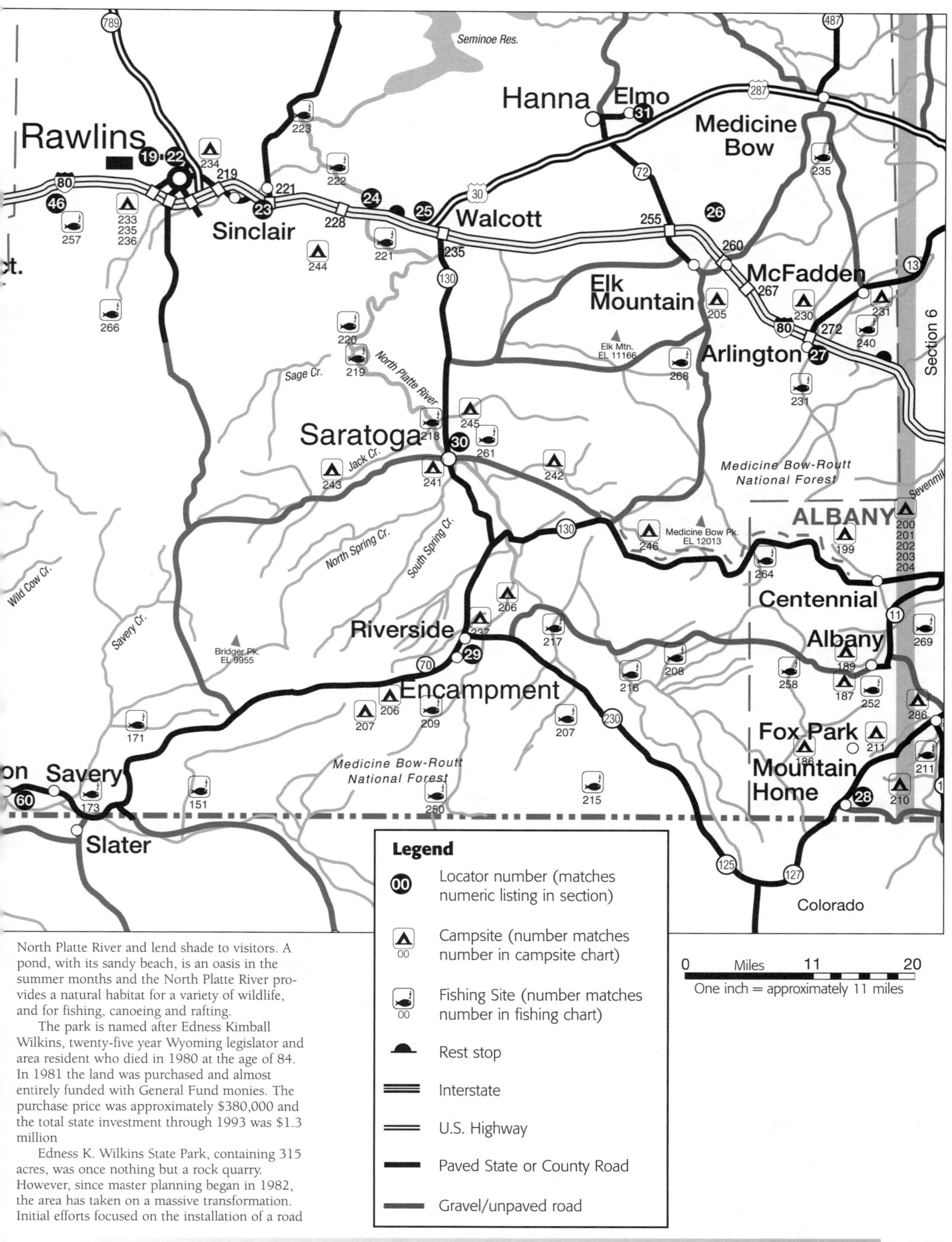

North Platte River and lend shade to visitors. A pond, with its sandy beach, is an oasis in the summer months and the North Platte River provides a natural habitat for a variety of wildlife, and for fishing, canoeing and rafting.

The park is named after Edness Kimball Wilkins, twenty-five year Wyoming legislator and area resident who died in 1980 at the age of 84. In 1981 the land was purchased and almost entirely funded with General Fund monies. The purchase price was approximately $380,000 and the total state investment through 1993 was $1.3 million

Edness K. Wilkins State Park, containing 315 acres, was once nothing but a rock quarry. However, since master planning began in 1982, the area has taken on a massive transformation. Initial efforts focused on the installation of a road

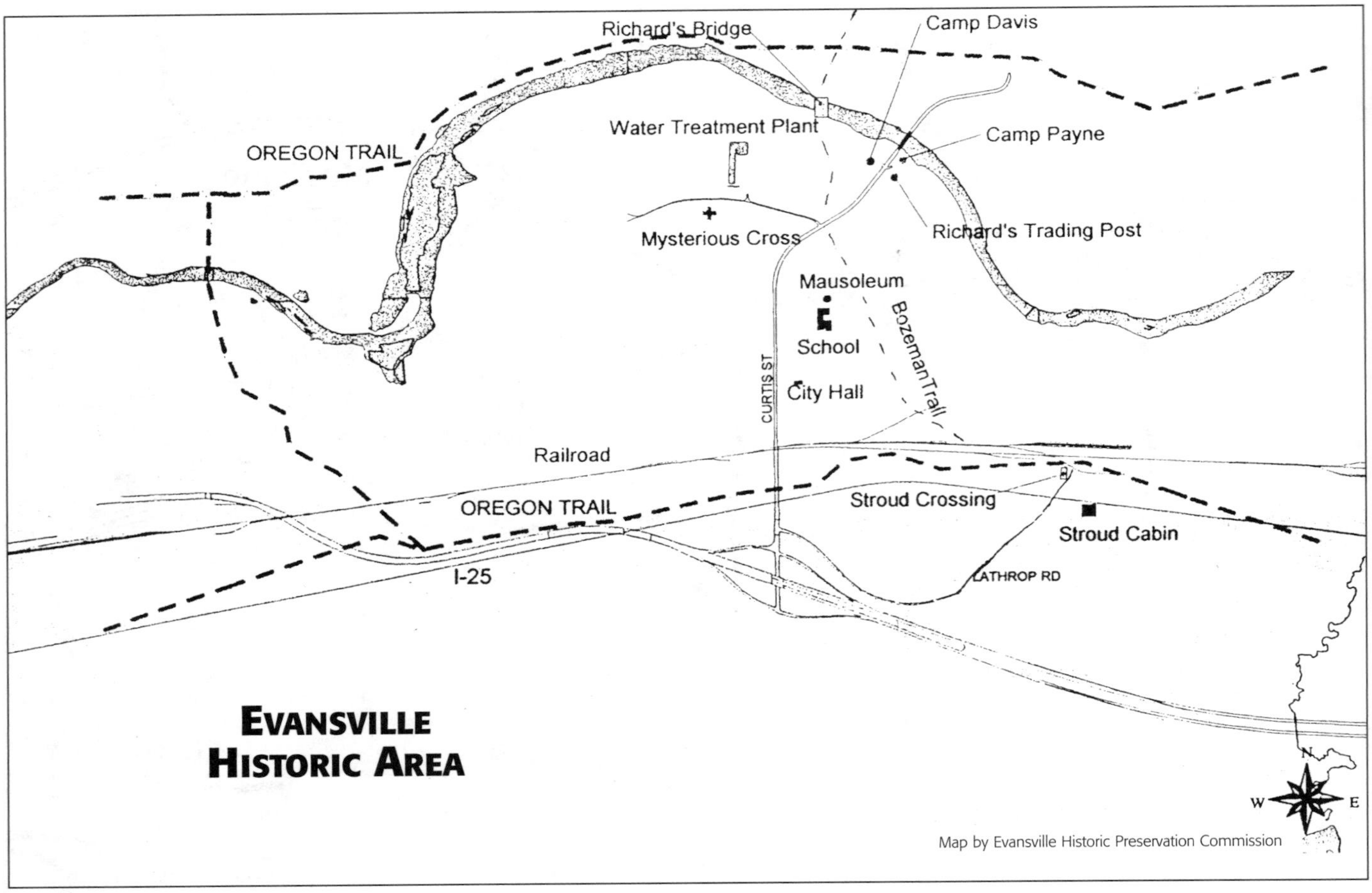

Evansville Historic Area

Richard's Bridge
Camp Davis
Water Treatment Plant
Camp Payne
OREGON TRAIL
Mysterious Cross
Richard's Trading Post
Mausoleum
School
City Hall
CURTIS ST
Bozeman Trail
Railroad
OREGON TRAIL
Stroud Crossing
Stroud Cabin
I-25
LATHROP RD
N
W
E

Map by Evansville Historic Preservation Commission

system and parking areas. Plantings, seeding and pruning improved the vegetation in the area. Barriers, fencing and signage allowed for continued use of designated roads while certain areas returned to their natural state. Like the master potter with a lump of unworked clay, the designers. planners and operators combined their energies to provide citizens with one of the most attractive small parks in the Wyoming state park system.

Today a visitor can utilize picnic tables, grills, group shelters, playgrounds and a launch- ing ramp for canoes or rafts. The handicapped accessible fishing pier, the only one like it in the state, has become one of the finest amenities provided to visitors. An additional nearly three miles of handicapped accessible hard-surfaced paths provide visitors with an opportunity to view some of the finest wildlife in the area. Anglers can try their fishing luck in the North Platte River and swimmers can take a refreshing dip at the park swimming area.

This park is a gem for birdwatchers where they can add to their life lists. The park contains several different habitats: it offers a river, a cottonwood grove and open areas. Therefore, many bird varieties are drawn to the park year round.

In a cooperative effort with the Wyoming Game & Fish Department, a variety of nesting ponds and wildlife viewing blinds have been developed in conjunction with the <I>Wyoming Wildlife Worth the Watching<I> program. A riparian habitat area for water-type birds has been included.

The local chapter of the National Audubon Society has identified over 50 different kinds of nesting birds and a list of over 200 different species of smaller birds. It is possible to see yellow billed cuckoos, cormorants, bald eagles, golden eagles, sharp shinned hawks and up to 16 species of ducks.

As you walk along the paths through the park, notice the many bird houses placed on trees at strategic heights to attract specific birds. Patient bird watchers may be rewarded with sightings of birds from both the eastern and western areas of the United States.

Courtesy of Wyoming State Parks and Historic Sites

H Reshaw's (Richard's) Bridge: National Historic Trail

Curtis Street at the North Platte River in Evansville.

This was the site used from 1852-1865 for a wooden toll bridge crossing the Platte River which served thousands of emigrants. The Reshaw Bridge put the Mormon Ferry at Platte Bridge Station out of business.

H Quintina Snodderly

On private land in Natrona County

A pioneer mother, Quintina Snodderly died near here on June 25, 1852. A native of Tennessee, Quintina, with her husband, Jacob, and their eight children (five girls and three boys) had lived in Clarinda County, Iowa, for several years before embarking on their trip across the plains. They were members of a wagon train captained by Rev. Joab Powell, which had left St. Joseph, Missouri, in the spring of 1852.

Quintina's grave was discovered and excavated in 1974. An examination of the skeleton revealed the cause of death. Most of the ribs had been crushed, probably by the heavy wheels of a covered wagon. The skeleton was in otherwise perfect condition, with fragments of a green ribbon bow still around the neck. The Powell wagon train probably crossed the North Platte River at this point and the accident may have occurred as the wagons climbed the river bluffs to enter the north bank trail.

Jacob and the children reached Linn County, Oregon, and several descendants still reside in that area.

The grave was restored and fence constructed here in 1987, by the Oregon-California Trails Association. It is a few feet from the original site.

L Shilo Inn

739 Luker Lane in Evansville. 237-1335 or 800-222-2244. www.shiloinnscom

The Shilo Inn 101 guestroom hotel with meeting/banquet space is located off I-25 at Curtis Road, near shopping, entertainment, and many indoor and outdoor parks, museums, and historical sites. Guestrooms include in-room ironing, hair dryer, data ports, first-run movies, entertainment, and cable. The hotel offers guest laundry, indoor pool, spa, sauna and steam room, free airport shuttle, and complimentary continental breakfast. Ample parking accommodates horse

Casper, Wyoming

trailers and trucks. AAA, senior, corporate, and government rates are available, and children 12 and under stay free with adult. Shilo Inns is reputed for cleanliness, friendliness, and a motto of "Affordable Excellence."

2 *Gas, Food, Lodging*

Casper

Pop. 50,000, Elev. 5,123

Known as the "Oil Capitol of the Rockies," Casper now has a broader economic base. The city still depends, however, largely on its refinery, tank farm, and host of oil fields for its income.

There has been a long-standing debate between Cheyenne and Casper regarding which city is Wyoming's biggest and most important. Casper prides itself on having the only statewide newspaper, the Casper Star-Tribune, Wyoming's biggest shopping center, the Eastridge Mall, and top-notch medical services at Wyoming Medical Center. There are a host of recreational activities to keep Casperites entertained, and educational and cultural opportunities to keep them enlightened. Casper is also rich in Western history.

Robert Stuart and a group of fur traders (sponsored by John Jacob Astor) were the first Europeans to travel near Casper. Stranded here during the cold, hungry winter of 1812, they built the first rock cabin in Wyoming and kept it warm with buffalo hides. There was enough game around to sustain them through the winter months, but a visit from a band of Arapaho convinced the party to head east towards Nebraska until spring.

The Astorians had blazed the trail, and the route through Casper now became frequently used. Crossing the North Platte River still proved challenging until 1847, when the Mormons arrived and built a ferry, the first business run in the area. The Mormon Ferry did not remain the only ferry for long, and in 1849 travelers crowded the shores of the Platte, eager to head west and find gold. Other businesses sprung up as well, including a Pony Express station and a telegraph office.

In 1852, French-Canadian trader John Baptiste Richard (pronounced "Reshaw" by locals) came up with the idea of building a toll bridge across the Platte, one of several bridge projects he spearheaded. First crossed in 1853, the bridge could save up to a week's travel time, and cost less than the ferries. It was not long before the ferries went out of business. During 1854, Richard made $17,000 from passing travelers, a considerable sum in those days.

Then, in 1859, Louis Guinard built a newer, longer bridge, first crossed in 1860. Travelers preferred to cross Guinard's bridge, because it seemed safer. After all, Richard's bridge had seen a lot of traffic in the preceding seven years. Guinard made so much money that myths arose regarding him sprinkling gold at travelers feet to repay them for the wealth they'd provided him.

The site became known as the Platte Bridge Station when the army arrived. Two dramatic battles took place here with members of the Lakota, Cheyenne, and Arapaho tribes in 1865. The first resulted in the heroic death of Lt. Caspar Collins,

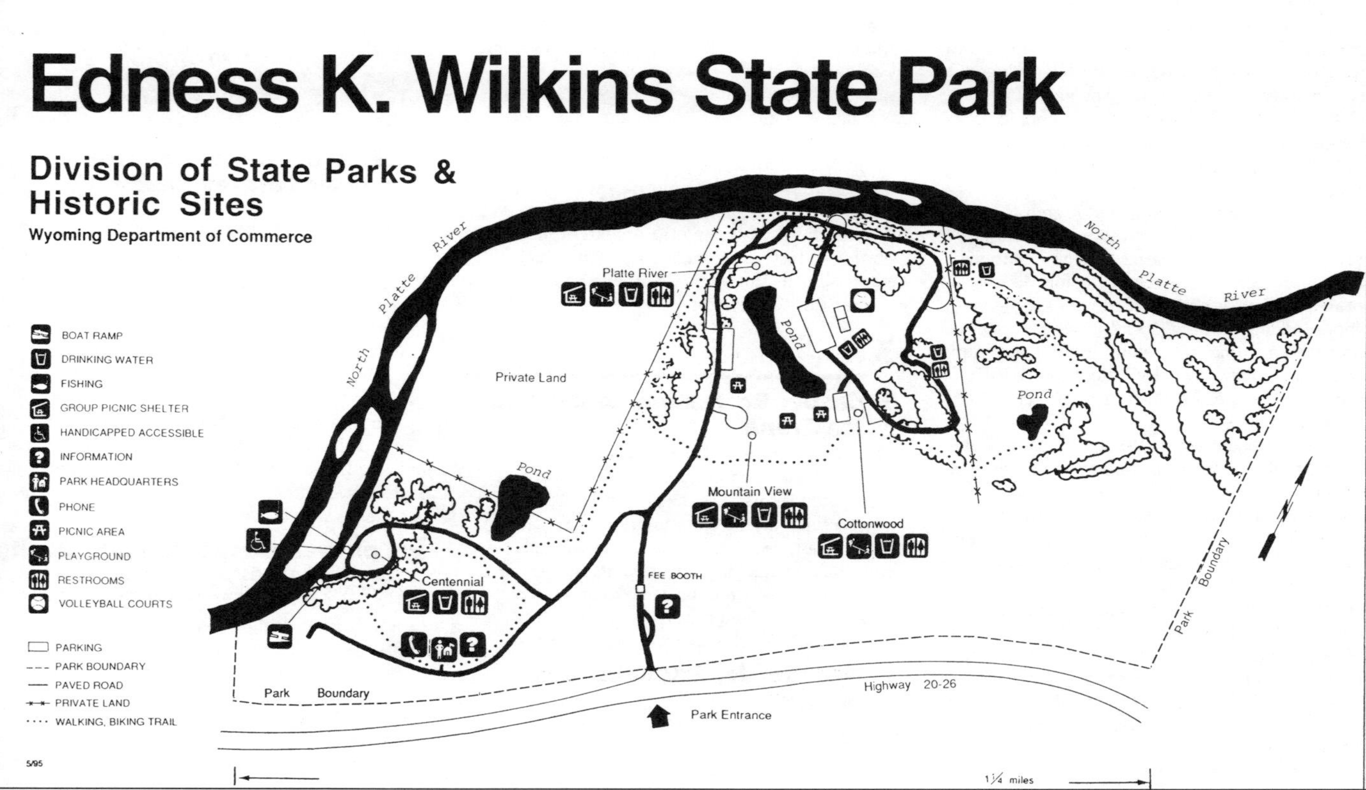

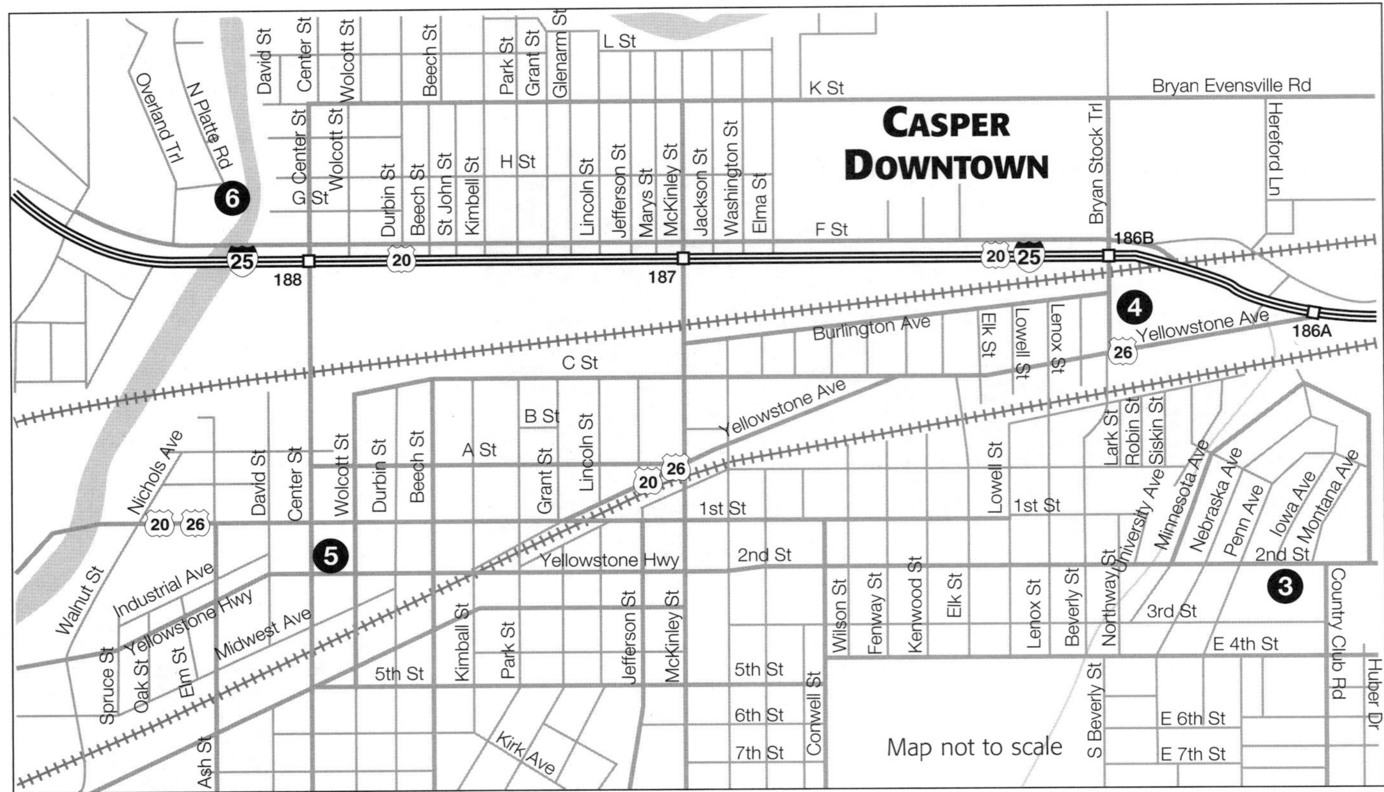

for whom the town was eventually named. Collins was said to have been trying to rescue a fellow soldier when his horse went the wrong way and carried him into the Indian throng. He went down with pistols blazing and was found later shot full of arrows, some accounts say half-buried. The second battle involved Sgt. Amos Custard, who also died along with his men in a fierce fight to protect the supply wagons they were bringing in. The name "Caspar" was misspelled when the information was telegraphed to the east, and so the newly established military base was dubbed Ft. Casper. The name Ft. Collins had already been used in Colorado, in honor of his father, William Collins. The elder Collins was commander at Ft. Laramie at the time.

Ft. Casper was closed in 1867, and its components were salvaged and moved to build Ft. Fetterman, which was easier to keep re-supplied from Ft. Laramie. So much of the fort disappeared so quickly that local rumors sprung up about Indians burning it. Old Ft. Caspar (spelled properly this time) was rebuilt in 1936 according to Caspar Collins' own 1863 floor plans. In 1971, it became listed on the National Register of Historical Places.

The railroad came in 1888, and the official town site developed three miles east of where the fort had been. In 1889, the city of Casper became incorporated. Many renegades were attracted to this wild place, and the air was often filled with gunfire. The first public building was a jail, and residents slept light. Vigilantism was rampant. Nearby, in what was to become the huge Salt Creek Field, oil was struck in 1889, and a flurry of claim jumpers rushed in, leaving behind the lives they'd known in the east for the promise of "black gold." The first refinery was built in 1895, and Casper would never again be free of the influence of oil.

With the oil came coarse workers, dishonest businessmen, prostitutes, gambling, and other threats to polite society. Honest people came too, including farmers, lumberjacks, and ranchers, and schools and churches emerged between the saloons. Women were only permitted to walk on the left side of Main Street, across from the saloons. Laws were passed to prevent the discharge of firearms within the city limits. The residents had big plans for Casper to become the capitol city of both Wyoming and the West as a whole. Some of the tallest buildings in Wyoming were built here in the early part of the 20th century. The town boomed until 1929, when the population diminished by half after the stock market crashed. World War II brought another boom, the 1960s a bust, the 1970s a boom, a bust again in the 1980s, and the cycle continues today.

Still, Casper is seeing the growth of more stabilizing industries, including tourism, which emphasizes its importance as the historic "Crossroads to the West."

3 *Gas, Food, Lodging*

T Casper Recreation Center and Ice Arena

The facility serves as a site for a wide variety of programs and drop in activities for Casper residents and visitors. It is the focal point of recreation services in the community. The Recreation Center features a gymnasium for basketball and volleyball, racquetball courts, weight room, fitness room, locker rooms, game room, indoor park and several multi-purpose rooms and meeting areas. The facility is open 7 days a week.

L Hearthside, Extended Stay Studios

111 S. Wilson in Casper. 232-5100 or 866-500-1110. www.hearthsidecasper.net

M Mary B. Moore, Coldwell Banker Lindsey Realty

2233 E. 2nd in Casper. 232-0132 or 866-232-0134. www.wyocoldwellbanker.com

Visit or call Mary B. Moore at Coldwell Banker Lindsey Realty and let this Atlanta, Georgia born gal show you a bit of the wonderful West. She knows that relocating to Casper in 1975 was one of the best moves she's ever made. Call her and see "why every move matters." Whether you are buying or selling real estate or need help with property management, Mary will help you. She is a firm believer that ethics and fairness are a must in every transaction. You can be assured that Mary is well qualified to show you why Wyoming is a great place to live.

M Coldwell Banker Lindsey Realty

2233 E. 2nd in Casper. 232-0132 or toll free at 866-232-0134. www.wyocoldwellbanker.com

Centrally located in Casper, Coldwell Banker Lindsey Realty offers full service brokerage in the form of residential, commercial, recreational farm and ranch and property management. Owners, Ceil and Dick Lindsey are living their dream in God's country, also known as Wyoming. They have lived, worked, and played in Wyoming since

Coldwell Banker Lindsey Realy

1978 and offer their vast experience. Ten full time agents at Coldwell Banker Lindsey Realty offer over 93 years of real estate experience. They will hold out a helping hand for all your real estate needs. Stop by for a cup of coffee or give them a call and get on their mailing list.

4 *Gas, Food, Lodging*

F Johnny J's Diner

1705 E. 2nd in Casper. 234-4204

Johnny J's serves great home style cooking 7 days a week from 6:30 a.m. to 9 p.m. Enjoy hearty breakfasts, lunches, and dinners or stop in for your favorite treat from a genuine soda fountain—hand dipped ice cream, shakes, malts, and sundaes. Great dinner favorites include items such as meatloaf, pot roast, and chicken fried steak. Try a burger—always served with a half-pound of fresh ground beef, and available with an array of toppings. Johnny J's fantastic desserts include fresh fruit and cream pies made fresh daily and award winning bread pudding. Hearty soups are made from scratch daily.

S Vivi's Artist's Choice Gallery

647 W. Yellowstone Highway in Casper. 234-7000 or 800-845-4553. www.vivicrandall.com

Vivi's Artist's Choice Gallery is the primary gallery for acclaimed wildlife artist, Vivi K. Crandall. Vivi's work is known for amazing detail, motion, and the lifelike appearance and soul of her wildlife subjects. Originals are highly sought after and rarely available. The large gallery features other Wyoming artists, and "top 20" print artists.

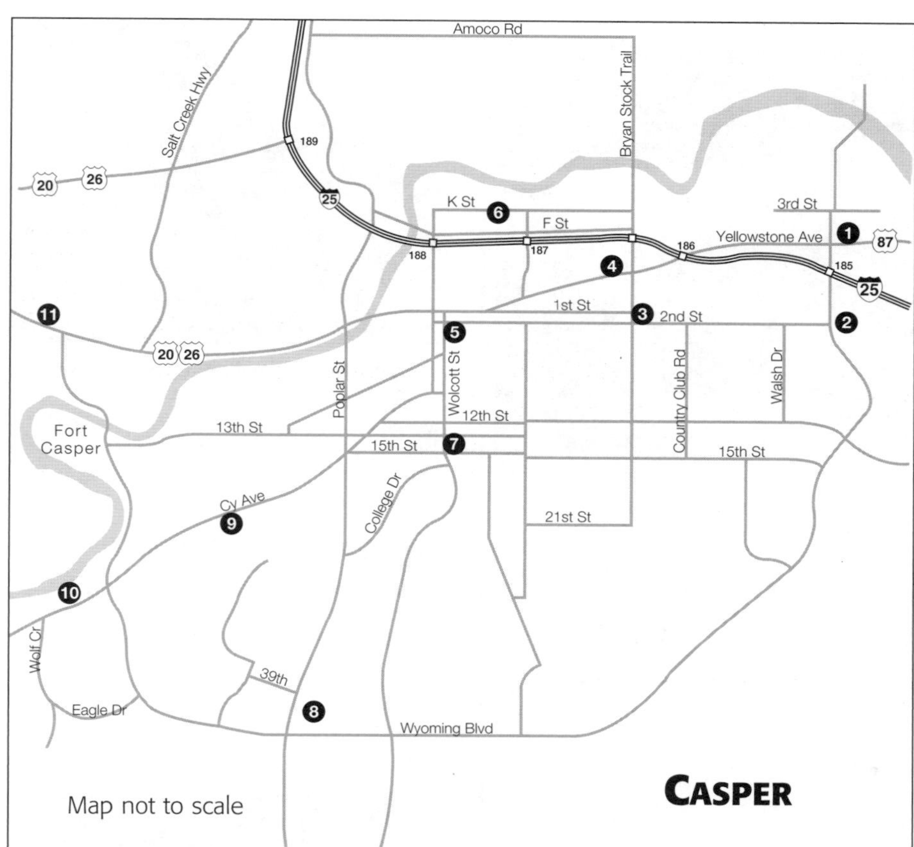

Vivi's Artist's Choice Gallery

Expert quality and custom framing is available at the gallery. The gallery is known for blue ribbon art in a blue jean ambiance. Enjoy fine art, a relaxed setting, and a cup or coffee or tea at Vivi's Artist's Choice Gallery.

5 *Gas, Food, Lodging*

T Nicolaysen Art Museum and Discovery Center

400 E. Collins Dr. in Casper. 235-5247

A refurbished power plant houses this collection of artwork, including both traditional and contemporary artists. New exhibits can be seen every couple of months in the six spacious galleries. Upstairs, kids can enjoy learning about both art and science, and how sometimes the two go hand in hand. Call ahead to find out about current guest speakers, visiting music ensembles, and other special events. Thursday nights, admission is free to all.

M Casper Area Convention & Visitors Bureau, Natrona County Travel & Tourism Council

330 S. Center, Suite 420 in Casper. 234-5362 or 800-852-1889. www.casperwyoming.info

S Blue Heron Books & Espresso

201 E. 2nd Street in Casper. 265-3774 or 800-585-3774 in Wyoming

F The Wonder Bar

256 S. Center in Casper. 234-4110.

If you'd like to experience some real Wyoming history visit the world famous Wonder Bar in the heart of downtown Casper. Outliving it's competition, prohibition, and several owners and name changes—it is back to it's origin and tradition where "A stranger is a friend we've never met." Today this historic landmark serves a great lunch and dinner menu with huge burgers and lots of different brews. They have a super salad bar that is included with a lot of the entree favorites. A long time resident of the area says, "It's great fun, great food, and even greater prices." Experience what Ernest Hemingway once did—a "World Famous" time at the Wonder Bar!

Wyoming Tidbits

In 1922, the Denver-based Producers and Refiners Corporation built an oil refinery in Carbon County. Located on the Union Pacific mainline at a cost of ten million dollars, the town of Parco included a central plaza with a fountain, buried electrical lines, and professional landscaping. The town was touted as "The Wonder Town of Wyoming."

F Jacquie's Garden Greek Cafe
251 S. Center in Casper. 265-9018

Jacquie's Garden Greek Cafe features delicious gourmet foods, specializing in good old fashioned home cooking fresh and wholesome foods that you can eat in or take out. This great delicatessen is known for fantastic breakfasts that feature Jacquie's homemade pita breakfast specials and sweet rolls and pastries. All menu items are prepared with fresh meats, fresh baked bread, imported and domestic cheeses, and Wyoming fresh grown herbs. Enjoy hearty soups, sandwiches piled high, and fresh salads for lunch. Jacquie's is open Monday through Saturday from 7 a.m. to 2 p.m. and Sunday, 8 am. To 2 p.m. Stop by for Sushi on Friday nights from 6 p.m. to 9 p.m.

F Campfire Cafe
137 E. 2nd in Casper. 472-1919

No one leaves the Campfire Cafe hungry. They serve up some of Casper's tastiest home cooking and that's a just fact. Enjoy wonderful fresh made dishes that are cleverly named after Wyoming's favorite camping areas and landmarks. You'll find a selection of delicious soups made from scratch, paninnis melts, vegetarian selections and a variety of fabulous salads. Mixed green salads are made with assorted fresh vegetables. The chicken salad is one of the most popular menu items. Tempting homemade desserts and cakes are made form scratch. Check for daily specials not on the menu.

F Botticelli Ristorante Italiano
129 W. 2nd in Casper. 266-2700

Dining at Botticelli's Ristorante Italiano will make you feel like you are stepping back into old Italy. Botticelli's has been open since 1999 and offers very affordable prices for every appetite. The menu is abundant with mouth watering selections from Northern Italian cuisine, served in an elegant, romantic and comfortable ambiance. They are open for lunch and dinner. Choose from an extensive selection of wines or your favorite cocktails and beers to accompany your meal. Unique artwork and original murals that surround diners are add to your pleasure. Once you've tried Botticelli's you'll be back for more. You can also enjoy Botticelli's in Rapid City, South Dakota.

Botticelli Ristorante Italiano

F PB's Fish Factory at Parkway Plaza
123 West E. Street in Casper. 235-1777.

F Parkway Cafe
123 West E. Street in Casper. 235-1777.

F Red's Bar-B-Que
147 E. 2nd in Casper. 261-9908

L Parkway Plaza Hotel & Convention Center
123 West E. Street in Casper. 235-1777 or 800-270-STAY(7829). www.parkwayplaza.net

S Alpenglow Natural Foods
109 E. 2nd Street in Casper. 234-4196. www.alpenglowfoods.com

Alpenglow Natural Foods has been a full-service health food store since 1963. Delight in their selection of over 450 bulk herbs and culinary spices. There are over 145 bulk items including grains, nuts, seeds, and more. They also carry a wide selection of fresh and frozen selections. Shop for wonderful wheat and gluten-free items as well. A personal care section offers skin care and cosmetics, aromatherapy items, essential oils, and candles. There's more—organic cotton clothing and bags of all sorts. They even have all natural cleaning supplies. Stop in for a great experience or visit them on the web.

S The Basement Branch Antique
201 E. 2nd, Suite 18, Atrium Plaza in Casper. 472-5092

S Lou Taubert Ranch Outfitters
125 E. 2nd in Casper. 234-2500 or 800-447-WEST(9378)

S Carriage House Antiques
520 South Ash in Casper. 266-2987. www.CarriageHouseOnline.com

Conveniently located near downtown Casper, Carriage House Antiques offers something for every collector. From fine art to primitives, art glass to kitchen collectibles, Louis XV furniture to Wild West memorabilia, Carriage House also has

Section 5

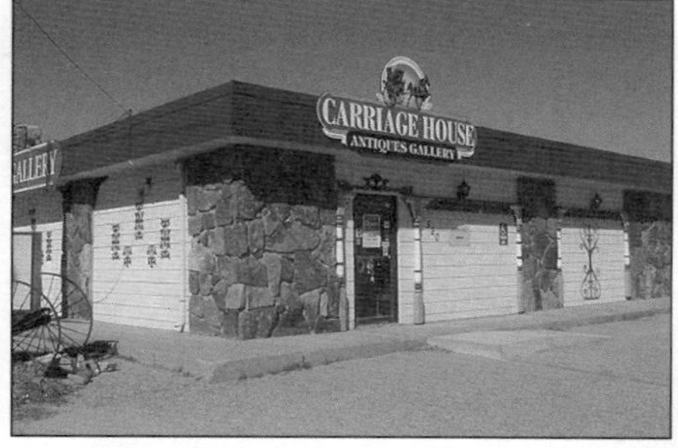

Carriage House Restaurant

a "man-tiques" section, featuring rustic tools, tack, knives, swords and many more items of interest to boys of all ages. Owned and operated by a lifelong antiques aficionado, Carriage House is one of Wyoming's finest antiques & collectibles stores. The shop is bright and clean with its wall-to-wall wares artfully displayed. Carriage House is a favorite haunt of many Casper residents and attracts repeat visitors from throughout the region.

S Toy Town
147 S. Center in Casper. 235-0550 or toll free at 888-695-5881

M America West Realty
304 N. Center in Casper. 472-9378. www.americanwestrealty.com

M Arrow Realty Co.
143 N. Kimball in Casper. 266-2320 or 800-448-2320 or email: gunars@prodigy.net. www.arrowrealty.net

6 *Gas, Food, Lodging*

T National Historic Trails Interpretive Center
1501 North Poplar in Casper, just north of I-25 Exit 189. 261-7700. www.wy.blm.gov/nhtic

The names are legend in western history. The Oregon Trail. The Pony Express Trail. The California Trail. The Mormon Pioneer Trail. They speak of the nation's expansion beyond the wide Missouri all the way to the Pacific. They conjure images of slow-moving covered wagon trains stretching to the distant horizon. They recall stories of hardy pioneers facing untold hardships in their quest for a better life on the other side of the shining mountains. All of these trails are now designated as National Historic Trails. All of them came through a place that would become Casper, Wyoming.

The National Historic Trails Interpretive Center in Casper tells the story of the pioneers and of the trails they traveled. The 27,000 square foot, multi-million dollar facility is dedicated to commemorate the emigrants who traveled westward in search of new lives, new land, new wealth or religious freedom in a raw, wild land few of them knew anything about. The story is told in the pioneers' own words taken from thousands of authentic emigrant diaries and journals.

Visitors to the Center's seven galleries will spend quality time with all of the people who played a role in America's west, ranging from the native peoples who established the travel routes the emigrants would later follow to the construction crews building the first transcontinental railroad, whose "Golden Spike" foretold the end of the American frontier. In between, visitors will meet fur trappers, mountainmen, missionaries, explorers and early hope-filled farm families in covered wagons headed for a rumored "land of milk and honey" in Oregon's Willamette Valley. Next they will encounter wild and reckless "Forty-Niners" in a rush to California's gold fields and thoughtful Mormon families pushing handcarts toward a new freedom in the valley of the Great Salt Lake. Young, wiry Pony Express riders, stagecoach drivers and telegraph construction crews round out the story.

Throughout the galleries, viewers are treated to historically authentic life-sized displays depicting life on the trails. Interactive exhibits allow visitors to experience first-hand what it was like to pull a handcart, cross the flood-swollen North Platte River in a covered wagon, feel the bone-chilling cold of a November night at Martin's Cove, sit in an Overland Stagecoach or mount a Pony Express horse.

A stop at the National Historic Trails Interpretive Center is the best first step in any traveler's personal mission of discovery and adventure in Wyoming. The Center is open 8 a.m. to 7 p.m. daily from April through October. Winter hours are 9 a.m. to 4:30 p.m.

Reprinted from museum brochure.

T **Casper Planetarium**

904 N. Poplar St. in Casper. 577-0310

Built in 1966 by the Casper school system, public programs are presented throughout the year. Open daily during the summer, shows start at 8 p.m. A nominal fee is charged.

T **Casper Events Center**

One Events Drive in Casper. 577-3030

This state-of-the-art complex is on a hill overlooking Casper and the scenic Platte River Valley. Hosting rodeos, circuses and major touring acts is just a part of the many events staged at this facility.

H **City of Casper**

At entrance to Parkway Plaza Motel

The city of Casper, established near the site of old Fort Caspar, formerly Platte Bridge Station, was named in honor of Lieut. Caspar Collins, who lost his life in an Indian battle there on July 26, 1865. The Fort was one of the small army posts which guarded the Oregon and Emigrant Trail and the transcontinental telegraph line during the mid-1800s. The first railroad came to Casper in 1888, and the town remained "Rail's End" until 1905 when the line was extended to Lander. Casper's early economy was based on cattle and sheep raising. Oil had been discovered in the vicinity and in 1895 the first oil refinery was built. The industry has developed since then until Casper is now the principal oil city in Wyoming.

Erected 1965 by Wyoming State Archives and Historical Department and the Wyoming State Historical Society.

F **La Cocina: Best Mexican Food Under The Sun**

1040 N. Center in Casper. 266-1414.
www.lococinawyo.com

Feel right at home at La Cocina: Best Mexican Under The Sun, where friends and families come to eat and enjoy a delightful dining experience. This family owned and operated restaurant is famous for personable and outstanding service in addition to excellent fresh food made daily. All dips, guacamole, rice, chili rellenos, and other delicious menu items are made on the premises. Accompany your meal with a frosty mug of cold beer or margaritas. On Thanksgiving Day they are open and dining is free to all and on this day proceeds from those who wish to pay are donated to charity. Mi casa est su casa!

FL **Radisson Hotel**

800 N. Poplar in Casper. 266-6000 or 800-333-3333. www.radisson.com/casper

The Radisson Hotel staff gives special attention to every aspect of your stay. Located in the center of Casper, you'll feel right at home the minute you step inside through your stay in one of the 229 newly renovated guest rooms and suites. All rooms feature in-room coffee, iron and board, hairdryer, voicemail, data ports, and 25" TV. They

Radisson Hotel

also offer an indoor pool, whirlpool, and exercise room for your added pleasure. Also on site is Legends Restaurant, Spirits Bar, and a gift shop. Complimentary airport and city shuttle service are available. There is plenty of free parking for all sizes of vehicles.

L National 9 Inn

100 W. F Street in Casper. 235-3711 or toll free at 866-999-1309. www.national9casper.com

L Holiday Inn

300 W. F St. in Casper. 235-2531 or 877-576-8636, www.holiday-inn.com

The staff at the Holiday Inn Casper recognizes that hospitality is their only business. Their professionally trained team is committed to customer service while providing many amenities for their guests. There are 200 spacious guest rooms offered at this riverfront location. Relax in the comfort of an indoor swimming pool, Jacuzzi, sauna, fitness center, and complimentary privileges to the Wyoming Athletic Club. Enjoy free in-room coffee. Other special services that will make your stay enjoyable include courtesy airport shuttle service, valet laundry service, and express check in/out. Drake's Restaurant and Lounge is on site for your added convenience. Kids eat, stay, and play free at the Holiday Inn Casper. Special group rates are available.

L Quality Inn & Suites

821 N. Poplar in Casper. 266-2400 or 800-4-CHOICE(246423)

M Century 21 Action Realty

800 Werner Court, Suite 230 in Casper. 237-4819 or 800-298-8826. www.actionc21.com

7 *Gas, Food*

T Tate Geological Museum

At Casper College.

The Tate Collection features dinosaur and other ancient fossil remains, petrified wood, meteorites, Paleo-Indian artifacts, and other intriguing and semi-precious stones, including an extensive assortment of jade samples.

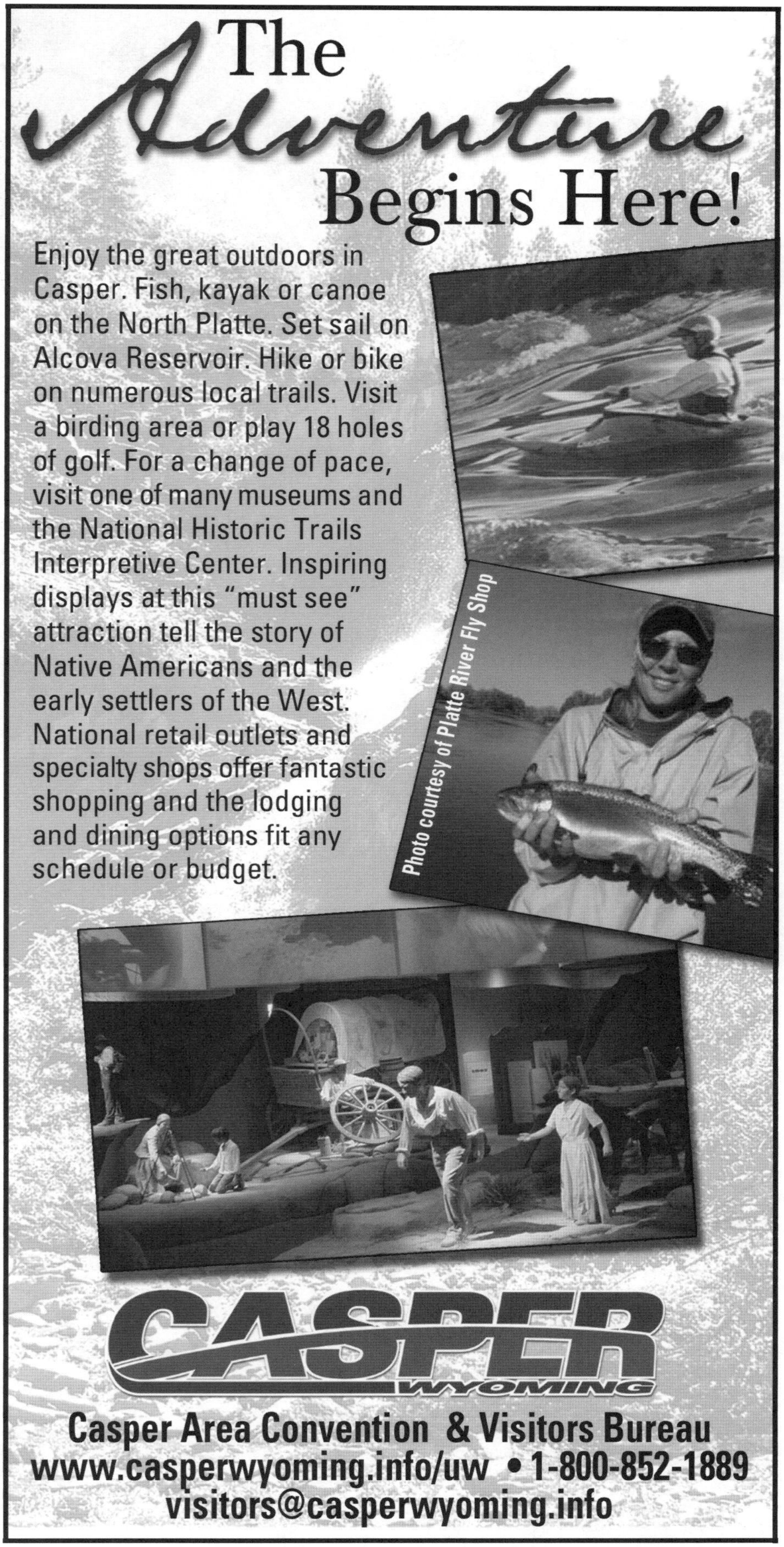

Section 5

H The Armory
Campus of Casper College in Casper

Casper's unique National Guard Armory was built here in 1930 to house the Headquarters Troop of the 115th Cavalry Regiment. The indoor field provided room for training both horses and men, and even hosted the occasional polo match until the regiment was called to active duty on February 24, 1941.

The first level housed the drill area, horse stalls, blacksmith shop, wagon shop, and equipment room. The second level contained the hay loft, a viewing area, and a ballroom with hardwood floors.

In 1987, the structure was razed to improve traffic flow around Casper College. This monument reflects the fond memories of Armory activities shared by many Casper citizens.

F Peaches' Family Restaurants
711 E. 2nd Street in Casper. 234-0951

Peaches' located in Casper and just down the road in Mills has been locally operated and owned since 1965. They are famous for fantastic French fries, but they offer a whole lot more. Specialty sandwiches and juicy hamburgers also bring on the compliments. No meal would be complete without one of their real fruit smoothies or old fashioned milk shakes. Other favorite menu items include chicken strips, fish sandwiches, and their fresh salads. You'll always enjoy the friendly atmosphere at Peaches'. There are only two Peaches Restaurants in the world. Be sure you don't miss them while you are in Wyoming.

M Casper College
125 College Drive in Casper. 268-2110 or 800-442-2963. www.caspercollege.edu

Casper College overlooks the city from the foothills of Casper Mountain. The college became Wyoming's first junior college in 1945 and was initially located on the third floor of Natrona County High School. The first fall enrollment was 73. As enrollment continued to climb, the college hired more faculty and expanded its curricular offerings and its facilities to meet the demands of steady growth. The campus now covers 125 acres with 27 buildings. In the fall semester 2000, the enrollment was 3,972; including 1,852 full-time and 2,120 part-time students. The student population came from all Wyoming counties, 36 other states, and 12 foreign countries.

M The Edgeworth Real Estate Firm, LLC
104 S. Wolcott, Suite 550 in Casper. 234-2000. www.jimedgeworth.com

M Equity Brokers Inc, GMAC Real Estate
145 S. Durbin, Suite 107, in Casper. 237-5757.

M Kathy Martin, Equity Brokers, GMAC
145 S. Durbin, Suite 107 in Casper. Direct line, 259-4446 or 237-5757. Email:realkitkat@hotmail.com

Kathy Martin of Equity Brokers, GMAC, believes that her job is to provide her clients with the best information possible, so they can make an intelligent decision. Kathy can help you with residential, farm, ranch, mountain property, or income producing properties. She will do whatever it takes, and will give you her time to help you find just what you are looking for. Kathy is a friendly outgoing person with a love of the outdoors, animals, and children. She is active in the Wyoming Association of Realtors and can help with properties in any county in Wyoming. As a Wyoming native Kathy is great source of information on the Wyoming outdoor lifestyle and activities she lives and enjoys.

8 *Gas, Food*

T Crimson Dawn Museum and Park
1620 Crimson Dawy Road south of Casper near the Hogadon Ski Area. 235-1303

This magical place atop Casper Mountain reflects the life and wondrous imagination of Neal Forsling: painter, storyteller, and one-time homesteader in these parts. Born in Missouri, she came here initially to marry a lawyer in the 1930s, but after a bitter divorce ended up making a life for herself and her children in this area. Later, she married rancher Jim Forsling, who joined in her frontier-style life on the mountain. When he died in a blizzard at the age of 38, she found herself alone again, but her love for the wilderness sustained her. This love was expressed in her artwork and stories, which she shared with area children and adults alike, especially on Midsummer's Eve. These involved a variety of mystical creatures who lived in the woods nearby, including leprechauns, witches, and forest spirits.

Neal gave her land and her cabin to the county shortly before she passed away in the 1970s. It is now a public park, where visitors may see shrines made by Forsling for her creatures. Her paintings can be seen in the cabin, and every Midsummer's Eve, a celebration of the mystical takes place here.

T Garden Creek Falls

State Highway 252 south of Casper

This 50 foot fall south of Casper is one of the only waterfalls in central Wyoming. A steep and very beautiful day hike. Off of State Highway 252, you can see the canyon cut by Garden Creek at the base of Casper Mountain, and several trails provide opportunities to explore.

H Reshaw's Bridge, 1852-65

Reshaw Park in Evansville

Thousands of emigrants following the Oregon-California Trail crossed the North Platte River over a bridge built here by John Richard (Reshaw). The $5 toll during high water saved swimming or ferrying across, and saved countless lives in the process.

Fort Clay, also known as Camp Davis, was established here in 1855 to protect the bridge. Camp Payne was also located here in 1858-59.

V Lee McCune Braille Trail

10 miles south of Casper in Casper Mountain Park

The trail was dedicated in 1975 "to the visually handicapped and the sighted of America to enjoy God's Unique World of Nature." The Trail was a dream come true for teacher Ed Strube. The Trail became a community effort and after four years and 8,000 hours of volunteer labor the hand-dug path was completed. The Trail was named for Casper Lions Club member, Lee McCune. The Casper Lions Club was the Trail's major benefactor. The Trail provides three bridges, a wide variety of plant life, and 37 stations with plaques printed in Braille and English, along with guide ropes. Each station vividly explains a unique part of nature's world. The Trail is a component of the National Trails System under the U.S. Department of the Interior.

9 *Gas, Food*

T Goodstein Foundation Art Gallery, Library, and Archives
At Casper College. 268-2269

T Wyoming Game and Fish Department, Casper
3030 Energy Lane in Casper. 473-3400

Come see the taxidermist displays of native Wyoming creatures, and find out more about wildlife, hunting, and fishing in the West.

S Cy Avenue Antique Mall
1905 CY Avenue in Casper. 237-2293

10 *Gas, Food, Lodging*

T The Oregon Trail Road
Take the Poison Spider Road west from Mills. Turn south on County Road 319 after 12 miles. Road re-joins State Highway 220 just north of Independence Rock.

Travelers willing to drive on improved dirt roads can follow the Oregon Trail Road as an alternative to State Highway 220. This road follows the actual trail ruts for 41.5 miles and includes such historic sites as Emigrant Gap (mile 8.5), Avenue of Rock (mile 19), Willow Spring (mile 27.5) and Prospect Hill (mile 29), the site of another BLM interpretive site. Try this in dry weather only. Inquire at Fort Caspar, the Casper Chamber of Commerce Information Center or BLM offices for advice and directions. The route is not well marked! *Source: BLM brochure.*

T Fort Caspar Museum and Historic Site
4001 Fort Caspar Road on west outskirts of Casper. 235-8462

This military post evolved from a previous site known as Mormon Ferry Post. Brigham Young established the first ferry service on the North Platte River near this location in June 1847 for the benefit of all trail travelers. When Louis Guinard spanned the North Platte with a 1,000-foot log bridge in 1859, the post became known as Platte Bridge Station. This site was one of the last opportunities the pioneers had to cross the river they had followed from central Nebraska. The army occupied the post from 1862-67. The present fort is constructed on the original site. It is the centerpiece of a City of Casper park complex.

This station was used as an overnight stage stop, where Richard Burton spent the night on August 16, 1860. "Our station lay near the upper crossing or second bridge, a short distance from the town. It was also built of timber at an expense of $40,000 about a year ago by Louis Guenot. . . . It was impossible to touch the squaw's supper: the tin cans that contained the coffee were slippery with grease, and the bacon looked as if it had been dressed side-by-side with 'boyaux'."

The Pony Express also established a station at this complex. Pony riders crossed the North Platte River on Guinard's Bridge, but the route stayed close to the north bank of the river until reaching Red Buttes Crossing, where another Pony Express station was located. In 1862, Lt. Col. William O. Collins sent one company of the 11th Ohio Volunteer Cavalry to protect the telegraph line at "Guinard's Bridge." The soldiers moved into Guinard's abandoned trading post/stage station complex, and named the garrison "Mormon Ferry Post."

It was renamed in honor of First Lieutenant Caspar Collins who was killed while protecting a supply train from Indian attack just north of the bridge. The fort continued to protected emigrant trails and the transcontinental telegraph line until its abandonment in 1867. Once the military departed, Indians quickly burned the post, but an excellent reconstruction marks the site.

Operated by the city of Casper, the fort has a museum/visitor center with interpretive exhibits. Source: National Park Service and BLM brochure.

H Fort Caspar Interpretive Signs
At Old Fort Casper

Fort Caspar

These fort buildings were reconstructed on the original site in 1936 by the Works Progress Administration. The WPA was a government program created during the Great Depression to provide jobs for the unemployed.

Prior to his death on July 26, 1885 Lt. Caspar W. Collins made several diagrams of military posts in Dakota Territory. This reconstruction was based on his diagram of the fort.

In November of 1865 the post known as Platte Bridge Station was officially renamed Fort Caspar in honor of Lt. Collins.

The Battle at Platte Bridge

Early on the morning of July 16, 1865 Lt. Caspar Collins led a troop of men to reinforce an army supply train coming into Platte Bridge Station. Only a mile west of the post, the group was ambushed by members of the Sioux, Cheyenne and Arapahoe nations.

The Indians were anxious to avenge the losses they sustained at the Sand Creek

Massacre the previous year. They hoped to destroy Platte Bridge Station in this attack.

The Indian force heavily outnumbered the group led by Collins. During the retreat, four men were killed including the twenty-year-old lieutenant.

The Army renamed Platte Bridge Station in honor of the young hero. Since a new post in Colorado had recently been named in honor of Caspar Collins' father, Col. W.O. Collins, the name Fort Caspar was chosen.

The Battle of Red Buttes
A desperate battle to save a supply train ended tragically the same day as the Battle at Platte Bridge. Sgt. Amos Custard and his men were bringing five supply wagons from the Sweetwater Station near Independence Rock. The group came into view of Platte Bridge Station from the direction of Red Buttes about noon on July 26, 1865.

Unaware of the morning's skirmish, Custard barely had time to assume a defensive position when a large group of Indians attacked. The four hour battle ended when the Indians overran the soldier's position.

The next day a detachment from Platte Bridge Station found the bodies of Sgt. Custard and 20 of his men. The only survivors were three of the five men on advance patrol from the supply train who made their way here to safety.

Casper Army Air Base
The summer of 1942 work was begun on an air base in the Casper area. In four months, four thousand workers constructed two hundred buildings, laid utility lines, built streets and laid out runways heavy enough for the largest military planes. On August 15, 1942, the first plane landed at the base. The official opening was on September 1, 1942. Major James A. Moore, a World War I veteran, was commanding officer. The base was built to handle four thousand military personnel. It became a training area for B-24 Liberators. A massive range was created to the west of the base for bombing practice. The air base was officially designated as the Casper Army Air Base. The base served as a training center until it was closed on March 7, 1945. The field became the Natrona County International Airport. This replaced the first airport, Wardwell Field. Many former base personnel stayed in the Casper area helping the city to prosper in the post-war years.

Eadsville
Eadsville, a mining ghost town, is situated 12 miles due south of Casper on top of Casper Mountain. It was founded by Charles W. Eads in 1891 after he had staked a 600' x 1,500' mining claim around a large spring. Word had spread that large deposits of precious minerals were found — gold, silver, lead, and copper. Lots were sold in the town in 1891 - 1892, and about a dozen cabins were built. Foundations of three cabins still remain today. Some 40 to 50 people lived there hoping to find a bonanza of gold and silver. Some copper was mined, and traces of gold and silver were found. Asbestos and feldspar were economically mined. The "spar" is still being mined today after nearly 100 years.

The miners finally gave up and abandoned the town in 1905-6. Numerous artifacts were uncovered in an archeological excavation of 7,800'.

Casper-Natron County-State Founding
On April 9, 1889, application was made to have the town of Casper incorporated. John Merritt made the application in Rawlins, Wyoming since Casper was in Carbon County at that time. On July 8, 1889, Casper was incorporated and George Mitchell was elected as the town's first Mayor.

The first act to separate Natrona county from Carbon County was presented to the Wyoming legislature in 1888. The county was officially organized on April 8 1890. Natrona County derives its name from the mineral, natron, which is carbonate of soda.

The Territory of Wyoming was formed on July 25, 1868, after separating from the Territory of Dakota. In 1869, the first Territorial Legislature passed the first Woman's Suffrage Bill in the Union, thus allowing women in Wyoming the right to vote. Wyoming became a state on July 10, 1890. The word, Wyoming, comes from a Delaware Indian word meaning "Upon the Great Plain."

Railroads
The first passenger train arrived in this area on June 15, 1888 as part of Fremont, Elkhorn & Missouri Valley Railroad System at the site of an "old town" that would later become Casper, Wyoming. A depot was built after the tracks were extended from the "old town" at present "A" & McKinley streets, to the area of Center and Collins streets. By 1891, extra cars were added in order to handle the traffic involved with mining ventures on Casper Mountain. The Fremont, Elkhorn & Missouri Valley, or locally called Wyoming central Railroad, extended passenger service on to Shoshoni, Riverton, and

Lander by 1906. The line eventually became part of the Chicago & North Western Railroad system.

The Chicago, Burlington & Quincy Railroad, commonly referred to as Burlington, reached Casper in October, 1913. The link through Wind River Canyon connected its Big Horn Basin line with the lines in southeastern Wyoming. Their depot in Casper was built in 1915. West of Casper, the consolidation of the parallel lines of the North Western and Burlington in 1942-23 made possible the salvage of 30,000 tons of rails for the war effort and the elimination of 87 miles of North Western Tracks. Burlington Northern now has 84.8 miles of track in Natrona County. This railroad has the distinction of being built from west to east in Natrona County.

The Mormon Ferry

Ella L. Watson ("Cattle Kate")
On Sturday, July 20, 1889, Ella L. Watson, popularly known as "Cattle Kate", was hanged with James Averell in Spring Canyon. The site is located 50 miles southwest of Casper near Independence Rock.

Ella and Jim had adjoining homesteads on Horse Creek which flows through the Pathfinder Ranch. This energetic couple had built up a sizeable herd of cattle, and Jim had established a road house on the Sweetwater River, located near the Oregon Trail and the Rawlins to Fort McKinney Stage Road.

One story of this hanging is that Jim Averell was a saloonkeeper who encouraged ranch hands to drink and carouse. Ella, in this story, raised a fine herd of cattle by exchanging her "favors" for young cattle "appropriated" by the ranch hands. The ranchers hung the two to rid the area of rustlers and troublemakers.

Another story claims Averell and Watson homesteaded on prime water rights and were honest law abiding citizens. Jim and Ella were hanged because the ranchers felt the land that was homesteaded was their own grazing land and wished to obtain the valuable water rights.

Guinard Bridge
The center piece of the Platte Bridge Station and Fort Caspar was the bridge built here by Louis Guinard in 1859-1860 and used until Fort Caspar was abandoned in 1867. The bridge superstructure stood on 28 timber cribbings filled with rock and gravel. Not counting the approaches, the bridge was 810 feet long and 17 feet wide. The total cost of construction was estimated at $40,000 dollars. The toll for wagons to cross was $1.00 to $6.00, determined by the height of the river. An additional toll was charged for animals and people. This bridge symbolized the changes being shaped by the expansion of America during the middle 19th Century.

Salt Creek Oil Field
The famous Salt Creek oil field is located in Natrona County, 40 miles north of Casper. Representative Stephen W. Downey was the first man to acquire land at Salt Creek in 1883, after the discovery of the Jackass Spring oil seep. The discovery oil well in the area was drilled in March of 1889 in the Shannon pool. Mr. Shannon later built a small oil refinery in Casper in 1895 to process his oil.

The main Salt Creek oil field was opened with the discovery of oil at the Dutch No. 1 location in October, 1908. It initally produced 150 barrels of oil per day. As the field was developed and expanded, many of the Salt Creek wells were famous for being gushers. After 20 wells were producing oil in Salt Creek, Franco-Wyoming Oil Company decided to build a 5,000 barrel of oil per day refinery on 20 acres located immediately east of Highland Cemetery. Transportation of large amounts of oil to the Casper refineries was a problem until the completion of two pipelines in December 1911.

For some time Salt Creek was the largest light oil field in the world. The Teapot Dome oil field of President Harding's tenure in the 1920s is located nearby.

Old Pioneer Military Cemetery
Lt. Caspar Collins was killed July 26, 1865 about three miles from this spot. His body was removed by relative to his old home in Hillsboro, Ohio. Bodies of soldiers killed from 1858 to 1867 were reburied at Fort D. A. Russell in 1899. Some still interred here are unknown. The roster shows of 103 men. 92 were under 23 years of age. Lt. Collins was not yet 21. Casper was named after Caspar Collins.

Platte Bridge Cemetery
You may be surprised that no one is buried under these stone markers. They represent some of the soldiers who died while stationed at Platte Bridge Station (Fort Caspar). The army removed the bodies originally located here and reinterred them at Fort D. A. Russell in 1899.

In 1926, members of the Civilian Conservation Corps unearthed three skeletons while working at this site. These bodies were reburied under the large monument to your left.

It is almost certain that other people are buried on the fort grounds. During the days of the great emigration along the Oregon Trail, this area served as a pioneer cemetery.

The "Mormon" Ferry
First commercial ferry on the Platte River was established 1/2 mile south of here in June 1847 by "Mormon" pioneers on their way to the valley of the Great Salt Lake. Brigham Young directed nine men to remain to operate the ferry. They wee Thomas Grover, Captain John S. Higby, Luke S. Johnson, Appleton M. Harmon, Edmund Ellsworth, Francis M. Pomeroy, William Empey, James Davenport and Benjamin F. Stewart. The first passengers were Missourians bound for Oregon. The ferry was made of two large cottonwood canoes fastened by cross pieces and covered with slabs. It was operated with oars. The ferry operated until 1852.

Site of old Platte Bridge
South side:

Built by Louis Guinard 1858-59. Immediately south and west are the sites of Platte Bridge Station. First overland telegraph, stage and Pony Express stations on the old Oregon Trail.

North side:

One half mile north and west across North Platte River on the tableland occurred Platte Bridge fight July 26, 1865 in which Lt. Caspar W. Collins, 11th Ohio Vol. Cav., and Privates George W. McDonald, Co. I, George Camp and Sebastian Nehring, Co. K., all of 11th Kan. Vol. Cav. were killed.

Also killed the same day near here were Privates James A. Porter and Adam Culp, both of Co. I, 11th Kan. Vol. Cav.

Goose Egg Ranch
The Goose Egg Ranch first received some notoriety when Owen Wister featured it in his book, The Virginian. In the novel, this is where the cowboys exchanged the babies' blankets, and after the dance, the mothers carried home the wrong children. The ranch and house site were located 10 miles south of Casper on the north bank of the North Platte River, at Bessemer Bend.

The Searight Brothers built the house in 1883 and lived there until 1886. The lumber, hardware, and materials used in the construction of the building was hauled by freight teams from Cheyenne, a distance of more than 225 miles. They then sold the ranch to J.M. Carey a future Governor of Wyoming.

The beautiful stone home slowly deteriorated, and despite efforts by local historians to save the ranch house, the building was demolished in July, 1951.

Bridger and Bozeman Trails
The discovery of gold in Montana in 1862 created a rush of miners traveling to Virginia city. The most direct routes were through Wyoming on the Bridger and Bozeman trails. In the spring of 1863, John Bozeman, a miner from Georgia, pioneered a route leaving the Oregon/California/Mormon Trail near Fort Fetterman and traveled east of the Big Horn Mountains through the Powder River Country. This area was hunting grounds claimed by the Sioux, Cheyenne, and Arapaho, who were determined to keep the white man out of this region. Except for Indian resistance, Bozeman's route was by far the easiest route to travel.

Jim Bridger, in 1864, aware of the Indians' determination to keep the emigrants out of the Powder River country, pioneered a route leaving the Oregon/California/Mormon Trail west of Platte Bridge Station. Traveling north through the Big Horn Basin and west of the Big Horn Mountains, Bridger's route passed through friendly Shoshoni and Crow lands The Bridger

Trail, though little used, proved to be a safe alternative to the more dangerous "Bloody" Bozeman Trail.

The determined resistance by the Sioux, Cheyenne, and Arapaho claimed many lives from 1863 to 1868, climaxing with the Fetterman disaster in December of 1866. The federal government consented to the Indians' demands with the Fort Laramie Treaty of 1868 by closing the Powder River country trails and forts.

Pony Express

Today you stand where the Pony Express ran in 1860-61, when daring riders on swift horses carried the mail between St. Joe, Missouri and Sacremento, California.

A January 30, 1860 news release read: "Have determined to establish a Pony Express to Sacramento, California, commencing 3rd of April. Time ten days." Horses had never crossed half the American continent in ten days. Stage stations, such as Platte Bridge Station, became a Pony Express Station, each averaging 12.5 miles apart. At these stations, tired horses were exchanged for fresh ones. Riders stayed at home stations, some 40 to 70 miles apart.

Young riders signed on the ride because of this San Francisco advertisement:

Wanted

Wanted skinny wiry fellows not over eighteen. Must be expert riders willing to risk death daily. Orphans preferred. Wages $25 per week. Apply, Central Overland Express....

Despite death defying rigors of summer heat, winter blizzards and Indian attacks, riders anxiously awaited the Pony's first run on April 3rd. Mail pouches, relayed from pony to pony at each relay station, were shuttled across the 1900 mile expanse on schedule, with letters and telegrams delivered on April 13th. Although it lasted a mere 19 months, it shall forever remain one of the truly remarkable feats of the old west.

Richard Bridge and Military Complex

The military camps and Richard Bridge were located in the bend of the North Platte River about one-mile north of Evansville, Wyoming. Locally known as Reshaw's Bridge, the area is marked by a historical sign.

John Richard (Reshaw) constructed a toll bridge in 1852-53 to offer a crossing for the Oregon/California/Mormon Trail emigrants. ON November 2, 1985, members of the 4th Artillery, 6th Infantry, and 10th Infantry arrived at the Richard trading post and established a military camp. In January, 1856, the camp became known as Fort Clay. From February through June the name was changed to Camp Davis. Special Order No. 9 on March 6, 1856, directed the garrison to "...protect the bridge and other interests in that part of the country." The camp at Richard Bridge was abandoned in November of 1856.

The area was again garrisoned by members of the 4th Artillery in July, 1858 when they established Post at Platte Bridge. The post was informally called Camp Payne by the troops and was abandoned in April, 1859. The next time troops were garrisoned in this area, they located at Fort Caspar near Guinard's Bridge.

The Mormons

Brigham Young led the first group of Mormons west from winter quarters in Nebraska in 1847, finally settling in the Salt Lake Valley. When these pioneers crossed the river here, they left nine men to operate a ferry. This ferry served fellow Mormons as well as Oregon and California bound emigrants and provided much needed money and supplies for the settlements in Utah.

In October of 1856 Natrona County's greatest tragedy began at what is now Bessemer Bend and continued to Martin's cove near Devil's Gate. The sixth Mormon Handcart Company, under Captain Edward Martin, struggled through an early Wyoming blizzard. Over 135 persons perished in this 50 mile stretch.

Of handcart travel, Chislett's narrative states, "Many a father pulled his cart, with his little children on it, until the day preceding his death. I have seen some pull their carts in the morning, give out during the day, and die before the next morning."

Oregon/California/Mormon Trails

From 1840 to 1869, over 350,000 emigrants traveled past this area on the Oregon/California /Mormon Trails. The promise of free land, sudden riches, or religious freedom caused these pioneers to endure great hardships. Thousands of persons died in the quest and are buried along this old pathway.

Only two graves in Natrona County are identified by name as trail dated burials. This is unusual due to the fact that hundreds of persons died while traveling through our county. Drowning, disease, and accidents took a toll in our area, especially between this point and Devil's Gate.

The peak of migration was in 1852 when 70,000 persons passed this spot, most on their way to the Callifornia gold fields. These trails contributed to the largest overland migration in history.

Military Explorers

John C. Fremont, the "Pathfinder", was born in 1813 and explored a large portion of central Wyoming including the Casper area. He made an independent survey to the Wind River Mountains of Wyoming in 1842, and the 13,743' Fremont Peak of the Wind Rivers is named in his honor. Fremont tried unsuccessfully to navigate the North Platte River through a canyon southwest of Casper in August of 1842. The boat capsized, resulting in the loss of important mapping equipment, journals, registers, maps and supplies. Subsequently, he received the dubious honor of having this area come to be known as Fremont Canyon. Through the recommendation of Fremont, the government purchased and garrisoned Ft. Laramie in 1849.

Benjamin L.E. Bonneville passed this point in the summer of 1832 during the exploration of the central Rockies. Bonneville, an American soldier, was born in France in 1796 and served with the 7th U.S. Infantry. In 1832 he led an expedition of 110 men and 20 wagons along the North Platte River, thus becoming the first to take wagons through South Pass. In 1833 he found an oil seep at Dallas Dome near present day Lander, wyoming. The drilling of the No. 1 Murphy well in 1884 kicked off the production of oil in Wyoming.

Robert Stuart Cabin Site

Approximately eight miles southwest of here, Robert Stuart built the first cabin in the state of Wyoming. The cabin was built in a three day period in early November,1812, at a site on the North Platte River at Bessemer Bend.

Robert Stuart was a member of the John Jacob Astor fur trading company that was under the command of William Price Hunt in 1812. After Astor's ship, the Tonquin, blew up in the Pacific Ocean and killed the crew, news was sent back to Astor via Robert Stuart. His route would take him over the Rockies from the mouth of the Columbia River to St. Louis.

Stuart's cabin was built of stone with a buffalo hide roof. According to his diary, it was 8' wide, 18' long, and 3' high. A hole in the center of the hide roof let the smoke escape. Following a visit by Arapahoes and learning of Crow Indians nearby, Stuart and his party abandoned their camp on December 13, 1812. They proceeded to present day Torrington, near the Wyoming-Nebraska border, where they spent the remainder of the winter.

Indians of Wyoming

At the time of the great migration of emigrants through Wyoming to the Pacific coast and Utah, Indians were the largest group of residents in wyoming. Many of these tribes such as Utes and Blackfeet, were semi-permanent and nomadic, traveling in and out of wyoming as warrior-hunting societies. The roaming buffalo supplied the Indians with all their subsistance, and the introduction of the horse provided the mobility to hunt the buffalo in great numbers.

The Shoshoni were located in the western part of Wyoming, generally in the Green River valley. The Crows were living in the Big Horn and Powder River Basins in northern Wyoming and southern Montana. The Cheyenne, Arapaho, and Sioux claimed the southeast part of Wyoming, an area heavily traveled during the emigrant migration.

The coming of the emigrants in great numbers was accepted peacefully by the Crow and Shoshoni, but the Sioux, with the help of the Cheyenne and Arapaho, resisted fiercely. From 1853 until 1877, the Sioux and their allies fought this intrusion in numerous battles until final defeat forced them to accept the invasion and reservation life. In Wyoming, the Wind River Indian Reservation is home for the Arapaho and Shoshoni.

Old Fort Caspar

Originally known to trappers and explorers (1830-1847) as Upper Crossing of the North Platte River, it became the Mormon Ferry in 1847. Guinard built a bridge here in 1858, and troops from Platte Bridge Station guarded the telegraph line and protected emigrants on the "Oregon Trail". July 26, 1865, the station was attacked by hordes of Indians. Lt. Caspar Collins led an heroic attempt to rescue Sgt. Custard's wagon train, but sacrified his life in aiding a fallen soldier. The station was renamed "Fort Caspar" in his honor. Abandoned in 1867 ,the fort and bridge were burned by Indians. The old fort was restored on its original foundations in 1936.

Mormon Ferry

Brigham Young arrived at a point near this site with the Mormon Pioneer 72-wagon company of 143 men, three women and two children on June 12, 1847. Strong winds and high water (150 yards wide and 10 to 15-feet deep) made crossing the river difficult and extrmely dangerous. After various attempts to cross and frustrated by slow progress, Brigham Young commissioned the construction of a larger ferry boat. After just three days, the ferry was com-

Section 5

Mormon Trail in the Casper Area

"All The Roads Were One..."

From the early 1840s until the completion of the railroad in 1869, all of the emigrant trails but the Overland Trail followed the North Platte River in Wyoming. Early trappers, explorers and missionaries forged this primitive highway, which subsequently served at least 200.000 pioneers bound for California. 50.000 bound for Oregon, and 70,000 Mormons bound for the deserts of Utah. Pony Express riders, freighters, soldiers and stage coach drivers also used the same well-worn Wyoming paths linking East and West.

"Casper was a significant point on the Mormon Trail for two reasons ..."

1. The "Last Crossing" of the North Platte took place near Casper.

A series of canyons upstream from Casper (southwest) remained virtually impassable until long after the pioneer period. Casper, then called the "Last Crossing," is significant in trail history because it is in this vicinity that all of the Mormon, California, and Oregon pioneers finally crossed and abandoned the North Platte River which had guided and sustained them through Nebraska and much of Wyoming. Crossing these swollen waters was a very dangerous undertaking that cost many lives.

In recent times, the construction of several upstream dams has regulated the spring runoff flow of the North Platte, but in the mid-19th century, the pioneers had to cross torrential waters up to a mile across. There were several alternative crossing points, in the short stretch between Deer Creek and Bessemer Bend near Casper where this perilous operation could be accomplished. Wind velocity, water level, and other seasonal variables influenced the particular crossing site selected.

2. Casper marked the northernmost point of the Mormon Trail.

Due to the peculiar deviation of the North Platte River around the mountains of south-central Wyoming (including Casper Mountain), the Casper area also marks the northernmost point along the Mormon Trail.

Three key events in Mormon history happened near Casper:

The region around Casper is significant in Mormon history because of three key events which took place here:

1. Establishment of the "Mormon Ferry" (1847);

2. Martin Handcart Company disaster (1856);

3. Attempt to establish a mail station in Glenrock which helped precipitate the "Utah War" (1857).

The Mormon Ferry (1847-1852)

As they approached the "Upper Crossing" of the North Platte, Brigham Young sent ahead a detachment of 40 men to secure a boat and prepare a way to ferry the wagons across the river. A Missouri company had preceded them, and arranged a contract with the Mormon ferry-builders to carry their wagons across for $1.50 per load in the "Revenue Cutter" – a leather boat which also served as a butcher wagon and pulpit which the pioneers had the foresight to bring from Winter Quarters. It had the capacity to carry cargoes weighing 1,500-1,800 pounds. Fees were paid in flour at the rate of $2.50 per hundred pounds when the going rate was $10 per hundred pounds elsewhere. Though they got 24 wagons across and earned $34 in this endeavor, they found that the wagons often rolled over in the currents, and the horses risked drowning. It was clear that a more efficient and reliable strategy for crossing these swollen currents had to be found.

Brigham Young arrived at the Upper Crossing of the North Platte with the rest of the 72-wagon company of 143 men, three women and two children on June 12, 1847. His party had to wait for the Missouri group to finish crossing. Then the Mormons ferried their emptied wagons while displaced provisions and personal belongings were carried across on the "Revenue Cutter." Strong winds and high water (150 yards wide and 10 to 15-feet deep) made the crossing difficult and extremely dangerous. After a long day, only 23 wagons rested safely on the other side of the river.

Frustrated by this slow progress, Brigham Young commissioned the construction of a larger ferry boat. Men were sent to locate two 23-foot cottonwood trees, which were hollowed out like canoes to serve as the base. Cross timbers were obtained from the mountain and slabbing for the floor from other cottonwoods. After just three days, the ferry was complete and had been provided as well with two oars and a rudder for control. Brigham Young realized that subsequent Mormon companies would require the ferry to cross the North Platte, and he also appreciated the revenue-generating potential of helping other pioneers cross the river. Wilford Woodruff recorded that " ... President Young thought it wisdom to leave a number of the brethren here and keep a ferry until our Company Came up. Emegrants will pay for ferrying $1.50 cnts per waggon ..." [sic].

After the Mormons had completed the crossing, other small wagon trains bound for Oregon contracted with the ferrymen to carry them across. On June 19, one week after their arrival, Brigham Young named nine men to remain and operate the ferry while he and the others pushed on to their new home in present-day Utah. A tenth, Eric Glines, elected himelf to stay behind with the ferrymen. These ten men possessed a variety of professional skills which were offered to other pioneers passing through. Mormon pioneers received these services free of charge; others paid $4-5 per wagon.

The original ferry was located near the present site of Fort Caspar, but a few days after Brigham Young's departure, in response to temporary competition, it was moved downstream-several miles. A sign post advertising the services provided by the Mormon Ferry was erected 28 miles downriver at Deer Creek (Glenrock). This was the first advertising sign in central Wyoming.

The Mormon ferry operation, established in 1847 by Brigham Young, marked the beginning of commercial ferrying in the Rocky Mountains. Every summer between 1848 and 1852, Mormon men returned to Casper from Salt Lake City to operate it during the "high water period" (between late May and July).

In 1847 and 1848, the Mormons enjoyed a near monopoly in the ferry business, but in 1849 at least three non-Mormon ferries began operating in the area. Even so, heavy traffic to the gold fields of California often created crossing delays that lasted up to a week. By this time, an ingenious rope and pulley system made it possible for the "Mormon Ferry" to carry a loaded wagon across the river in just five minutes.

Original Ferry Crew

Thomas Crover Captain (professional ferryman)
William Empey Assistant Captain
Appleton Harmon Carpenter/mechanic
Luke Johnson Doctor and hunter
James Davenport Blacksmith
James Highee Herdsman
Edmund Ellsworth Hunter
Francis Pomeroy Hunter
Benjamin Stewart Coal miner at Deer Creek
Eric Glines Crew member
Martin Handcart Company Disaster (1856)

In 1856 the financial burden associated with getting destitute European converts across the plains to join the Saints in Utah forced Mormon leaders to find ways to cut costs. Accordingly, Brigham Young instructed these converts to walk to "Zion" from the end of the railroad (which was then under construction), bearing their meager possessions in "handcarts" which could be pushed and pulled along the trail without the assistance of animals.

A handcart was a two-wheeled, wooden wagon, similar in design to an over-sized wheelbarrow. Each was about six-feet long, four-feet wide and five-feet deep when loaded to capacity with 400-500 pounds of provisions. Nevertheless, "handcart pioneers" could make the entire trip from Liverpool, England to the Salt Lake Valley for less than $45, in weeks less time, and with fewer casualties than those using costly covered wagons. In all, ten handcart companies with 2,962 pioneers – three percent of the total number of the Mormon emigrants - journeyed to the Salt Lake Valley between 1856 and 1860.

The first three handcart companies reached the Salt Lake Valley safely in 1856, but tragedy struck the Martin and Willie Handcart Companies which followed, as well as the Hunt and Hodgett wagon trains behind them. When they arrived at Iowa City (the departure point at the end of the railroad), these English and Scandinavian emigrants found that their handcarts were not ready as promised. Consequently, they were delayed as handcarts were hastily constructed of unseasoned wood, which would later shrink, warp, and crack as they were drawn along the trail in the summer heat. Determined to reach Utah rather than be stranded among strangers, James G. Willie's company left Iowa City on July 15; Edward Martin's left July 26. Almost a month later, August 11, the Willie Company pulled into Florence.

So late in the season, the question of proceeding was put to a vote. All but the experienced Levi Savage voted to travel on. Savage, with tears running down his cheeks, reportedly pleaded for "... the old, weak, and sickly to stop until another spring ... that if such undertook the journey at that late season of the year, that their bones would strew the way." He added,

"Brothers and Sisters, what I have said I know to be true; but seeing you are to go forward, I will go with you, will help you all I can, will work with you, will rest with you, will suffer with you, and, if necessary, I will die with you. May God in His mercy bless and preserve us."

As Savage predicted, a number of handcarts broke down. The cargo was redistributed on those remaining until they were grossly overloaded. Ironically, it was at Deer Creek, just two days from Casper, that the loads were reduced from 17 to 10 pounds per person, and the pioneers discarded the clothing, food, and blankets they would desperately need to sustain life within the week. Weak from fatigue and lack of food, many of the emigrants found themselves caught short of clothing and rations when the early and harsh winter storms of 1856 struck suddenly on October 19. One witness at Reshaw Bridge watched these impoverished pioneers ford the freezing river because they could not afford the bridge toll. This part of the ordeal hastened the death of many.

The Willie Company was caught near the sixth crossing of the Sweetwater River. Most of the losses from the Martin Company occurred between the North Platte crossing and Martin's Cove. When possible, the dead were wrapped in sheets and lowered into shallow graves, where they were then covered with stones to keep wolves away. However, much of the time the hard-frozen ground prevented burial, and corpses could only be covered with blankets and snow and left above-ground.

By the time a rescue party arrived from Salt Lake City on November 1, over 18 inches of snow had fallen, and temperatures had dropped to -14 F. Straggling survivors were picked up for nearly 60 miles along the trail from the Bessemer Bend area to Martin's Cove, near Devil's Gate, where the Martin Company survivors regrouped after the rescue party arrived. The Hunt and Hodgett wagon trains were caught in the same storm and added to the numbers gathering at Martin's Cove — ultimately about 800 people including the rescuers.

Sixty-seven of the Willie Handcart Company died before the remaining members reached Salt Lake City on November 9, 1856. Of the Martin Handcart Company, 145 died before the party finally reached Salt Lake at the end of November. Many more from both companies lost limbs or extremities. Others sustained lifelong physical impairments from the ordeal.

Attempt to Grow Crops and Establish a Mail Station Near Glenrock (1857)

Information is limited about the attempts of the Mormons to plant crops in Glenrock for the benefit of Mormon pioneers who would later pass through the area en route to Salt Lake City, but some believe their efforts began in the mid-1850s and persisted until the Utah War of 1857. By 1856, Hiram Kimball had secured a federal contract for delivering mail along the trail. In May 1857, Brigham Young announced the erection of a series of mail stations along the route, and dispatched crews from Salt Lake to build them that summer. One station was to be located at Deer Creek, and in anticipation of this development, a fort and thriving settlement were begun the same summer near Glenrock. However, this venture was quickly abandoned in August 1857 due to deteriorating relations between the Mormons and the federal government. The ensuing dispute known as the "Utah War" resulted in the cancellation of the mail contract and the subsequent dispatch of 2,500 federal troops to Utah under the command of Albert Sidney Johnson.

Reprint of article prepared by the Casper Wyoming Stake of The Church of Jesus Christ of Latter-day Saints

plete and had been provided as well with two oars and a rudder for control. Brigham Young realized that subsequent Mormon companies would require the ferry to cross the North Platte, and he also appreciated the revenue-generating potential of helping other pioneers cross the river. Wilford Woodruff recorded that "...President Young thought it wisdom to leave a number of the brethren here and keep a ferry until our Company Came up. Emigrants will pay for ferrying $1.50 cents per waggon..."(sic).

On June 19, one week after their arrival, Brigham Young named nine men to remain and operate the ferry.

"...A Company have gone back about three miles to make two canoes on which they intend to build a boat to be used here till the next company comes up. Another company also went about half a mile up the river to make slabs or puncheons to lay on the canoes. A while before dark the brethren returned from below with two good canoes twenty-five feet long each and nearly finished and ready to put together..."
William Clayton, 1847

"...I was called to go with 16 or 18 others down the river in search of Timber for Canoes, as the President said he was tired of experimenting with Raft after going about 3 miles we found two cottonwood trees near together of which we constructed two canoes 23 feet long, put them on the Wagons & hauled them up to camp at night..."
Norton Jacob, 1847

"....Meantime a set of hands was busy preparing two canoes, two and a half feet in diameter and 23 feet long, which, when coupled about five feet apart with cross timber covered with puncheons and manned with oars, made a boat with which three men could cross a wagon with its load..."
Erastus Snow, 1847

"....at first tried the plan of floating our wagons by extending ropes down the river and attaching them to the end of the tongue, but the current would roll them over as if they were nothing but a log, wheels and bows appearing alternately upon the surface of the water, and two lashed together by means of poles placed under them shared the same fate... The plan was abandoned as being too dangerous. The next plan was to try small rafts, but the difficulty of polling a raft in so deep and swift water was such that the wind, aiding the current, would not infrequently sweep them down from one to two miles before it would be possible to make the other shore... In attempting to drag rafts across the current with ropes, the current would draw them under... Prest. Young stript himself and went to work with all his strength, assisted by the Dr. and brethren, and made a first rate White Pine and White Cotton Wood Raft... The new raft was in operation all day and worked well..."
Wilford Woodruff, 1847

"...to the upper crossing of the Platte River. Here we had considerable trouble as the river was very high and rapid... It was decided to make two large canoes and lash them together for a ferry boat... We selected two large trees, three feet through. Of these we made two large canoes, 30 feet long. We then cut two other trees and hewed them down to two inches thick and straightened the edges, making planks of them 14"wide and 30' long... We then ran it across the river, which was quickly and easily done. In this way, the wagons were all soon over; the stock we swam across..."
Lewis Barney1847

Pioneer Party

"The boats were managed by means of large ropes stretched across the stream, then with pulley blocks working on the before named rope, then guy ropes attached to each end of the boat and to the two blocks with pulleys, then drop one end of the boat so that the force of the current pressing against it will push the boat across, then reverse the process and the boat will recross in about five minutes,"

11 *Gas, Food, Lodging*

Mills

Pop. 2,591, elev. 5,123

Now a suburb of Casper, this community was named for the Mills brothers, James, William, and Thomas, who planned the Mills-Baker addition to Casper in 1919.

H The Town of Mills

City Memorial Park in Mills

In 1919 the Mills Construction Company purchased a major portion of this area to mine sand and gravel from the floor plain of the North Platte River. This material was hauled by horse and wagon to the Midwest refinery (now Amoco) to build roads and tank farm dikes. By 1921 over a thousand people lived in the area along what is now Federal Street.

The people voted to incorporate the Town of Mills in April of 1921. George Boyle was elected Mayor and took office in May. The Town built a new town hall and a highly controversial bond election approved money for construction of a public water system. The Town's first water tank was built on this site in 1924 and stood here until 1975. Mills has grown over the years and today is over a square mile in size and has two thousand residents.

H Sgt. Custard Wagon-Train Fight

On private land near Casper

On July 26, 1865 near this site a U.S. Army Wagon Train under the command of Sgt. Custard, Eleventh Kansas Cavalry was attacked by Sioux, Cheyenne and Arapahoe Indians. In a vicious four hour fight, twenty troopers and an unknown number of warriors were killed. All the wagons were burned.

F Peaches' Family Restaurants

3550 W. Yellowstone in Mills. 265-6794

Bessemer Bend

12 *Gas, Food*

Bar Nunn
Pop. 936, elev. 5,282

Probably named for a rancher's brand, this little town is now a settlement outside of Casper.

H The Oregon Trail
On Horse Creek Road about 13 miles south of State Highway 220. At Ryan Hill Interpretive Site.

Ruts of the Oregon Trail are visible at this location. This trail was a great roadway for large covered wagon migrations to Oregon, California, and Utah. An estimated 350,000 people passed this way between 1843 and 1866. 1866 marked the end of the large migration parties; thereafter only small parties traveled the trail. The great migration ended in the 1880's. The trail remains an important transportation corridor today.

H Wildlife and Habitat
On Horse Creek Road about 13 miles south of State Highway 220. At Ryan Hill Interpretive Site.

The surrounding sagebrush/grassland habitat supports a variety of wildlife species today, just as it did during the active trail use days. Most of the plant and animal species observed and used by the early emigrants still inhabit this area. A notable exception is the buffalo, which is no longer found here. The grasses fed the emigrants' livestock, and the sagebrush fueled their fires, though not as satisfactorily a they might have wished. William G. Johnson noted in his journal on June 5, 1849, that it had drawbacks—it "sends forth great volumes of blinding smoke, particularly damaging to the eyes of the cook." The emigrants shot buffalo, sage grouse, and cottontail rabbits as they moved through the area, supplementing their meager diet with the fresh meat. With the exception of the roads, pipelines and other structures of human origin, this area appears today much as it did in the 1850's and 1860's.

H Ryan (Prospect) Hill
On Horse Creek Road about 13 miles south of State Highway 220. At Ryan Hill Interpretive Site.

Prospect Hill (now called Ryan Hill) derived its name from the view of the surrounding countryside, a view William Clayton called "pleasant" in his 1848 Emigrants' Guide." To the west, the emigrants got their first view of the Sweetwater Mountains and the route they would travel to Independence Rock and Devils Gate, some of the most spectacular sites along the trail. Those who could not make the 20 miles from here to Independence Rock in one day would usually camp at Horse Creek. Once at Independence Rock, they would follow the Sweetwater River for the next 90 miles, thus having access to a reliable water source.

Although this portion of the trail was repeatedly described as barren and rough, it was not desolate. Amelia Stewart Knight wrote in her journal on June 14, 1853, "There is no less than 150 wagons camped around us, but we have left most of the droves behind, and no end to the teams."

There are developed interpretive areas at Independence Rock, Devils Gate and Split Rock.

13 *No services*

H Emigrant Gap Historical Site
About 10 miles west of Mills on Poison Spider Road

Many emigrant pioneers passed through this gap, or opening, in Emigrant Ridge between the 1840's and the 1880's as they traveled the Oregon-Mormon Trail by oxen-drawn wagons, on horseback, or on foot. The trail generally followed the North Platte River from the Scottsbluff, Nebraska area to crossings near Fort Caspar (just eight miles east), which was active between 1862 and 1867. The trail departed from the North Platte River near Fort Caspar, meandering overland toward Willow Springs, Ryan (Prospect) Hill, the Sweetwater River drainage, Independence Rock, South Pass, and beyond to Utah, Oregon and California.

From this point the emigrants had a sweeping view to the west, the scene of their next week's journey. Emigrant Gap signified the departure from the North Platte River valley and the beginning of the ascent into the Rocky Mountains. The trail crossed over the Continental divide at South Pass.

From here you can follow Poison Spider Road to Oregon Trail Road which closely parallels the route of the Oregon-Mormon Trail.

H A Look Back
On Horse Creek Road about 13 miles south of State Highway 220. At Ryan Hill Interpretive Site.

Looking east from this point, the emigrants could see most of the route back to the North Platte River and Casper Mountain. From the oint where they left the North Platte River, they could travel to Willow Springs, at the base of Ryan (Prospect) Hill, in two or three days if they were not delayed by sickness or accients. Willow Springs, with its good water, was the customary campsite after they had passed through Emigrant Gap and Rock Avenue a day or two earlier.

There would be no reliable source of good water again until they reached Horse Creek, 10 miles beyond Willow Springs, on their way to the Sweetwater River near Independence Rock. Upon leaving Willow Springs they faced a 400-foot climb to this point at the top of what they called Prospect Hill, a trying task for draft animals pulling the belongings of emigrants.

From this vantage you can see the remains of the wagon ruts immediately to the north and east. Please stay on the posted foot trail—remember to enjoy and not destroy.

14 *No services*

T Bessemer Bend
Bessemer Bend Interpretive Site about 2 miles north of State Highway 220 on Bessemer Bend Road.

The distinctive Red Buttes stand above Bessemer Bend, the last fording site of the North Platte River on the Trail. This river, which the emigrants had followed for hundreds of miles, now turned to the south and became impassable. Toll ferries and bridges downstream of the Bend were established after 1847, but emigrants, including the handcart companies of 1856, who did not want to pay the tolls, used Bessemer Bend as a low-water crossing. There is a BLM interpretive site at the crossing. *Source: BLM brochure.*

H Bessemer Bend Interpretive Signs
Bessemer Bend Interpretive Site about 2 miles north of State Highway 220 on Bessemer Bend Road.

Bessemer Bend

Explorers, fur traders, mountain men and emigrants have camped at this site. Although the main route of the Oregon Trail is a few miles north of here, many emigrant travelers crossed the North Platte River at this site for the last time on their trek west. They preferred using this favorable ford rather than waiting in line and paying the tolls and ferry fees required at lower crossings. Ample grass, good water and pleasant surroundings made this a favorite campsite for some travelers, since the route to or from the Sweetwater River was three days of rough, dry country and poisonous alkali water.

Bessemer City, ("Queen of the Plains"),

flourished for a short time (1888-1891) a few miles west of the river. Bessemer City was founded by cattle kings anticipating the construction of a railroad This area was the hub of well-established stock-grazing ranches on major streams and rivers. The residents of Bessemer City staged a campaign for the Natrona County seat and in April of 1890 lost their bid to Casper, another nearby village. Bessemer City died and is now a field of waving alfalfa where once stood hotels, stores, churches and saloons.

Pony Express—April 4, 1860-October 24, 1861

Historic sites have been interpreted along the Pony Express Trail by the Bureau of Land Management in Wyoming, Utah and Nevada. This effort to enhance your understanding of our western heritage is in observance of the American Revolution Bicentennial. "Bessemer Bend" is one of three Bureau of Land Management sites in Wyoming. You are invited westward to the Sweetwater River to visit "Devil's Gate" near Independence Rock via Wyoming 220 and "Split Rock" via Wyoming 287. If you are the adventurous sort, trace the original path of the Pony Express or the Oregon Trail following the route of westward Expansion.

The Need was There

Competing with time, harsh climates, long distances, mountains, plains, deserts and the hostility of numerous Indian Bands, the Pony Express met the need to carry communication 1600 miles across the West. It was a triumph of organization, determination and courage and was vital to the life of the Nation. The Pony Express kept the far West informed and helped to keep Califonia in the Union at the outbreak of the Civil War, thus playing a part in holding the Nation together. During its eighteen-month life, the Pony Express operated at peak efficiency, speeding mail from either end at an average rate of only 10 days. The time was shorter for telegrams as the "talking wire" neared completion from east and west. From April 4, 1860 to October 24, 1861, the California Overland Mail and Pike's Peak Express (Pony Express) was the Nation's vital communication link with the far West.

How It Was Done

Relay stations were set up 10 to 15 miles apart along the route, each manned by two to four men and extra horses. In the desert west, relay stations were often much farther apart. About 500 of the hardiest western horses were bought at prices up to $200 each. Above all, the 80 riders were recruited from the most daring, determined and toughest "wiry young fellows" in the West. Lightly equipped and armed, each rider rode about 35 miles and back, exchanging horses at three relay stations. Over his saddle the rider carried the mochila, a leather cover with four mail pouches. Postage for a single letter was $1 to $5. Each rider rode at top speed to his relay stations. There the precious mochila was placed on a waiting horse and the rider was off again in two minutes. Day and night, good weather and bad, winter and summer, the "Pony" never stopped, averaging 10 to 15 miles an hour across the West.

The Pony's Echo

Completion of the Transcontinental Telegraph Line, October 24, 1861, put an end to the Pony Express. The wire now met the need for urgent communication. The Overland Mail Stage Coach service for letters had been intensified so that the high cost of Pony Express mail was no longer justified. In 18 months the story of the Pony Express had attracted world-wide attention that has not faded with time. Its backers, Russell, Majors, Waddell and Company, lost over $1million on the venture and never received federal support. Never the less, the Pony Express will remain as an outstanding example of American enterprise, endurance, courage and determination in the westward expansion of the Nation.

Red Butte

Goose Egg Ranch

The Goose Egg Ranch was established in this area of Wyoming by the Searight Cattle Company of Texas, which stocked it with 14,000 head of cattle trailed in from Oregon. Inspiration for the name of the ranch came when one of the cowboys found some goose eggs on an island in the North Platte River.

The ranch house, built in the fall of 1881, was a large native stone building with a living room, kitchen, five bedrooms and a cellar. Although most materials were freighted by wagon teams from Cheyenne, the stone was cut from nearby rocks.

Famous for its local dances and parties, the house was picked by Owen Wister as the setting for an incident in his western novel, "The Virginian". In this famous story the Virginian switched babies in clothing and cribs while their parents danced at the party. This prank was his reaction to being snubbed by the teacher, Molly Wood, after he rode 100 miles to attend the party.

The ranch house was one-quarter mile east of flourishing Bessemer City. It was once used as a hotel, advertised as "the best hotel in central Wyoming with accommodations unsurpassed".

When the Goose Egg Ranch was sold in 1886, it became part of J.M. Carey's spread. Carey and his son, Robert, both were Governor and Senator for Wyoming in the early 1900s. The house was razed in 1951 because it was felt to be a hazard.

Pony Express

Red Buttes Pony Express Station was located a few hundred feet from here on the ridge above the river. The station was constructed for the Overland Stage and shared by the Pony Express. It was also along this north bank of the river that the first transcontinental telegraph line was built.

William "Buffalo Bill" Cody, Pony Express rider, made the longest non-stop ride from this station. Completing his own run of 116 miles between Red Buttes and Three Crossings, he found his relief rider had met an untimely death, causing Cody to ride an extra 76 miles to Rocky Ridge Station. He immediately returned from Rocky Ridge to Red Buttes, completing the route in record time.

The Astorians

John Jacob Astor's "Astorians" are often given credit for finding the "South Pass" route to Oregon territory, later crossed by thousands on the Oregon Trail. Astor sent his "Astorians" by sea and land in 1810 to establish the Pacific Fur Company at the mouth of the Columbia River. Astor's dream was to establish a Pacific base for his fur trading business that would become a cornerstone for a great new American state. He intended to break the British fur monopoly in the Pacific Northwest and bring American territory under American control.

Wilson Price Hunt with his party of "Astorians" traveled west, crossing northern Wyoming in July of 1811. Robert Stuart, a partner in the company, traveled with others by sea. Stuart later returned to New York with dispatches for Astor. It was this journey which pioneered the route over South Pass, in October of 1812.

The Platte River, being a natural travel route across Wyoming and Nebraska, was first encountered by Stuart above Bessemer Bend. Stuart's party camped near here across the river, from November 1 to November 13, 1812, planning to winter in a crude cabin they built. Fearing Indian attack, the party abandoned the cabin and proceeded down the river.

Alcove Reservoir

Stuart's Diary Describes How He Found This Place

"…we reached a considerable mountain through which the River ran 4 miles, when the Country opening, it made a large bend to the north (Bessemer Bend), to the lower end of which we went in 2 more and encamped in a beautiful bottom of Cottonwoods surrounded with a thick growth of the common Willow—Our days journey was 24 miles NE."

Many explorers, mountain men and travelers stopped here, at what they referred to as "Red Buttes". Among them were Andrew Sublette, July 30, 1834, "bound for Laramy"s Fork", John Charles Fremont in 1842, and Howard Stansbury, July 27, 1852.

The Oregon Trail & California Trails

The Oregon Trail was the major corridor of westward migration—the main street of the West from the 1830 s to 1869 when the transcontinental railroad was completed. Restless Americans from all walks of life moved west along this corridor seeking a better life in a new land. The Mormons sought freedom from religious, social and economic intolerance and aggression. For others, the lure was land available for the taking. After the discovery of gold in California in 1848, bands of feverish fortune seekers sought the buried wealth of the West. An estimated 350,000 people passed this way between 1841 and 1866 on their way to western territories. For these thousands of men, women and children, the journey was 2,000 miles of plains, deserts and mountains—-one step at a time. Their visions of personal freedom and opportunity were vital to national expansion.

The long journey to Oregon took emigrants about six months, moving 10 to 20 miles a day with their wagons, carts and packs. Time, distance and hardships seasoned the travelers much as soldiers are seasoned by a long war. Those who crossed the North Platte River at this point had already traveled nearly 775 miles, most of it near the Platte River. Howard Stansbury passed through here in July 1852 and noted the difficulties encountered by those who had passed ahead of him. He witnessed eleven broken wagons and much discarded equipment, such as blacksmith's anvils, trunks, ploughs, ovens and grindstones.

H First White Man's Cabin in Wyoming

About 2 miles west of the Bessemer Road on State Highway 220. This marker no longer exists

Approximately 2 miles northwest from here is the location of the cabin built by Robert Stuart's party of Astorians. They were enroute from Astoria to St. Louis to report to John Jacob Astor the fate of his ship, which was destroyed by Indians, and the crew killed. Stuart and six companions left Astoria June 29, 1812, and reached Wyoming in November after winter had set in. Footsore and hungry, they found game plentiful here and built a cabin. They had planned to stay until spring, but after Indians discovered their cabin, they left in the night and continued eastward down the river.

15 *Gas*

Clarks Corner

16 *Gas, Food, Lodging*

Alcova

Planning to turn it into a health resort, an eastern company named this town for the hot springs, located in some coves nearby. The resort never came to pass, even though the water was considered very medicinal, because people in Wyoming were thought to bathe only on Saturday nights. The Alcova Reservoir covered the springs in 1933, but the heated water can still be enjoyed in an artesian well below the dam.

T Alcova Reservoir and Dam

About 30 miles west of Casper on State Highway 220

Sailboarders, kayakers and water skiers extol the virtues of this somewhat windy lake 30 miles southwest of Casper. Watch for golden eagles gracing the towering pines. Although Alcova's size does not rival that of the Pathfinder of Seminoe Reservoirs, its recreational opportunities make it a "must do" when traveling in the area.

H Bates Hole Stock Trail

About five miles north of State Highway 220 on County Road 316.

Stock Driveways were established under a provision of the 1916 Stockraising Homestead Act. Local ranch operators pay for trailing privileges along the Bates Hole Stock Driveway. Trailing occurs annually between May and November, with peak use occurring in June as herds travel to summer pastures in the Deer Creek Range, and in October as they return to home winter ranges. Your courtesy and cooperation towards the users of the stock trail is appreciated.

H Gray Reef Dam and Reservoir

About 30 miles west of Casper on State Highway 220.

Constructed to regulate rather than store water. Regulation of water flow in the North Platte River is of particular importance for power production, for full benefits for fish life, water quality, municipal and industrial water and irrigation.

Gray Reef Reservoir assures that releases can be made from Alcova Powerplant according to varying needs for power. It provides river flowage with a minimum of daily fluctuation.

The reservoir can store 1,800 acre-feet of water behind the earthfill dam which is 36 feet high and 650 feet long. The outlet gates are electronically controlled from Alcova Powerplant.

H Alcova Dam and Reservoir

About 30 miles west of Casper on State Highway 220.

Alcova Dam, 10 miles downstream from Pathfinder Dam, acts as a diversion structure and creates a reservoirs from which water is diverted into the Casper Canal for irrigating the Kendrick Project lands. The dam is an earth and rockfill embankment structure 265 feet high with a crest length of 763 feet.

Additional lands downstream are irrigated by water released through the Alcova Powerplant at the base of the dam, or over a controlled spillway. The storage capacity of Alcova Reservoir is 189,000 acre feet.

H Pathfinder Dam and Reservoir

About 30 miles west of Casper on State Highway 220.

Constructed for the storage of water on the North Platte River and for irrigation purposes in eastern Wyoming and western Nebraska.

This masonry, arch, gravity-type dam, structurally 214 feet in height with a crest length of 432 feet, is made of granite quarried from nearby hills. Constructed during 1905-1909, Pathfinder Dam is one of the first dams built under the Reclamation Law.

The storage capacity of Pathfinder Reservoir is 1,016,000 acre feet.

H Fremont Canyon Powerplant

At Pathfinder Dam.

Built to take advantage of a 350-foot 'head' between Pathfinder and Alcova Reservoirs, available water is used to generate electric power. The reinforced concrete powerplant contains two 24,000-kilowatt generators. Construction features also include a conduit 18 feet in diameter and three miles in length; a surge tank 40 feet in diameter and 246 feet (24 stories) high; and a vehicular tunnel 17 feet in diameter and 1,700 feet long for access to the powerplant.

H Alcova Reservoir

About 30 miles west of Casper on State Highway 220.

Alcova Reservoir, below you, created by Alcova Dam constructed by the Bureau of Reclamation and completed in 1938, is on the North Platte River .The reservoir is four miles long, has 2,500 acre surface area, and a normal water surface elevation of 5,500 feet. Water from this reservoir is diverted into Casper Canal for irrigating Kendrick Project lands.

Casper Canal with a capacity of 600 cubic feet per second, is 62 miles long and serves 201 miles of laterals and sub-laterals.

The principal crops grown on the 24,000 irrigable acres are corn, alfalfa and feed grains.

Lake shore Drive, 2 miles back, provides a more complete view of beautiful Alcova reservoir There you will find boat launching ramps, fishing, swimming areas, and picnic and camping sites.

H Pathfinder Cemetery

About one mile north of Pathfinder Dam

Seven grave sites dating from 1905 to 1912 are located in this tiny cemetery. Barney Flynn and Clint Moor, workers on the Pathfinder Dam, died February 9, 1912, in a construction accident. Five men were working on the concrete ladderway on the south side of the canyon when a tram cable directly above them gave way. As the cable fell it knocked the men from their scaffolding to the bottom of the canyon killing them.

The other graves are of residents of the area. The farthest to the right is that of infant Leslie Wolf(e) who died from eating poison meant for coyotes.

17 *No services*

T Martin's Cove

Just south of Independence Rock on Highway 220. 328-2953

A Mormon handcart company under the leadership of Edward Martin sought shelter from an early winter blizzard in a small cove in the flank of the Sweetwater Rocks about two miles west of Devil's Gate. The Martin Handcart Company, the last handcart expedition to attempt the Trail in 1856, forded the North Platte River near Red Buttes on October 19 and fought snow, wind and sub-zero temperatures to reach this place in early November. Rescuers sent from Salt Lake City found the company, "in perishing condition." The camp grounds became grave yards as the Martin Company buried their dead. Perhaps as many as 145 of the 576 members of the company froze or starved to death. (Access from the Sun Ranch at Devils Gate. Hiking is required with special consideration for handicapped access. Interpretation provided by the BLM and LDS Church.) *Source: BLM brochure.*

Mormon Pioneer Journals

On April 5, 1847, the vanguard of The Church of Jesus Christ of Latter-day Saints, the Mormons, headed west to the Great Basin. The pioneer company of 148 people, led by Brigham Young, was seeking the best route across the Rocky Mountains into the Valley of the Great Salt Lake. After years of violence and persecution in the Midwest, the Mormons sought an isolated area where they could permanently settle and practice their religion in peace. The Great Basin became their chosen "Zion."

The wagons pulled out of Winter Quarters (present-day North Omaha) and ascended the broad valley of the Platte River, traveling across Nebraska to Fort Laramie. Waiting at the fort to join the vanguard company were "Mississippi Saints," who had wintered over in Pueblo, Colorado, with Mormon Battalion members from the "Sick Detachments."

The pioneers followed the North Platte and Sweetwater Rivers across Wyoming to the crest of the continent at South Pass and descended to the Green River, where they were joined by a small group of Mormon Battalion members. This enlarged party traveled on to Fort Bridger, on Blacks Fork, arriving on July 7, 1847. They tarried at this "shabby" fort only long enough to do some trading and repair wagons.

The articles generally at Bridger's fort were at least one-third or one-half higher than at any other post in America that I ever saw.
-Wilford Woodruff

They now left the well-traveled Oregon-California Trail, which swung sharply northwest, following the faint, year-old track of the Donner-Reed party west-southwest along the Hastings Cutoff and into Echo Canyon.

There is a very singular echo in this ravine, the rattling of the wagons resembles carpenters hammering on boards inside the highest rocks.
-William Clayton

The final 116 miles from Fort Bridger, across the Wasatch Mountains, were the most difficult of the entire trip. Travel through the narrow willow-choked canyons and over the rocky crest of the Wasatch was so difficult that it took the pioneer company 14 days to complete this part of the journey.

Counselled the company not to go any further until they had spent several hours labour on the road over which we passed yesterday afternoon: all who were able to work laboured about two thirds of the day on the same.
-Orson Pratt

Crossed Canyon Creek 8 times—the road sideling, stumpy, bushy, etc.
-Eliza R. Snow

Orson Pratt led an advance party over Big Mountain and down Emigration Canyon, entering the valley on July 22, 1847. By the time Brigham Young, delayed by illness, entered the valley on July 24, the first crops were already in the ground.

On arriving there was much cheered by a handsome view of the Great Salt Lake.
-William Clayton

This forenoon commenced planing our potatoes, after which we turned the water upon them and gave them quite a soaking.
-Orson Pratt, July 24, 1847

In later years, this route from Fort Bridger to the Valley of the Great Salt Lake became a fundamental part of the wagon road to the Utah settlements and California. Emigrants headed to Oregon, by way of the Salt Lake Cutoff, argonauts seeking their fortunes in the California gold fields, and Pony Express riders galloping through on their way to Sacramento, California, or St. Joseph, Missouri, all passed along this route.

In Their Own Words

I rigged up my trout rod that I had brought with me from Liverpool, fixed my reel, & artificial fly & went to one of the brooks close by Camp to try my luck at catching trout ….
-Wilford Woodruff, 8 July, 1847

The power of the air rules and the dust is worse than intollerable.
-Eliza R. Snow, 24 September 1847

The day has been hot and sultery, and mosquitos are very troublesom…
-William Clayton, 13 July 1847

Very, very dirty thro brush & timber - up the Mt. where we met J.T who asked me if I had lately seen my face, his own being behind a black mask - we then went slash mash down over stumps, trees, etc, etc.
-Eliza R. Snow, 1 October 1847

The grass on this creek grows from six to twelve feet high… many signs of deer, antelope, and bears.
-William Clayton, 22 July 1847

…and beholding in a moment such as extensive scenery open before us, we could not refrain from a shout of joy which almost involuntarily escaped from our lips the moment this grand and lovely scenery was within our view.
-Orson Pratt, July 21, 1847

Hurra, hurra, hurra, there's my home at last!
-Thomas Bullock, 24 July 1847

Excerpted from brochure produced by Utah Historic Trails Consortium

T Mormon Handcart Visitor Center: National Historic Trail

55 miles southwest of Casper on Highway 220

This site commemorates the courage and suffering of Mormon pioneers who pulled their belongings in handcarts across the plains and mountains to avoid persecution in the East. The Visitor Center provides a host of information, from historic artifacts and pioneer journals to Family History Research assistance, and more. Visitors can also try their hand at pulling a cart along the trail once traversed by some of these pioneers.

Independence Rock

T Independence Rock

About 35 miles south of Casper on State Highway 220

The Register Of the Desert

This granite monolith is one of the more famous landmarks along the Oregon Trail and has served as a meeting place since the area was first inhabited.

Independence Rock was an important place for the Indians who first lived here. This giant igneous formation of feldspar and mica found its way into many native legends, and later, into the diaries of many westbound pioneers.

The first Europeans to visit the rock were members of Robert Stuart's expedition in 1812. It is Stuart who is generally credited with discovery of the route, which became known as the Oregon Trail. Stuart's diary indicated that he visited the site on October 30, 1812.

Stuart, however, did not name this giant rock. That honor is credited to William Sublette, who held an Independence Day celebration here on July 4, 1830, as he led the first wagon train to cross the new overland route. Before an audience of 80 pioneers, he christened the rock in honor of the birth date of our nation.

Independence Rock is most famous for the names inscribed on its face—the names and dates of people who passed by this place in search of a new life in the frontier.

Named for a fur trader's Fourth of July celebration, this huge rock became the most famous and anticipated of all trail landmarks. Here the trail met the cool, clean and clear Sweetwater River that would lead it to South Pass. The emigrants paused to inscribe their names on the "Great Register of the Desert" while they rested themselves and their livestock. They observed the national Independence Day (no matter the actual date) and congratulated themselves on reaching the perceived mid-point in their journey. Described by most as "looking like a great beached whale…," the Rock is now the site of a modern Highway Rest Area and State Interpretative Site.

It was the names carved in stone here that caused Father Peter J. DeSmet to appropriately name this place "The Register of the Desert" in 1840.

As you walk around the rock, you will see hundreds of names carved or chipped into the surface. Possibly one of the earliest signatures to be found here is that of "M.K. Hugh, 1824." Other early names include "Hanna Snow, 1844," "G. Gingham, 1846," "J. Bower, 1847," "Milo Ayer, age 29, 1849," "W.H. Collins, July 4, 1862," and "V.D. Moody, July 24, 1849."

The Names

Today, many names can still be found on this magnificent rock, although erosion and time have obliterated a good share of the pioneer's signatures. Just imagine what this rock must have looked like to Lydia Allen Rudd with signatures of travelers like herself:

"July 5, 1852 Came to independence rock about ten oclock this morning I presume there are a million of names wrote on this rock …"

Travelers climbed this rock not only to scrawl or carefully engrave their names on the surface, but many read it as if it were a lengthy letter written by their long absent friends or relatives. Although circumstances are quite different today, many of us will do this very same thing. We will climb the rock hoping to locate a name we learned in school or perhaps even a family name.

Lydia goes on to write:

"I saw my husbands name that he put on in 1849…"

She passed through this area three years after her husband. By locating his name here, she knew he had survived, at least to Independence Rock. What a wonderful feeling that must have been!

Only the greatest of imaginations can conjure up a realistic feeling of these terrible hardships experienced by so many. But the emigrant's most certain and greatest challenge, above all else, was that of staying alive.

Many who traveled this route, however, did not make it this far. There are some 39,000 emigrant graves out in these wide-open spaces along the trail, marked and, unmarked, with the largest percentage dying of cholera.

The Mormon Pioneer Trail

The initial movement of the Mormons from Nauvoo, Illinois, to the valley of the Great Salt Lake occurred in two segments—one in 1846 and one in 1847.

The first leg of the journey across Iowa to the Missouri River covered around 265 miles.

The second leg, from the Missouri River to the valley of the Great Salt Lake covered about 1,032 miles. The second leg of the journey began on April 5, 1847 and ended on July 24, 1847.

This part of the trip went smoother than the previous year's journey due to better organization, better provisions and beginning when the trail conditions were optimal. The lead pioneer party left with 148 people (143 men, 3 women and 2 young boys), 72 wagons, 93 horses, 66 oxen, 52 mules, 19 cows, 17 dogs, and some chickens.

This hand-picked group was organized into two large divisions and further split into companies of 50 and 10. This organizational structure was based on Brigham Young's plan for migrating West and included details on camp behavior and devotional practices to be followed.

At Fort Laramie the Mormons crossed to the south side of the river and joined the Oregon Trail. At Fort Bridger State Historic Site, they struck out on their own and followed the faint year-old tracks of the ill-fated Donner-Reed party.

The last 116 miles took 14 days to complete and were very demanding due to difficult terrain, weary travelers, worn wagons and weakened livestock. Upon arriving at the Valley, this first party began planting late crops, laying out streets, building shelters and preparing for winter. Mormon emigrants continued to arrive during the remaining weeks of summer and fall. Approximately 1,650 people spent their first winter in the valley. The next 20 years would see 70,000 Mormons traveling by wagon and handcarts over the Mormon Pioneer Trail.

Woodchoppers Jamboree and Rodeo

During the third week in June chain saws, axes, hand saws and loggers create plenty of action, along with bulls, broncs and cowboys. They all come together in Encampment for a unique two-day event full of activity and excitement. Starting on Friday night with a melodrama and continuing after Saturday morning's parade, the action gets under way with the woodchopping events. Events include axe throwing, pole throwing, log bucking, axe chopping, team and two-man cross-cutting and chainsaw contests, followed by a barbeque. The Wyoming Professional Rodeo sanctioned rodeo follows with a full slate of events including calf roping, team roping, break-away roping, barrel racing, bareback riding, saddle bronc, bull riding and steer wrestling. Saturday night brings casino night and dances throughout town. Get some rest though, Sunday brings the second day of both the woodchopping and rodeo events.

Rock Hard Facts

Independence Rock stands 6,028 feet (1,808.3 m) above sea level. The tallest point of the rock is 136 feet (40.8 m) above the surrounding terrain. If one were to walk around the base of this rock, the distance covered would be more than a mile, or 5,900 feet (1.8 km). The mass of Independence Rock is equal to an area of 24.81 acres (9.924 ha).

Many people believe that the shape of this highly polished round outcropping was created by glaciers. Not so. A process known to geologists as "exfoliation" is how the rock came to have its sleek and round form.

As Independence Rock was slowly uncovered by erosion, the immense pressures of the weight of overlying rock were gradually lessened. The rock then expanded outwardly shedding its surface layers like an onion. Layers of granite broke off, one after the other and formed the rounded shape you see today.

Windblown sand and silt have grooved the rock and polished it to a high gloss in a process called "windfaceting." It is because of this smooth surface that the pioneers were able to easily carve their names into the rock.

A Popular Stop

Trappers, emigrants, traders, religious leaders and followers, and just about everybody else who passed this way, stopped, walked around and allover this turtleshell-like outcropping of granite. That means that just about every person of the 550,000 or so now estimated to have used the Oregon Trail marveled at this uni ue formation. If it's July 4th, We're on time!

Each wagon train heading West tried to time its start so the spring grass would be sufficient to support the animals, without delaying too long to risk the early snows in the mountains. Conse quently, everyone was on the trail at the same time. The emigrants used the race to arrive at the rock by the Fourth of July. A huge celebration would then take place upon their arrival with sounds of gunfire, boisterous drinking, and patriotic oration.

New Beginnings

The sense of freedom, of new opportunities and of new beginnings must have been overpowering at times to the emigrants. Many chose to stay behind for a short time and build small communities along the route, one of which was here at the rock. These small communities, each one crowded, transitory, and unsanitary, came complete with its own graveyard.

Today, it is hard to believe this area once held such a community. With the passage of time, all traces of the "town" have been obliterated, recapturing the innocence of this area before the mass migration began, when the grasses were tall and the natives roamed these parts.

Trail Ruts

About ten miles north of Muddy Gap, on the north side of the highway, the ruts of the Oregon Trail are etched onto the solid cap rock and are visible from the highway. They are located on private property, but can easily be seen from your vehicle.

Devil's Gate and Split Rock

Just to the west of here are several more prominent natural features that were used as trail guides by the emigrants. As you follow Wyoming 220 South, to your right you will notice the Sweetwater River making an abrupt turn. At the point where the river flows through a granite ridge is the location of Devil's Gate. The river here has cut a chasm 330 feet (99 m) deep. It is 400 feet (120 m) wide at the top, but only 30 feet (9m) wide at the bottom!

Devil's Gate

There is a scenic turnout on the right side of the road a few miles south of Independence Rock. This turnout provides an excellent opportunity to view the Devil's Gate and the Sun Ranch. A few miles further south of this turnout you will see signs for the Sun Ranch. This is a one way road to your right that will lead you a few miles to the Sun Ranch headquarters. The Sun Ranch is a historic Wyoming ranch owned and operated by the Sun family for over 100 years. Recently the Mormon Church purchased the property as an interpretive center for this section of the Mormon Trail. Historic markers for the Pony Express, Oregon and California trails are located here as well as an excellent trail rut.

Of particular interest is the tragic story of the Willy/Martin Handcart Company. A stop at the Sun Ranch is certainly worth while. You will also find not only well informed but also very friendly folks on hand to make you feel welcome and answer your questions.

Twenty miles (32 km) south of Independence Rock is the Muddy Gap intersection. Turn north on Wyoming 789/U.S. Highway 287 and eight miles down the road (12.8 km) you will find another famous landmark known as Split Rock. Its summit elevation is 7,305 feet (2,191 m). The notch resembles a gun sight when viewed from either the east or west and it is visible for more than 50 miles.

Enjoy Your Visit, But Please Follow These Rules

Many of the travelers left their names on this rock, either carved or painted in axle grease. We ask you as modern day travelers to help us protect this historic landmark. Walk around the site and even on top to appreciate the view the pioneers would have seen as they passed through this area. But please do not take away the historical significance of this site by placing your signature on the rock or destroying the ones that are still visible. It's up to all of us to help save what remains here for future generations to appreciate and enjoy.

Park rules

- No defacing or writing on the rock.
- No gathering of artifacts (anything found must be left there or turned over to State Park personnel on site.)
- Metal detectors are not allowed.
- The discharge of firearms and fireworks is prohibited.
- Vehicle parking in designated areas only.
- Dogs, cats and other pets must be kept on a leash.
- No killing of wildlife, including rattlesnakes.
- Please pack out your own trash.
- Overnight camping by Special Use permit only.

Site Hours: open year 'round, sunrise to sunset. daily.

Reprinted from Wind River Country Brochure. and Wyoming State Parks and Historic Sites Brochure

T Devil's Gate

At interpretive site on State Highway 220 about 12 miles northeast of Muddy Gap

Devil's Gate is a narrow cleft carved by the Sweetwater River through a ridge called the Sweetwater Rocks-370 feet deep, 1,500 feet long, and only 50 feet wide in places.

Devil's Gate is among the more interesting geographical landmarks along the emigrant trails. This natural feature became visible approximately 15 miles to the east. The gorge was impassable to

Wyoming Tidbits

In 1874 a railroad car filled from the Rawlins red paint mines headed east, where its cargo was used to paint the Brooklyn Bridge.

Section 5

Steamboat Lake

wagons, and the trail passed to the south of the ridge, but this dark, gloomy canyon intrigued the emigrants. Many camped here, and almost all took the detour to inspect the gorge.

Osborne Cross recorded his delight on July 10, 1949. "This gap is truly wonderful, being a space not over twenty yards wide and about five hundred feet high, having very much the appearance of being chiseled out by the hand of man rather then the work of nature." More than 20 graves are thought to be located in the immediate vicinity, although only one is marked, and many emigrant inscriptions can still be found on the rock walls of the gorge.

This remarkable cleft in the east end of the Sweetwater Rocks drew diary comments from many pioneers. Many walked and waded in the Sweetwater River through the gorge while their wagons followed the trail through the pass to the east, a route now followed by an access road to the historic Sun Ranch. A BLM interpretive site is located just south of the Gate giving details of the long and colorful history of the area.
Source: National Park Service and BLM brochure.

T Pathfinder Reservoir and Dam

30 miles southwest of Casper on State Highway 220, onto County Rd. 409 for 10 miles

Pathfinder, the first dam in eastern Wyoming, is near the junction of the Sweetwater and North Platte Rivers. Much of the irrigation water supplied by the reservoir flows into Nebraska, but the dam itself was considered an engineering marvel when completed in 1909. The 214-foot granite structure is held together with cement, and steel was hauled in wagon teams from Casper. The dam is listed on the National Register of Historic Places.

The reservoir is a popular fishing spot with both locals and travelers. The crystalline blue waters are home to trout and walleye. The area also boasts some of Woming's best sailing and windsurfers take advantage of the consistent winds.

T Pathfinder Interpretive Center

30 miles southwest of Casper on State Highway 220, to County Road 409 for 10 miles

This quaint old stone building was once the home of the Pathfinder Dam tender; now it houses an assortment of exhibits and informative signs. Open in the summer on Saturday from 11-5 and Sunday 10-4.

H Steamboat Lake Interpretive Signs

Just north of Independence Rock Rest Area on State Highway 220

Riparian Habitat

Green band of life

Riparian vegetation, which is found along streams, rivers, lakes, and reservoirs, is more abundant and stays green longer than the vegetation characteristic of the drier uplands. Both waterfowl and songbirds depend on food and shelter provided by this plentiful vegetation that grows in and near the water.

Sedges, small grass-like plants, together with cattails and bulrushes, are often found in riparian areas. The riparian vegetation along the shores of Steamboat Lake provides important shelter and food for many bird species. Can you spot any birds along the shoreline?

Alkali Flat

A snow-lined lake in summer

Do you see a white ring around Steamboat Lake? During spring when water levels are high, wildlife can be seen in the early morning and late evening hours drinking at the water's edge. As the water level drops in late summer, glistening salts of alkaline deposits look much like snow along the shoreline. During this time, shorebirds and waterfowl continue to use the lake, but other wildlife need to look for fresh water.

Where do you think the animals go to find water if Steamboat Lake dries up in late summer? They might enjoy the cool waters of nearby Pathfinder Reservoir or its tributaries, the North Platte and Sweetwater Rivers.

Sagebrush Overflights

Soaring above the sage

Bird species such as Sage Grouse, Sage Sparrow, and Sage Thrasher are entirely dependent on healthy sagebrush habitat for meeting their life needs. These birds return the favor by spreading plant seeds and preying on insects.

The Prairie Falcon, American Kestrel, and Golden Eagle look for food within the healthy sagebrush habitat. They often prey upon small mammals, snakes, and other birds.

Sagebrush Critters

There's more out there than meets the eye!

Hidden in the sagebrush habitat is a variety of wildlife species. They include the swift pronghorn antelope, the chattering Richardson's ground squirrel, the slithering prairie rattlesnake, and the wily coyote.

Healthy sagebrush habitat includes young and old sagebrush stands, together with grassland openings. This habitat, referred to as a mosaic of vegetation, provides the proper mix of grasses and shrubs for sagebrush-dependent species to survive.

Steamboat Lake

Reservoir of life

This wetland provides a temporary resting place for many species of waterfowl, shorebirds, and songbirds. The wetland's water supply comes from seasonal springs and snowmelt, but by late summer, the water level recedes and the lake may even dry up.

Some of the migratory birds stay long enough to breed and raise their young here. Can you spot the man-made structures along the shoreline? These elevated platforms allow ducks and geese to nest above the reach of hungry foxes, weasels, coyotes, and raccoons.

Pathfinder National Wildlife Refuge

A safe haven for birds

Birds traveling long distances need to stop and rest along the way to gather strength for continuing their journey. Located in several parcels along the shores of Pathfinder Reservoir. Pathfinder National Wildlife Refuge (NWR) provides an important nesting area for migratory birds during their annual spring and fall migrations.

The National Audobon Society has joined with the partners listed below to ensure that this Refuge continues to provide a safe haven for migratory birds. Local citizens are helping to monitor the condition of the Refuge by surveying bird numbers and species. This information will tell us about the health of both the birds and the habitat on which they depend on their life needs.

How can you get involved in the Pathfinder conservation effort? Contact Wyoming Audubon at 235-3485 or your local Audobon Chapter for more information.

Migratory bird species in North America generally follow one of four migration routes known as "flyway." Pathfinder NWR is located within the Central Flyway. Birds stop to feed, nest, and breed near the Refuge waters. Can you spot Canada geese, mallards, and western grebes on the lake below?

You can discover the importance of three habitat types found on the Refuge by following the short pathway along the rim overlooking Steamboat Lake.

T Seminoe Reservoir and Dam

About 5 miles south of Pathfinder Reservoir

More than one million acre-feet of water is retained by this 295-foot-high concrete arch. completed in 1939, this is the farthest upstream of the North Platte dams. The reservoir winds through rugged pine-sprinkled mountains and white sand dunes. Horseshoe Ridge, a 500-foot cliff visible on the eastern shore of the reservoir, provides a ready subject for photographers.

The area has two state park developed campgrounds along its northwest shore, open from April through October.

Fish for trout and walleye, or hook on your water skis and enjoy this scenic recreational area.

T Seminoe State Park

About 5 miles south of Pathfinder Reservoir

History

The Seminoe Mountains around Seminoe State Park were once the site for gold prospecting during the late 1800s. The name "Seminoe" is commonly assumed to come from the Seminole tribe, but is an Americanized spelling of the French name Cimineau. Basil Cimineau Lajeunesse was a French trapper in the area in the 1800s.

Seminoe State Park, located on the northwest side of the reservoir, was established in 1965 through an agreement between the U.S. Bureau of Reclamation and the Wyoming Recreation Commission (predecessor to Wyoming State Parks and Historic Sites).

Facts & Figures

Seminoe Dam was completed April 1, 1939. The dam is a concrete arch construction and contains 210,000 cubic yards of concrete. It is 295 feet high, 530 feet long, 15 feet wide at the top, and 85 feet wide at the bottom. The crest elevation is 6,361 feet. The reservoir has 180 miles of shoreline and a reservoir capacity of 1,017,279 acre feet of water.

Wildlife

Wyoming wildlife is at its finest in and near Seminoe State Park. Patient visitors will be rewarded with a variety of creatures passing by—big horn sheep, elk, moose, mule deer, antelope, coyote, mountain lion, bobcat, fox, raccoon, skunk, jack rabbit and cottontail rabbit. Bird watchers may glimpse the American or Bald Eagle plus several types of waterfowl. Bring your binoculars, sit back and enjoy!

Fishing

Good river fishing can be found along the North Platte River from I-80 at Fort Fred Steele State Historic Site all the way to the Gray Reef Area below Alcova Dam. In between lies the famous "Miracle Mile," well- known for its blue ribbon fishing.

Seminoe Reservoir offers some great fishing, particularly in June and July, for both trout and walleye. Both species inhabit the entire reservoir though there are areas of greater concentration for each. State record walleye have been pulled from Seminoe in years past.

Fishing licenses are required and may be purchased at—Seminoe: The Seminoe Boat Club; Rawlins: Bi-Rite Drug Store & Sporting Goods and Trails West Taxidermy; Muddy Gap: Three Forks Muddy Gap Service (gas station); and Miracle Mile: Miracle Mile Ranch.

H Devil's Gate Interpretive Signs

At interpretive site on State Highway 220 about 12 miles northeast of Muddy Gap.

Esther Hobart Morris

Esther Hobart McQuigg was born in 1812 in the state of New York. Orphaned at the age of 14, she supported herself as a milliner until, at age 28, she married Artemus Slack, a civil engineer. Mr. Slack died not long after the marriage, leaving Esther with an infant son. She moved to Peru, Illinois in 1842, where she married John Morris, a merchant. In 1869 Mrs. Morris, along with twin sons, moved to South Pass City in the newly created Wyoming Territory, joining her husband who had opened a saloon there the previous year.

Mrs. Morris has been widely acclaimed as an influential figure in the events that established women's suffrage in Wyoming. However, her role in promoting suffrage legislation in the territory has been disputed. The record shows that in 1869, during the territory's first legislative session, William H. Bright introduced a women's suffrage bill. Although the legislation was received with some humor, it did pass and was signed into law by Governor John A. Campbell, thus according the young territory immediate fame as the first government to grant women the right to vote in all public elections.

Shortly after the legislative session, in February 1870, Wyoming achieved another "first" when three women were appointed to serve as justices of the peace. Esther Morris was selected to complete the term of the South Pass City justice, who had resigned. She is the only one of the three appointees known to have served, thereby winning accord as the first woman to hold a judicial position. Mrs. Morris served 81/2 months and handled 26 cases in a manner that was considered a credit to her position. In later years, following first separation from then death of her husband, Ms. Morris lived with her sons. She appeared at a number of women's rights gatherings and political affairs, though she was apparently not comfortable with making speeches. She died in 1902 in Cheyenne, Wyoming.

Mrs. Morris eventually became a symbol for the women's rights movement, and stories of her independent attitudes and support of women's issues have been circulated. As for the question of who was the main force behind the Women's Suffrage Act in Wyoming, the verifiable record favors William H. Bright, who introduced the bill. A story that Mrs. Morris had obtained a promise from Bright, also a South Pass City resident, at a tea party to introduce the suffrage bill surfaced decades after the fact and has been commonly repeated. Though this story and any direct involvement by Mrs. Morris in the drafting and introduction of the suffrage bill cannot be substantiated, Esther Morris is commonly regarded as one of the heroines of the women's suffrage movement. Her name became synonymous with equal rights, fame which led to her being chosen as Wyoming's representative in Statuary Hall in the Capitol Building in Washington, D.C. Her statue was presented in ceremonies at the Capitol in 1960.

Larson, T.A. History of Wyoming, 2nd edition, revised. University of Nebraska Press, 1978.

Courtesy of Wyoming State Archives

Sun Ranch

In front of you is the Sun Ranch, one of the first large open range ranches in Wyoming. The original ranch building, which today makes up part of the Mormon Handcart Visitor Center, was contructed in 1872.

Tom de Beau Soleil (a French Canadian name later anglicized to "Sun") came to Wyoming after the Civil War. He worked as a trapper and as a military scout with William "Buffalo Bill" Cody. He also cut railroad ties under a contract with the Union Pacific Railroad. The 1872 cabin was used as headquarters for a successful ranching and hunting guide business. It later became the "Hub and Spoke Ranch," with operations extending well into the Great Divide Basin. The Sun Ranch is a Registered National Historic Landmark.

Portions of the Sun Ranch were acquired by the Church of Jesus Christ of Latter-day Saints in 1997. The visitor center, constructed mostly by volunteer labor, opened its doors in the spring of 1997 as part of the celebration of the 150th anniversary of the 1847 Mormon Pioneer wagon train.

A Tribute to Hardship

Thousands of pioneers journeyed over 1,000 miles to reach this point. Illness and death were common. Everywhere along the trail people died and were buried.

It is estimated that one out of ten emigrants who started on the trail died before completing the trip. Roughly 90 percent of the deaths were caused by disease, the rest were from childbirth, accidents, and violence. In the late 1840s and early 1850s, cholera was reaching epidemic proportions on the trails. Cholera is caught by drinking tainted water. Symptoms include high fever, vomiting, and dehydration. In a few instances, almost entire wagon companies were wiped out by cholera's incredibly painful and rapid death.

Buried on this ridge, safe from trampling feet and iron-wheeled wagons, are over 20 known American Indian and emigrant graves.

The Emigrant Road

The Oregon Trail passed over the ridge to the east of Devil's Gate, Good grass, water and the shelter of the hills made this a popular campsite.

Explorer Brevet-Captain John C. Fremont, 1842:

"In about three miles, we reached the entrance of a kanyon where where the Sweet Water issues upon the more open valley we had passed over. The usual road passes to the right of this place…Wilderness and disorder were the character of the scenery…"

Oregon emigrant James Mathers stopped here July, 1846, and wrote:

"…encamped above the pass of the river, between high rocks. This is the most interesting sight we have met with on our journey."

Later, the Mormon Pioneer Trail and the California and Pony Express Trails came over this same ridge. Some 500,000 emigrants followed the Trail west. Many travellers called it the Emigrant Road.

THE 1856 HANDCART DISASTER

Cholera, childbirth, Indian attack, drowning at river crossings, accidents, even cannibalism. There were lots of ways for emigrants to die on western trails in the 1800s. However, mother nature was perhaps the most efficient killer of all. The largest, single disaster ever recorded on the Mormon Pioneer Trail, befell two parties of Mormon converts who were pulling handcarts in the late fall of 1856, and this time, it was weather that was the grim reaper.

The Mormon Exodus of 1846-47 to Utah Territory was only the beginning of emigrant travel on the overland route or the Mormon Trail to Utah. Thousands of converts followed in succeeding years. Besides religious freedom, moving to Zion offered the hope and opportunity of economic freedom, especially for displaced and poverty-stricken victims of Europe's industrial revolution.

Moving from Europe to Utah was expensive and not all converts had the money so the Latter Day Saints Church's Perpetual Emigration Fund financed expenses for tens of thousands of eager overseas emigrants.

A grasshopper plague descended on Utah in 1855 and funds were short. So, an earlier plan, which cut expenses for emigrants was given the go-ahead and the great handcart treks of 1856-1860 were underway. Instead of large wagons, handcarts held lighter loads and were pulled by humans, thus replacing expensive wagons and draft animals.

Almost 4,400 converts arrived in the United States during the winter 1855-56. They landed at New York and went by train to Iowa City, Iowa – the outfitting and jumping off point. The first three handcart "companies" of 1856 made it to Salt Lake without major incident. They paralleled the Missouri River from Iowa City to Florence, Nebraska; from there they followed the Platte and North Platte Rivers into Wyoming Territory to Fort Laramie. They continued on the "river road" following the Sweetwater to South Pass. From here, they went to Fort Bridger and on to Salt Lake, traveling part of the Hastings' Cutoff which the ill-fated Donner Party took in 1846.

The Willie Company (fourth) and the Martin Company (fifth) groups of handcart pullers ran into the same problem the Donners did—snow. The 500 people making up the Willie Company left Florence, Nebraska on August 18th, 1856 followed by 576 people in the Martin Company on August 25th, who were in turn followed by 385 people in the Hodgett Wagon Train.

The last half of August is much too late to travel hundreds of miles overland by wagon or by foot through Wyoming's high plains and expect to reach Salt Lake before the snow flies. Winter comes early and fast in the mountains and higher elevations around South Pass.

In fact, the Willie Company had a general vote at Florence and with the exception of one clearthinking man named Levi Savage, voted to continue on to Zion. For a lot of bad reasons, which were hotly debated later, over 1,000 emigrants continued their journey flying in the face of common sense and impending winter.

A fast-traveling group of Mormon missionary organizers who were headed west to Salt Lake overtook the Willie and Martin Companies. Although the missionaries had traveled the Trail themselves at least once east to west and back again, they encouraged the emigrants to press on, knowing what hardships could be in store for them. The missionary leader, Franklin D. Richards, purchased 100 buffalo robes at Fort Laramie and left instructions for them to be distributed to the emigrants upon their arrival. The missionaries continued to Salt Lake at good speed and arrived on October 1st. Richards immediately met with Mormon leader Brigham Young to apprise him of the situation.

In the meantime, early winter storms blasted eastern Wyoming and the cold, exposure, overwork, short rations, and bad decisions began to take their toll.

One man in the Willie Company, John Chislett, recorded ...*Cold weather, scarcity of food, lassitude and fatigue from over-exertion, soon produced their effects. Our old and infirm people began to droop, and they no sooner lost spirit and courage than death's stamp could be traced upon their features. Life went out as smoothly as a lamp ceases to burn when the oil is gone. At first the deaths occurred slowly and irregularly, but in a few days at more frequent intervals, until we soon thought it unusual to leave a campground without burying one or more persons.*

The Martin Company was several days and miles east of the Willie Company, and were in an even worse predicament than the others when the bad weather hit. Members of the Martin Company had made several serious errors in judgement, such as crossing a freezing river on foot rather than pay the toll even though they had the money, and by throwing away the buffalo robes purchased for them at Fort Laramie because they were too heavy to pull in the handcarts.

Once the emigrants realized their mistakes, it was too late to do anything about them. They hoped that help was on the way from Salt Lake, several hundred miles away. However, courage, stout hearts and their faith in God, didn't stop winter's relentless grip or the grim reaper's visits to their camps. Their journey to Zion had turned into a death march. For a lot of reasons—some good, some bad—and a bit of plain old bad luck, about 1,000 people were trapped on the high plains of Wyoming in danger of dying to the last man, woman and child.

By early October, the story of the Willie and Martin Handcart Companies had become three separate stories—the plight of the Willie Company east of South Pass; the Martin Company, who were even further east between Fort Laramie and Devil's Gate; and, the rescue efforts originating out of Salt Lake City.

When Brigham Young got word of the state of the handcart pilgrims on the eve of the Mormon Church's semi-annual conference, he wasted no time making a decision. Addressing members of the church, Young called for immediate action in no uncertain terms, ...*It is to save the people. This is the salvation I am now seeking for. To save our brethren that would be apt to perish, or suffer extremely, if we do not send them assistance. I shall call upon the Bishops this day. I shall not wait until tomorrow, nor until the next day, for 60 good mule teams and 12 or 15 wagons. I do not want to send oxen. I want good horses and mules...*

In addition to teams, supplies, and food, Brigham called for *40 good young men who know how to drive teams, to take charge of the teams that are now managed by men, women, and children who know nothing about them...*

By October 7th, the first rescue group left Salt Lake consisting of "16 good four-mule teams and 27 hardy young men headed eastward with the first installment of provisions." The people in Salt Lake realized the magnitude of the situation and kept a steady stream of wagons, supplies, and help headed east. By the end of October some 250 teams were on the road.

One member of the first rescue group, Harvey Cluff, recorded later, ... *Nine miles brought us down to the Sweetwater River where we camped for the night. On arising in the following morning snow was several inches deep. During the two following days, the storm raged with increasing fury until it attained the capacity of a northern blizzard. For protection of ourselves and animals, the company moved down the river to where the willows were dense enough to make a good protection against the raging storm from the north. The express team had been dispatched ahead as rapidly as possible to reach and give encouragement to the faultering emigrants, by letting them know that help was near at hand.*

The original 500 people making up the Willie Company were no longer 500. As they struggled westward on the Trail, each morning there were fresh corpses to bury. Captain Willie had left his charges and pressed on ahead to find the help he knew was on the way. Back at camp, John Chislett described the situation, ...*The weather grew colder every day, and many got their feet so badly frozen that they could not walk, and had to be lifted from place to place. Some got their fingers frozen; others their ears; and one woman lost her sight by the frost. These severities of the weather also increased our number of deaths, so that we buried several each day.*

On October 21, the first rescuers arrived and in Chislett's words, *Shouts of joy rent the air; strong men wept till tears ran freely down their furrowed and sun-burnt cheeks...Restraint was set aside in the general rejoicing, and as the brethren entered our camp the sisters fell upon them and deluged them with kisses.*

Half of the rescuers pressed on ahead to find the Martin Company while the remaining half reinforced the Willie Company people and got them on their way. By no means was their ordeal over, in fact, a few days later, while camped on present-day Rock Creek east of Atlantic City, 15 people died in a single 24-hour period and were buried in two graves.

The Willie Company continued their struggle west, meeting the supply trains headed east. They made to it Salt Lake City on November 9th. One individual story, though, stands out and embodies the determination and true grit of the emigrants.

One young Scotch woman—Margret Dalglish—continued to pull her handcart despite offers to load her meager possessions in a wagon and ride in relative comfort to Salt Lake. She toiled her way through snow and cold until she came to the overlook of the Salt Lake Valley. Seeing the end of her journey of thousands of miles from Scotland, she took her handcart loaded with all her earthly goods, pushed it over a cliff, and proudly walked into the valley owning only the clothes on her back.

The Willie Company's arrival in Salt Lake was cause for a huge celebration before harsh reality set in. Of the original 500 who had set out for Salt Lake, 67 were dead, and many other's had lost fingers or entire limbs to frostbite. And worse yet, over half the emigrants were still somewhere out on the plains in serious trouble.

The last of the handcart emigrants of 1856, the Martin Company and the Hodgett Wagon Train, were in dire straits by October. Winter had struck with a vengeance. Clothing was short, rations were shorter, people were dying of exposure, and hundreds of miles still loomed between them and safety. It was fast becoming a matter of logistics – getting enough provisions to hundreds of people facing extinction.

One of the rescuers, Harvey Cluff wrote, *On arriving at Devils Gate we found the express men awating (sic) our coming up, for as yet they had no word as to where the companies were. Here we were in a dilemma. Four or five hundred miles from Salt Lake and a thousand emigrants with handcarts on the dreary plains and the severity of winter already upon us...*

The first rescuers finally found the emigrants 65 miles east of Devil's Gate at Red Bluffs where they had been trapped by a blizzard. And they were in pitiful shape. Dan Jones recorded what he saw, ... *A condition of distress here met my eyes that I never saw before or since. The train was strung out for three or four miles. There were old men pulling and tugging their carts, sometimes loaded with a sick wife or children – women pulling along sick husbands – little children six to eight years old struggling through the mud and snow. As night came on the mud would freeze on their clothes and feet. There were two of us and hundreds needing help. What could we do?*

The rescuers bolstered spirits and encouraged the people along the Trail. Their immediate goal was to reach Devil's Gate where the decision would be made on whether to continue or to attempt to hole up for the winter.

Between the crossings of the North Platte and the first crossing of the Sweetwater, 65 people died. Once they arrived at Devil's Gate, they camped in a sheltered cove two miles west of that famous landmark. The spot is still known today as Martin's Cove.

More people died at the Cove and many others were near death. Because of the logistical problems involved in supplying what amounted to a small city throughout a long winter, the decision was made to press on. A small group of men were chosen to stay behind at the stockade at Devil's Gate to guard possessions which were left there until spring.

Ephraim Hanks one of the rescuers, described the horrors of tending to the wretched travelers, ...*Many of the immigrants whose extremities were frozen, lost their limbs, either whole or in part. Many such I washed with water and castile soap, until the frozen parts would fall off, after which I would sever the limbs with my scissors. Some of the emigrants lost toes, others fingers, and again others whole hands and feet...*

One young girl went to bed with her family, only to awaken screaming in pain in the night. A man was eating her fingers while she slept. He was dragged off into the snow, began eating his own fingers, and was found dead the next morning.

That one incident, which occurred at Willow Springs, is the only documented instance which even approached the unthinkable actions of the Donner Party—cannibalism.

Even with the aid of food and supplies, the deaths continued on the final leg, so many in fact that there is not an accurate count to this day. The figures range from 135 to 150 fatalities in the Martin Company alone. Add to that number the 67 deaths recorded in the Willie Company and uncounted deaths of the Hodgett Wagon Train, over 200 people or about one out of six perished. It was the greatest single tragedy in the entire history of the western migration.

Through sheer perseverance and unwavering support from Salt Lake, the emigrants finally made it to the Valley. On November 30, 1856, they arrived in Salt Lake.

Like so many other human disasters, even before all the emigrants were safely housed in Salt Lake, people started looking for someone to blame.

Somebody definitely had to be at fault, but who exactly? A few whisperings of criticism reached the ears of Brigham Young saying that the leadership of the Mormon Church was to blame. A dynamic leader and not given to taking criticism, Young exploded. In a speech given at the Tabernacle on Temple Square, he didn't mince any words, ... *If any man, or woman, complains of me or of my Counselors, in regard to the lateness of some of this season's immigration, let the Curse of God be on them and blast their substance with mildew and destruction, until their names are forgotten from the earth...*

That same year, 1856, was the eve of yet another fight for Mormon survival – the Utah War of 1857, when the Territory was "invaded" by soldiers of the United States. In many ways, Young was the leader of a sovereign nation, struggling to hold his people and his country together. He could not afford dissention in the ranks.

The best summary of the entire 1856 handcart disaster was written by Wallace Stegner in Collier's magazine, July 6, 1956, "Perhaps their suffering seems less dramatic because they bore it meekly, praising God, instead of fighting for life with the ferocity of animals and eating their dead to keep their own life beating, as both the Fremont and Donner parties did. And assuredly, the handcart pilgrims were less hardy, less skilled, and less well equipped to be pioneers. But, if courage and endurance make a story, if human kindness and helpfulness and brotherly love in the midst of raw horror are worth recording, this half-forgotten episode of the Mormon migration is one of the great tales of the West and of America."

Reprint of article by Mike W. Brown, Public Affairs Officer, Rock Springs District, Bureau of Land Management.

Following the River
From here to Split Rock, a day's trail journey west, the Oregon Trail followed two routes: one close to the Sweetwater River, the other a little further from it but more direct.

Capt. Howard Stansbury commented August 1, 1852:

"...Frost during the night; morning clear, calm and very beautiful. The road passing occasionally through deep, heavy sand continued up the right bank of the Sweetwater, ...The valley is here nearly two miles wide, with rolling hills between the two mountain ranges, which... form its limits."

Stansbury was a federal topographical engineer who was mapping both emigrant routes and a possible right-of-way for the railroad.

Granville Stuart in his book Forty Years on the Frontier, wrote this about the Sweetwater River in 1852:

"...its beautiful clear cold waters having a sweetish taste, caused by alkali held in solution...not enough , however, to cause any apparent injurious effects..."

Devil's Gate Mail Station
The U.S. Post Office Department contracted monthly mail delivery that passed here going between Independence, Missouri and Salt Lake City, Utah. This service normally used light-draft wagons in summer and pack mules in winter and remained the only mail delivery through here until late 1858. The Devil's Gate mail station was located one half mile south of the Gate.

Trails to Opportunity
The Oregon Trail was America's main street west. Building upon American Indian foot paths, emigrants bound for the Pacific Northwest used the trail. They were soon followed by Mormons fleeing persecution, gold seekers rushing to California and the thundering hooves of the Pony Express.

The Way West
Following Indian paths, fur trapping mountain men traveled west. Astor's Pacific Fur Company opened the trail through the Rockies at South Pass in 1812. Mountain men guided the first wagon train over it in 1841. Until the Transcontinental Railroad was completed in 1869 the Oregon Trail was the way west. As many as 500,000 men, women and children journeyed this way over some 2,000 miles of deserts, plains and moutains.

Yellow Metal
With the discovery of gold in California in 1848, the rush was on! By 1850, nearly 75,000 "49'ers" traveled through this valley. Numerous Trail cutoffs were developed that saved time or made for easier going. Some were pioneered by California emigrants and are known today as the California Trail.

Wyoming Tidbits

Mormon leader Brigham Young established the first commercial ferry operation in the Rocky Mountain area near the future town of Casper in 1874.

Popo Agie Wilderness

This piece of land is one of the loveliest in Wyoming. Along the western boundary, which Popo Agie (pronounced "po-po-zsha") shares with Bridger Wilderness, stands Wind River Peak, at 13,255 feet the highest point in the area. More than 20 other summits rise above 12,000 feet. The lowest elevation in the Popo Agie is the Middle Fork of the Popo Agie River at 8,400 feet on the eastern boundary. Bordering the north side is the Wind River Indian Reservation, outstanding country where visitors must first obtain a permit before entering.

More than 300 alpine and subalpine lakes and ponds, many filled with trout, send their waters down sparkling streams and over waterfalls to the Middle Fork and North Fork of the Popo Agie River and the South Fork of the Little Wind River. All the water eventually ends up in the Wind River. This rough land features high, jagged peaks; deep, narrow valleys and canyons; sheer granite walls; cirque basins; talus slopes; and perennial snowfields along its eastern side. The area, which abuts the Continental Divide, encompasses about 25 miles of the southern Wind River Mountain Range, with forests of lodgepole pine and Douglas fir, Engelmann spruce, and subalpine fir.

In a Smithsonian Institute report issued in 1879, it was said of the Wind River Mountains, "when a good Indian dies, he falls into a beautiful stream of bright, fresh water, and is carried to the pleasant grounds [of the Winds]. . . . " The temperature rarely exceeds 80 degrees Fahrenheit, but it may plunge to 40 below zero in the winter. Snow may fall any day of the year, and most of the precipitation is snow. There are occasional heavy rains in summer, and light afternoon thunderstorms are common.

Many miles of trails attract a relatively large number of visitors, which has led to a few restrictions on camping in some areas. Check with the district ranger.

Courtesy: US Forest Service

Seeking Zion

Church leader Brigham Young led the first Mormon wagon train west along the trail in 1846-47. He followed the Oregon Trail to Fort Bridger, taking the Hastings Cutoff into the Salt Lake Valley. At this time, the Valley was part of Mexico, a situation that was changed by the Mexican-American War (1846-48).

Days of Fleeting Glory

Starting in 1860, the California Overland Mail and Pikes Peak Express galloped into history and the legend of the Pony Express was born. For 18 months, "wiry young men" on fast horses carried the mail, covering the 1600 miles from St. Joseph, Missouri to Sacramento, California in 10 days.

Why Wyoming?

There was no other route across the west that provided the three essential things needed for travel; good water every day; a dependable supply of grass; and, a passable grade to and through the Rocky Mountains which can be found only at South Pass.

The Cleft in the Rock

Devil's Gate is a 370-foot high, 1,500-foot long fissure carved over the centuries by the Sweetwater River. It was a major landmark on the Oregon Trail...a pleasant change for weary travelers on the four day trek across the rough, dry country from the North Platte River.

Fr. Pierre-Jean DeSmet, S.J., 1841

"...Travelers have named this spot the Devil's Entrance [Devil's Gate]. In my opinion they should have rather called it Heaven's Avenue."

Goldrush 49'er, J.G.Bruff, wrote:

"...some of the boys clambered up the rocks on the north side of the Gate...where they fired pistols and threw down rocks, pleased with the reverberation, which was great. I made a careful sketch of this remarkable gorge."

Martin's Cove

Two miles to the northwest, nestled at the foot of the Sweetwater Rocks, is Martin's Cove. Here Captain Edward Martin's exhausted company of Mormon handcart emigrants sought shelter from an early winter storm in November of 1856. Of 576 men, women and children, 145 had died before rescue parties from Salt Lake City reached them.

"A condition of distress here meet my eyes that I never saw before or since. The (Mormon) train was strung out for two or three miles. There were old men pulling and tugging their carts, sometimes loaded with a sick wife or children, women pulling along sick husbands, little children six to eight years old struggling through the mud and snow. As night came on the mud would freeze on their clothes and feet. We gathered on to some of the most helpless with our riatas tied to the carts, and helped as many as we could into camp...Such assistance as we could give was rendered to all until they finally arrived at Devil's Gate fort, about the first of November. There were some 1,200 in all, about one half with handcarts and the other half with teams.

The winter storms had now set in in all their severity. The provisions we took amounted to almost nothing among so many people, many of them now on very short rations, some almost starving. Many were dying daily from exposure and want of food."

—*Daniel W. Jones, 1856*

Devil's Gate

Devil's Gate, the 370-foot high, 1500-foot long cleft, carved over the centuries by the Sweetwater River, was a major landmark on the Oregon Trail. A pleasant change for weary travelers coming across the rough, dry country from the North Platte River, a four day trek. Goldrush 49'er, J. G. Bruff, wrote of Devil's Gate: "...some of the boys clambered up the rocks on the north side of the Gate...where they fired pistols and threw down rocks, pleased with the reverberation, which was great. I made a careful sketch of this remarkable gorge."

Sweetwater River

From here to Split Rock, a day's trail journey west, the Oregon Trail followd two routes: one close to the Sweetwater River, the other further from it but more direct. Capt. Howard Stansbury comments August 1, 1852:

"...the road passing occasionally through deep, heavy sand continued up the right bank of the Sweetwater...the valley is here nearly two miles wide, with rolling hills between the two mountain ranges, which...form its limits. About a dozen burnt wagons and nineteen dead oxen passed today along the road; but the destruction has been by no means as great as upon the North Fork of the Platte and the crossing over to the Sweetwater."

The Pony Express and Overland Stage coaches followed these routes; the Pony Express changing horses at Plant's Station a few miles from here.

Legend of Devil's Gate

Shoshone and Arapahoe legend is one explanation of how Devil's Gate was formed. A powerful evil spirit in the form of a tremendous beast with enormous tusks ravaged the Sweetwater Valley, preventing the Indians from hunting and camping. A prophet informed the tribes that the Great Spirit required them to destroy the beast. They launched an attack from the mountain passes and ravines, and shot countless arrows into the evil mass. The enraged beast, with a mighty upward thrust of its tusks, ripped a gap in the mountain and disappeared through the gap, never to be seen again.

Robert L. Munkres, "Independence Rock and Devil's Gate" in Annals of Wyoming, April 1968.

The Oregon Trail

The Oregon Trail passed over the ridge to the right of Devil's Gate. Good grass, water and the shelter of the hills made this a popular campsite. Oregon emigrant James Mathers stopped here July 8, 1846, and wrote: "...encamped above the pass of the river, between high rocks. This is the most interesting sight we have met with on our journey."

Devil's Gate Mail Station

The Devil's Gate Mail Station was located here. The Post Office Department contracted monthly mail delivery along this route from independence, Missouri, to Salt Lake City, Utah. This service, using light wagons in summer and pack mules in winter, remained the sole mail service until late 1858. John M. hockaday and George Chorpenning established, under contract, this system of relay stations. These pack-mule stations preceded regular stagecoach service to Utah and California. Plant's Station, a few miles west of here, was used later as one of the stagecoach stations on the route to Utah and California.

H Independence Rock Interpretive Signs

At Independece Rock Rest Area on State Highway 220

Indepedence Rock: What is the Significance of Prospect Hill?

Left of Independence Rock on the horizon, sits a small but very important peak, Prospect Hill. This landmark is named because "... from the summit...is a grand prospect of the surrounding country. ..."

From atop Prospect Hill, the emigrants would have a good view of Independence Rock, Devil's Gate and Split Rock for the first time. These natural landmarks of the Sweetwater Valley allowed the travelers to make note of their progress along the trail.

Locating good water, forage for their animals and fuel for fires was the main concern each day for the emigrants crossing the prairie.

Wagons traveled between 16 and 20 miles a day, depending on the weather and terrain. They were built sturdy yet lightweight. Oxen were preferred over mules and horses for hauling the wagons. Though oxen were slower, they adapted better to the strenuous journy and various conditions on the trail.

Provisions had to last for a possible six month journey as supplies were scarce or very costly if purchased at stations along the way. Many emigrants took too many belongings and soon found their animals suffering. Possessions would be left along the trail to lighten the wagon load.

History Named in Stone

Independence Rock is one of the most famous landmarks on the Oregon Trail. Emigrants wanted to reach the rock by the Fourth of July to ensure passage over the western mountain ranges before winter snows.

Many theories vary about naming the rock but most versions originate with events that happened on the Fourth of July.

William Sublette, and early mountain guide, is credited with christening it in honor of our nation's birthdate on July 4th, 1830. One version was based on the Rock standing independent from the other rock formations on the plains.

Explorer John Fremont wrote in 1842 upon visiting the Rock, "…the rock is inscribed with…many a name famous in the history of this country…are to be found among those of traders and travelors…some of those have been washed away by the rain, but the greater number are not very "legible."

Names were sometimes painted with ordinary paint, wagon tar or with a mixture of black powder, buffalo grease and glue. Others were carved into the hard stone with tools carried for wagon repairs. Mormons stationed professional stone cutters at the rock to engrave names for one to five dollars a name.

Few names remain today, as lichen, weather and time are eroding them away.

Vandalism and graffiiti are also contributing to the destruction of this historic national landmark. Please preserve and respect our Wyoming heritage.

The Ox-Team Monument Expedition

In 1852 and estimated 50,000 pioneers passed Independence Rock on their way west. Among this number was the family of 21-year-old Ezra Meeker, recently of Eddyville, Iowa, but natives of Indiana. Meeker, his wife Eliza, and their infant son, arrived at Puget Sound, Washington Territory, in October 1852. They eventually settled in the Puyallup Valley, where over the years they experienced success and failure in farming, principally in raising hops.

Keenly aware of the national significance of the Oregon Trail in the development of the American Pacific Northwest, Meeker wrote several books on the subject. In 1906, greatly concerned that the Oregon Trail would fade from memory, he decided to retrace the old trail eastward with covered wagon and ox-team, for the purpose of permanently marking the trail. He called this journey the Ox-Team Monument Expedition.

The presence of the 75-year-old pioneer with his long white beard, his considerable promotional skills, and the enthusiasm he engendered brought about a generous response from communities along the old trail. As a result, a line of stone monuments now marks the course of the trail from The Dalles, Oregon, across the mountains and plains to Kansas.

Here at Independence Rock he wrote:

July 3 1906, We drove over to the "Rock", from the "Devil"s gate, a distance of six miles, and camped at 10:00 for the day…I selected a spot on the westward sloping face of the stone for the inscription, "Old Oregon Trail, 1843-57.", near the present traveled road, where people can see it…and inscribed it with as deep cut letters as we could make it with a dulled, cold, chisel, and painted, with sunken letters with the best of sign writer's painting oil. On this expedition, where possible, I have in like manner inscribed a number of boulders, with paint only, which, it is to be hoped, before the life of the paint has gone out, may find living hands to inscribe deep into the stone; but here on this huge boulder, I hope the inscription may last for centuries.

Meeker continued his 1906 odyssey through major eastern cities to Washington, D.C., where on November 29 he met with President Roosevelt. In subsequent years Meeker continued his promotion of the Oregon Trail. In 1916 he made the journey in a Pathfinder model automobile, and in 1924 he was flown over the trail by army pilots. The old pioneer died in Seattle, Washington, at the age of 97 on December 3, 1928.

Wyoming Landmarks on the Trail

Emigrants depended on known land marks and landscape features to guide them in their journey west. Guidebooks were available providing detailed descriptions and trail mileage. Even subtle features such as springs, alkali lakes, ravines, bluffs and aspen groves were noted with considerable detail to aid in the long trek.

Within the territory that is now Wyoming were some outstanding trail landmarks; Fort Laramie, Register Cliff, Red Buttes, Prospect Hill, Independence Rock, Devil's Gate, Split Rock, Three Crossings, Ice Slough, South Pass, Pacific Springs, Parting of the Ways, Church Butte and Fort Bridger.

Fort Laramie…a military post at the eastern foot of the Rockies and an essential supply and service depot.

Independence Rock and Devil's Gate…Imposing landmarks that were a Fourth of July meeting place for many emigrants and often described as "sublime" and "a natural curiosity."

Three Crossings… where the Sweetwater River had to be crossed three times within a mile and a half.

Ice Slough…a marshy area where water collected, froze and was kept insulated beneath the tundra-like sod. Ice could be dug a foot or more below the ground surface, providing travelers a luxury in the summer months.

South Pass…a gradual ascent over the continental divide. It marked the long-awaited Oregon country and the separation of waters into the Atlantic or Pacific Ocean.

Pacific Springs…a marshy meadow providing good grass and the first water flowing west.

Parting of the Ways…a fork in the trail allowing emigrants a choice: a shortcut or water and forage.

Sublette Cutoff…a shortcut through 50 waterless miles. The other fork went southwest to Ft. Bridger, adding 46 extra miles but favoring the livestock.

Church Butte…and eroded sandstone formation named for its shape.

Fort Bridger…an oasis where good water, grass and necessary supplies could be had.

Impressions at the Rock and Devil's Gate

Many emigrants recorded their daily struggles and observations in diaries, letters and journals while traveling the Oregon-California-Utah Trail. Enough of these documents survive that one can glimpse at the experiences of a variety of people, from teenage children to adults. Some entries are brief notations on travel conditions while others are very descriptive and informative.

Rachel Taylor, age 15, 1853

July 21st Started in good season and about noon reached the Sweetwater, a swift clear stream. Later in the day passed Independence Rock. We forded the river here and were somewhat hindered. Encamped near the river where grass is abundant. We have here a frightful as well as romantic situation. Just back of us Independence Rock stands out in bold relief, and in front of us yawns the Devils Gate.

July 22nd Today a party of us go to explore the Gate and found the place as wild and rugged as could be imagined.

Cecella Adams & Parthenia Blank, twin sisters, ages 23, 1852

25 Sun W.W. this morning we started at 3 o'clock to feed and get breakfast Sand very deep and dealt very troublesome Stoped for dinner opposit Independence Rock. It is a great curiosity but we were all so tired that we could not go to the top of it It is almost entirely covered with names of emigrants. Went on to the Devil's Gate and encamped, this is a great curiosity but we have not time to visit it and regret it very much. Passed 3 graves Forded the Sweet water M 16 "

Amelia Hadley, age 26, 1851

Monday June 16…This is an independent rock standing aloof from the rest of the mountains, and has a triangular appearance look like a great rock tooled down from the rest of the mountains. It has the appearunce of a court house standing in the centre with a block of I never seen any thing more splendid see a great many names whom I knew"

James Akin, Junior…

Friday July 2nd 1852 "Travel 18 miles-sandy road and dusty-pass Independence rock-cross sweet water-pass devils gate-camp near sweet water—not much grass"

Time and Understanding

Thousands of immigrants migrated past the point whre you are now standingon their way to settle the "new frontier" and begin new lives. They brought with them the coming of a new age.

The abundant wildlands and free-ranging wildlife seemed limitless to those early settlers. They believed such vast natural resources would last forever. Along with the settlers, however, came new ideas and technologies, railroads and more settlers. Soon, the natural resources of Wyoming were more readily available to the new settlers and the rest of the world.

The unrestricted use of these natural resources quickly lead to diminishing wildlife and wildlands. Eventually, conservation efforts

Section 5

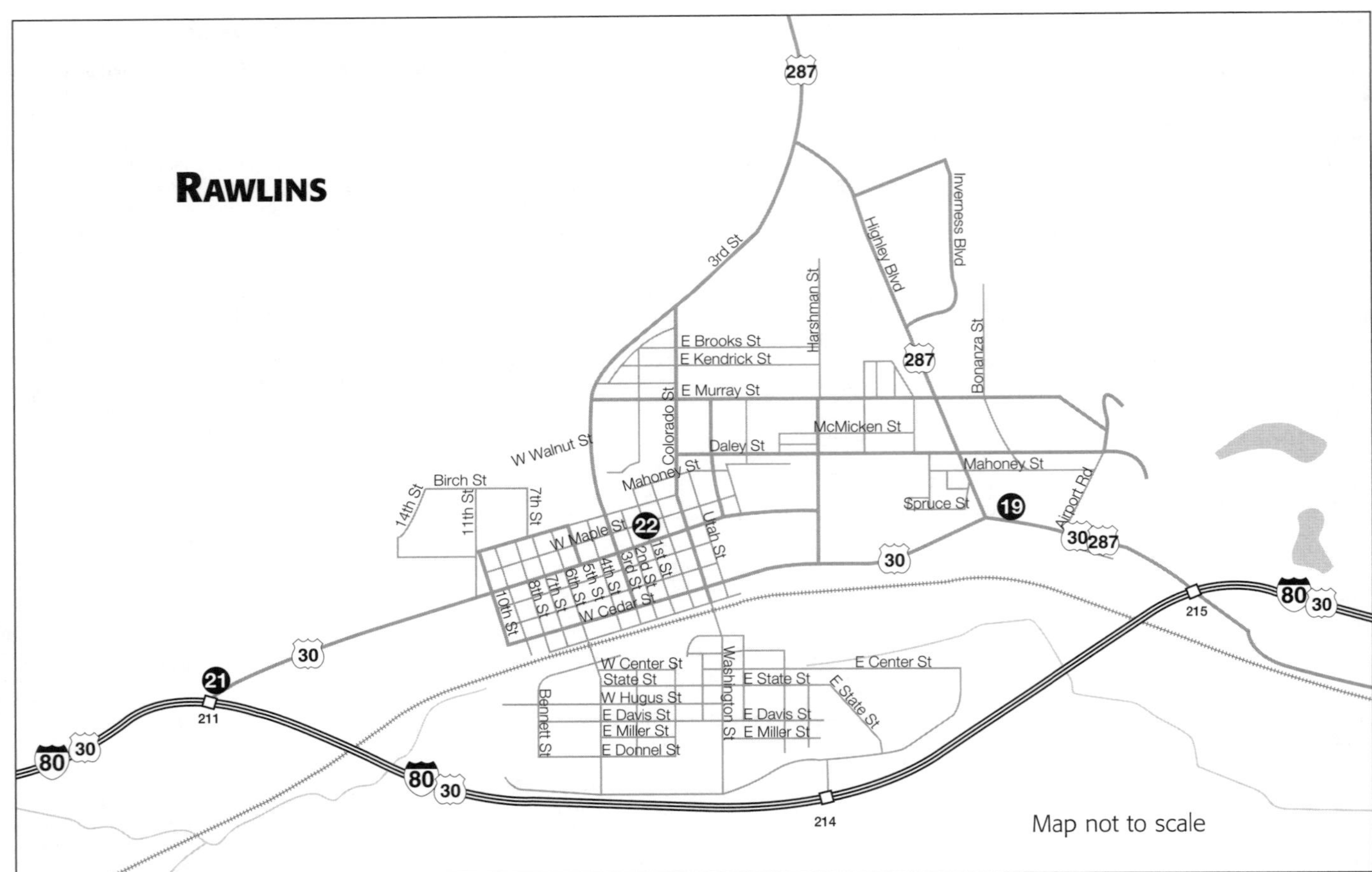

sprang up to preserve wildlife and the wildlands on which wildlife lived.

As we grow to understand our relationship with the earth, we realize that our future well-bing depends on our willingness and desire to act responsibly when we use the earth's precious natural resources-her soil, water, air, plants and animals.

Wyoming's vast natural wildlands are as important to people as they are to over 600 species of wildlife. A measure of our future may very well be reflected in our ability to responsibly conserve wildlife and preserve its habitat, for we all share the same space, food, shelter and water.

Independence Rock

Thousands who traveled the Oregon Trail in central Wyoming were unaware that they were the beneficiaries of a long series of geological events. The granite peaks around you are mountains that rose, sank and then were buried in sand and ashy sediments. Erosion exposed their summits and created the Sweetwater Valley, part of an east-west passageway through the Rockies. The route was used by game animals, Native Americans and fur trappers, followed at mid-century by wagon train and handcart emigrants, stagecoach passenger and Pony Express riders. For some this was the halfway point in a 2,000-mile trek from the Missouri River to the West Coast. Arriving here early in July, emigrants celebrated Independence Day. In July 1841, Jesuit missionary Pierre Jean De Smet wrote of this granite landmark: "The first rock which we saw, and which truly deserves the name, was the famous Independence Rock. It is of the same nature as the Rocky Mountains. At first I was led to believe that it had received this pompous name from its isolated situation and the solidity of its base; but I was afterward told that it was called so because the first travelers who thought of giving it a name arrived at it on the very day when the people of the United States celebrate the anniversary of their emancipation from Great Britain…lest it might be said that we passed this lofty monument of the desert with indifference, we cut our names on the south side of the rock under initials (I. H. S.) which we would wish to see engraved everywhere, and along with a great number of others, some of which perhaps ought not be found anywhere. On account of all these names, and of the dates that accompany them, as well as of the hieroglyphics of Indian warriors.

Independence Rock

Father DeSmet, early missionary, on July 5, 1841, surnamed this rock "The Great Record of the Desert" on account of the many names and dates carved on its surface.

It was an important landmark and camp site for the emigrants of the Oregon and Utah Trails crossing this territory from 1840 to 1869.

The first Masonic lodge held in Wyoming was opened on this rock on July 4, 1862.

The rock is of igneous origin consisting of red and white feldspar and mica. Marks on the sides show the action of the glacier, which crossed this part of the country in the Pre-Oligocene period.

Early Ranching

By 1869 people gradually began to settle this area. Cattle herds which had multiplied and overstocked Oregon range were driven back along the Oregon Trail to graze the empty plains. Other herds came to Wyoming, Montana and Colorado from the great Texas herds. The journey's end for many herds were well watered valleys such as along the Sweetwater River.

Although the Valley of the Sweetwater was once an active scene of westward migration, today it is a vast grazing land used by owners of working ranches. Independence Rock and the ruts of the Oregon Trail remain as evidence that a nation once passed this way.

Rawlins	Jan	Feb	March	April	May	June	July	Aug	Sep	Oct	Nov	Dec	Annual
Average Max. Temperature (F)	30.7	33.9	41.2	52.3	63.7	75.1	83.3	81.0	70.5	57.0	40.7	32.1	55.1
Average Min. Temperature (F)	12.5	14.9	20.3	27.7	36.5	44.7	51.4	50.0	40.9	31.2	20.3	13.9	30.4
Average Total Precipitation (in.)	0.50	0.53	0.68	1.05	1.33	0.91	0.76	0.75	0.80	0.82	0.58	0.49	9.21
Average Total SnowFall (in.)	7.9	7.5	7.8	7.1	1.6	0.2	0.0	0.0	1.2	3.4	7.7	7.5	51.9
Average Snow Depth (in.)	2	2	1	0	0	0	0	0	0	0	1	1	1

Military Involvement
Increased travel along the Oregon Trail and the construction of a telegraph line along this route led the Indians to the realization that their existence was threatened by another civilization. As a result, violence between emigrants and Indians increased. By 1860-61 several small military garrisons were built to protect travelers and keep the communication lines open.

The Three Crossing Station was located about 18 miles north and west of this site. It was a sturdy stockade, manned by one non-commissioned officer and 6 privates. Sweetwater Station, located about 2 miles northeast of Independence Rock was a telegraph relay station, military supply base, as well as a Pony Express and Overland Stage station. Both sites were abandoned in 1866.

The Great Emigration
Independence Rock was one of the most noted Oregon Trail landmarks. Between 1848 and completion of the transcontinental railroad in 1869, the trail was the major route followd by emigrants from Independence, Missouri to California, Utah and the Williamette Valley of Oregon.

Father Pierre DeSmet, a Jesuit missionary, dubbed the rock "The Register of the Desert" for at one time it had an estimated 40,000 names engraved on its surface. Almost all of the names, sometimes applied with a mixture of powder, buffalo grease and glue, are now coverd with lichens, mother nature's eraser, which is slowly decomposing the rock.

Fur Trade and Naming the Rock
Eastward-moving Astorian fur traders in 1812 were probably the first white men to discover Independence Rock. Regardless of the date of discovery, the rock was a well-known landmark to the fur trapping mountain men.

Theories about naming the rock vary, but one likely version states that on July 4, 1830, mountain man William Sublette, leader of the first wagon train to cross the overland route, christened Independence Rock in honor of the nation's birthdate.

Prehistory and Geology
The Sweetwater causeway was probably first used by animals. Early North American Indians, following migratory animal herds, also used this overland passage. When their descendants, including the Shoshone, Arapahoe, and other Plains tribes acquired the horse, the animal hooves and the poles of their travois wore the trail deeper and wider.

The geologic formation of Independence Rock is shown in the 3 diagrams at right.

Early Eocene Time, 50 million years ago.
The Granite Mountains were uplifted. Sedimentary rocks were stripped by streams from this rising fold, causing the granite core to be exposed, a part of which is Independence Rock, shown on the diagram as I.R.

Miocene Time, 15 million years ago.
The broad granite core of the Granite Mountains sagged downward several thousand feet. As a result, most of this once-majestic mountain range became lower than the basins to the north and south and was largely buried by enormous amounts of gray, windblown sand. In some places the sand accumulated to a thickness of 3000 feet.

Independence Rock as you see it today.
Most of the sediments that buried the rounded summits of the Granit Range have been stripped away. Summits such as Independence Rock have been re-exposed and appear today essentially as they were at the time of their burial 15 million years ago.

The Preservation of Independence Rock
An important landform like Independence Rock is protected and preserved only through the efforts of many people and organizations. Not all attempts at preservation and commemoration are acceptable by current standards, however, and some actions left permanent scars on the National Historic Landmark.

Past attempts to memorilize an event or person by the placement of a plaque on the Rock damaged the surface. Today, nine bronzed legends, bolted to this igneous summit are mute testimony to us about people of the immediate past and tell us what they believed to be important about their history.

A preservation ethic was fostered by public knowledge of the importance of the site. Public gatherings and celebrations held by the Rock over the years, including Independence Day commemorations, Mason Lodge celebrations, and a National Boy Scout Jamboree, helped build public awareness.

As part of the united States bicentennial celebration, the State of Wyoming established Independence Rock State Historic Site with administratie responsibilities given to the Wyoming Recreation Commission. In an effort to retain the undisturbed atmosphere surrounding the rock, development at the site was kept to a minimum. A fence placed around the area of the historical inscriptions reduces contemporary damage.

Hundreds and thousands of people stopped here to rest, to meet, and to picnic and the area continues to serve in the same capacity as Independence Rock State Historic Site, allowing visitors to enjoy the majestic beauty of the landmark while refreshing themselves.

First Lodge of Masons
The first lodge of Masons in what is now the State of Wyoming, was convened on Independence Rock on July 4, 1862 by a body of Master Masons who were traveling west on the Old Oregon Trail. To commemorate this event Casper Lodge, No. 15, A.F. & A.M. of casper, Wyoming, held memorial services here on July 4th, 1920.

H Pronghorns and Sagebrush
At turnout just south of Martin's Cove

Of all our magnificent big game animals, only the pronghorn antelope cannot be traced back to Eurasia. Other big game animals are believed to have migrated to the continent via the now sunken Bering land mass located between Siberia and Alaska. Thus, it can be said that the pronghorn is a true native of North America.

The pronghorn is not a true antelope and belongs to an entirely different family (Antilocapridae) than other antelope. The pronghorn is the only living representative of this family. Like other horned animals (i.e. cattle, sheep, goats) the pronghorn grows hollow horn sheaths composed of fused hairy fibers. It is the only horned animal in the world that sheds and regrows its sheaths annually and is the only horned animal with a branched or pronged horn. Members of the deer family (i.e. deer, elk, moose) grow antlers, not horns, of solid bone, which are also shed and regrown each year. The pronghorn is also one of the world's fastest animals and has been clocked at speeds up to 70 miles per hour.

Despite healthy population numbers today, the pronghorn once faced near extinction. Pressure from settlers and market hunters reduced a thriving population to about 5,000 pronghorns by 1903. From 1908-1915, the pronghorn hunting season in Wyoming was closed in order to allow the population to recover. Today, nearly two-thirds of all the world's pronghorn antelope are found within a three hundred mile radius of Casper and the state hosts a total pronghorn population of nearly a half-million animals.

Pronghorns depend on sagebrush for food in the winter and Wyoming features more vast expanses of sagebrush than any place in North America. Considering the relationship between pronghorns and sagebrush, it is not hard to see why Wyoming has more pronghorn antelope than any other place in the world.

18 *Gas, Food*

Bairoil
This was a company town for the Bair Oil Company, founded by Charles Bair in 1916. Prior to becoming an oilman, Bair made his money as a sheep mogul. Bairoil's claim to fame is a hang-gliding world record, set in 1989 by Kevin Christopherson, who rode an updraft 287 miles from here to North Dakota.

Lamont
Rancher James Lamont, who established several windmills in the area, gave his name to this little town. Its now in the heart of Lost Soldier Oil Field, so keep your eyes open for both windmills and oil pumps.

19 *Gas, Food, Lodging*

Rawlins
Pop. 9,006, Elev. 6,755

General John A. Rawlins aided General Grenville Dodge with protection of workers laying the Union Pacific Railroad in 1868. When Dodge discovered a spring here, Rawlins said he'd like to have a spring named for him, because they were so refreshing. Dodge obliged him then and there, and the town took the name of Rawlins Springs when it was established. It was later shortened to Rawlins, to avoid confusion with nearby Rock Springs.

In 1889, after the Wyoming Territorial Prison had burned down in Laramie, it was officially moved to Rawlins. The soon-to-be State Penitentiary (Wyoming achieved statehood in 1890) was not completed until 1901. During that time, the town had grown, and the prison ended up being in the middle of it. In 1981, a new prison site was established south of town, where inmates are housed today. The old Frontier Prison is now a museum and historic site.

Rawlins is also known for being the site of an iron oxide deposit mined for paint pigment. "Rawlins Red" paint is still used on barns and houses across America, and was the original paint chosen for the Brooklyn Bridge, which was approved by General Rawlins himself, then Secretary of War for the U.S. Government.

T Rawlins Uplift
Just north of town, this jutting ridge of stratified rock is full of fossils and a variety of minerals.

H Rawlins Paint Mines
Just north of Rawlins on U.S Highway 287

The hills located to the south and west (your left) are part of the Rawlins Uplift, a 40 mile long, north trending fold in the earth's crust. The geologic feature rises a thousand feet above the surrounding plains. Granite rocks that range in age from 2.6 billion years to 10 million years are exposed along its crest and slopes. The reddish rocks that comprise much of the distant hills are the Flathead Sandstone (Cambrian) which is 520 million years old. The gray strata that overlie the Flathead Sandstone are part of the Madison Limestone (Mississippian Period), a 360 million year old rock unit. Both the Flathead Sandstone and Madison Limestone were deposited in shallow seas which once covered this area. The Flathead Sandstone contains hematite, a red iron mineral, that was mined in this area from 1870 to the early 1900s.

The now abandoned mines were located in the rock outcrops located a mile to the south of this sign. Some of the mined hematite was used as a "barn red" paint pigment noted for its durability and covering qualities. This popular "Rawlins Red" enjoyed the distinction of being selected in 1893, as the paint for the newly constructed Brooklyn Bridge. Hundreds of tons of ore were extracted annually between 1879 and 1886, and the paint made from it was used all across the country on a wide variety of buildings and structures. Cost increases for extracting, shipping and processing the ore as well as technological advances in pain manufacture eventually led to permanent closure of the mines.

M Wyoming Ranch Company, LLC
Rawlins and Medicine Bow. Joe Stratton, 307-321-7777 or Bob Duca, 925-210-0560

20 *Gas, Food, lodging*

Rawlins I-80 Exit 214

21 *Gas, Food, Lodging*

Rawlins I-80 Exit 211

22 *Food, Lodging*

T Old Frontier Prison
5th and Walnut Street in Rawlins. 324-4422

While outlaws roamed the windswept high plains, canyons and mountains of post-Civil War Wyoming, the territorial legislature was planning a state-of-the-art penitentiary at Rawlins in anticipation of statehood. This new Wyoming State Penitentiary, which would serve from 1901 until 1981, would send a strong message to these free-wheeling desperados… Wyoming would no longer be a haven for the lawless!

The Old Pen, as the Wyoming Frontier Prison is affectionately called today, is "haunted by history" around every corner. Tales of great train robbers, wily escapes and of women driven to crimes of passion are told on the regularly scheduled guided tours offered daily from April thru October. Group tours and off-season tours are also avail- able.

Stand inside the tiny dark cells, sit in the gas chamber, fill your senses with the history of the wild west. Observe artwork with an ominous message, walk within the great stone walls. Visitors to the prison will see the place where 9 prisoners were hanged and 5 prisoners were executed by lethal gas. Be part of an unpleasant but necessary chapter in mankind's history of Wyoming.

Visitors may browse thru history in the prison museum where historical information sits side-by-side with confiscated inmate-made weapons and an exhibit of the movie, "Prison", filmed on location at the Old Pen. The Old Pen Gift Shop offers souvenirs and western gifts as well as inmate-made crafts of leather, horsehair items and jewelry. The proceeds from the tours and gift shop are returned to the Old Pen for historical and operational use.

Portions excerpted from prison brochure.

Photo credit: Old Pen Joint Powers Board

T Carbon County Museum
9th and Walnut in Rawlins. 328-2740

Carbon County in its original form was traversed by the Oregon Trail, The Bozeman Trail, Overland Trail, Cherokee Trail, the Outlaw Trail, the Union Pacific, the original Lincoln Highway and ultimately Interstate 80. Parts of Carbon County were in the Louisiana Purchase in 1803, the Mixican Secession in 1843, and the Texas Annexation in 1845.

Rawlins has always been the county seat of Carbon County. In 1870 a formal government was started in Carbon County and in 1890 Wyoming became a state. Rawlins has long been a transportation center. It served as a railhead for stage and freight lines serving Casper, the Big Horn Basin, the Wind River Basin and northwestern Colorado.

The museum contains artifacts telling the tales of the mining and ranching ventures in this area as well as the Thomas Edison expedition and an extensive photograph collection of early day scenes and people in Rawlins and the surrounding area.

Exhibits include the memorabilia of Dr. Lillian Heath, Wyoming's first woman physician, who practiced medicine from 1893 and maintained her license until her death in 1962 at the age of 96.

The Post Office and sign from Fort Fred Steele are on display. The Army used Fort Steele from 1868 to 1886 to protect the building of the railroad.

Also displayed are sheepwagons, various western saddles, sidesaddles, McClellan saddles and tack, a sample of brands from the area, one of 6 hand painted on silk original state flags, newspapers dating from 1879, a turn-of-the-century buggy, a 1920 American La France Hook 'n Ladder 52 foot long fire truck, a mystery safe that was found behind a wall of a building that was torn down in 1983, and shoes made from the skin of Big Nose George and the lower portion of his skull.

The museum is open year round and admission is free. Call for hours.

Excerpts from museum brochure.

T Wyoming Peace Officers Museum
5th and Walnut in Rawlins. 344-4422

This museum is located the Frontier Prison Museum. You will see descriptions and photos of various inmates who once occupied the facility. There are also various exhibits of artifacts relating to law enforcement, including memorials. There is a also a gift shop. The museum is open year around.

H Rawlins
At front of Rawlins City Hall in Rawlins

In the summer of 1867, a survey party led by General Grenville M. Dodge seeking a route for the Union Pacific Railroad, stopped one half mile southwest of here.

General John A. Rawlins, a member of the party, spoke of the spring there as the most gracious and acceptable of anything he had had on the march and said that if anything was ever named after him he wanted it to be a spring of water.

General Dodge replied: "We will name this Rawlins Springs."

H Wyoming State Penitentiary
5th and Walnut Streets in Rawlins

Before Wyoming was granted statehood, prisoners were incarcerated at the territorial prison located in Laramie. This was by Act of Congress of January 24, 1873 and the territorial prison was completed December 23, 1873. It housed 67 prisoners in a formidable stone barn with gabled roof and heavily barred windows. The National Territorial Building Act of 1888 provided that a penitentiary building for the use of the territory shall be erected in the City of Rawlins at a cost not exceeding $100,000.00 Construction of this territorial prison was begun July 23, 1888 and was named The Wyoming State Penitentiary by the Act of Admission July 10, 1890. It is situated on 65.31 acres of land within the City of Rawlins, Carbon County. Great slabs of stone and rock, observed on the outside structure, were wagoned from the Larson Stone Quarry south of Rawlins. The first prisoner recorded into this institution was on July 16, 1891. Starting in December of 1901 prisoners were transferred from Laramie to Rawlins and this transfer was completed in 1904. Of all prisoners incarcerated in this institution, probably the most publicized was Bill Carlisle the great train robber. The total capacity of inmates that could be incarcerated was 373.

23 *Gas, Food*

Sinclair
Pop. 423, Elev. 6,592

Established as a company town for the oil refinery in 1923, this town was originally named Parco, for the Producers Oil and Refinery Company (POR-co?). When the Sinclair Company bought the refinery in 1934, the name was changed to reflect the new ownership. It was not until 1967 that homes and public buildings were actually sold to the employees and the town government. A peaceful community with several mission style buildings, an ornate fountain in the center of town, and an inn listed as a National Historic Place, Sinclair is often overlooked by passing travelers.

T Parco/Sinclair Museum

At the Town Hall in Sinclair. 324-3058

Colorful exhibits of items from Wyoming's past are on display in this quaint museum which is housed in an old bank building. Self-guided tours introduce visitors to the history of Parco, the town whose name was changed when Sinclair Oil Company bought the refinery in 1934. Open 1-4 p.m. during summer months, the museum also welcomes visitors who stop at town hall next door if the museum is closed.

24 *No services*

Fort Steele

Located 12 miles east of Rawlins on Highway 80, then north two miles along the west bank of the Platte River, Fort Steele stands just across the Union Pacific tracks. It was established in 1868 as a fort to protect the Overland Stage Line and the Union Pacific railroad from Indian attacks. Four companies evolved comprised of three hundred men; the companies served to safeguard travelers and to construct the fort. Soon afterward, a town half-mile to the south was born, named Brownsville. Due to its numerous saloons and gambling joints, the Army forced Brownsville off government land. The town relocated three miles west of the fort and renamed itself Benton.

Records indicate that Fort Steele's Army never once encountered a battle. The west side of the fort was "Officers Row," and the east side contained the men's barracks, laundries, and a sawmill. Passing through on the south side was the railroad. In 1886, the fort was abandoned. Eight years later, the property was purchased by the Cosgriff Brothers for one hundred dollars. Soon after converting the buildings to stores and residences, fire destroyed much of the town, and the remaining buildings became the property of the Leo Sheep Company. Today, many of the buildings are foundations or depressions in the ground.

T Fort Fred Steele State Historic Site

I-80 Exit 228. Follow signs. 320-3013

History

Fort Fred Steele was established on June 20, 1868 and occupied until August 7, 1886 by soldiers who were sent by the U.S. Government to guard the railroad against attack from Indians. The construction of the transcontinental Union Pacific Railroad across southern Wyoming in 1867-1869, in turn, brought the cattlemen and sheepherders, loggers and tie hacks, miners and merchants who changed a wasteland into the Wyoming Territory.

Colonel Richard I Dodge, who selected this site on the west bank of the North Platte River, named the fort for Major General Frederick Steele, 20th U.S. Infantry, a Civil War hero.

Although the fort at first resembled a tent city, Colonel Dodge's military quartermaster quickly built the fort according to Army specifications by using local materials and labor. In fact, many of the 300 troops here at the time received extra pay for their help with this effort. Key civilians who were also employed at the post included a sawmill engineer, blacksmith, saddler and wheelwright. Like many other frontier outposts, the military relied, too, upon a licensed trader or sutler to supply fresh produce and mercantile goods for its personnel and dependents.

After the major Indian threat had passed, the War Department deactivated the post and transferred its troops to other military facilities throughout the United States. Only a guard was left to oversee this federal property.

Industry

After the fort was abandoned, a sparse population of civilians remained at what would be known only as Fort Steele. Prospering briefly as a logging center, millions of felled trees were floated down the North Platte River from the Medicine Bow and Sierra Madre Mountains to this small community where they were turned into railroad ties and fence posts. Later, a major sheep sheering plant was established to remove the animals' wool made thick and rich by the harsh Wyoming winters. The railway that passed through the community facilitated shipment of those bales to the east where the raw goods were processed and woven into material for fashionable garments for men and women.

America's First Transcontinental Highway

In 1912 the mighty Lincoln Highway was conceived as a transcontinental highway to parallel the original railroad that crossed this country. That dream became a reality in 1922 as the concrete ribbon was completed and linked the east and west coast. A brief economic revival for Fort Steele followed that achievement. The rerouting of the highway in 1939, plus the demise of the tie industry a year later was the village's death knell. *Excerpted from Wyoming State Parks and Historic Sites brochure.*

T Benton

Benton lies three miles west of Fort Steele and was known as the wildest town in Wyoming. Nothing remains, except wild stories and millions of broken bits of glass from thrown bottles.

Its proximity to the fort attracted several hundred troops. Benton was born on July 1, 1868 and died September, 1868 when the Army kicked it off its reservation. On weekdays, three thousand people lived in Benton. And during the weekends, five thousand people populated the town. Water was hauled from the Platte River, and it was sold for a dollar a barrel. Two popular institutions were the North Star Saloon and the Desert Hotel. In addition, twenty-three saloons served beer, with five dance halls contributing to this town's lively environment. During its wild three-month existence, one hundred people were killed.

T Carbon Timber Town

You will find Carbon Timber Town two miles from the rest area adjacent to Interstate 80 along a highway bridge that turns into a gravel road heading northward. Little is known about this company timber town's past.

The town's operation was comprised of ties coming down the North Platte River shortly after the establishment of Fort Steele in 1868. During a drive, the ties strung out for twenty miles. One half million ties required dozens of men to refloat those that became stuck or grounded. The process of transferring the ties from the mountains to the railroad took two months. These drives were conducted yearly up to 1931, with Saratoga serving as the halfway point.

H Fort Fred Steele Historical Overview

I-80 Exit 228 Fort Steele rest stop

The south central portion of Wyoming has long been a travel corridor for prehistoric and historic people. Native American tribes from the Great Basin region to the west crossed this area to hunt buffalo on the eastern plains.

From 1810 until the decline of the Rocky Mountain fur trade in the late 1830s, fur traders and trappers traversed this region on their way west in quest of beaver pelts, then retraced their route east laden with furs. These men left little evidence of their passing, but they explored the routes used by thousands of future settlers destined for locations west of Wyoming.

Although suggestions to build a transcontinental railroad had been made in the 1840s, no decision was reached until after the outbreak of the Civil War when Congress selected a central route through southern Wyoming. The Union Pacific Railroad, chartered by Congress, built track westward from Nebraska through Wyoming to Utah.

The military constructed a series of forts along the Union Pacific route to protect construction crews against attack by hostile Indians. Fort Fred Steele, named in honor of Civil War hero Major General Frederick Steele, was established in June, 1868 where the railroad crossed the North Platte River. Until 1886, when it was decommissioned, the garrison at Fort Fred Steele performed a variety of policing activities involving both Indians and civilians.

The railroad also promoted mercantile development, and livestock, lumber and mining industries. After the departure of the military, these industries continued and the town of Fort Steele survived. Completion of the transcontinental Lincoln Highway through Wyoming in 1922 contributed to a brief economic revival. However, rerouting of the highway in 1939 and the demise of the tie industry in 1940 ended the town's function as a commercial center.

H Fort Fred Steele Interpretive Signs

Just over a mile north of I-80 Exit 228

Bridge Tender's House

The bridge tender's house was constructed by the Union Pacific Railroad to serve as an employee surveillance point. The bridge tender could respond quickly to locomotive-caused fires and could remove flood debris which might damage the bridge and cause interruptions to railroad traffic.

Restored by the Wyoming Recreation Commission in 1983, the one and one-half story, clapboard-sided structure was probably built before 1887. The replacement of steam by diesel locomotives in the mid-1900's eliminated the necessity for a bridge tender and the house was abandoned.

Fort Fred Steele After 1886

Officially abandoned in 1886, the fort came under the jurisdiction of the Department of the Interior in 1887. In 1892 and 1893 most of the buildings were sold at public auction. In 1897 the land, opened to homesteading, was patented by the Union Pacific Railroad.

Primary industries in the town of Fort Steele

after the turn of the century were sheep ranching and tie processing. The Lincoln Highway, the nation's first transcontinental highway, passed through the town and boosted the economy between 1920 and 1939. When the highway was moved in 1939 most commercial activity ended. The number of residents declined rapidly and the town became practically deserted.

In 1973 the Wyoming Stage Legislature created the Fort Fred Steele State Historic Site. Although the number of structures has declined dramatically over the years what remains standing is mute testimony to the flourishing and subsequent passing of several frontiers.

Brownsville and Benton

During construction of the Union Pacific Railroad land speculators and a large contingent of undesirables kept pace with or moved ahead of the construction crews and their military escorts. Townsite speculators tried to anticipate depot locations, purchasing land, selling lots and constructing tent towns.

Before the railroad reached the North Platte crossing at Fort Fred Steele, speculators set up the town of Brownsville on the river's east bank. Commanding Officer, Major Richard I. Dodge, issued an order July 2, 1868 proclaiming all lands within a three mile radius of Fort Fred Steele to be part of the military reservation and prohibiting civilian residence. Benton thus grew up on the west edge of the reservation. In a matter of days Brownsville's population resided in Benton. The tent town of Benton lasted only a few months when its population moved west to Rawlins Springs.

Officers' Quarters

The collapsed sandstone building west of the sign is all that remains of the once imposing eight room, one and one-half story Commanding Officer's quarters. Residences for staff officers were four, wood-framed double quarters with a captain in one-half and two lieutenants in the other half. Compared to enlisted men's barracks, the officers' quarters were luxurious. Amenities included lath and plaster walls, kitchens with cellars and large enclosed yards.

Officers' salaries greatly exceeded those of enlisted men. They could hire servants and support a family, activities prohibited to the enlisted man. Social activities at Fort Fred Steele included dinner parties, card games, theatrical presentations, dances and outdoor activities such as fishing, hunting, ice skating and sledding. Even with these diversions, daily military life was monotonous. Opportunities for promotion were limited and usually occurred upon the retirement or death of a superior.

Fort Steele Schoolhouse

After the fort was decommissioned and the military buildings were sold at auction, the residents of the Fort Steele community converted some of the old structures into homes and businesses or built anew on top of bare foundations. The schoolhouse was built in 1919 over the foundation remains of the fort hospital. The one-story, gable-roofed structure with clapboard siding served as a library, church, and community meeting house as well as an education center for the town.

Work and leisure time at Fort Steele did not change drastically with the closing of the fort. The trains continued to stop daily supplying the community with fresh produce and other necessary goods while carrying local timber and wool to points beyond. The North Platte River still provided the town folk with a pleasant location for their leisure activities.

Enlisted Men's Barracks

Two stone foundations and chimneys remain of the five enlisted men's barracks once at Fort Fred Steele. The walls were constructed of logs and boards and battens while a shingled roof protected pine floor boards. Tar paper covered interior walls. Kitchens doubled as mess and washrooms, and iron bedsteads took up most of the floor space.

Enlisted life in the frontier army could only be characterized as boring, with inadequate salaries and a monotonous diet. Most soldiers spent their days drilling and digging ditches. Social activities for enlisted men were limited and alcohol consumption prompted periodic orders from the commanding officer restricting saloon activities.

In 1892 the barracks buildings, sold at auction with other fort structures, were purchased by private citizens. Only the two central barracks remained when the first transcontinental auto road, the Lincoln Highway, passed through the town of Fort Steele in the 1920s. The road bridged the Platte River directly north of the town and passed close by the old army barracks, one of which was given a new function as a gasoline station.

The last two barracks were destroyed by fires set by vandals on New Year's Eve, 1976.

Sheepherders' Community

Sheep were introduced to Wyoming in the 1850s near Fort Bridger, about 180 miles west of Fort Steele. By 1880 the number had grown to over 350,000 head ranging primarily along the route of the Union Pacific Railroad, The Cosgriff Brothers owned one of the largest sheep ranching operations in Wyoming at that time, and they established herds in the Fort Steele area in 1881. After the fort was decommissioned they acquired many of its buildings and in 1903 constructed one of the largest sheep shearing plants in Wyoming. In 1905 over 800,000 pounds of wool was shipped to Boston, the single largest shipment of wool ever sent out of Wyoming.

L. E. Vivion, owner of the Leo Sheep Company, purchased most of the Cosgriff land holdings including the land at Fort Fred Steele in 1915. The house, lean-to, and shed in this area are the remains of a sheepherders' community.

Powder Magazine

The powder magazine housed the fort's munitions and therefore was located away from the main military complex. Ironically, it is one of the few fort structures remaining. It replaced the original magazine, a dugout constructed when the post was established in 1868.

The structure was built in 1881 from locally quarried stone and from materials fabricated at the Department of the Platte Headquarters in Omaha and shipped by rail to Fort Fred Steele. With sturdy walls on random-coursed ashlar sandstone, the powder magazine remains essentially the same as it was in 1881, although the tin roof has been replaced with shingles and internal shelving has been removed.

Few artillery pieces and only small quantities of ammunition were kept at the post. Fort Fred Steele generally had only a single mountain howitzer, and sometimes a Gatling gun on hand. Other explosive and combustible materials such as powder, fuses and signaling fireworks probably also were stored in this building.

Major General Frederick Steele 1818-1868

General Steele commanded a division of the Union Army at Vicksburg. Later he commanded all Union forces on the line of the Arkansas, exercising President Lincoln's policy of conciliation and reconstruction. At the end of the war he served in Texas, on the Mexican border. He then was sent to Oregon and Washington as commander of the Department of the Columbia.

Shortly following his death, Fort Fred Steele was named in his honor,

Post Trader Residence

This site is the remains of the Post Trader's residence. The photograph taken of the building later in the army's occupation of the fort attests to the prosperity enjoyed by the Post Trader.

The Post Trader was appointed by the Secretary of War, and the position was highly prized because of its profit possibilities. In 1868 J. W. Hugus established dry goods, liquor, freighting and ferry operations, all welcomed by travelers and local residents including the fort's soldiers. Alcohol use apparently caused the Post Commander concern as he frequently ordered Hugus to limit sales to soldiers.

Hugus, one of the area's leading merchandisers, continued as Post Trader until 1884 when he sold his business to Fenimore Chatterton, a long-time employee. Chatterton later held the office of Wyoming Secretary of State and served as Acting Governor from 1903 to 1905.

Carbon Timber Company

Construction of the Union Pacific Railroad stimulated the growth of the timber industry in southern Wyoming. Two companies began supplying ties to the railroad in 1868, but the firm of Coe and Carter was the leading supplier to the Fort Fred Steele collection yards until 1896.

Cut and shaped in the Medicine Bow Mountains to the south, ties were floated downrivcr during spring run-off and were gathered behind a boom here. Coe and Carter also supplied timbers for coal mines at Carbon, Hanna, and Dana to the east, and lumber for buildings at Fort Fred Steele and the surrounding area. The Carbon Timber Company, successor to Coe and Carter, floated over 1.5 million timbers down the North Platte in 1909.

Directly across the North Platte River east of Fort Steele are the remains of the Carbon Timber Company tie processing facility, a privately-owned site.

Cemetery

The post cemetery served as a graveyard for soldiers, their dependents, and civilians during army occupation of Fort Fred Steele (1868-1886). Although some soldiers died during the Indian Wars of the 1860's and 1870's, most of the military deaths at the fort were the result of accidents and disease. Civilians and travelers who expired in the vicinity of Fort Steele also were interred in the cemetery.

Although the Fort Steele hospital provided medical services to military personnel and their dependents, the lack of refined medical techniques often resulted in death from infection and diseases like pneumonia and tuberculosis. The infant mortality rate was particularly high and 25% of the graves in the cemetery were occupied by children.

The 100' X 140' cemetery was enclosed by a picket fence and contained eighty irregularly spaced graves. Each grave was numbered, the

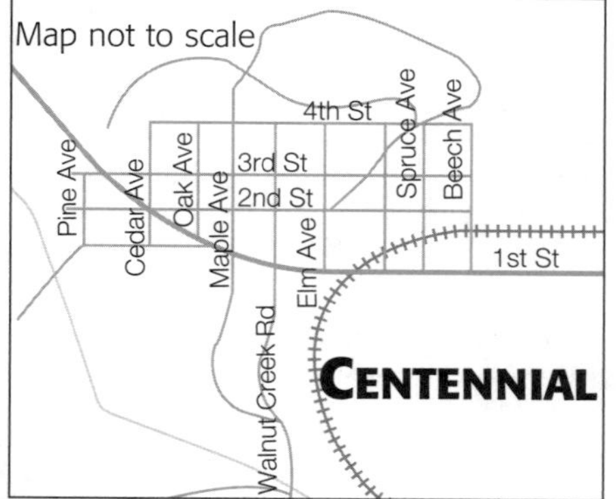

number appearing on a painted wooden peg at the foot of the plot. Gravesite markings included wood headboards for the military but they proved impractical as inscriptions soon became obliterated by weathering. Although few persons of historical fame were buried in the Fort Fred Steele cemetery, an exception was Jefferson J. Standifer, who participated in many western gold rushes including the brief 1867 boom at South Pass City, Wyoming.

Not all those who perished at Fort Steele were buried in the post cemetery. Rather than surrender their loved ones to an eternity on this wind-swept riverbank, some chose to ship the deceased by rail to other final resting places. Military families occasionally requested official assistance with the shipments. Officers reported civilian requests for coffins and embalming materials, complaining that to supply them was not a military responsibility.

When the post was decommissioned in 1886, the Secretary of the Interior declared the cemetery exempt from sale or transfer to public because of the military burials. In 1892 the graves of the soldiers, their dependents and some civilians were moved to Fort McPherson National Cemetery near Maxwell, Nebraska. Civilians continued to use the cemetery after the departure of the military and the last documented burial took place in the 1920's. The land occupied by the cemetery is still owned by the United States government.

25 *Gas*

T Walcott

Walcott known as "new highway Walcott" is seven miles east of the Fort Steele turnoff. The "railroad Walcott" is one mile north. In the railroad Walcott, you will find the old "Glub Saloon" with its false front. Across the tracks are a number of old cabins that are now used by the Vivian Sheep Company. Once a major shipping hub for the Union Pacific, especially during the copper boom, Walcott was named for a respected train conductor.

26 *Food, Lodging*

Elk Mountain

Pop. 192, Elev. 7,268

Once a stage station and then a railroad station, this town was named for the nearby mountain, part of the Medicine Bow elk feeding range.

H Wagonhound Tipi Rings

I-80 Exit 267 at rest area

The stone circles or "Tipi Rings" at this site mark the location of a prehistoric Native American campsite. The stones were probably used to anchor the skins of conical tents, known by the Sioux word "Tipi". The stones were placed around the base of the tipi to hold down the skins as well as to provide additional support to the tipi in high winds. After the introduction of the metal ax, wooden pegs gradually replaced the stones for holding down the skins.

The tipi was used for shelter and sleeping. Most daily activities occurred outside the structure. A hearth in the center of the tipi was used for heat and cooking in poor weather.

In prehorse times, tipis averaged approximately 12 feet in diameter, and poles used in their construction were up to 15 feet long. Eight to 12 buffalo hides were needed for the construction of a tipi. The hides of buffalo killed during the summer were preferred because they were thinner and lighter in weight. A smudge fire was built inside a new tipi, and the smoke was allowed to permeated the leather. This process waterproofed the leather and aided in its preservation.

It has been estimated that there are over 1 million tipi rings in the western United States. As such, they are one of the most common archaeological features to be found in this part of the country. The features at this rest area have been preserved by the Wyoming Highway Department and the Office of the Wyoming State Archaeologist for your benefit. Please feel free to inspect the tipi rings up close, but do not disturb the rocks.

27 *Gas, Food*

Arlington - Rock Creek Station

The Rock Creek Station, also known as Arlington or Rock Dale, was built in 1860, along the Overland Route. As a stage station known as a home station, Rock Creek became a commercial as well as "entertainment" center for immigrants. Rock Creek thrived as a supply and social center for growing agricultural and timber interests in the surrounding area. To serve the many needs of the travelers, Joe Bush, owner of the stage station operated a dancehall-saloon, general store, and blacksmith shop from one building. He also built a toll bridge. The block building is one of the original buildings still standing on Main Street. One of the oldest log cabins in Wyoming still stands in Arlington.

A post office was established in 1892 and Rock Creek or Rockdale was renamed Arlington. Arlington continued to operate as a commercial-agricultural center into the 20th century. As one of the earliest settlements in Carbon County, Rock Creek contributed in a commercial and social sense to the development of south central Wyoming. Arlington has been listed on the National Register of Historic Places since 1983. Today Arlington is mostly ranch country and mail comes to the post office in Rock River.

The Rock Creek Station is near where a wagon train was attacked by Cheyennes and Arapahoes. They captured two little girls—Mary Fletcher, 13, and Lizzie Fletcher, 2, after killing their mother and injuring the father and brothers. Mary was found and bought back by a white trader a short time later and was returned her to her father in Salt Lake City for a fee and supplies. Lizzie was not found until over 30 years later, living on the Wind River Reservation. Mary had settled in Iowa and read about Lizzie in a newspaper. She returned to Wyoming, identifying her sister. Lizzie was married and living with her Arapaho husband, John Brokenhorn. She spoke no English and enjoyied a high status in the community, chosing to stay on the reservation rather than reunite with her sister.

McFadden

Originally a railroad station, McFadden was once named Ohio City, but was renamed for an oil company official when oil was discovered nearby in 1917.

T Turbine Windmills

If you like wind, this is the place to be. One of the windiest places in the nation is now the home of one of the biggest wind farms. From miles away you can see the 69 towering white windmills which crank out 41,000 kilowatt-hours of electricity per day, powering 20,000 homes. Travelers on I-80 between Rawlins and Laramie will see one of the largest wind farms in the West outside of California. Energy is created for Utah, Oregon, Washington, and Wyoming. A project that was started in the 1990s, there are now 119 wind turbines capable of generating 91.4 megawatts of electricity. These generators have the capacity to supply electricity to 23,764 homes for an entire year. The largest rotors on these wind generators have a diameter of 57 feet. Imagine the wingspan of a Boeing 747 and you'll have an idea. The beauty of wind power is that there are no emissions and no waste to be managed.

28 *Gas, Food, Lodging*

Centennial

Pop. 50, Elev. 8,076

Named for the centennial of the Declaration of Independence, a gold mine was discovered here in 1876 by Col. Stephen W. Downey, pioneer and statesman. The gold ran out quickly, and only a few tough customers remained behind. Logging and ranching became the little town's livelihood, and in time, Centennial became a stopover for travelers on their way to the Snowy Range. The village provides a stunning view down into the Centennial Valley, and up the slopes of the tree-covered mountains, an especially lovely sight in autumn when the aspens turn gold.

Centennial

	Jan	Feb	March	April	May	June	July	Aug	Sep	Oct	Nov	Dec	Annual
Average Max. Temperature (F)	32.6	34.9	39.6	49.3	59.4	70.0	76.9	75.2	67.4	56.4	41.3	34.0	53.1
Average Min. Temperature (F)	12.3	13.9	16.9	24.3	32.7	40.5	46.8	45.1	37.6	28.9	19.1	13.9	27.7
Average Total Precipitation (in.)	1.10	0.87	1.06	1.32	1.65	1.38	1.53	1.22	1.20	0.79	0.99	1.08	14.20
Average Total SnowFall (in.)	17.8	14.4	18.2	13.8	6.1	0.7	0.0	0.0	1.8	5.4	14.1	19.3	111.5
Average Snow Depth (in.)	2	2	1	1	0	0	0	0	0	0	1	2	1

Grand Encampment Museum.

Albany

Like the county of the same name, Albany was named for the capitol city of New York by legislator Charles Bradley, who came from that area. Once a railroad stop, Albany is now the central point in a scenic valley of cabins and small ranches.

Fox Park

Once a gathering place for wild foxes, railroad officials chose this site as a stop due to its proximity to good lumber for ties. In 1906, a post office was established. Modern lumber companies continue to log in nearby Medicine Bow National Forest, although environmental concerns have changed the way the timber is harvested.

Mountain Home

Nestled at the foot of the Medicine Bow Range, this one-time stage station is now a traveler's playground.

T Nici Self Museum

2740 State Highway 130 in Centennial. 742-7158.

Partially housed in a 1907 Hahn's Peak and Pacific Railroad depot, the museum's exhibits depict the general history of the Centennial Valley. a range of topics are covered, including mining, ranching, lumbering, and railroading. A 1944 Union Pacific caboose and many large pieces of farming, ranching, and mining equipment are at the site. The museum is open from mid-June through Labor Day Friday through Monday from 1 p.m. to 4 p.m.

T Sugarloaf Recreation Area

Just east of the Snowy Range Pass in the Medicine Bow-Routt National Forest is this magnificant recreation area. Sharp spires carved from glaciers rise above small lakes and islands. Trails lead to various lakes and fragrant and colorful alpine meadows. A viewing platform provides panoramic vistas of Libby Flats, Medicine Bow Peak, and surrounding valleys.

29 *Gas, Food, Lodging*

Encampment

Pop. 443, Elev. 7,323

Encampment was named, like the nearby river, for being the site of Indian camps during hunting season. In the early 1800s, trappers and traders joined the Native Americans. The rendezvous site was officially called the Grand Encampment. The town developed in 1898 when copper was discovered and mined here. A sixteen-mile tramway, the longest in the world, was built to convey the ore to the smelter. The mine played out ten years later, and the community turned to ranching and logging. Now locals invite tourism, as the scenic mountains above draw those who crave the quiet life. Many of the early buildings have been restored, and provide a glimpse of the old mining days. Judge Charles E. Winter, author of the lyrics for the state song, "Wyoming," was from Encampment.

Riverside

Pop. 59, Elev. 7,137

Situated on the Encampment River, this was once part of the site of rendezvous for mountain men and Native Americans. Although Riverside was never a mining camp, it came into being in 1851 as the result of serving as the gateway to the mining district and as a neighbor to the prominent town, Encampment. Originally named after a man called Dogget who started a store and station, the town eventually came to be known as Riverside.

Soon, cabins were built, and sixty buildings followed. The most noted building being a forty-room hotel that burned and was rebuilt. The copper ran out and the town became a shell of its former glory. Recent growth in tourism has breathed new life into the one-time ghost town.

T Grand Encampment Museum

At Encampment. 327-5308

An abundance of fine pelts drew the first white men into this valley, long held sacred by the Indians. The trappers' day soon passed, and was succeeded by others, equally brief. Tie cutters, cattle barons, and hunting expeditions came and went. Thomas Edison accompanied one of these expeditions, and at Battle Lake he conceived the idea for the incandescent light. Homesteaders and ranchers, the first permanent residents, began to arrive in the 1870s.

The year of 1897 produced an electrifying change. A rich copper strike in the Sierra Madres precipitated the new city of Grand Encampment and several satellite settlements. A 16-mile aerial tramway—the longest in the world—supplied the smelter. Power was provided by water through a 4' wooden pipeline. The S & E Railroad was constructed, but its completion came a little late.

In 1908, the company, which had produced two million dollars in copper ore, was indicted for over-capitalization and fraudulent stock sales. The mines closed, and Rudefeha, Dillon, Copperton, Rambler, Battle and Elwood became ghost towns. Encampment and Riverside survived but the "Grand" was quietly dropped.

The museum captures some of this history through its collection. On the complex is the "Doc" Culleton Building. Inside you'll see a variety of displays including a folding oak bathtub and a square grand piano. Also at the complex is the George Kuntzman Building, the Wolfard School House, a U.S. Forest Service guard station, a Tiehack cabin, and the Lake Creek Stage Station.

One of the more unusual exhibits is the two-story outhouse. Though most dwellings in the mining communities in the hills above Encampment in the early days were settled on solid earth, many of the nearby Chic-Sale structures were designed in higher fashion, to overcome the problem of deep, drifting snows. Some of these outhouses were erected high atop a base of cribbed up logs; others were slender, silo-like creations with doors opening high up on their fronts; a few were even impressive with newly shingled exteriors. Most were approached by wooden steps leading up five or six feet to railed platforms in front of the doors; others were reached by railed ramps from building to outhouse. A two-story outhouse is part of the display at the Grand Encampment Museum complex.

The museum is open daily from Memorial Day weekend through September and on weekends through October. Call for hours. Admission is free. Brochures for a local walking tour can also be obtained here.

Excerpted from museum brochure.

T Old Encampment

Situated on the stream known as Encampment River nine miles above its junction with the North Platte lies what used to be Encampment. Numerous minerals, including gold and copper were found here in 1879. Unlike the other towns, no rush was forthcoming since the amounts discovered were minute. Several families built log homes and settled here, and eventually a tiny post office was built. A resident named Ed Haggerty discovered a copper mine in 1897, and from this discovery, the town slowly grew.

A stage service was started from Saratoga to the north over primitive, muddy roads. During its height, 5,000 people called Encampment home; it was one of the wildest and most boisterous camps in the State of Wyoming. At various points, four newspapers sprang up, with the Grand Encampment Herald surviving the longest of its following rivals: the Encampment Echo, Encampment Record, and the Valley Roundup.

The North American Copper Co. was created here. In 1898, the company acquired the largest mine, Rudefeha, for a half-million and then sold thousands of dollars worth of stock. The company built a twenty mile tramway—the longest in the world at that time—to carry ore from the mine to the reduction plant. The tram could carry 98 tons daily.

Wyoming Tidbits

Due to the winter storms that sweep across southern Wyoming, residents dubbed a portion of I-80 near Rawlins the Sno Chi Minh Trail. Complete whiteout conditions are not uncommon in the area.

The beginning of Encampment's demise started in 1906 when the mill at the largest smelter burned. Two years later, the remainder was destroyed. Although the railway came in 1908, the smelter had closed completely. Legal troubles soon followed as the company was accused of huge fraudulent stock sales and eventually endured the wrath of the court.

The famous tram was removed in 1910, and the railroad that once served the cattle shippers was soon replaced by trucks. The town died in June of 1962.

T Rambler

Rambler is nestled near a lake on the western slope of the Continental Divide. Today, only three buildings still stand as reminders of this copper boom town. Up until January 1, 1904, half a million pounds of copper was extracted in Rambler. All of the ore was hauled by mules over the Divide and down to Encampment smelter.

T Battle

High on the Continental Divide, approximately 10 miles west of Encampment, this ghost town was named for an 1841 confrontation between whites and Indians. The town was first a home to loggers and miners. Ore mined in the town was shipped to Encampment to be smelted.

T Copperton

Miners hoping to find copper in this area named the town. When the copper ore vein played out in the early 1900s, so did the town. Few remains are visible today of this once-thriving mining town.

T Dillon

Named for saloon owner Malachi Dillon, this town was founded after neighboring company town Rudefeha banned saloons. Soon afterwards, Dillon became the largest town in the Sierra Madres. Today, several buildings still stand, nestled among the trees. By 1907 Dillon was a ghost town along with Rudefeha.

T Rudefeha

East side of Bridger Peak summit northwest of Encampment

An abandoned mine shaft, tramway towers and several support buildings remain in this old mining company town in which the Ferris-Haggerty mine was located. When company officials banned saloons, bar owner Malachi Dillon moved a short distance away and built a spot for miners to wet their whistles. Rudefeha became a ghost town by 1907.

T Indian Bathtubs

One mile west of Riverside on State Highway 230

These intriguing rock basins collect rainwater and melting snow, and Native Americans came here to clean off after hunting. Take Blackhall Road about one mile to the trailhead, which takes you about another mile on foot to the bathtubs.

T Robert A. Peck Art Center, Central Wyoming College

2660 Peck Ave. in Riverton. 855-2202

The Robert A. Peck Arts Center presents touring performances, theater and music productions, and monthly art exhibits. Featured artists included are local, regional, and national recognized. Open Monday through Friday, 8 a.m. to 10 p.m. and Saturday and Sunday, from 12 p.m. to 6 p.m. Closed holidays.

H Thomas A. Edison

On State Highway 70 between Encampment and Savery overlooking Battle Lake

Camped near this spot in 1878, while on a fishing trip. It was here that his attention was directed to the fiber from his bamboo fishing pole which he tested as a suitable filament for his incandescent electric lamp.

Born February 11, 1847—Died October 18, 1931 Age 84.

H Encampment, Wyoming (Grand Encampment) Elevation 7,323 feet

At north end of town of Encampment

Gateway to the sites of ghost towns of the Copper Country. Once a favorite hunting ground of Prehistoric man, later "Camp le Grand" became a noted rendezvous of Indians and trappers. In 1897 the town site was laid out by Willis George Emerson and associates; in 1897 Ed Haggarty made his big strike on the Continental Divide. In 1902, during the mining boom, the longest aerial tramway in the world was built to convey ore 16 miles from the great Ferris-Haggarty mine to the smelter at Encampment. In 1908 the industry collapsed. Encampment is now a beef, timber, hunting, fishing and resort center.

H Battle Country

State Highway 70 between Encampment and Savery at Battle Lake Overlook.

The year is 1841. This country was teaming with beaver and other fur-bearing animals, and it was jealously guarded by Indians. Because the lure of beaver was so great, a group of American Fur Company trappers invaded these mountains determined to trap the streams.

On August 20, Henry Fraeb, with thirty-two trappers under his command, had a desperate battle with an overwhelming force of Cheyenne and Sioux Indians. On that day, ten men were sent out from camp to drive buffalo. Those remaining in camp would head off the bison after the ten started them running in their direction. By accident, the ten men ran onto a large body of Indians, and were attacked with great fury. One trapper was wounded badly in the fight and he turned his horse in the direction of camp, which he reached safely. Fraeb ordered twenty of his men to mount, and he led them to the rescue of the nine who were desperately fighting the unequal conflict. The arrival of the reinforcements decided the battle and the Indians retreated.

The Indians' resentment of their defeat was immediate. Retreating northeast, they fired the forest, thus serving notice that they would make the country a wasteland rather than let the white men take it. The immediate area was denuded.

From this trapper-Indian conflict, Battle Creek, Battle Lake, the town of Battle and Battle Mountain received their name.

The battle occurred where the creek in front of you joins the Little Snake River, about eight miles south.

Wyoming Tidbits

Wyoming author Owen Wister's classic novel The Virginian is the source for the famous line, "When you call me that, smile..."

Tom Horn

The legendary Tom Horn, most famous of the West's hired guns, and certainly Wyoming's, was born in Missouri on November 21, 1860. Considered an incorrigible youth his father, being of the old school persistently attempted to beat this badness out of the boy. After one such beating, Tom ran away from home and worked at various odd jobs as he roamed the West. By the time he was 17, he was employed by the Government as a U.S. Army scout. playing a prominent role in Geronimo's surrender in 1886. Horn was the man who managed to negotiate the terms of surrender with the notorious Apache Chief.

Tom Horn arrived in Wyoming during the Range Wars of the 1890s. He hired on as a stock detective with the Swan Land and Cattle Company located about 50 miles northwest of Cheyenne, Wyoming to scare would-be ranchers and farmers out of the Iron Mountain area. The cattle ranchers didn't take kindly to sheepmen or homesteader's who built homes in the middle of grazing land. While in this employment, Horn was supposedly responsible for eliminating a number of cattle rustlers in the area. Some true and some perhaps tall tales on Tom's part.

Horn saw himself as a benefactor of society. Getting rid of cattle thieves was considered to him on a par with killing a wolf or a coyote. For each cattle rustler he shot, he would charge the cattlemen $500 and, of course, receive their admiration. It was about this time that he was reported to have said that, "killing men is my specialty. I look at it as a business proposition, and I think I have a corner on the market." His trademark was a large rock, which he placed beneath the dead man's head.

In 1901 Horn was accused of the murder of a fourteen year old boy named Willie Nickell. Horn said he had mistaken the boy for his father who was trying to bring sheep into the Wyoming cattle ranges. Horn's demise came when he was arrested after bragging about the killing to the deputy U.S. Marshall while drinking. He was convicted by a jury in Cheyenne and sentenced to hang.

Horn escaped from the Cheyenne jail but was promptly recaptured. During his final days in jail he spent his time weaving the rope that would hang him in November of 1903 at the age of 42. His death ended the era of the "Outlaw West" in Wyoming, putting an end to gunfighters. road agents and rustlers.

Tom Horn is buried in the Old Pioneer Cemetery, which is part of the Columbia Cemetery in Boulder, Colorado. A reprieve came in 1993 when forensic experts and Amnesty International staged a retrial in which Horn was found not guilty—too late to actually do him any good.

Section 5

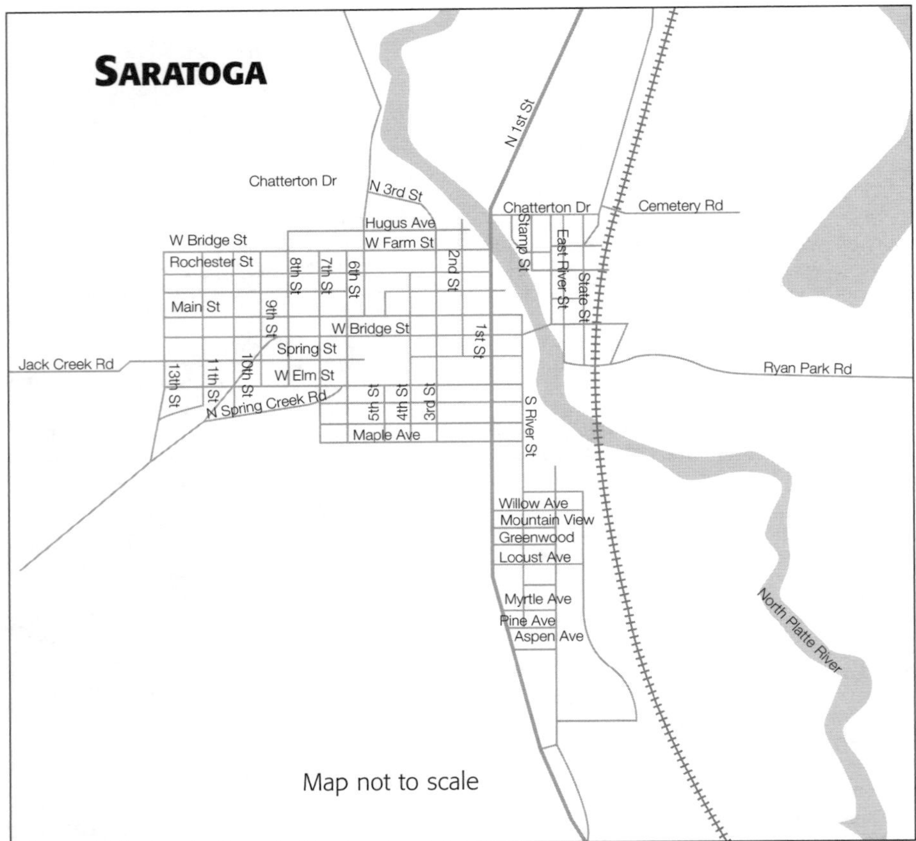

Saratoga

Pop. 1,726, Elev. 6,786

Local Native Americans called the hot springs here the "place of magic water" and often came here to find relief from illness. The first homesteader, William H. Cadwell, set up a bathhouse in the area, and travelers came from near and far to soak in the springs. Fennimore Chatterton, post trader at Fort Steele, hoped to turn this into a resort town, and thus named it for the renowned Saratoga Hot Springs in New York State. The town was established in 1878, but did not prosper until the railroad came in 1907. The copper boom also created growth, until the mines ran out. Today, Saratoga is largely an agricultural community, and also mills lumber from the nearby mountains. With the only "blue ribbon" trout stream in this part of the state, Saratoga is gaining increasing attention as a major tourist center.

T Saratoga Museum

104 Constitution Avenue in Saratoga. 326-5511

The Saratoga Museum, opened in 1980, is housed in the town's original c1915 Union Pacific Railroad Depot. The museum provides an opportunity for its visitors to explore the history of the Platte Valley. The museum exhibits tell the story of early man in the Americas and Saratoga's pioneer ranchers, merchants, tradesmen, loggers, clergy, dentists, physicians, educators and the women working beside them in the settlement of the Valley. Saratoga, Wyoming, originally called Warm Springs, was once neutral ground for the Indian tribes inhabiting the Platte Valley before the arrival of white settlers. In 1884, Fenimore C. Chatterton changed the name to Saratoga, a name derived from an Iroquois Indian word Sarachtogue, which translates to "place of miraculous water in the rock" Chatterton borrowed the name from Saratoga Springs, NY, a town he had visited in his youth. The town was later incorporated in 1890.

The museum's newest section is a natural history room featuring a world-class specimen collection and minerals of local historical importance as well as interpretive displays on the geologic history of the Valley.

Other exhibits at the museum include a caboose donated in 1982 by the Union Pacific Railroad, a sheep wagon, tie hack tools, a geology exhibit, and the Katharine Bakeless Nason Archaeology room.

Excerpted from museum brochure.

T Saratoga Hot Springs Hobo Pool

On State Highway 130 in Saratoga

A soaking pool bordered with a wall of moss rock greets swimmers. On the bank of the North Platte River, the pool is open all year, with water temperatures hovering around 105 degrees. Free to the public.

T Saratoga National Fish Hatchery

Four miles northeast of Saratoga, and 35 miles southeast of Rawlins

The Saratoga National Fish Hatchery is located in Southern Wyoming, four miles northeast of the town of Saratoga, and 35 miles southeast of Rawlins. The Hatchery was established in 1914 and has primarily served as an egg producing facility for most of its years of operation.

The current mission of the Hatchery is to provide four million Lewis Lake lake trout eggs to the Great Lakes restoration effort, and to provide 3.5 million Plymouth Rock brown trout eggs to other Federal, state and tribal programs. The Hatchery maintains the back-up broodstock for the McConaughy rainbow trout. We are also involved in rearing and breeding the endangered Wyoming toad for reintroduction into the wild. They are open year round, seven days a week, from 8:00 a.m. until 4:00 p.m. and provide guided group tours upon advanced request. Fish spawning activities can be observed from the end of September through October.

T Saratoga Petroglyphs

North of Saratoga along the North Platte River

Cliffs above the river bear reminders of the emigrants, who carved their names on the rock.

31 *Gas, Food, Lodging*

Elmo

Founded by a group of Finnish homesteaders, Elmo was named for one of their number who was killed in an Indian raid.

Hanna

Pop. 873, Elev. 6,777

Mark A. Hanna, for whom this town was named, was a politician and financier who once sat on the board of directors for the Union Pacific Railroad. This name was not given to the town until 1886, and by that time, the Hanna town site had already existed as a stage station and a coal mining camp since much earlier in the century. In fact, the first coal town established in Wyoming, in 1868, (Carbon) is now a ghost town a few miles to the east. A graveyard and a few ruins are all that remain.

Hanna is still primarily a coal town, being situated between two of the states biggest working coal fields: the Medicine Bow strip mine to the west, and the huge Cyprus Shoshone mine to the north.

Medicine Bow

Pop. 274, Elev. 6,353

Medicine Bow's birth is the result of the Central Pacific and Union Pacific Railroads tracks being laid in the bend of the Medicine River. A railroad station was built so that water could be pumped from the river and a tank supply kept for the engines.

Eventually, two saloons sprung up, and a general store owned by J.L. Klinkenbeard. Medicine Bow as incorporated in 1909; its first mayor was

Saratoga	Jan	Feb	March	April	May	June	July	Aug	Sep	Oct	Nov	Dec	Annual
Average Max. Temperature (F)	33.2	36.8	43.5	54.6	65.6	76.0	83.1	80.9	72.1	59.6	43.7	35.4	57.0
Average Min. Temperature (F)	10.4	13.2	19.3	27.1	35.5	43.4	49.3	47.1	38.5	28.8	19.0	12.1	28.6
Average Total Precipitation (in.)	0.47	0.44	0.73	0.94	1.39	0.95	0.94	0.92	0.87	0.98	0.56	0.44	9.61
Average Total SnowFall (in.)	8.9	7.7	9.5	5.6	1.7	0.1	0.0	0.0	1.1	3.4	8.1	8.2	54.3
Average Snow Depth (in.)	3	2	1	0	0	0	0	0	0	0	1	2	1

August Grimm. In 1913, one of the grandest hotels in the state, The Hotel Virginian, was built, whose walls were decorated by cowboy artist C.M. Russell.

On November 8, 1919, a train stopped at the Medicine Bow station was held up by an escaped convict, William Carlisle. Carlisle escaped, but was eventually apprehended in the Laramie Mountains and was returned to prison.

One individual who made the residents of Medicine Bow proud was Owen Wister, author of The Virginian. In gathering information for his popular book, Wister rode the land of Two Bar Ranch to capture the feel of the area.

Native Americans used to come to the Medicine Bow River for the ash wood that grew on its banks, which was especially good for making bows. The Indian conception of the English word "medicine" had multiple meanings, which included healing, good luck, and quality. Thus, a "medicine bow" was one that would assure good hunting.

Saratoga

T **Medicine Bow Museum**

405 Lincoln Highway in Medicine Bow. 739-2383

Located in an old railroad depot built in 1913, the museum is home to Old West and local history artifacts including a collection of cowboy chaps and branding irons.

T **Hanna Basin Museum**

502 Hanna Basin in Hanna. 325-9424

The Hanna Basin Museum is located in teh Old Community Hall on Front Street. The exhibits cover the general history of the Hanna area. There are a variety of exhibits including photos, documents, and artifacts on the coal camps, railroad, homesteading, and ranching. Hours are 1 p.m. to 5 p.m. Admission is free but donations are accepted.

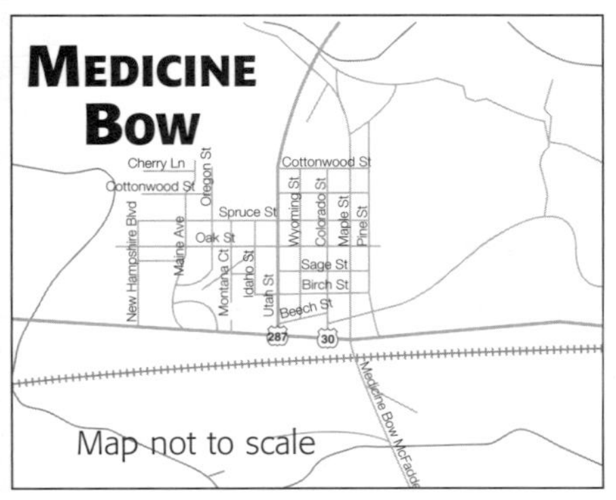

H **Owen Wister**

"When you say that, smile"

In Medicine Bow east of the train depot

Owen Wister whose writings acquainted the nation with pioneer Wyoming ranch life, made Medicine Bow the beginning of his most popular novel, "The Virginian".

Editor's note: The line, "When you call me that, smile!" is one of the most recognized lines from Western literature. It occured in Wister's novel during a saloon scene in Medicine Bow.

M **Wyoming Ranch Company, LLC**

Medicine Bow & Rawlins. Joe Stratton, 307-321-7777 or Bob Duca, 925-210-0560.

32 *No services*

H **Interconnected to all Life**

At rest area

In a time before time, only the natural forces of wind, water, weather and fire affected plant and animal life in Wyoming. In later times, Native Americans hunted, camped and lived in this basin. Since that time, the natural wildness of the land has changed. Yet the changes seen here over the past 200 years are not nearly as evident as those that have taken place elsewhere. Few places in the world still offer the diversity of native plant and animal species as do the sagebrush basins of Wyoming.

Many things that were here then are still here now. Sagebrush is still here, and sage sparrows still nest in its branches. Sage grouse still nest in tall prairie grasses near sagebrush plants, and pronghorn antelope still feed on tender sagebrush shoots. Over 250 species of wildlife still freely range across the sage-covered plains.

Despite their lasting wildness, the basins and prairies of Wyoming have not totally escaped change. The bison, wolf and grizzly bear are gone forever, never to return. The black-footed ferret, which once stalked through vast prairie dog towns in search of food, was nearly wiped out but may return to once again hunt the basin.

In fulfilling our present and future needs, we must not forget about the needs of the sagebrush, the little sage sparrow, the sage grouse and the pronghorn antelope. We are all interconnected to the land and water—we have to remember that their destiny is ours.

33 *Gas, Food, Lodging*

Natrona

Elev. 5,610

Natrona received it's name from the natural deposits of trona or carbonate of soda also known as soda ash. Trona is used to manufacture glass containers, fiber-glass, specialty glass, detergents, food additives, and photography, and pH control of water. Trona is one of the most widely used and important commodities in the United States.

Medicine Bow	Jan	Feb	March	April	May	June	July	Aug	Sep	Oct	Nov	Dec	Annual
Average Max. Temperature (F)	31.9	35.6	42.7	54.9	65.2	76.2	83.3	81.2	72.1	59.6	42.2	33.8	56.6
Average Min. Temperature (F)	11.3	13.4	18.3	26.0	34.5	42.3	47.4	45.3	36.2	27.1	18.5	12.7	27.8
Average Total Precipitation (in.)	0.45	0.50	0.70	1.12	1.61	1.23	1.17	0.84	0.94	0.81	0.53	0.42	10.32
Average Total SnowFall (in.)	6.5	6.0	6.3	5.8	1.3	0.1	0.0	0.0	1.5	2.6	5.4	4.9	40.4
Average Snow Depth (in.)	1	1	1	0	0	0	0	0	0	0	1	1	0

Hell's Half Acre

T Powder River

Pop. 50, Elev. 5,714

Named for the famous river, Powder River is in the heart of sheep country.

T Hell's Half Acre

A marvel of nature, this collection of intricately eroded rock formations in the midst of the prairie actually covers 320 acres. The colorful canyon walls of this convoluted geological wonderland served as a backdrop for the movie Starship Troopers in 1996. Captain Bonneville named the place the Devil's Kitchen when coal deposits here caught fire in the 1800s and burned for years, creating a sulfurous, smoky atmosphere within the red-walled maze.

H Hell's Half Acre

42 miles west of Casper at Hell's Half Acre turnout on U.S. Highway 20/26

This unique setting of natural beauty covers approximately 320 acres. Viewed from a point of maximum depth, its walls and pinnacles show soft and varied hues comparable to the Grand Canyon of the Yellowstone.

Investigation has confirmed that in former days the Indains drove great herds of buffalo into this depression for slaughter. Flint arrowheads and buffalo bones have been found here. A detachment of Captain B.L.E. Boneville's party visited this site in July 1833. This area has been dedicated to Natrona County by the Federal Government.

34 *No services*

Arminto

The post office here was named for Manuel Armenta, who owned the nearby Jack Pot Ranch. Union Pacific Railroad officials changed the spelling. Armenta was accused of being a horse thief, but also had a reputation for helping those in need, a sort of Western Robin Hood. The second incorporated town in Natrona County, Arminto once promised to rival Casper economically.

Ervay

Once a post office, this town was named for founder Jake E. Ervay in 1882.

Waltman

Once called Keg Springs, this town was named for Waltman Walters, who was the son of a Northwestern Railroad official.

H Bridger Road-Waltman Crossing

At Waltman Rest Area on U.S. Highway 20/26

Here the present-day highway crosses what remains of an all but forgotten road. That road led to the remote gold fields of western Montana, booming since 1862.

The Government, in 1859, ordered Captain W.F. Raynolds, Topographic Engineers, U.S. Army, to reconnoiter Rocky Mountain topography and potential routes leading to areas of indicated mineralization. Old Jim Bridger, noted explorer since fur trade days, was Raynolds' guide. In 1864 official energy was still concentrated on the Civil War and that most famous of mountain-men laid out this road himself.

The Oregon Trail was the trunk line of the western roads. Although Motnna's mines lay far north of its course, further west—in Idaho a branch-road turned off to those diggings. But that right-angle turn added some two hundred time-consuming, exhausting miles to the shortest feasible roadway. During 1863, John Bozeman had pioneered a road, east of the Big Horn Mountains and up the Yellowstone Valley, cutting across the angle, saving two weeks travel time. Still, by crossing Indian hunting grounds, his road increased the hazard of overland freight and travel.

Bridger's route—west of the Big Horns—reduced danger from indian attacks while saving ten days time. But the Bridger road was a compromise. It never was as well known as either of its alternatives. Later, it was important in the settlement of northwestern Wyoming.

H Mama Sage

At Waltman Rest Area

It is not coincidence that Wyoming supports over two-thirds of the world's population of pronghorn antelope and sage grouse. The only vast expanses of sagebrush-grassland habitat left on the North American continent are found in Wyoming, Nevada and Montana. Pronghorn antrelope and sage grouse require these extensive, uninterrupted native habitats to roam freely between summer and winter range.. Sagebrush provides the major food source for these species, especially in winter when snow covers most other vegetation.

Our state's sagebrush habitat also supports other unique life forms. The golden eagle, sage thrasher, cottontail rabbit, horned lark, sage lizard and western jumping mouse are just a few of the over 150 species of wildlife commonly found associated with sagebrush.

Wildlife agencies and state and federal land managers work with people using the land and its many resources to maintain these native habitats and free-ranging wildlife populations—so you and future generations can always enjoy "Mama Sage" and her wildlife.

While at first glance the sagebrush community takes on the appearance of "wasteland," it is an integral part of that magic formula which makes Wyoming a wildlife paradise.

35 *No services*

Lost Cabin

Named for a fabled gold mine where prospectors built a cabin. The cabin was never found after Indians scared them off. This little town grew up around the property of John B. Okie. Okie came to Wyoming as a penniless cowboy, then gradually got involved in the sheep industry, invested in a line of stores, and eventually became a millionaire. He built an elaborate mansion, which the Indians called "The Big Teepee", that had elegant chandeliers, marble fireplaces, Persian rugs, and extensive gardens tended by Japanese gardeners. It even boasted an aviary. His home had electric lighting while everyone else in the area still used kerosene lamps. The Okie mansion is privately owned today, but can be seen from the road.

Lysite

A prospector named Jim Lysaght (pronounced Lysite) gave his name to this town and the nearby Lysite Mountain. Indians killed him in 1876. John B. Okie had a warehouse here where he would stockpile wool until prices went up.

Shoshoni

	Jan	Feb	March	April	May	June	July	Aug	Sep	Oct	Nov	Dec	Annual
Average Max. Temperature (F)	Insufficient Data												
Average Min. Temperature (F)	Insufficient Data												
Average Total Precipitation (in.)	0.16	0.12	0.22	0.90	1.55	1.18	0.59	0.48	0.68	0.51	0.27	0.15	6.82
Average Total SnowFall (in.)	2.5	2.0	2.3	2.5	1.1	0.0	0.0	0.0	0.4	0.7	2.4	2.3	16.1
Average Snow Depth (in.)	2	1	0	0	0	0	0	0	0	0	0	1	0

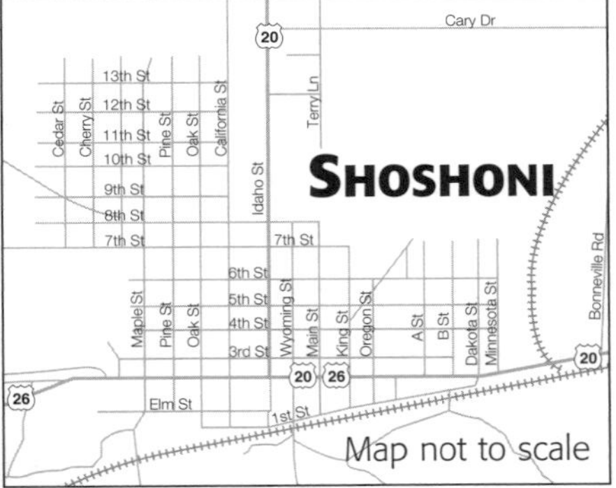

Moneta
Pop. 10, Elev. 5,428

Once called Big Springs, this town got its name from an Indian word, which means "running water."

36 *Gas, Food, Lodging*

Shoshoni jail.

Shoshoni
Pop. 635, Elev. 4,820

Named for the tribe, this is one of several variations on the spelling. The town became a stop on the Northwestern Railroad in 1904, and the surrounding land was opened for homesteading the following year. This was one of the towns in the area that needed help from federal troops to settle the furor over land rights that accompanied homesteading claims. Fires in 1907 and 1908 destroyed most of the original buildings. The drug store here is famous in the region for its milkshakes.

T Boysen State Park

Located north of Shoshoni, Boysen State Park was named for the Asmus Boysen who built the original dam on the Wind River in 1908. The massive reservoir and current dam built in 1951 is at the entrance to picturesque Wind River Canyon. Part of the original dam can still be seen adjacent to the tunnels in the Lower Wind River Campground.

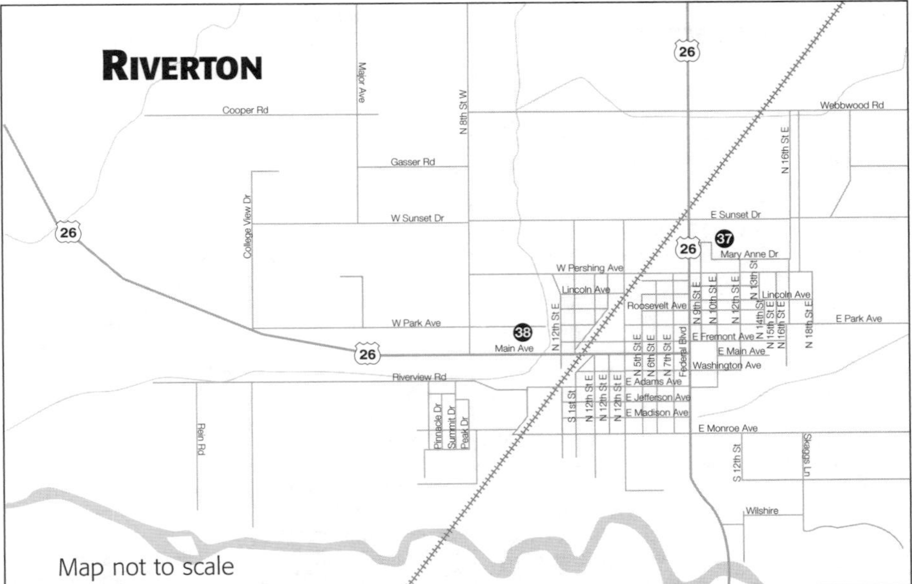

The area is popular with water skiiers and fishermen. Rainbow and brown trout, walleye, sauger, ling, catfish, bass, perch and crappie abound. Facilities at the state park including camp sites, restrooms, drinking water, picnic areas, boat ramps, marinas, and grocery stores.

The first white men passed through this area in 1825. The CB&O Railroad wen through the canyon in 1911 and the state highway went through in 1925. Boysen became a state park in 1956.

H Merritt's Pass Marker
Wind River Indian Reservation. Permission required to visit marker

Merritt's Pass, so named when Gen'l. Merritt, Commanding Fifth U. S. Cavalry, passed through these mountains in September of 1877 upon a scouting expedition. This monument is erected in memory of Col. George M. Sliney, W. N. G., who served under Gen'l. Merritt's command on this expedition. Col. Sliney was so impressed by the beauty and fertility of the Owl Creek Valley, as seen from this point, that he then and there determined to return and make his home in the valley. His plan materialized and on October 3, 1883, the Colonel returned and crossed through this pass accompanied by his wife and three daughters.

Wyoming Tidbits

President Gerald Ford's father, Leslie L. King, a lumber company executive in Riverton, and his grandfather, C.H. King, were two of the state's wealthiest men. Ford's mother divorced King and later married Gerald Ford. Sr. Born Gerry King, the future president legally changed his name to Gerald R. Ford., Jr. shortly after his 21st birthday.

L Desert Inn Motel
605 W. 2nd Street in Shoshoni. 876-2373. www.desertinnmotel.com

The Desert Inn Motel is located in the heart of excellent hunting and fishing country, It is renowned for walleye and trout fishing and is a hunter's and fisherman's paradise. Shoshoni was once the early shipping point for all livestock in the Wind River basin area. You'll find 52 newly remodeled motel rooms at the Desert Inn and your choice of two and three bedroom suites with full kitchens and dinettes or traditional single and double rooms. All rooms have refrigerators. The accommodations here are clean, comfortable, quiet. Pets are welcome and non-smoking rooms are also available. Great restaurants are nearby.

37 *Gas, Food, Lodging*

Riverton
Pop. 9,310, Elev. 4,956

Once a rendezvous site, Riverton was part of the Wind River Reservation when it was first established. Originally named Wadsworth for the Indian agent at Fort Washakie, Riverton was platted in 1906. A scuffle over homesteader claims resulted in federal intervention shortly thereafter. Over the first half of the twentieth century, extensive irrigation projects and well digging created a lush farmland. Dairy cattle were also brought here, and continue to be a mainstay of the economy. Wyoming's biggest dairy farm is located here.

During the 1960s, huge deposits of uranium

Riverton	Jan	Feb	March	April	May	June	July	Aug	Sep	Oct	Nov	Dec	Annual
Average Max. Temperature (F)	29.2	37.2	48.0	58.9	69.4	79.7	88.8	86.6	75.4	61.5	42.5	31.4	59.0
Average Min. Temperature (F)	-0.1	7.0	18.4	28.7	38.5	46.1	51.6	49.0	39.1	28.3	14.0	3.0	27.0
Average Total Precipitation (in.)	0.21	0.24	0.46	1.14	1.76	1.29	0.76	0.47	0.83	0.87	0.46	0.27	8.77
Average Total SnowFall (in.)	3.6	4.0	5.4	5.5	1.0	0.2	0.0	0.0	0.6	3.3	5.2	4.4	33.2
Average Snow Depth (in.)	1	1	0	0	0	0	0	0	0	0	0	1	0
Wind Speed (mph / kmh)	6 / 9	6 / 9	7 / 12	8 / 13	8 / 13	8 / 13	8 / 13	7 / 12	7 / 11	6 / 10	6 / 9	6 / 9	
Wind Direction	WSW	WSW	WSW	WSW	WSW	WSW	WSW	WSW	WSW	WSW	WSW	WSW	
Cloud Cover (out of 8)	5.0	5.0	5.1	5.2	5.2	4.2	3.6	3.6	3.6	4.2	4.9	4.6	

Riverton Rendezvous

As the site of the fur trade's 1830 rendezvous and 1838 rendezvous, Riverton played host to many of the legendary names of the mountain man era. Jim Bridger, William Sublette, Kit Carson, and Jedediah Smith are only a few of the legendary trappers and traders who met here in 1838. The most impressive of these was the 1838 event, which drew as many as 300 people including mountain men and traders, Native Americans and missionaries to a bench of cottonwood trees at the confluence of the Big Wind and the Little Wind. For several days, they traded and celebrated a season of trapping the mountains.

Riverton boasts the only rendezvous site that remains on original ground. The 1838 Rendezvous reenactment is held the third week of June. The event features men and women who demonstrate skills that were used by the mountain men that have otherwise been virtually lost through the decades. Events include live encampment, black powder shooting, beading, basket weaving, powwow, Indian dancing, and food. Later in July, the Riverton Rendezvous takes place at the same site. Both events bring in mountain men and women with historic food and crafts. The Riverton Rendezvous also features a car and bike show, rodeo, demolition derby, cowboy poetry, stock car races, and live music.

were discovered in the nearby Gas Hills. This boosted the economy, until nuclear power came under scrutiny in the 1970s. Central Wyoming Community College opened here in 1968.

Now Riverton has a diversified economic base, and its attractive location near the Wind River Mountains is inviting to tourists and new businesses alike.

T Riverton Museum

700 E. Park in Riverton. 856-4779

A local history museum, the Riverton tells the story of homesteaders who founded the town in 1906. Housed in a charming brick building (the former Riverton Methodist Church), the museum offers colorful displays and self-guided tours. No admission fee is charged, but donations are always welcome. Museum is open 10-4, Tuesday through Saturday, throughout the year, and is closed for major holidays. An extensive research library provides access to published and primary source materials about local and Wyoming history.

T Wind River Heritage Center

412 E. Freemont in Riverton. 856-0706

Dedicated to preserving the natural and human history of the West, the Wind River Heritage Center features lifelike displays of the Jake Korell Wildlife Collection and a collection of historic traps dating from 1804, from the fur trade era. The Korell Collection specializes in Wyoming wildlife including big-game species, predators and furbearers. Bison, bears and grey wolves are among the most popular exhibits. Colorful dioramas depicting the animals' natural habitat serve as backdrops for the mounts.

Wildlife play an important role in the Wind River Valley. The area has always been a prized hunting ground. Historically, wild animals provided meat, fur, bones, hides, horns, and even teeth. Today, they continue to be valued both for their aesthetic appeal and for their meat and hides. The Heritage Center displays provide a close-tip look at these animals that have been so vital in the settling of the American West.

In addition to its wildlife displays, the Heritage Center houses an extensive gift store specializing in Native American art and jewelry. Locally made beadwork and leather goods-trademarks of the Eastern Shoshone and Northern Arapaho tribes that inhabit the Wind River Indian Reservation-can be purchased at the store. The Heritage Center also sponsors slide shows, lectures and Native American dancing demonstrations throughout the year. The museum is open year round Monday through Saturday.

Reprinted from museum brochure.

T St. Stephens Indian Heritage Center

At the St. Stephens Mission.

St. Stephens mission was established in 1884 by a Jesuit missionary, and provided schooling for Arapaho children. Arapaho Chief Black Coal consented to its being built in 1888. The Center houses a museum which is open Mon.-Wed. and Friday, 9 a.m. -3:30 p.m. (closed 12-1 for lunch) and is open all year.

L Hi Lo Motel

414 N. Federal in Riverton. 856-9223

FL Sundowner Station–Motel, Restaurant & Lounge

1616 N. Federal Blvd. in Riverton. 856-6503 or 800-874-1116

L Super 8 Motel - Riverton

1040 N. Federal Blvd. in Riverton. 857-2400 or 800-800-8000. www.super8.com

The Super 8 Motel is right on your way to Yellowstone National Park and Teton National Park, and set in the center of Wyoming cowboy country. Each of the 32 unique and comfortably decorated rooms come with 19" remote control

Cowboy Poetry Roundup

The largest cowboy poetry event in the state takes place in October in Riverton. Cowpokes gather to tell tales and clever rhymes.

TV's with HBO and ESPN, individually controlled climate, data ports, and 24 hour front desk. Pets are allowed. Guests are served a complimentary continental breakfast with fresh baked muffins, donuts, bagels, coffee, and orange juice. There is a plenty of free parking for all sizes of vehicles. The atmosphere is perfect for every vacationer's traveling experience and convenient to the multitude of area recreation opportunities.

L Thunderbird Motel

302 E. Fremont Ave. in Riverton. 856-9201 or toll free reservations at 888-498-9201. www.T-Birdmotel.com

The Thunderbird Motel provides a quiet refuge one block off the highway and convenient to downtown Riverton. You are invited to inspect their rooms. The friendly motel offers direct dial phones, cable TV, 24 hour wake-up calls, winter plug-ins, non-smoking rooms, in-room temp control, guest laundry, and plenty of parking for large vehicles. Data ports are provided in every room. There is also a friendly hometown-type lounge to stop in for a Coke, conversation, or mixed drink. The Thunderbird is a perfect base camp while you enjoy all of the activities available in the surrounding area. Visit them on the web.

L Holiday Inn Riverton

900 E. Sunset in Riverton. 856-8100 or toll free 877-857-4834. www.blairhotels.com

Located in the heart of the Wind River Indian Reservation, the Holiday Inn-Riverton offers its guests a full service experience with the emphasis on service. Guests are welcome to enjoy any of their 121 deluxe sleeping accommodations as well as the facilities in the hotel. Facilities include an indoor Fundome with an indoor pool, exercise room, QT's Restaurant and the Bottoms Up Lounge. Conveniently located on Wyoming Highway 26, the hotel is en-route to Yellowstone and Grand Teton National Parks and participates in the Kids Eat Free/Kids Stay Free program. There is plenty of parking including space for oversized vehicles

38 *Food, Lodging*

S Wind River Gallery & Framing

310 Main Street in Riverton. 856-1402 or www.windrivergallery.net

Wind River Gallery and Framing features the work of many nationally recognized artists as well as local artists. The primary focus here is on Western and Wildlife Art. Explore the gallery and discover originals, limited edition prints, bronze and pewter sculptures, and unique collectibles. You'll also find Native American crafts and beadwork from the local Arapahoe and Shoshone Reservations. Some of the many artists represented by Wind River Gallery include: Lee Teter, Roy Kerswill, Vivi Crandall, Nancy Glazier, Tim Cox, Greg Beecham, and Bev Doolittle. The gallery also offers custom framing. Visit this exciting gallery on the web.

M Minter Realtors

213 W. Main Street in Riverton. 856-4755 or fax 856-4755

M Central Wyoming College

2660 Peck Avenue in Riverton.

The Central Wyoming College campus is located in Fremont County on the outskirts of Riverton. The campus and community lie in the Wind River Valley, a large lowland area bounded by mountains on threes sides. The mission of Central Wyoming College is to enhance the quality of life through innovation and excellence in education. The vision of Central Wyoming College is to provide lifelong learning opportunities beyond the boundaries of time and place. The student enrollment is approximately 1,600.

39 *Gas*

Kinnear

Pop. 44, Elev. 5,410

N.B. and Irene Kinnear, for whom this post office was named, were prominent figures in the valley. N.B. owned a ranch here and was a civil engineer; Irene was a respected school teacher on the Wind River Reservation. She was also a granddaughter of early mountain man, Jim Baker.

Wyoming Tidbits

In Encampment resides the state's only two-story outhouse. The upper level was used only when the snowdrifts were deep enough to bury the first level.

40 *No services*

Pavillion

Pop. 165, Elev. 5,609

This little town was named for the nearby butte that resembles a pavillion.

41 *Gas*

Ethete

This reservation fringe town began in 1887 as a post office, railroad station, and Episcopalian mission. The Arapaho name (pronounced Ee-thuh-tee), meaning "good," indicates the tribe approved of the development. It was important to have alternate gathering places for the different tribes, who still fostered old rivalries. The village is now a colorful hodge-podge of eclectic cobblestone and log buildings, dominated by the old mission, and decorated in artistic Arapaho splendor.

T Arapaho Cultural Museum

At St. Michael's Mission

This houses traditional tribal artifacts, including warrior implements, women's regalia, healing emblems, children's toys and tipi ornaments. There are also artifact demonstration and craft work areas. The museum offers great insight into the tribe and its traditions.

T St. Michael's Mission

The Episcopal Diocese of Wyoming purchases land from Yellow Calf and Wallowing Bull for the establishment of St. Michael's Mission at the site of the present community of Ethete. The mission, which was established in 1913, is laid out in a circle like an Arapaho encampment. The buildings are intact, although the mission is no longer active, and the Northern Arapaho Cultural Museum, which contains an impressive collection of traditional Arapaho clothing, implements, and ceremonial objects as well as an outstanding collection of photographs and portraits.

42 *Gas, Food*

Arapahoe

Named for the tribe, Arapahoe sits just off the edge of the Wind River Indian Reservation. In 1880, the Indian Service established the fist post office here. Annuities were distributed separately to the Arapaho and Shoshone people due to animosity between the tribes. The Crows actually gave the Arapaho the name by which we know them; it is their word for "tattooed." The Arapaho have no R sounds in their language. They called themselves He-nau-ana-nan-wan, "the chosen people."

Hudson

Pop. 407, Elev. 5,094

John G. Hudson was a rancher and legislator who promoted the railroad. He owned the land on which the town was built in 1905, where Indians, coal miners, and oil field workers could trade goods and services. The town was initially named

Lander

Alta, an Indian word meaning "swift water" for the nearby Little Popo Agie River. Coal was the main moneymaker here around 1912, which brought many European immigrants, especially many of Slavic descent.

43 *Gas, Food, Lodging*

Lander

Elev. 5,357, Pop. 7,500

Hailed by several publications as one of the "Best Small Towns in the West", Lander is a friendly mix of the old and the new. The Lander Valley was once the tribal territory of the Shoshones, and is still home to the sole reservation in the state, the Wind River Reservation. This area was a part of John Colter's excursions in 1807 and 1808, and next became a rendezvous spot for mountain men. Pioneers began settling in the valley in the late 1860s, and Major Noyes Baldwin established a trading post in 1868, which still stands on the creek of the same name. A military post, Fort Augur (later Fort Brown) was set up here to disperse commodities to the Shoshones. It was later moved farther north, closer to the reservation, and dubbed Fort Wahakie.

Disagreements over reservation boundaries inhibited settlement for a few years thereafter. In 1872, Chief Washakie renegotiated with the U.S. Government, and sold the land south of the North Fork of the Popo Agie (po-PO-zha) River. Many settlers came from the overflowing South Pass City, where gold had attracted the masses. The emerging town was dubbed Pushroot, due to the warm downdrafts from the Wind River Mountains that seemed to push crops from the ground earlier in spring than anticipated. When the town applied for a post office in 1875, the name Pushroot was rejected. Resident and former Pony Express rider Franklin Lowe suggested naming the town for Frederick W. Lander, who had engineered the nearby Lander Cut-off of the Oregon Trail in 1857.

Agriculture was the towns best source of revenue, and with the help of windmills, residents were able to effectively irrigate most of the valley. The population grew slowly but steadily over the next several years. The town became county seat when Fremont County was established in 1884. The streets had been designed extra wide to accommodate the freight wagons with their large ox teams, and they remained so even after the railroad arrived in 1906, effectively ending the need for the freighters.

Lander is known today as the "City of Bronze" for its bronze foundry, which has produced many bronze statues seen all over the US, including several that line the streets of Lander today. It is also an oil country hub, as well as being the first place in Wyoming where oil was discovered in 1833, by Captain Bonneville, who called a pool of oil he found here the "Great Tar Spring." When the "Spring" was drilled 51 years later, it proved to be a "spouter" capable of producing 200 barrels a day of top-notch crude. The area is now called the Dallas Dome Field.

Today, Lander provides a pleasant combination of Old West hospitality and New West style. From cowboy-style horseback riding to modern eateries, guest ranches to bed and breakfasts, the town has something to greet travelers of all tastes. The community continues to honor its agricultural and mountaineering traditions, but has also become the headquarters for several environmental groups, such as the Wyoming Outdoor Council and the Nature Conservancy. All in all, Lander is a place where balance is achieved in marvelous ways.

T Lander Children's Museum

The Lander Children's Museum was formed in 1999 and provides children the opportunity for innovative learning experiences that encourage them to interact with their surroundings. The museum is targeted toward the 3-12 age group. The museum offers a variety of hands-on exhibits, encompassing the fields of math, science, art, music and reading. The Museum provides a place where children and families can explore, learn and discover together. The museum is open on Saturdays from 10 a.m. to 4 p.m. A small admission is charged.

T Fremont County Pioneer Museum and Museum of the American West

636 Lincoln St. in Lander. 332-4137

This museum site includes a collection of structures and outdoor activity areas which take visitors through the history of the American West. Teepee camps, logs cabins, and an old pioneer cemetery are among the highlights. The museum grounds are still a work in progress, due to a major resoration and expansion program begun in 1998, when the original building was declared unsafe. The museum not only features traditional Western experiences, but provides glimpses into the past of immigrants from all over Europe, Asia, and Africa. Come and see what made the West the place everyone wanted to be.

T Sinks Canyon State Park Visitor Center

3079 Sinks Canyon Road. 332-3077

The visitor center has interpretive materials, an outlook to the Sinks, and nature trails.

T Sinks Canyon State Park

seven miles southwest of Lander. 332-6333

Sinks Canyon is so named because the Middle Fork of the Popo Agie River rushes out of the Wind River Mountains, down the canyon and then abruptly vanishes into a large cavern halfway down the canyon. The river is underground for 1/4 mile until it emerges in a large, calm pool on the other side of the canyon and then continues its course into the valley below.

The Sinks and Rise are natural occurrences that are not uncommon in limestone formations around the world. The uniqueness about the Sinks is its size and the length of time the water is underground.

The lower portion of the canyon is made up primarily of sandstone and limestone formations which are easily eroded by wind and water. The formation in which the river actually vanishes is

Lander	Jan	Feb	March	April	May	June	July	Aug	Sep	Oct	Nov	Dec	Annual
Average Max. Temperature (F)	31.8	37.4	45.6	55.6	66.0	77.1	86.1	84.5	73.1	59.7	42.7	33.4	57.8
Average Min. Temperature (F)	8.8	13.8	21.6	30.7	40.1	48.4	55.5	54.0	44.3	33.1	19.3	10.7	31.7
Average Total Precipitation (in.)	0.48	0.59	1.16	2.08	2.47	1.39	0.75	0.48	1.04	1.22	0.87	0.53	13.06
Average Total SnowFall (in.)	8.6	10.7	17.5	20.7	6.7	0.7	0.0	0.0	2.6	9.3	13.9	9.8	100.7
Average Snow Depth (in.)	5	5	2	1	0	0	0	0	0	0	2	3	2
Wind Speed (mph / kmh)	6 / 9	6 / 9	7 / 12	8 / 13	8 / 13	8 / 13	8 / 13	7 / 12	7 / 11	6 / 10	6 / 9	6 / 9	
Wind Direction	WSW	WSW	WSW	WSW	WSW	WSW	WSW	WSW	WSW	WSW	WSW	WSW	
Cloud Cover (out of 8)	5.0	5.0	5.1	5.2	5.2	4.2	3.6	3.6	3.6	4.2	4.9	4.6	

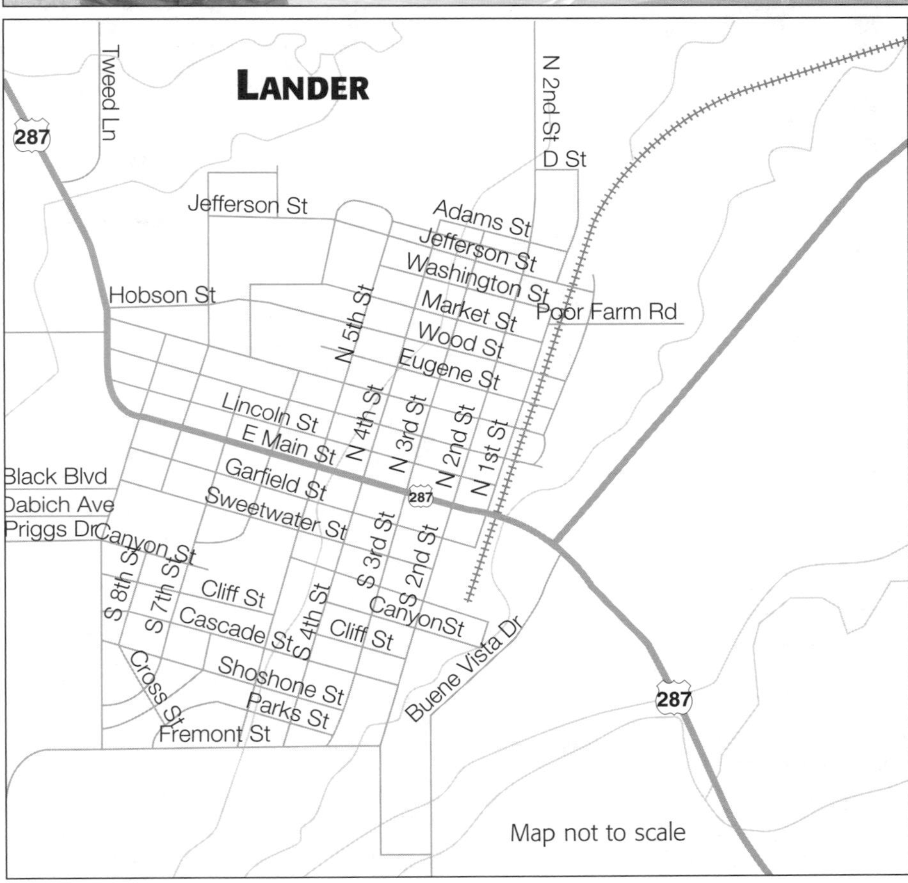

called Madison Limestone, a massive, off-white limestone formation that is very soft and soluble.

Geologists speculate that the Sinks could have been formed in two ways: either the cavern and cracks in the limestone already existed because of earth tremors and the river found and flowed into them; or the river naturally eroded the soft limestone creating its own passage underground. It's likely that a combination of these two events created the Sinks. For many years it was unknown if the water in the Rise was the same water flowing into the Sinks. Dye tests had been attempted on occasion but no conclusive evidence was found. In 1983 the U.S. Geological Survey and Sinks Canyon State Park staff conducted an official dye test using red dye.

The dye, called Rhodamine, was poured into the water above the Sinks and testing with a fluorometer was simultaneously started in the pool at the Rise. Samples were taken every five minutes but the first traces of dye were not detected until two hours after it had been dumped into the Sinks. When the testing was finished, nearly all of the dye had been recovered, leading the researchers to conclude that all of the water flowing into the sinks comes out at the Rise. However, two new facts were discovered during the testing: 1) MORE water comes out at the Rise than flows into the Sinks, and 2) the water that flows out into the Rise is a few degrees WARMER than the water entering the Sinks.

The central mystery of "where does the water go for over two hours?" has yet to be solved. Geologists speculate that there could be a large underground aquifer or lake that slows the progress of the water. There could also be a myriad of channels and passages that the water has to circulate though before it reaches the Rise. It is probable that a combination of these two geologic formations slows the progress of the water.

Rainbow Trout in the Rise

The huge trout in the Rise are not stocked. They have arrived there naturally and stay because it is a protected area with an extensive food supply. The fish are mainly Rainbow Trout, though some are Browns.

No one has weighed or measured the fish but some of the larger ones probably weigh up to 12 pounds. There is no fishing in the Rise, but visitors enjoy throwing fish food to the trout from the observation platform above the Rise.

What does Popo Agie mean?

The name Popo Agie (pronounced Po-Po Zshuh) comes from the Crow Indians and means "Tall Grass River." "Agie" means river in the Crow language and "PoPo" means tall grass or tall rye grass. The Crow named the river this because of the tall bunches of rye grass that grew along the banks of the river in the valley.

Wildlife, Flora and Fauna

Famous for the mysterious Sinks and Rise and its spectacular geology, Sinks Canyon is the home to a myriad of wildlife, birds and plants. There are three major habitats in the canyon and each is unique. The most dramatic contrast in habitats is between the heavily forested north facing slope and the drier, sagebrush and juniper covered south facing slope.

The north facing slope is in the shade much of the winter allowing heavy snow to accumulate. This snow provides moisture needed for Limber Pine and Douglas Fir trees. Birds such as the Western Tanager, the Mountain Chickadee, Blue Grouse and Townsend's Solitaire live in these thick, coniferous forests. Mammals such as the Pine Martin, Porcupine, Black Bear and the Red Squirrel prefer the forest. Wildflowers such as Heartleaf Arnica, Lupine and Phlox are also found.

The south facing slope receives a great deal of sunshine all winter which melts snow quickly. Lack of snow makes it excellent winter range for many animals because they don't have to struggle to find food. Bighorn Sheep and Mule Deer are commonly seen on this rocky slope in the winter. Golden Eagles and tiny Cliff Swallows can be seen souring above the cliffs. Green-tailed Towhees and Kestrels also make this place their home. Wildflowers such as Sego Lily, Hawksbeard and Arrowleaf Balsamroot are bright splashes of color among the blue-grey sagebrush.

The third Sinks Canyon habitat is the Riparian zone along the Popo Agie River. It is the moist area along either side of the river where thick stands of Aspen, Chokecherry and Willow grow. Moose are occasionally seen in the Riparian zone browsing on Willow or Red-Osier Dogwood. Birds such as the Lazuli Bunting, the Dipper, the Rufous Hummingbird and Black-headed Grosbeak can be seen in the heavy foliage. In this moist Riparian zone are wildflowers flouris such as Sticky Geranium, Yellow Monkeyflower and Columbine.

All of these habitats make Sinks Canyon a rich place to observe nature. Surrounding National Forest and wilderness areas extend the opportunity to experience Wyoming's beauty at its best. Remember, you are a visitor to the home of the Bighorn Sheep, Marmot and the Golden Eagle. Please respect the wildlife, observing them

Sinks Canyon State Park

Division of State Parks & Historic Sites
Wyoming Department of Commerce

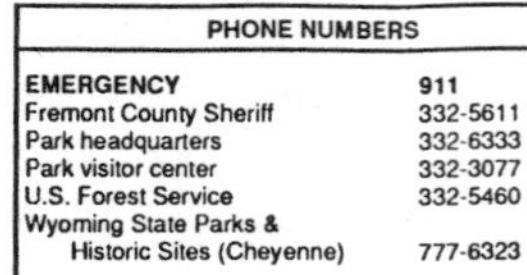

PHONE NUMBERS	
EMERGENCY	911
Fremont County Sheriff	332-5611
Park headquarters	332-6333
Park visitor center	332-3077
U.S. Forest Service	332-5460
Wyoming State Parks & Historic Sites (Cheyenne)	777-6323

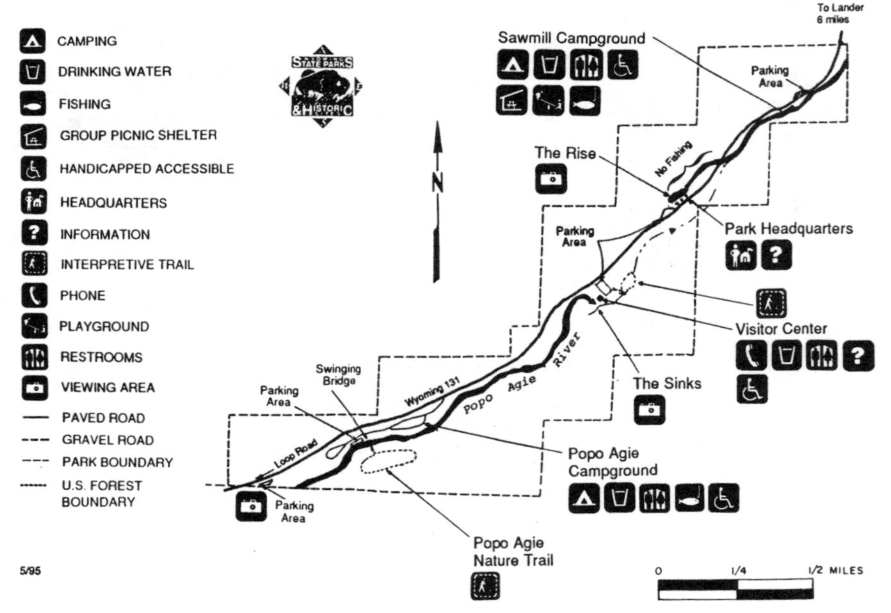

from a distance, and please leave the wildflowers for others to enjoy.

Reprinted from Wyoming State Parks and Historic Sites brochure.

H Sinks State Park

South of Lander.

"The Sinks" are a series of cracks and crevices at the back of the cavern before you. The water of the Popo Agie River flows into the Sinks. It then reappears at the "Rise of the Sinks", a large calm pool 1/4 mile down the canyon.

The Sinks are eroded into the soft white Madison Limestone formation. No spelunkers have explored very far into the sinks since the cracks narrow down to very small log and rock choked passages.

It is unknown exactly how old the Sinks are although they are likely an Ice-Age feature thousands of years old. The glaciers that carved the canyon exposed the soluble limestone and the billions of gallons of water from melting ice helped create the underground passages

For many years it was unknown whether the water flowing into the Sinks was the same water flowing out at the Rise. Dye test have proven the connection but have also revealed another mystery: it takes the water flowing into the Sinks over over 2 hours to reappear at the Rise. It was also discovered that more water flows out at the Rise than goes in at the Sinks. Why the water takes over two hours to make the journey and where it goes during that time is still a mystery.

The amount of water flowing into the Sinks varies throughout the year. Most of the time much of the limestone cavern is exposed and all of the river's water flows underground through the cracks and fissures in the rock.

The average flow of the Popo Agie into the Sinks is about 100 cubic feet per second. This level drops in the winter and jumps dramaticly during spring runoff. In late May and early June the river swells with melted snow from the mountains and the river fills the cavern completely. During run-off over 500 cubic feet per second of water flows into the cavern. The water is so high that logs and driftwood are jammed into cracks in the ceiling of the cave-high above where people stand when the water is low. The cracks in the limestone cannot handle all this extra water and the excess spills over into a seasonal streambed (called the overflow channel) to the left. Depending on how much snow is in the mountains, the Sinks can overflow from a few days to a few weeks. Every year during spring run-off there is water flowing both below and above ground between the Sinks and Rise.

H Sinks State Park: The Rise of the Sinks

Just past entrance to Sinks Canyon State Park

The Rise of the Sinks is a large spring where the water of the middle fork of the Popo Agie River reappears after flowing into a limestone cavern called the Sinks, located a quarter of a mile upstream.

The water flows underground folowing an unknown path. Geologists speculate the water travels through many cracks and fissures created in the water-soluble limestone until it rises to the surface in this calm pool.

The Rise is an active geologic formation that changes from year to year. Erosion in the river and underground alters water flow patterns and changes the amount of sand flowing into the pool. Some years the sandbar is almost gone and some years it takes up part of the upper end of the Rise.

Shaped by ice-age glaciers and the power of the river. Sinks Canyon has served as a natural travel corridor for wildlife and people for thousands of years. Known to Native Americans for centuries, the first white to see the Sinks and Rise were fur trappers. The name Popo Agie (pronounced Po-Po-zsha) is a Crow Indian word which means "Grass River."

The Rise was donated to the City of Lander in 1969 by Pacific Power and Light Company. The site is now part of Sinks Canyon State Park administered by Wyoming State Parks and Historic Sites.

H Sinks State Park: Geology

South of Lander.

Sinks Canyon offers an excellent opportunity to study geology. The Canyon, shaped by ice-age glaciers, cuts through 400 million years of geo-

The Popo Agie River disappears into this cavern at Sinks State Park just south of Lander.

The Geology of Sinks Canyon

Sinks Canyon cuts through some 600 million years of geological history and provides and excellent opportunity to see the layers of rock exposed because of the Wind River Uplift.

You have a unique opportunity to see the different geologic formations during your drive through the canyon. The youngest formation, about 280 millon years old is called Phosphoria and is at the top of the cliffs to your right. The Pre-Cambrian granite of over 600 million years ago is exposed at the bottom of the switchbacks about 4 miles from this point.

There is also evidence of the glacial action that was once a part of this area, including polishing and striation of rocks, glacial erratics or the large boulders carried down from higher elevations and deposited here as the glaciers melted, and the moraines or glacial debris (rocks and fine silt) left in long piles. You can see a medial moraine cross section revealed during road construction between the Visitor Center and Popo Agie Campground. Look for the road cut where you see the widest variety of rock sizes and types.

This canyon is a young one, and yet it shows us millions of years of rocks formations, exciting evidence of the glaciers and of the Sinks—where the Popo Agie River disappears into a cavern formed by erosion only to reappear in a trout filled pool called the Rise.

Source: Wyoming Recreation Commission

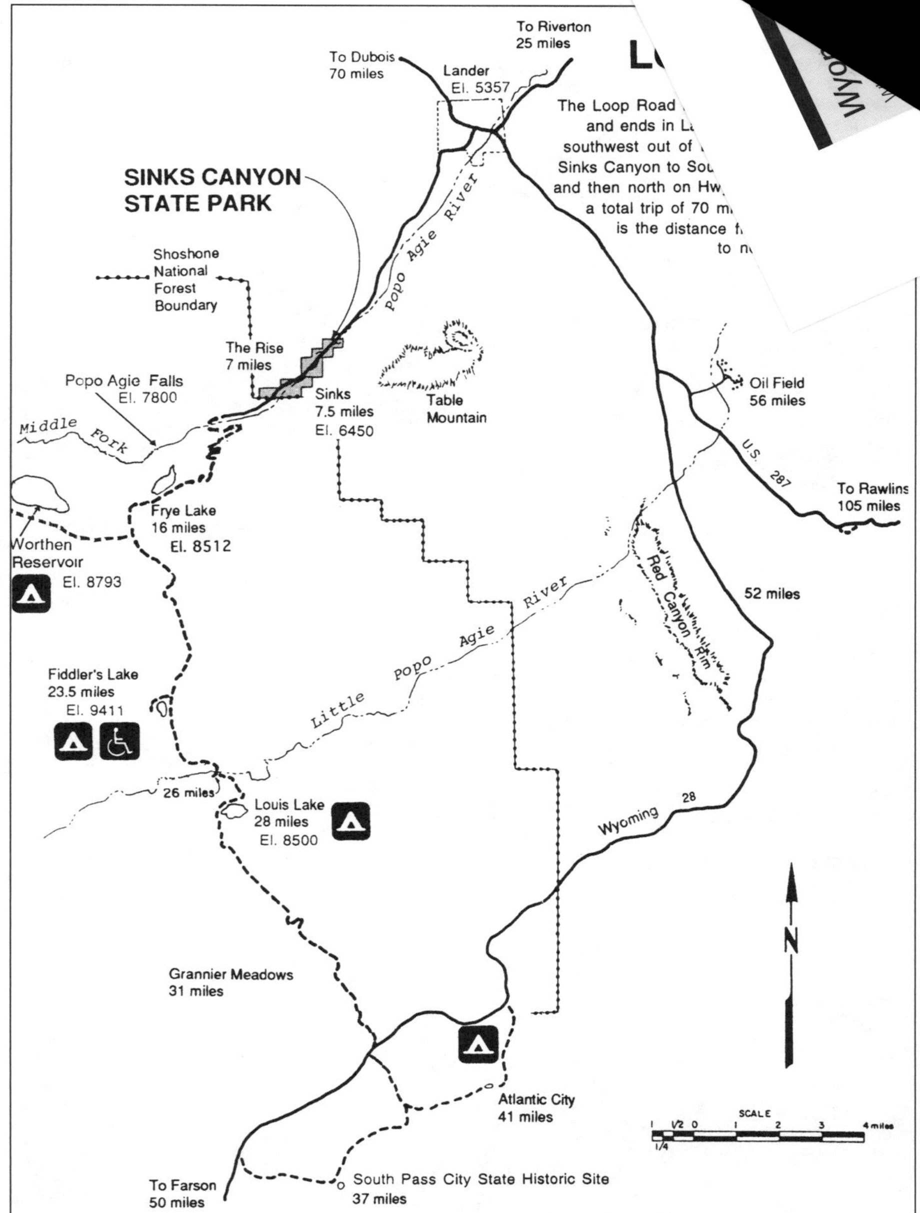

logical history. Some stratigraphy is visible above the Rise.

The uppermost formation, recognized by its light color and massive cliffs is the Tensleep Sandstone. The black and red streaks on the face of the cliffs are oxides of iron and manganese and are called "desert varnish." The next formation is the Amsden Formation but is difficult to see because it has eroded to a grass and tree-covered slope. Below this is Madison Limestone. Through this soft formation the Sinks and Rise occur. Water enters through fractures 1/4 mile upstrem at the Sinks, then moves laterally down through the formation These geologic features create the unique wildlife habitats found at Sinks Canyon.

Limestone can be dissolved by carbonic acid, a weak, naturally-forming acid created by the combination of water and carbon dioxide. This acid dissolves the limestone and continued water movement will create channels in the stone. In this fashion the Sinks were created. The water reappears here through small fractures around the sides of the pool and in the sandy bottom.

H Sinks State Park: Trout in the Rise

Just past entrance to Sinks State Park.

The Middle Popo Agie River is an excellent trout strem and here at the Rise two of the trout species in Wyoming are found. Both brown and rainbow trout inhabit the Rise.

Trout migrate upstream looking for suitable spawning areas, and the Rise acts as a natural barrier to any further upstream movement. The trout in the Rise arrived there naturally and stay because it is a protected area with an extensive food supply. The pool is deep enough and there is enough year-around water flow that it never freezes. It is unlikely that any fish travel through the fractures in the rock upstream to the river running into the Sinks cavern. No one has weighed or measured the fish in the Rise, but some of the larger ones probably weigh 9 to 10 pounds.

Trout swim by expanding their muscles on the side of their body while relaxing the muscles on the other side. In addition to what visitors feed them, the trout primarily eat aquatic insects, such as mayflies and stoneflies.

H Lander Valley Historical Sites

At junction of Highways 287/789 and 789 at roadside park.

Scouts and trappers visited this area in 1811 and rendezvous were held 1829, 1830, and 1838.

Camp Magraw, 1857, site 2.1 miles north.

Fort Thompson, 1857-1858, was located 4.4 miles north of here.

Camp Augur, 1869-1870, became the original Camp Brown, 1870-1871. Location was 1/2

Lander Jazz Festival

Lander's annual Labor Day Weekend event offers beautiful scenery, excellent music and an uncrowded, small town full of enthusiastic jazz fans. Typically the event begins with a Dixieland Extravaganza on Friday evening, outdoor venues on Saturday, local venues for Saturday Night Ramble, and Gospel on Sunday, and finishing with an afternoon and evening of music, food and fun. Big names and regional music are brought to town with events for the entire family.

Wyoming Tidbits

White men first discovered oil in 1824 at a site near Lander. Capt. Bonneville noticed oil during a fur trading expedition in 1832, but development didn't start until the mid 1880s.

mile west on the south side of Main Street.

Lander was named in 1875 in honor of Gen. Frederick West Lander.

H Oregon Trail-Lander Cutoff South Pass Area.

About 30 miles southwest of Highway 287/789 junction with State Highway 28.

This is an old trail used by the Indians and the trappers of the fur period, a short cut to the Snake River country. It was proposed an emigrant road by mountain man John Hockaday in 1854. No emigrant trails crossed the mountains north of here. It was improved as a wagon road for the government by F. W. Lander, in 1859 to avoid dry wastes of the roads to the south and to provide more water, wood and forage. Here it commenced the crossing of the south end of the Wind River Mountains and the Continental Divide and on to the Pacific Northwest. Thirteen thousand people and thousands of domestic animals passed this way in 1859 and for thirty years thereafter it was used heavily, setting the destiny of an empire. These wagon tracks and lonely graves for many miles beyond, a great landmark of history, have been recognized for preservation by: U.S. Department of the Interior, Bureau of Land Management, Sublette County Historical Society.

This trail has been marked at all accessible points with brass caps.

F Tony's Pizza

637 Main Street in Lander. 332-3900

Tony's Pizza has been delighting residents and Lander visitors with fresh Italian food and pizza for over 18 years. Each meal is prepared with baked items made on the premises order by order—breads, pastas, sauces, and salads. Build your own pizza with an extensive choice of toppings and sauces. Accompany your meal with your favorites from their beer and wine menu.

Wyoming Tidbits

Popo Agie (pronounced pu-POH-zah) means "beginning of waters" in the Crow Indian language.

Top off your meal with a delicious dessert. The warm and friendly atmosphere provides cozy quiet corners inside, rooftop dining, or outside deck dining. They also cater events such as weddings, reunions, and business meetings. Open for dine-in, take-out, or delivery.

FL Pronghorn Lodge and Oxbow Restaurant

150 E. Main in Lander. 332-3940 or toll free at 800-budhost (283-4678) or fax, 332-2651. email: pronghorn@wyoming.com. www.pronghornlodge.com

The Budget Host Pronghorn Lodge is located on the Popo Agie River at the base of the Wind River Mountains. The rustic style family facility offers both restaurant and conference hall on the premises. Kitchenettes, executive, and bridal suites are available along with handicapped accessible rooms. Large screen remote TV and phones are standard in all rooms, along with king or queen size beds. Other on-site amenities include whirlpool hot tub and exercise equipment. The Oxbow Restaurant serves delicious home-cooked style meals 7 days a week. Ample parking is available for all sizes of vehicles. The on-site Monarch Conference Hall can accommodate up to 150 people with bar and catering options available.

FL Maverick Motel, Restaurant & Lounge

808 W. Main in Lander. 332-2300 or toll free at 877-622-2300

The Maverick Motel, Restaurant and Lounge is conveniently located within walking distance of downtown Lander. They offer 31 newly remodeled rooms. Nonsmoking rooms are available and pets are allowed. A guest laundry is also on the premises. Motel guests are served a complimentary full breakfast. To satisfy your appetite before a good night's rest be sure and order one of their famous hand-cut steaks or succulent prime rib served nightly in the restaurant. Compliment your meal with your favorite cocktail or their delicious hand-crafted soups and desserts. They are open for lunch and breakfast with daily lunch specials.

L The Holiday Lodge National 9 Inn

210 McFarlane Drive in Lander. 332-2511, fax 332-2256, or toll free 800-624-1974

The Holiday Lodge sits next to the Popo Agie River (pronounced po-po'-zsha), in the midst of all the treasures in Wind River country. The Clark family has owned and operated the Lodge for 19 years. They don't consider themselves fancy, but do offer the things you remember from the old days—clean cozy rooms, friendly faces, and old fashioned hospitality. They have expanded cable TV, direct dial phones, spa, winter plug-ins, coin laundry, and riverfront camping for those hardy souls touring on bicycles or folks pulling a trailer. When you visit Lander, bring your family and stay with theirs!

C Sleeping Bear RV Park & Campground

715 E. Main in Lander. 332-5159 or 888-SLP-BEAR(757-2327). www.sleeping-rv-park.com

S Quilting Bee Quilts, Quilting, Quillows and Fabrics

637 Main Street in Lander. 332-4123

S Wild Bird Marketplace

645 W. Main Street in Lander. 332-7600, fax 332-2013 or toll free at 888-332-7600 (in-state). www.wyomingwildbirdplace.com

Wild Bird Marketplace is your outstanding source for backyard birding in Wyoming, providing proven products, local and national field guides, a large selection of gift items, and more. Birding information is one of their specialties, with over twenty years experience in birdwatching and identification. Wild Bird Marketplace is the longest established specialty birding store in Wyoming and they are proud to offer a large selection of feeders, nest boxes, birdbaths, Brunton binoculars, and many more items unique to Wyoming and the west. Why not add this warm and inviting shop to your Lander itinerary, or visit them on their secure web site at www.wyomingwildbirdplace.com.

S The Bear Guy

480 S. 9th Street in Lander. 332-4801 or cell, 349-1640. www.thebearguy.com

The Bear Guy, artist, Robert Waits, is a Wyoming native and has been creating chain saw carvings for 13 years. Add a little extra warmth and character to your home with one his bears, moose, raccoons, beavers, wood spirits, eagles, gnomes, and a few unexpected themes. Each piece is masterfully carved one at a time. The Bear Guy also builds and carves striking rustic furniture and accessories using various local woods such as aspen, juniper, pine, elm, Russian olive, and driftwood. Custom orders are welcome, major credit cards are accepted, and worldwide shipping is available. Visit them on the web!

S Bar-Bar-A's Art Gallery

555 W. Main St. in Lander. 332-7798

Bar-Bar-A's Art Gallery features the work of award winning artist and Wyoming native, Barbara Rieman. Barbara travels with her cameras, in hopes of finding the perfect view to paint or draw. In the process she has also become an accomplished and daring photographer. Original oils, pastels, charcoal, and photography by Barbara are available in the gallery. You'll also discover works by other local and not so local artists, including two of Barbara's sons, potter, Ken Rieman and painter photographer, Roderic Rieman. This exciting gallery offers artwork in all sizes with price ranges to suit every budget and taste.

44 *Gas*

T Sweetwater River

18.5 miles west of Jeffrey City on US-287.

The trail crossed the Sweetwater River for the sixth time about three miles southwest of the bridge on US-287. From this point, the Trail takes a southwesterly course directly toward Great South Pass at the southern end of the Wind River Mountains, the range that dominates the skyline to the west. US-287 turns to the northwest and leaves the trail corridor as it crosses Beaver Rim to drop into the Wind River valley. Sweetwater Station and a highway rest area offer visitor services and information at this point. Source: BLM brochure.

T Hudson-Atlantic City Road

This graveled road turns south from US-287 five miles west of Sweetwater Station and parallels the trail as it approaches South Pass.

Although this road stays some distance north of the actual trail, it does offer good overlooks to such historic locations as Rocky Ridge, Lewiston Lakes and the gash of Sweetwater Canyon. On the west end, the road connects with the South Pass — Atlantic City Historic Mining district near WYO-28. It is an interesting fair weather choice for travelers wishing to stay closer to the trail. Contact with the Lander BLM office or Chamber of Commerce is advised before starting out. Source: BLM brochure.

H The Sweetwater Valley

At junction of U.S. Highway 287/789 and State Highway 135 at Sweetwater Rest Area.

The Sweetwater Valley is the mid-section of the 2000 mile-long Oregon Trail. West of Casper, Wyoming, branches of that trail, meld into a single transportation corridor and here, paralleling the serpentine Sweetwater River, the trail approaches the base of South Pass. On the other side is "Oregon Country" where routes diverge toward Utah, California and Oregon.

For a week emigrants plodded this stretch of high altitude, semiarid desert. Everyday, more of the same alkali, sage and sand a continuing American Sahara. "How long for a timberd country" wrote one traveler. "...In a thousand miles I have not seen a hundred acres of wood. All that comes near to arborification is a fringe of cottonwood and willows along the banks of creeks and rivers. These everlasting hills have an everlasting curse of barrenness...."

For others, however, the Sweetwater was a relatively agreeable part of the journey. It was summer, the river was low and clear, and there was grass for stock. Days were bright and mild, and scenery was plentiful. "...Still by the Sweet Water. The valley is becoming more narrow and the stream more rapid. In advance and a little to the north of our trail we can see the Wind River Mountains. Their lofty summits are covered with snow, and in their dazzling whiteness appear truly sublime."

H Sweetwater Willows

At Sweetwater Station Rest Station

In summer, the trilling "Kroo-oo-oo" of the sandhill crane is heard along the Sweetwater River. The endangered whooping crane has been seen in the marshy meadows immediately south of this spot. The Sweetwater's wide floodplain, enhanced by the irrigated and naturally occurring wet meadows, supports wildlife as large as the 1,000 pound moose and as small as the 1/4 ounce pygmy shrew. The vegetation zone in the river's floodplain is called riparian habitat. Willows are often dominant woody vegetation in Wyoming's riparian habitats. Willows provide food and cover for moose in winter, food and dam building materials for the beaver, and streamside shade and insects for fish.

Willow roots also help stabilize streambanks. Without stabilizing vegetation, the streambanks erode and spring floods cut deeper into the riverbed. This accelerates erosion and affects wildlife. Unstable streambanks result in a loss of land, soil moisture, and vegetation growth. This affects wildlife and livestock, and ulltimately man. Willows are one of the valuable plants that help maintain a healthy and diverse wildlife community.

Wyoming Tidbits

The first oil well in Wyoming was dug in 1884 near Lander. Mike Murphy and two helpers used picks and shovels to dig into the Chugwater formation near the Popo Agie River.

Wyoming Tidbits

The Arapahoes, historically considered enemies of the Shoshone, began living on the Shoshone reserveration in 1878. The Shoshone are now outnumbered on the Wind River Reservation by the Arapahoes.

Wyoming Tidbits

Jade is the official stone of Wyoming. It is found along the Sweetwater River, and in areas of Fremont and Sweetwater counties.

45 *Food*

Jeffrey City

Elev. 6,324

This company town is named for Dr. Charles W. Jeffrey, a philanthropist who promoted mining in the area. The Jeffrey City area is famous for being the home of the Western Nuclear Company, which processes uranium from nearby mines. It is also the site of the biggest single chunk of jade ever unearthed in the world. Found by Verla Rhoades in 1943, it weighed 3,366 pounds. This part of Wyoming is the richest jade source in the world at present. Jeffrey City was also used as a scenic backdrop in the movie "Supergirl."

T Split Rock

Midway between Jeffrey City and Muddy Gap on U.S. Highway 287/789.

As the dominant landmark of the Sweetwater Valley, the unmistakable "gun sight" notch in the summit of Split Rock aimed the emigration directly at Great South Pass, still more than 75 miles to the west. A BLM interpretive site is at this location. A second highway turn-out a few miles west offers a better (although reverse) view of the "split" and also a look at the Old Castle, a smaller landmark south of the Trail and highway. Source: BLM brochure.

T Ice Slough

9.5 miles west of Jeffrey City on US-287.

While resting near this marshy spring, 49er J. Goldsborough Bruff wrote, "by digging a couple of feet, ice is obtained. The surface is dug up all around by travelers as much from curiosity as to obtain so desirable a luxury in a march so dry and thirsty..." The tundra-like turf that covers the marsh once provided enough insulation to preserve frozen sub-surface water well into the hottest summer months. For the pioneers, it was a minor miracle. Source: BLM brochure.

Split Rock

H Ice Slough

About 10 miles west of Jeffrey City on U.S. Highways 287/789

The Ice Slough is a tributary which drains into the Sweetwater River approximately five miles east of this point. Immediately before you is a slough or low lying wet area from which the tributary takes its name. This marshy expanse is created by a variety of grasses and related tufted marsh plants called sedges which form a patchwork of surface plant life. Water from the tributary flows through unseen beneath the peat-like vegetation. The water freezes solid in the winter and remains frozen during the spring and early summer because of the insulating peat.

Early explorers and the emigrants who traveled to Oregon and California stopped here often, welcoming the ice after having spent many days traversing the hot prairie. One forty-niner, Henry Tappan, wrote in his journal that it was a good place to enjoy a julep. Travelers who arrived late in the summer were disappointed to discover that the ice had finally melted. Today the Ice Slough is nearly dry and very little ice forms in the winter because much of the water has been drained off for irrigation.

H Split Rock

Midway between Jeffrey City and Muddy Gap on U.S. Highway 287/789

A famous natural landmark used by Indians, trappers and emigrants on the Oregon Trail. Site of Split Rock Pony Express 1860-61, stage, and telegraph station is on the south side of the Sweetwater. Split Rock can be seen as a cleft in the top of the Rattlesnake Range.

H Split Rock Interpretive Site Signs

Midway between Jeffrey City and Muddy Gap on U.S. Highway 287/789.

Split Rock

Split Rock was a relay station during the turbulent 18 month life of the Pony Express. The Express operated at a gallop, speeding mail across the West in only 19 days. However, because of the "talking wire," its days were numbered. The telegraph reached California by October 1861, ending a unique American experiment.

How it was done

Mail relay stations were set up 10 to 15 miles apart, each with two to four men and extra horses. About 500 of the hardiest western ponies were bought at prices up to $200 each. Most important of all, 80 riders were recruited from the most daring, determined and toughest "wiry young fellows" in the West.

Lightly equipped and armed, each rider rode about 70 miles round trip, exchanging horses at three relay stations. Over his saddle he carried the mochila, a leather cover with four mail pouches. Postage for a single letter varied from $1 to $5. Each rider rode at top speed to his relay stations where the precious mochila was placed on a waiting horse and he was off again in about two minutes. Day and night, good weather and bad, winter and summer, the "Pony" never stopped, averaging 10 to 15 miles an hour across the West.

The Pony's Echo

Completion of the transcontinental telegraph line on October 24, 1861 doomed the Pony Express. During its short life, the Express attracted world-wide attention that has not faded with time. Russell, Majors, Waddell and Company lost over $1 million on this venture. Nevertheless, the Pony Express stands tall as an outstanding example of American enterprise, endurance, courage and determination.

Split Rock Meadows

Shoshone, Arapaho, Crow and Sioux Indians occupied this pleasant valley long before the Oregon Trail, which changed their cultures and life styles forever. This led to tragic warfare and the eventual loss of country they had called their own.

Split Rock Relay Station, a crude log structure with a pole corral, was built at the base of the mass of rocks directly in front of you. It was used by both the Pony Express and the Overland Stage and until the early 1940s was a U.S. Post office.

The Pony Express generally followed the Oregon Trail through Wyoming to Fort Bridger which is located 185 miles west of here, then followed the existing mail route across Utah and Nevada to Sacramento, California.

A detachment of the 1st Independent Battalion Ohio Cavalry, which later became the 11th Ohio Cavalry, was garrisoned here in 1862. The troops provided escort for stagecoaches and emigrant wagon trains and protected the new telegraph lines.

Split Rock

Originally called the Emigrant Road, the Oregon Trail was the main route of westward expansion from 1812 to 1869. An estimated 500,000 people journeyed past here in search of new lands and new lives in the West.

Because of its unique shape, Split Rock was a well known trail landmark and navigation aid. Emigrants were guided by the rock for an entire day's travel from the east. It remained in view behind them for another two days. From Split Rock, it was about six days to South Pass, the gateway to the Great Salt Lake Valley, California's gold fields and the Pacific Northwest.

Emigrants on the Oregon and the Mormon Pioneer Trails coming from Devil's Gate, 12 miles east, often camped below this point on the Sweetwater River where good grass and water were available for stock. West of here, ruts carved in the rocks by iron wheeled wagons are still visible. Generally, Mormon emigrants tried to stay on the opposite side of the river from the main trail to avoid confrontations with others also heading West.

In 1844, James Clyman recorded this in his journal about this spot.

"(August) 17. Smokey But the sun rose over the Eastern Mountains in its usual majesty. Some recent Signs of a war party of Indians ware discovered yestarddy which caused some uneasiness...roled up the Steam on the South side...the most rugged bare granite rocks lay along the North side close to the water...saw some fine herds of Ibex or wild sheep some of which were taken and found to be very fine eating...This region seems to be the rufuses of the world thrown up in the utmost confusion."

Trails to Opportunity

The Oregon Trail was America's main street west. Building upon American Indian footpaths, emigrants bound for the Pacific Northwest used the trail. They were soon followed by Mormons fleeing persecution, gold seekers rushing to California and the thundering hooves of the Pony Express.

The Way West

Following Indian paths, fur trapping mountain men traveledd west. Astor's Pacific Fur Company opened the trail through the Rockies at South Pass in 1812. Mountain men guided the first wagon train over it in 1841. Until the Transcontinental Railroad was completed in 1869, the Oregon Trail was the way west. As many as 500,000 men, women and children journeyed this way over some 2,000 miles of deserts, plains and mountains.

The Red Desert and the Great Divide Basin

America's Heritage: The Red Desert

Hidden away in southwestern Wyoming lies one of the most unique and spectacular landscapes in North America—The Red Desert. A wondrous and incredible place: the desert's stunning rainbow-colored hoo-doos, towering buttes and prehistoric rock art define this rich landscape and provide a truly wild "home on the range" for the largest migratory game herd in the lower 48 states—over 50,000 pronghorn antelope in addition to a rare desert elk herd.

Since the settlement of the West and even long before, this region has played a special role in the lives of Native Americans and early settlers. For thousands of years the Red Desert has been a sacred place of worship for the Shoshone and Ute Tribes. Pioneers, Pony Express riders, Mormon settlers and mountain men also found important landmarks among the desert's features, guiding them west toward Oregon, Washington, Utah and California.

A Rich High Desert Landscape

The desert offers an unparalleled wilderness experience, with world-class wildlife viewing and hunting opportunities. Seven wilderness study areas (WSAs) including: Buffalo Hump, Sand Dunes, Alkali Draw, South Pinnacles, Honeycomb Buttes, Oregon Buttes and Whitehorse Creek, the largest cluster in Wyoming, lie within the Jack Morrow Hills area of the Red Desert. These WSAs make up the heart of a landscape that includes the largest active sand dune field in North America, ice-cold freshwater ponds, seasonal wetlands, aspen covered buttes, volcanic features and colorful clay hillsides for which the desert is famous.

Throughout the year these landscapes serve as home for thousands of animals and a paradise for humans to retreat from the world into a vast wilderness. In the springtime, thousands of sage grouse gather in the desert as they have done for centuries. In the fall, hunters and wildlife lovers descend on the region to track deer, antelope and elk through sixfoot stands of sage, limber pine and aspen. Rock hounds and paleontologists can find fossilized shark's teeth, tortoise shells and petrified wood scattered on the ground. Anthropologists can gaze at the sheer southern face of Steamboat Mountain, wander back in time and picture the land when it once was a favorite "Buffalo Jump" hunting area for Native Americans.

Heart of the West's History

Mountain men exploring the Rockies first set foot in the wild, wide open land of the Red Desert in 1825. During one of the earliest surveying expeditions of the west, in 1871, Dr. Ferdinand V. Hayden, passing through part of the Red Desert, noted the region's aspen groves and clear flowing springs upon Steamboat Mountain. Except for a few roads and the tragic loss of bison herds roaming the Great Divide Basin, the landscape looks very similar today as it did then.

On the northern edge of the Red Desert lies a historic gold mining area. Here, the old mining towns of South Pass City and Atlantic City remain today. Just south of them lies the Sweetwater River valley that provided an easy route to South Pass and the crossing of the Continental Divide. The pass served as the primary mountain gateway from the east to the west for hundreds of thousands of emigrants. Even today you can still see the imprints that their wagons left behind on their long journey along the Oregon, California and Mormon pioneer trails.

Prior to the arrival of early settlers and explorers, the desert was also home to many cultural and spiritual sites of the Shoshone people. Scattered throughout the landscape are two thousand-year-old rock art sites, and stone circles are said to be significant spiritual sites for the Shoshone people. Tipi rings, outlining ancient campsites of the Shoshone are evident throughout the region. A dramatically scenic black volcanic plug known as the Boar's Tusk that is strongly associated with the origins of their culture is also in the center of the region.

Losing Touch with the Land: Development Pressure Continues

The Red Desert is the largest unprotected and undeveloped high elevation desert left in the United States. Despite this distinction, the area has long been the focus of multinational oil, gas and mining corporations. According to the Bureau of Land Management, this pressure will continue to grow, with the industry hoping to turn southwestern Wyoming into the major natural gas producing region in the United States by 2015.

Over 90% of southwestern Wyoming's public land is available for oil and gas leasing and development. Thousands of gas wells sprawl throughout this region, linked together by a growing web of service roads, giant overhead powerlines and pipelines. These gas fields fragment wildlife habitat and disrupt animal behavior and migration. Emissions from generators and compressors degrade air quality, while contamination from spills can pollute surface and groundwater.

The Bureau of Land Management is responsible for developing a management plan for the region. It is within this plan that the future of the rare desert elk and the heart of the Red Desert itself will be decided. Permanently protecting 600,000 acres, out of 15 million acres of public land in southwestern Wyoming would safeguard at least one area of the state's magnificent wide-open landscape, an area that possesses all the qualities of a National Park.

Safeguarding Our Last Best Places

Citizens in Wyoming and around the country have attempted to permanently protect the Red Desert for over 100 years. Dr. Frank Durham launched the first effort in 1898 to designate the region as a "winter game preserve." His attempts were followed by Wyoming Governor Leslie Miller's 1935 campaign to designate the "great Divide Basin National Park." Despite many decades of support and numerous attempts the Red Desert has yet to be protected— leaving any decision about the future of the region to the BLM's current planning process.

This article reprinted with permission from Wyoming Outdoor Council. For more information on the Red Desert contact the Wyoming Outdoor Council, 262 Lincoln, Lander, WY 82520.

Section 5

Split Rock Station and Site Map
The Pony Express generally followed the Oregon Trail through Wyoming to Fort Bridger, then followed the existing mail route across Utah and Nevada to Placerville and Sacramento, California. Split Rock Relay Station, a crude log structure with a pole corral, was located at the base of the mass of rocks directly in front of you. Come view the site at a trail station a short walk from here.

William C. "Buffalo Bill" Cody exchanged horses at this site on a record ride from Red Buttes Station to Rocky Ridge Station and back. Due to another rider's untimely death, Cody was forced to add an extra leg to his normal relay and eventually covered a total distance of 322 miles in 21 hours and 40 minutes, using 21 horses in the process. On another occasion, Cody rode one horse at top speed for 24 miles when chased by Indians from Horse Creek Station east of Independence Rock to Plant's Station just east of here.

"Split Rock", the mass of rock on the skyline to the north, was an Oregon Trail landmark. It was visible for a day before it was reached from the east and for two days when it was viewed looking back from the west.

Wyoming Tidbits

The Red Desert in south central Wyoming drains neither to the east nor to the west. The continental divide splits and goes around the desert on all sides leaving the basin without normal drainage.

The Oregon Trail
The Oregon Trail, the main route of westward expansion from 1812 to 1869, passed through the valley below. An estimated 350,000 people journeyed past this point in search of new lands and new lives in the West.

Two routes of the Oregon Trail coming from Devil's Gate, twelve miles east, converged below this point on the Sweetwater River where good grass and water were available for the stock. Just west of here, ruts carved in the rocks by iron-tired wagons are still visible.

August 17. *Smokey But the sun rose over the Eastern Mountains in its usual majesty. Some recent Signs of a war party of Indians ware discovered yestardday which caused some uneasiness … roled up the Stream on the South side … the most ruged bare granite rocks lay along the North side close to the water … saw some fine herds of Ibex or wild sheep some of which ware taken and found to be verry fine eating … This region seems to be the refuses of the world thrown up in the utmost confusion.* —James Clyman, 1844

Split Rock Station
Split Rock Station, used by the Pony Express and the Overland Stage, was located in the meadow below. A small log building later served as the Split Rock Post Office until it was closed in the early 1940s.

Shoshone, Arapahoe, Crow and Sioux Indians occupied this pleasant valley before the Oregon Trail became heavily traveled. Their hunting patterns, culture and life style were changed forever. Friction between the tribes and the newcomers from the East led to tragic warfare and the loss to the Indians of the country they had known as theirs. It was due to such hostility that a division of the Sixth Ohio Cavalry was garrisoned at this site in 1862 to provide escort service for stagecoaches and emigrant wagon trains and to establish protection for the telegraph line.

The Sweetwater Rocks

The "Sweetwater Rocks" date back at least 1,400 million years and are some of the oldest found in the Rocky Mountain area. These Precambrian granites have been re-exposed in recent times by erosion of much younger Miocene and Pliocene sediments. When the sediment pressures were removed, granite slabs peeled off, producing the smooth rock knobs. Erosion along old fractures and shear zones left the large cracks in the rocks.

"Split Rock" served as a well known landmark and navigational aid because of its unique shape. Emigrants were guided by the rock for an entire day's travel when they were approaching from the east. It remained in view as a checkpoint behind them from the west for another two days.

46 *Gas, Food*

I-80 Exit 209

47 *No services*

I-80 Exits 184,187,196,201,204,206

H Continental Divide "The Backbone of the Nation" Elevation 7,178 feet above sea level

On I-80 Exit 184

The three principal river systems of the U.S. west of the Ohio have their source in Wyoming. The Mississippi thru the Missouri and its branches, the Madison, Gallatin and Yellowstone; the Columbia flowing into the North Pacific, by its longest branch, the Snake; the Colorado by its longest branch, the Green.

Precipitation falling west of this point finds it way into the Green and Colorado and eventually to the Gulf of California, and that falling east of this point finds its way to the Gulf of Mexico by way of the Mississippi drainage basin.

48 *Gas, Food, Lodging*

Wamsutter

Pop. 681, Elev. 6,709

Named for a UP bridge engineer in 1884, this settlement along the railroad had originally been called Washakie, until confusion with Fort Washakie forced them to change the name. The Hole-in-the-Wall gang once robbed a train nearby. Beautiful turritella agates, derived from ancient shelled invertebrates, can be found in the wild country to the south.

H Wamsutter

243 McCormick Street in Wamsutter

"On summer nights, this lonely place is merely a small group of lights set in blackness and silence. Over the immense darkness, stars shine brilliantly, neither dimmed by other lights nor hidden by smoke and dust in the air. A meteor flames against the sinking stars; an aeroplane, winging toward Cheyenne or Salt lake City, seems trying to imitate it. Wamsutter is on the edge of the Red Desert, where colors change hourly, according to the brilliance and direction of the sunlight." (from *Wyoming: A Guide to Its History, Highways and People, 1941.*) This is the Great Divide Basin. To the south and west the waters flow to the Pacific Oean. To the east and north they flow to the Atlantic. but here, atop the nation's Continental Divide, the waters drain inward, with no outlet to the sea. Ute and Shoshoni Indians once roamed this semiarid desert but were eventually forced out after the 1850s by increasing numbers of whites traveling along a transcontinental corridor containing the Overland Trail (15 miles south). Stage stations served as the first settlements until 1868 when the Transcontinental railroad was built. Wamsutter emerged as a section town on the mainline of the Union Pacific, and later developed as a railhead for shipping cattle and sheep with stockgrowers from Wyoming and colorado using the stock yards. In the early 1900s, as new lines were built, Wamsutter's importance began to decline. however, the Lincoln highway—which became U.S. 30 and then Interstate 80—brought many travelers and Wamsutter hung on as a service community. Eventually, oil, natural gas, and uranium were discovered, securing the town's existence. Wamsutter, the oldest continually occupied town within the basin, like many Wyoming communities expanded and contracted to accommodate economic realities and a microcosm of Wyoming history.

49 *No services*

I-80 Exits 168, 170

50 *Gas*

Red Desert

In the central part of the Great Divide Basin's Red Desert, this tiny town overlooks the biggest stretch of unfenced land in the lower 48 states.

51 *No services*

I-80 Exits 152, 154, 156, 158

Table Rock

Also known as Pulpit Rock, the stone pinnacle for which this railroad station was named was the site of a sermon given by Brigham Young in 1847 to Mormon pioneers headed for Utah. In 1876, the area achieved further notoriety when two prospectors salted the mines at Diamond Mesa and Ruby Gulch in order to swindle several easterners out of over a half million dollars.

53 *No services*

I-80 Exits 136, 139, 142, 146

Bitter Creek

A station on the Overland Stage Route, the town became a railroad grading camp in 1868. The creek for which it was named got its taste from the high alkali content of the water.

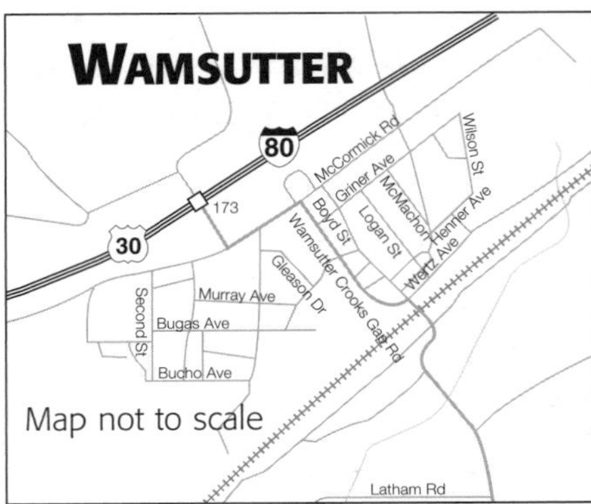

H Mama Sage

At rest area just east of Exit 142

Oh! "Mama Sage." It seems endless, the sage; the rolling sage-covered Wyoming hills. Sagebrush, the shrub that means survival to the world's largest populations of pronghorn antelope and sage grouse. Blown free of snow by the Wyoming winds, sagebrush is the major winter food for these species, and provides important habitat for a host of small mammals and birds.

The sagebrush deserts of the Great Divide, Green River, Bighorn River and Wind River basins also support large herds of wild, free-ranging mule deer and horses and over 150 other species of wildlife. The only elk herd in Wyoming associated entirely with a sagebrush desert is found immediately north of this area.

There are 13 species of sagebrush in our state. Sagebrush has a deep taproot, which enables it to survive in areas with as little as six inches annual precipitation. Sagebrush is a hearty shrub and an able provider for Wyoming's wildlife. That is why Wyoming works so hard to keep her sage-covered ranges productive. "Mama Sage" is a special part of the formula that makes our wildlife—worth the watching.

54 *Gas, Food*

Point of Rocks

Elev. 6,509

This was once the Almond Stage Station, serving as a stopover for those headed to the gold mines at South Pass and Atlantic Cities. Its name is taken from the nearby sandstone ridge overlooking the Bitter Creek. The station was established in 1862. Now, Point of Rocks is mainly a company town for the nearby Jim Bridger Coal Mine and Power Plant.

H Overland Stage Route

South side of 1-80 at Exit 130

Remains of old stage station can be seen on the other side of the railroad tracks at Point of Rocks exit southwest of exit against the hillside.

H Overland Stage Route

I-80 Exit 130 near Point of Rocks

At the beginning of the Civil War military strength in the West declined and often it was impossible to safeguard stage carrying the United States mail along the Oregon/California/Mormon Trail. Early in 1862 "Stagecoach King" Ben Holladay acquired the transcontinental stage business and the United States mail subsidy contract. He named his new company the Overland Stage Line and soon abandoned the central trail.

Holladay determined that a route further south was better because it would be safer, shorter and closer to Denver where economic growth was taking place due to the 1859 gold rush. The new route, established by trapper and explorers, became known as the Overland Trail.

The Overland split off from the older Oregon Trail near North Platte, Nebraska. From that point, coaches paralleled the South Platte, rolling west through Colorado before turning north to begin a steep and rocky climb into southern Wyoming where the trail flankd the medicine Bow Range before turning westward again. After crossing plains, rivers and streams and winding through mountain passes, the trail entered the Green River Basin. Traffic passed through this valley, following Bitter Creek to its confluence with the Green River. It then branched north to join the Oregon Trail near the junction of the Blacks Fork and Hams Fork Rivers. From there the trail continued west and south toward Salt Lake City and eventually Placerville, California.

The short, but exciting period of Overland Trail transportation lasted for several years until 1869 when the Union Pacific Railroad replaced the transcontinental overland stage as the major, east-west transportation system. Nevertheless, the emigrants and settlers continued to use the trail until after the turn of the century.

H Point of Rocks Monument

I-80 Exit 130 near Point of Rocks

Ruins of Almond Overland Stage Station, 1862-8. Located beyond railrod tracks, 1640 feet to southward of this marker. Erected by Wyoming Historical Landmark Commission 1947.

55 *Food*

Superior

Pop. 244, Elev. 6,700

Once a booming coal-mining town, Superior had a population of over 3000 when the original mines closed in the 1960s. Named for the Superior Coal Company, which in turn was named for the high quality of the coal here, Superior was the setting for the 1992 film Leaving Normal. Today, the nearby Jim Bridger Mines and Power Plant are revitalizing the area.

T Superior Community Center

27 Main in Superior. 382-7223

Once a bustling community of 3,000 people, Superior lost much of its population when the coal mines closed in 1963. Interpretive signs guide visitors through the history of the area.

H Superior

In Superior

This monument is dedicated to the miners who worked here and especially to those who lost their lives. It is also a monument to the living—those who have remained and exemplifiy the men and women whose independent character created this commuity.

The town of Superior, Wyoming had its origins in the coal boom days around the turn of the century. A prospecting team led by Morgan Griffiths entered Horse Thief Canyon in 1900, and established the site for the first of Superior's many coal mines. The town grew to its largest population of 2,700 in the mid 1940s when, during world War II, hundreds of workers came to the mines, living in quarters fashioned from boxcars.

The Superior Union Hall was built as a trapezoid.

The Superior mines produced nearly 24,000,000 tons of coal annually in their prime, second only to Rock Springs. There were eight mines in the area, all but two owned and operated by the Union Pacific Coal Company to supply their locomotives. The Premier and Copenhagen Mines were independents.

The Union Pacific mines were the last to close their mining operations, forbidden by law to sell their coal to the public, and having no great use for it themselves because of the advent of the diesel locomotive. The D.O. Clark Mine was closed in 1963.

The town of South Superior was an incorporated town, with a separate identity from the company town of Superior. This Hall and the standing buildings located north of here are all part of South Superior. The company-owned houses and stores have long since disappeared. These are the remnants of an independent venture built to serve the miners living in the area.

H Superior Interpretive Signs

At Superior Union Hall

Prospecting

In 1900, while prospecting was being carried on in the vicinity of Cumberland, Morgan Griffiths, Gus Paulsen and a party of prospectors went northeast from Rock Springs to prospect in Horse Thief Canyon, since outcrops of a promising deposit of coal were known to exist there.

Only twenty miles out, they established their camp in the picturesque canyon, named by early settlers who claimed that a gang of outlaws had made this their rendezvous and hiding place for their stolen horses. One of the crew was delegated cook for the party, with the understanding that anyone who complained about the cooking would immediately take over the job.

One morning when breakfast was especially inedible, a crew member spoke out unguardedly, stating that the biscuits were nothing but dough, the bacon burnt to a cinder, and the coffee not fit to drink. In the midst of his tirade, he remembered the agreement, and stopped with a smile. "You know, boys, I like everything cooked that way." The original cook kept his thankless job and the men continued to sit down to their less-than-delectable victuals.

With drinking water from the springs in the vicinity, and wild game, including deer, antelope, and sage chickens in abundance, the crew had all the necessities, and were not dependent on the day's drive by buckboard and mule to headquarters in Rock Springs.

Morgan Griffiths was a native Welshman who came to America in the late 1870s. Universally liked by all who knew him, he carried on much of the preliminary negotiation work when the United Mine Workers of America organized the miners of the Union Pacific Coal company.

Gus Paulsen, who later became Mayor of Superior and Outside Foreman of mines, had quite a reputation. The miners said he could take a meager lunch, a pocket compass, and a map of any district, no matter how difficult the terrain, and locate the section corners with unerring accuracy. He had the distinction of once refusing a raise in salary when it was offered him, stating that the company was then paying him all that he was worth.

Opening the Mines

Prospecting revealed that Seams Nos. 3, 1, 7, and 13, the latter also known as the Van Dyke Seam, were of sufficient thickness to justify the development of mines. Preliminary railroad surveys were made up the long canyon from Thayer Junction on the main line.

In the meantime, locations for mines had been selected and a town site laid out. On October 23, 1903, the drift into "C" Mine was started, and on February 24, 1906, the slope was begun. "A" and "B" Mines were opened April 30, 1906, and "D" Mine on June 30th of the same year. "A" Mine was opened on No. 7 Seam, and later included Seams Nos. 1 and 3.

The work was under comparatively light

cover, and haulage was carried on by mules, with a few electric locomotives. The haulage from Nos. 1 and 3 Seams was conducted by an endless rope haulage on an outside plane to the tipple, a distance of 3,500 feet. The coal was all undercut with electric mining machines, and drilled with electric drills.

"E" Mine was opened during 1910, and a modern steel screening plant was constructed that year. A shaft had been sunk for a distance of 100 feet from ground level, with a 200 HP electric hoist with full automatic control erected on the steel headframe that mounted the shaft. Self-dumping cages were used for hoisting purposes. By 1937, "E" 's reserves had been depleted and the mine closed down.

The first shaking conveyor installed in the Rock Springs district was put into operation in "C" Mine during 1927. About 1910 a gas producer plant was installed at "D" Mine, the gas being used to operate an electric generator, but the quantity of electric power developed was so small and the expense so great, that the plant was abandoned in 1922.

The Superior mines were originally opened by the Superior Coal Company, organized December 28, 1905, with a capital stock of 10,000 shares, with a par value of $100 each, headquarters located in Cheyenne, Wyoming. The company merged with the Union Pacific Coal Company on May 1, 1916.

In 1934, when it became evident that the coal reserves contiguous to the present Superior mines were nearing exhaustion, active prospecting was started in the vicinity of the mines. By mid 1936, reliable evidence indicating reserves of 40,000,000 tons justified the opening of a new mine of large capacity, with further substantial reserves partially prospected.

Put on a producing basis on New Year's Day 1939, the D.O. Clark Mine, was modern in every respect. Named for the man who did so much pioneer coal mining work in Wyoming, Utah, Colorado and Washington, it was designed for production of 7,500 tons per day of two shifts.

Premier Mine and Copenhagen Mine were opened and managed by private coal companies not directly associated with the UP Coal Company.

Town Development

This map shows the location of the Union Pacific coal mines and coal camps built in the years between 1906 and 1910. The town of South Superior is purposefully left off this map.

Wyoming Tidbits

The Shoshone Indians believe that deceased tribe members should take all their personal belongings with them. They often placed the deceased's iron bedstead atop the grave as a marker. At the Sacajawea Cemetery a few miles from Fort Washakie, there are still many iron bedsteads visible.

Wyoming Tidbits

Wyoming's first Indian reservation is also its only one. The Wind River Reservation was created in 1868 and is more than 2 million acres.

It was not owned by Union Pacific Coal Company and in this time period, "the company" as it was called, had little use for the future town. South Superior is located between "Superior" and "Japanese village" shown on this map. It was bordered on the west by Union Pacific's "B" Mine.

A number of dwelling houses and miscellaneous mine buildings were placed under construction as soon as the site for mining development was chosen, and during the life of "A" Mine, a store and schoolhouse were erected. In the main part of the town, store and office buildings were constructed.

The town was known as Reliance until, on July 14, 1906, the name was changed to Superior, after the Superior Coal Company which originally opened the mines.

While the company-owned homes were built adjacent to the mines, the town of South Superior was developed to house independently-minded individuals. At first a tent town, called various names such as "White City" and "Dog Town", it grew, and a relatively large commercial center developed.

56 *No services*

H Riverton Project

Just west of the junction of U.S. Highways 26 and 287 at Diversion Dam Junction rest area

Portions of the High Plains were not settled until the early 20th century because water was needed for irrigation. Responding to pressure for Western settlement, Congress created the Reclamation Service in 1902. Its purpose was to develop water resources making possible cultivation of what was considered desert wasteland. One effort was the Riverton Project. Located in the Wind River Basin it was undertaken by the Bureau of Reclamation in 1920.

The Midvale Irrigation District of the Riverton Project involves 73,000 acres, three dams—Bull Lake Dam to the south and Diversion Dam and Pilot Butte Dam to the east, 100 miles of canals and 300 miles of laterals. Diversion Dam, completed in 1923, diverts water from the Wind River to the Wyoming Canal. It is noteworthy as the first dam in the nation with a road incorporated into its structure and the first to contain a fish ladder.

Historian T. A. Larson describes the Riverton irrigation project as "a perennial object lesson in the formidable difficulties inherent in large-scale reclamation projects in the West." Initially posing financial and engineering problems, it came to involve legal and political issues. During the rise of Native American self determination the Arapaho and Shoshone tribes exercised their right to Wind River water, granted by an 1868 treaty. Court battles were fought over water used to irrigate land opened to homesteading by Congress in 1905. The struggle highlights the importance of water to the West.

H Wyoming Winds

At Diversion Dam rest area

This site lies at the northernmost extent of the Snowy Range Mountains, a spot where the high mountain peaks end and the winds begin. Winds here may exceed 70 mph at times, blowing winter snows, leaving ridges and slopes bare, and exposing grasses and shrubs to provide food for elk, mule deer and pronghorn antelope.

Elk and mule deer migrate from the high mountain summer range to these foothills and basins to winter. The Wyoming Game and Fish Department has acquired 12,870 acres of the wind blown slopes and basins along Wagonhound Creek to protect and maintain this crucial winter range.

The exposed vegetation provides important winter forage for elk, mule deer, and antelope These animals require both food and cover to survive the harsh winter conditions. Winter range in Wyoming is in critically short supply. If significant numbers of animals are to survive, winter range must be protected.

These winter ranges are managed to provide a balance of vegetation, including grasses and shrubs to provide forage, and conifers to provide cover from wind, sun and heat loss during cold periods. Wind and man interact on the land to free and protect your wildlife resource. As you travel, keep in mind the Wyoming wind is a friend!

57 *Gas*

Fort Washakie

Pop. 300, Elev. 5,570

Named for the great Shoshone Chief Washakie, who encouraged peaceful relations between whites and Native Americans, Ft. Washakie is the only fort ever named for an Indian chief. It is now the headquarters for the Wind River Reservation. Originally called Ft. Brown, and later Ft. Augur, it became a place of protection for the Shoshone people from the Arapaho and Sioux, their traditional enemies. Chief Washakie lived here until his death in 1900, when he was 102. The fort remained a protective entity until 1909, when hostilities between the Shoshone and Arapaho declined. Some of the original buildings still stand.

T Shoshone Tribal Cultural Center

The Shonshone Tribal Cultural Center is located in the Historic Fort Washakie exhibits of tribal crafts, art, Shoshone leaders treaty documents, maps, agreements, and other historical artifacts. There are also a displays of historical data and photographs. Vaious events such as walking

Fort Washakie	Jan	Feb	March	April	May	June	July	Aug	Sep	Oct	Nov	Dec	Annual
Average Max. Temperature (F)	32.4	40.7	46.7	56.9	67.4	77.4	85.6	84.2	74.3	62.1	45.0	36.5	59.1
Average Min. Temperature (F)	3.1	10.4	16.0	25.3	34.8	42.4	47.6	46.3	37.0	27.7	15.4	6.2	26.0
Average Total Precipitation (in.)	0.32	0.39	0.75	1.84	2.58	1.70	0.78	0.56	0.99	0.93	0.64	0.31	11.79
Average Total SnowFall (in.)	6.6	7.1	10.6	11.2	2.4	0.3	0.0	0.0	0.9	5.5	9.2	6.1	60.2
Average Snow Depth (in.)	2	2	2	1	0	0	0	0	0	0	2	2	1

tours, cultural classes, and workshops are held throughout the year. There is also a gift shop offering Native American handcrafted articles. The center is open Monday through Friday, 9 a.m. to 4 p.m.

T Washakie's White House

An interesting, history-filled building on the grounds of the Shoshone Tribal Cultural Center is Fort Washakie's historic White House, built in 1913. The Cultural Center is open M-F, 8-4:45. Admission is free, donations requested.

T Chief Washakie Plunge

A warm outdoor pool, jacuzzi, and private baths, located on the Wind River Indian Reservation.

T Fort Washakie Shoshone Cemetery

Fort Washakie

A number of notable individuals are buried here. Following are the names and inscriptions from their monuments. They can all be found in the southwest corner of the cemetery.

Sacajawea

Died-April 9, 1884

A guide with the Lewis and Clark Expedition 1805-1806. Identified, 1907 by Rev. J. Roberts who officiated at her burial.

Bazil

Son of Sacajawea Aged 86 years Died 1886. He was reburied here. January 12, 1925.

Baptiste Charbonneau

Dedicated in the memory of Baptiste Charbonneau papoose of the Lewis and Clark Expedition—1805-1806 Son of Sacajawea. Born Feb 11 1805. Died on this reservation 1885. Buried west in the Wind River Mountains.

Richards And Hall

Sacred to the memory of Mrs. Maggie Richards and Mrs. Hall.

Pioneer white settlers killed July 23rd, AD. 1873 by a raiding band of hostile Sioux Indians in their ranch home on the site of the present City of Lander, Wyoming

T Shoshone Episcopal Mission

See a collection of original structures from one of the earliest missions on the Wind River Indian Reservation still in use today.

H Fort Washakie

South of Fort Washakie on Highway 287 just past Ethete turnoff

Fort Washakie, headquarters of the Wind River Reservation, was originally established as Camp Augur, on the site of present-day Lander, in 1869, in accordance with the treaty with the Shoshone and Bannock Indians to protect them from Sioux, Arapahoe, Cheyenne and other hostile bands. In 1870 it was re-named Fort Brown, and in 1871 it was moved to the present location, built from adobe and from materials salvaged from the old fort. In 1873, the commanding officer headed a company assigned to explore toward the head of the Big Wind River for a possible wagon route. In compliment to the Shoshone chief, the post was named Fort Washakie in 1878. It was abandoned in 1908.

H The Shoshone-Episcopal Mission Boarding School 1890-1945

On Trout Creek Road south of Fort Washakie two miles west of Highways 26/287. Just north of the mission building.

The school was founded by the Reverand John Roberts. Born in Wales, in 1853, Roberts was a missionary to the Shoshones for 66 years.

'Our hope is in the children and the young people, the old people can't hear!" So spoke Washakie, Chief of Shoshones, when, in 1889, he gave this land—160 acres of hallowed Shoshone ground, traditional place of solemn assembly and religious ceremony—to his friend the "White Robe", the Reverend Mr. Roberts. Thus the unlettered warrior-statesman, nearing the end of a long life and heavy labors, bequeathed a share of his burdens to an Oxford educated ecclesiastic who, throughout a similarly long lifetime, would similarly labor to lighten the problems of people experiencing transition.

To that end the missionary established his school. Its cornerstone was laid in 1890 and, despite wilderness handicaps, the Georgian building was completed within a year. Here, on soil consecrated by former tribal rituals, Shoshone girls learned a Christian catechism. To their teacher's credit, new knowledge was imparted without disparagement of old beliefs.

Washakie, approaching his centenarian year and having studied the "White Robe's" procedure, submitted to baptism on January 25, 1897. Honored and respected, the Reverend John Roberts D.D., L.L.D. retired from office following 40 years of service. But only death, coming in 1949 in his 96th year, could end his work.

This school, largely self supporting through revenues from its farm lands, was in session 55 years. It closed in 1945.

H Washakie

At Fort Washakie on Blackcole Street

The great Shoshone Chief, and skilled hunter,

Chief Washakie

Chief Washakie is remembered as one the the most famous and beloved Native Americans. This last great chief was a pioneer in changing a course in American history by leading his people to a mutually cooperative relationship with the U.S. government. The date of Washakie's birth is unknown, but it is widely believed that when he died in 1900 he was at least 100 years old. His father was a Flathead and his mother was from one of the Shoshone tribal groups, probably a Lemhi. The future Shoshone chief was named Pina Quanah (Smell of Sugar) when he was born.

The surviving story of how Washakie became associated with the Shoshones relates that the Flathead village in which his family was living was attacked by Blackfeet Indians. Washakie's father was killed. The surviving villagers scattered. Washakie's family was eventually taken in by Lemhis. He and a sister remained with the Lemhis even after their mother and other family members rejoined the Flatheads.

Washakie later joined the Bannocks, a tribe hostile to white men. He lived with them five years before joining the Green River Snake Indians, who had peaceful relations with whites. Washakie became close friends with Jim Bridger during the 1830's and gave his daughter to Bridger in marriage. Perhaps this friendship influenced Washakie's decision to ally himself with the whites in exchange for their defense of his people against their Indian enemies.

Washakie became a noted warrior. Although the name by which he would be widely known has been translated in various ways, it apparently dealt with his tactics in battle. One story describes how Washakie devised a large rattle by placing stones in an inflated and dried balloon of buffalo hide which he tied on a stick. He carried the device into battle to frighten enemy horses, earning the name "The Rattle." Another translation of "Washakie" is "Shoots-on-the-Run."

By 1850 Washakie was head chief of the Shoshones, apparently earning the position by his deeds in battle and wise counsel, though there is no record to show exactly when and under what conditions the decision was made. It is thought that the various Shoshone tribes may have united under one chief to deal with threats by hostile tribes, such as the Sioux and Cheyenne.

Washakie became an ally of white men, deciding early that warfare was pointless and a policy of adaptation and mutual assistance should be followed. He assisted U.S. Army operations, with military forces and advice, against hostile tribes, particularly the Sioux and Cheyenne. Washakie granted right-of-way through Shoshone land in western Wyoming to the Union Pacific Railroad, aiding the completion of a coast-to-coast rail line.

Washakie's forces fought with General Crook against the Lakota and Cheyenne in the Battle of the Rosebud during the summer of 1876. Although the confrontation was a stand off, Washakie has received credit for influencing Crook's decision not to pursue the allied Indian armies further. He advised Crook to, "Leave them alone for a few days. They cannot subsist their large numbers in the camp and will have to scatter out for meat and pasturage. They will begin to fight among themselves and some will sneak away to their agencies." When General Custer confronted the massed Indian armies only one week later, he met with total defeat. Washakie's strategy of divide and conquer finally won the war.

The Shoshone chief also sought the best for his people, requesting schools, churches, and hospitals on Shoshone lands. He also pushed for a reservation in his beloved "Warm Valley" (Wind River Valley) which had been given to the Crows, enemies of the Shoshones, in the 1851 Fort Laramie Treaty. In 1868 the United States, determining that the Crows had broken treaty terms, gave the valley to the Shoshone Indians at the Fort Bridger Treaty Council. In 1896, Washakie ceded lands bounding mineral hot springs near Thermopolis for public use, requesting that a portion of the waters be set aside for free use by people of all races.

The famed leader and warrior died on February 20, 1900. He was buried with full military honors at Fort Washakie. Washakie is remembered for his clear vision and strong leadership in an extremely difficult era.

Courtesy of Wyoming State Archives

Section 5

Atlantic City

strategist, and warrior against his tribal enemies was noted for his friendship towards the white men. He united his people. He was born about 1804 and died February 20, 1900. Shoshone Indian Reservation was created by the Great Treaty of July 3, 1868. Fort Washakie 1879-1909, was a military post.

58 *Food, Lodging*

Atlantic City

Pop. 57, Elev. 7,675

Driving 27 miles south of Lander on Wyoming Highway 28, and then taking a gravel road left for roughly less than five miles, you arrive in Atlantic City, a century-old ghost town. Gold miners poured into this district in the late 1860s and, within a few months, created three typical frontier gold camps here — South Pass City, Atlantic City, and Miner's Delight. Today, Atlantic City can easily claim the title as boom/bust capital of Wyoming. Since its official platting in April 1868, the town has experienced a continuing series of mining booms and busts, all but one tied to the fortunes of gold.

In 1867, Atlantic City's population approached 300. When W.H. Jackson took his 1870 photograph of Atlantic City, the town sported a three block main street with business buildings on both sides and heavily populated residential areas on the hillsides and in Beer Garden Gulch.

Several miners from South Pass City in 1868 discovered "The Atlantic Ledge"—gold-bearing quartz several feet thick and thousands of feet long. The discovery spawned a boom of free-milling gold that resulted in a population of nearly two thousand in two years.

During the town's boom, it possessed a brewery, a beer garden, a large dance hall, and an opera house. After three years, the town consisted of a log school and a two-story stone building constructed by J.W. Anthony in which Robert McAuley operated a store. The ninety-foot upper story served as a dance hall where Calamity Jane conducted business. In 1862, Emil Granier, a French engineer, proposed a twenty-mile sluiceway to provide water. The ditch, built with $1,000.00 and three hundred Swedes, passed through miles of hard rock, circled around the town and angled south. Christina Lake, located at the head of the ditch, was dammed to create a vast water supply. Unfortunately, the grade had been laid out with too much slope, leaving the sluices wiped out and water spilling over. The result was a supply of "liquid gold" that had every miner rushing in, creating small bonanzas and heavy whiskey consumption.

Forlorn and defeated, Emil Granier returned to France to explain the project's failure and to request refinancing. Instead, Granier was jailed, tried, and sentenced to life imprisonment. Despite the Granier ditch failure, Atlantic City made the following additions: Mr. Giessler created a new store in 1898; the Carpenter family created a two-story log hotel in 1900; July 4, 1900 included a rodeo on Main Street; and in 1912, the log church was built which came to be known as "National Shrine."

By 1875, all of the gold had been harvested, and in 1920, all of the mines were shut down. During the Great Depression of the 1930s, Atlantic City experienced a small boom as the E.T. Fisher Company built and operated a dredge on the streams near Atlantic City where it took out seven hundred thousand dollars in gold. The two-man operation was comprised of a "traveling mill" mounted on rails. While one man controlled the dredge, the other handled the two-story gold washer, oiling bearings, and watched for nuggets. Along the way they left heaps of rock which are still visible today. Many of the nearby mines reopened. By the start of World War II, this short-lived excitement faded: When the government declared gold a non-strategic metal, the mines were forced to close. In their search for metal, scavengers came into the area and dismantled many of the mines in the district.

By the 1950s, Atlantic City was listed as a ghost town. During several winters in the 1950s and early 1960s, only three or four people remained in the town. In 1950, the only remaining business in operation was the Carpenter Hotel— a one-night stay in the cabin was one dollar and meals were fifty cents.

Later in the 1960s, interest in a different metal-iron ore brought hundreds of people to the area when U.S. Steel constructed a large, open pit mine three miles northwest of Atlantic City. Although most of the miners commuted from Lander, several settled in Atlantic City. This and the growing interest in vacation homes made the town slowly grow again. In the 1980s the U.S. Steel mine closed, and with economic hard times throughout Wyoming, most of the people in this community left to find jobs.

Each spring, the eternal hope of the gold mining community grows as geologists, promoters, and would-be investors drift in and out of Atlantic City. The wind of this old gold town always whispers of another boom on its way.

Atlantic City Tour

1. *Beer Garden Gulch.* To the east lies Beer Garden Gulch, so named because of the two breweries that operated during Atlantic City's early years. Nothing remains of the extensive saloons, gaming houses, and red light district. Only the stream, which provided the water for Wyoming's first brewery, still exists.

2. *Dexter Mill.* The large Dexter Mine and Milling Company's cyanide mill was built in 1904 at considerable expense, but it recovered little gold. The company eventually went bankrupt. In the late '20s, the buildings were moved to the Carissa Mine near South Pass City where they still stand today. A private residence was built on part of the foundation of the mill.

3. *School House.* Education was sporadic in early Atlantic City. The first recorded school was taught in a private home in 1869 by Miss Irwin. Some time later a schoolhouse was located here, but around the turn of the century, a cowboy riding through town knocked down a pupil, Jean Harsch. The citizens then moved the school to a safer location off of the main roads, east of the present location of the church.

4. *Sypes Barn.* The Sypes dairy barn dates to the early 1900s. Below the barn, the Sypes also built a huge, two-story house. Charley Sypes was a bookkeeper and caretaker for the Dexter Mining and Milling Company. In addition to running the dairy, he also served as postmaster for several years during the 1920s at the Granier building. When the Timba Bah Mining Company took over the Dexter interests, Sypes remained as its agent. He later committed suicide because of debts, and his large, white house was dismantled and moved.

5. *Gustafsen House.* Martha Harsch and Pete Gustafsen occupied this home after they married in 1912. Martha's sister, Nora, whose husband disappeared after their first year of marriage, also lived with them. The Harsch sisters were always called by their maiden name. Until Martha's death, the Harsch family had been an integral part of the town's history for almost a hundred years. Most of the family members are buried in the Atlantic City Cemetery on the hill east of town.

6. *Gratrix Cabin.* Reportedly the oldest building in Atlantic City, it was occupied by Judge Buck Gratrix, a late 1860s arrival who served as a Justice of the Peace. The building may have also served as the site of town meetings and a school. Gratrix boasted of having lived in three counties (Carter, Sweetwater and Fremont); two territories (Dakota and Wyoming); and one state (Wyoming)—all while living in this same house at this site.

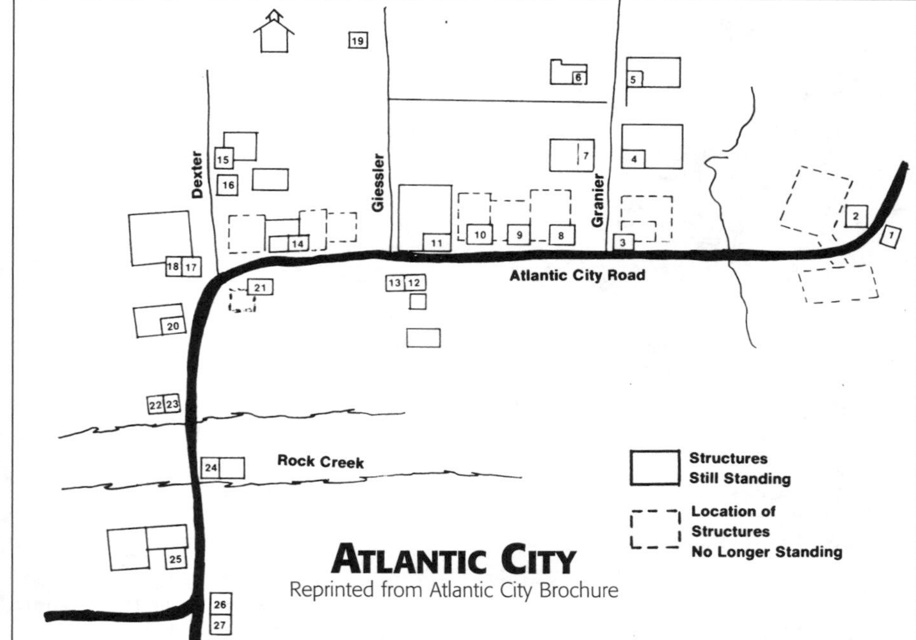

ATLANTIC CITY
Reprinted from Atlantic City Brochure

7. *Assay Building.* Early photographs of Atlantic City show the front part of this building, which may have been one of the several assay offices during the first boom. Presently it is a private residence.

8. *Granier building.* Emile Granier came to Atlantic City in 1884 before Atlantic City's second gold boom. A French capitalist, he supposedly invested almost a quarter of a million dollars in his hydraulic mining project. To the south and west of Atlantic City, one can still see evidence of the 25-mile ditch constructed to bring water down from Christina Lake, high in the Wind River Range, to Granier's claims east of Atlantic City. His ditch was completed in 1888 and operated for several years. In 1893, Granier's company went bankrupt, and he left. Ironically, Granier's dream of worthwhile gold recovery was realized by the Fischer-Crawford dredging operation in the 1930s; the dredge's gold was retorted into $10,000 bricks in Granier's former building, which burned down a few years later.

9. *Red Cloud Saloon.* The saloon was one of the earliest and most popular places in Atlantic City. An 1869 edition of the Sweetwater Mines newspaper noted that it was owned by Bill Long (Lawn) who was part Indian and was reportedly at one time kidnapped by Chief Red Cloud. Saloons were built before the church and schools, as in most frontier mining towns.

10. *Harsch House.* John Murphy, an early miner, built a house here in 1868 and operated it as the Atlantic Hotel, which was mentioned in James Chisholm's book <I>South Pass, 1868<I>. Murphy also owned a house of ill repute in South Pass City. Active in creating Wyoming Territory from the Dakota Territory, he served as the first sheriff of Carter County. He remained in the area and died in Lander, where the local newspaper obituary mentioned his "weakness for strong liquors."

Wyoming Tidbits

The first gold mining district in Wyoming was organized on November 11, 1865, at South Pass City.

11. *Giessler Store and Post Office (Atlantic City Mercantile).* After the success of an earlier store east of the McAuley Store, Lawrence Giessler constructed this building in 1893 out of adobe brick, covered with metal siding. The next year he built a large livery barn across the street, behind the store. For many years, Giessler successfully operated the store, a freighting business, and a ranch on Willow Creek. He installed the first telephone system in the area in 1904. After his death, his wife, Emma, operated a cafe and boarding house for the booming town. After the store closed in the late '30s, it was not opened again until the iron ore boom in the 1960s. A U.S. Steel worker, Lyle Moerer, restored the building. He and his wife, Jerrie, ran a store, gas station, and bar for several years. Since then, various owners have operated it as a bar and steak house. It is on the National Register of Historic Places.

12. *Drilling Rock.* While hand drilling holes for dynamite was dangerous and demanding work, the early miners enjoyed showing off their skill at drilling contests. This rock was quarried from nearby cliffs and brought to Atlantic City for contests. In recent years, there has been a national revival of drilling contests.

13. *Harsch Chicken House.* This structure, slowly being reclaimed by the elements, is easily spotted in early photo- graphs of Atlantic City. A long time resident of the town remembers it as the Harsch family's chicken house. It also probably served as an early home.

14. *Main Street.* This block contained a variety of businesses through the years, including a butcher shop, a general store, a drug store, and several saloons. The private residence in the middle of the block on the north side was once part of Blackie's Saloon. The Huff-Green saloon was located next to it.

15. *McAuley Cabin.* This cabin, where the Robert McAuley family lived for many years, dates back to the late 1860s. Many other families have occupied it through the years.

16. *Fisher Cabin.* Now abandoned, this cabin belonged to a bachelor by that name, according to several accounts. It may have also been used as a schoolhouse.

17. *McAuley Store (Hyde's Hall).* This building was constructed around 1869 by J.W. Anthony, who was never paid for his work, as happened with many of his jobs. Robert McAuley then opened a store here that supposedly also had gaming tables, a saloon, the post office, and one of the best dance floors in Wyoming. According to local legend, Calamity Jane, then living in the nearby settlement of Miner's Delight, was once a dance hall girl here. The second story was removed after being weakened by an earthquake in the early 1900s. Judge McAuley, the Justice of the Peace, was a well respected, imposing man of the community. In the 1920s, one of the local characters, Tom Hyde, who was famed for the many wives he wooed and lost through lonely hearts clubs, restored the building and renamed it Hyde's Hall. It served as a community dance hail for several years.

18. *Private Cemetery.* On the hillside behind the McAuley Store, on private land, is a small cemetery, sometimes called a children's cemetery. Only one headstone remains since most of the others were made of wood. The inscription reads: "Lydia Mae, only daughter of R. and L. McAuley, 1874."

19. *St. Andrews Episcopal Church.* In 1911, the Atlantic City residents began raising money through plays and dances to build the town's first church. It was consecrated in 1913, and for many years Miss Ellen Carpenter looked after it. By the 1960s, the church was beginning to show its age. Through a community effort, the new people of Atlantic City restored the building. Since then it has served as the ecumenical, community church. It is on the National Register of Historic Places.

20. *Third School House.* When the second school house — a cold, drafty building — began sliding down the hill in 1927, the town's people dismantled it to build this schoolhouse, which remained in use until the 1950s when the population of Atlantic City plummeted. Today this is a private residence.

21. *Huff Hotel.* Jake Huff built the Huff Hotel, one of the most imposing buildings of early Atlantic City, as well as a livery barn, candy store, and bunkhouse. Only the Huff Candy Store remains. Built later, about 1903, it was operated by the Huff sisters. Among the first settlers, Jake Huff had a financial interest in many of the businesses, including a brewery, saloon, gold mines, a stamp mill (west of town), and a lumber mill.

22. *Harsch Blacksmith Shop.* An early arrival in South Pass City, Philip Harsch had a blacksmith shop in that town until he moved to Atlantic City and opened this shop. His son, Henry, operated it until the 1920s. The dredging of the 1930s destroyed the remaining structures, but horseshoes still occasionally turn up in the vicinity.

23. *E.F. Cheney Blacksmith Shop (Located across the street).* This young man arrived in Atlantic City by stagecoach from Point of Rocks during a spring snowstorm in 1869. His diary, found at the Pioneer Museum in Lander, is one of the few day-by-day accounts of life in early Atlantic City. In the 1870s, he opened his own shop, but as the population of the town decreased, he moved his business to the growing community in Lander Valley.

24. *Atlantic City Volunteer Fire Department.* Atlantic

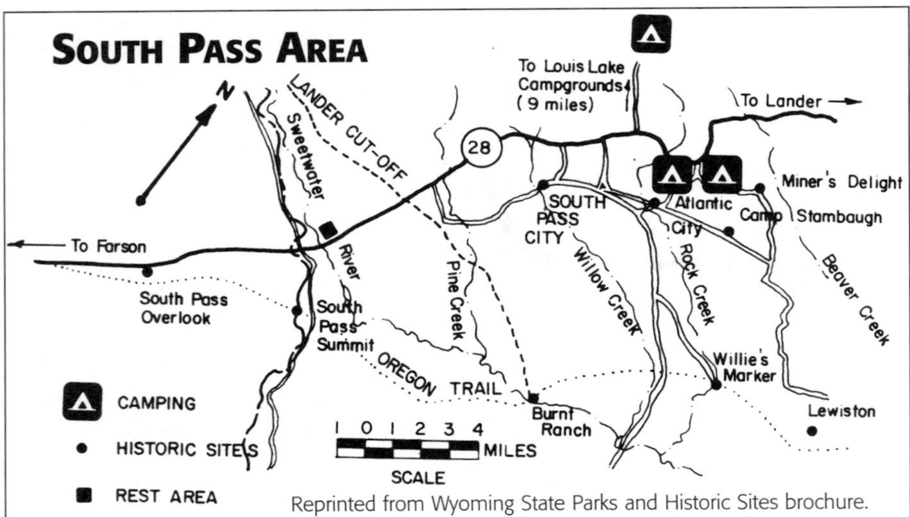

Reprinted from Wyoming State Parks and Historic Sites brochure.

City existed as a community for almost a hundred years without a fire department. With the influx of people during the iron ore boom, a volunteer fire department was organized. Local residents, including those from South Pass City, donate many hours to keep the fire department viable.

25. *Carpenter Hotel (Miner's Delight Inn).* The Carpenter family arrived in Atlantic City in October 1890 during an aborted attempt to reach the West Coast. Clarence Carpenter went to work for Emile Granier. The next year, his wife, Nellie, began serving meals to miners in their home on this location. Due to a small boom from the Dexter Mining Company in 1904, the Carpenters built a new addition, took in boarders, and put up the Carpenter Hotel sign. When Nellie became ill, her daughter, Ellen, took over most of the work. During the boom of the 1930s, the hotel was expanded again. "Miss Ellen" gained a wide following with her all-you-can-eat, family-style meals. Miss Ellen operated the hotel until her death in 1961. Former visitors of the hotel, New Yorkers Paul and Georgina Newman, bought and began restoring the hotel in 1963. For more than two decades the Miner's Delight Inn was recognized widely for its fine dining. After Paul's death in 1986, Gina kept the restaurant open. In 1997, Ken, Donna and Lester Ballard purchased the former hotel. Their love of the history of the area brought them to Atlantic City, where their historic building is presently a bed and breakfast.

26. *Diana Stamp Hall.* The first stamp mill in Atlantic City, a ten stamp mill, was constructed in 1869 by a man named Rice. Later the Diana Gold Company milled ore from various mines here. Because of metal scavengers, nothing remains of the mill. Local residents have always referred to the road and hill and Mill Hill, and it has been a favorite ski hill for decades.

27. *Toll Road.* In April 1869, the Carter County Commissioners approved the operation of a toll road between South Pass City and Atlantic City. The original site is probably in the draw, halfway up the hill. However, people were not inclined to pay a toll since other roads could be taken, and the toll was soon discontinued.

Portions of this article are reprinted from Atlantic City brochure.

T South Pass City

Pop. 17, Elev. 7,905

Sister city to Atlantic City, this gold mining town was built in 1866 when soldiers from Fort Bridger decided to prospect here. Before that, it had been a stopping place for wagon trains headed west, and then a stage and Pony Express station. It flourished until the gold ran out in the 1870s. The population once peaked at 2,000 in 1868. Periodic attempts to find more gold in the area have met with occasional success, but no great "mother lode" has been found since the early days. Calamity Jane worked here during the gold rush, and Esther Hobart Morris, the world's first female Justice of the Peace, upheld that office here. South Pass City still feels like a genuine Old West town, complete with false front buildings, thanks to restoration efforts since the 1960s.

South Pass City originated from a gold mining camp on Willow Creek in 1867 that quickly grew to become the largest town in the state. Within eighteen months, its population exceeded two thousand. And in 1870, South Pass City boasted a population of 4,000.

Unlike other gold-mining communities that evolved into saloon towns, South Pass City became a family-oriented community for miners with wives and children due to the Indian raids. During the raids, the town's women and children quickly headed towards a cell behind a local merchant's wine cellar. Continuing to join forces, the women of South Pass City also held meetings and discussed women's rights. Mrs. Esther Hobart Morris, was a strong advocate of women's right to vote. That same year, Mr. William Bright created a bill that passed, giving equal suffrage to women. After the bill's passage, Mrs. Esther Hobart Morris was appointed justice of the peace.

The town also claimed the first area bank, a school system, a newspaper, and a stage service. The following mines of South Pass City became highly productive: the Carissa Lode, the Franklin, the Shields, and the Jim Crow Hoosier Boy. However, when the largest of the mines, the Carissa Lode, dried out, so did the population. By 1880, South Pass City was nearly deserted. Today, the remaining buildings are the jail, the hat shop, and the Smith Sherlock store that has been recently converted into a museum. From the south, the graveyard overlooks the town, and to the north, you can see the Carissa Mine.

South Pass City

South Pass City	Jan	Feb	March	April	May	June	July	Aug	Sep	Oct	Nov	Dec	Annual
Average Max. Temperature (F)	25.7	28.3	33.5	45.1	57.4	67.3	76.6	74.6	65.4	53.1	37.2	28.1	49.3
Average Min. Temperature (F)	0.9	3.4	8.8	19.6	27.8	33.9	39.8	37.9	30.0	21.5	10.6	3.7	19.8
Average Total Precipitation (in.)	1.26	0.92	1.16	1.46	1.49	1.32	0.84	0.95	1.02	1.04	0.90	1.09	13.44
Average Total SnowFall (in.)	17.9	15.7	17.6	17.2	6.9	0.8	0.0	0.0	1.6	8.0	13.4	16.2	115.3
Average Snow Depth (in.)	18	19	17	7	1	0	0	0	0	0	4	9	

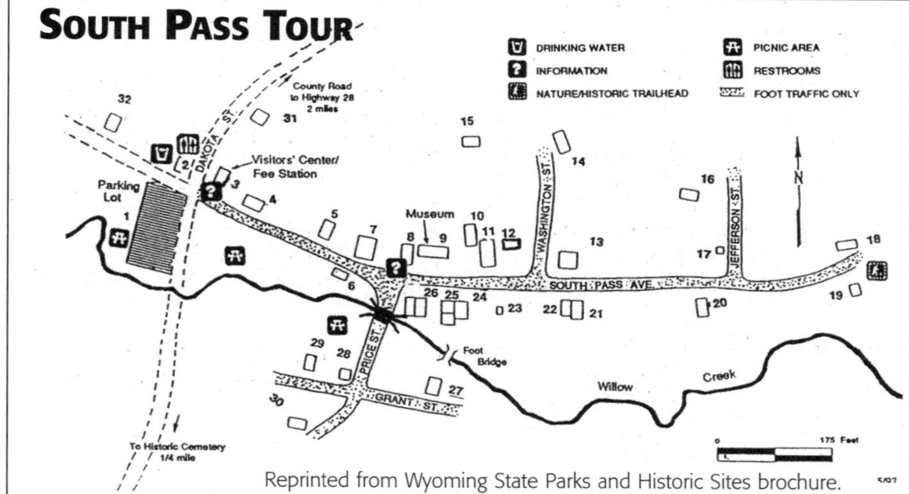

Reprinted from Wyoming State Parks and Historic Sites brochure.

T South Pass City State Historical Site

Travel 35 miles south of Lander on Highway 28, turning at the sign, and go another two miles to reach South Pass City. 352-0256. http://www.wy.blm.gov/rsfo/rec/trails.htm

Wyoming Tidbits

South Pass City is said to be haunted by the spirit of Polly Bartlett. An innkeeper, Polly supposedly laced her guests meals with arsenic and took their gold. Shot by a victim's relative, Polly was buried in an unmarked grave at the edge of town.

The South Pass gold rush started in 1867, and South Pass became the largest city in Wyoming. But the boom went bust almost as quickly as it started, and the region fell into decline. Today the partially restored ghost town of South Pass City is the center of the South Pass Historic Mining District with numerous historic sites.

South Pass City contains over 20 original structures, including a jail, livery stable, school, saloons, and home. The authentically furnished South Pass Hotel will give you a realistic glimpse of what it was like to stay in the real west during the late 1800s. At the Miner's Exchange Saloon, you can play billiards on a restored ca. 1840 billiard table, or you can visit the Smith-Sherlock General Store. At the Gold Mining Interpretive Center you'll gain historic insight on the gold mining practices during the late 1800s. Costumed interpreters can be seen at times throughout the summer, gold panning and black smithing.

Oregon Trail and South Pass

The Oregon Trail had several major destinations, including Utah and California. The first large emigration occurred in 1843 when over 1,000 people made the arduous 2,000 mile, six month trip. In total, nearly 500,000 individuals followed this route across the continent. The ruts of their wagons and the graves of those who died enroute are still visible nearby. The last recorded wagon crossed South Pass in 1912. South Pass is the gentle ascent where the trail crosses the Continental Divide called "Uncle Sam's backbone" by the emigrants. A stage and telegraph station where the trail made its final crossing of the Sweetwater River was established in 1850. That nearby site is now known as Burnt Ranch.

Gold

Many Oregon Trail emigrants were traveling to California in search of gold which had been discovered at Sutters Mill in 1848. Thousands of people hoped to strike it rich, but only a few succeeded. By the 1860s, gold and silver discoveries in Colorado, Nevada, Idaho and Montana resulted in hundreds of new boom towns. When the Carissa Mine began producing gold in 1867, a rush to the South Pass area began and South Pass City was founded. The boom continued in 1868 and Atlantic City and Miners Delight were quickly erected. The area's population soared to approximately 2,000 residents. Dozens of mines and hundreds of placer claims kept the miners busy.

A Busy, Dynamic Community

Businessmen arrived to fill the needs of the prospectors, and South Pass City soon developed a main street one half mile long. A resident could conduct business in general stores, butcher shops, restaurants, sawmills, clothing stores, sporting goods stores, a jewelry store and a furrier. Visitors could stay at one of seven hotels and seek an evening's entertainment at several saloons and "sporting houses" all supplied with liquid refreshments by two local brewers and a wholesale liquor establishment.

A miner could leave his horse at one of four livery stables and hire any of several blacksmiths to shoe the animal, sharpen his mining tools or mend his wagon. A gun could be purchased or repaired at the gun shop and be used at the shooting gallery. A miner lucky enough to "strike it rich" could deposit his gold at the local bank or ship it home on a Wells Fargo Stage. A stout jail held troublemakers, while a school saw to the educational needs of the children. Doctors and lawyers hung out shingles to serve the needs of the new frontier community. Ranchers and farmers soon moved nearby.

Booms and Busts

All booms must end. In 1872, a bust hit the Sweetwater Mining District. Most miners became discouraged over the absence of large gold deposits and the lack of sufficient capital. By 1875, less than one hundred people remained in the area. Even the nearby military post of Camp Stambaugh closed in 1878.

Many prospectors wandered to other boom towns to continue their relentless search for gold. Some folks moved to nearby settlements and played important roles in the founding of such towns as Lander, Pinedale and Thermopolis. However, a few persistent miners remained and helped start the area's future gold booms. A large hydraulic operation, a copper mine, a dredge, a strip mine and the continued gold speculation created South Pass mining rushes in the 1880s, 1890s, 1930s and 1960s. The population of Atlantic City and South Pass City bounced between a handful of people and as many as 500 residents. Today, a few prospectors continue to pan for gold and a couple of miners are still digging for ore.

Woman Suffrage

This rough and ready frontier community played a role in the woman suffrage movement. In the first territorial legislature, William Bright, a saloon keeper, mine owner and representative from South Pass City, wrote and introduced a woman suffrage bill. When this bill passed and

The Carissa Mine

the governor signed it in December 1869, Wyoming became the first territory or state to allow women the right to vote and hold office.

In February 1870, the county commissioners appointed Esther Morris as justice of the peace, making her the nation's first female judge. Even though her selection was controversial in South Pass City, she was an effective judge and tried twenty-six cases. Esther Morris represents the important and unique role that women played in frontier towns.

In 1966 the Wyoming 75th Anniversary Commission purchased South Pass City as a birthday present for the citizens of the state. The once dilapidated buildings are now restored to their splendor of 1898-1912 and most are open to the public. Many of the 30,000 artifacts in the site collections are original to the town and are exhibited in their original locations. The labor of many individuals and several state agencies have combined to create one of the most authentic historic sites in existence. Visitors can literally step back into another era to view the "Old West" as it really was at South Pass City.

South Pass City Tour

1. Public Parking Area.

2. *Restroom Area.* now located near the parking area and a uni-sex facility is located near the Sherlock House.

3. *Visitor Center.* This 1890 dance hall also functioned as a theater, community center and Sunday school for many years. A stage driver who lost a leg to frost-bite, got his wooden peg stuck in a knothole while tripping the light fantastic and had to be pulled free by several men. The dance hall now contains the fee counter, information center, video theater, exhibits and a gill shop. ALL VISITORS MUST PAY FEES HERE.

4. *Administration.* The original buildings include a liquor warehouse, residence, law office and store. This modern facility houses artifacts not currently on exhibit, research files, etc. Authorized personnel only.

5. *Tibbals Cabin.* The two stone dugouts at the rear were miner's residences in 1867-68. In the 1880s the existing front room was built and the kitchen was added in the 1890s which then incorporated the dugouts as additions to the kitchen. Barney Tibbals, manager of the Carissa Mine, lived in this cabin and later rented it to his employees.

6. *Carr Butcher Shop.* During the early 1900s William Carr operated a butcher shop here. Animals were killed and quartered at his corral in Slaughterhouse Gulch, about two miles south of town then processed at the shop.

7. *Carissa Saloon.* The Carissa dates to the 1890s and operated sporadically until 1949. An earlier saloon called the "White Swan" doubled as a whorehouse and was located next door to the east. The stone-walled remains of the "cribs" used by the Swan's "soiled doves" is visible in the hillside near the northeast corner on the Carissa.

8. *Smith Sherlock Co. Store.* Built in 1896 of logs salvaged from the 1870 Episcopal Church, this building was intended to replace the old Smith Store next door. The family operated this business, including the Post Office until 1948. Peter Sherlock blinded during an 1880s mining accident, was the clerk. He could find anything in the store and recognized patrons by the sound of their footsteps. The Friends of South Pass now operate a concession area here.

9. *Interpretive Center/Gold Mining Exhibit.* This general mercantile store was built by town constable Jim Smith about 1874. The store provided goods for local miners, residents and area cowboys. The building was used as a warehouse after 1896 for the Smith Sherlock Store. Today the building is utilized as a museum exhibit center.

10. *The Cave (Fort Bourbon).* The massive interior stone wall was built in 1868 to protect perishable food and liquor. Archaeologists found secretly buried gold in a cast iron pot near the back wall. Folklore says when townspeople feared Indian attacks, women and children were locked safely in the back while the men went out to fight.

11. *The John & Lida Sherlock House.* This was built during the 1890s and early 1900s. When the family had another child, they added another room. The original building on this lot was a large hotel which burned about 1877. The cabin currently is under restoration.

12. Restroom And Drinking Fountain.

13. *Ruins.* This collapsed cabin once stood across the street, west of the red garage. The original foundation is still visible and was moved to this location in the 1950s. The original building on this lot was a store, also used as a post office and court house during the 1860s and 1870s.

14. *Stamp Mill.* This huge device crushed gold bearing ore fed under the 1,000 pound pistons through chutes at the rear. The gold was then separated from the dust by a variety of methods. In 1869 this mill stood near the Franklin Mine a half mile upstream and was powered by a large overshot water wheel. Later, in Palmetto Gulch two miles east, it was run by steam. This is the only remaining mill of more than 20 used in the district. It was moved to this location to protect it from vandals. DO NOT CLIMB ON THE STAMP MILL.

15. *Wolverine Mine.* This small mine was dug searching for a vein of gold ore. Known as the Wolverine Mine it never found a paying quantity of gold and was soon abandoned. The exhibit allows visitors to safely enter a mine tunnel and experience the damp, enclosed atmosphere of a mine.

16 *Schoolhouse.* Citizens built this school just west of the parking lot (#1) about 1890. The building was moved away from the creek to this location in 1911. The school closed about 1948 when the last families with children moved away.

17. *Cody Cabin.* This small and hurriedly built cabin was constructed in the late 1890s. Archeological investigations done prior to restoration indicate that a married couple lived in this cabin for a brief period of time. Exhibit installation is planned in the near future.

18. *Reniker Cabin.* William Reniker, a Civil War veteran, lived in this cabin when not working his gold mine on Reniker Peak northwest of town. He moved the cabin to this spot from another location. Penciled numbers used to properly reassemble the cabin are still visible inside. Exhibit installation is planned in the near future.

19. *E. A. Slack Cabin.* Esther Morris was the first woman in the nation to hold political office. She served successfully as a justice of the peace in South Pass City in 1870. The five room cabin where she lived with her second husband and sons was located about 50 feet east of this reconstruction. E. A. Slack, Esther's son published his newspaper the "South Pass News" and lived in this house beginning in June 1871. The original building burned in December 1871 and Slack moved his press to Laramie, Wyoming where he published the "Laramie Daily Independent." The original Gordon Hand Press, which survived the fire is located in the northwest corner of the front room. It is on loan from the Univ. of Wyoming, American Heritage Center.

20. *Blacksmith Shop.* This 1915 shop contained a forge and tools to repair wagons and horsedrawn equipment. When automobiles became common, the smith had to learn new skills and obtain new types of tools and parts. This building was built of logs salvaged from the 1868 Ticknor Store located on Price Street just south of Willow Creek.

21. *Variety Theater.* Constructed on the foundation of an 1860s store, this modern theater is used for historic programs and speakers.

22. *Red Garage.* This garage, built in the 1920s to house one of the Sherlock family's first automobiles, was constructed of logs salvaged from the butcher William Carr's abandoned home and Jim Smith's 1868 cabin, located where the Collections Administration Building #3 is today.

23. *Ice House.* This small frame cabin was used to store ice for food preservation and later as a summer residence.

24. *South Pass Hotel.* Opened as the Idaho House in 1868, this was the finest of many hotels in South Pass City. It was acquired in 1873 by Janet Sherlock, the widowed mother of five children. A hotel was considered a respectable business for a proper woman to operate. The local stagecoach stop was at the front door and the office at times served as the town Post Office. Robert Todd Lincoln, General Phil Sheridan and many other notables stayed here. The Sherlock family quarters and kitchen are accessed from the rear.

25. *Restaurant.* Janet Sherlock Smith built the restaurant as an addition to the South Pass Hotel in 1899. The front room became the hotel's new lobby with the dining room and kitchen to the rear.

26. *Exchange Saloon & Card Room.* Beginning about 1873 the building was converted into the Exchange Saloon and operated as such, through the turn of the century. The lean-to next to the building was added to the saloon as a card room during the 1880s.

27. *Livery Stable.* This barn was built in the 1890s of logs salvaged from earlier structures. This part of town was the location of many stables which catered to miners, investors and locals who wanted to buy or rent horses, wagons or stable their own animals. It was also the scene of clandestine activities; many whiskey bottles and at least one gun was buried under the floor of this stable and later found in archaeological excavations.

28. *Miner's Exchange Saloon.* John Swingle, a county commissioner, building contractor, bar owner, stable owner and undertaker erected this structure in 1869. This was his popular Miners Exchange Saloon, where gold could be exchanged for whiskey. Later, the building was used as a residence. A millinery operated by two "tough women" in this building may have disguised a bordello in the rear.

29. *Sweetwater County Jail.* In answer to the needs of the raucous mining town, the county built this jail in 1870. One man who could not bear incarceration in the tiny, frigid, dark cells committed suicide; several others attempted to escape. No one was ever legally executed in South Pass City. County offices were moved to Green River in 1873, but use of this jail continued for several years. By the 1880s it was abandoned until the front room was appropriated for use as a school room. The alphabet is still visible on the wall above the front door.

30. *Libby/Pest House.* Harry Libby built this two room home in the spring of 1899 after being fired by Barney Tibbals from the Carissa Mine. Libby and his family left South Pass City in February 1900 and sold the cabin to Joe Blewett. In 1901 the cabin again sold to J. J. Marrin and Anna Tibbals. Some evidence suggests that this cabin may have been utilized as a Pest House or "isolation hospital" during a small pox epidemic in February 1901.

31. *Rock Cabin.* The hack room of this cabin was built about 1867. The family who lived here simply threw their trash on the ground outside the door. When the front room was added, the trash dump became their floor. Later, according to legend, the hack room was the first jail in South Pass City. There is no interior exhibit here.

32. *Masonic Lodge.* This is a private reconstruction of the Freund Brothers gun shop, agents for the Winchester 18-shot repeating rifle. The Ancient Free and Accepted Masons #28, U.D. Nebraska, now Wyoming Lodge #2, rented the second story of the building for a meeting place. The same organization (Lander, WY) reconstructed the building.

Reprinted from Wyoming State Parks and Historic Sites brochure.

Martha Jane "Calamity Jane" Canary

Sorting the fact from the fiction when it comes to Calamity Jane's colorful life isn't easy. Indeed, her autobiography written to raise money contains inaccuracies and, according to some who knew her, complete falsehoods!

Martha Jane Canary was born in 1852 in Missouri. Her mother abandoned the family soon after a younger child was born. The search for her had led the family to the gold fields of Virginia City, Montana Territory, where Martha Jane learned to shoot a rifle and ride a horse as well as any man. Martha Jane and her sisters saw destitution after their father's death, and she was forced to beg and use whatever means necessary to feed her siblings.

Although her claim to be a scout for General Custer was never substantiated, Martha Jane insists it was true. She moved on through Wyoming and Colorado, where she nursed miners infected with small pox. Some of the miners believed that where Martha Jane went, calamity followed. Thus the nickname by which she would be known the remainder of her life, was born. She had signed on for several military expeditions as a bullwacker but was fired when her gender was discovered.

She ultimately married Clinton Burk in El Paso and gave birth to a daughter. In 1896, after returning to Deadwood, Burk departed town after embezzling money. Jane's daughter was taken from her and placed in a convent to be reared by the sisters.

If Calamity Jane liked shooting and riding, she loved whiskey even more. Her binges were notorious, and she spent more than one night in local jails for drunken, disorderly conduct.

Her alleged love affair with Wild Bill Hickok is another point on which historians disagree. Some say they were a couple; others say Calamity Jane's imagination worked overtime in that regard. Whichever the truth, when Calamity Jane died in 1905, at just 52 years of age, her final wish to be buried next to Wild Bill in Deadwood was fulfilled. Her final words addressed to her daughter.

T Miner's Delight

12 miles northeast of Atlantic City

From Atlantic City, a gravel road leads toward Lander, where in a little over two miles, a dirt road branches to the east. If you drive another one and one-half miles, you will pass the Gold Dollar Mine, and a little more than a mile beyond, is the Miner's Delight cemetery. Take a left, go one quarter of a mile, and you will be on Main Street of Miners Delight.

Founded in 1867 by Herman Nickerson and friends, Miners Delight became a town when "color" was discovered in Spring Gulch. Originally, the town was called Hamilton City. The name was changed to Miners Delight when the mine by this name became successful. In its first year, the mine provided three hundred thousand dollars worth of gold. Since 1874, the mine has been dewatered and reworked seven times, with the last being 1927.

Miner's Delight was the childhood home of Calamity Jane.

Section 5

FARO

The most popular game in the Wild West. It was also one of the wildest games played in the saloons of the frontier. Saloons that offered Faro posted signs that read: "Buck the Tiger", Faro Played Here.

In the game of Faro, the dealer is also the banker. During the game, his personal fortune is at risk. One notorious episode in the history of Faro is the story of Black Jake. Black Jake owned a Faro table in Virginia City, Nevada in the 1860s. According to legend, he shot himself after losing $70,000 in one night. The next owner of the table lost his personal fortune in one night. He, too, shot himself. Considered bad luck, the table was stored until the 1890s when the Delta Saloon brought it out of retirement and turned it into a Blackjack table. As the story goes, a drunken gold miner, stinging from heavy losses at a neighboring saloon entered the Delta. He proceeded to wager his last possession, a gold ring, for $5. He won, and went on to win $86,000, a gold mine, and some horses. He wiped out the dealer's fortune. The dealer, as you would expect, shot himself. The table was retired and never used again. Thinking of playing Faro? Might want to unload your pistol if you're thinking of dealing.

The Rules of Faro

The following rules are paraphrased from "The Board Game Book":

Players: Any number.

Pieces: Gaming chips, 1 standard deck of 52 playing cards

Aim: Gambling game of pure chance

Rules:

The dealer is the banker, and sets the minimum and maximum bet amounts. The maximum bet limits refer to the wager amount for plain bets, and to the number of times a bet may be "parleyed".

Players place bets on a cloth-covered board containing the 13 card denominations (Ace, 2 thru 10, Jack, Queen, and King) displayed for a single suit (usually spades).

All bets are even-money bets; a bet may be declared against the given denomination by "coppering" it.

Various special bets are allowed. According to R.C. Bell:

"There are many esoteric methods of staking bets, but they add little to the game and tend to confuse the inexperienced, so they are omitted here."

One can imagine betting on two or four cards at a time, in a manner similar to Roulette.

After the initial bets are placed, the card deck is shuffled, and then placed face up inside a shoe.

The first top card is called the "soda", and neither wins nor loses. After play starts, the soda is discarded next to the betting board.

For 25 successive turns, the prior top card is discarded onto the soda pile. The next top card is a loser, and is discarded between the shoe and the soda. The next top card is a winner; it is left on the deck.

On successive turns, the prior winner card is discarded onto the soda pile.

Whenever the loser and winner cards are the same denomination for a turn, this is declared a "split". The dealer takes half of all bets staked for or against that denomination; this provides the house edge in a fair game.

After each turn, the dealer settles any bets on the winning and losing cards. All other bets are unaffected, and remain in place for the next turn.

Between turns, a player may modify any bet by declaring that he wants to "bar" a given bet for one turn.

A player may "halve" a bet by telling the dealer; such a declaration stays active until revoked by the player.

A player may also add or remove a copper from any bet.

After each turn, winning and losing bets are settled, and new bets can be made for the next turn.

When the deck is exhausted, a new deal is started, and play proceeds.

The last card in the deck is called the "hock", and is not used.

When there are only 3 cards left in the deck (one more turn), players may Call the Last Turn by guessing the order that the 3 denominations will appear. If the 3 cards are different, and the player guesses correctly, he wins 4 times the bet. If 2 of the three cards have the same denomination, he wins twice the bet.

Today, you can still see the standing head frame, and near the mine amidst deep brush, is the long row of miners' shacks. "Calamity Jane" grew up here. Orphaned at an early age, Martha Jane Canary (Calamity) was quickly adopted, and her new parents moved to Miners Delight during its first year of existence. A woman from the East persuaded "Calamity Jane" to visit New York, which she visited for a year. Martha returned educated and conducted business in the dance hall above McAuley's Store in Atlantic City. Miners Delight boasts the title of "Calamity Jane's home town."

T The Duncan

Traveling from Atlantic City, a gravel road winds up Mill Hill that levels off and heads southeast. At the crest one mile south of town, a dirt road branches to the right where the Mary Ellen Mine sits. Within one mile of the turnoff, "The Duncan" comes into view.

In 1911, the first rich strike of ore was made, resulting in forty thousand dollars' worth of ore being removed in three years. In 1914, the operation ran into financial difficulty and closed. Thirty-two years later, new owners made improvements, but only twelve tons of ore were processed that year, valued at a total of two thousand dollars.

The mine underwent another spurt of activity in 1956 when three thousand tons were shipped at twelve dollars per ton. During the height of its prosperity, "The Duncan" consisted of several dozen cabins, a small store, and a two-story dormitory.

T Lewiston

12 miles east of The Duncan

Lewiston, Wyoming is accessed by traveling south from Atlantic City up Mill Hill, passing The Duncan turnoff, and then heading eight miles east on a gravel road. To the side, you will spot a bronze monument on the banks of Rock Creek that tells the story of 13 Mormon emigrants traveling to Utah in October of 1865 who froze to death during a single night and were buried in one grave. Four miles east of this marker there is fork to the left—this is Lewiston. The two-remaining buildings are the old store and the livery. Founded in 1879, Lewiston once had more than twenty-five buildings and four saloons in its heyday. The most famous mine was Bullion Shaft, and one-half mile south of town lies the Hidden Hand Mine, the Iron Duke Shaft, and the Good Hope Mine.

T Fort Stambaugh

On private property just south of Miner's Delight

Established in 1870 to protect miners, this camp was named after Lt. Charles B. Stambaugh who was killed by Indians just a month before the post opened.

T Pacific Springs

12.5 miles southwest of South Pass City

Founded in 1853, Pacific Springs –once called the "Old Halter and Flick Ranch" –is commonly known as the muddiest spot on the Lander-Rawlins Stage Road as it sits on a swampy flat at an elevation 7,200 feet. During the spring rains, Main Street was deemed unsafe.

Today, five of the town's eight structures remain. A two-story barn sits on the north side that was used to shelter relay horses for the Pony Express. The Pacific Springs store stands intact without the false front, and now serves as a storage house for a nearby ranch.

This area, which was once a celebration spot on the Oregon Trail, marked the first camping spot for emigrants after crossing South Pass, which is seventy-four hundred feet high. Travelers typically celebrated the crossing and then woke up to three miles of mud.

By 1918, the town consisted of only a post office named Pacific. As you drive through Pacific Springs, you can see railroad tracks that pass on the edge of town. The tracks are used by U.S. Steel Corporation, and trains on this line haul iron ore from Atlantic City to the Union Pacific line.

T South Pass

From State Highway 28, take the dirt Oregon Buttes Road south from the summit of the first hill west of the Sweetwater bridge. Watch for Trail ruts and historic markers in 2.8 miles. Follow trail west to markers

This broad pass, the highest point on the trail is at the summit of an almost imperceptible approach to the Continental Divide and was the key to the entire trail system. Every emigrant wagon train and handcart company that went westward rolled through this Pass. There was no other way to go. No other path offered a depend-

The South Pass

able supply of grass and water plus an easy grade to and through the mountains. On crossing the Pass one pioneer woman noted that, "we have forever taken leave of the waters running toward the home of our childhood and youth..." Two-and-a-half miles farther west the emigration encountered Pacific Springs, the first water flowing westward. Stone monuments mark the Pass and honor Narcissa Whitman and Eliza Spalding, the first white women to cross South Pass. Source: BLM brochure.

T South Pass Overlook

4 miles southwest of Sweetwater Bridge on State Highway 28.

This BLM interpretive site offers information and a panoramic view of Pacific Springs, South Pass and the Oregon Buttes. American Indian, mountain man, fur trade, Oregon, Mormon, California and Pony Express Trail involvement with South Pass are all interpreted. Source: BLM brochure.

T South Pass

South Pass

South Pass was perhaps the most important landmark along the emigrant trails. It marked the end of the long ascent to the Continental Divide and the emigrants' arrival at the frontier of the Oregon country. It was also thought to be the halfway point along the trail.

South Pass dictated the location of the emigrant trail, for only via its gradual ascent was wagon travel over the Continental Divide practical for large-scale emigration. South Pass is the wide, flat summit of a long and gradually ascending plateau, with low ridges and hills on both sides and a wide sage and grass-covered saddle between. Many emigrants commented that they scarcely noticed the ascent or the crossing.

On July 12, 1846, Edwin Bryant made his way "up a very gentle ascent to the South Pass of the Rocky Mountains, or the dividing ridge separating the waters of the Atlantic and the Pacific. The ascent to the Pass is so gradual, that but for our geographical knowledge . . . we should not have been conscious that we had ascended to, and were standing upon the summit of the Rocky Mountains-the backbone . . . of the North American Continent."

T Willie Handcart Company Marker

At Rock Creek on the Lewiston road about 8 miles southeast of Atlantic City. Access via dirt roads. Make local inquiry for directions and road conditions.

A mass grave and plaque commemorate the fate of the Willie Handcart Company. Poorly supplied and traveling far too late in the season, the company was trapped by a winter storm as it approached South Pass in mid-October 1856. Before help arrived from Salt Lake City, about 67 of the 404-member party had starved or frozen to death. In terms of numbers of deaths, the combined Willie and Martin handcart companies disasters were the greatest ever suffered by any group traveling the trail. Source: BLM brochure.

H Meadows in the Sage

At South Pass Rest Area on State Highway 28, just south of South Pass City

With spring, the meadow grasses and broad - leaafed plants, called forbs, emerge green and succulent. Antelope, mule deer, and elk wintering south and west of here return each spring to the green grass and forb meadows found in the sagebrush desert and stream bottoms near the base of the Wind River Mountains.

These small green plants provide life-giving nutrients crucial to the last developmental stages of the embryo. Once born, the health and survival of the fawn or calf depends on the amount and quality of milk provided by the mother, which in turn depends on her intake of this succulent green feed.

Forbs and grasses also provide the moist conditions necessary for insect production. Insect production in the sagebrush and meadows are highest in May and June. Almost all bird life requires insect food to produce eggs and young. The newly hatched birds must consume large amounts of insects to acquire enough protein and calcium for their rapid growth.

Shrubs, such as sagebrush, provide fall and winter feed as well as yearlong cover for wildlife in this country. And so, it is the grass and forb meadows scattered throughout the sagebrush lands that are an important part of that special formula helping to keep Wyoming's wildlands abundant with wildlife.

H The Carissa Gold Mine

Just north of South Pass City

Soldiers from Fort Bridger discovered gold in Willow Creek in 1865. By 1867 the gold source was located and claimed in the gulch east of this sign. Development of the once famous Carissa Mine, visible across the gulch, began immediately.

Exaggerated stories of gold strikes and the Carissa's wealth spread across the West during the winter of 1867-1868. The following spring thousands of people rushed to this area hopin' to 'strike it rich.'

The miners established South Pass City, now a Wyoming State Historic Site, in the valley one third mile south of this spot. It is the second oldest town in Wyoming.

The Carissa produced an estimated 60,000-180,000 ounces of gold.

The Carissa Mine is private property. NO TRESPASSING.

H The Exchange Saloon

In South Pass City

This building was constructed in 1869 as The Exchange Bank. J.W. Hiff owned the bank and it operated until the fall of 1870. After 1870 it was operated as The Exchange Saloon and continued to operate it as a saloon and cardroom untill the mid 1900s. Butch Cassidy, Calamity Jane, and Wild Bill Hickok frequented this establishment.

H Butch Cassidy

In South Pass City

In 1901 or 1902 "I was probably 7 or 8 years old...I remember Butch Cassidy coming through the town, and he was quite a drinker and he'd get pretty well oiled down there and he'd be down to the bar...he'd wind up over right across from the Sherlock store where my dad had that bar leased...why, us kids would go down there and all to get nickels and dimes and silver dollars even and we'd holler 'Hello Uncle Butch' and he'd pitch them out in the dirt and us kids would just scramble to get them..."

–Oral interview with William Carr 1981

H Esther Morris

On grounds of South Pass City Historical Site adjacent to Esther Morris Cabin.

Controversy exists concerning Esther Morris and woman suffrage. In 1869, the legislature passed and Governor Campbell signed a woman suffrage bill authored by William Bright, a South Pass City resident. As a result, Wyoming became the first territory or state to allow women the right to vote.

For eight months in 1870, Esther Morris served as South Pass City's justice of the peace, making her the nation's first woman judge. After her death in 1901, some historians claimed that Mrs. Morris had helped Bright write the suffrage bill. Believing this theory, the Historical Landmarks Commission dedicated the adjacent marker in 1939 on the former location of the Morris family's five room cabin.

However, recent studies indicate that Bright was the only author of the suffrage bill, although he may have received some urging from his wife Julia and some help from Edward Lee, Secretary of the Territory. Morris probably held court in the county building near the center of town.

Today, Esther Morris is recognized as the nation's first woman justice of the peace. The monument and the nearby 1870 period cabin honor Mrs. Morris, who exemplified the spirit of frontier women.

H South Pass City Interpretive Plaques

South Pass City

The South Pass Hotel

This hotel opened in 1868 as the Idaho House. It advertised itself as "the only first class house in the city with commodious rooms comfortably fitted with new furniture." The dining room was constantly supplied with game and all other available luxuries.

Janet Sherlock began operating the hotel in 1873 to support herself and her children after the death of her husband. Hotels were seen as extensions of the home and, therefore, one of the few businesses socially acceptable for a woman to own.

Local businessmen who convinced her to buy the hotel were concerned for more than her welfare. They were worried the dubious sanitation of the filthy establishments run by competitors might scare away prospective mining investors.

The hotel was operated by the Sherlock-Smith family from 1873 to the mid-1920s when it closed. It was used as a private residence until the 1960s. This building was dismantled to replace rotted timbers and then safely reconstructed by the State of Wyoming using original material where possible.

South Pass Hotel

This hotel was purchased by Janet Sherlock-Smith in the early 1870s and was operated by her and her family through the 1940s. It is the only remaining hotel of five that was in town during the early boom years. At one time the Post Office for South Pass City was located in the hotel and the mail slot is visible in the eastern most front door. This hotel also served as a stage stop.

During the late 1890s and early 1900s the family made its residence in the rooms on the bottom floor of the hotel. The beds, dressers and washstands in these rooms are original to the hotel during this period. The portraits on the wall in this room are portraits of Janet's parents, Peter and Janet McOmie.

South Pass Hotel Rooms

Only one of the upstairs rooms was provided with heat. Guests in other rooms used several blankets and probably shared their beds with strangers who, like themselves, may not have bathed in many days. In winter, they may have awakened in the morning to find ice on their

A room at the South Pass Hotel

blankets.

The holes above the doors permitted air circulation between the rooms but did not help keep the rooms warm.

None of the rooms were supplied with plumbing. To wash, guests could take a sponge bath from the basins on the wash stands. They had to brave the cold winds and use the outhouse behind the hotel or use the chamber pots beneath the beds. The unpleasant daily task of cleaning the pots often fell to one of the girls in the proprietor's family.

The Saloon

Saloons were common gathering places for miners in Central and Northern Rocky Mountain mining camps. Men could catch up on news of the latest gold or silver strikes, discuss politics, or talk about the results of the latest championship boxing match. In many instances, saloons in the mining camps were also used for polling places, Sunday sermons, courtrooms, and town meetings.

Bitter cold and large amounts of snowfall during the winter months in the Central and Northern Rocky Mountains kept mining to a minimum. A feeling of isolation was prevalent in remote mining camps. This feeling was worse in the winter, due to sporadic mail and supply deliveries, as well as the difficulty involved in traveling long distances between towns. One winter resident wrote, "Everything is dead here…You cannot imagine the ennui I endure." Another wrote, "genius is taxed to provide amusement to pass the long winter evenings…." Saloons helped provide this badly needed amusement in the form of gambling, drinking and camaraderie; at least for the male portion of the population.

Faro

Faro is thought to have developed in France in the 17th Century. Throughout the 1800s, faro was an extremely popular game in the

Faro table

United States. One reporter called faro, "our national card game." Faro is a pure gambling game, with no skill involved. The player places a bet on a card or cards to win, or places a copper token on a card or cards to lose. Faro's popularity started to dwindle after 1900, and by the 1940s, the game could scarcely be found.

Tibbals Cabin

Barney Tibbals bought this cabin when he moved to South Pass City to manage the Carissa Gold Mine in 1896. After he married Anna Smith they moved into the managers quarters at the mine, and rented this cabin.

Emmett and Katie Connell rented this cabin from 1899 to aboout 1906. The first three of their six children were born while the Connells lived at South Pass City.

Emmett earned about $3.00 per day, working as a laborer in the Carissa Mine, while he paid about $7.50 per month for rent. The Connell family purchased supplies in the Smith-Sherlock Store and probably supplemented their food supply with wild game that could be hunted in the area.

Food Costs
50 lbs. flour $1.75
2 lbs. butter .70 cents
1 lbs. coffee .20 cents
31/2 lbs. bacon .60 cents
30 lbs. potatoes .75 cents
4 1/2 lbs. cheese .99 cents
1 can tomatoes .15 cents
1 can lobster .40 cents
1 gal syrup $1.00

Wood was the primary source of heat and cooking fuel and cost about $4.00 per cord. Archeological evidence also suggests that coal was used for heating and cooking, and probably obtained from coal mines in the Rock Springs area.

H On Top of the World

At South Pass Rest Area on Highway 28 just south of South Pass City.

From where you're standing South Pass doesn't look all that remarkable. But compared to the rugged Wind River Mountains, it can easily be recognized as a type of gateway.

Nevertheless, crossing the Continental Divide into "Oregon Country" was a task for all westward-bound travelers, and many described their feelings about the event. In 1852 Lucy Rutledge Cooke, a young woman with "California Fever" wrote:

"...This morn we arrived at the South Pass after which all water we see will be running to the Pacific. So we are now on the other side of the world..."

H South Pass

At South Pass Rest Area on State Highway 28, just south of South Pass City

Even after the rediscovery of South Pass in 1824, it was years before the route was used extensively. Fur trapper/trader William Sublette brought a small caravan of wagons to South Pass in 1828. While his party did not take wagons over the pass, they demonstrated the feasibility of using them.

Captain Benjamin Bonneville took the first wagons over South Pass in 1832. But it was U.S. Government explorer, Lt. John Charles Fremont, who was responsible for publicizing the South Pass route. Scattered references to an easy passage over the Rockies had appeared in newpapers for a decade, but in 1842 Fremont created enthusiasm for South Pass by explaining that a traveler could go through it without any "toilsome ascents".

As knowledge of South Pass became widespread, a great western migration commenced. Thousands of Mormons, and future Oregonians and Californians, would cut a wide swath along the route in the next twenty years.

H The Fur Trade

At South Pass Rest Area on Highway 28 just south of South Pass City.

The demand for beaver pelts in the early 1800s led to the exploration and eventual settlement of the American West. South Pass was part of a major thoroughfare through the Rockies and its discovery is significant to the era known as the fur trade.

South Pass was first crossed by white men in 1812. The Astorians, a small party of American Fur Company trappers led by Robert Stuart, used it as they traveled east with dispatches for company owner, John Jacob Astor. Even though Stuart noted South Pass in his diary and word of his journey was printed in a Missouri newspaper, it would be another decade before white men "rediscovered" it.

For Jedediah Smith and other mountain men working for fur entrepreneur William Ashley in the winter of 1823-24, the rugged Wind River Range in front of you was a barrier between them and the beaver-rich Green River Valley further west. Failing to negotiate these mountains through Union Pass further north, Smith and his men finally reached the Green River by traversing the southern end of the range at this gradual incline. Traveling west with supplies in 1825, Ashley initiated the Rendezvous, an annual event lasting until approximately 1840 when the demand for beaver played out.

H South Pass

At South Pass Rest Area on Highway 28 just south of South Pass City.

The South Pass, in which you are now located, is perhaps the most significant transportation gateway through the Rocky Mountains. Indians, mountain men, Oregon Trail emigrants, Pony Express riders, and miners all recognized the value of this passageway straddling the Continental Divide. Bounded by the Wind River Range on the north and the Antelope Hills on the south, the pass offered overland travelers a broad, relatively level corridor between the Atlantic and Pacific watersheds.

Mining plays a fundamental role in the history of the South Pass region. Gold may have been discovered as early as 1842, but gold fever did not strike until 1867 when a sample of South Pass ore arrived in Salt Lake City. News of the discovery spread swiftly and hordes of expectant millionaires descended on the new towns of South Pass City, Atlantic City, and Miner's Delight. The boom played out quickly. The easily obtained placer gold was rapidly exhausted and miners began leaving the area in the early 1870s.

Despite the brief duration of the boom, mining activity did not cease. In 1884, an enterprising Frenchman named Emile Granier began organizing the construction of a hydraulic gold mining system which employed many local residents over a ten year period. The Fisher Dredge Company recovered considerable gold ore from the bed of Rock Creek during the 1930s. More recently, the United States Steel iron ore mine operated near Atlantic City from the early 1960s until 1983. Hard rock mines also reopen periodically and some are presently operating. Until the next boom arrives, travelers can experience the flavor of a Rocky Mountain mining town by visiting nearby South Pass City, which has been restored by the State of Wyoming.

H The Corridor West

At South Pass Rest Area on State Highway 28, just south of South Pass City

The trail over South Pass is a transportation corridor which served many purposes. In addition to being the route to Oregon and California, it was used by Mormon pioneers and by the Pony express.

A great exodus to the Salt Lake Valley in 1847 was only the beginning of Mormon emigrant travel along the Oregon Trail. About 68,000 took the Utah branch of the trail from 1847 until 1869 when the completion of the Union Pacific Railroad ushered in a new phase of overland travel. The community of Zion at Salt Lake offered economic opportunity as well as religious freedom.

For a brief eighteen months beginning in April, 1860, eighty young men carried the nation's mail on horseback for 1600 miles from St. Joseph, Missouri to Sacramento, California. Riding day and night-regardless of weather - on the fastest horses available, Pony Express riders maintained a vital communication link between east and west at the beginning of the Civil War. The completion of the trascontinental telegraph line in October, 1861 marked the end of the Pony Express. Though the owners of the Express lost more than a million dollars, the venture captured the imagination of the entire world.

H The Sweetwater Mining Region

State Highway 28 at turnout to South Pass City

With the discovery of gold near Willow Creek in 1867, thousands of people rushed into this region, mined the streams and hills, and built some of the territory's first towns—South Pass City, Atlantic City, and Miner's Delight. Even though 3000 people lived in the area and more than 30 mines were operating by 1869, a bust soon occurred, and the towns dwindled in size. Since then, three more booms have sustained the area's mining tradition and sense of community.

The region's history still survives today. Besides several sites in and around Atlantic City, the South Pass City State Historic Site contains 24 historic structures and dozens of exhibits. Located just two miles along the adjacent dirt road, the site is open from May 15 to October 15 and is free of charge.

H Oregon Trail-Lander Cutoff-South Pass Area

Just south of South Pass City turnoff on Highway 28

This is an old trail used by the Indians and the trappers of the fur period, a short cut to the Snake River country. It was proposed an emigrant road by mountain man John Hockaday in 1854. No emigrant trails crossed the mountains north of here. It was improved as a wagon road for the government by F. W. Lander, in 1859 to avoid dry wastes of the roads to the south and to provide more water, wood and forage. Here it commenced the crossing of the south end of the Wind River Mountains and the Continental Divide and on to the Pacific Northwest. Thirteen thousand people and thousands of domestic animals passed this way in 1859 and for thirty years thereafter it was used heavily, setting the destiny of an empire. These wagon tracks and lonely graves for many miles beyond, a great landmark of history, have been recognized for preservation by:

U.S. Department of the Interior, Bureau of Land Management, Sublette County Historical Society.

This trail has been marked at all accessible points with brass caps.

H Willie's Handcart Company

About eight miles south of Atlantic City on the east bank of Rock Creek

Captain James G. Willie's Handcart Company of Mormon emigrants on the way to Utah, greatly exhausted by the deep snows of an early winter and suffering from lack of food and clothing, had assembled here for reorganization by relief parties from Utah, about the end of October, 1856. Thirteen persons were frozen to death during a single night and were buried here in one grave. Two others died the next day and were buried nearby. Of the company of 404 persons, 77 perished before help arrived. The survivors reached Salt Lake City November 9, 1856,

H Willie's Handcart Gravestone

About eight miles south of Atlantic City on the east bank of Rock Creek

In memory of those members of the Willie Handcart Co. whose journey started too late and ended too early and were buried here in a circular grave October 24 & 25, 1856.

William James, 46
Bodil Mortinsen, 9

Elizabeth Bailey, 52
Nils Anderson, 41
James Kirkwood, 11
Ole Madsen, 41
Samuel Gadd, 10
James Gibb, 67
Lars Wendin, 60
Chesterton Gilman, 66
Anne Olsen, 46
Thomas Gurldstone, 62
Ella Nilson, 22
William Groves, 22
Jens Nilson, 6

S South Pass Trading Co.

50 South Pass Main in South Pass City.
332-6810. www.south-pass.com
or info@cnlclothiers.com

The South Pass Trading Company is located along the Oregon trail and is in the midst of Western history–next to Wyoming's main historic sites. You'll especially enjoy the surroundings inside this exciting store, beginning with their friendly staff. Choose from an array of Wyoming-made products, souvenirs, gifts, snacks, and drinks. An extensive book department features western history, cowboy culture, children's books, and cookbooks. Maps of the historic migration trails nearby and old post cards, greeting cards and historic patterns are more examples of the goods you'll find. Visit their web site for an online catalog.

59 *No Services*

H "Parting of the Ways"

Just south of Sublette County line on U.S. Highway 28.

This marks a fork in the trail. Right to Oregon, left to Utah and California.

1812, Robert Stuart and east bound Astorians used South Pass Gateway.

1824, Eleven westbound Ashley-Henry men led by Jedediah Smith and Thomas Fitzpatrick.

1832, N. Wyeth and Capt. B.L.E. Bonneville parties.

1836, Missionaries M. Whitman and H.H. Spalding and wives.

1841, Bartleson-Bidwell party.

1852, Peak year, estimated 40,000 emigrants

H The Parting of the Ways

Just south of Sublette County line on U.S. Highway 28.

In July 1844 the California bound Stevens-Townsend-Murphy wagon train, guided by Isaac Hitchcock and 81-year old Caleb Greenwood,

Parting of the Ways Monument

passed this point and continued nine and one half miles west southwest from here to a place destined to become prominent in Oregon Trail history-the starting point of the Sublette Cut-off.

There, instead of following the regular Oregon Trail route southwest to Fort Bridger, then northwest to reach the Bear river below present day Cokeville, Wyoming, this wagon train pioneered a new route. Either Hitchcock or Greenwood, it is uncertain which, made the decision to lead the wagons due west, in effect along one side of a triangle.

It was the Gold Rush year of 1849 that brought this "Parting of the Ways" into prominence. Of the estimated 30,000 Forty-niners probably 20,000 travelled the Greenwood Cut-off which, due to an error in the 1849 Joseph E. Ware guide book, became known as the Sublette Cut-off.

In the ensuing years further refinements of the Trail route were made. In 1852 the Kinney and Slate Creek Cut-offs diverted trains from portions of the Sublette Cut-off, but until the covered wagon period ended, the Sublette Cut-off remained a popular direct route, and this "Parting of the Ways" was the place for crucial decisions.

A quartzite post inscribed *Fort Bridger S. Cut-off* and a Bureau of Land Management information panel now mark the historic "Parting of he Ways" site.

H The Parting of the Ways

Just south of Sublette County line on U.S. Highway 28.

Trail ruts at this site were mistakenly identified as the Parting-of -the-Ways where emigrant parties separated on their journeys to Oregon, California, or Utah.

The actual Parting-of-the-Ways is approximately 10 miles west of this spot. Where you are standing now is part of the main Oregon Trail over which 350,000 - 500,000 people passed on their way West between 1844 and 1869.

Look closely at the ground between the pullout fence and the monuments. The uneven "ridges" in the ground are trail ruts made by the passage of iron-wheeled freight wagons and stagecoaches on a road that connected south Pass with the Union Pacific Railroad in Green River, southwest of this spot. The freight road was used from about 1870 to 1900 - and the resulting ruts caused the confusion later with the actual Parting-of-the-Ways west of here.

Enjoy and appreciate your trail resources, but remember that they are very fragile. Please ensure that your visit doesn't result in any disturbance to the Trail.

H South Pass

On State Highway 28 about 6 miles southwest of the South Pass Rest Area.

John Jacob Astor's 'Astorians" are often given credit for the discovery of the "South Pass' ' route to western territories. Astor sent his "Astorians" by sea and land in 1810 to establish the Pacific Fur Company at the mouth of the Columbia River. He intended to break the British fur monopoly in the Pacific Northwest and bring American territory under American control. The overland party, led by Wilson Price Hunt, crossed northern Wyoming in July of 1811. Robert Stuart, a partner in the company, traveled with others by sea. Stuart later returned overland to New York with dispatches for Astor. It was this journey in October of 1812 which pioneered the route across this natural pass over the continental divide, later to become known as South Pass.

The discovery of South Pass, an important segment of the Oregon- California emigrant trails, hastened one of the greatest mass emigrations in the annals of American history. Restless Americans from all walks of life moved west, crossing this pass, seeking a better life in a new land. Among them were Mormons seeking freedom from religious, social and economic intolerance and aggression. For others, the lure was land available for the taking. The discovery of gold in California in 1848, attracted bands of feverish fortune seekers. An estimated 350,000 people passed this way between 1841 and 1866 on their way to western territories.

Chronology

1812 Discovery of South Pass by Robert Stuart and his group of Astorians

1826 First crossing of the pass by a wheeled vehicle

1832 First wagon train crossing, led by Army Captain B. L. E. Bonneville

1836 Narcissa P. Whitman and Eliza R. Spalding, first white women to cross South Pass

1843 Beginning of the great migration

1847 First wave of Mormon emigration

1849-1851 Peak period of emigration to the American West

1860 The Pony Express used this route for its brief nineteen month existence

H Oregon Buttes

Just south of South Pass on the Oregon Trail

To the south stand the Oregon Buttes, a major trail landmark. The name is significant because the Buttes were roughly the beginning of the Oregon Territory and also helped keep emigrants encouraged, even though there were still hundreds of miles of rough going ahead. Today, the Oregon Buttes are an Area of Critical Environmental Concern because of their cultural significance and important wildlife values.

The trail ruts of the pioneers are still clearly visible throughout much of southcentral Wyoming.

About twelve miles to the southwest of Oregon Buttes is the Tri- territory site. This site is the location where the Oregon Territory, Mexican Territory, and Louisiana Purchase had a common boundary. The large landmark, just to the south of where you are standing, is Pacific Butte. The great height and mass of the butte, combined with a ridge to the north paralleling the emigrant trails, helps to create a visual channel through which travelers migrated on their way through South Pass.

H South Pass

At South Pass on the Oregon Trail

South Pass was discovered in 1812 by a small party of Astorians led by Robert Stuart as they traveled east with dispatches for John Jacob Astor. It was "rediscovered" in 1824 by a party led by Jedediah Smith as they searched for a winter crossing through the Wind River Mountain Range. William Sublette led a small caravan of wagons to South Pass in 1828. While the party did not take the wagons over the pass, they proved that wagon travel was possible.

Captain Benjamin Bonneville took the first wagons over South Pass into the Green River Basin in 1832. But it was Lt. John Charles Fremont who would be credited with widely publicizing the route over South Pass as a result of his expedition in 1842. Scattered references to the easy passage over the Rocky Mountains had appeared in newspapers for a decade, but Fremont ignited enthusiasm for South Pass by explaining that a traveler could go through the pass without any "toilsome ascents."

With the discovery of South Pass, the great western migration began. Thousands of Mormons, future Oregonians and Californians would use the trail in the following years.

H Pacific Springs

From State Highway 28 take Oregon Buttes road about four miles west of South Pass to the Oregon Trail. Travel about one mile south on the Trail

For many emigrants, the first tangible evidence that they had crossed South Pass was Pacific Springs, "the fountain source of the Pacific streams," according to pioneer Joseph Goldsborough Bruff. The broad expanse of the pass from Pacific Springs was proof that the journey to the Pacific coast was geographically half over. But the event was only a slight consolation, the road ahead was still long and hard.

The springs was a major camping spot along the trail, providing good water and grazing. A number of pioneers also died here, most having succumbed to cholera contracted elsewhere along the trail. Several graves are known in the vicinity of Pacific Springs.

In the 1860's, a stagecoach and Pony Express station was located at the springs probably in the areas of the Halter and Flick Ranch. Some sources indicate that the station was burned by Indians in 1862. The exact location of the station is unknown.

Pacific Springs became an important water source for early livestock operators and they remain so today. The springs lie on private property owned by John Hay. The Hay family has been involved in ranching in southwestern Wyoming for five generations dating to the 1870s.

H Bennett Tribbett

Located on private land in Fremont County along the Oregon Trail

Private Bennett Tribbett was a nineteen-year-old soldier stationed here at Three Crossings Station. He was a member of Company B of the First Battalion, Sixth Ohio Volunteer Cavalry. On December 14, 1862, Tribbett died of an appendicitis. His burial was described by Pvt. Anthony Barleon in a letter written to Bennett's sister, Arviley, at home in Athens county, Ohio.

"We made a coffin of such lumber that we had which of course were rough boards but we planed them off as smooth as we could. We dressed him up in his best clothes which were new and clean, laid a blanket around him, and we tucked a blanket around the coffin which made it look a little better… When the time arrived for his burial he was bore off by the arms of 6 of his former associates accompanied by an escort of six men who performed the usual military escort and ceremony. When we arrived at the grave we put the coffin in and the escort fired three rounds over his grave. So he was buried with all the military honors of a soldier."

In July, 1863, four newly recruited companies were consolidated with the old battalion to form a new regiment, designated the Eleventh Ohio Volunteer Cavalry, which continued to serve on the frontier until the last companies were mustered out on July 14, 1866. By Civil War standards casualties in this regiment were light. Three officers and fifteen men died as a result of actions against Indians; one officer and fifty-eight men, like Bennett Tribbett, died of natural causes.

H Johnny Williams

On private land in Sweetwater County on private land

This is the probable gravesite of ten-year-old Johnny Williams, who died on or about June 20, 1851.

Johnny was riding in the rear of the baggage wagon when the oxen took fright and ran. Johnny went to the front of the wagon and clung to the driver but was thrown out; the wheels of the wagon ran over his head.

His mother wrote this in a letter to Johnny's grandmother: "We buried him there by the roadside, by the right side of the road, about one-half mile before we crossed the Fononelle. We had his grave covered with stones to protect it from wild animals and a board with his name and age and if any of our friends came through I wish they would find his grave and if it needs, repair it."

H Plume Rocks

About 2.5 miles west of State Highway 28 and the False Parting of the Ways Monument on the Oregon-Mormon Trail

In the days before man-made landmarks dominated the landscape, natural features such as Plume Rocks served as travelers signposts. J. Goldsborough Bruff noted in his journal on August 3, 1849, "… on right about 300 yards distant some low clay bluffs, of a dark dingy red hue, and singularily plume-formed projections on top from the effects of the elements."

While topographical features like Oregon Buttes served as navigational points on the horizon, minor features such as Plume Rocks served to keep emigrant travelerrs more precisely on course. They were especially critical in situations where it was not possible to sight between two navigational points on the horizon both ahead of and behind the travelers.

H Parting-of-the-Ways

About 12 miles west of the False Parting of the Ways Monument on the Oregon-Mormon Trail

This point on the trail is called the Parting-of-the-Ways. The trail to the right is the Sublette or Greenwood Cutoff and to the left is the main route of the Oregon, Mormon and California Trails. The Sublette Cutoff was opened in 1844 because it saved 46 miles over the main route. It did require a 50 mile waterless crossing of the desert and therefore was not popular until the gold rush period. The name tells the story, people who traveled a thousand miles together separated at this point. They did not know if they would ever see each other again. It was a place of great sorrow. It was also a place of great decision—to cross the desert and save miles or to favor their livestock. About two-thirds of the emigrants chose the main route through Fort Bridger instead of the Sublette Cutoff.

60 *Gas*

Baggs
Pop. 348, Elev. 6,245

Situated on a scenic bend of the Little Snake River, this little pastoral town was named for George and Maggie Baggs, major ranchers in the area. It's peaceful feel today belies its infamous past. Once a gathering place for outlaws in the 1880s and 90s, its isolation made it the perfect place to celebrate the latest heist. A rock fortress nearby was their hideout once the party was over. The Gaddis Matthews House, a refuge cabin built by Butch Cassidy's gang, still stands here.

Dixon
Pop. 79, Elev. 6,245

Robert Dixon, for whom this town was named, was a long-lived trapper. He hoped to live long enough to see a railroad train cross the Laramie Plains, but he died in an Arapaho raid the year before the Union Pacific arrived.

Savery
Once the stomping ground of mountain man Jim Baker, this tiny town is near his gravesite.

T Little Snake River Valley Museum
In Savery. 383-7262

The museum is housed in the former Savery School building. Exhibits include historical clothing, furniture, farm implements and books, as well as the Dr. Noyes Room and the John Terrill Room. There are restored historical buildings on the grounds including the Jim Baker cabin, Strobridge-Groshart-Hays house, Blair Cabin, and Dutch Joe School. Open Memorial Day through Labor Day, Wednesday through Saturday, 11 a.m.-5 p.m.

T Gaddis Matthews House
This old cabin was once a gathering place for Butch Cassidy and his cohorts.

H Jim Baker's Trading Post
At the Little Snake River Museum in Savery

This cabin was erected by Jim Baker, famous mountain man, plainsman, hunter, trapper, guide, scout, and Indian fighter on the Little Snake River in Carbon County, Wyoming, in 1873. Acquired by the State of Wyoming in 1917 and transported to Cheyenne, Wyoming, to be preserved as a lasting memorial to this brave pioneer citizen.
1977.

H Jim Baker
At the Baker Cemetery west of Savery

Here lies Jim Baker

Born in Illinois Dec. 19, 1819 Died May 15, 1898

One of the oldest Pioneers of the Rocky Mountains.

Contemporary of 'Kit" Carson, Jim Bridger, Freemont, and the rest who helped to civilize this district. A government scout, guide, and Indian fighter. His memory should be respected forever by those who live in all this region, the fighting land of the Indian tribes.

Scenic Drives

Wild Horse Viewing in Southcentral Wyoming

General Information

The Rawlins BLM Field Office is home to approximately 1,650 wild horses, the largest population of wild, free roaming horses outside of Nevada. While the horses generally inhabit the more remote and isolated portions of the field office, there is one area where you can see wild horses without leaving your vehicle. You need to keep in mind, however, that there is no guarantee you will observe wild horses on any given day. Even if you don't see any horses, your trip won't be in vain. You will pass through a variety of landscapes and habitat types and may encounter a variety of wildlife species and observe several of the uses of the public land.

The Land and Its Uses

The town of Rawlins is in the North Platte River drainage, part of the Mississippi River system. Eight miles north of Rawlins, you will cross the Continental Divide, but instead of crossing into the Pacific drainage, you will enter the Great Divide Basin—a large, high desert basin from which no water flows to either ocean's drainage. The Red Desert lies within this basin. Average annual precipitation in the basin ranges from six to nine inches. Nevertheless, the basin contains several natural playa lake systems that provide important habitat for migratory waterfowl and a myriad of other wildlife.

The viewing route will pass both historic and current signs of the area's considerable natural gas and uranium resources. In addition, rural agriculture is an important use of the area—Wyoming isn't called the Cowboy State without reason! Livestock grazing on the public land is managed by the BLM through the issuance of grazing permits. Depending on the time of year, you may encounter either sheep or cattle and the people who tend them.

You will probably see more pronghorn antelope than wild horses along the viewing route since there are more pronghorn in Wyoming than there are people. As a result of successful regulation of hunting by the Wyoming Game and Fish Department and careful use of the habitat by all users, the pronghorn antelope has returned from its near extinction at the turn of the century to its present level of abundance. During the fall, you will probably encounter many hunters in pursuit of pronghorn or other big game. Small animals are also abundant in the area. You might encounter a coyote hunting for its next meal of prairie dog, ground squirrel, or rabbit. The small birds which fly up in front of your car are horned larks. You may also see sage grouse and a variety of raptors such as hawks and eagles. But it is also possible that you may complete your entire trip without seeing another living being.

Points Along the Route

The viewing route begins 14 miles north of Rawlins at the intersection of U.S.Highway 287 and Carbon County Road 63 and ends at Jeffrey City. It's total length is 69 miles. About midway through the route, you can choose to travel on to Jeffrey City and subsequently Lander, Riverton, Casper, or Rawlins, or you can turn south and join I-80 at Wamsutter. It is only a few miles more from Rawlins to Lander via the viewing route than it is via U.S. Highway 287, but it will take longer due to the road. The route is paved for the first 30 miles and the rest is graveled. Consider purchasing the Bairoil 1:100,000 scale land ownership status map obtainable at any Wyoming BLM office for $4.00. The map shows all but the first three miles of the route and contains other information about the area. The yellow areas on the map show BLM-managed public land. The white and blue areas are private or state-owned lands. If you wish to leave the designated route, be sure to respect private property. The alternating white and yellow squares are known as the "checkerboard."

Before starting the route, make sure your vehicle is in good repair. If it has not rained recently, you can make this trip in any full or mid-sized passenger car. Make sure that your spare tire is usable and that you have drinking water and some basic emergency supplies with you. If you break down, it may be a long time before someone comes along to rescue you. A good pair of field glasses or perhaps even a portable spotting scope would also be handy. Do not attempt to make this trip during inclement weather. Be especially cautious when there is snow on the ground.

Even the horses with the most recent domestic origins have been roaming free for many generations. Although some horses are accustomed to traffic and may appear unconcerned when a vehicle approaches, you should not attempt to approach the horses. To do so might endanger yourself and cause unnecessary stress to the horses.

Two kinds of information follow. A point introduced by "22R" means that it is 22 miles from the start of the route and is on the right side of the road. A point introduced by "5-17" means that it encompasses the entire area between the 5th and 17th mile of the route.

0 Point of beginning at the junction of Carbon County Rd 63 and U.S. Highway 287. Set your trip odometer to zero. Stop at the turnoff and read the sign explaining the Shamrock Hills Raptor Concentration Area. The sign details the story of the successful management of the ferruginous hawk, a relatively rare species.

0-6 Greasewood/saltbush habitat type

6-69 The remainder of the route consists of the sagebrush/grass habitat type. Soils become somewhat sandier as you proceed toward the next crossing of the Continental Divide. The grass and forb (broad-leafed plants) species change throughout this area, but the sagebrush remains a constant feature of the landscape.

25.3R Intersection with BLM road 3215. Bairoil can be reached by following this road. Followed south, the road joins the Riner Road, crosses the Chain Lakes Desert Wetland Complex, and eventually intersects with Interstate 80. The wetland complex, consisting of many playa lakes, capillary springs, and bogs, is approximately five miles to the south. Do not attempt to explore the wetland area. It is possible to become hopelessly mired in what initially may appear to be a passable road or trail.

29.4R The Sweetwater Mill processed uranium ore into yellowcake during the uranium boom of the 1960s and 70s. It is one of the few mills in the U.S. designated by the Nuclear Regulatory Commission as being in standby status. This means that it could begin operating again in a short time period.

33.3 Intersection with Sweetwater County Road 23N. This point is almost exactly in the middle of

South of Lander

the Great Divide Basin. On a clear day, you can see the Oregon Buttes on the historic Oregon Trail (50 miles WNW), Continental Peak to the right of the buttes (50 Miles WNW), and the Wind River Range (70 miles NW). These features are situated at the western and northern edges of the Great Divide Basin along the Continental Divide. Turn right to continue the tour to Jeffrey City or turn left to reach Wamsutter and Interstate 80 23 miles to the south.

48.8 Intersection with Sweetwater County Road 22 which leads to Bairoil approximately 20 miles to the east and U.S. Highway 287 at Lamont a few miles further. Wild horses may be viewed along this road but it is very rocky in sections.

50 The numerous small dirt mounds are the result of uranium prospecting. At this point, you cross the Continental Divide at an elevation of 7,041 feet above sea level and leave the Great Divide Basin and re-enter the Platte River drainage. Five miles straight ahead is Crooks Peak. Crooks Mountain is to the west of Crooks Peak. Crooks Gap separates Crooks Peak and Green Mountain to the east. The features were named after famed Indian fighter General George Crook.

55.2L Intersection with Three Forks/Atlantic City Road—40 miles to Atlantic City and neighboring South Pass State Historic Site. This road is not regularly maintained. Crooks Creek is on the right side of the road.

58-63 These last few miles of the route cross mostly privately-owned lands. The streams and streamside areas are home to a rich diversity of plants and animals. You will see the remains of some of the original homesteads in the area and follow the route of the Rawlins-Ft. Washakie stage for a ways.

60-69 As you near Jeffrey City, pay close attention to the warning signs and be on the lookout for heavy equipment, especially large ore hauling trucks. Even though traffic is sparse, it is not non-existent.

69 At Jeffrey City, a thriving city of 8,000 during the uranium boom, you rejoin U.S. Highway 287. You can either turn left (west) and reach Lander or Riverton or turn right (east) and return to Rawlins to the south or travel north to Casper. With a little imagination, you can reverse all of these directions and begin your journey at Jeffrey City.

Seminoe/Alcova Scenic Backway

This is a 64-mile route passing through some of Wyoming's most arid country, but due to the dams and reservoirs built on the North Platte River, this country also boasts some of the most choice fishing and water recreation sports in Wyoming. There are no towns, stores, gas stations, or telephones between Sinclair and Alcova. Limited services are available at the marina store at Seminoe Reservoir. The road varies from two lane to single lane, with pullouts for passing as it goes through the Seminoe Mountains.

The Backway usually can be driven by a passenger car from May to December, depending on the amount of snow. In some places it is paved, and in other it is improved with gravel, but can get quite muddy, especially north of the Miracle Mile area. Because of the steepness of the road in a few spots, motor home and vehicles pulling large trailers are not advised to travel between Miracle Mile and Seminoe State Park. Driving time is about 2.5 miles, but can take longer depending on stops to enjoy the sights and varied recreation.

Some of the special features of this area include the Seminoe, Pathfinder, and Alcova Reservoirs, the North Platte River, and fishing at the Miracle Mile, Seminoe State Park, and the Seminoe, Pedro, and Haystack mountain ranges. The US Bureau of Reclamation manages the reservoirs, dams and campgrounds along the Miracle Mile and the banks of the reservoirs, except at Seminoe State Park.

Reprinted from Wyoming Department of Transportation Brochure

Battle Pass

This rarely traveled, 57-mile section of highway takes you from Baggs to Encampment by way of the Sierra Madre Mountains. There are no services between the two towns. From either end, the route follows Wyoming Highway 70, and passes below Bridger Peak, across Battle Pass at 9916 feet, by the ghost town of Battle, and past the Huston Park Wilderness. Along the way is some of the loveliest forest scenery in the state, including a side road (FDR 801) known as Aspen Alley. This features a drive through an extensive aspen grove, an especially enchanting place in spring and fall, when the colors are in transition. Views of both the Encampment and Little Snake River Valleys greet travelers at either end of the drive.

Pilot Butte Wild Horse Scenic Loop

This drive gives visitors a chance to see an abundance of wildlife, including antelope, elk, deer, rabbits, coyotes, hawks, eagles, and sage grouse. But the most visible is probably the wild horse. Most wild horses in Wyoming are located in the southwestern quarter of the state. The Rock Springs BLM is the headquarters for the management of the horses, which oversees about 2500 of the 6000 horses in the area. The existence of the wild herds is a credit to the private landowners here who do not fence their land, allowing the horses and other wildlife to wander as necessary for food, water, and shelter in the winter.

It takes about 2.5 miles to complete this drive if you do not stop to look at the sights. The road is mostly gravel, and conditions may vary, so high clearance vehicles are recommended. From Rock Springs, travel 14 miles north on Elk Street (Hwy. 191) to County Road 4-14 (Fourteen Mile Road). Turn left and continue 2.5 miles, then turn left again onto CR 4-53. Follow this road for 21.5 miles to Green River. The dirt road becomes Trona Drive. Follow Trona around the curve and turn right at its intersection with Hillcrest. Drive one block to Flaming Gorge Way. Downtown Green River will be to your left. You can also begin the tour here and return to Rock Springs.
Article courtesy of Bureau of Land Management.

Hikes

Wind River Mountains (East)

Bears Ears Trail #716

Distance: 16 miles
Climb: steep
Rating: very difficult
Usage: heavy
Location: Travel 15 miles northwest of Lander on Hwy. 26/287, then turn west at Trout Creek Road across from the Ft. Washakie historical marker, adjacent to a Conoco Station. Follow road southwest for 19 miles across Wind River Indian Reservation. Continue south (left) at the Moccasin Lake Dickinson Park junction for 1.7 miles to the signed Bears Ears Trailhead parking area.

The trail climbs some switchbacks, and at 3 miles, the double pronged stone outcroppings known as Bears Ears come into view. After five miles, you drop down from Adams Pass, cross a corduroy over marsh, proceed over a permanent snow field, and cross Sand Creek. At the head of the valley; the spectacular Wind River Peaks, which for the Continental Divide west, can be seen. In the Glacial cirques, numerous alpine lakes grace the terrain. Continue south over the rocky trail and come to the Lizard Head Trail junction at 9 miles. Fork right and descend into Valentine Meadows, past the moss Lake Trail (Dutch Oven) junction, and drop to the north side of Valentine Lake. The trail descends into the South Fork Little Wind River drainage and crosses the river. Here the trail connects with

Somewhere near Split Rock

Washakie Trail #718. The Bears Ears Trail heads north, and follows downstream past the junction of the Valentine Mountain Trail. The trail leaves the river, climbs west, and descends onto Grave Lake. On the north side of the lake, you'll pass the intersection with Onion Meadows Trail #902. On the northwest side of Grave Lake there is another junction with Baptiste Lake Trail #719, and the trail travels southwest, climbing Hailey Pass.

High Meadow Trail #712

Distance: 3 miles
Climb: steep
Rating: difficult
Usage: light
Location: This trail intersects with the Smith Lake Trail #715, and travels in a south/southeasterly direction to its junction with the North Fork Trail #710 in Sanford Park.

At the Junction of Smith Lake Trail #715, the High Meadow Trail heads south, crossing Smith Lake Creek. This junction is unmarked, as the trail is not maintained by the Forest Service. Just beyond this junction, the trail descends, dropping into the North Fork Drainage, and ending at its junction with the North Fork Trail #710 on the northwest side of Sanford Park.

Ice Lakes Trail #706

Distance: 7.2 miles
Climb: steep
Rating: difficult
Usage: light/ moderate
Location: In the southeast corner of Salt Cache Park, at a signed junction, turn northwest onto the Ice Lakes Trail. This trail begins at the intersection of the Tayo Lake Trail #707 and ends at its junction with the Pinto Park Trail #708.

This trail heads west, then begins a steep climb for another mile. From here, a good view of the Middle Popo Agie Valley is offered. The trail then drops down and you must follow cairns around a small pond, and once again begin climbing steeply. The view opens behind you, as Roaring Fork Mountain, Sweetwater Gap, and the Cirque above Little Mountain Sheep Lake in Mt. Nystrom are easily observed. After crossing the saddle, the Ice Lakes come into view. From this point, the trail drops steadily to the lakes. The trail continues north into the deep Creek Lakes area, then junctions with the Deep Creek cutoff trail#709 on the north side of the outlet of Lower Deep Creek Lake. The trail switches back as it climbs into the Bear Lakes, then continues along the west side of Echo Lakes, and ends at the junction of the Pinto Park Trail #708.

Smith Fork Trail #710

Distance: 15 miles
Climb: moderate
Rating: easy
Usage: light
Location: Travel 15 miles northwest of Lander on Hwy 26/287, then turn west at Trout Creek Road, across from the Ft. Washakie historical maker and adjacent to the Conoco Station. Follow this road southwest for 19 miles across the Wind River Indian Reservation. Continue south (left) at the Moccasin Lake/ Dickinson Park junction, and go 4.1 miles past the Dickinson Creek campground to signed trailhead parking area.

Follow the Smith Lake Trail across the corduroy and up the slope into the trees where it intersects with the North Fork Trail. This trail travels across a ridge and drops into the North Fork of the Popo Agie River Drainage, then heads upstream, past the junction with the Shoshone Lake Trail, and enters the Popo Agie Wilderness approximately one mile before the first river crossing. The trail crosses the river again at the lower end of Sanford Park, passes the junction of High Meadow Trail, then crosses High Meadow Creek. The trail crosses the river a third time at the upper end of Sanford Park and continues past the junction of the Pinot Park Trail. At 9.5 miles, you cross the North Fork for the last time. As the trail enters Lizard Head Meadows, just past the junction of Lizard Head Trail, there is a good view of Cirque of the Towers. The trail continues to Lonesome Lake and makes an easy climb to Jackass Pass.

Silas Creek Trail #722

Distance: 1.8 miles
Climb: gentle
Rating: easy
Usage: heavy
Location: Travel 23.4 miles southwest of Lander on Sinks Canyon Road (Hwy. 131). Then take FDR 300 to Fiddlers Lake. The Christina Lake Trail starts at the parking area on the South end of the lake. Follow the Christina Lake Trail to the Junction with Silas Lake Trail.

This trail travels west until Lower Silas Lake is visible from the trail, then it crosses Silas Creek. The trail continues upstream several hundred yards, then you must return by the same route.

Smith Lake Trail #715

Distance: 7.5 miles
Climb: gentle
Rating: easy
Usage: heavy
Location: Travel 15 miles northwest of Lander on Hwy 26/287, then turn west at Trout Creek Road, across from the Ft. Washakie historical marker and adjacent to the Conoco Station. Follow this road southwest for 19 miles across the Wind River Indian Reservation. Continue south (left) at the Moccasin Lake/ Dickinson Park Junction, and go 4.1 miles past the Dickinson Creek campground to the signed trailhead parking area.

This trail drops down to the marsh near Twin Parks Creek and crosses the corduroy before beginning a gradual climb up. Continue traveling on the road for 1/2 mile before reaching the Smith Lake/ North Fork junction. Go right onto the Smith Lake Trail and continue climbing. You will go southwest and drop across a creek at 3 miles. At 4.5 miles is the signed High Meadows Trail junction. Stay right on the trail and begin climbing steadily to the Cook Lake Trail junction. Say right and continue 100 yards to Middle Lake. To get to Cathedral Lake, follow the cairn-marked trail and climb west.

Stough Creeks Lake Trail #702

Distance: 7 miles
Climb: steep
Rating: difficult
Usage: heavy
Location: Travel 18 miles southwest of Lander on Sinks Canyon Road (Hwy. 131). Then take FDR 300 to Worthen Meadows Reservoir junction. Turn right and drive 2.3 miles to the Stough Creek Lakes Trailhead.

The trail begins climbing steadily up a rocky road 1/2 mile to Roaring Fork Lake, crossing the outlet of the lake, and then reaches a corduroy over a marsh at 1.7 miles. As you break out of the trees and begin to climb west, the trail crosses a tributary and swings across a meadow to an open alpine saddle, Roaring Fork Pass, at 5 miles. The view takes in Roaring Fork Mountain and Wind River Peak. The trail then drops steadily to a creek crossing, and continues to the junction at Stough Creek Basin Trail #704. At the junction the trail heads south to Big Stough and Shoal Lakes. You can stop here, or continue south through open country to reach the higher Stough Creek Lakes.

Tayo Lake Trail #707

Distance: 4.1 miles
Climb: steep
Rating: moderate
Usage: heavy
Location: This trail intersects with the Middle Fork Trail #700 at Tayo Park, and ends at Tayo Lake.

After entering Tayo Park, the trail crosses the Middle Fork of the Popo Agie River and climbs steeply to Salt Cache Park. The trail continues southwest past Poison Lake, then crosses Tayo Creek and intersects with Coon Lake Trail #705. From here, the trail heads northwest, crossing the Tayo Creek again and ending at Tayo Lake.

Encampment Area (including Platte River Wilderness, Encampment River Wilderness, and Savage Run Wilderness Areas)

(PRW) West of Encampment

Platte Ridge Trail #510

Distance: 7.9 to 8.4 miles
Climb: 900 feet
Rating: difficult
Usage: light
Location: Take Hwy. 230 to the eastern portion of the Wyoming/Colorado border crossing. Near the border will be FDR 898. Take this road about 8.5 miles to the Pelton Creek Campground. You will find the trailhead here.

This trail climbs steadily, then begins to drop down to Douglas Creek. After traveling about 7 miles, the trail forks to the east and west. The east fork intersects with the Douglas Creek Trail #506 and goes for about one mile, the west fork intersects with the Platte River Trail #473 and goes about 1.5 miles.

Platte River/ Six Mile Gap Trail #473

Distance: 8.4 miles
Climb: moderate
Rating: difficult
Usage: light
Location: Travel about 22 miles south of Encampment on Hwy. 230, and turn east onto FDR 492. Continue 2.1 miles to Six Mile Gap Campground. The trailhead is located here.

This trail follows the North Platte River through the lower end of the North Gate Canyon. Trail users should be aware that the trail crosses the North Platte River and Douglas Creek but has NO bridges. Check water conditions before starting out, and avoid crossing before July 1st, when water levels are at their highest.

Devil's Gate Trail #505

Distance: 2.8 miles
Climb: 1,000 feet (descent)
Rating: difficult
Usage: light
Location: Travel to Fox Park on Hwy. 230 and turn west on FDR 512. This road intersects with 506D. The trailhead is at the road's end. This is an extremely rocky, steep road that requires high clearance vehicles, and does not accommodate RV's or horse trailers. Early and late season snow may also limit access.

Although this is a relatively short hike, it is rated difficult for its steepness. After following the East Fork of Devil's Gate Creek, it crosses West Fork. Check runoff conditions before attempting this hike. The trail intersects with the Douglas Creek Trail #506 at the end.

Douglas Creek Trail #506

Distance: 9.1 miles
Climb: 800 feet (descent)
Rating: difficult
Usage: light
Location: Travel to Fox Park on Hwy. 230 and turn west on FDR 512. This road goes all the way to the northwest corner of the wilderness, where the trailhead begins. The road has many switchbacks, and requires a high clearance vehicle. Trailers and RV's are not recommended. Early and late season snow may also limit access

Baby Lake Trail #859

Distance: 4.2 miles
Location: Travel about 18 miles west of Encampment on Hwy .70. Turn south on FDR 811, by Lost Creek Campground. When road forks, take FDR 811.1A to gravel parking lot and trailhead.
Continental Divide Trail #412 (Red Mountain)
Distance: 13. 5 miles
Location: Travel 12 miles west of Encampment on Hwy. 70 to Battle Pass. South of here is the Huston Park Wilderness Area at Red Mountain. It is about 10 miles from here to the Continental Divide. The trail can also be accessed from Green Mountain Trailhead. Go two miles south on Green Mountain Trail to reach Huston Park Wilderness Area. Again, the Divide is about 10 miles additional traveling distance.

Green Mountain Falls Trail #478

Distance: 1.2 miles
Location: Travel 6 miles west of Encampment on Hwy. 70, then south on FDR 550, then west on FDR 406. Go 1.5 miles to the trailhead.
Roaring Fork Trail #860
Distance: 7.4 miles
Location: Travel 23 miles west of Encampment, then turn south on FDR 807. For about 6 miles do FDR 851, then continue east for 1.5 miles until the junction with FDR 851.1A. Take this road about 2 miles east to the trailhead. FDR 851.1A requires a high clearance vehicle.

Verde Mine Trail #858

Distance: 3.2 miles
Location: Travel 23 miles on Hwy. 70 west of Encampment to FDR 807. Go south about 6 miles to FDR 851. Continue 8.5 miles to FDR 851.1D. The trailhead is about 4 miles from this junction. This road requires a high clearance vehicle.

Green Mountain Trail #479

Distance: 1.2 miles
Location: Travel 6 miles west of Encampment on Hwy. 70, then go south on FDR 550 for 5.7 miles. Turn west on FDR 406, then go 1.5 miles to trailhead.

Encampment River Trail #470 (Commissary Park)

Distance: 15.6 miles
Location: Travel 6 miles west of Encampment on Hwy. 70, then go south on FDR 550 for about 14.5 miles to FDR 496. Turn southeast and go about 4 miles to reach trailhead.

Hog Park Creek Trail #475

Distance: 1.1 miles
Location: Travel 6 miles west of Encampment on Hwy. 70, then go south on FDR 550 for about 14.5 miles to FDR 496. Turn southeast and go about 2 miles to reach trailhead.

East Fork Trail #472

Distance: 6.7 miles
Location: Travel one mile east of Riverside on Hwy. 230. Go south on County Rd. 211 for 14.3 miles. This road becomes FDR 409 after the Forest Boundary is crossed. The road will reach the intersection with FDR 496. Stay on 409 past the intersection, and continue 3 miles to trailhead.

Purgatory Gulch Trail #477

Distance: 0.5 mile
Location: Travel one mile east of Riverside on Hwy. 230 then go south on County Rd. 211, which turns into FDR 409. After about 6 miles turn onto BLM Rd. 409.1B. The trailhead is about 2 miles southwest of this point. A high clearance vehicle is required.

Seminoe/ Pathfinder/Alcova Area

Pedro Mountains

Distance: varies
Climb: varies
Rating: varies
Usage: light
Location: South off of Hwy. 220 onto the Seminoe/Alcova Scenic Backway, about 25 miles, then west into the wilderness.

The bare granite Pedro Mountains dotted with ponderosa pine have no official hiking trails nor roads with legal public access. For that reason, they are not crowded and have great allure to the most adventuresome cross-country hikers and backpackers. Only those with extensive back-country experience in orienteering should attempt to go where there are no trails.

Cottonwood Creek Dinosaur Trail

Distance: 0.5 mile
Climb: steep
Rating: moderate/difficult
Usage: moderate
Location: South off of Hwy. 220 onto the Seminoe/Alcova Scenic Backway, about 5 miles, then west towards the reservoir.

In 1991, numerous dinosaur bones and the skeleton of a medium-sized dinosaur called Camarasaurus were discovered by 5th grade students from Casper. Most of the original skeleton now resides in a Casper museum. Today, a BLM trail runs through the sandstone ledges of the Morrison formation. Present along the trail are many vertabrate, invertabrate, and plant fossils. The slopes of the trail can be quite steep, and hikers should be in good physical condition before undertaking the walk.

Snowy Range Trails

Heart Lake Trail #101

Distance: 0.8 miles
Climb: 200 feet
Rating: easy
Usage: moderate
Location: Dipper Lake on forest road #103

Trail access is from Dipper Lake Trail #294. Very scenic alpine trail on the west side of Medicine Bow Peak.

Quealy Lake #102

Distance: 4. 1 miles
Climb: 500 feet
Rating: moderate
Usage: light
Location: By Quealy Lake on forest road #103.

Trail crosses sub-alpine terrain north of Medicine Bow ridge passing three lakes. Very scenic.

Vagner Lake Trail #103

Distance: 0.5 miles
Climb: 100 feet
Rating: easy
Usage: light
Location: By Quealy lake on forest road #103.
Spur from Quealy Lake Trail #102 to Vagner Lake.

North Gap Lake #108

Distance: 2.5 miles
Climb: 700 feet
Rating: moderate
Usage: light
Location: Off Lewis Lake Trailhead.

Trail follows a gentle grade past several high

mountain lake traveling across a few boulder fields.

Shelf Lakes Trail #109
Distance: 1.1 miles
Climb: 120 feet
Rating: easy
Usage: moderate
Location: Off Lewis Lake Trailhead.

Trail access is from the North Gap Lake Trail #108. Scenic alpine trail on the north side of Brown's Peak.

Lake Marie Falls #290
Distance: 0.2 miles
Climb: 50 feet
Rating: easy
Usage: moderate/ heavy
Location: off of Lake Marie West Parking Area.
Short scenic loop trail along South French Creek at the base of the peas of the Snowy Range.

Silver Lake #291
Distance: 1.6 miles
Climb: 280 feet
Rating: easy
Usage: moderate/ heavy
Location: Silver Lake Trailhead.

Loop trail around Silver Lake in sub-alpine terrain, with a short steep section to get to the lake.

Tipple #293
Distance: 2.1 miles
Climb: 400 feet
Rating: easy
Usage: moderate
Location: By Tipple Trailhead or Miner's Cabin Trailhead.

Trail traverses sub-alpine terrain with spectacular views of the Snowy Range and South French Creek.

Dipper Lake #294
Distance: 3.4 miles
Climb: 1400 feet
Rating: difficult
Usage: light
Location: By Dipper Lake on forest road #103

Trail passes Dipper Lake and climbs steeply to Medicine Bow Peak.

Medicine Bow Peak #297
Distance: 4.5 miles
Climb: 1600 feet
Rating: quite difficult
Usage: light/ moderate
Location: Off of Lake Marie West Parking Area of Lewis Lake Trailhead.

A very steep climb through open rocky alpine terrain with a panoramic view. Trail climbs to the top of Medicine Bow Peak, the highest point in the Medicine Bow National Forest.

Lakes #296
Distance: 1.8 miles
Climb: 900 feet
Rating: difficult
Usage: light
Location: Off of Mirror Lake Picnic Area

Trail goes through open alpine country past Lookout Lake with panoramic views of Medicine Bow Peak.

Meadow Falls #297
Distance: 2.7 miles
Climb: 350 feet
Rating: moderate
Usage: moderate
Location: Off of Silver Lake Trailhead.

Loop trail that passes through sub-alpine terrain with a 600 foot spur to view Meadow Falls. Ties into the Silver Lake Trail.

French Creek Canyon #298
Distance: 5.3 miles
Climb: 1600 feet
Rating: difficult
Usage: light
Location: off of Tipple of Miner's Cabin or French Creek Canyon Trailheads.

This trail starts at milepost 0.6 of the Tipple trail from the L ake Marie Trailhead or milepost 1.85 from the Miner's Cabin Trailhead, for a total mileage of either 5.9 or 7.1 miles. Trail follows South French Creek through sub-alpine forest, meadows, rock canyons, and past Sunshine Falls.

Lost Lake #395
Distance: 3.5 miles
Climb: 180 feet
Rating: moderate
Usage: light/ moderate
Location: off Lewis Lake Trailhead or Brooklyn Lake Campground.

Trail traverses through sub-alpine terrain passing through meadows and by high mountain streams and lakes.

Deep Lake #110
Distance: 0.5 miles
Climb: 180 feet
Rating: easy
Usage: moderate/ heavy
Location: Off Lewis Lake Trailhead or Brooklyn Lake Campground.

Trail traverses through sub-alpine terrain passing through meadow and by high mountain streams and lakes.

Miner's Cabin #201
Distance: 0.7 miles
Climb: 200 feet
Rating: easy
Usage: moderate/ heavy
Location: Off Medicine Bow Peak Overlook off Highway 130.

A self-guided loop trail which follows a gentle grade past the historic Red Mask mine and Cabin and includes several interpretive signs along the way.

Sheep Lake #389
Distance: 8.2 miles
Climb: 1300 feet
Rating: very difficult
Usage: light
Location: Off Sand Lake Trailhead or Sheep Lake Trailhead on forest road #317.

Trail passes through high flat sub-alpine country with many open parks, lakes and streams.

North Fork #390
Distance: 4.4 miles
Climb: 1300 feet
Rating: quite difficult
Usage: moderate
Location: Off North Fork Trailhead on forest road #317 or by North Fork Campground.

Trail follows the North Fork of the Little Laramie River for most of the route. Good fishing opportunities, and a good mountain bike trail from the west to east end.

Savage Run Wilderness Area

Savage Run Creek #501
Distance: about 10 miles
Climb: steep
Rating: quite difficult
Usage: light
Location: Off FDR #500 at marker 500.3 A.
Only high clearance vehicles can access this trailhead. Trail gradually follows the contour of Savage Run Creek through mostly forested land. It dead-ends at private property, which isn't accessible to the public. An extension trail (#501 A) leaves the main trail, just south of the main fork on Savage Run Creek, beyond the Cottonwood Creek Trail, to connect with FDR #512.

Cottonwood Creek #501
Distance: 1.5 miles
Climb: steep
Rating: difficult
Usage: light
Location: Off FDR #512 (Platte Access Road) at marker 512 V.

Trail descends down and across Cottonwood Creek, and over another hill which descends into the Savage Run Creek Trail.

INFORMATION PLEASE

Tourism Information

National Historic Trails Interpretive Center 261-7700
Casper Area Convention & Visitors Bureau, Natrona County Travel & Tourism Council 234-5362
Lander Chamber of Commerce 332-3892
Rawlins-Carbon Country Chamber of Commerce 324-4111
Chamber of Commerce of Riverton 856-4801
Saratoga-Platte Valley Chamber of Commerce 326-8855

Government

BLM Casper Field Office 261-7600
Wyoming Game and Fish Department, Casper 473-3400
BLM Lander Field Office 332-8400
BLM Rawlins Field Office 328-4200
BLM Resevoir Management Group 261-7600
BLM Wyoming State Office 775-6256
MedicineBow-Routt National Forests Thunder Basin National Grassland 745-2300
Shoshone National Forest - Washakie Ranger Districts 527-6241
Medicine Bow-Routt National Forests Thunder Basin National Grassland - Brush Creek/Hayden Ranger District 745-2300

Car Rentals

Hertz • Riverton 856-2344
Aries Car Rentals • Casper 234-3501
Around Town Rent-A-Car • Casper 265-5667
Avis Rent A Car • Casper 237-2634
Hertz • Casper 265-1355
Enterprise • Casper 234-8122
Jim's Aircraft Service & Car Rental • Riverton 856-3599
Price King Rent-A-Car • Casper 472-7378
Quality Auto Rentals • Rawlins 324-7131
Rent A Wreck • Lander 332-9965

Hospitals

Lander Valley Medical Center • Lander 332-4420
Riverton Memorial Hospital • Riverton 856-4161
Memorial Hospital of Carbon County • Rawlins 324-2221
Wyoming Medical Center • Casper 577-7201

Airports

Riverton 856-7063
Casper 472-6688

Golf

Casper Golf Club • Casper 234-2405
Lander Golf & Country Club • Lander 332-4653
Renegade Golf Course • Riverton 857-0117
Links at Casper Golf Club • Casper 234-2405
Saratoga Inn, Hot Springs & Golf Resort • Saratoga 326-5261
Rawlins Municipal Golf Course • Rawlins 328-4573
Riverton Country Club • Riverton 856-4779

Ski Areas

Hogadon Basin Ski Area 235-8499

Guest Ranches

Miracle Mile Ranch • 325-6710
Overland Trail Guest Ranch • Arlington 378-2400
Mountain Meadow Guest Ranch • Centennial 742-6042
Rustic Mountain Lodge • Encampment 327-5539
Twin Creek Ranch and Lodge • Lander 335-7485
Black Mountain Ranch • Lander 332-6442
Resort at Louis Lake • Lander 332-5549
Allen's Diamond 4 Ranch • Lander 332-2995
Willow Creek Inn • Lander 332-7396
Hart Ranch Hideout • Lander 332-3836
VR Halawasa Ranch • Pavillion 857-2057
Hat 2 Wranglers • Pavillion 856-1993
Strathkay Wranglers Ranch • Riverton 856-2194
Wolf Hotel Restaurant & Lounge • Saratoga 326-5525
Brush Creek Guest Ranch • Saratoga 327-5241
Medicine Bow Guest Ranch • Saratoga 326-3439
Sierra Madre Guest Ranch • Saratoga 326-5261
Battlecreek Outfitters • Savery 383-2418
Antelope Retreat • Savery 383-2625

Lodges and Resorts

North Platte Lodge • Alcova 237-1182
Snowy Mountain Lodge • Centennial 742-7669
Grand & Sierra Bed and Breakfast Lodge • Encampment 327-5200
Spirit West River Lodge • Riverside 327-5753
Mountain Hideaway Lodge • Saratoga 326-5887
Saratoga Inn, Hot Springs & Golf Resort • Saratoga 326-5261

Vacation Houses, Cabins & Condos

Dredge Station • Atlantic City 339-7404
Atlantic City Mercantile • Atlantic City 332-5143
Valley's End Guest House • Centennial 742-5715
Middle Mountain Guest Cottage • Centennial 755-0696
TNT Guest House • Fox Park 755-5050
Outlaw Cabins • Lander 332-9655
High Country Guest House • Lander 332-2106
Mountain Rose Cabin • Lander 332-2830
Bear Trap Bar, Cafe, & Cabins • Riverside 327-5277
Three River Cottages • Saratoga 326-8750

Bed and Breakfasts

Miner's Delight B&B • Atlantic City 332-0248
The Bunk House • Lander 332-5624
Wolf Hotel Restaurant & Lounge • Saratoga 326-5525
Rustic Mountain Lodge • Encampment 327-5539
Cottage House of Squaw Creek • Lander 332-7485
Far Out West B&B • Saratoga 326-5869
Hood House B&B Inn • Saratoga 326-8901
Delfelder Inn B&B • Riverton 857-3100
Blue Spruce Inn B&B • Lander 332-8253
Sand Creek Ranch • Alcova 234-9597
Edna's B&B • Lander 332-3175
Whispering Pines B&B • Lander 332-9735
Willow Creek Inn • Lander 332-7396
Brooksong B&B • Saratoga 326-8744
Antique Bed Inn • Casper 265-2304
Ivy House Inn • Casper 265-0974
Baldwin Creek B&B •Lander 332-7608
Outlaw B&B • Lander 332-5624
Centennial Trust Co. • Centennial 721-4090
Brooklyn Lodge B&B • 924-1236
Old Depot B&B • Riverside 327-5277
Kingfisher House • Saratoga 326-8217

Outfitters and Guides

Name	Type	Phone
Lander Llama Company	G	332-5624
The Bunk House	G	332-5624
Teton Horseback Adventures & Swift Creek Outfitters	E	856-3628
Battlecreek Outfitters	H	383-2418
Wildhorse Country Tours	E	383-2015
BJ Outfitters	H	472-7956
Paradise Outfitters	EG	856-2950
Rocky Mt. Horseback Adventures	EG	332-4502
Sweetwater Fishing Expeditions	F	332-3986
Great Rocky Mountain Outfitters	FR	326-8750
Hack's Tackle & Outfitters	FH	326-9823
Horseback Adventures	E	326-5569
Medicine Bow Drifters	F	326-8002
Wyoming Trout Company	FR	327-5444
Meadow Lake Outfitters	HF	332-6158
Dan Artery's Rimrock Hunts	H	332-2029
Saratoga Outfitters	H	327-5504
A Cross Ranch	H	327-5794
AJ Outfitters	H	473-1196
Big Game Outfitters	H	856-3364
Diamond J Outfitters	H	326-8259
Wyoming Trophy Outfitters	H	234-6167
7D Ranch Outfitting	FHEG	587-9885

Section 5

NOTES:

Dining Quick Reference

Price Range refers to the average cost of a meal per person: ($) $1-$6, ($$) $7-$11, ($$$) $12-up. Cocktails: "Yes" indicates full bar; Beer (B)/Wine (W), Service: Breakfast (B), Brunch (BR), Lunch (L), Dinner (D). Businesses in bold print will have additional information under the appropriate map locator number in the body of this section.

MAP#	RESTAURANT	TYPE CUISINE	PRICE RANGE	CHILD MENU	COCKTAILS BEER WINE	MEALS SERVED	CREDIT CARDS ACCEPTED
1	Applebee's	American	$$	Yes	Yes	L/D	Major
1	Roadway Husky	Family	$$	Yes		L/B/D	Major
1	Country Mill Restaurant	Family	$$	Yes	Yes	L/D/B	Major
1	Dori Lou's Restaurant	Family	$$	Yes		B/L/D	Major
1	Home Town Buffet	Family	$$			L/D	Major
1	Pammy Jo's Java Coffee	Coffee Drive Thru				B/L	
1	Sandwich Bar	Sandwiches	$	Yes		L	
1	Mountain View Sub Shop	Sandwiches	$$	Yes		L/D	
1	Old House Restaurant	Homestyle	$$	Yes		L	Major
1	Great American Deli	Deli	$$	No		L/D	Major
1	Blimpie's Subs & Salads	Sandwiches	$	Yes		D/L	Major
1	Crazy Buffalo Steakhouse	Steakhouse	$$$	Yes	Yes	L/D	Major
1	El Jarro	Mexican	$$	Yes	B	L/D	M/V
1	Hamburger Stand/Tasty Freeze/Wienerschnitzel	Fast Food	$	Yes		L/D/B	M/V
2	La Costa Mexican Restaurant	Mexican	$$	Yes	B	L/D	M/V
2	Cookery/Pepperoni's	Family	$$	No		L/D/B	Major
2	Hot Dog on a Stick	Fast Food	$			L/D	
2	1 Potato 2	Fast Food	$	Yes		L/D	
2	Java Jitters Espresso	Coffee	$			L/D	
2	Flaming Wok	Chinese	$$	Yes		L/D	M/V
2	Pretzelmaker	Pretzels	$			L/D	
2	Pic-a-Piece Pizza	Pizza	$			L/D	
2	Mrs. Fields Cookies	Bakery	$			L/D	
2	Taco Bell	Fast Food	$	Yes		L/D	
2	Taco John's	Fast Food	$	Yes		L/D	
2	Mongolian Grill	Mongolian	$	Yes		L/D	M/V
2	Domino's Pizza	Pizza	$$$/$$	No	Yes	D/L	Major
2	Wendy's	Fast Food	$	Yes		D/L	Major
2	Pizza Hut	Pizza	$$	Yes	B	L/D	Major
2	Red Lobster	Seafood	$$$	Yes	Yes	L/D	Major
3	Godfather's Pizza	Pizza	$$	Yes	B/W	D/L	Major
3	South Sea Chinese Restaurant	Chinese	$$	No	W/B	L/D	M/V
3	Subway	Sandwiches	$	Yes		L/D	M/V
4	**Johnny J's Diner**	Homestyle	$$			B/L/D	Major
4	Subway	Sandwiches	$	Yes		L/D	M/V
4	Red & White Café	Family	$$	Yes		L/B/D	Major
4	Ghost Town Restaurant	Family	$$	No		D/L/B	Major
4	Yellowstone Grill & Daylight Donuts	Family	$$	No	Yes	L/D/B	Major
4	Western Grill Restaurant	Family	$$	Yes		D/L/B	
4	Pizza Place	Pizza	$$	Yes		L/D	
4	Sherrie's Place	Family	$$	Yes		B/L	Major
4	Plow's Diner	Family	$$	Yes		L/D/B	
5	**The Wonder Bar**	American	$$/$$$	Yes	Yes	L/D	Major
5	**Campfire Café**	Homecooking	$$/$			L	Major
5	**PB's Fish Factory at Parkway Plaza**	Family	$$	Yes	Yes	L/D	Major
5	**Parkway Café**	Family	$$	Yes	Yes	L/D/B	Major
5	**Botticelli Ristorante Italiano**	Northern Italian	$$	No	Yes	L/D	Major
5	**Red's Bar-B-Que**	Bar-B-Que	$$	Yes	W/B	L/D	Major
5	**Jacquie's Garden Greek Café**	Delicatesssen	$/$$	Yes		B/L	Major
5	Daddy O's Chicago Grill	American/Italian	$$	Yes	B/W	L/D	Major
5	Sanford's Grub & Pub	Brew Pub	$$	Yes	Yes	D/L	Major
5	Don Jaun Mexican Restaurant	Mexican	$$	No	W/B	L/D	Major
5	Sandwich Bar	Sandwiches	$	Yes		L	
5	Barry's Italian Restaurant	Italian	$$$	No	Yes	D/L	Major
5	Cattleman's Supper Club	Steakhouse	$$$	No	Yes	D	Major
5	Delices De France	Family	$$	No	Yes	L/D/B	Major
5	Fajita Cantina	Mexican	$$	Yes		L/D	
5	First Street Bakery	Bakery	$$	Yes		L/B	Major
5	Eagle Bowl & Café	American					
5	Golden Dragon	Chinese	$$	Yes		L/D	M/V

Dining Quick Reference-Continued

Price Range refers to the average cost of a meal per person: ($) $1-$6, ($$) $7-$11, ($$$) $12-up. Cocktails: "Yes" indicates full bar; Beer (B)/Wine (W), Service: Breakfast (B), Brunch (BR), Lunch (L), Dinner (D). Businesses in bold print will have additional information under the appropriate map locator number in the body of this section.

MAP#	RESTAURANT	TYPE CUISINE	PRICE RANGE	CHILD MENU	COCKTAILS BEER WINE	MEALS SERVED	CREDIT CARDS ACCEPTED
5	Cheese Barrel	Vegetarian	$$	Yes		B/L	M/V
5	Cottage Café	Family	$$			L/D	Major
6	**La Cocina:Best Mexican Food Under The Sun**	Mexican	$$		B	L/D	Major
6	**Radisson Hotel**	Family	$$	Yes	Yes	B/L/D	Major
6	Metro Coffee Company	Coffee/bakery	$	Yes		L/D	M/V
6	Drakes	Family	$$	Yes	Yes	L/D/B	Major
6	Subway	Sandwiches	$			L/D	M/V
6	JB's Restaurant	Family	$$	Yes		B/L/D	Major
6	Dairy Queen	Fast Food	$	Yes		L/D	Major
6	Casper's Good Cooking	Family	$$	0No		B/L/D	Major
6	Sidelines Sports Bar & Grill	American	$$	No	Yes	L/D	Major
6	TCBY	Fast Food	$			L/D	
6	Hardee's	Fast Food	$	Yes		B/L/D	
6	Poor Boy's Steakhouse	Family	$$		Yes	L/D	Major
7	**Peaches' Family Restaurants**	Fast Food	$	Yes		L/D	
7	Sunrise Coffee	Coffee Drive Thru	$			L/B	
8	Elkhorn Canyon Café	Family	$$	Yes		L/D	
8	Sedars Colonial Restaurant	Fine Dining	$$$	No	Yes	D	Major
8	TCBY	Fast Food	$	No		L/D	Major
8	Village Inn	Family	$$	Yes		L/D/B	Major
8	Pizza Hut	Pizza	$$	Yes	B	L/D	Major
9	Quizno's	Sandwiches	$	Yes		L/D	
9	Guadalajara	Mexican	$$		Yes	L/D	Major
9	Adam's Rib & Steakhouse	Steakhouse	$$$	No	Yes	D/L	Major
9	New Moon Café	Chinese	$$			L/D	Major
9	Subway	Sandwiches	$	Yes		L/D	Major/M/V
9	Moxie Java			No			
9	Taco Bell	Fast Food	$	Yes		L/D	
9	Wings & Things	Fast Food	$	Yes		L/D	Major
9	Don's Fireside Restaurant & Lounge	Steakhouse	$$$		Yes	D	Major
9	Quizno's	Sandwiches	$	Yes		L/D	Major
10	Armor's Silver Fox Lounge	Steak/Seafood	$$$		Yes	D/L	Major
10	West Side Café	American	$$	Yes		B/L/D	Major
10	Goose Egg Inn	Steakhouse	$$$	No	Yes	D	Major
10	Westside Café	Family	$$	Yes		B/L/D	V/M/D
10	Pizza Hut	Pizza	$$	Yes	B	L/D	Major
12	Chatters Bar & Grill	American	$$		Yes	L/D	Major
13	Peaches' Family Restaurants	Fast Food	$	Yes		L/D	
13	Taco John's	Fast Food	$	Yes		L/D	
13	Buzy B'Z	Family	$$	Yes		L/B	
13	Fort Java Outpost	Coffee House	$	No		L/B	
13	Subway	Sandwiches	$	Yes		L/D	M/V
13	TCBY	Fast Food	$	Yes		L/D	Major
13	Bid's Place	Sandwiches	$$	Yes		L/D	Major
13	Kopper Kettle Restaurant	Family	$$	Yes		L/D/B	Major
13	Herbo's	Family	$$/$	Yes		L/B	M/V
14	The Breadboard	Sandwiches	$			L/D	
16	Alcova Lakeside Marina & Restaurant	Family	$$$/$$	Yes	Yes	B/L/D	Major
16	Sunset Grill	Family	$$	Yes	Yes	B/L/D	Major
19	Peppermill Bar & Grill	American	$$			L/D	Major
19	Wendy's	Fast Food	$			B/L/D	
19	Taco Bell	Fast Food	$	Yes		L/D	
19	Subway	Sandwiches/	$	Yes		L/D	Major
19	Aspen House Restaurant	American	$$			B/L/D	
19	China Panda	Chinese	$$			L/D	
19	Rustlers Family Restaurant	Family	$$			B/L/D	Major
19	Taco John's	Fast Food	$	Yes		L/D	
20	Subway	Sandwiches	$	Yes			Major
20	JB's Big Boy Restaurant	Family	$	Yes		B/BR/L/D	Major
21	Cappy's Drive In Restaurant	Fast Food	$			L/D	
22	Pantry Restaurant	Family	$/$$			B/L/D	Major

Section 5

Dining Quick Reference-Continued

Price Range refers to the average cost of a meal per person: ($) $1-$6, ($$) $7-$11, ($$$) $12-up. Cocktails: "Yes" indicates full bar; Beer (B)/Wine (W), Service: Breakfast (B), Brunch (BR), Lunch (L), Dinner (D). Businesses in bold print will have additional information under the appropriate map locator number in the body of this section.

MAP#	RESTAURANT	TYPE CUISINE	PRICE RANGE	CHILD MENU	COCKTAILS BEER WINE	MEALS SERVED	CREDIT CARDS ACCEPTED
28	Old Corral Hotel	Steakhouse	$$/$$$	Yes	Yes	D/B	Major
28	Mountain View Historic Hotel	Family	$$	Yes		B/L	D/M/V
28	Albany Lodge Restaurant	Family	$$		Yes	L/D	Major
28	Three Horned Rhino	Family	$$/$$$	Yes	Yes	B/L/D	Major
28	Beartree Tavern & Café	Family	$$	No	Yes	L/D/BR	V/M
28	Friendly Store Café	Family	$	Yes	Yes	L/D/B	Major
29	Airport Café	Family	$$	Yes		L/D/B	Major
29	Oriental Palace Chinese Restaurant	Chinese	$$	Yes		L/D	M/V
29	Perrett's	Pizza	$$	Yes	B/W	L/D	M/V
29	QT's Restaurant	Family	$$	Yes		L/D/B	Major
29	Country Cove Restaurant	Family	$$			L/B	Major
29	Bear Trap Cafe & Bar	American	$/$$	Yes	Yes	L/D/B	M/V
29	Pine Lodge Bar	Bistro	$	No	Yes		Major
29	Sugar Bowl	Family	$	No			
29	Grand & Sierra Bed and Breakfast Lodge	Family	$$/$$$			B	Major
29	Bear Trap Bar, Cafe, & Cabins	Family	$$		Yes	D/L/B	Major
30	Wolf Hotel Restaurant & Lounge	Steakhouse	$$	Yes		L/D/B	Major
30	Mom's Kitchen	Family	$/$$	Yes		B/L/D	
30	Bubba's Bar-B-Que Restaurant	Barbeque	$$	Yes		L/D	Major
30	Lollypops	Ice Cream	$				
30	Lazy River Cantina & Lounge	Fine Dining	$/$$		Yes	L/D	V/M
30	Donut Ranch Bakery	Bakery & Desserts	$			B/L	
30	Corral Restaurant	Family	$/$$	No		B/L/D	M/V
30	Wilder Stumpy's Eatery	American	$/$$	No		L/D	Major
30	Saratoga Inn, Hot Springs & Golf Resort	Fine Dining	$$$		Yes	L/D	Major
31	Dip Bar & Diner	Family	$$	No	Yes	L/D	
33	Hell's Half Acre	Family	$$	Yes	Yes	B/L/D	Major
33	Sanford's Tumble Inn	Family	$$	Yes	Yes	L/D	Major
35	Steelman's Brite Spot	Tavern	$		Yes	L/D	
36	Hot Stuff Pizza	Pizza	$	No		L/D	
36	Wrangler Cafe	Family	$/$$	Yes		B/L/D	Major
37	**Sundowner Station Restaurant & Lounge**	Family	$$	Yes	Yes	L/D	Major
37	Burger King	Fast Food	$	Yes		D/L/B	M/V
37	China Panda	Chinese	$$	Yes		D/L	Major
37	Dairy Queen	Fast Food	$	Yes		D/L	
37	El Durango	Mexican	$$		B/W		Major
37	Golden Corral Family Restaurant	Family	$$	Yes		L/D	Major
37	Kentucky Fried Chicken	Chicken	$	Yes		L/D	Major
37	Pizza Hut	Pizza	$$	Yes	B	L/D	Major
37	Taco Bell	Fast Food	$	Yes		L/D	
37	Trailhead Family Restaurant	Family	$$	Yes		D/L/B	Major
37	Wendy's	Fast Food	$	Yes		D/L	Major
37	Pony Expresso	Coffee Shop	$			L/B	
37	JB's Restaurant	American	$$	Yes		L/D/B	Major
38	Arby's	Fast Food	$	Yes		D/L/B	Major
38	Bull Steakhouse	Steak/Seafood	$$$		Yes	L/D	Major
38	Domino's Pizza	Pizza	$$	Yes		D/L	Major
38	McDonald's	Fast Food	$	Yes		L/D/B	
38	Subway	Sandwiches	$	Yes		L/D/B	Major/M/V
38	Taco John's	Fast Food	$	Yes		L/D	
38	Broker Restaurant	Steak/Seafood	$$$		Yes	D/L	Major
38	Daylight Donuts	Coffee Shop	$	No		L/B	
38	The Depot	Mexican	$$$		Yes	L/D	Major
38	Good Time Charlie's	Bar & Grill	$$	Yes	Yes	L/D	Major
39	La Cantina Restaurant	Mexican/American	$$	Yes	Yes	L/D	Major
42	Club El Toro	Steakhouse	$$$	Yes	Yes	D	
42	Svilar's Dining Room	Fine Dining	$$$	No	Yes	L/D	
42	El Toro	Fine Dining	$$$	No	Yes	D	
43	**Pronghorn Lodge and Oxbow Restaurant**	American	$$	Yes	Yes	B/L/D	Major
43	**Tony's Pizza**	Pizza/Italian	$$		W/B	L/D	Major

Dining Quick Reference-Continued

Price Range refers to the average cost of a meal per person: ($) $1-$6, ($$) $7-$11, ($$$) $12-up. Cocktails: "Yes" indicates full bar; Beer (B)/Wine (W), Service: Breakfast (B), Brunch (BR), Lunch (L), Dinner (D). Businesses in bold print will have additional information under the appropriate map locator number in the body of this section.

MAP#	RESTAURANT	TYPE CUISINE	PRICE RANGE	CHILD MENU	COCKTAILS BEER WINE	MEALS SERVED	CREDIT CARDS ACCEPTED
43	**Maverick Motel, Restaurant & Lounge**	Western Steakhouse	$$/$$$		Yes	B/L/D	Major
43	Arctic Circle	Fast Food	$	Yes		L/D	Major
43	Wildflower Bakery & Espresso	Bakery	$$			B/L/D	
43	Subway	Sandwiches	$			L/D	Major
43	Silver Spur BBQ & Deli	BBQ	$$			L/B	
43	Showboat Diner	Steaks/American	$$	Yes		L/D/B	
43	Pizza Hut	Pizza	$$	Yes	B	L/D	Major
43	Judd's Grub	Burgers	$	Yes		L/D	
43	Hitching Rack	Fine Food	$$$	No	Yes	D	Major
43	El Sol Mexico	Mexican	$$	No	B	D/L	Major
43	Domino's Pizza	Pizza	$$	No		D/L	Major
43	Cowfish	Steak/Seafood	$/$$$	Yes	Yes	D/L	Major
43	China Garden	Chinese	$$	No		D/L	M/V
43	Big Noi Family Restaurant	Thai	$$	No		D/L/B	
43	Breadboard	Soup/Sandwich	$	No		D/L	
43	The Magpie	Family	$$/$	Yes		B/L	
43	The Oxbow	Family	$$	Yes		B/L/D	Major
43	Ray Lake Campground & Café	Family	$$	Yes		D/BR/B	
43	JB's Wild Wyoming	Barbeque	$$	Yes		L/D	
43	Dairy Land Drive In	Fast Food	$	No		D/L	
43	Mom's Malt Shop	Ice Cream	$				
43	Taco Bell	Fast Food	$	Yes		L/D	
45	High Plains Bar & Café	Family	$$	Yes	Yes	B/L/D	
46	Flying J-The Cookery	American	$	No			Major
48	Broadway Cafe	Family	$	Yes		B/L/D	Major
54	Point of Rocks Café	Family	$$		Yes	B/L/D	M/V
55	Canyon Bar	Tavern	$		Yes		
58	Atlantic City Mercantile	Steak/Family	$$$	Yes	Yes	L/D	Major
60	Wagon Wheel Cafe	Family	$	No		B/L/D	V/M

NOTES:

Motel Quick Reference

Price Range: ($) Under $40 ; ($$) $40-$60; ($$$) $60-$80, ($$$$) Over $80. Pets [check with the motel for specific policies] (P), Dining (D), Lounge (L), Disabled Access (DA), Full Breakfast (FB), Cont. Breakfast (CB), Indoor Pool (IP), Outdoor Pool (OP), Hot Tub (HT), Sauna (S), Refrigerator (R), Microwave (M) (Microwave and Refrigerator indicated only if in majority of rooms), Kitchenette (K). All Wyoming area codes are 307.

MAP #	HOTEL	PHONE	NUMBER ROOMS	PRICE RANGE	BREAKFAST	POOL/ HOT TUB SAUNA	NON SMOKE ROOMS	OTHER AMENITIES	CREDIT CARDS
1	**Shilo Inn**	237-1335	101	$$/$$$	CB	IP/HT	Yes	P	Major
1	Comfort Inn	235-3038	56	$$$	CB	IP/HT	Yes	P/DA	Major
3	**Hearthside, Extended Stay Studios**	232-5100	66	$$			Yes	P/D/R/M/K	Major
4	Topper Bob's Motel	237-8407	20	$$			Yes	P/K/M/R	M/V
4	Yellowstone Motel	234-9174	17	$			Yes	P/R/M/K	Major
4	Virginian Motel	266-3959	18	$$			Yes	P/DA/K	D/M/V
4	Sage & Sand Motel	237-2088	31	$		OP	Yes	P/K	Major
4	Colonial House Motel	577-1263	20	$$	CB	OP	Yes	P/K/M/R	Major
4	Bel Air Motel	472-1930	10	$			Yes	K	M/V
5	**Parkway Plaza Hotel & Convention Center**	235-1777	300	$$$		IP	Yes	P/K/DA	Major
6	**Radisson Hotel**	266-6000	229			IP/HT	Yes	P/D/L/DA	Major
6	**Holiday Inn**	235-2531	200	$$$$		IP/HT/S	Yes	D/L/P	Major
6	**National 9 Inn**	235-2711	47	$$	CB		Yes	P	Major
6	**Quality Inn & Suites**	266-2400	92	$$$	CB		Yes	P/DA	Major
6	Motel 6	234-3903	111	$$		OP	Yes	P/K	Major
7	Ivy House Inn	265-0974	31	$		OP	Yes	P/K	Major
8	Red Arrow Motel	234-5293	10	$			No	P/M/R	Major
9	CY Motel Complex	473-2202	9	$	CB		Yes	P/DA/M/R	M/V
9	Westridge Motel	234-8911	28	$$	CB		Yes	P	Major
10	Super 8 - Casper	266-3480	66	$$	CB		Yes		Major
10	All American Inn	235-6688	38	$		OP	Yes	P/M/R	Major
10	Royal Inn	234-3501	36	$		OP	Yes	P/DA/K	Major
11	Ranch House Motel	266-4044	12	$			Yes	P	Major
19	Days Inn	324-6615	118	$$		HT/IP	Yes	P/D/L/DA	Major
19	Lodge at Rawlins	324-2783	132	$$		IP	Yes	P/D/L	Major
19	Key Motel	324-2728		$			No		
19	1st Choice Inn	328-1401	50	$				P	V/M
19	Sleep Inn	328-1732	81	$/$$			Yes	P	Major
21	Super 8 Motel	328-0630	47	$$/$			Yes		Major
21	Best Western Cottontree Inn	324-2737	122	$$		HT/IP/S	Yes	L/D/P/DA	Major
21	Motel 7	324-2263	32	$			No	P/D	Major
21	Budget Inn	328-1600	62	$	CB		Yes	P/R/M	Major
21	Bucking Horse Lodge	324-3471	42	$/$$	CB		Yes	P/R/M/K	Major
21	Ideal Motel	324-3451	59	$			Yes	P/R/M	D/V/M/Major
21	Best Motel	324-3456	26	$			Yes	P/R/M	Major
22	Rawlins Motel	324-3456	24	$$			Yes	P	Major
26	Elk Mountain Hotel	348-7774	12	$$/$$$	CB		Yes	D/DA/R	Major
28	Old Corral Hotel	745-5918	16	$$$	FB		Yes	L/P/D	
28	Mountain View Historic Hotel	742-5476	6	$$$			Yes	P/K/D	Major
28	Friendly Motel	742-6033	8	$$			No	L/DA/P	Major
29	El Rancho	856-7455	24	$$			Yes	P	M/V
29	Vacher's Bighorn Lodge	327-5110	13	$$$				P/K	Major
29	Riverside Garage & Cabins	327-5361	9	$$			Yes	P/K	Major
30	Wolf Hotel	326-5525	9	$$			Yes	L/D	Major
30	Hacienda Motel	326-5751	32	$$				P/K	V/M/D
30	Sage & Sand Motel	326-8333	18	$			No	P	
30	Riviera Lodge	326-5651	30	$/$$			Yes	P	Major
30	Silver Moon Motel	326-5974	14	$$$			Yes	P/K	Major
31	Trampas Lodge	379-2280	18	$				P/R	M/V
31	Golden Rule Motel	325-6525	21	$$			Yes	P	Major
33	Hell's Half Acre	473-7773	11	$$			Yes	P/DA/L/D	Major
33	Motel 20/26	234-7205	3	$$			Yes	K/P/R/M	V/M
36	**Desert Inn Motel**	876-2373	52	$				P/K/R	
36	Shoshoni Motel	876-2216	12	$				P	M/V
37	**Sundowner Station–Motel**	856-6503	61	$$		S	Yes	P/D/L	Major
37	**Hi Lo Motel**	856-9223	23	$$			Yes	P/R/M/K	Major
37	**Super 8 Motel - Riverton**	857-2400	32	$$	CB		Yes	P/DA	Major
37	**Thunderbird Motel**	856-9201	45	$			Yes	P/L	Major
37	**Holiday Inn Riverton**	856-8100	123			IP	Yes	D/L/P/DA	Major
37	Jackpine Motel	856-9251	19	$$			Yes		Major

Motel Quick Reference-Continued

Price Range: ($) Under $40 ; ($$) $40-$60; ($$$) $60-$80, ($$$$) Over $80. Pets [check with the motel for specific policies] (P), Dining (D), Lounge (L), Disabled Access (DA), Full Breakfast (FB), Cont. Breakfast (CB), Indoor Pool (IP), Outdoor Pool (OP), Hot Tub (HT), Sauna (S), Refrigerator (R), Microwave (M) (Microwave and Refrigerator indicated only if in majority of rooms), Kitchenette (K). All Wyoming area codes are 307.

MAP #	HOTEL	PHONE	NUMBER ROOMS	PRICE RANGE	BREAKFAST	POOL/ HOT TUB SAUNA	NON SMOKE ROOMS	OTHER AMENITIES	CREDIT CARDS
37	Paintbrush Motel	856-9238	23	$$			Yes	P/K	Major
37	Roomers Motel	857-1735	16	$$			Yes	P/DA	Major
37	Inn El Rancho/	856-7455	23	$$			Yes	P/K	Major
38	Days Inn	856-9677	33	$$			Yes	P	Major
38	Driftwood Inn	856-4811	28	$$			Yes	P	Major
38	Tomahawk Motor Lodge	856-9205	32	$$			Yes	P/DA/K	Major
38	Mountain View Motel	856-2418	20	$			Yes	P/K	M/V
43	**Pronghorn Lodge**	332-3940	56	$$$/$$	CB	HT	Yes	K/M/R/DA/P/D	Major
43	**Maverick Motel, Restaurant & Lounge**	332-2300	31	$$	FB			P/D/L/K	Major
43	**The Holiday Lodge National 9 Inn**	332-2511	40	$$	CB	HT	Yes	P/K	Major
43	Western Motel	332-4270	13	$				K	M/V
43	Rock Shop Inn	332-7396-1	8	$$				D/L/P	Major
43	Silver Spur Motel	332-5189-1	25	$$		OP	Yes	P	Major
43	Downtown Motel	332-3171	16	$					Major
43	Best Western Inn at Lander	332-2847	100	$$$	CB	OP/HT	Yes	K/DA/P	Major
43	Teton Motel	332-3582	16	$$		OP	Yes	P/K	M/V
43	Horseshoe Motel	332-4915	15	$$			Yes	K/D/L	Major
45	JC Motel	544-9317	18	$				P	
48	Sagebrush Motel	328-1584	8	$			No	P	V/M
60	Country Inn Motel	383-6448	11	$$			No	P/R/M/K	V/M
60	Drifters Inn	383-2015	41	$/$$			Yes	P/D/L/R/M	Major

Notes:

NOTES:

SECTION 6

SOUTHEAST AREA

INCLUDING CHEYENNE, LARAMIE AND DOUGLAS

State Capitol Building

1 *No services*

Redbird

The owner of the store out of which the post office ran here was named Red Bird.

2 *No services*

Lance Creek

Native Americans used the wood from ash trees that grew along the creek here for arrows and spears, or "lances", as the early European explorers called them. Thus the name. The town of the same name grew up around the oil industry. This is also one of the first places dinosaur bones were unearthed in Wyoming, in the 1880s, although there is nothing to commemorate the finds at present.

3 *No services*

T Fort Hat Creek Stage Station

U.S. Highway 85, 13.5 miles north of Lusk

The Fort Hat Creek Stage Station is 15 miles northeast of Lusk off US Highway 18-85, near the border from Nebraska, on the banks of Sage Creek. The fort also known as Camp Hat Creek, was built by the Army in 1875, under the leadership of Captain James Egin on the banks of Sage Creek. The group thought they were at Hat Creek, Nebraska, hence the name. First established as a sub-post of Fort Laramie, its purpose was to secure communications to the Black Hills. The first mission was to discourage settlers and prospectors from sneaking illegally into the Black Hills. Custer found gold there in 1874 and a rush was on, in spite of Fort Hat Creek. After the resulting Indian troubles had been settled in the white man's favor, the fort became a stage stop on the Cheyenne to Deadwood Stage Route and then became known as Hat Creek Station. The general store/roadhouse built in the 1880s, after the original building burned, still stands, and the entire station is in the process of being restored. The site is located about 15 miles northeast of Lusk off US Highway 18-85.

Fort Hat Creek Stage Station

H Fort Hat Creek

About 14 miles north of Lusk on U.S. Highway 18/85

In 1875 soldiers went from Fort Laramie to establish an outpost on Hat Creek in Nebraska.

Confused, they bilt a fort of logs on Sage Creek in Wyoming. The gold rush to the Black Hills started the Cheyenne-Deadwood Stage Route in 1876.

Bullwhackers freighting salt pork and whiskey to Deadwood, armored coaches hauling gold bricks and passengers to Cheyenne, Indians, and road agents brought adventure to Hat Creek Stage station. A two story log structure was built near the fort for a telegraph station, post office, blacksmith shop, hotel and store.

This building, still standing and used as a ranch home, is two miles east and one mile south.

Source: Wyoming Recreation Commission.

4 *Gas, Food, Lodging*

Lusk

Pop. 1,447, Elev. 5,015

As the county seat of the least populous county in Wyoming, Lusk contains over half of the people living in Niobrara County. Each person in the county is matched by 524 acres of land. The oil industry once created a boom and bust cycle around here, but the town has returned to its agricultural roots to thrive. The economy has also been boosted by an influx of retail, service, and governmental employers.

Named for Frank Lusk, an early rancher who donated land for the town to be established, Lusk was once a stop on the Cheyenne Deadwood Stage Line. It is also close to the Texas Trail, a route commonly used by cattle ranchers moving stock from Texas to Wyoming, Montana, and the Dakotas to take advantage of the open range. Ranching continues to be one of the area's primary economic bases, as well as oil production and dry farming.

Node

Originally a post office and store named for a cattle brand.

Van Tassell

Schuyler Van Tassell, a major rancher in the area,

Lusk	Jan	Feb	March	April	May	June	July	Aug	Sep	Oct	Nov	Dec	Annual
Average Max. Temperature (F)	35.4	39.6	45.9	56.5	66.4	77.3	85.9	84.6	74.8	61.7	46.3	37.6	59.3
Average Min. Temperature (F)	11.0	15.1	20.0	28.8	38.3	47.3	53.3	51.2	41.2	31.1	20.9	13.5	31.0
Average Total Precipitation (in.)	0.51	0.54	0.96	2.11	2.78	2.50	1.74	1.07	1.21	1.03	0.63	0.55	15.63
Average Total SnowFall (in.)	7.3	7.1	9.7	8.9	1.9	0.2	0.0	0.0	0.5	2.6	6.2	7.5	51.8
Average Snow Depth (in.)	2	2	1	0	0	0	0	0	0	0	1	2	1

Section 6

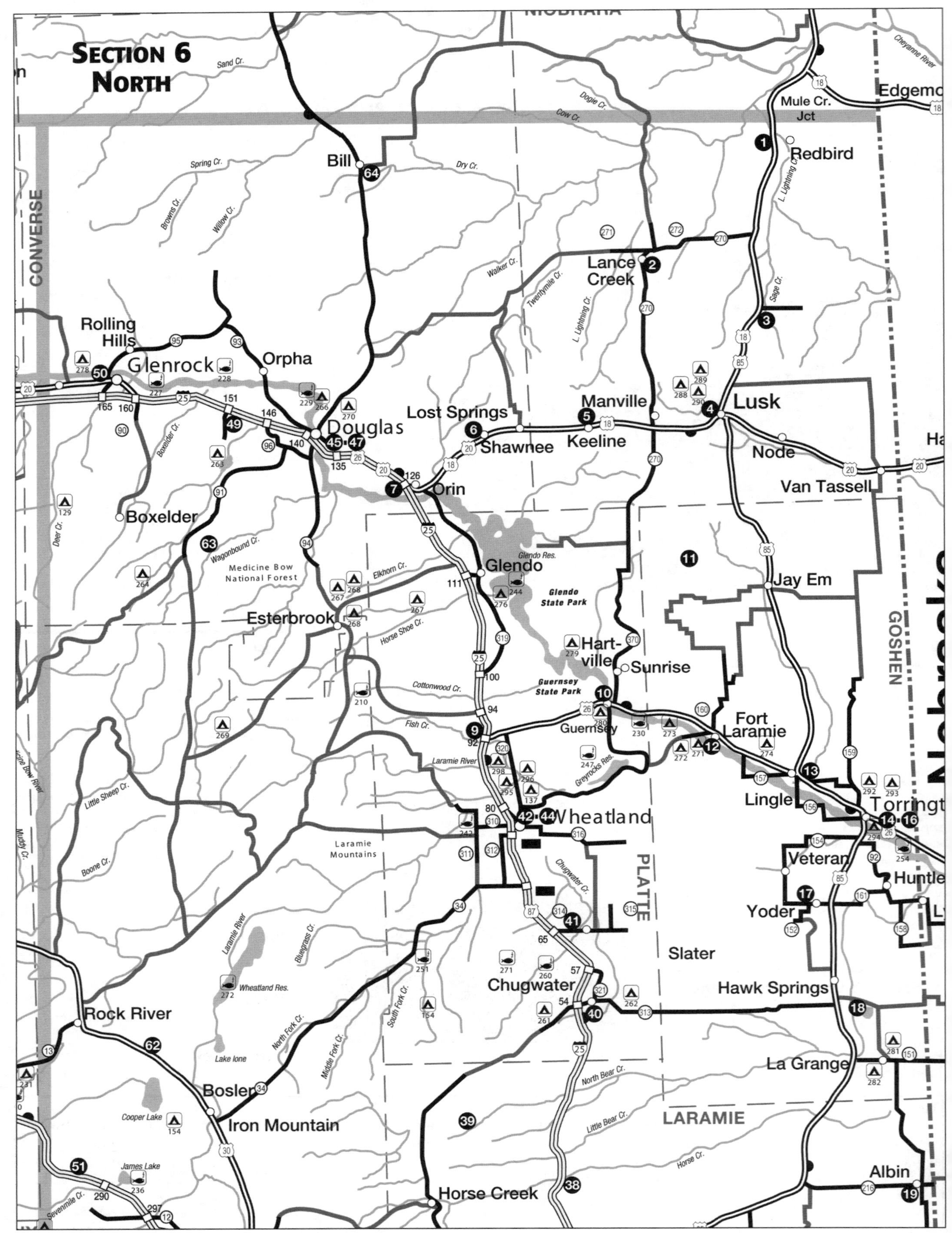
SECTION 6 NORTH
CONVERSE
PLATTE
GOSHEN
LARAMIE
Bill
Rolling Hills
Glenrock
Orpha
Douglas
Lost Springs
Shawnee
Manville
Keeline
Lance Creek
Mule Cr. Jct
Redbird
Edgemont
Lusk
Node
Van Tassell
Orin
Glendo
Glendo State Park
Boxelder
Medicine Bow National Forest
Esterbrook
Jay Em
Hartville
Sunrise
Guernsey State Park
Guernsey
Fort Laramie
Lingle
Torrington
Wheatland
Laramie Mountains
Veteran
Huntley
Yoder
Slater
Chugwater
Hawk Springs
Rock River
La Grange
Bosler
Iron Mountain
Albin
Horse Creek
Wheatland Res.
Lake Ione
Cooper Lake
James Lake
Glendo Res.
Greyrocks Res.
Spring Cr.
Sand Cr.
Dogie Cr.
Cow Cr.
Dry Cr.
Browns Cr.
Willow Cr.
Walker Cr.
Twentymile Cr.
L. Lightning Cr.
Sage Cr.
Cheyenne River
Boxelder Cr.
Deer Cr.
Wagonbound Cr.
Elkhorn Cr.
Horse Shoe Cr.
Cottonwood Cr.
Fish Cr.
Laramie River
Little Sheep Cr.
Boone Cr.
Chugwater Cr.
Bluegrass Cr.
North Fork Cr.
Middle Fork Cr.
South Fork Cr.
North Bear Cr.
Little Bear Cr.
Horse Cr.
Sevenmile Cr.
Muddy Cr.

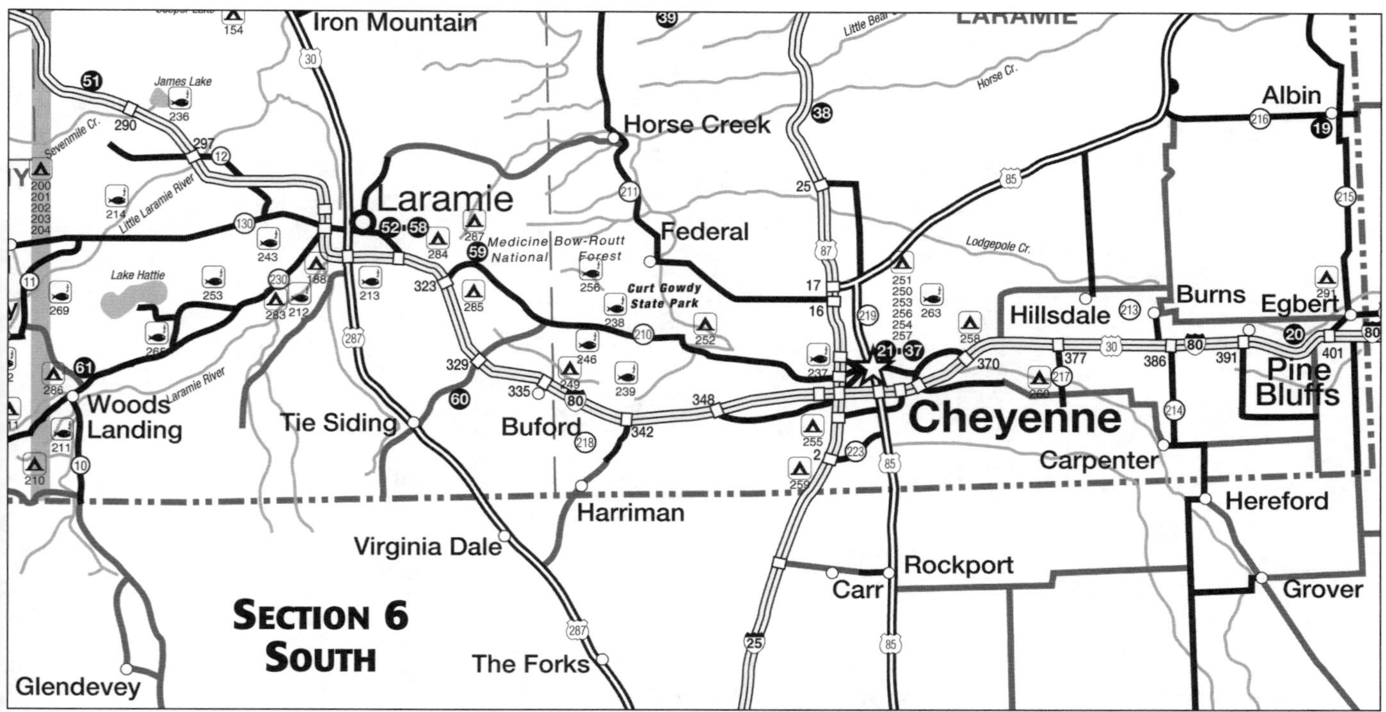

0 Miles 15 27
One inch = approximately 10 miles

Legend

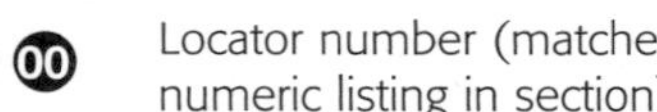
Locator number (matches numeric listing in section)

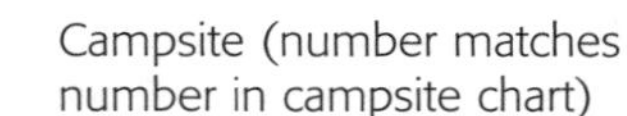
Campsite (number matches number in campsite chart)

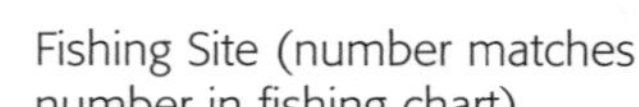
Fishing Site (number matches number in fishing chart)

Rest stop

Interstate

U.S. Highway

Paved State or County Road

Gravel/unpaved road

objected to having a railroad station named after him. He persisted in utilizing Cheyenne for shipping purposes, ignoring the much closer stop. Ferdinand Branstetter, the first US soldier to die in the trenches in World War I, was from Van Tassell. The American Legion opened its first post here in 1919, naming it after Branstetter. The Ferdinand Branstetter Post Number One is on the National Register of Historic Places.

T Niobrara Chamber of Commerce

119 W. 3rd in Lusk. 334-2950
or 800-223-LUSK(5875).
www.luskwyoming.com

T Stagecoach Museum

In Lusk

Highlighting this museum is a Cheyenne/Black Hills Stage Line stagecoach built in 1863 by Abbott & Downing of Concord, New Hampshire. In addition to the old buggies, wagons and Indian artifacts are a some museum oddities, too: a two-head calf, a bedpan collection, and a Barbie doll dressed like Barbara Bush.

T Legend of Rawhide

In Lusk

This is an annual celebration of the history, legend and wester heritage of Niobrara County. More than 400 volunteers contribute to make this production possible. Events include a dance, auction, golf tournament, rodeo, barbecues, a pancake breakfast, art show, history presentations, and a parade. The pageant festivities are held on the second weekend in July every year. This event attracts a lively crowd to Lusk, so lodging reservations are encouraged.

H Cheyenne-Deadwood Trail

Just west of Lusk on Hwy. 18 at Rest Stop

Here you stand on the Cheyenne-Deadwood Trail over which freight wagons and stagecoaches traveled between Cheyenne and the Black Hills gold mining area from 1876 to 1887. One of these stages may be seen in the Lusk Museum. The nearby monument is at the grave of George Lathrop, pioneer stage driver. South you can see Rawhide Buttes, west of which was located the home station of the Cheyenne and Black Hills Stage Lines. One and a half miles northeast was Running Water or Silver Cliff's stage station, forerunner of Lusk. Last straggler of the great Buffalo herds in this area was killed nearby in recent years.

H George Lathrop Monument

West of Lusk on U.S. Highway 18 at Rest Stop on the south side of U. S. Hwy 18/20. About 1.7 miles west of the junction of U. S. Hwys 20/85 and 18/20. Adjacent to Cheyenne-Deadwood Trail informative Sign (Niobrara County #2).

In Memory of George Lathrop

Pioneer of the West, Indian fighter, veteran stage driver. Born at Pottsville, Pa., December 24, 1830. Died at Willow, Wyoming, Dec. 24, 1915. Buried here. A good man whose life was filled with stirring events.

Marking the Cheyenne and Black Hills Trail.

This marker is erected on the old Cheyenne and Black Hills Stage Road, in memory of the operators of the line and the pioneers who trav-

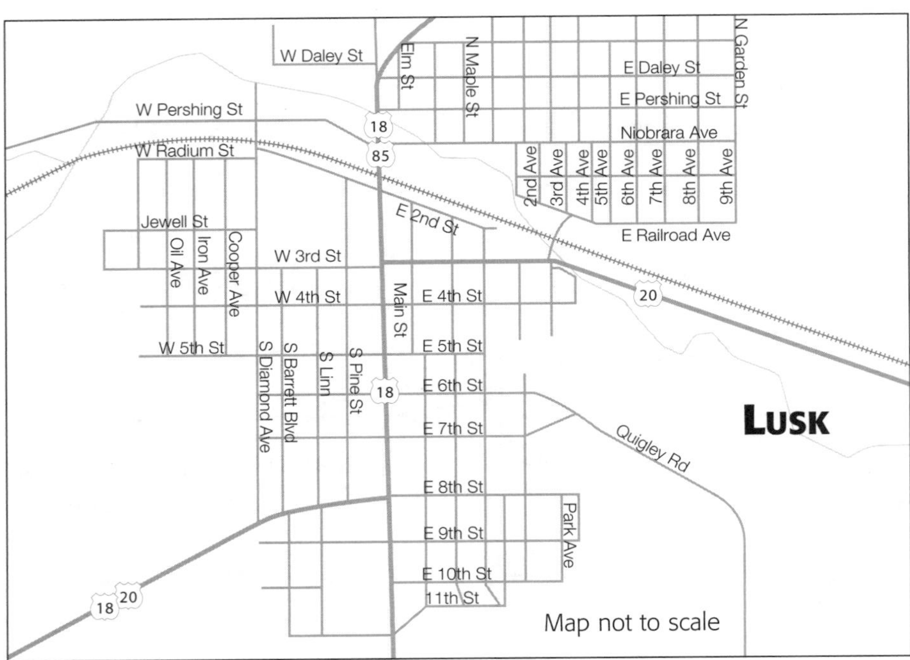

eled it. Operators of the stage line: Luke Voorhees, Russell Thorp. Sr.

H Redwood Water Tank

North side of U.S. Highway 20 just east of Lusk

The redwood water tank was built to furnish water for the Fremont, Elkhorn and Missouri Valley Railroad steam engines. This line, which was part of the northwestern line, and later became the Chicago Northwestern Railroad, came to Lusk on July 13, 1886.

The original site was several hundred feet to the west of the present location. Water was furnished from a well by a windmill. Later, it came from a hand-dug well by hand and steam power. The tank is one of six left standing in the U.S.

The historical society has been working to preserve the tank since 1971. We had assistance from Chicago Northwestern Railroad, Town of Lusk, and numerous other contributions.

H Breaks in the Prairie

Just west of Lusk on U.S Highway 18 at rest stop

Rawhide Buttes in front of you is an island habitat within the shortgrass prairie. Because the Buttes contain forest habitat, they support different species of wildlife than the surrounding prairie.

Elk, deer, turkeys, bobcats and mountain lions are found on the buttes. Historically, elk were native to this area but were killed off as food when the area was settled. In the 1960s, the Game and Fish Department transplanted elk to reestablish the herd. The elk continue to thrive in their native environment.

Both mule deer and white-tailed deer are found in this area. Mule deer were not found here until the 1920s; and white-tailed deer appeared in the 1950s. Changes in the area due to agricultural development provided additional water sources, forage and predator control for wildlife.

Mountain lions, also called cougars, pumas or panthers, can be found in various habitats throughout Wyoming. The key to the presence of mountain lions is the existence of deer or elk. Mountain lions may kill sick or injured animals, thus improving the overall health of elk and deer herds.

H American Legion - Ferdinand Branstetter Post No. 1

U.S. Highway 20 at west end of Van Tassell

The American Legion, founded at Paris, France in 1919 holds a long and enviable record of service to the nation and to the veterans of the nation's wars.

Covering those formative years of rapid growth, Legion records are not always exact, but it is determinable that Van Tassell, Wyoming was among the first four posts organized within the nation, their charters all signed on the same day.

Named for Ferdinand Branstetter, resident of Van Tassell community and among the first to cross broad seas and fall on the field of honor, Post No. 1 has led the role of chartered posts throughout the history of the Legion's Wyoming department. It has led that role honorably in service to community, state and nation.

H Mother Featherlegs Shepherd

Turn south and go 10 miles on dirt road about 1.7 miles west of junction of U.S. Highway 20/85 and 18/20

Here lies Mother Featherlegs Shepherd

So called, as in her ruffled pantalettes she looked like a feather-legged chicken in a high wind. Was a roadhouse ma'am here on the Cheyenne-Black Hills Stage Line.

An outlaw confederate, she was murdered by "Dangerous Dick Davis, the Terrapin" in 1879 for a $1500 cache.

Dedicated May 17, 1964.

H Rawhide Buttes

About 10 miles south of Lusk to west of U.S. Highway 85

Rawhide Buttes, visible west of this point, once served as a favorite camping spot of Indians and fur trappers. Several different tales explain the origin of the name. One account holds that this locale served as a departure point from which trappers sent fur pelts, or "rawhides," east to St. Louis. Another story tells of a reckless young man who killed an Indian woman while journeying to California during the 1849 gold rush. Attempting to avoid trouble, his fellow travelers surrendered the man for punishment and then watched in horror as the Indians skinned him alive at the base of the buttes—thus the name "Rawhide Buttes."

In 1874, a military expedition led by Lieutenant Col. George A. Custer discovered gold in the Black Hills of Dakota Territory. Hoping to capitalize on the ensuing rush of prospectors, the entrepreneurial team of John Gilmer, Monroe Salisbury and Mathewson Patrick organized the Cheyenne and Black Hills Stage and Express line in 1876. The company soon began leasing ranch buildings located at Rawhide Buttes for use as a stage station. When Russell Thorp, Sr. purchased the Rawhide Buttes station in November 1882, the bustling stage stop had grown to include a grocery and dry good store, stage barn, post office and blacksmith shop.

The arrival of the Chicago and North Western Railroad led the demise of stage coaching. The last Black Hills-bound stage departed from Cheyenne's Inter-ocean Hotel on February 19, 1887. With the stage no longer rolling, the buildings clustered at the base of Rawhide Buttes reverted from stage station to ranch headquarters. The end of an era had arrived.

H Spanish Diggings

West edge of Lusk

The greatest prehistoric workshop on the American Continent lies twelve and one half miles to the South. Covering an area thirty miles long and ten miles wide, it presents a panorama of hundreds of stone shops surrounded by huge piles of chippings left by generations of prehistoric arrow and spearhead makers.

Hundreds of specimens of perfect pottery have been removed from this site to Eastern Museums, many more probably remain for the searcher of today.

L Town House Motel

525 S. Main in Lusk. 334-2376
or 800-484-5782, ext. 8963.
www.lusktownhouse.com

The Town House Motel is conveniently located near downtown Lusk. This super friendly family owned and operated motel offers lovely cozy rooms with your total comfort in mind. They have been in the area for three generations and can tell you about all the great activities in the surrounding area. You'll feel right at home. Refrigerators and microwaves are available on request. Guests are treated to a complimentary continental breakfast from May through September. Be sure and ask about corporate, senior, and weekly rates. They do accept pets and provide ample parking for all sizes of vehicles. Visit them on the web for more information.

L Rawhide Motel

805 South Main in Lusk. 334-2440 or toll free at 888-679-2558.

M Denny & Associates, LLC

201 S. Main in Lusk. 334-4021 or 334-2372.
Email: ludenny@coffey.com

Denny & Associates is an outstanding company to see for real estate in Wyoming. Lee Denny has over 30 years experience in banking and real estate in Wyoming. He represents his clients' interests exclusively and offers the highest standards of professional and personalized service. Whether you are looking for a working ranch, recreational property or just a nice home, call Lee Denny at Denny & Associates and find your piece of heaven in Wyoming.

5 *Gas, Food*

Keeline

Elev. 5,377

George A. Keeline, the owner of the 4J Ranch, gave his name to this little community.

Manville

Pop. 197, Elev. 5,245

H.S. Manville, a founder of the Converse Cattle Company, gave his name to this little town. Manville may have the smallest post office building in Wyoming.

H Jireh

Five miles west of Manville on U.S. Highway 18; two miles east of Keeline, where U.S. Highway 18/20 intersects with the Jireh Road

The townsite of Jireh and the campus of the Jireh College, 1909-1920, lying to the northeast, marked the location of a pioneer Denominational Preparatory School and Junior College in Wyoming. Both townsite and campus were established during homesteading days to serve the residents of the Eastern Wyoming Area with the opportunity for an advanced education. Envisioned was not only a Christian College, but also a sympathetic Christian Community. Herein was engendered both the pioneering spirit of the early West and a missionary spirit of the dedicated. Jehovah-Jireh: Genesis XXII 14 "The Lord will provide."

6 *No services*

Lost Springs

Pop. 4, Elev. 4,996

Named for a disappearing stream nearby, this is the smallest incorporated town in the US with a post office.

Shawnee

Elev. 4,996

Shawnee is an unincorporated community named for the Indian tribe of the same name. The tribe migrated from Georgia and the name means "Southern".

7 *Gas, Food*

H Cottonwoods: Home Along the Prairie River

At Orin rest area

Take a good look at those big old trees down along the river. You know, the ones with the big limbs and huge trunks. Those old cottonwoods are special trees. They have grown tall with their roots spreading as grand as their limbs. Their roots reach down to the water level and help hold the riverbank soil, keeping it from washing away during heavy spring flows. Grass grows tall and lush where the cottonwoods hold the soil. Along these grassy riverbanks, wildlife flourishes.

A variety of birds nest and raise their young in the mighty old cottonwoods. Bald eagles nest in the strongest branches above the riffles where fish spawn. Old, dead limbs, where wood is soft, becomes home to woodpeckers, like the northern flicker. Other birds like finches and wrens live in the abandoned woodpecker holes. Other birds nest in the willows and buffaloberry bushes that grow beneath the cottonwoods. Look closely and you might see a yellow-billed cuckoo, brown thrasher, robin or several mourning doves. A Merriam's turkey

Mother Featherlegs

It's a ten mile unpaved journey from Lusk over 8-inch deep muddy furrows and ruts to find it. Here you'll see a pink granite slab paying tribute to Wyoming's most famous prostitute. The inscription is wearing down and there are no bawdy statuary or explicit images in relief on the stone.

Mother Featherlegs earned her name after the local cowboys observed her riding through town with tiers of lace ruffles on her pantaloons fluttering in the breeze as she straddled her horse. "Them ruffled drawers make the old gal look like a feather legged chicken." There weren't many ruffles in Wyoming at that time!

Forever after known as Mother Featherlegs, she arrived in Wyoming in 1876 and established a bawdyhouse on the Cheyenne-Black Hills trail. Her place also became a refuge for outlaws ambushing stagecoaches. Acting as a go-between for the road agents, Mother Featherlegs was entrusted with the loot of money and jewelry until the bandits could safely dispose of the stolen booty.

In 1979 Mother Featherlegs was found dead, murdered while filling a bucket of water at her spring. She was buried at the site of her cabin. Footprints around the spring pointed to Dangerous Dick, an old friend, who had apparently skipped the country with the woman's money and jewelry.

Davis had returned to his old haunts and criminal activity in the swamps of Louisiana. He was captured and charged with murder and robbery a few years later. Before he was lynched, Davis confessed to killing Mother Featherlegs and revealed that her name was actually Mrs. Charlotte Shepard.

The story Davis told was; "Ma'am" Shepard was one of a gang of cutthroats that operated in the swamps of northern Louisiana after the Civil War. Eventually all the gang members had been hunted down and eliminated, except for Mrs. Shepard and Davis, known in Louisiana as "The Terrapin." Ma'am Shepard fled north to a healthier climate after her sons, Tom and Bill, were honored guests at a vigilante necktie party.

That might have been the end of the story, except in 1964 Lusk residents Jim Griffith and Bob Arrow, along with the residents of Lusk dedicated the monument during the reenactment of the Denver to Deadwood stage run. One of the major contributors was Del Burke, whose Yellow Hotel brother in Lusk was still in operation at that time.

A marker stands at the site of her cabin, and her famous ruffled pantaloons have had adventures of their own. Stolen from the site in 1964, they ended up in a Deadwood saloon until 1990, when a determined posse of Lusk residents raided the saloon and retrieved that garment. They now have a permanent home in the Stagecoach Museum in Lusk.

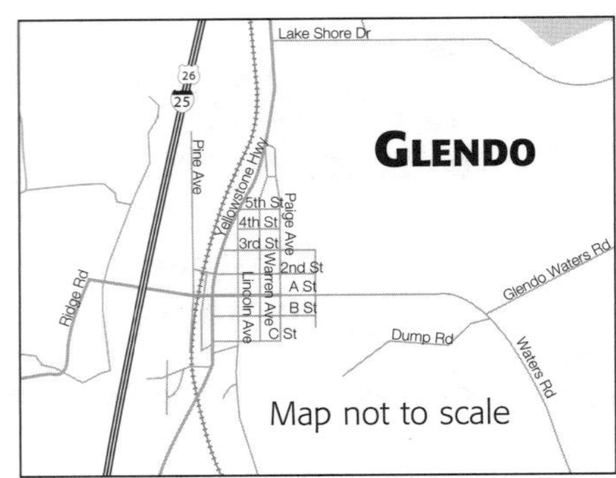

may make its nest on the forest floor. In all, more than 150 species of birds nest in the healthy cottonwood forest—from the forest floor all the way up to the top of the trees. The variety of bird species occurs because of the lush growth and variety of plants present in this forest.

Birds are not the only critters which make their homes in the cottonwood forest. Fox squirrel, white-tailed deer, opossum, raccoon, beaver and mink also live here. The old cottonwood forests, where they stand tall and strong, are important parts of a formula, making "Wyoming's Wildlife—Worth the Watching."

8 *Gas, Food, Lodging*

Glendo

Pop. 229, Elev. 4,718

When the railroad arrived here in 1887, they named the site for the pretty glen in which it was nestled. Prior to this, the Horseshoe Creek Stage Station had been situated here, established by Mormons in the 1850s.

T Glendo Historical Museum

In Glendo

This charming museum, housing exhibits of paleontology, Native American culture and regional history, is open Monday through Friday, 8 a.m. to Noon and 1-4 p.m. Free admission, with donations gratefully accepted.

T Glendo State Park

Near Glendo

Tipi rings and cultural artifacts left behind by the Arapaho and Cheyenne Indians highlight this park. Activities are offered May through September, with the park best known for its excellent boating opportunities.

T Glendo State Park - History

Glendo State Park is located in one of the most historic areas in the state. The reservoir inundates several miles of historic trails. Two or more branches of the Oregon-Utah- California Trail passed where the water now lies. Some of the state's early farming and ranching was conducted in this area.

The Spanish Diggings, a large area of aboriginal activity, lies just a few miles east of the reservoir. Also rising out of the reservoir's east side at Sandy Beach are a series of sand dunes that reach from the Great Divide Basin and the Green River, east to the sand hills of Nebraska. The Arapahoe and Cheyenne Indians arrived in southeastern Wyoming and the North Platte River Basin in the 18th century. The Oglalla and Brule Sioux arrived in the 1830s, moving into eastern Wyoming from South Dakota. Tipi rings and a variety of cultural artifacts are still uncovered in Glendo State Park and the surrounding area (remember, it is unlawful to remove any artifacts you find).

The Platte River meanders through Glendo State Park.

Glendo dam was begun in 1954. The dam was completed in 1957 and the power plant in 1958. The dam is an earth fill structure 2,096 feet long and 167 feet high.

Courtesy of Wyoming State Parks and Historic Sites

9 *No services*

T Laramie Peak

West and south of U.S. Highway 26 & 1-25, between Ft. Laramie and Douglas.

Geology

The Laramie Range was formed when an uplift thrust ancient granite rock through overlying sandstones and limestones. Remnants of these sedimentary rocks, formed from the ancient seas that once covered Wyoming, are visible on the east range. Massive granite rocks characterize the top of Laramie Peak, which is the highest point on the mountain range, visible for more than 100 miles at 10,200 feet above sea level.

History

Evidence reveals that the Laramie Mountains have been occupied by humans for at least 11,000 years. Several Indian tribes are known to have migrated through or lived in the Laramie Peak area; Arapaho, Sioux, Cheyenne, Ute, Shoshone and Crow.

The first Euro-Americans to enter the Laramie Peak area were the fur trappers. From the early 1820s to around 1840, these hardy men co-existed with the Indians and trapped beaver in the mountain streams. One of the most famous among these mountain men was Jacque La Ramie. His legacy lives on in the place names of the area including Laramie Peak and the North Laramie River. Other geographic features in the area such as LaBonte Creek (meaning bountiful goodness) and LaPrele Creek (meaning the ferns) reflect the predominance of the French/Canadian fur trappers who lived here.

Today

In 1935, a summer long forest fire ravaged thousands of acres of timber and rangelands. As a direct result of the need for fire control, on August 20, 1935, the Laramie Peak Ranger Division was added to the Medicine Bow National Forest by an Act of Congress. This later became the Douglas Ranger District, Laramie Peak Unit.

Today, Laramie Peak is still a landmark for weary travelers. It is also a popular recreation area, with a rigorous 5- mile trail to the peak, and Friend Park campground at its base. The trail was originally built for ATV use in the 1960s to access an antennae site, owned by Western Wireless. Hikers discovered the beauty of this "industrial" trail, and have made it their own. However, it will always remain an ATV access trail to the towers at the peak.

Know where you are when recreating on the Laramie Peak Unit, as there is scattered landownership. Purchase a forest map and watch for signs. It is illegal to trespass on private property.

For more information on the recreation opportunities found on Laramie Peak, contact the Douglas Ranger Station at 358-4690, or pick up one of the Converse County/Douglas Ranger District brochures at numerous outlets throughout the state.

Courtesy of National Forest Service

H Wildland Diversity

Dwyer Jct. Exit 1-25 rest area

The Laramie Mountains provide a striking contrast for those traveling through the primarily flat to rolling prairies of southeastern Wyoming. Mountains are important to wildlife in Wyoming. As you go up in elevation, the average annual temperature declines, and the average annual precipitation increases. The rugged terrain in the mountains provides south-facing slopes that get very little. As you travel, take note of the fact that most trees grow on the north slope, where snow accumulates and soil moisture lasts longer. Rough, rugged terrain provides a variety of holes, cracks and crevices which can be used by animals as dens or nesting areas, and places out of the wind where soil accumulates and different plants can grow. These, in turn, attract a variety of animals. A greater variety of habitats or homes means a greater variety of animals.

Contrasting vegetation, topography and large wide-open spaces make Wyoming a home to over 600 species of wildlife, which are "Worth the Watching."

10 *Gas, Food, Lodging*

Guernsey

Pop. 1,147, Elev. 4,354

Incorporated in 1902, this town was named for Charles A. Guernsey, author of Wyoming Cowboy Days. Guernsey was also a noted rancher, legislator, and mining promoter. Located between both the Oregon and Mormon Trails, you can see wagon ruts on either side of town.

Hartville

Pop. 76, Elev. 4,500

Major Verling K. Hart, once an officer at Ft. Laramie, gave his name to this town when he opened the copper mine here. It became the first incorporated town in Wyoming in 1884. Copper mining brought Italian and Greek immigrants, and with them, a taste of southern European culture, including a Dante Alighieri Society and an opera house. The miners had homes in nearby Sunset, which is now a ghost town. The old buildings still stand, but you need local permission to look around, as they are not officially

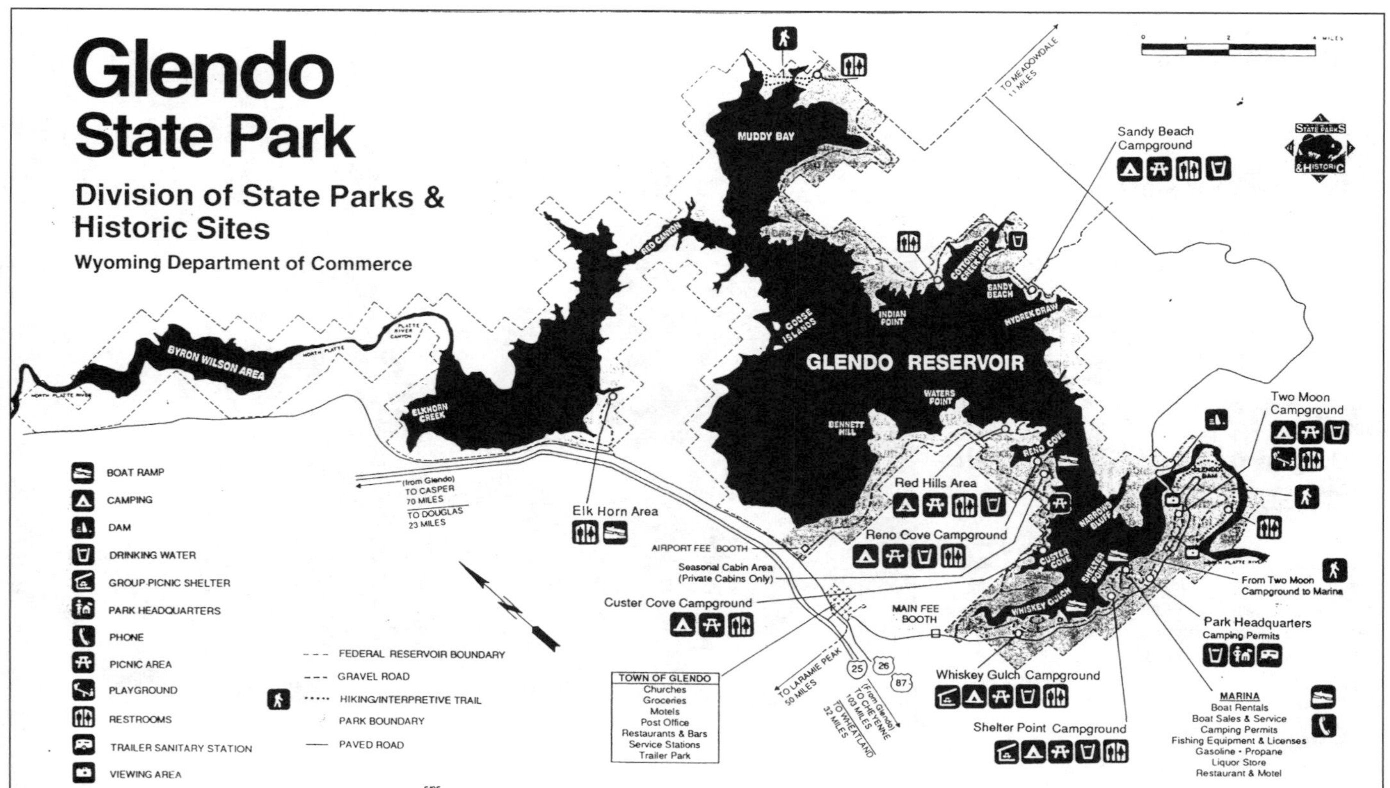

open to the public.

By 1887, gold and silver had also been mined here in small amounts. The copper had mostly run out, but then miners discovered one of the world's most extensive deposits of pure iron. Native Americans had used the red-pigmented mineral for war paint. The area became the first open pit mine in the world, named the Chicago Mine, or "The Glory Hole," a name that is still used for other open pit mines. The Chicago Mine went 650 feet deep, deep enough to fit the United Nations Building inside, and is still one of the largest open pit mines the world has ever seen. Production here peaked in 1942, reaching a million tons, but then tapered off. The mine officially closed in 1984. Environmental reclamation of the area has been an ongoing project.

Hartville gave its name to a geological formation. A Hartville Uplift is one that is rich in ores and semi-precious stones. Recent archeological digs have uncovered that, in addition to the metals mentioned above, Native Americans came here to find jasper, moss agate, onyx, chalcedony and flint for arrowheads. The area has been a gathering place due to its mineral treasures for nearly 11,000 years now.

Wyoming Tidbits

The Homestead Act of 1862 gave 160 acres of government land to each settler. To own the land, settlers had to live on the homestead and improve it within five years. The first homestead in Wyoming was filed by Mrs. Margaret Dolan, a widow and mother of six children, near Egbert.

GUERNSEY

Map not to scale

T Sunrise

One mile east of Hartville lies the mining ghost town of Sunrise. In 1887, a rich vein of iron ore was discovered that led the Colorado Fuel and Iron Corp. to begin open-pit mining. The 650-foot pit was at that time the world's largest.

T Guernsey State Park Civilian Conservation Corps Museum

On State Highway 317 east of I-25 near Guernsey. 836-2334

The park features one of the finest examples of Civilian Conservation Corps (CCC) work in the Rocky Mountain Area. Hiking trails, roads, bridges and a museum are all products of the CCC's efforts. Buildings made of local sandstones are extraordinary and are recognized for their architectural significance. The Castle, a massive picnic shelter, faces the reservoir and Laramie Peak. Work was started in 1933 and approximately 85% completed before the CCC was disbanded in 1936. Visitors can now enjoy Guernsey museum. The museum is located on a high cliff, overlooking the water. The building itself, made of hand hewn timbers and hand forged iron, has been called one of the finest examples of CCC building and architecture in the United States .

T North Platte Valley Overlook
U.S. Highway 26, about 3 miles east of Guernsey

This rest area and viewpoint highlight several historic sites.

T Register Cliff State Historic Site
Two miles past turn-off to Oregon Trail Ruts south of Guernsey

About one-day's wagon travel west of Fort Laramie, emigrants took the time to leave a record of their progress. The sandstone cliff is covered with the names of pioneers who passed this way on their journeys during the 1840s, 5Os and 60s. Most names include a hometown, state and date. Some even left a message. Source: BLM brochure.

T Oregon Trail Ruts State Historic Site
Follow signs from the central Guernsey intersection. Go south across North Platte River.

The Signature Ruts of the trail system are located at a place where terrain forced the emigrant wagons to cross a sandstone outcrop. Thousands of wagon wheels wore ruts into the soft stone to a depth of five feet in some places. Visitors can still see places where the wheel hubs rubbed against the rut walls. Source: BLM brochure.

T Emigrant Hill
Just outside of Guernsey you will find amazing deep ruts along the Morman Trail where those pioneers struggled to hoist their wagons up the very steep slope.

T Spanish Diggings
About 10 miles northeast of Hartville

The Spanish Diggings is actually a Paleo-Indian quartzite quarry, dating to 10,000 years ago. Pits 30 feet deep were dug into the solid quartzite with stone tools. The area was discovered by cowboy A.A. Spaugh in 1879, who thought the Spaniards had dug for gold at the site. Some four hundred square miles of quarries, teepee rings, hearths, chipping stations, and locality markers exist in the quarries. Many significant artifacts have been recovered at the site. Scientists dated the site by the existence of slow growing lichens on the mined rocks. Caches of crude tools and the distinctive lavender and golden quartzite have been found as far away as Ohio and Indiana indicating the extensive trade and travel of prehistoric people. The quarries are located on the Patten Creek Site which is a prehistoric lithic procurement and workshop area listed on the National Registry of Historic Places.

T Guernsey State Park
15 miles ast of I-25 Exit 52 on U.S. Highway 26; one and a half miles north on State Highway 317

Guernsey State Park consists of 6,227 land acres and 2,375 water surface areas. The elevation of the reservoir shoreline is 4,420 feet. Construction of Guernsey Dam and Power plant began on June 1, 1925 and was completed in July 1927. Guernsey Dam is a diaphragm-type embankment with a structural height of 135 feet and a length of 560 feet along its crest. The original capacity of the reservoir was 73,810 acre feet, but this has been greatly reduced by silt deposits to about 46,000 acre feet. The PowerPoint contains two generating units, each with a capacity of 2,400 kilowatts. Guernsey State Park provides seven campgrounds (142 campsites), three day use areas and four boat ramps.

Register Cliffs State Historic Site

Oregon Trail Ruts at Guernsey

Source: Wyoming State Parks & Historic Sites brochure.

H Enough Water To Go Around?
At Guernsey Rest stop 2.5 miles east of Guernsey

The Platte River has two forks, both originate in the high Colorado Rockies. This is the north fork of the Platte. The northfork and south fork join in western Nebraska and eventually flow into the Missouri River. As human populations have grown throughout the world, so has their need for water. Platte River water irrigates croplands in Wyoming, Colorado, and Nebraska—part of our nation's breadbasket. It provides drinking water for over four million people and as many domestic animals. Competition for this water is fierce. Fish and wildlife also rely on this water to survive. Upstream and downstream wildlife use the water from the river for drinking and as a home. It is particularly important as a resting place for millions of ducks and geese as well as the nation's largest single gathering of sandhill cranes. Vegetation growing along the river's banks is lush because of the deep soils and available water. This vegetation, when protected and conserved, grows deep roots which hold river bank soils together, keeps the river from eroding the banks and filters soil out of the water before entering the river. River bank vegetation helps keep the river water clean for humans, fish, and wildlife.

All humans along the Platte are responsible for the river's water. We control the destiny of humans and wildlife on the Platte. Part of our responsibility to Wyoming's resources is its wild places and wild things.

H Oregon Trail Ruts Interpretive Signs
At Oregon Trail Ruts State Historic Site

The Road West

Settlement of new agricultural land, freedom from religious persecution, the quest for personal riches, and the need for improved communications and commerce across the country. These are all reasons for the Road West. America's emigrant trails began along the Missouri River in Missouri, Iowa , Nebraska, and Kansas.They came into central Wyoming along the banks of the North Platte River. Along the way to their intended destinations in California, Oregon and Utah, these trails crossed unbroken plains, rugged hills, steep mountains and waterless deserts. As trail use intensified and critical resources were depleted, conflicts arose with Native Americans. Though some emigrants died in skirmishes, many more lives were lost due to the rigors of the journey, including shortages of food and water, adverse weather, drownings, accidents and disease.

Although overlaps occur between the various uses, four general trail eras can be identified.

The Oregon Trail
The Bidwell-Bartleson wagon train left Independence, Missouri in the spring of 1841. Bound for the fertile valleys of Oregon and Washington, they pioneered the westward migration. Their 2,400 mile journey ended in Oregon near the Columbia River Valley, Oregon City area.

The California Trail
Started around the same time as the Oregon Trail, this trail achieved prominence in 1848 with the discovery of gold in California. In 1849, approximately 30,000 "Forty-Niners" used it to reach the gold fields. Many more emigrants followed in subsequent years. Starting at various points along the Missouri River, the main trail extended from the American Midwest to the Sierra Nevada Mountains and interior valleys of California. A more southerly route began near Tahlequah, Oklahoma. Known as the Cherokee/Overland Trail (1849-1850). It followed the Arkansas River westward into central Colorado, then turned north into Wyoming. It rejoined the main California route near Fort Bridger in southwestern Wyoming.

The Mormon Pioneer Trail
Seeking feedom to practice their religious beliefs, Brigham Young led the followers of Mormonism from the banks of the Mississippi into the western wilderness. In 1846 they left Nauvoo, Illinois, and wintered along the Missouri River near present-day Omaha, Nebraska. In the spring of 1847, the lead party departed from Fort Bridger, Wyoming for the Great Salt Lake of Utah. By late July, the pioneers completed their 1,400 mile trek. Inspired by this first group of 148 emigrants, nearly 70,000 Mormons follwed the trail in the next 20 years, most heading for sanctuary in the Salt Lake Valley.

The Pony Express Trail
The Pony Express Trail was the first major inland communications route linking the eastern United States with the new setlements of the West. Beginning in April of 1860, riders carried mail from St. Joseph, Missouri, to San Francisco, California. With a series of stations along the route supplying fresh horses and men, the 2,000 mile trek could be completed in only ten days. Although service was discontinued in November of 1861-due in part to the construction of the transcontinental telegraph line-the Pony Express provided a vital link between east and west.

It is estimated that approximately 500,000 people ventured westward over the trails to settle and develop the vast resources of the American West. Soon, however, the trails waned in importance.With the completion of the transccontinental railroad in 1869, the 2,000 mile cross country journey, which once took four to six months by wagon or on foot, could be accomplished by rail in a mere two weeks.

Today, by car…,a few days; by plane…, a few hours.

Through a Narrow Passage….
at the crest of the hill, thousands of people and wagons eventually wore the deep ruts into the soft stone. Within a day's journey of Ft. Laramie, livestock and riders struggled through the rocky terrain before making camp at Warm Springs or Cold Springs just to the west. Some chose to stop for the night at Register Cliff (three miles east) before proceeding on, depending on the condition of teams and travelers.

While the North Platte River provided critical water for stock and emigrants, it also posed a barrier to overland travel. The river's waters, then untamed by dams could be swift and treacherous, especially in the spring/early summer. Not easily viewed from this vantage point, a deep meander channel of the river lies about a hundred feet to the east. It was easier to traverse the rugged landscape above than risk fording the river below. Childs Cutoff, established in 1850, coursed along the north side of the Platte from Ft. Laramie. It rejoined the main route of the trail at present-day Casper without having to cross the river. Still, the majority of emigrants followed the south bank path.

Listed as a National Historic Landmark in 1966, this site was dedicated as a State Historic Site in 1970. The numerous trail remnants found here, some vivid, some obscure, serve as a tribute to the passing of pioneers and the westward expansion of the country.

Forts, Stations and Camps
There were four forts, numerous stations and camps along the Oregon-California-Mormon Trails in Wyoming during the mid 1800s. In 1849, Fort Laramie was specifically established to protect emigrants traveling west.The post was abandoned on March 2, 1890. Fort Clay was established October 1855 and redesignated Camp Davis February 1856. Fort Bridger was purchased in 1858 and closed November 6, 1890.

Fort Casper was originally established in May 1862 and named Platte Bridge Station. It was designated a fort November 21, 1865 and was officially abandoned October 19, 1867.

Most miltary camps and stations were established near Pacific telegraph stations located near river, creek, or springs. The soldiers at those stations were responsible for protecting emigrants, delivering mail, protecting and repairing the telegraph line. All stations were constructed by the 11th Ohio Volunteer Calvalrly Regiment from 1862 to 1864. Buildings were constructed of logs or sod and had dirt or wood floors. All stations had enclosed corrals. Tents were also used for housing.

Camp Marshall, had wood buildings and was located just east of La Bonte Creek Station. It was established by E Company, 2nd Battalion in 1864. Named after Captain Levi G. Marshall, the camp was officially abandoned in the Spring of 1866.

Camp Dodge was established April 1865 by the 11th Kansas volunteer Cavalry Regiment, four miles east of Platte Bridge Station on present day Garden Creek, Casper, Wyoming. It was composed of tents. The camp was abandoned in June 1865.

Post at Platte Bridge/Camp Payne
Payne was established at the Camp Davis site. The post was to maintain communications for the Army's 1858 Utah Expedition and to protect emigrants using the trail. Companies D and E, 4th Artillery Regiment, under the command of Captain Joseph Roberts and Captain G.W. Getty, were assigned there.

All of the stations were abandoned in Fall of 1866 when the last battalion of the 11th Ohio Volunteer Cavalry Regiment and the 3rd U.S. Volunteer Infantry Regiment were finally mustered out of service.

Fort Clay, later named Camp Davis, was established to protect Richard's Bridge. The post was officially abandoned in November of 1856. At its peak, no more than 53 soldiers were assigned there.

Fort Laramie to Horseshoe Creek Station, (S. of Glendo) 43 miles

Horseshoe to Camp Marshall (on La Bonte Creek) 20 miles

Camp Marshall to La Prele Creek Station 18 miles

La Prele to Deer Creek Station (Genrock) 17 miles

Nellie Tayloe Ross

Nellie Tayloe Ross was born November 29,1876 near St. Joseph, Missouri. She was educated in public and private schools, and attended a kindergarten training school in Omaha, Nebraska. She taught school for a few years in Omaha before coming to Cheyenne in 1902, following her marriage to William B. Ross. Mr. Ross began a law practice in Wyoming and eventually became active in politics. He was elected as Wyoming's governor in the 1922 election.

Mrs. Ross was an avid supporter of her husband. When he died in office in October, 1924, the Secretary of State, as Acting Governor, called for a special election. The Democratic party nominated Mrs. Ross to complete her husband's term. She initially declined, but upon reflection accepted the nomination. She felt she was the best qualified to understand her husband's goals and work to realize them. Mrs. Ross won the election handily and became the first woman governor in the United States when she was inaugurated 16 days before Miriam A. Ferguson of Texas. She served from January 5, 1925 to January 3, 1927, losing a bid for reelection.

Following her defeat Mrs. Ross continued to be a much sought speaker. She was appointed as a vice-chairman of the Democratic National Committee in 1928, and directed the party's women's division. She campaigned extensively for Franklin D. Roosevelt in 1932. Following his inauguration in 1933, Roosevelt appointed Mrs. Ross to the position of Director of the United States Mint, a position she held until 1953. After her retirement she continued to reside in Washington, D.C., and kept busy with speaking engagements. She died in 1977 at the age of 101. Interment was in Cheyenne, Wyoming.
Courtesy of Wyoming State Archives

Deer Creek Station to Camp Davis, (Evansville) 24 miles

Camp Davis to Camp Dodge (Garden Creek, Casper 4 miles

Camp Dodge to Platte Bridge Station (Casper) 4 miles

Platte Bridge Station to Sweetwater Station (Sweetwater River) 45 miles

Sweetwater Station to 3 Crossings of the Sweetwater Station 36 miles

3 Crossings to Saint Mary's Station (Rocky Ridge) 38 miles

St. Mary's to South Pass Station (Burnt Station) 18 miles

Total Miles 267 miles

Encampments in the Guernsey Area
By wagon, encampments in the Guernsey area, are a day's trek from Fort Laramie. Emigrants had three choices of camp sites in the Guernsey area: Register Cliff, Warm Springs or Cold Springs, the farthest encampment.

Lieutenant John C. Fremont's Camp Site
In 1842, Lieutenant John C. Fremont, lead a mapping expedition of the Oregon Trail. According to Fremont's map maker, Charles Preuss, the flat area just below this sign is most likely where the expedition camped on 21-22 July 1842. While camped here, Fremont noted in his report to Congress that Fort Laramie would be a suitable place of a military post.

Warm Springs Camp Site
Many period documents describe this area as the Emigrant's Wash or Laundry Tub, due to the natural warm water temperature. Warm Springs is located approximately 1.25 miles to the west, up the drainage you are facing. In 1842 Lieutenant John C. Fremont wrote "At the distance of ten miles from the fort, we entered the sandy bed of a creek, a place where, on the left bank, a very large spring gushes with considerable noise and force out of the limestone. On the opposite side, a little below the spring, is a lofty limestone escarpment, partially shaded by a grove of large trees." Today, the site remains much the same.

Cold springs Pass and Camp Site
Cold Springs Pass is located approximately three quarters of a mile and just to the left of the highest point you see. The Pass was used to get to Cold Springs Camp Site. The camp site is observable from a pull out on Highway 26 and is located approximately 2 miles west of Guernsey.

Register Cliff
Register Cliff is located 2 miles to the East The camp site was located on the flats below a mile long cliff of soft sandstone used as a name register by thousands of emigrants from 1847 on. It's interesting that no emigrant ever mentions inscribing names or initials on the cliff in diaries. Also located near Register Cliff was the War and Guerrier Trading Post (1852-1855), Mills and Janis Trading Post (1858-1860), and the Sandy Point Pony Express Station (1860 -1861).

The United States Army and the Oregon Trail
The U.S. Army's Role in Protecting the Oregon Trail in Wyoming 1842 to 1870.

Lieutenant John C. Fremont lead an expedition west in 1842 to map a route to Oregon Territory. The Scout, Kit Carson, guided the expedition. Lieutenant Fremont's report and Charles Preuss's maps were used by many emigrants.

In June of 1849, the first Army Post in Wyoming was established at Fort Laramie, also known as Fort John. Fort John was an old American Fur Company trading post located near the confluence of the Laramie and North Platte Rivers. The mission of Army units stationed at Fort Laramie was to protect emigrants travelling the Oregon Trail.

East of Fort Laramie at the confluence of Horse Creek and North Platte River, the first Fort Laramie Treaty (1851) was signed by representatives of the Sioux, Cheyenne, Arapaho, Gros Ventre, Mandan, Assiniboin and Crow Nations to allow Whites safe passage along the Oregon Trail.

On August 19, 1854, an emigrant's lame cow was killed and eaten by members and guests of a Brule-Sioux village located approximately nine miles east of Fort Laramie. This lead to an event known as the "Grattan Massacre". Lieutenant John Grattan's badly mishandled attempt to arrest High Forehead, a Miniconjou-Sioux, who had killed the cow, resulted in the deaths of Grattan, 29 soldiers and Brule Chief Conquering Bear.

Near present day Casper, Wyoming, the Army established Camp Payne in 1858 and abandoned it in 1859. In 1862, Platte Bridge Station was established nearby. Two separate battles would occur near the station on July 26, 1865 involving Cheyenne, Sioux, and Arapaho warriors and the US. Army. In the first, Lieutenant Caspar W. Collins and four troopers are killed. Sergeant Amos J. Custard and twenty-two troopers were killed in the final battle. Sixty warriors involved in the battles were estimated to have been killed. Platte Bridge Station was renamed Fort Casper in honor of young Lieutenant Collins.

With the completion of the Continental Railroad in 1869, and the relocation of the telegraph line, the use of the Oregon Trail dramatically decreased and so did the Army's role in protection of the trail.

The Wyoming Army National Guard, in cooperation with the Advisory Council on Historic Preservation, U.S. Department of Interior, Wyoming State Historic Preservation Office, and Wyoming State Parks & Historical

Tens of thousands of pioneer wagons wore the trail down through solid stone.

Sites, has provided interpretive signage to meet its responsibilities under the National Historic Preservation Act.

The U.S. Army's Role in Protecting the Oregon Trail in Wyoming 1842 to 1870

The U.S. Army's role in protecting the Oregon Trail is best described by the soldiers.

"Who is the cause of all this trouble now? Just one bad man. "The man who killed the cow." The Great Father does not care about a cow but that fellow was a bad fellow, and was not given up, this caused all the difficulty. It was a very little thing, yet see how it spread over the whole Sioux nation from one bad fellow. I hope all the red people will remember this." General William S. Harney, Commander of the Punitive Expedition against the Sioux for the August 1854 Grattan Fight. Fort Pierre Peace Council March 1-5, 1856.

"We are so busy now building and getting ready to pass the winter comfortably that I can't write as interesting letters as I could other wise. When we get done building we go to hauling wood and then as soon as it will do we will go to making hay. We can get eight dollars per ton for cutting and curing hay. The weather is so warm that we sleep out doors in wagons. We spread out gum blankets and bed ticks over the bows for a cover and it is as dry and cool in there as any where." Private Hervey Johnson, Company"G", 11th Ohio Volunteer Cavalry, June 24, 1864, Deer Creek Station.

"Cold dreary wind and cloudy all night; very chilly cold and windy. Most of the men are in their tents, overcoats on to keep comfortable. Captain Green of "B" Company and detachment just starting for Deer Creek. Snowing like forty thousand devils; ground covered with snow; still pouring down the near way; very cold, wet snow. Quit snowing but clears after dinner; cool northwest wind. Lieut. Clancey starts fo South Pass this evening." First Sergeant Isaac B. Pennock, Company "I", 11th Kansas Volunteer Cavalry, June 17, 1865, Platte Bridge Station.

"If it is in comtemplation to keep open the communications with Oregon Territory, a show of military force in this country is absolutely necessary; and a combination of advantages renders the neighborhood of Fort Laramie the most suitable place, on the line of the Platte, for the establishment of a military post." Brevet Captain John C. Fremont, Leader of the 1842, 43-44, Oregon Trail Mapping Expeditions, 1845.

"Your Great Father...has sent me with a handful of braves to visit you...I am opening a road for your white brethren, and your Great Father directs that his red children shall not attempt to close it up. There are many whites now coming on this road, moving to the other side of the mountains.... You must not disturb them...Should you do so, your Great Father would be angry with you although he is the enemy of all bad Indians, he is the friend of those who are good." Colonel Stephen W. Kearny, Commander of Presidential directed Military Show of Force Expedition, June 16, 1845, Council meeting with Brule, Ogalala, and Arapaho near Fort Platte, Wyoming.

"I regret the necessity which obliged me to kill any of your people, but under similar circumstances I will always act precisely in the same manner. I am now willing to forget what has passed, and receive you as friends; provided, you promise to behave yourselves here after; otherwise, I shall regard you as enemies, and am ready and able to meet you as such...you might escape at the time, and even for years, yet sooner or later, the day of retribution would certainly come." First Lieutenant Richard B Garnett, Commanding Officer Fort Laramie, June 1853, Fort Laramie Ferry Incident between Chief Little Brave's Miniconjou Souix and Fort Laramie's Garrison.

"It was a race of life. Nehring, a private of Company K, 11th Kansas, not understanding the order, dismounted to fight from a deep washout in the road. Cpl. Grimm, looking around, yelled to him in German "to the bridge." That was the last that was seen of poor Nehring. Camp, lost his horse and then ran for dear life, but within a few rods of safety was overtaken and tomahawked. Sergeant HankHammer's horse was wounded but carried him safely to the bridge and then dropped. It was a miracle that any man escaped." Private Stephen H. Fairfield, Company K, 11th Kansas Volunteer Cavalry, July 26, 1865, Platte Bridge Battle.

"Long trains of wagons were winding their way over the plains, the mysterious telegraph wires were stretching across their hunting grounds to the mountains, engineers were surveying a route for a track for the iron horse, and all without saying as much as 'By your leave' to the Indians. Knowing that their game would soon be gone, that their hunting grounds taken from them, and that they themselves would soon be without a country, they had resorted to arms to defend their way of life and themselves." Sergeant Stephen H. Fairfield, Company K, 11th Kansas Volunteer Cavalry, reflecting on the Indian War of 1865, 1903.

"No sir; we don't stop here. We are going into Platte Bridge in spite of all the redskins this side of Hell....I don't care a damn. You Ohio fellows, decked out in buckskin and fringe think you know too much about this Injun business. We have been South, where fighting is done, and we know how to do it. You fellows are skeered. We will go on, and if you want to be safe, go on with us. We will cut our way through, or go to Hell a-trying. Forward, Men!" Commissary Sergeant Amos J. Custard, Company H, 11th Kansas Volunteer Cavalry, July 26, 1865, Sergeant Custard Army Supply Train Fight.

H Oregon Trail Ruts

Oregon Trail Ruts State Historic Site

Wagon wheels cut solid rock, carving a memorial to Empire Builders. What manner of men and beasts impelled conveyances weighing on those grinding wheels? Look! A line of shadows crossing boundless wilderness

Foremost, nimble mules drawing their carts, come poised Mountain Men carrying trade goods to a fur fair – the Rendezvous. So, in 1830, Bill Sublette turns the first wheels from St. Louis to the Rocky Mountians! Following his faint trail, a decade later and on through the 1860s, appear straining, twisting teams of oxen, mules and heavy draft horses drawing Conestoga wagons for Oregon pioneers. Trailing the Oregon-bound avant garde but otherwise mingling with those emigrants. Inspired by religious fervor, loom foot sore and trail worn companies – Mormons dragging or pushing handcarts as they follow Brigham Young to the Valley of the Salt Lake. And, after 1849 reacting to a different stimulus but sharing the same trail, urging draft animals to extremity, straining resources and often failing, hurry gold rushers California bound.

A different breed, no emigrants but enterprisers and adventurers, capture the 1860's scene. They appear, multi-teamed units in draft – heavy wagons in tandem, jerkline operators and bullwackers delivering freight to Indian War outposts and agencies. Now the apparition fades in a changing environment. Dimly seen, this last commerce serves a new, pastoral society: the era of the cattle baron and the advent of settlement blot the Oregon Trail

Wyoming Tidbits

The "Glory Hole" was one of the largest open pit iron mines in the world. It began operations at Sunrise in 1887 and operated until 1974.

H Register Cliff

Register Cliffs State Historic Site.

The wayfarers penchant for inscribing names and dates on prominent landmarks excites the interest of his descendants. Regrettably, marks of historic value are often effaced by later opportunists.

Along the Oregon Trail, famed transcontinental route of the 19th century, pertinent dates are from the 1820s through the 1860s. Three outstanding recording areas exist within Wyoming: Register Cliff here; Independence Rock 180 miles west; and Names Hill a further 175 miles along the Trail's wandering course. Register Cliff and Names Hill are self-evident titles; Independence Rock derives from a July 4th, 1825 observance which, according to some authorities, was staged by Mountain Men of Fur Trade fame.

Register Cliff invited emigrants because broad river bottoms offered pleasing campsites and excellent pasture. Hardship and illness were inevitable to Trail travel; of 55,000 emigrants during a peak year some 5,000 died enroute. Cliffside graves attest to the high mortality. This being their lot, travelers eagerly sought and singularly valued recuperative lay overs. Here, rest offered the opportunity to register.

But not all who registered were worn and grieving emigrants. Early inscriptions were by Mountain Men inured to wilderness life–many descendants of two centuries of French Fur Trade. One reads; "1829 This July 14". Does it denote an observance? If the American Independence Day was celebrated in 1825 at Independence Rock could the French trappers have noted Bastille Day at Register Cliff in 1829?

Settlement and Homesteaders

In the 1870s and 1880s, ranchers and homes leaders gradually moved into this territory, and Fort Laramie was abandoned as a military post in 1890. Charles A. Guernsey came into Wyoming Territory in June of 1880, trailing cattle from Colorado. Heading north, he passed through this area along the old Black Hills freight and stage route. The Guernsey Cattle

FRANCIS E. WARREN

Francis E. Warren was born in Hinsdale, Massachusetts on June 20, 1844. He served as a private and noncommissioned officer during the Civil War, earning a Medal of Honor. He farmed and raised stock for a short time in Massachusetts before heading west to what would be Wyoming, but was then part of Dakota Territory, in 1868. He engaged in several business ventures, including real estate, livestock, mercantile, and promotion of the first lighting system in Cheyenne. In 1871 Warren married Helen M. Smith, also of Hinsdale, and they made their home in the young town of Cheyenne, Wyoming Territory.

Warren's political career was marked by a steady rise in influence. He was a member of the Cheyenne City Council in 1873 and 1874. In 1873 Warren was also elected to the Council of the Territorial Assembly. The Council elected him as their president. Warren was appointed to two terms as Territorial Treasurer. He was again elected to the Territorial Council in 1884, and to the office of Mayor of Cheyenne in 1885. In the same year, he was appointed by President Chester Arthur to fill the unexpired term of governor William Hale. A second appointment as governor was made by President Benjamin Harrison in 1889.

Warren was elected Wyoming's first state governor in October, 1890, but served only about six weeks before being elected by the state legislature as one of Wyoming's first United States Senators, beginning a highly distinguished career in that capacity. Tragedy struck the family in 1915 when daughter Frances Warren Pershing, wife of General John J. Pershing, and three granddaughters died in a fire at the Presidio in San Francisco.

Warren served in the Senate until his death in Washington, D.C. on November 24, 1929, a tenure longer than any other senator's to that time. He was buried in Cheyenne.

Courtesy of Wyoming State Archives

Company was formed the next year and the 999 (Three Nine) brand became its trademark. Guernsey's land holdings later included ranches on the Laramie, Cheyenne and North Platte rivers.

When Wyoming was admitted as a state in 1890, the first application for purchase of state school land adjoining the present town site of Guernsey was made by C.A. Guernsey. Under the Warren Act, several thousand acres of land lying south of the North Platte in the Warm Springs area were also granted to Guernsey upon statehood. This land is still held with the present ranching operation.

Guernsey established his ranch at the base of Register Cliff and continued to operate it until 1926, when the Henry Frederick family acquired the land and began a ranching operation that still continues today. The cave that you see in the cliff face was initially blasted out for the storage of potatoes raised on the ranch, as the stone walls would insulate the produce and keep it from freezing in the winter. Later, the cave was used for machinery storage. It is not currently in use.

Henry Fredrick gifted a portion of the Register Cliff historic site to the State of Wyoming in 1932, and the site was listed on the National Register of Historic Places in 1970. It is through the generosity of the Frederick Family that the site is open to the public, as most of the land is still under their ownership. Chet Frederick, the son of Henry and a fourth generation Wyomingite, lived on this ranch during most of his life until his death in 1995. He always shared his knowledge and admiration for this area with family and friends alike, including much of the information above. Today, Register Cliff continues to be a stopping point for thousands of visitors each year, as it was during the western migration in the 1800s.

What Lies Ahead…"

With the change in the geological formation leaving Fort Laramie, the whole face of the country has entirely altered its appearance. Eastward of that meridian, the principal objects which strike the eye of a traveler are the absence of timber, and the immense expanse of prairie, covered with the verdure of rich grasses, and highly adapted for pasturage. Whenever they are not disturbed by the vicinity of man, large herds of buffalo give animation to this country. Westward of Laramie river, the region is sand, and apparently sterile; and the place of the grass is usurped by the artemesia and other odiferous plants, to whose growth the sandy soil and dry air of this elevated region seem highly favorable." (Van Tramp, John C., Prairie and Rocky Mountain Adventures; or, Life in the West. Columbus: J&H Miller, 1885)

For emigrants who reached this portion of the Oregon, California, Mormon Pioneer and Pony Express trails between 1841-1868, the landscape was changing and new challenges lay ahead. Rested and resupplied with provisions from Fort Laramie, emigrants bound for destinations in Utah, California and Oregon now encountered increasingly difficult travel conditions as they made their journey westward. It would be 368 miles to the next major supply point, Fort Bridger, or further if other trail cutoffs were taken.

Within a day's travel of Ft. Laramie, Register Cliff or "Sand Point" was one of the overnight camp locations in this area, with others approximately 3 miles further west. As a record of their passing, guests occasionally "registered" at this site by engraving their names and sometimes the date of their visit into the soft sandstone wall. Young Alvah H. Unthank, age 19 and bound for the California gold fields, left his mark here in 1850. His name, along with those of two of his relatives, O.N. Unthank who served as telegraph operator at Ft. Laramie from 1869 to 1874, and O.N.'s son, can be found low on the cliff near the east end of the walking path (can you find it?).

Unfortunately, Alvah Unthank never made it to California. His fortunes were lost about 75 miles down the trail when, like hundreds of other emigrants, he succumbed to cholera. Several graves of unknown emigrants are found here at the site, enclosed by the fence to the south.

In the mid-1850s, Misters Ward and Guerrier operated a small trading post just west of the cliff, offering goods to the emigrants. Later, a pony express station was based here, known as Sand Point or Star Ranch Station.

The importance of the Oregon, California, Mormon Pioneer and Pony Express trails dwindled for the emigrants with completion of the transcontinental railroad in 1869. However, the trail was still utilized by a few travelers as well as the military, especially after Ft. Laramie became a hub for military operations during the Indian Wars period in the West.

H Olinger's Overlook Interpretive Signs

At Guernsey Rest Stop two and a half miles east of Guernsey

Olinger's Overlook-North Platte Valley

The valley of the North Platte River offers the most advantageous approach to the easiest crossing of North America's continental backbone-the Rocky Mountain Cordillera. This is a geographic fact understood by prehistoric and historic man since time immemorial.

The route was first trekked by migratory foragers of western arid land, themselves burdened and aided by packed and travois-trailing dogs. Later, from agrarian regions to the eastward, came Stone Age artisans to mine hematite (for paint colors) and quarry flint (for implements) in the famous "Spanish Diggings" of the Hartville Uplift, which here forms the valley's northern flank.

At the dawn of historic times and attributable to acquisition of the horse, here developed and flourished migratory tribes whose common culture has been designated Plains Indian. Then, fully recorded by history, came civilized man: first, like the foragers, weary pedestrians, second, like Plains Indians, mounted; and third, a new scene for the Platte, riding in wagons. Later, they drove cattle, laid rails, dug pipelines and built super highways. To the right and left, signs and siting devices point out landmarks relating to man's activities in the valley.

D. J. Olinger, Wyoming Highway Department engineer and amateur historian.

Fort Laramie

This sighting device points to the crest of a ridge separating the North Platte and Laramie Rivers. directly down the opposite slope, on the banks of the Laramie about a mile above the confluence of the streams, stands Fort Laramie. it is about eight miles from here as the crow flies, but twelve miles by road.

Founded in 1834 by fur traders William Sublette and Robert Campbell, who named their log structure Fort William, the post was acquired by the American Fur Company in 1841. That company built an adobe-walled complex nearby which they named Fort John, but the mountain men called it Fort Laramie. This latter name stemmed from the river on which it was located and which, in its own turn, got its name from the trapper Jacques LaRamie, who is believed to have trapped and died in the area in the early 1800s.

The government purchased Fort Laramie in 1849. In the next forty years it became the most famous military post protecting the Oregon Trail and served as a forward base for many campaigns of the Indian Wars. The fort was deactivated in 1890, the land sold into private ownership and the buildings sold at auction or abandoned and allowed to fall into ruins. In 1937 the State of Wyoming purchased the property–land and building ruins–from private owners and gave it back to the federal government. by presidential proclamation in 1938 Fort Laramie National Historic Site became a unit of the National Park System.

Mexican Hill

Spotted through the right-hand sight is Mexican Hill. at Mexican Hill the covered wagon emigrants, having turned into the fort on the Laramie River for information, supplies or repairs, cut over the intervening ridge to regain the Platte River route. There, wagon ruts worn into bedded rock attest to the volume of westward traffic traversing the Oregon Trail during the years 1840 to 1870.

Coming down Mexican Hill's steep slope, drivers roughlocked wheels to keep wagons from running into their own backward-holding though forward-moving teams. here, besides the animals iron-shod hooves, it was their singular stiff-legged, sliding step—adapted to hold against the forward thrust of heavily loaded wagons—which, together with the locked and sliding, steel-rimmed wheels, contributed to the extraordinary depth of the ruts.

In 1841 Mexican artisans were engaged by the American Fur company to build the adobe trading post later known as Fort Laramie. This hill took its name from the craftsmen who settled permanently in the vicinity and constructed an irrigation system at the foot of the hill to water their extensive gardens. They sold the produce to fur traders, soldiers and passing emigrants for whom it was a welcome supplement to diets otherwise lacking any fresh foods other than meat.

North Platte River

In 1739 the brothers Pierre and Paul mallet, earliest explorers along this river's lower course, named it after the French word for flat. although the sighting tube aims at a wide, strong flowing current, the North Platte is not navigable.

It is unlikely that prehistoric foragers, habituated to arid environs, would have attempted a journey on water. But flint quarriers and hematite miners, accustomed to cruising midwestern rivers and burdened with the products of their labors, might have tried the Platte. In 1812 Robert Stuart's party of eastbound Astorians, recorded discoverers of this ancient, transmontane route of aborigines, wintered a short distance downstream. They fashioned dugout canoes and embarked on the spring floods of 1813, but their craft soon stranded on sandbars and they finished their journey on foot. Eleven years later Tom Fitzpatrick and other trappers again put a boat in the Platte. They encountered wild waters between canyon walls, and though experienced voyageurs, lost a part of Ashley's valuable furs. Thereafter, mountain men stuck to their horses.

The Platte's chief historical significance, other than as a natural route for transcontinental travel and commerce, relates to the "arid-lands culture theory" of John Wesley Powell, 19th century explorer, ethnologist, engineer and statesman. An agency created through his instigation, the U. S. Bureau of Reclamation, constructed along the Platte one of the west's first great irrigation systems. The prosperity resulting from the regulated spreading of North Platte waters over formerly arid lands is visible for hundreds of miles along the river's course.

The Burlington-Northern Railroad

Pointed out by the sight, Burlington-Northern tracks are in close view. That railroad's forerunner, the Burlington and Missouri, laid rails up the North Platte Valley in 1900. With a view to eventually reaching the Pacific, the company surveyed beyond immediate construction goals—on through South Pass.

Primarily laid down as a supplement to existing feeder lines in Iowa and Nebraska, this branch line was intended for moving Wyoming range livestock to midwestern feedlots and, following fattening, on to metropolitan packing plants. Further considerations were developing possibilities for transporting Platte Valley iron ore, petroleum products and irrigated field crops to established centers of processing and distribution.

Subsequent consolidations have made the Burlington and Missouri a part of a vast railroad network. Therein, one of the most profitable sectors connects gulf coast ports—via the Platte Valley here and the Yellowstone Valley in Montana—with the Pacific Northwest. Thus the Burlington finally reached the western ocean, but not throng the easy grades via South pass as originally projected.

Though gradual grades were as important to railroad engineer as to wagon train mater, the more abundant timber for ties and coal for fuel found south and north of the famous pass met the railroader's needs better than the wildlife, grass and water which were essential to the emigrant wagoners following the Oregon Trail through central Wyoming.

Guernsey Pipeline Station

This site points to the Guernsey Pipeline Station, jointly owned by the Platte Pipeline Company, the American Oil company and the continental Oil Company. Most of the structures under view were built in 1952 although, owing to the river's favorable grade and southeasterly course, the first pipeline through this vicinity was delivering Platte Valley petroleum wealth to Midwestern urban centers as early as 1918. Technologically, this station is capable of interchanging crude oil among several carrier lines and moving it south to Cheyenne and Denver or east to mid-continent refineries.

Aborigines, from the early foraging societies through the heyday of the Plains Tribes, exploited the North Platte Valley both as a route of travel and commerce and for its own natural wealth. But fur traders, conducting most of their operations further west in the mountains, were chiefly interested in the North Platte as a route of commerce; for covered wagon emigrants, the North Platte was only a necessarily traveled route lying between their past and their future; for Pony Express, stage and telegraph enterprises it was a pathway between the inhabited regions wherein they provided a connecting link; livestock men did exploit the valley's riches but preferred that someone else provide transportational services; railroaders found some local business but that was incidental to their basic operation—the transcontinental haul.

Petroleum concerns, however, like the aborigines before them, have existed on both the valley's natural wealth and its transportational potentials. They have exploited its availability as a route for commerce to increase the value of its products through delivery to areas of maximum demand.

Register cliff

Register Cliff stands in plain view after it is singled out by the sighting device. This natural landmark, enrolled in the national Register of Historic Places, is a developed area with parking and rest facilities, foot trails and informative signs. A fence protects the earliest names registered on the cliff face. Also fenced is a little cemetery originated by covered wagon emigrants.

The Cliff's historic significance stems from the large number of emigrants names and dates carved in the sandstone-limestone formation. However, it also bears names of early fur traders, Indian Wars participants and names and dates of pioneer ranchers. Some early names have been obliterated by more recent carving, and this made it necessary to fence a portion of the cliff where signatures are most concentrated.

Register Cliff can be reached by a paved and well-marked country road extending three miles southeast from Guernsey.

Sand Point

A monument marking Sand Point appears as a white dot in the center of the sight. Sand deposits caused by currents at a bend in the river evidently gave the site its name. The surrounding meadows have been favorite campsites since prehistoric time.

Seth Ward and William Guerrier established an Indian trade post at Sand Point in 1852. It was an ideal location for trading in hides and furs as well as for supplying Oregon Trail travelers who camped nearby. In 1852 a lady diarist wrote, "We are now encamped directly on the bank of the river, under two fine trees. The station, about a mile below, is in a handsome bend of the stream and consists of two or three log buildings, with a large one of stone, about half erected."

In 1855, Ward and Guerrier moved to Fort Laramie, where Ward soon became post sutler—a position leading to accumulation of a great fortune. Until his death in 1858, Guerrier handled the Fort's Indian trade. Thereafter, B.B. Mills and Antoine Janis managed that trade, moving its headquarters back to Sand point. later, under Jules Coffey, the post became a stage station and, in 1860 and 1861, it was a Pony Express Station. By 1822, Sand Point was a ranch homestead, and Charles Guernsey acquired the property in 1891.

The country road from Guernsey to Register Cliff passes by Sand Point.

Guernsey-Frederick Ranch

The sight centers on the headquarters buildings of the Guernsey-Frederck Ranch. That these buildings stand almost in the shadow of Register Cliff is symbolic of the valley's heritage. Here, history emphasizes the Oregon Trail; such other epochs as the storied Cattleman's Frontier are subordinated by memories and the visual landmarks of that nationally famous emigrant road.

Since the days of "open range" and "free grass" the Guernsey-Frederick Ranch has been representative of Wyoming's always important livestock industry. The place is, however, also significant in its own right. it brings together two pioneer ranching family names which also relate to such other facets of state history as frontier military life, political activity, governmental organization and the development of railroads, mines, irrigated lands, schools, churches and banks.

Favorably located and progressively operated, the ranch is as significant in modern times as ever it was in the past.

Oregon Trail Ruts

Although the sight aims at the general location, the Oregon Trail Ruts National Historic

Cheyenne Deadwood Stage

Driving north of Lusk you can still see the deep ruts worn on the famous Cheyenne-Deadwood Stage Route. The trail connected the Union Pacific Railroad in Cheyenne with the gold mining region in the Black Hills of Dakota Territory.

Often a dangerous and desolate trail for travelers in the 1870s through the 1880s. The coaches were routinely besieged by horse thieves, stage coach robbers, Sioux warriors protecting their own land, along with a a host of other problems and invaders.

Along the rough and tumble trail, travelers were tossed about the coach, wheels often broke on the rocks, and blizzards swept across the prairie. The spirits of Persimmons Bill Chambers and "Big Nose" George Parrott, outlaws, Stuttering Brown, a hired agent for the stagecoach company, along with those of the robbers, and Sioux warriors, might still be felt along stretches of the trail. There are possibly echoes of famous passengers such as Buffalo Bill, Calamity Jane, and Wild Bill Hickok. Hat Creek Station, along with Robbers Roost were busy stops along the trail.

Imagine riding from the hard benches and the breathing the choking prairie dust as one bumped along on the rutted and rocky trails. The stage left Cheyenne every Monday and Thursday, with returning stages leaving Deadwood on Tuesdays and Saturdays. It was a little less than 200 miles one way. Top speed of travel was about eight miles per hour.

The route was blazed by freighters, seduced by the lure of gold in the Black Hills. Most of the land the trail covered was owned by the Sioux Indians. Eager to partake of the latest gold rush, this fact was largely ignored by the miners, settlers, and government, thus inviting trouble for trespassing.

Some of the trails heaviest use occurred during the United States military's last campaign against the Sioux, Cheyenne, and Arapaho Indians at the Battle of the Little Big Horn when Sioux warriors under Crazy Horse and Sitting Bull destroyed most of George A. Custer's command.

In the early 1900s, the stage itself, gained much notoriety traveling with Buffalo Bill Cody's Wild West Show. The Stagecoach Museum in Lusk exhibits an original coach used in the show.

The Road is marked by monuments and informative signs at intersections with public roads. Most of the actual trail is on private land, but much of the route is paralleled by improved county and state roads, near Cheyenne, Chugwater, Lusk, and Newcastle. US Highway 85, also known as the the CanAm Highway, links Canada with Texas, using the Old Deadwood-Cheyenne Stage Line in several locations.

Landmark cannot be seen from here. Like Register Cliff, it is a developed historic site, accessible by a good country road.

The terrain here forced travelers to follow a single set of tracks along a relatively soft sand rock formation. over the years, the volume of emigrant wagon traffic cut ruts so deep as to leave marks of turning wheel-hubs which extend over a length of several hundred feet.

The ruts are reached by a country road out of Guernsey. It is the same road leading to Register cliff but, just beyond a bridge over the North Platte, a sign directs the visitor to a side road which brings him, at the end of half a mile, to the parking area. From there, a short foot trail leads to the ruts.

Laramie Peak

The sight points to Laramie Peak, altitude 10,247 feet, the highest elevation in the Laramie Range. These mountains were originally called the Black Hills, a name deriving from the dark appearance of their evergreen forests as noted from far to the eastward by westward journeying mountain men. Only the northern end of the range, in northeastern Wyoming and western South Dakota, is now known as the Black Hills.

Although the name of that more legendary than historic figure, Jacques Laramie, has been given to numerous features of Wyoming geography, apparently this mountain was the first to be so designated. Looming on a distant horizon, that major natural landmark won historic significance through being cited time and again—in the journals, diaries and letters of Oregon Trail travelers—as first evidence of a successful high plains crossing and impending entry into the rocky Mountains.

One who so recorded a sighting of Laramie Peak, and whose transit triangulations would later make the mountain an important cartographic reference point, was famed Dr. Francis V. Hayden of the U.S. Geological Survey. He wrote, in 1869: "From our camp on the Laramie we enjoyed one of the beautiful sunsets which are not uncommon in this western country. But this was a rare occasion, for the sun passed directly behind the summit of Laramie Peak. The whole range was gilded with golden light, and the haziness of the atmosphere gave to the whole a deeper beauty. Such a scene as this could occur but once in a lifetime."

H Register Cliff

U.S. Highway 26 just east of Guernsey

Emigrants participating in the great continental migrations of the mid-nineteenth century left enduring traces of their arduous passage along trails. On soft rock faces they inscribed their names and dates of passing. These etchings no only confirm their prsence on the frontier, they are evidence of the pioneers' realization that they were participants in a dramatic process; the settlement of the trans-Mississippi west. After the first day out of Fort Laramie emigrants paused to mark their passing at Register Cliff, a sandstone bluff one and a half miles southeast of here.

Register Cliff can be observed more closely by traveling 2.5 miles southeast of downtown Guernsey.

H Grave of Lucindy Rollins, 1849-1934

At Oregon Trail Ruts State Historic Site

Dedicated to the pioneer women of Wyoming, erected by the Historical Landmark Commission of Wyoming 1934.

H Warm Springs

On private land in Platte County

Wagon trains heading west found these springs a convenient one-day's travel twelve miles beyond fort Laramie. There were two main routes from the fort and emigrants traveling either could utilize this campground. Though well known to early mountaineers trapping local streams, Warm Springs was first described by John C. Fremont who stopped here on July 21, 1842.

Sometimes called the "Big Springs" by emigrants, Warm Springs is best known in Wyoming folklore as "the Emigrant's Laundry Tub". This later term can be confirmed by at least one account, that of Pusey Graves who camped nearby on June 24, 1850. he wrote, "After I finished my letter to send back to the Fort, I proceeded to the spring a distance of 1 1/2 miles with my bucket of dirty clothes."

Early settlers found this area littered with wagon train debris and many graves. Of the graves, only one remains to be seen today. It is located across the draw southwest of here.

H Elva Ingram

On private land in Platte County

On April 15, 1852, James and Ritta Ann Ingram with their nine children left Salem, Henry County, Iowa, for Pleasant Valley, Oregon. The wagon train, consisting of forty people in four families, reached the Fort Laramie area June 21, 1852.

Here on the North Bank (Childs') road, on Wednesday, June 23, 1852, their daughter, four-year-old Elva Ingram, died. The cause of her death is unknown. On that day eighteen-year-old James Akin, Jr., wrote: "Travel 12 miles very hilly bad roads pine and cedar bluffs—cloudy rainy weather, Elva Ingram died. Camp in good place. Plenty wood no water."

There were seven more deaths in the Richey-Ingram-Akin wagon train, which reached the Williamette Valley late in October 1852. Research and signing by Oregon-California Trails Association, funding by Dr. Jack Ingram and Family, Medford, Oregon 1987.

11 *No services*

Jay Em

Just off highway 85, halfway between the towns of Lingle and Lusk, sits the near-ghost town of Jay Em. A few people still live there, fifteen by last count. When homesteaders began to flood into the area at the turn of the nineteenth century, Lake Harris, a man of vision, saw the need for several businesses to service the newcomers. As the demand for goods and services grew, so did the town. In addition to overseeing the towns creation and growth, he was, at different times, a newspaper publisher, banker, postmaster, and land commissioner. Today his children and grandchildren give tours of the town and its buildings.

The town took its name from local cattle rancher James Moore whose ranch was situated two miles north of the town site. His brand "JM" was transformed from initials to words and the town was named., Mr. Moore had a colorful career as a Pony Express rider, a drover, and a freighter before settling down to ranch.

A number of the original buildings are still standing and are a photographer's delight.

Hardware Store

Built in 1920 it was called "J.M. Hardware." People traveled as much as 100 miles to get ranch supplies here, always knowing they would be able to get what they needed. Mr. Harris even kept parts for one complete windmill; just to be sure he had what the customer needed. The hardware was more than a supply store though, it also had a soda fountain and gas pumps. Town meetings, socials, and even rifle practices were held in the hall above the store.

Grocery Store

Built in 1935, this building replaced the grocery store that was originally in Lake's home and then later in the mill building. People were allowed to charge their groceries and dry goods. The hall above this store was used for Sunday school, church club meetings, and as apartments.

Cream Station

Now located between the grocery and hardware store, this small, but mighty, cream station at one time shipped out more cream than any other station in Wyoming.

Gas Station / Garage

James Shoults was the first proprietor, from 1928–1945, calling it "Shoults Garage." From 1946–1960 it ran as "Wolfes Repair." A blacksmiths shop was located in the rear.

Jay Em Stone Shop

The first blacksmith shop was west of Harris's home. Bill Bradbury was village blacksmith. After it was flooded out it was then moved to this site around 1919 and later became a garage. In 1935 Lloyd Damrow and Oscar Bradbury opened a business called Jay Em Onyx & Gem Co. Through the years it was also known as the Wy. Marble & Stone Inc., and Jay Em Stone Shop. Here they made head stones, fireplace mantels, tabletops, paperweights, salt & pepper shakers, ash trays, candle stick holders, and jewelry.

Lumber Yard / Mill Building

The mill building was first called Jay Em Store and then General Store. In 1917 this building housed the grocery, hardware, drugstore, livestock feed, and lumberyard. Lumber and equipment came by train to Ft. Laramie or Lingle.

Bank / Post Office

Farmers State Bank of Jay Em opened for business in 1920. It was sold to the 1st National Bank of Torrington in 1945. In 1933, after President Roosevelt's inauguration, he issued a proclamation closing all banks and embargoing all gold, this to prove the governments power to cope with the financial crisis of the Depression. The Jay Em bank did not receive word of this so it stayed open. The bank was robbed in 1935.

The first Post Office for this area was established in 1899 in William (Uncle Jack) Hargraves cabin just north of town. The Postal inspector reprimanded Mr. Hargraves for being lax in his duties so Uncle Jack told him to take the post office back. In 1908 Silas Harris (Lake's father) sent a request to Washington D.C. to have a post office in the area again. Lake Harris carried mail by horseback three times a week for three months, free of charge, to show he was worthy of running a Post Office. On February 10, 1909 Mrs. C.H. Thornton was appointed postmistress. Lake was not old enough, but in 1914 he was appointed postmaster, and again in 1931 until he retired in 1959. The Post Office was located in a front corner of the Bank building.

Portions excerpted from Goshen County Chamber brochure.

T Goshen County

Goshen County is home to antelope, deer, wild turkey, geese, ducks and other game birds. The region enjoys mild winters and an abundance of wildlife. In the 1920s, the Union Pacific Railroad expanded into Goshen County, allowing the principle industry of agriculture to flourish. Over 200,000 cattle are raised and marketed in Goshen county. Potatoes, beans, corn and other grains, and alfalfa are among the crops produced. Sugar beets are grown and processed locally. Anglers can catch trout in the North Platte and Laramie Rivers; perch, walleye and catfish abound in the smaller streams and reservoirs.

Excerpted from Goshen County Chamber of Commerce brochure

H Babe "Little Sweetheart of the Prairie" April 1906–June 14, 1958

25 miles north of Torrington on private land

This monument was erected in memory of "Little Babe"—The Worlds Oldest Horse.

Black and white shetland—Height 37 in,

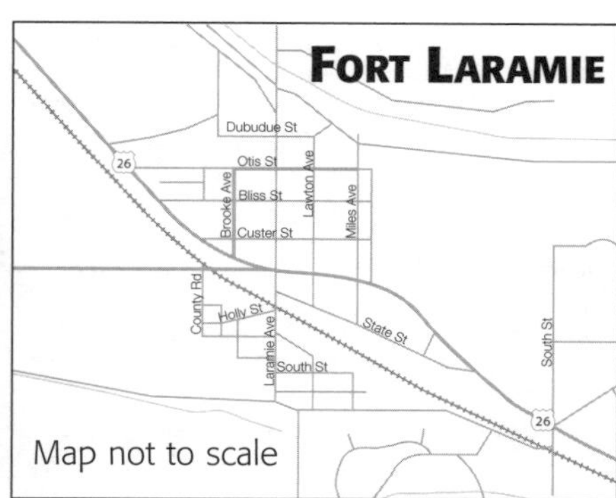

weight 330 lbs. She was famous the world over for her unusual age of 52 years and was extremely intelligent. She was active, good eyesight, good hearing until the time of her death. Her fame for her age had spread across the nation. When she became 50 years old, tourists traveling through Wyoming would make special efforts to see the spotted black and white pony.

Babe was the pet of the community. Owned by Velda and Wayne Childers

12 *Gas, Food, Lodging*

Fort Laramie, the town

Pop. 243, Elev. 4,230

Like the river, Ft. Laramie was named for French-Canadian trapper Jacques La Ramie, who explored much of eastern Wyoming. As well as being an auxiliary stop to the old Fort site, the town has its own share of historical significance. Wyoming's oldest post office was established here in the 1880s, and the old iron bridge here, built in 1875, was funded by a $15,000 congressional appropriation for the express purpose of accommodating the Cheyenne-Deadwood Stage.

T Fort Laramie National Historic Site

Three miles southwest of the Town of Fort Laramie. Follow signs off U.S. Highway 26. 837-2221

One of the most significant outposts on the trail was officially established as Fort William in 1834 by fur traders William Sublette and Robert Campbell. An adobe fort was built in 1841 by the American Fur Company and named Fort John. The U. S. Military purchased the Fort in 1849 as a base to protect and supply the growing emigration on the trail. Fort Laramie became a major link in the Pony Express, Overland Stage and transcontinental telegraph systems and served as an operations base for the Plains Indian Wars. Today, the site is operated by the National Park Service and is open year around with extended hours and living history programs during summer months. Many related historic sites are in the vicinity. *Source: BLM brochure.*

H Henry Hill

Located on private land in Goshen County along the Oregon Trail

At least three grave markers, each with conflicting data, have marked this grave of Henry Hill. A wood headboard was found here in the 1870s. In 1972 a headstone was found among the stone debris inscribed HENRY HILL June 8 [?] 1852 59 M.

From the date of his death and the numeral 59, presumed to be his age at death, it is believed that this is indeed the grave of Henry Hill, born in Caroline County, Virginia, in 1793. A veteran of the War of 1812, he sold his 399-acre farm in Monroe County, Missouri, in April 1852, to accompany his daughters, Martha and Clemencia, and son Joseph, with their families to California.

From the North Platte ferry area, on June 15, 1852, in-law James Hill wrote: "...about thirty five miles below Fort Larame we was called on to pay the last tribute of respect to old Father Hill." The cause of death was a cholera-like illness. "next morning we buried little black boy Billy."

Henry's daughter, Clemencia, died on Forty-mile Desert in Nevada. Nancy J. Hill, the sister-in-law of his son, Joseph, died July 5, 1852, on the Sublette Cutoff. Her marked grave is located northwest of Kemmerer, Wyoming.

H The Journey West Continues

About two miles west and northwest of Fort Laramie National Historic Site on the Oregon Trail.

"We proceeded (westward from Fort Laramie) and encamped outside the boundaries of Uncle Sam." So wrote Dr. J. S. Shepard in 1851 as he began the second leg of his journey west. "To leave Fort Laramie was to cast off all ties with civilization. It was an alien land," he noted.

The emigrants' elation at reaching the "civilization" of the Fort after 650 miles of monotonous, difficult overland travel was soon tempered by the realization that even more troublesome trail conditions lay ahead over the final two-thirds of the journey. "Here comes the ascent to the Rocky Mountains," wrote an apprehensive Cornelius Conway at mid-century.

To lighten their loads many travelers cast off thousands of dollars worth of food and equipment. This was especially true of the "49ers" who, in their haste to reach the gold fields, often invested little effort in planning their trip. Joseph Berrien reached Fort Laramie early, May 30, 1849, yet still referred to it as "Camp Sacrifice" because of the large quantities of abandoned gear and foodstuffs he saw nearby.

Between 1849 and 1854 an annual average of some 31,000 overlanders passed through or near the fort on their journey to Oregon, California, or Utah. Most passed on a trail marked by the ruts before you. Wagon travel near the Platte River, just to the north, was difficult due to seasonal high water and progressively more difficult terrain.

H Cheyenne-Black Hills Stage Monument

U.S. Highway 26 about five miles west of Fort Laramie

The Cheyenne-Black Hills Trail passed near this point between 1876 and 1887. Built to supply the Dakota gold camps, the road was constructed in violation of the Ft. Laramie Treaty of 1868 which reserved the Black Hills for Sioux Indians. Stagecoaches and wagons carrying passengers, freight and gold bullion rumbled through nearby Ft. Laramie, an important stopping point along the line, until the arrival of the Chicago and North Western Railroad rendered the route obsolete.

H The Greatest Ride In History

About a quarter mile from the entrance of the Fort Laramie National Historic Site on Fort Laramie Road

In memory of the thoroughbred horse ridden by John "Portugee" Phillips from Fort Phil Kearny Wyoming to Fort Laramie Wyoming December 24 and 25, 1866. When he sought aid for the garrison at Fort Phil Kearny, which was surrounded by Indians, after the battle with Lieutenant Colonel William F. Fetterman, resulting in the death of Lieutenant Colonel Fetterman and 80 men. The horse died from exhaustion soon after arriving at Fort Laramie, having gone 236 miles in two days, through a blizzard with the temperature below zero.

13 *Gas, Food*

Lingle

Pop. 510, Elev. 4,165

Hiram Lingle, who promoted development of the area, gave his name to this little agricultural town. It lies just across the Platte River from the site of the Grattan Massacre of 1854.

T Western History Center

Highway 26 five miles west of Lingle. 837-3052

The Western Plains Historic Preservation Association (WPHPA) was conceived in 1980 when an 1860's cemetery was accidentally unearthed near Lingle during a land-leveling project. The site contained human burials and thousands of artifacts. The land owner notified a professional archeologist who organized a group of concerned residents to salvage the site. When a similar incident occurred later that year, the volunteers were again called to action and it became obvious that more latitude was necessary to address the magnitude of the resources present. The WPHPA was established as a nonprofit entity

and began a wide range of historic preservation activities including the formation of the Western History Center. Exhibits include local fossils, mammoth tusks, various artifacts and historic items on display from local sites.
Excerpted from museum brochure.

H Grattan Fight Site

State HIghway 157 three miles west of Lingle

This monument marks the location of one of the earliest conflicts between the American Indians and soldiers in Wyoming. The fight broke out when Brevet 2nd Lt. John L. Grattan and 28 soldiers attempted to arrest a Sioux Indian for killing a crippled cow belonging to a Mormon wagon train. An allegedly drunken interpreter, who had grievances against the Indians, apparently mistranslated an offer by Chief Conquering Bear to replace the cow with a sound pony of his own. Grattan ordered his men to fire and when the gun smoke cleared, Grattan, almost his entire command and the chief lay dead. This August 1854 incident led to years of intermittent hostility along the trail. An Oregon Trail crossing monument is located just beyond the Grattan marker. Source: BLM brochure.

H Wyoming Rural Electrification

U.S. Highway 26 about one mile east of Lingle at rest area

In the early 1930s, fewer than one out of ten rural families in Wyoming had electric power.

The year 1985 marked the 50th anniversary of organized efforts to deliver electric service to the countryside. It began with President Franklin D. Roosevelt's executive order creating the Rural Electrification Administration (REA) on May 11, 1935.

Electrical service was widely available in towns, but rural residents struggled to bring water to their homes in buckets while their children studied by the light of smokey kerosene lanterns.

Cooperatives were formed by people who were determined to have electricity even though many thought it was not economically practical to build and maintain lines to isolated farms and ranches.

Wyrulec Company in Lingle was the first cooperative formed in Wyoming to bring electricity to the rural people. It started in October of 1937 to supply power to 101 member/consumers in Goshen County and the surrounding area.

In 1985, there were fourteen rural electric systems in Wyoming. Because of the rural electrification program, nearly everyone in rural America can receive electric power.

H Agriculture and Wildlife

At rest stop just east of Lingle

As you travel across Wyoming, its beauty, wide-open spaces and mountains may beckon to you. Many people have chosen to live in Wyoming because of its splendor. As we settle the land we must continue to keep in mind that humans are not the only inhabitants.

The area around you has been used by people for a very long time. Native American tribes traveled across the plains hunting the migrating bison, elk and pronghorn. The native people had little impact on the land because they seldom settled in one area. They lived off the land and shared it with all forms of wildlife. They knew they must treat the land well so it would return a living to them.

Today we have built houses, cities and roads throughout these wildlands. These are areas we must share with the native plants and animals, which are adapted to this environment. We have taken a diverse prairie community and turned it into fields of alfalfa, corn and wheat. Cropland is needed by all of us. Even though it has decreased available food and habitat for some wildlife, it has benefited other wildlife.

Acknowledging the fact that we need to share all resources with other forms of life is the first step we can take towards improving our own environment.

14 *Gas, Food, Lodging*

Torrington

Pop. 5,776, Elev. 4,104

Situated near the Platte River along the Oregon and Mormon Trails, the Cheyenne/ Deadwood Stage Route, and the Texas Trail, Torrington is now a busy farming community reminiscent of the Midwest. When William G. Curtis opened the post office out of his ranch here, he named it for his hometown of Torrington, Connecticut. When the Burlington Railroad arrived in 1900, the town was relocated off ranch property, and was officially platted in 1907.

With two major waterways diverted from the river (Fort Laramie Canal and Interstate Canal), Torrington was excellent property for homesteaders. The town grew with the production of sugar beets, dry beans, corn, hay, alfalfa, and oats, and continues to depend on these crops today. The Holly Sugar Factory, which processes the sugar beets grown in the area, is the town's number one employer.

T Homesteader's Museum

495 Main St. in Torrington.

The Homesteader's Museum is located at the crossroads of world famous trails: the Oregon Trail, Morman Trail, Cheyenne to Deadwood Stage Route, Fort Laramie Trail and Texas Cattle Trail. From the Homesteader's Museum.

The most interesting attraction of the Homesteader's Museum is the museum building—it is truly a show piece in itself. The Union Pacific Depot was built in 1925 and opened its doors to both passengers and freight service to

the world at that time. It is one of two "Spanish" style depots remaining in the North Platte valley.

The museum is actually a complex of buildings and exhibits. Here one can experience "homestead life" as was lived on the barren prairies of Southeastern Wyoming in Goshen County.

The Trout Homestead Shack was built in 1910 by Ben Trout. It is 12'7" X 12'8" and was occupied by the family for 12 years. It was located north of present day Hawk Springs Reservoir in southern Goshen County.

The Yoder Family Memorial Home houses hundreds of items from the old 4A Ranch (Yoder) which was established in 1882 by Phillip and Cinderella Yoder and their seven children. This ranch was located on Bear Creek, west of the town site of LaGrange, Wyoming. The Yoder children were involved in ranching, banking, politics and rodeo.

The Midway School House was built in 1928 and closed in 1949. This building is one of the last of its kind remaining in Goshen County.

Enjoy the saddles and rodeo memorbilia of Carl Sawyer. See the F. A. Meanea saddles of Odessa Dearing and Eunice Cameron Everling. Also see the veterinary medical equipment of 'Doc' Fuller, early homestead veterinarian. Visit the Union Pacific Caboose Gallery of railroad photographs and railroad memoribilia. Both Union Pacific and burlington Northern items are on display. Both railroads run through Torrington.

See the Knowlton family's International Harvester Auto-Buggy which was brought to Goshen County in 1908. This was the first car in the area at that time. 'Wil' Knowlton, first elected County Assessor, used the car to travel the new county (1913) as he assessed homesteaders in the area. The car was acclaimed the best 'hill climber' of its time.

Enjoy fashions and costumes from the late 1890s through 1945. See how style changes in women's clothes foretold the changes in social and political issues of the period.

Browse the Merrill and Marie Potter Collection of early Plains Indians arrowheads, knives, scrapers, drill, hammerheads and more. Approximately 11,000 plus pieces collected when walking the plains of Goshen, Platte and Niobrara Counties.

The museum is open year round. Call for hours.

Reprinted from museum brochure.

F The Java Jar

1940 Main in Torrington. 532-8541

M Eastern Wyoming College

3200 West C Street in Torrington. 532-8200 or 800-658-3195. http://ewcweb.ewc.cc.wy.us/

Eastern Wyoming College was established in September 1948 as the Southeast University Center. It is located in the North Platte River Valley in the southeast Wyoming town of Torrington. After a reorganization in 1956 growth of the institution continued steadily. Today the college serves over 1600 students in credit courses and over 8000 students in noncredit activities.

Torrington

	Jan	Feb	March	April	May	June	July	Aug	Sep	Oct	Nov	Dec	Annual
Average Max. Temperature (F)	40.3	45.1	51.0	61.8	71.2	81.6	89.2	87.4	78.0	66.1	51.1	42.3	63.8
Average Min. Temperature (F)	10.9	15.3	21.5	30.7	40.9	49.9	55.7	53.1	42.3	30.6	20.2	13.0	32.0
Average Total Precipitation (in.)	0.29	0.36	0.69	1.69	2.54	2.47	1.66	1.11	1.14	0.95	0.49	0.37	13.75
Average Total SnowFall (in.)	4.2	4.9	5.8	3.3	0.6	0.0	0.0	0.0	0.3	1.6	4.4	5.3	30.6
Average Snow Depth (in.)	1	1	0	0	0	0	0	0	0	0	0	1	0
Wind Speed (mph / kmh)	12 / 19	12 / 19	13 / 21	13 / 21	12 / 19	11 / 17	10 / 15	9 / 15	10 / 16	10 / 16	10 / 17	11 / 18	
Wind Direction	WNW	WNW	WNW	WNW	WNW	SE	ESE	ESE	ESE	WNW	WNW	WNW	
Cloud Cover (out of 8)	5.0	5.0	5.4	5.1	5.1	4.1	3.6	3.6	3.6	4.1	4.9	4.8	

The college sponsors outreach programs in Converse, Crook, Niobrara, Platte, and Weston counties. Eastern Wyoming College is a student-centered, comprehensive public community college committed to providing accessible, post-secondary education for its students. Students are from 19 states and 3 foreign countries.

15 *Food, Lodging*

T Torrington Livestock Market

Auctions take place every Friday at 10am.

T Torrington Botanical Park

1st Ave. and S. Main in Torrington

A small park laced with paths and plants for the enjoyment of the community and visitors.

H Stuart Campsite

On U.S. Highway 26 about 5 miles east of Torrington

East of Torrington, near the Wyoming/Nebraska state line, is the camp site of Robert Stuart and his party of Astorians. They were the men who laid out and first traveled the route from the West Coast to St. Louis, which later became known as the Oregon Trail. Leaving Astoria, John Jacob Astor's fur trading post at the mouth of the Columbia River, the Astorians got as far as present-day Torrington by December, 1812. According to Stuart's diary, the party constructed a small shack and spent the rest of the winter on the bank of the North Platte River.

16 *Food, Lodging*

H Cold Springs

On the east side of U. S. Highway 85 about one and a half miles south of the intersection of U. S. Highways 85 and 26 in Torrington. Adjacent to Oregon Trail marker

Cold Springs 3/4 mile east from this point

Cold Springs was a popular camping ground on the Overland Emigrant Trail to California, Oregon, Utah, and other points in the far west.

It was a stage station along the Overland Stage route 1854-1862 and also a pony express relay stop 1860-1861. Station tender was M. Reynal.

17 *No services*

Huntley

This town received its name from a civil engineer with the Union Pacific railroad.

Veteran

Pop. 19, Elev. 4,100

Veterans of WWI who drew lots for parcels of land established this little town in the 1920s. The community is centrally located to water recreation.

Yoder

Pop. 169, Elev. 4,245

Frank and Jesse Yoder were local landowners who gave this town its name.

T Downar Bird Farm

U.S. Highway 85 about 17 miles south of Yoder. 532-3449

The Wyoming Fish and Game Department runs this interesting project which raises over 11,000 pheasants each year. There are over 27 different breeds. The birds are released each fall for the pleasure of area hunters. Although the ring-neck pheasant is abundant in the Midwest and western states it is native to China. Call the farm for information on visiting.

Prairie dog city near Hawk Springs

18 *Food, Lodging*

LaGrange

Pop. 332

The oldest town in Goshen County, (incorporated in 1889), LaGrange was named for local rancher, Kale LaGrange. The first Texas cattle came through this area in 1886. It is now a quiet agricultural community with a cozy town park, tennis courts and rodeo grounds to entice visitors.

Hawk Springs

Pop. 100

"Black" Hawk, a saloonkeeper, gave his name to this town and the nearby springs. Hawk operated a stagecoach station in the early 1900s. The springs were covered by the reservoir.

T Hawk Springs State Recreation Area

Five miles southeast of Hawk Springs, between 66 Mountain and Bear Mountain

History

Hawk Springs reservoir and the surrounding area is owned by the Horse Creek Conservation District. When the word began to spread about the recreational opportunities at Hawk Springs, visitation increased dramatically. The Wyoming Game & Fish Department began to enforce regulations for recreational water usage (fishing and boating) and installed 12 picnic tables and fire grills, the boat ramp and two toilets.

The site was named a state recreation area in 1987 at which time the Wyoming Recreation Commission (now called the Division of State Parks and Historic Sites, Wyoming Department of State Parks and Cultural Resources) agreed to administer the site. In 1989 the agency further improved the site with additional tables and fire grills, a sprinkler drip system for trees donated by the Hawk Springs boat club and many other trees were planted. In 1990 camping fees were first collected.

Bird Watchers

Hawk Springs reservoir boasts a blue heron rookery. At the south end of the reservoir in the reeds, patient bird watchers will be rewarded by a glimpse of the blue heron. This may only be accessed by boat. Other birds in the area include the Canada Goose, mallard, blue-winged and green-winged teal, gadwall, pintail, wood duck, avocet and great horned owl.

Fishing

Fisherman have long known that fishing is good at Hawk Springs. Game fish include walleye, large mouth bass, yellow perch, channel catfish and black croppie. Walleye fishing is best in June and July. A valid fishing license is required by both residents and nonresidents. Winter ice fishing is also good at the park. Keep in mind, however, that the roads are not maintained during the winter, so be cautious when driving.

Reprinted from Wyoming State Parks & Historic Sites brochure.

H Of Birds and Bluffs

At the rest area south of LaGrange on U.S. Highway 85

Notice that you are in a depression surrounded by bluffs as you observe the landscape. This is the southern part of an area called "Goshen Hole." It is also the western edge of the North American short-grass prairie.

The bluffs were formed by deposition of materials from the Laramie Mountains, located to the west. These bluffs consist mainly of siltstone and are capped by sandstone. The entire area supports a variety of wildlife. The bluffs and associate prairie provide habitat for raptors, including Swainson's and ferruginous hawks, prairie falcons. American kestrels and burrowing owls. Mule deer, coyotes, prairie dogs and meadowlarks are a few of the other inhabitants. One population, which has recently increased its numbers, is the sharp-tailed grouse. Sharptails eat grains, forbs (non-woody, flowering plants), grasses, buds and fruit. They also eat insects such as grasshoppers, especially when the birds are young.

Grouse need a variety of habitats to survive throughout the year. Prairies and shrubby draws are crucial for their survival, providing breeding habitat, cover and a winter food source. In the past, declines in sharp-tailed grouse populations were due to competition with agriculture, which changed the prairie. Many landowners now

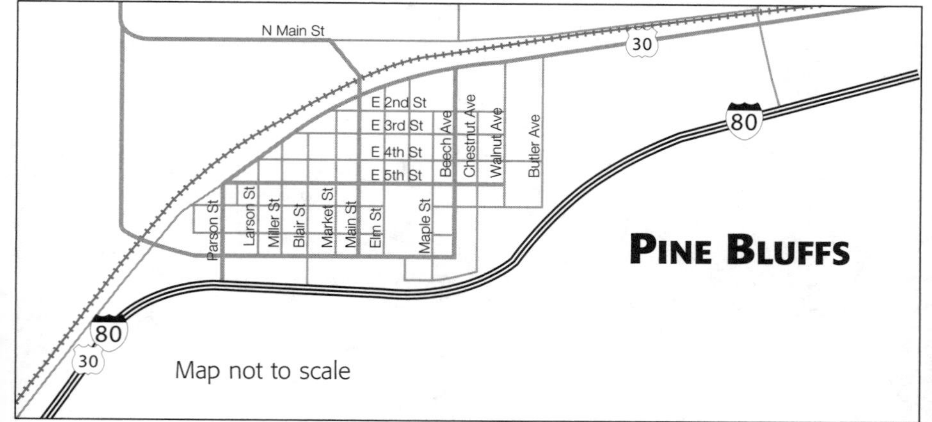

plant shelter belts and leave tall grass cover which are used by grouse and other wildlife for food and shelter. Wildlife also search grain fields for seeds. Keeping remaining native prairies intact will help ensure prime habitat for these birds and other wildlife in the future.

19 *Gas*

Albin

Pop. 120, Elev. 5,334

This little town was named for John Albin Anderson, the first local postmaster in 1905, whose father owned the ranch nearby. Keep your eyes out for the old frontier sod house.

Wyoming Tidbits

Niobrara County was named for an Omaha Indian word meaning "flat or broad river".

20 *Gas, Food, Lodging*

Burns

Pop. 285, Elev. 5,455

Originally named Luther (for Martin Luther) by the German emigrants who settled it in 1907, Burns name was changed by UP officials to honor a division engineer. The emigrants, displaced from Iowa, had hoped to begin a Lutheran colony. Uinta County, unfortunately, already had a post office named Burns, so a dispute arose until the other Burns post office closed in 1910. In due time, Burns became a provisional stop for nearby farmers and ranchers.

Carpenter

no services

On the Colorado-Wyoming border, this town was named for real estate promoter J. Ross Carpenter. He sold 160-acre plots of land to many Iowa immigrants. Settled homesteaders came here in the early days to stock up on winter supplies.

Wyoming Tidbits

When Calamity Jane set out with horse and buggy for Cheyenne's Fort D. A. Russell, according to the Cheyenne Leader, ..."*indulgence in frequent and liberal potations completely befogged her not very clear brain, and she drove right by the place until she reached Chugwater, 50 miles distant. Continuing to imbibe in bug-juice at close intervals and in large quanitities throughout the night, she woke up the next morning with the vague idea Fort Russell had been removed.*"

Egbert

Dan and Augustus Egbert were railroad workers who chose this site for a station in 1868.

Hillsdale

This little town was named for Lathrop Hills, an engineer for the railroad, who lead a survey team in 1867. Hills was killed here when a group of Indians attacked the party. A memorial for him was erected in 1973.

Pine Bluffs

Pop. 1,153, Elev. 5,047

This border town was once a stop on the Texas Trail. The town was established when the railroad came in 1867, and by the 1880s, Pine Bluffs became the major shipping hub for the cattle industry. More cattle boarded trains here than anywhere else in the world. Originally called Rock Ranch, the name was later changed to reflect the pine-covered bluffs south of the town site. Pine Bluffs is now primarily a farming community, with several silos and a variety of crops growing around the town.

T University of Wyoming Archeological Museum & Archeological Site

1001 Muddy Creek Dr. in Pine Bluffs. 245-3746

Housing more than 50,000 cataloged fossil, rock, and mineral specimens, this is an important source of information for researchers throughout the world. The museum functions to support both public education and educational research.

T Texas Trail Park and Museum

201 W. 3rd Street in Pine Bluffs. 245-3695

This museum is housed in Pine Bluffs original power plant. It preserves and displays historic treasures of the area, town, cattle ranches, and homesteads. There is even a fully complete boarding house interior. The Transportation of Time Exhibit showcases the importance of Pine Bluffs Crossroads in the development of Pine Bluffs and the West. It is open the first week of May through the third week of September, Monday through Saturday 11 a.m. to 4 p.m.

T Our Lady of Peace Shrine

On the north side of I-80 on U.S. Highway 30 at Pine Bluffs. 632-0100

Our Lady of Peace Shrine, is the dream of a Wyoming couple, Ted and Marjorie Trefren of Cheyenne. The dream came from Marjorie's visit to the Old World holy shrines of Medjugorge, Yugoslavia, Lourdes, and Fatima, where visions of the Blessed Mother have appeared. Although Marjorie saw no visions, she returned to Wyoming with the dream of a Marian Shrine in her home state. For several years, the couple sought a site for the shrine, and formed the non-profit Out Lady of Peace Shrine Organization, with the blessing of the local Catholic Diocese.

Finally, the Pine Bluffs site was chosen and the work by sculptor Robert Fida began. The statue was rendered in rubber, fiberglass, and foam before a laser generated cast was filled with marble cement, a mixture of marble dust, sealant, and additives. The marble was taken from a Wyoming quarry in Wheatland. The completed sculpture stands 5-stories high, and weighs 180 tons, one of the largest Marian statues in the U.S.

H Pine Bluffs Interpretive Signs

Archeological site at rest stop off I-80 exit 401

Wildflowers

Wildflowers emerge in early spring when the soil warms and the rains begin. The Bluffs area is colored with the white and yellow of low growing species such as western yarrow, mountain lily, and pasque flower.

Pine Bluffs

	Jan	Feb	March	April	May	June	July	Aug	Sep	Oct	Nov	Dec	Annual
Average Max. Temperature (F)	39.6	43.2	48.1	58.8	68.8	79.9	88.5	86.6	77.2	64.4	49.4	41.3	62.2
Average Min. Temperature (F)	12.7	16.0	20.9	29.7	39.6	48.3	54.6	52.9	43.0	32.2	21.3	14.8	32.2
Average Total Precipitation (in.)	0.33	0.31	0.84	1.64	2.46	2.65	2.13	1.90	1.26	0.85	0.48	0.36	15.21
Average Total SnowFall (in.)	3.2	3.3	6.1	4.3	0.7	0.0	0.0	0.0	0.1	1.4	4.2	3.8	27.1
Average Snow Depth (in.)	1	1	0	0	0	0	0	0	0	0	1	1	0

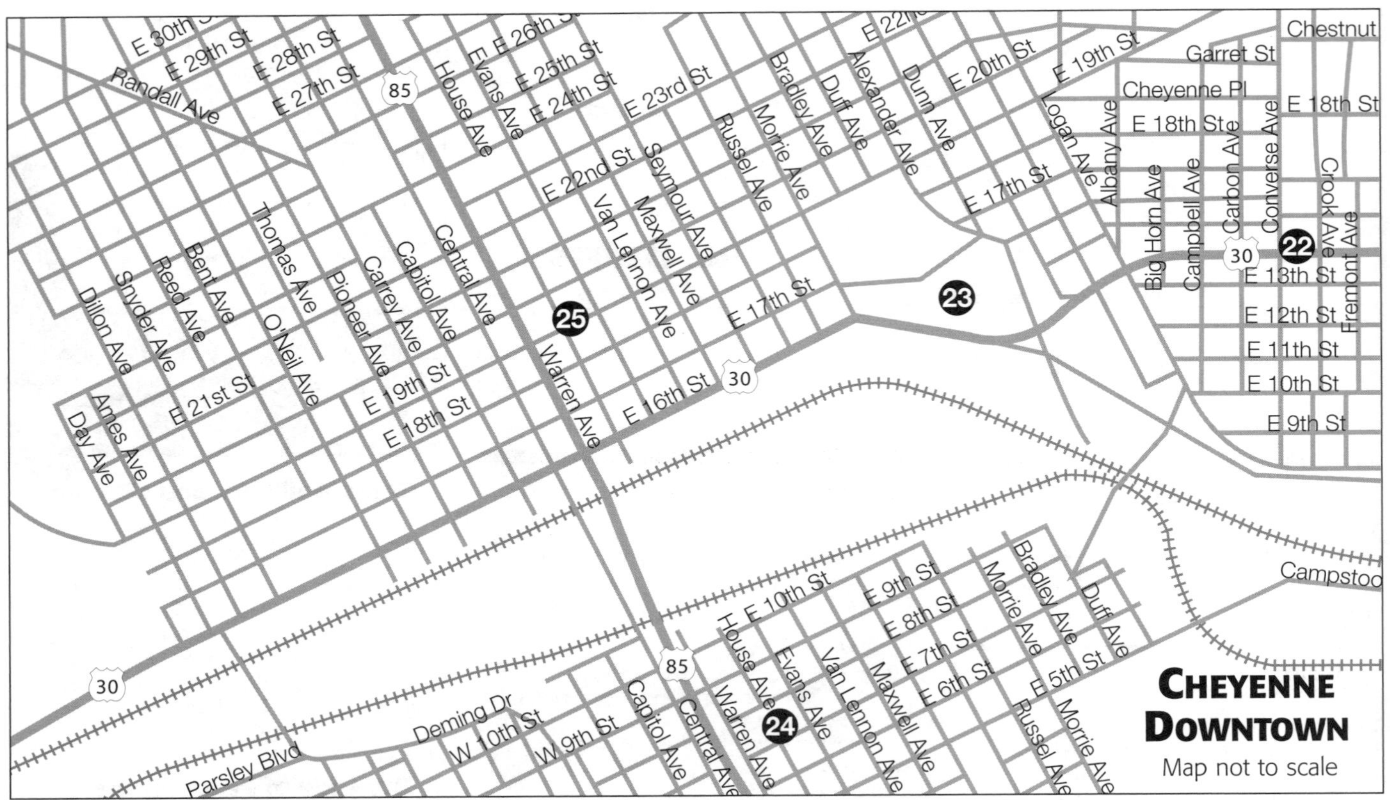

These early spring bloomers struggle for light and warmth and after a few weeks of vigorous activity, they disappear or sometimes persist in the shade of other plants long into the summer.

May and June is a colorfest as the wildflowers rush to finish their work before the blistering days of summer. Now there are flowers to be made and seeds to spread. The prairie buck bean, rock sandwort, sego lily, prairie phlox as well as the prairie ragwort can be seen with their bright yellow or white flowers basking in the sun. This is an excellent time to hunt and identify wildflowers in the area.

In the summer months when moisture is scarce, the prickly pear, large flower to sedum lanceolatum, beards tongue, sawsepal penstemon, standing milk vetch, death camas (which is possibly the most poisonous plant in the area and looks a lot like a wild onion), western yarrow and lupines are in full bloom.

In the later part of summer and into fall, flowers such as the sunflower, asters, goldenrods, and some species of the Gentian family are in bloom. These are but a few of the wildflowers found in the Pine Bluffs area.

The succulent green growth of wildflowers are an important source of protein to the doe mule deer nursing her fawns. Bird life of the area rely on the insects, hatched in the shade of wildflowers as a source of calcium and protein for producing eggs. Young birds also require this insect food in early stages of growth.

With a wildflower field guide and some time in the field you can discover a whole new world. You will see that wild beauty in the eye of humans is also an important part of the formula making Wyoming's wildlife a nation.

Wyoming Tidbits

Cheyenne's second mayor was a dairy farmer named Sloan. When Duke Alexis of Russia visited the city in 1872, Mayor Sloan hauled the visiting royal through town in a milk wagon preceded by a band with four horns and a drum.

Tipi Rings

The classic plains lifestyle often depicted in the movies developed after the European introduction of the horse which provided more mobility, allowing the Indians to follow buffalo (bison) herds, increased trade and contact with other Indian tribes and Euro-American traders and explorers. Archaeological sites of this time period are often recognize by the presence of spaced stone circles or "tipi rings."

Actually several thousand years ago, Native American Indian groups developed a conical leather tent, or "tipi," which was ideally suited to a nomadic life on the High Plains. With a shape offering low wind resistance, ventilating flaps for catching the breeze in warm weather, and other features. No better design has ever been developed.

The bottom edge of the hide covered tipis was often held down with a circle of rocks which were left in place when the tent was moved. Some of these "tipi rings" are relatively complete and obvious to anyone, while others, with just a few rocks, require identification and verification by professional archaeologists. These stone circles or "tipi rings" are found throughout the Pine Bluffs area and Plains in general are one of the lasting legacies of the rich history of the human occupation of the High Plains.

The Prairie Rattlesnake

Less conspicuous than the pronghorn antelope and the golden eagle is an even more ancient inhabitant of the high plains and valley of Wyoming, the prairie rattlesnake. Feared by many and respected by most, these pit vipers (so-called because of their heat–sensing facial pits used to detect warm bodied prey) are common in the eastern two-thirds of the state in all but alpine habitats. During winter these snakes hibernate in underground dens for up to eight months. In spring they migrate away from the dens in search of food (typically rodents and other small mammals) and mates. Studies show that they move from the den in virtually a straight-line path covering perhaps several miles until they find a food source. They stay on their fixed-angle course by using the sun as a navigational aid. When the temperature cools in fall, the snakes return to the same den.

The habitat around you no doubt contains many of these secretive and fascinating reptilian hunters, but there is really very little to fear. Though they are poisonous and seemingly hostile, evidence indicates that chances of being bitten are virtually nil, as long as the snake is not touched, provoked, or frightened. Since rattlesnakes are deaf and cannot actually hear rattling, this behavior is believed to be defensive. A rattling rattlesnake is simply trying to warn or drive off another creature if it perceives to be a threat.

If you encounter a prairie rattlesnake, give it plenty of room and you will be in no danger–its probably more frightened than you are. Allow the snake to go on its way and hunt prey like its ancestors have done in this area for thousands and thousands of years. The prairie rattler may not earn you admiration, but it deserves respect as a fascinating and important element of Wyoming's wildlands.

Archaeological Site

Archaeology is the scientific study of prehistoric peoples, and deals with lifeways, subsistence practices, settlement patterns, and prehistoric technology. The bluffs extending east and south from Pine Bluffs incorporate one of the largest concentrations of archaeological sites on the western plains. Although perhaps not as impressive as the archaeological record of many other regions, the Pine Bluffs area contains a rich prehistoric legacy. This scattering of chipped stone artifacts, burned rock, stone circles, (tipi rings), and other materials represents and accumulation from over 11,000 years of occupation by small groups of nomadic Native American Indian peoples.

The Pine Bluffs Site, one of the largest sites in the area, is located on and around the bluff on the west side of the I-80 Rest Area. Excavations by archaeologists from University of Wyoming have revealed cultural levels which include the entire range of occupation, from early historic plains Indian tribes such as the Arapaho, Kiowa, Cheyenne, and Dakota back to the earliest Pleistocene (ice age) big game hunters.

These archaeological excavations revealed the remains of butchered buffalo (bison), deer, antelope, rabbits, and other small mammals. Plant remains have also been found which together indicate these prehistoric ancestors of the modern American Indians lived by hunting the wild animals inhabiting the prairies and from gathering wild plants. Although a wide range of plant and animal resources were used by prehistoric inhabitants of the Pine Bluffs area, evidence reveals that bison were the preferred game animal. The Pine Bluffs site is a "master key" for the study of the prehistoric occupation of the entire region.

H Lathrop Hills, Surveyor for the first transcontinental railroad, killed by Indians

South of the Post Office in Hillside

On June 11, 1867, Lathrop Hills led a party of surveyors up the nearby Lodgepole Creek, staking out the location for the Union Pacific Railroad, the first transcontinental railroad. Hills was riding out in front of the group when he was attacked by Indians and killed. Within minutes his men drove off the Indians and later reported they found 19 arrow wounds in his body. He was 35.

Hills' work lived after him. By November 14, 1867, the track layers had reached Cheyenne and 18 months later a golden spike was driven at Promontory, Utah, completing the first railroad connection between the East and West and opening millions of acres for settlement. The railroad reduced travel time from six months required by wagon train to five days from Omaha to San Francisco.

21 *Gas, Food, Lodging*

Cheyenne

Pop. 53, 011, Elev. 6,062

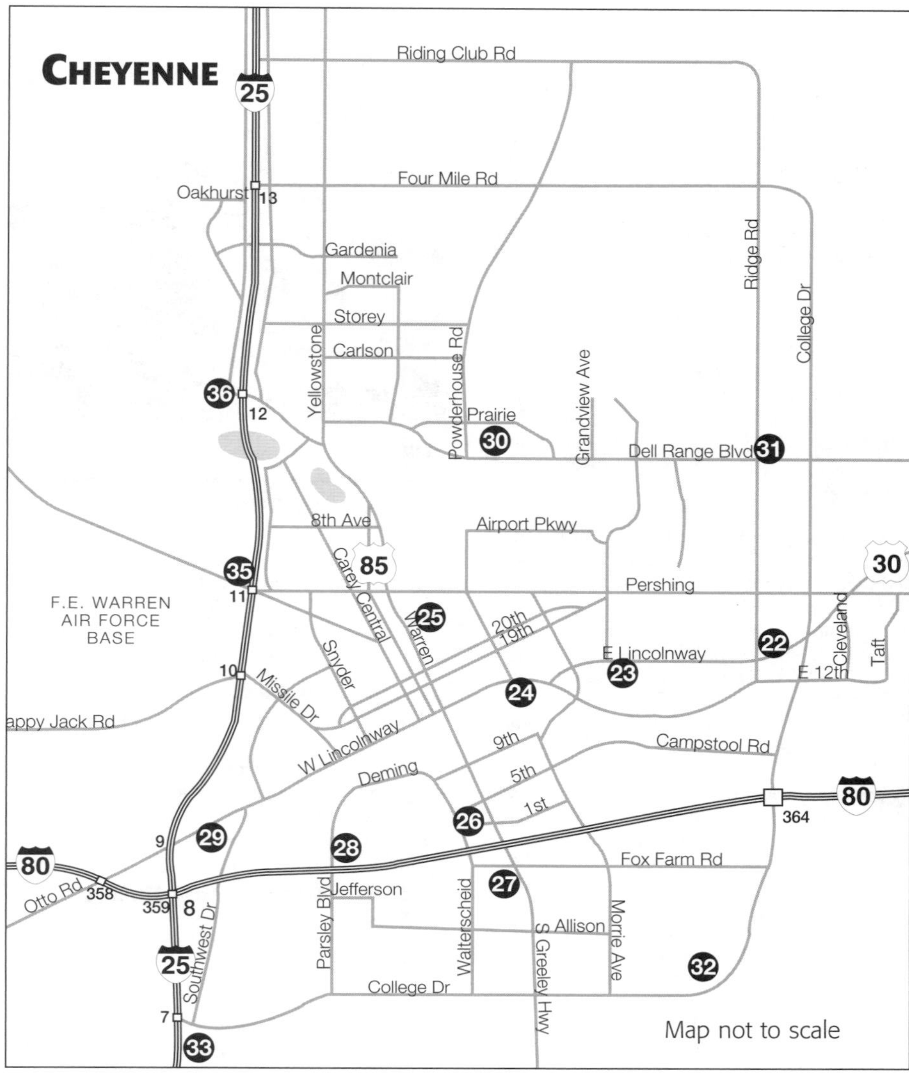

Situated in the southeast corner of the state, Cheyenne is the gateway to Wyoming from both Nebraska and Colorado. At the intersection of I-80 and I-25, all kinds of transportation meet here and send people in every direction across the state. To the east lie the Great Plains, and brilliant thunderstorms can be viewed over the prairie on summer nights. To the south and west loom the Rocky Mountains in all their glory, awing newcomers with their splendor. Cheyenne is becoming increasingly urban, as its political and economic connections put it more and more on the map of the American West. As the state capitol, and home of Francis E. Warren Air Force Base, governmental support helps tremendously. The shopping and tourist industries have boosted the city's prospects as well. Frontier Days, one of the most widely known Western attractions, is held here every July.

Named for the Indian tribe, Cheyenne is actually the French trappers' spelling for the Sioux phrase "sha hi ye na," which means "speakers of a strange language." The Cheyenne called themselves "tsis tsistas", meaning "The People." They inhabited most of the southeast quarter of the state of Wyoming before the eastern influx of immigrants.

Cheyenne became a "hell on wheels" tent city in 1867, established by Gen. Grenville Dodge for workers on the UP railroad. The fast and furious race to lay down tracks brought laborers from all parts of the world, especially many from famine-ravaged countries like Ireland and China. The town grew so fast it became known as "The Magic City of the Plains." The Cheyenne-Deadwood Stage carried gold-hungry workers between the railroad and the gold fields of South Dakota. Law and order were loosely maintained, mostly by

Cheyenne	Jan	Feb	March	April	May	June	July	Aug	Sep	Oct	Nov	Dec	Annual
Average Max. Temperature (F)	37.6	40.2	44.4	53.7	63.6	74.6	82.5	80.4	71.5	59.7	46.4	39.6	57.9
Average Min. Temperature (F)	15.5	17.6	21.6	29.7	39.1	48.1	54.5	53.0	43.9	33.7	23.5	17.7	33.2
Average Total Precipitation (in.)	0.44	0.52	1.06	1.74	2.45	2.02	2.03	1.65	1.29	0.91	0.62	0.45	15.18
Average Total SnowFall (in.)	5.9	6.9	11.2	9.8	3.1	0.2	0.0	0.0	0.7	3.8	7.1	6.3	55.1
Average Snow Depth (in.)	1	1	1	0	0	0	0	0	0	0	1	1	0
Wind Speed (mph / kmh)	15 / 24	15 / 23	14 / 23	14 / 23	13 / 21	11 / 18	10 / 17	10 / 17	11 / 18	12 / 19	13 / 21	15 / 23	
Wind Direction	WNW	WNW	WNW	WNW	WNW	WNW	WNW	WNW	WNW	WNW	WNW	WNW	
Cloud Cover (out of 8)	4.7	4.9	5.2	5.1	5.3	4.3	4.1	4.0	3.8	3.9	4.6	4.6	

vigilante groups. The military was sent in to keep the peace, and Ft. D.A. Russell was established to protect the railroad from both outlaws and Indians. It eventually displaced Ft. Laramie as the strategic headquarters in that area.

Cheyenne was among the few such towns to survive the completion of the railroad and become a train station city. Not only did it end up being the half-way point between Omaha, Nebraska, and Ogden, Utah, but its location just before the highest point on the Transcontinental Railroad made it the perfect place to tune up engines before the big climb. In 1869, Cheyenne was declared the unofficial capitol of the Wyoming Territory.

As the Indians were sent to the reservations, and the buffalo diminished, the range opened up. The trains brought homesteaders of Scandinavian, German, Slavic, English, and Basque decent, to name just a few. Many wealthy aristocrats also took advantage of the opportunities the open range promised. As a shipping hub, Cheyenne naturally became a place to socialize for the pre-eminent ranchers and businessmen in the area, and the Cactus Club became the local hotspot. Later renamed the Cheyenne Club, it ultimately hosted many of the elite, some of whom only resided in Cheyenne in the summer.

By 1880, Cheyenne was known as the wealthiest city per capita in the world. In 1882, it became one of the first cities in the nation to have incandescent electric lighting. In 1886, the first public county library was established here. Then in 1887-88, the country's economy crashed, and many cattlemen were forced to leave the area. The Cheyenne Club went out of business, and was burned to the ground in 1936.

In the meantime, Cheyenne remained Wyoming's largest city, and became the official capitol when Wyoming became a state in 1890. In 1920, Buck Chiffron flew the first Transcontinental Air Mail flight from the hills of Cheyenne westward. First Governor and long-time US Senator Francis E. Warren died in 1930, and Ft. Russell was renamed Ft. Warren in his honor. The new-fangled Air Force acquired the fort in 1947, and it received the name it has today, Francis E. Warren Air Force Base. The base became important in 1958 as the site of the nation's first strategic nuclear missile silos.

Cheyenne continues to be a lively community of events and opportunities for lovers of the Old West and modern consumers alike.

Campstool
13 miles east of Cheyenne

Named after the Camp Stool Ranch, the town was founded shortly after the Civil War.

H Swan Land and Cattle Company

Among the most famous of all cattle operations in Wyoming, this was founded in 1883 by brothers Alexander and Thomas Swan. Backed by Scottish investors, the company ran more than 100,000 cattle on nearly one million acres. Lawsuits and the devastating winter of 1886-87 pushed the company into the verge of bankruptcy. The company reorganized and survived for another 50 years, raising sheep instead of cattle after 1903. By 1950, profits were dwindling and the operation was liquidated. The ranch complex has been designated a National Historic Landmark.

L Howdy Pardner Bed & Breakfast
1920 Tranquility Road in Cheyenne. 634-6493. www.howdypardner.net

22 *Gas, Food, Lodging*

F Estevan's Cafe
1820 Ridge Road in Cheyenne. 632-6828

The family owned and operated Estevan's Cafe has been serving outstanding Mexican food for over 17 years. They will make you feel at home with great food, great service, and great prices in a quaint Mexican atmosphere. This popular restaurant serves daily specials and homemade specials that are loved by locals and visitors alike. Some say the homemade tortillas and deep-fried tacos "are to live for." The prices are the same for lunch and dinner. A wide range of authentic dishes and combinations will delight your palate. Accent your meal with beer, wine, and margaritas. Don't forget to try the fried ice cream or fluffy sopapillas.

S Sierra Trading Post Outlet Store
5025 Campstool Road in Cheyenne. 775-8090 or 800-713-4534. www.SierraTradingPost.com

23 *Gas, Food, Lodging*

H Merci Boxcar Train
Northeast of downtown at the corner of Lincolnway and Big Horn in front of the American Legion Hall

This Boxcar is just one of forty-nine presented to each of the forty-eight states and one to Washington D.C. and Hawaii in 1949.

The Train was an expression of thanks from the citizens of France to the people of the United States for aid rendered during and after World War II. This boxcar was laden with gifts which were distributed throughout the State of Wyoming.

This Boxcar is both a rarity and a remembrance to the Gallant Men and Women who served. The cars were built between 1872 and 1885 and ferried troops, horses, and equipment during both World Wars.

Donated by Republique De France to; The State of Wyoming in care of the Grand Voiture Du Wyoming La Societe Des 40 Hommes Et 8 Chevaux. (40 Hommes—40 Humans, 8 Chevaux—8 Horses)

Voiture Locale

Cheyenne 851 Casper 321 Lander 1437

24 *Food*

T "Big Boy" Steam Engine
Southeast of downtown Cheyenne in Holiday Park

Old Number 4004, the world's largest steam locomotive, was retired from active duty by the Union Pacific in 1962 after logging over 1,029,507 miles. Overall length: 132 feet, 9-1/4 inches and weighs about 600 tons. Big Boy, is considered by many to be the largest, most successful articulated steam locomotive ever built. "Articulated" refers to the flexibility of the locomotive which is crucial to successfully handling curves on the track.

H Big Boy Locomotive
Southeast of downtown Cheyenne in Holiday Park

"Big Boy'—The world's largest steam locomotive.

Built in 1941 Big Boy was designed especially for use by the Union Pacific Railroad on its rugged Cheyenne to Ogden, Utah run. The mighty 4004 was one of a series of only 25 locomotives of this type ever built. It was retired from service on December 21, 1956.

Total weight 1,208,750 lbs. Overall length-132' 93/8". Fuel capacity—28 Tons. Water capacity—25,000 Gals.

25 *Food, Lodging*

T Cheyenne Area Convention and Visitors Bureau
309 W. Lincolnway in Cheyenne. 778-3133 or 800-426-5009. www.cheyenne.org

T The Nelson Museum of the West
1714 Carey Ave. in downtown Cheyenne. 635-7670 www.nelsonmuseum.com

This museum has 11,000 square feet of displays including an eclectic collection of cowboy and Indian collectibles and wildlife trophies from around the world. It is open year round. Call for hours. There is an admission fee.

T Wyoming State Museum
2301 Central Avenue just north of downtown Cheyenne. 777-7022

Founded in 1895, and located in the Barrett Building just south of the State Capitol Building, the Wyoming State Museum is the only museum in the world dedicated to the entire history of Wyoming. The museum also hosts several temporary exhibits throughout the year.

In the Wyoming's Story gallery visitors can view artifacts from many eras of Wyoming's history. The Blocks of Time exhibit compares the significant amount of time involved in the state's natural history and the relatively small amount of time the state's human history occupies. A large interactive map highlights archaeological sites, trails, military forts, mountain man rendezvous sites, and military battles. It is the focal point of the gallery and allows visitors to mentally orient themselves.

The Wild Bunch gallery attempts to acquaint visitors with some of the state's more common wildlife. The exhibit examines the impact that humans can have on wildlife populations. A diorama depicting a scene from central Wyoming with flora and fauna specimens is the highlight of the exhibit

The Swamped With Coal gallery educates the visitor about the importance of the mining industry to the state. Swamped With Coal also describes the geologic events in the distant past, which created modern Wyoming's vast mineral wealth. A large model reminds visitors that the swamps of ancient times are the coal mines of today.

Younger visitors love the Hands-on History, but all ages can benefit from a visit here. Touchable reproduction artifacts, a curiosity cabinet filled with objects to examine, a chuck wagon, and a child-sized tipi are just some of the many features that bring Wyoming's history to life in this gallery.

Wyoming is a dinosaur graveyard and the state's dinosaur and other fossils can be found in museums throughout the world. The R. I. P. - Rex in Pieces gallery tells of fossil discovery competitions in the nineteenth century, and examines some of the state's earliest prehistoric residents. R. I. P. - Rex in Pieces features a cast (reproduction) of a full-sized Camptosaurus skeleton. Camptosaurus was one of the first dinosaurs found in the state. Another highlight is a cast of a huge leg bone from an Apatosaurus.

Highlights of Wyoming's Common Wealth gallery include the silver service from the battleship USS Wyoming, fine Native American beadwork and quillwork, a marble sculpture depicting the state's animals and plants, firearms, and a diorama made in the 1950s of Wyoming cowboys at work branding calves.

The Drawn to This Land gallery looks at the reasons why certain industries and peoples have been drawn either permanently or temporarily to what is now Wyoming. Its six sections tell the story: animal management, retail, tourism, agriculture, the military, transportation and mining.

The living in Wyoming gallery focuses on six themes to address the social history of Wyoming: the home, Wyomingites, traditions, government, education, and recreation. This is the largest permanent gallery in the museum.

Prestigious temporary exhibits rotate through The Changing Exhibits Gallery each year. Some recent ones included the Wyoming Game & Fish Department Conservation Stamp Art Competition, Show & Sale in the spring and the Governor's Capitol Art Exhibition in the summer. Throughout the year, other temporary exhibits related to Wyoming's history are on display here, as well as temporary exhibits created through the museum's From the People of Wyoming program.

The museum is open Tuesday through Saturday year round. Call for hours. Admission is free.

T Wyoming Arts Council Gallery

2320 Capitol Ave. in Cheyenne. 777-7742

Features a variety of changing and traveling exhibits throughout the year.

T Wyoming Transportation Museum & Learning Center

1701 Capitol Ave. in Cheyenne. 637-3376

Visit this museum to learn about the many ways that people have crossed the state over the years. Exhibits in the museum recreate the history of people on the move throughout the American West. The building is considered by many to be the most beautiful railroad station between Omaha and Sacramento. Call for hours.

T Historic Lakeview Cemetery

2501 Seymour Ave. in Cheyenne. 637-6402

Established in the 1800s when the Union Pacific Railroad came to Cheyenne, this nest of Old West history offers self-guided tours. Open Monday through Friday, 8 a.m. to 5 p.m.

T Martin Luther King Park

17th Street and Ames in Cheyenne

Named for the famed Civil Rights leader, this verdant park offers a picnic area and playground, as well as tennis and basketball courts.

T Cheyenne Street Railway Trolley

309 W. Lincolnway in Cheyenne. 778-3133

Hear tales of the area's rich past on this two hour trolley tour of Cheyenne and F.E.Warren AFB. Operates daily with boarding at 16th and Capitol from Mid-May through September.

T Frontier Hotel

1901 Central Ave. in Cheyenne

Throughout the country, Art Deco designers embellished their buildings with local images and created a unique American architectural expression. The Frontier Hotel, built in 1937, is a fine example of Art Deco style. Plains Indian tipis frame the terra cotta entrances, and a portrait of rodeo cowboy Pete Knight flanks the south entrance. Under windows, stepped brickwork contrasts with geometric terra cotta blocks. Bands of stylized floral motifs ring the building and finish vertical panels.

T Lane House

1721 Warren Ave. in Cheyenne

This modest family cottage is representative of early Cheyenne residences. Its Queen Ann styling features include fish scale siding, arched bay windows, and a central chimney. A part of the Rainsford Historic District, this home demonstrates the natural expansion of community development and the supportive role the neighborhood has with the economic center of Cheyenne.

T Nagle-Warren Mansion

222 E. 17th St. in Cheyenne. 637-3333

This Romanesque residence, built by Erasmus Nagle of stone rejected for use in the State capitol, underwent a stucco facade when the stone face deteriorated. The mansion's stained glass windows, parquet floors and woodwork of cherry, oak and maple highlight the interior, as do copper and bronze fireplaces and papier mache ceiling embellishments. Less than a year after the home's completion Nagle died, and the new owner was Francis Warren. Among Warren's guests was frequent visitor President Theodore Roosevelt.

T The Whipple House

300 E. 17th St. in Cheyenne. 638-3551

Ithamar Whipple constructed this Italianate mansion during Cheyenne's golden age, 1880-1890. A Cheyenne merchant, Whipple became a founder of the Wyoming Stock Growers' Association. He later sold this home to Territorial Supreme Court Justice John Lacey. The building was later used by a private men's club and fell into disrepair before being restored to its original grandeur in 1986. Listed on the National Register of Historic Places.

T Lincoln Theater

1615 Central Ave. in Cheyenne. 637-7469

The Lincoln Theater formerly opened with the Orpheum Circuit's Centennial bill, the "Peer of all Vaudeville". In 1990, the building was restored to its 1953 elegance, boasting a vintage neon marquee and a proscenium arch framed with rococco flourishes.

T Cheyenne Railroad Depot

Capitol Ave. in Cheyenne. 778-3133

The beautiful old Union Pacific Railroad Depot on Capitol Avenue is one of the finest examples of architecture in the west. Built in 1886 of red and gray sandstone, the depot was at one time Wyoming Teritory's largest building. The structure contains an elegant clock tower and romanesque arches. Look behind the depot at the enormous roundhouse still used to maintain locomotives.

T Cattle Baron's Row

E. 17th St. in Cheyenne. 634-2021

Gracing 17th Street are a series of Victorian "painted ladies"; the ornate homes of cattlemen that give the area the moniker "Cattle Baron's Row." The Whipple House and the Nagle-Warren Mansion are just two of the elegant mansions in this neighborhood. Call for information on walking tours.

T St. Mark's Episcopal Church

1908 Central Ave. in Cheyenne. 634-7709

The first resident rector, the Reverend Joseph W. Cook, arrived in Cheyenne January 14, 1868 and when the congregation outgrew the first building the plans for the present structure were started. The design was for a stone building in old English style, with pointed arches, massive buttresses and plain finishing. Construction was begun in the summer of 1886. The structure also contains a number of stunning stained glass windows, including a Tiffany. In 1988, a century after the original dedication, the cornerstone was opened up and the contents are on display at St. Mark's today.

Wyoming Tidbits

Cattle drives not only added romance to the history of Wyoming, they were a vital part of the territory's growth. Stock prices were high and grazing land was free. In 1867, the Union Pacific finished its line to Cheyenne and cattle could now be shipped to eastern slaughter houses.

T St. Mary's Catholic Cathedral

2107 Capitol Ave. in Cheyenne. 635-9261

This Gothic Revival style building was built in 1907 of Wyoming sandstone. It is reknowned for its acoustical clarity.

T First United Methodist Church

108 E. 18th In Cheyenne. 632-1410

The First United Methodist Church was begun in 1890 and completed in 1894. The church building was designed by Architect J. P. Julien, whose name appears on the cornerstone, and was constructed by Moses Patrick Keefe. Keefe was the builder of many early homes and offices in Cheyenne. His work includes Saint Mary's Catholic Cathedral, several structures at Fort D. A. Russell, and the second phase of construction on the Wyoming State Capitol. The building was constructed of Wyoming red sandstone. Listed on the National Register of Historic Places.

T Wyoming State Archives

2301 Central Ave. in Cheyenne. 777-7826.
http://wyoarchives.state.wy.us

Located in the Barrett Building, the archives is open Monday through Friday 8 a.m. to 4:45 p.m. daily Monday through Friday, closed holidays. State and local government records documenting the activities of government in Wyoming and information about state history are available for research and copying. There is also a large collection of newspapers, Western books, periodicals, maps, military records, historical photographs and other important documents are available.

T Governor's Mansion - Tour

300 E. 21st St. in Cheyenne. 777-7878

Designing the Mansion

Fourteen years after achieving statehood in 1890, the State of Wyoming built its first governors' mansion in 1904. The state purchased the vacant corner lot at 21st and House Avenue in an established, middle class neighborhood, five blocks from the State Capitol. The lot was surrounded by beautiful Queen Anne houses, built in the mid-1880s, such as those located just east and catty-corner from the Mansion.

The architect was Charles Murdock of Omaha, Nebraska. Although stately, the Colonial Revival residence he designed was modest compared to the mansions built in Cheyenne by the cattle barons in the 1880s and 1890s on Carey Avenue and in what is now downtown Cheyenne.

The mansion was never intended to be a show place, intimidating in size or location. Thus it was never enclosed by a fence and it never had on-site security. It was intended to be a comfortable, gracious residence that the people of Wyoming provided their governors and first families. The mansion's front facade was enhanced by the portico supported by four Corinthian columns cast in sections and installed on-site.

Construction began in the spring of 1904 and was completed that fall. The final cost of the two and one-half story house with a full basement and separate carriage house was $33,253.29. this figure included the cost of the lot ($3,000), the landscaping ($2,036), and all the original furnishings. The house was modern in most respects because it had central plumbing, hot water heat, and combination gas and electrical fixtures throughout.

From 1905 to 1976, the mansion was the residence of nineteen Wyoming first families. Governor Bryant B. Brooks and his family were the first occupants. Brooks, a Natrona County rancher, and his wife, Mary Naomi Brooks had five children-four daughters, Jean, Lena, Abby and Melissa; and a son, Silas, who was the youngest child. The children brought their pet pony from the V-V Ranch with them. The pony was quartered in the carriage house and tended by the resident horse groom. The Brooks were the largest and youngest family ever to occupy the mansion.

The last family to occupy the mansion was also Wyoming's first three-term governor, Ed Herschler and his wife, Casey. The Herschlers have the distinction of being the last first family to live in the mansion and the first to live in the new Governors' Residence located in Frontier Park. The Herschlers lived here for almost two years, from January 1975 until October of 1976.

In July 1977, the Historic Governors' Mansion opened to the public as a historic house museum.

First Floor

Entrance Hall

The ceramic tile floor is original. The pair of combination, brass ceiling fixtures are like the originals. When frequent brown-outs or electrical failures occurred, the gas arm was lit as a back-up system. The elevator chair on the staircase was originally installed for First Lady Casey Herschler who had multiple sclerosis. The steer horn chair, dating from 1900, is an example of organic furniture. Photographs of the Wyoming Territorial and State First Ladies hang on the staircase walls.

Library

The actual library collection was moved to the new Governors' Residence in 1976. The photos of the Territorial (bottom row) and State Governors (top three rows) were hung when the house became a museum. A twenty minute introduction and tour video can be viewed at any time.

Drawing Room

Two pieces of furniture the mahogany library table and the cane-topped side table-are original furnishings from 1905. The Chickering concert grand piano, made in 1869 in Boston, replaces the original one that was moved to the new residence in 1976. The upholstered furniture was purchased by the state in 1937 at the Chicago Furniture Mart. None has its original fabric. The photo collections shows the first families, 1905-1976. The wallpaper and silk curtains are Scalamandre fabrics installed in 1963. The 1915 oak mantel and over-chimney piece replaced the originals. The round pedestal table, made of inlaid woods identified in the center silver band, was made by local rancher Johnnie Gordon for the Wyoming exhibit at the 1904 St. Louis World's Fair.

Dining Room

The dining room furniture in the Chippendale style, was made in Rockford, Illinois. The leather upholstery is original. The set, purchased in 1937 at the Chicago Furniture Mart, includes a sideboard, chest of drawers, and a cabinet-on-stand.

Breakfast Room

This room was added in 1937 as a family dining room. The set of French pottery plates with rabbits dates from 1901.

Kitchen

The metal cabinets with stainless steel counter tops were installed in 1937. The Tappan Range and Thermadore ovens and bread warmer were installed in 1959. The GE dishwasher, the third in the mansion, was installed in 2001. The inlaid stone pattern seen in the vinyl floor is the same pattern of linoleum that was installed in the 1920s.

Staff Dining Room/Sitting Room

The mansion usually had two full-time, live-in employees, a cook and a housekeeper. Additional help was employed for special events. The room is now used as the museum office.

Governors' Den

Last redecorated during Milward Simpson's term (1955-59), the furniture was made in Cody, Wyoming by Tom Molesworth, a well-known Wyoming furniture maker who attended the Art Institute of Chicago. The upholstered arm chairs show the Indian Paintbrush in punch embroidery. The floor lamp shade is made of unborn calf skin. The table lamps have lamb skin shades.

Second Floor

The double window is original stained glass showing a fleur de-lis design. Originally this floor had six bedroom and two full baths. In 1937, the floor was remodeled to its present state of four bedrooms, each with a full bath and closets. The Pioneer Club of Cheyenne donated its 1990 Wyoming Centennial Quilt which hangs in the hallway.

Children's Bedroom

The room is interpreted to reflect its first occupants—Lena and Melissa Brooks, who chose this bedroom so that they could be close to the carriage house to hear their pet pony.

The red and white "calling card" or "memory" quilt, depicting the names of 800 Cheyenne residents, was made in 1908 by the Presbyterian Aid Society as a fund-raising project. The names of three Brooks children, including the younger brother Silas, appear on the quilt. The oval photograph shows the Brooks' daughters. The room is furnished with American Eastlake furniture, after Sir Charles Lock Eastlake, an English painter and Keeper of the National Art Gallery in London.

State Guest Bedroom

The walnut twin poster beds have been here since 1937. The handworked oriental rug was made in the 1920s in Persia (present day Iran) in the Sarouk pattern.

Fireplace Bedroom

This room was intended to be the master bedroom and was the only bedroom that furniture is American Eastlake in cherry wood with mahogany panels. The setee and matching chair are Art Nouveau style. The wool patchwork quilt is in the bow tie design.

Second Master Bedroom

The Renaisance Revival furniture is from the estate of Governor Joseph M. Carey. An antique crazy quilt covers the bed. The Campbell County Woolgrowers Auxiliary donated the pelt.

Sunporch

In 1955, Governor Milward Simpson created an open-air patio over the roof of the kitchen and staff dining room. The ceramic tile floor was laid and the retaining wall built. In 1959, during the term of John J. Hickey, the patio was enclosed with aluminum windows and corrugated fiberglass panels. During the administration of Stanley K. Hathaway, Wyoming's first governor to complete a second term (1967-75), the room was refurbished with redwood paneling and Andersen windows. The Hathaways lived in the mansion for eight years, longer than any other first family. Mrs. Hathaway placed the set of Heywood-Wakefield wicker furniture.

Third Floor

The back staircase and the landing that traverses the window, allowing daylight to reach both sides of the landing, are original.

The third floor was used as the maids' quarters until an apartment was built in the basement of the mansion in 1930.

The wallpaper, curtains and remodeled bathroom date from the early 1970s. The carpeting on the stairs was installed in 1998.

Reprinted from Museum Brochure

T Wyoming State Capitol Building

Between Capitol and Warren Streets at 24th Street in Cheyenne

The arrival of the Union Pacific crews in 1867 as they laid the tracks westward changed Cheyenne from a village to a city in a matter of months, and the seat of the new Territorial government was established in 1869.

In 1886, the Ninth Territorial Legislative Assembly authorized construction of the State Capitol; to be erected in the City of Cheyenne at a cost not to exceed $150,000.

A five-member Commission, appointed by Governor Francis E. Warren, was charged with the selection and purchase of the site, selection of an architect and accepted the lowest bids for construction of the building. The Commission chose the firm of David W. Gibbs & Company, Architects, to draw plans and specifications. These were accepted in July 1886, and the contract was awarded to the lowest bidder, Adam Feick & Brothers, who bid $131,275.12 and broke ground on September 9, 1886.

The architecture of the building is pseudo-Corinthian, reminiscent of the National Capitol Building in Washington, D.C.

The first two courses of the building proper are of sandstone from the quarries of Fort Collins, Colorado the remainder of the building is of sandstone from the quarries at Rawlins, Wyoming.

The building's cornerstone was laid on May 18,1887, with maps, a roster of territorial officers and other papers placed within the cornerstone. During the Centennial of the Capitol in 1987, the cornerstone was removed and these documents replaced and the cornerstone reset.

The Tenth Territorial Legislative Assembly convened in the still-to-be completed building. The second portion of the building, small wings on the east and west, was completed in April 1890. Crowded conditions persisted with the growth of the state and in 1915, the Thirteenth State Legislature approved the construction of the House and Senate Chambers, which were completed in March 1917.

The Dome of the Capitol is real gold leaf. The 24-carat gold leaf dome is visible from all roads entering the city. It has been gilded six times, the first in 1900 and the last in 1988. A highly skilled person is needed to put this leaf in place because, if touched by fingers in handling, it will disintegrate. The peak of the dome is 146 feet high, and the base is 50 feet in diameter.

The 42nd Legislature in 1974 appropriated funds for the first phase of a renovation of the Capitol. At a cost of $7.6 million, the project was completed in 1980. Work included stripping and staining all woodwork, painting walls in the original designs, replacing wooden floor beams and floors with steal and concrete and modernizing the wiring, heating, plumbing and air conditioning.

Dome Interior

While standing in the center of the rotunda, look upward at the base of the dome directly overhead and see the blue and green stained glass, Imported from England. It sparkles with blue and green hues from underneath, but the upper side glistens with red, orange and yellow shades. Normal sunlight cannot penetrate and Illuminate the glass. Electric spotlights were installed in the dome to shine downward.

Four of Wyoming's five elected officials — Governor, Secretary of State, Auditor and Treasurer — have their offices surrounding the Capitol Rotunda on the first floor. The Superintendent of Public Instruction is housed In the Hathaway Building.

The mounted Bison specimen on display in the hallway was raised with the state herd In Hot Springs State Park near Thermopolis. While living, the animal weighed approximately 3,000 pounds and holds the distinction of being the third largest bison ever to be enrolled in the Boone and Crocket Book of Records. In 1985, the state legislature enacted a bill designating the American Bison as the State Mammal of Wyoming. This American Bison is an excellent specimen of Wyoming's monarch of the plains. The Bison was a key to the Indian economy, and when it began to disappear because of the white man, the Indian's independence diminished.

"Here in this Rocky Passage " an oil painting by Wyoming artist, John Giarrizzo, hangs in the rotunda near the Secretary of State's Office. The painting, which honors the diverse national and ethnic groups who settled the State of Wyoming, was formally unveiled on February 22, 1988.

Chief Washakie

"Washakie stood for bravery and courage, he was a peacemaker a strong leader and above all a wise and generous man." John Washakie, Chairman, Eastern Shoshone Business Council

As you leave the first floor, mention should be made of the wood used in the Capitol. The wood in the basement is maple, while the wood In the rotunda is cherry. In the House and Senate the wood is oak.

House Of Representatives

The House of Representatives Chamber is in the East Wing, and was completed In March 1917. Allen True painted the four murals. Two oil paintings were done by William Gollings who has many paintings featured in the Whitney Gallery of western art in Cody, Wyoming. In the ceiling, the State Seal is embedded in Tiffany stained glass.

Wyoming presently has 60 representatives. The 40th Legislature, in 1969, had a woman Speaker of the House for the first time in the state's history. She was Miss Verda James of Casper. Representatives come from the state's 23 counties and are elected to two-year terms. They must be 21 years old and a United States citizen and must have lived in the county for at least 12 months. The number of members is controlled by legislative apportionment. The number is never to be less than twice nor more than three times the members of the Senate. The House has the sole power of Impeachment of state and judicial officers except justices of the peace. All revenue bills must originate in the House.

Senate

The Senate Chamber is housed in the West Wing, which was also completed in March 1917. The four murals were painted by Allen True. The State Seal is embedded In the Tiffany stained glass in the ceiling. (See House Gollings Information)

Wyoming currently has 30 Senators, who are elected for four-year terms. To be eligible to run for the Senate, a person must be 25 years old, a resident of Wyoming and a United States citizen. The Governor's appointments are confirmed by the Senate. It sits as a Court of Impeachment of state and judicial officers (except for justices of the peace) after charges are brought by the House.

Balconies

The balconies are usually open for visitors at all times. Again, you should note the Corinthian architecture here, which the columns graphically depict. The Tenth Legislature was the first to convene in the Capitol in 1888. The First State Legislature convened in November 1890.

Stained Glass Ceilings

The ceilings of both House and Senate chambers are inlaid with beautiful Tiffany-style glass and the Wyoming State Seal is prominently displayed in the center.

Allen Tupper True Murals

The Senate and House of Representatives chambers are in the building's two wings—the Senate In the West and the House of Representatives in the East. Each chamber has four large murals depicting industry, pioneer life, law and transportation. The Senate murals are titled "Indian Chief Cheyenne," "Frontier Cavalry Officer," "Pony Express Rider," and "Railroad Builders/Surveyors" Those in the House are named "Cattlemen", "Trappers," "Homesteaders:' and "Stagecoach." They are the works of Allen True who contracted to paint them In August 1917 for a price of $500 each.

Legislative Conference Room 302

Ornate and uniquely designed hinges were installed during the construction of the Capitol in 1887, Their beauty and craftsmanship add to the handsome cherry wood doors found on entering Room 302.

A 1,000-lb. tiffany chandelier, which was originally located elsewhere in the Capitol, hangs beneath a beautiful four-pane stained glass ceiling insert.

The 8' by 22' mural painted by artist Mike Kopriva, a Wyoming native dominates the north wall. Entitled "Wyoming, the Land of the People, Past and Present" the art work depicts "real Wyoming and also some secrets".

Outside Points of Interest

A replica of the Liberty Bell stands on the Capitol grounds at the corner of 24th and Carey. Wyoming is one of the few states given a replica of the Liberty Bell that keeps it outside for all to see. On the Capitol grounds at the corner of 24th and Central Avenue stands a statute dedicated to those who served in the Spanish American War.

Spirit Of Wyoming

Conceived as a symbol to represent Wyoming's people, "The Spirit Of Wyoming" depicts a cowboy and his horse at odds against nature and it's elements. This handsome bronze statue stands prominently near the Capitol and the Herschler Building and is the work of national and international award winning sculptor and artist Edward J. Fraughton. The statue weighs nearly 4,500 pounds and stands on a five-foot, precast base for a combined height of over 18 feet.

Bison

On the east lawn of the Capitol grounds stands a bronze bison statue. It was a gift to the State of Wyoming made possible by donations from Wyoming citizens. The handsome statue is the work of Cheyenne native Dan Ostermiller.

Esther Morris Statue

Commanding a prominent position in front of

Cheyenne Frontier Days

This annual event, held the last full week of July, celebrates the spirit of the Old West with a PRCA rodeo, carnival and concert. A free pancake breakfast downtown kick-starts the festivities and an Indian village showcasing Native American culture is free to the public. Square dancing sets feet stomping, and you'll get a chance to cheer the hero and hiss the villain at a good old-fashioned melodrama. Several rodeos are held during this 10 day event.

the Capitol is a statue of Esther Hobart Morris, a replica of which stands in Statuary Hall in the U.S. Capitol. Mrs. Morris played a role in granting women equal suffrage. The Act to grant women suffrage was introduced November 27, 1869, during the First Territorial Assembly and was signed by Governor J.A. Campbell on December 10, 1869. Wyoming was the first government in the world to grant women suffrage and was thus named the "Equality State". A resident of South Pass City and later Cheyenne, Mrs. Morris was appointed the first woman Justice of the Peace in 1870.

Tree Walk

In 1876 Mrs. Nannie Steel reported that there were only 12 trees in Cheyenne! Almost all of the trees in Cheyenne today were planted by someone. The Wyoming State Forestry Division provides a guide to the specimens around the Capitol grounds. The guide is available at the Capitol Information Desk.

Capitol Tours

The Capitol is open to the public from 8 a.m. to 5 p.m., Monday through Friday. Visitor's services are provided at the Information Desk between 8:30 am. and 4:30 p.m. All tours for groups and schools require prior notice. Tours are available year round. Groups can call 777-7220 for reservations.

Wyoming State Flag

The Wyoming State Flag, designed by Mrs. A.C. Keyes, Casper, was adopted by the 14th Legislature on January 31, 1917. The original sketch is in the possession of the Wyoming State Archives and Historical Department.

The Great Seal of the State of Wyoming is the heart of the flag. On the bison, once the monarch of the plains is the seal representing the custom of branding. The colors of the flag are the same as those of the United States Flag. The red border represents the Red Men, also the blood the pioneers shed in giving their lives to claim the soil. White is the emblem of purity and uprightness over Wyoming. Blue, the color of the sky and mountains, is symbolic of fidelity, justice and virility.

The State Seal

The Great Seal of the State of Wyoming was adopted in its present design by the second state legislature in 1893. The original design was submitted in 1891, but the main objection to the seal was that the figure of the woman was unclothed. Therefore, for two years, the state was without an official state seal. The two dates of the seal, 1869 and 1890, commemorate the organization of the Territorial Government and Wyoming's admission into the Union. The number 44 signifies that Wyoming was the 44th State to be admitted to the Union. The draped figure in the center symbolized the political status women have always enjoyed in the state. The male figures typify the livestock and mining industries of Wyoming.

The motto displayed on the Territorial seal was "Cedant Arma Togae, "translated: "Let arms yield to the gown," or more literally, "Force must yield to law."

Reprinted from State of Wyoming brochure.

H Old Governor's Mansion

300 East 21st Street in Cheyenne

The 1902 Wyoming Legislature authorized an Executive Mansion and appropriated $40,000 for that purpose. Under architect Charles W. Murdock, this Georgian style building was completed late in 1904 at a total cost, including site, landscaping, construction and furnishings, of $33,253.29.

Governor and Mrs. Bryant B. Brooks were the Mansion's first occupants. A society-news item from the Cheyenne Daily Leader, January 4, 1905, said: "Mrs. B. B. Brooks will return from Casper on Friday evening accompanied by her children. Every effort is being made by the decorators and furnishers to have the Executive Mansion in readiness to receive the family Saturday."

The Mansion got its housewarming in official and formal style when, on January 23, 1905, Governor and Mrs. Brooks entertained at a reception in honor of State Legislators, State Officials and their wives. Next day, the Wyoming Tribune reported the affair in a page one story which said, "A Happy Throng of Guests Assemble at Executive Mansion to meet the Legislature." Other accounts proclaimed the occasion "one of brilliance" and stressed the "stately Mansion ablaze with lights."

State Executive Mansions were customary structures long before Wyoming got around to building this one as a home for its governors. Still, this Mansion had one "first." When Mrs. Nellie Tayloe Ross became Governor of Wyoming in 1925, this was the first Executive Mansion in the Nation to become the home of a woman governor.

H The Cheyenne Club

17th Street and Warren Avenue in downtown Cheyenne

The Cheyenne Club was built on this site in 1882. Most of the members were wealthy cattle barons from the East and Europe. The Club gained world-wide fame. After the blizzard of 1886-1887 the cattle business was ruined, and the Club lost its glamour. The building became the headquarters for the Cheyenne Chamber of Commerce. It was razed in 1936.

H Cheyenne–Fort Laramie–Deadwood Trail

22nd Street and Capitol Avenue in downtown Cheyenne

The Cheyenne–Fort Laramie–Deadwood Trail started from the corner of Capitol Ave. & 16th Street and ran 88 miles north to Ft. Laramie, the most historic fort in the Rocky Mountain west. In 1876 it was extended to Deadwood and the Black Hills gold fields 266 miles from Cheyenne. Indians, trappers, traders, pack trains, cavalry, freighters, cowboys, and stage coaches traveled this way. Road agents and Indians added to the hazard of the road.

H Cheyenne Opera House And Territorial Library

North of corner of 17th Street on Capitol Avenue in downtown Cheyenne. On the side of the old J.C. Penney store

The Cheyenne Opera House and Territorial Library was erected on this site in 1882. For twenty years, it was the center of civic, and cultural activity.

In 1902, a fire destroyed the auditorium and stage of the building.

In 1905, the annex was built on the site adjoining the remaining portion of the opera house. The two buildings were razed in 1961.

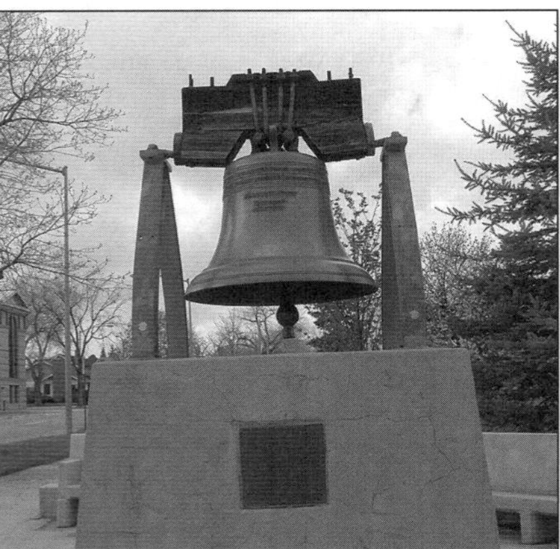

H Liberty Bell Model

24th Street and Capitol Avenue on the capitol lawn in Cheyenne

DEDICATED TO YOU, A FREE CITIZEN IN A FREE LAND

This reproduction of the Liberty Bell was presented to the people of WYOMING by direction of the HONORABLE JOHN W. SNYDER, Secretary of the Treasury, as the inspirational symbol of the United States Savings Bonds Independence Drive from May 15 to July 4, 1950, it was displayed in every part of the state.

The dimensions and tone are identical to those of the original Liberty Bell when it rang out our independence in 1776.

In standing before the symbol, you have the opportunity to dedicate yourself, as did our founding fathers, to the principle of the individual freedom for which our nation stands.

This bell is one of fifty-three cast in France in 1950, and given to the United States Government by:

American Smelting and Refining Company

Miami Copper Company

Anaconda Copper Mining Company

Phelps Dodge Corporation Kennicott Copper Company

The American Metal Company

Steel Supports by U.S. Steel Corporation's American Bridge Company.

This plaque donated by Revere Copper and Brass Incorporated.

H Esther Hobart Morris Statue

In front of Capitol Building in Cheyenne.

South face

Esther Hobart Morris

Proponent of the legislative act which in 1869 gave distinction to the Territory of WYOMING as the 1st government in the world to grant WOMEN EQUAL RIGHTS.

North face

A grateful people honors this stalwart pioneer who also became the 1st woman justice of the peace.

H St. Mark's Episcopal Church

1908 Central Avenue in downtown Cheyenne

Finding "the wickedness unimaginable and appalling," the Rev. Joseph Cook organized St. Mark's Parish Jan. 27, 1868, in Cheyenne, Dakota Territory, then a railroad winter camp. The first church at 18th and Carey Avenue was dedicated in August 1868 and was the first church building erected and dedicated in Wyoming.

This present edifice was constructed in 1886 and was patterned after Stoke Poges Church, Buckinghamshire, England.

The ministry of St. Mark's is historically linked with the settling and development of the frontier west. The church register records the burial service of the cavalrymen killed by Indians, the wedding of an acting governor, and use of the Parish Hall as a social and cultural center.

The Rev. George Rafter, Rector, was asked to "pray over" Tom Horn during his public hanging in November of 1903.

In August 1915, the wife and three daughters of the General John J. Pershing were buried with solemn military rites from this church. They lost their lives in a tragic fire at the Presidio, San Francisco. Hundreds of cavalry troops from Fort D. A. Russell participated in the burial procession.

On Sunday, Oct. 11, 1936, President and Mrs. Franklin D. Roosevelt worshipped here.

H Castle Dare 1886

Just east of Pioneer Avenue and 20th Streets in Cheyenne.

Castle Dare was designed by architect J. P. Julien and built by R. W. Bradley, pioneer stonemason and contractor. The original house was commissioned by cattle baron Alexander Swan as a wedding present for his daughter Louise. Construction was begun in 1886, but the terrible blizzard of that winter caused Swan such financial reverses that the house was sold to David D. Dare who undertook its completion and furnishing. It was for Dare that the house was named.

Later, the house became the property of Bradley, who built the barn carriage house. Both buildings were done in a combination of Norman Revival and Richardson Romanesque architecture. The characteristics include ashlar masonry and towers with crenelated battlements or conical roofs.

The main house served as a boarding house, funeral parlor, and lodge hall until it was razed in 1963 to make way for a parking lot. The carriage house has been used as a private club, shops, and professional offices.

It is a reflection of Cheyenne during the height of the cattle baron days and is representative of the town when it was referred to as the richest small town in America. Renovation of the carriage house began in 1979 and was done almost entirely by volunteer labor.

H Cheyenne Architectural Heritage Map

Corner of W. Lincolnway and Capitol Avenue in downtown Cheyenne.

August 29, 1986, this Cheyenne Architectural Heritage Map was donated to the City of Cheyenne by the X-JWC Federated Women's Club. The purpose of the map is to preserve the memory of the beautiful historical buildings in the downtown area of Cheyenne. Artists William A. Little Jr., and Randy Hurst. Photographs Courtesy of: Wyoming State Archives, Museums and Historical Department. Constructed by: Western Specialty Mfg. Corp.

Wyoming State Capitol
24th & Capitol Avenue

The Territorial Legislature authorized 150,000 for the construction of the Capitol's first phase in 1886. The Wyoming Capitol is one of ten gold domed U.S. state capitols.

Union Pacific Depot
121 West 15th Street

Construction began in 1886, and included a Romanesque clock tower that was a prominent landmark for railroad travelers approaching Cheyenne at the turn of the century.

Tivoli Building
301 West 16th Street

A fine bar and restaurant was established here in 1883. Ladies, with or without escorts, were welcomed. The present building was constructed in 1892.

Atlas Theatre
213 West 16th Street

Constructed in 1887, the Atlas is the oldest standing theatre in Cheyenne. Home to vaudeville performances, in the 1980s the Atlas stage presents live theatre.

St. Mark's Episcopal Church
1908 Central Avenue

Begun in 1886, the 1887 collapse of the cattle industry postponed completion of the church's interior until 1888, Windows include Tiffany stained glass.

St. Mary's Cathedral
2107 Capitol Avenue

St. Mary's neo-gothic cathedral, constructed 1906-09. features nine major stained-glass windows. The largest, above the choir loft, was inspired by Raphael's Sistine Madonna.

First United Methodist Church
NE Corner 18th Street & Central Avenue

The cornerstone of the red sandstone church was laid in 1890, the year Wyoming became a state. Wild Bill Hickock married Agnes Lake Thatcher on this site in 1870.

First Presbyterian Church
220 West 22nd Street

The limestone church erected 1923-24. includes Centennial Doors depicting the stained glass Wyoming's great seal, state flag. territorial seal and the Union Pacific emblem.

Whipple House
300 East 17th Street

This Italianate brick residence was built in 1883 by Ithamar C. Whipple, Cheyenne merchant, financier and cattleman. Later this was home to Judge John Lacey, distinguished Wyoming counselor.

Nagle-Warren Mansion
222 East 17th Street

Built in l887-88 for Erasmus Nagle, faulty sandstone rejected by state Capitol contractors was installed here. Later this mansion was home of U.S. Senator Francis E. Warren.

Phoenix Block
SW Corner 16th Street & Capitol Avenue

Completed in 1882 by Francis F. Warren at a cost of $35,000. the Phoenix boasted three stories and a complete plumbing system with water and gas.

Hynds Building
1600 Capitol Avenue

Built in 1922 by Harry P. Hynds. a prominent Cheyenne businessman and philanthropist, this was the site of the historic Interocean Hotel.

Idleman Building
NE Corner 16th Street & Carey Avenue

Constructed in 1884 for wholesale liquor business, customers could walk among barrels and siphon samples through a tube, buying whatever they fancied.

Commercial Building
200 block West 16th Street

Constructed in 1883. this building housed federal government offices until 1905. U S. Deputy Marshall Joe LeFors heard hired gunman Tom Horn's alleged confession here.

Warren Mercantile
SE corner 16th Street & Capitol Avenue

You are standing on the site of the 1884 Warren Mercantile Company building. 1887 to 1932 Burlington Railroad occupied part of the building for depot use.

Rocky Mountain Telephone Building
1623 Capitol Avenue

Constructed in 1906 for the new telephone exchange, John Arp purchased this building in 1930 to create a comfortable hotel with running water and private baths.

Dinneen's Garage
400 West 16th Street

Designed and built in 1927 for W.E. Dinneen. the building includes a water-powered elevator for lifting automobiles to the second floor, still in use in the 1980s

Historic Governor's Mansion
300 East 21st Street

Constructed in 1904, the residence was the home of twenty Wyoming first families between 1905 and 1876 Notable visitors were Theodore Roosevelt. Harry Truman and William "Buffalo Bill" Cody.

Majestic Building
1601 Capitol Avenue

The Majestic Building was constructed in 1907

for the First National Bank. The emergency exit became a social passage, known as Peacock Alley, between the Paramount Theatre and the Plains Hotel.

Plains Hotel
1600 Central Avenue

The Plains Hotel opened in 1911 and was the focus of Cheyenne's social and political events for fifty years. Chief Little Shield's picture became the hotel trademark.

Masonic Temple
1820 Capitol Avenue

The cornerstone was placed by the Masons in 1901, Following a fire in 1903, the interior was rebuilt. The stained-glass windows still show fire damage.

Ferdinand W. LaFrentz House
2015 Warren Avenue

The LaFrentz house is representative of the frame cottages built in Cheyenne during the 1880's when Cheyenne was reputed to be the richest little city in the world.

Corson House
209 East 18th Street

Designed in 1883 by George D. Rainsford, this whimsical cottage is almost unchanged in appearance and has been the home of three generations of Corsons.

Castle Dare
1920 Carey Avenue

Construction started in 1886. R. W. Bradley moved into the mansion after sales to both Alexander Swan and D. D. Dare failed to close. In 1963 all but the carriage house was razed.

Knights of Pythias
312 West 17th Street

Constructed in 1884, Knights of Pythias Hall was the home of the Ninth Territorial Legislative Assembly in 1886. Portions of the elaborate cornice are still visible.

Davis Building
320 West 17th Street

Five Cheyenne streets' names titled by General Dodge were changed. The Davis Building, constructed in 1895, remembers Eddy Street by a sign on the west side of the building.

Boyd Building
1720 Carey Avenue

Designed by Frederick H. Porter in 1912, the building originally housed the Citizens' National Bank. H. N. Boyd purchased the structure after the bank failed in 1924.

Nettford Apartments
215 East 18th Street

The Greek Revival red brick structure graced with white columns was opened in 1911 as apartments. It was owned by Arthur C. Kingsford and named for his wife, Nettie.

County Building
NW corner 19th Street & Carey Avenue

Construction began in 1917. This edifice replaced the first Laramie County Court House where, in 1903, the famous hanging of Tom Horn took place.

Grier Furniture
1601 Central Avenue

Erected in 1911 by Cheyenne businessman and politician, Francis E. Warren, this commercial structure was later the funeral home and furniture store of Hobbs, Huckfeldt and Finkbiner.

F The Whipple House
300 E. 17th Street in Cheyenne. 638-3551

The Whipple House is a fine dining establishment located in an 1883 building listed on the National Register of Historic Places. This restaurant offers an exceptional menu selection with daily luncheon and dinner features. Accompany your meal with a choice from their menu of fine wines and hand-crafted cocktails. On Sundays they offer a wonderful brunch. A special late night menu on Fridays and Saturdays features crepes, omelets, and fondues. Top your meal with special selections such as creme brulee or Tiramisu made by their in-house pastry chef. The Whipple House is a lovely choice for parties, banquets, or meetings up to 50.

F Poor Richard's, Eating & Drinking Establishment
2233 E. Lincolnway in Cheyenne. 635-5114

Poor Richard's is an eating and drinking establishment, locally owned and operated by the same family since 1977. At Poor Richard's you'll enjoy warm and comfortable casual dining with a taste of elegance. The restaurant is well known for their large menu that includes aged beef, juicy prime rib, fresh seafood, formula-fed veal, and chicken. Check out daily chef specials for lunch or dinner. They also feature fresh soups and an extensive salad bar. Relax with a cocktail or glass of wine from their extensive bar menu or a yummy appetizer. Poor Richard's also can accommodate large groups and banquets.

F Zen's Bistro
2606 E. Lincolnway in Cheyenne. 635-1889.
www.zensbistro.com

Visit Zen's Bistro for breakfast, lunch, dinner, or a relaxing coffee break. Enjoy their great coffee and teas along with sandwiches, soups, salads, and desserts. There are several vegetarian selections. Relax in a friendly, tranquil atmosphere. They also feature changing menus of live music, open microphone, poetry readings, and local artists' exhibits. Stop in for a game of chess or checkers. There is even a pillow room where people can lounge Moroccan style. Start you day right with breakfast at the Bistro or unwind after a busy day of play or work. They also have a drive up window and delivery service.

FL The Plains Hotel
1600 Central Avenue in Cheyenne. 638-3311 or 866-2PLAINS(275-2467).
www.theplainshotel.com

The Historic Plains Hotel has been a landmark in downtown Cheyenne since it was built in 1911. The newly renovated hotel offers 130 elegant rooms, as well as exquisite food in the Capitol Grille. The Trail Coffee Shop proudly brews Starbucks Coffee and offers quick lunches. In addition, the facility offers a wealth of history for the visitor to experience, and downtown convenience. For the business visitor, the hotel offers 9,000 sq. ft. of meeting space as well as banquet facilities. All suites have high-speed Internet access. There is also a fitness center available to all guests. Experience the new stained glass skylight in the lobby. For more information, visit the hotel's website: www.theplainshotel.com.

F The Cheyenne Smokehouse
Corner of House Avenue at 18th Street in Cheyenne. 773-8621 or 866-896-4834

> *Wyoming Tidbits*
>
> A former Wells Fargo agent in Cheyenne and later restaurant critic who had a cake mix named for him in 1949 was Duncan Hines.

L Nagle Warren Mansion Bed & Breakfast
222 E. 17th Street in Cheyenne. 637-3333 or 800-811-2610. www.naglewarrenmansion.com

The Nagle Warren Mansion, one of Cheyenne's most elegant residences, was built by Erasmus Nagle in 1888. In 1910 it became the home of Francis E. Warren, businessman, Governor, and U.S. Senator. It is conveniently located on the edge of the downtown Cheyenne business district. Owner Jim Osterfoss invites you to share in the rich western history and contemporary comfort of this elegant bed and breakfast. Every room in the house has been decorated to recreate the elegance of the Victorian West. This bed and breakfast offers 12 guest rooms with private baths, central air conditioning, 2 line telephones, dataports, and television. Enjoy their unparalleled comfort and accommodations for business, getaways, or special events. Visit them on the web.

L Rainsford Inn Bed & Breakfast
219 E. 18th Street in Cheyenne. 638-2337. Email: tobeds@sisna.com or www.rainsfordinnbedandbreakfast.com

S Deselms Fine Art & Custom Framing
303 E. 17th Street in Cheyenne. 432-0606. www.deselmsfineart.com

Since 1992, Deselms Fine Art and Custom Framing has featured fine original art by local and regional artists, many with national acclaim. Located in one of Cheyenne's oldest homes, they offer art in many different styles and medias, for your private art collection or corporate office needs. Large or small, Deselms Fine Art can fill your custom framing needs. Originals, prints, and shadow box treatments will be cared for and presented beautifully. On Thursday evenings join them for Artists Hangout, when various artists display their talents for everyone to enjoy. Visit Deselms Fine Art on the web and learn more about changing exhibits and special events.

S Just Dandy Outstanding Clothing & Accessories
212 W. 17th Street in Cheyenne. 635-2565. www.justdandyonline.com

26 *Gas, Food, Lodging*

27 *Gas, Food, Lodging*

28 *Gas, Food*

29 *Gas, Food, Lodging*

H The Gangplank
About 16 miles west of Cheyenne on I-80

The granite rocks to the west are more than a billion years old (Pre-Cambrian in age). The sedimentary rocks to the east are some 10 million years old (Late Miocene in age). After the mountains were elevated, some 20,000 feet of rocks were eroded from their crest. Later the younger sedimentary rocks were deposited against the flank of the range.

The time between the formation of the granite to the west and the deposition of the onlapping sediments to the east is measured in terms of more than ten hundred million years. You are now standing on the gangplank.

L Super 8 Cheyenne
1900 W. Lincolnway in Cheyenne. 635-8741 or 800-800-8000. www.super8.com

The Super 8 Motel in Cheyenne is conveniently located near Cheyenne exits at I-25 and I-80. They are near family dining and area attractions. The motel is open year round and offer plenty of parking for large vehicles, including outside outlets. Children age 18 and under stay free and all guests receive a complimentary SuperSTART breakfast. Additional services you will appreciate include free local calls, cribs, copy and fax service, and movie and VCR rentals, cable TV with HBO, and a 24 hour front desk. King rooms are available that include a recliner and a Microfridge.

S Wyoming Home
210 W. Lincolnway in Cheyenne. 638-2222. www.wyominghome.com

S Hemispheres: Trading Crafts from South to North
315 W. Lincolnway in Cheyenne. 432-9000 or toll free at 877-369-3200. www.tradingcrafts.com

Hemispheres: Trading Crafts from South to North, Inc., markets unique handmade crafts from Africa through its Cheyenne store and worldwide Web site. By providing selected African artisans with a market for their carefully made, wonderfully imaginative crafts, Hemispheres hopes to bring economic progress to the artisans home villages without harming the environment for future generations. Visit Hemispheres to find stylish casual clothing including vests and jackets; personal accessories such as unusual jewelry, scarves, and hats; home decor items including brightly patterned cushions, table cloths, place mats, and beautiful baskets from at least a dozen African countries; and decorative arts—hand blown glass, gorgeous wall-hangings, and masks—that are perfect for gift-giving and receiving

30 *Gas, Food, Lodging*

F Avanti Italian Ristorante

4620 Grandview, next to Wal-Mart in Cheyenne. 634-3432

The family owned Avanti Italian Ristorante has been in business since 1983 and specializes in serving dishes made from recipes handed down in the Mancini and the DiMarzio families. Select from an extensive menu or enjoy their popular all-you-can-eat Italian Buffet with daily specials. You will enjoy the large variety of wines and beers, or your favorite cocktail, to accompany your meal. They also offer a banquet room for up to 100 people and cater for any occasion, large or small. Avanti has been selected as Cheyenne's favorite Italian restaurant for six years in a row by Wyoming Tribune-Eagle Readers' Choice. Enjoy distinctive dining in a relaxed and friendly setting.

31 *Food, Lodging*

L The Storyteller Pueblo Bed & Breakfast

5201 Odgen Road in Cheyenne. 634-7036. www.storyteller-pueblo-bnb.com

Slip into history at The Storyteller Pueblo Bed and Breakfast while enjoying the present. Surround yourself with Native American art, pottery, baskets, beadwork, and rugs representing over 50 tribes. The home also features a lifetime collection of country antiques. Relax on cool nights in front of warm fireplaces. Chose a sitting room to curl up with a book or visit with friends. Beverages and snacks are always available and a full breakfast is served at your convenience. Enjoy the modern home atmosphere while visiting the past through the lovely furnishings. The Storyteller is conveniently located to historic Cheyenne's great shopping, restaurants, and attractions. Advance reservations recommended.

> ***Wyoming Tidbits***
>
> The William C. Irvine mansion in Cheyenne was purportedly the first American home wired for electricity.

32 *No services*

T Laramie County Community College Fine Arts Gallery

At Laramie Community College

M Laramie County Community College

1400 East College Drive in Cheyenne. 778-5222 or 800-522-2993. www.lccc.cc.wy.us/

Laramie County Community College was established in 1968. The campus is near the Medicine Bow National Forest and an hour and a half from many of the outdoor activities of Colorado. It is a full-service, comprehensive community college with campuses in Cheyenne and Laramie and an outreach center in Pine Bluffs. A wide range of academic, vocational, and continuing education/community service programs provided. The 271 acre campus includes 20 buildings, most of which are connected by enclosed walkways. Annual enrollment is approximately 2,556.

33 *Gas, Food, Lodging*

H Wyoming's Wildlife Heritage

At I-25 Exit 7 rest stop

Welcome to wonderful Wyoming! As you travel through the state, your visit will be more enjoyable and interesting if you stay alert to one of Wyoming most precious treasures – an abundance and diversity of free ranging wildlife. The large expanses of wildlands make Wyoming unique and well worth exploring.

Wyoming is most famous for large mammals. Free-ranging pronghorn, elk, mule deer, bighorn sheep, moose and grizzly bear grace our wild places. Over half of the world's population of pronghorn (also called antelope) reside here and the largest concentration of bighorn sheep in the country can be found each winter on Whiskey Mountain near Dubois. The world's largest concentrations of elk can be found in the northwest part of the state. When it comes to large native wildlife, Wyoming is blessed with both quantity and quality.

As you drive through the state, your chances are excellent for seeing a variety of interesting wildlife species. Watch for coyotes, badgers, sage grouse and red foxes. Scan the skies for golden eagles, prairie falcons and other unique non-game wildlife. If your travels include wetland areas, be on the lookout for great blue herons, shore-birds, sandhill cranes and white pelicans.

In your travels, you will find interpretive signs at highway rest areas calling your attention to wildlife-habitat relationships unique to each area. Pick up a loop tour guide and increase your viewing opportunities and learning experiences. Visit the Game and Fish Department Visitor Center in Cheyenne.

We hope your visit here is most memorable and we also believe you will agree, Wyoming wild life – is "worth the watching".

H The Greeting and The Gift

At the information center rest area just south of I-25/I-80 junction.

The scene depicts a typical meeting of the Indian and the Mountain Man on the open plains of WYOMING during the time of western discovery and exploration in the early 1800s.

At such meetings offerings of friendship would take place. The Indian is holding out a ceremonial buffalo horn filled with Rocky Mountain "sweetwater" while the Mountain Man brings several beaver skins stretched on rounds of aspen branches.

Note that the Mountain Man holds his Muzzle Loading "long rifle" well away from his body with his hand over the muzzle to assure that it is harmless.

The Indian stands 126' and weighs 3,000 pounds. The Mountain Man, whose raised hand reaches to 14', weighs 2,500 pounds.

34 *Food, Lodging*

I-25 Exit 2

35 *No services*

T Warren ICBM & Heritage Museum, F.E. Warren AFB

On F.E. Warren AFB, just west of Cheyenne. 773-2980

The Museum is in historic Building 210, which was the Army commander's headquarters at the turn of the century. You will find exhibits in the first floor rooms, as well as the museum annex building 211, depicting the history of missiles and that of the 90th Space Wing. On the second floor of Bldg. 210 are rooms that create a look back into the life of the men and women stationed at the post/base. National Park Service excavated an archeology site in 1991-1992, and the base has a Archeology Interpretive Center near Crow creek.

The museum is open to the public. Please call for our hours and procedures.

Genealogy Researchers: there are no personnel or old unit records kept on this installation. You must contact the National Archives, in Washington D.C. Thank You.

Courtesy F.E. Warren website

T FE Warren Air Force Base

Francis E. Warren AFB is the longest continuously active base in the USAF inventory; it is also home to the most powerful missile wing in the free world.

In 1867 Fort D.A. Russell was established to protect workers building the western link of the trans-continental railroad. Over the years Fort Russell (later Fort Warren in1930) was host to units of infantry, cavalry and field artillery.

The Air Force assumed command in1947 and in 1949 the fort was renamed F.E. Warren AFB. During the first ten years as an Air Force base, the installation was used as a training facility. In 1958 the 4320 Strategic Missile Wing was established with responsibility for the first twenty-four Atlas missile sites under Strategic Air Command (SAC). On 2 Sep 1960 the 564th Strategic Missile Sqn at

F.E. Warren AFB was declared the first fully operational ICBM squadron.

Two years later the new ICBM Minuteman replaced the Atlas. On 1 July 1963, the 90th Strategic Missile Wing was activated. The wing was redesignated the 90th Space Wing on 4 Sep 1997.

Since 1986, F.E. Warren AFB has maintained 150 Minuteman IIIs and is home to the Air Force's only 50 Peacekeeper ICBMs.

From the early days of the United States western expansion, through two world war's, the cold war and beyond, F.E. Warren AFB has been in the forefront of America's proud military history. F.E. Warren AFB remains a major presence in our nation's military defense.

Warren was placed on the National Register of Historic Places in 1975. The red brick buildings, built between 1885 and 1930, remain structurally unchanged and are currently occupied by members of the Air Force.

The Base Cemetery is the final resting place of more than 850 deceased military personnel and dependents. Burials date from November 1867 and include an Italian and 8 German POWs who died here during WWII

Courtesy of Warren AFB website

H Camp Carlin

Just west of Cheyenne on State Highway 210

Camp Carlin or Cheyenne Depot, 1867-1890, was 2nd largest quartermaster depot in the United States. In Wyoming it supplied Forts Russell, Sanders, Steele, Bridger, Washakie, Fetterman, Laramie, McKinney and Phil Kearny; in Nebraska, Forts Sidney, Omaha Robinson; in Utah, Fort Douglas; in Idaho, Fort Hall; and Meeker Colorado. It supplied annuity goods for Indian tribes, Particularly the Red Cloud and Spotted Tail Agencies. Site 1/4 mile west. 1/4 mile south. Erected by the Historical Landmark Commission of Wyoming 1957

L A. Drummond's Ranch Bed & Breakfast

399 Happy Jack Road just west of Cheyenne. 634-6042. www.cruising-america.com/html

The A. Drummond's Ranch Bed & Breakfast is nestled on the south side of a hill looking south to the Colorado Rockies. A quiet, gracious retreat on 120 acres bordered by the National Forest and State Park. Drummond's is a true retreat to tranquility with terry robes, outdoor hot tubs, complimentary homemade snacks, fresh fruits, and beverages always available. Dine on fine silver, crystal, and china. Sourdough waffles are served on Sunday. This retreat with awesome views provides privacy with personalized service. Bring your horse, hunt or fish, rent a mountain bike, take a llama to lunch, go for a hike, or just relax. Spend a night or a week to suit your needs.

L Windy Hills Guest House & Spa

393 Happy Jack Road, near Cheyenne. 632-6423 or toll free 877-946-3944. www.windyhillswyo.com

Experience a hearty Wyoming welcome at Windy Hills Guest House and Spa. This secluded hideaway rests 7,200 feet atop a stony rolling vista overlooking Granite Lake. The solace and charm will invigorate your sense and dash away your worries. Windy Hills was founded on a "don't hurry, don't worry" philosophy. The property offers a ranch-style two-bedroom guest house and a three-level log house with three bedrooms and two Spa Houses feature a great room living space. Guest suites have private entrances and are surrounded with cozy western amenities. Breakfast is an experience with out of the ordinary tantalizing entrees. Whether you are planning a family reunion, professional meeting, or romantic getaway, Windy Hills is the perfect place to gather. Visit them on the web.

36 *Gas, Lodging*

T Wyoming Game and Fish, Cheyenne Visitor Center

5400 Bishop Blvd. in Cheyenne. 777-4600

View dioramas of Wyoming wildlife while you find information about hunting and fishing.

T Cheyenne Botanic Gardens
710 South Lions Park Drive in Frontier Park, Cheyenne. 637-6458. www.botanic.org

The Cheyenne Botanic Gardens is a 6,800 square-foot, three-sectioned greenhouse conservatory. The greenhouse is 100% passively solar-heated and partially solar-powered. It is one of the region's largest and most unique solar energy demonstrations. Meander through the greenhouse and follow the paths through a fragrant herb garden, past the softly trickling waterfall, and under exotic vines and tropical trees including angel's trumpet, citrus trees, a cactus garden and a variety of ornamental flowers. If you're lucky, the towering fig tree and banana plant will display their unusual fruits. Discover the world of herbs used in cooking, dyes, fragrances and medicines.

Winter is one of the most colorful times inside the Cheyenne Botanic Gardens with fragrant stocks, snapdragons and freesias along with the interesting blooms of thunbergia, bougainvillea and assorted forced bulbs. By the small waterfall, you'll see a tall bamboo plant and papyrus along with Koi goldfish, a turtle and a frog. In late winter, you will see bedding plants destined for the Cheyenne park system, grown and maintained by the Garden's volunteers.

The Gardens are open daily.

Excerpted from Botanic Gardens brochure.

T Old West Museum
4810 N. Carey Avenue in Cheyenne at Frontier Park. 778-7290. www.oldwestmuseum.org

Rotating exhibits capture the spirit and rigorous life of the Cowboys, Pioneers and Native Americans whose challenges and courage shaped the West as we know it today. Travel through time with the third largest carriage collection in the country. Pique your imagination with their outstanding collection of Western art, which includes bronzes, oils, watercolors and more. The "Hole in the Wall" Kids Room delights children of all ages. The museum is open daily year round. Call for hours. An admission fee is charged.

Excerpted from museum brochure.

> **Wyoming Tidbits**
>
> An 1875 territorial law forbade the wearing of firearms within the limits of Wyoming's towns, but it was rarely enforced. "In Cheyenne, it's gettin' easier to kill a man than to steal his horse," the Cheyenne Daily Leader commented.

H Railing from Riner Viaduct In service from 1929 to 1982
In the entrance of the Wyoming State Transportation Department in Cheyenne

This piece of wrought iron railing is about all that remains of the historic Riner Viaduct that once bridged Cheyenne's north and south sides separated by the Union Pacific Railroad yards.

Originally an all-wood structure, Riner Viaduct first carried travelers over the railroad yards in 1892. At that time, a significant portion of Cheyenne's commercial district was located immediately south of where the viaduct was built.

Although named after J. S. Riner, Cheyenne's mayor from 1887 to 1891, the structure has also been called the Central Avenue Viaduct. Riner was in his second term when the Kansas City Structural Steel Co. of Kansas City, Mo., replaced the original viaduct with a steel structure in 1929. The replacement was a joint venture by the railroad, Laramie County and federal government.

However, after many years of heavy use and weathering, deterioration set in. Use restrictions became necessary, and replacement became inevitable.

On the morning of July 15, 1982, the last vehicle passed over Riner Viaduct because the first of twin replacement viaducts was ready for traffic. Riner Viaduct was razed during the 1982-83 winter to make way for construction of the second viaduct.

M Coldwell Banker Team Real Estate
7350 Stockman Street, Suite B, in Cheyenne. 635-9171 or 800-733-9171. www.cheyennerealestate.com

37 *Gas, Food*

T Wyoming Hereford Ranch
1114 Hereford Ranch Road, five miles east of Cheyenne. 634-1905

Covering nearly 60,00 acres, the ranch has been in operation for over one hundred years. The current residents, the Hales, are the first owner-operators to live on the Wyoming Hereford Ranch, originally claimed in 1883 as part of the famed Swan Land and Cattle Co. Wyoming Hereford Ranch is revered throughout the American West for its cattle. A visitors center covers the history of the ranch and tours of the many vintage buildings are available.

M Frontier Properties
5920 Yellowstone Road in Cheyenne. 638-1313 or toll free at 866-638-1313. www.frontierpoperties.net

38 *Gas (Exit 17 only)*

Exits 16, 17, 21, 25, 29, 34, 39, 47

H Little Bear Monument
About 27 miles north of Cheyenne on I-25.

Cheyenne, Fort Laramie, Deadwood Trail, 1867-1887, started from Camp Carlin and Fort D. A. Russell on the west edge of Cheyenne. This road first ran to Ft. Laramie and in 1876 was extended to Deadwood, Dakota Territory, and the Black Hills gold fields. It also joined the Bozeman Road to Montana. Little Bear stage station, 150 yards east, was opened as a road ranch by Isaac Bard, May 4, 1875. It became a stage station in 1877.

> **Wyoming Tidbits**
>
> A ribbon of gold leaf 67 feet long and one-half inch wide is used in the delicate process of gilding the Wyoming State Capitol Building dome.

39 *No services*

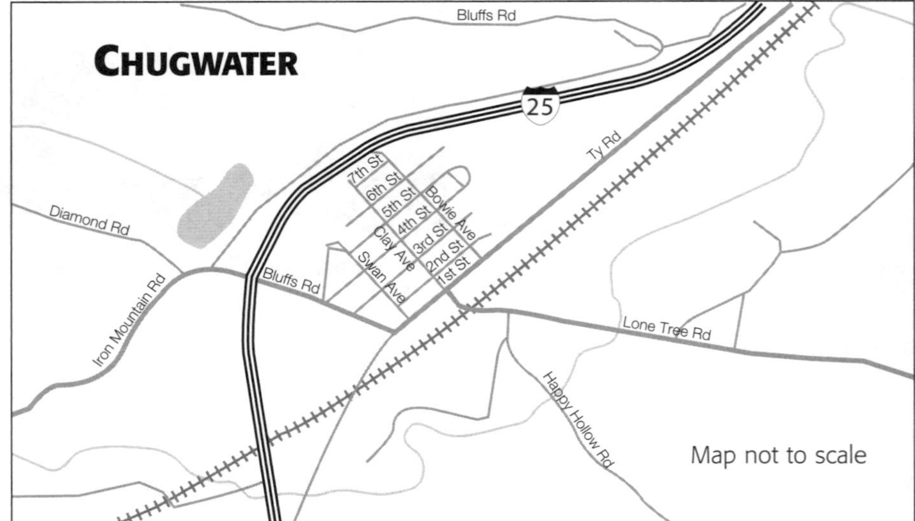

Edward and Jane Ivinson

Edward Ivinson was born in 1830 at Three River Estates on St. Croix in the Virgin Islands. He was educated at the Croft House Academy in Brampton, England, and arrived in London on Queen Victoria's coronation day in 1837. He returned to St. Croix, and after a time, emigrated to New York where he served as an apprentice at Lord and Taylor, learning the mercantile business. He married Jane Wood in 1854, in New Jersey, shortly after her arrival in the United States. She was born in Bolton, England, in 1840.

The young couple started west in 1856, and after various business ventures in Pennsylvania, Tennessee, and Illinois, arrived in Laramie City, Dakota Territory, in May, 1868. With them they had the necessary stock to open a grocery and general mercantile business. Accompanying them was their daughter, Margaret, whom they had adopted in Peoria. In addition to his mercantile business, Edward Ivinson became the chief purveyor of ties and timber for the Union Pacific Railroad, and this enterprise was the base of his future fortune. In 1871, he purchased a bank and expanded his real estate holdings. It was said that for fifty years he walked past the bank every night at exactly 8:30 to see that all was well with the institution, which held his millions. In addition to his business interests, Ivinson was active in a great number of civic enterprises. He was Treasurer of the University of Wyoming's first Board of Trustees; Vestryman and Senior Warden of St. Matthew's Episcopal Cathedral parish; Mayor of Laramie, and an unsuccessful gubernatorial candidate in the second state election in 1892.

Jane Ivinson was instrumental in forming the Episcopal parish, the first Sunday School, the first public school, and was involved in a wide range of educational and charitable activities. She died in 1915, not long after the couple had celebrated their sixtieth wedding anniversary. In her memory, Ivinson built a hospital, a home for aged ladies, deeded their mansion to the Episcopal Church to house a girls' school, and completed the towers, the clock and the chimes of St. Matthew's Cathedral. He died in Denver in 1928 at the age of 98.

Reprinted from Laramie Plains Museum brochure.

Wyoming Tidbits

In 1959, construction began on underground missile silos in southestern Wyoming as part of the Atlas and Minuteman missile systems. Warren Air Force Base became a Strategic Air Command Center.

Federal

The Federal Land and Securities Company gave this town the land it is on, as well as its name. Developer J. Ross Carpenter was responsible for the town's establishment, as well as for the settlement, which bears his name (Carpenter).

Horse Creek

This creek and the town were named for a Crow raid on a white trapping party, in which all the white's horses were stolen. The party, passing through in 1824, included Jedediah Smith, Thomas Fitzpatrick, and William Ashley. Another creek named Horse Creek can be found in Sublette County, west of Daniel. It was named for wild horses, which roamed in the area.

40 *Gas, Food, Lodging*

Chugwater

Pop. 244, Elev. 5,288

Nearby Chug Springs, at the head of Chugwater Creek, was once the site of an Indian buffalo jump. According to legend, chasing buffalo off a cliff, instead of hunting them, was the idea of a young chieftain. He was known as "The Dreamer," because he was a man of thought, not action. Derived from the sound the buffalo made when they fell into the water, the Indians called the place "water where the buffalo chug." Immigrants shortened this to Chugwater, and so it remains to this day. Today Chugwater is best known for Chugwater Chili which was created by local residents and is now sold and famous worldwide.

A lively place for such a small town, Chugwater was once the central headquarters for the Swan Land and Cattle Company, the biggest Wyoming cattle concern for many years, covering over 500,000 acres. It was also an important stop for the Cheyenne-Deadwood Stage. John "Portugee" Phillips, of Fetterman Fight fame, became the first postmaster here, and opened the Chugwater Ranch in 1876.

Chugwater is also the source of an important geologic term: Chugwater Formation. This is a telltale combination of red gypsum and shale discovered here which gives a specific Triassic dating to the rock wherever it's found.

Slater

Named for homesteader Ellis Slater, there was once another post office named Slater in Sheridan County, as well as one just across the Colorado border south of Savery.

T Chugwater Community Museum

In Chugwater

This collection of Western artifacts includes ranch brands, farm machinery, and railroad items, including an old train caboose. Research materials include homestead locations and area maps. Open Memorial Day to Labor Day. Admission is free with donations accepted.

H Chugwater Rock Outcroppings

Chugwater Rest Area at I-25, Exit 54

Rugged rock outcrops, like those nearby, are clearly visible on the otherwise treeless and lonely plains of Wyoming. Sculpted by years of wind and weather, the rock formations provide a pleasing contrast to the often stark prairie scenery. The rock formations also offer a diversity of habitats, which provide homes for a variety of wildlife, including some animals not normally found on the prairie.

More than 13 species of mammals live in, on or around the rocky formations. Cottontail rabbits, yellow-bellied marmots and least chipmunks are common sights at the outcrops. Other more secretive residents, like plains harvest mice, deer mice, bushy-tailed wood rats and bats, are nocturnal. Reptiles like snakes, lizards and skinks reside in cracks and crevices. Some predators—like the long-tailed weasel, striped skunk and bobcat—hunt the smaller mammals, birds, reptiles and insects that live on the rocks.

Many different species of hawks and owls use the rocky outcroppings as nest sites. Red-tailed hawks and golden eagles nest on ledges, and ferruginous hawks nest on boulders and

Chugwater	Jan	Feb	March	April	May	June	July	Aug	Sep	Oct	Nov	Dec	Annual
Average Max. Temperature (F)	39.6	42.8	48.4	58.5	68.1	78.7	86.9	85.5	76.6	64.4	49.4	41.7	61.7
Average Min. Temperature (F)	14.9	16.9	20.8	28.5	37.3	45.6	51.3	49.5	39.8	30.3	21.8	16.4	31.1
Average Total Precipitation (in.)	0.52	0.57	1.02	1.91	2.81	2.24	1.80	1.37	1.24	1.05	0.68	0.64	15.85
Average Total SnowFall (in.)	7.7	8.0	11.3	10.8	2.7	0.1	0.0	0.0	1.2	4.0	8.5	8.7	63.0
Average Snow Depth (in.)	2	1	1	0	0	0	0	0	0	0	1	1	1

pillars. The prairie falcon and great-horned owl nest in holes and crevices. These raptors, or birds of prey, help keep small mammal populations in balance. Smaller insect-eating birds, like Say's peobe, cliff swallows and rock wrens, also nest in and around the rocky cliffs. Other birds, like the rosy finch and raven, come to the rocks in winter, seeking shelter from the wind and cold.

The rocks add contrast to Wyoming's wildlands scenery, and provide essential habitat for a variety of wildlife.

FS Chugwater Soda Fountain
314 First Street in Chugwater. 422-3222.

The Chugwater Soda Fountain is one of Wyoming's oldest operating soda fountains. Stop in for all of your old fashioned favorites, relax, and enjoy the cozy atmosphere. Try a fantastic old fashioned malt, sundae, cone, banana split, or root beer float, all made with hand dipped ice cream. While you are at the shop check out their great T-shirts, collectibles, gifts, and Wyoming treasures. They open the be beer garden during the summer for even more fun. Enjoy the views and great deli sandwiches, fresh salads, yummy soups, and sizzling burgers. Refresh yourself with a ice cold beer, a favorite cocktail, or frosty root beer.

F Miss Kitty's Buffalo Grill
98 Buffalo Drive in Chugwater. 422-3463

Miss Kitty's Buffalo Grill is large enough to serve the whole family and small enough to know you as a friend. Miss Kitty's is popular for homemade pies, turnovers, and cinnamon and caramel rolls, but they serve a whole lot more. The famous Chugwater Chili and awesome homemade Green Chili keep people coming back for more. The extensive menu offers something for every appetite from hamburgers, chicken, and steaks to delicious homemade soups made from scratch. Every meal is served with pleasant, courteous service that always comes with a smile. There is plenty of parking for all sizes of vehicles.

S Chugwater Chili Corporation
210 First Street in Chugwater. 422-3345 or 800-972-4454. www.chugwaterchili.com

The Chugwater Chili Corporation was formed to offer the "gourmet spice of western life." Chugwater is not just another small town peppered on the prairie. It is, in fact, the spiciest spot along the trail with the explosion of the famous Chugwater Chili. Five farm and ranch families formed the Chugwater Chili Corporation promoting the award-winning Chugwater Chili—a delicious rich gourmet blend of herbs and spices, made of all natural seasonings—no preservatives or additives. From the original blend, three additional products have been developed. Be sure and try the Chugwater Chili Dip and Dressing Mix, Chugwater Chili Red Pepper Jelly, and Chugwater Chili Nuts. Visitors are welcome to stop in at their headquarters and enjoy a free sampling.

41 *No services*

Exits 65, 66, 68, 70, 73

T Sybille Wildlife Research Center
On Highway 34, about 20 miles west of Wheatland. 322-2784

The Sybille Wildlife Research Center is one of the West's best facilities for the study of Wyoming's many large ungulates and other native species, especially those who are endangered. Besides providing a home for moose, elk, deer, antelope, and bighorn sheep, there are also black-footed ferrets and Wyoming Toads who are being researched here.

Studies at Sybille are directed to the needs of game and habitat management, and include a focus on wildlife diseases. Founded in 1972, when an epidemic among cattle threatened Wyoming's ungulates, Sybille has contributed more than 170 research projects to conservation. With easy access, adequate space for pastures and confinement areas, and possessing diverse terrain, cover and weather conditions, its proximity to the University and supporting facilities also make its location optimal. The development of the research facility began in 1952 under the direction of Floyd Blunt and continues today.

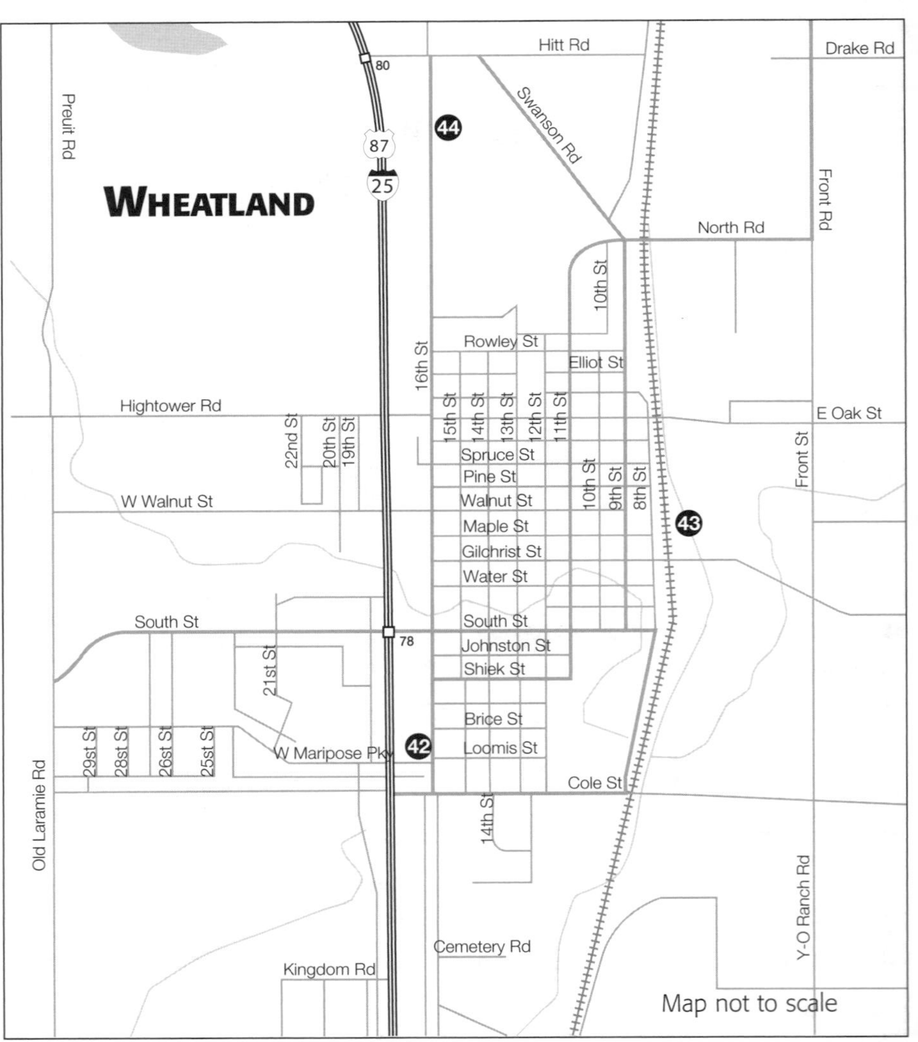

42 *Gas, Food, Lodging*

Wheatland

Pop. 3,548, Elev. 4,733

Once called Gilchrist, for a local rancher, this town got the name Wheatland when an irrigation project brought farming to the area. Francis E. Warren and Joseph M. Carey spearheaded the building of a dam on the Big Laramie River to create canals for homesteaders. Bill Bodley is thought to have been the first settler to break the sod to plant wheat. A flourmill and a sugar beet factory created a stable economy for a time, but both closed. Oil, gas, and a power plant created prosperity in the 1970s, but the 80s were less productive. Wheatland has returned to its agricultural roots, and is home to one of the state's largest hog farms.

L Motel West Winds

1756 South Road in Wheatland. 322-2705

43 *Food, Lodging*

L Wyoming Motel

1101 9th Street in Wheatland. 322-5383 or 800-839-5383. www.wyomingmotel.com or email: cstenson@communicomm.com

S Wheatland Mercantile

875 Gilchrist in Wheatland. 322-1727 or 800-620-7897. www.wheatlandmercantile.net

Step back in time at the old Wheatland Mercantile originally built in 1890. Destroyed by fire in 1903, it was rebuilt in 1909 with locally made brick. Today, walk on straight sided oak floors, under the original ceiling of pressed tin. Gas chandeliers were replaced with electric lights in the 1930's. Enjoy collections of old artifacts—some for sale. Shop for new items that range from 100% cotton quilt fabrics, lace making supplies, locally grown wool, and other dry goods items for all your stitchery projects. The store has a gunsmith/knifesmith, selling hand made guns and knives. They also do gun and knife repairs. Bead lovers will find a large selection of beads. They also carry model cars, planes, and miniature furniture, and First Day Covers for collectors of postal items.

> ### *Wyoming Tidbits*
>
> Wyoming's State Fair is held in late August each year in Douglas. The first fair was held with a $10,000 appropriation from the State Legislature.

M Graves Realty, L.C.

1253 South Street in Wheatland. 322-9395 or toll free at 888-201-1299. www.gravesrealtywyo.com

44 *Gas, Food, Lodging*

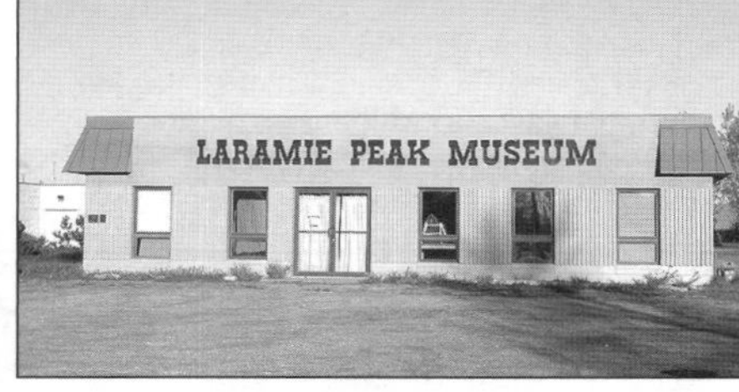

T Laramie Peak Museum

1601 16th St. in Wheatland. 322-2052

Features historical artifacts from the Platte County area. A number of items dating back to the late 1800s tell the story of the Oregon Trail, the cattle baron era, and the first settlers in the area. Open third Monday of May through second week of September.

H In Honor of Jacques LaRamie

State Highway 320 north of Wheatland

Free trapper, who came to this region around 1815 and met an unknown fate, probably at the hands of Indains, about 1820, on one of the rivers bearing his name between which this monument stands. Tradition says he was an honest, just and courageous leader and trader. His name is perpetuated by three Laramie Rivers, Fort Laramie, the Laramie Plains, Laramie Peak, Laramie City, and Laramie County.

45 *Gas, Food, Lodging*

Douglas

Pop. 5,288, Elev. 4,815

Hometown of the Jackalope, and the county seat of Converse County, Douglas was named for Stephen A. Douglas, Abraham Lincoln's famous opponent. Once a railroad tent town, Douglas prospered in true renegade fashion (there were 21 saloons) until Casper became the end of the line, and the community settled into a peaceful rural existence. Like so many other Wyoming towns, though, this would not be the only boom and bust cycle. Through the years, the discovery of coal, oil, natural gas, and even uranium brought prosperity and disappointment to the community's fortunes. Today, the town relies mostly on energy and ranching concerns, but welcomes tourism with a number of historic sites, services, and amenities.

T Sir Barton Burial Monument
Washington Park in Douglas

The first Triple Crown Winner, Sir Barton began racing in 1918. After retiring to a Wyoming ranch, the noble steed died of colic in 1937. A statue is erected over his grave in Washington Park.

FLS Plains Motel and Trading Post Restaurant
628 East Richards in Douglas. 358-4484. Restaurant, 358-4489.

The past comes alive at the Plains Trading Post Complex where the late Neil Goodrich preserved all or part of 40 historic western buildings to construct a unique western complex. The property continues to be improved by the Hegglund family, preserving the essence of the Old West. The Ice Cream Parlor and Gift Shop are located in an 1880s country barn. The restaurant is housed in the old Trading Post built in the 1920s. You'll marvel at the history preserved in the lounge, dance hall, and grounds. Plan to stay at the Plains Motel and step back in time. Enjoy the warmth that emanates from the labor of love that comprises the Plains Complex.

46 *Food, Lodging*

T Douglas Area Chamber of Commerce
121 Brownfield in Douglas. 358-2950. www.jackalope.org

T Douglas Railroad Interpretive Center
311 North 5th in Douglas. 358-9684

Parked outside the old Chicago Elk Horn Railroad depot which now houses the Chamber of Commerce, seven train cars make up the Interpretive Center. Included in the car collection are a sleeper, dining, baggage, coach, cattle car, a caboose and a steam locomotive. Volunteers staff the car Saturday and Sunday, 9 a.m. through 5 p.m. from May through September.

T Converse County Tourism Promotion Board
121 Brownfield in Douglas. 358-2950. www.conversecountytourism.com

T Wyoming Pioneer Memorial Museum
400 W. Center St. near Downtown Douglas. 358-9288.

This fine western history museum houses one of the largest collections of historical memorabilia, which will stir your imagination and take you on a trip back through time to an era when buffalo roamed free, the Indians were the undisputed rulers and the pioneers struggled in a hostile and unchartered land.

The original Wyoming Pioneer Memorial Museum was built in 1925. The log structure was used until a new, modern facility was erected adjacent to it and dedicated in 1956. Since then the museum has been enlarged three times and many new exhibits have been added.

Among the exhibits you will see: the saddle of Range Detective Tom Horn, the mittens worn by "Portugee" Phillips on his historic ride, artifacts from the Johnson County Cattle War, and the original bar from the historic LaBonte Inn. As you tour the museum you will find everything from dolls and dishes to guns and harness. Traveling on the trails and life on the frontier was packed full of trials and hardships. Having very little to work with, they carved their futures out of next to nothing. Their strong will and hard work made settlement of Wyoming possible.

Over the years the museum has acquired a fine collection of art depicting life in the West, past and present. It also hosts various traveling exhibits and the permanent collection from the Cowboy State Art Spectacular. The museum is also the home of the annual Douglas Invitational Art Show and Sale.

Reprinted from museum brochure.

T Plains Complex
628 E. Richards in Douglas. 358-4489

See several historic buildings moved to the site from all over Wyoming. There are officer's quarters from Fort Fetterman, a POW camp building, and an ice cream parlor with a colorful history.

T Christ Episcopal Church
411 Center Street in Douglas. 358-5609

Listed in the National Register of Historic Places, this church was built in 1896.

T Douglas Park Cemetery
9th and Ash in Douglas

This graveyard is the final resting place of several interesting Western characters, including outlaws "Doc" Middleton and George W. Pike. The chamber of commerce provides information for a walking tour.

H Wyoming State Fair
400 W. Center in Douglas. 358-2398

In 1905, Chicago Northwestern Railroad donated the fairgrounds on the condition that a fair beheld in Douglas each year. The great Depression, a polio outbreak in 1937 and World War II caused the cancellation of a State Fair in those years. There has been a Wyoming State Fair every year since the end of WWII.

Some of the more interesting entertainment over the years has included

The Girl in Red, a member of Professor Carver's High Diving Girls, jumping her diving horse from a platform into a pool below and Baxter Adams with his airplane stunts and motorcycle racing.

Premium list advertisers in the early days included DeLaval Cream Separators, MicaAxle Grease and Chloro-Naptholeum Dip and Disinfectant.

Speaking of the first state fair in 1905, M.C. Barrow, early day publisher of "Bill Barlow"s Budget," said: "...There was plenty doing each day, uptown, on the grounds each afternoon and

Douglas

	Jan	Feb	March	April	May	June	July	Aug	Sep	Oct	Nov	Dec	Annual
Average Max. Temperature (F)	36.9	40.7	47.0	57.9	67.5	78.3	87.2	84.8	74.7	61.9	47.4	39.0	60.3
Average Min. Temperature (F)	11.1	15.5	21.3	30.5	39.5	48.3	55.2	52.7	42.4	31.6	21.4	14.2	32.0
Average Total Precipitation (in.)	0.48	0.58	0.82	1.84	2.39	1.86	1.37	1.10	1.29	1.26	0.63	0.51	14.14
Average Total SnowFall (in.)	6.4	7.3	8.4	9.6	1.7	0.2	0.0	0.0	0.6	3.5	6.5	7.3	51.7
Average Snow Depth (in.)	1	1	1	0	0	0	0	0	0	0	1	1	0
Wind Speed (mph / kmh)	17 / 27	16 / 25	15 / 23	13 / 22	12 / 20	11 / 18	11 / 17	11 / 17	12 / 19	13 / 21	15 / 24	17 / 27	
Wind Direction	SW	SW	SW	SW	SW	WSW	WSW	SW	SW	SW	SW	SW	

Wheatland

	Jan	Feb	March	April	May	June	July	Aug	Sep	Oct	Nov	Dec	Annual
Average Max. Temperature (F)	40.7	44.1	50.7	61.0	70.5	81.1	89.4	87.7	78.0	65.7	50.7	42.6	63.5
Average Min. Temperature (F)	17.0	19.5	23.9	32.0	41.4	49.7	55.9	53.8	44.0	34.6	25.4	19.4	34.7
Average Total Precipitation (in.)	0.26	0.35	0.67	1.64	2.41	2.08	1.51	1.08	1.24	0.90	0.45	0.36	12.96
Average Total SnowFall (in.)	5.2	5.8	7.5	6.9	1.1	0.0	0.0	0.0	0.8	2.7	5.2	5.9	41.1
Average Snow Depth (in.)	1	0	0	0	0	0	0	0	0	0	0	1	0

at night a half dozen attractions served to keep everybody amused and entertained according to his or her inclination."

H Jackalopes

It is believed that the first jackalope sightings on United States soil first occurred while lonesome cowboys were relaxing at the end of long hard day on the range and singing songs around their campfires. Now that would probably have been around and near Douglas, Wyoming.

The origin of the American Jackalope is attributed to Douglas Herrick, a native of Douglas, Wyoming. Why it must be true for he had a great reputation as one fine taxidermist. Jackalope have literally popped up everywhere. Since the 1930s in magazine articles have been written, movies made, found for sale in gift shops, truck stops and in plenty of taxidermy shops. Douglas even has an annual festival, Jackalope Days, held every June. In 1965, the state of Wyoming trademarked the name and you can even buy hunting licenses, good between midnight and 2 a.m. on 31 June any year. In 1985, Governor of the State of Wyoming, proclaimed Douglas to be the "Home of the Jackalope." Like snipe hunts, jackalope hunts have been used as a ritual form of hazing in rural communities. When you see a jackalope what you are most likely to find is a jackrabbit mounted with the antlers of a young antelope or deer.

On an interesting side note, Jackalopism, is created by a naturally occurring North American disease in rabbits called papillomatosis, where certain growths caused by a parasite harden. A papillomavirus is the same sort of disease that causes the growth of warts on humans. The disease is very common in cottontails. When such growths occur on the top of a rabbit's head, they may resemble horns, thus leading to the birth of the Jackalope legend.

S Whistle-Stop Mercantile: New & Used Books, Wyoming Souvenirs and Gifts

One block from Jackalope Square in Douglas. 358-3663. www.whistlestopbooks.com

M Aspen Realty Co.

1125 W. Yellowstone in Douglas. 358-3586. www.aspen-realty.com

47 *Gas, Food, Lodging*

T Odd Fellows Hall Murals

115 S. Riverbend Dr. in Douglas. 358-2421

Section 6

Largest Infrared Observatory

The largest infrared telescope in the continental United States is in Albany County. Located 25 miles southwest of Laramie the telescope sits on top of Jeb Mountain. This site was chosen for dry air, low pollution, and dark skies. The observatory was funded jointly by the Wyoming State Legislature and the National Science Foundation in 1975 and became operational in 1977. It ranks as one of the premier infrared observatories in the world. For more information call the University of Wyoming Department of Physics and Astronomy at 766-6250.

This building was once the Officer's Club for the POW camp officers. Italian prisoners of war, held here during World War II, painted the murals that line the walls inside.

T Douglas WWII POW Camp

During World War II Douglas hosted a large POW camp that housed approximately 3,000 prisoners. The only remnants left today are the murals that Italian POW's painted in the old officer's club, now the local Odd Fellows Hall.

Little remains today of the original Fort Fetterman.

48 *No services*

T Fort Fetterman State Historic Site

State Highway 93 about seven miles northwest of Douglas. 684-7629

Fort Fetterman is preserved as an homage to the winning of the west. It features restored officers' quarters, an ordinance warehouse, and parade grounds. The fort, built in 1867, was an Army supply post. Exhibits allude to regional history of the Army and Fetterman City.

Fort Fetterman — Its History

Fort Fetterman, located approximately eleven miles northwest of Douglas, Wyoming, is situated on a plateau above the valleys of LaPrele Creek and the North Platte River.

The fort was established as a military post on July 19, 1867 because of conditions that existed on the Northern Plains at the close of the Civil War. Civilization was advancing across the frontier along the line of the Union Pacific Railroad and the fort was needed as a major supply point for the army operating against the Indians. On July 31, 1867, the post was named Fort Fetterman in honor of Captain William J. Fetterman who was killed in a fight with Indians near Fort Phil Kearny, December 21, 1866.

Major William McEnery Dye, with Companies A, C, H, and I, 4th Infantry was assigned to build the post. In a letter to the Adjutant General, Major Dye described the post and surrounding country as "...situated on a plateau above the valley of the Platte, being neither so low as to be seriously affected by the rains or snow; nor so high and unprotected as to suffer from the winter winds."

Unfortunately, Major Dye's optimistic view of the site did not hold true for winter months.

In November of 1867, Brigadier General H.W. Wessells became commanding officer at the fort. According to his report to the Department of the Platte, "...officers and men were found under canvas exposed on a bleak plain to violent and almost constant gales and very uncomfortable..."

The garrison managed to get through the winter and the fort continued to grow and develop until, by 1870, it was well established arid destined to play a conspicuous part in the Indians wars for the next few years. Jim Bridger, Wild Bill Hickock, Calamity Jane and "Buffalo Bill" Cody were among the colorful personalities of the time whose activities and travels took them to Fort Fetterman.

In accordance with the Treaty of 1868, Forts Reno, Phil Kearny and Smith, (along the Bozeman Trail) were abandoned. Fort Fetterman, alone, remained on the fringe of the disputed area. As an outpost of civilization on the Western frontier, the fort represented protection and was a haven to travelers.

Fort Fetterman was always considered a hardship post by officers and men stationed there. On May 18, 1874, Captain F. Van Vliet, of Company C, 3rd Cavalry, felt so strongly about the hardships on his men that he wrote to the Adjutant General requesting his company be transferred because there was "...no opportunity for procuring fresh vegetables, and gardens are a failure. There is no female society for enlisted men ...the enlisted men of the company are leaving very much dissatisfied, as they look upon being held so long at this post as an unmerited punishment... whenever men get to the railroad there are some desertions caused by dread of returning to this post..."

Desertions were common and the post frequently lacked adequate supplies and equipment. Supplies had to be hauled from Fort Laramie to the southeast or from Medicine Bow Station on the Union Pacific Railroad. Luxuries were scarce and pleasures few. However the soldiers found some diversion from the garrison life at a nearby establishment known as the "Hog Ranch."

During the mid-1870s, Fort Fetterman reached its pinnacle of importance when it became the jumping-off place for several major military expeditions. It was the base for three of General George Crook's Powder River Expeditions and Colonel Ranald Mackenzie's campaign against Dull Knife and the Cheyenne Indians. These events contributed to the end of the resistance by the Plains Indians who shortly after were confined to reservations. With the passing of Indians from the scene, the fort had outlived its usefulness.

When the military abandoned the fort in 1882, it did not die immediately. A community grew up at the post and after 1882, it was an outfitting point for area ranchers and wagon trains. The boom was short-lived, however, and in 1886, the town of Douglas was founded a short distance to the south. The old fort, in a state of decay, lost out as a town and declined rapidly. Most of the buildings were sold, dismantled or moved to other locations.

Fort Fetterman is open to the public during the summer. A restored officers' quarters and an ordnance warehouse are original buildings. They stand among the visible foundations of the fort and Fetterman City. These two buildings house interpretive exhibits and artifacts of the fort's history, Fetterman City and Its Indian predecessors. You are encouraged to walk the grounds where interpretive signs describe the fort's buildings and activities.

The fort is open daily between Memorial Day and Labor Day from 9 a.m. to 5 p.m. The grounds are open from sunrise to sunset.
Courtesy of Wyoming State Parks and Historic Sites

H Fort Fetterman

I-25 Exit 140

The federal government established Fort Fetterman on July 19, 1867. Situated on the south bank of the North Platte River at the point where the Bozeman Trail left the river and turned north, the Fort's purpose was to protect emigrants and control the Sioux and other tribes who resented the miners and settlers passing through their lands. The Bozeman Trail, which crossed through the northeast quadrant of present day Wyoming, pierced Sioux, Cheyenne and Arapaho hunting territories. By

1866 warfare broke out between Indians and whites along the Bozeman Trail. In response, the government built a series of army posts: Forts Reno, Phil Kearny and C.F. Smith. The most dramatic episode of "Red Cloud's War" occurred December 21, 1866 near Fort Phil Kearny. The Sioux and their allies killed Captain William J. Fetterman and a detachment of 80 men. Fort Fetterman, constructed the following summer, was named in honor of the fallen captain. In the summer of 1868 the government's peace commissioners abandoned the northern posts and yielded the Bozeman Trail as part of the Fort Laramie Treaty of 1868.

The army did not evacuate Fort Fetterman, however, which experienced only minor skirmishing throughout the conflict. The 1873 Post Commander described the fort: "this being one of the most remote and…one of the most uninhabitable posts in the Department…" The two sides remained at peace until the Sioux War of 1876 when the army launched three expeditions under the command of General George Crook from Fort Fetterman. The military abandoned Fort Fetterman in November 1882, selling many of its buildings. The old post became the nucleus for a hell-raising cattle town. Eventually that too declined when Douglas was founded in 1886. Ft. Fetterman State Historic Site is located ten miles northeast on WY 93.

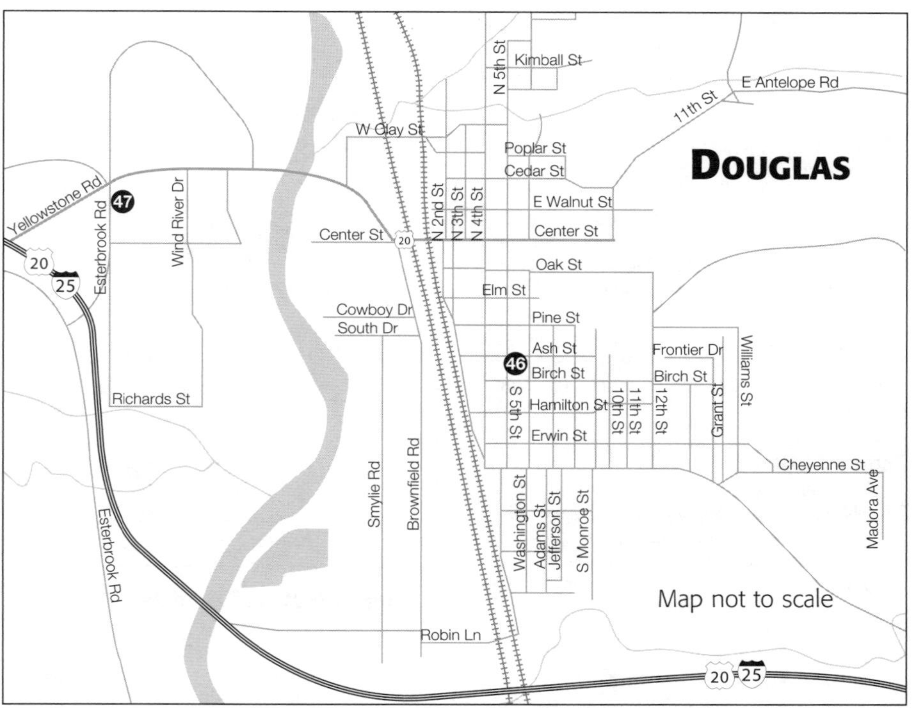

H Fort Fetterman Plaques

At Fort Fetterman Historic Site

Post Traders' Store

To the garrison of a frontier army post the Trader's Store was a commercial and social enterprise which today is duplicated by the separate functions of Post Exchange, Officers' Club, NCO' Club and Enlisted Men's Club. In addition, the store was an unofficial headquarters for civilian scouts, news reporters, trappers, Indians and other travelers desiring to trade for goods or seeking business or social contact with members of the military command. Depicted below is the south side of the parade ground.

Communications

Depicted above are: on the left, the site of the once-busy guard house; and on the right, the still-standing ordnance building. Headquarters, located nearby, was connected by telegraph to higher commands in the east. The left view-sight points to the route of that line as it approached this post from Fort Laramie. Most of the line was part of the original 1861 transcontinental telegraph link along the Oregon Trail. This line had been abandoned, but was patched up and extended to this point for military use.

The device on the right locates the former route of the heavily-used wagon road out of Rock Creek, which was once a Union Pacific Railroad station 80 miles to the south. It was from Rock Creek that most supplies were freighted to Fort Fetterman. According to records, wagons traveling this road required a military escort, at times more for protection against outlaws than Indians.

Barracks

Three identical enlisted men's barracks stood in a row parallel to the walk. Bunks were double-decked, with springs made of rope stretched on a wooden frame. Mattresses consisted of large bags filled with prairie hay. Clothing and other gear was hung on pegs or stored on wall shelves near each bunk.

Soldier's Rations

Behind the row of barracks which paralleled this walkway, were kitchens and mess halls. Cooking duties were supposedly rotated; actually the most competent man usually held the job. Campaign food customarily consisted of the unleavened biscuit called hardtack; wild game when available, otherwise salt-pork; bacon, often moldy and/or wormy; and a watery soup ladled from a stock of canned vegetables mixed and boiled with hardtack. In garrison, baked bread, occasionally beef, and fruits such as raisins and dried apples and peaches offered variety. Raw onions were used as a means of preventing and curing scurvy, supplemented at established posts by fresh vegetables from the garden.

Bozeman Trail

From this point, the Bozeman Trail wound a long, twisting northwesterly route to the Montana gold fields. Also leaving the fort at this point was the telegraph line to Fort Reno about 75 miles northwest. Later, with the abandonment of that fort in 1868, the line ended here until it was extended to Fort McKinney, established in 1878, near the present town of Buffalo.

Stables and Shops

Fort Fetterman had extensive stables, with corrals enclosed by a six-foot adobe fence. Teamsters' quarters were also located within the walls. Due to the isolation of the fort, there was provision for all types of repair work.

Hog Ranch

"Hog Ranch" was a common frontier term used to describe certain off-post facilities which catered to the lonely soldier's desire for wine, women and song. A cluster of cabins, the "ranch" was typical of similar establishments located outside the bounds of many western military reservations. The nearby one was among the most notorious in the history of the west. Below, on the North Platte River, is a probable former site of a ferry crossing. Because the Hog Ranch was off-limits, soldiers who desired to visit it usually swam the river. Later a bridge was built not far from the present highway crossing.

Water Supply

From this location, where the water reservoir once stood, one can see several interesting points. The sighting device points out the location of the pump used during later years to supply the fort with water. Prior to installation of the pump the water detail was usually a punishment duty, water having been dipped from the river and hauled in a wooden tank wagon to the fort. There were never any wells on the grounds of the post.

Bill Nye

Bill Nye, born Edgar Wilson "Bill" Nye, was one of America's most famous and beloved humorists and journalists He was born in Maine around 1850 and raised in Wisconsin. He moved to Wyoming from Wisconsin in 1876 and became a lawyer, postmaster, justice of the peace, and later becoming a judge. He founded and edited the Laramie Daily Boomerang, named in honor of his mule. Nye soon achieved national fame for his poker faced, tongue-in-cheek editorials and his humorous comments and yarns of frontier life as a correspondent for several national newspapers. He remained in Wyoming until 1886, then moving to New York City and continued writing, authoring several books and plays. His highly successful life was cut short when he died of a stroke in North Carolina in 1896.

Crook's Campaign
It was from this post that General Crook, in the spring of 1876, led the southern unit of the three-pronged Big Horn and Yellowstone Expedition against the Sioux, Cheyenne and Arapaho Indians. Severe losses were sustained by Crook on June 17th, in the stand-off Battle of the Rosebud. Shortly thereafter, on June 25th, the same Indians annihilated Lt. Col. George A. Custer and the 220 men of the 7th Cavalry which he personally led in the Battle of the Little Big Horn. Fort Letterman figured prominently in the final wars with these tribes and, following termination of hostilities, the post was abandoned in 1882. The sighting device points to Crook's camp at the beginning of his campaign.

Letterman Hotel
Located here was a triplex officer's quarters, usually occupied by the younger bachelor officers. Following abandonment by the army in 1882, the post was converted by civilians into the town of Letterman. That town was given a notorious reputation under the name "Drybone" in stories by Owen Wister, the founder of the western novel and author of "The Virginian". The building was known as the Letterman Hotel at that time. Letterman began to die when, in 1886, the town of Douglas was established by the westward-building predecessor of the Chicago North Western Railway.

Post Hospital
The post hospital once stood near this point. Due to its frontier isolation and location on an exposed plateau, Letterman received the dubious honor of being called a hardship post. Here the relentless wind carrying biting sand or stinging snow gave the fort a reputation for being desolate, a reputation due to the unfavorable location of the fort rather than the general climate of the region. Because of these conditions and the hard duty, more soldiers were treated for mental disorders, or physical injuries received in brawling, than those hospitalized due to wounds received in combat.

H Herman Werner 1892-1973
Fort Fetterman Site Memorial Shelter

Born here, at Fort Fetterman, son of an emigrant soldier serving on the Western Frontier, Herman Werner commenced his career as an open range cowboy and went on to develop one of the most notable ranching operations recorded in Wyoming's history.

Prominently known throughout the state as a rancher, a businessman, a sportsman and a philanthropist, Herman Werner remained at heart a cowboy. Surely, in his own estimation, his greatest success was that ranch workers everywhere recognized him to be "one of the boys".

49 *No services*

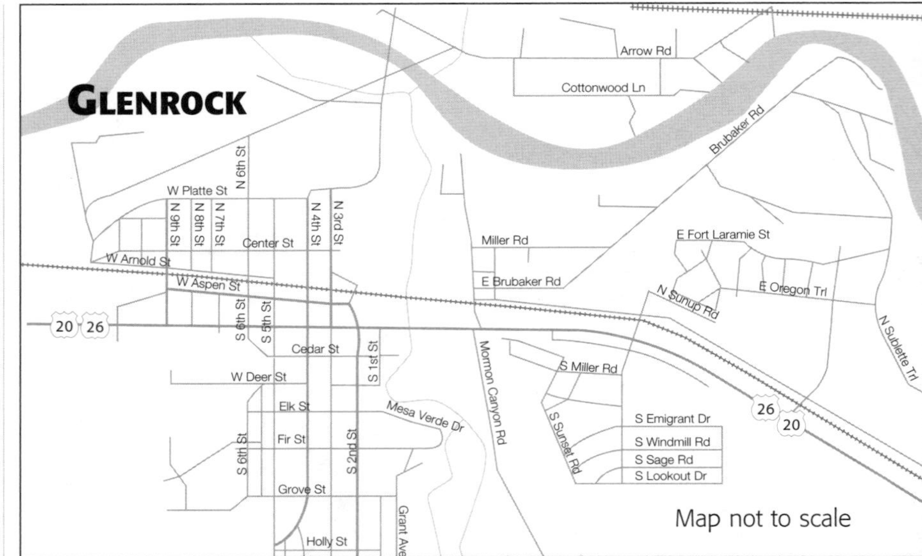

T Ayres Natural Bridge
11 miles west of Douglas on I-25 to Natural Bridge Exit 151, then 5 miles south

One of nature's wonders, Ayres Natural Bridge is one of the few natural bridges in the world that has water flowing under it. The Bridge is part of the Casper Sandstone Formation which was laid down during the Pennsylvanian Age more than 280 million years ago. Time and water eroded a hole in the rock allowing the stream now known as LaPrele Creek to flow through.

The bridge arch above the water is 50 feet high and 100 feet long. It sets in an amphitheater of red sand stone walls with tree-shaded picnic grounds for a pleasant visit.

Indian lore tells of the time that an Indian brave was struck by lightning near the bridge and was killed instantly. His people believed that an evil spirit, "King of Beasts," lived beneath the bridge and had swallowed the life of this warrior. From then on, the Indians would not go near the bridge. It became a sanctuary for people fleeing the Indians. If they could make it to the bridge, they would be safe because the Indians wouldn't follow for fear of the evil spirit.

In 1882, Alva Ayres, an early day freighter and bull whacker, settled on the land which included the bridge on LaPrele Creed. Alva's son, Andrew Clement Ayres, gave a deed for 15 acres of land to Converse County in May 1920. This land included the bridge and was to be known as Ayres Natural Bridge Park. In later years, Glen Edwards donated more land to the county to be added to the park.

The old two-story cement building near the entrance to the park was built by the North Platte Valley Irrigation Company in the early 1900s. When completed, it was to be a power house that would furnish electricity to pump water out of North Platte River for 40,000 acres north of the river. LaPrele Dam, located two miles south of the power house, would have supplied water for the installation. The company went bankrupt before the power project was completed.

Ayres Natural Bridge Park is located four miles south of Interstate 25 at the end of county Road #13. The Natural Bridge interchange is 11 miles west of Douglas, Wyoming at Exit 151.
Reprint of Converse County Brochure.

H Ayres Natural Bridge Park
South of I-25 Exit 151 on Natural Bridge Road

Ages ago Wyoming was covered by seas. Through a period of millions of years the land gradually rose, leaving the present landscape of plains, mountains and rolling hills. As the land emerged, erosion began and through eons of time, formed Ayres Natural Bridge as it exists today.

The bridge is 20 feet high and has a 90 foot span at the base. A trout stream flows beneath. The setting is in the center of a high red sandstone walled amphitheater, which provides a fine shady picnic ground.

All facilities are free and maintained by Converse County. Visitors welcome.

The bridge is 4-3/4 miles south from this point on an all weather road.

50 *Gas, Food, Lodging*

Glenrock
Pop. 2,231, Elev. 5,009

Named for "The Rock in the Glen," a Deer Creek landmark that is now by the old railroad station, pioneers often camped here between 1843 and 1887. The rock now bears many of their names, and some solitary graves are scattered nearby. The Mormons turned the place into an official way station in 1850. Shortly thereafter, it became the Deer Creek Overland Stage Station, telegraph office, and Pony Express stop. The station was burned by Indians in 1866, and never rebuilt. It acquired the name Mercedes for a while, and then was briefly named Nuttell, for coal developer William Nuttell.

Glenrock

	Jan	Feb	March	April	May	June	July	Aug	Sep	Oct	Nov	Dec	Annual
Average Max. Temperature (F)	37.6	41.5	48.1	58.7	69.0	80.2	88.9	87.1	76.5	63.3	47.2	39.2	61.4
Average Min. Temperature (F)	15.2	19.0	23.7	31.5	40.8	49.5	55.7	53.8	43.7	33.5	24.2	17.5	34.0
Average Total Precipitation (in.)	0.41	0.43	0.77	1.57	2.34	1.71	1.13	0.71	1.04	1.02	0.59	0.33	12.06
Average Total SnowFall (in.)	4.7	3.6	3.8	1.7	0.2	0.0	0.0	0.0	0.2	1.3	3.0	3.1	21.4
Average Snow Depth (in.)	1	0	0	0	0	0	0	0	0	0	0	0	0

T Glenrock Chamber of Commerce

506 Birch Street in Glenrock. 436-5652.

Glenrock is situated roughly at the confluence of the North Platte River and Deer Creek where rich history evolved as pioneers traveling the spacious and beautiful Wyoming Territory decided to stay. Today, Glenrock is a unique place to live and raise a family in harmony with nature. Families live without the hindrances of pollution, congestion, and explosive growth, while making lifelong friendships. The area provides year round recreation, abundant wildlife, and excellent museums. Highly acclaimed educational facilities in Glenrock have demonstrated progressiveness in the buildings and programs. The Glenrock Diagnostic and Treatment Center offers a total health care center for the community. Visit Glenrock and it is easy to see why the pioneers decided to go no further.

T Glenrock Deer Creek Historical Museum

935 West Birch in Glenrock, 436-2810

The building housing this museum was formerly the church of Our Redeemer Lutheran. It was moved from Kinnear, Wyoming to its present location in 1976.

The museum displays articles and artifacts from the prehistory of the Indians thru the immigration days on the Oregon-California Trail and early settlement. The cattle industry, mining and oil played a large part in the development of Wyoming which is also represented.

The museum is a free museum and is open from 10:00 a.m. to 4:00 p.m. every day except Wednesday and Thursday, from Memorial Day through Labor Day, and is handicapped accessible.

Excerpted from Glenrock Historical Commission brochure

T Deer Creek Station and Pony Express Station

In the Town of Glenrock

Ayres Natural Bridge

In 1857 a major trading post, consisting of a stage coach station, a store, a blacksmith shop and a post office, was established at the point where the trails crossed Deer Creek just above the creek's junction with the North Platte River. This was a very popular emigrant camping and resting place and an important stop on the stage line to Salt Lake City. The Station served the Pony Express and the telegraph before being burned by Indians in 1866.

Originally a pioneer and Indian trading post during the 1850s, the settlement first took the name of "Deer Creek Station" as a relay terminal for the Overland Stage system. In 1860, it became a "home station" for the Pony Express.

A remarkable feat of courage by pony rider Henry Avis took place here, resulting in the Pony Express Co. paying him a bonus of $300 for exceptional bravery. Upon reaching Horseshoe Station (about a mile south of present-day Glendo, Wyoming) Avis found the relay rider unwilling to carry the mail. Up ahead marauding Sioux Indians were on the warpath, making the trail a veritable death trap. Undaunted, Avis changed horses ... and rode into the night. He reached Deer Creek only to find the station abandoned, the station keeper missing and all relay mounts stolen. To compound matters, the eastbound pony rider arrived, he too refusing to ride further. So, once more Avis took the saddle, returning to Horseshoe Station. Without a rest, he had covered 220 dangerous and bone-weary miles.

Telegraph Station

During 1861, construction crews raced to string a single strand of wire, which when completed would link the eastern states with far-off California. Completed on Oct. 18, the first telegraphic message was sent from Salt Lake City. It read: "Utah has not seceded, but is firm for the Constitution and laws of our once happy country." Oscar Collister, telegrapher at Deer Creek Station (1861-1864) relayed the message to the Pacific Telegraph Company's office in Cleveland, Ohio. (Electrical current for transmitting messages was so weak that signals could only travel short distances, requiring many relay stations across the continent.) Shortly, a message came back, signed by President "A. Lincoln:" "The completion of the telegraph to Salt Lake City is auspicious ... and the government reciprocates your congratulations."

The telegraph was in business. And just as quickly, the fate of the Pony Express was sealed.

Military Outpost

As Indian depredations grew worse, the U.S. government found it necessary to station military troops at strategic locations along the Oregon, California and Mormon trails. From Fort Laramie west, troops were garrisoned at several of the old Overland Stage Stations including Deer Creek Station (1862-65). Military duties included guarding wagon trains, keeping the telegraph line in repair, and chasing after bad Indians.

Attacks grew worse. By 1865, the Indians were engaged in open warfare. More troops were brought in. Nine companies of the 11th Kansas Cavalry were at Deer Creek on April 18 when Collister received a message telling of the assassination of President Lincoln. On July 27, following the attack on Platte Bridge Station, two companies of troops were dispatched from Deer Creek to reinforce its sister station to the west (shortly renamed "Fort Caspar, where Casper, Wyoming now stands).

In August of 1866, Indians burned the telegraph station to the ground. It was never rebuilt. Traffic on the old trails dwindled. And Deer Creek Station became a part of the past.

Excerpted from Glenrock Historical Commission brochure.

T Glenrock Paleontological Museum

506 West Birch in downtown Glenrock. 436-2667. www.paleon.org

The museum started in 1994 after the discovery of a Triceratops skull just outside of Glenrock. Since then it has grown to incorporate a wide variety of fossil material. Displays include parts of numerous Wyoming dinosaurs such as Triceratops, Torosaurs, Nanotyrannus, Camarasaurs, Apatosaurus, Allosaurus, and T-rex. It also includes displays of fossil mammals, small reptiles, and fish from throughout the world.

Displays are constantly changing and visitors will likely see something different every time they visit. The museum is the repository for Dr. Bakker's collection of Jurassic-age dinosaur bones from the Como Bluff area in south central Wyoming. Summer hours: 9:00 a.m. to 5:00 p.m., Tuesday through Saturday. Winter hours: 1:00 p.m.-5:00 p.m., Tuesday through Saturday. Admission is free and donations are accepted.

T Ada MaGill Grave

About 5 miles west of Glenrock. Next to the railroad tracks about one third mile southwest of old brick building at Parkerton

Mr. and Mrs. G. M. Magill, with their two small children, joined up with a Kansas wagon train enroute to Oregon. While camped at Fort Laramie, their daughter, Ada, came down with dysentery. A hundred miles of jolting torture later, the feverish little body reached Deer Creek. That night her condition worsened and five miles west of Glenrock at a favorite " nooning" spot (wagons stopped to rest during the heat of the day), Ada Magill passed away.

There, beside the Oregon Trail, July 3, 1864, the grieving family laid Ada to rest, a little tombstone over her head, with stones piled high upon the grave to discourage the wolves from digging up her remains. But the Magill's grief was not over. Before reaching their destination, their 2-year old boy would eat a poisonous weed, and he too would die … and be left behind … another victim of the trail.

Excerpted from Glenrock Historical Commission brochure.

T A. H. Unthank Grave

Old U.S. Highway 20-26-87 east out of Glenrock. Turn left after four miles onto a paved road leading to the Dave Johnston Power Plant (just before reaching the interstate). One-half mile east, his grave can be seen 50 yards to the south

Traveling with friends and relatives, Alvah Unthank left West Port (now Kansas City), Missouri, bound for the gold fields of California. Not yet turned 20, he carefully carved his name in the sandstone of Register Cliff (east of Guernsey, Wyoming) only to be struck down within the week by dreaded cholera. His Uncle Joe placed a stone bearing these words on his grave: A H Unthank Wayne Co. Ind. Died July 2, 1850." He also took time to set a footstone (an exception on the Oregon Trail) bearing the initials "A H U."

Excerpted from Glenrock Historical Commission brochure.

T Brigham Young Mail Station (BYX)

Just south of I-25 Glenrock Exit 165

Anxious to obtain better mail service from the States, Hyrum Kimball, acting as agent for the Mormon BYX operation with headquarters at Salt Lake City, was low bidder for a U.S. Postal contract to carry the mail between western Missouri and that city. The contract was formally awarded Oct. 9, 1856. (Notice was not delivered until the following spring.)

Construction of a "Mail Station" at Deer Creek (south of present-day Glenrock) began the following spring. Elder John Taylor reported progress of construction, July 24, 1857: Fifteen acres had been planted to crops, a corral had been completed "… 150 feet square made of logs 12-1/2 feet long with their ends in the ground and dovetailed together near the top, and a stockyard adjoining of the same dimensions nearly completed … the fort is 320 feet square … with a stockage enclosing 42 houses …" (not yet completed). A survey plat prepared by Thomas D. Brown for the Mormons, dated July 11, 1857, showed the "Trading Station" (Bissonette's Trading Post) to be 3-1/2 miles to the north (on the Oregon Trail). As fate would have it, the project was never completed.

The United States government, acting on a false belief that Mormons were taking over the West, ordered federal troops to march against Utah that very summer. Upon learning of Col. Albert Johnson's advancing army, the Mormons hastily withdrew from Deer Creek, returning to the sanctuary of Salt Lake Valley.

Twiss Indian Agency

A major influence in shaping the decision of President Buchanan was a letter written by Major Thomas S. Twiss, Indian agent for the Upper Platte District located at Ft. Laramie. It read: "On the 25th May (1857) a large Mormon colony took possession of the valley of Deer Creek, one hundred miles west of Fort Laramie, and drove away a band of Sioux Indians whom I had settle there in April …" He estimated the settlement contained "… houses sufficient for the accommodation of five hundred persons …" He summed up by saying, "I am powerless to control this matter, for the Mormons obey no laws enacted by Congress."

No sooner had the Mormons left than Agent Twiss penned a letter to Washington, dated Nov. 7, 1857, showing his return address as: "Indian Agency of the Upper Platte, Re: Deer Creek." It began, "I have the honor to report that I have arrived at this post on the 29th ultimo and shall remain here for the present." And remain he did, conducting all Indian affairs business from his Deer Creek headquarters for several years thereafter, including the distribution of yearly annuities to various Indian tribes, even entering unto a treaty which would have made Deer Creek valley into an Indian Reservation had the treaty been ratified by Congress.

Lutheran Indian Mission

Sharing the Twiss Agency were several Lutheran missionaries who established an Indian Mission within its stockade, later building five structures 1-1/2 miles above the old fort. History records that these missionaries conducted the first formal Christmas ceremony (1859) in what would later become Wyoming. Their efforts enjoyed only limited success and the mission was officially closed in 1867.

Excerpted from Glenrock Historical Commission brochure.

T Emigrant Crossing

Just north of Glenrock at the Platte River

A narrow gorge a few miles west of present day Casper, Wyoming, forced all pioneers traveling the south bank of the North Platte to cross to the other side. Three such crossings were in general use near old Fort Caspar, but with the hordes of 49ers glutting the trails during the California Gold Rush, wagon trains were forced to wait for days to be ferried across.

Impatient gold-seekers, unwilling to waste precious time, began crossing just above the mouth of Deer Creek. Imprudent prospectors attempted to swim across, resulting in a long list of drownings reported daily. More cautious pioneers took time to build adequate ferries.

Such was the case when J.G. Bruff reached Deer Creek on July 16, 1849: "…which we crossed, passing through hundreds of tents, wagons, camp fires and people of every age, sex, congregated on its banks … camped on the banks of Platte, at the Ferry … " He described the ferry being of eight dugout canoes. On July 25 of the same year, Capt. Howard Stansbury paid to have his troops transported across the Platte for $2.00 per wagon, describing the raft as being made of seven canoes. Yet another ferry was mentioned in Charles Gould's diary as being "… constructed of six 'dug-outs' fastened together, worked by oars …"

Sensing fat profits, in 1851, John Richard (pronounced "Reshaw"), a squaw-man, along with four other French traders, built the first bridge to span the North Platte River just above the mouth of Deer Creek. Although it was washed out in the spring flood of '52, it holds the distinction of being the first such enterprise in Wyoming.

Excerpted from Glenrock Historical Commission brochure.

T Hayden Pioneer Monument

Downtown Glenrock behind Higgins Hotel in Kimball Park.

The only known granite monument erected to the memory of Dr. F.V. Hayden was placed at Glenrock, Wyoming, thanks to the tireless efforts of renowned photographer William H. Jackson. Dr. Hayden first came to the Deer Creek area while attached to a military operation called the "Expedition of the Yellowstone." As a doctor, he looked after the medical needs of the troops wintering at the Twiss Indian Agency (1859-60). As a geologist (his first love), he did scientific research for the government.

Credited with later founding the U.S. Geological Survey, he began writing annual geological reports, the first published in 1867. He visited Deer Creek in both 1870 and 1871, observing that "… the coal bed … on fire in the winter of 1859-60 … is still on fire" and had baked the earth" to a brick red color."

Accompanying Hayden both years was none other than pioneer photographer Wm. H. Jackson, who on Aug. 17, 1870, made the first photograph of Converse County's "Natural Bridge." More importantly, the following year he accompanied Dr. Hayden on an official expedition to explore the Yellowstone country. There, Jackson recorded the first photographs ever taken of the wonders of that region. Now, armed with graphic evidence, the marvels of Yellowstone could no longer be disputed (for 6-1/2 decades the outside world had scoffed at the tales of rumblings in the ground, boiling mud, hissing geysers and the like). Upon returning to Washington, Hayden and Jackson put their talents to work, convincing Congress that a bill should be passed, preserving the natural state of the region forever. As a result of their concerted efforts, Yellowstone National Park came into existence, March of 1872, the first such park in the United States of America.

Excerpted from Glenrock Historical Commission brochure.

T Mormon Mines

East of Glenrock on Morman Canyon Road

The first group of Mormons to reach Deer Creek, that balmy June 10th, 1847, described it as a "…lovely place to camp. Swift current, clear water and abundance of fish. Nice grove of timber on the banks, and a coal mine about a quarter mile up, on the east side." One of the party, William Empey, recalls in his own words "…the country is more beautiful then we saw it since we

Left winter quarters; Brother B. Young says he will have a few famley farms on it on Deer Creek for it is a Delightful place."

Upon reaching the crossing place over the Platte (near old Ft. Caspar), where mountain men suggested crossing, they encountered a river running high from spring run-off, making it necessary to build a ferry to float their wagons across. Mr. Empey relates in his own words "... on the 13 of june we washed our faces with snow (part way up Casper Mountain) we came back with our poles at 9 oclock at night it being 7 miles to the mountains ... on the 14 june we commenced ferrying across the platte takeing 2 waggons side of each other."

Like a blessing out of the blue, another wagon train arrived and, like the Mormons, needed to cross. A bargain was struck. The wagons would be ferried over in exchange for foodstuff and other supplies. (Money was of little value so far removed from civilization.) Another train arrived — and Wm. Empey wrote "... Brother Brigham young gave us in struct how to proceed with the jentiles. " (Gentiles were anyone who was not a Mormon.) As a result, 9 men were left behind to man the ferry, the others going on to Salt Lake Valley.

Having finished ferrying on the 20th, "... Capt grover chosed too men to go to Deer creek for a load of coal ..." and even though Wm. Empey found it " ... Disagreeable on account of Indians ..." and he didn't want to go, in true pioneering spirit he states: "... but we went." Then, having gotten their coal "... on the 23 we arrived to our Ferry." Thus is recorded the first coal mined in what would 22 years later become the Territory of Wyoming.

Excerpted from Glenrock Historical Commission brochure.

T Rock in the Glen

Just west of Glenrock

On the south face of this landmark for the Oregon-California Trail are carvings of some of the names and dates of only a few of the estimated 350,000 immigrants that passed this way from 1841-1869.

Lt. John Charles Fremont and his first expedition to the far West camped here on July 26, 1842. The "Pathfinder" was following the trail used by trappers and traders since 1 812 and Indians since pre-history.

The sand laden winds are slowly eroding the names away but history will forever record what these people did to promote development in the West.

Take a short walk to the outcropping on the right behind the farm. Walk around to the far side to find some carvings. Be careful walking on the sand stone as it is very slippery.

T Parker-Ringo Grave

About 2 miles west of Glenrock on Hwy. 20/26

At this spot stands two sandstone markers, silent sentinels over the final resting place of two more victims of the old trails. One simply reads, "J.P. Parker, Died July 1, 1860, Age 41 Yrs., Iowa."

The other bears only the name "M. Ringo," nothing more. And yet, research brings to light a fascinating tale: Martin Ringo, veteran, wagonmaster and freighter during the war with Mexico, was enroute to California with his family. While camped near Deer Creek an accident caused his gun to discharge, mortally wounding him. To John, his 14-year old son, fell the distasteful task of burying his father. John continued with his family, successfully reaching California. But perhaps the traumatic experience of his father's death proved his undoing, for Martin's son reportedly grew up to be the notorious gunman and outlaw of the southwest, Johnny Ringo. (Research by Mr. Ed Bartholomew of Fort Davis, Texas.)

Reprinted from Glenrock Historical Commission brochure.

H Big Muddy Oil Field

About 10 miles west of Glenrock on I-25

Big Muddy oil field is a typical Wyoming oil producing structure. The field, discovered in 1916, has produced over 30 million barrels of high quality oil. Strata here were arched upward at the time the Rocky Mountains originated about 60 million years ago, to form an anticline, or dome. Because oil is lighter than water, it rose to the crest of the dome where it was trapped in pore spaces between sand grains. The Wall Creek sand lies at a depth of near 3,000 feet and the Dakota sand at about 4,000 feet.

The first oil well in Wyoming was drilled in 1884. There are now about 100 oil fields in the state.

H Mary J. Hurley

This Oregon-California Trails Association marker is on private land in Converse County

On July 12, 1864, a small Montana-bound wagon train was attacked by Sioux Indians a half-mile east of Little Box Elder crossing. The four men buried here were killed immediately: Noah Taylor of Coffey County, Kansas; Mr. Sharp, a Methodist minister probably from Wilson Co., Kansas; one unknown; and Franklin, sixteen-year-old Negro servant of Josiah and Fanny Kelly.

The Kellys, from Allen, Co., Kansas, were accompanied by their niece, seven-year-old Mary J. Hurley. Fanny and Mary, with Sarah Larimer, and son, were taken captive. Mary escaped that night and found her way back to the trail near here but was overtaken and killed just as she was about to be rescued by passing soldiers. Her body was discovered and buried here a few days later.

These graves were identified and restored in 1946 by W. W. Morrison of Cheyenne. When the dam across Little Box Elder was built in 1954, the remains of the four men were removed from their original burial place in the valley and reinterred beside the grave of Mary Hurley.

H Deer Creek Station

Cedar and 4th Streets in Glenrock

Deer Creek Station, which once stood on the site of present- day Glenrock near the confluence of Deer Creek and the North Platte River, became a familiar landmark along the Oregon-California-Mormon Trail between 1857 and 1866.

The station began with Joseph Bissonette's Trading Post, also known as Dakota City. The mountain man's store, post office, blacksmith shop, corrals, and hotel-saloon, served the needs of a variety of visitors. They included photographer William Henry Jackson during his days as a freighter, stage passengers such as British author, Sir Richard Burton, a party of Lutheran missionaries who remained in the area from 1859-1864, troops en route to Salt Lake City during the Utah war and in the winter of 1859-1860, an expedition of the Army Corps of Topographical Engineers under Captain William F. Raynolds. From 1857 to 1861, the post also was a trading center for the nearby Upper Platte Indian Agency, located about three and a half miles upstream along Deer Creek.

Beginning in April of 1860, Pony Express Riders exchanged mounts here at Deer Creek Station. The Pony Express experiment, however, ended abruptly in October 1861. The completion of the first transcontinental telegraph meant that clicking telegraph keys quickly replaced pounding hooves.

Indian-white hostilities escalated after the Civil War began, prompting troops from Fort Laramie to erect a military installation across the road from the trading post in 1862. From Deer Creek, troops sought to protect the telegraph line and travelers along the trail. Intensifying conflicts between the soldiers and Indians ultimately forced Bissonette to abandon his establishment in the fall of 1864. Indians finally burned Deer Creek Station on August 18, 1866. This incident marked the closing of an important chapter of Wyoming's early history.

H McKinstry Ridge

This is located on private land in Converse County

On June 26, 1850, portions of two emigrant companies, the Upper Mississippi Ox Company and the Wisconsin Blues, passed this way enroute to the gold fields of California. They are believed to be the first wagon trains to follow a route beyond Fort Laramie that remained north of the N. Platte River. This trail segment, ending at the ferries of the Platte at present-day Glenrock and Casper, is known as Child's Cutoff, named for Andrew Childs of Waukeshaw, Wisconsin, whose emigrant guidebook was published in 1852.

School teacher Byron N. McKinstry of McHenry County, Illinois, was, like Andrew Childs, a member of the Upper Mississippi Ox Company. His diary entry for June 26 describes this stretch of trail:

"After following the river for 5 or 6 m. we crossed some very rough ground. Following a kind of divide first rising in a Northerly direction to the summit, then turning SW. and descending to the Platte–the crookedest road possible. These hills are bare and have a wild savage appearance, but little vegetation on them. Camped on the Platte. Poor grass. 20 m."

McKinstry's diary, published in 1975 and edited by his grandson, Bruce L. McKinstry, has become a classic trail account. This stretch of Childs Cutoff, described so vividly by Byron, is named McKinstry Ridge in his honor and also for grandson Bruce, who, by tracing his grandfather's journey across the country, has made an invaluable contribution to trail scholarship.

H Martin Ringo

Located on private land in Converse County

On May 18, 1864, Martin and Mary Peters Ringo left their home in Gallatin, Missouri, intending to settle in California. With them went their five children, John, Albert, Fanny, Enna, and Mattie.

The wagon train they traveled with–some seventy wagons grouped together for mutual protection–camped here on the night on July 29. Early the next morning, as Ringo climbed up his wagon, his shotgun went off in his own hands, killing him instantly. He was forty-five years old.

A friend, William Davenport, wrote: "He was buried near the place he was shot, in as decent a manner as was possible with the facilities on the plains."

The family eventually reached San Jose, California, the home of Coleman and Augusta Younger, brother-in-law and sister of Mary Ringo. Mary Enna Ringo, daughter of Martin and Mary Ringo, became an outstanding teacher in the San Jose school system for over fifty years.

Buried next to Ringo is J. P. Parker. Parker's tombstone tells all that is known of his life and death.

H Joel Hembree

Located on private land in Converse County

Joel Jordan Hembree, his wife Sara (Sally) and their eight sons from McMinnville, Tennessee, were part of the estimated 1,000 men, women and children who left Fitzhugh's Mill near Independence, Missouri, in May 1843, for Oregon.

On July 18, between Bed Tick Creek and here at LaPrele Creek, six-year-old Joel Hembree, the second youngest son, fell from the wagon tongue on which he was riding and was fatally injured.

Diarist William T. Newby wrote, July 18: "A very bad road. Joel J. Hembrees son Joel fel off the waggeon tung & both wheels run over him. Distance 17 miles." July 19: "Lay buy. Joel Hembree departed this life about 2 o'clock." July 20: "We buried the youth & ingraved his name on the headstone." Dr. Marcus Whitman described the fatality as "a wagon having passed over the abdomen." This is the oldest identified grave along the Oregon Trail.

Joel's body, originally buried 1/4 miles east, was moved here March 24, 1962, and placed beside Pvt. Ralston Baker, who was killed in an Indian skirmish on May 1, 1867.

North 400 feet is the site of the 1860's LaPrele Stage and Pony Express station.

V Glenrock Recreation Complex

Mormon Canyon Road on the east side of town, turn south and go under the interstate and turn right at park area

This beautiful free campground is located just south of Glenrock, and includes access to a stream of water, a rodeo arena, a play area with swings and a jungle gym and slide for children.

There are public rest rooms, water hydrants and a waste dump for trailers and campers. Also barbecue facilities at each trailer space. Furnish your own fuel. Please do not cut or break the trees for burning and deposit your trash in the receptacles furnished when you leave.

Excerpted from Glenrock Historical Commission brochure.

Wyoming Tidbits

Among the instructions given stagecoach drivers on the Cheyenne-Deadwood run were these:

1. If ladies are present, gentlemen are urged to forego cigars and pipes as the odor of same is repugnant to the gentle sex. Chewing tobacco is permitted, but spit WITH the wind, not against it.

2. Abstinence from liquor is requested. But if you must drink, share the bottle. To do otherwise makes you appear selfish.

3. Do not hog the buffalo robes.

F Fort Diablo Steak House & Saloon

1136 Hwy. 87-26-20, east of Glenrock. 436-2288.

There are plenty of reasons why the Fort Diablo Steakhouse and Saloon is so popular. The folks around Glenrock will tell you its because of the great food, and a comfortable and friendly atmosphere. If you are just passing through you will be treated just like an old friend. Diners enjoy their traditional favorite steaks, along with buffalo steaks, and seafood. On Friday and Saturday nights they feature prime rib. The restaurant was opened in the 1950's as the El Diablo. Open for dinner 7 days a week. Reservations are recommended on weekends. Wedding parties, reunions, and banquets are welcome.

FL Hotel Higgins & Paisley Shawl Restaurant

416 W. Birch in Glenrock. 436-9212 or 800-458-0144. www.hotelhiggins.com

The Hotel Higgins is one of the oldest continuously operated hotels Wyoming. The wonderful lobby is graced with antiques and fixtures that will take you back in time setting the tone for your visit. The Paisley Shawl Restaurant provides elegant dining in a romantic setting. The mouth watering menu includes steaks, veal, seafood, pasta, duckling and other exquisite entrees. They offer an extensive wine and champagne list. The cozy pub features 25 brands of beer on ice and a light bar menu. During the summer months enjoy dining on the outdoor patio. The Hotel Higgins is an excellent location for weddings, reunions, or a special getaway.

S Glenrock Gift & Book Emporium

409 W. Birch in Glenrock. 436-8291

The Glenrock Gift and Book Emporium will intrigue and inspire you. Visit this delightful store to explore the world of the whimsical and fantastic to the world of the Old West. A large selection of toys and games for children, as well as adults, includes dinosaur themed items, books, toys, puzzles, games, and porcelain dolls. Items to accent your home include picture frames, lamps, and wind chimes. A wonderful selection of Indian and Western art and other gift collections are also available. If you are looking for fairies, angels, dragons, and swords you'll be pleased with the items they carry. They also carry incense and scented oils.

Glenrock Gift & Book Emporium

S Just-A-Jug

134 Millar Lane in Glenrock. 436-2797 or 800-283-5847.

Just-A-Jug is a wonderful country store well worth a short trip off the beaten path. This great hideaway is a treasure trove of unique and special gifts for any occasion. "Just-A-Jugs" are glass jugs that are hand cut and fitted with redwood sections. Each section can be used to store anything from beans to buttons to treats or snacks. A unique and functional addition to your home or special gift. Watch out for bears, moose, chickens, and other clever critters in the store. Discover their gift baskets, handmade candles and soaps, wax-melt pots, and picture frames. They also carry rustic barn wood items such as benches, planters, and birdhouses. Call for color brochure

51 *Gas, Lodging*

Exit 290

52 *Gas, Food, Lodging*

Laramie

The city of Laramie, known as the "Gem City of the Plains", looks like a handful of precious stones nestled in a black velvet jewel box when approached from any direction at night. Surrounded by the Snowy Range to the west and the Laramie Mountains to the east, the Laramie Valley is wide enough to be considered a high plain. Its local high school's mascot is the Plainsman, a nod to explorer/trapper Jacques LaRamee, for whom the town is named. One of the highest incorporated cities in the US, at an

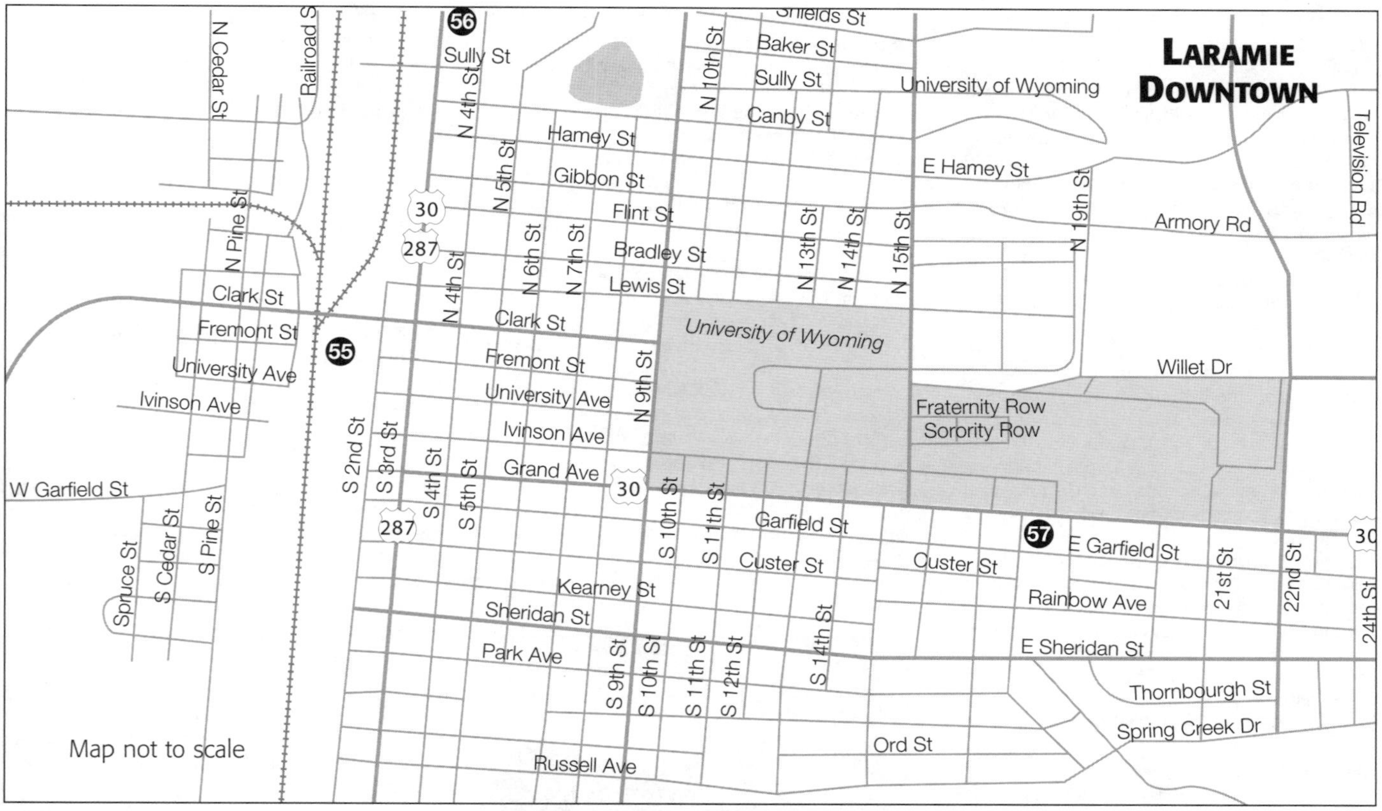

Laramie Downtown

Map not to scale

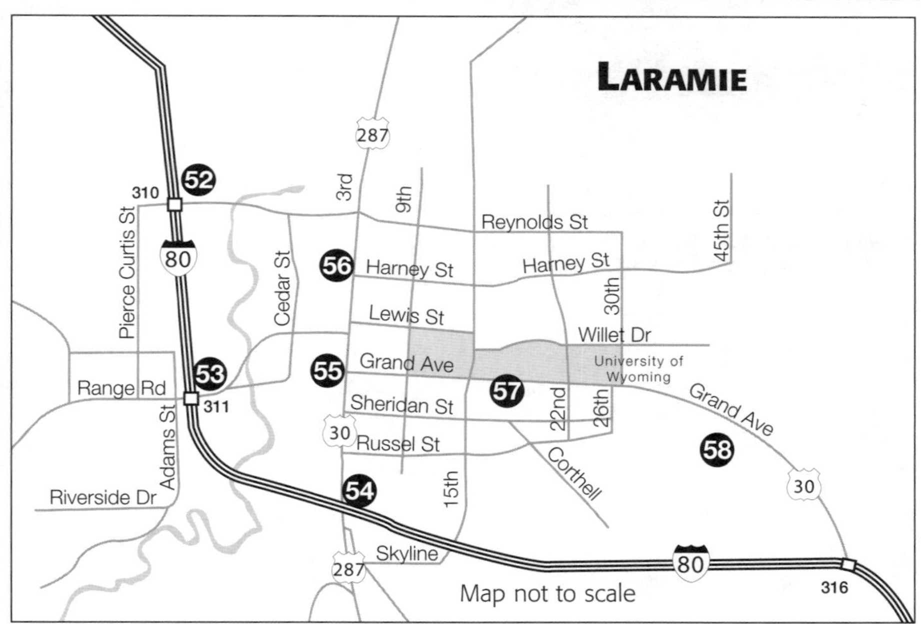

elevation of nearly 7,200 feet, Laramie is also near the highest point in the US on I-80. Lincoln Monument, at 8,640 feet, is about 10 miles to the east of town.

With the Laramie River running through it, the area has been a stopping place for travelers for millions of years, as the remains of dinosaurs and other ancient creatures here has proven. Native Americans, including the Sioux, Shoshones and Teton-Dakotas, have been camping here since about 8, 000 years ago. Jacques LaRamee was probably the first white man to come to the area between 1810 and 1820, as well as building the first European habitation in the area, a cabin at the confluence of the Platte and Laramie Rivers.

A few settlers left the Oregon and Mormon Trails in the 1840s and 50s to settle in the valley, which resulted in some Indian hostility. The US Army established a fort for protection, Fort Sanders (originally named Fort Buford) in 1866. In 1868, Indian troubles decreased for a time and the railroad came. General Grenville Dodge established the town site for Laramie, just north of the fort, as a camp for Union Pacific workers. An artesian spring with pristine drinking water and ample timber from the nearby Medicine Bow forest made this an ideal location.

The early days were typical of an "end of the tracks" town, with a lot of wild and rough individuals. By the end of 1868, Laramie sustained 23 saloons, one hotel, and not a single church. Law-abiding citizens became fed up after a while and formed a "vigilance committee" to keep the lawlessness to a minimum. After a few well-displayed hangings, and a little help from the federal government, the town settled into a more peaceful existence.

The year 1870 put Laramie in the history books, when the first woman in the world to ever vote in a general election, "Grandma" Louisa A. Swain, cast her ballot. That same year, the world's first female jurors took their place in a trial in Laramie, despite taunts of "Baby, Baby, don't be in a hurry. Your mama's gone to sit on the jury." At

Laramie	Jan	Feb	March	April	May	June	July	Aug	Sep	Oct	Nov	Dec	Annual
AAverage Max. Temperature (F)	32.5	35.5	40.9	50.7	61.6	72.9	79.9	78.1	69.2	57.0	41.7	34.0	54.5
Average Min. Temperature (F)	9.1	11.5	16.7	24.3	33.5	41.8	47.8	46.2	37.7	27.7	16.9	10.7	27.0
Average Total Precipitation (in.)	0.42	0.42	0.71	0.95	1.52	1.30	1.53	1.19	0.95	0.74	0.56	0.39	10.68
Average Total SnowFall (in.)	5.6	5.7	8.4	7.2	3.2	0.4	0.0	0.0	1.1	3.7	6.7	6.5	48.5
Average Snow Depth (in.)	2	2	1	0	0	0	0	0	0	0	1	1	

the same trial, the Andrew Howie Case, Mrs. Martha Atkinson became the first female bailiff in the world.

In 1873, the Wyoming Territorial Prison was built near Laramie, and later housed many famous outlaws, including Butch Cassidy and "Big Nose" George Parrott. The 1870s and 1880s brought the advent of the cattle industry in the Laramie area, as herd after herd came up from Texas. In 1886, Wyoming University opened its doors. Now called the University of Wyoming, it remains the only four-year institution of higher learning in the state, although it has branches in several towns.

As other railroad towns went the way of the wind, the stability provided by the university, the prison, and the timber and ranching industries gave the town a niche as a permanent stop on the railway line, even though Cheyenne was only fifty miles away. The Old Laramie Depot continues to be a functioning depot today, and the town is a significant crossroads for both passenger and freight lines.

The territory became a state in 1890, and the prison (then penitentiary) burned down and was relocated to Rawlins. But the lumber, cattle, and educational advantages of Laramie kept the area strong while other towns in the state went through several boom and bust cycles.

Today, Laramie is most strongly influenced by the University, and the students and faculty from all parts of the country and the world who are drawn to this rich, windswept landscape. They bring to it their own skills, talents, tastes and perspectives to enrich the local milieu. Like many other Wyoming communities, Laramie is able to embrace both its historical ties to Western history and the new and increasingly global character of Wyoming's lifestyle.

Location

Laramie stands astride a pair of the nation's most significant transcontinental transportation arteries: I-80 and the Union Pacific main line. The point of highest elevation, (8,640 feet above sea level) on I-80 is just east of the city at the Lincoln Monument in the Pole Mountain area. West of Laramie, Medicine Bow Peak rises to 12,013 feet.

The diversity of altitude creates diversity of habitat and life. From the pronghorn antelope beside the Interstate to the moose in the marshes on the high ground, the presence of wildlife adds to the pleasure of living here.

The city is built on the sun-dappled plain between two units of the Medicine Bow National Forest. The granite Snowy Range mountains west of Laramie and the unusual sandstone formations of Vedauwoo to the east provide unparalleled opportunities for outdoor recreation.

Day to Day Living

Every place in the world has its own quality of life, the characteristics which make it unique. Laramie is distinguished by its variety.

The influence of the University of Wyoming, the state's only four-year institution, is marked. Faculty and students come from everywhere. Their skills, talents and tastes enrich the local milieu. The University also has impact on the local business environment, providing a well-educated labor force and employers spun off from University-related research projects. This is enhanced by two more post-secondary education providers: Laramie County Community College's Albany County campus, and Wyoming Technical Institute, a highly-regarded vocational school.

The urban environment is highlighted by a charming downtown area with lovingly restored buildings. Some of the most remarkable characteristics of Laramie, however, don't come into play until you leave the city limits. The Snowy Range Mountains to the west shelter a family downhill ski area, 80 mountain lakes, innumerable ice-cold mountain streams, and all the room in the world for snowmobiling, mountain biking, cross-country skiing - all manner of mountain delights!

The Wyoming Territorial Park also makes its home in Laramie, centered on the Wyoming Territorial Prison, restored to the glory of its first life in the 1870s. The park also hosts special events like the Valentine's Day Territorial Sweetheart Ball, Beerfest, Halloween Haunted Prison and the Lumberjack competition.

The Old West lives on in modern-day Laramie. The broad plain on which the city lies supports big cattle ranches and with them, the singular blend of reliance on community and proud individualism which typifies life on the land.

Portions excerpted from Laramie Chamber of Commerce brochure

53 *Food, Lodging*

T Wyoming Territorial Prison, Old West Park, and US Marshall's Museum

At I-80 Exit 311 in Laramie. 745-6161

The inspiration and cornerstone of the Wyoming Territorial Park is the beautifully restored Wyoming Territorial Prison Museum, built in 1872, now a showpiece of the National Historic Register. The arrival of the Union Pacific Railroad to Laramie City brought not only prosperity, but also problems in the form of unscrupulous ruffians to the area. The need for law and order, along with a place to house criminals, was quickly recognized. In December of 1869, a bill was passed by the territorial legislature approving the construction of the penitentiary. Federal funding was approved on July 15, 1870 for the construction of the Wyoming Territorial Prison.

During its use as a federal penal facility (1872 to 1903), more than 1,000 men and 12 women served sentences at the Wyoming Territorial Prison. Some of the West's most notorious outlaws, including Butch Cassidy, spent part of their lives in this place that was "dedicated to evil doers of all classes and kinds." Discover how the prison had a civilizing effect not only on the prisoners, but the "hell on wheels" railroad town of Laramie. Listen carefully and you can almost hear the clanking of the leg irons or the damnable bang of the cell doors closing.

When Wyoming became a state, a new penal institution was built in Rawlins and the prison was turned over to the University of Wyoming for use as an experimental stock farm. It was as a stock farm that the prison had its most use – 70+ years until it was restored as a museum. Today, the prison brings those famous legends to life through state-of-the-art displays and interactive exhibits on frontier law and justice, and other facets of Western history. Well-versed tour guides take you through the old building, giving you a glimpse into the colorful past of this unique institution and its residents.

Courtesy of Territorial Museum and the University of Wyoming

T National U.S. Marshalls Museum

At I-80 Exit 311 in Laramie. 745-6161.
www.wyoprisonpark.org

Law and order prevail in an impressive collection of artifacts saluting the steadfast courage of the nation's oldest law enforcement agency. Over 200 years of service is commemorated in this unique exhibit that pays tribute to the men and women who enforced the Constitution of the United States.

Reprinted from museum brochure.

T Hutton Lake National Wildlife Refuge

Hwy. 230, 12 miles south of Laramie

Avid bird watchers take great pleasure in the assortment of ducks, migratory birds, and shorebirds, along with other wildlife that gathers here. The peaceful, park-like setting is surroundeb by mountains and consists of five small lakes, covering nearly 2,000 acres.

H Construction History

At Wyoming Territorial Prison

The building of the Wyomming Territorial Prison was fraught with political infighting charges of fraud, delays, faulty construction practices and much finger pointing. Yet, several of the original structures have stood for more then a century of use conversion, and abandonment to eventually become historic land marks unlike any others in the United States.

In 1871, Melville C. Brown was appointed "Superintendent of Construction of the Penitentiary for Wyoming Territory." Brown oversaw a lengthy bidding process that included accusations of favoritism and fraud. Promising to give the merchants of Laramie an "opportunity to bid." Judge Brown finally awarded the construction job on April 14, 1872, to Samuel Livingston and George Schram of Denver for $31,450. Then, on July 15, some of Laramie's citizens laid the cornerstone, placing in it mementoes such a copies of local Newspapers, speeches by natonal politicians, merchants' business cards, photographs of Laramie's leading society, and a bottle of old bourbon. The gathering dedicated the building to "evil doers of all classes and kinds." The first phase of construction took just six months to complete.

The original penitentiary included only the north wing and kitchen addition of the existing structure. It contained 42 brick cells on three tiers. Walls were of stone masonry two feet thick and a massive steel and wood plank door measuring 4x8 feet formed the entrance. Barely seven months after the first prisoners arrived, much of the original woodwork and roof were destroyed in a fire resulting from faulty construction of one of the chimney flues.

In 1875, convict labor built the warden's quarters of stone quarried from the banks of the Big Laramie River outside the prison grounds. That same year saw improvements of the addition of a 12 foot high stockade to reduce the number of escapes, an irrigation canal, brickyard, and ice house. Then, in 1889, the capacity of the penitentiary was doubled with the addition of the central area and south wing. In 1892, the first wing of the broom factory was built with additions following in subsequent years.

H **Prisoners**

At Wyoming Territorial Prison

In the thirty years prisoners were incarcerated at the Wyoming Territorial Prison, they were a good representitive cross-section of the American West. They came from all corners of the U.S.from Europe, Canada, Mexico, and China. Among them were Native Amercans, African Americans, and a variety of European ethnicities. They were Protestants, Catholics, Jews, Mormons and atheists. Though a few were well educated, most had little, if any, education. Their crimes ranged from shop lifting to murder, though the greatest number were guilty of cattle or horse rustling. Sentences were from one year to life. Prisoners attributed their lawless ways to avarice, intemperance, wantoness, ignorance, gambling, association with prostitutes, and general depravity.

Once in the prison, their lives were difficult, though not without small pleasures. Prisoners would would rise at 5:30 or or 6:00 a.m; clean their cells; have a breakfast of hash or stew; work for five hours (when season permitted and work was available); take a midday meal of roasted or boiled meats, fresh baked breads, and vegetables, if available; return to work for another five hours; and end their day with a dinner of simpler fare. They had to observe a strict code of silence except when working outside. Tobacco, for either smoking or chewing, was distributed each week and the prisoners were permitted to partake of it in their cells.

Forever promoting prisoner uplift, Laramie citizens collected books and magazines for a prison library that at one time held some 1,200 volumes. Likewise, community ministers held weekly services, and university faculty gave periodic instructive lectures to guide prisoners back to the right path. Baths were taken weekly, more often in warm weather. Uniforms were routinely laundered. Those who exhibited notably good behavior were granted up to five days off their sentence for each of the calendar months in which they qualified.

Common punishments consisted of living in total darkness; loss of tobacco or library privileges; bread and water diets; and forfeiture of good time or time off. In more extreme cases, a prisoner might be manacled to his cell door; and hung by both hands from the ceiling of the cell for two to four hours; placed in the solitary cell or "dungeon", or subjected to a high pressure water dousing for up to fifteen minutes at a time.

This was unusual, though as it was the intention of the prison administration to reform the prisoners, to have them "go out from here better, both morally and physically". And so with a good serviceable suit of clothes to the value of $15 and a cash gratuity of $5 they went forth to rejoin productive society.

H **One Mile South**

About 5 miles southwest of Laramie on Highway 230.

Section 6

Site of Big Laramie Stage Station and river crossing of Overland Trail, 1862-68 which became in 1869 part of the first established cattle ranch on Union Pacific Railroad. This ranch known as Hutton or Heart Ranch was owned by a Charles Hutton, Tom Alsop and Edward Creighton after completing a Union Pacific grading contract.

54 *Gas, Food, Lodging*

M Laramie Area Chamber of Commerce

800 S. 3rd Street in Laramie. 745-7339 or toll free at 866-876-1012. www.laramie.org

The Laramie Area Chamber of Commerce Visitor Information Caboose is located at I-80, exit 313, at the corner of Third Street and I-80. The Caboose is open Memorial Day through Labor Day. Stop in and get tourist information for Laramie, Albany County and the State of Wyoming. The rest of the year, head a few blocks up the street to the office of the Laramie Area Chamber of Commerce, at 800 S. 3rd Street. The friendly staff will assist you in finding that perfect spot to spend the day or order a relocation packet if Laramie is where you would like to hang your hat.

T Fort Sanders

Off U.S. Highway 287 about two miles south of Laramie.

Originally christened Fort Buford, Fort Sanders was established by Captain Henry Mizner of the 18th U. S. Infantry in 1866. The first permanent settlement in this area. At one time 600 soldiers were housed here, but numbers dropped with fear of Indian attacks. The military reservation covered 81 square acres of southeastern Wyoming in its heyday, protecting travelers over the Overland Trail and later Union Pacific Railroad workers. The post headquarters was located two miles south of present-day Laramie. Very little remains of the settlement which was abandoned in 1882.

T Fort Sanders Monument

About 2 miles south of Laramie on Hwy. 287.

The first army outpost established in the Laramie area by General Dodge, Fort Sanders provided protection for railroad workers during the late 1860s. Although most of the fort has long since been overrun by the construction of the highway and housing developments, you can still find the monument and a couple of old buildings. One of the buildings was moved to LaBonte Park in Laramie, on 9th and Harney, where it serves as a community center for arts and crafts.

H Fort Sanders Marker

About 2 miles south of I-80 Exit 313 on Highway 287. Located in a fenced enclosure on Kiowa Street just northeast of the cement plant.

This monument marks the site of Fort Sanders established September 5, 1866. Abandoned May 18, 1882. Named in honor of Brigadier General William P. Sanders.

H Laramie

1502 S. 3rd in Laramie just north of I-80 Exit 313.

Founded in 1868 upon the arrival of the Union Pacific Railroad, Laramie was named after the fur trader Jacques LaRamie, The first female juror served here in 1870 after Wyoming Territory, in 1869, for the first time in history, gave women full rights of suffrage. Humorist Bill Nye founded his Boomerang newspaper in 1881, and the University of Wyoming opened its doors in 1887. At the south edge of the city lie the ruins of Fort Sanders, 1866-1882. West of the city can be seen the first intermountain ranch (1869) and the ruts left by Ben Holladay's stagecoaches on the old Overland Trail.

L Motel 6

621 Plaza Lane in Laramie. 742-2307 or 800-4-MOTEL6 (446-8356). www.visitmotel6.com

L Sunset Inn

1104 S. 3rd Street in Laramie. 742-3741 or 800-308-3744

55 *Food, Lodging*

T Albany County Tourism Board

210 Custer in Laramie. 745-4195 or 800-445-5303. www.laramie-tourism.org

T Laramie Plains Museum

603 Ivinson Ave in Laramie. 742-4448

In 1870 when Edward Ivinson bought a city block of land for his future home, Laramie City was only two years old—barely past vigilante days and frontier justice "necktie parties."

By 1892, the town had become a staid community and Banker Ivinson a wealthy man. That year he and his wife, Jane, built a handsome Victorian mansion on the block originally purchased from the Union Pacific Railroad. The home was built for the then princely sum of $40,000. The house had central heating, electric lights and running water, as well as the most elegant appointments of any house in town.

Jane Ivinson designed the interior of the house. She selected the variety of hardwoods used to enhance the mansion's rooms, and in 1892 and 1893, she visited Chicago to select furnishings, hardware and fixtures, including doorknobs, lighting fixtures, the bathroom appointments, and stained-glass windows.

By 1921, Ivinson had been a widower for six years, and he deeded his home to the Episcopal Missionary District of Wyoming. The mansion became the Jane Ivinson Memorial Hall, used as a church-run boarding house originally for teen-age girls who lived on ranches and had trouble getting to town to attend high school. Because of vastly improved transportation methods, the girls school closed in 1958.

The splendid old home stood empty for over a decade when the non-profit Laramie Plains Museum Association spearheaded a drive for funds which netted $74,450—a remarkable achievement in the Laramie Plains and surrounding area which totals about 5,000 square miles with a population under 30,000.

A Federal Historic Preservation Grant enabled the Association to buy the Ivinson property for $100,000, and the Laramie Plains Museum opened its doors in its new historic location in 1973. In 1992, a yearlong celebration of the centennial of the Ivinson Mansion was observed with special events and programming.

Nearly eighty years after its completion, the Ivinson Mansion and grounds were enrolled on the National Register of Historic Places because of the building's distinctive architecture and the Ivinsons' contribution to pioneer Wyoming.

The beautiful Ivinson Mansion interior is a fitting background for a wide variety of artifacts attractively arranged throughout its many restored, Victorian-era rooms. The large collection includes historic items used in the Laramie Plains area as well as those items, which aid in interpreting the area's rich history.

Among the many items you'll se are intricately hand-carved furniture made at the Wyoming Territorial Prison; lovely textiles, which present a fascinating history of fashion; a well-outfitted kitchen displaying century-old appliances; a formal dining room filled with elegant dishes; a restored drawing room, opulent with its fine appointments; an extensive photo collection and archives; memorabilia from early Laramie history—political, social, cultural and economic; a room filled with toys of yesteryear—much to the delight of visitors of all ages; a cowboy line cabin, extensive saddle collection, many ranching implements, and artifacts which tell the story of the area's sheep industry; and a one-room schoolhouse still used by area teachers to the delight of their students.

The museum is open year round. Call for hours. An admission fee is charged.

Reprinted from museum brochure.

T St. Matthew's Cathedral

104 South 4th Street in Laramie. 742-6608

One of Laramie's first large structures, St. Matthew's was built in 1868 and funded by Edward Ivinson. Made of limestone quarried in the area, this sizeable church has all the appointments of a classic cathedral in high Victorian style.

H Laramie City Historical Signs

Located on grounds of Ivinson Mansion at 603 Ivinson Avenue in Laramie

Laramie Woman's Club

Laramie Woman's Club, organized in 1898, honors Laramie's "First Ladies" who pioneered civic and political responsibility by woman in this country and the world.

Louisa Gardner Swain made world history as the first woman to vote in a general election. She cast her ballot early in the morning of September 6, 1870 in Laramie, Wyoming.

Mary Godat Bellamy

Mary Godat Bellamy, the first woman elected to the Wyoming State Legislature, represented Albany County in 1911. She worked effectively for laws benefiting woman and children and became a nationally known speaker for woman suffrage.

Martha Symons-Boies

The first woman bailiff in the world, Mrs. Martha Symons-Boies, was appointed to arrange accommodations for the first woman jurors when the Grand Jury met in a building located at First and Garfield Streets in Laramie, March, 1870.

West side of pillar

World wide attention focused on Laramie in March, 1870 when the first women in history to serve on a jury dealt stern justice in cases of murder, horse-stealing, and illegal branding. They were Miss Eliza Stewart, Mrs. Amelia Hatcher, Mrs. G. F. Hilton, Mrs. Mary Mackel, Mrs. Agnes Baker, and Mrs. Sarah A. Pease.

F Coal Creek Coffee Company
110 Grand Avenue in Laramie. 745-7737.
Wholesale at 800-838-7737.
www.coalcreekcoffee.com

The Coal Creek Coffee Company opened in 1993 and has been roasting coffees on the premises since 1999. Only the coffees meeting the highest industry standards are offered by Coal Creek, with a large selection of organic coffees. In addition to great coffee, there are sandwiches, soups, and salads, and fresh bakery items are made on the premises daily. Compliment their great food and coffee with a beverage from their selection of beers and wines. Weekends at Coal Creek Coffee feature live music from regional and national artists. Coffee businesses will appreciate the wholesale equipment, products, and training available from Coal Creek. Stop in for a great cup of coffee or visit them on the web.

The Life and Times of Big Al

The Late Jurassic dinosaur Allosaurus has been known for over 100 years. However, it was not until 1991 when Big Al, a young, 95 percent complete Allosaurus fragilis skeleton with numerous injured bones was discovered, that one of the most fascinating paleontological mysteries began to unfold. The skeleton was found on public lands administered by the Bureau of Land Management near Shell, Wyoming, in the Upper Jurassic Morrison Formation. Research on this specimen has provided exciting new information on Allosaurus (the dominant predator of the Late Jurassic of North America), as well as the environment in which he lived. Big Al has gained international recognition as the story of his tragically painful life, early death, and rapid burial has been told through interactive exhibits and state-of-the-art television programs at the University of Wyoming Geological Museum.

Excerpted from museum brochure.

F Jeffrey's Bistro
123 Ivinson in Laramie. 742-7046.
www.jeffreysbistro.com

Jeffrey's Bistro is a cozy little oasis conveniently located in downtown Laramie for over 20 years. You'll find a menu offering a wide variety of eclectic dishes including a good selection for the Vegetarian. All foods are prepared or baked on the premises, using the finest ingredients available. Unique salad entrees filled with nutrient rich leafy greens are served in large bowls with extra room for tossing. All meals include homemade bread and the desserts are out of this world. For a fresh and healthy meal, you'll surely enjoy lunch or dinner at Jeffrey's in a smoke-free environment.

LS Ranger Motel, Lounge, & Liquor Mart
453 N. 3rd in Laramie. 742-6677

The Ranger Motel offers quiet comfortable rooms in easy walking distance to historic downtown Laramie. A lounge and drive-up liquor store are located on the premises. It is conveniently situated with numerous restaurants nearby, the University campus within close proximity and a grocery store just across the street. The motel features the first Wyoming wellness room equipped with the Nikken Kenko Dream Sleep System including mattress, bedspread, pillows, and PiMag Shower. All rooms have air conditioning, HBO, direct-dial phones, refrigerators, microwaves, and free in-room coffee. Be sure to ask the on-staff wellness consultant for a demonstration of other Nikken products.

L TraveLodge
165 N. 3rd Street in Laramie. 742-6671 or 800-942-6671. www.travelodge.vcn.com

S Alexander's Fine Jewelry
205 S. 2nd Street in Laramie. 745-4266 or 800-531-4266

Alexander's Fine Jewelry in historic downtown Laramie is where you will discover five generations of excellence—polished to perfection. As one of Laramie's oldest established downtown businesses, Alexander's was started when the owner's great grandfather emigrated from Denmark as a clock maker. Today, shopper's can still enjoy a large selection of quality clocks, along with watches and other fine gifts. Custom jewelry is featured, specializing in Elk ivory and gold creations. You will also see breathtaking fine diamond jewelry with many pieces designed and custom made on the premises. You will appreciate Alexander's warm hometown service while shopping for a special gift for yourself or a loved one.

S Antique Fever, Early American Oak Furniture
211 S. 2nd Street in Laramie. 721-8398

M Saulcy Real Estate
306 S. 2nd Street in Laramie. 721-2802 or toll free at 888-716-SOLD (7653). www.ShowMeLaramie.com

Saulcy Real Estate Corporation makes it easy to "shop after hours" at their illuminated Window on Real Estate located in Historic Downtown Laramie. This technologically advanced real estate firm also provides their web site to view pictures of homes for sale or request a relocation packet. You can also be on an email notification list when properties matching your parameters come on the market. Use their web site to have a virtual market analysis performed on your current property. Saulcy Real Estate has over 10 associates and 4 offices in southeast Wyoming. Their team can benefit the buyer or seller with superior access to inventory and superior exposure. Saulcy is a "House-Sold" word!

M Golden Key Realty
107 S. 5th in Laramie. 742-8131 or 800-578-1027.

M Wayne Rauer, Realty Executives of Laramie
318 Bradley Street in Laramie. 755-200 or 745-8092. Toll free at 877-929-2003

Wayne Rauer, an Associate Broker of Realty Executives of Laramie, has earned an excellent reputation as an experienced realtor, providing excellent customer service. He is available nights and weekends for busy buyers and sellers seeking or selling residential, farm, commercial, or mountain properties in Laramie and the surrounding area. Wayne is well grounded in the area and is a member of the Laramie Real Estate Board and the National Real Estate Association.

M Donna Emery/Real Estate Executives
318 E. Bradley Street in Laramie. 745-1586 or 877-929-2003. Email: DonnaEmery1@aol.com

56 *Food, Lodging*

T Wyoming Children's Museum & Nature Center
968 North 9th Street in Laramie. 745-6332

The Wyoming Children's Museum and Nature Center offers hands-on activities for children ages 3-12. Exhibits include topics such as the Oregon Trail and Native Americans. There is also a nature center, a discovery center, and pottery and ceramic youth classes. The Nature Center emphasizes wildlife and environmental awareness. Open year around with a modeset admission charge.

L Gas Lite Motel
960 N. 3rd Street in Laramie. 742-6616 or reservationains at 800-942-6610. www.laramie-gaslitemotel.com or email: gaslitemotel@fiber-pipe.net

The Gas Lite Motel offers an opportunity to live like a cowboy in clean, quiet, and comfortable accommodations. The cowboy decor throughout the motel and in each unique room is accented

Gas Lite Motel

with original paintings and large hand painted murals. Some items are for sale by resident artist, Mark Garrett.. Rooms are also equipped with HBO, Cable, DVD, refrigerators, microwaves, irons, hair dryers, and free local calls. Guests also appreciate the indoor pool, free local shuttle service and ample and safe parking for all sizes of vehicles. Pets are welcome. The Gas Lite Motel has a 24 hour desk with friendly family personalized service. They are close to shopping, dining, and the University. Visit them on the web.

57 *Food, Lodging*

T University of Wyoming
Laramie. 766-1121 or 800-342-5996. www.uwyo.edu

The University of Wyoming in Laramie is set in the idyllic backdrop of southeastern Wyoming's Snowy Range and Medicine Bow Mountains and high plains. Established in 1886 it is the state's only provider of baccalaureate and graduate education, research, and outreach services. UW combines major-university benefits and small-school advantages, with more than 180 programs of study, an outstanding faculty, and world-class research facilities. The main campus is located in Laramie, approximately two hours north of Denver. The university also maintains the UW/Casper College Center, nine outreach education centers across Wyoming, and Cooperative Extension Service centers in each of the state's 23 counties and on the Wind River Indian Reservation. There are nearly 9,900 students enrolled at the Laramie campus with nearly 6,000 students served at the other locations.

T The University of Wyoming Art Museum
In the Centennial Complex on the UW Campus. 766-3497

The museum is located in the dramatic new Centennial Complex on the university campus in Laramie. The Centennial Complex, which also houses the American Heritage Center, was designed by internationally recognized architect Antoine Predock.

Museum exhibitions offer something for everyone and are displayed in an exciting environment. Nine expansive galleries and a dramatic outdoor sculpture terrace offer a variety of exhibition experiences. The permanent collection is a primary source for exhibitions in addition to those on loan from other institutions, galleries, and artists. Contemporary art and art of the 18th, 19th and 20th centuries fill the galleries. Exhibitions include paintings, drawings, prints, sculptures, crafts and ethnographic arts from America and around the world.

The museum has a diverse collection of over

The University of Wyoming Art Museum and American Heritage Center

6,000 objects. Significant holdings include European and American paintings, prints, and drawings; 19th century Japanese prints; 18th and 19th century Persian and Indian miniature paintings; 20th century Persian and Indian miniature paintings; 20th century photography; decorative art; crafts; and African and Native American artifacts. The museum is open year round from Tuesday through Sunday.
Excerpted from museum brochure.

T University of Wyoming Geological Museum

Near the northwest corner of the UW campus. 766-2646. www.uwyo.edu/geomuseum

This is Wyoming's oldest museum, established in 1887. Exhibits include: Big Al, the most complete skeleton of Allosaurus ever found; displays featuring the Red Gulch Dinosaur Tracksite in northern Wyoming, the largest tracksite in the State, with over 1,000 meat-eating dinosaur footprints preserved; a 75-foot-long, mounted Apatosaurus (Brontosaurus) skeleton, one of only six on display in the world; a skull cast of Wyoming's State Dinosaur, Triceratops; the largest, complete, freshwater fossil fish on display in the world, a 50-million-year-old garfish from Wyoming's Green River Formation; the fluorescent mineral room, featuring specimens from Wyoming and all around the world; and a one-of-a-kind, life-size, copper-plated Tyrannosaurus rex statue, along with a skull cast of T.rex and the story of the world's first T.rex found in northeastern Wyoming in 1900.

The museum is open daily from 8 a.m. to 5 p.m. weekdays and 10 a.m. to 3 p.m. weekends. Admission is free.
Excerpted from museum brochure.

T American Heritage Center

At the Centennial Complex on the UW campus in Laramie. 766-3520

The American Heritage Center is a major research facility and repository of manuscripts, photographs, rare books, and artifacts. It holds materials related to the history of Wyoming and the American West and various aspects of the American experience.

Named for Eleanor Chatterton Kennedy, daughter of former Wyoming Governor Fenimore Chatterton, and Joe and Arlene Watt, descendants of Wyoming pioneer families and long involved in cattle ranching in the state, the AHC occupies 60% of the Centennial Complex on the UW campus. Designed by architect Antoine Predock of Albuquerque, New Mexico, the building is an abstract representation of the surrounding Wyoming landscape. The cone, that houses the AHC, represents a mountain, the UW Art Museum resembles a village at the foot of the mountain, and the Sculpture Court represents the Laramie Plains.

The 127,000 square-foot building took three years to build at a cost of nineteen million dollars (half state funds and half private donations). Groundbreaking for the building took place on October 6, 1990. Wyoming Governor Mike Sullivan and UW President Terry Roark cut the ribbon officially opening the facility on September II, 1993.

The Rentschler Room is an exact replica of the library of George Rentschler, a New York industrialist and collector of Western art. Born in 1892 in Fairfield, Ohio, Rentschler attended Princeton University and served as an aviator in World War I. After the war, he joined the family foundry business and expanded it into shipbuilding, railroad equipment, armaments and other heavy machinery. Rentschler often hunted in Wyoming's Powder River Basin and his love of the West influenced the art he purchased. After Rentschler's death in 1972, his family agreed to donate the paintings to the American Heritage Center. Lights are subdued to protect the paintings but still open to the public.

Hanging in the room is a portrait of Shoshone Chief Washakie by George DeForest Brush, and paintings by Western artist Henry Farny, who was Mr. Rentschler's favorite artist. Farny produced more than 100 pieces of Western art.

The Storer Loggia represents an early forest with columns that resemble giant trees surrounding a welcoming fire. The Loggia contains paintings by famous Western artist Alfred Jacob Miller. Through his paintings he documented an 1837 expedition to the fur-trading region of Wyoming. Presenting a romantic view of the West Also in the Loggia are artifacts including the saddles of

Section 6

William "Hopalong Cassidy" Boyd, The Cisco Kid, and Jack Benny's violin. Tub Loggia also features a variety of rotating exhibits.

The Toppan Rare Books Library is home to UW's rare books collection, consisting of more than 40,000 items. The majority of the materials are printed books, although there are newspapers, magazines, illuminated manuscripts, and other materials. Subjects collected include the American West, British and American literature, history, early exploration, religion, hunting and fishing, natural history, women authors, and examples of the book arts.

The Colket Room is located in the Toppan Library. C. Howard Colket (1859-1924) traveled the world beginning in 1879 when he journeyed by horseback from Beirut to Baghdad, visiting the ancient cities of Telloh, Corinth, Ninevah, Baalbek, Tell Billa, and Rayy, collecting many artifacts, curios, and mementos. Some of the artifacts acquired during these travels, and the cases built to house them, are on display thanks to the generosity of Mr. and Mrs. T. C. Colket, II.

The American Heritage Center Exhibit showcases principal collecting areas of the AHC. These are Wyoming and the American West, UW Archives, Environment and Conservation, Mining & Petroleum Industries, 20th Century American Culture, Journalism, Politics & World Affairs, Rare Books, and Transportation. The AHC holds collections such as the papers of U.S. Senator Gale McGee, Barbara Stanwyck, Admiral Husband Kimmel, pioneer aviator Roscoe Turner, and the Anaconda Mining Company.

The LaBarre Business History Center (turn left as you exit the elevator and pass through the door labeled "Public Gallery") is the only public area on the fifth floor. Displayed are photographs of Laramie and the University of Wyoming campus. Views of the Loggia, Laramie, and the Snowy Range Mountains are available from this floor.

The Reliquary contains exhibits that are drawn from the AHC's collections. Located on either side of the Reliquary are the Meg and Fred Karlin Audio-Visual Room and The Anaconda Reading Room. The Anaconda Geological Document Collection is the country's largest collection relating to geological exploration. These rooms are available by appointment only and are not part of the self-guided tour.

The Center is open Monday through Friday from 8 a.m. to 5 p.m. Admission is free.
Reprinted from Heritage Center walking tour brochure.

T University of Wyoming Anthropology Museum
14th and Ivinson on the UW campus in Laramie. 766-5136

The Anthropology Museum has collections and displays that highlight Wyoming, Northwest Plains Indian and other North American Indian cultures. It is open year round Monday through Friday from 8 a.m. to 5 p.m.

T University of Wyoming Insect Gallery
Room 4018 College of Agriculture Building on UW campus.766-2298

The Gallery Room includes a variety of exotic and native insect displays, educational exhibits, live insect zoo, insect artifacts, insect hand stamps, insect models, kid's book corner, and a mural and display explaining the importance of insects in forest ecosystems (student artists are continuing to work on this). Included in the insect zoo are Madagascar hissing cockroachs, tropical millipedes, water striders, crickets, grasshoppers, tarantula, darkling beetles, and other seasonal displays. It is open to the public Monday through Friday from 9 a.m. to 4 p.m. Admission is free.

T University of Wyoming Gallery 234
On the UW campus. 766-6340

Open M-F from 8-5, the gallery boasts an eclectic collection of student, contributing and visiting artist projects.

T Cooper Mansion
Grand Ave. and 15th St. in Laramie

The Cooper Mansion was built in 1921 and designed by architect, Wilbur Hitchcock. The beautiful building is an interesting combination of styles including; modern and classical styles, part pueblo and mission, and part art deco. It has been listed on the National Register of Historic Places since 1983. As the Cooper family home the mansion serves as tangible evidence to the extent and character of British economic colonialism in the western United Stated during the late 19th century. Beginning in the 1870s many wealthy young men from Britain came to Wyoming and purchased huge tracts of land on which they sought to establish virtual empires. Collectively called the "Cattle Barons," on the Laramie Plains, Frank Cooper was the leading member of the foreign-born contingent. It is currently serves as the home to the American Studies Program at The University of Wyoming.

T University of Wyoming Rocky Mountain Herbarium and Williams Botany Conservatory
In the Aven Nelson building on the UW campus. 766-2236

These collections of plant life are among the most extensive in the nation. The Herbarium, located on the Third Floor of the Aven Nelson Building, is open only by prior arrangement. The Conservatory is open every weekday at 10 am, closing at 4pm Monday - Thursday, at 3pm on Friday. During the winter, it is open on Saturdays from 10am - noon.

L University Inn
1720 Grand Avenue in Laramie. 721-8855 or 800-869-9466

The University Inn is conveniently located in the heart of Cowboy Country with easy access to all points of interest in the Laramie area. They are just minutes from the Snowy Range Mountains and just a little north of the Colorado border. When traveling to town for events at the University of Wyoming you'll appreciate the fact that the Inn is a short walk away, directly across from the campus. They are located in a quiet neighborhood and offer clean comfortable rooms with microwaves, refrigerators, and free local calls. Family sized rooms are also available.

58 *Gas, Food*

59 *No services*

T The Ames Monument
Near the summit between Cheyenne and Laramie approximately 1.5 miles south of I-80, exit 329

This 60-foot tall limestone pyramid was built in 1881 to honor Oliver and Oakes Ames, two brothers who were largely responsible for the financing of the Union Pacific Railroad. A great deal of scandal accompanied some of their methods for appropriating funds. A congressional investigaton failed to account for missing money.

The Tree Rock

Costing some $65, 000 to build, in the days when a large mansion cost less to build, the monument itself caused quite an uproar. The railroad that the Ames brothers helped to build once passed nearby, but when it was rerouted to the south, both the monument and the little town of Sherman were abandoned. The Ames brothers died under a cloud of suspicion. Only the monument and a small cemetery remain.

T Sherman

Built in the 1860s at the highest point along the transcontinental railroad, Sherman was a major stop. It sported a five stall roundhouse and turntable. Most of the buildings have fallen, but several foundations remain.

T Vedauwoo Recreation Area

Southeast of Laramie on I-80

Spectacular granite rock formations welcome climbers, hikers and mountain bikers.

T Lincoln Monument

I-80 between Cheyenne and Laramie

A 13-foot bronze bust of the famous president marks the highest point on Interstate 80 on Sherman Hill. Commissioned in 1959, it is one of the largest busts in the U.S. The monument originally stood on the Lincoln Highway, which traversed America before the building of the intestates. It was moved to its present location in 1969. Sculptor Robert Russin was a professor of sculpture at the University of Wyoming whose work was nationally known. More of his work can be seen on and around the UW campus.

T Devil's Playground

Off I-80 southeast of Laramie

Located in the Medicine Bow National Forest, Devil's Playground is a jumbled pile of granite boulders. The area was named in 1929 by businessmen from Cheyenne who were promoting the area as a tourist attractions.

H Sherman Mountains

At pullout on I-80 between Exits 329 and 335

The Sherman Mountains are erosional remnants rising above the general level of the surface of the Laramie Range. The flat topped characteristic of the range resulted from beveling during an ancient erosion cycle. Bedrock here is granite, a crystalline rock made up of pink feldspar, glassy quartz, black mica and hornblende, which originated deep in the earth's crust over a billion years ago.

The peculiar rock forms of the Sherman Mountains are controlled by three sets of joints, or planes of weakness, cutting the granite and dividing it into large blocks. Weathering has rounded off corners and has enlarged joint planes, resulting in irregular blocky rock masses, many of which are capped by balance rocks.

H Gateway to the Rockies

At Exit 323 rest area

Tall trees, short trees, shrubs, grasses, and flowering plants—mountains, canyons, river bottoms, and prairies—all intermingle to form the landscape. The greater the variety of landforms and vegetation, the more homes or habitats there are for wildlife.

The large expanses of native wildland habitats make Wyoming unique and the home to over 600 species of native wildlife.

Here at the Gateway to the Rockies you will see animals of the conifer forest. The golden-crowned kinglet is found nesting and feeding atop the forest canopy in the older, taller evergreen trees. Other birds nest and feed here, some in shrubs and some on the ground. Woodpeckers hammer on trees building nest cavities. Other species of birds and mammals use these holes for nesting and shelter. Birds consume insects, which can harm trees.

Dead trees, both standing and fallen, provide homes for wildlife, too. A last contribution before nutrients are returned to the soil.

Elk and mule deer feed at dusk and again at dawn in forest openings. The nearby forest is used as cover.

Beyond this gateway we pass into the rich land and plant diversity offered by the Rocky Mountains and its many basins. The Rocky Mountains are beautiful, majestic and powerful, but they are also a crucial part of this fragile formula. These Rocky Mountain habitats are the reason for much of Wyoming's wildlife.

H The Ames Monument

Near the summit between Cheyenne and Laramie approximately 1.5 miles south of I-80, exit 329.

Completed in 1882 at a cost of $65,000, this monolithic, 60 foot high granite pyramid was built by the Union Pacific Railroad Company. It stands on the highest elevation (8,247 feet) of the original transcontinental route. Until 1901, when the railroad was relocated several miles to the south, it passed close by the north side of the monument where once stood the rail town of Sherman.

The monument serves a memorial to the Ames brothers of Massachusetts, Oakes (1804-1873) and Oliver (1807-1877), whose wealth, influence, talent, and work were key factors in the construction of the first coast to coast railroad in North America. The contribution made by Oakes was especially significant even though in 1873 he was implicated in a scandal relative to financing the construction of the railroad.

Ames Monument was designed by the distinguished American architect Henry Hobson Richardson (1838-1886). Located further west than any of his works, this memorial typifies the

Ranching is still a way of life for many in southeastern Wyoming. Photo courtesy of Laramie Area Chamber of Commerce.

Richardsonian style by its energetic elemental characteristics. His love for native construction materials is demonstrated by the monument's great, rough hewn granite blocks, quarried from "Reeds rock" one-half mile west. A Richardson biographer has called the monument "perhaps the finest memorial in America... one of Richardson's least known and most perfect works. The bas-relief medallions of the Ames brothers were done by the prominent American sculptor, Augustus Saint-Gaudens.

H Tree Rock

At pullout on I-80 between Exits 329 and 335

This small pine tree that seems to be growing out of solid rock has fascinated travelers since the first train rolled past on the Union Pacific Railroad. It is said that the builders of the original railroad diverted the tracks slightly to pass by the tree as they laid rails across Sherman Mountain in 1867-69. It is also said that trains stopped here while locomotive firemen "gave the tree a drink" from their water buckets. The railroad moved several miles to the south in 1901 and the abandoned grade became a wagon road.

In 1913 the Lincoln Highway Association was formed "To procure the establishment of a continuous improved highway from the Atlantic to the Pacific." The Lincoln Highway was an instant success in a nation enamored with the newfangled automobiles and eager for a plae to drive them. The Lincoln passed right by Tree Rock as did U.S. 30 in the 1920's and Interstate 80 in the 1960s. At this place the road was approaching the 8,835-foot Sherman Summit, the highest point on the Lincoln. The view of the surrounding mountains was like nothing that westbound easterners had ever seen. Still, they noticed the little tree, which became the favored subject of many early postcards and photographs. It still is.

The tree is a somewhat stunted twisted limber pine (Pinus Flexilis), a type of tree commonly found in this area where ponderosa and limber pines dominate the landscape. The age of the tree is unknown, although limber pines can live as long as 2000 years. The tree grows out of a crack in a boulder of Precambrian era pink Sherman granite formed more than 1-4 billion years ago.

H Father of the Interstate Highway System

I-80 Exit 323 at Summit rest area

In August, 1973, the U.S. Congress designated a cross-country stretch of Interstate as the "Dwight D. Eisenhower Highway" in tribute to President Eisenhower's early recognition of the need for a national network of highways to enhance the mobility of a growing nation. His dream originated in 1919 on an Army convoy from Washington, D.C. to San Francisco, California, a journey that took sixty-two days.

On June 29, 1956, President Eisenhower signed the historic legislation that created the national system of Interstate and Defense Highways and the Federal Highway Trust Fund, the pay-as-you-go mechanism through which U.S. motorists have funded the construction and upkeep of the U.S. Highway system. Today, that system stands as a monument to Eisenhower's vision as a young Army officer—a legacy of safety and mobility that has brought all Americans closer together.

This sign commemorating the Eisenhower Highway was made possible by the following organizations: American Traffic Safety Services Association and the Road Information Program. LOCATION: Summit Rest Area on the north side of 1-80 between Cheyenne and Laramie.

60 *Gas*

T Curt Gowdy State Park

I-80 Exit 329 north to Highway 210, east on 210. 632-7946.

History of Curt Gowdy: State Park

Curt Gowdy State Park, named after the well-known sportscaster, was established in 1971 through a lease agreement with the City of Cheyenne and the Boy Scouts. Today it is administered by the Division of State Parks and Historic Sites, Wyoming Department of Commerce.

This region was a favored camping area for the Comanche, Pawnee, Crow and Shoshone during their search for bison. Other tribes including the Iowa, Cheyenne, Arapaho and Sioux are thought to have roamed the area also. The arrival of the Union Pacific construction crews in the 1860s caused Native Americans to be pressured onto the ever-shrinking hunting lands and their presence diminished into oblivion on the lands now known as Curt Gowdy State Park.

The Terrain

The seven sections of richly varied landscape that comprise the park include flora and fauna on the foothills of the Laramie Mountains halfway between Cheyenne and Laramie. In fairly close proximity to the Colorado border, 12 miles directly south, and the Nebraska border, 61 miles east, the beautiful attractions within Curt Gowdy State Park are also near the crossroads of two major interstates, I-80 and I-25. Several historic sites of note lie nearby, including Ames Monument.

In addition to two reservoirs, the park includes Hynds Lodge which is listed on the National Register and an amphitheater available for concerts, theater and other cultural activities. Both are available by reservation.

The area is one of low-lying meadows, gently rolling hills and massive steep granite formations. Wildlife abounds and both reservoirs are stocked by the Wyoming Game & Fish Department.

The elevation varies from a low of 6,450 feet to a high of over 7,500 feet.

Hynds Lodge

The lodge is named for noted Cheyenne philanthropist and capitalist, Harry P. Hynds, who built and donated the structure in 1922-23 to Cheyenne's Boy Scout movement.

The building is open to both large and small groups on a reservation-only basis (reservations may be made starting on the first working day of January each—call park headquarters). A covered porch, large kitchen, dining area, recreational and sleeping accommodations, a hiking trail and amphitheater are all part of the lodge complex. *Reprinted from Wyoming State Parks and Historical Sites brochure.*

Buford

Pop. 2, Elev. 8,000

This one-time railroad station, established in 1867, was named after General John Buford, who was in charge at nearby Ft. Sanders in 1866. The post office remains, and Buford marks the halfway point between Laramie and Cheyenne. Keep your eyes open for the Tree in the Rock Monument, a marvel of nature just to the east of Buford.

Tie Siding

When the post office was built here, which still stands, the outside of the building was lined with surplus railroad ties; thus, it has "tie siding". The ties were shipped through here from the Medicine Bow Forest from 1868 on. With the completion of the railroad, the small community remained to provide goods and services to area ranchers.

61 *Food, Lodging*

Woods Landing

Col. Samuel S. Woods came to Wyoming as a

freighter. He came with his family from Atlantic, Iowa in 1883 and stayed to settle, building a sawmill. He and his wife became known for their extensive hospitality and often hosted parties and dances, first in their home, and later in a community hall built for such purposes. Their property was further developed by a couple from Indiana. In 1927 a hall was built on top of 24 boxcar springs and even today is reputed to be the best dance floor in southeastern Wyoming. The dance hall was placed on the National Register of Historic Places in 1986. The present resort community at Woods Landing continues to reflect this celebratory spirit.

T University of Wyoming Infrared Observatory on Jelm Mountain

2 miles east of Woods Landing. 766-6150. faraday.uwyo.edu/observatories/wiro/

WIRO is located 25 miles SW of Laramie, two miles east of Woods Landing, and situated atop Jelm Mountain at 9656 feet (2943m.) The site was chosen because of : (1) the dryness of the air (an important consideration when doing infrared astronomy since moisture absorbs IR radiation,) (2) comparatively low turbulence in the air above the mountain, (3) low air and light pollution levels, (4) proximity to the University of Wyoming, and (5) the site had pre-existing electricity, phone lines, and a road to the top (Jelm was formerly used by the US Forest Service and BLM as a fire look-out station.) This ranks as one of the premier infrared observatories in the world. Call to arrange for a private tour.

62 *Food, Lodging*

Bosler

This tiny town was named for Frank Bosler, owner of the Diamond Ranch and prominent figure in Albany County for many years. Before his tenure at the Ranch, it was the headquarters for Tom Horn, an infamous hired gun who was hung in Cheyenne after killing a boy by mistake.

Iron Mountain

Named for a nearby mountain rich in iron ore, this town was once a railroad station and post office. It is most notorious for being the place where hired gun Tom Horn allegedly shot a 13 year-old boy, Willie Nickell, whom he mistook for the boy's father. Horn paid for the crime at the end of a rope, one of the last hangings in Wyoming. There is still much debate about whether or not Horn really committed the murder.

Rock River

Pop. 235, Elev. 6,892

This railroad town once thrived after the Rock Creek Station (now Arlington) was closed in 1900. Some accounts say it was the same community, just moved downstream. Como Bluff, just northwest of Rock River on Hwy. 30, is one of the most significant paleontological sites in the world, where diplodocus fossils, the largest animal ever known, were first found.

T Como Bluffs

Highway 30/287 just north of Rock River

This ordinary looking rock formation was once the most significant dinosaur find in America. The fossils found here impacted paleontology in the late 1800s like never before. Leading researchers from Yale came to unearth the unprecedented fossil remains, which included many species of dinosaurs and ancient mammals that were new to science. Rivalry over who found what first resulted in many fossils being destroyed to prevent others from getting them. The dig sites are now quite thoroughly cleaned out, and what was there is now housed in a number of museums on the East Coast, including the Smithsonian, the Museum of Natural History (NY) and the National Museum in Washington D.C., but there still remains "The World's Oldest Building," a locked-up gift shop constructed of dinosaur bones. The dig site is currently closed to the public. Fossil Cabin Museum is open during the summer months eight miles east of Medicine Bow on State Highway 30.

Medicine Bow Peak. Photo courtesy of Laramie Area Chamber of Commerce.

T Rock River Museum

212 D Street in Rock River. 378-2386

View phosphorescent rocks, dinosaur bones, and local pioneer memorabilia alluding to the area's Wild West history, in this small museum, open Tues-Sun. 10-3, June through August.

H Dinosaur Graveyard

U.S. Highway 30/287 at the Carbon/Albany County line.

The bluff lying 1.3 miles to the north is Como Ridge, just beyond the crest of which lies 'The Dinosaur Graveyard", one of the greatest fossil beds of dinosaur skeletons in the world. One of the largest skeletons ever unearthed, measuring 70 feet in length, was taken from this fossil bed. Hundreds of dinosaur skeletons and the bones of early mammals were unearthed and shipped from this area between 1880 and 1890. These dinosaurs lived from about one hundred million to two hundred million years ago.

63 *No services*

Boxelder

Named for the trees, which grew along Boxelder Creek, the canyon walls protected the Pony Express riders who stopped here. The post office was discontinued in the 1940s.

Esterbrook

Like the creek of the same name, this town was named for Mrs. Ester Cooper, an important Wyoming pioneer, in 1897 (see the Cooper Mansion in Laramie). It had a short stint as a copper mining town.

64 *No services*

Bill

Four men named Bill had homesteads that came together here. One of the last skirmishes between Indians and whites took place just east of here, about halfway to Lance Creek, when some Newcastle lawmen encountered a band of Sioux on October 3, 1903.

Scenic Drives

Snowy Range Scenic Byway

This road crosses the Medicine Bow Mountain Range and includes 27 miles of the Medicine Bow National Forest along Wyoming Highway130. Located in southern Wyoming, this route can be reached by exiting Interstate 80 at Laramie or at Walcott Junction, approximately 22 miles east of Rawlins. Driving time along the Snowy Range Scenic Byway from one forest boundary to the other depends on the interest of the visitor. Driving straight through during the summer tourist season will take about an hour. Stopping to enjoy the magnificent scenery, the many points of interest, or adventures like camping and fishing can extend travel time by several hours, or even days. Approached from the west or east, the route rises from 800 feet on the valley floor to an elevation of 10,847 feet above sea level. At Snowy Range Pass, nearby Medicine Bow Peak towers to 12,013 feet.

The highway over the Snowy Range is one of the shortest of Wyoming's Scenic Byways, both in length and in the number of months it can be driven. It is a two-lane highway, leading over the second highest mountain pass in Wyoming, and when open is drivable by passenger cars. Snow usually closes the highest section of the road about mid-November . Snowplows then traditionally open the road in May before the

Wyoming State Fair

Enjoy the Cowboy State at its finest at the Wyoming State Fair held in mid-August. You'll find everything you expect at a state fair here. The pure Wyoming hospitality will treat you to great exhibits from the garden to the livestock to cooking and art. For the adventuresome there is always a midway, demolition derby, paintball wars, and even an arm wrestling tournament. Plenty of special activities include everything from sheet shearing to horse competitions to police dog demonstrations. Great entertainment is featured nightly at the grandstand. Of course, there are plenty of rodeos too. Spend a day or a few, enjoy great entertainment, and a variety of food. This is a great leisurely fair for the whole family to enjoy, especially if you are seeking refuge from the fast paced city life. The fairgrounds are handicapped accessible with plenty of shade and large grassy areas. The Wyoming Pioneer Memorial Museum is conveniently located on the fairgrounds. Call the Wyoming State Fair Office for more information and current schedules.

Memorial Day weekend. The east and west extremes of the Byway are drivable during the winter mothers because there is less snow accumulation at the lower elevations.

On this drive, travelers are close enough to medicine Bow Peak to feel the chill from its year-round glaciers. Even deep in summer it is easy to see how the Snowy Range got its name. Watch for wildlife while driving this byway, because deer and elk and the many other creatures that live in this forest may cross the road at any time, especially in the early morning or late evening hours. *Reprinted from Wyoming Department of Transportation Brochure*

Happy Jack Road

This 27-mile stretch of two lane highway, with sections of three lanes for passing, climbs over the Laramie Mountain Range and through the Medicine Bow National Forest between Cheyenne and Laramie on a route parallel to Interstate 80. It can be reached off of I-80 at the Lincoln Monument/ Summit Rest Area, or from Cheyenne at the Happy Jack exit.

This route is usually open year round, and is often passable even when the interstate is closed. It crosses over a broad stretch of open grassland at the eastern end, passing by Curt Gowdy State Park and Veedauwoo Rocks before it begins a dramatic ascent up the tree-lined mountains, terminating at Lincoln Monument before reconnecting with the interstate above Telegraph Canyon. Several opportunities to stop and view the scenery, as well as campgrounds, short hikes, and recreational opportunities, can be found along the way.

Sybille Canyon

Passing over the Laramie Mountains and past the Sybille Wildlife Center, this 52-mile paved highway offers beautiful views of the mountains and the canyon, as well as opportunities to fish, hike, and scout for wildlife. This route heads east off of US 30/287, about 18 miles north of Laramie, where it intersects with Wyoming Highway 34. There are services in both Laramie and Wheatland. The route takes you across a grassy plain before climbing up into the foothills of the Laramie Range and through the gouged out rock walls of the canyon.

As you pass the Wildlife Center, keep your eyes open for elk, moose, deer, and bighorn sheep which are fostered here. Another climb higher into the mountains takes you through a hill-lined valley and some ranch land before connecting with Interstate 25 to Wheatland.

Hikes

Laramie Range Trails

Black Mountain Lookout

Distance: 2.5 miles
Climb: moderate
Rating: easy
Usage: moderate
Location: From Wheatland, head north on I-25 to El Rancho exit. Follow signs to Harris Park to the Boy Scout Camp, and turn left. Turn right on FDR 667 and proceed until the marked Forest Service boundary (prior to that is private land). Park within the Forest boundary.

The "trail" is a road that is not for passenger cars. As you reach journey's end, the Black Mountain Lookout comes into view. It is a 13 by 13 metal, flat-roofed structure with a catwalk located atop a rock knob, reached by a metal stairway. You are invited to stroll the catwalk, but remember that, while it is staffed, the lookout is also a residence, so enter only if invited.

Laramie Peak Trail #602

Distance: 5 miles
Climb: 3000 feet
Rating: difficult
Usage: light
Location: Take Hwy. 94 south from Douglas for 17 miles, continue south on County Road 5 for 11 miles, then southwest 15 miles. Turn left (SE) on FDR 671 and drive 2 miles to FDR 661. Continue 1 mile to trailhead.

The trail is relatively flat for the first mile, as it follows along Friend Creek. As the climb increases, the trail affords views of the nearby rock hills. Friend Falls is a small waterfall about 2 miles up the trail and provides a convenient resting or turnaround point. As the hiker climbs further, the trail rises 2500 feet over approximately 3 miles. Panoramic views can be seen from the summit of Laramie Peak. Once can see several states, mountain ranges, and cities.

Salt Lick Trail #606

Distance: 4.4 miles
Climb: 100 feet
Rating: moderate
Usage: light
Location: From Wheatland, head north on I-25 to El Rancho exit. Follow signs to Harris Park to the Boy Scout Camp and turn left. Then take FDR 667 through the camp about one mile to the Harris Park Trailhead. FDR 667 is rough; you will need a high clearance vehicle. At the end of the Harris Park Trail, the Salt Lick Trail begins and travels south along the Salt Lick Creek.

This trail travels through an area of beetle-killed, blown-down timber and provides some camping opportunities along meadows near Salt Lick Creek. This trail connects with the Black Mountain Trail, which turns northeast and ends at Black Mountain Lookout.

Friend Park Trail #609

Distance: 4 miles
Climb: 800 feet
Rating: moderate/difficult
Usage: light
Location: Take Hwy. 94 south from Douglas for 17 miles. Continue south on County Road 5 for 11 miles, then southwest for 15 miles. Turn left (SE) on FDR 671 and drive 2 miles to FDR 661. Continue 1 mile to trailhead.

This trail leaves the Laramie Peak Trail about 1/8 mile below the campground and travels south towards Arapahoe Creek. Due to a bark beetle epidemic that killed many of the pines in the area during the late 1980s, one can expect to find blown-down, dead trees across the trail.

Harris Park Trail #616

Distance: 2.8 miles
Climb: 1000 feet
Rating: moderate/difficult
Usage: light
Location: From Wheatland, head north on I-25 to El Rancho exit. Follow signs to Harris Park to the Boy Scout Camp and turn left. Then take FDR 667 through the camp about a mile to the trailhead. FDR667 is rough; you will need a high clearance vehicle

This trail travels up Fall Creek through ponderosa pine stands and rocky outcroppings for the firsts mile. The trail then descends the rest of the way into a very scenic camping area along Ashenfelder Creek. Black bears, mountain lions , mule deer, and elk may be seen in this area. Please be cautious.

Twin Peaks Trail #618

Distance: 2.5 miles
Climb: 1400 feet
Rating: moderate/difficult
Usage: light
Location: From Douglas ,take Hwy. 91 west then south. After 25 miles, the pavement ends and the road becomes County Rd. 24. Continue south and southwest on CR 24 for about 11 miles to the Twin Peaks Trailhead.

This trail heads west into Roaring Fork Creek. The first 1/2 mile is through private land, so please stay on the trail. The next mile passes through State Land where day use is allowed but overnight camping is prohibited. The last 1 1/2 miles to the base of Twins Peaks leaves Roaring Fork Creek and gains elevation more rapidly. Views of the Laramie Mountains can be enjoyed from the top of Twin Peaks.

North Laramie River Trail #625

Distance: 2.5 miles
Climb: 1000 feet (descent)
Rating: moderate
Usage: moderate
Location: Take I-25 north from Wheatland to the El Rancho exit. Follow the signs to Fletcher Park. Follow the Fletcher Park Road west past Camp Grace. Signs to the trailhead can be found at the intersection of Fletcher Park Road and Cow Camp Road.

This trail provides public access to 3.5 miles of the North Laramie River, which offers good fishing of primarily brown and rainbow trout, ranging in size form 6 to 15 inches. Upstream the canyon becomes very narrow and steep. Most of the year the river has to be crossed to reach its upper portions. Downstream the canyon opens up where bighorn sheep, deer, and elk may be seen. You will also notice the large fire that swept through this area. In July of 1996, 7000 acres were burned as the result of a lightning strike.

Watch the area regrow as the years go by. In the bottom of the canyon is an old homestead, built in the 1920s. It was developed into a resort, known as the Rainbow's End, and includes 15 buildings scattered along the river. Some of these structures are unsafe so please use care around them. They are part of our cultural heritage, so please help protect them and don't injure or disturb them or any artifacts.

Curtis Gulch and La Bonte Canyon Trail #624
Distance: 4.1 miles, 3.7 miles
Climb: 1300 feet, 700 feet
Rating: difficult/moderate
Usage: light
Location: Take Hwy. 91 west then south from Douglas for 20 miles, then County Rd. 16 south for 14miles, and northeast on FDR 658 for one mile. Curtis Gulch Trailhead is just 50 yards west f Curtis Gulch Campground, on the north side of the road. La Bone Canyon Trailhead is in the campground.

Steep canyon sides, along with patches of aspen and conifers, make this area one of the most scenic on the Douglas Ranger District. The canyon bottom is about 6000 feet in elevation, and has granite rock formations for climbing and photography.

Sunset Ridge Trail #680
Distance: 1.6 miles
Climb: 1400 feet
Rating: moderate
Usage: moderate
Location: Take Hwy. 94 south from Douglas for 17 miles, then 11 miles south on County Road 5, and 3miles east on FDR 633. The trailhead is adjacent to campsite #3.

As a moderate loop trail, this one offers a terrific opportunity for families to discover a panoramic view of Glendo, the Wheatland Area, and Laramie Peak.

Black Mountain Trail #683
Distance: 1.8 miles
Climb: 3000 feet (descent)
Rating: moderate
Usage: light
Location: From Wheatland, head north on I-25 to the El Rancho exit. Follow signs to Harris Park to the Boy Scout Camp and turn left. Then take FDR 667 through the camp about one mile to the Harris Park Trailhead. This road leads to a staffed Forest Service Lookout Tower where visitors are welcome. The trail provides a hiking link between the lookout and the Salt lick Trail within the Ashenfelder Basin, the largest block of contiguous National Forest lands in the Laramie Range.

This trail travels through very rugged, steep country with large rocky outcroppings and an abundance of blown-down, beetle-killed ponderosa pine. Drainages in the area offer cascading water over rocks and numerous pools within a very remote, secluded setting.

INFORMATION PLEASE

Tourism Information

Cheyenne Area Convention and Visitors Bureau 778-3133
Douglas Area Chamber of Commerce 358-2950
Converse County Tourism Board 358-2950
Glenrock Chamber of Commerce 436-5652
Albany County Tourism Board 745-4195
Laramie Area Chamber of Commerce 745-7339
Niobrara Chamber of Commerce 334-2950
Goshen Chamber of Commerce 532-5612

Government

Wyoming Game and Fish, Cheyenne Visitor Center 777-4554
Wyoming State Parks and Historic Sites 777-6324
Medicine Bow-Routt National Forests Thunder Bas National Grassland - Laramie District 745-2300
Medicine Bow-Routt National Forests Thunder Bas National Grassland - Douglas Ranger District 358-4690

Car Rentals

Price King Rent-A-Car • Cheyenne 638-0688
Price King Rent-A-Car • Laramie 721-8811
Affordable Rent A Car • Cheyenne 632-1907
Enterprise • Laramie 721-9876
Hertz • Laramie 745-0500
Ford Rental • Wheatland 322-2355
Hertz • Cheyenne 634-2131
McCarty Rent-A-Car • Laramie 745-8921

Hospitals

Community Hospital • Torrington 532-4181
Memorial Hospital of Converse County • Douglas 358-2122
Niobrara Memorial Hospital • Lusk 334-2711
United Medical Center-West • Cheyenne 634-2273

Airports

Wheatland 322-9909
Cheyenne 634-7071
Douglas 358-4924
Guernsey 836-2661
Laramie 742-4164

Golf

Glen Red Jacoby Golf Club • Laramie 745-3111
Niobrara Country Club • Lusk 344-9916
Wheatland Golf Club • Wheatland 322-3675
Glenrock Golf Course • Glenrock 436-5560
Trail Ruts Golf Club • Guernsey 836-2255
Douglas Country Club • Douglas 358-5099
Leaning Rock Golf Course • Pine Bluffs 245-3236
Little America Hotels & Resort • Cheyenne 775-843
FE Warren AFM Golf Club - Military • FE Warren AFB 773-3556
Cheyenne Country Club • Cheyenne 637-2230
F. E. Warren Golf Club • Cheyenne 773-3556
Kingham Prairie View Golf Club • Cheyenne 637-6418
Torrington Municipal Golf Course • Torrington 532-3868

Guest Ranches

Vee Bar Guest Ranch • Laramie 745-7036
Terry Bison Ranch • Cheyenne 634-4171
Diamond Guest Ranch • Chugwater 422-3564
LaBonte Canyon Ranch • Douglas 358-2447
The Ogalalla Ranch • Douglas 358-3786
Powderhorn Ranch • Douglas 358-0549
Spearhead Ranch • Douglas 358-2694
Grey Rocks Guest Ranch • Guernsey 532-4419
Double Mule Shoe Ranch • Laramie 742-5629
Mill Iron 7 Ranch • Lusk 334-2951
Dodge Creek Ranch • Rock River 322-2345
Rockin 7 Ranch • Shawnee 334-2309
Two Bars Seven Ranch • Tie Siding 742-6072
Grant Ranch • Wheatland 322-2923
Laramie Peak Ranch • Wheatland 664-1298
Kamp Dakota • Wheatland 322-2772

Lodges and Resorts

Windy Hills Guest House & Spa • Cheyenne 632-6423
Rainbow Valley Resort • Centennial 745-0368
Glendo Marina • Glendo 735-4203
Lakeview • Glendo 735-4461
Hubbard's Mountain Cupboard • Wheatland 322-4520
Woods Landing Resort • Woods Landing 745-9638
Little America Hotels & Resort • Cheyenne 775-8430

Bed and Breakfasts

Rainsford Inn B&B • Cheyenne 638-2337
Nagle Warren Mansion B&B • Cheyenne 637-3333
Howdy Pardner B&B • Cheyenne 634-6493
The Storyteller Pueblo B&B • Cheyenne 634-7036
A. Drummond's Ranch B&B • Cheyenne 634-6042
Windy Hills Guest House & Spa • Cheyenne 632-6423
Hotel Higgins & Paisley Shawl Restaurant • Glenrock 436-9212
Carriage House B&B • Douglas 358-2752
Morton Mansion B&B • Douglas 358-2129
Bear Mountain Riding Ranch B&B • LaGrange 834-2492
The Inn at Bear Creek • LaGrange 834-2398
Adventure's Country B&B •Cheyenne 632-4087
Avenue Rose B&B • Cheyenne 635-2400
Double M & N B&B •Cheyenne 778-7021
Porch Swing B&B • Cheyenne 778-7182
Heaven's Little Wonder B&B •Albany 742-2247
Deer Forks Ranch • Douglas 358-2033
Two Creek Ranch • Douglas 358-3467
Bit-O-Wyo Ranch B&Bt • Cheyenne 638-8340
Annette's B&B • Guernsey 836-2148
Bear Mountain Back Trails • LaGrange 834-2281
Sage & Cactus Village • Lusk 663-7653
Blackbird Inn B&B • Wheatland 322-4540
Gentry Guest House • Torrington 532-5774
Home Ranch B&B • Laramie 745-6010
Prairie Breeze B&B • Laramie 745-5482
Alpine House • Jackson 739-1570
Ronnie & Tal's Hunting B&B • Torrington 532-4107

Outfitters and Guides

Wyoming Outfitters & Guides Association FHERG 265-2376
LaBonte Canyon Ranch H 358-2447
88 Ranch Outfitters H 358-5941
Mike Tillard Outfitters H 436-8555
Grant Ranch Outfitting H 436-2421
Wyoming Professional Hunters H 436-8655
Rough Country Outiftters & Guides HFRE 436-2304
Chug Creek Outfitters H 422-3372
Milliron T.J. Outfitting H 632-6848
Snowy Range Snowmobile Tours G 632-4075
Timberline Outfitters H 635-7288
Jim & Lorrie Werner Hunting H 358-2633
Spearhead Ranch H 358-2694
Rockin 7 Ranch H 334-2309
Ronnie & Tal's Hunting H 532-4107
A.J. Rosa's Fat Boy Fishing F 733-3061
Grizzly Bear Outfitters H 736-2277
Dodge Creek Ranch HF 322-2345
Jones Outfitters HFE 721-2133
Monster Critters Outfitting FH 745-5196

Dining Quick Reference

Price Range refers to the average cost of a meal per person: ($) $1-$6, ($$) $7-$11, ($$$) $12-up. Cocktails: "Yes" indicates full bar; Beer (B)/Wine (W), Service: Breakfast (B), Brunch (BR), Lunch (L), Dinner (D). Businesses in bold print will have additional information under the appropriate map locator number in the body of this section.

MAP#	RESTAURANT	TYPE CUISINE	PRICE RANGE	CHILD MENU	COCKTAILS BEER WINE	MEALS SERVED	CREDIT CARDS ACCEPTED
3	Cavalryman Supper Club	Steak/Seafood	$$	Yes	Yes	D	
4	Taco Bell/KFC	Fast Food	$	Yes		L/D	
4	Orin Junction Truck Stop	American	$/$$	Yes		B/L/D	
4	JD's Italian Reatuarant	Italian	$$	Yes		L/D	Major
4	Outpost Café	Family	$	Yes		B/L/D	Major
4	B-Q Corral	Fast Food	$	Yes		L/D	
4	Fireside Restaurant & Cowboy Bar	Family	$$	Yes	Yes	B/L/D	Major
4	El Jarro	Mexican/American	$$	Yes	B	L/D	M/V
4	Cowboy Bar & Rose Butte Supper Club	Family	$$	Yes	Yes	B/L/D	Major
4	Val's Western Café	Family	$	Yes		L/D/B	
8	Diamond A's Bar & Grill	American	$$		Yes	L/D	Major
8	Pair-A-Dice Grill	American	$$	Yes		B/L/D	M/V
8	Mike's Place	Family	$$	Yes		B/L/D	M/V
8	Rooster's Old Western Saloon	American	$$/$$$		Yes	L/D/B	Major
10	Bob's Riverview Restaurant	Family	$$			L/D	Major
10	One-Eyed Jack's Bar & Grill	American	$$	No	Yes	L/D	Major
10	Burrito Brothers	Mexican	$$			L/D	M/V
10	Lunch Box LLC	Family	$			L/D/B	
12	Outfitters Restaurant	American	$$	Yes	B/W	B/D/L	
12	Garhart's Pioneer Inn	American	$$		Yes	L/D/B	
13	Stagecoach Inn Café	Family	$$/$	Yes		B/L/D	Major
13	Real McCoy	Bakery	$			B/L	
13	Stagecoach Café	Family	$$			B/L	Major
13	Lira's Mexican Restaurant	Mexican	$$			L/D	
14	**The Java Jar**	Espresso /Soup & Sandwich	$			L/B	
14	Arby's	Fast Food	$	Yes		D/L/B	Major
14	Chuckwagon Café	Family	$	Yes		L/D/B	
14	Granpa Chuy's Mexican Restaurant	Mexican	$	Yes	Yes	L/D	Major
14	Peking Garden	Chinese	$$	Yes		L/D/B	Major
14	Subway	Steak/Seafood	$$$	Yes	Yes	D	M/V
14	Taco John's	Fast Food	$	Yes		D/L	
14	Bake Haus	Bakery	$			B/L	M/V
14	Buck's Pizza	Pizza/sandwiches	$$	No		L/D	Major
14	Cabbage Patch Cuisine	German/American	$$	No		L/D/B	
14	Carmelita's	Mexican	$$	Yes	Yes	L/D	Major
14	Pep's Restaurant	Family	$$	Yes		L/D/B	M/V
14	Hardee's	Fast Food	$	Yes		L/D/B	
14	Jose Palzanio's	Fine Dining	$$/$$$	Yes	W/B	L/D	Major
14	King's Inn Restaurant	Family	$$/$$$	Yes	Yes	L/D/B	Major
14	Lorena's Restaurant	Family	$$/$$$	Yes		L/D/B	M/V
15	Burger King	Fast Food	$	Yes		L/D/B	M/V
15	Pizza Hut	Pizza	$$	Yes	B	L/D	Major
15	State Line Oasis Bar & Grill	Steak/Seafood	$$$	Yes	Yes	D	M/V
15	Chicken Hut	Chicken/Burgers	$	Yes		L/D	
15	Ten Pen Tropics	American	$$		Yes	L/D	
15	Little Moon Lake Supper Club	Steakhouse/	$$$	Yes	Yes	D	Major
16	Deacon's Restaurant	American	$$	Yes		B/L/D	M/V
16	La Familia Prado	Mexican	$$			L/D	
17	Yoder Bar	American	$$	No	Yes	D/L	D/V/M
18	Long Branch Saloon & Steakhouse	Steakhouse	$$$		Yes	D	Major
18	Long Horn Grocery & Café	Family	$$	Yes		B/L/D	
18	Longhorn Café	Family	$	Yes		B/D/L	
18	Grandma's Café	Family	$	Yes		B/L	
20	Ampride	Family	$	Yes		B/L/D	Major
20	A&W	Fast Food	$	Yes		L/D	
20	Subway	Sandwiches	$	Yes		L/D	M/V
20	Wild Horse Restaurant	American	$$	Yes		L/D/B	Major
20	Uncle Fred's	American	$$	Yes		B/L/D	M/V
20	Rock Ranch Steakhouse	Steakhouse	$$	Yes	Yes	L/D	Major
20	Taco Bell	Fast Food	$	Yes		L/D	

All Wyoming Area Codes are 307

Section 6

Dining Quick Reference-Continued

Price Range refers to the average cost of a meal per person: ($) $1-$6, ($$) $7-$11, ($$$) $12-up. Cocktails: "Yes" indicates full bar; Beer (B)/Wine (W), Service: Breakfast (B), Brunch (BR), Lunch (L), Dinner (D). Businesses in bold print will have additional information under the appropriate map locator number in the body of this section.

MAP#	RESTAURANT	TYPE CUISINE	PRICE RANGE	CHILD MENU	COCKTAILS BEER WINE	MEALS SERVED	CREDIT CARDS ACCEPTED
21	Crazy Irishman Bar Bee Q	Barbeque	$$	Yes		L/D	Major
21	Pete's Pizza	Pizza	$$			L/D	
21	Sapp Bros. Big C Hot Stuff Pizza	Pizza	$$	Yes		L/D	Major
21	T. Joe's Steakhouse & Saloon	Steakhouse	$$$		Yes	D	Major
21	Great American Real Food Fast	Family	$$	Yes		L/B	
21	Flying J Travel Plaza	Fast Food	$			L	
22	**Estevan's Cafe**	Mexican	$$	Yes	W/B	L/D	D/M/V
22	Casa de Trujillo	Mexican	$$	Yes	Yes	L/D	Major
22	Shari's	Family	$$	Yes		L/D/B	Major
22	Pie Lady	American	$			B/L/D	Major
22	Armadillo Restaurant	Family	$$	Yes	Yes	L/D	Major
22	Parkway Pizza	Pizza	$				
23	Burger King	Fast Food	$	Yes	Yes	L/D/B	M/V
23	Korean House	Korean	$$	Yes		L/D	Major
23	Las Salsas	Mexican	$$	Yes	Yes	L/D	Major
23	Little Philly	Sandwiches	$	Yes		D/L	Major
23	Pizza Hut	Pizza	$$	Yes	B	L/D	Major
23	Subway	Sandwiches	$	Yes		L/D	Major
23	Wendy's	Fast Food	$	Yes		D/L	Major
23	Zanna's Drive Thru Espresss	Coffee	$			B/L	
23	Burger Inn	Burgers	$	Yes		B/L/D	
24	Papa John's Pizza	Pizza	$$	No		L/D	Major
24	Village Inn	Family	$$	Yes		L/D/B	Major
24	Arby's	Fast Food	$	Yes	Yes	L/D	Major
24	Good Friends Chinese Restaurant	Chinese	$$	Yes		L/D	Major
24	Hardee's	Fast Food	$	Yes		L/D/B	
24	Blackjack Pizza	Pizza	$$			D/L	D/M/V
25	**The Plains Hotel**	Fine Dining	$$	Yes	Yes	B/L/D	Major
25	**The Cheyenne Smokehouse**	Barbecue	$$			L/D	V/M
25	**The Whipple House**	Fine Dining	$$$	No	Yes	L/D	Major
25	**Poor Richard's, Eating & Drinking Estab.**	Steaks & Seafood	$$$	Yes	Yes	L/D/BR	Major
25	**Zen's Bistro**	Sandwich/Salads	$$	Yes		B/L/D	Major
25	Driftwood Cafe	Home Cooking	$$	No		L/B	
25	Dynasty Café	Chinese/Vietnamese	$$	No		L/D	Major
25	Subway	Sandwiches	$	Yes		L/D	Major/M/V
25	Twin Dragon	Chinese	$$	Yes		D/L	Major
25	Western Gold Dining Room & Grille	Fine Dining	$$$	No	Yes	L/D	Major
25	Grand Hotel Plaza	Family	$$		Yes	B/L/D	Major
25	Peppercorn Restaurant	American	$$	Yes	Yes	B/L/D	Major
25	Taco John's	Mexican	$	Yes		L/D	
25	Albany Restaurant Bar	Steakhouse	$$$	No	Yes	L/D	Major
25	Egg & I	Family	$$	Yes		L/B	Major
25	Quizno's	Sandwiches	$	Yes		L/D	Major
25	Teriyaki Grill	Oriental	$$	Yes		L/D	
25	Laus Kitchen	Chinese	$$			L/D	
26	Los Amigos Mexican Restaurant	Mexican	$$	Yes	Yes	D/L	Major
26	Diamond Horseshoe Restaurant	Family	$	Yes		L/B	
27	Burger King	Fast Food	$	Yes	Yes	L/D/B	M/V
27	Domino's Pizza	Pizza	$$	No		L/D	Major
27	Sandlewood Restaurant	Family	$$	Yes	Yes	B/L/D	Major
27	Sonic Drive In	Fast food	$	Yes		L/D	
27	Taco John's Franchise Support Center	Mexican	$	Yes		L/D	
28	Hitching Post Inn & Restaurant	American	$$	Yes		L/D/B	Major
28	Mildreds Coffee Shop	American	$$	Yes		B/L/D	Major
28	Cheyenne Cattle Company Steakhouse	Steakhouse	$$$	Yes	Yes	L/D	Major
28	WYCOLO Lodge Restaurant	Family	$$	Yes	Yes	L/D/B	M/V
28	Sanford's Grub & Pub	Brew Pub	$$/$$$	Yes	Yes	D/L	Major
28	R&B Breakfast Club	Family	$	Yes		L/D/B	
28	Sagebrush Sandwich Co.	Sandwiches	$$	Yes		L	
29	Outback Steakhouse	Steakhouse//	$$$	No	Yes	D/L	Major

Section 6

Dining Quick Reference-Continued

Price Range refers to the average cost of a meal per person: ($) $1-$6, ($$) $7-$11, ($$$) $12-up. Cocktails: "Yes" indicates full bar; Beer (B)/Wine (W), Service: Breakfast (B), Brunch (BR), Lunch (L), Dinner (D). Businesses in bold print will have additional information under the appropriate map locator number in the body of this section.

MAP#	RESTAURANT	TYPE CUISINE	PRICE RANGE	CHILD MENU	COCKTAILS BEER WINE	MEALS SERVED	CREDIT CARDS ACCEPTED
29	Crossroads Café	Family	$$	Yes		L/D/B	Major
30	**Avanti Italian Ristorante**	Italian	$$	Yes	Yes	L/D	Major
30	Guadalajara	Mexican	$$	Yes	Yes	L/D	Major
30	Perkins	Family	$$	Yes		L/D/B	Major
30	C.B. & Potts Restaurant & Brewery	American	$$	Yes	Yes	L/D	Major
30	Country Buffet	Buffet	$$	Yes		L/D	Major
30	Applebee's	American	$$$/$$	Yes	Yes	L/D	Major
30	Chick-Fil-A	Fast Food	$	Yes		L/D	
30	Chili's Grill & Bar	American	$$	Yes	Yes	L/D	Major
30	China Buffet	Chinese	$$	Yes		L/D	Major
30	China Wok	Chinese	$$	Yes		L/D	Major
30	Hardee's	Fast Food	$	Yes		L/D/B	
30	La Costa Mexican Restaurant	Mexican	$$	Yes		L/D	Major
30	Tan's Kitchen	Chinese	$$	Yes		L/D	Major
30	Lexie's Café	American	$$	Yes		L/D/B	Major
30	Ling's Café	Chinese	$$	Yes		L/D	V/M
30	L' Osteria Mondello Italian Cucina	Italian	$$	Yes	W/B	D/L	Major
30	Quizno's	Sandwiches	$	Yes		L/D	Major
30	Shari's	Family	$$	Yes		L/D/B	Major
30	Subway	Sandwiches	$	Yes		L/D	Major/M/V
30	Subway	Sandwiches	$	Yes		L/D	M/V
30	Texas Roadhouse	Steakhouse	$$$		Yes	D	Major
30	Wendy's	Fast Food	$	Yes		D/L	Major
30	Bagelmakers	Bagels	$$/$	Yes		B/L/D	Major
30	Penny's Diner	Family	$$/$	Yes		L/D/B	
30	The Bread Basket	Sandwiches	$	Yes		B/L/D	Major
30	Taco Bell	Mexican	$	Yes		L/D	
30	Papa John's Pizza	Pizza	$$			L/D	Major
30	Pete's Pizza	Pizza	$$			L/D	
30	Red Lobster	Seafood	$$$	Yes	Yes	L/D	Major
30	Sun Dog Restaurant	Chinese	$$$	No	Yes	L/D	
30	Blimpie Subs & Salads	Sandwiches	$	Yes		D/L	Major
30	CJ's The Whole Enchilada	mexican	$$	Yes		L/D	M/V
30	Double Eagle Diner	Family	$	Yes		L/B	
30	Gold Room, Little America Hotel	Fine Dining	$$$/$$	Yes	Yes	D/L	Major
30	Herschler Building Cafeteria	Family	$$	Yes		L/B	
30	Oom-Pah Taco	Mexican	$	Yes		L/D	
30	Patsy's Pantry	Homecookiing	$/$$	Yes		L/D/B	
30	Pizza Time	Pizza	$$	Yes		L/D	Major
30	Player's Restaurant	American	$$	Yes	Yes	D	Major
30	Renzio's Greek Food	Greek	$	Yes		L/D	
30	Sandwich & More	Sandwiches	$	Yes		L	
30	Scooter's Scoreboard Bar	American	$$	Yes	Yes	L/D	Major
30	Pretzel-time Inc.	Family	$	Yes		L/D	
30	Taco John's	Mexican	$	Yes		L/D	
30	Sbarro Italian	Italian	$$				Major
33	McDonald's	Fast Food	$	Yes		D/L/B	Major
34	Senator's & Brass Buffalo Saloon	Family	$$$	Yes	Yes	D/L	Major
37	Godfather's Pizza	Pizza	$$	Yes	B/W	L/D	Major
37	McDonald's	Fast Food	$	Yes		D/L/B	Major
37	Pizza Hut	Pizza	$$	Yes	B/W	L/D	Major
38	Little Bear Inn	Steak/Seafood	$$$	Yes	Yes	D	Major
40	**Chugwater Soda Fountain**	Deli	$$/$	Yes	Yes	L/D	Major
40	**Miss Kitty's Buffalo Grill**	Family	$$	Yes		B/L/D	Major
40	The Steak Out	American	$/$$	Yes	Yes	L/D	
40	River Rocks Steak House	Steaks/Seafood	$$$		Yes	D	Major
42	Silver Dragon Chinese Restaurant	Chinese	$$	Yes	W/B	L/D	Major
42	Taco John's	Fast Food	$	Yes		L/D	
42	Wheatland Inn Family Restaurant	Family	$$	Yes		B/L/D	Major
42	Arby's	Fast Food	$	Yes		D/L/B	Major

Dining Quick Reference-Continued

Price Range refers to the average cost of a meal per person: ($) $1-$6, ($$) $7-$11, ($$$) $12-up. Cocktails: "Yes" indicates full bar; Beer (B)/Wine (W), Service: Breakfast (B), Brunch (BR), Lunch (L), Dinner (D). Businesses in bold print will have additional information under the appropriate map locator number in the body of this section.

MAP#	RESTAURANT	TYPE CUISINE	PRICE RANGE	CHILD MENU	COCKTAILS BEER WINE	MEALS SERVED	CREDIT CARDS ACCEPTED
42	Burger King	Fast Food	$	No		D/L/B	M/V
42	Subway/TCBY	Sandwiches/	$$/$	No		D/L	Major
42	Terra Grano Pizza	Pizza	$$			L/D	M/V
42	TCBY	Fast Food	$	No		L/D	Major
42	Terra Grand Pizza	Pizza	$$			L/D	M/V
43	El Gringo's	Mexican	$$			L/D	Major
43	Yvonne's Little Brown Derby Café	Family	$$	Yes		B/L/D	Major
43	Marie's Bakery & Restaurant	Bakery	$$	Yes		B/L	
43	Daylight Donuts	Coffee Shop	$			B/L	
44	El Rancho Steakhouse & Tavern	Steakhouse	$$$/$$		Yes	L/D	M/V
44	A&W and Chester's Fried Chicken	Fast Food	$	Yes		D/L	
44	Pizza Hut	Pizza	$$	No	B	D/L	Major
44	Casey's Timberhaus Restaurant & Lounge	American	$$$/$$	Yes	Yes	B/L/D	Major
45	**Plains Motel and Trading Post Restaurant**	Family	$$			B/L/D	Major
45	Pizza Hut	Pizza	$$	Yes	B	L/D	Major
45	A&W/Subway	Fast Food	$	Yes		L/D	Major
45	Taco John's	Fast Food	$	Yes		L/D	M/V
45	Clementine's Cattle Company Restaurant	Steakhouse	$$/$$$	Yes	Yes	B/L/D	Major
45	Village Inn	Family	$$	Yes		L/D	Major
45	Four Seasons Chinese Restaurant	Chinese	$$			L/D	Major
46	Arby's	Fast Food	$	Yes		L/D	Major
46	Subway	Sandwiches	$	Yes		L/D/B	M/V
46	Bright's Café	American	$			B/L	
46	Douglas Community Club Restaurant	American	$$	Yes	Yes	L/D	Major
46	La Costa Mexican Restaurant	Mexican	$$	Yes	W/B	L/D	M/V
47	Subway	Sandwiches	$	Yes		L/D/B	M/V
47	Broken Wheel Truck Stop & Restaurant	Family	$$	Yes		B/L/D	Major
47	Chutes Eatery & Saloon	Regional	$$	Yes	Yes	B/L/D	Major
47	McDonald's	Fast Food	$			B/L/D	
50	**Hotel Higgins & Paisley Shawl Restaurant**	American Bistro	$$$	Yes	Yes	L/D	Major
50	**Fort Diablo Steak House & Saloon**	Steakhouse	$$$	No	Yes	D	Major
50	Four Aces Supper Club	Steakhouse	$$$/$$	Yes	Yes	D/B/L	Major
50	Grandma's Kitchen	Family Dining	$$	Yes		D/B/L	Major
50	Classsic Café & Pizza	American	$$/$	Yes	B	L/D	Major
50	Fireside Grill & Pizza	American	$	Yes		L/D/B	M/V
50	Subway	Sandwiches	$	Yes		D/L	M/V
52	C.K. Chuckwagon	Family	$$	Yes		L/D/B	Major
52	Rose Café	Chinese/American	$$	Yes	W/B	L/D	Major
52	JJ North's Western Family Restautant	American	$$	Yes		L/D/B	D/M/V
52	Iron Skillet	Family	$$	Yes		L/D/B	Major
52	Horse Barn Dinner Theatre (seasonal)	Family	$$	Yes		L/D	Major
52	Harmony Station Restaurant	Family	$	Yes	B	L/D	
52	Wendy's	Fast Food	$			B/L/D	Major
53	Vee Bar Guest Ranch Restaurant	Family	$$$	No	Yes	L/B/D	Major
53	Beanery	Mexican/American	$$	Yes		L/B	Major
53	Bernie's Mexican Restaurant	Mexican	$$	Yes	Yes	L/D	Major
53	Foster's Restaurant and Country Inn	Family	$$	No	Yes	L/B/D	Major
53	McDonald's	Fast Food	$	Yes		L/D/B	
53	Gramma's Olde Ice Cream Parlor	Family	$	Yes		B/L/D	
54	Corona Village Restaurant	Mexican	$$	Yes	Yes	D/L	Major
54	New Great Wall Restaurant	Chinese	$$	No	W/B	L/D	M/V
54	Sports Bar & Grill, Holiday Inn	Steak/Burgers	$$$	No	Yes	L/D	Major
54	Steakhouse, Holiday Inn	Steak/Seafood	$$$	No	Yes	L/D	Major
55	**Coal Creek Coffee Company**	Coffeehouse/Bakery	$$/$		W/B	D/L/B	M/V
55	**Jeffrey's Bistro**	Eclectic	$$	Yes	Yes	L/D	Major
55	Altitude Chophouse & Brewery	Family	$$	Yes	Yes	L/D	Major
55	Lovejoy's Bar & Grill	Steak/Burgers	$$	No	Yes	L/D	Major
55	Bagelmakers	Bagels	$	No		L/B	
55	Cactus Jacks	Mexican/American	$$	Yes	Yes	L/D	Major
55	El Conquistador	Mexican	$$	No	Yes	L/D	Major

Dining Quick Reference-Continued

Price Range refers to the average cost of a meal per person: ($) $1-$6, ($$) $7-$11, ($$$) $12-up. Cocktails: "Yes" indicates full bar; Beer (B)/Wine (W), Service: Breakfast (B), Brunch (BR), Lunch (L), Dinner (D). Businesses in bold print will have additional information under the appropriate map locator number in the body of this section.

MAP#	RESTAURANT	TYPE CUISINE	PRICE RANGE	CHILD MENU	COCKTAILS BEER WINE	MEALS SERVED	CREDIT CARDS ACCEPTED
55	Grand Avenue Pizza	Pizza	$$	No	W/B	L/D	Major
55	Overland Fine Eatery	Family	$$$	No	Yes	L/D	Major
55	Subway	Sandwiches	$	No		L/D	M/V
55	Sweet Melissa Vegetarian Café	Vegetarian	$$$/$$	No		L/D	Major
55	Third Street Bar & Grill	Family	$	Yes	Yes	L/D	
55	Daylight Donuts	Bakery	$	No		B/L	Major
55	Chelo's Mexican Cuisine	Mexican	$$	No	Yes	D/L	Major
55	O'Dwyer's Grub & Pub	Burgers	$$	No	Yes	L/D	
56	Hardee's	Fast Food	$	Yes		L/D/B	
56	Shari's	Family	$$	Yes		L/D	Major
57	Arby's	Fast Food	$	Yes		L/D	Major
57	Domino's Pizza	Pizza	$$	No		D/L	Major
57	Library Restaurant & Brewing Co.	Steaks/Seafood	$$	Yes	Yes	L/D	Major
57	New Mandarin	Chinese	$$	No	W/B	L/D	M/V
57	Papa John's Pizza	Pizza	$$$/$$	No	Yes	L/D	Major
57	Peking Chinese Restaurant	Chinese	$$	Yes	W/B	L/D	Major
57	Pizza Hut	Pizza	$$	Yes	B	L/D	Major
57	Subway	Sandwiches	$	Yes		L/D	M/V
57	Taco Bell	Fast Food	$	Yes		L/D	
57	Taco John's	Fast Food	$	Yes		L/D	
57	T's Wings & Barbecue	Barbecue	$$	No	B	L/D	
57	Cherrie's Ice Cream & Grill	Family	$	Yes		B/L/D	M/V
57	Vitale's Italian Cowboy	Italian	$$$	Yes	Yes	D	Major
57	Village Inn	Family	$$	Yes		B/L/D	Major
57	Old Town Bagel & Ice Cream Shop	Fast Food	$	Yes		L/D	
57	First Story Café	Family	$$	Yes		L/D	
57	Little Caesars Pie Guys	Pizza	$			L/D	
58	Wingers	American	$$	Yes	B	L/D	Major
58	Applebee's	American	$$	Yes	Yes	L/D	Major
58	Godfather's Pizza	Pizza	$$	Yes	Yes/B/W	L/D	Major
58	McDonald's	Fast Food	$	Yes		L/D/B	
58	Wendy's	Fast Food	$$			B/L/D	Major
58	Burger King	Fast Food	$			L/D/B	M/V
58	Teriyaki Bowl	Chinese	$$	No		L/D	Major
58	Bailey's Restaurant & Patio	American	$$	Yes		L/D	Major
62	Longhorn Motel & Restaurant	Family	$$	Yes		L/D/B	V/M

NOTES:

Motel Quick Reference

Price Range: ($) Under $40 ; ($$) $40-$60; ($$$) $60-$80, ($$$$) Over $80. Pets [check with the motel for specific policies] (P), Dining (D), Lounge (L), Disabled Access (DA), Full Breakfast (FB), Cont. Breakfast (CB), Indoor Pool (IP), Outdoor Pool (OP), Hot Tub (HT), Sauna (S), Refrigerator (R), Microwave (M) (Microwave and Refrigerator indicated only if in majority of rooms), Kitchenette (K). All Wyoming area codes are 307.

MAP #	HOTEL	PHONE	NUMBER ROOMS	PRICE RANGE	BREAKFAST	POOL/ HOT TUB SAUNA	NON SMOKE ROOMS	OTHER AMENITIES	CREDIT CARDS
2	Hi Country Inn	885-3856	30	$$$		HT/OP	Yes	P	Major
4	**Town House Motel**	334-2376	20	$$	CB		Yes	P	Major
4	**Rawhide Motel**	334-2440	18	$			Yes		Major
4	LaBonte Canyon Ranch	358-2447							
4	Hospitality House Motor Hotel	334-2120	12	$$		IP		K	Major
4	Covered Wagon Motel	334-2826	51	$$$		IP/HT/S	Yes	K/DA	Major
4	Best Western Pioneer Court	334-2640	30	$$$/$$		OP	Yes	K/DA	Major
4	Trail Motel	334-2530	22	$$		IP			Major
8	Howard's Motel & General Store	735-4252	6	$$			Yes	D	M/V
8	Lakeview Motel & Campground	735-4461	12	$$			No	P	M/V
8	Hall's Marina Motel	735-4216	6	$$$			Yes	P/D/L	Major
10	Bunkhouse Motel	836-2356	30	$$	CB		Yes	P	V/Major
10	Sage Brush Motel	836-2331	12	$			Yes	R	Major
10	Guernsey Hotel	836-2998	3	$	CB		No	R/P	V
12	Fort Laramie Motel	837-3063	6	$				K	
14	Maverick Motel	532-4064	13	$			Yes	P/K	Major
14	Blue Lantern Motel	532-8999	14	$			Yes	P/K	Major
14	Super 8	532-7118	56	$$		IP		P/DA	Major
14	Western Motel	532-2104	20	$$					M/V
15	Oregon Trail Lodge	532-2101	20	$$			Yes	P	Major
15	Holiday Inn Express	532-7600	62	$$$	CB	IP	Yes	DA	Major
16	King's Inn	532-4011	52	$$$	CB	IP	Yes	DA/L/D/P	Major
20	Gators Travelyn Motel	245-3226	31	$$				P	Major
20	Sunset Motel	245-3591	14	$$				P/K	M/V
21	**Howdy Pardner Bed & Breakfast**	634-6493	4	$$$	FB		Yes	P	M/V
22	Fleetwood Motel	638-8908	20	$	CB	OP	Yes	P	Major
23	Cheyenne Motel	632-6802	31	$		OP	Yes	K	M/V
23	Home Ranch Motel	634-3575	37	$			Yes	R	Major
23	Firebird Motor Hotel	632-5505	50	$		IP	Yes	R/M	Major
24	Rodeo Inn	634-2171	66	$		OP	Yes	DA/P/K	Major
24	Roundup Motel	634-7741	36	$		OP	Yes	K	Major
25	**The Plains Hotel**	638-3311	130	$$$$			Yes	P/D/L/DA	Major
25	**Rainsford Inn Bed & Breakfast**	638-2337	7	$$$	FB		Yes	P/D/DA	Major
25	**Nagle Warren Mansion Bed & Breakfast**	637-3333	12			HT			
25	Grand Hotel Plaza	637-0100	88	$$		IP	Yes	P/D	Major
26	Lariat Motel	635-8439	16	$			Yes	DA/P	Major
27	Holiday Inn	638-4466	244	$$$		IP/HT	Yes	P/D/L/DA	Major
28	Hitching Post Inn	638-3301	166	$$$		IP/HT/S	Yes	D/L/DA/R	Major
28	Frontier Motel	634-7961	40	$			Yes	DA	Major
28	Ranger Motel	634-7995	22	$			Yes	P/R/M	D/M/V
28	Lincoln Court	638-7921	64	$$	CB	OP	Yes	DA/P	Major
28	Atlas Motel	632-9214	31	$			Yes	K/R	Major
28	Stage Coach Motel	634-4495	25	$			Yes		V/M
29	**Super 8 Cheyenne**	635-8741	61	$$	CB		Yes	P/DA	Major
29	Motel 6	635-6806	108	$		OP	Yes	P/DA	Major
29	Express Inn	632-7556	60	$$	CB	IP/HT	Yes	DA/P	Major
29	Best Western Hitching Post Inn	638-3301	166	$$/$		IP/HT	Yes	L/D/R/DA	Major
29	Hampton Inn	632-2747	64	$$$		IP	Yes	D/M/R/DA	Major
29	Pioneer Hotel	634-3010	50	$			Yes	DA/P	M/V
29	Guest Ranch Motel	634-2137	32	$			Yes	M/R/P	Major
29	The Sands Motel	634-7771	50	$			Yes	R/P	Major
29	La Quinta Inn & Suites	634-7117	105	$$$			Yes	P/DA	Major
29	Days Inn	778-8877	72	$$	CB	HT	Yes	DA	Major
30	Oaktree Inn	778-6620	60	$$			Yes	D/P/K	Major
30	Quality Inn	632-8901	105	$$	CB	OP	Yes	DA/P	Major
31	**The Storyteller Pueblo Bed & Breakfast**	634-7036	4	$$$	FB				
31	**Historic Virginian Hotel**	379-2377	32	$$			Yes	P/D/L/R	M/V
31	Big Horn Motel	632-3122	14	$				K	M/V
31	Fairfield Inn	637-4070	62	$$	CB	IP	Yes	DA	Major
33	Comfort Inn	638-7202	77	$$	CB		Yes	DA/P	Major

Motel Quick Reference-Continued

Price Range: ($) Under $40 ; ($$) $40-$60; ($$$) $60-$80, ($$$$) Over $80. Pets [check with the motel for specific policies] (P), Dining (D), Lounge (L), Disabled Access (DA), Full Breakfast (FB), Cont. Breakfast (CB), Indoor Pool (IP), Outdoor Pool (OP), Hot Tub (HT), Sauna (S), Refrigerator (R), Microwave (M) (Microwave and Refrigerator indicated only if in majority of rooms), Kitchenette (K). All Wyoming area codes are 307.

MAP #	HOTEL	PHONE	NUMBER ROOMS	PRICE RANGE	BREAKFAST	POOL/ HOT TUB SAUNA	NON SMOKE ROOMS	OTHER AMENITIES	CREDIT CARDS
35	**A. Drummond's Ranch Bed & Breakfast**	634-6042	4	$$$	FB	HT/S	Yes		M/V
35	**Windy Hills Guest House & Spa**	632-6423	9	$$$$	FB	HT/S	Yes	P/DA/M/R/K	M/V
36	Luxury Inn	778-8113	32	$$/$			Yes	DA	Major
40	Super 8 of Chugwater	422-3248	24	$$			Yes	P/D	Major
42	**Motel West Winds**	322-2705	30	$$			Yes	P/R/M	Major
42	Motel 6	322-1800	45	$/$$			Yes	P/DA/R/M	Major
42	Parkway Motel	322-3080	13	$			Yes	K	Major
42	Vimbo's Dusty Boots	322-3842	42	$$			Yes	K/P/L/D	Major
42	Plains Motel	322-3416	11	$			Yes	P	M/V
42	Western Motel	322-9317	8	$				K	
43	**Wyoming Motel**	322-5383	26	$$/$			Yes	P	Major
44	Best Western Torchlite Motor Inn	322-4070	50	$$		OP/HT	Yes	P/R/D	Major
45	**Plains Motel and Trading Post Restaurant**	358-4484	39	$				P/D/L/K	Major
45	Alpine Inn	358-4780	40	$$			Yes	P/DA	Major
45	Four Winds Motel	358-2322	13	$$/$			Yes	P	M/V
45	First Interstate Inn	358-2833	43	$$/$			Yes	P	Major
45	Chieftain Motel	358-2673	20	$			Yes	P	V/M
46	Hotel La Bonte	358-9856	20	$$	CB		Yes	P/L/D	Major
47	Super 8 - Douglas	358-6800	37	$$$			Yes	P	Major
47	Best Western Douglas Inn	358-9790	118	$$		IP/HT/S	Yes	D/L/P/DA/R/M	Major
50	**Hotel Higgins & Paisley Shawl Restaurant**	436-9212	10	$$	CB			D/P/L	Major
50	All American Inn	436-2772	23	$$				P/R/M/K	Major
50	Glenrock Motel	436-2772	17	$$				P/K	Major
52	Super 8 Motel	745-8901	42	$$$/$$			Yes	DA	Major
52	Days Inn	745-5678	53	$$$/$$	CB	OP	Yes	P/DA	Major
53	Foster's Restaurant and Country Inn	742-8371	112	$$/$$$		HT/IP	Yes	P/D/DA/R/M/K	Major
53	Best Value Inn	745-8901	33	$$			Yes	P/DA	Major
53	Howard Johnson Inn	742-8371	112	$$$		IP/HT	Yes	P/D/L/DA	Major
54	**Motel 6**	742-2307	99	$$		OP	Yes	P	Major
54	**Sunset Inn**	742-3741	51	$$		OP	Yes	P/DA	Major
54	1st Inn Gold	800-642-4212	79	$$	CB	OP/HT	Yes	DA	Major
54	Holiday Inn	743-6611	100	$$$		IP/HT	Yes	P/D/L/DA	Major
54	Motel 8	745-4856	64	$$			Yes	P	Major
54	Camelot Motel	721-8860	33	$$			Yes	DA/P	Major
55	**TraveLodge**	742-6671	30	$$	CB		Yes	P	Major
55	**Ranger Motel, Lounge, & Liquor Mart**	742-6677	30	$$			Yes	L/P/R/M	Major
55	Travel Inn	745-4853	34	$$			Yes	DA/R	Major
56	**Gas Lite Motel**	742-6616	30	$$	CB	OP	Yes	P/DA/R/M	Major
56	Econo Lodge	745-8900	52	$$$/$$	CB	IP	Yes	P/DA	Major
57	**University Inn**	721-8855	37	$$			Yes	P/R/M	Major
57	Thunderbird Lodge	745-4871	42	$$$			Yes	DA	Major
58	Comfort Inn	721-8856	55		CB	IP	Yes	DA	Major
62	Longhorn Motel & Restaurant	378-2555	8	$			Yes	D/L/P	M/V
63	Deer Forks Ranch	358-2033							

NOTES:

Section 6

Fort Laramie

National Historic Site

Fort Laramie parade grounds

Fort Laramie in Brief

Fort Laramie—the Crossroads of a Nation Moving West. This unique historic place preserves and interprets one of America's most important locations in the history of westward expansion and Indian resistance.

In 1834, where the Cheyenne and Arapaho travelled, traded and hunted, a fur trading post was created. Soon to be known as Fort Laramie, it rested at a location that would quickly prove to be the path of least resistance across a continent. By the 1840s, wagon trains rested and resupplied here, bound for Oregon, California and Utah.

In 1849 as the Gold Rush of California drew more westward, Fort Laramie became a military post, and for the next 41 years, would shape major events as the struggle between two cultures for domination of the northern plains increased into conflict. In 1876, Fort Laramie served as an anchor for military operations, communication, supply and logistics during the "Great Sioux War."

Fort Laramie closed, along with the frontier it helped shape and influence in 1890. Its legacy is one of peace and war, of cooperation and conflict; a place where the west we know today was forged.

Email: FOLA_Superintendent@nps.gov
Fax: 307-837-2120
Write to: HC 72, Box 389, Fort Laramie, WY 82212

Headquarters Phone: 307-837-2221

Operating Hours, Seasons

The Fort grounds are open from 8:00 am until dusk every day of the year. The Fort museum and Visitor Center is open daily at 8:00 am with extended hours during the Summer, May 26 through September 30.

Accessibility

Park entrance, grounds and visitor center accessible. Many historic structures are partially accessible.

Getting Around

Walking tours of grounds, features and historic buildings. Mobility assistance available. Contact visitor center.

Fees/Permits

Entrance Fee: $3.00 for 7 Days; $15.00 for Annual; Visitors 16 and under are free.
Fort Laramie Visitor Center: Open All Year 8 a.m.–4:30 p.m. Memorial Day weekend to Labor Day weekend 8 a.m.–7 p.m. 837-2221
Closures: Visitors Center closed annually on Thanksgiving,Christmas and New Years Days, but park grounds remain open.
Special Programs: 18 minute fort history video shown daily.
Exhibits: Uniforms, weapons, and artifacts relate the varied and influential history of Fort Laramie in the 19th century western frontier.
Available Facilities: Includes visitor orientation, auditorium, museum and exhibits, as well as the Fort Laramie Historical Association Bookstore.

Fort Laramie History

Fort Laramie, the military post, was founded in 1849 when the army purchased the old Fort John for $4000, and began to build a military outpost along the Oregon Trail.

For many years, the Plains Indians and the travelers along the Oregon Trail had coexisted peacefuly. As the numbers of emigrants increased, however, tensions between the two cultures began to develop. To help insure the safety of the travelers, Congress approved the establishment of forts along the Oregon Trail and a special regiment of Mounted Riflemen to man them. Fort Laramie was the second of these forts to be established.

The popular view of a western fort, perhaps generated by Hollywood movies, is that of an enclosure surrounded by a wall or stockade. Fort Laramie, however, was never enclosed by a wall. Initial plans for the fort included a wooden fence or a thick structure of rubble, nine feet high, that enclosed an area 550 feet by 650 feet. Because of the high costs involved, however, the wall was never built. Fort Laramie was always an open fort that depended upon its location and its garrison of troops for security.

In the 1850's, one of the main functions of the troops stationed at the fort was patrolling and maintaining the security of a lengthy stretch of the Oregon Trail. This was a difficult task because of the small size of the garrison and the vast distances involved. In 1851, a treaty, the Treaty of 1851, was signed between the United States and the most important tribes of the Plains Indians. The peace that it inaugurated, however, lasted only three years. In 1854, an incident involving a passing wagon train precipitated the Grattan Fight in which an officer, an interpreter, and 29 soldiers from Fort Laramie were killed. This incident was one of several that ignited the flames of a conflict between the United States and the Plains Indians that would not be resolved until the end of the 1870s.

The 186's brought a different type of soldier to Fort Laramie. After the beginning of the Civil War, most regular army troops were withdrawn to the East to participate in that conflict, and the fort was garrisoned by state volunteer regiments, such as the Seventh Iowa and the Eleventh Ohio. The stream of emigrants along the Oregon trial began to diminish, but the completion of the transcontinental telegraph line in 1861 brought a new responsibility to the soldiers. Inspecting, defending, and repairing the "talking wire" was added to their duties. During the latter part of the

Fort Laramie	Jan	Feb	March	April	May	June	July	Aug	Sep	Oct	Nov	Dec	Annual
Average Max. Temperature (F)	40.4	46.4	47.8	61.1	67.9	78.6	88.7	88.2	79.5	67.5	53.6	42.7	63.5
Average Min. Temperature (F)	7.7	12.3	16.6	26.4	38.1	46.6	51.3	48.9	39.6	28.1	18.0	11.1	28.7
Average Total Precipitation (in.)	0.27	0.24	0.53	1.34	2.42	2.37	1.57	0.94	1.13	0.62	0.32	0.31	12.08
Average Total SnowFall (in.)	4.0	3.7	6.7	6.8	1.0	0.1	0.0	0.0	0.3	2.4	3.2	4.7	33.0
Average Snow Depth (in.)	1	0	0	0	0	0	0	0	0	0	0	1	0

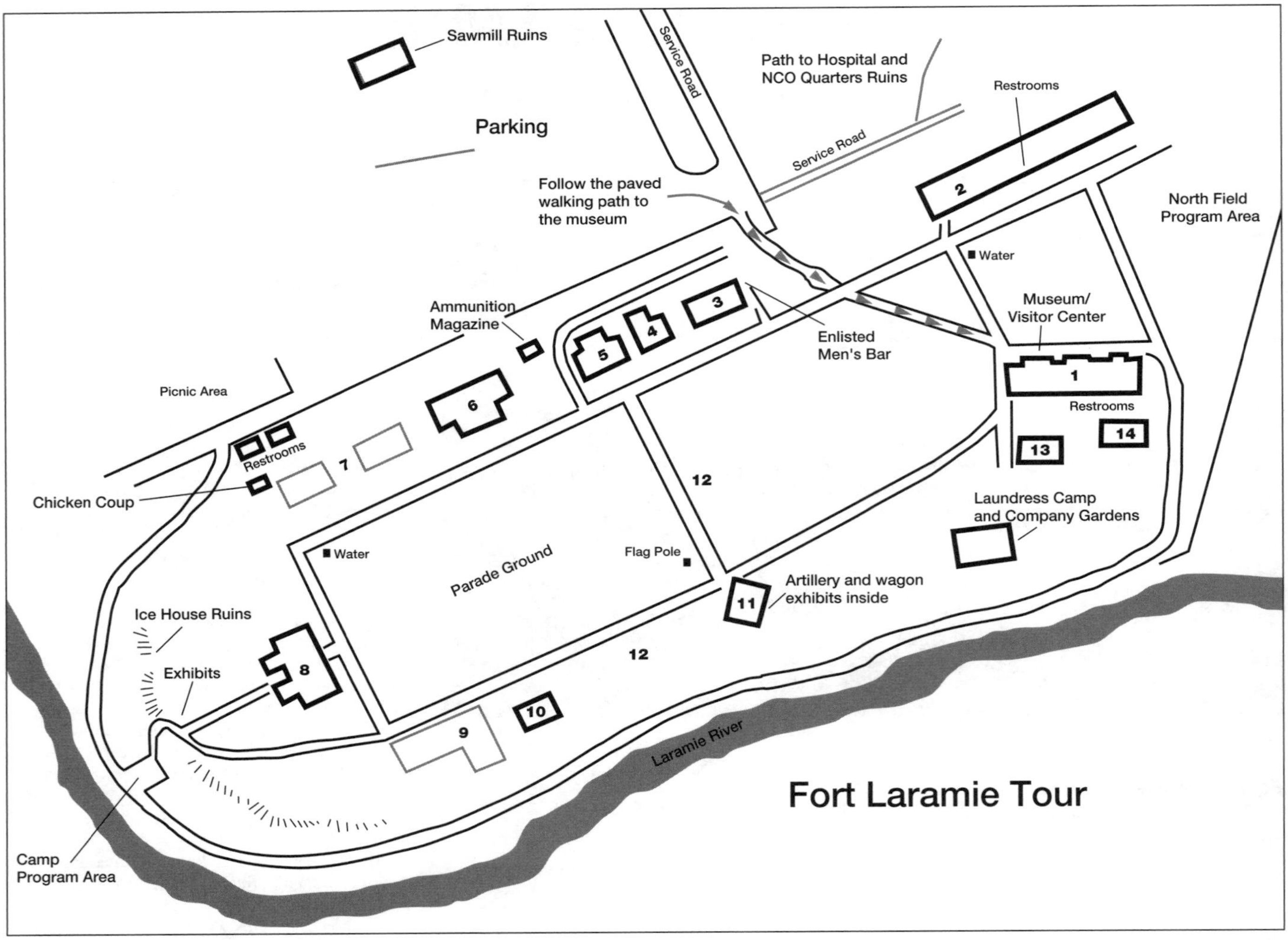

Fort Laramie Tour

Sawmill Ruins
Service Road
Path to Hospital and NCO Quarters Ruins
Restrooms
Parking
Service Road
Follow the paved walking path to the museum
2
North Field Program Area
Water
Museum/ Visitor Center
Ammunition Magazine
3
4
5
Enlisted Men's Bar
1
Restrooms
Picnic Area
6
13
14
Restrooms
7
Chicken Coup
12
Laundress Camp and Company Gardens
Water
Parade Ground
Flag Pole
Artillery and wagon exhibits inside
11
Ice House Ruins
Exhibits
8
12
10
9
Laramie River
Camp Program Area

1860s, troops from Fort Laramie were involved in supplying and reinforcing the forts along the Bozeman Trail, until the Treaty of 1868 was signed.

Fort Laramie in 1876

Unfortunately, the Treaty of 1868 did not end the conflict between the United States and the Plains Indians and, by the 1870s, major campaigns were being mounted against the plains tribes. The discovery of gold in the Black Hills, in 1874, and the resultant rush to the gold fields had violated some of the terms of the treaty and antagonized the Sioux who regarded the Hills as sacred ground. Under leaders such as Crazy Horse and Sitting Bull, they and their allies chose to fight to keep their land. In campaigns such as the ones in 1876, Fort Laramie served as a staging area for troops, a communications and logistical center, and a command post.

Conflicts with the Indians on the Northern Plains had abated by the 188's. Relieved of some of its military function, Fort Laramie relaxed into a Victorian era of relative comfort. Boardwalks were built in front of officers' houses and trees were planted to soften the stark landscape.

By the end of the 1880s, the Army recognized that Fort Laramie had served its purpose. Many important events on the Northern Plains had involved the Fort, and many arteries of transport and communication had passed through it. Perhaps the most important artery, however, the Union Pacific Railroad, had bypassed it to the South. In March of 1890, troops marched out of Fort Laramie for the last time. The land and buildings that comprised the Fort were sold at auction to civilians.

Fort John

Fort John, constructed in 1841, replaced Fort William, the original wooden stockade fort. Part of the impetus for its construction was competition from Fort Platte, built by a rival fur company less than two miles away. Constructed of adobe brick, Fort John stood on a bluff overlooking the Laramie River. It was named for John Sarpy, a partner in the American Fur Company, but was more commonly called Fort Laramie by employees and travelers.

The business of the fort was the Buffalo Robe Trade with local indian tribes. However, soon after the fort's completion, emigrants heading West began to use the fort as a stopping place for rest and resupply. By 1849, the press of increasing immigration resulted in the sale of the fort to the Army. With the arrival of Company E of the First Regiment of Mounted Riflemen, the army's 41 year history at Fort Laramie began.

Virtual Tour

The map is a view of the grounds of Fort Laramie National Historic Site. The buildings whose outlines are in heavy black have been restored and refurnished to a particular period in the history of the Fort. These buildings are open to Fort vistors during the day.

Buildings number 1 and number 11 are restored, but not refurnished to a historical period. They are the Old Commissary that houses the Vistor Center and the 1876 Guardhouse that contains artillery pieces and military transport vehicles.

Buildings whose outlines are gray are ruins with standing walls but no restoration. Several officer's residences, the Post Hospital, and the 1885 Administration Building may be viewed as ruins. Foundations (number 12) mark the locations of barracks along the Parade Ground.

2. Cavalry Barracks

The building designated as the Cavalry Barracks is a two-company barracks built in 1874. The designation is somewhat misleading, however, because at various times it housed infantry as well as cavalry soldiers.

It is the only surviving enlisted mens' barracks on the post. Two other barracks, along the North end and East side of the parade ground, housed three companies and two companies of

All Wyoming Area Codes are 307

Chronological List of Fort Laramie History

1812 - Robert Stuart and the returning Astorians are the first recorded white men to pass by what will become Fort Laramie. While camped at the mouth of the Laramie River they leave the first recorded description of the area. Without knowing it they discover what will become the Oregon Trail.

1821 - Jacque LaRamee is killed on the Laramie River somewhere near the present site of Fort Laramie. Several geographical landmarks later take his name.

1830 - Smith, Jackson, and Sublette haul supplies to the annual rendezvous by wagon, thus becoming the first to pass the future site of Fort Laramie and the first on what will become the Oregon Trail.

1834 - William Sublette and Robert Campbell establish a log-stockaded fort at the confluence of the Laramie and North Platte rivers to trade with the Indians, and name it Fort William (the first Fort Laramie).

1835 - Fort William is sold to Jim Bridger, William Fitzpatrick, and Milton Sublette.

1836 - Fort William is sold to the American Fur Company.

1836 - Elizabeth Spaulding and Narcissa Whitman visit Fort Laramie, and become the first white women to pass over the Oregon Trail, and the first known white women in the future state of Wyoming.

1841 - A rival fort, adobe-walled Fort Platte is built on the Platte River within a mile of Fort William. In response to the construction of Fort Platte, the American Fur Company replaces deteriorating log Fort William with a new fort, Fort John, also made of adobe (the second Fort Laramie).

1841 - The Bidwell-Bartelson party passes Fort Laramie enroute to California, the first true wagon train bound for California.

1842 - Lieutenant John C. Fremont passes on his first exploratory trip to the Rockies.

1843 - The Cow Column passes Fort Laramie. This train represented the first of the wagon trains to Oregon.

1845 - Colonel Stephen W. Kearny councils with the Indians at Fort Laramie to insure safe passage for the growing tide of emigrants traveling along the trail. This is the first peace council at Fort Laramie.

1845 - Fort Platte is abandoned

1846 - The Donner Party passes through Fort Laramie on their fateful trip to the west.

1847 - Brigham Young leads the first of the Mormon emigrants through Fort Laramie in search of their Zion, the valley of the Great Salt Lake.

1849 - Fort John (Fort Laramie) is purchased by the Army for $4,000 on June 26th. The first garrison is comprised of two companies of Mounted Riflemen and one company of the 6th Infantry.

1850 - The high tide of emigration passes Fort Laramie, nearly 50,000 people.

1851 - Fort Laramie Treaty of 1851 (Horse Creek Treaty) is signed.

1853 - The Platte Ferry, just north of Fort Laramie, is seized by the Sioux. A skirmish results between Fort Laramie soldiers and the Sioux with the result of three Indians killed, three wounded, and two taken prisoner.

1854 - The Grattan Fight takes place on August 19th, after Brevet Second Lieutenant Grattan tries to arrest a Miniconjou brave for the killing of an emigrant's cow, eight miles east of Fort Laramie. All whites at the fight died. This is the first major battle of the Northern Plains Indian Wars.

1856 - Mormon emigrants pass Fort Laramie using "handcarts," the first of many handcart pioneers.

1857 - A large column of troops move through Fort Laramie enroute to Utah to suppress the rebellious Mormons.

1860 - April 6th, the Pony Express starts its express mail delivery through Fort Laramie.

1861 - The continental telegraph line is completed. The telegraph runs through Fort Laramie. The Pony Express ceases operations.

1864 - The only recorded attack on Fort Laramie. A scout detachment unsaddled their mounts on the Parade ground and approximately 30 warriors dashed through the fort, stealing the command's horses. No injuries or loss of life were reported.

1865 - Powder River Expedition is organized at Fort Laramie under General Patrick E. Connor to punish Indians in the region.

1866 - Peace Council is held at Fort Laramie to secure the right to use the Bozeman Trail. The peace council fails after Colonel Henry B. Carrington arrives with troops to establish Bozeman Trail forts. Start of Red Cloud's War.

1866 - Fetterman Fight takes place on December 21, and 81 soldiers die at the battle. John Phillips and Daniel Dixon start their ride to Deer Creek Station. Phillips continues on to Fort Laramie, arriving (so goes the legend) during a Christmas Night party at Old Bedlam.

1868 - Red Cloud wins his war with the government and a peace council is held at Fort Laramie, resulting in the signing of the Treaty of 1868, which sets aside the Great Sioux Reservation.

1874 - Gold is discovered in the Black Hills, causing a rush of miners to travel through Fort Laramie up the Cheyenne-Deadwood Trail.

1875 - A bridge is built over the North Platte River, the first iron bridge in Wyoming.

1876 - The campaign of 1876 begins, involving troops from Fort Laramie under the command of General George Crook. Fort Laramie troops fight in the Reynolds Fight of March 17th, and the Battle of the Rosebud on June 17th.

1883 - Last cavalry company leaves Fort Laramie, only infantry troops remain.

1889 - Order to abandon Fort Laramie is issued August 31.

1890 - Last garrison of the post marches away on March 2nd. A public auction is held on April 9th to sell the remaining property and buildings. On April 20th the fort is officially abandoned.

soldiers, respectively. Mess halls and mess kitchens would have been sited in separate buildings behind the barracks buildings. Only the foundations of these two barracks and their accompanying structures survive.

The Cavalry Barracks was a more modern structure than the other, older barracks buildings, built in 1866 and 1867. It was constructed as a two- story structure designed to house the soldiers living areas as well as their mess halls, mess kitchens, and other facilities.

The North end of the barracks building is currently being used, adaptively for Park support facilities and curative laboratories, but the South end has been restored and refurnished to the Summer of 1876 when it would have housed Company K of the Second Cavalry. The second floor contains the squad bay where the company would have lived and slept. Visitors can view the soldiers' beds, uniforms, weapons, and other military equipment. The company kitchen, mess hall, wash room, armory, orderly room, and First Sergeant's room occupy the lower floor.

3. Post Trader's Store

The building identified as the Post Trader's Complex on the map of the grounds was the site of a commercial enterprise on the Post that was operated by the Sutler or Post Trader. (The title Sutler was used until shortly after the Civil War when it was changed to Post Trader.) Between 1849 and 1890 several traders would operate the enterprise.

The Post Trader was a civilian who was given a license to operate a store on the Post. He was an important asset to the Fort because he supplied the soldiers with items that supplemented the bare necessities provided by the Army. In addition to military personnel, he also supplied emigrants traveling along the Oregon and Bozeman Trails and stocked items that appealed to officers' wives and other civilians in the area. In the 1850's and 1860's, Indians would also trade at his store. Although the prices of items in his store were regulated to some extent by the Army, the Post Trader still made a tidy profit.

Interior of Post Trader's Store

There are three sections to the store: an adobe section built in 1850, a stone section added in 1852, and a segment added in 1883 that housed

Where Myth and Reality Merge

As children, we are brought up on a steady diet of western folklore. Cowboys and Indians, soldiers, fur trappers and emigrants are all familiar characters to us. For the most part, they are nothing more than myth - fleeting characters on the big screen or the family television set. There was a place, however, where myth and reality merged; a place where the great events of the opening of the frontier were played out on a grand scale; a place where the list of characters who passed through read like a Who's Who of western history. This place was Fort Laramie, truly the crossroads of the American West.

an officer's club and an enlisted men's bar. The complex has been restored to its appearance in 1876 when the adobe portion housed the store and the stone section contained the trader's headquarters and the post office. The enlisted men's bar has been refurnished as a bar, and sells sarsaparilla and non- alcoholic beer to vistors.
Lieutenant Colonel's Quarters

4. Lt. Colonel's Quarters

The officer's house designated on the Fort map as the Lt. Colonel's Quarters is a two-story officers quarters that was constructed in 1884. It is somewhat unique in that, aside from he commanding officer's house, it is the only single-family dwelling on the post. Most officers and their families lived in duplexes.

Although occupied by several officers and their families at various times, it has been restored to 1887-1888 when it was the home of Lt. Colonel Andrew Sheridan Burt, his wife Elizabeth, and their children, Reynolds and Edith. Lt. Col. Burt was second in command at Fort Laramie during most of his tenure in this house.

When the building was restored and refurnished, the National Park Service had the good fortune to have the assistance of Reynolds Burt. Although only fourteen when he lived at Fort Laramie with his parents, Reynolds was able to remember the furnishings in the house and their arrangement. Some of the original items in the house have been donated by the Burt family and are placed in their original locations.

5. Post Surgeon's Quarters

The Surgeon's Quarters is an officer's duplex that was constructed in 1875. During most of the period from its completion until the decommission of the Fort in 1990, the South half of this residence was the home of a succession of Post Surgeons.

The Post Surgeon assumed many roles at frontier posts such as Fort Laramie. He was the surgeon and physician to the enlisted men, officers, and laundresses at the Fort. He also administered to the medical needs of officer's wives and children and to the other civilians in the area. Only a small amount of his professional duties would involve battle wounds. Most of his practice would be devoted to caring for victims of accidents and treating diseases. The medical practices of the 19th century were primitive, however, and he often treated the symptoms rather than the causes of diseases.

In addition to his medical duties, the Surgeon also functioned as the local scientist. He logged the daily weather records, and recorded other scientific events of interest such as comets and meteor showers. He would also maintain a list of flora and fauna that he might encounter near the Post, and even collect and prepare scientific specimens to be sent back East to the Army Medical Museum and the Smithsonian Institution.

The Surgeon's Quarters have been refurnished to the years 1880-1882. They depict a Victorian residence of an officer of above-average means, his wife, and four children.

Old Hospital

The hospital in this photograph was built in 1873 on the site of an old cemetary used by the army until 1868. It contained a dispensary, a kitchen, a dining room, isolation rooms for quarantined or critical patients, and even a surgeon's office. There were only 12 beds, however, and no operating rooms or laboratories.

The hospital staff included a hospital steward, a matron, and one or more attendants (nurses). The steward was a regularly appointed non-commissioned officer who would most likely be permanently attached to the medical corps. He would be the wardmaster, record keeper and pharmacist. Only one steward was allotted to a hospital.

The matron (a woman) would assist the attendants and do laundry. One matron was allotted per hospital (two for posts with five or more companies in residence.)

The hospital attendants were ordinary soldiers, usually privates, who were detailed for hospital duty. One attendant was recommended for every two companies of soldiers stationed at the post. Attendants were exempt from most of the other normal duties of a soldier, but had to attend parades and weekly inspections. Hospital duty was not popular among the soldiers.

6. Old Bedlam

The building identified as Old Bedlam on the map of the Fort grounds was built in 1849 and is the oldest military building at Fort Laramie. To many people it is and was the symbol of Fort Laramie. It was originally designed to be a bachelor officers quarters, but served many other purposes during the 41-year history of the Fort. For

several years it was Post Headquarters. Most of the people important in the drama of the westward expansion of the United States stood in its rooms or walked its halls.

The North side of Old Bedlam has been restored to the early 1854-1855 when it was a bachelor officer's quarters. The furnishings reflect the spartan atmosphere of the Fort at that time. The officers would have employed an enlisted man, called a striker, to cook their meals, order their quarters, and assist them with daily tasks. The striker's room has also been restored.

The South side of the building has been refurnished to the years 1863-1864 when it was Post Headquarters and the residence of the Post Commander, Colonel William O. Collins of the Eleventh Ohio Volunteer Cavalry. At that time, the Civil War was raging back East and Regular Army troops had been withdrawn from the frontier forts to serve in that conflict. State volunteer regiments supplied troops for Fort Laramie. The lower floor of this side of Old Bedlam housed Post Headquarters and the officer's mess. The top floor was the residence of Colonel Collins and his wife.

8. Captain's Quarters

The building designated Captain's Quarters was built in 1868-1870 and was originally designed to be the Post Commander's house. The Commander, however, preferred another house, and upon hearing this, the Fort Laramie Quartermaster converted the structure into a duplex.

The building was constructed at a time when the garrison at Fort Laramie was increasing and housing for officers was in short supply. If a new officer was assigned to the Fort, he could rank out of quarters any officer junior to him, appropriating the house for his own. Some very junior officers and their families were ranked into halls or even tents for short periods of time.

The building has been refurnished to its appearance in the year 1872. The East side of the duplex has been restored to reflect the residence of a Captain and his family. The West side has been furnished to show how a Lieutenant of more modest means might live.

10. The 1866 Guardhouse

The 1866 guardhouse was the second of three such structures built at Fort Laramie. It served

two important functions, the headquarters of the guards or sentries at the Fort, and the incarceration center for soldiers who ran afoul of Army discipline and the rules of conduct outlined in the Articles of War. The building was constructed of stone.

Each day a group of soldiers would be selected to serve as guards or senties at the Fort. They would serve in this capacity for 24 hours and would be attired in dress uniforms with white Berlin gloves. A formal ceremony, on the Parade Ground, would be held each morning to mark the changing of the guard. The new guards would be inspected by the Officer of the Day and given the password for the day.

The guards were usually split into two shifts, with one shift assuming sentry duties at strategic positions around the Post, and the other one remaining in a state of readiness in the upper level of the guardhouse. At two-hour intervals, the two shifts would switch roles.

The lower level of the guardhouse was the Fort's jail. The prisoners were usually forced to work at hard labor jobs during the day, under guard and often with ball and chain. At night they were confined to the jail. A general confinement room could hold up to 40 prisoners, and two solitary confinement cells were provided for incorrigibles. There was no stove or fireplace in the confinement area, so a soldier had only his two army-issue blankets to keep him warm, even on the coldest nights.

13. 1876 Post Bakery

The building designated as the 1876 Bakery on the map was one of four bakeries in use at various times at Fort Laramie. Bakeries were important because bread was a staple of a soldier's diet while he was in garrison. A loaf af bread was baked for every soldier at the Fort every day.

The baker was usually an ordinary soldier from the garrison detailed to bakery duty for ten days. At the end of his ten-day stint, he would be moved on to other duties and someone else would be rotated into the baker role. It was probable that most of the bakers had no previous baking experience and even possible that some would be illiterate and unable to read the bread recipe. The baker's job would have been relatively easy when the number of soldiers at the Fort was small, but challenging during the brief periods when the garrison was above 700.

This bakery was in use from 1876 to 1883 when its two ovens became faulty and it had to be replaced by another structure. The building has been restored to this time period and has been refurnished with a replica of one of the original ovens and with period utensils that the baker would have used.

Significant Characters Who Passed Through Fort Laramie

Robert Stuart

The first known white person to visit the site that would eventually become Fort Laramie. Stuart and his traveling companions camped at the mouth of the Laramie River on December 22, 1812 on their return trip to St. Louis from Fort Astoria, Oregon. Stuart inadvertently discovered the route that would later become the Oregon Trail.

Jacques Laramee

A French fur trapper, rumored to have been killed by Indians on the stream that would take his name. Laramee is a shadowy character of whom we know very little. However, he now has a river, fort, town, city, county, mountain range, a peak, and plains all named after him.

Jedediah S. Smith

Famous mountain man and one of the first to exploit the fur resources of the Fort Laramie region. He led William H. Ashley's expedition into the central Rocky Mountains in 1823.

Thomas Fitzpatrick

Also known as Broken Hand, co-led the Ashley expedition with Jed Smith. Fitzpatrick became one of the best known of the mountain men. He purchased Fort William with his associates in the spring of 1835. Later he served as a guide for the first true emigrant wagon train, the Bidwell-Bartelson party, in 1841. In 1847, he was appointed as Indian Agent to the Cheyenne, Arapaho, and Sioux, and in 1851, was instrumental in the success of the "Horse Creek" Treaty.

James Bridger—Probably the most famous of the mountain men and a frequent visitor to Fort Laramie. Bridger gained most of his fame as a fur trapper but was also much sought after as a competent guide by emigrants and military alike. In his later years, Bridger spent many hours at Fort Laramie, "spinning yarns" for anybody who would listen. He is rumored to have had a room in the Post Trader's Store, where he wintered in 1867 while recovering his health.

Kit Carson

Although Carson's fame was gained mostly on the Southern Plains, he nevertheless passed through Fort Laramie on many different occasions. Like most of the other famous guides of the period, Carson got his start in the fur trade. One of the little known phases of Carson's career was as a sheepman. He passed through Fort Laramie in 1853 with 6,500 head in route to California where he could turn a 100% profit.

Robert Campbell & William Sublette

Formed a partnership in 1832 to compete in the fur trade. After being driven from the Upper Missouri, the partners became active in the central Rocky Mountain fur trade. Sensing a change in the fur trade industry, Campbell and Sublette decided to erect a fixed trading post to take advantage of the buffalo trade with the local natives. Campbell and Sublette selected the junction of the North Platte and Laramie Rivers for their new post—Fort William, the first Fort Laramie. Campbell later went on to become active in Indian affairs. He attended the Treaty Council of 1851 and was appointed to the Board of Indian Affairs in 1869. Sublette added to his fame as a guide when he led Sir William Drummond Stewart's party in 1843.

Alfred Jacob Miller

Accompanied Sir William Drummond Stewart on his 1837 expedition. Miller was an accomplished artist. Among Miller's portraits of the western landscape through which he passed, are drawings and paintings of Fort William. Thus, he became the first artist to record the Fort Laramie landscape. His work now resides in some of the most renowned art galleries in the country.

Donner Party

This famous company of emigrants passed through Fort Laramie in 1846. They were destined to be remembered because of the fateful decision to take the Hastings Cutoff south of the Great Salt Lake. This decision caused travel delays that allowed the train to get caught in the mountain snows of the High Sierra. Of the original 81 in the party, only 45 survived the tribulations of the winter. Thirty-six members of the company either froze or starved to death.

Francis Parkman - At age 23, he made his famous journey on the Oregon Trail, "a tour of curiosity and amusement." As a product of this trip, he published The Oregon Trail, in 1849, an American classic. During this trip, he stopped at Fort Laramie and left a vivid description of life at the post. Parkman later went on to write an eight volume history of France and England in North America, as well as the History of the Conspiracy of the Pontiac.

John C. Fremont

United States Army officer, passed through Fort John—the second Fort Laramie—in July of 1842 on his first expedition to the Rocky Mountains. Fremont recommended the site of Fort Laramie in his report of the expedition as a logical choice for a military post. Fremont visited Fort Laramie again in 1847, while being escorted east for his court martial by General Stephen Watts Kearny.

Colonel Stephen W. Kearny

In the spring of 1845, Kearny was detailed to take five companies of dragoons as far as South Pass to impress the Indians and to study problems associated with overland travel. On June 16th he met 1200 Sioux at Fort Laramie and told them not to disturb the emigrants or molest their persons or property. He then "fired several shots with his howitzer, followed at darkness by a burst of rockets to tell the Great Spirit that they had listened to his words."

Brigham Young

Leader of the Mormon pioneer movement. He led the first group of Mormons to their Zion, the valley of the Great Salt Lake, in 1847. Young and this first group of pioneers camped near Fort Laramie on June 1, 1847. Brigham Young conceived and implemented the handcart system in 1856.

Whitmans and Spauldings

Dr. Marcus Whitman, his wife Narcissa, Reverend Henry Spaulding and his wife Elizabeth, were members of a missionary party that traveled West with a group of traders in 1836. On this trek they became the first party to take a wagon overland to Oregon. Narcissa and Elizabeth were the first white women to visit Fort Laramie. It was Dr. Whitman who, on his first trip to the west in 1835, surgically removed a three-inch arrowhead from the back of Jim Bridger at the rendezvous that year. The Whitmans and Spauldings went on to establish a Presbyterian mission in Oregon. In November, 1847, the Whitman mission was attacked by Cayuse Indians. Marcus and Narcissa were killed in the raid.

Bidwell-Bartelson Party
Passed through Fort Laramie on June 22, 1841, en route to California. This group of emigrants would constitute the vanguard of the migration to the West Coast.

Father Pierre Jean DeSmet S.J.
Probably the most notable of all the missionaries who ventured into the Great American West. Father DeSmet first visited Fort Laramie (Fort William) on June 4, 1840—the last year that fort existed. On July 25, 1840, Father DeSmet celebrated the first Catholic mass in Wyoming. DeSmet returned to Fort Laramie in 1851, to attend the treaty council, and was instrumental in successfully completing the negotiations. While at the council, he baptized no less than 988 participants.

Lieutenant Daniel P. Woodbury
Officer of the Corps of Engineers, detailed to locate a fort somewhere in the vicinity of Laramie's Fork on the North Platte River. After surveying a number of sites in the vicinity, Woodbury choose the site occupied by Fort John—the second Fort Laramie. On June 26, 1849, Woodbury purchased the old fur trading post for $4,000, and thus it officially passed into the hands of the U.S. Army and became Fort Laramie.

Fort Laramie Firsts

First Permanent settlement in state of Wyoming - Fort William, 1834.

First Drunk Driving Fatality in Wyoming - 1841; the Sioux chief Susu-ceicha fell off his horse and broke his neck after riding back and forth between Fort John and Fort Platte, "receiving strongly drugged liquor."

First Military Post in State of Wyoming - 1849; with the purchase of fur-trade post Fort John by the Army, becoming Fort Laramie, a military installation.

First School in the State of Wyoming - as early as 1856; formal classes taught at Fort Laramie - the first recorded teacher was Post Chaplain Reverend Vaux.

First Post Office in the State of Wyoming - established on March 14, 1850; the oldest continuously operating post office in Wyoming.

First Major Indian Battle of the Northem Plains Indian Wars - Grattan fight, 1854.

First Iron Bridge in state of Wyoming - Army Iron Bridge constructed in 1875 on the North Platte River.

Brevet 2nd Lieutenant John L. Grattan
Impetuous young officer of the Sixth U.S. Infantry. On August 19, 1854, Grattan was put in command of a detachment of 29 enlisted men and an interpreter and was sent to arrest a Miniconjou Indian for supposedly stealing and killing an emigrant's cow in a Brule Indian camp eight miles east of Fort Laramie. It is unknown exactly what transpired at the Indian village, which may have contained as many as 4,000 people. Fighting broke out, claiming the life of Chief Conquering Bear, Grattan, the 29 enlisted men, and the interpreter. Most historians acknowledge this to be the first major battle of the Northern Plains Indian Wars.

General William S. Harney
On September 3, 1855, Harney lead his troops to Ash Hollow, Nebraska, where Little Thunder and his band of Brules were encamped on Blue Water Creek. Harney attacked the village in retaliation for the Grattan fight a year earlier. Harney killed 86 Indians and took another 70 women and children captive. Harney then proceeded to Fort Laramie for a council with a delegation of Sioux chiefs. Harney threatened the Indians with continuing military action if any further depredations occurred along the trail. Harney again played a significant role in Plains Indian affairs in 1868 as part of the Indian Peace Commission held at Fort Laramie.

Ordnance Sergeant Leodegar Schnyder
One of the least known but most significant figures in the history of Fort Laramie. Schnyder arrived at Fort Laramie with Company G, 6th U.S. Infantry, on August 12, 1849. He was appointed as assistant post librarian on September 17, 1851. Schnyder was promoted to the rank of Post Ordnance Sergeant on December 1, 1851. On September 17, 1859, he was appointed Garrison Postmaster, concurrent with his other duties. Despite requesting transfers on numerous occasions, Schnyder did not leave Fort Laramie until the fall of 1886. Schnyder retired in 1890. Ordnance Sergeant Schnyder holds the record for the longest term of service at Fort Laramie, 37 years, and is among the record holders for the longest term of service in the U.S. Army for an enlisted man—a total of 53 years. Spotted Tail (Sinte Galeska)—Chief of the Brule Sioux. Spotted Tail was bom in 1823, and frequented the Fort Laramie region both as a child and as an adult. Spotted Tail was considered one of the greatest Sioux chiefs of his period. He was a brilliant orator, as well as a distinguished warrior. Lt. Eugene Ware states that Spotted Tail had counted 26 coups in personal combat. Spotted Tail was considered a peace chief. After witnessing the destruction of his village by General Harney in 1855, he recognized the futility of war with the whites. However, he was consistently an outspoken advocate for the rights of his people. Perhaps the most notable of Spotted Tail's many visits to Fort Laramie occurred in 1866, when he came to bury his daughter.

Wheat Flour (Ah-ho-ap-pa)
Ah-ho-ap-pa was the daughter of the Brule Chief Spotted Tail. Legend has it that she was enamored by the white way of life. She reputedly fell in love with an army officer at Fort Laramie, but was separated from him when he was transferred to another post. Apparently one of Ah-ho-ap-pa's favorite pastimes was watching the soldiers at formal dress parades. Although much of her life is a mystery, we do know that in keeping with his daughter's wishes, Spotted Tail brought her to Fort Laramie for burial. Colonel Henry Maynadier provided a military escort for the burial party and arranged to have a scaffold erected on the high ground overlooking the fort to the north. Maynadier issued orders to provide full military honors to the girl. After the tumultuous events of 1876, Spotted Tail retrieved his daughter's bones and took them to the reservation for reburial.

Red Cloud (Mahpialuta)
Chief of the Oglala Sioux. Red Cloud was one of the most influential of the Sioux leaders. Red Cloud consolidated his leadership of the Oglala and was considered their principle leader by 1865. He was a frequent visitor to the Fort Laramie area. From 1866-1868 he led the Sioux in opposing white encroachment into the Powder River country. "Red Cloud's War," as it. became known, proved to be very costly to the U.S. Army and white emigrants on the Bozeman Trail. Red Cloud won the war by forcing the government to abandon the Bozeman Trail forts and negotiate a treaty—the only such victory the Sioux could claim throughout the Indian Wars period. Thinking the whites would now keep their word, Red Cloud signed the Fort Laramie Treaty of 1868. He continued to be a champion of Indian rights and to oppose any further encroachment of Indian lands.

Crazy Horse (Tashunka Witco)
Probably the greatest of the Sioux leaders and still considered to be a sacred personage among the Sioux. Although legend states that Crazy Horse never visited the "white man's" fort on the Laramie, he certainly passed through the area very near Fort Laramie. As a boy, in 1851, Crazy Horse witnessed the Grattan Fight eight miles east of Fort Laramie. He became a powerful military leader among his people, playing a decisive role in the Indian victories at the Fetterman Fight in 1866, The Battle of the Rosebud in 1876, and the Custer Fight in 1876. Crazy Horse was killed during an altercation at Fort Robinson on September 5, 1877, while being arrested by soldiers.

Colonel Henry Carrington
Commanding officer of the 18th U.S. Infantry. Carrington passed through Fort Laramie on June 13, 1866, with his troops, en route to the Powder River country to establish forts along the Bozeman Trail. Unfortunately peace negotiations were in progress at Fort Laramie during this time for the purpose of securing the right of travel on the trail. After learning of the soldier's mission, the peace council failed, and Red Cloud began his war. Colonel Carrington was in command of Fort Phil Kearny at the time of the Fetterman Fight. The serious losses incurred during the fight cost Carrington his command and forever tarnished his reputation.

Lieutenant Caspar Collins
Son of the Post Commander, William 0. Collins, and officer of the 11 th Ohio Volunteer Cavalry. Collins left detailed accounts of life at Fort Laramie during the Civil War period. Unfortunately for young Collins, he became most well-known in death. On July 25, 1865, Collins led a group of 25 soldiers out of Platte River Bridge Station to relieve a detachment of ten soldiers guarding a supply train that was approaching the station. Indians closed in on the soldiers; Collins's horse bolted and ran into the group of Sioux. Collins and four other soldiers were killed. Platte River Bridge Station was soon renamed Fort

Caspar. The city of Casper, Wyoming now stands on the site.

Colonel Thomas Moonlight
Moonlight was probably the most incompetent of the long list of officers who commanded Fort Laramie. Of all the tragic blunders that Moonlight made, the hanging of Chiefs Two Face and Black Foot in 1865 was probably the most infamous. Two Face and Black Foot brought white captive Mrs. Eubank and her baby to Fort Laramie to turn them over to the Army. Mrs. Eubank had been taken captive during a raid by the Cheyenne on the Little Blue the proceeding year. Apparently the chiefs had bought Mrs. Eubank's freedom to gain the favor of the whites. Instead, they received death. Despite protests from several individuals, Colonel Moonlight had the chiefs hung with chains and left their bodies hanging for months as an example to other chiefs. Of course Moonlight's action brought further hostilities to the area. Moonlight went on to become Territorial Governor of Colorado in 1887.

General William T. Sherman
Civil war hero and commanding general of the Army after the election of U.S. Grant to the presidency. Sherman's Indian policy shaped the role that the Army would play during the height of the Indian Wars. Sherman was at Fort Laramie as part of the 1867-1868 peace commission.

General Phillip Sheridan
Lieutenant General of the army, Commander of the Division of the Missouri, and also a well-known Civil War hero. Sheridan spent time at Fort Laramie during the uneasy summer of 1876, at times making it his base of operations. Sheridan eventually went on to become commanding general of the Army.

General George Crook
Commanding general of the Department of the Platte and one of the most effective of the Indian Wars generals. General Crook was at Fort Laramie on many occasions, particularly in 1876. Crook was well known for his use of mules in the field and for his "horse meat" or "mud march" in 1876. Crook's character as a hard campaigner who also understood the Plains Indians made him effective as a general. It was Crook who ordered the arrest and confinement of Crazy Horse in 1877. He later went on to direct a successful campaign against the Apaches in the southwest.

John "Portugee" Phillips (Manuel Filipe Cardoso)
Phillips made the legendary ride from Fort Phil Kearney to Fort Laramie (December 21 to 25, 1866) to deliver messages to the commanding officer of the post following the Fetterman Fight. Much has been written of the ride to Fort Laramie, most of it myth. Phillips was hired to make the journey to Deer Creek Station along with Daniel Dixon for $300.00 each. Phillips was given an additional message at Fort Reno to carry to Colonel Palmer at Fort Laramie. The ride took four days. Most accounts make no mention of Indians chasing Phillips and Dixon. There is also no contemporary documentation supporting the story that Phillip's horse died after he arrived at Fort Laramie.

Martha Jane Cannary (Calamity Jane)
Frequented the Fort Laramie area and was an employee of the famous Three Mile or "Hog" Ranch (a house of ill repute just outside Fort Laramie Military Reservation). Calamity Jane's exploits are legendary. On one occasion, Calamity Jane dressed as a male and joined the Jenny expedition of 1875, to the Black Hills. She disguised herself as one of the cavalry troopers escorting the expedition. When discovered, Colonel Dodge ordered her out of the column, but she hid amongst the cargo in one of the wagons and later turned up in the Black Hills. There she reportedly made herself so useful as a forager that she was permitted to stay with the column. In 1876, she was discovered masquerading as one of General Crook's mule skinners, placed under arrest, and sent packing back to Fort Laramie. Calamity probably would not have been discovered had it not been for the fact that "her language when addressing the animals was not up to the usual standards of vituperative eloquence."

Wild Bill Hickok (James Butler Hickok)
Passed through Fort Laramie enroute to the Black Hills on the Cheyenne-Deadwood Stage line. Wild Bill was famous as a gunfighter, lawman and gambler. Hickok was later murdered in a saloon in Deadwood by Jack McCall.

Mark Twain (Samuel Clemens)
Unfortunately for history, Mark Twain passed through Fort Laramie in the summer of 1861, during the night on the stagecoach. Undoubtedly, had he passed through in the daylight hours he would have left a vivid written picture of life at the Fort.

Wyatt Earp
Earp was a noted gunfighter and lawman (sometimes concurrently.) Earp took part in the famous "Gunfight at the OK Corral." He passed through Fort Laramie in 1877, as a special shotgun messenger for a gold shipment on the Cheyenne-Deadwood Stage.

Buffalo Bill Cody (William F. Cody)
Cody passed through Fort Laramie in 1876, while en route north with the Fifth Cavalry. Cody was a well known frontiersman, Pony Express rider, buffalo hunter, scout, and showman. Shortly after passing through Fort Laramie, Cody had his famous duel with Yellow Hair at the War Bonnet Creek Fight on July 17th, 1876. Cody took Yellow Hair's scalp—an event widely touted as "the first scalp for Custer."

Plains Indians

During most of its early history, Fort Laramie was a social and economic center for several tribes of Plains Indians. The Native Americans came to trade, to visit, and later to sign treaties and receive annuities.

Early relations between the traders at the Fort and the Indians were amicable, but as the tide of emigrants swelled along the Oregon Trial, resentments and friction began to emerge. In an effort to end hostilities, a council attended by representatives of the United States and more than 10,000 Indians was called near Fort Laramie in 1851. The council give birth to the Treaty of 1851 that was signed by the United States and tribal representatives. In return for $50,000 per year of annuities, the Indians agreed to stop harassing the wagon trains.

The Treaty was not effective, however, and subsequent incidents resulted in deaths of Native Americans, emigrants, and soldiers alike. The Bozeman Trail, which headed North to the gold fields of Montana, was soon swarming with emigrants who passed through the prime bison hunting lands of the Sioux and the Cheyenne tribes. The Army constructed three Forts along the Trail to provide for the safety of the travelers. The Native Americans resented the intrusions, and the high plains were soon aflame with conflict. A new treaty, the Treaty of 1868 was signed in which the Army agreed to withdraw from the Bozeman Trail and evacuate the forts along it. It addition, the treaty provided a reservation for the Indians along with rights to their traditional hunting grounds.

The Treaty of 1868 did not bring a lasting peace to the high plains. In 1874, gold was discovered in the Black Hills and miners soon flocked to the area. Attempts by the U.S. Army to keep prospectors out of the area were unsuccessful. The influx angered the Sioux, because the Black Hills region was a sacred area and it was also part of the reservation lands guaranteed to the Indians by the Treaty of 1868. Under leaders such as Sitting Bull and Crazy Horse, they fought the Army in engagements such as the ones at the Rosebud and the Little Bighorn. Hostilities reached their peak in the Summer of 1876 and did not end until the Native Americans were forced onto their reservations.

The Tribes

There were three tribes of Native Americans that called the high plains around Fort Laramie home: the Sioux, the Cheyenne, and the Arapaho.

Red Cloud-Oglala Chief. National Park Service Photo.

The Sioux

The dominant tribe on the high plains near Ft. Laramie were the Sioux. The name Sioux refers to a large group of Native Americans speaking a common or similar language. They are often divided into three groups based on their geographic distribution. In the 1800's the Western group, called the Lakota or Teton Sioux, were the dominant tribe in the region around Fort Laramie. They were represented by several bands, the Oglala Sioux, the Brule Sioux, the Hunkpapa Sioux, and the Minneconjou Sioux. The Lakota Sioux were a nomadic people who hunted the buffalo that roamed the high plains in huge herds. The buffalo provided them with food, clothing, the covering for their dwellings, and the raw material for many of their tools. The Sioux could be peaceful or, when the occasion demanded, they could be formidable warriors. The spiritual power, Wakan, and the Summer Sun Dance ceremony played important parts in their lives.

The Cheyenne

The Cheyenne were another well-known tribe that played a part in the pagent of Ft. Laramie. Originally from what is now northern Minnesota, they had migrated to the high plains by the early 1800's and ranged from the Missouri River in the North to the Arkansas River in the South. They were divided into two branches, the Northern Cheyenne and the Southern Cheyenne. The Northern group spent much of their time on the high plains of Colorado and Wyoming, not far from Fort Laramie.

Like the Sioux, with whom they were often allied, the Cheyenne were horsemen and buffalo-hunters who obtained most of their physical needs from the shaggy bison. Also, like the Sioux, they celebrated the Summer Sun Dance, in which men would dance for several days in a ritual of spiritual cleansing and empowerment.

The Arapaho

The Arapaho, although a distinct tribe, were very similar to their close allies, the Cheyenne. Like the Cheyenne, they spoke an Algonquin language and were originally from what is now northern Minnesota. They migrated westward and divided into Northern and Southern branches. The Northern branch lived on the high plains and were more relevant to the historical events played out at Fort Laramie. The Arapaho were mounted bison-hunters who depended on the buffalo for much of their livelihood. They also celebrated the Sun Dance.

The following history of the fort is a reprint of "Fort Laramie" by David L. Heib, a National Park Service Historical Handbook Series No. 20, Washington,D.C., 1954.

Early Fur Trade on the Platte

On the level land near the junction of the Laramie and North Platte Rivers stands Fort Laramie, long a landmark and symbol of the Old West. Situated at a strategic point on a natural route of travel, the site early attracted the attention of trail-blazing fur trappers, who established the first fort. In later years it offered protection and refreshment to the throngs who made the great western migrations over the Oregon Trail. It was a station for the Pony Express and the Overland Stage. It served as an important base in the conquest of the Plains Indians, and it witnessed the development of the open range cattle industry, the coming of the homesteaders, and the final settlement which marked the closing of the frontier. Perhaps no other single site is so intimately connected with the history of the Old West in all its phases.

Early Fur Trade on the Platte, 1812-30

American and French Canadian fur traders and trappers, exploring the land, traveled the North Platte Route intermittently for over two decades before the original fort was established at the mouth of the Laramie River. First to mention the well-wooded stream flowing into the North Platte River from the southwest was Robert Stuart, leader of the seven "Returning Astorians" on their path-breaking journey from Astoria at the mouth of the Columbia River to St. Louis, by way of South Pass in the Rockies and the valley of the Platte, during the winter of 1812-13. They journeyed eastward over what was to become the greatest roadway to the West, thus entitling them to recognition as the discoverers of the Oregon Trail.

Records of actual fur trade activity in this area for the next 10 years are extremely meager, but many geographical names bear witness to the gradual westward movement of the beaver hunters, some of them undoubtedly of Canadian origin. Among them was Jacques La Ramee who, according to tradition, was killed by Indians in 1821 on the stream which now bears his name and which was destined to become the setting of Fort Laramie. Famous only in death, his name was to be given also to a plains region, a peak, a mountain range, a town, a city, and a county in Wyoming.

In 1823, Jim Bridger, Jedediah Smith, and other enterprising trappers of the Rocky Mountain Fur Co., going overland from the upper Missouri, rediscovered South Pass and the lush beaver country west of the Continental Divide. In 1824, while taking furs back to "the States," a band of "mountain men" under Thomas Fitzpatrick became the first Americans of record to pass the mouth of the Laramie after the Astorians. For 15 years thereafter the St. Louis traders sent supply trains up the North Platte route to the annual trappers' rendezvous, usually held in the valleys of the Green or Wind Rivers. In 1830, William Sublette, with supplies for the rendezvous on the Wind River, took the first wagons over the greater part of what was to become the Oregon Trail.

The Laramie and its tributaries were also the homes of the prized beaver, and much trading was done at the pleasant campsites near its mouth. Here, too, was the junction with the trappers' trail to Taos.

Fort William, the first Fort Laramie, in 1837. From a painting by A. J. Miller. Courtesy Mrs. Clyde Porter.

Fort William, the First "Fort Laramie," 1834

The advantages of the site were readily apparent to William Sublette and Robert Campbell, when, in 1834, they paused en route to the annual trappers' rendezvous to launch construction of log-stockaded Fort William. This fort, named for Sublette, was the first fort on the Laramie. In 1835, Sublette and Campbell sold Fort William to Jim Bridger, Thomas Fitzpatrick, and Milton Sublette, and a year later these men in turn sold their interests to the monopolistic American Fur Co. (after 1838, known officially as Pierre Chouteau, Jr. and Company).

Rev. Samuel Parker and Dr. Marcus Whitman, early missionaries to Oregon, traveling with a company of fur traders, paused at "the fort of the Black Hills" in July 1835. Reverend Parker has left a vivid description of activities at the fort, including near-fatal fights between drunken trappers, a council with the chiefs of 2,000 Oglala Sioux gathered at the fort to trade, and a buffalo dance, regarding which Parker commented, "I cannot say I was much amused to see how well they could imitate brute beasts, while ignorant of God and salvation . . ."

Marcus Whitman again traveled westward in 1836 with a fur traders' caravan, this time accompanied by his bride and Rev. and Mrs. Henry H. Spalding. The ladies, the first to travel the Oregon Trail, were extended all possible hospitality at Fort William. Especially remembered were chairs with buffalo skin bottoms, no doubt a most welcome change from the ordeal of saddle or wagon box.

To an artist, A. J. Miller, who traveled with Sir William Drummond Stewart, we are indebted for the only known pictures of Fort William. Made during his visit to the fort in 1837, these paintings depict a typical log stockade which Miller's notes describe further as being

"of a quadrangular form, with block houses at diagonal corners to sweep the fronts in case of attack. Over the front entrance is a large blockhouse in which is placed a cannon. The interior of the fort is about 150 feet square, surrounded by small cabins whose roofs reach within 3 feet of the top of the palisades against which they abut. The Indians encamp in great numbers here 3 or 4 times a year, bringing peltries to be exchanged for dry goods, tobacco, beads and alcohol. The Indians have a mortal horror of the "big gun" which rests in the blockhouse, as they have had experience of its prowess and witnessed the havoc produced by its loud "talk". They conceive it to be only asleep and have a wholesome dread of its being waked up."

The fur traders came to be more and more dependent upon the fort on the Laramie as a base of supplies and a refuge in time of trouble. Similarly, early travelers and missionaries found it a most welcome haven in the wilderness. In 1840, the famous Father de Smet paused at this "Fort La Ramee" where he was favorably impressed by a village of Cheyennes.

Fort Platte and Fort John on the Laramie

Late in 1840 or early in 1841, a rival trading post appeared. This was Fort Platte, built of adobe on the nearby banks of the North Platte River by L. P. Lupton, a veteran of the fur trade in what is now Colorado, but later operated by at least two other independent trading companies.

Abandonment of the rendezvous system after 1840 increased the importance of fixed trading posts. The deterioration of Fort William prompted the American Fur Co. to replace it in 1841 with a more pretentious adobe-walled post which cost some $10,000. Christened Fort John, presumably after John Sarpy, a stockholder, the new fort, like its predecessor, was popularly known as "Fort Laramie."

Competition in the declining fur trade led to open traffic in "fire water," and the debauchery of the Indians around Forts Platte and Laramie was noted by many travelers of the early 1840's. Rufus B. Sage vividly describes the carousals of one band of Indians which ended with the death and burial of a Brule chief. In a state of drunkenness, this unfortunate merrymaker fell from his horse and broke his neck while racing from Fort Laramie to Fort Platte.

Trade goods for the rival posts came out in wagons over the Platte Valley road from St. Joseph or over the trail from Fort Pierre on the upper Missouri. On the return trip, packs of buffalo robes and furs were sent down to St. Louis. In addition to wagon transportation, cargoes were sent by boat down the fickle Platte, which often dried up and left the boatmen stranded on sandbars in the middle of Nebraska.

The First Emigrants

Up to 1840, traders, adventurers, and missionaries dominated the scene. The first party of true covered-wagon emigrants, whose experiences were recorded by John Bidwell and Joseph Williams, paused at Fort Laramie in 1841. The following year Lt. John C. Fremont visited the fort on his first exploring trip to the Rocky Mountains. Recognizing its strategic location and foreseeing the covered-wagon migrations, Fremont added his voice to those recommending the establishment of a military post at the site.

In 1843, the "cow column," first of the great migrations to Oregon, reached the fort under the guidance of Marcus Whitman. This group numbered nearly 1,000 persons. Thereafter, the emigrants with their covered wagons became a familiar sight each May and June. Impressions of the swift-flowing Laramie River, the white-walled fort, the populous Indian tepee villages, the "squawmen" at the fort, and the dances held on level ground beneath nearby cottonwoods were frequently recorded by diarists.

More than 3,000 Oregon-bound emigrants paused at the fort in 1845, intermingling peacefully with the numerous Sioux Indians encamped there. Later that summer, peace still prevailed when Col. Stephen Watts Kearny arrived with five companies of the First Dragoons, encamped on the grassy Laramie River bottoms, and held a formal council with the Indians between the two forts. Here the Indians were warned against drinking "Taos Lightning" or disturbing the emigrants and were assured of the love and solicitude of the Great White Father. They were also duly impressed with his power as symbolized in a display of howitzer fire and rockets.

While Fort Platte was abandoned by its owners in 1845, trade was brisk at Fort Laramie during the winter of 1845-46, and it is recorded that during the following spring a little fleet of Mackinaw boats, under the leadership of the veteran factor P. D. Papin, successfully navigated the Platte with 1,100 packs of buffalo robes, 110 packs of beaver, and 3 packs of bear and wolf skins. Thus, it was a moderately prosperous Fort Laramie in the waning days of the fur trade which the young historian Francis Parkman visited in the spring of 1846 and described so vividly in his book The Oregon Trail:

"Fort Laramie is one of the posts established by the American Fur Company, which well-nigh monopolizes the Indian trade of this region. Prices are most extortionate: sugar, two dollars a cup; five-cent tobacco at a dollar and a half; bullets at seventy-five cents a pound. The company is exceedingly disliked in this country; it suppresses all opposition and, keeping up these enormous prices, pays its men in necessities on these terms. Here its officials rule with an absolute sway; the arm of the United States has little force, for when we were there the extreme outposts of her troops were about seven hundred miles to the eastward. The little fort is built of bricks dried in the sun, and externally is of an oblong form, with bastions of clay in the form of ordinary blockhouses at two of the corners. The walls are about fifteen feet high, and surmounted by a slender palisade. The roofs of the apartments within, which are built close against the walls, serve the purpose of banquette. Within, the fort is divided by a partition: on one side is the square area, surrounded by the storerooms, offices, and apartments of the inmates; on the other is the corral, a narrow place encompassed by the high clay walls, where at night or in the presence of dangerous Indians the horses and mules of the fort are crowded for safekeeping. The main entrance has two gates with an arched passage intervening. A little square window, high above the ground, opens laterally from an adjoining chamber into this passage; so that, when the inner gate is closed and barred, a person without may still hold communication with those within through this narrow aperture. This obviates the necessity of admitting suspicious Indians for purposes of trading into the body of the fort, for when danger is apprehended the inner gate is shut fast, and all traffic is carried on by means of the window. This precaution, though necessary at some of the company's posts, is seldom resorted to at Fort Laramie, where, though men are frequently killed in the neighborhood, no apprehensions are felt of any general designs of hostility from the Indians."

While here, Parkman also witnessed the arrival of the Donner party, who paused at the fort to celebrate the Fourth of July. Many of this party later met a tragic fate in the snow-locked passes of the Sierras.

The Mormon Migrations, 1847-48

While many of the early visitors to Fort Laramie were missionaries, mass emigration motivated by religion was not in evidence until 1847. That spring the pioneer band of Mormons, led by Brigham Young, passed up the north bank of the Platte to its confluence with the Laramie, and crossed near the ruins of Fort Platte. They paused there for a few days to repair wagons and record for future emigrants the facilities available at Fort Laramie, of which James Bordeaux was then in charge. This party of 143 men, 3 women, and 2 children seeking a new Zion in the Salt Lake Valley were but pathbreakers for more than 4,000 Mormons who almost monopolized the trail in 1848.

Like emigrants of all sects, the Mormons enjoyed a respite from travel on arrival at the great way station of Fort Laramie. A variety of activities engaged the emigrants during their brief stopover. Men engaged in blacksmithing and general repair, traded at the fort, or went fishing. The women busied themselves with washing and baking or gathered chokecherries or currants.

The Mormons at this time conceived a plan which was used for several years at Fort Laramie. Wagon supply trains from Utah, drawn by teams acclimated to mountain travel, met emigrating "Saints" from the East, and teams were exchanged. Thus, they avoided the serious losses of stock often resulting when tired low-country teams encountered the high altitudes of South Pass and the rough mountain trails into Utah.

Meanwhile, despite a moderately brisk business with the emigrants, trading at Fort Laramie continued to suffer from the general decline of the fur market and the competition of independent dealers in "Taos Lightning." Conditions were now ripe for the early retirement of the American Fur Co.

Fort Laramie Becomes a Military Post

For some years the Government had considered establishing military posts along the Oregon Trail for the protection of emigrants, and this site at the mouth of the Laramie had often been recommended. In December 1845, such action was proposed by President Polk and in May 1846 the Congress approved "An Act to provide for raising a regiment of Mounted Riflemen, and for establishing military stations on the route to Oregon." Funds were provided to mount and equip the troops, to defray the expenses of each station, and to compensate the Indian tribes on whose lands these stations might be erected.

The Mexican War delayed the projected building of forts on the Oregon Trail, but in 1847 a battalion of Missouri Mounted Volunteers was recruited. Early in 1848 this battalion established Fort Kearny, the first of the posts on the trail, on the south bank of the Platte near the bead of Grand Island. In November, they were mustered out, being relieved by the Mounted Riflemen.

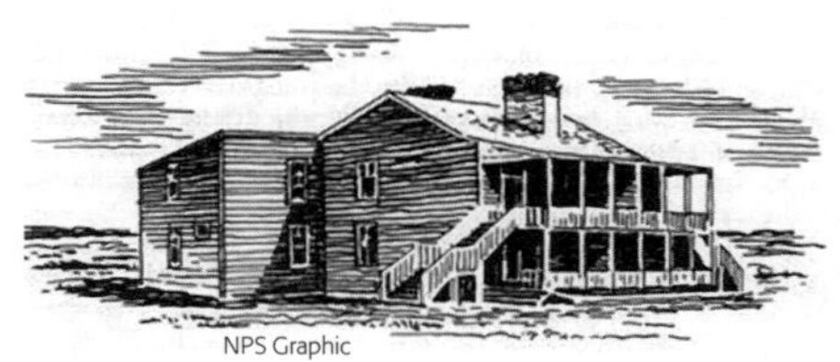
NPS Graphic

During the following winter the news of the discovery of gold in California was published throughout the land, and the resulting fevered preparations to trek westward the next spring increased the urgency of completing the chain of forts.

In March, United States Adj. Gen. Roger Jones directed Gen. D. E. Triggs at St. Louis to carry out establishment of the second post "at or near Fort Laramie, a trading station belonging to the American Fur Company." Lt. Daniel P. Woodbury, of the Corps of Engineers, was authorized to purchase the buildings of Fort Laramie "should he deem it necessary to do so." Companies A and E, Mounted Riflemen, and Company G, Sixth Infantry, were designated as the first garrison of the new post with Maj. W. F. Sanderson, Mounted Riflemen, in command.

Major Sanderson with 4 officers and 58 men of Company E, Mounted Riflemen, left Fort Leavenworth early in May and arrived at the Laramie on June 16 without incident. On June 27 he wrote to the adjutant general reporting that after making a thorough reconnaissance of the neighborhood he had found this to be the most eligible site and that at his request Lieutenant Woodbury had, on June 26, purchased Fort Laramie from Bruce Husband, agent of the American Fur Co., for $4,000. He reported further that good pine timber, limestone, hay, and dry wood were readily available and that the Laramie River furnished abundant good water for the command.

Company C, Mounted Rifles, consisting of 2 officers and 60 men, arrived at the post on July 26, and on August 12 the 2 officers and 53 men of Company G, Sixth Infantry, completed the garrison and joined in the work of preparing additional quarters.

The California Gold Rush

Meanwhile, these troops had been preceded, accompanied, and followed over the trail by some 30,000 goldseekers bound for California, a few thousand Mormons en route to Utah, and additional troops of Mounted Riflemen pushing west to establish a post at Fort Hall in Idaho.

Many of those who trekked westward from the Missouri did not even reach Fort Laramie. The dread Asiatic cholera took a terrible toll along the banks of the Platte. Fresh graves, averaging one and a half to the mile, marked the 700-mile trail from Westport Landing to the Laramie. Beyond Fort Laramie the ravages of disease abated, but already many trains were short of men and stock. These conditions and the rougher roads ahead frequently forced the abandonment of wagons, personal property, and stocks of provisions. However, not all of the westward surging throng reached Fort Laramie with surplus supplies. Many were thankful to be able to replenish dwindling supplies at the commissary as well as to obtain fresh draft animals, repair failing wagons, and mail letters to "the States."

While purchase of the adobe trading post provided the Army with a measure of shelter for men and supplies, it was far from adequate. In late June 1849, Major Sanderson reported that the entire command was already employed in cutting and hauling timber and burning lime. Stone was also quarried and a horse-powered sawmill placed in operation. By winter, a two-storied block of officers' quarters (to become known as "Old Bedlam"), a block of soldiers' quarters, a bakery, and two stables had been pushed near enough completion to be occupied.

That winter was mild and uneventful at Fort Laramie, but by early May 1850 the high tide of westward migration began. Goldseekers and homeseekers bound for California, Oregon, or Utah thronged the trails on both sides of the Platte and converged on the fort, where, by August 14, a record had been made of 39,506 men, 2,421 women, 2,609 children, 9,927 wagons, and proportionate numbers of livestock. Also, 316 deaths en route were recorded, for cholera again raged along the trail in Nebraska. The graves along the trail east of Fort Laramie were only outnumbered by the bodies of dead draft animals and piles of abandoned property westward toward South Pass.

Meager blacksmithing and repair facilities were available to the emigrants at Fort Laramie. Supplies could be purchased at the commissary and at the sutler's store, whose adobe walls were first noted that year. The sutler, John S. Tutt, also had brisk competition from numerous oldtime mountain men who set up shop along the trails nearby.

The post commander reported further progress in new construction during 1850. The stonewalled magazine was probably completed that year, "Old Bedlam" neared completion, and a two-storied barracks was begun. Lured by gold, however, troops as well as civilian artisans deserted the post to such an extent that Mexican labor was imported for building and experimental farming.

In 1851, the gold fever subsided somewhat, but Mormon emigrations increased and in all probability 20,000 emigrants trekked westward past the fort. Cholera was not epidemic and emigration was less eventful, but the fort was busy preparing to play host to other visitors.

The Fort Laramie Treaty Council, 1851

Early in 1851, the Congress had authorized holding a great treaty council with the Plains Indians to assure peaceful relations along the trails to the West. D. D. Mitchell and Thomas Fitzpatrick, the commissioners, chose Fort Laramie as the meeting place and summoned the various Indian tribes to come in by September 1. For days before that date, Indians gathered at the fort. The Sioux, Cheyennes. and Arapahoes mingled freely, but tension mounted as their enemies, the Snakes and Crows, made their appearance. Peace prevailed, however, and the sole major difficulties were a grazing problem and the late arrival of a wagon train of gifts. The countless ponies accompanying 10,000 Indians required so much forage that the vast assemblage had to move to the meadows at the mouth of Horse Creek, 30 miles east of the fort. Chiefs representing many other tribes arrived. Parades of Indian hordes in full array were held, speeches made, presents distributed, the pipe of peace smoked, and by September 17 it had been agreed that peace should reign among the red men and between them and the whites. The white men were to be free to travel the roads and hold their scattered forts, and the Indians were to receive an annuity of $50,000 in goods each year. The council was considered a great success and gave promise of a lasting peace on the plains.

Fort laramie in 1853. From a sketch by Frederick Piercy. Courtesy National Park Service.

The Emigrant Tide and Indian Troubles, 1852-53

In 1852, the emigrant tide again swelled to nearly 40,000, over 10,000 of which were Mormons. The emigrants were encouraged to depend on supplies available at Fort Laramie and other posts along the trail. A toll bridge over the Laramie River, a mile below the fort, eliminated one obstacle on the trail, and disease took a much lighter toll of lives.

Beginning in 1850, many of the emigrants on the north bank, or Mormon Trail, stopped crossing to the south bank trail at Fort Laramie and followed a rough, but shorter, route westward along the north side of the river. Those who did not cross with their wagons, however, still found the old ferry across the North Platte a welcome means of visiting the fort for mail and supplies. In 1853, this ferry figured in the first serious Indian trouble near the fort.

The Sioux were becoming alarmed by the great numbers of whites using the Oregon Trail, with resulting destruction of game, and the ravages of new diseases among the tribes. On June 15, a group of Sioux seized the ferry boat, and one of them fired on Sergeant Raymond, who recaptured it. Lt. H. B. Fleming and 23 men were dispatched to the Indian village to arrest the offender. The Indians refused to give up the culprit and fired on the soldiers. In the resulting skirmish, 3 Indians were killed, 3 wounded, and 2 taken prisoner. The Miniconjou Sioux were incensed by this action, but after a full explanation by Capt. R. Garnett, commander of the fort, they accepted their annuities from the indian agent and no further hostilities resulted that year.

In spite of this incident and considerable begging and thievery by Indians, the emigrants had been in little real danger of Indian attack. All this was changed by an unfortunate occurrence late in the summer of 1854.

The Grattan and Harney Massacres, 1854-55

Until August 18, summer emigration in 1854 appears to have been unaffected by trouble with the Indians. On that day a Mormon caravan passed a village of Brule Sioux 8 miles east of Fort Laramie, and a cow ran into the village where it was appropriated by a visiting Miniconjou brave. This matter was reported at the fort by both the Mormons and the chief of the Brules. Lt. John Grattan, Sixth Infantry, with 29 soldiers, 2 cannon, and an interpreter, was dispatched to the village to arrest the offending Indian. Unfortunately, the interpreter was drunk and the young officer was arrogant. The Indian offender refused to give himself up and a fight was precipitated in the Indian village, resulting in the annihilation of the military party.

The enraged Indians then pillaged Bordeaux's nearby trading post and helped themselves to both annuity goods and company property at the American Fur Co.'s post 3 miles up the river. Fortunately, no attack was made on the small remaining garrison of Fort Laramie to which neighboring traders and others rushed for protection. All Sioux immediately left the vicinity of the fort, and the Cheyennes and Arapahoes waited only for the distribution of treaty goods before moving away.

During the following year, Indians committed many small-scale depredations along the Oregon Trail. However, despite greatly exaggerated alarms, the emigrants of 1855 were for the most part unmolested. Meanwhile, the Army had become convinced that the Indians must be punished, and a force of 600 men under Gen. W. S. Harney marched westward from Fort Leavenworth. The Indian agent at Fort Laramie warned all friendly Indians to come to the south side of the Platte—a warning heeded by many bands. On September 2, General Harney arrived at Ash Hollow, 150 miles below Fort Laramie, and located Little Thunder's band of Brule Sioux some 6 miles north on the Blue Water. Early the next morning, after rejecting protestations of friendship by Little Thunder, his troops attacked the village from two sides, killing 86 Indians and capturing an almost equal number of women and children. At Fort Laramie, General Harney issued a stern warning to other Sioux bands, then proceeded overland through Sioux territory to establish a military post at Fort Pierre on the upper Missouri River.

Handcart to Pony Express, 1856-61

In 1856, in an effort to reduce the cost of emigration to Utah, the Mormons introduced the handcart plan. Two-wheeled handcarts, similar to those once used by street sweepers, were constructed of Iowa hickory and oak. One cart was assigned to each four or five converts who walked and pushed or pulled their carts over the long trek from the railhead at Iowa City to the Salt Lake Valley. Livestock was driven with the parties and at times 1 ox-drawn wagon to each 100 emigrants was provided to carry additional baggage and supplies.

The first handcart parties were very successful, but the last two, in 1856, started too late in the summer and were snowed in near Devil's Gate. There, more than 200 of the 1,000 or more in the two parties perished from cold and hunger before the survivors could be rescued by wagon trains sent out from Utah. From 1856 to 1860 some 3,000 Mormons made the journey to Utah in 10 handcart companies, and to these footsore travelers Fort Laramie was indeed a haven in the wilderness.

Early in 1857, the War Department decided to abandon Fort Laramie, but events forced the cancellation of the order before it could be carried out, and the fort again demonstrated its strategic importance. First, it served as a supply base for a punitive expedition led by Col. E. V. Sumner against the Cheyennes between the Platte and Arkansas Rivers. Then, as that campaign drew to an inconclusive end, the fort became a vital base for the Army which marched toward Utah that fall to subdue the reportedly rebellious Mormons.

By the next year, the Utah Campaign involved some 6,000 troops, half of whom were in or near Utah, with Fort Laramie their nearest sure source of supply.

In spite of this warlike activity, thousands of emigrants continued to roll westward by covered wagon, the great travel medium of the plains. To these the fort was a vital way station, as it was to the great firm of Russell, Majors, and Waddell, freighting contractors who carried supplies to the Army in Utah. In 1858, this enterprise alone involved 3,500 wagons, 40,000 oxen, 1,000 mules, and 4,000 men.

Beginning in 1850, mail service of varying frequency and reliability linked Fort Laramie with the States to the east and Salt Lake City to the west. Interrupted in the summer of 1857 by the Utah Campaign, a new and improved weekly mail service was organized in 1858 bringing news only 12 days old from the Missouri River to the fort.

In 1858, the discovery of gold at Cherry Creek, 200 miles south of Fort Laramie, precipitated the Colorado gold rush. That winter Fort Laramie was the nearest link between the gold miners clustered about the site of Denver, Colo., and the outside world. An informal mail express to the fort was organized and carried by old trappers.

These developments were soon overshadowed by the spectacular Pony Express. The first westbound rider galloped into Fort Laramie on April 6, 1860, just 3 days out from St. Joseph, Mo. This remarkable system of relays of riders and ponies carried up to 10 pounds of mail from St. Joseph to San Francisco in 13 days, at the rate of $5 in gold for a half-ounce letter. Later, a Government subsidy, begun on July 1, 1861, reduced the rate to $1 for one-half ounce. On that same date daily overland mail coaches began operating from St. Joseph to San Francisco, via Fort Laramie, on an 18-day schedule.

Meanwhile, the poles and wires of the first transcontinental telegraph were stretching out across the plains and mountains. Reaching Fort Laramie in September, the telegraph was completed to Salt Lake City and connected with the line from the west coast on October 24, 1861. That date also marked the end of the pony express which, although a financial failure that cost W. H. Russell his fortune, had proved the practicability of the central route to California for year-round travel.

The Civil War and the Uprising of the Plains Indians

The outbreak of the Civil War led to the reduction of garrisons at all outposts. This, coupled with a bloody uprising of the Sioux in Minnesota in 1862, inspired the Plains Indians, nursing many grievances, to go on the warpath. In the spring of 1862, many stage stations along the Platte route were raided and burned, To meet this threat, volunteer cavalry from Utah rushed east to the South Pass area, and the Eleventh Ohio Volunteer Cavalry under Col. Wm. O. Collins was ordered west to Fort Laramie. These raids

Fort Laramie in 1863. Note "Old Bedlam" to the right of the flagpole From a sketch in the University of Wyoming Archives by Bugler C. Moellman, 11th Ohio Volunteer Cavalry. Courtesy National Park Service.

also prompted the moving of the overland mail and stage route south to the Overland Trail and the establishment of Fort Halleck 120 miles to the southwest. During this period, troops at Fort Laramie continued to protect the vital telegraph line through South Pass and a still considerable volume of travelers, principally to Utah.

The next winter was fairly peaceful at Fort Laramie, and of social life at the post young Caspar Collins wrote to his mother: "They make the soldiers wear white gloves at this post, and they cut around very fashionably. A good many of the regulars are married and have their wives and families with them." He also indicated that they had a circulating library, a band, amateur theatricals, and an occasional ball. However, the dangers of the frontier were ever present, and, later that winter, troops en route from Fort Laramie to Fort Halleck encountered weather so severe that several were frozen to death.

Indians continued to steal horses from the overland mail stations, freighters, and ranchers; and incidents provoked by both whites and Indians piled up until the whole region was in a state of alarm. Efforts were made to call the Indians into the forts to treat for peace, but with little success.

At this time the difficulty of detecting the movements of Indian war parties was demonstrated at Fort Laramie. Returning from a 3-day scout, without finding a sign of hostile Indians, a large detachment of troops unsaddled their horses and let them roll on the parade grounds. Suddenly, at midday, a daring party of 30 warriors dashed through the fort, drove the horses off to the north and escaped, with all but the poorest animals, despite a 48-hour pursuit. The fort's commander, Major Wood, was described by his adjutant as "the maddest man I ever saw."

Later in 1864, after another attempt to make peace with the northern Indians had failed, Gen. R. B. Mitchell ordered the strengthening of the defenses along the road to South Pass. Several former stage and pony express stations were strengthened and garrisoned. Fort Sedgwick, near Julesburg, and Fort Mitchell, at Scottsbluff, were among those established. Fort Laramie became headquarters of a district extending from South Pass east to Mud Springs Station. Meanwhile, Indian raids along the South Platte River virtually cut off Denver from the east for 6 weeks.

Continuing efforts to seek peace with the Indians were made unsuccessful by the Sand Creek Massacre in November 1864, which united the southern bands of Sioux, Cheyenne, and Arapahoe on the warpath, Early in January 1865, they raided Julesburg, sacking the station, carrying off great quantities of foodstuffs, and almost succeeding in destroying the garrison of Fort Sedgwick. Efforts to burn out the Indians by setting a 300-mile-wide prairie fire brought them swarming back to the attack, destroying the South Platte road stations and miles of telegraph line, sacking and burning Julesburg a second time, and driving off great herds of livestock. While troops from Fort Laramie arrived at Mud Springs Station in time to fight off the Indians there, all efforts by troops from Fort Laramie and the east failed to prevent the Indians from escaping with their booty across the North Platte, near Ash Hollow.

Termination of the Civil War in April 1865 released many troops for service against the Indians, and plans were laid for extensive punitive expeditions, especially in the country to the north of the North Platte River.

In May, the fort's commander, Col. Thomas Moonlight, led 500 cavalrymen on a 450-mile foray into the Wind River Valley, but failed to find the Indians. Meanwhile, there were several raids on stations westward to South Pass. An effort to move a village of friendly Brules from Fort Laramie to Fort Kearny resulted in a fight at Horse Creek where Captain Fouts and four soldiers were killed as these Indians escaped to join the hostiles. In pursuing them, all of Colonel Moonlight's horses were stolen, and he returned to Fort Laramie in disgrace.

The major Indian raids of the summer centered on Platte Bridge Station, 130 miles above Fort Laramie, where late in July a large force of Indians wiped out a wagon train and killed 26 white men, including Lt. Caspar Collins who led a small party from the station in a valiant rescue effort.

In the meantime, a great campaign against the Indians, known as the Powder River Expedition, got under way with 2,500 men, directed by Gen. R. E. Connor. Of three columns planned to converge on the Indians in the Powder River country, the first, under Colonel Cole, started from Omaha, marched up the Loup River Valley, thence east of the Black Hills and on to the Powder River in Montana. The second, under Lieutenant Colonel Walker, left Fort Laramie, marched north along the west side of the Black Hills, and joined Colonel Cole's column as planned. The third, under General Connor, marched about 100 miles up the Platte from Fort Laramie, then north to the headwaters of Powder River where a small fort, Camp Connor, was established; thence, down the Powder River, where he destroyed the village and supplies of a large band of Arapahoes, but failed to meet the other two columns. The other commanders, lacking adequate supplies and proper knowledge of the country, lost most of their horses and mules in a September storm and, beset by fast-riding Indians, were forced to destroy the bulk of their heavy equipment. They were finally found and led to Camp Connor just in time to prevent heavy losses by starvation and possible destruction by Indians. The expedition straggled back to Fort Laramie, a failure.

Peace Talk and War on the Bozeman Trail, 1866-68

Officials at Washington now decided to try peaceful measures with the Indians of the Fort Laramie region, and General Connor was succeeded in command by General Wheaton. Emissaries were sent to the tribes, inviting them to a general peace council at Fort Laramie in June 1866.

In March of that year, Col. Henry Maynadier, then in command at Fort Laramie, reported, as auguring success of the peace council, that

Fort Laramie in 1867. From a sketch by Anton Schoenborn. Courtesy of National Park Service.

Spotted Tail, head chief of the Brule Sioux, had brought in the body of his daughter for burial among the whites at Fort Laramie. Her name was Ah-ho-ap-pa, which is Sioux for wheat flour, although modern poets have referred to her as Fallen Leaf. In the summer of 1864, she was a familiar figure at Fort Laramie. While she haughtily refused the crackers, coffee, and bacon doled out to the Indian women and children at that time, she spent long hours on a bench by the sutler'sstore watching the white man's way of life. She was particularly fond of watching the guard mount and the dress parade, and the officer in charge was often especially decked out in sash and plumes for her benefit. She refused to marry one of her own people, attempted to learn English, and told her people they were fools for not living in houses and making peace with the whites. When the Sioux went on the warpath in 1864, however, Spotted Tail and his daughter were with them and spent the next year in the Powder River country. There the hard life weakened her, and she sickened and died during the following cold winter.

The grave of Spotted Tail's daughter near Fort Laramie, about 1881.

Courtesy Wyoming Historical Department.

Having promised to carry out her express wish to be buried at Fort Laramie, her father led the funeral procession on a journey of 260 miles. Colonel Maynadier responded gallantly to Spotted Tail's request. In a ceremony which combined all the pageantry of the military and the primitive tradition of the Sioux, her body was placed in a coffin on a raised platform a half mile north of the parade grounds. Thus, a long step had been taken toward winning the friendship of a great chief.

By June, a good representation of Brule and Oglala Sioux being present, the commissioners set about negotiating a treaty. In the meantime, unfortunately, the War Department sent out an expedition instructed to open the Bozeman Trail through the Powder River country to the Montana gold mines. Colonel Carrington and his troops arrived at Fort Laramie in the midst of the negotiations and caused serious unrest among the Indians. One chief commented, "Great Father send us presents and wants new road, but white chief goes with soldiers to steal road before Indian say yes or no," and a large faction, led by Red Cloud and Man-Afraid-of-His-Horses, withdrew in open opposition to all peace talk. Nevertheless, the remaining Indians agreed to a treaty which provided for the opening of the Bozeman Trail.

In late June the troops under Colonel Carrington marched up the trail, garrisoned Camp Connor (later moved and named Fort Reno), and began building Fort Phil Kearny at the foot of the Bighorn Mountains and Fort C. F. Smith farther north in Montana. Immediately, it became evident that the peace treaty was meaningless. Fort Phil Kearny was the scene of almost daily Indian attacks on traders, wagon trains, wood-cutting parties, and troops. These attacks were climaxed on December 21 when Capt. William Fetterman and 80 men were led into an ambush and annihilated by Indians led by Crazy Horse and Red Cloud. The fort and its remaining garrison were in danger of being overwhelmed, and the nearest aid lay at Fort Laramie, 236 miles away. At midnight, John "Portugee" Phillips, trader and scout, slipped out into a blizzard on the colonel's favorite horse and in 4 days made his way across the storm-swept, Indian-infested plains to Fort Laramie in one of the truly heroic rides of American history. While his gallant mount lay dying on the parade ground, Phillips interrupted a gay Christmas night party in "Old Bedlam" to deliver his message, and a relief expedition was soon on its way.

The severe weather made an attempted winter campaign against the Indians unsuccessful, and there was no important fighting until summer. On August 2, 1867, the Indians again attacked a woodcutting party near Fort Phil Kearny, but the small detachment led by Captain Powell was armed with the new 1866 Springfield breech-loading rifles and fought off repeated charges by the Indians in the famous Wagon Box Fight.

The Treaty of 1868

Again, the peace advocates in Washington were in the ascendancy, and in the summer of 1867 the Congress provided a commission to treat with the Indians, but authorized recruiting an army of 4,000 men if peace was not attained. Treaties with the southern tribes were concluded at Fort Larned in October, and the commissioners came to Fort Laramie in November to treat with the northern tribes. However, few came in and the hostiles, led by Red Cloud, sent word that no treaty was possible until the forts on the Bozeman Trail and in the valley of the Powder River were abandoned to the Indians. They did agree to cease hostilities and to come to Fort Laramie the next spring. In April 1868, the commissioners came again to Fort Laramie and were prepared to grant the Indians' demands, including abandonment of the Bozeman Trail. By late May, both the Brule and Oglala Sioux had signed the treaty, but Red Cloud refused to sign until the troops had left the Powder River country and his warriors had burned the abandoned Fort Phil Kearny to the ground.

This treaty gave the Indians all of what is now South Dakota west of the Missouri River as a reservation. It also gave them control and hunting rights in the great territory north of the North Platte River and east of the Bighorn Mountains as unceded Indian lands. The Indian agencies were to be built on the Missouri River. Many of the Indians, however, objected to giving up trading at Fort Laramie as had been their custom, and, in 1870, a temporary agency for Red Cloud's band was established on the North Platte River 30 miles below the fort, at the present Nebraska-Wyoming line. Finaly, in 1873, after he and other chiefs had twice been taken to Washington and New York to view the numbers and power of the white men, Red Cloud agreed to having his-agency moved north to a site on White River away from Fort Laramie and the Platte Road.

In the meantime, peace prevailed on the high plains, and, in 1872, it was reported that not a white man was killed in the department of the Platte.

Later in 1873, however, the attitude of many Indians toward their agents at the Red Cloud and Spotted Tail agencies became so hostile that the agents requested that troops be stationed at the agencies. Although the Indians protested this as a violation of their treaty rights, Camp Robinson and Camp Sheridan were established at these respective agencies in 1874. At the same time, funds were obtained for an iron bridge over the North Platte at Fort Laramie. Its completion, early in 1876, gave the troops there ready access to the Indian country.

The Fight for the Black Hills

Rumors of gold in the Black Hills of South Dakota had persisted for many years, which induced the Government to send an expedition under Col. George A. Custer from Fort Abraham Lincoln on the upper Missouri to investigate the area. Proceeding without opposition from the Indians, the expedition confirmed the presence of gold in the hills and sent out word of their discoveries to Fort Laramie in August 1874. The resulting rush of prospecting parties was at first forbidden by the military, who rounded up several and imprisoned some of theirleaders at Fort Laramie, while other parties were attacked by the Indians for flagrant violation of the treaty of 1868.

A second expedition, led by Col. R. I. Dodge and Prof. W. P. Jenney, set out from Fort Laramie the next spring to explore and evaluate the gold deposits in the Black Hills. Miners also thronged the hills, and efforts to make them await negotiations with the Indians were only partly successful. Meanwhile, the Government did make an effort to buy the Black Hills from the Sioux; but the Indians, led by Chief Spotted Tail, set a justly high price on the area, which the Government refused to meet. Moreover, the wild bands of Sitting Bull and other chiefs refused to sell at any price and warned the whites to stay out. No longer restrained by the Army, the miners now swarmed into the hills, which became a powder keg.

Ignoring existing treaties, the Government decided to force the wild Sioux onto their reservation, and when the order for them to come in was not instantly complied with, the Army prepared for action. A double enveloping campaign was planned, to be led by Gen. George Crook with troops based at Fort Laramie and Fort Fetterman, and by Gen. Alfred H. Terry with Custer's Seventh Cavalry from Fort Abraham Lincoln and Col. John Gibbon's command from Fort Ellis, Mont. In March, Crook marched north from Fort Fetterman, 80 miles northwest of Fort Laramie, with 12 companies of soldiers. His cavalry surprised a large village of Sioux and Cheyenne on the Little Powder River in Montana, but Crazy Horse rallied the Indians and forced the troops to retreat. Again in late May, Crook moved north with 20 companies of men plus 300 friendly Shoshones and Crows, and once more, on June 17, on the Rosebud, he was defeated by a great array of warriors led by Crazy Horse. Retreating to his supply camp, Crook again decided to send for reinforcements.

Meanwhile, General Terry's command had marched west from Fort Abraham Lincoln and met Colonel Gibbon's detachment on the Yellowstone River. Again dividing his forces, Terry sent Custer and the entire Seventh Cavalry up the Rosebud River, while he and Gibbon, with 12 companies of infantry and four troops of cavalry, proceeded up the Bighorn River.

On the morning of June 25, 1876, Custer's scouts sighted the Indian village in the valley of the Little Bighorn. He divided his command to attack the village from three directions. The Indians, however, first met Maj. Marcus A. Reno's contingent of three troops in the afternoon in overwhelming numbers and forced them to retreat to a defensive position, where they were joined by a similar detachment under Capt. Frederick W. Benteen and the pack train. Meanwhile, the great part of the Indians had swung away to meet and wipe out Custer's personal command of five troops. Again the warriors attacked Reno, but since he was on favorable ground he was able to fight them off until the next day when their scouts detected the approach of General Terry. Firing the grass, the Indians moved off into the Bighorn Mountain, leaving over 260 soldiers dead on the battlefield. It was an empty victory, however, as the Indians were compelled to scatter to hunt for food. By winter, reinforced armies under General Crook and Colonel Miles had defeated bands led by Dull Knife and Crazy Horse, forcing them to return to the reservation and surrender, while Sitting Bull's band fled north into Canada.

In the meantime, the Government had decreed that no annuities should be paid to the hostile bands or to any Sioux until they had ceded the coveted Black Hills to the whites. A commission succeeded in getting the Sioux to sign an agreement effecting that end when it became law in February 1877.

The Northern Cheyennes were taken south to the Indian territory in 1877, but they broke away the next year, led by Dull Knife and Little Wolf, and headed north for their old home in the Dakotas. After hard campaigning by troops from Fort Laramie and other posts, many of Dull Knife's band were killed and all others were captured. These, however, were permitted to remain on the northern reservation.

The rush to the Black Hills gave new importance to Fort Laramie, for, with its bridge across the North Platte, it was the gateway to the gold-mining region via the trail leading north from Cheyenne, whose merchants advertised the route as being well guarded. Although the troops from the fort were virtually all engaged in the effort to combat Indian depredations and provide escorts, travel to the gold fields was in fact extremely hazardous. Regular service by the Cheyenne and Black Hills stage line was impossible, until conditions improved in the fall of 1876. But no sooner had Indian raids on the trail lessened than the activities of "road agents" threatened the traveler. Even armored coaches with shotgun guards failed to deter the bandits seeking gold shipments.

Last Years of the Army Post, 1877-90

Beginning in the late 1870's, other changes took place around Fort Laramie. With the Indians removed to reservations, ranchers and other settlers came in, and great herds of cattle replaced the buffalo on the Wyoming plains. To many of these settlers the fort on the Laramie was a supply center, as well as insurance against Indian outbreaks and lawless white men.

During these same years, Fort Laramie was assuming a false air of permanence as many of the old buildings of frame, log, and adobe construction were replaced by sturdy new structures with lime-concrete walls. A water system changed the parade ground from a gravelly flat to a tree-shaded greensward. The last cavalry unit to be stationed at the fort rode away in 1883 with Col. Wesley Merritt. Part of the Seventh Infantry, commanded by Colonel Gibbon, then garrisoned the post.

Fort Laramie's importance had been threatened by construction of the Union Pacific Railroad 100 miles to the south. Its fate was now sealed by construction, in the late 1880's, of the Northwestern Line 50 miles to the north. This made Fort Robinson the logical guardian of the Indian reservations to the north, and by 1886 Col. Henry Merriam, then commanding officer of the Seventh Infantry and Fort Laramie, was ready to agree that further development of the old post was unwise. Not until August 31, 1889, however, was abandonment of the proud old fort decreed. At the request of Wyoming's Governor Warren, troops remained at the post until March 2, 1890, when the last two companies of the Seventh Infantry marched away. A few men were left to ship movable property, while a detachment from Fort Robinson dismantled some of the structures and on April 9, 1890, auctioned off the buildings and fixtures. At that auction, Lt. C. M. Taylor of the Ninth Cavalry sold the buildings of historic Fort Laramie at prices ranging from $2.50 to $100. Thirty-five lots of buildings and much miscellaneous furniture and fixtures brought a total of $1,395.

The Homesteaders Take Over

In June 1890, the military reservation of some 35,000 acres was turned over to the Department of the Interior and opened to homesteading. John Hunton was appointed custodian of the abandoned military reservation for the General Land Office. He first came to Fort Laramie in 1867 to work for the sutler. Later, he became a ranch operator, and in 1888 he succeeded John London as post trader. Hunton was a major buyer at the final auction and managed to homestead the northwest side of the old parade grounds of the fort, continuing to operate the sutler's store briefly, and living next door in the former officers' quarters for nearly 30 years.

Another of the major purchasers at the auction was one Joe Wilde, who also homesteaded part of the fort grounds, including the commissary storehouse and the cavalry barracks. He converted the buildings into a combination hotel, dance hall, and saloon and operated them as a social center for North Platte Valley residents for over 25 years. The west end of the parade grounds and the site of the old adobe trading post which the Army had demolished in 1862 was homesteaded by the widow of Thomas Sandercock, a civilian engineer at the fort, who made her home in the officers' quarters which had been built in 1870.

A dozen or more buildings used by these civilian owners were preserved with some alterations; but the bulk of the buildings were soon dismantled for lumber by their purchasers, and the old fort became a part of many a ranch home, homestead shack, or barn.

Efforts to Preserve the Fort

John Hunton and a few other citizens recognized the historic importance of the old fort and expressed regret at its decay. In 1913, despairing anything better, they erected a monument commemorating its long service as a military post on the Oregon Trail.

Lands and buildings changed hands. Absentee landlords, tenants, and souvenir hunters contributed much to the destruction of the historic buildings and to the scattering of priceless relics. Creation of the Wyoming Historical Landmark Commission in 1927 initiated efforts to achieve public ownership and to protect this historic site. Ten years later the State of Wyoming appropriated funds for the purchase and donation to the Federal Government of 214 acres of land, including the surviving buildings. By Presidential proclamation, this became Fort Laramie National Monument on July 16, 1938, under the administration of the National Park Service of the United States Department of the Interior.

H Visitor's Center Interpretive Signs

Fort William 1834-1841

The mountain man was a frontiersman of the first order-an adventurer, loner, and a part-time diplomat. But he was also an entrepreneur, seeking to make a living in the perilous Rocky Mountain fur trade, where many of those who went into the mountains were never heard from again.

Conflicts between Indians and trappers were relatively rare. Instead, mountain men often took Indian wives and established themselves in Indian families. Trade was mutually beneficial and, for the most part, honestly conducted.

Competition for Indian trade did not become ruthless and unscrupulous until large fur trading corporations arrived, each company trying to drive the others out of business. Fort William, the first fort at the confluence of the North Platte and Laramie Rivers, was established in 1834 in this atmosphere of competition and company rivalry.

Though the heyday of the fur trade lasted only 20 years, the changes it wrought were immense. The mountain men were truly the vanguard of the great migration West. The letters, reports, and tall tales that filtered east excit-

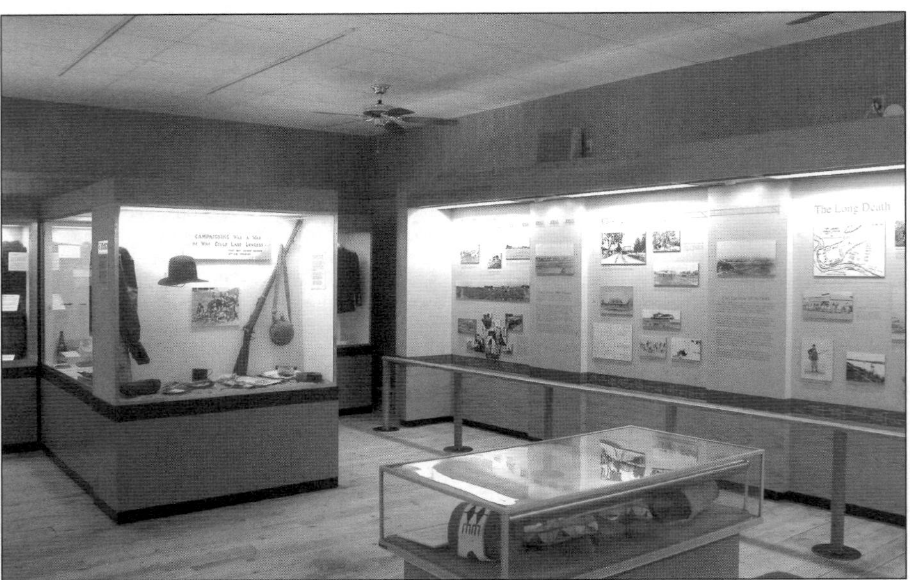

Fort Laramie Museum and Visitor's Center

ed a nation to the seemingly limitless land, wealth, and possibilities that awaited in the West.

Fort John 1841-1849

By the late 1830s, the mountain men had opened trails through the Rocky Mountains and shown the practicality of wagon travel over the Platte River route. Missionaries, scientists, explorers, and sportsmen began filtering west. Their letters, reports, and stories painted a glowing picture of the paradise of Oregon and California. These glorified accounts of life beyond the Rocky Mountains filled the imaginations of the American people, inspiring the greatest mass overland migration the world had ever seen.

Many emigrants gave up everything they knew and owned to make the journey west. The goodbyes said to family and friends were known to be final, for in all likelihood, the emigrants would never return to see loved ones again. The travelers then plunged into the great unknown, into a wild and forbidding country called the "great American desert."

The travails of the journey were many. People and animals were pushed to their limits as they struggled to cross desert and mountain before thirst, snow, and starvation overtook them. Suffocating dust, quagmires of mud, violent thunderstorms, heat, and cold were everyday occurrences. In spite of severe hardship, most persevered and completed the journey. Only a few "saw the elephant" and turned back.

At Fort John, the second Fort Laramie, farmers heading for Oregon, Mormons seeking religious freedom near the Great Salt Lake, and argonauts bound for the California gold fields, mingled with mountain men from another era, and Indians, through whose land the emigrants passed. Tlhe Oregon, California, and Mormon nation moving west.

Fort Laramie 1849-1859

By the 1850s, the trickle of westbound emigrants had become a flood. Few episodes in history can rival the drama that unfolded along the emigrant routes. Tens of thousands of people choked the dusty trails with masses of bawling farm and draft animals.

Destruction followed in their wake. As thousands of wagons passed over the trails, game was killed and driven off, depriving the Indians of subsistence. Emigrants' livestock destroyed the grass for several miles in all directions. The trail corridor scarred the land, and remains visible over one hundred and fifty years after its carving.

Soldiers and emigrants desired good relations with the Indians, and in 1851 a peace council secured safe passage for travelers and compensated the Indians for their trail-related losses. The Fort Laramie Treaty of 1851, called the "Horse Creek Treaty," was the largest known gathering of Northern Plains tribes in history. More than 10,000 people from virtually all of the plains Indian nations gathered at Horse Creek to make peace with the whites and end intertribal warfare. The headmen of each tribe and representatives of the U.S. government met and pledged peace to each other from that time forward. Unfortunately, the peace would last but a few short years.

The Platte River Ferry incident and the Grattan Fight brought peace to an abrupt end, and the resulting Northern Plains Indian wars would rage for the next 25 years. By the late 1850s, waning emigration and rising tensions with the Indians had changed Fort operations against the Northern Plains tribes.

Fort Laramie 1859-1869

The 1860s were tumultuous years for the nation and Fort Laramie. On the eve of the Civil War, Fort Laramie stood as a vital supply and communications link between the east and west coasts.

Almost 500,000 Americans now lived west of the Rocky Mountains. Rapid, dependable communication between east and west have become a necessity. The first transcontinental express mail service was launched in the spring of 1860; the celebrated Pony Express. Yet shortly after the first hoofbeats were heard, workmen began stringing miles of galvanized iron wire to tie the nation together. With the completion of the Transcontinental Telegraph in October, 1861, messages now flashed almost instantly from shore to shore.

At the outbreak of the Civil War, troops were withdrawn from most western forts and sent east. Volunteer units at Fort Laramie faced the daunting task of keeping hundreds of miles of telegraph line and the Central Overland mail route open and operating.

Between 1864 and 1868, Indian attacks on miltary outposts, telegraph stations, mail stages, and civilians increased. The opening of the Bozeman Trail infringed on Indian territorial rights. When three new forts were built along the trail in 1866, the Indians struck back. By 1868, Red Cloud and his Sioux warriors had forced the abandonment of the "bloody Bozeman" and driven the federal government to the peace table once more.

The Fort Laramie treaties of 1868 held the promise of lasting peace on the plains. Resrvations were organized, and promises were made to keep out trespassers. Once again, peace was fleeting. The pattern of empty promises and broken treaties continued.

Fort Laramie 1869-1879

The opening years of th 1870s offered hope of lasting peace on the Northern Plains. Destruction of the buffalo herds by hide hunters left the Indians with little choice but to settle on the new reservations in Dakota, where food and supplies were promised. Despite Red Cloud's pleas to remain near Fort Laramie, the government moved his agency to the White River in Nebraska. After 1873, Fort Laramie was no longer the traditional center of trade between the whites and the Sioux.

News of gold in the Black Hills electrified the nation in 1874. Despite government attempts to preserve Indain treaty rights, miners poured into the region. Submitting to public pressure, in the spring of 1876, the army launched the Bighorn—Yellowstone Expedition to force the Indians back to their agencies. Several major battles ensued, culminating in the defeat of Lieutenant Colonel George A. Custer at the Little Bighorn. The fate of a people was sealed.

Relentlessly pursued by the army throughout the following winter and summer, bands of warriors surrendered one by one. The Indians were no longer a proud, free roaming people, but starving, ragtag refugees, and prisoners in their own land.

By the late 1870s, the Northern Plains Indian Wars were essentially over. Settlers now made their homes on former Indian lands, and ranchers acquired great expanses of territory, where cattle replaced the buffalo. Fort Laramie was no longer a strategic outpost in the wilderness, but a fort whose military purpose was waning, a remnant of the old frontier.

Fort Laramie: 1879-1890

The 1880s were the golden years of Fort Laramie. A false sense of permanence prevailed as major building and public works projects were undertaken. Many old frame, log, adobe, and stone buildings were replaced by new lime grout structures. Streetlights, board walks, picket fences, and birdbaths lined Officers' Row.

While the enlisted soldiers were occupied with routine drill, fatigue details, and occasional field maneuvers, officers spent many hours socializing, hunting, fishing, picnicking, and staging amateur theatricals. By the mid-1880s, a railhead within thirty miles of Fort Laramie brought all the amenities of late Victorian life.

The last cavalry unit rode away in 1883, leaving only the infantry to garrison the fort. In

1886, the construction of a new railroad near Fort Robinson, Nebraska, made the closure of Fort Laramie inevitable. On August 31, 1889, General Orders 69 ordered the abandonment of the "Grand Old Post." The remaining buildings and land were sold at public auction and in April, 1890 the army marched away for the last time.

1890, the end of an era: Fort Laramie abandoned, Wyoming proclaimed a state, the last major Indian conflict on the Northern Plains at Wounded Knee Creek, and the Superintendent of the Census declared that the American frontier had ceased to exist.

Fort Laramie 1890-Present

Life continued at Fort Laramie after the 1890 public auction. The old post was homesteaded by three local families and the fort remained the social and economic center of the area's civilian community.

In 1900, a rail line was built on the north side of the North Platte River, and a new community was established, taking the name "Fort Laramie." As the town grew, the importance of the old fort declined, and time took its toll on the remaining structures. A few early visionaries recognized the historic importance of Fort Laramie. In 1937, their preservation efforts convinced the state of Wyoming to purchase 214 acres and the old post's surviving buildings. Since 1938, the National Park Service has preserved and interpreted this historic site.

We hold the past in trust for the future. Thanks to the far-sighted preservation efforts of a few concerned citizens, Fort Laramie is as alive today with visitors, researchers, staff, and neighbors as it ever was as a trading post, emigrant way station, fort, and homestead center. They saved this place for us, we must save it for the future.

Fort Laramie and the Fur Trade

In the early 1800s the wealth of the wilderness was measured in the furs of wild animals, and the beaver was the most important. During that period a new breed of western explorer appeared upon the scene, the mountain man. Essentially a trapper of beaver, he was a staunch individualist and romantic adventurer who roamed the mountains and explored the rivers.

The river below, once abundant with beaver was named for one such trapper-explorer, a French-Canadian, Jacques La Ramee, (Laramie). His arrow-pierced body was found in the spring of 1821 near the mouth of the river that bears his name.

In the 1830s silk replaced beaver in fashionable hat styles. This combined with the increasing scarcity of beaver, signaled the end of the trapping era and the mountain's rendezvous, (where trappers and traders met to exchange furs for goods). A flourishing trade in buffalo hides and robes soon took its place and the need for permanent trading posts to store the bulky hides became apparent. Thousands of buffalo hides were shipped east from Fort Laramie in the 1840's.

In 1834, during the decline of the beaver trade, Robert Campbell and William Sublette established the first Fort Laramie, christened Fort William, the small fort constructed of cottonwood logs remained in existence for eight years. Fort William was then replaced by Fort John (1841). Like its predecessor it was commonly known as Fort Laramie.

Fort Laramie and the Westward Movement

In addition to being an important fur trading post and, later, a strategic military installation, Fort Laramie was the most significant outpost of civilization on the Oregon Trail.

The first (true) covered wagon party embarked from what is now Kansas City, Missouri in 1841. Between 1841 and 1867 an estimated 350,000 emigrants crossed the continent on their way to Oregon, California and the Salt Lake Valley.

Fort Laramie was a place to replenish supplies, repair wagons, mail letters (home) and acquire fresh animals for the trail ahead. Here many abandoned their cumbersome wagons and continued the journey with pack mules or on foot. Others lightened their loads, keeping only bare essentials.

As you look across the river you will notice a large, flat, open area. This was a choice campsite for weary travelers.

Imagine, (as far as you can see) covered wagons, cattle and horses grazing and the activities of the evening camp—men unyoking oxen and discussing the trail ahead, women and children building fires and making preparation for the evening meal.

Construction of the first transcontinental railroad in 1867 diminished animal powered overland travel along the trail and led to its eventual abandonment.

H Fort Laramie National Historic Site Interpretive Signs

Fort Laramie National Historic Site

Sawmill

Through a succession of accidental fires, Fort Laramie's sawmills gained a reputation of being ill-fated. The lime-grout building erected upon this site in 1887 was the last of several such structures that sheltered steam engines used for sawing wood and pumping water.
Site of Cheyenne-Deadwood Stage Station

Cheyenne 93 Miles (arrow pointing to the right)

213 Miles (arrow pointing to the left)
Deadwood

The Rustic Hotel

The Rustic Hotel opened in 1876. During that year it probably provided the best accommodations for travelers between Cheyenne and the Black Hills. It also served as a station for the Cheyenne-Black Hills State and Express Line.

By 1883, when this photograph was taken one lady traveler found "horrid little bugs" in the sheets. Three years later, the stage station corrals were polluting the fort's water supply and had to be removed.

The Post Hospital

These walls are all that remain of a twelve-bed hospital built on this in 1873-1874. The 1888 photograph shows the hospital in better days, with spacious verandas, flower gardens and picket-fenced yard. Posing in the garden is Post Surgeon Brechemin and enlisted men of the Medical Department. The site selected for the hospital had been used as a post cemetery prior to 1867. Six burials found within the lines of construction were first moved to a nearby cemetery, and finally to Fort McPherson National Cemetery in Nebraska.

Noncommissioned Officers Quarters

A six-unit apartment, built on this site in 1884, was the best housing available for married enlisted men until the abandonment of the post in 1890. Pictured in 1885, it usually housed ranking NCOs such as Chief Post Musician, Post Quartermaster Sergeant or Regimental Quartermaster Serveant.

Post Ordnance Sergeant Schnyder and his family lived in the next-to-last apartment during the final two years of his 35-year Fort Laramie residency.

Site of Workshops, Storehouses and Stables

Extending from here to the river was a succession of storehouses and workshops that supplied goods and services to the army. As much as 500,000 pounds of grain were stored here in addition to coal, oil, paint, hay, wood and other quartermaster supplies.

Since soldiers were seldom skilled workers, as many as 100 civilians were hired in Denver, Omaha and Cheyenne to serve as wheelwrights, blacksmiths, carpenters, saddlers and laborers. These men received rations and shelter in addition to $30 to $100 a month.

To the left once stood stables, a constant source of aggravation to the shovel-wielding soldier.

Cavalry Barracks

The building before you is the only surviving enlisted men's barracks at Fort Laramie. The building proper was completed in late 1874 and was designed to provide quarters and other needed support facilities for two companies of soldiers. The veranda, although originally planned, was not added until 1883. As constructed the entire second floor was made up of only two equal, large rooms. These were the company dormitory bays or squad rooms where the enlisted soldiers lived. Each could house about sixty soldiers or one company. On the first floor below each squad room, the building was divided into a kitchen, messroom, cook's room, storage room, wash room, library, armory and orderly room for the N.C.O. 's and non-commissioned officers room.

The Sutler's House

The Victorian-style cottage, built in 1863 and shown in this 1868 photograph, must have been a strange sight on the untamed Northern Plains.

Sometime between 1875 and 1882, the cottage was replaced by a much larger lime-grout structure, used by the Sutler or his agents until the abandonment of the post in 1890.

Commissary Storehouse

This building was completed in 1884. It was built as a commissary storage facility. As such it would have been primarily divided into two large storerooms: one for meat and one for flour, rice, and beans. Three or four smaller rooms would have been used as offices, an "issue room" and a storage room for canned goods. This building also had a partial cellar with a trap door for use with a hand-operated elevator. Rations and other official Army food items were issued from this building. A commissary officer and sergeant ran the operation.

The Post Bakeries

Four different bakeries operated successively at Fort Laramie. The remains of two bakeries stand before you. The nearer, built in 1876, was used until 1884, when it was converted into a school. A bakery built upon the far site operated from 1884 until 1890. Army bakers produced one eighteen-ounce loaf daily for each man at the fort. With a garrison numbering as many as 700 men, imagine the production that resulted!

Site of Army Bridge
The Laramie River was unpredictable and unchecked by dams. High water during the spring of the year often damaged or washed away existing bridges; therefore, from 1853 to post abandonment in 1890 the river was spanned by several successive bridges on or near this site. The first was constructed by a private firm

Fort Laramie and The Fur Trade
In the early 1800s the wealth of the wilderness was measured in the furs of wild animals, and the beaver was the most important. During that period a new breed of western explorer appeared upon the scene, the mountain man. Essentially a trapper of beaver, he was a staunch individualist and romantic adventurer who roamed the mountains and explored the rivers.

The river below, once abundant with beaver was named for one such trapper-explorer, a French-Canadian, Jacques La Ramee (Laramie). His arrow-pierced body was found in the spring of 1821 near the mouth of the river that bears his name.

In the 1830s silk replaced beaver in fashionable hat styles. This combined with the increasing scarcity of beaver, signaled the end of the trapping era and the mountain's rendezvous, (where trappers and traders met to exchange furs for goods). A flourishing trade in buffalo hides and robes soon took its place and the need for permanent trading posts to store the bulky hides became apparent. Thousands of buffalo hides were shipped east from Fort Laramie, in the 1840s.

In 1834, during the decline of the beaver trade, Robert Campbell and William Sublette established the first Fort Laramie, christened Fort William. The small fort constructed of cottonwood logs remained in existence for eight years. Fort William was then replaced by Fort John (1841). Like its predecessor it was commonly known as Fort Laramie.

Officers' Quarters
Here stood a frame duplex built in 1858.

Ice Houses
During the winter months ice blocks were cut from the Laramie and Platte Rivers and hauled to ice houses at this and other sites. Thick walled and partially underground, the frame or sod structures could each store as much as 150 tons of ice. Ice distribution began with the onset of warm weather and, if carefully rationed, ice could last until September.

Officers, enlisted men and laundresses, as well as the hospital and butchershops, were among the recipients. The post commander determined who could receive ice and in what order and amount. Immediately after reveille, often on alternating days, those entitled could come to the ice houses to receive their shares.

At left is the headquarters circular of April 20, 1876, announcing the first of ice and determining a generous daily allotment.

CO.'s Chicken Coop (Built in 1881)
High ranking officers commonly kept chickens for their own use. The consumption of chickens and eggs provided a welcome change from meals of wild game and tough army beef. Individual soldiers and cooks utilizing company funds could purchase chickens and eggs from civilians. However, such items were a luxury which seldom appeared on the enlisted man's table.

Refinement at Fort Laramie
Fort Laramie began as a dusty, drab frontier outpost as pictured above in the 1868 photograph. However, by the 1880's, the Army had embarked upon a major cleanup and improvement campaign. The delightful results are evident in the 1887 view—trees and grass, gaslights, boardwalks, picket fences and vine-covered verandas, modern, comfortable quarters... even birdbaths!

Officers Quarters
This 1885 photograph (on plaque) shows the buildings constructed on this site in 1881. Previous adobe structures, built in 1855, were left standing as rear wings. On the far left was the Commanding Officer's residence. Between 1881 and 1890 it was successively occupied by the families of Colonels Merritt, Gibbon, and Merriam and the only one equipped with inside plumbing, with a full bathroom upstairs and water pipes into the kitchen. The other two buildings were customarily occupied by Lieutenants or Captains and their families.

Old Bedlam
This graceful old structure, built in 1849, is the oldest standing building in Wyoming. It was nicknamed "Old Bedlam" because of boisterous sounds supposedly heard while it was occupied by bachelor officers.

Shown in an 1889 photograph, "Old Bedlam" is generally regarded as a Bachelor Officers Quarters. However, the left half was used as Post Headquarters and Commanders Apartment in the 1860's, and at various times, the building was occupied by married officers.

John (Portugee) Phillips
Here on December 25, 1866 John (Portugee) Phillips finished his 236 mile ride to obtain troops for the relief of Fort Phil Kearny after the Fetterman Massacre.

Magazine (Built in 1849)
Restored here to the 1850-1862 period, the magazine is among the oldest surviving structures at Fort Laramie. It was during this early period that George Balch, 1st Lieutenant Ordnance Corps, sent the following report to the Assistant Adjutant General:

"I find all the ordnance property with the exception of the field guns and their cartridges stored in the magazine arranged with much order and preserved with great care. The different kinds of ammunition piled together in such positions as to be easily reached, and the artillery implements and equipments, the small arms and their equipments properly disposed of on shelves and in boxes."

Infantry Barracks
In answer to the perpetual need for housing, construction of an enlisted men's barracks commenced at the opposite end of these foundation ruins. The barracks were extended in this direction as more men were assigned. Kitchens, mess halls, laundress' quarters and latrines were built behind (to your left).

Home to about 150 men, the two-story barracks were sparsely furnished. Bunks, made of wood by the quartermaster, were two tiers high with each tier accommodating two men. The Indian wars term "Bunkie," referring to a soldier's closest comrade, derived from this sleeping arrangement.

The two-story barracks were replaced in 1868 by a one-story barracks.

"Officers Row"
This 1889 winter scene (on plaque) shows buildings along the west side of the Parade Ground which housed Fort Laramie's officer complement—hence "Officers Row."

Right to left, the "Burt" House, the "Surgeon's" quarters, two adobe quarters and "Old Bedlam".

The surgeon's eminent position in the social line at Fort Laramie is reflected in this 1888 view (left).

The Sutler's Store
Parts of this building date from the earliest periods at Fort Laramie. The adobe portion on the left, built in 1849, housed the Post Trader's Store.

In 1852, the right section was added and used at various times as the Sutler's office, the Post Office and a game room. The photograph shows an 1877 view.

The rear portion was built in 1883. The Enlisted Men's Bar and a rustic saloon were on the right; The Officers Club on the left housed the Sutler's Store in 1875. (Courtesy University of Wyoming Archives and Western History Dept.)

Fort Laramie Army Bridge
This bridge was constructed in 1875. It is believed to be the oldest existing military bridge west of the Mississippi River.

Once the then-broad and turbulent North Platte River was spanned, the Cheyenne to Deadwood Route was considered the best road to the Black Hills gold fields. The bridge also influenced the establishment of the famous Cheyenne and Black Hills Stage and Express Line. The bridge remained in use until 1958.

Fort Laramie and The Transcontinental Telegraph
The transcontinental telegraph reached Fort Laramie from the east on August 5, 1861. From then until May, 1869, Fort Laramie was a major station on the telegraph line. Soldiers from Fort Laramie protected the line, made repairs, and operated remote repeater stations from Julesburg, Colorado (150 miles to the east) to South Pass, Wyoming (300 miles to the west).

Electrical Engineering Milestone Transcontinental Telegraph
Between July 4 and October 24, 1861, a telegraph line was constructed by the Western Union Telegraph Co. between St. Joseph, Missouri, and Sacramento, California, thereby completing the first high speed communication link between the Atlantic and Pacific coasts. This service met the critical demand for fast communication between these two areas. This telegraph line operated until May, 1869, when it was replaced by a multi-wire system constructed with the Union Pacific and Central Pacific Railroad Lines.

Grand Teton National Park

Youngest Range in the Rockies

Mt. Moran. National Park Service Photo.

Towering more than a mile above the valley of Jackson Hole, the Grand Teton rises to 13,770 feet. Twelve Teton peaks reach above 12,000 feet and support a dozen mountain glaciers. The west side of the range slopes gently, showing the angle of tilt of the Earth's crust. The Teton Range is the youngest range in the Rockies and displays some of North America's oldest rocks.

History of Grand Teton National Park

The Earliest Visitors

Archeological studies established human occupation of Jackson Hole for at least 11,000 years. Knowledge of early people is extremely limited. Data suggests that they used the area from spring to fall, based on seasonal availability of resources. Prehistoric people crossed the passes into Jackson Hole en route to seasonal hunting grounds in the region. In historic times, Indian tribes such as the Shoshoni, Gros Ventre, Flathead and Blackfeet knew the Teton country.

Days of Mountain Men

The splendor of the Teton Mountains first dazzled fur traders. Although evidence is inconclusive, John Colter probably explored the area in 1808. By the 1820s, mountain men followed wildlife and Indian trails through Jackson Hole and trapped beaver in the icy waters of the valley.

The term "hole" was coined by fur trappers of the 1820s to describe a high altitude plateau ringed by mountains. Thus, Jackson Hole is the entire valley, 8 to 15 miles wide and 40 miles long. The valley was named for David E. Jackson, a trapper who reputedly spent the winter of 1829 along the shore of Jackson Lake.

After the decline of the fur trade in the late 1830s, America forgot Jackson Hole until the military and civilian surveys of the 1860s and 1870s. Members of the Hayden Survey named many of the area's features.

The First Tourists

The region acquired a national reputation for its splendid hunting and fishing in the 1880s and 1890s. Many settlers supplemented their incomes by serving as guides and packers for wealthy hunters. A few, such as Ben Sheffield, made it a full-time occupation. He acquired a ranch at the outlet of Jackson Lake in 1902 to use as a base for outfitting his expeditions. The ranch became the town of Moran.

Others recognized that dudes winter better than cows and began operating dude ranches. The JY and the Bar BC were established in 1908 and 1912, respectively. By the 1920s, dude ranching made significant contributions to the valley's economy. At this time some local residents realized that scenery and wildlife (especially elk) were valuable resources to be conserved rather than exploited.

Evolution of a Dream

The birth of present-day Grand Teton National Park involved controversy and a struggle that lasted several decades. Animosity toward expanding governmental control and a perceived loss of individual freedoms fueled anti-park sentiments in Jackson Hole that nearly derailed establishment of the park. By contrast, Yellowstone National Park benefited from an expedient and near universal agreement for its creation in 1872. The world's first national park took only two years from idea to reality; however Grand Teton National Park evolved through a burdensome process requiring three separate governmental acts and a series of compromises:

The original Grand Teton National Park, set aside by an act of Congress in 1929, included only the Teton Range and six glacial lakes at the base of the mountains.

The Jackson Hole National Monument, decreed by Franklin Delano Roosevelt through presidential proclamation in 1943, combined Teton National Forest acreage, other federal properties including Jackson Lake and a generous 35,000-acre donation by John D. Rockefeller, Jr. The Rockefeller lands continued to be privately held until December 16, 1949 when impasse for addition to the national park was resolved.

On September 14, 1950, the original 1929 Park and the 1943 National Monument (including Rockefeller's donation) were united into a "New" Grand Teton National Park, creating present-day boundaries.

An Idea is Born

As early as 1897, Colonel S.B.M. Young, acting Superintendent of Yellowstone, proposed to expand Yellowstone's boundaries southward to encompass portions of northern Jackson Hole and protect migrating elk herds. In 1898 Charles D. Walcott, head of the U.S. Geological Survey, made a similar proposal, suggesting that the Teton Range be included as well as northern

Grand Teton National Park	Jan	Feb	March	April	May	June	July	Aug	Sep	Oct	Nov	Dec
Average Max. Temperature (F)	26	32	38	48	60	70	80	78	68	56	38	28
Average Min. Temperature (F)	5	8	10	24	31	38	42	41	34	26	16	7
Extreme High (F)	55	60	64	75	85	98	95	96	93	84	65	58
Extreme Low (F)	-60	-63	-43	-28	0	18	24	18	7	-20	-36	-52
Days above 90°	0	0	0	0	0	0	1	1	0	0	0	0
Days below 32°	31	27	30	26	19	6	2	4	14	26	28	31
Average Total Precipitation (in.)	1.4	0.8	1.1	1.3	1.9	2.2	1.2	1.4	1.3	1.0	1.1	1.2
Maximum Precipitation (in.)	3.8	1.8	3.0	2.8	2.9	4.0	2.2	3.9	3.7	2.6	2.5	4.1
Maximum SnowFall (in.)	42	30	32	24	14	6	6	2	8	18	23	31
Days with measurable precipation	14	12	12	10	10	10	7	8	8	9	10	13
Average No. Thunderstorms	0	0	0	1	5	11	14	12	2	0	0	0

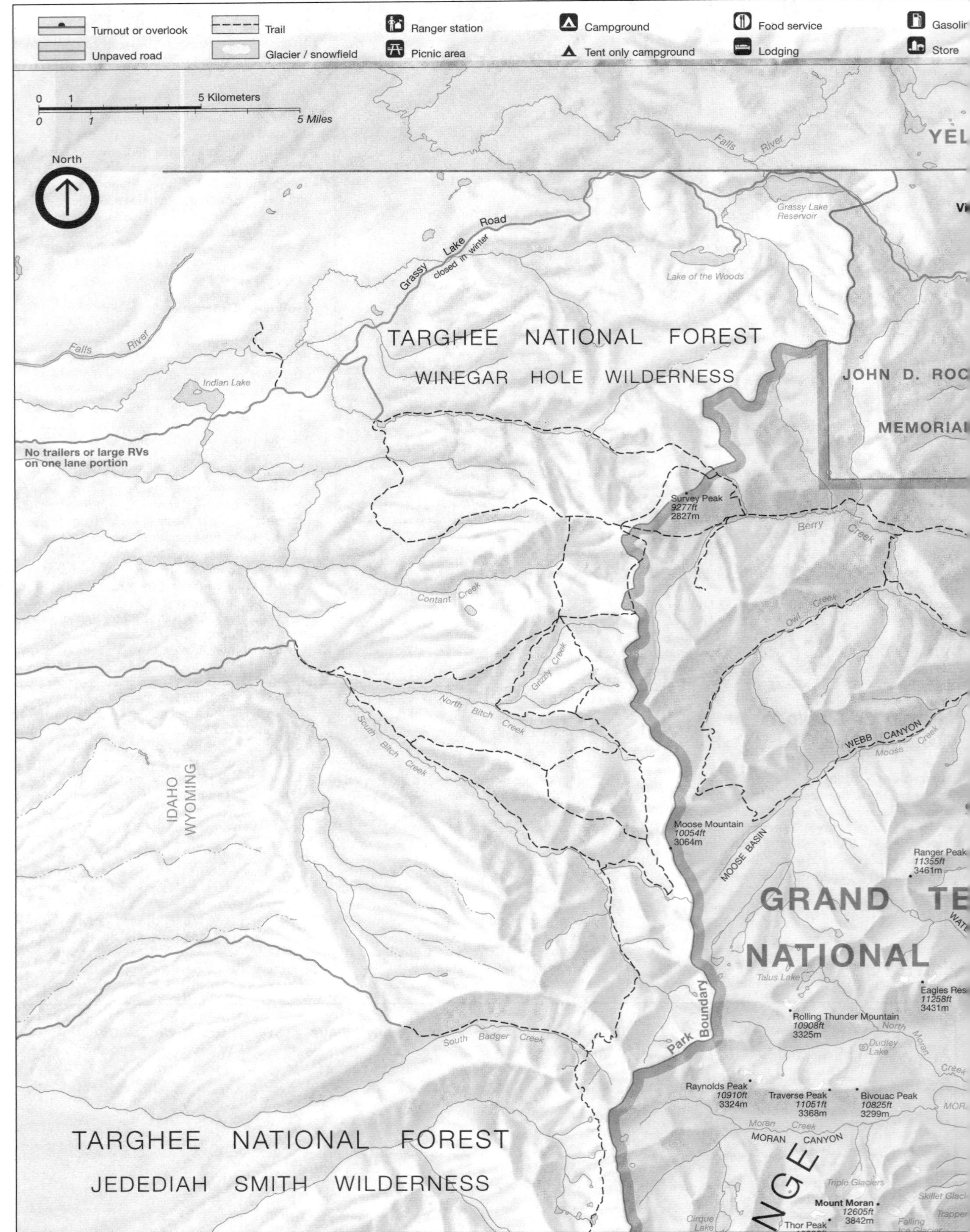

Turnout or overlook
Unpaved road
Trail
Glacier / snowfield
Ranger station
Picnic area
Campground
Tent only campground
Food service
Lodging
Store
5 Kilometers
5 Miles
North
Falls River
Grassy Lake Road
closed in winter
Grassy Lake Reservoir
Lake of the Woods
TARGHEE NATIONAL FOREST
WINEGAR HOLE WILDERNESS
JOHN D. ROC
MEMORIAL
Indian Lake
No trailers or large RVs on one lane portion
Survey Peak 9277ft 2827m
Berry Creek
Conant Creek
Owl Creek
Grizzly Creek
North Bitch Creek
South Bitch Creek
WEBB CANYON
Moose Creek
IDAHO
WYOMING
Moose Mountain 10054ft 3064m
MOOSE BASIN
Ranger Peak 11355ft 3461m
GRAND TE
NATIONAL
Talus Lake
Eagles Res 11258ft 3431m
Rolling Thunder Mountain 10908ft 3325m
North Moran Creek
Dudley Lake
Park Boundary
South Badger Creek
Raynolds Peak 10910ft 3324m
Traverse Peak 11051ft 3368m
Bivouac Peak 10825ft 3299m
Moran Creek
MORAN CANYON
TARGHEE NATIONAL FOREST
JEDEDIAH SMITH WILDERNESS
Triple Glaciers
Skillet Glaci
Mount Moran 12605ft 3842m
Cirque Lake
Thor Peak

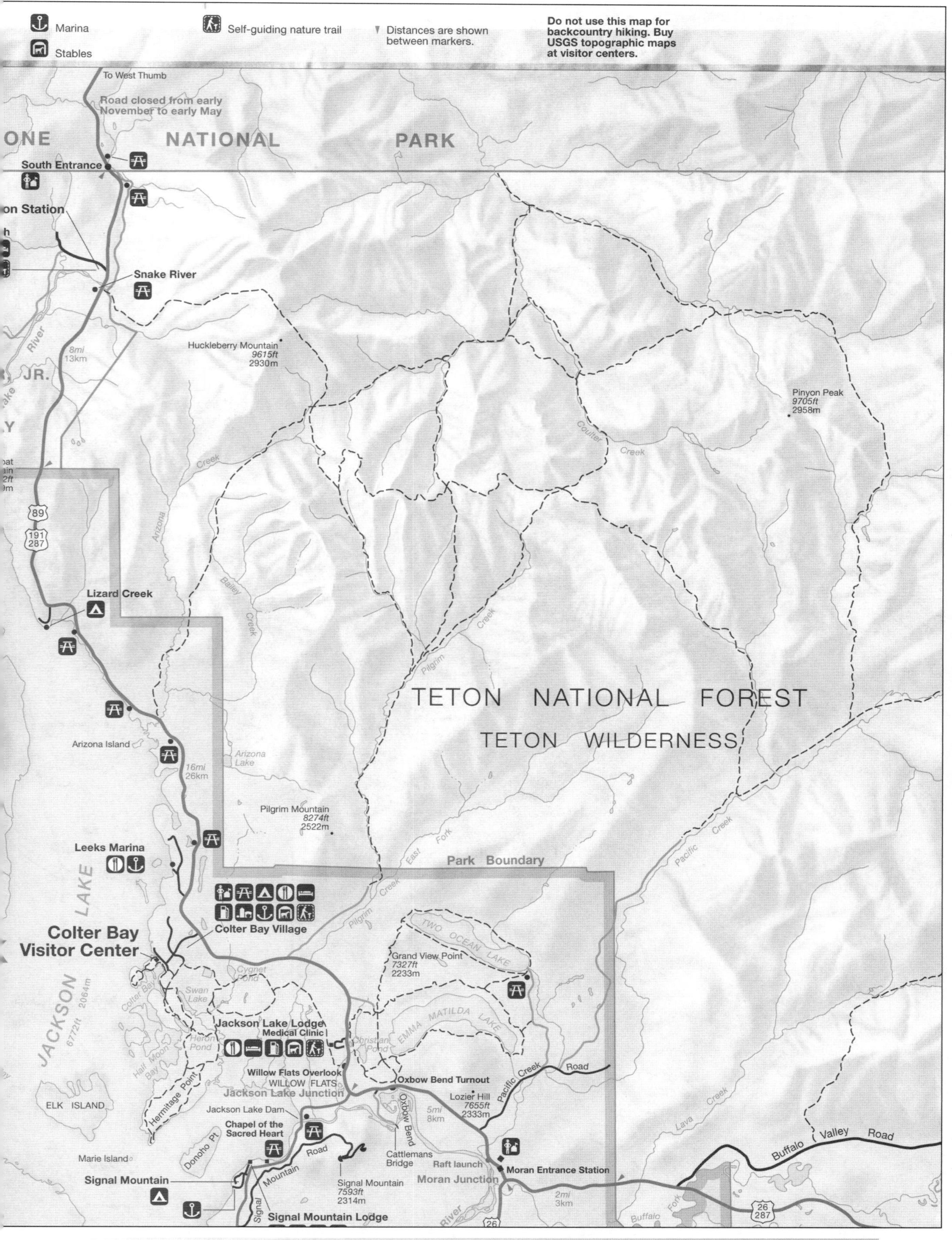
Marina
Stables
Self-guiding nature trail
Distances are shown between markers.
Do not use this map for backcountry hiking. Buy USGS topographic maps at visitor centers.
To West Thumb
Road closed from early November to early May
ONE NATIONAL PARK
South Entrance
Snake River
Huckleberry Mountain 9615ft 2930m
8mi 13km
Pinyon Peak 9705ft 2958m
TETON NATIONAL FOREST
TETON WILDERNESS
Lizard Creek
Arizona Island
16mi 26km
Arizona Lake
Pilgrim Mountain 8274ft 2522m
Leeks Marina
Park Boundary
Colter Bay Visitor Center
Colter Bay Village
JACKSON LAKE 6772ft 2064m
TWO OCEAN LAKE
Grand View Point 7327ft 2233m
EMMA MATILDA LAKE
Jackson Lake Lodge
Medical Clinic
Willow Flats Overlook
WILLOW FLATS
Jackson Lake Junction
Oxbow Bend Turnout
Lozier Hill 7655ft 2333m
5mi 8km
ELK ISLAND
Hermitage Point
Jackson Lake Dam
Chapel of the Sacred Heart
Donoho Pt.
Marie Island
Signal Mountain
Signal Mountain Road
Signal Mountain 7593ft 2314m
Signal Mountain Lodge
Cattlemans Bridge
Raft launch
Moran Junction
Moran Entrance Station
2mi 3km
Pacific Creek Road
Buffalo Valley Road
Lava Creek
Pacific Creek
Coulter Creek
Pilgrim Creek
Bailey Creek
Arizona Creek
East Fork
89
191 287
26 287
26

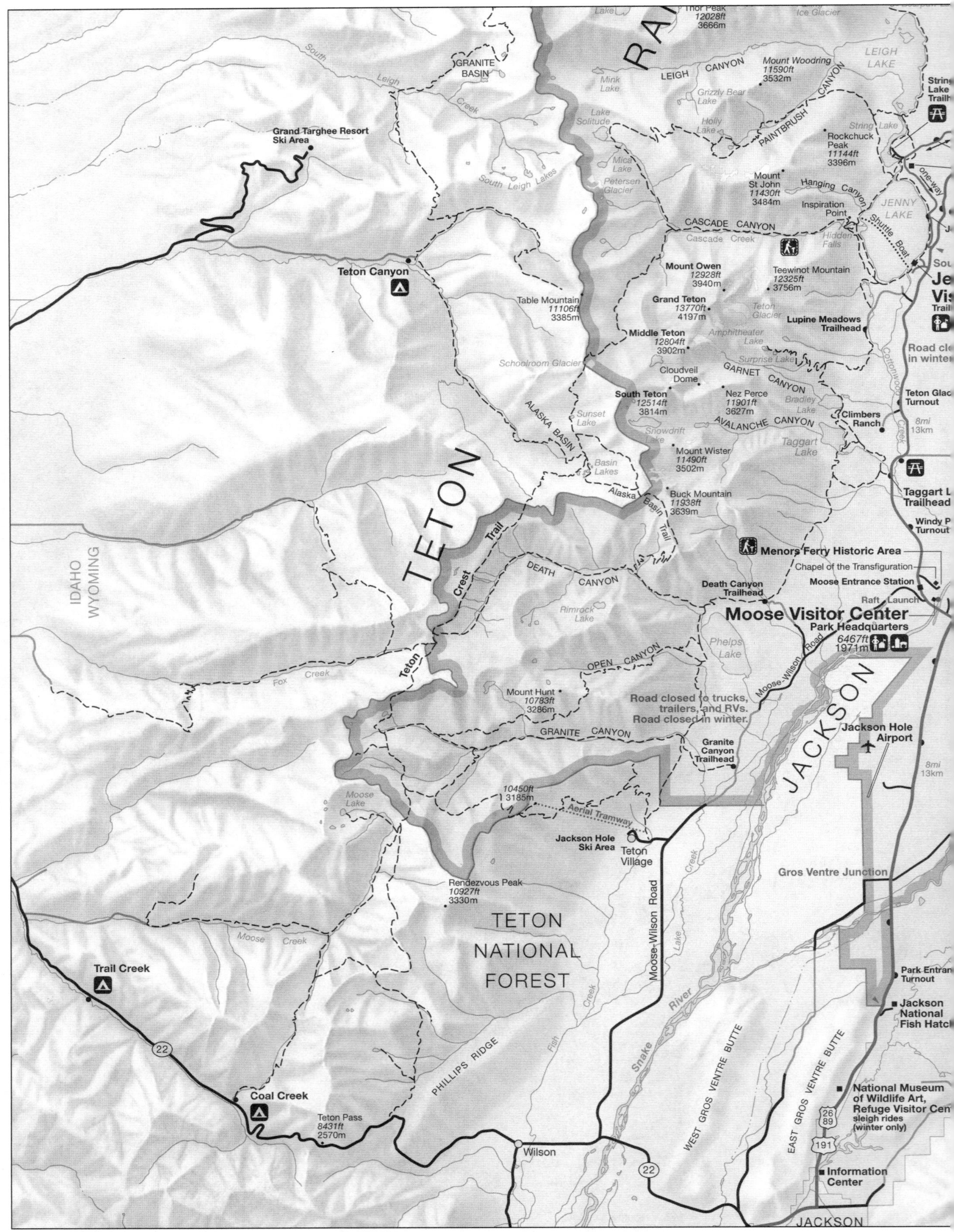
Thor Peak
12028ft
3666m
Ice Glacier
LEIGH LAKE
GRANITE BASIN
South Leigh Creek
Grand Targhee Resort Ski Area
Mink Lake
LEIGH CANYON
Mount Woodring
11590ft
3532m
Grizzly Bear Lake
Holly Lake
PAINTBRUSH CANYON
String Lake
Rockchuck Peak
11144ft
3396m
Lake Solitude
Mica Lake
Petersen Glacier
South Leigh Lakes
Mount St John
11430ft
3484m
Hanging Canyon
Inspiration Point
JENNY LAKE
Shuttle Boat
one-way
CASCADE CANYON
Cascade Creek
Hidden Falls
Teton Canyon
Mount Owen
12928ft
3940m
Teewinot Mountain
12325ft
3756m
Table Mountain
11106ft
3385m
Grand Teton
13770ft
4197m
Teton Glacier
Lupine Meadows Trailhead
Middle Teton
12804ft
3902m
Amphitheater Lake
Surprise Lake
Schoolroom Glacier
Cloudveil Dome
GARNET CANYON
South Teton
12514ft
3814m
Nez Perce
11901ft
3627m
Bradley Lake
Climbers Ranch
Sunset Lake
ALASKA BASIN
AVALANCHE CANYON
Snowdrift Lake
Mount Wister
11490ft
3502m
Taggart Lake
Basin Lakes
Alaska Basin Trail
Buck Mountain
11938ft
3639m
TETON
Teton Crest Trail
IDAHO
WYOMING
DEATH CANYON
Menors Ferry Historic Area
Chapel of the Transfiguration
Moose Entrance Station
Death Canyon Trailhead
Rimrock Lake
Raft Launch
Moose Visitor Center
Park Headquarters
6467ft
1971m
Phelps Lake
OPEN CANYON
Fox Creek
Mount Hunt
10783ft
3286m
Moose-Wilson Road
Road closed to trucks, trailers, and RVs. Road closed in winter.
JACKSON
Jackson Hole Airport
GRANITE CANYON
Granite Canyon Trailhead
8mi
13km
Moose Lake
10450ft
3185m
Aerial Tramway
Jackson Hole Ski Area
Teton Village
Gros Ventre Junction
Rendezvous Peak
10927ft
3330m
TETON NATIONAL FOREST
Moose Creek
Trail Creek
Lake Creek
Snake River
Fish Creek
PHILLIPS RIDGE
WEST GROS VENTRE BUTTE
EAST GROS VENTRE BUTTE
22
Coal Creek
Teton Pass
8431ft
2570m
Wilson
National Museum of Wildlife Art, Refuge Visitor Cen
sleigh rides (winter only)
26
89
191
Information Center
JACKSON
Park Entran Turnout
Jackson National Fish Hatc
Taggart L Trailhead
Windy P Turnout
Teton Glac Turnout
Road cl in winte
Cottonwood Creek
8mi
13km

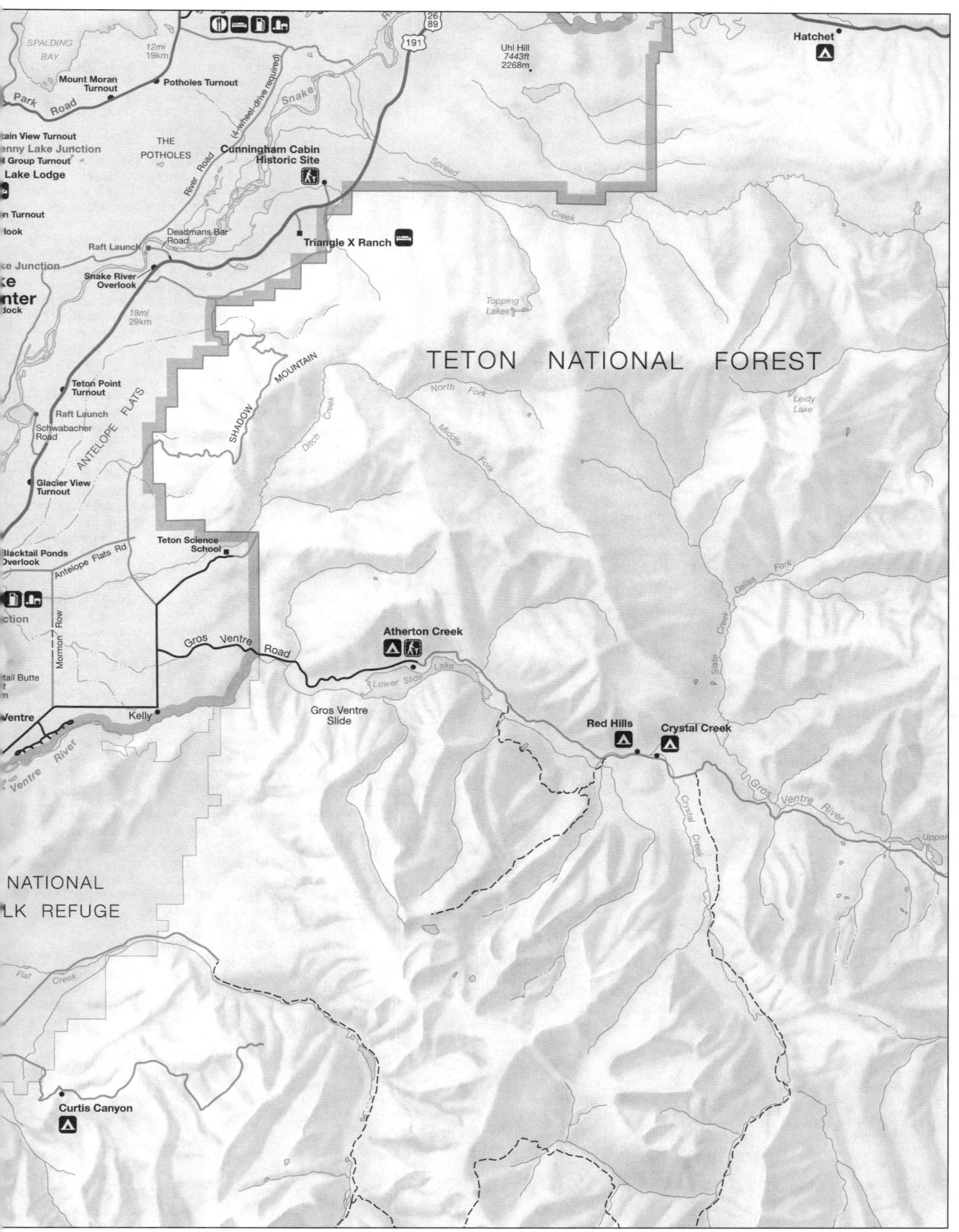

SPALDING BAY
12mi 19km
Mount Moran Turnout
Potholes Turnout
Park Road
(4-wheel-drive required)
Snake
THE POTHOLES
River Road
Cunningham Cabin Historic Site
Uhl Hill 7443ft 2268m
Hatchet
Spread Creek
Deadmans Bar Road
Raft Launch
Triangle X Ranch
Snake River Overlook
18mi 29km
Topping Lakes
SHADOW MOUNTAIN
TETON NATIONAL FOREST
Teton Point Turnout
Raft Launch
Schwabacher Road
ANTELOPE FLATS
Ditch Creek
North Fork
Middle Fork
Leidy Lake
Glacier View Turnout
Teton Science School
Blacktail Ponds Overlook
Antelope Flats Rd
Mormon Row
Dallas Fork
Slate Creek
Gros Ventre Road
Atherton Creek
Lower Slide Lake
Gros Ventre Slide
Kelly
Gros Ventre River
Red Hills
Crystal Creek
Crystal Creek
Gros Ventre River
NATIONAL ELK REFUGE
Flat Creek
Curtis Canyon

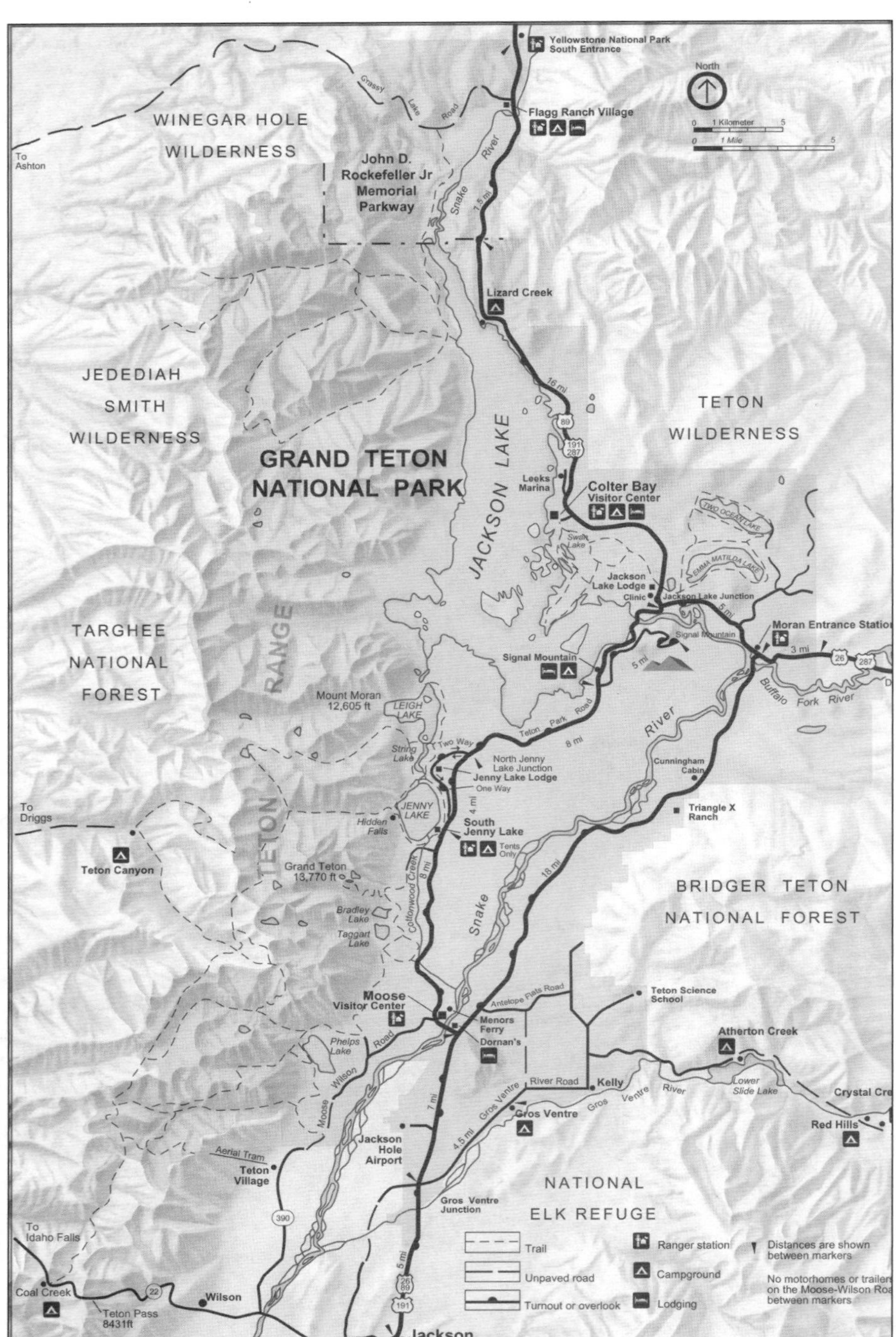

Jackson Hole. Neither the Interior Department nor Congress acted on either of these proposals.

In 1916, a new bureau called the National Park Service was created within the Department of Interior. This bureau could promote park ideas both locally and at the national level with the creation of a Washington DC office. Director of the National Park Service, Stephen Mather and his assistant, Horace Albright affirmed their commitment toward park expansion in a 1917 report to Secretary of the Interior, Franklin Lane. The report stated that adding part of the Tetons, Jackson Lake, and headwaters of the Snake River to Yellowstone National Park is "one of seven urgent needs facing the Park Service." Mather and Albright worked with the Wyoming congressional delegation to draft a bill addressing expansion of Yellowstone's boundaries into the Teton country. Congressman Frank Mondell of Wyoming introduced the bill in 1918. The House unanimously approved a revised bill in 1919. However, the bill died in the Senate when Idaho Senator John Nugent feared the loss of sheep grazing permits with expanded park service jurisdiction.

As historian Robert Righter states, "an opportunity had been lost. Never again would park extension be so non-controversial."

A Fledgling Park Emerges

In addition to Idaho sheep ranchers, other groups opposed park extension, these included regional U.S. Forest Service personnel, Jackson Hole businessmen, and some area ranchers. In 1919 Yellowstone Superintendent, Horace Albright was unaware of the pervasive anti-park attitude in Jackson Hole. As a result, he was practically "run out of town" when he traveled to Jackson to promote his park enlargement vision. Ranchers worried that park extension would reduce grazing allotments; Forest Service employees feared the loss of jurisdiction on previously managed forest areas; and local dude ranchers were against improved roads, hotel construction and concessioner monopolies.

Proposals emerged to dam outlets of Jenny Lake and Emma Matilda and Two Ocean Lakes in 1919. Alarmed businessmen and ranchers felt that some form of protection by the National Park Service might be their only salvation from commercialization and natural resource destruction. Eventually, local and National Park Service interests merged at an historic meeting in Maud Noble's cabin on July 26, 1923. Participants included Yellowstone Superintendent, Horace Albright; Bar BC dude ranchers, Struthers Burt and Horace Carncross; newspaperman, Dick Winger; grocery storeowner, Joe Jones; rancher, Jack Eynon; and ferry owner, Maud Noble. They devised a strategy. Their plan sought to find private funds to purchase private lands in Jackson Hole and create a recreation area or reserve that would preserve the "Old West" character of the valley, basically creating a "museum on the hoof." With the exception of Horace Albright, the attendees did not support a national park, "because they wanted traditional hunting, grazing, and dude-ranching activities to continue." In 1928, a Coordinating Commission on National Parks and Forests met with residents of Jackson and reached consensus for park approval. Local support and the Commission's recommendations led Senator John Kendrick of Wyoming to introduce a bill to establish Grand Teton National Park. Senator Kendrick stated that once he viewed the Tetons he "realized that some day they would become a park dedicated to the Nation and posterity…" Congress passed Senator Kendrick's bill. On February 26, 1929, President Calvin Coolidge signed this bill creating a 96,000-acre park that included the Teton Range and six glacial lakes at the base of the peaks. Since this fledgling 1929 park did not safeguard an entire ecosystem, Albright and the other participants of the 1923 meeting continued to pursue their dream of seeking private funds to purchase private lands in Jackson Hole.

Rockefeller's Interest Grows

John D. Rockefeller, Jr. became involved in the Jackson Hole Plan after a visit to Teton country in 1924 and again in 1926. These visits highlighted not only spectacular Teton scenery, but also shabby developments littering the roadway from Menor's Ferry to Moran and along Jenny Lake's south and east shores. Yellowstone Superintendent Albright seized an opportunity to explain to Rockefeller the essence of the Noble cabin meeting and the hope of protecting and preserving "this sublime valley" from unsightly commercial development. Rockefeller decided to purchase offending private properties with the intention of donating these lands for National Park designation. He created the Snake River Land Company as a purchasing agent to mask his association and keep land prices affordable, since landowners would have undoubtedly inflated their asking prices had they known of his involvement.

The Snake River Land Company launched an ambitious campaign to buy more than 35,000 acres for approximately $1.4 million. What seemed like a simple and straightforward plan became 20 years of bitter debate, nearly tearing

Facts about the park:

Teton Range
An active fault-block mountain front, 40 miles long (65 km), 7-9 miles wide (11-14.5 km).

Highest peak
Grand Teton, elevation 13,770 feet (4198 m). Twelve peaks over 12,000 ft (3658 m) in elevation.

Jackson Hole
Mountain valley, 55 miles long (89 km), 13 miles wide (21 km), average elevation 6,800 feet (2073 m). Lowest elevation at south park boundary, 6350 feet (1936 m).

Climate
Semi-arid mountain climate.
Extreme high: 93 degrees F (34 degrees C).
Extreme low: -46 degrees F (-43 degrees C).
Average snowfall: 191 inches (490 cm).
Avg. rainfall: 10 inches (26 cm).

Snake River
Headwaters of the Columbia River system, 1056 miles long. Approximately 50 miles lie within Grand Teton NP. Major tributaries: Pacific Creek, Buffalo Fork, and Gros Ventre River.

Lakes
Seven morainal lakes at the base of the Teton Range: Jackson, Leigh, String, Jenny, Bradley, Taggart, and Phelps. Jackson Lake: 25,540 acres (10,340 hectares) maximum depth 438 feet (134 m). Over 100 alpine and backcountry lakes.

Wildlife
17 species of carnivores (black and grizzly bears)
6 species of hoofed mammals
3 species of rabbits/hares
22 species of rodents
6 species of bats
4 species of reptiles (none poisonous)
5 species of amphibians
16 species of fishes
300+ species of birds
numerous invertebrates (no poisonous spiders)

Flora
7 species of coniferous trees
900+ species of flowering plants

apart the Jackson Hole community. Intense hostility surrounded land acquisitions; attempts by Rockefeller to gift these properties to the National Park Service met resistance. Economic hardships suffered by ranchers during the 1920s helped ease some land acquisitions. Many ranchers were actually relieved to sell and get out of business during a time of economic difficulty. In 1925, ranchers circulated a petition in support of the private buyout countering anti-park opinions in Jackson Hole. Ninety-seven ranchers endorsed the petition's statement, "that this region will find its highest use as a playground...The destiny of Jackson's Hole is as a playground, typical of the west, for the education and enjoyment of the Nation, as a whole." Perhaps this quote has more credibility as a tacit admission that ranching in northern Jackson Hole was difficult, if not impossible, than it has as a genuine altruistic gesture by the ranchers.

A Valley in Discord

Because allegations were made that the Snake River Land Company used illegal tactics during the purchase of properties, a Senate Subcommittee convened hearings in 1933 to investigate. When the hearings concluded, it was clear that claims about unfair business dealings by the Snake River Land Company and the National Park Service were groundless and both were exonerated. In 1934, Wyoming Senator Robert Carey introduced a bill in the Senate once again to expand park boundaries. One compromise of this bill dealt with reimbursement to Teton County for lost tax revenues. This bill and another drafted in 1935 failed. The tax issue and objections to including Jackson Lake because of dam and reservoir degradation fueled anti-park sentiments anew. During 1937 and 1938, the National Park Service prepared a document outlining the history of park extension and defending the importance of park status upon tourism. Again, anti-park sentiments flared and the expansion issue grew politically hotter. A group of locals calling themselves the Jackson Hole Committee vehemently opposed the park plan and encouraged the Wyoming delegation and Congress to do so as well. The park dream remained bruised and battered as controversy over enlargement continued into the 1940s.

After purchasing 35,000 acres and holding the land for 15 years, John D. Rockefeller, Jr. became discouraged and impatient with the stalemate surrounding acceptance of his gift. In an historic letter to President Franklin Delano Roosevelt, he wrote that if the federal government did not want the gift of land or could not "arrange to accept it on the general terms long discussed...it will be my thought to make some other disposition of it or to sell it in the market to any satisfactory buyers." This threat persuaded FDR to use his presidential power to proclaim 221,000 acres as the Jackson Hole National Monument on March 15, 1943. Robert Righter believes that Rockefeller threatened to sell in order to provoke governmental action. This bold action by Roosevelt provided a chance to circumvent obstacles created by Congress and the Wyoming delegation.

Local backlash immediately followed as park opponents criticized the monument for being a blatant violation of states' rights. They also believed the monument would destroy the local economy and county tax base. Hoping to force a confrontation, armed and defiant ranchers trailed 500 cattle across newly created monument land. The Park Service ignored this stunt but the drive focused national attention on the monument. Controversy grew more vocal and bitter, causing Wyoming Congressman Frank Barrett to introduce a bill abolishing the Jackson Hole National Monument; it passed both House and Senate. President Roosevelt exercised a pocket veto, killing the bill. The state of Wyoming responded to the veto by filing suit against the National Park Service to overturn the proclamation. The suit failed in the court system but the acrimonious local rift continued. The proclamation directed transfer of acreage from the Teton National Forest to the National Park Service. Since forest service administrators opposed the monument, the transition between jurisdictions provoked several vindictive deeds; one vengeful act involved gutting the Jackson Lake Ranger Station before turning it over to park staff. Local park supporters often faced hostilities and boycotts of their businesses throughout these turbulent years.

The Storm Passes

After World War II ended, the sentiment began to change in Jackson Hole. Between 1945 and 1947, bills were introduced in Congress to abolish the monument, but none passed. Local citizens began to realize that tourism offered an economic future for Jackson Hole. Eventually, attitudes became more agreeable toward park enlargement. By April 1949, interested parties had gathered in the Senate Appropriation Committee chambers to work out a final compromise. Though it took decades of controversy and conflict, discord and strife, the creation of a "new" Grand Teton National Park finally occurred on September 14, 1950, when Harry S. Truman signed a bill merging the 1929 park with the 1943 monument to form an enlarged 310,000-acre park. Preservation of the Teton Range, Jackson Lake, and much of Jackson Hole was finally placed in the hands of the National Park Service as a more complete ecosystem.

Difficulties of park-making define Grand Teton National Park and emphasize the visionary ideology of Horace Albright, John D. Rockefeller, Jr. and several pro-park residents. Legislation for the new park contained significant compromises: 1) protection of existing grazing rights and stock driveways; 2) reimbursement to Teton County for lost tax revenues; 3) provision for the controlled reduction of elk within park boundaries; 4) agreement that in the future presidential proclamation could not be used to create a national monument in Wyoming; and 5) allowance for continuation of certain existing uses and access rights to forest lands and inholder properties.

Heritage Preserved

Congress enlarged the park to its present size in 1950, "...for the purpose of including in one national park, for public benefit and enjoyment, the lands within the present Grand Teton National Park and a portion of the lands within Jackson Hole National Monument." The conservation battle for Jackson Hole coupled with the philanthropic dedication of John D. Rockefeller, Jr. shapes the character of this valley to the present day. Imagine how different the Teton landscape would look if unbridled development had prevailed over preservation of natural resources. In celebrating the Fiftieth Anniversary of Grand Teton National Park, we recognize and honor the dedication, perseverance and aspirations of visionary men and women who believed that the greatest good for the Teton countryside was as a "public park or pleasure ground for the benefit and enjoyment of the American people." As Crucible for Conservation author Robert Righter suggests, what these visionaries achieved was "perhaps the most notable conservation victory of the twentieth century."

The Creation of Grand Teton National Park was written in January 2000 by Jackie Skaggs, 50th Anniversary Coordinator, with research, references, and quotations taken from A Place Called Jackson Hole by John Daugherty, Park Historian 1980-1991 and from Crucible For Conservation by Robert Righter, currently research professor of history at Southern Methodist University in Texas.

Nature and Science

Located in northwestern Wyoming, Grand Teton National Park protects stunning mountain scenery and a diverse array of wildlife. Rising over 7,000 feet above the valley known as

Wolves in the Tetons

In October of 1998, the howling of wolves could be heard in Grand Teton National Park for the first time in over fifty years. Two years after being reintroduced to Yellowstone, wolves began expanding their range south to encompass the sagebrush flats, forested hillsides, and river bottoms of Grand Teton National Park and the valley of Jackson Hole. Their return represents the restoration of an important part of this ecosystem.

Although their present distribution is limited to Canada, Alaska, and a few isolated areas in the northern United States, wolves once roamed the tundra, forests, and high plains of North America from coast to coast. By 1930, human activities, including extensive settlement, unregulated harvest, and organized predator control programs, had pushed the gray wolf to the brink of extinction in the United States. The last known wild wolf in the Yellowstone area was killed in the 1940s.

In 1987, the United States Fish and Wildlife Service recommended establishing three core wolf recovery areas in the Northern Rocky Mountain region: northwestern Montana, central Idaho, and Yellowstone. Biologists suggested allowing wolf populations to recover naturally in northwestern Montana while reintroducing wolves in central Idaho and Yellowstone.

In accordance with this plan, wolves captured in Canada were transported to the U.S. and released in central Idaho and Yellowstone National Park in 1995 and 1996.

Ecology

The gray wolf is a critical player in the Greater Yellowstone Ecosystem, which encompasses Yellowstone and Grand Teton National Parks and surrounding National Forests. Wolves are highly efficient and selective predators, preying on young, old, weak, and sick animals. By culling the herds of their prey species in this manner, wolves are important agents of natural selection, encouraging survivorship of those animals best suited to their environment–the fastest, strongest, and healthiest.

In the Greater Yellowstone Ecosystem, wolves usually prey on elk, although they will occasionally take moose, bison, pronghorn, bighorn sheep, and beavers. Wolf populations are naturally regulated by prey availability, which prevents decimation of prey species populations.

Although wolves do make surplus kills when convenient, the carcasses do not go to waste. They are either cached for later consumption or left for scavengers, including coyotes, ravens, magpies, golden and bald eagles, crows, bears, wolverines, fishers, mountain lions, and lynx.

Wolf Biology

The gray or timber wolf, Canis lupus, is the largest wild canid in existence, ranging from 60 to 175 pounds. Despite its common name the gray wolf may be white, silver/gray, or black in color. Wolves have been clocked at speeds in excess of thirty miles per hour and have been known to travel over a hundred miles in a day, although travels are more often ten or twenty miles per day. Wolves may live up to fifteen years in the wild.

Wolves are highly social animals, functioning primarily in packs. The social structure of the pack is based on a breeding pair comprised of an alpha male and female, followed by a hierarchy consisting of betas (second rank, males and/or females), subordinates, pups, and occasional omegas (outcasts, generally recipients of aggressive behavior from other pack members).

Because only the alpha pair breeds, subordinate wolves of reproductive age must disperse from their packs and form new associations in order to breed. Pack size is ultimately determined by hunting efficiency, which in turn depends on the size, type, and density of prey species available. Wolf packs average five to ten members.

Wolf packs defend home ranges of up to several hundred square miles. During the spring denning season, wolves are especially aggressive in defending core territories around their den sites. In the Greater Yellowstone Ecosystem, wolves generally breed in February and give birth in late April, after a gestation period of about 63 days. The alpha female usually remains at the den site with the pups, while the alpha male and other pack members bring food back to the den. When pups reach approximately two months of age, they are moved to an outdoor nursery referred to as a rendezvous site. By October, pups are usually traveling and hunting with the rest of their pack.

Eradication History

Wolves have long been the target of aggressive eradication efforts by humans. In 1630, the Colony of Massachusetts enacted the first bounty on wolves in what is now the United States. Wolves were effectively eliminated from the eastern United States by the end of the eighteenth century. With settlers' westward expansion, populations of predator and prey species were greatly reduced due to human development and unregulated harvest.

The decline in wild prey populations, especially bison, led many people to believe that wolves posed an unacceptable threat to domestic livestock. These beliefs fueled government-sanctioned, bounty-driven efforts to destroy the wolf in the west. From approximately 1850 through 1930, thousands of wolves were trapped, shot, and poisoned each year in the western U.S.

Government hunters destroyed the last known wolf in the Yellowstone area in the 1940s. By 1930, wolves were virtually absent from the contiguous U.S., except Minnesota and remote areas of northwestern Montana. Sizeable wolf populations remained in Canada and Alaska.

Recovery

1973 marked the passing of the federal Endangered Species Act (ESA), a pivotal event in the history of wildlife preservation. Under the ESA, the gray wolf is listed as endangered throughout the contiguous United States except Minnesota, where it is listed as threatened. The ESA defines an endangered species as one "in danger of extinction throughout all or a significant part of its range" and a threatened species as one "likely to become endangered" in the foreseeable future.

The Endangered Species Act requires the U.S. Fish and Wildlife Service (FWS) to create recovery plans for all listed species. In 1987, the FWS published a recovery plan for the gray wolf in the Northern Rockies, which recommended establishing three gray wolf populations, in northwestern Montana, central Idaho, and Yellowstone, respectively. Biologists predicted that wolves from Canada would naturally recolonize northwestern Montana. However, because central Idaho and Yellowstone were isolated from existing wolf populations, biologists determined that it was impractical to expect natural recolonization of these areas in the near future. Therefore, the Fish and Wildlife Service recommended reintroducing wolves into central Idaho and Yellowstone, while encouraging natural wolf recovery in northwestern Montana.

In 1995, wolves captured in Canada were transported to the U.S. and released in central Idaho and Yellowstone National Park. Because the central Idaho and Yellowstone area wolves are reintroduced populations, they are defined as "experimental" according to the Endangered Species Act. This designation allows more flexibility in managing these populations than is normally allowed for populations of endangered species.

Delisting/Reclassification of the Gray Wolf in the Northern Rocky Mountains

The minimum criteria for removal of the gray wolf from the endangered species list requires the establishment of ten breeding pairs, about 100 wolves, in each of three northern Rocky Mountain population areas (Yellowstone, central Idaho, and northwestern Montana) for three consecutive years. As a prerequisite for delisting from federal protection, the individual states within the recovery area must establish wolf management plans approved by the FWS. These state plans could allow for wolves to be managed in a manner similar to that in which individual states currently manage other large predators, such as bears and mountain lions.

Wildlife managers predicted that recovery goals for the northern Rocky Mountain region would be achieved by the year 2002 or 2003, andit seems that the restoration program is on track. In 1998, there were nine breeding pairs/packs in the Yellowstone area, ten in central Idaho, and seven in northwestern Montana.

Your Park Visit

As with all wildlife, it is smart to keep your distance from wolves in order to avoid disturbing the animals or endangering yourself. Many wild animals will attack people if provoked. However, according to wolf expert L. David Mech, there has never been a documented case of a healthy, wild wolf killing or seriously injuring a human in the Western Hemisphere.

There have been five documented cases of pets being killed by wolves in the Yellowstone area since the reintroduction, and rates of wolf attacks on pets have been similarly low in other areas inhabited by wolves. Grand Teton National Park regulations restrict pets to areas open to motorized vehicles, and require that pets be restrained on a leash at all times.

Jackson Hole, the Teton Range dominates the park's skyline. Natural processes continue to shape the ecosystem against this impressive and recognizable backdrop.

The elevation of the park ranges from 6,400 feet on the sagebrush-dominated valley floor to 13,770 feet on the windswept granite summit of the Grand Teton. Between the summit and plain, forests carpet the mountainsides. During summer, wildflowers paint meadows in vivid colors. Crystalline alpine lakes fill glacial cirques, and noisy streams cascade down rocky canyons to larger lakes at the foot of the range. These lakes, impounded by glacial debris, mirror the mountains on calm days. Running north to south, the Snake River winds its way down the valley and across this amazing scene.

Long, snowy, and bitterly cold winters make the climate of Jackson Hole unforgiving. The coldest temperature ever recorded in Grand Teton National Park was –63°F, and snow often blankets the landscape from early November to late April. Brief, relatively warm summers provide a respite from the rigors of winter and a time of renewal and rebirth. In cooperation or competition, the plants and animals adapt to this harsh climate and dramatic elevation change as each finds ways to survive.

Animals

It seems that wildlife is never far away in Grand Teton National Park. High in the mountains, a yellow bellied marmot whistles a warning as a golden eagle soars above. Searching for insect larvae, a black bear rips into a rotten lodgepole pine log. On the valley floor, a herd of bison graze as a coyote trots among the sagebrush, looking for a meal. Along the Snake River, an osprey dives into the water with talons extended, rising with a cutthroat trout. In a nearby meadow, a moose browses the tender buds of willows that grow in this water-rich environment.

Animals relate to and shape the environment in which they survive; they are also connected one with another. Some of these relationships are obvious, while others are much less so. These relationships and connections cross park boundaries. Grand Teton National Park's 310,000 acres lie at the heart of the Greater Yellowstone Area. The Greater Yellowstone Area encompasses over eleven million acres and is considered one of the few remaining, nearly intact, temperate ecosystems on earth. The animals that inhabit Grand Teton National Park depend on this vast area for survival, residing in and migrating to different areas depending on the season.

Forget-me-nots, the official park flower. National Park Service Photo.

Amphibians

While most visitors don't come to Grand Teton National Park seeking amphibians, they are some of the most unique and important species found in the park. The word amphibian comes from the Greek words meaning "double life", and refers to their unusual two-stage life cycle. An

List of Mammals

Insectivora (Insect-eaters)
c Masked Shrew *Sorex cinereus*
c Vagrant Shrew *Sorex vagrans*
r Dwarf Shrew *Sorex nanus*
u Northern Water Shrew *Sorex palustris*

Chiroptera (Bats)
c Little Brown Bat *Myotis lucifugus*
u Long-eared Myotis *Myotis evotis*
u Long-legged Myotis *Myotis volans*
u Silver-haired Myotis *Lasionycteris noctivagans*
r Hoary Bat *Lasiuris cinereus*
u Big Brown Bat *Eptisicus fuscus*

Lagomorpha (Rabbits and Hares)
c Pika *Ochotona princeps*
c Snowshoe Hare *Lepus americanus*
u White-tailed Jackrabbit *Lepus townsendii*

Rodentia (Gnawing Mammals)
a Least Chipmunk *Tamias minimus*
c Yellow Pine Chipmunk *Eutamias amoenus*
u Uinta Chipmunk *Tamias umbrinus*
c Yellow-bellied Marmot *Marmota flaviventris*
a Uinta Ground Squirrel *Spermophilus armatus*
c Golden-mantled Ground Squirrel *Spermophilus lateralis*
a Red Squirrel *Tamasciurus hudsonicus*
u Northern Flying Squirrel *Glaucomys sabrinus*
u Northern Pocket Gopher *Thomomys talpoides*
a Beaver *Castor canadensis*
a Deer Mouse *Peromyscus maniculatus*
u Bushy-tailed Woodrat *Neotoma cinerea*
c Southern Red-backed Vole *Clethrionomys gapperi*
c Heather Vole *Phenacomys intermedius*
a Meadow Vole *Microtus pennsylvanicus*
a Montane Vole *Microtus montanus*
u Long-tailed Vole *Microtus longicaudus*
c Richardson Vole *Microtus richardsoni*
r Sagebrush Vole *Lemmiscus curtatus*
c Muskrat *Ondatra zibethicus*
c Western Jumping Mouse *Zappus princeps*
c Porcupine *Erethizon dorsatum*

Carnivora (Flesh-eaters)
Ursidae – Bear Family
c Black Bear *Ursus americanus*
u Grizzly Bear *Ursos arctos*

Canidae – Dog Family
a Coyote *Canis latrans*
u Gray Wolf *Canis lupus*
r Red Fox *Vulpes vulpes*

Mustelidae – Weasel Family
c Marten *Martes americana*
u Short-tailed Weasel *Mustela erminea*
r Least Weasel *Mustela nivalis*
c Long-tailed Weasel *Mustela frenata*
u Mink *Mustela vison*
r Wolverine *Gulo gulo*
c Badger *Taxidea taxus*
u Striped Skunk *Mephitis mephitis*
c River Otter *Lutra canadensis*

Felidae – Cat Family
r Mountain Lion *Felis concolor*
r Lynx *Felis lynx*
r Bobcat *Felis rufus*

Procyonidae – Raccoon Family
r Raccoon *Procyon lotor*

Artiodactyla (Even-toed Hooves)
Cervidae – Deer Family
a Elk (wapiti) *Cervus elaphus*
c Mule Deer *Odocoileus hemionus*
r White-tailed Deer *Odocoileus virginianus*
a Moose *Alces alces*

Antilocapridae – Pronghorn Family
c Pronghorn *Antilocapra americana*

Bovidae – Cattle Family
c Bison *Bison bison*
x Mountain Goat *Oreamnos americanus*
u Bighorn Sheep *Ovis canadensis*

Key to Symbols
a – Abundant – likely to be seen in appropriate habitat and season.
c – Common – frequently seen in appropriate habitat and season.
u – Uncommon – seen irregularly in appropriate habitat and season.
r – Rare – unexpected even in appropriate habitat and season.
x – Accidental – out of known range, or reported only once or twice.
? – Questionable – verification unavailable.

Abundance categories are based on the park and parkway wildlife database, research projects and observations by biologists and naturalists.

Bird Finding Guide

Grand Teton National Park and the John D. Rockefeller, Jr., Memorial Parkway encompass a range of habitats, from alpine meadows to sagebrush flats, from lodgepole pine forests to mountain streams. Birds use habitats that meet their needs for food, water, shelter and nest sites. Some birds frequent only one habitat type while others occupy a variety of habitats. This guide will acquaint you with some habitat types of the park and parkway as well as specific locations to look for birds. Use it in conjunction with the park map and the various bird identification books available at any of our vistor centers. Please report any sightings of birds listed as rare or accidental on the bird checklist.

Lodgepole Pine Forests

Lodgepole pine grows in dense forests covering much of the valley and the lower slopes of the mountains. Expect olivesided flycatchers, yellow-rumped warblers, ruby-crowned kinglets, mountain chickadees, white-crowned and chipping sparrows and dark-eyed juncos (especially in developed areas within lodgepole forests such as Colter Bay).

Aspens

Aspens occur chiefly in pure stands, often on hillsides. Many of the aspen stands in the park and parkway have rotting trunks that attract numerous woodpeckers. Sawwhet owls, house wrens, mountain and black-capped chickadees, tree swallows and violet-green swallows nest in old woodpecker cavities.

Sagebrush Flats

Sagebrush covers most of the valley called Jackson Hole. Despite the hot dry conditions existing where sagebrush grows, some species flourish. Look for sage grouse, vesper sparrows, Brewer's sparrows and sage thrashers.

Alpine

Above 10,000 feet, severe conditions limit vegetation to low-growing forms. Birds that nest above treeline migrate south or to lower elevations for winter. Watch for golden eagles, Clark's nutcrackers, rosy finches, white-crowned sparrows and water pipits.

Aquatic and Riparian

Numerous rivers, creeks, lakes and ponds provide habitats where Canada geese and other waterfowl nest and osprey and bald eagles hunt for fish. Common snipe, white-crowned and Lincoln sparrows, yellow and MacGillivray's warblers and common yellowthroats nest and forage in adjacent wet meadows. American dippers search for insects in fast-moving streams.

Bird-Watching Etiquette

Enjoy birds but be a responsible birder.

• Nesting birds of all species are easily disturbed. If an adult on a nest flies off at your approach or circles you or screams in alarm, you are too close to the nest. Unattended nestlings readily succumb to predation or exposure to heat, cold and wet weather.

• Good birding areas often attract other wildlife. Maintain a safe distance (300 feet) from large animals such as moose, bears and bison. Do not position yourself between a female and her offspring.

Cascade Canyon.

Glaciers gouged out Cascade Canyon thousands of years ago. Today Cascade Creek carries melted snow through conifer forests and meadows of wildflowers, while the Teton peaks tower above. American dippers frequent Cascade Creek near Hidden Falls. Western tanagers, ruby-crowned kinglets and yellow-rumped warblers nest near the trail. Also look for golden eagles, Steller's jays, gray jays, golden-crowned kinglets, dark-eyed juncos and occasional Townsend's warblers. Secretive harlequin ducks sometimes nest along the creek.

Taggart Lake Trail

In 1985 a lightning-caused forest fire burned most of the trees on the glacial moraine surrounding Taggart Lake. Insects feeding on the decaying trees attract woodpeckers. Look for blackbacked and three-toed woodpeckers. Abundant insects also attract mountain bluebirds, tree swallows, olive-sided and dusky flycatchers, western wood-pewees and yellow-rumped warblers. Calliope hummingbirds frequently perch in willows near the base of the moraine.

Antelope Flats – Kelly Road.

Large hayfields attract raptors that search the fields for abundant small rodents. Look for American kestrels, prairie falcons, redtailed hawks, Swainson's hawks and northern harriers. Check fence posts for western meadowlarks, western and eastern kingbirds and mountain bluebirds. Scan irrigated pastures for long-billed curlews and savannah sparrows.

Menor's Ferry at Moose

Follow the self-guiding trail to homesteader cabins along the Snake River. Bird life abounds due to riparian habitat. Violet-green, tree, cliff and barn swallows scoop insects out of the air as western wood-pewees, dusky flycatchers and mountain bluebirds hawk for flying insects. Yellow warblers glean insects from cottonwood trees and willow and silverberry shrubs lining the Snake River. Calliope, broad-tailed and rufous hummingbirds seek nectar from wildflowers. Kingfishers, common mergansers, ospreys and bald eagles catch fish in the river.

Phelps Lake Overlook

The trail to the overlook traverses a lateral glacial moraine where mixed conifers and aspens grow. Because the trail follows a small creek, expect abundant birdlife. Look for western tanagers, MacGillivray's warblers, northern flickers, Lazuli buntings, ruby-crowned kinglets and greentailed towhees. Listen for the sweet songs of hermit and Swainson's thrushes. Calliope and broad-tailed hummingbirds feed on scarlet gilia below the overlook.

Grand View Point.

Old growth Douglas firs support Williamson's sapsuckers, red-naped sapsuckers and other woodpeckers. Common songbirds include mountain chickadees, red-breasted nuthatches, dark-eyed juncos, western tanagers and Townsend's solitaires. Blue grouse and ruffed grouse nest here. At the summit, look up for red-tailed hawks, white pelicans and other soaring birds.

Christian Pond

Several species of waterfowl nest here. Look for ruddy ducks, ring-necked ducks, American wigeon and American coots. Trumpeter swans occasionally nest on the pond. Because human presence interferes with the swans' nesting effort, remain on the trail on the west side of the pond, at least 300 feet from the edge of the pond, and obey all posted closures.

Willow Flats

Extensive willow thickets merge with wet grassy meadows. Small creeks and beaver ponds provide riparian and aquatic habitats. Look for cinnamon teal, greenwinged teal and American wigeon in ponds and creeks. Sandhill cranes, northern harriers, American bitterns, common snipes and soras nest here. Calliope hummingbirds feed on scarlet gilia growing near Jackson Lake Lodge. Red-naped sapsuckers and other woodpeckers abound. Frequently seen songbirds include willow flycatchers, cliff swallows, yellow warblers, MacGillivray's warblers, common yellowthroats, Wilson's warblers, fox sparrows, white-crowned sparrows, pine siskins and yellow-headed blackbirds. Lazuli buntings and greentailed towhees use the drier hillsides adjacent to Willow Flats.

Oxbow Bend

A slow-moving, cut-off meander of the Snake River, Oxbow Bend supports lush underwater plant growth and abundant fish, food for aquatic birds. Great blue herons and osprey nest here. White pelicans, double-crested cormorants, common mergansers and bald eagles fish in the shallow water. Because of Oxbow Bend's proximity to Willow Flats, the birdlife is quite similar.

Two Ocean Lake

Western grebes, trumpeter swans, common mergansers and occasional common loons summer on the lake. Western tanagers, pine grosbeaks, Cassin's finches and other songbirds abound in the open coniferous forests and aspen stands surrounding the lake.

Blacktail Ponds Overlook This overlook is just north of Moose Junction and is situated at the transition of three different plant communities: Sagebrush flats, the coniferous forest of Blacktail Butte, and the willow and cottonwood lined wetlands of the Snake River flood plane. Looking down on the wetlands from the overlook gives you a great vantage point to observe waterfowl such as American wigeons, blue-winged teal, mallards, and goldeneyes. Up to six species of swallows can also be seen at eye level as they skillfully fly through the air catching insects. Raptors such as bald eagles and osprey can be seen in the high cottonwoods. Strewn through out the willows, yellow warblers, song sparrows and willow flycatchers among others can be seen and heard. An occasional greentailed towhee flutters through the sagebrush near the overlook and evening grosbeaks visit from the forest. Partners in Flight

Bull Elk. National Park Service Photo.

amphibian begins life as an egg, laid either in water, or in some other damp environment. The larvae hatch and spend their time in water breathing through gills. They then undergo a metamorphosis into an adult form, and the adults breathe using lungs. While adults are considered terrestrial, amphibians continue to spend most of their lives near water. Unlike reptiles that have dry scaly skin, amphibians have moist, smooth, glandular skin with no scales, and they have no claws on their toes.

Amphibians are cold-blooded and cannot regulate their body's temperature like mammals and birds, so in the park, the cold annual temperatures, high elevation, and dry climate limits amphibian diversity and numbers. The park is home to six species of amphibians: spotted frogs, boreal chorus frogs, boreal toads, tiger salamanders, northern leopard frogs (unfortunately, these are now believed to be extinct in the area), and bullfrogs (which were introduced just outside the park).

The best places to find amphibians are near the rivers, streams, and lakes along the valley floor. Good places to look for spotted frogs include String Lake, Schwabacher's Landing (along the Snake River), and Taggart Lake. Chorus frogs are easiest to find in late May and early June because the males are actively calling during their breeding season, moist valley meadows are great spots to look and listen for these frogs at dusk. The boreal toad seems to be disappearing from their historic range; sightings of these, as well as leopard frogs, should be reported to any of the park's visitor centers.

Take some time on your visit to search for these interesting creatures; they can be readily seen if one knows where to look. They are key links in the food web—providing food for many other animals including birds, otters, and fish. Amphibians are also important predators of insects. Finally, they are excellent indicators of overall ecosystem health. Their dependence on water and the dual life cycle they lead makes them extremely sensitive to changes in environmental conditions.

Birds

Grand Teton National Park has a number of diverse habitats which support a host of birds in the area. Within the park boundaries some of the largest and smallest North American birds can be found. The calliope hummingbird, the smallest North American bird, weighs less than a tenth of an ounce. This bird can be found around blooming scarlet gila and near willow. The trumpeter swan, the largest water fowl in North America, can be seen in the area of Swan Lake as well as near the National Elk Refuge. These birds are usually found in pairs that mate for life.

Two birds that can be found around areas of water are the osprey and bald eagle. A sighting of either of these birds catching fish is a special treat. Ospreys are distinguishable from other birds by the streamlined manner in which they carry a fish in their talons. The talons are typically turned so that the fish can be carried parallel to the bird's body.

The Western Tanager is one of the most colorful birds in the Tetons and can be found in forested areas. In the summer the male is red, orange, yellow, and black. Another impressive bird sighting in the area of the Tetons is the Sage Grouse. If you visit the park during the spring months you may see the courtship display which occurs near the Jackson Hole airport. The tail feathers of the male Sage Grouse can spread over a 280-degree angle. This display, along with brightly colored expanded air sacs on the chest which produce a popping sound, may help to attract a female.

Birdwatchers are reminded to view birds from a distance, preferably with binoculars. Also, as with all wildlife, birds are not to be harassed or disturbed. This descriptive list is only a sampling of the birds that can be found in the Jackson Hole area.

Fish

The world inhabited by the fishes of Grand Teton National Park seems to be a world apart. While the rivers, lakes, and ponds are wonderful visual features of the landscape, the processes and life forms that exist beneath the waters' surface are not so readily observed. For many of us the most familiar creatures of these underwater worlds are the fishes. Although sometimes the victims of "out of sight, out of mind" thinking, the fishes are crucial to the health of the regions ecosystem.

The fish species present in Grand Teton come in a range of shapes and sizes. The species have a variety of eating habits. The mountain sucker feeds almost exclusively on algae; the cutthroat trout, named for its markings not its temperament, feeds mainly on insects and smaller fish. The species favor different zones in which to live within the waters. The Utah chub is typically found in warm, shallow, slow-moving water; the mountain whitefish prefers cold, deep, fast-moving water. Despite their many differences, a common thread that connects the various fish species is their importance as a food source. Fish are the primary food of several species of birds, mammals, and other fish. The threatened bald eagles are dependent on fish for their survival. Many other animals, including human beings, consume fish as a secondary food source. Fish in turn control plant and animal, especially insect, populations through their eating habits. Because of their unique physiology the well being of fishes worldwide is precarious. Pollution, loss of habitat, and overfishing are continuous threats.

Grand Teton National Park has a worldwide reputation for its excellent trout fishing. Interestingly, of the five species of trout present in the park only one, the Snake River cutthroat trout, is native to the region. In total there are more than a dozen species of fish that make the waters of Grand Teton National Park home.

Native Species

Snake River cutthroat trout
Utah sucker
Longnose dace
Redside shiner
Paiute sculpin
Mountain whitefish
Speckled dace
Mountain sucker
Mottled sculpin
Non-Native Species
Rainbow trout
Eastern brook trout
Lake trout
Brown trout
Utah chub
Arctic grayling
Bluehead sucker

Mammals

Mammals hold a special place in our perception of wild nature. They warm our hearts, inspire our imaginations, and thrill our senses. They are big and small, friendly and malicious, inquisitive and reclusive. They are always engaging and thrilling to see. The sixty-one species of mammals that live beneath the towering peaks of the Teton Range in Grand Teton National Park are no exception. They are found in each of the four major habitats in the park: the alpine, coniferous forests, sagebrush flats, and wetlands, and in each they have secured a place for themselves that has allowed them to live and prosper no matter what the conditions.

Mammals share two characteristics that make them unique among the world's animals: they have hair, and they nurse their young. In addition, there are several other characteristics that have allowed mammals to live successfully in almost any habitat. First, mammals are warm-blooded. They rely on metabolism to maintain a

Flowering Times of Selected Flowers and Shrubs

White Flowers	Valley	Canyons	Alpine
Huckleberry	Jun	Jul	
Mountain Ash		Jul	
Birchleaf Spirea	Jul	Jul	
Chokecherry	Jun		
Woodlandstar	Jun		
Richardson Geranium	Jun – Aug	Jun – Aug	
Thimbleberry		Jun – Jul	
Green Gentian	Jun – Jul	Jul – mid Aug	
Snowbrush Ceanothus	Jun – Jul		
Cowparsnip	late Jun – mid Aug	Jul – Aug	
Serviceberry	Jun		
American Bistort	Jun	Jul	Aug
Ladies-tresses	Aug – mid Sep	Aug – Sep	
White Bog-Orchid	late Jun – mid Aug	Jul – Aug	
Manyflowered Phlox	Jun – mid Jul	mid Jun – Jul	
Colorado Columbine		late Jun – Aug	
Marsh Marigold		Jun – mid Jul	Jun – Jul
Yampah	Jul – mid Aug	mid Jul – Aug	
Engelmann Aster		Jul – Aug	
Yarrow	Jul – early Aug	mid Jul – late Aug	Aug
Yellow Flowers			
Mules-ear Wyethia	mid Jun – Jul		
Hymenoxys			Jul – Aug
Sunflower	mid Jul – Aug		
Balsamroot	Jun – mid Jul		
Rabbitbrush	mid Aug – Sep		
Heartleaf Arnica	mid Jun – mid Jul	late Jun – late Jul	
Shrubby Cinquefoil	Jun – Sep		
Yellow Monkey-flower	Jun – mid Jul	mid Jun – mid Aug	
Lanceleaved Stonecrop	Jun – Aug		
Glacier Lily		Jun – Jul	Jul
Western Wallflower		Jun – Jul	
Subalpine Buttercup		Jul – Aug	
Deathcamas	Jun	mid Jun – early Aug	mid Jul – Aug
Oregongrape	May – Jun		
Sulfur Buckwheat	mid Jun – mid Aug		
Bracted Lousewort	late Jun – mid Jul	Jul	
Yellow Columbine	late Jun – Jul	Jul – late Aug	
Yellow Fritillary	mid May – mid Jun		
Butterweed Groundsel	late Jul – Sep		
Pink – Red Flowers			
Springbeauty	May	Jun – mid Jul	
Sticky Geranium	Jun – Aug		
Parry's Primrose		Jul – Aug	Aug
Prairiesmoke	Jun – early Jul		
Globemallow	Jul – mid Aug	mid Jul – Aug	
Steershead	late May – mid Jun	late Jun – mid Jul	
Subalpine Spirea		mid Jul – Aug	
Shooting Star	Jun	late Jun – late Aug	
Ladysthumb Knotweed	Aug		
Lewis Monkeyflower		late Jun – Aug	
Mountain Snowberry	Jun – Jul	Jul	
Spreading Dogbane	Jul – Aug		
Mountainheather		Jul – Aug	Aug – Sep
Fireweed	mid Jul – Aug		
Moss Campion			Jul – mid Aug
Calypso Orchid	Jun		
Elephanthead	late Jun – Jul	mid Jul – Aug	
Indian Paintbrush	Jun – Jul	Jul – Aug	mid Jul – early Sep
Striped Coralroot	Jun – Jul		
Skyrocket Gilia	mid Jun – Jul		
Blue – Purple Flowers			
Wild Blue Flax	July – Aug		
Rock Clematis	Jun	Jul	
Sky Pilot			July – Aug
Monkshood	late Jun – mid Jul	mid Jul – mid Aug	
Low Larkspur	mid May – Jun		
Mountain Bluebell		mid Jul – early Sep	
Fringed Gentian	late Jul – mid Aug	Aug – early Sep	
Harebell	mid Jun – early Sep		
Lupine	Jun – Jul		
Mountain Bog Gentian		late Jul – early Sep	
Silky Phacelia	late Jun – Jul	mid Jul – late Aug	late Jul – early Sep
Blue Camas	Jun		
Alpine Forget-me-not			Jul – early Aug

constant body temperature instead of depending on the environment to keep them warm. This allows mammals to live in areas that cold-blooded animals cannot tolerate. Secondly, mammals have well-developed sensory systems and specialized tooth structures that allow them to find and eat different foods depending on their requirements. Also, different modes of travel, such as climbing, swimming, running, gliding, and flying, have allowed mammals to inhabit a variety of niches in every ecosystem. Finally, mammals stress quality over quantity in regard to reproduction. Instead of utilizing energy to produce vast numbers of offspring, mammals instead produce a smaller number of young and concentrate their efforts on ensuring the survival and success of those young. Thanks to a combination of these characteristics, mammals have successfully adapted to almost every environment found on Earth.

In Grand Teton National Park, mammals make up the largest part of the wildlife that people travel hundreds of miles to see. Large ungulates like moose, elk, mule deer, bison, and pronghorn are commonly seen from roadside vantage points. However, large predatory mammals like grizzly bears, black bears, wolves, and mountain lions are often more sought after sightings. Uinta ground squirrels, least chipmunks, and red squirrels tend to show up where ever you go in the park, but you'll have to keep your eyes open to find less commonly viewed mammals like badgers, pine martens, long-tailed weasels, and wolverines. In rocky regions, pikas, yellow-bellied marmots, and golden mantled ground squirrels will probably cross your path, and in the waters of Grand Teton National Park, you may be lucky enough to spy a muskrat, beaver, or river otter. No matter where you go in Grand Teton National Park, a mammal will not be far away. Their success in adapting to a variety of conditions has made their dispersal throughout the park possible, and their ubiquitous presence in Grand Teton National Park has made this beautiful place even more exciting and rewarding to visit.

The Snake River flows in the shadows of the Teton Range. National Park Service Photo.

Reptiles

Grand Teton National Park is home to a diverse array of wildlife including several species of reptiles. Reptiles are a highly successful group of animals with dry, scaly skin that either lay eggs or bear live young. Although reptiles cannot maintain a constant body temperature like mammals, they can regulate their body temperature behaviorally, such as moving into or out of sunlight. The park's cold mountain climate limits the diversity, distribution, and abundance of reptile species found here.

There are currently four confirmed species of reptiles in Grand Teton National Park. Along with one species of lizard, there are three species of snakes. The most common reptile in the park is the wandering garter snake (Thamnophis elegans vagrans). The valley garter snake (Thamnophis sirtalis fitchi) and the rubber boa (Charina bottae) are much less commonly encountered. All three species of snakes typically live near areas of water. There are no species of poisonous snakes in the

Menor's Ferry

Menor's Ferry once belonged to William D. Menor who came to Jackson Hole in 1894, taking up a homestead beside the Snake River. Here he constructed a ferryboat that became a vital crossing for the early settlers of Jackson Hole Valley.

Jackson Hole was isolated by its surrounding mountains and had such a harsh climate that it was one of the last areas of the lower 48 states to be settled. Homesteaders came here, mainly from Idaho, beginning in the late 1880s. Most early settlement in the valley took place in the south, or on a few scattered areas with fertile soil on the east side of the Snake River. Menor was alone on the west side of the Snake for more than ten years.

Rivers are often important transportation corridors. However, the Snake River was a natural barrier that divided the valley. In dry months the river could be forded safely in several locations, but during periods of high water even the most reliable fords were impassable. After 1894, Menor's Ferry became the main crossing in the central part of Jackson Hole. Residents crossed on the ferry to hunt, gather berries and mushrooms, and cut timber at the foot of the mountains.

Bill Menor built the original ferryboat and cableworks. Today's ferry and cableworks are replicas. The ferry is a simple platform set on two pontoons. The cable system across the river keeps the ferry from going downstream, while allowing it to move sideways. By turning the pilot wheel, the rope attaching the boat to the cable is tightened and points the pontoons toward the opposite bank. The pressure of the current against the pontoons pushes the ferryboat across the river in the direction the pontoons point. This type of ferry existed in ancient times and was used elsewhere in the United States.

Menor charged 50¢ for a wagon and team and 25¢ for a rider and horse. Pedestrians rode free if a wagon was crossing. When the water was too low for the ferry, Menor suspended a platform from the cable and three to four passengers could ride a primitive cablecar across the river. In later years, Menor and his neighbors built a bridge for winter use, dismantling it each spring.

Menor sold out to Maude Noble in 1918. She doubled the fares, hoping to earn a living from the growing number of tourists in the valley. Noble charged $1 for automobiles with local license plates, or $2 for out-of-state plates. In 1927, a steel truss bridge was built just south of the ferry, making it obsolete. Maude Noble sold the property to the Snake River Land Company in 1929.

Bill Menor and his neighbors homesteaded here thinking of the local natural resources as commodities for survival, but many of them grew to treasure the beauty and uniqueness of Jackson Hole. In 35 short years, from Bill Menor's arrival until the establishment of the original park in 1929, this land passed from homestead to national treasure.

park.

The only confirmed species of lizard in Grand Teton National Park is the northern sagebrush lizard (Sceloporus graciosus graciosus). Amazingly, this lizard species, which lives in dry, rocky sagebrush habitat, was not confirmed to exist within the 310,000-acre park until 1992. Although Grand Teton is a heavily visited jewel of the National Park Service, and much is known about its larger mammal species, this recent "discovery" points to our deficiency of knowledge of smaller invertebrate and vertebrate species within the park, including reptiles. Since the possibility exists that other reptile species, including the Great Basin gopher snake (Pituophis catenifer deserticola), may someday be found in the park, further study on the reptiles of Grand Teton National Park is needed.

Plants

Over 1000 species of vascular plants grow in Grand Teton National Park and the surrounding area. Soil conditions, availability of moisture, slope, aspect, and elevation all determine where plants grow. Plants that require similar conditions are often found growing in the same area. These associations form various plant communities. It is useful to divide the plants of Grand Teton National Park into the following communities: sagebrush flats, riparian corridors and wetlands, forests, and alpine areas.

The valley floor of Jackson Hole is comprised of loose rocky soil through which water percolates easily. In these conditions the silvery-green big leaf sagebrush is conspicuous. Although at first glance it appears that only sage grows on the flats, this area is remarkably diverse.

Moisture-loving plants find suitable growing conditions along the Snake River, its tributaries, and other wetland areas. Narrow leaf cottonwood and willows, both of which thrive in wet areas, grow along the watercourses, creating ribbons of light green across the landscape. Wet meadows provide the conditions suited to grasses, sedges, and wildflowers.

The canyons, mountainsides, and hills created by glacial debris, called moraines, contain deeper soils that are capable of holding moisture. These conditions support the growth of trees. Conifers dominate these areas, coloring the slopes a dark green.

Although they appear gray and lifeless, the high alpine reaches of the park support plants specially adapted to the harsh growing conditions found there. Wind, snow, lack of soil, increased ultraviolet radiation, rapid and dramatic shifts in temperature, and a short growing season all challenge the hardy plants that survive here. Most plants adapt by growing close to the ground in mats like the alpine forget-me-not.

Natural Features and Ecosystems

Artists create a mosaic by setting small colored pieces of tile into mortar to create a decorative design or picture. While each piece of tile is unique and colorful in its own right, the artist creates something greater than the individual parts by carefully combining and arranging each small piece.

While the Teton Range dominates the landscape, it is the interplay of mountains, faults, glaciers, forests, rivers, lakes, wetlands, and geologic features that create the overal grandeur of Grand Teton National Park. Taken individually, each feature is fascinating and worthy of protection, but when combined as they are in Grand Teton, they create a mosaic that is inspiring beyond compare.

Flood Plains

It is normal for river levels to fluctuate throughout the year. The flood plain is the area around a river that experiences flooding while water levels are high. In the park you can see the Snake River meander through its flood plain, creating a braided effect.

Wetlands and marshes can be found in the flood plain and provide vital plant and animal habitat. A great place to view wildlife in the flood plain is Schwabacker's Landing, where you can observe an active beaver colony. (Don't get too close, beavers are very shy.)

Flooding brings nutrients to the flood plain because rivers carry rich sediments and material that serves as fertilizer. Efforts to control natural flooding often leads to worse flooding in other areas. Wild rivers without levees or dams are becoming increasingly hard to find.

Forests

Everyone knows that forests contain trees, but each forest is unique in it's own way, and every forest has an intricate story to tell. The forest type is dependent on many factors, including climate, topographical conditions, geographical location, and soil type. Forests may contain just one or two species of trees in large stands, or mix hundreds of different species together! Along with the trees comes various other species of plants and animals that are all interconnected in the forest ecosystem.

In Grand Teton National Park, there are a variety of forest types, containing different tree species as well as associated wildlife. Some trees, such as the whitebark and limber pines, subalpine fir, and engelmann spruce can survive the cold windy slopes and alpine zone high up in the Tetons to around 10,000 feet. Other evergreens, like the lodgepole pine, douglas fir, and blue spruce, are more commonly found on the valley floor, while the aspens, cottonwoods, alders, and willows prefer the moist soils found along the rivers and lakeshores.

Grand Teton forests generally contain two or three different types of trees growing together in a specific habitat type. These forests merge into one another in zones called ecotones, which creates edge habitat for various species of wildlife. Some animals, like the red squirrel, pine marten, and black bear spend most of their time in the forests. Others, such as moose, elk, and wolves, seek the forest for shade and shelter during the day and move out to the sagebrush or meadows to feed in the early mornings and evenings. Forests are a very important part of the Grand Teton ecosystem. They stabilize the soil, create homes and

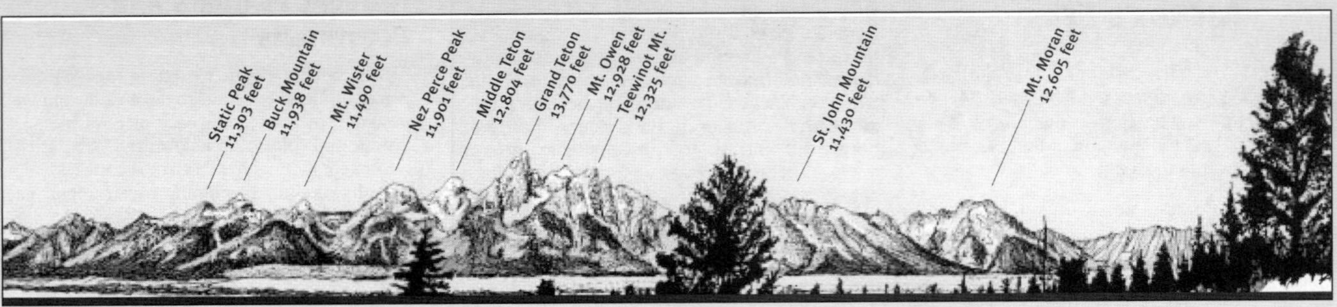

Peak Names

From the book Origins by Hayden and Nielsen.

Static Peak In the Teton Range north of Death Canyon. So named because it is so often hit by lightning.

Buck Mountain Named for George A. Buck, recorder for T.M. Bannon's 1898 mapping party. Bannon gave the name "Buck Station" to the triangulation station he and George Buck established on the summit in 1898.

Nez Perce Named for an Indian tribe whose well-known leader was Chief Joseph. Sometimes referred to as Howling Dog Mountain because of the resemblance when seen from the north.

The Grand Teton Highest mountain in the Teton Range. Named by French trappers. Upon viewing the Teton Range from the west, the trappers dubbed the South, Middle and Grand, Les Trois Tetons, meaning "the three breasts." Wilson Price Hunt called them "Pilot Knobs" in 1811 because he had used them for orientation while crossing Union Pass. In his Journal of a Trapper, Osborne Russel said that the Shoshone Indians named the peaks "Hoary Headed Fathers."

Mount Owen Neighboring peak of the Grand Teton to the northeast. Named for W.O. Owen, who climbed the Grand Teton in 1898 with Bishop Spalding, John Shive, and Frank Petersen.

Teewinot Mountain Towers above Cascade Canyon and Jenny Lake. Its name comes from the Shoshone word meaning "many pinnacles." Teewinot probably once applied to the entire Teton Range, rather than just this one peak. Fritiof Fryxell and Phil Smith named the peak when they successfully completed the first ascent of the mountain in 1929.

Mount Saint John Between Cascade and Indian Paintbrush canyons. Actually a series of peaks of nearly equal height. Named for Orestes St. John, geologist of Hayden's 1877 survey, whose monographs on the Teton and Wind River ranges are now classics. MOUNT MORAN Most prominent peak in the northern end of the Teton Range. Named by Ferdinand V. Hayden for the landscape artist Thomas Moran, who traveled with the 1872 Hayden expedition into Yellowstone and into Pierre's Hole on the western side of the Teton Range. He produced many sketches and watercolors from these travels.

food for wildlife, provide nutrients and carbon dioxide to the ecosystem, and create beauty and enjoyment for us all.

Fossils

When one views the Teton Range visions of vast, ancient seas do not usually come to mind. The peaks of the Tetons seem so powerful, so imposing, that it may be difficult to imagine this area as an almost featureless underwater plain. Both of these scenes, however, describe chapters in the geologic history of Grand Teton National Park. One of the most revealing clues for geologists unraveling the mystery of the Tetons' past is the existence of fossils. Fossils are the mineralized remains or impressions of plants or animals from past geologic ages.

Fossils are typically found in sedimentary rock. One way that sedimentary rock forms is through the settling of suspended material (sand, gravel, or mud) from water. The settling material forms horizontal layers that thicken and lithify (harden to rock) over time. Sand, gravel, and mud are not the only material that settles to the bottom of aquatic bodies. Plant and animal material settles too. Once this organic material—perhaps the remains of an ancient fish—has settled, it is covered by the ongoing sedimentation process. In time the seas recede and the sedimentary layers are exposed to erosive forces such as wind, rain, and gravity. These forces break down the rock formations exposing successive underlying layers. Eventually, the fossil remains of a creature once buried under tons of sediment are exposed at the earth's surface.

In the northern, southern, and, most dramatically, in the western portions of Grand Teton National Park are extensive formations of sedimentary deposits, some over a thousand feet thick. These formations contain the fossil remains of oceanic organisms. The presence of the fossils leads geologists to conclude that the area now occupied by the Tetons was once the floor of ancient seas. The seas were inhabited by algaes and corals, brachiopods (clamlike in appearance), and early ancestors of the crayfish—trilobites. Fossil records in Grand Teton date back to at least the Cambrian age approximately 500 million years ago.

Fossils do more than provide us with a fascinating look at prehistoric life forms. They are useful tools in dating geologic features, analyzing past climates, and tracing evolutionary processes. If you are fortunate enough to find a fossil during a visit to one of the national parks, please look but do not touch. Leave them to be rediscovered by the visitors and scientists of the future.

Glaciers / Glacial Features

A quilt of white blankets Grand Teton National Park in the winter. As spring approaches that white blanket dwindles in size. However, even in the heat of summer, snow and ice are present in the form of glaciers and snowfields.

Glaciers carry rocks, soil, sand, and other debris from higher to lower elevations. This material can be carried on the surface, inside, or even frozen to the bottom of the glacier. In this park, the glaciers are wet-based, meaning they move on a thin plane of water like an ice skater.

One major feature you may see on a glacier is a crevasse. These are deep, V-shaped structures found in the uppermost layer of the glacier. This part of the glacier breaks easily as the ice moves, causing crevasses to open and close.

Glaciers have had a weighty impact on the Teton Range. Ice, over 3,000 feet thick, moved across the valley floor. Today the mottled beauty of the mountains is punctuated by a contrast of dark and light. Exposed rock lies adjacent to snow or ice. Currently there are numerous snowfields and twelve glaciers in the park. These masses of moving ice have names like Schoolroom, Teton, Middle Teton, Triple, and Skillet Glacier.

Lakes and Ponds

Most of the lakes in the park were created thousands of years ago. As the glaciers moved they pushed aside soil and dug into the ground. When they melted they left behind an indentation in the ground that filled with water from the melting glacial ice. These became the lakes that we see today. Jackson Lake, the park's largest lake, is a natural lake that has been altered by a human-made dam.

Ponds can be formed like lakes but may also be the result of part of a river being blocked, beavers building a dam, natural sinkholes in the ground, or even human activity. The plant and animal life in a pond area is very diverse and productive.

Ponds and lakes provide for a variety of habitat in and around them. From cutthroat trout to crawfish, from great blue herons to moose, almost all wildlife in the park derive some benefit from lakes and ponds.

Ponds and lakes also provide recreational opportunities for visitors. Some of the easiest and most popular hikes are around lakes and ponds. All of the lakes are open to swimming and non-motorized boating. Jackson Lake also allows motorized boats for recreational use.

Mountains

Grand Teton National Park inspires your sense of wonder. Magnificent mountains tower over a valley bisected by the Snake River. This beautiful valley, overlooked on the western edge by an impressive skyline, is known as Jackson Hole. The Teton Range dominates the landscape of the park.

The range began rising 2 to 13 million years ago. There were numerous earthquakes that released tension along the Teton Fault to create a vertical offset of 23,000 feet. However, when you view the range you will see that the Grand Teton at 13,770 feet, stands only about 7,000 feet above the valley floor. Most of the elevation change has been buried in this gravity driven environment. Erosion is filling the valley in but it also bestowed the Teton Range with a rugged appearance. The terrain and lack of foothills allures outdoor enthusiasts of all types to visit this area. Climbers can find at least 12 peaks in the Teton Range over 12,000 feet high with varying degrees of difficulty.

Watersheds

A watershed is a topographic region in which all precipitation flows from an area of uplift toward a central valley. The North American continental divide bisects the continent as the landmass' most consistent high point, usually found near the Rocky Mountains. Precipitation that falls east of the continental divide flows toward the Atlantic Ocean watershed, while precipitation that falls to the west of the divide flows west toward the Pacific Ocean watershed.

In Grand Teton National Park, the most apparent watersheds are located east and west of the Teton Mountain range. Precipitation falling on the eastern side of the range flows toward the Jackson Hole valley watershed. However, the rate of uplift of the Teton Range is occurring so quickly that the mountain peaks do not act as the dividing line between the two watersheds. In reality, the watershed is two kilometers west of the peaks due to the rate of erosion not occurring as quickly as the rate of uplift. Nonetheless, precipitation falling on the west side of the mountains flows into eastern Idaho. The Snake River Valley is its own watershed, collecting precipitation that falls on or near the Snake River.

Two Ocean Lake, in the northeastern portion of the park near Moran, was originally named due to the misbelief that the continental divide ran through the center of the lake forcing waves to move toward opposite shores and opposite watersheds. Subsequent mapping has determined that the divide is many miles to the northwest of Two Ocean Lake, yet the name remains.

Wetlands, Marshes and Swamps

Wetlands, marshes, and swamps are abundant in Grand Teton National Park. These areas are fed by numerous mountain streams, springs, or seeps and provide vital habitat for a wide variety of plants and animals. Vegetation such as pond lilies, willows, and cattails supply wildlife with food and shelter.

It is very common to see wildlife browsing in these areas where the water meets the land. Oxbow Bend and Willow Flats provide excellent habitat for moose that graze on willow and other aquatic vegetation.

Beyond providing habitat for plants and animals, wetlands help filter water and temper flood waters. Whether they are created by a beaver's dam at Schwabacher's Landing or are naturally occuring along the Snake, wetlands are an integral component of the ecosystem.

Geology

Read the past as you view the Teton Range today. The ancient geologic processes that shaped the mountains and valley have left visible marks. Watch millions of years of dynamic geology unfold before you while exploring Grand Teton National Park.

Two rectangular blocks of the Earth's crust moved like giant trap doors, one swinging skyward to form the mountains, the other hinging downward to create the valley. Wind, rain, ice, and glaciers constantly eroded the rising range. Meanwhile, enormous glaciers and torrential meltwaters flowed southward carrying cobbles, gravel, and coarse sand and periodically re leveled the floor of the sinking valley.

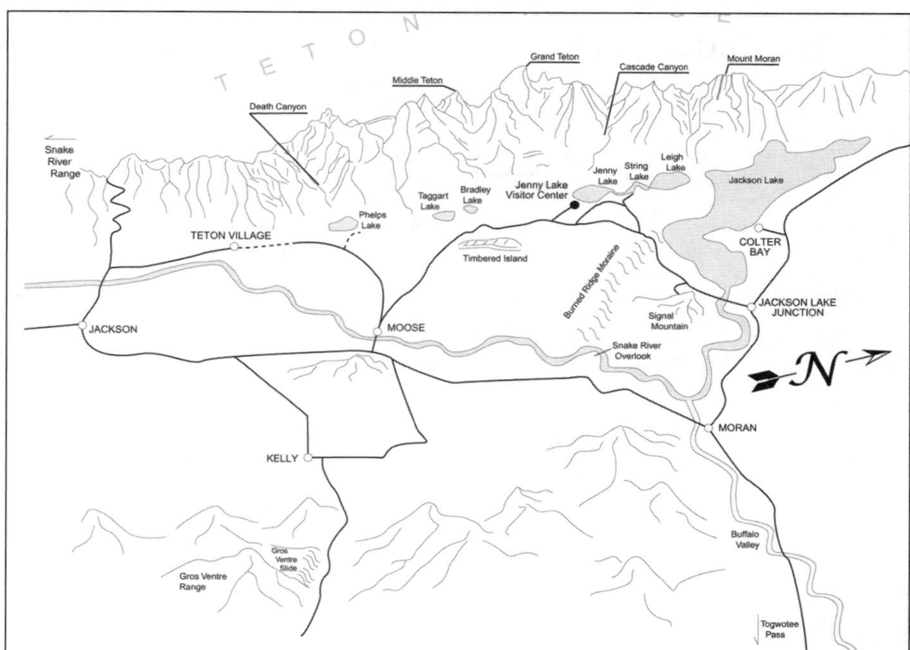

Collecting Rocks

Federal law prohibits collecting in National Parks. Please leave rocks where you find them so that others may enjoy the intact geologic story.

Rock Formation

The geologic story of the Teton Range starts with the formation of the rocks that make up the mountains, rocks far older than the mountains themselves. The process began over 2.5 billion years ago when sand and volcanic debris settled in an ancient ocean. For millions of years, additional sediment was deposited and buried within the earth's crust. Heat and pressure metamorphosed (changed) the sediment into gneiss, the rocks that comprise the main mass of the Teton Range. The stress of metamorphosis caused minerals to segregate. Today, alternating light and dark layers identify banded gneiss, readily seen in Death Canyon and other canyons in the Teton Range.

Next, magma (molten rock) forced its way up through cracks and zones of weakness in the gneiss. This igneous (formed by heat) rock slowly cooled, forming light-colored dikes of granite, inches to hundreds of feet thick. Look for larger dikes as you view the mountains from the Jenny Lake and String Lake areas. Uplift and erosion have exposed the granite that now forms the central peaks of the range.

Diabase, a dark-colored igneous rock, 1.3 billion years ago flowed up through the gneiss and granite, resulting in the prominent vertical dikes seen today on the faces of Mt. Moran and the Middle Teton. The diabase dike on Mt. Moran protrudes from the face because the gneiss surrounding it erodes faster than the diabase. The diabase dike on the Middle Teton is recessed because the granite of the central peaks erodes more slowly than the diabase.

Shallow seas that covered the Teton region 600 million to 65 million years ago have left sedimentary formations, still visible at the north and south ends of the Teton Range and also on the west slope of the mountains. Marine life, especially tiny trilobites, corals and brachiopods, flourished in the shallow seas covering this area. The seas repeatedly advanced and retreated. During retreat of the younger seas, this area became a low-lying coastal plain frequented by dinosaurs. Fossilized bones of a horned dinosaur, the Triceratops, have been found east of the Park near Togwotee Pass.

Mountain Building

Compression of the earth's crust 80 million to 40 million years ago caused uplift of the Rocky Mountain chain, from what is now Mexico to Canada. While the mountains on the south and east formed during this period, the rise of the Teton Range as we now see it had not yet begun. Stretching and thinning of the earth's crust caused movement along the Teton fault to begin about 6-9 million years ago.

Every few thousand years, when the elasticity of the crust stretches to its limit, a fault (or break) of about 10 feet occurs, relieving stress in the earth's crust. The blocks on either side of the fault moved, with the west block swinging skyward to form the Teton Range, the youngest and most spectacular range in the Rocky Mountain chain. The east block dropped downward, forming the valley called Jackson Hole. The valley block has actually dropped down four times more than the mountain block has uplifted. Total vertical movement along the Teton fault approaches 30,000 feet. Evidence for the amount of move-

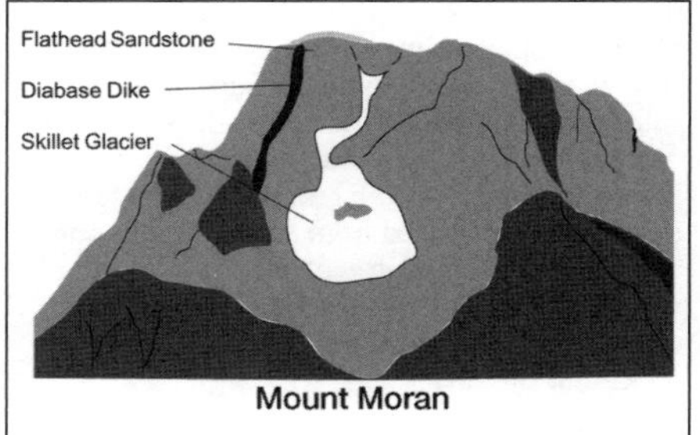

Mount Moran

The Colter Stone

The Colter Stone, discovered near Tetonia, Idaho in 1933, is a piece of rhyolite carved in the shape of a human head. It is engraved on one side with the name "John Colter", on the other side is the year "1808". If authentic, it represents the only solid proof of the route followed by trapper and explorer John Colter.

Colter explored the greater Yellowstone area during the winter of 1807-8, perhaps the first white man to do so. His route, however, is uncertain as no clear maps or records exist. Colter set out from a fur trapping fort in present-day southern Montana and headed south to near today's Cody, Wyoming. On his return he passed through what is now Yellowstone National Park. The middle section of his journey is a matter of conjecture. One theory indicates he traveled via Togowtee Pass. The other commonly held view traces Colter's route through Jackson Hole, over Teton Pass, and north along the west side of the Teton Range. No evidence exists to substantiate either route. The only available sources of information are vague accounts and maps derived from interviews with Colter after his return.

Thus, the significance of the Colter Stone becomes clear. The location of its discovery, the west side of the Teton Range, would prove that John Colter had traveled the Teton Pass route. But the Stone has not been fully authenticated, so the Colter Stone remains a fascinating piece of the puzzle yet to fit into the mystery of John Colter's pioneering sojourn through this region.

ment comes from the present location of the Flathead Sandstone. Activity along the Teton fault separated this formation on the opposing blocks.

On the summit of Mt. Moran 6,000 feet above the valley floor, lies a pink cap of Flathead Sandstone, visible when the snow has melted. On the valley side of the fault, this formation lies buried at least 24,000 feet below the surface.

Early nineteenth century fur trappers referred to high mountain valleys as "holes". When they named this valley Jackson Hole, they were geologically correct! Today the sheer east face of the Teton Range, rising abruptly more than a mile above the valley, captures our attention more than the valley does. Rocks and soil, thousands of feet thick, transported into the valley over the past several million years, mask the subsidence of the valley. Some of the deposits filling Jackson Hole contain innumerable rounded rocks varying in color from white to pink and purple. These quartzite rocks eroded from an ancestral mountain range probably located 20 to 70 miles northwest of the Teton Range. Rivers rounded the quartzite into cobblestones as they carried the rocks into this area.

Volcanism

Vast clouds of volcanic ash blew into the Teton region from the west and north, beginning more than 20 million years ago. White ash accumulated on the sinking floor of Jackson Hole 9 million to 10 million years ago, leaving deposits nearly one mile thick. Between 6 million and 600 thousand years ago, fiery incandescent clouds of gaseous molten rock originated in what is now central Yellowstone Park and flowed southward on both sides of the Teton Range. Remnants of this flow are exposed on Signal Mountain and on the north end of the Teton Range.

Glaciation

The sculpturing influence of ice has provided a final spectacular touch to a scene that already boasted mountains rising sharply from a broad, flat valley. About 150,000 years ago this region experienced a slight cooling that allowed an accumulation of more and more snow each year. Eventually glaciers (masses of ice) began to flow from higher elevations. Over two thousand feet thick in places, the ice sheet flowed from north to south through Jackson Hole. The glacier finally halted south of the town of Jackson and melted about 100,000 years ago.

About 60,000 years ago the glaciers returned, first surging from the east down the Buffalo Valley, stopping near the Snake River Overlook. The most recent ice advance flowed from the Yellowstone Plateau south down the Snake River drainage and east from the canyons in the Teton Range, about 20,000 years ago. The Yellowstone ice mass gouged out the depression occupied today by Jackson Lake. Smaller glaciers flowing eastward down the Teton Range broadened the V-shaped stream canyons into U-shaped canyons, typical evidence of glaciation. Ice flowed from the canyons into Jackson Hole, then melted to form the basins that small lakes occupy today. Glacial lakes include: Phelps, Taggart, Bradley, Jenny, String, and Leigh. As glaciers flowed down the canyons, rocks and ice smoothed and polished canyon floors and walls. Look for glacial polishing today in Cascade and other canyons. Other telltale signs of glaciation include cirque lakes high up in the canyons, such as Lake Solitude in the north fork of Cascade Canyon.

The peaks of the Teton Range became more jagged from frost-wedging, where water freezing in the rocks exerted a prying force, eventually chiseling the rocks free, leaving the sharp ridges and pinnacles seen today.

Although the last great ice masses melted about 15,000 years ago, a dozen re-established glaciers still exist in the Teton Range. Mt. Moran exhibits five glaciers: Triple Glaciers on the north face, prominent Skillet Glacier on the east face and Falling Ice Glacier on the southeast face. Teton Glacier lies in the shadow of the Grand Teton. One way to view a glacier up close involves a ten-mile hike (twenty miles round trip) up the south fork of Cascade Canyon to Schoolroom Glacier. It demonstrates all the features of a classic glacier.

Moraines (deposits of glacially-carried debris) accumulated at the terminus of each ice surge. Because moraines contain a jumble of unsorted rocks and soil that retains water and minerals, glacial debris today supports dense lodgepole pine forests. To locate moraines, look for large stands of pines on ridges projecting above the valley floor, such as Timbered Island and Burned Ridge. Glacial moraines also surround the lakes at the base of the peaks. Where glacial meltwater washed away most of the soil, the cobbles and poor, thin soil left behind cannot retain moisture or nutrients. Sagebrush, certain wildflowers and grasses can tolerate such desert-like growing conditions. Thus the geologic history of a region determines the vegetation and ultimately the wildlife, too.

Accessibility

Facilities for visitors with disabilities include restrooms, picnic tables, and a limited number of campsites.

There are approximately 100 miles of park roads and 200 miles of trails throughout the park. Most park trails are rough rock or dirt and are not accessible to visitors with disabilities.

There are many asphalt trails in the Jenny Lake area, some of which are accessible. Some trails may begin as asphalt and change to dirt or gravel shortly thereafter

Weather

www.mountainweather.com Teton Forecast

Avalanche Forecast
(307) 733-2664 recorded information
(307) 733-2759 report obsreved avalanche activity

Jackson Hole has long, cold winters. The first heavy snows fall by November 1 and continue through March; snow and frost are possible during any month.

Mid-April, May, June
Mild days and cool nights alternate with rain and occasional snow. Valley trails are snow covered until late May.

July and August
Warm days and cool nights prevail, with afternoon thundershowers common.

September, October, November
Sunny days and cold nights alternate with rain and occasional snow storms.

December through mid-April
Between storms the days are sunny and nights are frigid. Snow blankets mountains and valley. Travel is not advised and roads may be closed during blizzards.

Recommended Clothing

Raingear is recommended during spring, summer, and fall. Sub-zero temperatures are common throughout winter and demand multi-layered clothing, hats, mittens and cold weather boots.

Fees

Fees are established annually. Call the Park or consult their website for current fees. 2003 fess were:

Park Entry
$20.00 entrance fee covers both Yellowstone and Grand Teton National Parks.

Camping
$12.00 per night, per site

Other Fees
Fees are also charged for watercraft, backcountry reservations (not permits) and snow planes.

Pets in the Park

Grand Teton National Park is a protected area where wildlife is free to roam undisturbed. Park visitors should be able to enjoy native wildlife in their natural environment without the disruption of other people's pets. For this reason pet restrictions are enforced.

A good rule is a pet may go anywhere a car may go: roads and road shoulders, campgrounds and picnic areas, parking lots, etc. Pets must be on a leash and under physical restraint. Pets are not permitted on any park trails or in the park backcountry. Pets are not considered pack animals.

Regulations

You are responsible for clean-up and disposal of all pet feces.

Pets must be kept under physical control at all times — caged, crated, or restrained on a leash

Photography is one of the most popular pastimes in the park. National Park Service Photo.

not to exceed six feet in length.

Pets are prohibited in the backcountry and on park trails.

Pets are prohibited from public buildings and swimming beaches, except for guide dogs.

Pets are prohibited from riding in boats on park waters, except for Jackson Lake.

Pets must stay within 50 feet of any roadway.

Pets must not be left unattended and/or tied to an object.

Pets are prohibited from making unreasonable noise or frightening wildlife.

Pets running-at-large may be impounded and their owner charged for the care and feeding of the animal.

Kennels

If you are planning on exploring areas of the park that are closed to pets, we recommend that you place your pet in a kennel.

Jackson, Wyoming
Alpha Animal Care
(307) 733-5352

Babysitting by the Tetons
(307) 733-0754

Critter Camp
(307) 733-4279

Kindness Kennels
(307) 733-2633

Spring Creek Kennels
(307) 733-1606

Idaho
The Hairball Hotel
(208) 787-2806

Petstoppe Ranch
(208) 787-2420

Bear Safety

Allowing a bear to obtain human food, even once, often results in aggressive behavior. The bear then becomes a threat to human safety and must be removed or destroyed. Help keep park bears wild and safe. Do not feed the bears for any reason! Failure to follow park regulations is a violation of federal law and may result in citations and fines.

Keep a Clean Camp

After eating and before leaving camp or sleeping, check to be sure you have a clean, bear-proof campsite:

All food, containers, and utensils must be stored in a bear box or in a closed, locked vehicle with windows rolled up. The only exceptions are during the transport, preparation, and eating of food.

Trash and garbage must be stored in the same manner as food, or placed in bear-proof trash cans or dumpsters.

Treat odorous products such as soap, deodorant, sunscreen, and perfumes in the same manner as food.

For your safety absolutely no food, foodstuffs, garbage, or odorous products may be stored in tents or sleeping bags.

Ice chests, thermoses, water containers, barbecue grills, stoves, dishes, and pans must be stored in the same way as food — inside a locked vehicle or bear box.

Grizzly bear. Best to watch from a (long) distance. National Park Service Photo.

Bear Etiquette

If you encounter a bear, do not run. If the bear is unaware of you, detour quickly and quietly away. If the bear is aware but has not acted aggressively, back slowly away while talking in an even tone.

Never approach a bear for any reason.

Never allow a bear to get human food. If approached while eating, put food away and retreat to a safe distance (100 yards/91 meters).

Never abandon food because of an approaching bear. Always take it with you.

Never throw your pack or food at a bear in an attempt to distract it.

Never bury food scraps, containers, or fish entrails. Put them in trash cans.

Never leave food, containers, or garbage unattended in camp. Bears are active both day and night.

You Can Make a Difference

Since 1996, seven bears have been destroyed in this park due to irresponsible human behavior that led to the bear's habituation to human food. Please help to ensure that similar situations are not repeated. Your actions while on park trails and in the campground will affect the chances of these bears survival.

If you encounter a bear, *do not approach it for any reason.* Bears are unpredictable and should be watched only from a safe distance of at least 100 yards (91m). Report all bear sightings to a ranger.

Wildlife Viewing

Always Keep a Safe Distance When Viewing Wildlife

All animals require food, water, and shelter. Each species also has particular living space, or habitat, requirements. To learn more about wildlife habitats and animal behavior, attend ranger-led activities.

Oxbow Bend

One mile east of Jackson Lake Junction. Slow-moving water provides habitat for fish such as suckers and trout, which become food for river otters, ospreys, bald eagles, American white pelicans, and common mergansers. Look for swimming beavers and muskrats. Moose browse on abundant willows at the water's edge. Elk occasionally graze in open aspen groves to the east.

Timbered Island

A forested ridge southeast of Jenny Lake. Small bands of pronghorn antelope, the fastest North American land animal, forage on nearby sagebrush throughout the day.

Elk leave the shade of Timbered Island at dawn and dusk to eat the grasses growing among the surrounding sagebrush.

Mormon Row

East of Highway 26-89-91, one mile north of Moose Junction. Along Mormon Row and Antelope Flats Road, bison and pronghorn can be seen grazing in spring, summer, and fall. Also watch for coyotes, Northern harriers, and American kestrels hunting mice, Uinta ground squirrels, and grasshoppers. Sage grouse, sage thrashers, and sparrows also frequent the area.

Snake River

Jackson Lake Dam south to Moose. Elk and bison graze in grassy meadows along the river. Bison also eat grasses in the sagebrush flats on the benches above the river. Bald eagles, ospreys, and great blue herons build large stick nests within sight of the river. Beavers and moose eat willows that line the waterway.

Cascade Canyon

West of Jenny Lake. Look for, but do not feed, golden-mantled ground squirrels at Inspiration

Point. Pikas and yellow-bellied marmots live in scattered boulder fields.

Mule deer and moose occasionally browse on shrubs growing at the mouth of the canyon. Listen for the numerous songbirds that nest in the canyon.

Blacktail Ponds

Half-mile north of Moose on Highway 26-89-191. Old beaver ponds have filled in and now support grassy meadows where elk graze during the cooler parts of the day. Several kinds of ducks feed in the side channels of the Snake River. Moose browse on willows growing along the river.

Be a Responsible Wildlife Observer

Use binoculars, spotting scopes or long lenses for close views and photographs. Always maintain a safe distance of at least 300 feet from large animals such as bears, bison, moose, and elk.

Never position yourself between an adult and its offspring. Females with young are especially defensive.

It is illegal to feed wildlife, including ground squirrels and birds. Feeding wild animals makes them dependent on people, and animals often bite the hand that feeds them.

Do not harass wildlife. Harassment is any human action that causes unusual behavior, or a change of behavior, in an animal. Repeated encounters with people can have negative, long-term impacts on wildlife,including increased levels of stress and the avoidance of essential feeding areas.

Nesting birds are easily disturbed. For wildlife, raising young is a private affair. If an adult bird on a nest fl.ies off at your approach, or circles you or screams in alarm, you are too close to the nest. Unattended nestlings readily succumb to predation and exposure to heat, cold, and wet weather.

Allow other visitors a chance to enjoy wildlife. If your actions cause an animal to flee, you have deprived other visitors of a viewing opportunity. Use an animal's behavior as a guide to your actions, and limit the time you spend with wildlife, just as you would when visiting a friend's home.

A trip into the backcountry requires advance planning. Download the Backcountry publication for more details.

Backcountry Regulations

• Pets, weapons, bicycles, and vehicles are not allowed on trails or in the backcountry.

• All overnight camping requires a permit.

• Carry out all your garbage.

• Prevent erosion by hiking on established trails erosion.

• Horses have the right-of-way. Step off the trail and remain quiet while horses pass.

• Observe and photograph wildlife from a safe distance. Do not approach or feed animals.

•Prevent contamination of waterways by burying feces in a hole 6-8 inches deep at least 200 feet from streams and lakes. Pack out used toilet paper, tampons, sanitary napkins, and diapers in sealed plastic bags. Do not bury or burn them.

For your safety

• This is bear country. Make bears aware of your presence and avoid surprising them by making loud noises like shouting or singing.

John D. Rockefeller,Jr. Memorial Parkway

Located at the heart of the Greater Yellowstone Ecosystem, the Rockefeller Parkway connects Grand Teton and Yellowstone National Parks. The late conservationist and philanthropist John D. Rockefeller, Jr. made significant contributions to several national parks including Grand Teton, Acadia, Great Smoky Mountains, and Virgin Islands. In 1972 Congress dedicated a 24,000 acre parcel of land as the John D. Rockefeller, Jr. Memorial Parkway to recognize his generosity and foresight. Congress also named the highway from the south boundary of Grand Teton to West Thumb in Yellowstone in honor of Rockefeller.

The Rockefeller Parkway provides a natural link between the two national parks and contains features characteristic of both areas. In the parkway, the Teton Range tapers to a gentle slope at its northern edge, while rocks born of volcanic flows from Yellowstone line the Snake River and form outcroppings scattered atop hills and ridges.

• Carry drinking water.

• Be prepared for rapid weather changes; bring rain gear and extra clothing.

•High elevation may cause breathing difficulties; pace yourself.

• Snow melts gradually, leaving valley trails by mid-June, canyon trails by late July. Be careful crossing snowfields and streams.

• Tell someone where you are going and when you expect to return.

• Solo hiking and off-trail hiking are not recommended.

•Check with a ranger for current information on trail conditions.

Avoid Crowds

During July and August trailhead parking areas fill early, especially at South Jenny Lake, String Lake, Lupine Meadows, Death Canyon, and Granite Canyon. Parking on natural vegetation results in permanent damage to plants; violators will be ticketed.

In paved parking lots, parking illegally will also result in a ticket. An early start will help you avoid parking problems.

Scenic Drives

Many turnouts along park roads offer exhibits on park geology, wildlife, and plants. Turnouts also provide safe places to enjoy scenic views and take photographs. Do not stop in the middle of the road to view wildlife.

The Teton Park Road follows the base of the Teton Range from Moose to Jackson Lake Junction.

The Jenny Lake Scenic Drive skirts Jenny Lake and provides spectacular views of the peaks; the scenic drive is one-way and begins just south of String Lake.

The Signal Mountain Summit Road climbs 800 feet (242 meters) to panoramic views of the Teton Range, Jackson Hole valley, and Jackson Lake.

Driving Safely

Watch for large animals on the road. Drive slowly at night. Elk, bison and mule deer frequently migrate at night and may be difficult to see. Moose use roads as travel corridors. Hitting a large animal at highway speeds has resulted in fatal accidents. Careful driving protects you and wildlife. Always wear your seatbelt.

Half-Day Activities

You can do all of these activiites in a half-day.

Colter Bay Visitor Center and Indian Arts Museum

Visit the museum to view art created by native peoples and gain a glimpse of 19th century American Indian life. American Indian and wildlife videotapes and a park orientation slide program are shown throughout the day. Ranger-led activities include museum tours, park orientation talks, natural history hikes and evening amphitheater programs.

Signal Mountain Summit Road

This 5-mile drive starts one mile south of Signal Mountain Lodge and Campground. The road winds to the top of Signal Mountain, 800 feet above the valley. Summit overlooks provide panoramic views of the entire Teton Range, Jackson Lake and most of Jackson Hole. The road is narrow and parking at overlooks is limited, so no trailers or large motorhomes, please.

Jenny Lake Scenic Drive

Turn at North Jenny Lake and drive south-west. Stop at the Cathedral Group Turnout for a spectacular view of the Grand Teton (13,770'), Teewinot and Mt. Owen. The road is two-way as far as String Lake and Jenny Lake Lodge. South of String Lake, the road becomes one-way and provides a relaxed lakeshore drive with views of Jenny Lake. Rejoin the Teton Park Road near South Jenny Lake.

Menors Ferry & the Chapel of the Transfiguration

Turn off the Teton Park Road 0.5-mile north of Moose. The Menor's Ferry Trail, less than 0.5-mile long, affords a look at homesteading and pioneer life in Jackson Hole. Visit Bill Menor's cabin and country store. Ride a replica of the ferry that crossed the Snake River at the turn of the century (the ferry is launched after high water in the spring, usually after the 4th of July). The altar window of the Chapel of the Transfiguration frames the tallest Teton peaks. Please be respectful, the chapel is a house of worship.

Whole-Day Activities

If you have a whole day add the following stops to those suggested for the half day visit:

Willow Flats

Stop at the Willow Flats Turnout, 6 miles south of Colter Bay, for a view of an extensive freshwater marsh that provides excellent habitat for birds, beavers and moose. Jackson Lake and the Teton Range for the backdrop.

Oxbow Bend

Located one mile east of Jackson Lake Junction, this cut-off meander of the Snake River attracts a wide variety of wildlife. Mount Moran, the most massive peak in the Teton Range, dominates the background.

Jackson Lake Dam Overlook

Jackson Lake Dam, one mile west of Jackson Lake Junction on the Teton Park Road, raises the level of Jackson Lake a maximum of 39 feet. In addition to being a reservoir, Jackson Lake is also

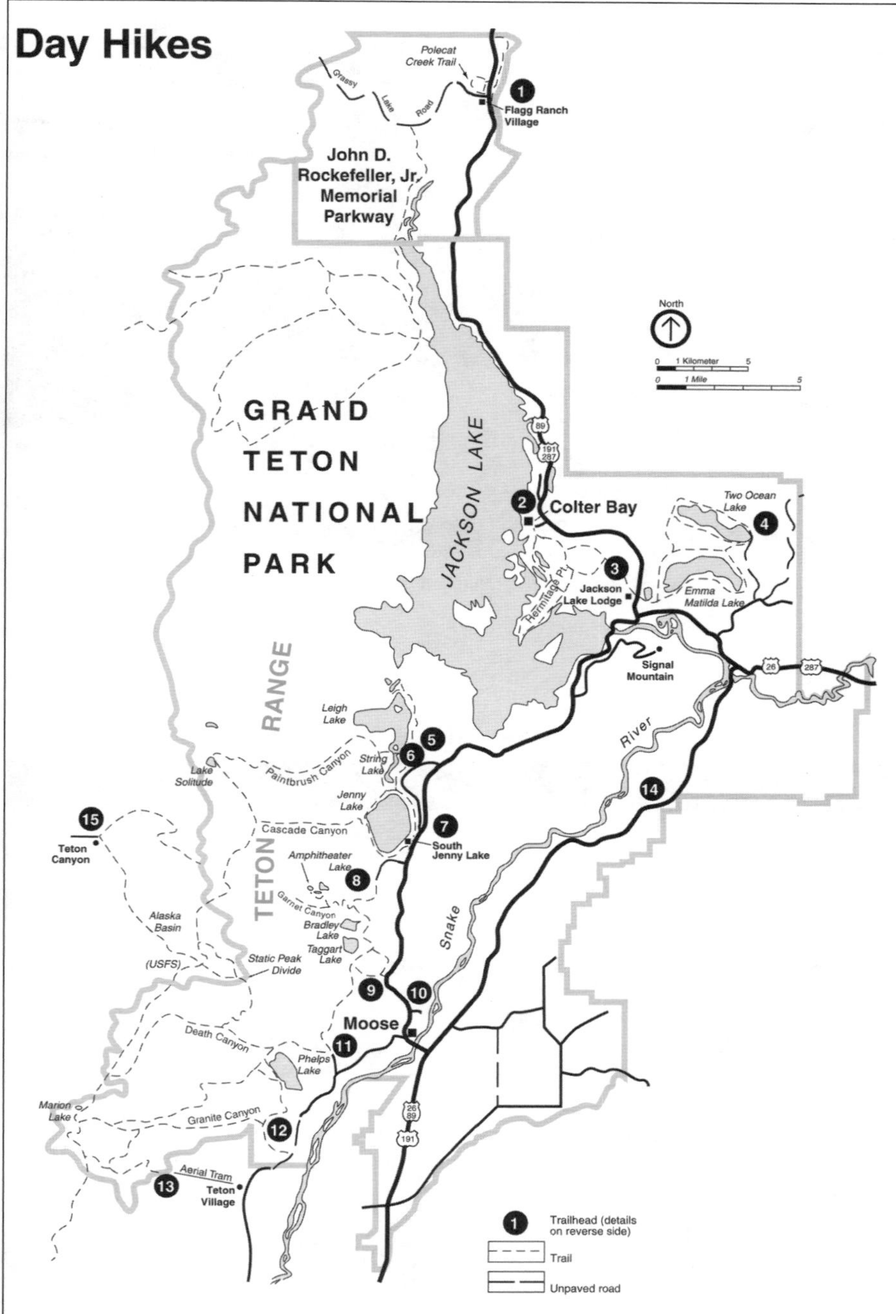

a natural lake formed by an immense glacier that once flowed from Yellowstone National Park. Park on the southwest side of the dam and take a short walk for a peaceful view of Jackson Lake and Mount Moran.

South Jenny Lake

Park at South Jenny Lake and take a short walk to view glacially-carved Jenny Lake nestled at the base of the tallest Teton peaks. A 6-mile hiking trail encircles Jenny Lake. Shuttle boats (early June through late September) provide easy access to the west shore of the lake and trails to Hidden Falls, Inspiration Point and Cascade Canyon. Parking is limited and the trail becomes crowded, so plan to arrive early or late in the day. A midday arrival will be frustrating.

Antelope Flats-Kelly Loop

At Gros Ventre Junction, 5 miles south of Moose Junction on Highway 26-89-191, turn east. Follow the road to the small town of Kelly. To see the Gros Ventre Slide, turn at the sign marked national forest access. The Gros Ventre Slide occurred in 1925 when earthquakes and rain caused the north end of Sheep Mountain to break off and dam the Gros Ventre River, forming Lower Slide Lake. Follow the Antelope Flats Road along hayfields and ranches to rejoin Highway 26-89-121.

Multi-Day Activities

If you have more than one day, try some of these ideas in addition to the half-day and whole-day suggestions:

Attend Ranger-Led Activities

Join a ranger for a visitor center talk, museum tour, stroll, hike or evening program. From early June to Labor Day a full schedule of activities is conducted daily. Consult a park newspaper, available at visitor centers and entrance stations, or various bulletin boards in the park. Attend the activities of your choice and learn more about the natural and human history of the park and parkway.

Take a Hike

Over 200 miles of hiking trails in the park and parkway range from level and easy trails on the valley floor to steep, arduous trails into the mountains. At visitor centers, ask a ranger for recommended hikes and look at or purchase maps and trail guides. Parking areas at popular trail heads fill as early as 11:00 a.m., from late June to early September.

Go Rafting

Park and parkway concessioners and operators provide a variety of floating and fishing trips on the Snake River. Equipment is also available for rent in Jackson from several sources.

Ride a Bike

The Teton Park Road has wide shoulders and superb views of the Tetons. The Antelope Flats-Kelly Loop provides riding opportunities on secondary roads. Ride bikes only where cars can legally go; bicycles are not allowed on trails or in the backcountry. Equipment is available at Dornans and in Jackson from several sources.

Climb a Mountain

The Teton Range offers many opportunities for climbers and mountaineers. The Jenny Lake Ranger Station is the center for climbing information and climbers are encouraged to stop in and obtain information on routes, conditions and regulations. Registration for day climbs is not required, while all overnight stays require a backcountry permit. The Jenny Lake Ranger Station is open from early June to mid-September, 8 a.m. to 6 p.m.

Go Horseback Riding

Park concessioners offer horseback rides at Colter Bay and Jackson Lake Lodge. A publication is available for Saddle and Pack Stock.

Day Hikes

The following hikes are shown on the accompanying map.

1. Flagg Ranch

Polecat Creek Loop Trail, 2.5 miles roundtrip, 2 hours, EASY.

West side of level loop follows ridge above a marsh, habitat for waterfowl and other wildlife.

Flagg Canyon, 5.0 miles roundtrip, 3-4 hours, 40-foot elevation change, EASY.

Access from east side of Polecat Creek Loop Trail. Spectacular views of the Snake River.

2. Colter Bay

Lakeshore Trail, 2.0 miles roundtrip, 1 hour, EASY.

Level trail follows east and north shoreline of Colter Bay then follows perimeter of a forested peninsula jutting into Jackson Lake, providing views of the northern part of the Teton Range.

Heron Pond & Swan Lake, 3.0 miles roundtrip, 2 hours, 40-foot elevation change, EASY

Follow mostly level trail to ponds to see birds and other wildlife. Brochure available.

Hermitage Point, 8.8 miles roundtrip, 4 hours, 100-foot elevation change, EASY

Forests, meadows, ponds, and streams along trail provide wildlife habitat. Terrain is gently rolling.

3. Jackson Lake Lodge

Lunch Tree Hill, 0.5 mile roundtrip, 1/2 hour, 80-foot elevation change, EASY.

Short trail with interpretive signs leads to top of hill overlooking Willow Flats and Teton Range.

4. Two Ocean Lake

Two Ocean Lake, 6.4 miles roundtrip, 3 hours, 80-foot elevation change, MODERATE.

Traverses conifer forests along the south shore; aspens and meadows on the north shore.

Emma Matilda Lake, 9.1 miles roundtrip, 5 hours, 440-ft elevation change, MODERATE.

Follows lakeshore with views of the Tetons.

Two Ocean & Emma Matilda Lakes, 12.9 miles roundtrip, 7 hours, 710-foot elevation change, MODERATE.

Follows north shore of Two Ocean Lake, climbs to Grand View Point for a panoramic view, then follows south shore of Emma Matilda Lake looping back to Two Ocean Lake.

5. Leigh Lake

Leigh Lake, 2.0 miles roundtrip, 1 hour, 40- foot elevation change, EASY.

Bearpaw Lake, 7.4 miles roundtrip, 4 hours, 40-foot elevation change, EASY

Follows forested shore of Leigh Lake, with close views of Mount Moran.

6. String Lake

String Lake, 3.3 miles roundtrip, 3 hours, 120-foot elevation change, EASY.

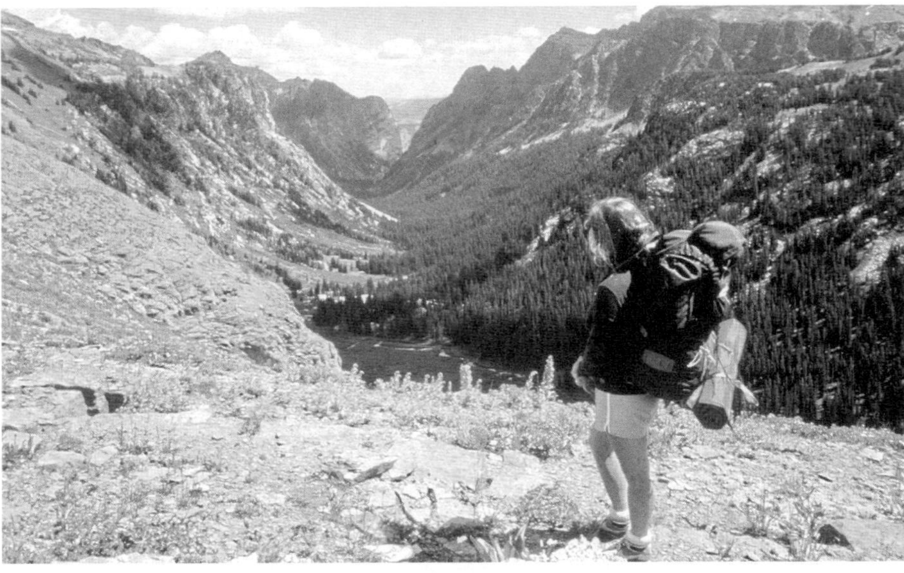

Backcountry travel is uncrowded and rewarding. National Park Service Photo.

Hermitage Point, Two Ocean & Emma Matilda Lakes Trails

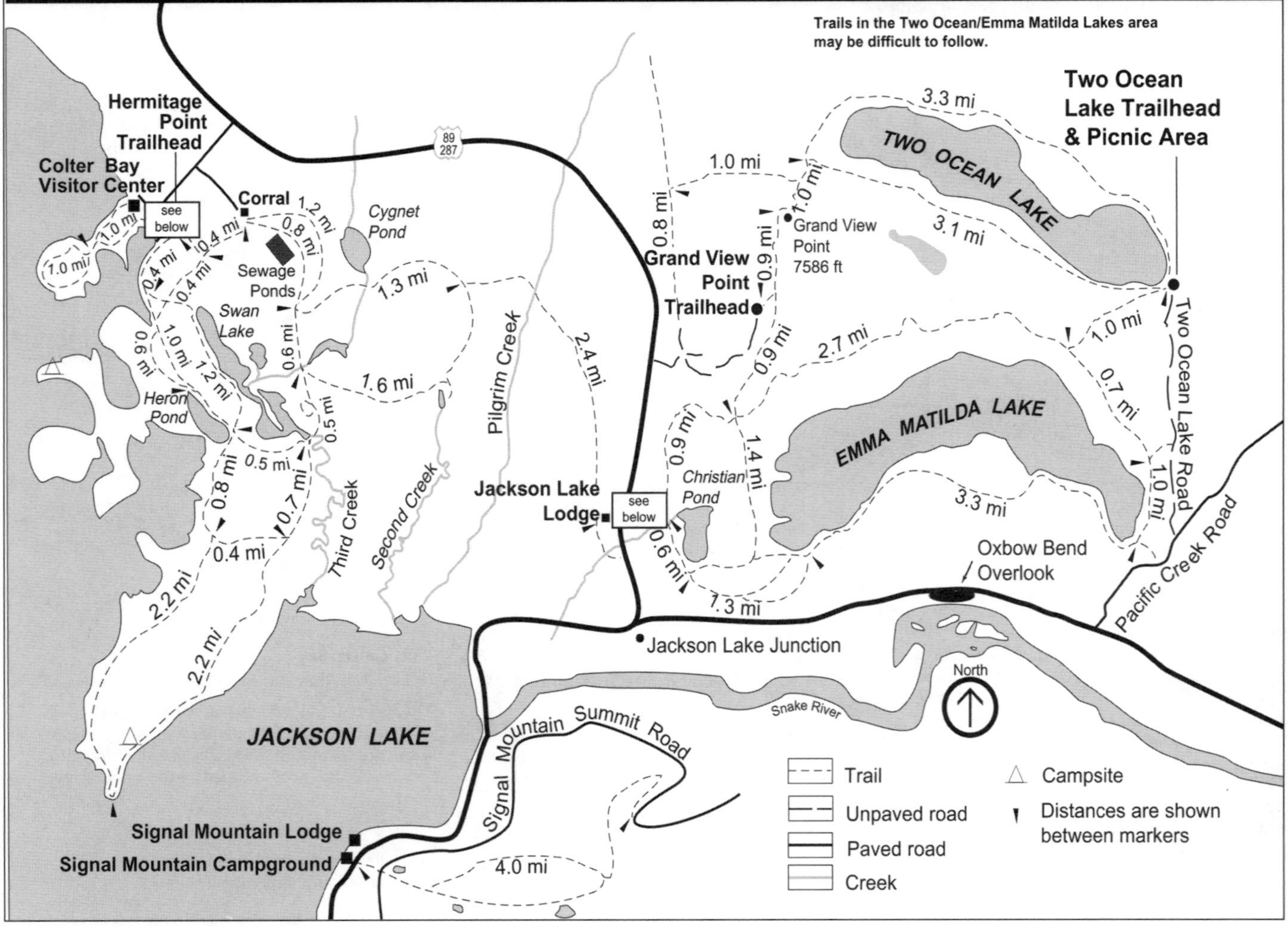
Trails in the Two Ocean/Emma Matilda Lakes area may be difficult to follow.
Two Ocean Lake Trailhead & Picnic Area
Hermitage Point Trailhead
Colter Bay Visitor Center
see below
Corral
Cygnet Pond
Sewage Ponds
Swan Lake
Heron Pond
Third Creek
Second Creek
Pilgrim Creek
Grand View Point Trailhead
Grand View Point 7586 ft
TWO OCEAN LAKE
EMMA MATILDA LAKE
Christian Pond
Jackson Lake Lodge
Oxbow Bend Overlook
Jackson Lake Junction
Two Ocean Lake Road
Pacific Creek Road
89 287
Snake River
North
JACKSON LAKE
Signal Mountain Summit Road
Signal Mountain Lodge
Signal Mountain Campground
1.0 mi
0.4 mi
0.6 mi
1.2 mi
0.8 mi
1.3 mi
1.6 mi
0.5 mi
0.7 mi
2.2 mi
2.4 mi
3.3 mi
3.1 mi
2.7 mi
0.9 mi
1.4 mi
7.3 mi
4.0 mi
Trail
Unpaved road
Paved road
Creek
Campsite
Distances are shown between markers

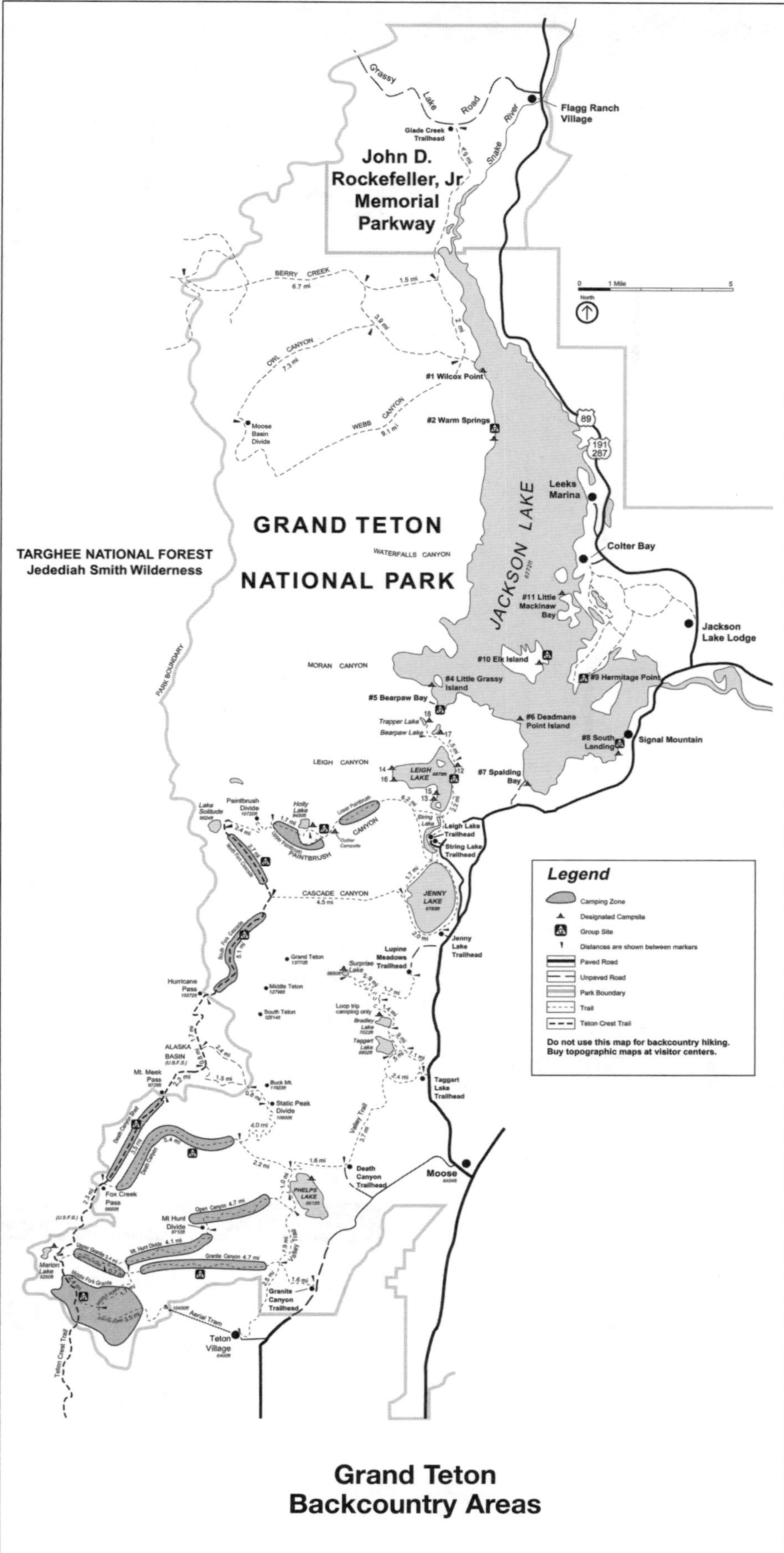

Grand Teton Backcountry Areas

Trail circles the lake through a burned area just below Rockchuck Peak and Mt. St. John.

Holly Lake, 12.4 miles roundtrip, 8 hours, 2535-foot elevation change, STRENUOUS.

Follow Paintbrush Canyon trail through seasonally abundant wildflowers.

Paintbrush-Cascade Loop, 19.2 miles roundtrip, 14 hours, 3845-foot elevation change, VERY STRENUOUS.

Hike up Paintbrush Canyon, over Paintbrush Divide, and down Cascade Canyon. An ice axe may be necessary until August.

7. Cascade Canyon

Jenny Lake Loop, 6.6 miles roundtrip, 4 hours, 100-foot elevation change, EASY

Mostly level trail skirts shoreline, with views of the Teton Range. Brochure available.

Hidden Falls, 5.0 miles roundtrip, 3 hours, 150-foot elevation change; via shuttle boat (fee charged): 1.0 mile, 1-1/2 hours, 150-foot elevation change, MODERATE.

Popular trail follows Jenny Lake's south shore, then climbs to view of 200-foot cascade.

Inspiration Point, 5.8 miles roundtrip, 4 hours, 417-foot elevation change; via shuttle boat (fee charged): 2.2 miles roundtrip, 2-1/2 hours, 417-foot elevation change, MODERATE-STRENUOUS.

Follow trail to Hidden Falls, then continue up to Inspiration Point overlooking Jenny Lake

Forks of Cascade Canyon, 13.0 miles roundtrip, 7 hours, 1057-foot elevation change; via shuttle boat (fee charged): 9.0 miles roundtrip, 5 hours, 105-foot elevation change, MODERATE-STRENUOUS.

Popular trail leads into Cascade Canyon with views of the Grand, Mt. Owen, and Teewinot.

Lake Solitude, 18.4 miles roundtrip, 10 hours, 2252-foot elevation change; via shuttle boat (fee charged): 14.4 miles roundtrip, 8 hours, 2252-foot elevation change, STRENUOUS.

Follow popular Cascade Canyon trail. North Fork leads to Lake Solitude and views of the Grand and Mt. Owen.

South Fork of Cascade Canyon, 23.2 miles roundtrip, 12 hours, 3589-foot elevation change; via shuttle boat (fee charged): 19.2 miles roundtrip, 11 hours, 3589-foot elevation change, STRENUOUS

Follow popular Cascade Canyon trail. South Fork leads to Hurricane Pass and views of Schoolroom Glacier.

8. Lupine Meadows

Amphitheater and Surprise Lakes, 9.6 miles roundtrip, 8 hours, 2958-foot elevation change, STRENUOUS

Hike up to glacial lakes surrounded by subalpine meadows. Horses not allowed.

Garnet Canyon, 8.2 miles roundtrip, 7 hours, 2160-foot elevation change, STRENUOUS

Trail leads to the mouth of Garnet Canyon. Horses not allowed.

9. Taggart Lake

Taggart Lake, 3.2 miles roundtrip, 2 hours, 277-foot elevation change, MODERATE.

Trail traverses area burned in 1985 to reach Taggart Lake.

Bradley & Taggart Lakes

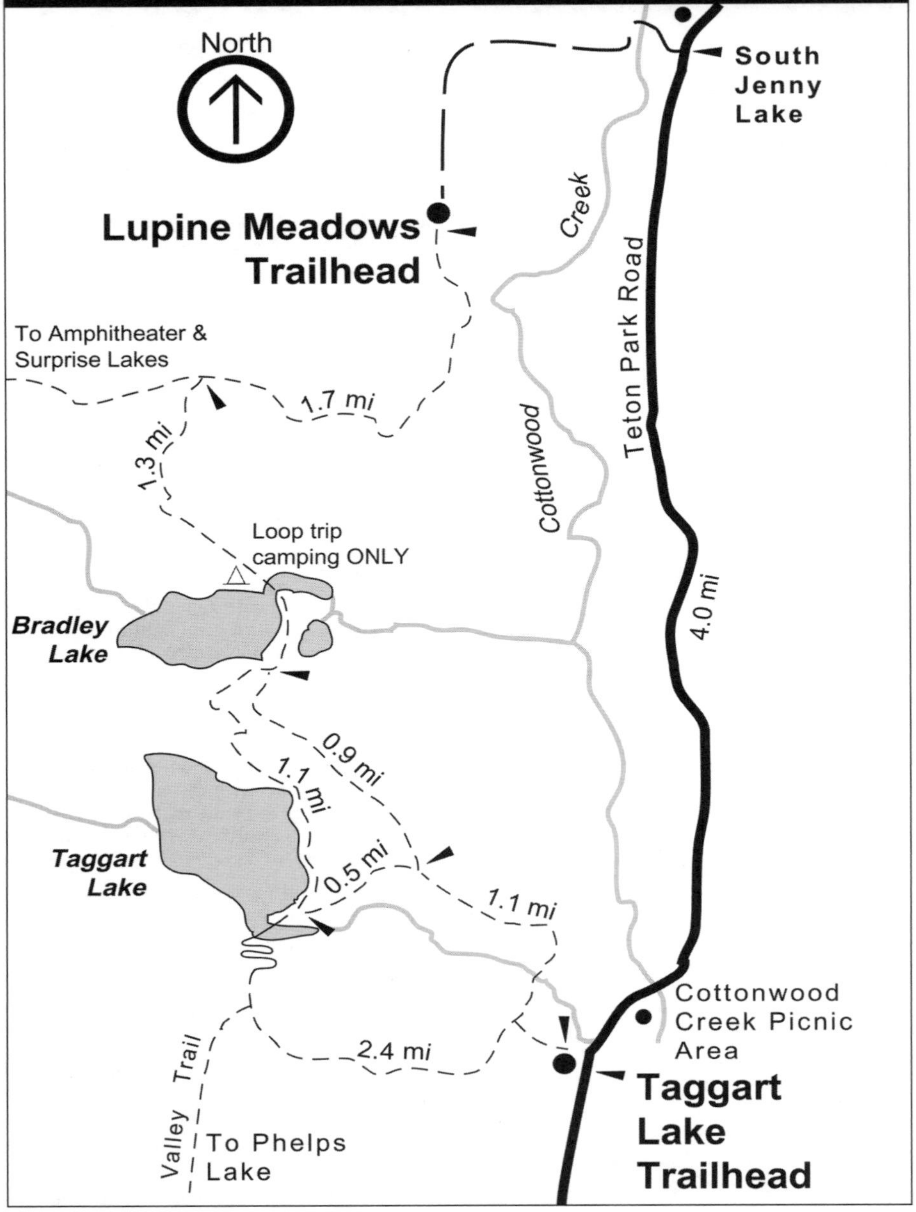

North
South Jenny Lake
Lupine Meadows Trailhead
To Amphitheater & Surprise Lakes
1.7 mi
1.3 mi
Loop trip camping ONLY
Bradley Lake
Cottonwood Creek
Teton Park Road
4.0 mi
0.9 mi
1.1 mi
Taggart Lake
0.5 mi
1.1 mi
Cottonwood Creek Picnic Area
2.4 mi
Valley Trail
To Phelps Lake
Taggart Lake Trailhead

Bradley Lake, 4.0 miles roundtrip, 3 hours, 397-foot elevation change, MODERATE.

Trail climbs through area burned in 1985, then down a glacial moraine to Bradley Lake.

Taggart Lake-Beaver Creek, 4.0 miles roundtrip, 3 hours, 277-foot elevation change, MODERATE.

Trail traverses area burned in 1985 and climbs glacial moraines surrounding Taggart Lake.

10. Chapel of the Transfiguration
Menor's Ferry, 0.5 mile roundtrip, 1/2 hour, 10-foot elevation change, EASY.

See an original homestead on the banks of the Snake River. Brochure available.

11. Death Canyon
Phelps Lake Overlook, 1.8 miles roundtrip, 2 hours, 420-foot elevation change, MODERATE.

Trail climbs moraine to overlook Phelps Lake. Phelps Lake, 4.0 miles roundtrip, 4 hours, 987-foot elevation change, STRENUOUS.

Trail climbs to overlook, then descends to Phelps Lake. Return involves steep hike up to overlook.

Death Canyon-Static Peak Trail Junction, 7.6 miles roundtrip, 6 hours, 1061-foot elevation change, STRENUOUS.

Trail climbs up and then down to Phelps Lake, followed by a climb into Death Canyon.

Static Peak Divide, 15.6 miles roundtrip, 10 hours, 4020-foot elevation change, VERY STRENUOUS.

Switchbacks through whitebark pine forest to impressive views. Ice axe may be necessary until August.

12. Granite Canyon
Marion Lake, 20.8 miles roundtrip, 12 hours, 2880-foot elevation change, STRENUOUS.

Follow Granite Creek to subalpine meadows around Marion Lake.

13. Top of the Tram
Fee charged for tram. Visitors are allowed to hike trails leading from the tram after snow has melted sufficiently to allow safe travel.

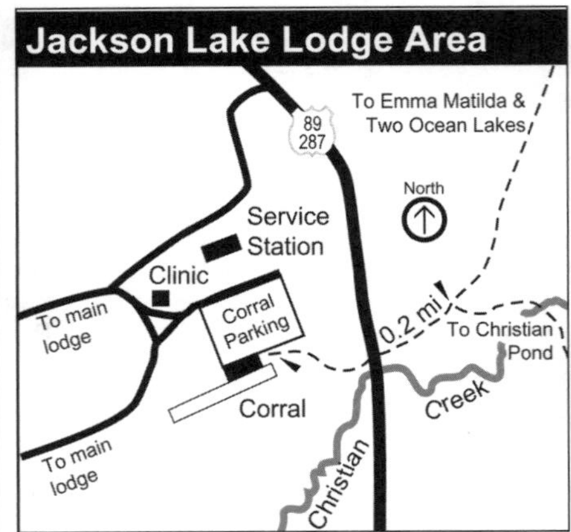

Marion Lake, 11.8 miles roundtrip, 7 hours, 1206-foot elevation change, MODERATELY STRENUOUS.

Hike through alpine and subalpine terrain to Marion Lake and return to the tram.

Granite Canyon, 12.4 miles roundtrip, 7 hours, 4135-foot elevation change (downhill), MODERATE.

Start at the top and hike down through alpine meadows to Teton Village.

14. Cunningham Cabin
Cunningham Cabin, 0.75 mile roundtrip, 1 hour, 20-foot elevation change, EASY.

Follow short trail to see early homestead. Trail leaflet available at trailhead and at visitor centers.

15. Teton Canyon
Targhee National Forest/Table Mountain, 11.0 miles roundtrip, 7 hours, 4151-foot elevation change, STRENUOUS.

Steep trail follows Teton Creek and ends 0.5 mi. below the summit. Ascend summit by scrambling up talus slope. (Brochure available).

BACKCOUNTRY

Planning Your Trip
This guide contains general information regarding Grand Teton National Park's backcountry. For specific information obtain a topographic map of the park or a hiking guide. The map on the other side of this guide is only for planning purposes and selecting campsites. As you plan your trip, consider every member of your party. Also con-

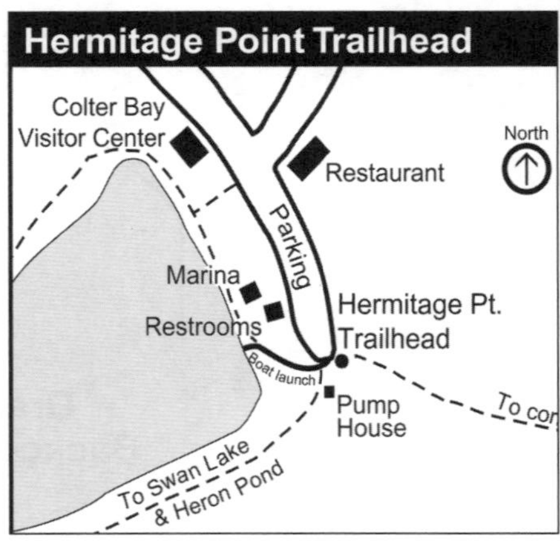

Flagg Ranch Area Trails

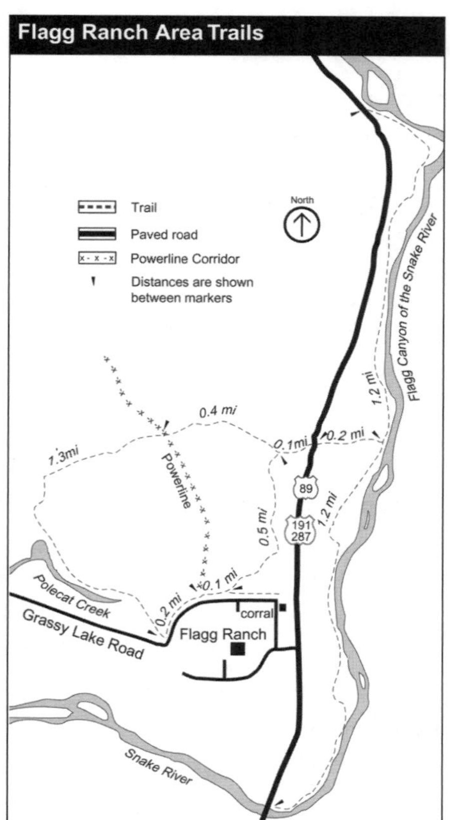

sider the distance and elevation gain to your destination. There is no shuttle service in the park.but taxi services are available from the local community. If you have only one vehicle, you may want to plan a loop trip that returns to the same trailhead. July and August are the busiest times because there is less snow in the high country. Weekends and holidays are busiest for boaters on Jackson Lake.

Getting A Permit

Permits are required for all overnight trips. To minimize impacts on park resources, backcountry permits are limited. One-third of the backcountry campsites and all of the groupsites may be reserved in advance. The rest are filled first-come, first-served at park permit offices.

Reservations

The park backcountry is very popular. Reservations are recommended. Requests are accepted by mail, fax or in person from January 1st to May 15th. Requests are processed in the order received. Include your name, address, and daytime telephone number, the number of people, and your preferred campsites and dates. It is best to include alternate dates and campsites. Write to Grand Teton National Park, Permits Office, P.O. Drawer 170, Moose, WY 83012 or fax to 307 739-3438. Reservations may be made in person at the Moose Visitor Center, open daily from 8 a.m. to 5 p.m. We will return written confirmation within two weeks. Phone reservations are not accepted. Call 307 739-3309 or 739-3397 for more information. A non-refundable service fee of $15 will be charged for each reservation.

Picking Up Your Permit

A reservation holds your permit but does not replace your permit. Obtain permits in person at the Moose and Colter Bay Visitor Centers or the Jenny Lake Ranger Station in the summer. During winter, permits may be picked up only at the Moose Visitor Center. You may get a permit as early as the day before your trip begins. Have alternate destinations and dates in mind in case your first choice is full. A reserved permit must be picked up by 10 a.m. the morning of your trip or it will become available to others. You may call to inform us if you will be late. If you know you will not be using your permit, please cancel your reservation as soon as possible.

Permit Parameters

By signing the backcountry permit you agree to respect the backcountry. Printed on the back of your permit are some of the backcountry regulations. Read and abide by them. Failure to comply with regulations may result in fines and revocation of the permit.

Group Size

Individual parties consist of 1 to 6 people. Groups of 7 to 12 people are limited to camping in designated Groupsites able to withstand the impact of larger groups. In winter, parties are limited to 20 people.

Backcountry Conditions

Snow usually melts from valley trails by mid-June but remains in the high country through much of the summer. Safe travel over Paintbrush, Static Peak, and Moose Basin Divides and Hurricane, Mt. Meek, and Fox Creek Passes requires an ice axe and knowledge of its use until as late as August. Snow conditions vary from year to year. Check with a ranger for current information. Trails begin at about 6800 feet in elevation. Expect to encounter horses and yield to them by stepping off the uphill side of the trail and standing quietly until they pass. Boaters should be aware of strong afternoon winds.

Mountaineering

Permits are not required for mountaineering, but climbers on overnight trips must have a backcountry permit to camp or bivouac. Ask for the Mountaineering brochure. Current and detailed information is available at the Jenny Lake Ranger Station in the summer, 307 739-3343. In the winter call 307 739-3309. From June through September, all Garnet Canyon permits and permits for any trip involving technical climbing or mountaineering should be picked up at the Jenny Lake Ranger Station.

Fishing

A Wyoming state fishing license is required to fish in the park. There are established creel limits. For specific fishing rules and regulations ask for the Fishing brochure. Fishing licenses are available at the Colter Bay, Moose, Flagg Ranch and Signal Mountain camp stores.

Boating

All vessels must be registered with the park annually. A fee is required. Permits may be purchased at the Moose or Colter Bay Visitor Centers. Lakeshore campsites are located on Jackson Lake and Leigh Lake. Camping is not permitted on the Snake river. For specific information regarding the use of watercraft in the park ask for the Boating brochure.

Horses and Llamas

Stock may be used on established trails, however some trails are closed to horses and llamas. There are special campsites and rules for overnight stock use. Ask for the Stock Use brochure.

Stay Limits

Campers may stay in a camping zone or designated sites for two consecutive nights. On

Phelps Lake

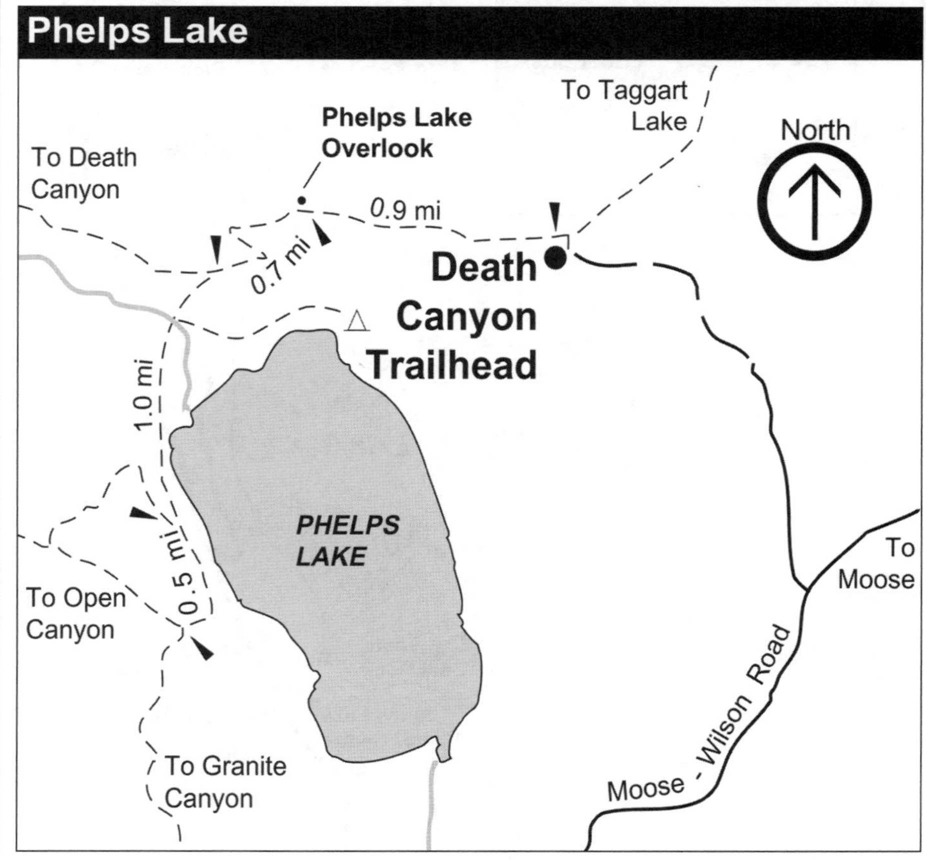

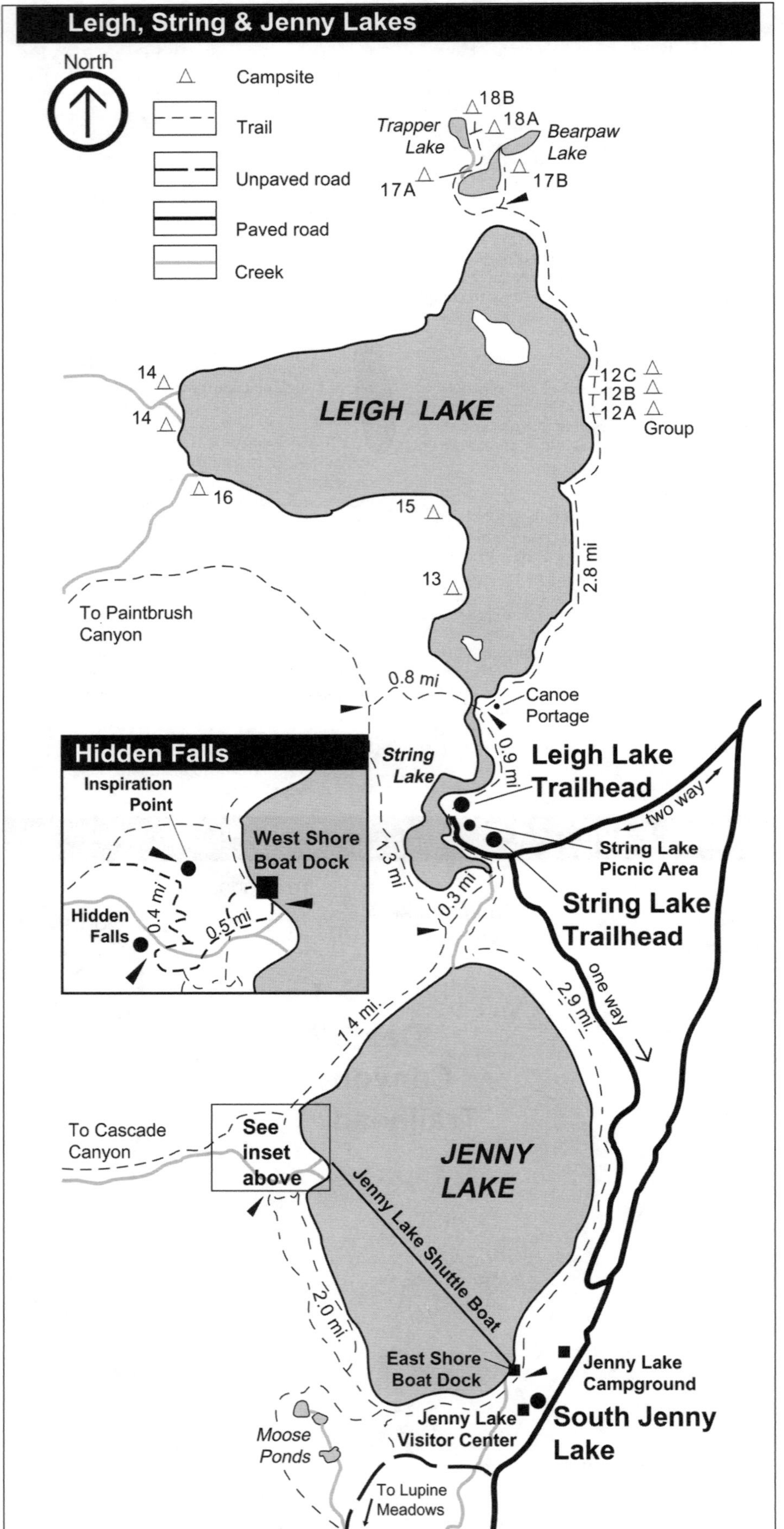

Jackson Lake the limit is 3 nights. Between June 1 and September 15 campers may stay in the backcountry a maximum of 10 nights. In winter, the length of stay is 5 nights in one site.

Maps and Books

Maps and guidebooks are available from the Grand Teton Natural History Association, a nonprofit organization that supports the interpretive, educational, and scientific programs in the park. Call 307- 739-3403 for details. This table characterizes the lower elevation areas of the park. Most of the park is at higher elevations and temperatures will average at least 5 degrees colder. Precipitation will be much greater; the precipitation on the high windward slopes can be expected to be twice that shown here. Be aware that mountain weather changes quickly. Check the weather forecast before starting your trip. In The Backcountry

Managing Backcountry Use

The permit system helps ensure protection of park resources while providing a quality backcountry experience. In popular areas, designated campsites are selected for their durability and are spread apart to minimize disturbance to other campers. Canyons that receive less use are divided into camping zones. A limited number of people are allowed to camp in each zone.

Leave No Trace

- No trace means not leaving litter, scraps of food, fire rings, buried trash, or toilet paper.
- Camp in designated sites where required. In camping zones, where improved sites are not provided use an existing bare ground site at least 200 feet from water and out of sight and sound of others if possible.
- In pristine areas camp on a durable surface such as rock, snow, or bare ground. Dry grass or bare duff can stand a little use, but wildflowers and shrubs are fragile. In any camp, pick bare rock or ground for social gathering and cooking.
- One foot leaves little trace, but many feet combined degrade resources quickly. Stay on existing trails. Feet trample plants and compact soil, leading to erosion. Be sure not to trample new areas. One misplaced step can destroy a tiny 100-year-old plant.
- Shortcutting switchbacks causes erosion and is prohibited.
- Where no trail exists, walk abreast, not single file. It's better to trample many plants a little than a few plants a lot. Walk on rock, snow, or non-vegetated surfaces when possible.
- Be aware that loud voices and radios disturb those who are seeking solitude.
- Your camping impact, added to everyone else's, can remove vegetation from an area.
- Removing flowers, plants, rocks and other natural or cultural objects is prohibited. Please leave them for others to enjoy.
- Strive to avoid resource damage, and be aware that past damage must be remedied. You may see trails rerouted or campsites closed so scars from overuse may heal. Please respect these efforts by staying out of closed areas and by using existing trails. Please help keep Grand Teton's backcountry looking "grand." The scenery that you came here to experience needs to be preserved for your next visit and for generations to come.

Water

Giardia, campylobacter and other harmful organisms that cause intestinal disorders with severe diarrhea can be transmitted through untreated water. To be certain that your water is safe, treat backcountry water by boiling or filtering with a portable water filter.

Sanitation

Prevent contaminated waterways. Urinate at least 200 feet away from any water source in rocky places that won't be damaged by animals digging for the salts and minerals found in human urine. Bury feces in soil 6-8 inches deep and at least 200 feet from lakes, streams, and wetlands. Pack out toilet paper in a sealed plastic bag or use natural options such as rocks, snow, or vegetation. Store used tampons, sanitary napkins, and diapers in sealed plastic bags.

Backcountry Regulations

Regulations are needed to protect resources and ensure a high quality backcountry experience. Your cooperation is needed in understanding and abiding by all park rules. Help eliminate the need for more restrictions by hiking and camping responsibly.

The following key regulations are strictly enforced.

Permits are required for all overnight stays. The permit is valid only for the location and dates indicated.

Campsite "improvements" such as the construction of rock walls, log benches, tree bough beds, new fire rings, and trenches are prohibited.

Fires are permitted only at designated lakeshore sites. Where permitted, fires must be confined to metal fire grates.

Keep fires small and do not leave them unattended. Downed and dead wood may be collected. Gas stoves are encouraged.

Pets, bicycles, wheeled vehicles, motorized equipment, weapons, and explosives including fireworks are not allowed in the backcountry.

Anglers must have a Wyoming State fishing license in possession.

Horse, mule and llama use is limited to established trails and stock camps. Use hitch rails where provided. Carry stock feed; grazing is not allowed.

Shortcutting trail switchbacks is prohibited.

Keep a safe distance from wildlife. Feeding wildlife interferes with their natural diet and is harmful to their health. Please don't feed the animals.

This is bear country. Follow the food storage regulations in the In Bear Country section of this brochure.

Prevent pollution by not washing dishes or bathing in or near streams or lakes.

Carry out all trash and food scraps. When possible, carry out trash left by others. Never bury trash or attempt to burn aluminum.

Black bears and grizzly bears live in the park and parkway. Follow these guidelines to make your hike and camp safer. They are for your protection and for the preservation of the bears, one of the true signs of wild country.

Camping Zones

With a permit, you may stay within the indicated camping zone, unless assigned to a designated site.

- Signs mark the beginning and end of each zone. If there are groupsites or improved campsites inside the zone, they are marked with signs.

Jackson Lake

- In non-designated sites, camp out of sight of trails and other campers. Camp on previously impacted campsites.
- Camp at least 200 feet from lakes and streams, where possible.
- Group campsites may only be used by groups specifically assigned to them. Groupsites are marked with signs.
- Fires are prohibited, use a stove.
- Bears are common. Properly hang your food using the counter-balance method. Food storage poles or boxes are available at some sites.

Berry Creek, Webb Canyon & Canyons Without Trails

Bears, including grizzlies, are frequently observed in this area. Hiking includes difficult and dangerous stream crossings without bridges. Safe travel requires good physical condition and experience with map and compass. Hikers must be prepared for selfevacuation in case of problems. Horse and llama camping is permitted only at Hechtman Stock Camp.

Lower Paintbrush Canyon Zone

Begins 3 miles from the String Lake Parking Area below the first crossing of Paintbrush Creek. The upper camping zone boundary is 1.5 miles below the lower Holly Lake Trail Junction. The "Outlier" campsite is I mile below Holly Lake and is a designated site.

Upper Paintbrush Canyon Zone

Extends from about 0.1 mile above the lower Holly Lake Trail Junction to the Paintbrush Divide headwall, on the main canyon trail. From the lower end of the zone to the upper Holly Lake Trail Junction, camp only on the south side of the trail (the left side as you hike up the canyon). From the upper Holly Lake Trail Junction to the Paintbrush Divide headwall, you may camp on either side of the trail.

Holly Lake Designated Sites

Follow the Holly Lake Trail to the trail marked "Holly Lake Campsites" that begins at Holly Lake. This trail leads north to two designated campsites, each marked with a sign. Group and stock site is 0.25 mile below Holly Lake.

North Fork Cascade Zone

Extends from the second bridge above the fork to where the trail crosses the stream Lake Solitude. Groupsite is 0.5 mile above the lower boundary of the zone on terraces east of the trail.

South Fork Cascade Zone

Begins 1 mile above the Cascade Canyon trail fork and ends 0.5 mile below Hurricane Pass. Groupsite is 1.75 miles above the trail fork, east of the trail.

Death Canyon Zone

Starts 4.5 miles from the Death Canyon Trailhead 1/4-mile above the bridge crossing of Death Canyon Creek. The lower zone boundary is 0.5 mile west of the Death Canyon Patrol Cabin (not staffed). The upper boundary is 0.5 mile below Fox Creek Pass. Groupsite is between the trail and creek, 2 miles west of the patrol cabin.

Death Canyon Shelf Zone

Extends from just above Fox Creek Pass to Mt. Meek Pass. Groupsite is 2 miles north of Fox Creek Pass.

Marion Lake Designated Sites

Three sites are just east of the lake. A spur trail leads east from the lake. Please camp on tent pads.

North Fork Granite Canyon Zone

Lower boundary is 0.25 mile above the Middle/North Fork trail junction. The upper boundary is where the trail crosses the North Fork Creek.

South-Middle Forks Zone

Lower boundary is 0.75 mile above the upper Middle/North Fork trail junction. On the north, the boundary is the ridge between the North and Middle Forks. The east boundary is 1.5 miles from the top of the tram. Groupsite is 4.6 miles

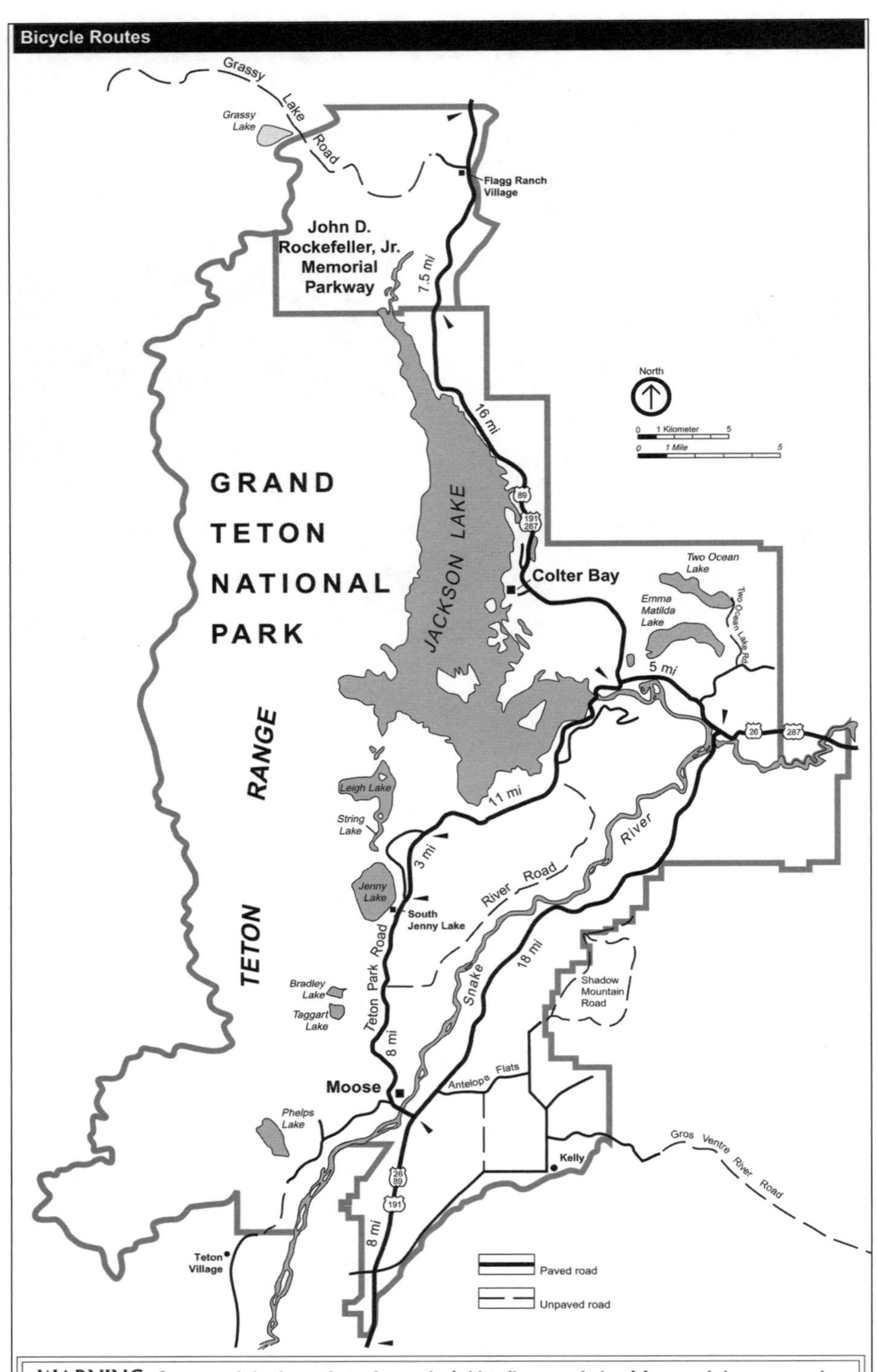

WARNING: Some roads in the park predate today's bicycling popularity. Most roads have a paved marked shoulder, providing limited space for safe bicycling. ***Some roads have only a very narrow shoulder, or lack one altogether.* USE EXTREME CAUTION.**

from the top of the tram and 1.4 miles south of Marion Lake. Site is in trees 150 yards east of where the trail crosses the Middle Fork Creek.

Lower Granite Canyon
Upper boundary is just below the Middle/North Fork trail junction. Groupsite is south of the trail, 3.4 miles west of the Granite Canyon trail junction with the Valley Trail.

Mt. Hunt Divide Zone
Upper boundary is just south of Mt. Hunt Divide and extends down to 0.75 mile above the Granite Canyon trail.

Open Canyon Zone
Extends from where the trail crosses Open Canyon Creek to just north of Mt. Hunt Divide.

Lakeshore Sites

Jackson Lake
• Bears are common. Bear boxes are provided at each site and must be used for food storage. Coolers are not bear-proof.

• Fires are allowed only in fire grates.

• Pets are not allowed in Jackson Lake campsites except at Spalding Bay. Pets must be physically restrained at all times and are not allowed out of boats.

• Beware of waves caused by afternoon winds on the lake.

Leigh Lake
• Bears are common. Bear boxes are provided at each site and must be used for food storage.

• Fires are allowed in fire grates only.

• Pitch tents on tent pads, where provided.

• Beware of waves caused by afternoon winds on the lake.

Phelps Lake
• Bears are common. Bear boxes are provided at each site and must be used for food storage.

• Fires are prohibited.

• Pitch tents on tent pads.

Trail Combination & Mileages

Tram to Granite Canyon via Marion Lake 17.1 miles. Trailhead: Teton Village – 1 night. Fee charged for tram.

Cascade Canyon/Paintbrush Canyon loop (Note: This is an extremely busy trail July through August) 19.2 miles. Trailhead: String Lake parking area – 1 night.

Granite Canyon/Open Canyon loop via Valley Trail 19.3 miles. Trailhead: Granite Canyon parking area – 1 night.

Tram/Death Canyon loop via Valley Trail 23.1 miles. Trailhead: Teton Village – 1 to 2 nights. Fee charged for tram.

Cascade Canyon/Death Canyon via Static Peak Divide 24.8 miles. Trailheads: South Jenny Lake parking area and Death Canyon parking area – 1 to 2 nights.

Granite Canyon/Death Canyon loop via Valley Trail 25.7 miles. Trailhead: Granite Canyon Parking Area – 2 nights.

Tram to Cascade Canyon via Teton Crest Trail 28.5 miles. Trailheads: Teton Village and South Jenny Lake parking area – 2 to 3 nights. Fee charged for tram.

Death Canyon/Cascade Canyon via Teton Crest Trail 29.5 miles. Trailheads: Death Canyon parking area and String Lake parking area – 2 to 3 nights.

Death Canyon/Paintbrush Canyon via Teton Crest Trail 36.0 miles. Trailheads: Death Canyon parking area and String Lake parking area – 3 to 4 nights.

Granite Canyon/Paintbrush Canyon via Teton Crest Trail 37.9 miles. Trailheads: Granite Canyon parking area and String Lake parking area – 4 nights.

BICYCLING

Most of Jackson Hole, a 40-mile long, 15-mile wide valley surrounded by mountains, lies within Grand Teton National Park and the John D. Rockefeller, Jr., Memorial Parkway. Within the park and parkway, approximately 100 miles of paved roads await the bicyclist. Numerous scenic turnouts provide spectacular views of the impressive Teton Range. To enter or leave the valley, bicyclists may need to cross one or more mountain passes.

Some roads in the park predate today's bicycling popularity. Most roads have a paved marked shoulder, providing limited space for safe bicycling. Some roads have only a very narrow shoulder, or lack one altogether. Use extreme caution.

Mountain Biking Suggested Routes

Two-Ocean Lake Road
Three miles of dirt road lead from the Pacific Creek Road to Two-Ocean Lake for a short but scenic ride over rolling terrain.

River Road
A gravel road parallels the west side of the Snake River for approximately 15 miles between Signal Mountain and Cottonwood Creek. Watch for wildlife. Maintain a safe distance (300 feet minimum) from large animals, such as bison, that frequent this area.

Grassy Lake Road
Travel an old American Indian route through the transition between Grand Teton and Yellowstone National Parks. Ride all or part of the 52-mile road that starts west of Flagg Ranch and continues to Ashton, Idaho.

REMEMBER: Bicycles are not allowed on any trails in Grand Teton National Park or the John D. Rockefeller, Jr., Memorial Parkway, but you can ride your fat-tired bicycle on any unpaved roads where cars can legally go.

CAUTION: Unpaved roads are narrow. Ride on the right side of the road and be alert for vehicular traffic. Dry weather causes unpaved roads to become extremely dusty.

Road Biking Suggested Routes

Teton Park Road Recent road construction from Moose to North Jenny Lake Junction included widening the road shoulders. The adjacent 3-mile Jenny Lake Scenic Drive provides spectacular views of the tallest Teton peaks.

Antelope Flats – Kelly Area
Bicycle secondary roads through sagebrush flats with spectacular views of the Teton Range.

For More Information

Obtain information concerning bicycling, bicycle routes, facilities, and services from the park visitor centers at Moose, Jenny Lake and Colter Bay. A recorded message provides information about the park's weather, activities and park facilities 24- hours a day all year long. Call (307) 739- 3611.

Bicycles may be rented in the park at Dornans' in Moose. Bicycle rentals, parts and service are also available from several shops nearby in the town of Jackson.

Floating the Snake River

General Information

Floating the Snake River offers a chance to experience an outstanding natural area. Flowing west from its source in the Teton Wilderness, the river enters Yellowstone National Park, then flows south through the John D. Rockefeller, Jr., Memorial Parkway, and into Jackson Lake in Grand Teton National Park. Regaining its free-flowing character at the Jackson Lake Dam, the river winds through the park.

The Snake is a complex river to float. The

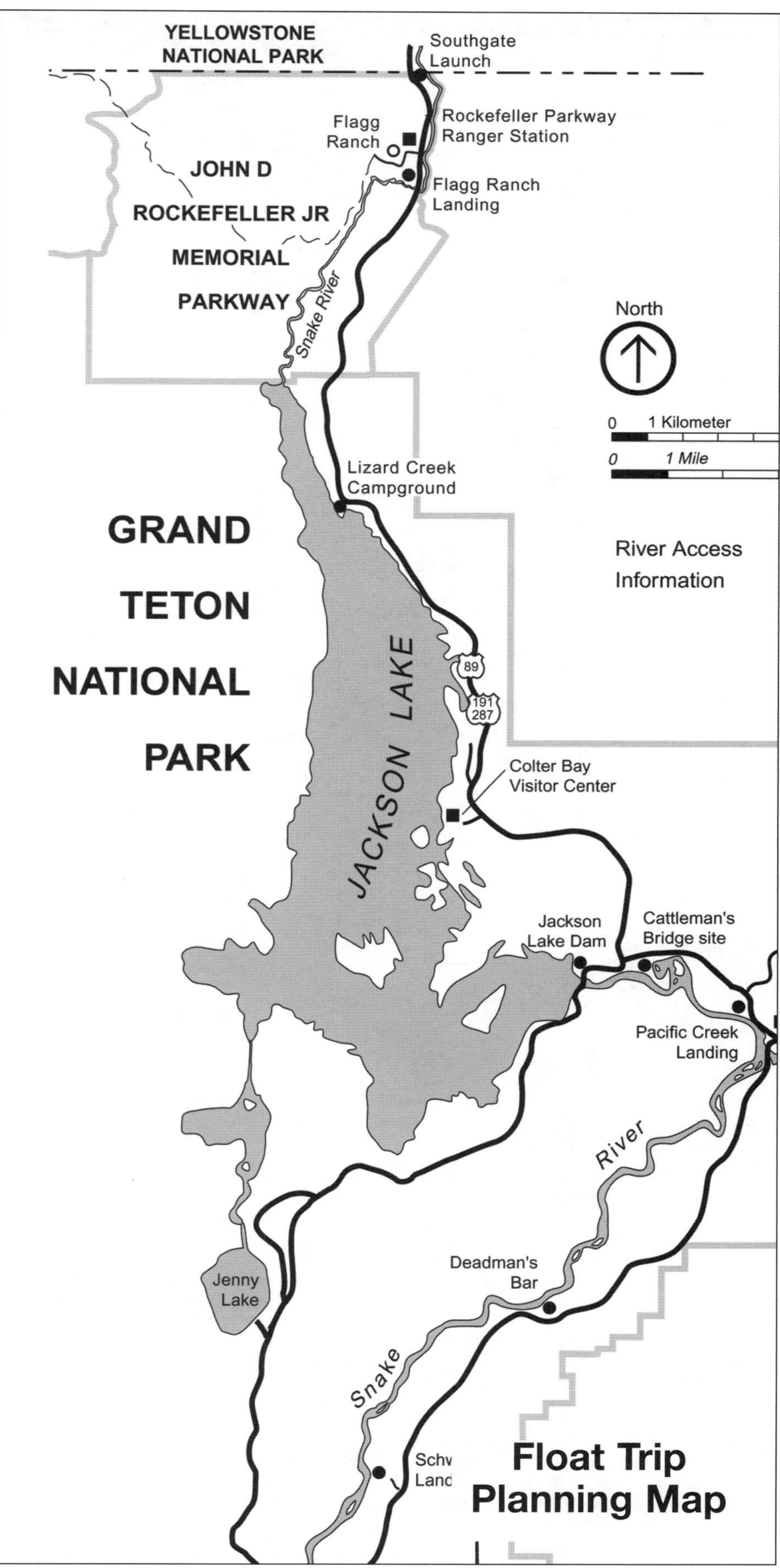

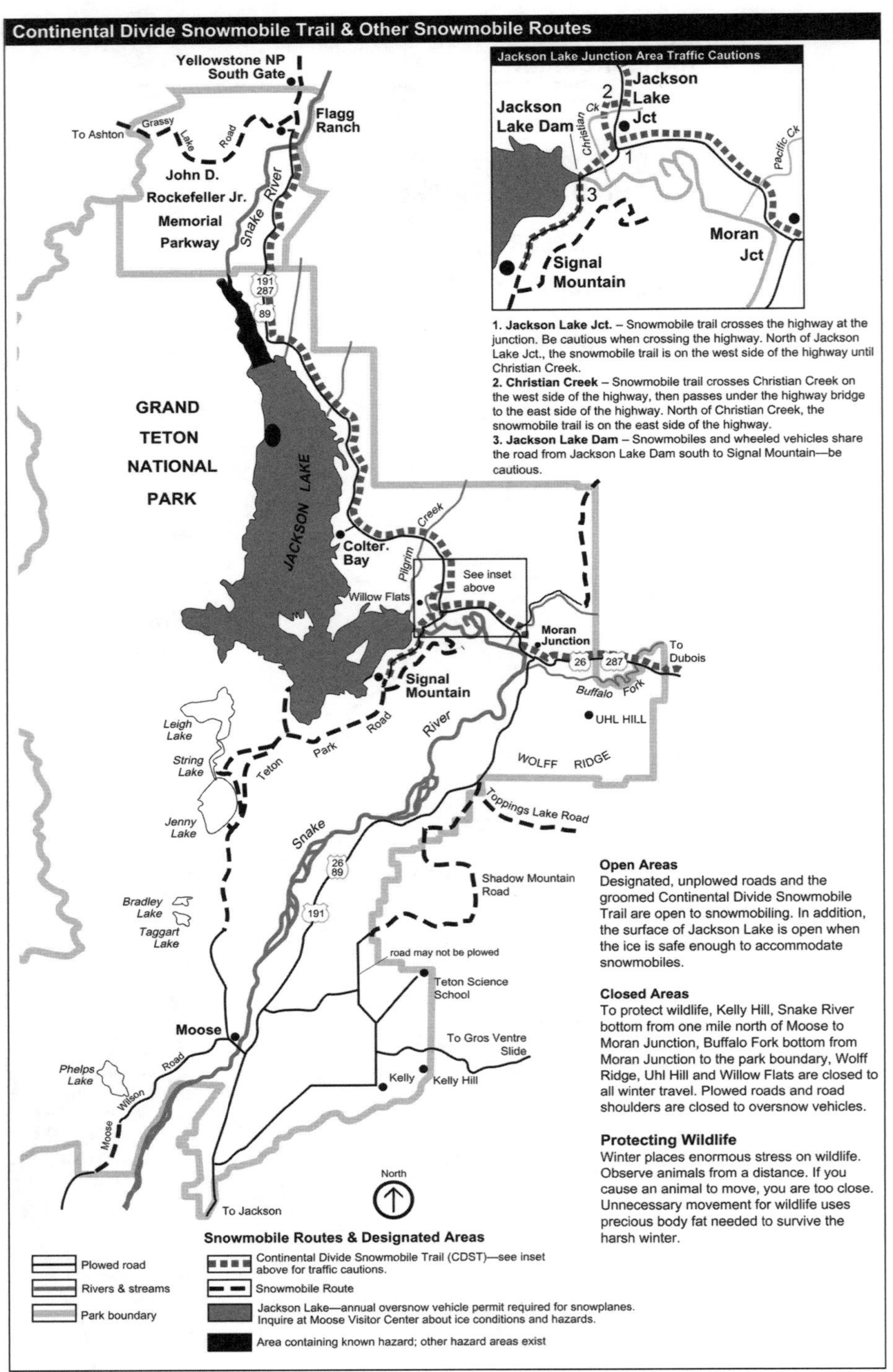

beauty and lack of whitewater often lull floaters into inattentiveness. A tangle of channels and constant shifting of logjams present difficulties found on few whitewater rivers. Accidents occur often. Use caution whenever you float.

Information on flow rates and additional caution areas are posted at river landings, visitor centers, the Rockefeller Parkway and Buffalo Fork Ranger Stations. Reports are updated weekly or whenever significant change in river conditions occur. Even boaters frequently floating the Snake should check conditions before every trip, as the river can change overnight. River flow varies greatly throughout the summer. Water depths average 2 to 3 feet, but exceed 10 feet in a few locations. Boulders and bottom irregularities cause standing waves up to 3 feet high. Typically, spring flows will be muddy, extremely cold, and very high, increasing the difficulty of all river sections. As snowmelt diminishes, volume decreases and waters clear. In spite of reduced flow, the current stays deceptively strong. Logjams and tight turns remain. Always set up maneuvers well in advance and make decisions early. Take into consideration traditionally strong upstream winds, especially when canoeing.

River Etiquette

The quality of float trips depends largely on the wildness of the river. The very presence of other boaters threatens this quality. Help preserve the tranquility of the river scene. Reduce congestion at landings by preparing craft away from launch slips. Launch when other boats are out of sight, and maintain this interval throughout the trip. Excessive noise disrupts the solitude others seek. Silence is especially important when passing wildlife. When encountering other boaters and anglers, respect their rights by steering clear of their boats and lines.

Rangers regularly patrol the river during the summer. Patrol boats carry first aid gear and two-way radios. If you have any questions or need assistance, contact the River Patrol Rangers. Information and assistance are available year-round at the Moose Visitor Center and in summer (May through September) at the Buffalo Fork Ranger Station in Moran, the Rockefeller Parkway Ranger Station at Flagg Ranch and the Colter Bay Visitor Center.

Equipment should include an extra paddle or oar, a waterproof container with extra clothes, a first aid kit and a waste receptacle. Attach all gear securely. Inflatable boats should have an air pump, bucket for bailing and patch kit.

Do not drink the water unless you boil or treat it first. Swimming in the river is not recommended.

For information on Snake River flows, call 1-800-658-5771; internet address http://wy.water.usgs.gov/rt-cgi/ gen_tbl_pg/ For information on floating the Snake outside the park contact: Jackson Hole Chamber of Commerce, Box E, Jackson, WY 83001, phone 307-733- 3316; or Bridger-Teton National Forest, Box 1888, Jackson, WY 83001 307- 739-5500 or 739-5417.

Regulations

Detailed boating regulations are available at visitor centers and ranger stations.

Beginner Level

Jackson Lake Dam to Cattleman's Bridge Cattleman's Bridge to Pacific Creek

These stretches provide scenic views, calmer water and the fewest obstructions. Fast water at the Pacific Creek landing requires boaters to land their craft in quiet waters about 100 yards upstream from the actual landing.

Intermediate Level

Pacific Creek to Deadman's Bar

More difficult than the preceding section, this stretch of river drops significantly, increasing the current. Braided channels make routefinding difficult and require more skill. Boating experience on lakes has proven to be of little help to river runners on the Snake.

Flagg Ranch to Lizard Creek Campground

The braided channel makes route-finding a challenge. After the Snake River winds through the Rockefeller Parkway for 6 miles, it flows into Jackson Lake. During the remaining 4 miles on the lake, the predominant southwest winds can be moderate to strong and strenuous rowing or paddling is required. Afternoon thunderstorms and strong lake winds can produce high waves that can swamp rafts and canoes. Motorized craft are prohibited on the river; however, motors can be carried on vessels and used on Jackson Lake.

Advanced Level

Deadman's Bar to Moose Landing

Most river accidents occur on this section, the most challenging stretch of the river in the park. The river drops more steeply, with faster flows than in other sections south of Pacific Creek, giving boaters very little time to maneuver their

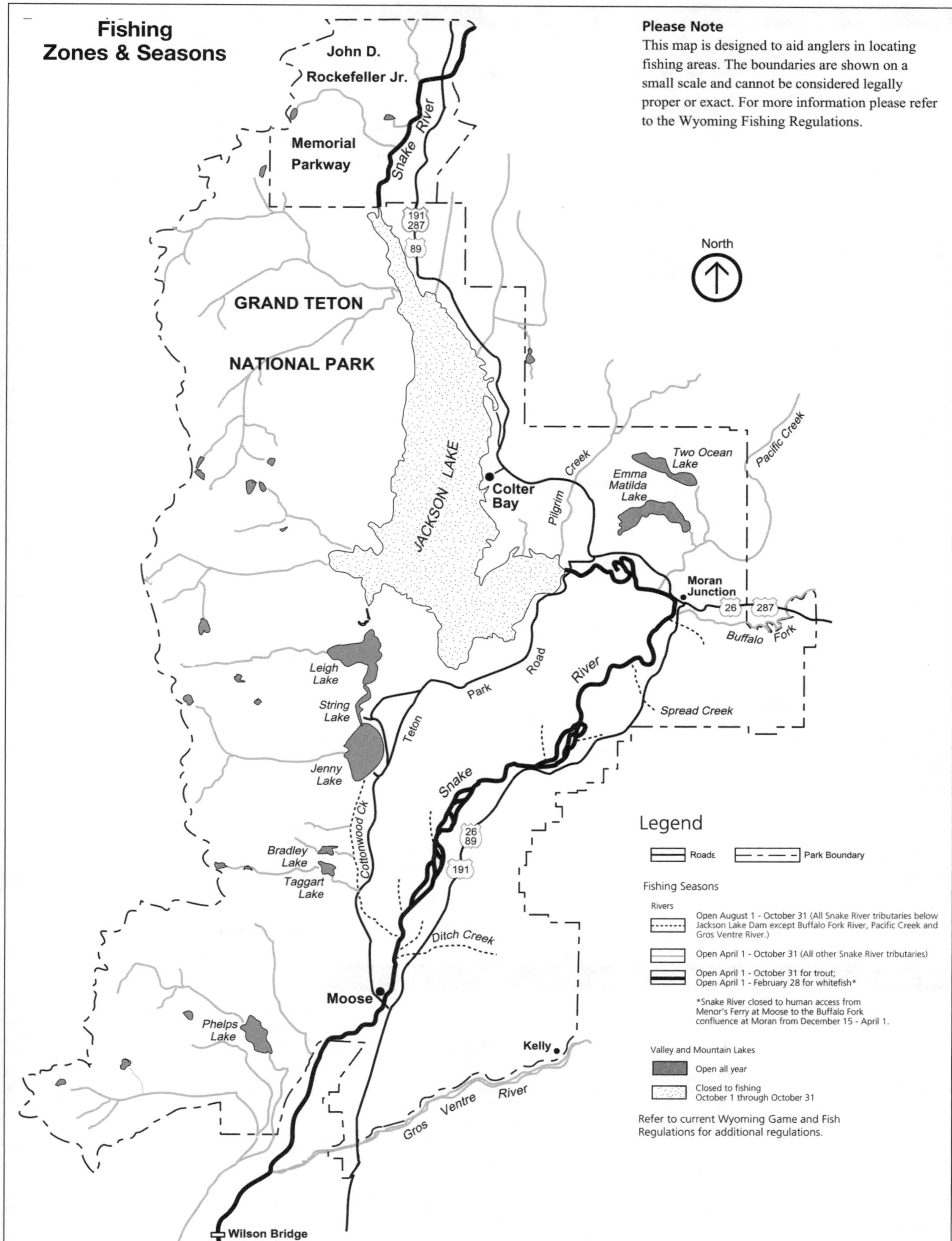

Grand Teton National Park

X-Country Ski Trails from Taggart Lake Parking Area

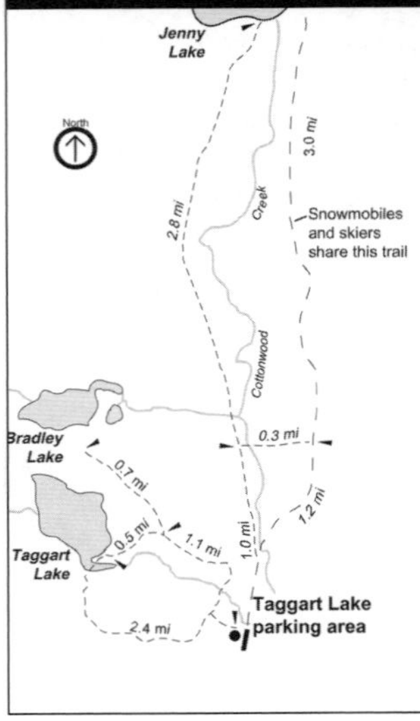

Taggart Lake Parking Area
Drive 4.5 mi. northwest of Moose Junction on the Teton Park Road to the Taggart Lake parking area at the end of the plowed road.

Jenny Lake Trail
Easy. Roundtrip: 7.6 mi., Elevation change: 100'. Follow the unplowed road 1/4-mile to Cottonwood Creek (be alert for snowmobiles), then ski north along the creek. The trail follows the west side of the creek and crosses several large meadows, then gently climbs a low ridge of glacial moraine and ends at an overlook of Jenny Lake. On clear days, the trail provides close views of the snow-draped peaks as it skirts the base of the Teton Range. The terrain is mostly level and is excellent for beginners. Skiing on Cottonwood Creek is not recommended. Return via the same trail. Another option is to follow the unplowed road (not flagged) to the east side of Jenny Lake (be alert for snowmobiles). To reach the flagged ski trail from the unplowed road, cross the bridge over Cottonwood Creek and head west along the edge of Jenny Lake.

Taggart Lake-Beaver Creek Loop
Difficult. Taggart Lake and return – roundtrip: 3.2 mi., elevation change: 277'. Taggart Lake/Beaver Creek Loop – roundtrip: 4 mi., elevation change: 397'. This loop through a forest that burned in 1985 has steep sections. From the parking area, ski directly toward the mountains. Turn north (right) and follow the trail as it climbs over the moraine (ridge of glacial debris). The trail forks in about one mile. The right fork climbs 0.7 mile for a view down to Taggart Lake. The left fork takes you directly to Taggart Lake nestled at the foot of the Tetons. If you return the way you came, you will encounter a steep, treelined section that is at times icy and treacherous, requiring downhill skiing ability. Another option from Taggart Lake is to turn south, cross the bridge over the lake outlet, and follow the trail that climbs the moraine. Then ski down the steep open slope and follow the trail to the east to return to the parking area.

craft. Complex braiding obscures the main channel. Strong current can sweep boaters into side channels blocked by logjams.

Moose to South Park Boundary

This section of the river is as difficult as the preceding section. Fast moving water, braiding, channel selection, logjams and route finding require advanced boating skills. The park boundary extends 5 miles downriver of Moose on the west bank and 2 miles downriver on the east bank; there is no take out or access to the river at the park boundary. The next take out is at Wilson, 12 miles downstream from Moose.

Southgate to Flagg Ranch

Southgate Launch is 1/2-mile south of the South Entrance of Yellowstone National Park. The river slopes steeply and the narrow riverway provides challenging whitewater for rafts and kayaks. In spring, increased water volume creates large standing waves, haystacks, laterals and large holes capable of flipping rafts. It can be scouted by walking the canyon rim trail along the west bank of the river. During flows greater than 4000 cfs, the whitewater rapids are Class III and are not recommended for canoes. Below 4000 cfs, only canoeists with advanced white water skills should attempt this section.

Mileages

Southgate Launch to Flagg Ranch	3.0
Flagg Ranch to Lizard Creek Campground	10.0
Jackson Lake Dam to Cattleman's Bridge	2.0
Cattleman's Bridge to Pacific Creek	3.0
Pacific Creek to Deadman's Bar	10.5
Deadman's Bar to Moose Landing	10.0
Moose to Wilson	12.0

Snowmobiling in the Tetons

When snow depth is sufficient, snowmobile routes including the Continental Divide Snowmobile Trail (CDST) will be opened within Grand Teton National Park and the John D. Rockefeller, Jr., Memorial Parkway. For the unplowed portion of the Teton Park Road, the snowmobile season is generally mid-December through mid-March. The season for the CDST is considerably shorter. Travel on Jackson Lake is not recommended because of numerous hazards. See the map on the reverse side for the location of snowmobile trails.

Snowmobile regulations in Yellowstone National Park differ from those in Grand Teton National Park and the Rockefeller Parkway. For Yellowstone information call 307-344-7381.

The CDST connects Dubois, Lander and the Togwotee Pass areas with Yellowstone National Park.

The CDST is a groomed trail and may be closed periodically for grooming. For current information on trail conditions, please call 307-739-3612; ask at the Moose Visitor Center and the Flagg Ranch Information Station; or check bulletin boards located along the CDST at the East Entrance to Grand Teton, at Signal Mountain and the Snake River Bridge at Flagg Ranch.

The CDST is located immediately adjacent to the plowed road and follows Highway 26- 287 from the east park boundary to Moran Junction, then follows Highway 89 to the south entrance of Yellowstone National Park. From the east park boundary to Jackson Lake Junction, the CDST is located on the north side of the highway. At Jackson Lake Junction the trail crosses the highway to the west side and follows an old roadbed north to Christian Creek. After crossing Christian Creek, the trail passes under the highway bridge and continues north to Flagg Ranch on the east side of the highway.

A spur trail from Jackson Lake Junction south connects the CDST with the Teton Park Road snowmobile route. This spur trail follows the north side of the Teton Park Road to Jackson Lake Dam. From Jackson Lake Dam to Signal Mountain, snowmobiles must share the roadway with wheeled vehicles, so snowmobile operators must be extremely cautious. The snowmobile route from Signal Mountain south to Taggart Lake parking area follows the unplowed road and is not groomed.

Open Areas

Designated, unplowed roads and the groomed Continental Divide Snowmobile Trail are open to snowmobiling. In addition, the surface of Jackson Lake is open when the ice is safe enough to accommodate snowmobiles.

Closed Areas

To protect wildlife, Kelly Hill, Snake River bottom from one mile north of Moose to Moran Junction, Buffalo Fork bottom from Moran Junction to the park boundary, Wolff Ridge, Uhl Hill and Willow Flats are closed to all winter travel. Plowed roads and road shoulders are closed to oversnow vehicles.

Protecting Wildlife

Winter places enormous stress on wildlife. Observe animals from a distance. If you cause an animal to move, you are too close. Unnecessary movement for wildlife uses precious body fat needed to survive the harsh winter.

Trail Distances

Moran Junction to Jackson Lake Junction	5 mi
Jackson Lake Junction to Signal Mountain	3 mi
Signal Mountain–Taggart Lake parking	15 mi
Signal Mountain summit road	5 mi
Jackson Lake Junction to Colter Bay	6 mi
Colter Bay to Flagg Ranch	15 mi
Flagg Ranch to Grassy Lake	11 mi
Moose-Wilson road	2 mi

Campgrounds

Five National Park Service campgrounds are available on a first-come, first-served basis within the park. The fee is $12.00 per night, per site. Maximum length of stay is 14 days, 7 days at Jenny Lake Campground. These campgrounds do not have electrical hook-ups.

Gros Ventre Campground
South of Moose
360 sites and a trailer dump station; generally fills in the evening, if at all.

Jenny Lake Campground
North of Moose
49 sites, tents only; full by 8 a.m.

Signal Mountain Campground
North of Jenny Lake
86 sites and a trailer dump station; no vehicles

X-Country Ski Trails from Moose-Wilson Road Area

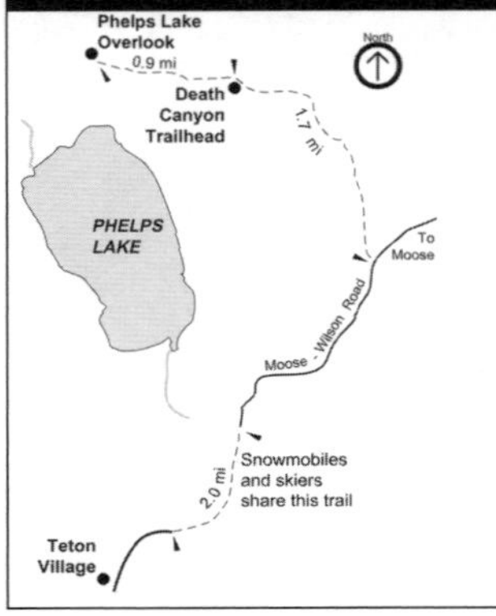

Moose-Wilson Road Area
The Moose-Wilson Road connects Moose and Teton Village, but plowing of the road ends one mile north of Teton Village. The trailhead for Phelps Lake is located 3.1 mi. south of Moose on the (west) right side of the Moose-Wilson Road and is accessible by vehicle only from Moose at the north end. The skiable section of the Moose-Wilson Road starts 6 mi. south of Moose and may also be reached by driving one mile north of Teton Village.

Phelps Lake Overlook
Moderate. Roundtrip: 5.2 mi., elevation change: 520'. The trail follows a narrow unplowed road through a forest of mixed conifers for the first 1.7 mi., making a gradual ascent to the Death Canyon trailhead. Then the trail climbs westward through a lodgepole pine forest and over an open slope to reach the overlook of Phelps Lake framed by towering Douglas firs. Do not continue beyond the overlook because of high avalanche hazard. The return trip is all downhill. When the trail is well packed, skiing can be fast.

Moose-Wilson Road
Easy. Roundtrip: 4 mi., elevation change: 100'. Park at either end of this unplowed portion of road. The trail follows a winding unplowed road (be alert for snowmobiles) and is mostly flat but has enough changes in terrain and scenery to make it interesting. This trail through conifer and aspen forest is a good choice for beginners.

X-Country Ski Trails from Colter Bay and Signal Mountain Areas

Colter Bay Area
Colter Bay is 10 mi. north of Moran Junction. Trailhead is located 300 ft. south of the Colter Bay Ranger Station. Park in front of the Ranger Station or near the trailhead on the spur road from the main highway.

Swan Lake-Heron Pond Loop
Easy. Roundtrip: 2.6 mi., elevation change: 40'. The trail first crosses an unplowed parking area, then passes the summer Hermitage Point Trailhead. Continue to the right of the trailhead sign and follow an old road for the first 0.4 mile. The trail then forks to either Swan Lake or Heron Pond. Ski 2.2 mi. in either direction on the gently sloping loop trail to return to this junction. Skiing on the ponds is not recommended. View the jagged Teton Range and Jackson Lake from the edge of Heron Pond. Beyond Heron Pond, unflagged trails lead to Hermitage Point; this loop adds 5.8 mi. (60' elevation) to the trip.

Signal Mountain Area
Signal Mountain is located 26 mi. north of Moose Junction (8 mi. west of Moran Junction). To reach the trailhead, follow Highways 26-89-191 north to Moran Junction, then 5.0 mi. west to Jackson Lake Junction and south 3.0 mi. on the Teton Park Road.

Signal Mountain Summit Road
Moderate. Roundtrip: 12 mi., elevation change: 700'. Park near Signal Mountain Lodge (closed in winter). Ski the unplowed road (be alert for snowmobiles) southward for approximately one mile until you reach the unplowed road that goes eastward (left) to the summit of Signal Mountain. The Signal Mountain Summit Road winds gradually uphill through conifer forests. The summit affords panoramic views of Jackson Hole and the Teton Range. The return trip is all downhill.

over 30 feet;full by 10 a.m.

Colter Bay Campground
North of Jackson Lake Junction
350 sites with showers, laundry, and dump station; full by noon.

Lizard Creek Campground
At the north end of the park
60 sites; no vehicles over 30-feet; full by about 2:00 p.m.

Concessioner-Operated Campgrounds

A concessioner-operated campground is available at Flagg Ranch in the John D. Rockefeller, Jr. Memorial Parkway, just south of Yellowstone National Park. To make reservations contact:

Flagg Ranch Resort
PO Box 187
Moran, WY 83013
(800) 443-2311 or (307) 543-2861
www.flaggranch.com

For information on the Colter Bay RV Park & Tent Cabins contact:

Grand Teton Lodge Company
PO Box 250
Moran, WY 83013
(307) 543-2811
www.gtlc.com

Group Camping

Only organized groups such as youth, religious, and educational groups may use the group sites. Colter Bay Campground has 10 group campsites and Gros Ventre Campground has five. Site capacities range from 10 to 75 people.

The nightly use fee is $3.00 per person plus a $15.00 non-refundable reservation fee.

Advance reservations are required. Requests for reservations should be made between January 1 and May 15 by writing to:

Campground Reservations
Grand Teton National Park
PO Drawer 170
Moose, WY 83012

Trailer Villages

Colter Bay and Flagg Ranch Trailer Villages are concessioner-operated trailer facilities with full hook-ups, showers, and laundry.
Flagg Ranch Trailer Village has 100 trailer sites and 75 tent sites. To make reservations contact:

Flagg Ranch Resort
PO Box 187
Moran, WY 83013
(800) 443-2311 or (307) 543-2861
www.flaggranch.com

Colter Bay RV Park has 112 sites. For more information and to make reservations contact:

Grand Teton Lodge Company
PO Box 250
Moran, WY 83013
(307) 543-2811
www.gtlc.com

X-Country Ski Trails from Flagg Ranch Area

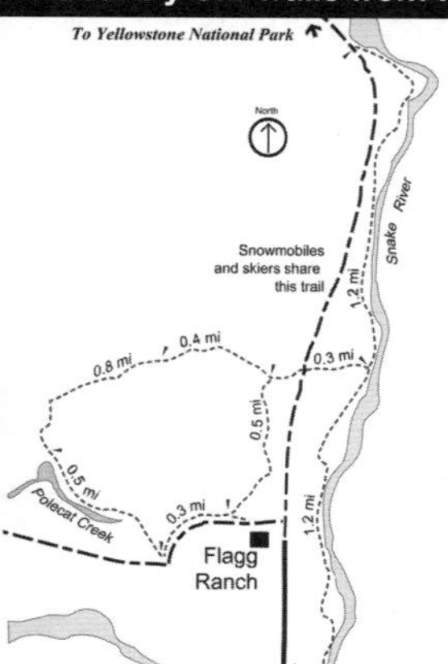

Flagg Ranch Area
Flagg Ranch is 26 mi. north of Moran Junction. The trailhead is located near the northwest corner of the Flagg Ranch parking area.

Polecat Creek Loop Trail
Easy. 2.5 mi., elevation change: 50'. Take the loop in either direction. The south side of the loop parallels the Grassy Lake road, which is open to snowmobiles. The west side of the loop follows a bench above Polecat Creek, kept open by thermal activity. The north and east sides of the loop traverse a dense conifer forest of lodgepole pines, sub-alpine firs and Engelmann spruce.

Flagg Canyon Trail North
Difficult. Roundtrip 4.0 mi., elevation change: 120'. Follow the east side of the Polecat Creek Loop Trail and travel north for 0.5 mi. Turn east (right) at the marked trail junction. The trail crosses the groomed snowmobile trail; use caution and watch for snowmobiles and snowcoaches. The flagged trail continues on the east side of the road and leads to the Flagg Canyon Trail, which follows the Snake River. Take the Flagg Canyon Trail north (left) to reach the South Gate of Yellowstone National Park. This section of trail contains a few short steep sections that can easily be avoided. **Use caution and avoid cornices where the trail follows the edge of the cliff above the Snake River.** Return via the same route or take the groomed snowmobile trail.

Flagg Canyon Trail South
Easy. Roundtrip 4.0 mi., elevation change: 40'. Reach the Flagg Canyon Trail as described for Flagg Canyon Trail north. At the junction with the Flagg Canyon Trail, turn south (right). The southern half of the Flagg Canyon Trail leads 1.2 mi. to end at the highway near the bridge over the Snake River. The trail follows rolling terrain and is suitable for beginners. Return via the same route.

Commercial Services

The National Park Service does not make concession reservations. Please make direct contact with the service of your choice.

Opening and closing dates are approximate.

The listing of authorized concessions operating float trips, horseback riding and mountaineering guide services is rotated within each category in a prescribed manner unrelated to quality.

A permit is required for conducting any commercial activity in Grand Teton National Park and the John D. Rockefeller, Jr. Memorial Parkway.

Flagg Ranch Resort (*open in winter)
Open for summer season May 15 – Oct. 15. Open for winter season Dec. 15 – Mar. 12. Hours of operation subject to change before June 1 and after Sept. 15. Call 307-543-2861 or toll free 1-800-443-2311. Write Box 187, Moran WY 83013.

Accommodations – Log style lodging units with 2 queen beds or 1 king bed (open summer and winter).

Restaurant and Espresso Bar – Open daily. Breakfast, lunch & dinner. Home style menu.

Camper & Trailer Services – Campground with full hookups, tent sites, 24-hour launderette, showers and restrooms.

Gift Shop – National park gifts, souvenirs, clothing, American Indian jewelry & children's items.

Service Station – Phillips 66. Diesel available. Emergency gas available year-round.

Grocery Store – Essentials, camping/fishing supplies, package beer, ice & firewood.

Float Trips – see Float Trip section.

Horseback Riding – See Horseback Riding section.

Spirits – Burnt Bear Saloon & package goods.
Snowmobiling and Snowcoach Tours – Self-guided and guided snowmobile trips into Yellowstone. Daily snowcoach tours to Old Faithful with an interpretive guide. Dec. 15 – Mar. 12.

Leek's Marina
Call 307-543-2494.
Pizza Restaurant – Pizza, sandwiches & beer. Open daily 11:00 a.m–9:00 p.m. June 4–Sept. 6.

Marina – On Jackson Lake. Gas dock, overnight buoys. May 22 – Sept. 19.

Colter Bay Village
Reservations today call 307-543-2811, for cabins 543-2828; future 543-3100. Write Grand Teton Lodge Co., Box 240, Moran, WY 83013.

Accommodations – Colter Bay Cabins Open May 28 – Oct. 3. Tent Village open June 4 – Sept. 6.

RV Park – Open daily May 21 – Oct. 3 with all hookups available. Reservations advised.

Restaurants and Snack Bar – Chuckwagon Restaurant Open daily May 28 – Oct. 3. Table and buffet service for breakfast, lunch & dinner. *Colter Bay Cafe Court* Open daily 6:30 a.m. – 10:00 p.m., June 11 – Sept. 6.

General Stores and Gift Shops – Colter Bay Village General Store open daily 7:30 a.m. – 10:00 p.m., May 28 – Oct. 3. Hours subject to change. ATM machine. *Colter Bay Highway Convenience Store* Open daily May 7 – Oct. 20. Groceries, soft drinks, beer, film, gifts & firewood.

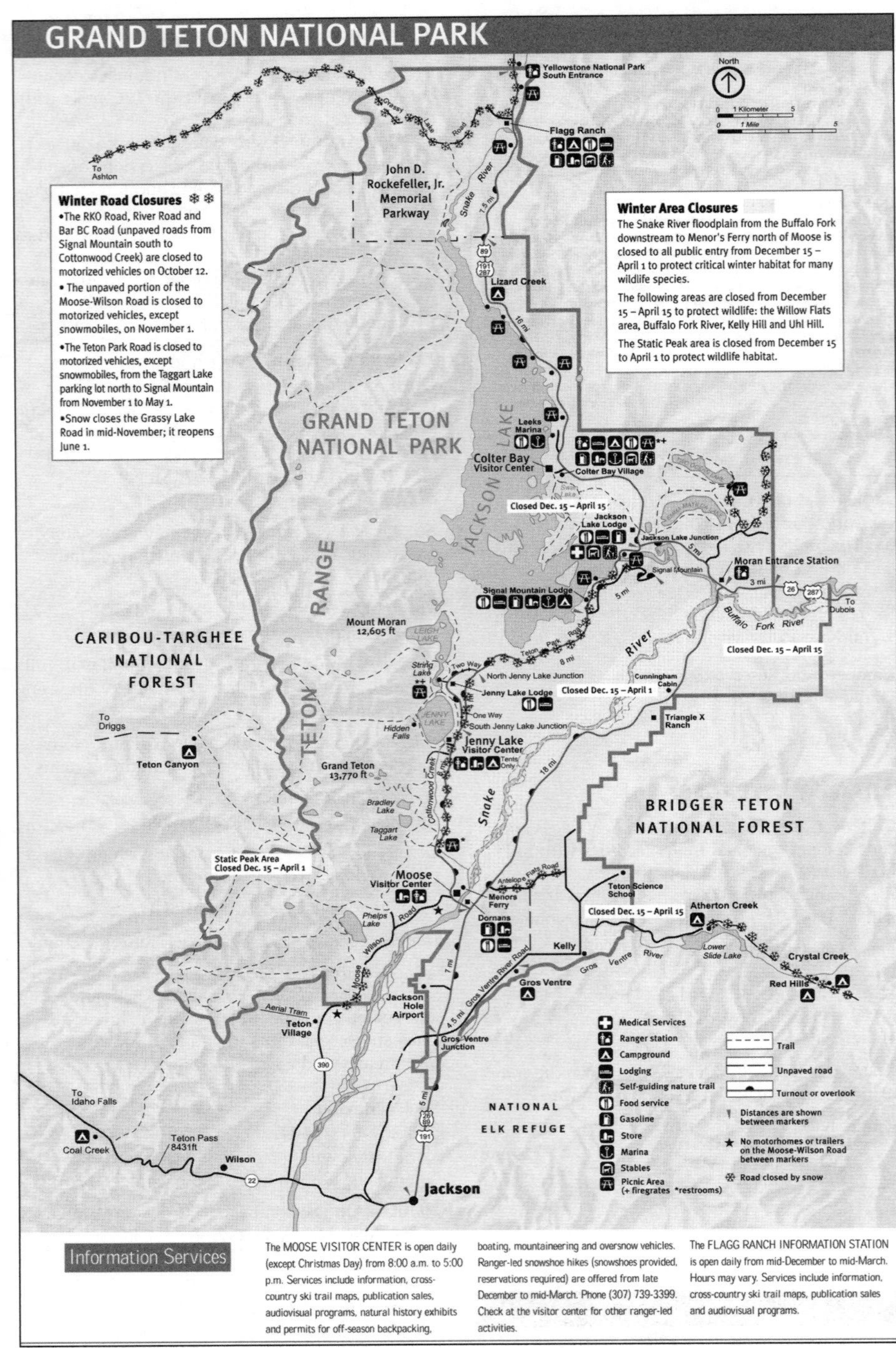

Service Stations – Colter Bay Highway Chevron Station Open daily 7:30 a.m. – 10:30 p.m., May 7 – Oct. 20. Automotive fuel, including diesel fuel. Self-service. *Colter Bay Village Chevron* Open daily May 29 – Sept. 19. Self-service. RV accessories and service. Dump station.

Marina –Activities May 28 – Oct. 3. Daily breakfast &1-1/2 hr. scenic, narrated cruises. Sat. and Wed. evening steak fry cruises, (dates subject to change depending on weather & lake levels). Guided lake fishing, boat & canoe rentals, overnight buoys, fuel & discharge pump, tackle & WY fishing licenses. Marina Store May 28 – Oct. 3. Fishing tackle, film, outdoor apparel, snack food & beer.

Float Trips – see Float Trip section under Grand Teton Lodge Co.

Horseback Riding – See Horseback Riding section.

Public Showers – Open daily 7:30 a.m. – 9:00 p.m. May 28 – Oct. 3. Hours subject to change.

Launderette – Open daily 7:30 a.m. – 9:00 p.m. May 28 – Oct. 3. Hours subject to change.

Jackson Lake Lodge

Call 307-543-2811. Reservations today: 543-2811; future 543-3100. Write Grand Teton Lodge Co., Box 240, Moran WY 83013.

Accommodations – May 16 – Oct. 13.

Restaurants – Mural Room Breakfast 7:00 a.m. – 9:30 a.m. Lunch noon – 1:30 p.m. Dinner 6:00 p.m. – 9:00 p.m. May16 – Oct. 13. *Pioneer Grill* Open daily 6:00 a.m. – 10:30 p.m. May 16 – Oct. 13. Pool Open daily 11:30 a.m. – 3:30 p.m. lunch & snacks; poolside BBQ dinner 6:00 – 8:00 p.m. July 1 – Aug. 31. Weather permitting.

Gift and Apparel Shops – Open daily 8:00 a.m. – 10:30 p.m. May 16 – Oct. 13.

Newsstand – Sundries, magazines, books, cigars. 7:00 a.m. – 10:30 p.m. May 16 – Oct. 13.

ATM Machine – Hotel registration area.

Service Station – Self-service Chevron station. Diesel fuel available. Open daily 7:30 a.m. – 6:00 p.m. May 16 – Oct. 13.

Horseback Riding – See Horseback Riding section.

Float Trips – see Float Trip section under Grand Teton Lodge Co.

Spirits – Blue Heron Lounge open daily 11:00 a.m. – midnight (Sun. noon – 10:00 p.m.). May 16 – Oct. 12. *Package Store* open daily 8:00 a.m. – 10:00 p.m. (Sun. noon – 10:00 p.m.) May 16 – Oct. 12.

Signal Mountain

Call 307-543-2831. Write Box 50, Moran WY 83013.

Accommodations – Lakefront apartments with kitchenettes, log cabins (some with fireplaces) & motel units (some with fireplaces) on Jackson Lake. May 8 – Oct. 16.

Restaurants – Aspens Dining Room open daily Breakfast 7:00 – 11:00 a.m. Lunch 11:00 a.m. – 2:30 p.m. Dinner 5:30 – 10:00 p.m. May 8 – Oct. 9. Hours subject to change before May 18 & after Sept. 21. *Cottonwood Cafe* open daily Lunch 11:00 a.m. – 5:30 p.m. Dinner 5:30 p.m. – 10:00 p.m. May 8 – Oct. 9. Hours subject to change before May 18 & after Sept. 21.

Gift & Apparel – Gift Shop National park gifts, mountain home accessories and American Indian jewelry. Open daily 8:00 a.m. – 10:00 p.m. May 8 – Oct. 3. *Teton Traditions* Mountain-inspired clothing and accessories. Open daily 9:00 a.m. – 8:30 p.m. May 8 – Oct. 3. Hours of both stores subject to change before May 18 & after Sept. 21.

Service Station and Convenience Store – Open daily 7:00 a.m. – 10:00 p.m. May 8 – Oct. 6. Hours subject to change before May 18 & after Sept. 21. Emergency gas available year-round.

Marina – On Jackson Lake. Canoes, fishing boats, pontoon boats and deck cruiser rentals. Guest buoys available. Guided lake fishing trips. Gas and courtesy docks. Open May 22 – Sept. 19.

Float Trips – see Float Trip section.

Spirits – *Aspens Bar & Lounge* open daily noon – midnight. May 8 – Oct. 9. Hours subject to change before May 18 & after Sept. 21.

Jenny Lake Lodge

Call 307-733-4647. Write Grand Teton Lodge Co., Box 240, Moran WY 83013.

Accommodations – Modified American Plan. June 2 – Oct. 10.

Dining Room – Breakfast 7:30 – 9:00 a.m. Lunch noon – 1:30 p.m. Dinner 6:15 – 9:00 p.m. Reservations suggested for breakfast & lunch; reservations required for dinner. June 2 – Oct. 10.

South Jenny Lake Area

General Store – Jenny Lake Store – Open daily May 13 – Sept. 26. Camping & hiking supplies, outdoor clothing, t-shirts, groceries, film & gifts.

Boat Shuttles & Cruises - Teton Boating Co. - On Jenny Lake. Scenic cruises, shuttle service, fishing boat rentals. Open 8:00 a.m. – 6:00 p.m. June 8 – Sept. 12. Closing date is subject to water levels. Call 733-2703.

Mountaineering – Exum Mountain Guides & School of American Mountaineering See Mountaineering section.

Moose Village
General Store & Tackle Shop – Open daily May 22– Sept. 12. 8:00 a.m. – 6:00 p.m. Guided fly-fishing trips. Call 733-3471.

Dornans at Moose
Open all year. Call 307-733-2415. www.dornans.com For accommodations call 733-2522 or write Spur Ranch Cabins, Box 39, Moose WY 83012.

Accommodations - Spur Ranch Cabins. New log cabins located on the Snake River. Year-round availability, fully equipped kitchens, hand-crafted lodgepole furnishings.

Restaurants – Chuckwagon open daily for breakfast 7:00 a.m. – 11:00 a.m. Lunch noon – 3:00 p.m. Dinner 5:00 – 8:45 p.m., June 12 – Sept. 5. *Moose Pizza & Pasta Company* open noon – 9:00 p.m., June 15 – Sept. 15; 11:30 a.m. – 6:30 p.m., Sept. 15 – June 15, with pizza to go service. Families welcome.

Gift Shop – Open daily May 15 – Sept. 15. Souvenirs, local crafts, gifts. Winter hours, Sept. 16 – May 14.

Service Station – Open daily 8:00 a.m. – 8:00 p.m., June – Sept., 8:00 a.m. – 6:00 p.m., Sept. – June.

Grocery Store – Open daily 8:00 a.m. – 8:00 p.m. Winter hours 8:00 a.m. – 6:00 p.m. Firewood available. ATM machine.

Spirits – Moose Bar Lounge & view deck open daily 10:00 a.m. – 11:00 p.m.; 10:00 a.m. – 7:00 p.m., Sept. 15 – June 1. *Wine and Package Shop* – Large selection of wines. Open daily 10:00 a.m. – 11:00 p.m. June 1 – Sept. 14; 10:00 a.m. – 7:00

p.m., Sept. 15 – June 1.

Sports Equipment Rentals – Dornans Adventure Sports – Bicycle, canoe and kayak rentals. Repairs and accessories. 8:00 a.m. – 8:00 p.m., May 1 – October 15. 733-3307.

Fishing – Snake River Anglers – Spin & flyfishing, camping equipment. 8:00 a.m. – 6:00 p.m., May 1 – Sept. 30. 733-3699. Fishing licenses available year-round.

Mountaineering Shop - Moosely Seconds Open 9:00 a.m. – 8:00 p.m. summer.

Triangle X Ranch
Call 307-733-2183. Write Box 120T, Moose WY 83012.

A dude ranch (weekly; American Plan) with horseback riding, hikes, float trips, western cookouts, meals, fishing, dancing, & other western ranch activities for ranch guests. May 20 – Nov. 10. Winter activities include cross-country skiing, snowmobiling, snowshoeing & sightseeing. American Plan includes lodging, meals and guides. December 26– March 31.

Teton Science School
Field Natural History Seminars – One- to four-day naturalist-led field trips in Grand Teton National Park and throughout the Greater Yellowstone Ecosystem (May- August). Write Box 68T, Kelly, WY 83011; call 307-733-4765, fax 307-739-9388, e-mail info@tetonscience.org or on the web www.tetonscience.org

Gros Ventre Slide In
Gifts, American Indian crafts, snacks, ice & firewood. Open daily May 1 – Sept. 15. 7:30 a.m. – 8:30 p.m. Write Box 101, Kelly WY 83011.

Snake River Float Trips
The season for most companies is between mid-May and mid-September depending on weather and river-flow conditions.
All trips interpretive. Fishing season extends later.

Jack Dennis Fishing Trips – Guided fishing float trips; fly or spin fishing; lunch, instruction and equipment included. Call 733-3270 or write to Box 3369, Jackson WY 83001.

National Park Float Trips – 10-mile scenic wildlife trips, departing throughout day. Group arrangements available. Write Moose WY 83012. Call 733-6445 or 733-5500.

Heart Six Ranch Float Trips – 10-mile scenic trips and sunrise wildlife trips. Guided fishing trips for ranch guests. Write Box 70, Moran WY 83013. Call 543-2477.

Signal Mountain Lodge – 10-mile scenic trips, guided fishing trips. Write Box 50, Moran WY 83013. Call 543-2831.

Triangle X-Osprey Float Trips – 5- & 10-mile scenic trips scheduled throughout the day; sunrise & evening wildlife trips, supper floats, & breakfast and lunch floats for groups. Fishing trips. Moose WY 83012. Call 733-5500 or 733-6445. FAX 733-8685.

Barker-Ewing Float Trips – 10-mile scenic trips, including morning & late evening wildlife trips. Departures throughout the day. May 9 – Sept. 30. Dinner trips available weekdays June 15 – Aug. 20. Write Box 100T, Moose WY 83012; Call 733-1800 or 1-800-365-1800.

Fort Jackson Float Trips – Scenic rafting trips depart daily May through Sept. Sunrise trips, short trips (3 hours). Long trips with meal (5 hours). Also guided fishing trips, full & half day, equipment & transportation included. Call 733-2583 or 1-800-735-8430.
Flagg Ranch Float Trips – Whitewater & scenic wildlife trips—only trips north of Jackson Lake. Whitewater trips depart every two hours starting at 10 a.m.; scenic trips 10:00 a.m. and 2:00 p.m., depending on weather. Call 543-2861. June 1 – Labor Day.

Grand Teton Lodge Company – (Colter Bay Village & Jackson Lake Lodge) 10-mile scenic trips with several morning & afternoon departures daily; some trips include lunch or dinner cookout at Deadman's Bar; morning departures daily; guided fishing trips. Write Box 240, Moran WY 83013. Call 543-2811.

Solitude Float Trips – 5- & 10-mile scenic trips. Guided fishing trips. Write Box 112, Moose WY 83012. Call 733-2871.

River & Lake Multi-Day Trips
O.A.R.S. (Outdoor Adventure River Specialists) – Offers 2-, 3- and 5-day sea kayaking excursions on Jackson Lake, and 2-day scenic float trips on the Snake River through Grand Teton National Park. Wilderness camping, hiking, fishing, fun and relaxation. Call 1-800-346-6277 for information or reservations. www.oars.com

Mountaineering
Exum Mountain Guides & School of American Mountaineering located at Jenny Lake. Daily basic & intermediate schools at Hidden Falls. Guided ascents of Grand Teton & all peaks & routes in Teton Range. Summer & winter. All skill levels. Rock, ice and snow. Private guides available for individuals or groups. AMGA accredited. Call 733-2297. Write Box 56, Moose WY 83012.

Jackson Hole Mountain Guides & Climbing School – Guide service for individuals and small groups. All peaks & routes in the Teton Range. Year-round. Daily schools on rock, ice, snow; all ability levels, certified guides; member U.S. Mountain Guide Federation; AMGA accredited. Office in downtown Jackson. Box 7477, 165 N. Glenwood, Jackson WY 83001; call (307) 733-4979.
Climbers' Ranch/American Alpine Club – Dormitory accommodations, cooking area and showers for climbers. Call 733-7271.

Horseback Riding
Flagg Ranch Resort – One-hour trail rides. June 15 – Sept. 1. Call 543-2861.

Colter Bay Village Corral – Breakfast & dinner rides, wagon seats available. Trail rides of various lengths. 543-2811. June 4 – Sept. 6. Weather permitting.

Jackson Lake Lodge Corral – Breakfast & dinner rides, wagon seats available. Trail rides of various lengths. Call 543-2811. May 29 – Oct. 12. Weather permitting.

Bus Tours and Transportation
Grand Teton Lodge Co. - Call 543-2811 for bus tours, charters, & transportation to & from Jackson, Yellowstone, intrapark. May 16 – Oct. 13.

Medical
Grand Teton Medical Clinic – Near Chevron station at Jackson Lake Lodge. Open daily 10:00 a.m. – 6:00 p.m. May 16 – Oct. 13. Call 543-2514. Other hours call 733-8002.
Medical Services - St. John's Hospital in Jackson WY 83001. Call 733-3636.

Other Services Outside the Park
The town of Jackson is 13 miles south of park headquarters at Moose. All services are available. For a complete listing of accommodations and attractions outside the park, stop at the multi-agency Visitor Information Center at 532 North Cache, call 733-3316, or write Jackson Hole Chamber of Commerce, Box E, Jackson WY 83001; http://www.jacksonholechamber.com Stores and services are also available at Teton Village. Some services are located 6-8 miles east of Moran Junction. For information on Dubois, 52 miles east of the park, call the Dubois Chamber of Commerce, 455-2556.

NOTES:

Yellowstone

The First National Park

NPS Photo

Basic Data

Area: approximately 2.2 million acres or 3,472 square miles in Wyoming, Montana, and Idaho.

Elevations: 5,300 ft (1,608 m) at the North Entrance to almost 11,358 feet (3,640 m) at Eagle Peak on the east boundary; most roads lie at 7,500-8,000 feet (2,275-2,427 m).

Speed limit: 45 mph (73 kph) or lower where posted.

Yellowstone Lake: about 110 miles (170 km) of shoreline and approximately 136 square miles (354 sq km) of surface area.

Thermal features: About 10,000 thermal features are known, including more than 300 geysers.

Grand Loop Road provides access to major scenic attractions. Some, such as Old Faithful Geyser or the Grand Canyon, can only be seen by parking and walking to the feature. 142 miles (229 km) total around; Upper Loop, 70 miles (113 km); Lower Loop, 96 miles (155 km).

Quick tour: Explore one area instead of seeing the entire park from the road. Many people believe that to fully appreciate just the major attractions in Yellowstone, you must spend at least three days.

General park information: 307-344-7381 (long distance from some park locations).

Lodging and services: 307-344-7311 (long distance from some park locations).

Yellowstone National Park Official Web Site: www.nps.gov/yell.

In Brief

By Act of Congress on March 1, 1872, Yellowstone National Park was "dedicated and set apart as a public park or pleasuring ground for the benefit and enjoyment of the people" and "for the preservation, from injury or spoilation, of all timber, mineral deposits, natural curiosities, or wonders. . . and their retention in their natural condition." Yellowstone is the first and oldest national park in the world.

The commanding features that initially attracted interest, and led to the preservation of Yellowstone as a national park, were geological: the geothermal phenomena (there are more geysers and hot springs here than in the rest of the world combined), the colorful Grand Canyon of the Yellowstone River, fossil forests, and the size and elevation of Yellowstone Lake.

The human history of the park is evidenced by cultural sites dating back 12,000 years. More recent history can be seen in the historic structures and sites that represent the various periods of park administration and visitor facilities development.

Operating Hours, Seasons

Summer: Park entrances open on different dates when snow crews are able to clear the roads. Visit the following Web address to learn the projected dates for this year. (http://www.nps.gov/yell/planvisit/orientation/travel/roadopen.htm) The season runs from mid-April to late-October. Once an entrance/road opens it is open 24 hours. The only exceptions are caused by road construction and weather-caused restrictions.

Winter: The season runs from mid-December to mid-March. The road for the North Entrance at Gardiner, MT to the Northeast Entrance at Cooke City, MT is open to wheeled-vehicle use year around. Only over-snow vehicles are allowed on other park roads.

Visitor Information Stations

Albright Visitor Center, Mammoth: Daily, year-round, 9 a.m.-6 p.m., through Sept. 24; 9 a.m.-5 p.m. thereafter. Information, bookstore, and exhibits on wildlife, early history, exploration, and establishment of the park. Films on the national park idea and artist Thomas Moran are shown throughout the day. Call 307-344-2263.

Norris Geyser Basin Museum: Daily, through Oct. 9, 9 a.m.-5 p.m.. Information, bookstore, and exhibits on the geothermal features of Yellowstone. Call 307-344-2812.

Museum of the National Park Ranger, Norris: Daily, through Sept. 30, 9 a.m.-5 p.m. Exhibits at historic soldier station trace development of the park ranger profession; video shown. Chat with former National Park Service employees who volunteer at the museum.

Madison Information Station: Daily, through Oct. 9, 9 a.m.-5 p.m.. Information and bookstore. Call 307-344-2821.

Canyon Visitor Center: Daily, through Oct. 9, 9 a.m.-6 p.m.. Information, bison exhibit, and bookstore. Call 307-242-2550.

Grant Visitor Center: Daily, through Oct. 1, 9 a.m.-6 p.m. Information, bookstore, exhibits, video on the role of fire in Yellowstone. Call 307-242-2650.

Fishing Bridge Visitor Center: Daily, through Oct. 1, 9 a.m.-6 p.m.. Information, bookstore, and exhibits on the park's birds and other wildlife. Call 307-242-2450.

Old Faithful Visitor Center: Daily, 8 a.m.-6 p.m., through Sept. 30; 9 a.m.-5 p.m. thereafter. Information, bookstore, and geyser eruption predictions. A short movie on thermal life is shown throughout the day. Call 307-545-2750.

West Thumb Information Station: Daily, through Oct. 1, 9 a.m.-5 p.m. Information and bookstore.

Weather & Climate

Summer: Daytime temperatures are often in the 70s (25C) and occasionally in the 80s (30C) in lower elevations. Nights are usually cool and temperatures may drop below freezing at higher elevations. Thunderstorms are common in the afternoons. Winter: Temperatures often range from zero to 20F(-20 to -5C) throughout the day. Sub-zero temperatures over-night are common. The record low temperature is -66F (-54C). Snowfall is highly variable. While the average is 150 inches per year, it is not uncommon for higher elevations to get twice that amount. Spring & Fall: Daytime temperatures range from the 30s to the 60s (0 to 20C) with overnight lows in the teens to single digits (-5 to -20C). Snow is common in the Spring and Fall with regular accumulations of 12" in a 24 hour period. At any time of year, be prepared for sudden changes. Unpredictability, more than anything else, characterizes Yellowstone's weather. Always be equipped with a wide range of clothing options. Be sure to bring a warm jacket and rain gear even in the summer.

Spring Weather

Cold and snow linger into April and May, although temperatures gradually climb. Average daytime readings fall in the 40s to 50s (5-15C), reaching the 60s and 70s (15-25C) by late May and June. Over-night temperatures fall below freezing and may plunge near zero (-20C). These are statistical averages; actual conditions can be vastly different from longterm "norms." At any time of year, be prepared for sudden changes; unpredictability, more than anything else, characterizes Yellowstone's weather. Storms in late May and early June may result in significant accumulations of snow—up to a foot of snow in 24 hours is not uncommon.

We recommend that you bring a warm jacket and rain gear. Spring visitors should be prepared for any type of weather. Call ahead for current weather and road information since sudden storms may result in cold temperatures, snow and/or temporary road closures. Yellowstone's weather is always unpredictable. Carry extra clothing when hiking. Good walking shoes and layers of clothing are recommended throughout the year.

Summer Weather

Average maximum summer temperatures are usually in the 70s (25C) and occasionally in the 80s (30C) in the lower elevations. Nights are cool and temperatures may drop into the 30s and 40s (0-10C). Depending on the elevation, temperatures may even fall into the 20s (-5C) with a light freeze. June can be cool and rainy; July and August tend to be somewhat drier, although afternoon thundershowers and lightning storms are common. During lightning storms get off water or beaches and stay away from ridges, exposed places, and isolated trees. At any time of year, be prepared for sudden changes; unpredictability, more than anything else, characterizes Yellowstone's weather.

We recommend that you bring a warm jacket and rain gear even in the summer. If you plan to visit Yellowstone during spring or fall, call ahead for current weather and road information since sudden storms may result in cold temperatures, snow and/or temporary road closures. In summer, stop at visitor centers or ranger stations for weather forecasts. Always carry extra clothing when hiking. Good walking shoes and layers of clothing are recommended throughout the year.

Autumn Weather

Autumn weather can be pleasant, although temperatures average 10 to 20 degrees lower than summer readings—highs in the 40s to 60s (5-20C). Over-night temperatures can fall into the teens and single digits (-10 to -20C). Snowstorms increase in frequency and intensity as the weeks go by. At any time of year be prepared for sudden changes; unpredictability, more than anything else, characterizes Yellowstone's weather.

Sudden storms can cause a drop in temperature or result in precipitation. Always carry extra clothing when hiking. Good walking shoes and layers of clothing are recommended throughout the year. If you plan to visit Yellowstone during spring or fall, call ahead for current weather and road information since sudden storms may result in cold temperatures, snow and/or temporary road closures.

Winter Weather

Winter temperatures often hover near zero (-20C) throughout the day but may reach highs in the 20s (-5C). Subzero over-night temperatures are common. Occasionally, warm "chinook" winds will push daytime temperatures into the 40s (5-10C), causing significant melting of snowpack—especially at lower elevations. Yellowstone also typically experiences periods of bitterly cold weather. The lowest temperature recorded in Yellowstone was -66F (-54C) near West Yellowstone on February 9, 1933. Annual snowfall averages near 150 inches (380cm) in most of the park. At higher elevations, 200-400 inches (5-10m) of snowfall have been recorded. At any time of year, be prepared for sudden changes; unpredictability, more than anything else, characterizes Yellowstone's weather.

Snowmobilers and skiers should always check on temperatures and wind chill forecasts; subzero weather can make travel dangerous even with proper gear. Always carry extra clothing when hiking, skiing, or snowmobiling. Take advantage of the warming huts (heated shelters) provided in some park areas. Good walking shoes and layers of clothing are recommended throughout the year, but in the winter you'll also need warm boots. Cross-country skis or snowshoes are a 'must' in winter if you plan to go beyond the main roads and boardwalks.

The Roosevelt Arch at the North Entrance to the park at Gardiner. This is the only year round entrance to the park. NPS photo.

You Need to Know

Anglers and Boaters: Yellowstone National Park's fishing season opens the Saturday of Memorial Day weekend and closes the first Sunday in November. Boats and float tubes require permits.

Back Country Permits: *Permits are required for overnight backcountry use* and may be obtained in person up to 48 hours in advance from any ranger station. Rangers will provide information on weather, trails and other conditions.

Bicycling: Bicycling is permitted on established public roads, parking areas, and designated routes. There are no bicycle paths along roadways. Bicycles are prohibited on backcountry trails and boardwalks.

We strongly recommend that safety gear, including helmet and high visibility clothing, be worn by all bicyclists. Park roads are narrow and winding; most do not have a shoulder, or shoulders are covered with gravel. During April, May, and June, high snowbanks make travel more dangerous. Road elevations range from 5,300 to 8,860 feet (1,615-2,700 m); relatively long distances exist between services and facilities.

Motorists frequently do not see bicyclists or fail to give them sufficient space on the road. Drivers sometimes pass on hill crests, blind curves or in oncoming traffic. Vehicles, especially motor homes or those towing trailers, may have wide mirrors, posing an additional hazard. For more information about bicycling in Yellowstone, inquire at a visitor center.

Falling Trees: Following the fires of 1988, thousands of dead trees, known as snags, were left standing in Yellowstone. These snags may fall with very little warning.

Be cautious and alert for falling snags along trails and roadways, and in campsites and picnic areas. Avoid areas with large numbers of dead trees. Again, there is no guarantee of your safety.

Weapons: No firearms or weapons, including state-permitted concealed weapons, are allowed in Yellowstone. However, unloaded firearms may be transported in a vehicle when the weapon is cased, broken down or rendered inoperable, and kept out of sight. Ammunition must be placed in a separate compartment of the vehicle.

Pets: Pets must be leashed. They are prohibited on any trails, in the backcountry, and in thermal basins. Pets are not allowed more than 100 feet from a road or parking area. Leaving a pet unattended and/or tied to an object is prohibited.

Traffic: Yellowstone has more than 350 miles (564 km) of roads. Most are narrow rough, and busy! Some sections are steep with sharp drop-offs. Drive cautiously and courteously; **slow moving vehicles must use pullouts to observe**

wildlife or scenery and to allow safe passing by other vehicles. Watch for animals on the road, especially at night.

Bicycles and motorcycles present special hazards. Drive defensively and wear seat belts. *Yellowstone has a mandatory seat belt requirement for all passengers.* Be especially cautious of ice and road damage; cool temperatures may occur any time of the year. *The maximum speed limit is 45 mph (73 kru per hour) unless otherwise posted,* and they will stop you. Rangers are constantly patrolling the road with radar. The tickets are expensive and next to impossible to argue.

High Altitude: Visitors with a cardiac or respiratory medical history should be aware that most park roads range between 5,300 to 8,860 feet (1,615-2,700 m) in elevation. We recommend contacting a physician prior to your visit.

Be aware of your physical limitations, Don't over exert and drink plenty of fluids to forestall the dehydrating effects of the park's dry climate. Stop and rest frequently.

Picnic Areas: Overnight camping is not allowed in any of the park's picnic areas. Fires may be built only in fire grates available in picnic areas at Snake River, Grant Village, Bridge Bay, Cascade, Norris Meadows, Yellowstone River, Spring Creek, Nez Perce, and the east parking lot of Old Faithful. Liquid fuel stoves may be used for cooking at other locations. Most picnic areas have pit toilets, but none have drinking water.

Avoid These Situations

Your visit may be marred by tragedy if you violate park rules. Law enforcement rangers strictly enforce park regulations to protect you and the park. Please help keep their contacts with you pleasant by paying special attention to park regulations and avoiding. these problems:

- speeding (radar enforced)
- driving while intoxicated (open container law is enforced)
- off-road travel by Vehicle or bicycle
- improper food storage
- camping violations
- pets off leash
- littering
- swimming in thermal pools
- removal or possession of natural (flowers, antlers, etc.) or cultural (artifacts) features
- feeding or approaching wildlife
- spotlighting (viewing animals with artificial light)
- boating and fishing violations
- failure to remove detachable side mirrors when not pulling trailers.

Getting Around

Most visits use private vehicles to get around inside Yellowstone National Park. There is no public transportation service provided within the park.

AmFac Parks & Resorts provides bus tours within the park during the summer season. The Lower Loop Tour departs from locations in the southern part of the Park only. The Upper Loop Tour departs from Lake Hotel, Fishing Bridge RV Park, and Canyon Lodge to tour the northern section of the park only. The Grand Loop Tour departs from Gardiner, MT and Mammoth Hot Springs Hotel to tour the entire park in one day. During the winter season, they provide several snowcoach tours from various locations. Please call 307-344-7311 for information or reservations.

Traffic jams like this usually indicate that there are watchable wildlife nearby. NPS photo.

During the summer season, commercial businesses offer tours originating from many area towns and cities. During the winter season, some businesses provide snowcoach tours for most park roads or bus transportation on the Mammoth Hot Springs to Cooke City road.

Seasonal Road Opening and Closing Schedule

Winter: The winter season of snowmobile and snowcoach travel runs from the third Monday of December to mid-March. All roads and entrances, with one exception, are closed to motor vehicle travel and are groomed for oversnow vehicles. The exception is the North Entrance and the road from Gardiner, MT, through the Northeast Entrance to Cooke City, MT, which is open only to wheeled vehicles. Plowing stops at Cooke City, so you must return to the North Entrance to leave the park.

Spring: Plowing begins in early March. Depending on weather, the first stretches of road to open to motor vehicles include Mammoth-Norris, Norris-Madison, and West Yellowstone-Old Faithful; these roads open in mid-April. Roads on the east and south sides of the park, including East and South Entrances, typically open in early May. The Sunlight Basin Road, between Cooke City, MT and Cody, WY and Craig Pass, between Old Faithful and West Thumb, open by early May as conditions allow. Dunraven Pass, between Tower and Canyon Junctions, and the Beartooth Highway, connecting Cooke City to Red Lodge, MT generally open by Memorial Day weekend. Weather can especially affect road openings over the higher passes. Spring storms may cause restrictions or temporary closures on some roads.

Summer: Park roads are generally open for travel, barring accidents, rock/mud slides or road construction.

Fall: Storms may cause temporary restrictions (snow tire or chain requirements) or closures of park roads. Large road reconstruction projects are underway in Yellowstone resulting in some closures of major sections of road. (See Road Construction Information.) The Beartooth Highway, connecting Cooke City to Red Lodge, MT closes for the season in mid-October. Depending on weather, park roads close for the season on the first Sunday of November. The only exception is the year round road from Gardiner to Cooke City, MT. The winter season of snowmobile and snowcoach travel begins in mid-December.

Trip Checklist

- Barring road construction, most park roads are open to automobiles from about May 1 to the first Sunday in November; please plan with this in mind.
- Make lodging reservations as early as possible.
- Plan your arrival to secure your campsite early in the day.
- Review park regulation and permit information before your arrival.
- Pack clothes that can be layered and that are appropriate for the season of your visit.
- Get up-to-date road and weather information close to your time of visit by calling 307-344-7381.

Bicycling in Yellowstone

Bicycles are not available for rent at the park. If you plan to bring one, remember it is subject to the same traffic rules as automobiles. Bicycling is permitted on established public roads, parking areas, and designated routes. Bikes are prohibited on backcountry trails and boardwalks.

Use extreme caution when riding on park roads; roads are winding and narrow while shoulders are either narrow or nonexistent. Vehicle traffic is heavy most of the time. There are no bicycle paths along roadways.

We strongly recommend that safety gear, including helmet and high visibility clothing, be worn by all bicyclists. During April, May, and June, high snowbanks make travel more dangerous. Road elevations range from 5,300 to 8,860 feet (1615 to 2700 meters), and services and facilities are relatively far apart—typically 20 to 30 miles (37 to 56 kilometers).

Motorists frequently do not see bicyclists or fail to give them sufficient space on the road. Drivers sometimes pass on hill crests, blind curves, or in oncoming traffic. Vehicles, especially motor homes or those towing trailers, may have wide mirrors, posing an additional hazard. For more information about bicycling, stop at a visitor center.

Before the roads open to general automobile traffic in the Spring, some of them are opened to bicycling.

Boating in Yellowstone

Private Boats A permit is required for all vessels (motorized and non-motorized including float tubes) and must be obtained in person at any of the following locations: South Entrance, Lewis Lake Campground, Grant Village Visitor Center, Bridge Bay Ranger Station, and Lake Ranger Station. At Canyon and Mammoth Visitor Centers, only non-motorized boating permits are available. The fee is $20 (annual) or $10 (7 day) for motorized vessels and $10 (annual) or $5 (7 day) for non-motorized vessels. A Coast Guard approved wearable personal flotation device is required for each person boating.

Grand Teton National Park's boat permit will be honored as a one-time 7 day permit or can be applied toward a Yellowstone annual permit.

All vessels are prohibited on park rivers and

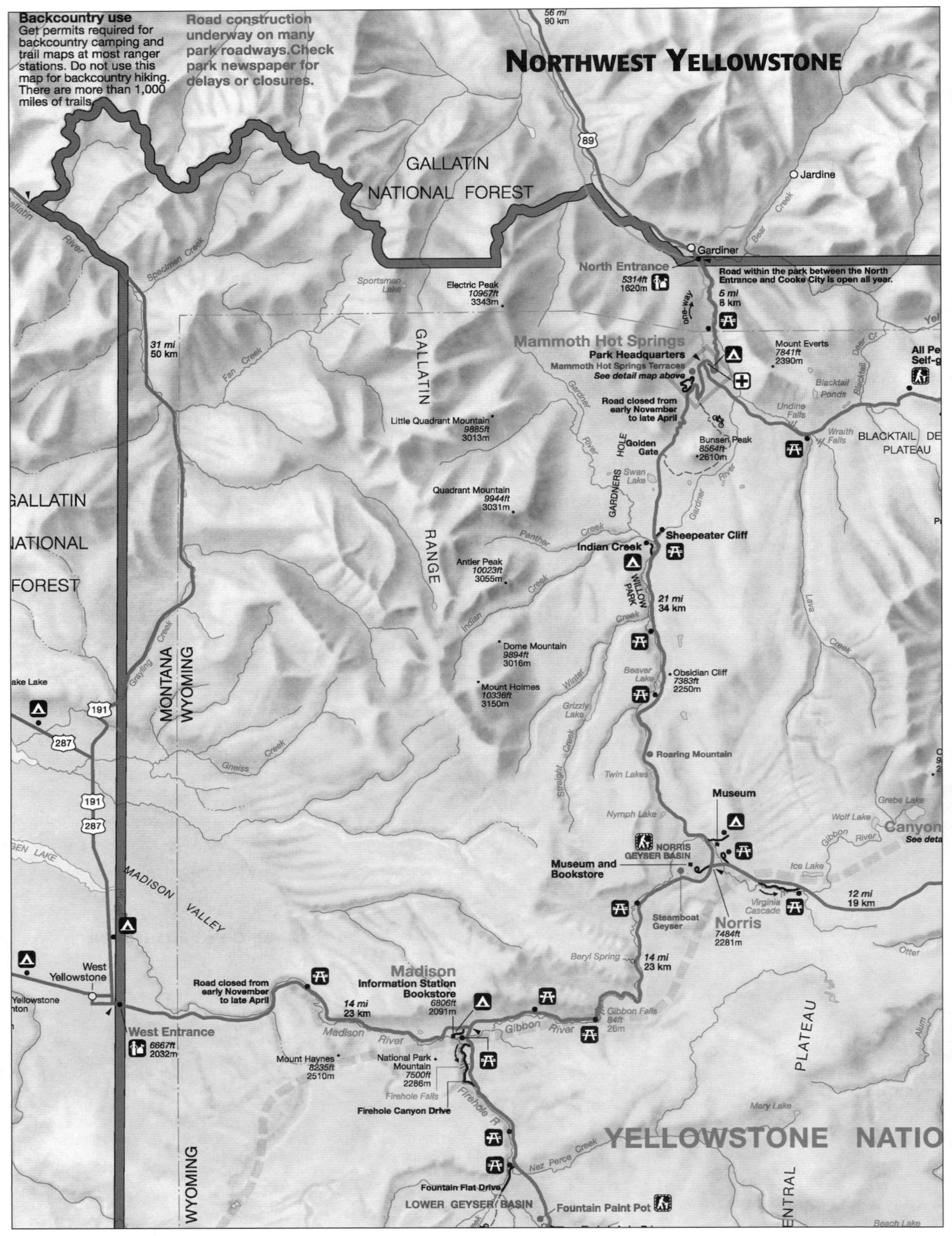

Backcountry use
Get permits required for backcountry camping and trail maps at most ranger stations. Do not use this map for backcountry hiking. There are more than 1,000 miles of trails.
Road construction underway on many park roadways. Check park newspaper for delays or closures.
56 mi
90 km
NORTHWEST YELLOWSTONE
89
GALLATIN
NATIONAL FOREST
Jardine
Gardiner
North Entrance
5314ft
1620m
Road within the park between the North Entrance and Cooke City is open all year.
5 mi
8 km
one-way
Mammoth Hot Springs
Park Headquarters
Mammoth Hot Springs Terraces
See detail map above
Mount Everts
7841ft
2390m
Blacktail Ponds
Undine Falls
Wraith Falls
BLACKTAIL DE
PLATEAU
Road closed from early November to late April
Golden Gate
Bunsen Peak
8564ft
2610m
Swan Lake
GARDNERS HOLE
Gardner River
Sportsman Lake
Electric Peak
10967ft
3343m
GALLATIN
RANGE
Specimen Creek
Gallatin River
31 mi
50 km
Fan Creek
Little Quadrant Mountain
9885ft
3013m
Quadrant Mountain
9944ft
3031m
Panther Creek
Sheepeater Cliff
Indian Creek
Antler Peak
10023ft
3055m
WILLOW PARK
21 mi
34 km
Dome Mountain
9894ft
3016m
Mount Holmes
10336ft
3150m
Beaver Lake
Obsidian Cliff
7383ft
2250m
Grizzly Lake
Winter Creek
Roaring Mountain
Twin Lakes
Straight Creek
Lava Creek
GALLATIN
NATIONAL
FOREST
Grayling Creek
MONTANA
WYOMING
191
287
Gneiss Creek
Museum
Nymph Lake
NORRIS GEYSER BASIN
Museum and Bookstore
Grebe Lake
Wolf Lake
Gibbon River
Canyon
Ice Lake
Virginia Cascade
12 mi
19 km
Steamboat Geyser
Norris
7484ft
2281m
MADISON VALLEY
West Yellowstone
West Entrance
6667ft
2032m
Beryl Spring
14 mi
23 km
Otter
Madison
Information Station
Bookstore
6806ft
2091m
Road closed from early November to late April
14 mi
23 km
Gibbon Falls
84ft
26m
Madison River
Gibbon River
Mount Haynes
8235ft
2510m
National Park Mountain
7500ft
2286m
Firehole Falls
Firehole Canyon Drive
Firehole R.
PLATEAU
Mary Lake
YELLOWSTONE NATIO
Nez Perce Creek
Fountain Flat Drive
LOWER GEYSER BASIN
Fountain Paint Pot
WYOMING
CENTRAL
Beach Lake

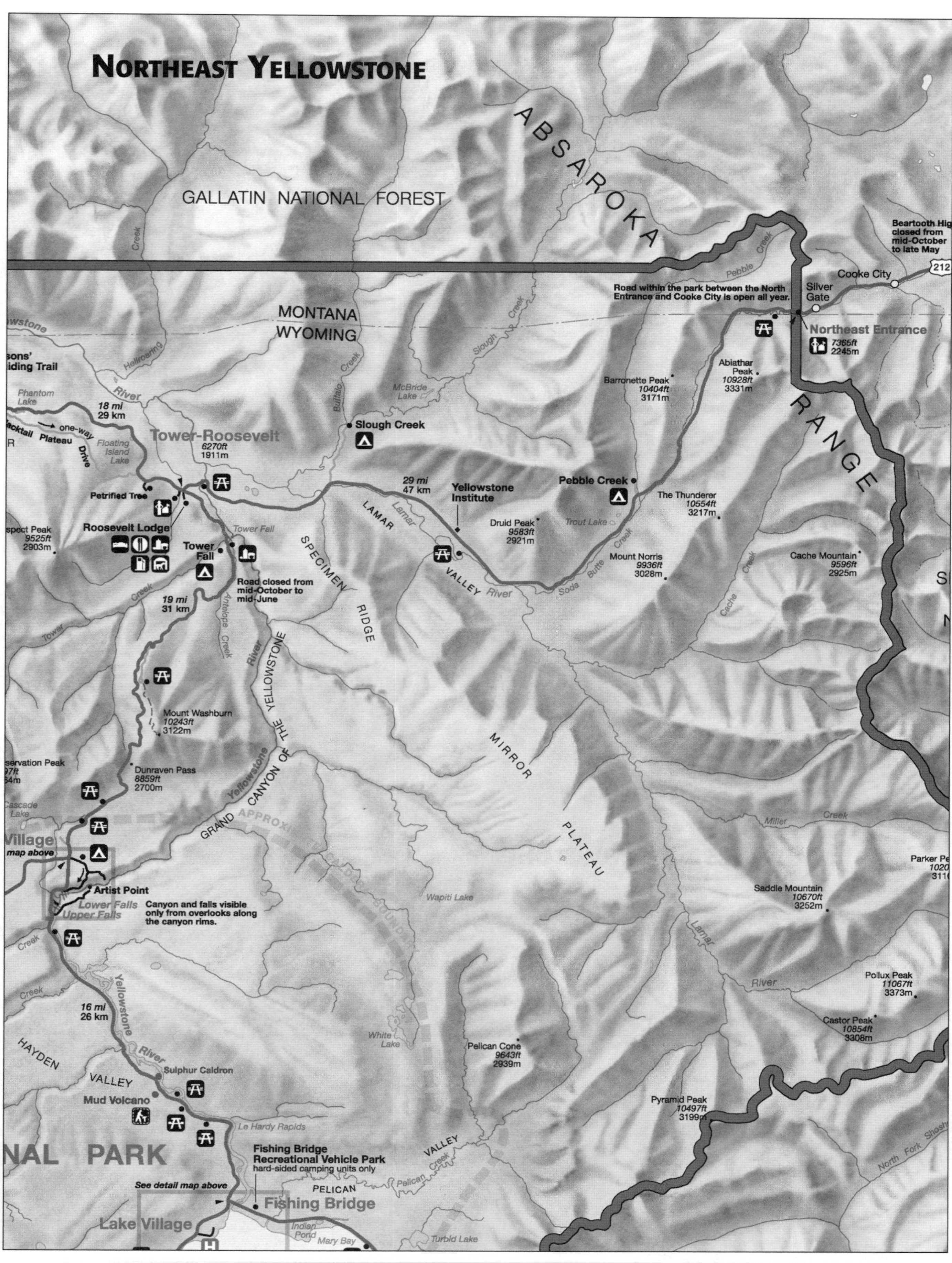

Yellowstone

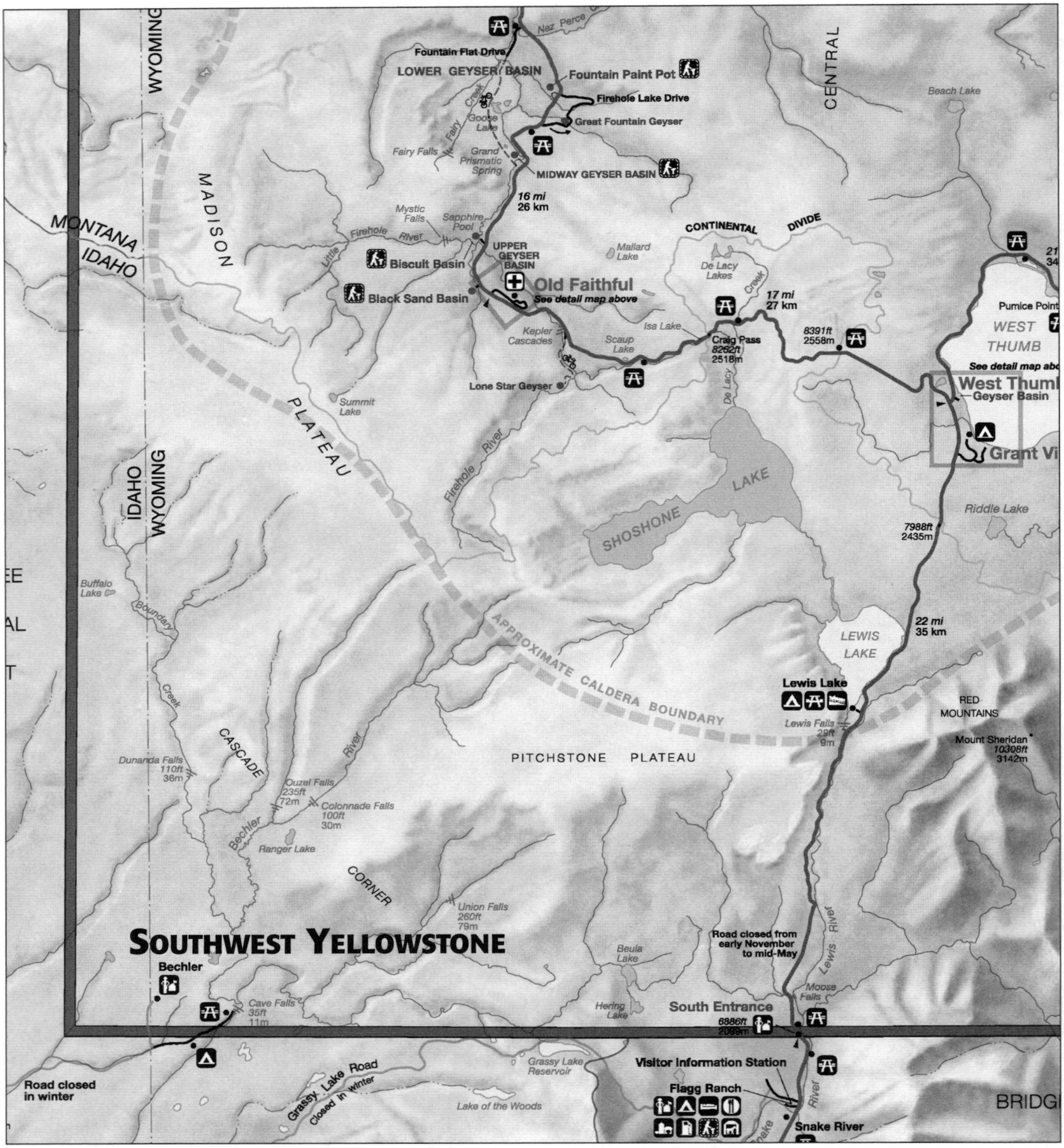

Southwest Yellowstone

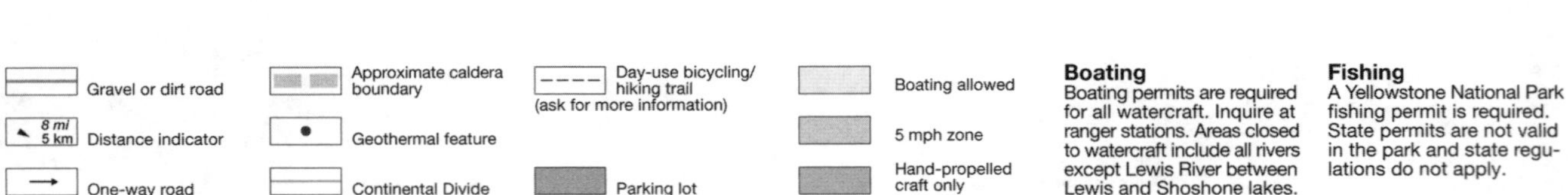

Boating
Boating permits are required for all watercraft. Inquire at ranger stations. Areas closed to watercraft include all rivers except Lewis River between Lewis and Shoshone lakes.

Fishing
A Yellowstone National Park fishing permit is required. State permits are not valid in the park and state regulations do not apply.

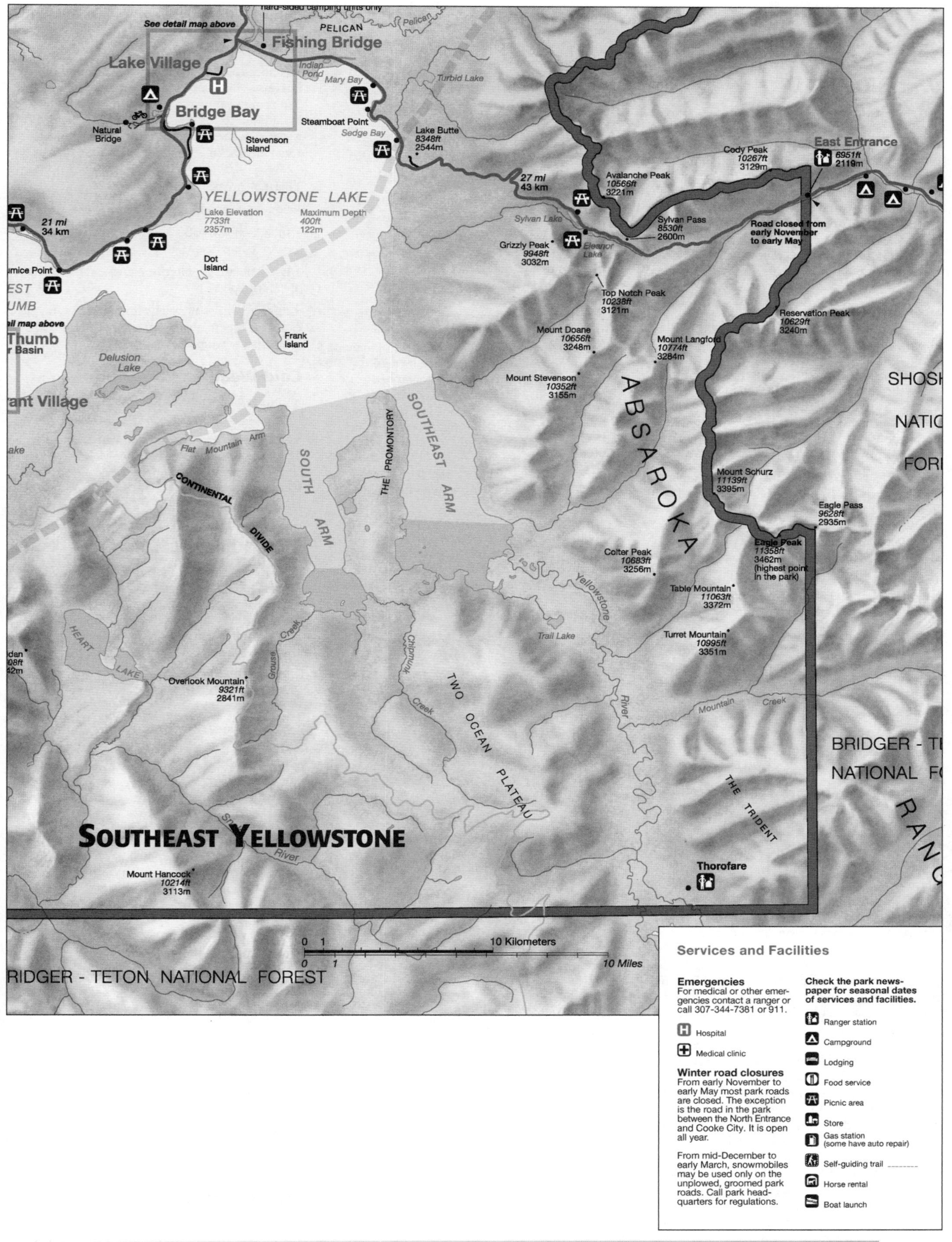

Southeast Yellowstone
See detail map above
PELICAN
Pelican
Fishing Bridge
Lake Village
Indian Pond
Mary Bay
Turbid Lake
Bridge Bay
Natural Bridge
Steamboat Point
Stevenson Island
Sedge Bay
Lake Butte
8348ft
2544m
27 mi
43 km
YELLOWSTONE LAKE
Lake Elevation
7733ft
2357m
Maximum Depth
400ft
122m
21 mi
34 km
Dot Island
Pumice Point
Frank Island
Delusion Lake
Thumb
Flat Mountain Arm
CONTINENTAL DIVIDE
SOUTH ARM
THE PROMONTORY
SOUTHEAST ARM
HEART LAKE
Grouse Creek
Overlook Mountain
9321ft
2841m
Chipmunk Creek
TWO OCEAN PLATEAU
Snake River
Mount Hancock
10214ft
3113m
Sylvan Lake
Eleanor Lake
Grizzly Peak
9948ft
3032m
Avalanche Peak
10566ft
3221m
Sylvan Pass
8530ft
2600m
Cody Peak
10267ft
3129m
East Entrance
6951ft
2119m
Road closed from early November to early May
Top Notch Peak
10238ft
3121m
Reservation Peak
10629ft
3240m
Mount Doane
10656ft
3248m
Mount Langford
10774ft
3284m
Mount Stevenson
10352ft
3155m
ABSAROKA
Mount Schurz
11139ft
3395m
Eagle Pass
9628ft
2935m
Eagle Peak
11358ft
3462m
(highest point in the park)
Colter Peak
10683ft
3256m
Table Mountain
11063ft
3372m
Yellowstone River
Trail Lake
Turret Mountain
10995ft
3351m
Mountain Creek
THE TRIDENT
Thorofare
BRIDGER - TETON NATIONAL FOREST
10 Kilometers
10 Miles
Services and Facilities
Emergencies
For medical or other emergencies contact a ranger or call 307-344-7381 or 911.
Hospital
Medical clinic
Winter road closures
From early November to early May most park roads are closed. The exception is the road in the park between the North Entrance and Cooke City. It is open all year.
From mid-December to early March, snowmobiles may be used only on the unplowed, groomed park roads. Call park headquarters for regulations.
Check the park newspaper for seasonal dates of services and facilities.
Ranger station
Campground
Lodging
Food service
Picnic area
Store
Gas station (some have auto repair)
Self-guiding trail
Horse rental
Boat launch

streams except the channel between Lewis and Shoshone Lakes, where only hand-propelled vessels are permitted.

Where Do I Go?

Geysers & Hot Springs: An unparalleled array of geothermal phenomena—geysers, hot springs, mudpots, and steam vents—are evidence of a volcanic past and the active earth beneath our feet. Many of the most famous features can be found between Mammoth Hot Springs and Old Faithful. Thermal areas include Mammoth Hot Springs, Norris Geyser Basin, Fountain Paint Pot, Midway Geyser Basin, and the Old Faithful area. West Thumb Geyser Basin is 17 miles east of Old Faithful; Mud Volcano is north of Yellowstone Lake.

Grand Canyon: The Grand Canyon of the Yellowstone extends from Canyon Village north to Tower Junction. The most famous and spectacular section, including the Upper and Lower Falls of the Yellowstone River, is seen from overlooks along the North and South Rim roads in the Canyon Village area. The northernmost extent of the canyon is visible from Tower Falls and Calcite Springs overlooks, 19 miles (31 km) north of Canyon Village.

The road between **Tower Junction and Canyon Village** goes over Dunraven Pass, the highest road in the park at 8,600 feet (2700 m). Along the way you will find spectacular views of the Absaroka Mountains, the Yellowstone caldera, and, on a clear day, the Teton Range to the south.

Lake Area: Yellowstone Lake is North America's largest high-altitude lake. The area is prime habitat for a variety of birds and mammals.

Viewing Wildlife: Yellowstone is home to a variety and abundance of wildlife unparalleled in the lower 48 states. The numbers and variety of animals you see are largely a matter of luck and coincidence, but the viewing tips on page 8 can help.

Please be safe when you stop: Use pullouts, never stop in the middle of the road or block traffic.

Photographing Yellowstone

Photography has always played an important role in Yellowstone's history.

To help prove that the natural oddities described by mountain men and explorers did indeed exist, Ferdinand Hayden hired William Henry Jackson to produce photographs of the scenery, waterfalls, canyons, and thermal features viewed by the Hayden Expedition of 1871. Jackson used two cameras, and a bulky, time-consuming method of photography known as the wet plate process. One camera measured 6-1/2 inches by 8-1/2 inches, and the other was 8 inches by 10 inches. Due to slow shutter speeds of five to 15 seconds, the camera needed to be held steady by a heavy tripod. Just prior to taking a photograph, Jackson would prepare a light-sensitive emulsion layer to coat a piece of glass the same size as the camera. After exposing the glass plate negative, Jackson would immediately develop the negative in his darkroom tent before the emulsion layer dried. The average time to make a single photograph was 45 minutes.

Jackson carried hundreds of pounds of fragile glass plates, chemicals and solutions, cameras and tripod on pack mules. He would frequently take his equipment to some very difficult and sometimes precarious locations to get just the view he wanted.

The photographs taken by Jackson in 1871 were instrumental in persuading Congress to establish Yellowstone as the world's first national park in 1872.

Frank J. Haynes was another important photographer in the early days of the park, first journeying here in 1881. Haynes recognized the unique beauty of Yellowstone and realized that this first look would lead to some significant changes in his own career and life.

Haynes was the official photographer for Yellowstone National Park from 1884-1916. By 1897, Haynes had two photo studios in Yellowstone. The first was located in the Upper Geyser Basin, and the second at Mammoth Hot Springs. The Haynes studios sold black and white photographs, and hand-tinted postcards and stereocards to park visitors.

One of Haynes' most important accomplishments was documenting the early development of Yellowstone Park to accommodate increasing numbers of visitors. Haynes photographed park roads and bridges, stagecoaches, steamships on Yellowstone Lake, train stations in Gardiner and West Yellowstone, hotels, lodges, campgrounds, and visitors. Haynes also photographed the natural beauty of Yellowstone. Some of these photographs are of particular importance as they show thermal features displaying activity that differs from today.

Photography still plays an important role today in Yellowstone. Even though nearly every visitor today has a still or video camera, there remains the importance of recording today's cultural, natural and historical features, documenting gradual changes, and events of significant importance such as the restoration of the wolf.

Photo by Corinne Gaffner

Taking Great Photos in Yellowstone

The Basics

• Pay attention to light. At noon or with a bright background, use the flash to even out the light and bring out people's features.

• Take photos early or late in the day. The light is warmer, people I aren't squinting, crowds have thinned, animals are more active.

• Be careful with metering, whether automatic or manual. Sunlit reflective surfaces such as snow, or bright backgrounds such as a thermal basin, can cause inaccurate readings.

• Take photos in all kinds of weather. For example, colors are brighter on cloudy, damp days.

Learn about your subject. To take great photos of elk, read about their behavior, talk to park rangers about the best places to observe elk, etc.

Home Video

• Reduce camera shake by using a tripod or image stabilizer, or filming at lower magnification. Use zoom sparingly. Show where the wildlife live in addition to the animals themselves. Remember to get in scenes yourself! Hand the camera to someone else in your group from time to time.

Thermal Areas

• For extra mood, take pictures early in the day.

• Include boardwalks for extra depth and people for size comparison.

• Use a polarizing filter to increase the brilliance of colorful algae.

• Protect your camera lens from geyser spray; it can leave a permanent deposit if not removed immediately with lens tissue.

Cold Weather

• Cold is hard on batteries, so start with new batteries and carry spares.

• Keep your camera, film, and batteries in a warm place, such as inside your jacket. Avoid sudden temperature changes. Keep the lens and viewfinder free of fog and spray; expose as little glass as possible.

Fishing in Yellowstone

Yellowstone National Park is managed as a natural area to protect plants, wildlife, geology, and scenery. Angling has been a major visitor activity for over a century. Present regulations reflect the park's primary purposes of resource protection and visitor use. The objectives of the fishing program are to:

1. Manage aquatic resources as an important part of the ecosystem.

2. Preserve and restore native fishes and their habitats.

3. Provide recreational fishing opportunities for the enjoyment of park visitors, consistent with the first two objectives.

In Yellowstone, bald eagles, ospreys, pelicans, otters, grizzly bears, and other wildlife take precedence over humans in utilizing fish as food. None of the fish in Yellowstone are stocked, and populations depend on sufficient number of spawning adults to maintain natural reproduction and genetic diversity. In Yellowstone National Park, we place less emphasis upon providing fishing for human consumption and put more emphasis upon the quality for recreational fishing. Anglers, in return, have the opportunity to fish for wild trout in a natural setting.

Because of the increasing number of anglers in the park, more restrictive regulations have been adopted in Yellowstone. These restrictions include: season opening/closing dates, restrictive use of bait, catch-and-release only areas, and number/size limits according to species. A few places are closed to the public to protect threatened and endangered species, sensitive nesting birds, and to provide scenic viewing areas for visitors seeking undisturbed wildlife.

Permits and Fees

A permit is required to fish in Yellowstone.

Anglers 16 years of age and older are required to purchase either a $10 ten-day or $20 season permit. Anglers 12 to 15 years of age are required to obtain a non-fee permit. Children 11 years of age or younger may fish without a permit when supervised by an adult. The adult is responsible for the child's actions. Fishing permits are available at all ranger stations, visitor centers, and Hamilton General Stores. No state fishing license is required in Yellowstone National Park.

Fishing Season

Yellowstone's fishing season generally begins on the Saturday of Memorial Day weekend and continues through the first Sunday of November. Major exceptions: Yellowstone Lake opens June 1; Yellowstone Lake's tributary streams open July 15; Yellowstone River and its tributaries between Canyon and Yellowstone Lake open July 15.

Boats & Float Tubes

You also must obtain a permit in person for boats and float tubes from the following locations: South Entrance, Lewis Lake Campground, Grant Village backcountry office, Bridge Bay Marina, and Lake Ranger Station. Non-motorized boating permits only are available at the Canyon, Mammoth, and Old Faithful backcountry offices, Bechler Ranger Station, and West and Northeast Entrances. You must have a Coast Guard approved "wearable" personal flotation device for each person boating.

Non-toxic Fishing

Yellowstone National Park has implemented a non-toxic fishing program. Nationwide, over three million waterfowl die from lead poisoning through ingestion. Because lead from fishing tackle concentrates in aquatic environments, tackle such as leaded split shot sinkers, weighted jigs, and soft weighted ribbon for fly fishing are prohibited. Only non-toxic alternatives to lead are allowed.

Releasing Fish

The following suggestions will insure that a released fish has the best chance for survival:

1. Play fish as rapidly as possible, do not play to total exhaustion.

2. Keep fish in water as much as possible when handling and removing hook.

3. Remove hook gently—do not squeeze fish or put fingers in gills. The use of barbless hooks is encouraged to make release easier.

4. If deeply hooked—cut line—do not pull hook out. Most fish survive with hooks left in them.

5. Release fish only after its equilibrium is maintained. If necessary, gently hold fish upright, facing upstream.

6. Release fish in quiet water, close to area where it was hooked.

7. Never release lake trout. They are an exotic threat to the fishery. All lake trout you catch must be kept and killed.

Bears, Backcountry, and Anglers

Yellowstone is bear country, and there is no guarantee of your safety. Bears often utilize trails, streams, and lakeshores. Entry into some areas may be restricted; check with a ranger for specific bear management information. Traveling alone in bear country is not recommended. Make enough noise to make your presence known to bears. If you should encounter a bear, give it plenty of room, detour if possible, or wait for the bear to move on. If a bear should charge or attack and the situation allows, climb a tree. If you are caught by a bear, try playing dead. Do not run; this may excite the bear. Carefully read all bear country guidelines and regulations and be prepared for any situation.

Yellowstone Park provides some of the finest angling in the world.

Garbage Disposal and Fish Cleaning

Please pick up all trash, including items such as monofilament fishing line and six pack holders, which may cause injury to wildlife, and properly dispose in trash receptacles.

When fish cleaning and disposal areas are not provided, dispose of fish entrails by puncturing the air bladder and dropping into deep water.

Camping in Yellowstone

First Come—First Served Campsites: There are 12 campgrounds in Yellowstone National Park. Seven of these campgrounds are operated by the National Park Service: Indian Creek, Lewis Lake, Mammoth, Norris, Pebble Creek, Slough Creek, and Tower Fall. Sites at these campgrounds are available on a first-come, first-served basis.

Reserved Campsites: Yellowstone National Park Lodges operates campgrounds at Bridge Bay, Canyon, Grant Village, Madison, and Fishing Bridge RV Park. Same day reservations can be made by calling 307-344-7901 or by asking at lodging activities desks. Future reservations can be made by calling 307-344-7311 or by writing Yellowstone National Park Lodges, P.O. Box 165, YNP, WY 82100; www.travelyellowstone.com. Fishing Bridge RV Park is the only campground offering water, sewer, and electrical hookups, and it is for hardsided vehicles only (no tents or tent trailers are allowed).

Make your reservations early and/or plan on securing your campsite as early in the day as possible; campgrounds may fill by early morning.

Camping Rules: Camping or overnight vehicle parking in pullouts, parking areas, picnic grounds, or any place other than a designated campground are not permitted, and there are no overflow camping facilities. However, camping is often available in neighboring communities and forests outside the park.

Camping is limited to 14 days between June 15 and September 15 and to 30 days the rest of the year; there is no limit at Fishing Bridge RV Park. Check-out time for all campgrounds is 10 AM.

Guest Hours: Camping in Yellowstone is a special experience. Each visitor deserves the opportunity to hear the birds, wildlife, and streams in this beautiful environment. Respect the rights of other campers and comply with the law by adhering to quiet hours, 8 p.m. to 8 a.m. (10 p.m.-7 a.m. at Fishing Bridge RV Park). No generators, loud audio devices, or other noise disturbances will be allowed during this time. Generators are only permitted in six campgrounds and the Fishing Bridge RV Park.

Holders of Golden Age and Golden Access passes will be given approximately 50% discount on camping fees; this discount does not apply at the Fishing Bridge RV Park.

Group Camping: Group camping areas are available at Madison, Grant, and Bridge Bay campgrounds from late May through closing date for large organized groups with a designated leader such as youth groups or educational groups. The fees range from $40-$70 per night, depending on the size of the group. Advance reservations are required and can be made by writing Yellowstone National Park Lodges, P.O. Box 165, YNP, WY 82190 or by phoning 307-344-7311.

Wildlife Viewing

Yellowstone's abundant and diverse wildlife are as famous as its geysers. Habitat preferences and seasonal cycles of movement determine, in a general sense, where a particular animal may be at a particular time. Early morning and evening hours are when animals tend to be feeding and thus are more easily seen. But remember that the numbers and variety of animals you see are largely a matter of luck and coincidence. Check at visitor centers for detailed information.

Wild animals, especially females with young, are unpredictable. Keep a safe distance from all wildlife. Each year a number of park visitors are injured by wildlife when approaching too closely.

Approaching on foot within 100 yards (91 m) of bears or within 25 yards (23 m) of other wildlife is prohibited. Please use roadside pullouts when viewing wildlife. Use binoculars or telephoto lenses for safe viewing and to avoid disturbing them. By being sensitive to its needs, you will see more of an animal's natural behavior and activity. If you cause an animal to move, you are too close!

Where to Watch Wildlife

Yellowstone National Park is home to one of the greatest concentrations of free-roaming, large mammals in the lower 48 states. With the restoration of the gray wolf, the variety of species found here now includes all those large mammals present when Euro-Americans first arrived here.

Habitat preferences and seasonal cycles of movement determine, in a general sense, where a particular animal may be at a particular time. Generally, you are more likely to see mammals in the early morning and late evening hours when they tend to feed.

Grizzly bears: Look around sunrise or sunset in the open meadows of the Lamar and Hayden valleys, Lake and Fishing Bridge areas, and along the road from Tower to Canyon. Also look along the road to the East Entrance. Backcountry travelers should be alert for bears at all times.

Black bears: Look in small openings within or near forested areas, especially along the roads from Mammoth to Tower and the Northeast Entrance, and in the Old Faithful, Madison, and Canyon areas. Black bears may also be seen on any backcountry trail.

Wolves: Most active at dawn and dusk; most often seen in the open areas along the Lamar River and Soda Butte Creek.

Elk: Look around Mammoth Hot Springs, Lamar Valley, Hayden Valley, and the north slope of Mount Washburn.

Pronghorn: Look in the grasslands between Mammoth and the Northeast Entrance.

Moose: Look for this elusive animal in willow thickets bordering streams, especially between Mammoth and Norris, near Lake, and along the road to the Northeast Entrance.

Mule deer: Look during cooler parts of the day near edges of forests.

Mountain Lion: Rare sightings occur at night, especially along the road to the Northeast Entrance.

Bighorn Sheep: Look on cliffs along the Gardner River and between Calcite Springs and Tower Fall, and on Mount Washburn.

Beaver: May be seen early mornings and evenings in streams and ponds such as at Willow Park and Harlequin Lake.

Be a Wise Wildlife Watcher

Remember that you are a guest in the home of wildlife.

• Stay at least 100 yards (91 m.) away from bears and at least 25 yards (23 m.) from all other animals.

• Stop in a pullout instead of the middle of the road.

• Turn off your engine.

• Always talk quietly.

• To find out what people are observing, get out of your car, approach them, and speak quietly. Never call or shout from your car.

Call of the Wild

As you travel through Yellowstone in autumn, stop often to listen for one of the most haunting sounds in nature—the bugle of a bull elk. His high pitched, melodic call echoes off of the canyons and hills of the park, and the final grunts finish off his vocal advertisement to all around that he is ready for the rut, or the mating season.

To a female elk, known as a cow, the bugle provides clues to the size and fitness of a bull. Each bull's bugle is different, but generally the older, larger bulls bugle more loudly than younger bulls.

Bugling often precedes a sparring match. During these matches, bulls lock antlers and shove each other until one retreats. Their sparring matches are shows of strength, not battles to the death.

All this action begins in September and goes on through the month, tapering off into October. Enjoy the sounds and sights of the elk mating season, but remember to keep yourself safe. Stay far away from them and use binoculars to view the action.

Keeping the Wild in Wildlife

Animals in Yellowstone are ***wild***; they are not like animals in zoos or on ranches and farms. Respect their need for undisturbed space, and you will be rewarded by seeing more of their natural activities and discovering how they live in the wild. You'll also expand your opportunities and have a safer, more rewarding visit.

When an animal is disturbed:

• It may move from a good feeding area to a less desirable area, thereby losing vital nourishment.

• Its heart rate increases due to stress, costing the animal vital energy.

• Through time and large numbers of human contacts, it becomes habituated to humans and is less likely to run from a potential poacher.

It may become annoyed and charge the photographer, sometimes causing serious injury.

Minimize your impact:

• Consider your impact before you approach.

• Use an appropriate telephoto lens to take photos of an animal acting naturally in its own environment.

Do not approach animals closely. In Yellowstone, you are required to stay 100 yards (91 m) from a bear and 25 yards (23 m) from all other animals-including the "friendly" elk around Mammoth Hot Springs.

• Pull off the road and use your vehicle as a photo blind.

• Do not bait animals or tempt them with handouts, It's against the law and harms the animals.

Unpredictable Wildlife—Keep

Campground	Sites	Dates	Fee	Elev (ft)	Toilet	Showers/ Laundry Nearby	Dump Station	Generators Permitted (8 AM-8 PM)
Bridge Bay*	430	5/26-9/17	$15.00**	700	Flush		X	X
Canyon*	272	6/2-9/10	15.00**	8,000	Flush	X	X	X
Grant Village*	425	6/21-10/1	15.00**	7,800	Flush	X	X	X
Madison*	280	5/5-10/22	15.00**	6,800	Flush		X	X
Mammoth	85	All Year	12.00	6,200	Flush			X
Norris	116	5/19-9/25	12.00	7,500	Flush			X
Indian Creek	75	6/9-9/18	10.00	7,300	Vault			
Lewis Laki	85	6/23-11/5	10.00	7,800	Vault			
Pebble Creek	32	6/2-9/25	10.00	6,900	Vault			
Slough Creek	29	5/26-10/31	10.00	6,250	Vault			
Tower Fall	32	5/19-79/25	10.00'	6,600	Vault			
Fishing Bridge RV*	340	5/12-9/24	27.00"t	7,800	Flush	X	Sewer	X

*Reserve through Yellowstone National Park Lodges; call 307-344-7311 or TDD 307-344-5305.
**Plus sales tax
† 1-4 people
Dates are approximate and may change because of weather or resource management concerns.
Bridge Bay, Canyon, Grant Village, and Madison campgrounds all contain accessible sites.

Your Distance

You will see more of an animal's natural behavior and activity if you are sensitive to its need for space. Do not approach any wildlife, especially those with young. View them from the safety of your vehicle. If an animal reacts to your presence, you are too close.

Each year a number of park visitors are injured by wildlife when they approach animals too closely. You must stay at least 100 yards (91 m) away from bears and at least 25 yards (23 m) away from all other large animals—bison, elk, bighorn sheep, deer, moose, wolves, and coyotes.

Bison may appear tame and slow but they are unpredictable and dangerous. They weigh up to 2,000 pounds (900 kg) and sprint at 30 miles per hour (48 kph)—three times faster than you can run! Every year visitors are gored, and some have been killed.

Coyotes quickly learn bad habits like roadside begging. This may lead to aggressive behavior toward humans.

Bears—be alert for tracks and sign. The best way to avoid being injured by a bear is to take all necessary precautions to avoid surprise encounters.

If precautionary measures fail and you are charged by a bear, you can usually defuse the situation. Pepper spray is a good last line of defense, it has been effective in more than 90% of the reported cases where it has been used. Become familiar with your pepper spray, read all instructions, and know its limitations. Pepper spray must be instantly available, not in your pack. Remember, carrying pepper spray is not a substitute for vigilance and good safety precautions.

If you are injured by a bear (regardless of how minor), or if you observe a bear or bear sign, report it to a park ranger as soon as possible. Someone's safety may depend on it.

Bighorn Sheep

Bighorn sheep (*Ovis canadensis*) once numbered in the millions in western United States and were an important food source for humans. The "Sheepeaters", related to the Shoshoni tribe, lived year-round in Yellowstone until 1880. Their principal food was bighorn sheep and they made their bows from sheep horns. By 1900, during an "*epoch of relentless destruction by the skin hunters*" (Seton 1913), bighorn numbers were reduced to a few hundred in the United States. In 1897 Seton spent several months roaming the upper ranges of Yellowstone Park and did not see any, although about 100-150 were estimated to be present. He reported that by 1912, despite a disease (scab) contracted from domestic sheep, bighorns in the park had increased to more than 200 and travelers could find them with fair certainty by devoting a few days to searching around Mt. Everts, Mt. Washburn or other well-known ranges. In winter, small bands of sheep could then be seen every day between Mammoth and Gardiner … "*4 great rams with about 40 other sheep…so tame that one could get pictures within ten feet…*"

Bighorn sheep are named for the large, curved horns borne by the males, or rams. Females, or ewes, also have horns, but they are short with only a slight curvature. Sheep range in color from light brown to grayish or dark, chocolate brown, with a white rump and lining on the back of all four legs. Rocky Mountain bighorn females weigh up to 200 pounds, and males occasionally exceed 300 pounds. During the mating season or "rut", occurring in November and December, the rams butt heads in apparent sparring for females. Rams' horns can weigh more than 40 pounds, and frequently show broken or "broomed" tips from repeated clashes. Lambs, usually only one per mother, are born in May and June. They graze on grasses and browse shrubby plants, particularly in fall and winter, and seek minerals at natural salt licks. Bighorns are well adapted to climbing steep terrain where they seek cover from predators such as coyotes, eagles, and mountain lions. They are susceptible to disease such as lungworm, and sometimes fall off cliffs.

By 1914 there were about 210 sheep in Yellowstone and by 1922 there were 300 (Seton 1929). Censuses since the 1920s have never indicated more than 500 sheep. In recent years, bighorns have been systematically counted by aerial surveys in early spring. An annual ground count is also conducted on the winter range in the northern part of the park.

In the winter of 1981-82, an outbreak of pinkeye occurred among bighorns in the Mt. Everts area. Many sheep were blinded and/or killed on the adjacent park road or by falling from cliffs. No evidence of the disease, a natural occurrence, has been seen since. Winter visitors to the park still enjoy watching and photographing bighorns along the cliffs between Gardiner and Mammoth, as they did 80 years ago. Annual surveys of bighorn indicate that the resident herd on Yellowstone's northern range consists of at least 150-225 animals.

In 1997, a new study done by researchers at Montana State University began to investigate bighorn population status and behavior in northern Yellowstone. Of particular interest to these investigators is the effect of road use on the bighorns' ability to use their summer and winter range. Sheep are commonly seen along the road through the Gardner River Canyon, where visitors should be alert for bighorns crossing between their preferred cliffs and the river where they drink.

Summering bands are found in the Gallatin and Washburn Ranges, the Absarokas, and occasionally in the Red Mountains. On Dunraven Pass, a section of the Grand Loop Road in the park, a band of ewes and lambs has become somewhat habituated to summer traffic. These bighorns cause numerous traffic jams and are sometimes illegally fed by visitors, posing traffic hazards and danger to sheep. Park staff and visitors are encouraged to educate others about the importance of the "no feeding" regulation to the long-term welfare of wild animals.

Bison

Bison are the largest mammals in Yellowstone National Park. They are strictly vegetarian, a grazer of grasslands and sedges in the meadows, the foothills, and even the high-elevation, forested plateaus of Yellowstone. Bison males, called bulls, can weigh upwards of 1,800 pounds. Females (cows) average about 1,000 pounds. Both stand approximately six feet tall at the shoulder, and can move with surprising speed to defend their young or when approached too closely by people. Bison breed from mid-July to mid-August, and bear one calf in April and May. Some wolf predation of bison is documented in Canada and has recently been observed in Yellowstone.

Yellowstone is the only place in the lower 48 states where a population of wild bison has persisted since prehistoric times, although fewer than 50 native bison remained here in 1902. Fearing extinction, the park imported 21 bison from two privately-owned herds, as foundation stock for a bison ranching project that spanned 50 years at the Buffalo Ranch in Yellowstone's Lamar Valley. Activities there included irrigation, hay-feeding, roundups, culling, and predator control, to artificially ensure herd survival. By the 1920s, some intermingling of the introduced and wild bison had begun. With protection from poaching, the native and transplanted populations increased. In 1936, bison were transplanted to historic habitats in the Firehole River and Hayden Valley. In 1954, the entire population numbered 1,477. Bison were trapped and herds periodically reduced until 1967, when only 397 bison were counted parkwide. All bison herd reduction activities were phased out after 1966, again allowing natural ecological processes to determine bison numbers and distribution. Although winterkill takes a toll, by 1996 bison numbers had increased to about 3,500.

A bison bull. NPS Photo

Bison are nomadic grazers, wandering high on Yellowstone's grassy plateaus in summer. Despite their slow gait, bison are surprisingly fast for animals that weigh more than half a ton. In winter, they use their large heads like a plow to push aside snow and find winter food. In the park interior where snows are deep, they winter in thermally influenced areas and around the geyser basins. Bison also move to winter range in the northern part of Yellowstone.

Bison are enjoyed by visitors, celebrated by conservationists, and revered by Native Americans. Why are they a management challenge? One reason is that about half of

The Grizzly Bear

NPS Photo

The Yellowstone ecosystem provides vital habitat for grizzlies in its two national parks (Yellowstone and Grand Teton), six national forests, state lands, and private lands. Some bears live either totally inside or outside of Yellowstone National Park; others may use portions of various different agency holdings.

Because grizzly bears range widely and are usually solitary, they are difficult to count. Biologists estimate their population within the Yellowstone ecosystem to be 280-610 bears.

The Yellowstone ecosystem is unique among areas inhabited by grizzly bears in North America because of the foods it provides. Here, grizzly bears depend more on animals, ranging from ants and moths to elk and bison. Bears here and elsewhere also eat large amounts of plants, but Yellowstone lacks the lush vegetation and berries found in northern Montana.

When Yellowstone grizzly bears emerge from hibernation in March and April, there is still a lot of snow and very little vegetation in most of the park. The bears move to the low country where elk and other ungulates (hoofed mammals) spent the winter. There, the bears feed on carcasses of ungulates that died during the winter. (Never approach a carcass-a bear may be nearby and it will often defend its food source.) Bears are not the only animal that depends on winter-killed ungulates for survival. Wolves, coyotes, wolverines, badgers, foxes, eagles, ravens, magpies, and carrion beetles also feed on the carcasses.

Grizzly bears prey on elk calves in the spring, usually from mid-May through early July. After early July, most elk calves can outrun bears. Some bears will feed on spawning cutthroat trout in the Yellowstone Lake area during the early summer. Bears also dig for small rodents (primarily pocket gophers), ants, roots, and tubers. Later in the summer, grizzly bears feed on army cutworm moths and whitebark pine nuts at high elevations. Despite their small size, these foods are important, high-protein foods for grizzly bears, especially as autumn approaches.

The restoration of wolves to the park appears to be providing bears more opportunities to obtain meat. During the years since the 1995 release of wolves into the park, bears have been observed successfully taking wolf-killed ungulates away from wolf packs. Will this new opportunity increase the grizzly bear population in Yellowstone? No one knows.

Yellowstone's bison have been exposed to brucellosis, a bacterial disease that came to this continent with European cattle and may cause cattle to miscarry. The disease has little effect on park bison and has never been transmitted from wild bison to a visitor or to domestic livestock. Despite the very low risk to humans and livestock today, since the possibility of contagion exists, the State of Montana believes its "brucellosis-free" status may be jeopardized if bison are in proximity to cattle. Although the risk is very low, if cattle become infected, ranchers can be prevented from shipping livestock out of state until stringent testing and quarantine requirements are met. Although scientists are studying new possibilities, there is yet no known safe, effective brucellosis vaccine for bison. Ironically, elk in the ecosystem also carry the disease, but this popular game species is not considered a threat to livestock.

Yellowstone wildlife freely move across boundaries set a century ago without knowledge of each animal's habitat needs. But bison are not always unwelcome outside the park. In the park managers have tried to limit bison use of lands outside the park through public hunting, hazing bison back inside park boundaries, capture, testing for exposure to brucellosis, and shipping them to slaughter. Since 1990, state and federal agency personnel have shot bison that leave the park. During the severe winter of 1996-1997, nearly 1,100 bison were sent to slaughter. The carcasses sold at public auction, or shot and given to Native Americans. These actions reduced the bison population to about 2,200 in 1997-1998. In the mild winter of 1997-1998, only 11 bison were killed in management actions, all in January, and all from the West Yellowstone area. Six bison were shot and five were sent to slaughter. Through the winter another 21 bison are known to have died, 12 of natural causes, and 9 from other causes such as collisions with vehicles.

The NPS, U.S.D.A. Forest Service, U.S.D.A. Animal and Plant Health Inspection Service, and the State of Montana completed a Draft Environmental Impact Statement for the Interagency Bison Management Plan for the State of Montana and Yellowstone National Park for public release on June 12, 1998. The purpose is to maintain a wild free-ranging bison population and to address the risk of brucellosis transmissions to protect the economic interest and viability of the livestock industry in Montana. Alternatives being considered range from: allowing bison to freely range over a large portion of public land inside and outside the park; managing bison like elk and other wildlife through controlled hunting outside park boundaries; and attempting to eradicate brucellosis by capturing, testing, and slaughtering infected bison at numerous facilities constructed inside the park. Additional options include purchase of additional winter range; attacking brucellosis with a (yet unknown) safe and effective vaccine for bison; and quarantine of animals at appropriate locations such as Indian Reservations or other suitable sites outside Yellowstone.

Bobcats

Bobcats (*Felix rufus*) are small wild cats with reddish-brown or yellowish-brown coats, streaked with black or dark brown. They have prominent, pointed ears with a tuft of black hair at the tip. Females average 20 pounds and males weigh from 16 to 30 pounds. They breed in late winter or early spring and have a gestation period of about two months. A female may have one to six kittens each year. Although adapted to a variety of habitats across the country, they do not tolerate the deep snows found in much of Yellowstone, and thus they are usually reported in the northern portion of the park. Bobcats move about their home ranges most actively in the hours near dawn and dusk, hunting small mammals such as mice, rabbits, hares, and deer. They seek cover in conifer stands and on rocky ledges.

In the early years of this century, bobcats were reported as "somewhat common" in the park. In the last 64 years, there have been at least 43 reports of bobcats sighted in the park, 9 to 14 reports in each decade since 1960. These sightings have occurred throughout the park; about 80 percent have occurred in the northern half. Bobcats have been reported in about equal numbers during all seasons. In 1960, a bobcat was killed by a car near Squaw Lake (now Indian Pond) on the north shore of Yellowstone Lake; its skull was deposited in the Yellowstone Museum collection. Other roadkilled bobcats were reported in 1993 and 1996. In 1960, a young bobcat was reported on the porch of the administration building at Mammoth; other young bobcats have been reported at Pebble Creek bridge (Feb. 1977) and at Canyon campground (July 1986), where one accompanied an adult bobcat.

No research has been conducted in Yellowstone to determine the numbers or distribution of this elusive animal that usually is solitary, nocturnal, and widely scattered over its range.

Unlike lynx, which they resemble, bobcats elsewhere have been highly adaptable to human-caused changes in environmental conditions; some biologists believe that there are more bobcats in the United States today than in colonial times. Yellowstone has many rock outcrops, canyons bordered by rock ledges, conifer forests, and semi-open areas that seem to offer conditions favorable for bobcats—adequate shelter, a variety of rodents, rabbits, hares, birds, and other small animals as well as seasonal carrion, for food.

Park rangers are one of your best sources of information while visiting the park.

Carrion is seldom used if live prey is available. Studies elsewhere have shown that bobcats also may kill both young and adult antelope and deer; they stalk bedded adults and may be carried long distances while biting their prey in the neck.

Bobcats are known to hole-up and wait out severe winter storms elsewhere, but whether they are able to tolerate the severe midwinter conditions of the park interior is unknown. These elusive cats are most active at night, so even those who study them seldom have an opportunity to see one. If you are so fortunate, look for the black bars on the inside of the forelegs. Black bars mean bobcat, and not the similar-looking lynx! If you see tracks, measure and photograph them carefully, then consult a track field guide. Bobcat tracks seldom exceed 2 1/4 inches in length; lynx tracks usually are longer than 3 1/2 inches.

If you see a bobcat or bobcat tracks, please report them promptly to a ranger or visitor center. For animals so seldom recorded, every observation is useful and important.

Hiking and Camping in Bear Country

Although the risk of an encounter with a bear is low, there are no guarantees of your safety. Minimize your risks by following the guidelines below.

A Fed Bear is a Dead Bear

Do not leave packs containing food unattended, even for a few minutes. Allowing a bear to obtain human food even once often results in the bear becoming aggressive about obtaining such food in the future. Aggressive bears present a threat to human safety and eventually may be destroyed or removed from the park.

While Hiking

Make bears aware of your presence on trails by making loud noises, shouting, or singing. This lessens the chance of sudden encounters, which are the cause of most bear-caused human injuries in the park. Hike in groups and use caution where vision is obstructed. Do not hike after dark. Avoid carcasses; bears often defend this source of food.

If You Encounter a Bear

Do not run. Bears can run 30 mph (48 kph), or 44 feet/second (13 m/second), which is faster than Olympic sprinters. Running may elicit an attack from an otherwise nonaggressive bear. If the bear is unaware of you, keep out of sight and detour behind and downwind of the bear. If the bear is aware of you and nearby, but has not acted aggressively, slowly back away.

Tree climbing to avoid bears is popular advice, but not very practical in many circumstances. All black bears, all grizzly cubs, and some adult grizzlies can climb trees. Plus, running to a tree may provoke an otherwise uncertain bear to chase you.

If A Bear Charges or Approaches You

Do not run. Some bears will bluff their way out of a threatening situation by charging, then veering off or stopping abruptly at the last second. Bear experts generally recommend standing still until the bear stops and then slowly backing away. If you are attacked, lie on the ground completely flat. Spread your legs and clasp your hands over the back of your neck. Another alternative is to play dead: drop to the ground, lift your legs up to your chest, and clasp your hands over the back of your neck.

When Camping

Never camp in an area that has obvious evidence of bear activity such as digging, tracks, scat, or where animal carcasses are present.

Odors attract bears. Avoid carrying or cooking odorous foods or other products. Keep a clean camp; do not cook or store food in your tent. All food, garbage, or other odorous items used for preparing or cooking food must be secured from bears. Hang all such items at least 10 feet (3 m) above the ground and at least 4 feet (1.2 m) out from tree trunks. Treat all odorous products such as soap, deodorant, or toiletries in the same manner as food.

Sleep a minimum of 100 yards (91m) from where you hang, cook, and eat your food. Keep your sleeping gear clean and free of food odor. Don't sleep in the same clothes worn while cooking and eating; hang those clothes in plastic bags.

Coyotes are some of the more common critters seen in Yellowstone.

Coyotes

Yellowstone's coyotes (*Canis latrans*) are among the largest coyotes in the United States; adults average about 30 lbs. and some weigh around 40 lbs. This canid (member of the dog family) stands less than two feet tall and varies in color from gray to tan with sometimes a reddish tint to its coat. Coyotes live an average of about 6 years, although one Yellowstone coyote lived to be more than 13 before she was killed and eaten by a cougar. A coyote's ears and nose appear long and pointed, especially in relation to the size of its head. It can generally be distinguished from its much larger relative, the gray wolf, by its overall slight appearance compared to the massive 75 to 125-pound stockiness of the bigger dog. The coyote is a common predator in the park, often seen alone or in packs, traveling through the park's wide open valleys hunting small mammals. But they are widely distributed and their sign can also be found in the forests and thermal areas throughout Yellowstone. They are capable of killing large prey, especially when they cooperatively hunt.Yellowstone's coyotes (Canis latrans) are among the largest coyotes in the United States; adults average about 30 lbs. and some weigh around 40 lbs. This canid (member of the dog family) stands less than two feet tall and varies in color from gray to tan with sometimes a reddish tint to its coat. Coyotes live an average of about 6 years, although one Yellowstone coyote lived to be more than 13 before she was killed and eaten by a cougar. A coyote's ears and nose appear long and pointed, especially in relation to the size of its head. It can generally be distinguished from its much larger relative, the gray wolf, by its overall slight appearance compared to the massive 75 to 125-pound stockiness of the bigger dog. The coyote is a common predator in the park, often seen alone or in packs, traveling through the park's wide open valleys hunting small mammals. But they are widely distributed and their sign can also be found in the forests and thermal areas throughout Yellowstone. They are capable of killing large prey, especially when they cooperatively hunt.

Mountain Lions

The mountain lion (*Felis concolor*), also called the cougar, is the largest member of the cat family living in Yellowstone. Mountain lions can weigh up to 200 pounds, although lions in Yellowstone are thought to range between 140 and 160 pounds

Mountain lions are seldom seen, but ever present. NPS photo

for males and around 100 pounds for females. Two to three kittens may be born at any time of year, although most arrive in summer and fall. For reasons that are not clear, only about 50 percent of kittens survive their first year. The current population of lions in Yellowstone is estimated to be 18-24 animals and is thought to be increasing.

Mountain lions are rather secretive, consequently, most visitors are unaware of their existence in Yellowstone. Lions probably live throughout the park in summer. In winter, difficulty of movement and lack of available prey causes most lions to move to lower elevations. Lions are territorial and will kill other lions. The dominant animals reside in the northern range

A bison herd grazes in a meadow. NPS Photo

areas of the park where prey is available year-round. Mountain lions prey chiefly upon elk and deer, although their diet probably varies based upon opportunity, porcupines provide an important supplement to the lion's diet.

Mountain lions were significantly reduced by predator control measures during the early 1900s. It is reported that 121 lions were removed from the park between the years 1904 and 1925. At that time, the remaining population was estimated to be 12 individuals. Mountain lions apparently existed at very low numbers between 1925 and 1940. Reports of lions in Yellowstone have increased steadily from 1 each year between 1930 and 1939 to about 16 each year between 1980 and 1988. However, increases in visitor travel in Yellowstone and improvements in record keeping during this period probably contributed to this trend.

In 1987, the first study of mountain lion ecology was initiated in Yellowstone National Park. The research documented population dynamics of mountain lions in the northern Yellowstone ecosystem inside and outside the park boundary, determined home ranges and habitat requirements, and assessed the role of lions as a predator in the ecosystem. In recent years in other areas of the West, mountain lions have occasionally attacked humans. No documented lion/human confrontations have occurred in Yellowstone.

Elk

Elk (*Cervus elaphus*) are the most abundant large mammal found in Yellowstone; paleontological evidence confirms their continuous presence for at least 1,000 years. Yellowstone National Park was established in 1872, when market hunting of all large grazing animals was rampant. Not until after 1886, when the U.S. Army was called in to protect the park and wildlife slaughter was brought under control, did the large animals increase in number.

More than 30,000 elk from 7-8 different herds summer in Yellowstone and approximately 15,000 to 22,000 winter in the park. The subspecies of elk that lives here are found from Arizona to northern Canada along the Rocky

Elk are the most commonly observed animal in Yellowstone.

Mountain chain; other species of elk were historically distributed from coast to coast, but disappeared from the eastern United States in the early 1800s. Some other subspecies of elk still occupy coastal regions of California, Washington, and Oregon. Elk are the second largest member of the deer family (moose are larger). Adult males, or bulls, range upwards of 700 pounds while females, or cows, average 500-525 pounds. Their coats are reddish brown with heavy, darker-colored manes and a distinct yellowish rump patch.

Bulls grow antlers annually from the time they are nearly one year old. When mature, a bull's "rack" may have 6 to 8 points or tines on each side and weigh more than 30 pounds. The antlers are usually shed in March or April, and begin regrowing in May, when the bony growth is nourished by blood vessels and covered by furry-looking "velvet." Antler growth ceases each year by August, when the velvet dries up and bulls begin to scrape it off by rubbing against trees, in preparation for the autumn mating season or rut. A bull may gather 20-30 cows into his harem during the mating season, often clashing or locking antlers with another mature male for the privilege of dominating the herd group. By November, mating season ends and elk generally move to their winter ranges. Calves weighing 25-40 pounds are born in late May or early June.

Climate is the most important factor affecting the size and distribution of elk herds here. Nearly the whole park—approximately 2.2 million acres—provides summer range for elk. However, winter snowfalls force elk and other ungulates to leave the greater part of the park. Only the northern, lower-elevation portion of Yellowstone, where temperatures are more moderate and snowfall less than in the park interior, can support large numbers of wintering elk. Annual precipitation, which occurs mostly as snow, averages as high as 75" in the southern, high-mountain plateaus of the park; minimum temperatures there are often well below 0° F, and have been as low as -66° F. In contrast, most of the northern range averages less than 30" of precipitation annually, and winter temperatures are considerably warmer.

Bull moose lock antlers. NPS photo

Moose

Moose (*Alces alces shirasi Nelson*), the largest member of the deer family, were reportedly very rare in northwest Wyoming when Yellowstone National Park was established in 1872. Subsequent protection from hunting and wolf control programs may have contributed to increased numbers but suppression of forest fires probably was the most important factor, since moose here depend on mature fir forests for winter survival.

Moose breed from early September to November and one to three calves are born in May or June. Calves weigh 25 to 35 pounds at birth but grow rapidly; adult females (cows) weigh up to 800 pounds and males (bulls) up to 1300 pounds. Bulls are readily identified by their large, palmate antlers, which are shed annually, and their bells, an apparently useless dewlap of skin and hair that dangles from the throat. Moose live mostly solitary lives, and die from disease, starvation, or predation by wolves and, occasionally, by grizzly bears.

Surveys in the late 1980s suggested a total park population of fewer than 1000 moose.

Research on radio-collared moose in northern Yellowstone has shown that when snow depth forces moose from low-elevation willow stands in November, they move up to as high as 8500 feet, to winter in mature stands of subalpine fir and Douglas-fir. They browse fir almost exclusively during the deep-snow winter months. Tyers (unpubl. data) found that moose ate 39.6 percent subalpine fir, 25.5 percent willows, 10.6 percent lodgepole pine, 4.6 percent gooseberry, and 4 percent buffaloberry. Snow is not as deep under a canopy of conifer branches since some snow remains on them, and a crust that may restrict moose movements is less likely to form on shaded snow. However, Tyers found that moose could winter in areas where snow considerably deeper than that which elk could withstand.

The moose calf crop has been declining since

the fires of 1988. During that summer there was also high predation of moose by grizzly bears in small patches of surviving timber. The winter following the fires many old moose died, probably as a combined result of the loss of good moose forage and a harsh winter. The fires forced some moose into poorer habitats, with the result that some almost doubled their home range, using deeper snow areas than previously, and sometimes browsing burned lodgepole pines. Unlike moose habitat elsewhere, northern Yellowstone does not have woody browse species that will come in quickly after a fire and extend above the snowpack to provide winter food. Therefore, the overall effects of the fires were probably detrimental to moose populations. Park managers, in cooperation with staff from the adjacent Gallatin National Forest and the Montana Department of Fish, Wildlife and Parks continue to seek good methods to monitor the status of moose in northern Yellowstone. Aerial surveys of willow habitats in spring have shown some promise of providing an index of moose population trends in Yellowstone, although their current population and distribution remain largely unknown.

Moose are commonly observed in the park's southwestern corner along the Bechler and Falls rivers, in the riparian zones around Yellowstone Lake, in the Soda Butte Creek, Pelican Creek, Lewis River, and Gallatin river drainages, and in the Willow Park area between Mammoth and Norris. Summer moose migrations from south and west of the park into Yellowstone have been confirmed by radiotelemetry.

Self-Guiding Trails

Slow down and stretch your legs on these self-guiding trails. At each location, you can purchase a trail guide with a map, photos, and information.

Mammoth Hot Springs. Visitors marvel at the surreal appearance of these travertine terraces. As an early visitor described them: "the hot springs fall over a lofty hill of snowy whiteness, resembling cascades." The trail winds through the area, and you can also drive through the Upper Terraces.

Fort Yellowstone Historic Trail. Most of the buildings constructed in Mammoth during the time that the U.S. Army managed the park (1886-1918) are now used by the National Park Service as its headquarters.

Norris Geyser Basin. Explore the hottest, most dynamic geyser basin in the park. Porcelain Basin features hundreds of geothermal features in an open area; Back Basin trail winds through more forested terrain past a number of springs and geysers. Steamboat, the world's tallest geyser, erupted in May 2000—its first eruption since October 1991.

Fountain Paint Pot. Active, ever-changing mudpots; constant geysers; hissing fumaroles; and colorful, boiling hot springs await you on this trail and on Firehole Lake Drive. Park in the large parking area 8 miles (12.9 km) north of Old Faithful on the road to Madison Junction.

Upper Geyser Basin. The world's largest concentration of geysers is located here, including Old Faithful. View that famous feature, then walk the trails that wind past hundreds of geysers and hot springs. Names such as Beehive, Grotto, Castle, Riverside, and Morning Glory hint at the wonders you will see.

Grand Canyon of the Yellowstone. The Canyon and the Upper and Lower Falls can be seen from overlooks along the rims, which you can reach by car or foot. See for yourself why viewpoints are named Inspiration, Grandview, and Artist Point.

West Thumb Geyser Basin. The boiling springs in this basin, including the famous Fishing Cone, discharge their waters into chilly Yellowstone Lake. With mountains as a backdrop to the east, this is one of the prettiest self-guiding trails.

Mud Volcano Area. Discover turbulent and explosive mudpots, including Mud Volcano and Dragon's Mouth. View—and smell—Sulphur Caldron. Located on the road between Lake and Canyon, 6 miles (9.6 km) north of Fishing Bridge Junction.

Natural Highlights of the Mammoth Area

Mammoth Hot Springs

Mammoth Hot Springs are the main attraction of the Mammoth District. These features are quite different from thermal areas elsewhere in the park. Travertine formations grow much more rapidly than sinter formations due to the softer nature of limestone. As hot water rises through limestone, large quantities of rock are dissolved by the hot water, and a white chalky mineral is deposited on the surface.

Although visitors are sometimes confused by the rapidly shifting activity of the hot springs and disappointed when a favorite spring appears to have "died," it is important to realize that the location of springs and the rate of flow changes daily, that "on-again-off-again" is the rule, and that the overall volume of water discharged by all of the springs fluctuates little.

The Gardner River and Gardner River Canyon

The North Entrance Road from Gardiner, Montana, to Mammoth Hot Springs, Wyoming, runs along the Gardner River. The road winds into the park, up the canyon, past crumbling walls of sandstone and ancient mudflows. The vegetation is much thicker in the canyon than on the open prairie down below, the common trees being Rocky Mountain juniper, cottonwood, and Douglas-fir. Low-growing willows also crowd the river's edge in the flatter, flood-prone sections of the canyon.

Watch for wildlife in season: eagles, osprey, dippers, and kingfishers along the river and bighorn sheep in the steeper parts of the canyon.

45th Parallel Bridge and Boiling River

A sign near where the road crosses the Gardner River marks the 45th parallel of latitude. The 45th parallel is an imaginary line that circles the globe halfway between the equator and the North Pole. This same line passes through Minneapolis-St. Paul, Ottawa, Bordeaux, Venice, Belgrade, and the northern tip of the Japanese islands. It is, here in Yellowstone, roughly aligned with the Montana-Wyoming border.

A parking area on the east side of the road is used by bathers in the "Boiling River." Bathers must walk upstream about a half mile from the parking area to the place where the footpath reaches the river. This spot is also marked by large clouds of steam, especially in cold weather. Here, a large hot spring, known as Boiling River, enters the Gardner River. The hot and the cold water mix in pools along the river's edge. Bathers are allowed in the river during daylight hours only. Bathing suits are required, and no alcoholic beverages are allowed. Boiling River is closed in the springtime due to hazardous high water and often does not reopen until mid-summer. The Yellowstone Park Foundation funded the Boiling River Trail Project. They are a non-profit organization whose mission is to fund projects and programs that protect, preserve and enhance Yellowstone National Park.

Mt. Everts

Mt. Everts was named for explorer Truman Everts of the 1870 Washburn Expedition who became separated from his camping buddies, lost his glasses, lost his horse, and spent the next 37 days starving and freezing and hallucinating as he made his way through the untracked and inhospitable wilderness. Upon rescue, he was, according to his rescuers, within but a few hours of death. Everts never made it quite as far as Mt. Everts. He was found near the "Cut" on the Blacktail Plateau Drive and was mistaken for a black bear and nearly shot. His story, which he later published in Scribner's Monthly Magazine, remains one of Yellowstone's best known, lost-in-the-wilderness stories. It has also been published in book form, edited by Yellowstone's archivist Lee Whittlesey under the name *Lost in the Yellowstone*.

Mt. Everts is made up of distinctly layered sandstones and shales—sedimentary rocks deposited when this area was covered by a shallow inland sea, 70 to 140 million years ago.

Bunsen Peak

Bunsen Peak and the "Bunsen burner" were both named for the German physicist, Robert Wilhelm Bunsen. Although most people are familiar with the "Bunsen burner," few people know why his students gave the burner that name. He was involved in pioneering research about geysers, and a "Bunsen burner" has a resemblance to a geyser. His theory on geysers was published in the 1800s, and it is still believed to be accurate.

Bunsen Peak is 8,564 feet high (2,612 meters) and may be climbed via a trail that starts at the Golden Gate. Another trail, the old Bunsen Peak road, skirts around the flank of the peak from the YCC camp to the Golden Gate. This old road may be used by hikers, mountain-bikers, and skiers in winter.

The peak is also interesting because it burned in the 1880s and then again in 1988. A series of old photos show the creep of trees up Bunsen following the 1880 fires, and the new patterns of open space created by the fires of 1988.

Geological Overview of the Mammoth Area

Mammoth Hot Springs

Mammoth Hot Springs are a surficial expression of the deep volcanic forces at work in Yellowstone. Although these springs lie outside the caldera boundary, their energy is attributed to the same magmatic system that fuels other Yellowstone thermal areas. Hot water flows from Norris to Mammoth along a fault line roughly associated with the Norris to Mammoth road. Shallow circulation along this corridor allows Norris' super-heated water to cool somewhat before surfacing at Mammoth, generally at about the travertine that forms the terraces.

Terrace features can change rapidly in appearance. Don't be surprised to find that some of these features look very different if you visit in person.

Opal Terrace

Opal Spring flows from the base of Capitol Hill, which is across the road from Liberty Cap. After years of dormancy, this spring became active in 1926 and began depositing up to one foot (0.3m) of travertine per year. In 1947, a tennis court was removed to allow natural expansion of the terrace. Further growth threatens the historic home next to Opal Terrace. Designed by Robert Reamer and built in 1908, the house is an example of Prairie Style architecture. Among Reamer's other designs are the Old Faithful Inn and the Roosevelt Arch at Yellowstone's North Entrance. Today sandbags and an earthen wall protect the house. The National Park Service strives to protect both historic and natural resources. At Opal Terrace both types of resources must be considered.

NPS photo

Palette Spring

Water flows from a flat area and then down a steep ridge, creating a colorful hillside palette of brown, green, and orange (the colors are due to the presence of different heat-tolerant bacteria). This effect is much the same as an artist would achieve by allowing wet paint to run down a vertical surface.

Liberty Cap

This 37-foot (11-m) hot spring cone marks the northern portion of Mammoth Hot Springs. Liberty Cap was named in 1871 by the Hayden Survey party because of its marked resemblance to the peaked caps worn during the French Revolution. Its unusual formation was created by a hot spring whose plumbing remained open and in one location for a long time. Its internal pressure was sufficient to raise the water to a great height, allowing mineral deposits to build continuously for perhaps hundreds of years.

Minerva Terrace

Minerva Spring is a favorite not only because of its wide range of bright colors but also for its ornate travertine formations. Since the 1890s, when records were first kept on the activity of Mammoth Hot Springs, Minerva has gone through both active and inactive periods. For several years in the early 1900s, it was completely dry, but by 1951 reports state that Minerva was again active.

During some cycles of activity, water discharge and mineral deposition have been so great

Wolves

As of August 2000, about 115-120 wolves inhabit the Yellowstone ecosystem. Approximately eighty-three known wolf mortalities have occurred in the ecosystem since wolf restoration began six years ago. There are about fourteen packs or groups in the ecosystem, most of which inhabit territories within the Yellowstone National Park or Grand Teton National Park. There are currently about eleven breeding pairs in the ecosystem.

Northern Rocky Mountain wolves, a subspecies of the gray wolf (Canis lupus), were native to Yellowstone when the park was established in 1872. Predator control was practiced here in the late 1800s and early 1900s. Between 1914 and 1926, at least 136 wolves were killed in the park; by the 1940s, wolf packs were rarely reported. By the 1970s, scientists found no evidence of a wolf population in Yellowstone; wolves persisted in the lower 48 states only in northern Minnesota and on Isle Royale in Michigan. An occasional wolf likely wandered into the Yellowstone area; however, no verifiable evidence of a breeding pair of wolves existed through the mid 1990s. In the early 1980s, wolves began to reestablish themselves near Glacier National Park in northern Montana; an estimated 75 wolves inhabited Montana in 1996. At the same time, wolf reports were increasing in central and north-central Idaho, and wolves were occasionally reported in the state of Washington. The wolf is listed as "endangered" throughout its historic range in the lower 48 states except in Minnesota, where it is "threatened."

National Park Service (NPS) policy calls for restoring native species when: a) sufficient habitat exists to support a self-perpetuating population, b) management can prevent serious threats to outside interests, c) the restored subspecies most nearly resembles the extirpated subspecies, and d) extirpation resulted from human activities.

The U.S. Fish & Wildlife Service 1987 Northern Rocky Mountain Wolf Recovery Plan proposed reintroduction of an "experimental population" of wolves into Yellowstone. In a report to Congress, scientists from the University of Wyoming predicted reductions of elk (15%-25%), bison (5%-15%), moose, and mule deer could result from wolf restoration in Yellowstone. A separate panel of 15 experts predicted decreases in moose (10%-15%) and mule deer (20%-30%). Minor effects were predicted for grizzly bears and mountain lions. Coyotes probably would decline and red foxes probably would increase.

In October 1991, Congress provided funds to the U.S Fish & Wildlife Service (USFWS) to prepare, in consultation with the NPS and the U.S. Forest Service, an Environmental Impact Statement (EIS) on restoring wolves to Yellowstone and central Idaho. After several years and a near-record number of public comments, the Secretary of Interior signed the Record of Decision on the Final Environmental Impact Statement (FEIS) for reintroduction of gray wolves to both areas. Staff from Yellowstone, the USFWS, and participating states prepared to implement wolf restoration. The USFWS prepared special regulations outlining how wolves would be managed as a nonessential experimental population under section 10(j) of the Endangered Species Act. These regulations took effect in November 1994. As outlined in the Record of Decision, the states and tribes would implement and lead wolf management outside the boundaries of national parks and wildlife refuges, within federal guidelines. The states of Idaho, Wyoming, and Montana have begun preparation of wolf management plans.

Park staff assisted with planning for a soft release of wolves in Yellowstone. This technique has been used to restore red wolves in the southeastern United States and swift fox in the Great Plains and involves holding animals temporarily in areas of suitable habitat. Penning of the animals is intended to discourage immediate long-distance dispersal. In contrast, a hard release allows animals to disperse immediately wherever they choose, and has been used in Idaho where there is limited access to the central Idaho wilderness.

In the autumn of 1995 at three sites in the Lamar Valley, park staff completed site planning, and archaeological and sensitive plant surveys. Approximately 1 acre was enclosed at each site with 9-gauge chain link fence in 10' x 10' panels. These enclosures could be dismantled and reconstructed at other sites if necessary. The fences had a 2' overhang and a 4' skirt at the bottom to discourage climbing over or digging under the enclosure. Each pen had a small holding area attached, to allow a wolf to be separated from the group for medical treatment. Inside each pen were several plywood security boxes to provide shelter. For the 1996 release, one pen was relocated to Blacktail Plateau and another was constructed in the Firehole Valley in central Yellowstone. Subsequently pens have been relocated from Lamar to other areas in the park interior to facilitate releases into other geographic areas or the park or special circumstances that require the temporary penning of wolves.

USFWS and Canadian wildlife biologists captured wolves in Canada and released them in both recovery areas in 1995 and 1996. As planned, wolves of dispersal age (1-2 years old) were released in Idaho, while Yellowstone released pups of the year (7+ months old), together with one or more of the alpha pair (breeding adults). Young pups weigh about 75 lbs. and are less likely to have established a home range. The goal was to have 5-7 wolves from one social group together in each release pen.

Each wolf was radio-collared when captured in Canada. For about 8-10 weeks while temporarily penned, the wolves experienced minimal human contact. Approximately once each week, they were fed roadkills. They were guarded by rangers and other volunteers who minimized the amount of visual contact between wolves and humans. The pen sites and surrounding areas were closed and marked to prevent unauthorized entry. Biologists used radio-telemetry to check on the welfare of wolves.

Although concern was expressed about the wolves becoming habituated to humans or to the captive conditions, the temporary holding period was not long in the life of a wolf. In Alaska and Canada, wolves are seldom known to develop the habituated behaviors seen more commonly in grizzly bears. Wolves, while social

The wolf is the subject of more stories, myths, and legends than any other creature that exists today.
NPS Photo

among their own kind, typically avoid human contact. They are highly efficient predators with well-developed predatory instincts. Their social structure and pack behavior minimizes their need to scavenge food or garbage available from human sources. Compared to bears, whose diet is predominantly vegetarian, wolves have less specific habitat requirements. The wolves' primary need is for prey, which is most likely to be elk, deer, and other ungulates in these recovery areas.

In 1995, fourteen wolves were released into Yellowstone National Park. In 1996, seventeen more wolves were brought from Canada and released. After release, several thousand visitors were lucky to view wolves chasing and killing elk or interacting with bears during spring. A park ranger and a group of visitors watched a most exciting encounter between two packs which likely resulted in one young wolf's death. This was not the first fatal encounter between wolves, although human-caused mortalities still outnumber inter-pack strife as a cause of wolf deaths.

Yellowstone's first fourteen wolves bore two litters totalling nine pups. In 1996, four packs produced fourteen pups. After the wolves' release in 1996, plans to transplant additional wolves were terminated due to reduced funding and due to the wolves' unexpected early reproductive success.

In early 1997, ten young wolves, orphaned when their parents were involved in livestock depredation on the Rocky Mountain Front in northwestern Montana, were released into the park. In the spring of the wolf restoration project's third year, nine packs of wolves produced 13 litters of 64 pups. Three of the packs produced multiple litters which, while documented in the literature, is still unusual. Alpha male wolves generally do not breed with their own offspring, possibly to prevent inbreeding. However, as wolves were matched up during temporary periods of penning and as pack members shifted or were killed and replaced by other dispersing wolves, the occasional result has been packs in which one or both of the alpha pair were not the parents of subordinate pack members. Consequently, the alpha males probably had less incentive to breed with only one female, especially since food was abundant and the packs were still in the early stages of establishing their territories. Lone wolves continued to roam widely, but most of the wolves remained primarily within the boundaries of Yellowstone National Park

An estimated 20,000 park visitors have observed wolves since their return in 1995. The program's visibility has resulted in opportunities to educate audiences about predator-prey relationships, endangered species restoration, and the importance of maintaining intact ecosystems. The program has also generated numerous partnerships with private groups and individuals who generously donated their time and money—critical in an era of reduced budgets and staff downsizing.

For both Idaho and Yellowstone, wolf population recovery is defined as having about 100 wolves, or approximately 10 breeding pairs, established in each area for 3 successive years. The goal to restore wolves and begin delisting them by approximately 2002 appears within reach. The return of the only species known to be missing from the world's first national park for the past half-century has been a milestone in ecological restoration. It has not only restored the wildlife complement of greater Yellowstone; it has been a symbolic victory for conservationists who patiently and persistently reversed the once-dominant attitude against predators to one of acceptance. We believe that Aldo Leopold would be proud that so many humans have come to respect even these "killer creatures" with whom we share the Earth.

170° F.

Thermal activity here is extensive both over time and distance. Terrace Mountain, northwest of Golden Gate, has a thick cap of travertine. The Mammoth Terraces extend all the way from the hillside where we see them today, across the Parade Ground, and down to Boiling River. The Mammoth Hotel, as well as all of Fort Yellowstone, is built upon an old terrace formation known as Hotel Terrace. There was some concern when construction began in 1891 on the Fort site that the hollow ground would not support the weight of the buildings. Several large sink holes (fenced off) can be seen out on the Parade Ground. This area has been thermally active for several thousand years.

The Mammoth area exhibits much evidence of glacial activity from the Pinedale Glaciation. The summit of Terrace Mountain is covered with glacial till, thereby dating the travertine formation there to earlier than the end of the Pinedale Glaciation. Several thermal kames, including Capitol Hill and Dude Hill, are major features of the Mammoth Village area. Ice-marginal stream beds are in evidence in the small, narrow valleys where Floating Island Lake and Phantom Lake are found. In Gardner Canyon, one can see the old, sorted gravel bed of the Gardner River covered by unsorted glacial till.

Mammoth Tour

Several key ingredients combine to make the Mammoth Hot Springs Terraces: heat, water, limestone, and a rock fracture system through which hot water can reach the earth's surface.

Today's geothermal activity is a link to past volcanism. A partially molten magma chamber, remnant of a cataclysmic volcanic explosion 600,000 years ago in central Yellowstone, supplies one of the ingredients, heat.

Hot water is the creative force of the terraces. Without it, terrace growth ceases and color vanishes. The source of the water flowing out of Yellowstone's geothermal features is rain and snow. Falling high on the slopes in and around Yellowstone, water seeps deep into the earth. This cold ground water is warmed by heat radiating from the magma chamber before rising back to the surface.

Hot water must be able to reach the earth's surface in relatively large volumes to erupt as a geyser or flow as a hot spring. In Yellowstone, many conduits remain from the collapse of the giant caldera; frequent earthquakes keep this underground "plumbing" system open. Even though Mammoth lies north of the caldera ring-fracture system, a fault trending north from Norris Geyser Basin, 21 miles (34 km) away, may connect Mammoth to the hot water of that system. A system of small fissures carries water upward to create approximately 50 hot springs in the Mammoth Hot Springs area.

Another necessary ingredient for terrace growth is the mineral calcium carbonate. Thick layers of sedimentary limestone, deposited millions of years ago by vast seas, lie beneath the Mammoth area. As ground water seeps slowly downward and laterally, it comes in contact with hot gases charged with carbon dioxide rising from the magma chamber. Some carbon dioxide is readily dissolved in the hot water to form a weak carbonic acid solution. This hot, acidic solution dissolves great quantities of limestone as it works up through the rock layers to the surface hot springs. Once exposed to the open air, some of the carbon dioxide escapes from solution. As this happens, limestone can no longer remain in solution. A solid mineral reforms and is deposited as

Liberty Cap. NPS photo

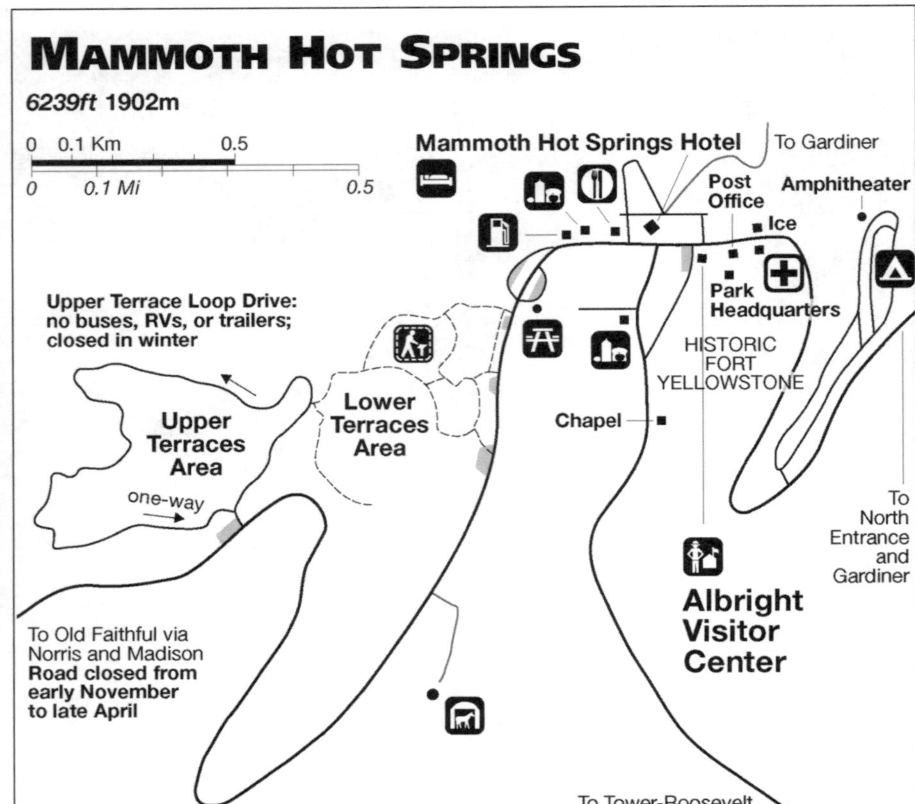

that boardwalks have been buried beneath mounds of newly deposited travertine. Consequently, an elevated and movable boardwalk now spans the hill in the vicinity of Minerva. In recent years, hot spring activity has shifted dramatically from Minerva to other features on the Lower Terraces, and back again.

Cleopatra Terrace

Due to confusion related to the intermittent nature of many of the springs in the Mammoth Area, the name Cleopatra Spring has been given to at least three different springs over the years. As the confusion developed the original Cleopatra Spring came to be called Minerva Spring

Jupiter Terrace

Jupiter Terrace displays cycles of activity and has been dry since 1992. When active, its color and intricate terraces make Jupiter an appealing spring.

Overlook

From the Overlook visitors have a great view of the Main Terrace and the surrounding mountains.

Main Terrace

Looking across the Main Terrace the red-roofed buildings of historic Fort Yellowstone are visible in the distance. The fort was built and occupied by the U.S. Cavalry during their tour of duty here from 1886 to 1918.

Canary Spring

So named for its bright yellow color, Canary owes its brilliance to sulfur dependent filamentous bacteria. The colors blend here in delicate tints on the creamy rock face.

Prospect Terrace

This terrace was referred to as the "Eleventh Terrace" by Dr. Peale in 1872. In the late 1880s a U.S Geological Service party led by Arnold Hague gave it the name Prospect Terrace. While the reason for its receiving this name is uncertain, it is likely that it was named simply because of the spectacular "prospective" views it affords.

New Highland Terrace

Tree skeletons, engulfed by travertine, stand as monuments to a landscape created in the 1950s. In recent years, activity has shifted to other locations.

Orange Spring Mound

Bacteria and algae create the streaks of color on Orange Spring Mound. It is noticeably different from many of the other terrace formations nearby. Its large mounded shape is the result of very slow water flow and mineral deposition.

Bath Lake

At the bottom of a short but very steep hill lies Bath Lake, named by some of the local residents in the 1880s. Through the years, this "lake" has been empty as often as full. Though soldiers in the late 1880s once bathed in this pool, we now know that such activity destroys fragile formations and may cause dramatic changes in the behavior of thermal features. Bathing in any of Yellowstone's thermal features is unsafe and unlawful.

White Elephant Back Terrace

Here, a long ridge replaces the terrace shape seen so frequently elsewhere in Mammoth. Water flowing from a rift in the earth's crust has built the mounded formation, which someone thought looked like the vertebral column of an elephant. Portions of the Upper Terraces beyond White Elephant Back are very old and have been inactive for hundreds of years.

Angel Terrace

Known both for the pure white formations and colorful microorganisms of its active periods, Angel Terrace is one of the area's most unpredictable features. For decades it was dry and crumbling. More recently, hot springs have been intermittently active in parts of the formation.

Historic Highlights of the Mammoth Area

Due to its year-round access and comparatively mild winters, Mammoth has always been the headquarters for the park. The hot springs were an early commercialized attraction for those seeking relief from ailments in the mineral waters. Two historic events taking place at Mammoth were the Nez Perce flight in 1877 and President Teddy Roosevelt's visit in 1903.

Archaeological Resources

There are several wickiups in the vicinity as well as the Bannock Indian trail, roasting pits, and the Obsidian Cliff quarry site. In 1959, a Clovis point that was dated to more than 10,000 years ago was found at the site of the old Gardiner post office.

Fort Yellowstone

All of the red-roofed, many-chimneyed buildings in the Mammoth area are part of historic Fort Yellowstone. Beginning in 1886, after 14 years of poor civilian management of the park, the Cavalry was called upon to manage the park's resources and visitors. Because the Cavalry only expected to be here a short while, they built a temporary post near the base of the Terraces called Camp Sheridan. After five cold, harsh winters, they realized that their stay in the park was

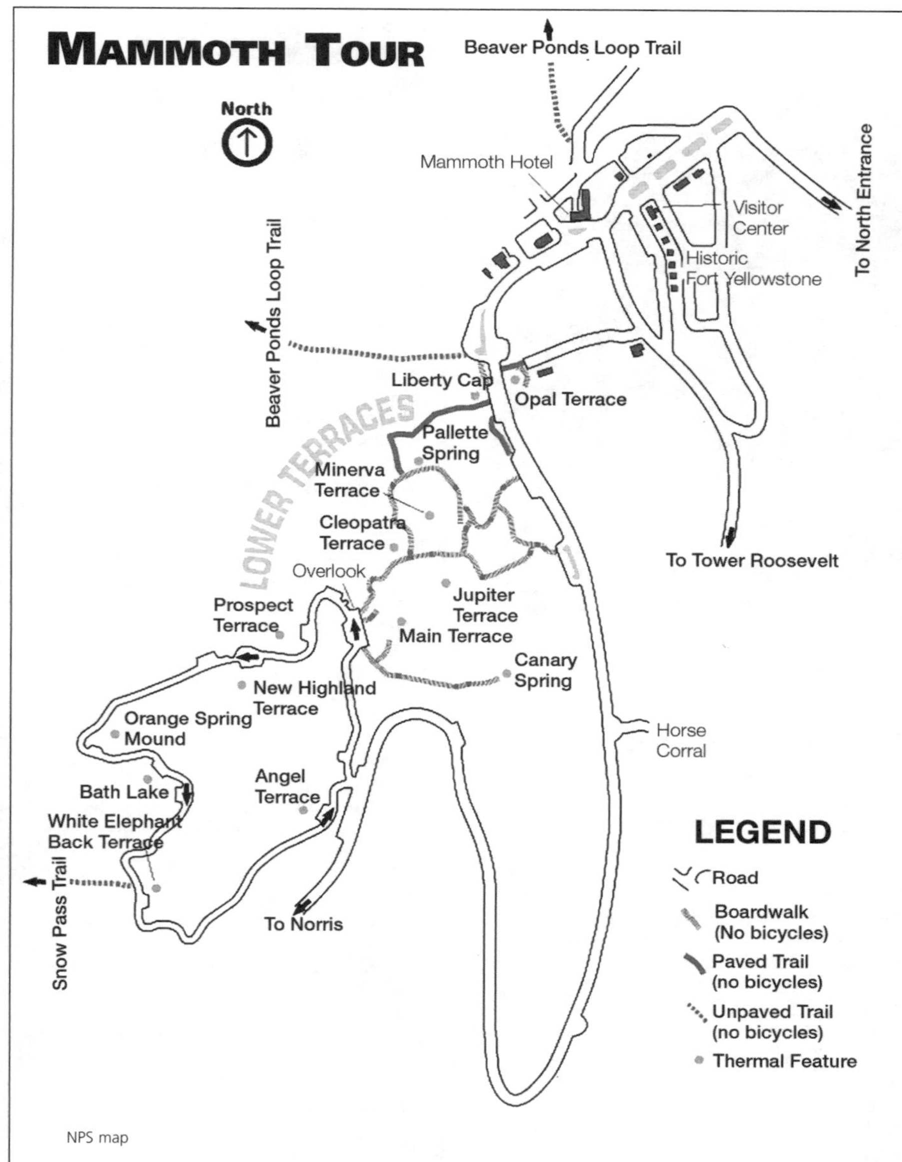

NPS map

Fort Yellowstone. NPS Photo.

going to be longer than expected, so they built Fort Yellowstone, a permanent post.

In 1891, the first building to be constructed was the guard house because it directly coincided with the Cavalry's mission—protection and management. There were three stages of construction at Fort Yellowstone. The first set of clapboard buildings were built in 1891, the second set in 1897 as the Fort expanded to a two-troop fort, and, finally, the stone buildings were built in 1909 making the fort's capacity 400 men or four troops. By 1916, the National Park Service was established, and the Cavalry gave control of Yellowstone back to the civilians. After a short time away, the Cavalry returned in 1917 and finished their duty completely in 1918. Since that time, historic Fort Yellowstone has been Yellowstone's headquarters.

Roosevelt Arch

The first major entrance for Yellowstone was at the north boundary. Before 1903, trains would bring visitors to Cinnabar, Montana, which was a few miles northwest of Gardiner, Montana, and people would climb onto horse-drawn coaches there to enter the park. In 1903, the railway finally came to Gardiner, and people entered through an enormous stone archway. Robert Reamer, a famous architect in Yellowstone, designed the immense stone arch for coaches to travel through on their way into the park. At the time of the arch's construction, President Theodore Roosevelt was visiting the park. He consequently placed the cornerstone for the arch, which then took his name. The top of the Roosevelt Arch is inscribed with "For the benefit and enjoyment of the people," which is from the Organic Act of 1872, the enabling legislation for Yellowstone National Park.

Obsidian Cliff

Obsidian Cliff is located 11 miles south of Mammoth Hot Springs and rises 150-200 feet above Obsidian Creek. The wayside exhibit here is one of the first of its kind in Yellowstone, built in the 1920s. Obsidian is created when lava cools so quickly that it does not have time to form crystals. A massive outcrop the size of Obsidian Cliff is quite rare because obsidian is usually found as small sections of other rock outcrops. Obsidian Cliff probably formed because the molten rock that erupted from the earth had very little water. The absence of water discourages the nucleation of atoms and causes faster cooling. Obsidian can be dated by measuring the hydration rate (absorption of water) of the rock. Because there are so few outcrops of obsidian, matching a projectile point to an outcrop is fairly easy.

For centuries, many Native Americans made their projectile points from obsidian. The rock itself is dark and glassy in appearance and, when broken, fractures into round pieces with sharp edges. Projectile points found as far away as Ohio have had their origin traced back to the Obsidian Cliff area. Tracking obsidian from Yellowstone to the Midwest indicates that the quality of obsidian found here was very good. In 1996, Obsidian Cliff was named a National Historic Landmark.

Other Historic Sites

The list includes: the Engineer's office, designed in 1903 by Hiram Chittenden of the U.S. Army Corps of Engineers; Scottish Rite Chapel, 1913; Capitol Hill, former site of Superintendent Norris' headquarters blockhouse; Kite Hill cemetery, 1880s, containing graves of early settlers and employees; Reamer House, designed in 1908 by well-known architect Robert Reamer, an example of Prairie-style architecture; Haynes Picture Shop, photographic studio used by the Haynes family; old roads, railroad beds, bridges; and historic structures in Gardiner.

Natural Highlights of the Norris Area

Norris Geyser Basin

Norris Geyser Basin is the hottest, oldest, and most dynamic of Yellowstone's thermal areas. The highest temperature yet recorded in any geothermal area in Yellowstone was measured in a scientific drill hole at Norris: 459°F (237°C) just 1,087 feet (326 meters) below the surface! There are very few thermal features at Norris under the boiling point (199°F at this elevation). Norris shows evidence of having had thermal features for at least 115,000 years. The features in the basin change daily, with frequent disturbances from seismic activity and water fluctuations. The vast majority of the waters at Norris are acidic, including acid geysers which are very rare.

Steamboat Geyser, the tallest geyser in the world (300 to 400 feet) and Echinus Geyser (pH 3.5 or so) are the most popular features. The basin consists of three areas: Porcelain Basin, Back Basin, and One Hundred Springs Plain. Porcelain Basin is barren of trees and provides a sensory experience in sound, color, and smell; a 3/4 mile dirt and boardwalk trail accesses this

Bunsen Peak with Aspens Looking East from Fawn Pass Trail. NPS Photo

area. Back Basin is more heavily wooded with features scattered throughout the area; a 1.5 mile trail of boardwalk and dirt encircles this part of the basin. One Hundred Springs Plain is an off-trail section of the Norris Geyser Basin that is very acidic, hollow, and dangerous. Travel is discouraged without the guidance of knowledgeable staff members. The area was named after Philetus W. Norris, the second superintendent of Yellowstone, who provided the first detailed information about the thermal features.

Roaring Mountain

Located just north of Norris on the Norris-Mammoth section of the Grand Loop Road, Roaring Mountain is a large, acidic thermal area (solfatara) that contains many steam vents (fumaroles). In the late 1800s and early 1900s, the number, size, and power of the fumaroles was much greater than today.

Gibbon River

The Gibbon River flows from Wolf Lake through the Norris area and meets the Firehole River at Madison Junction to form the Madison River. Both cold and hot springs are responsible for the majority of the Gibbon's flow. Brook trout, brown trout, grayling, and rainbow trout find the Gibbon to their liking. The Gibbon River is fly-fishing only below Gibbon Falls.

Virginia Cascades

A three-mile section of the old road takes visitors past 60-foot high Virginia Cascades. This cascading waterfall is formed by the very small (at that point) Gibbon River.

Norris-Canyon Blowdown

This is a 22-mile swath of lodgepole pine blown down by wind-shear action in 1984. It was then burned during the North Fork fire in 1988. This is the site where a famous news anchor said, "Tonight, this is all that's left of Yellowstone." A wayside exhibit there tells the story.

Geological Overview of the Norris Area

Norris sits on the intersection of three major faults. The Norris-Mammoth Corridor is a fault that runs from Norris north through Mammoth to the Gardiner, Montana, area. The Hebgen Lake fault runs from northwest of West Yellowstone, Montana, to Norris. This fault experienced an earthquake in 1959 that measured 7.4 on the Richter scale (sources vary on exact magnitude between 7.1 and 7.8). These two faults intersect with a ring fracture that resulted from the Yellowstone Caldera of 600,000 years ago. These faults are the primary reason that Norris Geyser Basin is so hot and dynamic. The Ragged Hills that lie between Back Basin and One Hundred Springs Plain are thermally altered glacial moraines. As glaciers receded, the underlying thermal features began to express themselves once again, melting remnants of the ice and causing masses of debris to be dumped. These debris piles were then altered by steam and hot water flowing through them.

Madison lies within the eroded stream channels cut through lava flows formed after the caldera eruption. The Gibbon Falls lies on the caldera boundary as does Virginia Cascades.

Historic Highlights of the Norris Area

The Norris Soldier Station

The Norris Soldier Station (Museum of the National Park Ranger) was an outlying station for soldiers to patrol and watch over Norris Geyser Basin. It was among the longest occupied stations in the park. A prior structure was built in 1886, replaced after fire in 1897, and modified in 1908. After the Army years, the building was used as a Ranger Station and residence until the 1959 earthquake caused structural damage. The building was restored in 1991.

World's Tallest Geyser Erupts

With a thunderous roar, the world's tallest geyser erupted on the morning of May 2, 2000 for the first time in more than eight years. Steamboat—in Norris Geyser Basin—blasted water 300 feet (30 stories!) into the air for about a half hour, then settled into a steam phase that reached hundreds more feet into the sky. During a major eruption, Steamboat ejects several hundred thousand gallons of water. Much of the water falls to the slope above the geyser and collects in torrents of mud, sand, and rock that rush back into the vent and are blown back out again and again. Water rushes downhill, carving wide gullies and washing away trees.

Most of Steamboat's power comes from the steam that follows the eruption of water. Geysers release energy via steam and hot water. Some geysers release copious amounts of water but run out of energy before they run out of water. Steamboat, on the other hand, has so much energy that it cannot be dissipated by hot water alone and thus much steam is released.

After its massive eruption on May 2, Steamboat roared with steam for hours. The clouds billowed and condensed, falling as mist that shifted with the breeze. Water dripped off hoods and hats, benches and signs. People looked straight up and still could not see the top of the steam.

Steamboat's massive eruptions were first recorded by Park Superintendent P.W. Norris: *"The new crater which burst forth in the Norris Geyser Plateau, with such upturning and hurling of rocks and trees, August 11, 1878, ... seems this year to have settled down to business as a very powerful flowing geyser, having in common with many others, a double period of eruption, one some 30 feet high about each half hour, and another 100 feet and long continued, each 6 or 7 days, and is doubtless still changing."*

Will Steamboat blow again? No one knows. Even so, it's still an impressive feature. The summer of 2000, Steamboat was splashing water higher than most of the park's geysers. So stop by Norris Geyser Basin and check out Steamboat. As Yellowstone's geyser observers like to say, "Go, Steamboat, Go!"

The Norris Geyser Basin Museum

The Norris Geyser Basin Museum is one of the park's original trailside museums built in 1929-30. It has always been a museum. It is an outstanding example of stone-and-log architecture.

Archeological Resources

Digs by the Midwest Archaeological Center in Norris and Madison campgrounds reveal that people have camped in these areas for at least 10,000 years. Campfire remnants, obsidian flakes, and chips and bone fragments show that these campgrounds have always been favorites! Other such sites abound throughout the Norris area, particularly along the Solfatara Trail that connects Norris Campground with the Obsidian Cliff area.

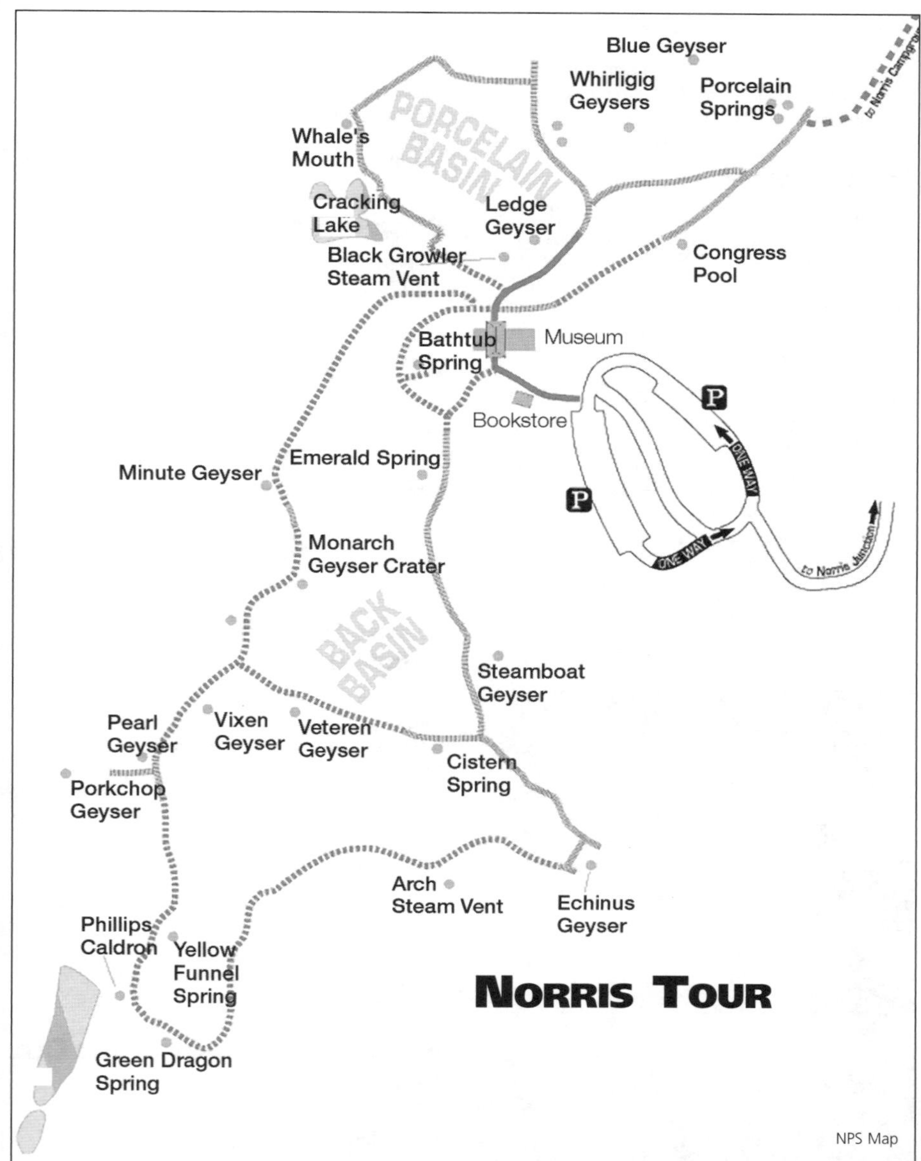

NPS Map

Norris Tour

Norris Geyser Basin is the hottest and most changeable thermal area in Yellowstone. We will explore many of the features you would see if you walked the 2 1/4 miles (3.6 km) of trails. Discover the location of the tallest active geyser, colorful hot springs, and microscopic life in one of the most extreme environments on earth.

Our tour starts at the Norris Museum. The museum houses exhibits relating to the origins of the geothermal features found at the basin. Two loop trails leave from here. They provide a safe route for viewing the Porcelain Basin and Back Basin.

Rainbow Colors, hissing steam, and pungent odors combine to create an experience unique in Yellowstone. Porcelain Basin is open terrain with hundreds of densely packed geothermal features; in contrast, Back Basin is forested and its features are more scattered and isolated.

Porcelain Basin

Parts of the whitish rock-sheet before you pulsate from the pressure of steam and boiling water beneath them. A number of geysers and other features here have been born suddenly in small hydrothermal explosions. Some features are ephemeral, their activity lasting a few hours, days, or weeks. A few others have become relatively permanent fixtures in the scene.

NPS photo

Congress Pool

A visit most times of the year will show a Congress Pool that appears pale blue in color. Due to the variable nature of Norris features it is possible to see the same pool looking muddy and boiling violently.

At Norris, "disturbances" of geothermal activity take place annually. No other thermal area in Yellowstone exhibits this phenomenon. Mysteriously features throughout the Norris area undergo dramatic behavioral changes literally overnight. Clear pools become muddy and boil violently, and some temporarily become geysers. These "disturbances" often occur in late summer and early fall but have been observed throughout the year.

Features that typically behave as geysers may display altered eruption cycles or temporarily cease erupting. New features may be created during a disturbance, although they seldom remain long-term attractions at the basin. Disturbances tend to last from a few days to more than a week. Gradually, most features revert to "normal" activity.

Why this happens is not fully understood. Further study will no doubt yield new clues that will help unravel the mystery of this phenomenon and lead to a greater understanding of the earth's hidden geologic forces.

Black Growler Steam Vent

The hottest of Yellowstone's geothermal features are steam vents (fumaroles). Black Growler Steam Vent, on the hillside in front of you, has measured 199 to 280 degrees F (93 to 138 degrees C). A plentiful water supply would help cool these features; however, steam vents are usually found on hillsides or higher ground, above the basin's water supply. They rapidly boil away what little water they contain, releasing steam and other gases forcefully from underground.

NPS photo

Ledge Geyser

Ledge is the second largest geyser in the Norris Geyser Basin, capable of shooting water 125 feet into the air. Because it erupts at an angle, however, the water will sometimes reach the ground 220 feet away. It has at times in the past erupted at regular intervals of 14 hours. The geyser became inactive between 1979 and late 1993. It erupted on a fairly regular cycle of every four to six days in 1994 and 1995.

Hot Springs of Porcelain Basin

The milky color of the mineral deposited here inspired the naming of Porcelain Basin. The mineral, siliceous sinter, is brought to the surface by hot water and forms a sinter "sheet" over this flat area as the water flows across the ground and the mineral settles out. This is the fastest changing area in Norris Geyser Basin, and siliceous sinter is one of the agents of change. If the mineral seals off a hot spring or geyser by accumulating in its vent, the hot, pressurized water may flow underground to another weak area and blow through it.

Siliceous sinter is also called geyserite. Deposits usually accumulate very slowly, less than one inch (2.5cm) per century, and form the geyser cones and mounds seen in most geyser basins.

Colorful Water

Many of Norris' features release acidic water. Amazingly living organisms thrive even in the extreme environments of these acid hot springs! The overflow channels of geysers and hot springs are often brightly colored with minerals and microscopic life forms. Hardy, microscopic, lime-green Cyanidium algae thrives in these warm acid waters. Orange cyanobacteria may be found in the runoff streams in Porcelain Basin. From a distance these bacteria look like rusty, iron-rich mineral deposits.

These and other microscopic life forms are links to the emergence of life on earth billions of years ago. They are also a focus of research in the fields of medicine and criminal investigation. New tools for use in such complex areas as AIDS research and DNA "fingerprinting" have been developed from the microscopic thermal organisms found in Yellowstone's hot springs.

Blue Geyser

Blue Geyser was called Iris Spring in 1886. Due to a misread map label, in 1904 the feature was inadvertently given its current name. It was observed to erupt to heights of over 60 feet from 1993 to 1996. It became almost dormant in 1997 and has remained very quiet ever since. Blue Geyser's last observed eruption was in February of 1997.

Whirligig Geysers

Little Whirligig got its name because of its close proximity to Whirligig Geyser. Whirligig was so named because while erupting its water swirls in its crater. The orange-yellow iron oxide deposits around Little Whirligig make it one of the most colorful features in Porcelain Basin. It has been dormant for several years.

Cistern Spring

Cistern Spring and Steamboat Geyser are linked underground. During a major eruption of Steamboat, the water in Cistern Spring's pool drains. Normally Cistern is a beautiful blue pool from which water continually overflows. It is quite creative, depositing as much as 1/2 inch (12mm) of grayish sinter each year. By comparison Old Faithful Geyser and many other thermal features may build at the rate of 1/2 to 1 inch (12–25mm) per century. Cistern Spring's influence expands throughout the lodgepole pine forest below. This forest has been slowly flooded with silica rich water since 1965. The pioneering lodgepole pine forest at Norris is in constant flux, retreating here and in other areas of increasing heat while advancing in places of diminished thermal activity.

Emerald Spring

A hot spring's color often indicates the presence of minerals. In a clear blue pool, the water is absorbing all colors of sunlight except one, blue, which is reflected back to our eyes. Here in Emerald Spring's pool, another factor joins with light refraction to give this spring its color. The 27-foot (8 meter) deep pool is lined with yellow sulfur deposits. The yellow color from the sulfur combines with the reflected blue light, making the hot spring appear a magnificent emerald green.

Hot spring water can dissolve and transport sulfur from underground. The mineral can deposit and crystallize at the earth's surface, sometimes in hot spring pools.

Echinus Geyser

Echinus (e-KI-nus) Geyser was a perennial crowd-pleaser which typically erupted every 35 to 75 minutes. Late in 1998 this geyser altered its interval and now erupts only a few times per day at best. Its pool fills gradually with water; then suddenly, bursts of steam and water explode 40 to 60 feet (12 to 18 m) skyward. Eruptions usually last about 4 minutes but in the past major eruptions have lasted as long as 118 minutes. The major eruptions were believed to be caused by a secondary water source which has mysteriously vanished. There has not been a major eruption in 3 years. In late 1998 Echinus' performance diminished and became erratic. As of mid-1999 its eruptions remain unpredictable.

Echinus is the largest acid-water geyser known. Its waters are almost as acidic as vinegar with a pH ranging from 3.3 to 3.6 . Acid geysers are extremely rare with the majority of the planet's total being found here at Norris Geyser Basin.

NPS photo

Steamboat Geyser

The world's tallest active geyser, Steamboat can erupt to more than 300 feet (90m), showering viewers with its mineral-rich waters. For hours following its rare 3 to 40 minute major eruptions, Steamboat thunders with powerful jets of steam. As befitting such an awesome event, full eruptions are entirely unpredictable. Recently, Steamboat had one major eruption on May 2, 2000. More commonly, Steamboat has minor eruptions and ejects water in frequent bursts of 10 to 40 feet.

Porkchop Geyser

Dramatic behavioral changes have characterized Porkchop Geyser during the last decade. Once a small hot spring that occasionally erupted, Porkchop Geyser became a continuous spouter in the spring of 1985. The force of the spray caused a roar that could be heard at the museum over 660 yards (603m) away. On September 5, 1989, Porkchop Geyser exploded. Rocks surrounding the old vent were upended and some were thrown more than 216 feet (66m) from the feature. Porkchop Geyser is now a gently rolling hot spring.

Green Dragon Spring

Except on warm summer afternoons, steam frequently fills the cavern of this intriguing hot spring. Visitors must wait patiently for a glimpse of the sulfur-lined cave and boiling green water.

Whale's Mouth

This hot spring was named by a park naturalist in 1967 because its shape "resembles the mouth and gullet of a giant fish".

Crackling Lake

The name of this thermal feature was proposed by Ed Leigh in 1967 because of popping sounds from nearby springs on its southern shore. It was formerly simply called Spring #39 in Dr. Peale's publication entitled Gibbon Geyser Basin.

Minute Geyser

Minute Geyser's eruptions have changed dramatically. Its larger west vent is clogged with rocks tossed in by early visitors when the park's main road was near this trail and passed within 70 feet of the geyser. Minute once erupted every 60 seconds, sometimes to heights of 40 to 50 feet (12 to 15 meters). Eruptions now are irregular and originate from its smaller east vent. Removal of the west vent's mineral-cemented rocks would require the use of heavy equipment resulting in severe damage.

Minute Geyser's destruction stands today as a sad reminder of thoughtless behavior on the part of some visitors.

Natural Highlights of the Old Faithful Area

The Upper Geyser Basin

Yellowstone, as a whole, possesses close to 60 percent of the world's geysers. The Upper Geyser Basin is home to the largest numbers of this fragile feature found in the park. Within one square mile there are at least 150 of these hydrothermal wonders. Of this remarkable number, only five major geysers are predicted regularly by the naturalist staff. They are Castle, Grand, Daisy, Riverside, and Old Faithful. There are many frequent, smaller geysers to be seen and marveled at in this basin as well as numerous hot springs and one recently developed mudpot (if it lasts).

Lower Geyser Basin

This large area of hydrothermal activity can be viewed by foot along the boardwalk trail at Fountain Paint Pots and by car along the three mile Firehole Lake Drive. The latter is a one-way drive where you will find the sixth geyser predicted by the Old Faithful staff: Great Fountain. Its splashy eruptions send jets of diamond droplets bursting 100-200 feet in the air, while waves of water cascade down the raised terraces. Patience is a virtue with this twice-a-day geyser, as the predictions allow a 2 hour +/- window of opportunity.

Fountain Flats Drive departs the Grand Loop

Fire: a Natural Force

Fire, climate, erosion, and a vast assortment of life forms ranging from microbes to insects to mammals, including humans, have all played roles in the creation of the vegetative landscape of Yellowstone. Vegetation here has adapted to fire and, in some cases, may be dependent on it.

Ecologists have known for many years that wildfire is essential to the evolution of a natural setting. Records kept in Yellowstone since 1931 show that lightning starts an average of 22 fires each year. Large-scale fires burn through the conifer forests of the Yellowstone plateau every 250 to 400 years and take place in the low-elevation grass-lands on average every 25 to 60 years. When fires are, suppressed the habitat gradually becomes less diverse. This, in turn, affects the variety of animals able to successfully inhabit a particular area.

In the first few decades after Yellowstone was established as the world's first national park in 1872, no effective fire fighting was done. Then, during the Army administration of Yellowstone (1886-1918), fire suppression occurred most frequently on the grass lands of the northern range. Throughout the rest of the park, which is largely covered by a lodgepole pine forest, reliable and consistent fire suppression began with the era of modern airborne fire-fighting techniques of the past 30 to 40 years.

In natural areas such as Yellowstone National Park, preserving a state of wildness is a primary goal of management. In 1972, Yellowstone was one of several national parks that initiated programs to allow some naturally caused fires to burn. By 1988, scientists had learned much about the occurrence and behavior of fire. Tens of thousands of lightning strikes simply fizzled out with no acreage burned. While 140 lightning strikes produced fires, most burned only a small area. Eighty percent of the lightning starts in this period went out by themselves.

The Historic Fires of 1988

The summer of 1988 was the driest on record in Yellowstone. Though substantial precipitation fell during April and May, practically no rain fell in June, July, or August—an event previously unrecorded in the park's 112-year written record of weather conditions. In early summer, about 20 lightning-caused fires had been allowed to burn, and eleven of these fires burned themselves out.

But fires that continued to burn into the extremely dry weeks of late June and July met dramatically changed conditions. By late July, moisture content of grasses and small branches had dropped as low as 2 or 3 percent, and downed trees measured at 7 percent (kiln-dried lumber is 12 percent). After July 15, no new natural fires were allowed to burn and after July 21, all fires were fought.

The extreme weather conditions and heavy, dry accumulations of "fuel' (vegetation of various types) presented even the most skilled professional fire fighters with conditions rarely observed. Typical firefighting techniques were frequently ineffective because fires spread long distances by "spotting," a phenomenon in which wind carries embers from the tops of 200-foot flames far across unburned forest to start spot fires well ahead of the main fire. Fires routinely jumped barriers that normally stopped them such as rivers, roads, and major topographic features such as the Grand Canyon of the Yellowstone River. Fires advanced rapidly, making frontal attacks dangerous and impossible.

By the last week of September, about 50 lightning-caused fires had occurred in the park, 8 of which were still burning. More than $120,000,000 had been spent on fire control efforts in the greater Yellowstone area, and most major park developments—and a few surrounding communities—had been evacuated at least once as fire approached within a few miles of them. At the operation's peak, 9,000 firefighters (including Army and Marine units), more than 100 fire engines, and dozens of helicopters participated in the complex effort to control the fires and protect developments. It was the largest such cooperative effort ever undertaken in the United States.

Changes Since 1988

Changes in both the natural landscape of Yellowstone and the management of naturally-caused fires have taken place since the historic fires of 1988. Scientists knew that the vegetative cover of Yellowstone was, in large part, the product of fires that had burned for millennia before the arrival of European humans. The growth of new plants and entire plant communities began immediately. In most places, plant growth is unusually lush because minerals and other nutrients are released by fire into the soil and because increased light stimulates growth in what was previously shaded forest floor.

These fires did not annihilate all life in their paths. Burning at a variety of temperatures, sometimes as ground fires, sometimes as crown fires (burning through treetops), fires killed many lodgepole pines and other trees but did not kill most other plants. Instead, they burned off the tops, leaving roots to regenerate. The fires created a mosaic of burns, partial burns, and unburned areas that provide new habitats for plants and animals.

Yellowstone National Park is one of the greatest living laboratories on the planet. Here, we can observe the effects of fire and other natural forces and processes, and learn from them. And what we learn is that change is constant in the natural world, flowing from the past into the present—continuing into the future to outcomes both predictable and mysterious,

Facts About the Fires of 1988

Why They Occurred

Conditions occurred that were never before seen in the history of Yellowstone: extended drought & high winds.

Statistics

- 9 fires caused by humans
- 42 fires caused by lightning
- 36% of the park burned (793,880 acres)
- Fires begun outside of the park burned more than half of the total acreage
- About 400 large mammals, primarily elk, perished
- $120 million spent fighting the fires
- 25,000 people employed in these efforts

Fighting the Fires

- Until July 21, naturally-caused fires allowed to burn.
- After that, all fires fought, regardless of their cause.
- Largest fire-fighting effort in the history of the U.S.
- Effort saved human life and property, but probably had little impact on the fires themselves.
- Rain and snow finally stopped the advance of the fires.

After the Fires

- Enormous public controversy occurred.
- Several high-level task forces formed to review NPS fire policies.
- Their recommendations reaffirmed the importance of natural fire in an ecosystem.
- They recommended additional guidelines be established to manage natural fire in Yellowstone.

Road just south of the Nez Perce picnic area and follows along the Firehole River to a trailhead 1.5 miles distant. From there, the Fountain Freight Road hiking/biking trail continues along the old roadbed giving hikers access to the Sentinel Meadows Trail and the Fairy Falls Trail. Also along this path is the only handicapped-accessible backcountry site in the Old Faithful district at Goose Lake.

Midway Geyser Basin

This geyser basin, though small in size compared to its companions along the Firehole River, holds large wonders for the visitor. Excelsior Geyser reveals a gaping crater 200 x 300 feet with a constant discharge of more than 4,000 gallons of water per minute into the Firehole River. Also in this surprising basin is Yellowstone's largest hot springs, Grand Prismatic Spring. This feature is 370 feet in diameter and more than 121 feet in depth.

Lone Star Geyser Basin

This backcountry geyser basin is easily reached by a 5-mile roundtrip hike from the trailhead south of Old Faithful. Lone Star Geyser erupts about every three hours. There is a logbook, located in a cache near the geyser, for observations of geyser times and types of eruptions.

Shoshone Geyser Basin

Shoshone Geyser Basin is reached by a 17-mile roundtrip hike that crosses the Continental Divide at Grant's Pass. This basin has no boardwalks, and extreme caution should be exercised when travelling through it. Trails in the basin must be used. Remote thermal areas, such as this, should be approached with respect, knowledge, and care. Be sure to emphasize personal safety

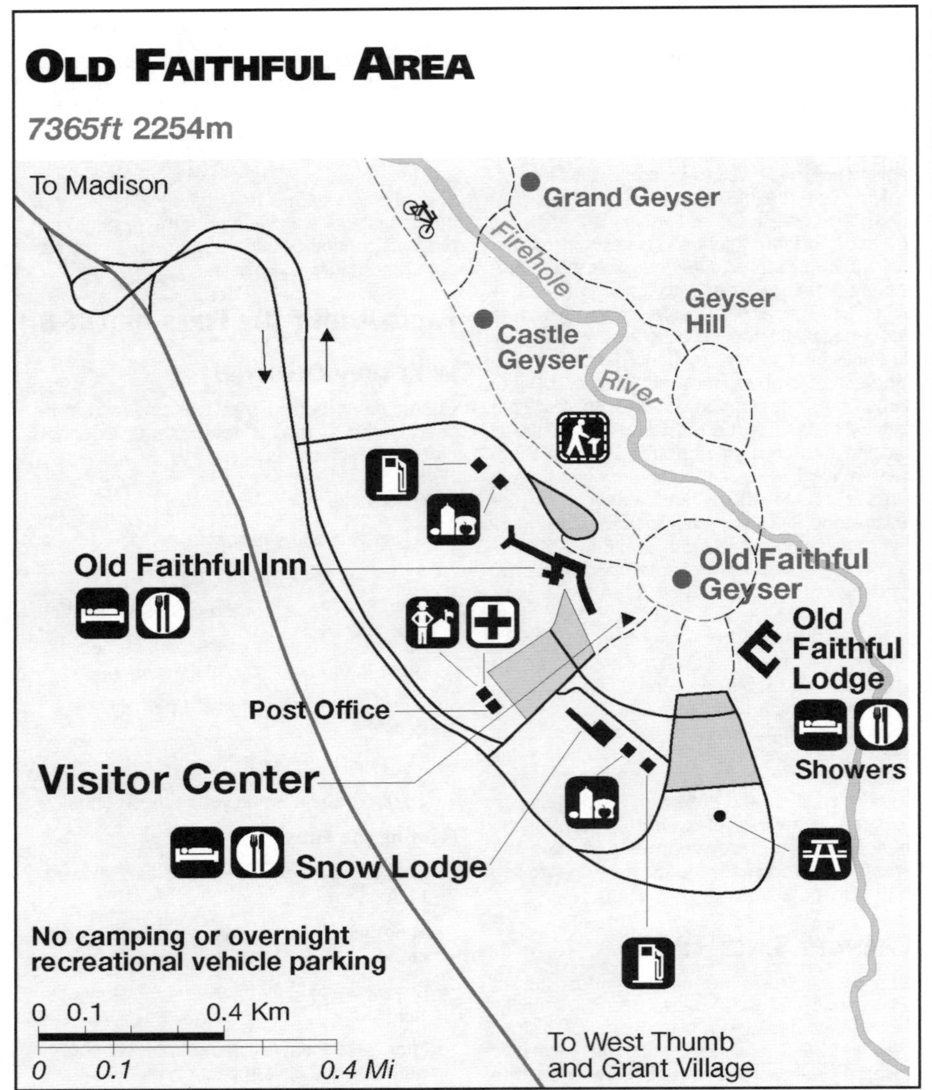

and resource protection when entering a backcountry basin.

Firehole River

The river derives its name from the steam (which they thought was smoke from fires) witnessed by early trappers to the area. Their term for a mountain valley was "hole," and the designation was born. The Firehole River boasts a world-famous reputation for challenging fly-fishing. Brown, rainbow, and brook trout give the angler a wary target in this stream.

Craig Pass/Isa Lake

Both names are used to describe the same location seven miles south of Old Faithful on the Grand Loop Road. At 8,262 feet along the Continental Divide, Isa Lake is a uniquely confusing feature. During spring runoff, it drains into both the Atlantic and Pacific Oceans at the same time! (And backwards, too!) The west side of the lake flows into the Firehole drainage and, eventually, the Atlantic throughout the year. The east side, during spring, flows toward the Snake River drainage and the Pacific.

Waterfall

Kepler Cascades is the most easily reached waterfall in the district. A marked pullout just south of Old Faithful and a short walk from the car offers the visitor easy access to view this 125-foot cascade.

Geological Overview of the Old Faithful Area

Evidence of the geological forces that have shaped Yellowstone are found in abundance in this district. The hills surrounding Old Faithful and the Upper Geyser Basin are reminders of Quaternary rhyolitic lava flows. These flows, occurring long after the catastrophic eruption of 600,000 years ago, flowed across the landscape like stiff mounds of bread dough due to their high silica content.

Evidence of glacial activity is common, and it is one of the keys that allows geysers to exist. Glacier till deposits underlie the geyser basins providing storage areas for the water used in eruptions. Many landforms, such as Porcupine Hills north of Fountain Flats, are comprised of glacial gravel and are reminders that as recently as 13,000 years ago, this area was buried under ice.

Signs of the forces of erosion can be seen everywhere, from runoff channels carved across the sinter in the geyser basins to the drainage created by the Firehole River.

Mountain building is evident as you drive south of Old Faithful, toward Craig Pass. Here the Rocky Mountains reach a height of 8,262 feet, dividing the country into two distinct watersheds.

Yellowstone is a vast land containing a landscape that is continually being shaped by geological forces.

Historic Highlights of the Old Faithful Area

Old Faithful Historic District

This designation applies to the developed area adjacent to Old Faithful Geyser, which contains many historic structures.

NPS photo

Old Faithful Inn

Built during the winter of 1903-04, the Old Faithful Inn was designed by Robert C. Reamer, who wanted the asymmetry of the building to reflect the chaos of nature. The lobby of the hotel features a 65-foot ceiling, a massive rhyolite fireplace, and railings made of contorted lodgepole pine. Wings were added to the hotel in 1915 and 1927, and today there are 327 rooms available to guests in this National Historic Landmark.

Old Faithful Lodge

Unlike the Inn, the current Old Faithful Lodge is a result of numerous changes dating back to the early days of tent camps provided by companies like Shaw and Powell Camping Company and Wylie Permanent Camping Company. These camps were erected throughout the park and offered shelter before hotels and lodges were built. Both companies had facilities at Old Faithful. By 1917, auto traffic into the park was increasing, and it was decided that some camps could be eliminated. Yellowstone Park Camping Company emerged and operated on the old site of the Shaw and Powell camp, the present day site of the Lodge. In 1918, a laundry was built on the site and construction continued on the facility until 1928 when the Lodge reached its present configuration.

Cabin-style accommodations are available at Old Faithful Lodge. Often confused with the other two hotels in the area, Old Faithful Lodge houses a cafeteria, gift shop, coffee shop, and the front desk where guests check in.

Lower Hamilton Store

Built in 1897, this is the oldest structure in the Old Faithful area still in use. The "knotty pine" porch is a popular resting place for visitors, providing a great view of Geyser Hill. (The oldest building at Old Faithful was built as a photo studio in 1897 for F. Jay Haynes. Originally located 700 feet southwest of Beehive Geyser and about 350 feet northwest of the front of the Old Faithful Inn, it now stands near the intersection of the Grand Loop Road and the fire lane, near the crosswalk.)

The lobby of the Old Faithful Inn. NPS photo

Nez Perce Creek Wayside

This exhibit tells the story of the flight of the Nez Perce through Yellowstone in 1877. A band of 700 men, women, and children entered the park on the evening of August 23rd, fleeing 600 Army regulars commanded by General O.O. Howard. The Nez Perce had been told to leave their homeland and move to a reservation. They fled their ancestral home in the Wallowa Valley in northeastern Oregon on June 17, 1877, and by the time they entered the park, several battles, including a fight at Big Hole (another NPS site), had occurred.

During the two weeks they were in the park, the Nez Perce bumped into all 25 known people visiting the new park at that time, some more than once. Camps were plundered, hostages taken, and several people were killed or wounded.

After leaving the park, the Nez Perce tried reaching the Canadian border but were stopped by General Nelson Miles, who had reinforced General Howard's command. Some Nez Perce were able to slip into Canada, but the remaining 350 tribal members led by Chief Joseph surrendered to General Miles. This is where Chief Joseph gave his famous speech, "I will fight no more forever." The 1,700-mile flight that included Yellowstone National Park had come to an end. Today, Nez Perce Creek and the nearby wayside exhibit are reminders of their visit.

Howard Eaton Trail

Named for an early park outfitter and guide, the Howard Eaton Trail paralleled the Grand Loop Road in many places. Remnants of this old horse trail are maintained and used by hikers today. Here in the Old Faithful District, the trail provides a less traveled route to Lone Star Geyser from the developed area.

Old Faithful Tour

The largest concentration of geysers in the world is in the Upper Geyser Basin. Several of the more prominent geysers and hot springs are included on this tour with information concerning their eruption patterns, names, and relationships with other geothermal features.

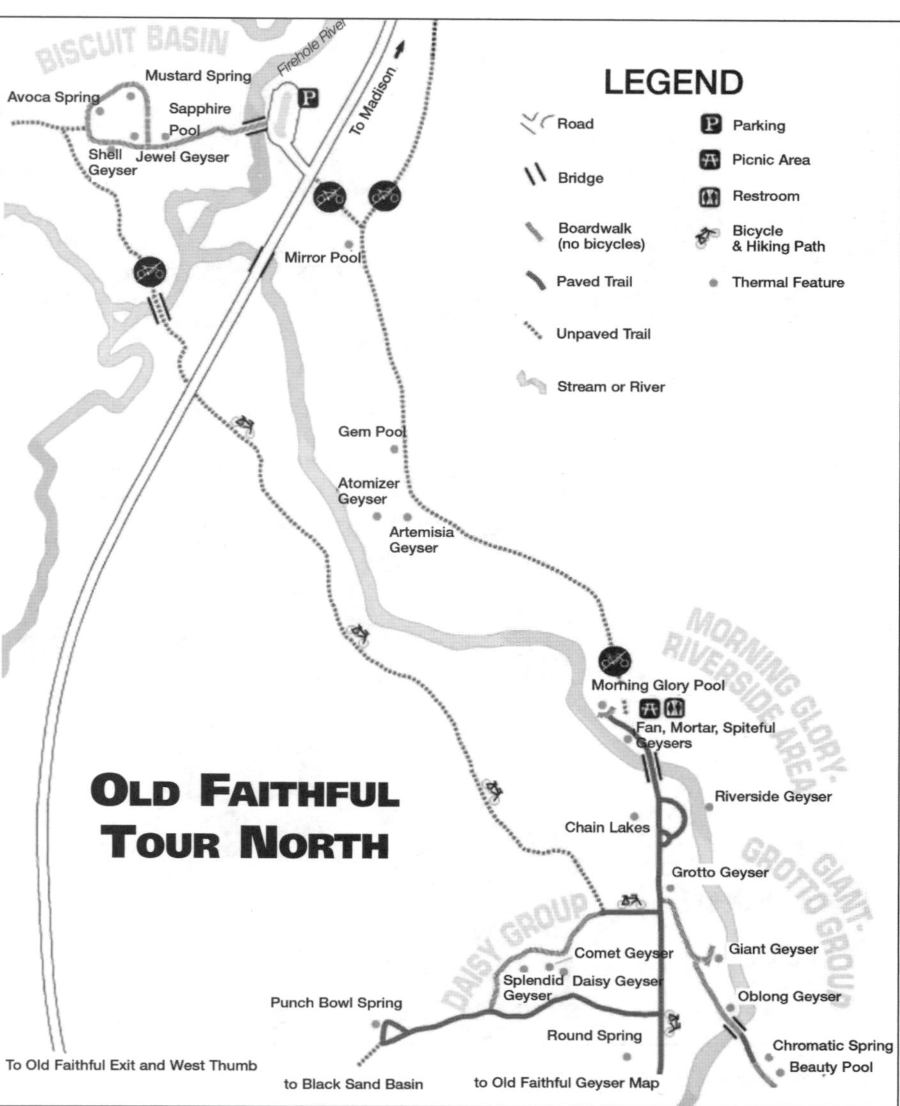

NPS photo

Old Faithful Geyser

Old Faithful erupts more frequently than any of the other big geysers, although it is not the largest or most regular geyser in the park. Its average interval between eruptions is about 76 minutes, varying from 45–110 minutes. An eruption lasts 1 1/2 to 5 minutes, expels 3,700–8,400 gallons (14,000–32,000 liters) of boiling water, and reaches heights of 106–184 feet (30–55m). It was named for its consistent performance by members of the Washburn Expedition in 1870. Although its average interval has lengthened through the years (due to earthquakes and vandalism), Old Faithful is still as spectacular and predictable as it was a century ago.

The largest active geyser in the world is Steamboat Geyser in the Norris Geyser Basin.

Solitary Geyser

When Yellowstone National Park was established this feature was known as Solitary Spring and it did not erupt. Water was diverted from the spring to a swimming pool which lowered the water level sufficiently to start eruptions. Even though the diversion channel was filled and the water returned to its original level in the late 1940s, this thermal feature has not returned to its stable hot spring condition. A temporary change in the water level has led to a long-term change in the nature of this portion of the geyser basin illustrating the delicate nature of these geothermal systems. Most eruptions today occur every 4–8 minutes and last about 1 minute. They are typically less than 6 ft in height.*

**This information was found in the book The Geysers of Yellowstone, by: T. Scott Bryan.*

Giantess Geyser

Infrequent but violent eruptions characterize Giantess Geyser. This fountain-type geyser erupts in several bursts 100–200 ft (30–60m) high.

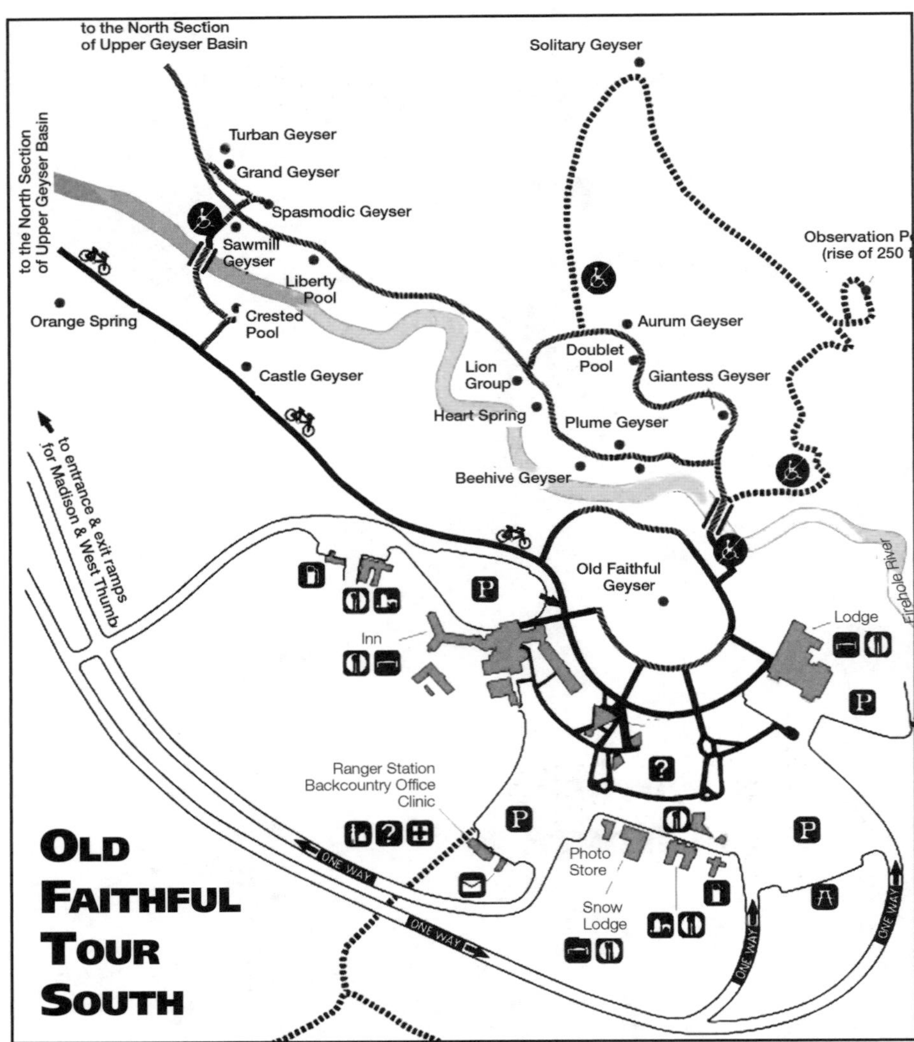

Eruptions generally occur 2–6 times a year. The surrounding area may shake from underground steam explosions just before the initial water and/or steam eruptions. Eruptions may occur twice hourly and continue for 12–43 hours.

Doublet Pool

Especially striking for its complex series of ledges, elaborate border ornamentation, and deep blue waters, Doublet Pool is an attractive subject for photographers. Occasionally, Doublet produces periodic vibrations underfoot, surface wave motion, and audible thumping. This is most likely the result of collapsing gas and steam bubbles deep underground.

View from Observation Point

Climbing the hill to Observation Point allows you to take in one of the best views of the Upper Geyser Basin. From this vantage point 250 ft above Old Faithful the panorama is spectacular.

Plume Geyser

Plume Geyser erupts about every 20 minutes. Its 3–5 quick bursts can reach heights of 25 ft (8m). This is a relatively young geyser that came into existence when a steam explosion created its vent in 1922.

Beehive Geyser

Beehive Geyser is magnificent. Eruptions usually occur twice each day with displays lasting 4–5 minutes. During an eruption, the narrow cone acts like a nozzle, projecting the water column to heights of 130–190 ft (40–55m).

The Lion Group

The Lion Group consists of four geysers: Lion, Lioness, Big Cub, and Little Cub, which are all connected underground. Of these Lion has the largest cone and eruptions. Active phases normally occur each day. Eruptions of Lion Geyser last 1–7 minutes and are often preceded by sudden gushes of steam and a deep roaring sound, hence the name Lion.

Heart Spring

Heart Spring was named by park geologist George Marler in or about 1959 apparently because its shape resembles a human heart. It is 7-1/2 by 10 feet at the surface and 15 feet deep.

Sawmill Geyser

Sawmill Geyser's eruptions are highly variable, some lasting only 9 minutes while others may last over 4 hours. The typical interval between eruptions is 1–3 hours. Overall it is erupting about 30% of the time. Sawmill received its name because water spins in its crater as it erupts looking somewhat like the rotating circular blade of a lumber mill.

Grand Geyser

An eruption of Grand Geyser, the tallest predictable geyser in the world, occurs every 7–15 hours. A classic fountain geyser, Grand erupts from a large pool with powerful bursts rather than a steady column like Old Faithful. An average eruption lasts 9–12 minutes and consists of 1–4 bursts, sometimes reaching 200 feet (60m).

Crested Pool

Crested pool is 42 feet deep and is constantly superheated. At times the temperature drops to a mere simmer but it occasionally comes to a full rolling boil as well. When boiling violently the water may dome to heights of 8–10 feet.

NPS photo

Castle Geyser

Castle Geyser has the largest cone and may be the oldest of all geysers in the basin. Its eruption pattern has changed considerably throughout its recorded history. Castle is currently erupting about every 10–12 hours. A water eruption frequently reaches 90 feet (27m) and lasts about 20 minutes. The water phase is followed by a noisy steam phase lasting 30–40 minutes.

Beauty Pool

Truly deserving its name, Beauty Pool is noted for its rich, blue water framed by rainbow-colored bacteria. It's plumbing system is closely related to the neighboring Chromatic Spring. Click "Next Stop" below for more details.

Chromatic Spring

Chromatic Spring is closely related to Beauty Pool. During periodic energy shifts the level of one spring descends while the other rises and overflows. The time interval between shifts has ranged from a few weeks to several years.

Giant Geyser

Giant Geyser was dormant for many years after the energy shift in 1955. Since then, it has slowly become active again. During 1997, its eruptions

Geothermal Features and How They Work

With half of the earth's geothermal features, Yellowstone holds the planet's most diverse and intact collection of geysers, hot springs, mudpots, and fumaroles. Its more than 300 geysers make up two thirds of all those found on earth. Combine this with more than 10,000 thermal features comprised of brilliantly colored hot springs, bubbling mudpots, and steaming fumaroles, and you have a place like no other. Geyserland, fairyland, wonderland—through the years, all have been used to describe the natural wonder and magic of this unique park that contains more geothermal features than any other place on earth.

Yellowstone's vast collection of thermal features provides a constant reminder of the park's recent volcanic past. Indeed, the caldera provides the setting that allows such features as Old Faithful to exist and to exist in such great concentrations.

Hot Springs and How They Work

In the high mountains surrounding the Yellowstone Plateau, water falls as snow or rain and slowly percolates through layers of porous rock, finding its way through cracks and fissures in the earth's crust created by the ring fracturing and collapse of the caldera. Sinking to a depth of nearly 10,000 feet, this cold water comes into contact with the hot rocks associated with the shallow magma chamber beneath the surface. As the water is heated, its temperatures rise well above the boiling point to become superheated. This superheated water, however, remains in a liquid state due to the great pressure and weight pushing down on it from overlying rock and water. The result is something akin to a giant pressure cooker, with water temperatures in excess of 400°F.

The highly energized water is less dense than the colder, heavier water sinking around it. This creates convection currents that allow the lighter, more buoyant, superheated water to begin its slow, arduous journey back toward the surface through rhyolitic lava flows, following the cracks, fissures, and weak areas of the earth's crust. Rhyolite is essential to geysers because it contains an abundance of silica, the mineral from which glass is made. As the hot water travels through this "natural plumbing system," the high temperatures dissolve some of the silica in the rhyolite, yielding a solution of silica within the water.

At the surface, these silica-laden waters form a rock called geyserite, or sinter, creating the massive geyser cones; the scalloped edges of hot springs; and the expansive, light- colored, barren landscape characteristic of geyser basins. While in solution underground, some of this silica deposits as geyserite on the walls of the plumbing system forming a pressure-tight seal, locking in the hot water and creating a system that can withstand the great pressure needed to produce a geyser.

With the rise of superheated water through this complex plumbing system, the immense pressure exerted over the water drops as it nears the surface. The heat energy, if released in a slow steady manner, gives rise to a hot spring, the most abundant and colorful thermal feature in the park. Hot springs with names like Morning Glory, Grand Prismatic, Abyss, Emerald, and Sapphire, glisten like jewels in a host of colors across the park's harsh volcanic plain.

Mudpots & How They Work

Where hot water is limited and hydrogen sulfide gas is present (emitting the "rotten egg" smell common to thermal areas), sulfuric acid is generated. The acid dissolves the surrounding rock into fine particles of silica and clay that mix with what little water there is to form the seething and bubbling mudpots. The sights, sounds, and smells of areas like Artist and Fountain paint pots and Mud Volcano make these curious features some of the most memorable in the park.

Fumeroles (Steam Vents) and How They Work

Fumaroles, or steam vents, are hot springs with a lot of heat, but so little water that it all boils away before reaching the surface. At places like Roaring Mountain, the result is a loud hissing vent of steam and gases.

NPS photo

Mammoth Hot Springs Terraces and How They Work

At Mammoth Hot Springs, a rarer kind of spring is born when the hot water ascends through the ancient limestone deposits of the area instead of the silica-rich lava flows of the hot springs common elsewhere in the park. The results are strikingly different and unique. They invoke a landscape that resembles a cave turned inside out, with its delicate features exposed for all to see. The flowing waters spill across the surface to sculpt magnificent travertine limestone terraces. As one early visitor described them, "No human architect ever designed such intricate fountains as these. The water trickles over the edges from one to another, blending them together with the effect of a frozen waterfall."

How They Work

As ground water seeps slowly downward and laterally, it comes in contact with hot gases charged with carbon dioxide rising from the magma chamber. Some carbon dioxide is readily dissolved in the hot water to form a weak carbonic acid solution. This hot, acidic solution dissolves great quantities of limestone as it works up through the rock layers to the surface hot springs. Once exposed to the open air, some of the carbon dioxide escapes from solution. As this happens, limestone can no longer remain in solution. A solid mineral reforms and is deposited as the travertine that forms the terraces.

Geysers and How They Work

Sprinkled amid the hot springs are the rarest fountains of all, the geysers. What makes them rare and distinguishes them from hot springs is that somewhere, usually near the surface in the plumbing system of a geyser, there are one or more constrictions. Expanding steam bubbles generated from the rising hot water build up behind these constrictions, ultimately squeezing through the narrow passageways and forcing the water above to overflow from the geyser. The release of water at the surface prompts a sudden decline in pressure of the hotter waters at great depth, triggering a violent chain reaction of tremendous steam explosions in which the volume of rising, now boiling, water expands 1,500 times or more. This expanding body of boiling superheated water bursts into the sky as one of Yellowstone's many famous geysers.

There are more geysers here than anywhere else on earth. Old Faithful, certainly the most famous geyser, is joined by numerous others big and small, named and unnamed. Though born of the same water and rock, what is enchanting is how differently they play in the sky. Riverside Geyser shoots at an angle across the Firehole River, often forming a rainbow in its mist. Castle erupts from a cone shaped like the ruins of some medieval fortress. Grand explodes in a series of powerful bursts, towering above the surrounding trees. Echinus spouts up and out to all sides like a fireworks display of water. And Steamboat, the largest in the world, pulsates like a massive steam engine in a rare, but remarkably memorable eruption, reaching heights of 300 to 400 feet.

occurred every 3–10 days. This spectacular geyser's eruptions last about an hour and can reach heights of 180–250 feet (55–76m). During eruptions small geysers nearby may also erupt.

Comet Geyser

Comet Geyser is a member of the Daisy Group which also contains Daisy and Splendid Geysers. Comet has the largest cone of the three but has, by far, the smallest eruptions. The nearly constant splashing of Comet over a long period of time has resulted in its large cone. Eruptions rarely exceed 6 feet in height.

Splendid Geyser

Splendid Geyser's eruptions are at times over 200 feet in height, making it among the tallest geysers in Yellowstone. Its eruptions are infrequent and difficult to predict except for the fact that it is more likely to erupt when a storm front rapidly reduces the barometric pressure in the area. This slightly reduces the boiling temperature in the plumbing system and occasionally triggers a splendid eruption.

Punch Bowl Spring

This boiling, intermittent spring has produced a sinter lip that raises it above the basin floor. That "punch bowl" appearance gave this feature its name.

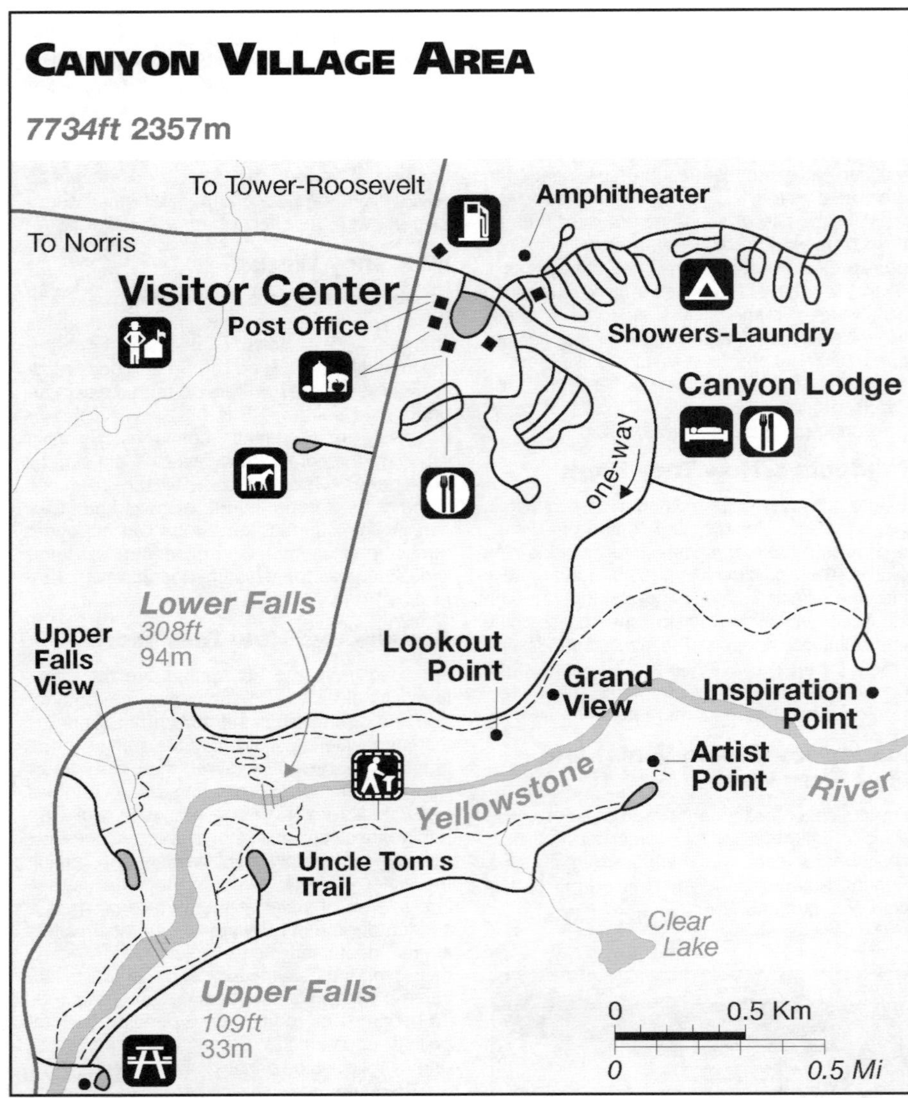

Daisy Geyser

Daisy Geyser erupts at an angle to a height of 75 feet (23m) for 3–5 minutes. Typically, Daisy is quite predictable, with eruption intervals of 90–115 minutes. An exception to this is when nearby Splendid Geyser erupts.

Grotto Geyser

Grotto Geyser erupts about every eight hours. It splashes to a height of 10 feet (3m) for 1 1/2 to more than 10 hours. The weirdly shaped cone, that gives this geyser its name, may have resulted from geyserite covering the trunks of trees that once grew there.

Morning Glory Pool

Long a favored destination for park visitors, Morning Glory Pool was named in the 1880s for its remarkable likeness to its namesake flower. However, this beautiful pool has fallen victim to vandalism. People have thrown literally tons of coins, trash, rocks, and logs into the pool. Much of the debris subsequently became embedded in the sides and vent of the spring, affecting water circulation and accelerating the loss of thermal energy. Through the years Morning Glory's appearance has changed as its temperature dropped. Orange and yellow bacteria that formerly colored only the periphery of the spring now spread toward its center.

Riverside Geyser. NPS photo.

Riverside Geyser

Situated on the bank of the Firehole River, Riverside Geyser is one of the most picturesque geysers in the park. During its 20-minute eruptions, a 75 foot (23m) column of water arches gracefully over the river. Eruptions are about 5-1/2 to 6-1/2 hours apart. There is water runoff over the edge of Riverside's cone for an hour or two before each eruption. Many geysers have similar "indications" that they are about to erupt.

Fan & Mortar Geysers

Fan and Mortar Geysers are in close proximity to one another and almost always erupt in concert. The interval between eruptions ranges from 1-1/2 days to months. Most eruptions last about 45 minutes. Mortar Geyser, pictured here, erupts to heights of 40–80 feet while Fan can reach heights of 100–125 feet.

Sapphire Pool

Three miles north of Old Faithful is Biscuit Basin, named for the unusual biscuit-like deposits formerly surrounding Sapphire Pool. Following the 1959 Hebgen Lake earthquake, Sapphire erupted, and the "biscuits" were blown away. Other notable colorful features in the basin are Jewel Geyser, Shell Geyser, Avoca Spring, and Mustard Spring.

Natural Highlights of the Canyon Village Area

The Grand Canyon of the Yellowstone

The Grand Canyon of the Yellowstone is the primary geologic feature in the Canyon District. It is roughly 20 miles long, measured from the Upper Falls to the Tower Fall area. Depth is 800 to 1,200 ft.; width is 1,500 to 4,000 ft. The canyon as we know it today is a very recent geologic feature. The present canyon is no more than 10,000 to 14,000 years old, although there has probably been a canyon in this location for a much longer period. The exact sequence of events in the formation of the canyon is not well understood, as there has been little field work done in the area. The few studies that are available are thought to be inaccurate. We do know that the canyon was formed by erosion rather than by glaciation. A more complete explanation can be found in the Geological Overview section. The geologic story of the canyon, its historical significance as a barrier to travel, its significance as destination/attraction, and its appearance in Native American lore and in the accounts of early explorers are all important interpretive points. The "ooh-ahh" factor is also important: its beauty and grandeur, its significance as a feature to be preserved, and the development of the national park idea.

The Upper and Lower Falls of the Yellowstone

The falls are erosional features formed by the Yellowstone River as it flows over progressively softer, less resistant rock. The Upper Falls is upstream of the Lower Falls and is 109 ft. high. It can be seen from the Brink of the Upper Falls Trail and from Uncle Tom's Trail.

The Lower Falls is 308 ft. high and can be seen from Lookout Point, Red Rock Point, Artist

Point, Brink of the Lower Falls Trail, and from various points on the South Rim Trail. The Lower Falls is often described as being more than twice the size of Niagara, although this only refers to its height and not the volume of water flowing over it. The volume of water flowing over the falls can vary from 63,500 gal/sec at peak runoff to 5,000 gal/sec in the fall.

A third falls can be found in the canyon between the Upper and Lower falls. Crystal Falls is the outfall of Cascade Creek into the canyon. It can be seen from the South Rim Trail just east of the Uncle Tom's area.

The Yellowstone River

The Yellowstone River is the force that created the canyon and the falls. It begins on the slopes of Yount Peak, south of the park, and travels more than 600 miles to its terminus in North Dakota where it empties into the Missouri River. It is the longest undammed river in the continental United States.

Hayden Valley

Hayden Valley is one of the best places in the park to view a wide variety of wildlife. It is an excellent place to look for grizzly bears, particularly in the spring and early summer when they may be preying upon newborn bison and elk calves. Large herds of bison may be viewed in the spring, early summer, and during the fall rut, which usually begins late July to early August. Coyotes can almost always be seen in the valley.

Bird life is abundant in and along the river. A variety of shore birds may be seen in the mud flats at Alum Creek. A pair of sandhill cranes usually nests at the south end of the valley. Ducks, geese, and American white pelicans cruise the river. The valley is also an excellent place to look for bald eagles and northern harriers.

Mt. Washburn

Mt. Washburn is the main peak in the Washburn Range, rising 10,243 ft. above the west side of the canyon. It is the remnant of volcanic activity that took place long before the formation of the present canyon. It is an excellent example of sub-alpine habitat and is very accessible to the average visitor. Bighorn sheep and an abundance of wildflowers can be found on its slopes in the summer. Mt. Washburn was named for Gen. Henry Dana Washburn, leader of the 1870 Washburn-Langford-Doane Expedition.

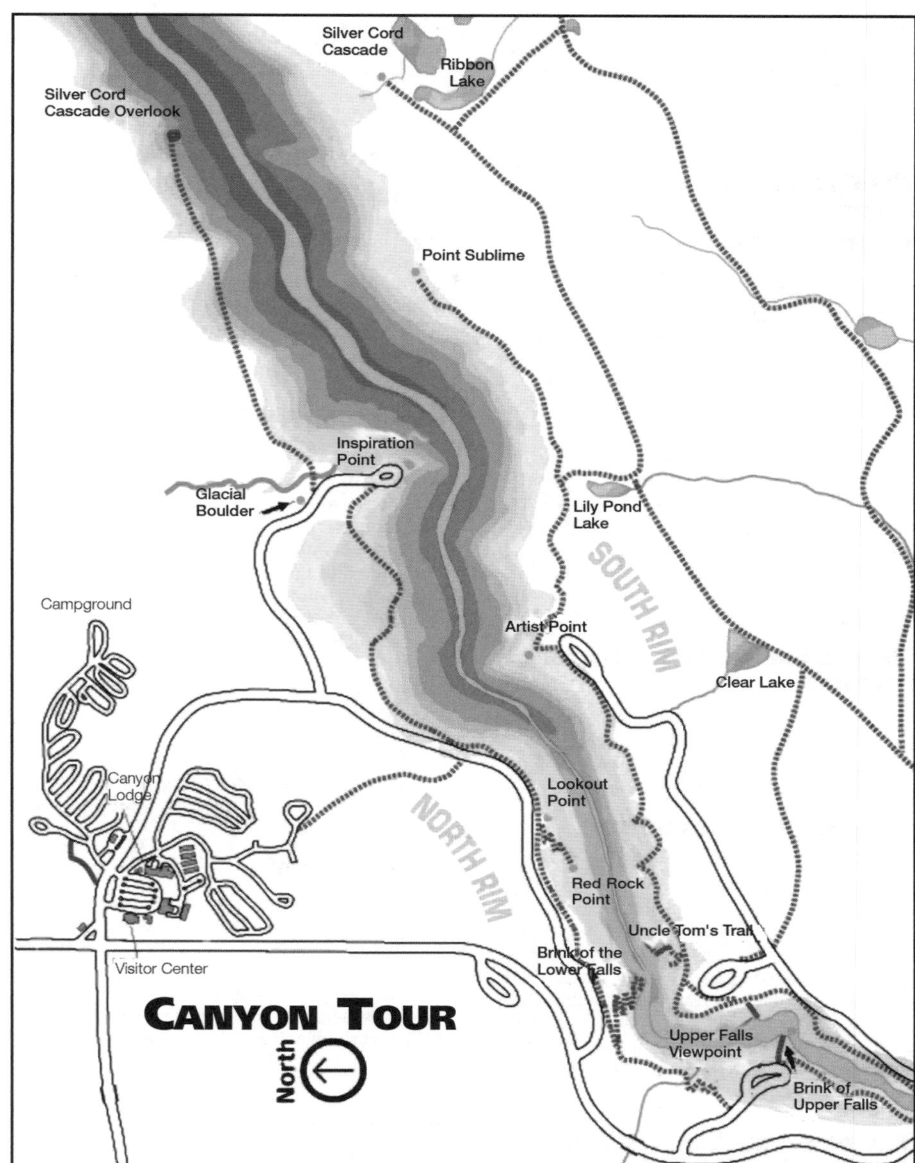

Geological Overview of the Canyon Area

The Grand Canyon of the Yellowstone

The specifics of the geology of the canyon are not well understood, except that it is an erosional feature rather than the result of glaciation. After the caldera eruption of about 600,000 years ago, the area was covered by a series of lava flows. The area was also faulted by the doming action of the caldera before the eruption. The site of the present canyon, as well as any previous canyons, was probably the result of this faulting, which allowed erosion to proceed at an accelerated rate. The area was also covered by the glaciers that followed the volcanic activity. Glacial deposits probably filled the canyon at one time, but have since been eroded away, leaving little or no evidence of their presence.

The canyon below the Lower Falls was at one time the site of a geyser basin that was the result of rhyolite lava flows, extensive faulting, and heat beneath the surface (related to the hot spot). No one is sure exactly when the geyser basin was formed in the area, although it was probably present at the time of the last glaciation. The chemical and heat action of the geyser basin caused the rhyolite rock to become hydrothermally altered, making it very soft and brittle and more easily erodible (sometimes likened to baking a potato). Evidence of this thermal activity still exists in the canyon in the form of geysers and hot springs that are still active and visible. The Clear Lake area (Clear Lake is fed by hot springs) south of the canyon is probably also a remnant of this activity.

According to Ken Pierce, U.S. Geological Survey geologist, at the end of the last glacial period, about 14,000 to 18,000 years ago, ice dams formed at the mouth of Yellowstone Lake. When the ice dams melted, a great volume of water was released downstream causing massive flash floods and immediate and catastrophic erosion of the present-day canyon. These flash floods probably happened more than once. The canyon is a classic V-shaped valley, indicative of river-type erosion rather than glaciation. The canyon is still being eroded by the Yellowstone River.

The colors in the canyon are also a result of hydrothermal alteration. The rhyolite in the canyon contains a variety of different iron compounds. When the old geyser basin was active, the "cooking" of the rock caused chemical alterations in these iron compounds. Exposure to the elements caused the rocks to change colors. The rocks are, in effect, oxidizing; the canyon is rusting. The colors indicate the presence or absence of water in the individual iron compounds. Most of the yellows in the canyon are the result of iron present in the rock rather than sulfur, as many people think.

Historic Highlights of the Canyon Area

Canyon Village

The Canyon Village complex is part of the Mission 66 project in the park. The Visitor Center was completed in 1957, and the new lodge was open for business in the same year. Though some people consider the development representative of the architecture of the time, none of the present buildings in the complex can be considered historic. There are, however, still remnants of the old hotel, lodge, and related facilities. These constitute the cultural resources of the district.

The Canyon Hotel (no longer standing)

The old Canyon Hotel was located about 1 mile south of Canyon Junction at the present site of the horse corrals. It was a huge building, nearly a mile around its perimeter. It was dismantled and burned in 1962. See Aubrey Haines' account of this in *The Yellowstone Story, Vol. II.* Photographs of the hotel are available for viewing in an album at the Visitor Center and in the park's historic photo collection. Little if anything is left of the hotel building itself, but the hotel's cistern and the dump remain. The winterkeeper's house, in which Steve Fuller (a concession employee) lives, is also from this era. The cistern is being studied for removal, the dump is an archeological site that must be evaluated before further action is taken, and the house is being considered for the National Register of Historic Places.

The Old Canyon Lodge (no longer standing)

The old Canyon Lodge was located at the present site of Uncle Tom's parking lot and in the meadows just east of the rest rooms. Remnants of this complex can still be found in the meadows.

Other Cultural Resources

The remaining cultural resources associated with earlier developments are far from the public eye and not easily accessible. One has to know where to look for them. They include, but are not limited to, the Ram pump on Cascade Creek, the concrete apron (for water supply) on Cascade Creek, the hotel water tank, and the water tank at the Brink of the Upper Falls. All are slated for some kind of mitigation, depending upon funding, staffing, and priority by the resource management staff.

Yellowstone-Canyon Tour

About 600,000 years ago, huge volcanic eruptions occurred in Yellowstone, emptying a large underground magma chamber. Volcanic debris spread for thousands of square miles in a matter of minutes. The roof of this chamber collapsed, forming a giant smoldering pit. This caldera was 30 miles (45 km) across, 45 miles (75 km) long, and several thousand feet deep. Eventually the caldera was filled with lava.

One of these lava flows was the Canyon Rhyolite flow, approximately 590,000 years ago which came from the east and ended just west of the present canyon. A thermal basin developed in this lava flow, altering and weakening the rhyolite lava by action of the hot steam and gases. Steam rises from vents in the canyon today and the multi-hued rocks of the canyon walls are also evidence of hydrothermally altered rhyolite.

Other lava flows blocked rivers and streams forming lakes that overflowed and cut through the various hard and soft rhyolites, creating the canyon. Later the canyon was blocked three different times by glaciers. Each time these glaciers formed lakes, which filled with sand and gravel. Floods from the melting glaciers at the end of each glacial period recarved the canyon, deepened it, and removed most of the sand and gravel.

The present appearance of the canyon dates from about 10,000 years ago when the last glaciers melted. Since that time, erosional forces (water, wind, earthquakes, and other natural forces) have continued to sculpt the canyon.

Glacial Boulder

Along the road to Inspiration Point there is a house-sized granite boulder sitting in the pine forest alongside the road. It was plucked from the Beartooth Mountains by an early Pinedale Glacier and dropped on the north rim of the Grand Canyon of the Yellowstone nearly 80,000 years ago. Continued glacial advances and retreats led to the present-day appearance of the canyon and surrounding area.

Inspiration Point Platform

Inspiration Point is a natural observation point. It is at a location where the canyon wall juts far out into the canyon allowing spectacular views both upstream and down.

A member of the Washburn party in 1870, Nathanial P. Langford, used these words to describe his visit to this point:

"The place where I obtained the best and most terrible view of the canyon was a narrow projecting point situated two to three miles below the lower fall. Standing there or rather lying there for greater safety, I thought how utterly impossible it would be to describe to another the sensations inspired by such a presence. As I took in the scene, I realized my own littleness, my helplessness, my dread exposure to destruction, my inability to cope with or even comprehend the mighty architecture of nature."

Lookout Point

This was a popular lookout for many early visitors to the park. Noticing that it got regular visitation, in 1880 Superintendent P.W. Norris built a railing here and the location has been called Lookout Point ever since. It is likely that this was the superintendents preferred name for the spot. It had been called many things prior to 1880 including Point Lookout, Lookout Rock, Mount Lookout, and Prospect Point.

Red Rock Point

Red Rock Point is near the tall reddish pinnacle of rock below the Lower Falls. Iron oxide is the cause of this rock's red pigmentation. The pinnacle has had several names relating to its color including Red Pinnacles and Cinnabar Tower. It was finally given its present-day name of Red Rock by the 1886 Park Photographer, F. Jay Haynes.

Brink of the Lower Falls

The Lower Falls is the tallest waterfall in the park at 308 feet. The arrow at the top of the photo points at a group of visitors on the platform at the Brink of the Lower Falls.

Over the years the estimates of the height of this falls has varied dramatically. In 1851 Jim Bridger estimated its height at 250 feet. One outrageous newspaper story from 1867 placed its height at "thousands of feet". A map from 1869 gives the falls its current name of Lower Falls for the first time and estimates the height at 350 feet.

It mattered little how tall the observers thought the falls was. They consistently write journal entries that comment on its awe-inspiring nature. A member of the 1870 Washburn party N. P. Langford gave this brief but poetic description: *"A grander scene than the lower cataract of the Yellowstone was never witnessed by mortal eyes."*

The Lower Falls of the Yellowstone. NPS photo.

The Brink of the Upper Falls

This is the smaller of the two famous waterfalls on the Yellowstone River at 109 feet tall. To get a feel for its magnitude notice that the arrow at the top of the photo points at three people standing on the platform at the Brink of the Upper Falls.

This falls was called the "upper falls" for the first time by members of the 1869 Folsom party who estimated its height at 115 feet. Visitors to the Brink of the Upper Falls have throughout time found the power of the experience worthy of detailed description.

In 1870 N.P. Langford of the Washburn party wrote of his visit to the brink:

"Mr. Hedges and I made our way down to this table rock, where we sat for a long time. As from this spot we looked up at the descending waters, we insensibly felt that the slightest protrusion in them would hurl us backwards into the gulf below. A thousand arrows of foam, apparently aimed at us, leaped from the verge, and passed rapidly down the sheet. But as the view grew upon us, and we comprehended the power, majesty and beauty of the scene, we became insensible to the danger and gave ourselves up to the full enjoyment of it."

Upper Falls Viewpoint

Of the two famous Yellowstone River waterfalls this one stands at a higher elevation, but it is considerably shorter in height than its downstream neighbor, the Lower Falls. The height of the Upper Falls is 109 feet.

According to a companion, the famous mountain man Jim Bridger visited this waterfall in 1846. Word spread of its existence and in the 1860s some prospectors went out of their way to visit it.

View of the Lower Falls from Uncle Tom's Trail

Uncle Tom's Trail was first constructed in 1898 by "Uncle" Tom Richardson. The five years following its construction, Uncle Tom led visitors on tours which included crossing the river upstream from the present day Chittenden Bridge, and then following his rough trail to the base of the Lower Falls. The tour was concluded with a picnic and a return trip across the river.

Today Uncle Tom's Trail is very different from the simple trail used by Mr. Richardson and his visitors. It is still, however, a very strenuous walk into the canyon. The trail drops 500 feet (150 m) in a series of more than 300 stairs and paved inclines.

Artist Point

Many people thought that this was the point where Thomas Moran made the sketches he used to produce his famous painting of the canyon in 1872. In fact those sketches were made from the north rim in a location known today as Moran Point.

The name Artist Point is believed to have been given to this location around 1883 by Park Photographer F. Jay Haynes. The name appeared in print for the first time in Mr. Haynes guidebook, published in 1890.

Point Sublime

When the Cook-Folsom expedition stepped out of the woods on the south rim of the canyon in 1869 the staggering view prompted Folsom to use the following adjectives in his description of it: "pretty, beautiful, picturesque, magnificent, grand, sublime, awful, terrible". It is thought to be that description which prompted the naming of Point Sublime in the early 1920s.

Silver Cord Cascade

Surface Creek flows passed this overlook and then falls abruptly in a long series of falls down to the river. While not a single waterfall, this cascade may well have given rise to the stories of a waterfall over 1000 feet tall that was hidden in the mountains.

Members of the Washburn party discovered the cascade in 1870 and named it Silverthread Fall. In 1885 the USGS Hague parties gave it the name that survives today, Silver Cord Cascade.

Natural Highlights of the Tower-Roosevelt Area

Specimen Ridge

Specimen Ridge, located along the Northeast Entrance Road east of Tower Junction, contains the largest concentration of petrified trees in the world. There are also excellent samples of petrified leaf impressions, conifer needles, and microscopic pollen from numerous species no longer growing in the park. Specimen Ridge provides a superb "window" into the distant past when plant communities and climactic conditions were much different than today.

Petrified Tree

The Petrified Tree, located near the Lost Lake trailhead, is an excellent example of an ancient redwood, similar to many found on Specimen Ridge, that is easily accessible to park visitors. The interpretive message here also applies to those trees found on Specimen Ridge.

Petrified trees in the park are evidence of its volcanic history. Trees buried by volcanic ash slowly had their organic structure replaced by minerals. These tree trunks were literally turned to stone. The petrified tree pictured here was placed behind the fence to protect it from vandals

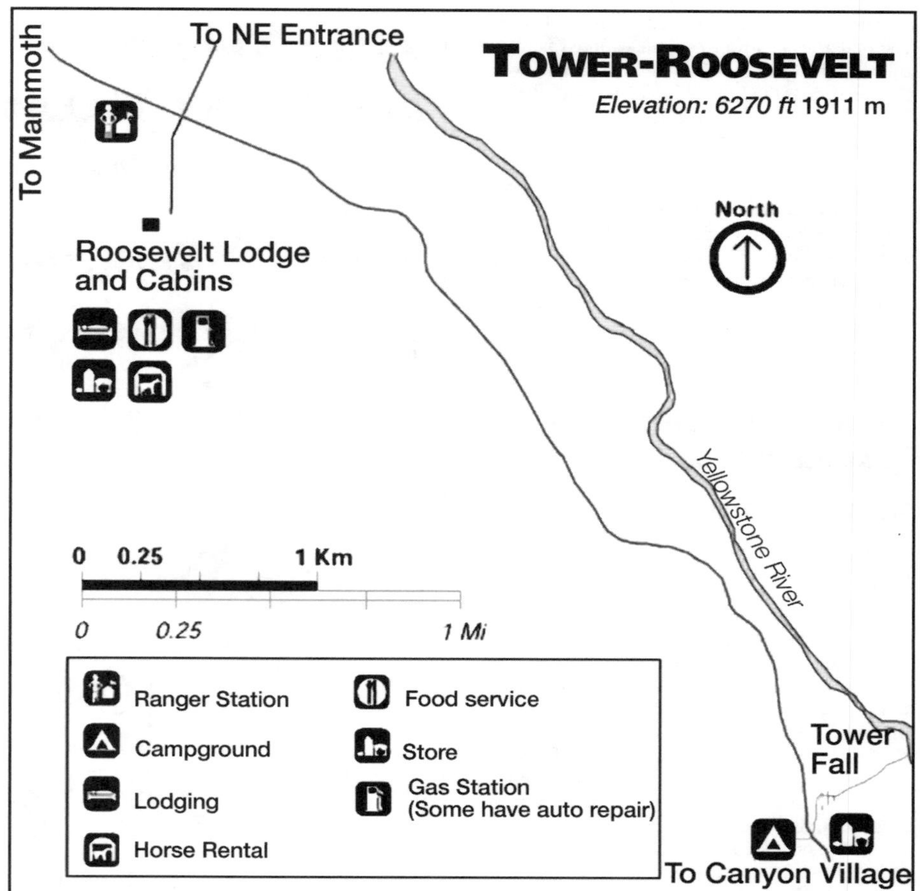

and collectors. Two other petrified trees that were nearby were totally removed one piece at a time by thoughtless visitors in the past.

Tower Fall

Tower Fall is the most recognizable natural feature in the district. The 132-foot drop of Tower Creek, framed by eroded volcanic pinnacles has been documented by park visitors from the earliest trips of Europeans into the Yellowstone region. Its idyllic setting has inspired numerous artists, including Thomas Moran. His painting of Tower Fall played a crucial role in the establishment of Yellowstone National Park in 1872. The nearby Bannock Ford on the Yellowstone River was an important travel route for early Native Americans as well as for early European visitors and miners up to the late 19th century.

Calcite Springs

This grouping of thermal springs along the Yellowstone River signals the downstream end of the Grand Canyon of the Yellowstone. The geothermally altered rhyolite inspired the artist Moran; his paintings of this scene were among those presented to Congress in 1872, leading to the establishment of the park. The steep, columnar basalt cliffs on the opposite side of the river from the overlook are remnants of an ancient lava flow, providing a window into the past volcanic forces that shaped much of the Yellowstone landscape. The gorge and cliffs provide habitat for numerous wildlife species including bighorn sheep, red-tailed hawks, and osprey.

Yellowstone River and its Tributaries

The Yellowstone River and its tributaries provide habitat for numerous bird and fish species.

Geological Overview of the Tower-Roosevelt Area

The geology of the Tower district is incredibly varied. Major landforms are expressions of geologic events that helped shape much of the Yellowstone area. Absaroka volcanics, glaciation, and erosion have left features as varied as Specimen Ridge's petrified trees to the gorges along the Yellowstone River's Black Canyon and the Grand Canyon of the Yellowstone.

Mt. Washburn and the Absaroka Range are both remnants of ancient volcanic events that formed the highest peaks in the Tower District. Ancient eruptions, perhaps 45 to 50 million years ago, buried the forests of Specimen Ridge in ash and debris flows. The columnar basalt formations near Tower Fall, the volcanic breccias of the "towers" themselves, and numerous igneous outcrops all reflect the district's volcanic history.

Later, glacial events scoured the landscape, exposing the stone forests and leaving evidence of their passage throughout the district. The glacial ponds and huge boulders (erratics) between the Lamar and Yellowstone rivers are remnants left by the retreating glaciers. Lateral and terminal moraines are common in these areas. Such evidence can also be found in the Hellroaring and Slough creek drainages, on Blacktail Plateau, and in the Lamar Valley.

The eroding power of running water has been

at work in the district for many millions of years. The pinnacles of Tower Fall, the exposed rainbow colors of the Grand Canyon of the Yellowstone at Calcite Springs, and the fearsome gorge of the Black Canyon all are due, at least in part, to the forces of running water and gravity.

In the Lamar River Canyon lie exposed outcrops of gneiss and schist which are among the oldest rocks known in Yellowstone, perhaps more than two billion years old. Little is known about their origin due to their extreme age. Through time, heat and pressure have altered these rocks from their original state, further obscuring their early history. Only in the Gallatin Range are older outcrops found within the boundaries of the park.

Historic Highlights of the Tower-Roosevelt Area

The Buffalo Ranch

The Lamar Buffalo Ranch was built in the early part of the century in an effort to increase the herd size of the few remaining bison in Yellowstone, preventing the feared extinction of the species. Buffalo ranching operations continued at Lamar until the 1950s. The valley was irrigated for hay pastures, and corrals and fencing were scattered throughout the area. Remnants of irrigation ditches, fencing, and water troughs can still be found. Four remaining buildings from the original ranch compound are contained within the Lamar Buffalo Ranch Historic District (two residences, the bunkhouse, and the barn) and are on the National Register of Historic Places. In the early 1980s, old tourist cabins from Fishing Bridge were brought to Lamar to be used for Yellowstone Institute classes. In 1993, a cabin replacement project, funded by the Yellowstone Association, was begun. At this time all of the old cabins have been replaced with new insulated and heated structures. The facility is also used in the spring and fall for the Park Service's residential environmental education program,

Tower Falls. NPS photo

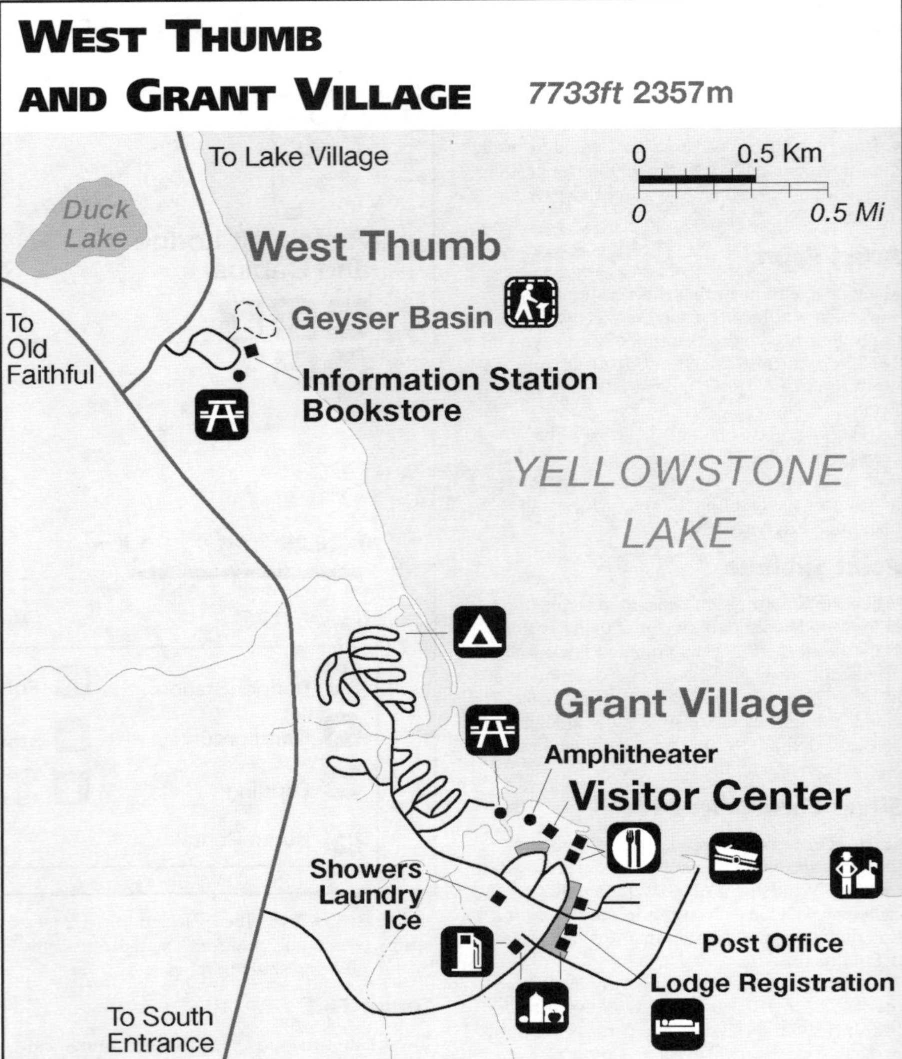

Expedition: Yellowstone!

You are welcome to drive by to view the historic buffalo ranch, however, there are no facilities open to the general public at this location.

The Tower Ranger Station & Roosevelt National Historic District

The Tower Ranger Station, though not on the National Register of Historic Places, is a remodeled reconstruction of the second Tower Soldier Station, which was built in 1907. The Roosevelt Lodge was constructed in 1920 and has been determined eligible for the National Register of Historic Places. The Roosevelt National Historic District also includes the Roosevelt cabins. Interestingly, one of the reasons Roosevelt Lodge was nominated for the National Register was due to its important role in early park interpretation.

Pleasant Valley

Pleasant Valley was the sight of "Uncle John" Yancey's Pleasant Valley Hotel, one of the earliest lodging facilities in Yellowstone. The hotel and outbuildings were built between 1884 and 1893 and served early park visitors as well as miners passing through en route to the mining district near Cooke City. Currently, the site is used by the park's main concessioner, Amfac, for their "Old West" cookouts. None of the original buildings remain.

The Northeast Entrance Ranger Station

The Northeast Entrance Ranger Station was constructed in 1934-35 and is a National Historic Landmark. It's rustic log construction is characteristic of "parkitecture" common in the national parks of the west during that period.

The Bannock Trail

The Bannock Trail, once used by Native Americans to access the buffalo plains east of the park from the Snake River plains in Idaho, was extensively used from approximately 1840 to 1876. A lengthy portion of the trail extends through the Tower District from the Blacktail Plateau (closely paralleling or actually covered by the existing road) to where it crosses the Yellowstone River at the Bannock Ford upstream from Tower Creek. From the river, the trail's main fork ascends the Lamar River splitting at Soda Butte Creek. From there, one fork ascends the creek before leaving the park. Traces of the trail can still be plainly seen in various locations, particularly on the Blacktail Plateau and at the

Lamar-Soda Butte confluence.

Archeological Resources

There are many archaeological sites in the Tower District. In fact, sites are found in a greater density here than in most other areas of the park. Unfortunately, most have yet to be extensively catalogued or studied.

Natural Highlights of the West Thumb and Grant Village Areas

Yellowstone Lake

The park's largest lake is Yellowstone Lake. This "matchless mountain lake" was probably seen by John Colter on his famous winter trip of discovery in 1807-1808. Before that, Native Americans surely camped on its shores every summer. Although it is unlikely that Native Americans lived here, many arrowheads, spearheads, and other artifacts have been found near the lake.

William Clark's map of 1806-1811 showed what was probably Yellowstone Lake as "Eustis Lake," the name of the Secretary of War under President Jefferson. An 1814 map maker changed Clark's "Lake Biddle" (probably Jackson Lake) to "Lake Riddle," and it may at times also have referred to Yellowstone Lake. The name "Bridger Lake" (now applied to a small lake southeast of the park) may also have applied at times to Yellowstone Lake. In 1826, a party of fur trappers that included Daniel Potts, Bill Sublette, and Jedidiah Smith called Yellowstone Lake "Sublette Lake," and some historians credit Sublette with discovering the lake. Daniel Potts, one of the chroniclers of that 1826 trip, wrote to his family on July 8, 1827, and said that near the headwaters of the Yellowstone River is "a large fresh water lake...on the very top of the mountain which is about one hundred by forty miles in diameter and as clear as crystal" (letter, Yellowstone Park Research Library). Trapper Warren Ferris knew the name "Yellow Stone Lake" by 1831, and he showed it on his map of 1836. By the 1860s, Yellowstone Lake was well-known among former fur trappers, army personnel, and other frequent western explorers.

The 1871 Hayden Survey was the first to sail a boat, the Anna, on the waters of Yellowstone Lake, although some fur trappers or Indians may have floated rafts on the lake much earlier. Other early boats used to explore the lake were the Topping in 1874 (see Topping Point), a raft containing government surveyors in 1874, the Explorer in 1880 (see Explorer's Creek), a USGS boat destroyed by lightning in 1885, the Zillah in 1889, and the E.C. Waters (test runs only) in 1905. A boat piloted by Billy Hofer and William D. Pickett made at least one trip on the lake in 1880.

Yellowstone Lake covers 136 square miles and is 20 miles long by 14 miles wide. It has 110 miles of shoreline. The lake is at least 320 feet deep in the West Thumb area and has an average depth of 140 feet. Situated at an elevation of 7,733 feet, the lake remains cold the year-round, with an average temperature of 41°F.

Yellowstone Lake is the largest natural freshwater lake in the United States that is above 7,000 feet and is one of the largest such lakes in the world. Because of its size and depth and the area's prevailing winds, the lake can sometimes be whipped into a tempestuous inland ocean.

During late summer, Yellowstone Lake becomes thermally stratified with each of several water layers having a different temperature. The topmost layer rarely exceeds 66°F, and the lower layers are much colder. Because of the extremely cold water, swimming is not recommended. Survival time is estimated to be only 20 to 30 minutes in water of this temperature.

The lake has the largest population of wild cutthroat trout in North America. Just how these Pacific Ocean cutthroat got trapped in a lake that drains to the Atlantic Ocean puzzled experts for years. There is now a theory that Yellowstone Lake once drained to the Pacific Ocean (via Outlet Canyon to Snake River) and that fish could pass across the Continental Divide at Two Ocean Pass. Lake trout, an illegally introduced, exotic species, is now found in Yellowstone Lake and threatens the existence of the native cutthroat trout.

Yellowstone Lake freezes over completely in winter, with ice thicknesses varying from a few inches to more than two feet. The lake's basin has an estimated capacity of 12,095,264 acre-feet of water. Because its annual outflow is about 1,100,000 acre-feet, the lake's water is completely replaced only about every eight to ten years. Since 1952, the annual water level fluctuation has been less than six feet.

West Thumb of Yellowstone Lake

Members of the 1870 Washburn party noted that Yellowstone Lake was shaped like "a human hand with the fingers extended and spread apart as much as possible," with the large west bay representing the thumb. In 1878, however, the Hayden Survey used the name "West Arm" for the bay; "West Bay" was also used. Norris' maps of 1880 and 1881 used "West Bay or Thumb." During the 1930s, park personnel attempted to change the name back to "West Arm," but West Thumb remains the accepted name.

West Thumb Geyser Basin

While many of the park's features had been described by mountain men and other explorers, the West Thumb area was the first Yellowstone feature to be written about in a publication. Daniel T. Potts, a trapper in the Yellowstone region in the 1820s, wrote a letter to his brother in Philadelphia, Pennsylvania, regarding his experiences in this area. The letter was later corrected for punctuation and spelling and printed in the Philadelphia Gazette on September 27, 1827. Part of the letter describing the northern part of the West Thumb Geyser Basin, which is currently known as "Potts Basin" follows:

...on the south borders of this lake is a number of hot and boiling springs some of water and others of most beautiful fine clay and resembles that of a mush pot and throws its particles to the immense height of from twenty to thirty feet in height[.] The clay is white and of a pink and water appears fathomless as it appears to be entirely hollow under neath. There is also a number of places where the pure sulfur is sent forth in abundance[.] One of our men visited one of those whilst taking his recreation[.] There at an instant the earth began a tremendous trembling and he with difficulty made his escape when an explosion took place resembling that of thunder. During our stay in that quarter I heard it every day[.]

In 1869, the first scientific expedition to explore the Yellowstone area, the Folsom-Cook-Peterson Expedition, visited the West Thumb Geyser Basin. David Folsom described the area as follows:

"Among these were springs differing from any we had previously seen. They were situated along the shore for a distance of two miles, extending back from it about five hundred yards and into the lake perhaps as many feet. There were several hundred springs here, varying in size from miniature fountains to pools or wells seventy-five feet in diameter and of great depth. The water had a pale violet tinge, and was very clear, enabling us to discern small objects fifty or sixty feet below the surface. A small cluster of mud springs near by claimed our attention. These were filled with mud, resembling thick paint of the finest quality, differing in color from pure white to the various shades of yellow, pink, red and violet. During the afternoon they threw mud to the height of fifteen feet... ."

Historically, visitors travelling to Yellowstone would arrive at West Thumb via stagecoach from the Old Faithful area. At West Thumb, they had the choice of continuing on the dusty, bumpy stagecoach or boarding the steamship "Zillah" to continue the journey to the Lake Hotel. The boat dock was located near the south end of the basin near Lakeside Spring.

The West Thumb area used to be the site of a large campground, cabins, a photo shop, a cafeteria, and a gas station. This development was located immediately next to the geyser basin with the park road passing between the two. In an effort to further protect the scenic quality and the very resource that visitors were coming to see, the National Park Service removed this development in the 1980s.

Abyss Pool

In 1935, Chief Park Naturalist C.M. Bauer named Abyss Pool, a hot spring of the West Thumb Geyser Basin, for its impressive deepness. Bauer may have taken the name from Lieutenant G.C. Doane's 1870 description of a spring in this area: "*the distance to which objects are visible down in [its] deep abysses is truly wonderful*" (Bonney and Bonney, *Battle Drums*, p. 330). Abyss Pool may also be the spring that visitors referred to during the 1880s as "Tapering Spring" because of its sloping walls.

Nineteenth century observers were impressed with the pool's beauty. In 1871, F.V. Hayden reported that this spring's "ultramarine hue of the transparent depth in the bright sunlight was the most dazzlingly beautiful sight I have ever beheld" (*Preliminary Reports*, p. 101). And W.W. Wylie observed in 1882 that the spring's walls, "*coral-like in formation and singular in shape, tinted by the water's color, are surely good representations of fairy palaces*".

Fishing Cone

Fishing Cone is a hot spring located in the West Thumb Geyser Basin. The Folsom party probably saw it in 1869, but the first recorded description of Fishing Cone comes from the 1870 Washburn Expedition. Party member Walter Trumball wrote about Cornelius Hedges's experience fishing:

"A gentleman was fishing from one of the narrow isthmuses or shelves of rock, which divided one of these hot springs from the [Yellowstone] lake, when, in swinging a trout ashore, it accidentally got off the hook and fell into the spring. For a moment it darted about with wonderful rapidity, as if seeking an outlet. Then it came to the top, dead, and literally boiled (Overland Monthly, June 1871, p. 492)."

From that time on, and perhaps even earlier, visitor after visitor performed this feat, catching fish from the cold lake and cooking them on the hook. Hayden Survey members did it in 1871, and the next year they named the spring "Fish Pot" or "Hot Spring Cone." Later names were "Fisherman's Kettle," "Fish Cone," "Fishpot Spring," "Crater Island," and "Chowder Pot." The name Fishing Cone came about gradually through the generic use of the term in guidebooks.

The cooking-on-the-hook feat at Fishing Cone soon became famous. For years, Park Superintendent P.W. Norris (1877-1882) demonstrated it to incredulous tourists, and in 1894 members of Congress hooted at their colleagues who described the process. A national magazine reported in 1903 that no visit to the park was complete without this experience, and tourists often dressed in a cook's hat and apron to have their pictures taken at Fishing Cone. The fishing and cooking practice, regarded today as unhealthy, is now prohibited.

Fishing at the cone can be dangerous. A known geyser, Fishing Cone erupted frequently to the height of 40 feet in 1919 and to lesser heights in 1939. One fisherman was badly burned in Fishing Cone in 1921.

Lodgepole Pine Forests & Fire

This area is in a lodgepole pine forest, and the fires of 1988 greatly affected this part of the park. Several trails including the Lake Overlook Trail, Duck Lake Trail, and Riddle Lake Trail provide excellent opportunities to examine the various stages of lodgepole pine forest succession and development as well as fire ecology.

On July 12, 1988, a small fire started near the Falls River in the southeastern corner of the park. For several weeks, the fire grew slowly as crews attempted to contain it. On August 20, the winds picked up. This day would later become known as "Black Saturday" because more acres burned on this day alone than in the entire history of Yellowstone prior to this day. During that week, high winds drove the fire for miles until it approached the Lewis River. Defying all conventional understanding of fire behavior and driven by 60 mph winds that gusted to 80 mph, the fire blew all the way across the Lewis River Canyon on August 23.

Firefighters were astounded. Even the most experienced Incident Commanders had never seen fire burn like it did in 1988. While the fires shocked the nation and the world, scientists had long known that a fire of this magnitude would burn through a lodgepole pine forest like Yellowstone's on an average of once every 300 years. In fact, lodgepole pine forests are adapted to fire. Some of the pine cones need the intense heat of fire to open the cones and drop the seeds for the next generation of forests. While fire is often difficult for people to understand, for the lodgepole pine forests it is as important and necessary as other natural processes like rain and sunshine, death and rebirth.

Cutthroat Trout Spawning Streams

Big Thumb Creek and Little Thumb Creek along with several other intermittent streams serve as cutthroat trout spawning streams, thus as major feeding areas for both grizzly and black bears during spawning season.

Heart Lake

Lying in the Snake River watershed west of Lewis Lake and south of Yellowstone Lake, Heart Lake was named sometime before 1871 for Hart Hunney, an early hunter. The name does not refer to the heart-like shape of the lake. During the 1890s, historian Hiram Chittenden learned from Richard "Beaver Dick" Leigh, one of Hunney's cronies, about the naming of the lake. Evidently, Capt. John W. Barlow (see Barlow Peak), who explored Yellowstone in 1871, made the incorrect connection between the lake's name and its shape. Chittenden wrote to Barlow, who could recall nothing about the naming, but Leigh "was so positive and gave so much detail" that Chittenden concluded that he was right. Chittenden petitioned Arnold Hague of the USGS to change the spelling back to "Hart Lake," but Hague refused, convinced the shape of the lake determined the name.

As for Hart Hunney, Leigh said that Hunney operated in the vicinity of Heart Lake between 1840 and 1850 and died in a fight with Crow Indians in 1852. Chittenden thought it was possible that Hunney was one of Capt. Benjamin Bonneville's men.

NPS photo

Isa Lake

Hiram Chittenden of the U.S. Army Corps of Engineers claimed to have discovered this lake on the Continental Divide at Craig Pass in 1891. Chittenden, who built many early roads in Yellowstone, was searching for a practicable route to locate his new road between Old Faithful and West Thumb. It was not until 1893 that Northern Pacific Railroad (NPRR) officials named the lake for Isabel Jelke of Cincinnati. Little is known about Jelke or about her relationship to Chittenden, the NPRR, and Yellowstone. Chittenden's 1916 poetic tribute to the lake and his discovery includes the puzzling line: "Thou hast no name; pray, wilt thou deign to bear/The name of her who first has sung of thee" (Verse, p. 53). Perhaps Isabel Jelke was already associated with the lake when Chittenden "discovered" it. Isa Lake is noteworthy as probably the only lake on earth that drains naturally to two oceans backwards, the east side draining to the Pacific and the west side to the Atlantic.

Craig Pass

Craig Pass, at 8,262 feet on the Continental Divide, is about eight miles east of Old Faithful on the Grand Loop Road. In 1891, road engineer Captain Hiram Chittenden discovered Craig Pass while he was surveying for the first road between Old Faithful and West Thumb. It was probably Chittenden who named the pass for Ida M. Craig (Wilcox), "the first tourist to cross the pass" on Chittenden's new road, on about September 10, 1891. At the time that her name was given to the pass, Ida Wilcox (1847-1930) had been married 24 years. So why did Chittenden use her maiden name? Perhaps it was to honor her singularly for being the first tourist to cross the pass. It is also possible that through his connection with the military, Chittenden knew her father (Gen. James Craig) or her brother (Malin Craig, Sr.) and was really honoring the Craig family.

DeLacy Creek

DeLacy Creek flows south from DeLacy Lakes to Shoshone Lake. Park Superintendent P.W. Norris named the creek in 1881 for Walter Washington DeLacy (1819-1892), the leader of a prospecting expedition that passed through the Yellowstone region in 1863. DeLacy, a surveyor and engineer, compiled the first accurate map of the Yellowstone area in 1865.

In 1863, DeLacy led a group of prospectors from Jackson Hole across the Pitchstone Plateau and discovered Shoshone Lake, which he named "DeLacy's Lake." He was the first to note the "strange" drainage of that lake south to the Snake River rather than west to the Madison River. But he did not publish his discoveries until 1876, which kept him from receiving credit for being the man who discovered Yellowstone and from leaving his name on present-day Shoshone Lake.

DeLacy also recognized the importance of Yellowstone's thermal features. In a published letter in 1869, he wrote: "At the head of the South Snake, and also on the south fork of the Madison [present-day Shoshone Lake and Firehole River], there are hundreds of hot springs, many of which are 'geysers'" (Raymond, "Mineral Resources," p. 142). In 1871, Hayden changed the name of "DeLacy's Lake" to "Madison Lake." In 1872, Frank Bradley criticized DeLacy for the "numerous errors" on his map and named the lake Shoshone.

Park Superintendent P.W. Norris felt sorry for DeLacy and named the present stream for him in 1881, stating:

"The . . . narrative, the high character of its writer [DeLacy], his mainly correct descriptions of the region visited, and the traces which I have found of this party [campsite remains, etc.], proves alike its entire truthfulness, and the injustice of changing the name of De Lacy's Lake [to Shoshone Lake]; and fearing it is now too late to restore the proper name to it, I have, as a small token of deserved justice, named the stream and Park crossed by our trail above the Shoshone Lake after their discoverer (Fifth Annual Report, p. 44)."

Factory Hill

Factory Hill is a 9,607-foot-high peak in the Red Mountains. By 1876, the peak was called "Red Mountain," a name that had originally been given to present-day Mount Sheridan by members of the 1871 Hayden Survey. Eventually, the name "Red" was applied to the entire small mountain range.

Members of the Hague parties named Factory Hill in about 1885 because N.P. Langford's description of steam vents near the mountain. In the June 1871 issue of Scribner's, Langford had written: "Through the hazy atmosphere we beheld, on the shore of the inlet opposite our camp, the steam ascending in jets from more than fifty craters, giving it much the appearance of a New England factory village" (p. 120).

Lewis River

This river drains Shoshone and Lewis lakes and is a tributary of the Snake River. In 1872, members of the second Hayden survey called the river "Lake Fork" because it was a fork of the Snake that began in those two lakes. An 1876 map showed the river marked "Lewis Fork" (of the

Snake), named from Lewis Lake.

Red Mountains

This small range of mountains, located just west of Heart Lake, is completely contained within the boundaries of Yellowstone National Park. In 1871, F.V. Hayden named present-day Mount Sheridan "Red Mountain." In 1872, members of the second Hayden Survey transferred that name to the entire range. The name was "derived from the prevailing color of the volcanic rocks which compose them" (Hayden, Twelfth Annual Report, p. 470). In 1878, Henry Gannett reported that there were 12 peaks in the range, with 10,308-foot-high Mount Sheridan being the highest.

Riddle Lake

This small lake is located about three miles south of the West Thumb bay of Yellowstone Lake. Rudolph Hering (see Hering Lake) of the Hayden Survey named Riddle Lake in 1872. Frank Bradley of the Survey wrote:

"Lake Riddle" is a fugitive name, which has been located at several places, but nowhere permanently. It is supposed to have been used originally to designate the mythical lake, among the mountains, whence, according to the hunters, water flowed to both oceans. I have agreed to Mr. Hering's proposal to attach the name to the lake, which is directly upon the [Continental] divide at a point where the waters of the two oceans start so nearly together, and thus to solve the insolvable "riddle" of the "two-ocean water" (in Hayden, Sixth Annual Report, p. 250).

This "insolvable riddle" of the "mythical lake among the mountains" where water flowed to both oceans probably originated from (or at least was fueled by) "Lake Biddle," which appeared on the Lewis and Clark map of 1806 (named after their editor, Nicholas Biddle). The lake then appeared on the Samuel Lewis version of the map in 1814 as "Lake Riddle." Riddle Lake is not "directly on the divide"; it drains to the Atlantic Ocean by way of its outlet, Solution Creek, which flows to Yellowstone Lake. Thus, the name was the result of a mapping error combined with fur-trapper stories of two-ocean water.

Shoshone Lake

Shoshone Lake, the park's second largest lake, is located at the head of the Lewis River southwest of West Thumb. It is possible that fur trapper Jim Bridger visited this lake in 1833, and fellow trapper Osborne Russell certainly reached the lake in 1839. According to James Gemmell, he and Bridger visited the lake in 1846 (in Wheeler, "*The Late James Gemmell*," pp. 131-136). Gemmell referred to it then as "Snake Lake," a name apparently used by the hunters.

Fr. Pierre-Jean DeSmet's 1851 map showed a "DeSmet's L." in the approximate position of present-day Shoshone Lake. In 1863, prospector Walter DeLacy visited the lake and named it "DeLacy's Lake." The lake was also called "Madison Lake" because it was erroneously thought to be the head of the Madison River. Cornelius Hedges of the 1870 Washburn Expedition named the lake after the party's leader, Gen. H.D. Washburn. By 1872, Shoshone Lake had already borne four or five names when Frank Bradley of the second Hayden Survey added a sixth. Bradley wrote: "Upon crossing the divide to the larger lake, we found it to belong to the Snake River drainage, and therefore called it Shoshone Lake, adopting the Indian name of the Snake [River]" (American Journal of Science and Arts, September 1873, p. 201). Bradley's name thus returned in spirit to Gemmell's and the fur trappers' name "Snake Lake."

Park Superintendent P.W. Norris thought that the name Shoshone Lake was "a fitting record of the name of the Indians who frequented it" (Fifth Annual Report, p. 44). The Shoshones lived mainly to the west and south of present-day Yellowstone National Park, but there is evidence that they occasionally entered the area and may have visited the lake each summer. Their arrowheads and other artifacts have been found in various places around the park.

The meaning of "Shoshone" has long been debated. Some authorities believe that the word represented an uncomplimentary Sioux expression given to the tribe by their Crow neighbors. David Shaul, a University of Arizona linguist, believes that the word literally translates as "those who camp together in wickiups" or "grass house people."

Shoshone Lake is 205 feet at its maximum depth, has an area of 8,050 acres, and contains lake trout, brown trout, and Utah chubs. Originally, Shoshone Lake was barren of fish owing to waterfalls on the Lewis River. The two types of trout were planted beginning in 1890, and the Utah chub was apparently introduced by bait fishermen. This large lake is the source of the Lewis River, which flows to the Pacific Ocean via the Snake River system. The U.S. Fish and Wildlife Service believes that Shoshone Lake may be the largest lake in the lower 48 states that cannot be reached by road. No motorboats are allowed on the lake.

Shoshone Point

This point on the Grand Loop Road is located halfway between West Thumb and Old Faithful. It was named in 1891 because Shoshone Lake could be seen from here. In that year, Hiram M. Chittenden began constructing the first road between Old Faithful and West Thumb, and he probably named the point himself.

Shoshone Point was the scene of a stagecoach holdup in 1914. One bandit, armed and masked, stopped the first coaches of a long line of vehicles and robbed the 82 passengers in 15 coaches of $915.35 and about $130 in jewelry. Edward Trafton was convicted of the robbery and sentenced to five years in federal prison at Leavenworth, Kansas.

Snake River

The Snake River is a major tributary of the Columbia River and has its headwaters just inside Yellowstone on the Two Ocean Plateau. Various stretches of this important river have had at least 15 different names. The name, which comes from the Snake (Shoshone) Indians, was applied to the river as early as 1812, making it one of the oldest place names in the park. Shoshone Indians referred to some parts of the stream as "Yampa-pah," meaning "stream where the Yampa grows" (yampa is a food plant) and later as "Po-og-way" meaning "road river" (a reference to the Oregon Trail, which followed sections of the river) or, less often, "sagebrush river."

In 1872, the second Hayden Survey to Yellowstone gave the name "Barlow's Fork" (of the Snake) to the part of the river above the mouth of Harebell Creek, honoring J.W. Barlow who had explored that area in 1871. The group thought that Harebell Creek was the Snake River's main channel, an interpretation of the stream that was changed by the Hague surveys during the 1880s. Frank Bradley of the 1872 survey gave the name "Lewis Fork" (of the Snake) to the present-day Lewis River. The Snake name comes from sign language—a serpentine movement of the hand with the index finger extended—that referred to the weaving of baskets or grass lodges of the Snake or Shoshone Indians.

The source of the Snake River was debated for a long time. The problem was to find the longest branch in the Two Ocean Plateau, which is thoroughly crisscrossed with streams. Current maps show the head of the Snake to be about 3 miles north of Phelps Pass, at a point on the Continental Divide inside Yellowstone National Park. In 1926, John G. White showed a photo in his hand-typed book Souvenir of Wyoming of the "true source of the Snake," writing that "it is near the Continental Divide upon two ocean plateau. A number of springs gush forth upon the hillside. Uniting, they form a small stream, which, at an altitude of two miles above sea level, begins its arduous journey…to the Pacific" (p. 309). The Snake River is the nation's fourth largest river; 42 miles of it are in Yellowstone National Park.

Geological Overview of the Grant Village & West Thumb Areas

West Thumb Geyser Basin

The West Thumb Geyser Basin, including Potts Basin to the north, is unique in that it is the largest geyser basin on the shores of Yellowstone Lake. The heat source of the thermal features in this location is thought to be relatively close to the surface, only 10,000 feet down! The West Thumb of Yellowstone Lake was formed by a large volcanic explosion that occurred approximately 150,000 years ago (125,000-200,000). The resulting collapsed volcano, called a caldera ("boiling pot" or caldron), later filled with water forming an extension of Yellowstone Lake. The West Thumb is about the same size as another famous volcanic caldera, Crater Lake in Oregon, but much smaller than the great Yellowstone caldera which formed 600,000 years ago. It is interesting to note that West Thumb is a caldera within a caldera.

Ring fractures formed as the magma chamber bulged up under the surface of the earth and subsequently cracked, releasing the enclosed magma. This created the source of heat for the West Thumb Geyser Basin today.

West Thumb Thermal Features

The thermal features at West Thumb are found not only on the lake shore, but extend under the surface of the lake as well. Several underwater geysers were discovered in the early 1990s and can be seen as slick spots or slight bulges in the summer. During the winter, the underwater thermal features are visible as melt holes in the icy surface of the lake. The ice averages about three feet thick during the winter.

Historic Highlights of the West Thumb & Grant Village Areas

West Thumb Ranger Station

Built in 1925, with the open breezeway enclosed

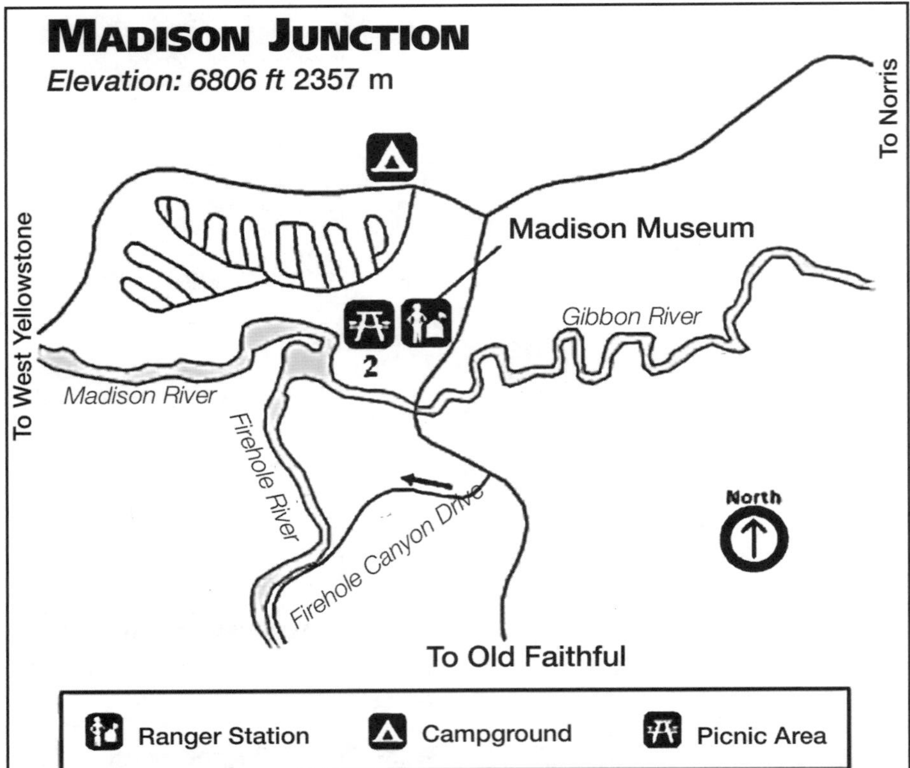

in 1966, the West Thumb Ranger Station is an excellent example of historic architecture associated with ranger stations in Yellowstone.

Archeological Resources

The shoreline of West Thumb is the location of several Native American hearth sites providing evidence that native peoples once used this area as a travel route, camping ground, and food-gathering area.

Natural Highlights of the Madison Area

Gibbon Falls

This 84-foot (26-meter) waterfall tumbles over remnants of the Yellowstone Caldera rim. The rock wall on the opposite side of the road from the waterfall is the inner rim of the caldera.

NPS photo

Artist Paint Pots

Artist Paint Pots is a small but lovely thermal area just south of Norris Junction. A one-mile round trip trail takes visitors to colorful hot springs, two large mudpots, and through a section of forest burned in 1988. Adjacent to this area are three other off-trail, backcountry thermal areas: Sylvan Springs, Gibbon Hill Geyser Basin, and Geyser Creek Thermal area. These areas are fragile, dangerous, and difficult to get to; travel without knowledgeable personnel is discouraged.

Firehole River

The Firehole River starts south of Old Faithful, runs through the thermal areas northward to join the Gibbon and form the Madison River. The Firehole is world famous among anglers for its pristine beauty and healthy brown, brook, and rainbow trout.

Firehole Canyon Drive and Firehole Falls

Firehole Canyon Drive, a side road, follows the Firehole River upstream from Madison Junction to just above Firehole Falls. The drive takes sightseers past 800-foot thick lava flows. Firehole Falls is a 40-foot waterfall. An unstaffed swimming area here is very popular in the warmest of the summer season. Cliff diving is illegal.

Monument Geyser Basin

This small, nearly dormant basin lies at the top of a very steep one-mile trail. Thermos-bottle shaped geyser cones are remnants of a much more active time.

Madison River

The Madison River is formed at the junction of the Gibbon and Firehole rivers, hence Madison Junction. The Madison joins the Jefferson and the Gallatin rivers at Three Forks, Montana, to form the Missouri River. The Madison is a blue-ribbon fly fishing stream with healthy stocks of brown and rainbow trout and mountain whitefish.

Terrace Springs

The small thermal area just north of Madison Junction. This area provides the visitor with a short boardwalk tour of hot springs.

National Park Mountain

The mountain is actually part of the lava flows that encircle the Madison Junction area. Near this site, in 1870, the Washburn-Langford-Doane Expedition is said to have camped and discussed the future of the region they were exploring. Legend has it that this was where the idea of the national park was discussed. It should be noted that there is no evidence of the campfire conversation ever taking place, and there is certainly no evidence to show that the idea of a national park was discussed.

Natural Highlights of the Lake, Bridge Bay and Fishing Bridge Areas

Yellowstone Lake

With a surface area of 136 square miles, Yellowstone Lake is the largest lake at high elevation (i.e., more than 7,000 ft.) in North America. It is a natural lake, situated at 7,733 ft. above sea level. It is roughly 20 miles long and 14 miles wide with 110 miles of shoreline. It is frozen nearly half the year. It freezes in late December or early January and thaws in late May or early June.

Recent research by Dr. Val Klump of the Center for Great Lakes Research and the University of Wisconsin has revolutionized the way we look at Yellowstone Lake. Figuratively, if one could pour all the water out of Yellowstone Lake, what would be found on the bottom is similar to what is found on land in Yellowstone; geysers, hot springs, and deep canyons. With a small submersible robot submarine, the researchers found a canyon just east of Stevenson Island which was 390 ft. deep. Prior to this finding, the deepest spot in the lake was thought to be 320 ft. at West Thumb. Underwater geysers, hot springs, and fumaroles were found at West Thumb and Mary and Sedge bays. The hottest spot in the lake was found at Mary Bay where the temperature was recorded at 252° F (122° C). Hollow pipes, or chimneys of silica, several feet in height, were found rising up from the lake bottom at Mary Bay. It is thought that these are the old plumbing systems of now dormant geysers. Rock spires up to 20-feet tall were found underwater near Bridge Bay. Samples of this rock are being analyzed, though it is believed that these features are probably related to underwater thermal activity.

This group of researchers also found that the conditions in Yellowstone Lake are similar to those that occur near the famous hydrothermal vents on the Pacific Ocean's mid- ocean ridge. Nutrient- and mineral-rich submarine fountains support incredible plant and animal communities, including bacterial mats, sponges, and earthworms.

Yellowstone River

The Yellowstone River is the last major undammed river in the lower 48 states, flowing 671 miles from its source southeast of Yellowstone into the Missouri River and then, eventually, into the Atlantic Ocean. It begins in the Absaroka Mountain Range on Yount Peak. The river enters the park and meanders through the Thorofare region into Yellowstone Lake. It leaves the lake at Fishing Bridge and flows north over LeHardy Rapids and through Hayden Valley. After this peaceful stretch, it crashes over the Upper and Lower falls of the Grand Canyon. It then flows generally northwest, meeting it's largest tributary, the Lamar River, at Tower Junction. It continues through the Black Canyon and leaves the park near Gardiner, Montana. The Yellowstone River continues north and east through the state of Montana and joins the Missouri River near the eastern boundary line of the state. The Missouri River eventually joins the Mississippi River, which flows into the Atlantic Ocean at the Gulf of Mexico.

In addition to the Yellowstone River, many of the spawning streams in the Lake/Fishing Bridge/Bridge Bay area provide critical food sources for grizzly bears in the spring time. Therefore, ecologically speaking, these river and streams are a primary resource in the district. The LeHardy Rapids are a cascade on the Yellowstone River, three miles north of Fishing Bridge. Geomorphologically, it is thought that this is the actual spot where the lake ends and the river continues it's northward flow. In the spring, many cutthroat trout may be seen here, resting in the shallow pools before expending bursts of energy to leap up the rapids on the their way to spawn under Fishing Bridge.

The rapids were named for Paul LeHardy, a civilian topographer with the Jones Expedition in 1873. Jones and a partner started off on a raft with the intent of surveying the river, planning to meet the rest of their party at the Lower Falls. Upon hitting the rapids, the raft capsized, and many of the supplies were lost, including guns, bedding, and food. LeHardy and his partner saved what they could and continued their journey to the falls on foot.

The rapids became a popular visitor attraction when a boardwalk was built in 1984 providing access to the area. Due to increased visitation, a group of harlequin ducks, which once frequented this area in spring, have not been seen for several years. The boardwalk has consequently been closed in early spring to protect this sensitive habitat, but the harlequins have not returned.

Mud Volcano/Sulphur Caldron

When the Washburn Expedition explored the area in 1870, Nathaniel Langford described Mud Volcano as "greatest marvel we have yet met with." Although the Mud Volcano can no longer be heard from a mile away nor does it throw mud from it's massive crater, the area is still eerily intriguing.

The short loop from the parking lot past the Dragon's Mouth and the Mud Volcano is handicapped accessible. The half-mile upper loop trail via Sour Lake and the Black Dragon's Caldron is relatively steep. Two of the most popular features in the Mud Volcano front country are the Dragon's Mouth and the Black Dragon's Caldron. The rhythmic belching of steam and the flashing tongue of water give the Dragon's Mouth Spring it's name, though its activity has decreased notably since December 1994. The Black Dragon's Caldron exploded onto the landscape in 1948, blowing trees out by their roots and covering the surrounding forest with mud. The large roil in one end of the Caldron gives one the sense that the Black Dragon itself might rear it's head at any time.

In January 1995, a new feature on the south bank of Mud Geyser became extremely active. It covers an area of 20 by 8 feet and is comprised of fumaroles, small pools, and frying-pan type features. Much of the hillside to the south and

Fishing Bridge, Lake Village and Bridge Bay

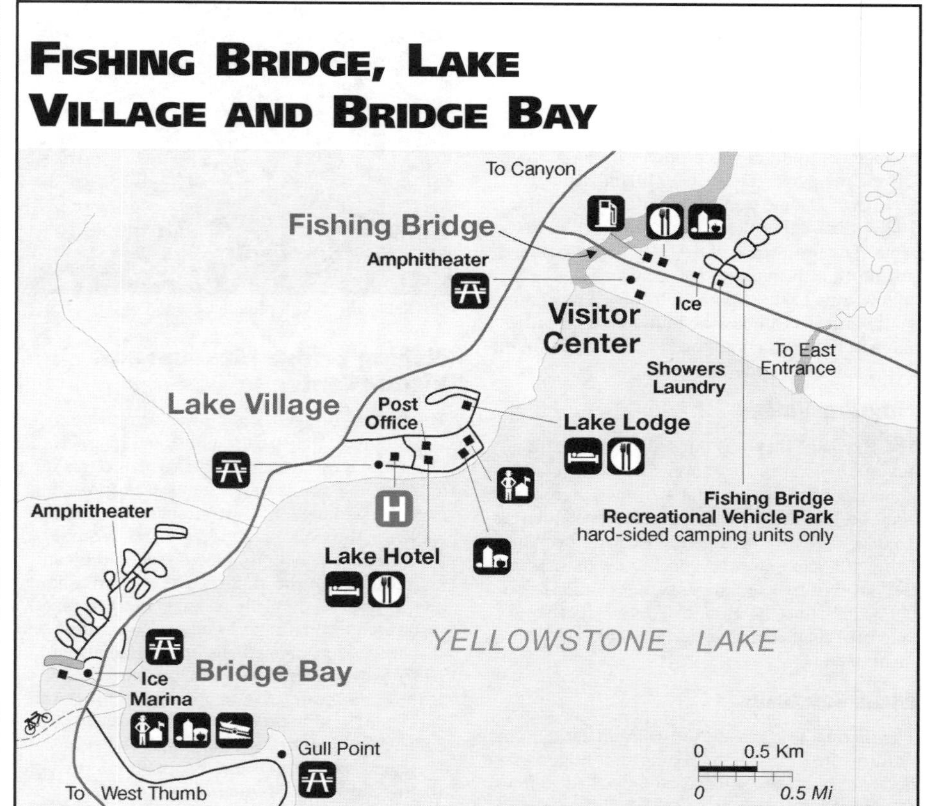

southwest of Mud Geyser is steaming and hissing with a few mudpots intermixed. This increase in activity precipitated a great deal of visitor interest and subsequent illegal entry into the area.

The most dramatic features of the Mud Volcano area however, are not open to the public. The huge seething mud pot known as the "Gumper" is located off-boardwalk behind Sour Lake. The more recent features just south of the Gumper are some of the hottest and most active in the area. Ranger-guided walks are offered to provide visitors an opportunity to view this interesting place.

Farther in the backcountry behind Mud Volcano, several features are being tested for the existence of thermophilic microbes, which may offer insights into origin of life theories as well as having medical/environmental applications.

The Sulphur Caldron area can be viewed from a staging area just north of Mud Volcano. The Sulphur Caldron is among the most acidic springs in the park with a pH of 1.3. Its yellow, turbulent splashing waters bring to mind images of Shakespeare's soothsayers. Other features which can be viewed from this overlook are Turbulent Pool (which is no longer "turbulent") and the crater of a large, active mudpot.

For more specific information on the features of the Mud Volcano/Sulphur Caldron area, consult the annual reports that are available in the Ranger Naturalist Office adjacent to the Fishing Bridge Visitor Center.

Hayden and Pelican Valleys

The Hayden Valley is located six miles north of Fishing Bridge Junction. The Pelican Valley is situated three miles east of Fishing Bridge. These two vast valleys comprise some of the best habitat in the lower 48 states for grizzly bears, bison, elk, and other wildlife species.

Natural Bridge

Located just south of Bridge Bay Campground, it is an easy one-mile walk to the Natural Bridge. There is also a bicycle trail leading to the bridge. The Natural Bridge was formed by erosion of this rhyolite outcrop by Bridge Creek. The top of the bridge is approximately 51 ft. above the creek. A short switchback trail leads to the top, though travel across the bridge is now prohibited to protect this feature.

Geological Overview of the Lake, Bridge Bay & Fishing Bridge Areas

Yellowstone Lake

Geologists indicate that large volcanic eruptions have occurred in Yellowstone on an approximate interval of 600,000 years. The most recent of these (600,000 years ago) erupted from two large vents, one near Old Faithful, the Mallard Lake Dome, and one just north of Fishing Bridge, the Sour Creek Dome. Ash from this huge explosion, 1,000 times the size of Mt. St. Helens, has been found all across the continent. The magma chamber then collapsed, forming a large caldera filled partially by subsequent lava flows. Part of this caldera is the 136-square mile basin of Yellowstone Lake. The original lake was 200 ft. higher than the present-day lake, extending northward across Hayden Valley to the base of Mt. Washburn.

It is thought that Yellowstone Lake originally drained south into the Pacific Ocean via the Snake River. The lake currently drains north from its only outlet, the Yellowstone River, at Fishing Bridge. The elevation of the lake's north end does not drop substantially until LeHardy Rapids.

Therefore, this spot is considered the actual northern boundary of Yellowstone Lake.

In the last decade, geological research has determined that the two volcanic vents, now known as "resurgent domes", are rising again. From year to year, they either rise or fall, with an average net uplift of about one inch per year. During the period between 1923 and 1985, the Sour Creek Dome was rising. In the years since 1986, it has either declined or remained the same. The resurgence of the Sour Creek dome, just north of Fishing Bridge is causing Yellowstone Lake to "tilt" southward. Larger sandy beaches can now be found on the north shore of the lake, and flooded areas can be found in the southern arms.

Hayden Valley

The Hayden Valley was once filled by an arm of Yellowstone Lake. Therefore, it contains fine-grained lake sediments that are now covered with glacial till left from the most recent glacial retreat 13,000 years ago. Because the glacial till contains many different grain sizes, including clay and a thin layer of lake sediments, water cannot percolate readily into the ground. This is why the Hayden Valley is marshy and has little encroachment of trees.

Mud Volcano

The thermal features at Mud Volcano and Sulphur Caldron are primarily mud pots and fumaroles because the area is situated on a perched water system with little water available. Fumaroles or "steam vents" occur when the ground water boils away faster than it can be recharged. Also, the vapors are rich in sulfuric acid that leaches the rock, breaking it down into clay. Because no water washes away the acid or leached rock, it remains as sticky clay to form a mud pot. Hydrogen sulfide gas is present deep in the earth at Mud Volcano. As this gas combines with water and the sulfur is metabolized by cyanobacteria, a solution of sulfuric acid is formed that dissolves the surface soils to create pools and cones of clay and mud. Along with hydrogen sulfide, steam, carbon dioxide, and other gases explode through the layers of mud.

A series of shallow earthquakes associated with the volcanic activity in Yellowstone struck this area in 1978. Soil temperatures increased to nearly 200° F (93° C). The slope between Sizzling Basin and Mud Geyser, once covered with green grass and trees, became a barren landscape of fallen trees known as "the cooking hillside."

Historic Highlights of the Lake, Bridge Bay, and Fishing Bridge Areas

Fishing Bridge

The original bridge was built in 1902. It was a rough-hewn corduroy log bridge with a slightly different alignment than the current bridge. The existing bridge was built in 1937. The Fishing Bridge was historically a tremendously popular place to fish. Angling from the bridge was quite good, due to the fact that it was a major spawning area for cutthroat trout. However, because of the decline of the cutthroat population (in part, a result of this practice), the bridge was closed to fishing in 1973. Since that time, it has become a popular place to observe fish.

Hayden Valley. NPS photo

Fishing Bridge Museum and Visitor Center

The Fishing Bridge Museum was completed in 1931. Built of native rock and stone, it appears to rise out of a rock outcrop. The structure was built to reflect the beauty of nature itself. Approaching from the parking lot, it was designed so that one could see through the building to Yellowstone Lake, hence the notion of focussing on the natural resource that the building was created to interpret. It would eventually become a prototype of rustic architecture in parks all over the nation and was declared a National Historic Landmark in 1987. When automobiles replaced stagecoaches as the main means of transportation through the park, people were no longer accompanied by a guide. The Museum was built as a "Trailside Museum," allowing visitors to obtain information about Yellowstone on their own.

Lake Village

The buildings comprising historic Lake Village are figuratively, and literally in some cases, landmarks in the history of the Yellowstone story.

NPS photo

The Lake Yellowstone Hotel

Built on a site long known as a meeting place for Indians, trappers, and mountain men, the Lake Yellowstone Hotel was ready to serve guests in 1891. At that time, it was not particularly distinctive, resembling any other railroad hotel financed by the Northern Pacific Railroad.

In 1903, the architect of the Old Faithful Inn, Robert Reamer, masterminded the renovation of the Hotel, designing the ionic columns, extending the roof in three places, and adding the 15 false balconies, which prompted it to be known for several years as the "Lake Colonial Hotel." A number of further changes by 1929, including the addition of the dining room, porte-cochere (portico), and sunroom as well as the refurbishing of the interior created the gracious landmark we see today.

By the 1970s, the Hotel had fallen into serious disrepair. In 1981, the National Park Service and the park concessioner, TW Recreational Services, embarked upon a ten-year project to restore the Lake Hotel in appearance to its days of glory in the 1920s. The work was finished for the celebration of the hotel's centennial in 1991. The Hotel was placed on the National Register of Historic Places that year.

The hotel is currently operated by AmFac Parks & Resorts. Information regarding room availability and reservation procedures is available through their website.

The Lake Ranger Station

After a decade of military administration in Yellowstone, Congress created the National Park Service in 1916. Ranger stations began to replace soldier stations throughout the park. The Lake Ranger Station was completed in 1923. The first Director of the National Park Service, Steven Mather, suggested that the station should blend in with its natural and cultural environment. A local woodsman used pioneer building techniques to give the station its "trapper cabin" style. With park architects, Superintendent Horace Albright designed a large octagonal "community room" with a central stone fireplace. This rustic hall served an informational function by day, and, in the evening, it became the scene of a folksy gathering around a log fire.

NPS photo

The Lake Lodge

The advent of the auto in the park in 1915 created a great influx of visitors. The need arose for an intermediate style of lodging between the luxury of the Lake Hotel and the rustic accommodations of the tent camps. In 1926, the Lake Lodge (also a Robert Reamer design) was completed, one of four lodges in the park. The park was no longer primarily accessible to only affluent "dudes" or hearty "sagebrushers." Democracy had come to Yellowstone.

The lodge is currently operated by AmFac Parks & Resorts. Information regarding room availability and reservation procedures is available throughout their website.

Archeological Research

For compliance purposes associated with the reconstruction of the East Entrance Road, recent archeological research has been conducted by the Mid-West Archeological Center of the National Park Service. Preliminary studies indicate that indigenous people inhabited the Lake area 9,600 years before present. Numerous projectile points have been found in addition to a hearth (cooking) structure, middens, and a bison harvest site.

Winter Activities

Skiing in Yellowstone

Most of Yellowstone is backcountry and managed as wilderness; many miles of trails are available for skiing. Track is set only on a few trails. All unplowed roads and trails are open to cross country skiing and showshoeing. When skiing on unplowed roadways used by snowmobiles, keep to the right to avoid accidents.

There are dangers inherent in wilderness: unpredictable wildlife, changing weather conditions, remote thermal areas, deep snow, open streams, and rugged mountains with extreme avalanche danger. When you choose to explore Yellowstone, you experience the land on its own terms; there is no guarantee of your safety. Be prepared for any situation. Carefully read all backcountry guidelines and regulations, and know the limit of your ability.

Most trails are marked with orange metal markers attached to trees. Few streams have bridges. Parties venturing into the backcountry should carry a USGS topographic map and a compass and know how to use them. Even on a well-marked trail, it is easy to get lost in a "white-out" or blizzard. Only skiers thoroughly familiar with the area should attempt off-trail travel. When planning your trip, get specific information on conditions from rangers at a ranger station or visitor center.

Park elevations with adequate skiable snow range from 7,000 to 10,000 feet (2133 - 3048 meters.) Skiers and snowshoers who live at lower elevations should take a short day or overnight trip to test their capabilities before attempting longer outings.

A Backcountry Use Permit is required for all overnight ski trips. Contact a park ranger at a ranger station or visitor center before you begin a ski trip— whether for a few hours or several days. Trip planning should include allowances for limited daylight, snow conditions, temperature extremes, and the number of people in the group, their experience and physical condition. Overnight ski and snowshoe trips during December and January are difficult due to short days, extreme temperatures, and soft snow. Learn as much as you can about winter survival. Talk with park rangers before you leave on any trip.

Choose skis and boots made for touring or mountaineering. Narrow racing skis won't provide enough surface area to break trail.

Many of Yellowstone's roads are groomed and open to snowmobiles though this may change soon. Personal snowmobiles may be brought into the park or they may be rented in several different locations. Businesses with permits to rent snowmobiles or conduct guided snowmobile tours can be found on our Permitted Winter Businesses page. the park's lodging concessioner, Amfac Parks & Resorts, also provides snowmobile tours & rentals along with various other winter services and activities.

Snowmobile Regulations & other Safety Tips

Snowmobile operators must have a valid state motor vehicle driver's license in their possession. Persons possessing a learners permit may operate a snowmobile when supervised one-to-one within line of sight (but no more than 100 yards) by a licensed person 21 years old or older.

Operate snowmobiles as you would an automobile. Use hand signals when turning or stopping. Allow enough distance in between snowmobiles when traveling. Passing is allowed only when safe. If you turn around, you must do so within the road width.

Maximum speed limit is 45 mph (72 kph) or less where posted or as conditions warrant. Speed is checked by radar. Obey all speed limit signs and stop signs.

Cross Country skiing is one of the more "personal" ways to enjoy the park in the winter. NPS photo

Drive on the right side of the road and in single file. When stopping, pull to the far right and park in single file. Stay to the right even if the roads are rough.

Snowmobiles may be driven on designated roads only. Sidehilling, berm-riding, or any off-road travel is prohibited and carries a fine of up to $5000. Report accidents to a ranger.

Operating a snowmobile while intoxicated is illegal. Possession of open alcoholic beverage containers, including botabags, is illegal.

Snowmobiles must be registered according to applicable state law. Muffler, lights, and brakes must be in good working condition.

Snowmobile exhaust and muffler systems must be in good working order. The maximum noise allowed is 78 decibels when measured during full acceleration at a distance of 50 feet. Most stock exhaust systems meet this standard; "after-market" ("piped") exhaust systems often do not. Snowmobiles exceeding the decibel standard will be denied entry into the park.

The future of snowmobiles in the park is under discussion at this time. NPS photo

Thermal basins, viewpoints, and walkways are snowpacked and icy during winter; fog reduces visibility. When walking, stay on boardwalks or maintained trails; walk carefully. Watch your children. Your hand or voice may be too far away if your child leaves your side.

Wild animals have the right of way. Wildlife are dangerous and unpredictable. Winter is a time of great stress. When you force an animal to move, it uses energy which is vital to its survival. Approaching, chasing, molesting, or feeding animals is prohibited.

If bison or other wildlife are on the road, stop at least 25 yards away and/or pull your machine as far as possible to the opposite side of the road; give them a chance to get off the road. If they run toward you, and you can confidently turn around, do so and move to a safe place to reassess the situation. If they walk or run toward you, and you cannot turn around, get off your machine and stand to the side of it, keeping the machine between you and the animal(s). If they are standing calmly, inch toward them and access their behavior. If they remain calm, pass on the opposite side of the road at a moderate speed. Do not make sudden or erratic movements; use groomed pullouts where possible. If the animal(s) appear agitated, do not attempt to pass as any advance may cause the animal(s) to charge. Do not chase animals or cause them to stampede. There is no guarantee of your safety.

Winter Services

Snowmobile Fuel is available at Old Faithful, Canyon, Fishing Bridge, and Mammoth Hot Springs.

Lodging is available at the Old Faithful Snow Lodge and Mammoth Hot Springs Hotel. Reservations are strongly recommended; call 307-344-7311.

Restaurants are available at the Old Faithful

Snowcoaches are a great way to enjoy Yellowstone in the winter. NPS photo

Snow Lodge and Mammoth Hot Springs Hotel Dining Room. Dinner reservations are required; call 307-344-7901.

Fast Food is available at the Old Faithful Snow Lodge - Geyser Grill and at the Canyon and Madison warming huts.

Lunch Counter & Groceries are available at Hamilton's Store at Mammoth Hot Springs.

Restrooms: Heated restroom facilities are located at Mammoth Hot Springs campground, Mammoth Visitor Center, Old Faithful Visitor Center, Madison warming hut, and Canyon warming hut. Vault toilets are found at other locations throughout the park.

Camping: The only campground open in winter is located at Mammoth Hot Springs. A backcountry permit is required for camping at any other location, including the winter camping area at Old Faithful. Permits may be obtained at ranger stations open in winter.

Clinics: Mammoth Clinic open weekdays 8:30 AM - 1 PM and 2-5 PM; closed Wednesday afternoons; call 307-344-7965. Old Faithful Clinic open every other Friday starting December 29th.

Snowcoach Tours: Tours depart from Mammoth Hot Springs, Old Faithful Snow Lodge, West Yellowstone, and Flagg Ranch outside the South Entrance.

Snowmobile Rentals & Tours: Depart from Mammoth Hot Springs Hotel, Old Faithful Snow Lodge, and nearby communities.

Ski and Snowshoe Rentals and Tours: Bear Den Ski Shops at Mammoth Hot Springs Hotel and Old Faithful Snow Lodge.

Equipment and Clothing

Choose skis and boots made for touring or mountaineering. Narrow racing skis won't provide enough surface area to break trail. Low shoes won't give enough ankle support. Before you rent or borrow equipment, check for fit and suitability for wilderness use. Equipment that fits both you and park conditions can make or break your trip.

Winter temperatures are severe in Yellowstone, but you can be comfortable and confident if you are properly dressed. Prepare for changing conditions by wearing clothes in several adjustable layers. It is as important to prevent overheating as it is to prevent chilling.

Be sure your clothing includes a windproof hooded outer layer with wool or other insulated garments underneath. Wool or synthetic trousers and long underwear will help to keep your legs warm and dry in deep snow. Wind or rain-pants are lightweight and provide extra warmth on windy days. Avoid cotton jeans and sweatshirts. Thick wool socks and gaiters over boots help to keep your feet warm and dry. Wear gloves or wool mittens with shells that breathe to allow moisture to escape from sweaty hands.

Since you lose more heat through your head than any other part of your body, wear a face mask-style stocking cap or parka hood when you need maximum protection. Dark sunglasses are a must for sunny days. High altitude sunlight reflected from snow is much more intense than at lower elevations; snow-blindness may occur if sunglasses are not worn. Apply sunscreen lotion to exposed skin to avoid sunburn.

Backcountry Rules

To preserve Yellowstone's backcountry and enhance your wilderness experience, the National Park Service has established the following regulations and guidelines. **Contact a park ranger before you begin a day hike or overnight trip.**

Permits

Yellowstone National Park has a designated backcountry campsite system; permits are required for all overnight trips. Permits must be obtained at a ranger station no more than 48 hours before your camping date. Advance reservations for some backcountry campsites may be made in writing or in person for a $15 fee. To obtain the necessary forms, write the Backcountry Office, P.O. Box 168, YNP, WY 82190 or check at a ranger station.

You must also have a permit for fishing, boats, and float tubes.

Limits

Each designated campsite has a maximum limit for the number of people and stock allowed per night. The maximum stay per campsite varies from I to 3 nights per trip. To protect resources and visitors, some hiking and camping restrictions may apply. Firearms, pets, motorized equipment, and any type of wheeled vehicle (except wheelchairs) are prohibited in the backcountry.

Campfires

Campfires are permitted only in established fire pits. Burn only dead-and-down wood. Wood and ground fires are not allowed in some campsites. Your fire must be attended at all times and be completely extinguished before you leave.

Pack It In-Pack It Out

All refuse must be carried out of the backcountry. This includes items partly burned in fire pits (foil, tin, glass, etc).

Sanitation

Bury human waste 6 to 8 inches (15-20 cm) below the ground and a minimum of 100 feet (30 in) from water. Waste water should be disposed of at least 100 feet (30 in) from water or a campsite. Do not pollute lakes, ponds, rivers, or streams by washing yourself, clothing, or dishes in them.

Should You Drink the Water?

Intestinal infections from drinking untreated water are increasingly common. Waters may be polluted by animal and/or human wastes. When possible, carry a supply of water from a domestic source. If you drink water from lakes or streams, boil it a minimum of two minutes to reduce the chance of infection or disease.

Storms

Yellowstone's weather is unpredictable. A sunny warm day may become fiercely stormy with wind, rain, sleet, and, sometimes snow. Lightning storms are common; get off water or beaches and stay away from ridges, exposed places, and isolated trees.

Without adequate clothing and gear, an easy day hike or boat trip can turn into a battle for survival. Exposure to wind, rain, or cold can result in hypothermia. This rapid loss of body heat can cause death if not treated. Early warning signs include shivering, slurred speech, memory lapses, drowsiness, and exhaustion. Cold water is a special hazard to anglers and boaters. Get into dry clothes and drink warm fluids at the first signs of hypothermia.

Stock Use

Overnight stock (horses, mules, burros, and llamas) use is not permitted prior to July 1, due to forage conditions and/or wet trail conditions. Horses are not allowed in frontcountry campgrounds.

Stream Crossings

Fording a stream can be hazardous, especially during spring snow melt or high water. Check at local ranger stations for current trail and stream conditions.

Trails

Yellowstone has more than 800 miles (1,280 km) of trails, allowing access to all major backcountry lakes, numerous waterfalls, mountain peaks, and thermal areas. Trails are minimally marked in keeping with the wilderness nature of the backcountry. Cross country travel is difficult because of the terrain and the amount of downed trees.

Backcountry hikers should carry a map and compass, and know how to use both.

Day Hiking in Yellowstone

Yellowstone National Park, encompassing 2.2 million acres, is one of America's premier wilderness areas. Most of the park is backcountry and managed as wilderness. Over 1,100 miles (1770 km) of trails are available for hiking. However, there are dangers inherent in wilderness: unpredictable wildlife, changing weather conditions, remote thermal areas, cold water lakes, turbulent streams, and rugged mountains with loose, "rotten" rock. Visiting wilderness means experiencing the land on its terms. If you choose to explore and enjoy the natural wonders of Yellowstone, there is no guarantee of your safety. Be prepared for any situation. Carefully read all backcountry guidelines and regulations.

There are numerous trails suitable for day hiking. Begin your hike by stopping at a ranger station or visitor center for information. Trail conditions may change suddenly and unexpectedly. Bear activity, rain or snow storms, high water, and fires may temporarily close trails. At a minimum, carry water, a raincoat or poncho, a warm hat, insect repellent, sunscreen, and a first aid kit. It is recommended that you hike with another person. No permit is required for day hiking.

Electric Peak, Snow-covered Gallatin Mountain Range. NPS Photo

Day Hikes Near Mammoth

Begin your hike by stopping at a ranger station or visitor center for information. Trail conditions may change suddenly and unexpectedly. Bear activity, rain or snow storms, high water, and fires may temporarily close trails.

Beaver Ponds Loop Trail
The trail follows the creek up Clematis Gulch, climbing 350 feet through Douglas-fir trees. The beaver ponds are reached after hiking 2.5 miles through open meadows of sagebrush and stands of aspen. Elk, mule deer, pronghorn, moose, beaver dams and lodges, and the occasional beaver and black bear may be sighted in the area. There are spectacular views as you wind your way back to Mammoth.
Trailhead: Clematis Gulch between Liberty Cap and the stone house (Judge's house)
Distance: 5 mile (8 km) loop
Level of Difficulty: Moderate

Bunsen Peak Trail
This gradual 1,300 foot climb to the summit of Bunsen Peak provides a panoramic view of the Blacktail Plateau, Swan Lake Flats, Gallatin Mountain Range, and the Yellowstone River Valley. Return by the same route or take the trail down the back side to Osprey Falls trailhead (about 2 miles) and return via the Old Bunsen Peak Road Trail. Or visit Osprey Falls (an additional 2.8 miles, see below). Please plan for the additional mileage.
Trailhead: Entrance of the Old Bunsen Peak Road, five miles south of Mammoth toward Norris
Distance: 10 miles (16.1 km) roundtrip depending on side trips, 2 miles to the summit.
Level of Difficulty: Moderate

Osprey Falls Trail
The trail follows the old roadbed for 2.5 miles through grassland and burnt forest. The Osprey Falls trail veers off the old road and follows the rim of Sheepeater Canyon before descending in a series of switchbacks to the bottom of Sheepeater Canyon. The Gardner River plunges over a 150-foot drop, forming Osprey Falls. Vertical cliffs rise 500 feet above you, making it one of the deepest canyons in Yellowstone.
Trailhead: 5 miles south of Mammoth on the Old Bunsen Peak Road Trail
Distance: 8 miles (12.9 km) roundtrip
Level of Difficulty: Difficult

Lava Creek Trail
This trail follows Lava Creek downstream past Undine Falls (50 feet), descending gradually. Lava Creek meets the Gardner River farther downstream. The trail crosses a foot bridge on the Gardner River, and there is one final ascent to a pullout on the North Entrance Road just north of the Mammoth Campground.
Trailhead: The bridge at Lava Creek picnic area on the Mammoth-Tower Road
Distance: 3.5 miles (5.6 km) one way; 7 miles (11.3 km) roundtrip
Level of Difficulty: Moderate

Rescue Creek Trail
This trail follows the Blacktail Deer Creek trail for the first 3/4 mile until meeting Rescue Creek trail. The trail climbs gradually through aspens and open meadows before beginning a 1,400 foot descent to the Gardner River. The trail crosses a foot bridge over the river and ends one mile south of the North Entrance Station.
Trailhead: Blacktail Trailhead on the Mammoth-Tower Road, seven miles east of Mammoth
Distance: 8 miles (12.9 km) on way; 16 miles (25.7 km) roundtrip
Level of Difficulty: Moderate

Sepulcher Mountain Trail
This trail follows the Beaver Ponds Trail to the Sepulcher Mountain Trail junction. This trail rises 3,400 feet through pine trees and open meadows until the 9,652 foot summit of Sepulcher is reached. To complete the loop, continue along the opposite side of the mountain through a broad open slope to the junction of the Snow Pass Trail. Continue down until you reach the junction with the Howard Eaton Trail. This will lead you west of the Mammoth Terraces and back to your original trailhead.
Trailhead: Clematis Gulch between Liberty Cap and the stone house
Distance: 11 mile (17.7 km) loop trail
Level of Difficulty: Strenuous

Wraith Falls
This short, easy hike through open sagebrush and Douglas-fir forest to the foot of Wraith Falls cascade on Lupine Creek.
Trailhead: Pullout 1/4 mile east of Lava Creek Picnic area on the Mammoth-Tower Road
Distance: 1 mile (1 km) round trip
Level of Difficulty: Easy

Blacktail Deer Creek-Yellowstone River Trail
This trail follows Blacktail Deer Creek as it descends 1,100 feet through rolling, grassy hills and Douglas-fir where it reaches the Yellowstone River. The trail continues across the Yellowstone River on a steel suspension bridge and joins the Yellowstone River Trail. The trail continues downriver, passing Knowles Falls and into arid terrain until it ends in Gardiner, Montana.
Trailhead: Blacktail Trailhead on the Mammoth-Tower Road, seven miles east of Mammoth
Distance: 12.5 miles (21 km) one way
Level of Difficulty: Moderate due to length

Day Hikes near Norris

Begin your hike by stopping at a ranger station or visitor center for information. Trail conditions may change suddenly and unexpectedly. Bear activity, rain or snow storms, high water, and fires may temporarily close trails.

Grizzly Lake
This trail passes through a twice-burned lodgepole pine stand (1976 and 1988) and through nice meadows. The lake is long, narrow, and heavily wooded. It can be difficult to access beyond the trail end of the lake. Marshiness and mosquitoes can make travel difficult early in the season. The lake is popular with anglers due to a strong population of small brook trout.
Trailhead: 1 mile (1 km) south of Beaver Lake on the Mammoth-Norris road
Distance: 4 miles (6 km) roundtrip

Level of difficulty: Moderate with some short, steep climbs and rolling terrain. A log jam crossing is required to continue past Grizzly Lake.

Solfatara Creek
The trail follows Solfatara Creek for a short distance to the junction with Ice Lake Trail, it then parallels a power line for most of the way to Whiterock Springs. It climbs a short distance up to Lake of the Woods (difficult to find as it's off trail a bit) and passes Amphitheater Springs and Lemonade Creek (don't drink it). These are small, but pretty thermal areas in the otherwise nondescript lodgepole pine forest. The trail then continues on to meet the road. There is no trail connection back to the campground except the way you came. Parking a car at both ends is desirable. This is a good place for folks who don't want to see many other hikers, but it can be under bear restrictions so check before starting out.
Trailhead: Beginning of Loop C in Norris Campground and 3/4 mile south of Beaver Lake Picnic Area on the Mammoth-Norris road
Distance: Campground to trailhead on the Mammoth-Norris road it is 13 miles (20 km) roundtrip
Level of Difficulty: Easy to moderate with one climb and descent of about 400 feet.

Ice Lake Trail (direct route)
Ice Lake is a lovely, small lake nestled in the thick lodgepole pine forest. Some of the area was heavily burned in 1988. Hikers can continue from Ice Lake to Wolf Lake, Grebe Lake, and Cascade Lake, and then on to Canyon.
Trailhead: 3.5 miles east of Norris on the Norris-Canyon road
Distance: 0.3 miles (0.5 km)
Level of Difficulty: Easy, handicapped accessible backcountry site on lake, may need assistance to reach lake due to some terrain level change

Wolf Lake Cut-off Trail
The trail follows the Gibbon River for at least 1 mile (1 km), passing Little Gibbon Falls. Dense, partially burned lodgepole pine forest is your main companion the rest of the way to Wolf Lake. Trailhead: Big pull-out about 1/4 miles east of Ice Lake Trailhead on Canyon-Norris Road. There is no trailhead sign due to lack of regular maintenance on the trail, but orange markers can be seen once hikers cross the road from the trailhead.
Distance: 6 miles (10 km) roundtrip; 1 mile (1.6 km) to junction with Wolf Lake Trail, then 2+ miles to Wolf Lake
Level of Difficulty: Moderate due to stream crossings and downfall; trail may be difficult to find at times

Cygnet Lakes Trail
This trail travels through intermittently burned lodgepole pine forest and past small marshy ephemeral ponds to the lush meadows surrounding Cygnet Lakes (small and boggy). Day use only! Trail not maintained beyond Cygnet Lakes.
Trailhead: Pullout on south side of Norris-Canyon road approximately 5.5 miles west of Canyon Junction
Distance: 8 miles (14.4 km) roundtrip
Level of Difficulty: Easy

Artist Paint Pots
This is one of the overlooked yet wonderful short hikes of Yellowstone. The trail winds across a wet meadow on boardwalk then enters a partially burned lodgepole pine forest. The thermal area within the short loop at the end of the trail contains some of the most colorful hot springs and small geysers found in the area. Two mudpots at the top of the hill allow closer access than Fountain Paint Pots. Caution for flying mud! Remind folks to stay on the trail throughout the area.
Trailhead: 4.5 miles south of Norris on the Norris-Madison road
Distance: 1 mile (1 km) roundtrip
Level of Difficulty: Easy with one steep uphill/downhill section, trail erodes easily so may be rutted after rains.

Monument Geyser Basin
This trail meanders along a gentle gradient following the Gibbon River then it turns sharply uphill and climbs 500 feet in 1/2 mile to the top

Electric Peak with Stream in Foreground Gallatin Mountain Range. NPS Photo

NPS photo

of the mountain! Footing is on eroding geyserite and rhyolite, somewhat reminiscent of ball bearings. The geyser basin is a very interesting collection of dormant cones of varying sizes. One resembles a thermos bottle! Most of the activity here has dried up; hikers looking for exciting thermal activity will be disappointed, but those looking for adventure will find it. Remind folks to stay on trail!
Trailhead: 5 miles south of Norris Junction on the Norris-Madison road, just after Gibbon River Bridge
Distance: 2 miles (3 km)
Level of Difficulty: Deceptively easy, then difficult!

Day Hikes Near Madison

Begin your hike by stopping at a ranger station or visitor center for information. Trail conditions may change suddenly and unexpectedly. Bear activity, rain or snow storms, high water, and fires may temporarily close trails.

Purple Mountain
This trail ascends through intermittent burned lodgepole pine forest and ends with a nice view of the Firehole Valley and lower Gibbon Valley; some views of the Madison Junction area are also visible. Close to Madison Campground.
Trailhead: 1/4 mile north of Madison Junction on the Madison-Norris road, limited parking
Distance: 6 miles (10 km) roundtrip
Level of Difficulty: Moderate with steady climb of 1,500 feet

Harlequin Lake
This is a gentle ascent through burned lodgepole pines to a small, marshy lake popular with mosquitoes and waterfowl (but not harlequin ducks). Nice quick hike to escape the road for a little bit.
Trailhead: 1.5 miles west of Madison Campground on the West Entrance road
Distance: 1 mile (1 km) roundtrip
Level of Difficulty: Easy

Two Ribbons Trail

This is a completely boardwalked trail that winds through burned lodgepole pine and sagebrush communities next to the Madison River. Good examples of fire recovery and regrowth as well as buffalo wallows. There are no interpretive signs or brochures other than the wayside exhibits at the trailheads.
Trailhead: Approximately 5 miles east of the West Entrance, no marked trailhead, look for wayside exhibits next to boardwalk in large pull-outs
Distance: Approximately 1.5 miles (2 km) roundtrip
Level of Difficulty: Easy, mostly accessible

Gallatin Area

There are many excellent hiking opportunities in the Gallatin area. Most of these, however, are longer and steeper than the average day hike. They include Daily Creek, the Sky Rim, Black Butte, Specimen Creek, Crescent Lake/High Lake, Sportsman Lake, Bighorn Pass and Fawn Pass. For more information, consult a Visitor Center or one of the hiking trail guides available from the Yellowstone Association.

Day Hikes Near Old Faithful

Begin your hike by stopping at a ranger station or visitor center for information. Trail conditions may change suddenly and unexpectedly. Bear activity, rain or snow storms, high water, and fires may temporarily close trails.

Geyser Hill Loop Trail
This short loop trail gives visitors a good chance of seeing a variety of geysers, from the ever-entertaining Anemone with its short intervals of 5-10 minutes to the impressive Beehive with its unpredictable eruptions reaching 100-150 feet!
Trailhead: Boardwalk in front of Old Faithful Visitor Center
Distance: 1.3 mile (1.2 km) loop
Level of Difficulty: Easy

Numerous other combination loops or one-way walks can be chosen in the Upper Geyser Basin. Features such as Castle, Grand, Riverside, and Daisy geysers along with Morning Glory Pool are easily accessed using the Old Faithful self-guiding trail map. Details on geyser prediction times may be obtained by stopping by the visitor center.

Observation Point Loop Trail
This trail gains about 200 ft. in elevation to a prominent overlook providing a great view of the Upper Geyser Basin.
Trailhead: Firehole River footbridge behind Old Faithful Geyser
Distance: 1.1 mile (1 km) loop
Level of Difficulty: Moderate

Mallard Lake Trail
This trail climbs through lodgepole pine forest (some burned areas from the 1988 fires) and along meadows and rocky slopes before terminating at Mallard Lake.
Trailhead: Old Faithful Lodge cabin area
Distance: 6.8 miles (5.3 km) roundtrip
Level of Difficulty: Moderate

Lone Star Geyser Trail
This mostly level trail follows an old service road along the Firehole River through unburned forests of lodgepole pine. The geyser, which erupts approximately every 3 hours, puts on a delightful show. This trail can be accessed by bicycle with the final approach to the geyser on foot.
Trailhead: 3.5 miles southeast of the Old Faithful area, just beyond Kepler Cascades parking area.
Distance: 5 miles (8 km) roundtrip
Level of Difficulty: Easy

Black Sand and Biscuit Basin Trails
Easily accessed by boardwalks less than a mile in length, Emerald Pool, Sunset Lake, Jewel Geyser, and Sapphire Pool are among the features found in these less visited basins. Both areas are included in the Old Faithful area trail guide.
Trailhead: 0.5 and 2 miles north of Old Faithful area, respectively
Distance: Less than 0.5 (0.5 km) miles each
Level of Difficulty: Easy

Midway Geyser Basin Trail
The boardwalk leads visitors by impressive features including Excelsior Geyser and Grand Prismatic Spring.
Trailhead: Parking area 6 miles north of Old Faithful
Distance: 0.5 mile (0.5 km) loop
Level of Difficulty: Easy

Fountain Paint Pot Trail
Yellowstone's four types of thermal features can be seen in one short walk along this loop trail: geysers, hot springs, mudpots, and fumaroles. A trail guide is available for this area, which also includes the Firehole Lake Drive area.
Trailhead: Parking area 8 miles north of Old Faithful
Distance: 0.5 mile (0.5 km) loop
Level of Difficulty: Easy

Mystic Falls Trail
This trail follows a lovely creek through a lodgepole pine forest before reaching the 70- foot falls. By following a series of switchbacks, an overlook of the Upper Geyser Basin can be reached before looping back to join the main trail.
Trailhead: Back of the Biscuit Basin boardwalk
Distance: 2.4 miles (4 km) roundtrip
Level of Difficulty: Moderate

Fairy Falls Trail
At 200 feet high, Fairy Falls is an impressive backcountry sight. It can be reached from two different trailheads. The first trailhead, 1 mile south of the Midway Geyser Basin, begins at a steel bridge across the Firehole River and follows the Fountain Freight Road hiking/biking trail for approximately 1 mile before the hiking-only trail to Fairy Falls branches off on the left. The second trailhead, 1/2 mile south of the Nez Perce picnic area on the Fountain Freight Road, follows the hiking/biking path from the northern end, 1-3/4 miles to the junction with the Fairy Falls trail.
Trailhead: 1) Steel Bridge parking area 1 mile south of the Midway Geyser Basin
2) Fountain Freight Road parking area 1 mile south of Nez Perce picnic area on the Fountain Freight Road
Distance: 5 miles (8 km) from trailhead #1; 7 miles (5.5 km) from trailhead #2
Level of Difficulty: Easy

Day Hikes near Grant Village & West Thumb

Begin your hike by stopping at a ranger station or visitor center for information. Trail conditions may change suddenly and unexpectedly. Bear activity, rain or snow storms, high water, and fires may temporarily close trails.

West Thumb Geyser Basin Trail
Stroll through a geyser basin of colorful hot springs and dormant lakeshore geysers situated on the scenic shores of Yellowstone Lake. Trails and boardwalks are handicapped accessible with assistance.
Trailhead: West Thumb Geyser Basin, 1/4 mile east of West Thumb Junction
Distance: 3/8 mile (1 km) roundtrip
Level of Difficulty: Easy; boardwalk trail with slight grade as trail descends to and climbs up from the lake shore

Yellowstone Lake Overlook Trail
Hike to a high mountain meadow for a commanding view of the West Thumb of Yellowstone Lake and the Absaroka Mountains.
Trailhead: Trailhead sign at entrance to West

Hiking a wildflower-covered hillside Rescue Creek Trail. NPS photo

Park Ranger assisting visitors Canyon Visitor Center information desk. NPS photo

Thumb Geyser Basin parking area
Distance: 2 miles (3 km) roundtrip
Level of Difficulty: Moderate; mostly level terrain with a moderately strenuous 400-foot elevation gain near the overlook.

Shoshone Lake Trail (via DeLacy Creek)
Hike along a forest's edge and through open meadows to the shores of Yellowstone's largest backcountry lake. Look for wildlife in meadows.
Trailhead: Trailhead sign at DeLacy Creek, 8.8 miles west of West Thumb Junction
Distance: 6 miles (10 km) roundtrip
Level of Difficulty: Moderate; flat trail with no steep grades

Riddle Lake Trail
Crossing the Continental Divide, hike through small mountain meadows and forests to the shores of a picturesque little lake. Look for moose in the marshy meadows and for birds near the lake. Bear Management Area—trail opens July 15.
Trailhead: Approximately 3 miles south of the Grant Village intersection, immediately south of the Continental Divide sign
Distance: 5 miles (8 km) roundtrip
Level of Difficulty: Moderate; level walking

Lewis River Channel/Shoshone Lake Loop Trail
Get a feel for Yellowstone's backcountry…hike through a forested area to the colorful waters of the Lewis River Channel. Look for eagles and osprey fishing for trout in the shallow waters. For an all-day hike, follow the channel to Shoshone Lake and return via the forested Dogshead Trail.
Trailhead: Approximately 5 miles south of Grant Village intersection, just north of Lewis Lake on west side of the road
Roundtrip Distance: To channel outlet—7 miles (11 km) roundtrip; Loop—11 miles (17.5) roundtrip
Level of Difficulty: Moderate; mostly level, some rolling terrain

Duck Lake Trail
Climb a small hill for a view of Duck and Yellowstone lakes and explore the effects of the 1988 fires that swept through this area. Trail descends to lakeshore.
Trailhead: Trail begins in West Thumb Geyser Basin parking area, across the lot from Lake Overlook trailhead.
Distance: 1 mile (1.6 km) roundtrip
Level of Difficulty: Moderate

Day Hikes Near Lake Village

Begin your hike by stopping at a ranger station or visitor center for information. Trail conditions may change suddenly and unexpectedly. Bear activity, rain or snow storms, high water, and fires may temporarily close trails.

Pelican Creek Trail
This short but diverse trail passes through the forest to the lakeshore before looping back across the marsh along Pelican Creek to the trailhead. It is a scenic introduction to a variety of Yellowstone's habitats and a good place for birding.
Trailhead: West end of Pelican Creek Bridge, 1 mile (1.5 km) east of Fishing Bridge Visitor Center
Distance: 1 mile (1.5 km) loop
Level of Difficulty: Easy

Natural Bridge Trail
The natural bridge is a 51 ft. (18 m) high cliff of rhyolite rock that has been cut through by the erosional forces of Bridge Creek. The trail from the campground meanders through the forest for 1.2 mile (0.8 km). It then joins the road and continues to the right (west) for 1 mile (1.5 km) before reaching the Natural Bridge. The short but steep switchback trail to the top of the bridge starts in front of the interpretive exhibit. To protect this fragile resource, the top of the bridge is closed to hiking. However, good views may be attained next to the bridge. The bicycle trail to the bridge begins just south of the marina off the main road.

The trail is closed from late spring to early summer due to bears feeding on spawning trout in Bridge Creek. Inquire at the Visitor Center about trail closures before hiking or bicycling these trails.
Trailhead: Bridge Bay Marina parking lot near the campground entrance road
Distance: 3 miles (5 km) roundtrip
Level of Difficulty: Easy

Storm Point Trail
This trail begins in the open meadows overlooking Indian Pond and Yellowstone Lake. The trail passes by the pond before turning right (west) into the forest. It continues through the trees and out to scenic, windswept Storm Point. The rocky area near the point is home to a large colony of yellow-bellied marmots. Following the shoreline to the west, the trail eventually loops through the lodgepole pine forest and returns to Indian Pond.
Trailhead: Pullout at Indian Pond, 3 miles (5 km) east of Fishing Bridge Visitor Center
Distance: 2 mile (3 km) loop
Level of Difficulty: Easy

Elephant Back Mountain Trail
This trail climbs 800 ft (244 km) in 1-1/2 miles (2.4 km) through a dense lodgepole pine forest. After a mile, the trail splits into a loop. The left fork is the shortest and least steep route to the top. The overlook provides a sweeping panoramic view of Yellowstone Lake and the surrounding area.
Trailhead: Pullout 1 mile (1.5 km) south of Fishing Bridge Junction
Distance: 3 mile (5 km) loop
Level of Difficulty: Moderately strenuous

Howard Eaton Trail
From the east side of Fishing Bridge, the trail follows the Yellowstone River for a short distance before joining a service road; the trail continues on the road for 1/4 mile (0.4 km). Leaving the road, the trail meanders for three miles (5 km) through meadow, forest, and sagebrush flats with frequent views of the river. Wildlife and waterfowl are commonly seen here. The last mile (1.5 km) passes through a dense lodgepole pine forest before reaching an overview of LeHardy Rapids.

To return, follow the same trail back to the trailhead. The trail does continue on for another 12 miles (19 km) to the South Rim Drive at Canyon, but is not well maintained. This trip would require planning for a full day's hike and a return ride to the trailhead.
This area is good grizzly bear habitat, and the trail is closed when bears are known to be in the area. Inquire at the Visitor Center before hiking.
Trailhead: Parking lot on east side of Fishing Bridge
Distance: 7 miles (11.3 km) roundtrip
Level of Difficulty: Easy

Avalanche Peak Trail
This trail climbs steeply (1,800 ft in 2.5 miles) without the benefit of switchbacks. It passes through the forest and into an old avalanche slide area. It continues through the whitebark pine forest to a small meadow at the base of the bowl of Avalanche Peak, affording some of the best panoramic views in the park. The trail continues up a scree slope along the narrow ridgeline of Avalanche Peak. An unmarked trail drops down the northeast side of the bowl and returns to the meadow. Since whitebark pine cones are a favored food of grizzly bears in the fall, avoid this trail at that time.
Trailhead: West end of Eleanor Lake across the road to the east of the small creek
Distance: 5 miles (8 km) roundtrip
Level of Difficulty: Strenuous

Pelican Valley Trail
This trail winds through the Pelican Valley providing views of the broad open valley and forest,

some of the best grizzly habitat in the lower 48 states. It reaches the footbridge in 3 miles (5 km). The trail continues on through the valley. Due to grizzly bears in the area, the trail is not open until July 4th, and then it is recommended (not required) for use by groups of four people or more.
Trailhead: Dirt road 3 miles (5 km) east of Fishing Bridge Visitor Center, across the road from Indian Pond
Distance: 6 miles (10 km) roundtrip to footbridge
Level of Difficulty: Moderate

Day Hikes Near Canyon Village

Begin your hike by stopping at a ranger station or visitor center for information. Trail conditions may change suddenly and unexpectedly. Bear activity, rain or snow storms, high water, and fires may temporarily close trails.

Canyon Rims

There are numerous trails and viewpoints of the canyon falls, both from the north and south rim.

Mary Mountain Trail

This trail climbs gradually up over Mary Mountain and the park's Central Plateau to the Nez Perce trailhead between Madison and Old Faithful. Elk and bison can sometimes be seen in the distant meadows. The trail through Hayden Valley is often difficult to follow as bison regularly knock down the trail markers.
Trailhead: North of Alum Creek pullout, 4 miles south of Canyon Junction
Distance: 21 miles one way
Level of Difficulty: Moderately strenuous due to length

Howard Eaton Trail

This hike, with little vertical rise, will take 2-8 hours. It passes through forest, meadow, and marshland to Cascade Lake (3 mi; 4.8 km), Grebe Lake (4.25 mi; 6.8 km), Wolf Lake (6.25 mi; 10 km), Ice Lake (8.25 mi; 13.7 km), and Norris Campground (12 mi; 19.3 km). Most years, this trail remains very wet and muddy through July. Insects can be very annoying.
Trailhead: 0.5 miles (0.8 km) west of Canyon Junction on the Norris-Canyon Road
Distance: From 3-12 miles one way, depending on destination
Level of Difficulty: Moderately easy

Cascade Lake Trail

This hike takes 3 hours and is an enjoyable walk through open meadows and over small creeks for those with limited time. Look for wildlife and wildflowers in season. Most years, this trail remains very wet and muddy through July.
Trailhead: Cascade Lake Picnic Area, 1.5 miles north of Canyon Jct. on the Tower-Canyon Road.
Distance: 4.5 miles (7.2 km) roundtrip
Level of Difficulty: Easy

Observation Peak

Hike to Cascade Lake from either of its two trailheads. From the lake, this strenuous, 1,400 foot climb in 3 miles will take roughly 3 hours. The hike takes you to a high mountain peak for an outstanding view of the Yellowstone wilderness. The trail passes through open meadows and some whitebark pine forests. Past Cascade Lake, no water is available along the trail. Not recommended for persons with heart and/or respiratory problems.
Trailhead: Cascade Lake Picnic Area, 1.5 miles north of Canyon Jct. on the Tower- Canyon Road. The other trailhead is accessed from a pullout 1/4 mile west of Canyon on the Norris-Canyon Road.
Distance: 11 miles roundtrip
Level of Difficulty: Strenuous

Grebe Lake Trail

There is little vertical rise on this 3-4 hour hike. This trail follows an old fire road through meadows and forest, some of which burned during the fires of 1988. Once at the lake you can connect with the Howard Eaton Trail.
Trailhead: 3.5 miles (5.6 km) west of Canyon Junction on the Norris-Canyon Road
Distance: 6 miles (9.7 km) roundtrip
Level of Difficulty: Moderately easy

Seven Mile Hole Trail

This hike takes 6-8 hours to complete. Following the Canyon Rim for the first 1.5 miles (2.4 km), you will be rewarded with views of Silver Cord Cascade. Continue north another 0.5 mile (0.8 km) to join the Washburn Spur Trail; at 3 miles (4.8 km), the trail drops off to Seven Mile Hole, a 1.5 mile (2.4 km), 1,400 foot (425 m) drop. Hike it carefully, watch your footing, and conserve your energy. Depending on your condition and the weather, it can be a long hike back out. Be especially careful where the trail passes both dormant and active hot springs. Off-trail travel is prohibited. Not recommended for persons with heart and/or respiratory problems.
Trailhead: Glacial Boulder Trailhead on Inspiration Point Road
Distance: 11 miles (17.7 km) roundtrip
Level of Difficulty: Strenuous

Washburn Trail/Washburn Spur Trail

This hike begins at the Dunraven Pass trailhead to Mount Washburn and ends at the Glacial Boulder on Inspiration Point Road. This strenuous hike takes 6-8 hours to complete. Starting at the Washburn Trailhead at Dunraven Pass, you ascend Mt. Washburn on a trail complete with (in season) wildflowers, bighorn sheep, and spectacular views. After this three mile ascent, the Washburn Spur Trail descends very steeply from the east side of the Fire Lookout to Washburn Hot Springs in another 3.7 miles (6 km). Here you will find some interesting thermal features, including mud pots. Continue past the turnoff to Seven Mile Hole and follow the trail to the Glacial Boulder and the Canyon area. Not recommended for persons with heart and/or respiratory problems.
Trailhead: Dunraven Pass, Washburn Trailhead, 4.5 miles north of Canyon Junction
Distance: 11.5 miles (18.5 km) one way
Level of Difficulty: Strenuous

Day Hikes near Tower-Roosevelt

Begin your hike by stopping at a ranger station or visitor center for information. Trail conditions may change suddenly and unexpectedly. Bear activity, rain or snow storms, high water, and fires may temporarily close trails.

Lost Lake Trail

This loop trail departs from behind Roosevelt Lodge and climbs 300 feet (91 m) onto the bench. Here the trail joins the Roosevelt horse trail and continues west to Lost Lake. (If you take the trail east, you loop back to the Roosevelt corrals on the horse trail or continue on to Tower Fall Campground.) From Lost Lake, the trail follows the contour around the hillside to the Petrified Tree parking area. Cross the parking lot and climb the hill at its northeast end to loop back behind Tower Ranger Station. Cross the creek and return to the Roosevelt Lodge cabins.

Offering views of Lost Lake, waterfowl, wet meadows, sagebrush hilltops, wildflowers, and quite often black bears, this trail has a bit of everything. Parts of the trail are used by horse parties. For your safety when meeting horses, we recommend you move to the downhill side of the trail and remain still until they have passed.
Trailhead: Behind Roosevelt Lodge
Distance: 4 miles (6.4 km) roundtrip
Level of difficulty: Moderately strenuous

Garnet Hill and Hellroaring Trails

To access the Garnet Hill Loop Trail, park in the large parking area to the east of the service station at Tower Junction. Walk down the road toward the Northeast Entrance Road (approximately 100 yards/91 m) and head west on the dirt stagecoach road about 1.5 miles to the cookout shelter.

Visitors on the boardwalk at LeHardy Rapids on the Yellowstone River. NPS photo

Continue north along Elk Creek until nearly reaching the Yellowstone River. Here the trail divides, with the west fork joining the Hellroaring Trail and the east fork continuing around Garnet Hill and eventually returning to the Northeast Entrance Road where it is a short walk back to Tower Junction.

The Hellroaring Trail can be reached from the fork of Garnet Hill Trail (see above) or you can start from the Hellroaring parking area 3.5 miles (5.6 km) west of Tower Junction. Follow the trail over the Yellowstone River Suspension Bridge, cross a sagebrush plateau, and drop down to Hellroaring Creek. The Yellowstone River and Hellroaring Creek are both popular fishing areas. Note: This trail can be hot and dry during the summer months. Please remember to take water! Also, watch your footing if you go off-trail and onto the smooth river boulders along the Yellowstone River.

Trailhead: Tower Junction or 3.5 miles (5.6 km) west of Tower Junction

Distance:

1) Garnet Hill Loop: 7.5 miles (11.8 km) roundtrip

2) To Hellroaring Creek and back via Garnet Hill: 10 miles (16 km) roundtrip

3) To Hellroaring Creek and back via Hellroaring Trailhead: 4 miles (4.6 km) roundtrip

Level of difficulty: Moderately strenuous

Yellowstone River Picnic Area Trail

This often overlooked trail along the east rim of the Yellowstone River offers views of the Narrows of the Yellowstone, the Overhanging Cliff area, the towers of Tower Fall, basalt columns, and the historic Bannock Indian Ford. Tower Fall itself is not visible, but the store and highway across the river can be seen for reference purposes. The trail ties into the Specimen Ridge Trail above the Bannock Ford. (Continue up to Specimen Ridge only if you are prepared for a longer hike with few trail markers.) Otherwise continue north about one mile (1.6 km) to the Specimen Ridge Trailhead. Walk west along the road for another 0.7 mile (1.1 km) to the Yellowstone River Picnic Area. Watch for bighorn sheep along this trail but please don't approach them! Use caution along the river canyon with its steep dropoffs.

Trailhead: Yellowstone Picnic Area, 1.25 miles (2 km) northeast of Tower Junction on the road to the Northeast Entrance and Cooke City

Distance: 3.7 miles (5.9 km) roundtrip

Level of difficulty: Moderately strenuous

Slough Creek Trail

This is both a scenic walk and a fishing trail, a favorite of catch-and-release anglers from around the country. The trail follows a historic wagon trail up Slough Creek through several meadows and over Plateau and Elk Tongue creeks. From the trailhead, the trail switchbacks up a moderately steep trail and rejoins Slough Creek in about 2 miles (3.2 km) at the first meadow. While wildlife do not abound in this meadow during the summer, moose are commonly seen. Grizzly and black bears also use this valley. As on all Yellowstone trails, be alert for the possibility of bears in the backcountry. You may encounter the horse drawn wagons of Silver Tip Ranch, a private ranch north of the park boundary that has a historic right of access.

Trailhead: Near the vault toilet on the road to Slough Creek Campground

Distance: 2 miles (3.2 km) one way to First Meadow; 5 miles (8 km) one way to Second Meadow

Level of difficulty: Moderately strenuous for first 1.5 miles (2.4 km), then easy.

Mt. Washburn Trail

The hike to the top of Mt. Washburn is one of the most popular hikes in Yellowstone. Two trails, each 3 miles (4.8 km) in length, switchback to the summit where expansive views of much of Yellowstone unfold below on clear, summer days. An enclosed observation area allows you to get out of the wind. Bighorn sheep are seen quite frequently during the summer on the upper parts of the trails. Harsh alpine conditions contribute to short growing seasons for the fragile alpine vegetation on the mountain. Please stay on the trails and do not approach sheep or other wildlife to help preserve the wildness of this area.

The northern trail begins at the Chittenden Road parking area. The southern trail begins at Dunraven Pass parking area. More parking is available at the Chittenden Road Trailhead, although hikers using this trail may encounter bicycles and occasionally vehicles accessing Mt. Washburn for maintenance purposes.

Trailheads: Chittenden Road Parking Area, 8.7 miles (13.9 km) or Dunraven Pass Parking Area, 13.6 miles (21.8 km) south of Tower Junction on the Tower-Canyon Road

Distance: 6 miles (9.6 km) roundtrip

Level of difficulty: Moderately strenuous.

The contents of this section are reprinted from National Park Service information publications.

NOTES: